T H E

LIFE APPLICATION® BIBLE FOR

Students

NEW TESTAMENT
WITH
PSALMS AND PROVERBS

LIVING BIBLE

Tyndale House Publishers, Inc.
WHEATON, ILLINOIS

Library of Congress Cataloging-in-Publication Data

Bible. English. Living Bible. 1992.
  Life application Bible for students : the Living Bible.
    p.   cm.
  Includes indexes.
  Summary: Background information, personality profiles, life
application notes, charts and maps, and other special features
accompany this modern language translation of the Old and
New Testaments.
    ISBN 0-8423-2741-X (softcover).
    ISBN 0-8423-2742-8 (hardcover).
    ISBN 0-8423-2814-9 (denim blue bonded).
    ISBN 0-8423-2815-7 (burgundy bonded).
    ISBN 0-8423-2884-X (hardcover indexed).
    ISBN 0-8423-2885-8 (denim blue bonded indexed).
    ISBN 0-8423-2886-6 (burgundy bonded indexed).
    ISBN 0-8423-2888-2 (New Testament/Psa and Prov)
    I. Tyndale House Publishers.   II. Title.
BS551.2.B474   1992
220.5'208—dc20   91-39392

The publisher gratefully acknowledges the role of Youth for
Christ/USA in preparing the Life Application Notes and Bible
Helps.

The Bible text used in this *Life Application Bible for Students* is
The Living Bible.

Printed in the United States of America

02 01 00 99 98 97 96 95
8   7   6   5   4   3   2   1

CONTRIBUTORS

Design Team
Dr. Bruce B. Barton
Ron Beers
Dr. James Galvin
LaVonne Neff
David R. Veerman

Senior Editor
David R. Veerman

Associate Editor
Karen Ball

Assistant Editors
Linda Taylor
Karen Voke

Graphic Design
Timothy R. Botts
Janet Cameron
Dan Beery
Tan Nguyen

WRITERS

Richard R. Dunn
Chairman, Department of Youth Ministry
Trinity College, Deerfield, Illinois

Terry Prisk
Youth Communicator/Consultant
Executive Director of Contemporary
    Communication
Detroit, Michigan

Kent Keller
Director of Single Adult Ministry
Key Biscayne Presbyterian Church
Miami, Florida

Jared Reed
Minister of Youth
Key Biscayne Presbyterian Church
Miami, Florida

Len Woods
Former Editor of Youthwalk
Minister to Students, Christ Community Church
Ruston, Louisiana

Greg Johnson
Former Editor, Breakaway
Focus on the Family
Currently an Associate with Alive Communications
Colorado Springs, Colorado

Byron Emmert
Speaker and seminar leader
Youth for Christ
Mt. Lake, Minnesota

Diane Eble
Associate Editor, Campus Life Magazine
Wheaton, Illinois

Neil Wilson
Pastor, Eureka United Methodist Church
Omro, Wisconsin

Bill Sanders
Author and speaker
Kalamazoo, Michigan

David R. Veerman
Veteran youth worker and author
Vice President, Livingstone Corporation
Naperville, Illinois

Thank you to the young people from the following youth groups for their invaluable assistance with this project.
Southern Gables Church (Denver, Colorado)
Spring Hill Camps (Evart, Michigan)
Pekin Bible Church (Pekin, Illinois)
Ward Presbyterian Church (Livonia, Michigan)
First Baptist Church (Holdrege, Nebraska)
Naperville Presbyterian Church (Naperville, Illinois)

NOTES AND FEATURES

Book Introductions
Jared Reed
Len Woods
David R. Veerman

Personality Profiles
Neil Wilson

Moral Dilemma Notes
Len Woods

"I Wonder" Notes
Greg Johnson

"Here's What I Did" Notes
Terry Prisk
Diane Eble

Megathemes and Discussion Questions
Richard R. Dunn
Dr. Bruce B. Barton

Ultimate Issues
Kent Keller

Life-Changer Index
Bill Sanders
Linda Taylor

Maps
Adapted from the *Life Application Bible*

Charts
Adapted from the *Life Application Bible*
Tan Nguyen

Memory Verses
Timothy R. Botts
Tan Nguyen
David R. Veerman
Karen Ball

Bible Reading Plan
Neil Wilson

Follow-Up/Appointments with God
Byron Emmert

Life Application Notes
Adapted from the *Life Application Bible*
David R. Veerman

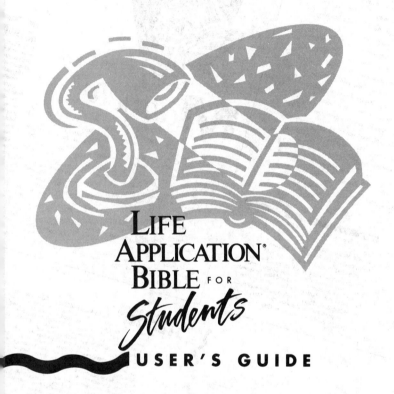

LIFE APPLICATION® BIBLE FOR *Students*

USER'S GUIDE

Welcome to the *Life Application Bible for Students New Testament with Psalms and Proverbs*. God gave us his Word to tell us about himself and his plan for our life. When we read the New Testament, as well as the rest of God's Word, we see his love in action, and we learn about what he wants us to do.

In addition to reading, however, we should be studying God's Word. Then we can discover what he wants us to do and do it. That's what the word *application* means—putting into practice, obeying, *doing* biblical principles.

That's why the *Life Application Bible for Students New Testament with Psalms and Proverbs* was written—to help you understand and apply God's Word. It is easy to use and packed with helpful notes and other features. You will find the notes within the text, at the beginnings of books, and at the endings of books. These special features *are not* God's Word—only the Bible text itself speaks with God's authority. The notes and other features *are* a valuable help in understanding God's truth and seeing how the biblical principles apply to life, your life, today.

The following spread is a quick look at each of the special features.

BOOK INTRODUCTIONS To get an interesting overview of a specific Bible book, read the introduction material containing interesting summaries, timelines, and stats (the who, what, where, and when of the book).

CHARTS These compare, contrast, and list important information to help you visualize difficult concepts or pull together related Bible facts.

Matthew

W ho would you put on a list of the most influential people of all time? Think beyond singers, stars, or athletes. We're talking the real "heavyweights of history." People who took civilization by the scruff of the neck and shook it. Folks about whom we say, "Because of his/her presence, the world will never be the same." ■ Using that criteria, your list probably would feature Julius Caesar, Karl Marx, Martin Luther King, Jr., William Shakespeare, Adolf Hitler, Napoleon, Abraham Lincoln, Genghis Khan, Elvis Presley, Mohammed, Buddha, Alexander the Great, Mohandas Gandhi, or Henry Ford. ■ Those people—and many others—deserve to be on such a list. But if you're looking for one person who changed the world more than anyone, look at Jesus Christ. ■ Of course, naming a first-century carpenter and itinerant preacher "the most influential person of all time" probably won't sit well with some people. They may prefer to put Jesus on an list of influential "religious" figures. But here's why the founder of Christianity cannot be ignored: ■ Two thousand years ago, Jesus of Nazareth launched a spiritual revolution that is still going strong. He has been the motivation behind more songs and sermons, more works of charity, and the object of more affection than all the other great figures of history combined. And don't forget the inspiration underlying more works of charity, and the object of more affection than all the other great figures of history combined. And don't forget the millions of lives that have been transformed by his timeless touch. ■ Dive into the Gospel of Matthew. See for yourself how Jesus succeeded in turning ancient Israel on its ear. In the process, you'll also begin to see why he still rocks the planet.

STATS

PURPOSE: To prove that Jesus is the Messiah, the eternal King

AUTHOR: Matthew (Levi)

TO WHOM WRITTEN: Especially for the Jews

DATE WRITTEN: Probably between A.D. 60–65

SETTING: Matthew was a Jewish tax collector who became one of Jesus' disciples. This Gospel forms the connecting link between the Old and New Testaments because of its emphasis on the fulfillment of prophecy.

KEY PEOPLE: Jesus, Mary, Joseph, John the Baptist, disciples, religious leaders, Caiaphas, Pilate, Mary Magdalene

KEY PLACES: Bethlehem, Jerusalem, Capernaum, Galilee, Judea

CHAPTER 1 JESUS' FAMILY TREE. These are the ancestors of Jesus Christ, a descendant of King David and of Abraham: ²Abraham was the father of Isaac; Isaac was the father of Jacob; Jacob was the father of Judah and his brothers. ³Judah was the father of Perez and Zerah (Tamar was their mother); Perez was the father of Hezron; Hezron was the father of Aram; ⁴Aram was the father of Amminadab; Amminadab was the father of Nahshon; Nahshon was the father of Salmon; ⁵Salmon was the father of Boaz (Rahab was his mother); Boaz was the father of Obed (Ruth was his mother); Obed was the father of Jesse; ⁶Jesse was the father of King David. David was the father of Solomon (his mother was the widow of Uriah); ⁷Solomon was the father of Rehoboam; Rehoboam was the father of Abijah; Abijah was the father of Asa;

⁸Asa was the father of Jehoshaphat; Jehoshaphat was the father of Jehoram; Jehoram was the father of Uzziah; ⁹Uzziah was the father of Jotham; Jotham was the father of Ahaz; Ahaz was the father of Hezekiah; ¹⁰Hezekiah was the father of Manasseh; Manasseh was the father of Amos; Amos was the father of Josiah; ¹¹Josiah was the father of Jechoniah and his brothers (born at the time of the exile to Babylon). ¹²After the exile: Jechon Shealtiel; Shealtiel was the ¹³Zerubbabel was the was the father of Eliakim of Azor;

NO LIMITS

1:1-17 In the first of Matthew we ... people spanning ... All were ances ... but they varied ... in personalitie ... and experience ... heroes (such ... faith ... Ruth, the ... shady ... Rahab ... ordina ... Arono ... wes ...

STEPHEN

The book you hold in your hand is there today because thousands of Christians throughout history have given their lives to carry the gospel around the world. They died for the Good News. It is important for us to remember, though, that a person cannot give his life for the gospel until he has learned to live his life for the gospel. Stephen was just that kind of person.

One way God trains his servants is to have them do jobs that don't seem very important or glamorous. We meet Stephen in the New Testament when he is appointed with others to manage the distribution of food among Christians in Jerusalem. Because many people lost jobs and belongings, and when they became Christians, it became necessary for all Christians to share what they had with each other. Stephen and others were asked to make sure that the available food was handed out fairly. It was probably a job with more headaches than thank-yous.

Stephen also proved himself as a powerful speaker. When he was honored in the Temple by several troublemakers about his faith, he responded calmly and clearly. His logic devastated their arguments. Stephen was hauled before the official religious court where he used a summary of the Jews' own history to show that Jesus was the Savior. The court was unable to answer him, so they decided to silence him. They stoned him to death while he prayed for their forgiveness. Stephen's first short show how much he had become like Jesus in a few moments. His death had a lasting effect on a young Paul, who would later change from fiercely destroying the faith to radically defending it.

Stephen's life is a continual challenge to Christians. Because he was the first to die for the faith, his sacrifice raises questions: How many risks do we take in being Jesus' followers? Would we be willing to die for him? Are we really willing to live for him?

LESSONS: Striving for excellence in small assignments prepares a person for greater responsibilities.

Real understanding of God always leads to practical and compassionate actions toward people.

KEY VERSES: "And as the murderous stones came hurling at him, Stephen prayed, 'Lord Jesus, receive my spirit.' And he fell to his knees, shouting, 'Lord don't charge them with this sin!' and with that, he died" (Acts 7:59-60).

Stephen's story is told in Acts 6:3–8:2. He also is mentioned in Acts 11:19; 22:20.

UPS:
• One of seven leaders chosen to supervise food distribution to the needy in the early church
• Known for his spiritual qualities of faith, wisdom, grace, and power, and for the Spirit's presence in his life
• Outstanding leader, teacher, and debater
• First to give his life for the gospel

STATS:
• Church responsibilities: Deacon—distributing food to the needy
• Contemporaries: Paul, Caiaphas, Gamaliel, the apostles

MAPS Located in the text, the maps help you find Bible locations quickly and easily.

KEY PLACES IN ACTS

300 MI.

300 Km.

The apostle Paul, whose missionary journeys fill much of this book, traveled tremendous distances as he tirelessly spread the gospel across much of the Roman Empire. His combined trips, by land and ship, total more than 13,000 airline miles, to say nothing of the circuitous land routes he walked and climbed.

Judea Paul ascended to heaven from the Mount of Olives outside Jerusalem, and his followers returned to the city to await the fulfilling of the Holy Spirit, which occurred on Pentecost. Peter gave a powerful sermon that was heard by Jews from across the empire (1:1–2:59).

Samaria After Stephen was martyred for his faith by Jewish leaders, who did not believe in Jesus (1:1–7:59). ...

PERSONALITY PROFILES
These are character sketches of key Bible people—both heroes and villains— highlighting their strengths, weaknesses, successes, failures, and life-lessons.

... John 8:... Luke 7:47-50
the paralyzed man lowered on a stretcher through the ...
the woman caught in adultery ... John 8:...
the woman who anointed his feet with oil ... Luke 7:47-50
Peter, for denying he knew Jesus ... John 18:15-18, 25-27; 21:15-19
the thief on the cross ... Luke 23:39-43
the people who crucified him ... Luke 23:34

US AND FORGIVENESS

Jesus forgave

Jesus not only taught frequently about forgiveness, he also demonstrated his own willingness to forgive. Here are several examples of his willingness to recognize his should help us to recognize his willingness to forgive us also.

HIGHLIGHTED MEMORY VERSES

Key verses are artistically highlighted to help impress them in your mind.

"HERE'S WHAT I DID" notes

After interviewing tons of kids, we took some of their stories and included them here. These notes tell how other young people used the principles of God's Word in specific situations in their lives.

ULTIMATE ISSUE notes

An "ultimate issue" is a tough question about life or God. These full-page notes bring up difficult questions and then give clear and helpful answers.

THE WHOLE BIBLE WAS GIVEN TO US BY INSPIRATION FROM GOD and is useful to teach us what is TRUE and to make us realize what is wrong in our lives; IT straightens us out and helps us do what is RIGHT.

2 TIMOTHY 3:16-17

LUST

Last year, thirteen-year-old Danny found a secret stash of pornographic magazines in his older brother's bedroom. Since then, he's developed a system. Each time his brother goes out for the evening, Danny sneaks one of the magazines into his own bedroom. There he'll stay for two hours fantasizing about being with each of the beautiful models. After a few days, he smuggles the much-studied magazine back into its place, whereupon he takes another one and repeats the process.

Each time he yields to these lustful temptations, Danny is overcome by a wave of guilt. After the short-term pleasure, Danny experiences only feelings of emptiness and loneliness. Even so, he rationalizes it this way:

"It's better to do what I'm doing than to be like my friends and actually go out and have sex! At least this way, I won't get myself or anybody else in trouble. Besides, I can't help it if I have a healthy sex drive. And anyway, I'm not sure I can stop."

What about Danny's ideas on lust? Are they sound arguments? Is it OK to stare at pictures (or real people) and imagine having sex with them? Take a look at Colossians 3:5 for God's thoughts on the issue.

AIDS: WHAT WOULD JESUS DO?

There are few more explosive topics in America than that of AIDS. Conservatives believe AIDS is God's judgment on certain sinners. Gay rights groups and others scream just as loudly that this is a medical issue, not a moral one. Who's right? And how should Christians respond to this overwhelming problem? In one sense, AIDS (Acquired Immune Deficiency Syndrome) is primarily a medical issue. The AIDS virus attacks the body's immune system, making the body defenseless against the diseases a healthy person's immune system would destroy. AIDS is an "equal opportunity" nightmare: it affects everyone: young, old, male, female, gay, or straight. But this is only a part of the picture. Since the majority of people in our country infected with AIDS are homosexual men and IV drug abusers and junkies, many people believe that AIDS must be a special judgment on those homosexuals and junkies. Is this a reasonable belief? Did God get "fed up" with gays and junkies—too, pointing to passages like Romans 1 or 1 Corinthians 6:9) as evidence of God's special displeasure on the sin of homosexuality. Is this a reasonable belief with this belief. First, "judgment bandwagon," too, pointing to passages like Romans 1 or 1 Corinthians 6:9) as evidence of while male homosexuals seldom contract it. Does this mean that God hates male gays, but female gays are OK? That is obviously inconsistent. As for drug abusers, those who don't use or homosexuals against the diseases everyone. There are a number of problems with this belief. First, intravenously and share their needles with one another often contract the AIDS virus. Those who inject drugs share needles don't get it nearly as frequently. So does God only hate those drug abusers who inject drugs community and IV drug abusers so hard? That's clearly illogical. If AIDS isn't a punishment from God, why has it hit the male gay activities that pass the virus from person to person very affectively. God hasn't singled out particular groups for special judgment; rather, those people engage in activities that are particularly risky as regards the you will—like it or not—encounter it. There are natural laws governing human behavior, too. One such law is that your body is not made for sexual promiscuity. Violate that law and you risk contracting AIDS or other diseases (syphilis, gonorrhea, herpes, etc.). Likewise, your body was not made to handle large amounts of drugs. Continually inject them into your veins and you probably will experience a lot of physical problems— one of which may be AIDS. So it's not that God is using AIDS to "get" certain kinds of people. AIDS simply is a natural—though terrifying—result of human behavior that goes against God's design for our own sin. As the Psalmist wrote in Psalm 143:1-2, "Hear my prayer, O Lord; answer my plea because you are faithful to your who believe AIDS is a special divine judgment simply don't understand the reality of their own sin.

"Here's what I did..."

I used to struggle a lot with doubt. Was God real? Did he really care about what happens to me? Is the Bible relevant? Then someone challenged me to actively try to apply a passage from the Bible every day for two weeks and see if that made any difference. I did. I read some of the Psalms and found that they were wonderfully relevant. When I felt lonely and had no one to turn to, I found that David's words perfectly expressed my feelings. Another passage I came across reminded me that God has promised never to leave us. Then when I came across Jesus' words in Matthew 7:24-27, I realized that his Word is the only solid thing we have to build our lives on. The Matthew passage, and my two-week experiment, motivated me to try to live out what I only through obeying and applying God's Word that we know he's real. His read more and more every day.

Laura AGE 17

UNPOPULAR

19:1-10 Tax collectors were among the most unpopular people in Israel. Jews by birth who chose to work for Rome were considered traitors. Besides, it was common knowledge that tax collectors made themselves rich by gouging their fellow Jews. No wonder the crowds were displeased when Jesus went home with the tax collector Zacchaeus. But despite the fact that Zacchaeus was both dishonest and a turncoat, Jesus loved him—and in response, the little tax collector was converted. In every society, certain groups of people are considered "untouchables" because of their politics, immoral behavior, or life-style. We should not avoid these people. Jesus loves them, and they need to hear his Good News.

MORAL DILEMMA notes

These are real-life case studies, situations where kids like you had to make important decisions. In each of these notes, you will be told where to find a Bible passage that will help you understand what God has to say about the situations you face.

Now that I am a Christian, how should I act around my friends and family who are not believers?

The most important thing you have going for you in both sets of relationships is that you already have a "relational bridge." Your friends and family knew what your life was like before you met Christ. Now they will have the chance to see you afterward.

In Mark 5:1-20, Jesus recognized that this was the case with the man he had just cleansed from demon possession. So he sent him back to his home instead of asking him to leave those who knew him best.

Another passage calls us Christ's ambassadors to our world (2 Corinthians 5:17-20). This means we are his hand-picked representatives! If people want to know what God is like, all they have to do is look at us.

God does not expect you to be perfect, but he does expect your faith to grow (Romans 10:17), and he expects you to try to live more like Jesus Christ would (Romans 12:1-2).

The people around you will be able to relate to your progress, not to perfection. Progress may be slow at first, but eventually, as you give areas of your life to Christ's

MEGA Themes

I WONDER...

SALVATION Salvation is a gracious gift from God. God chose us out of his love for us. Jesus died to pay the penalty for our sin, and the Holy Spirit cleansed us from sin when we believed. Eternal life is a wonderful privilege for those who trust in Christ.

Our safety and security are in God. If we experience joy in relationship with Christ now, how much greater will our joy be when he returns and we see him face-to-face? Such a hope should motivate us to serve Christ even more.

1. What are the blessings of our salvation that have been revealed to us through Jesus?
2. Why would this be such an important message for Jewish Christians who had been suffering for their faith?
3. What does it mean to you to be saved? Include your feelings, the present benefits, and your hope for the future.
4. How can you communicate this through your life to someone who is without Christ? Why is it important that others come to know Christ?

2. Who are the people who have ministered Christ's love and grace to you? In what ways have they provided this love and grace?
3. Why is it necessary for you and other believers to be providers of his love to one another?
4. In what two ways will you become a part of God's love and grace in the life of fellow believers?

FAMILY LIFE Peter encouraged the wives of unbelievers to submit to the authority of their husbands as a means of winning them to Christ. He urged all family members to treat others with sympathy, love, tenderness, and humility. Though it's never easy, willing service is the best way to influence our loved ones. To gain the needed strength, we must pray for God's help. Relationships with parents, brothers and sisters, and spouses are important aspects of Christian discipleship.

1. In 1 Peter, what principles do you find for a godly

LIFE APPLICATION notes

On just about every page you'll find these concise mini-lessons. Each note helps explain a specific Bible passage and then tells ways you can put it into practice.

"I WONDER" notes

If you've ever wondered about what the Bible has to say about something, or about some aspect of the Christian life, you'll probably find your questions repeated in these notes. And you'll also find interesting and thoughtful answers.

MEGATHEMES

At the end of each Bible book the main themes are presented. With each theme there is a set of questions that can be used for individual or group study.

At the back of the New Testament you will discover . . .

NEW TESTAMENT, PSALMS, AND PROVERBS READING PLAN
By following this simple plan, you will read all the major biblical themes and stories from the New Testament, Psalms, and Proverbs in a year.

FOLLOW-THROUGH COURSE This course takes new believers through the basics of the Christian faith. Use it yourself or share it with a friend.

LIFE-CHANGER INDEX More than 100 topics are listed in this index. Each topic has a selection of relevant Bible passages and the notes that relate. (The Scripture references listed for the notes in this section are given only to help you find the note. It may or may not actually relate to the Scripture listed.)

INDEXES FOR MORAL DILEMMA, "I WONDER," AND ULTIMATE ISSUE NOTES; CHARTS; PERSONALITY PROFILES; MAPS; AND "HERE'S WHAT I DID" NOTES Again, Scripture references listed for these notes are to help you locate the notes easily. The notes may or may not actually relate to the Scripture listed.

"WHERE TO FIND IT" INDEX Thirty of the best-known New Testament passages and stories are listed in this index, along with Jesus' parables and miracles. Use either the Scripture references or the page numbers to find the story, parable, or miracle you want quickly and easily.

It's all here. Just about everything you will need to help you understand and apply God's Word. The next step—actually taking time to read and study the New Testament with Psalms and Proverbs—is yours. *GO FOR IT!*

NEW Testament

Who would you put on a list of the most influential people of all time? Think beyond singers, stars, or athletes. We're talking the real "heavyweights of history." People who took civilization by the scruff of the neck and shook it. Folks about whom we say, "Because of his/her presence, the world will never be the same." ■ Using that criteria, your list probably would feature Julius Caesar, Karl Marx, Martin Luther King, Jr., William Shakespeare, Adolf Hitler, Napoleon, Abraham Lincoln, Genghis Khan, Elvis Presley, Mohammed, Buddha, Alexander the Great, Mohandas Gandhi, or Henry Ford. ■ Those people—and many others—deserve to be on such a list. But if you're looking for one person who changed the world more than anyone, look at Jesus Christ. ■ Of course, naming a first-century carpenter and itinerant preacher "the most influential person of all time" probably won't sit well with some people. They may prefer to put Jesus on a list of influential "religious" figures. But here's why the founder of Christianity cannot be ignored: ■ Two thousand years ago, Jesus of Nazareth launched a spiritual revolution that is still going strong. He has been the motivation behind more songs and sermons, the inspiration underlying more works of charity, and the object of more affection than all the other great figures of history combined. And don't forget the millions of lives that have been transformed by his timeless touch. ■ Dive into the Gospel of Matthew. See for yourself how Jesus succeeded in turning ancient Israel on its ear. In the process, you'll also begin to see why he still rocks the planet.

STATS

PURPOSE: To prove that Jesus is the Messiah, the eternal King

AUTHOR: Matthew (Levi)

TO WHOM WRITTEN: Especially for the Jews

DATE WRITTEN: Probably between A.D. 60–65

SETTING: Matthew was a Jewish tax collector who became one of Jesus' disciples. This Gospel forms the connecting link between the Old and New Testaments because of its emphasis on the fulfillment of prophecy.

KEY PEOPLE: Jesus, Mary, Joseph, John the Baptist, disciples, religious leaders, Caiaphas, Pilate, Mary Magdalene

KEY PLACES: Bethlehem, Jerusalem, Capernaum, Galilee, Judea

Matthew

NO LIMITS

1:1-17 In the first 17 verses of Matthew we meet 46 people spanning 2,000 years. All were ancestors of Jesus, but they varied considerably in personality, spirituality, and experience. Some were heroes (and heroines) of faith—like Abraham, Isaac, Ruth, and David. Some had shady reputations—like Rahab and Tamar. Many were ordinary—like Hezron, Aram, and Achim. Others were evil—like Manasseh and Abijah. God's work has never been limited by human failures or sins; he works through ordinary people. God used all kinds of people to bring his Son into the world; he uses all kinds today to accomplish his will.

CHAPTER 1 JESUS' FAMILY TREE. These are the ancestors of Jesus Christ, a descendant of King David and of Abraham:

²Abraham was the father of Isaac; Isaac was the father of Jacob; Jacob was the father of Judah and his brothers.

³Judah was the father of Perez and Zerah (Tamar was their mother); Perez was the father of Hezron; Hezron was the father of Aram;

⁴Aram was the father of Amminadab; Amminadab was the father of Nahshon; Nahshon was the father of Salmon;

⁵Salmon was the father of Boaz (Rahab was his mother); Boaz was the father of Obed (Ruth was his mother); Obed was the father of Jesse;

⁶Jesse was the father of King David. David was the father of Solomon (his mother was the widow of Uriah);

⁷Solomon was the father of Rehoboam; Rehoboam was the father of Abijah; Abijah was the father of Asa;

⁸Asa was the father of Jehoshaphat; Jehoshaphat was the father of Jehoram; Jehoram was the father of Uzziah;

⁹Uzziah was the father of Jotham; Jotham was the father of Ahaz; Ahaz was the father of Hezekiah;

¹⁰Hezekiah was the father of Manasseh; Manasseh was the father of Amos; Amos was the father of Josiah;

¹¹Josiah was the father of Jechoniah and his brothers (born at the time of the exile to Babylon).

¹²After the exile: Jechoniah was the father of Shealtiel; Shealtiel was the father of Zerubbabel;

¹³Zerubbabel was the father of Abiud; Abiud was the father of Eliakim; Eliakim was the father of Azor;

Jesus' earthly story begins in the town of Bethlehem in the Roman province of Judea (2:1). A threat to kill the infant King led Joseph to take his family to Egypt (2:14). When they returned, God led them to settle in Nazareth in Galilee (2:22-23). At about age 30, Jesus was baptized in the Jordan River (3:13) and was tempted by Satan in the Judean wilderness (4:1). He set up his base of operations in Capernaum (4:12-13) and from there ministered throughout Israel, telling parables, teaching about the Kingdom, and healing the sick. He traveled to the country of the Gadarenes and healed two demon-possessed men (8:28ff); fed over 5,000 people with five small loaves of bread and two fish on the shores of Galilee near Bethsaida-Julias (14:15ff); healed the sick in Gennesaret (14:34ff); ministered to the Gentiles in Tyre and Sidon (15:21ff); visited Caesarea Philippi where Peter declared him to be the Messiah (16:13ff); and taught in Perea, across the Jordan (19:1). As he set out on his last visit to Jerusalem, he told the disciples what would happen to him there (20:17ff). He spent some time in Jericho (20:29), then stayed in Bethany at night as he went back and forth into Jerusalem during his last week (21:17ff). In Jerusalem he would be crucified, but he would rise again.

The broken lines (– · – ·) indicate modern boundaries.

---

[14] Azor was the father of Zadok; Zadok was the father of Achim; Achim was the father of Eliud;

[15] Eliud was the father of Eleazar; Eleazar was the father of Matthan; Matthan was the father of Jacob;

[16] Jacob was the father of Joseph (who was the husband of Mary, the mother of Jesus Christ the Messiah).

[17] These are fourteen of the generations from Abraham to King David; and fourteen from King David's time to the exile; and fourteen from the exile to Christ.

[18] These are the facts concerning the birth of Jesus Christ: His mother, Mary, was engaged to be married to Joseph. But while she was still a virgin she became pregnant by the Holy Spirit. [19] Then Joseph, her fiancé, being a man of stern principle, decided to break the engagement but to do it quietly, as he didn't want to publicly disgrace her.

[20] As he lay awake considering this, he fell into a dream, and saw an angel standing beside him. "Joseph, son of David," the angel said, "don't hesitate to take Mary as your wife! For the child within her has been conceived by the Holy Spirit. [21] And she will have a Son, and you shall name him Jesus (meaning 'Savior'), for he will save his people from their sins. [22] This will fulfill God's message through his prophets—

²³'*Listen! The virgin shall conceive a child! She shall give birth to a Son, and he shall be called "Emmanuel" (meaning "God is with us").'*"

²⁴When Joseph awoke, he did as the angel commanded and brought Mary home to be his wife, ²⁵but she remained a virgin until her Son was born; and Joseph named him "Jesus."

CHAPTER **2** **WISE MEN VISIT BABY JESUS.** Jesus was born in the town of Bethlehem, in Judea, during the reign of King Herod.

At about that time some astrologers from eastern lands arrived in Jerusalem, asking, ²"Where is the newborn King of the Jews? for we have seen his star in far-off eastern lands and have come to worship him."

³King Herod was deeply disturbed by their question, and all Jerusalem was filled with rumors. ⁴He called a meeting of the Jewish religious leaders.

"Did the prophets tell us where the Messiah would be born?" he asked.

⁵"Yes, in Bethlehem," they said, "for this is what the prophet Micah wrote:

⁶"O little town of Bethlehem, you are not just an unimportant Judean village, for a Governor shall rise from you to rule my people Israel.'"

⁷Then Herod sent a private message to the astrologers, asking them to come to see him; at this meeting he found out from them the exact time when they first saw the star. Then he told them, ⁸"Go to Bethlehem and search for the child. And when you find him, come back and tell me so that I can go and worship him too!"

⁹After this interview the astrologers started out again. And look! The star appeared to them again, standing over Bethlehem. ¹⁰Their joy knew no bounds!

¹¹Entering the house where the baby and Mary, his mother, were, they threw themselves down before him, worshiping. Then they opened their presents and gave him gold, frankincense, and myrrh. ¹²But when they returned to their own land, they didn't go through Jerusalem to report to Herod, for God had warned them in a dream to go home another way.

¹³After they were gone, an angel of the Lord appeared to Joseph in a dream. "Get up and flee to Egypt with the baby and his mother," the angel said, "and stay there until I tell you to return, for King Herod is going to try to kill the child." ¹⁴That same night he left for Egypt with Mary and the baby, ¹⁵and stayed there until King Herod's death. This fulfilled the prophet's prediction,

"I have called my Son from Egypt."

¹⁶Herod was furious when he learned that the astrologers had disobeyed him. Sending soldiers to Bethlehem, he ordered them to kill every baby boy two years old and under, both in the town and on the nearby farms, for the astrologers had told him the star first appeared to them two years before. ¹⁷This brutal action of Herod's fulfilled the prophecy of Jeremiah,

¹⁸"Screams of anguish come from Ramah,
Weeping unrestrained;
Rachel weeping for her children,
Uncomforted—
For they are dead."

¹⁹When Herod died, an angel of the Lord appeared in a dream to Joseph in Egypt and told him, ²⁰"Get up and take the baby and his mother back to Israel, for those who were trying to kill the child are dead."

²¹So he returned immediately to Israel with Jesus and his mother. ²²But on the way he was frightened to learn that the new king was Herod's son, Archelaus. Then, in another dream, he was warned not to go to Judea, so they went to Galilee instead ²³and lived in Nazareth. This fulfilled the prediction of the prophets concerning the Messiah,

"He shall be called a Nazarene."

AFRAID

2:16-18 Herod was afraid that this newborn king would one day take his throne. But Jesus wanted to be king of Herod's life. Jesus wanted to give Herod eternal life, not take away his present life. Today people often are afraid that Christ wants to take things away when, in reality, he wants to give them real freedom, peace, and joy.

And she will have a Son, and you shall name him **JESUS** *(meaning "Savior"), for* **he will save his people** *from their sins sins sins sins sins sins sins sins sins*

MATTHEW 1:21

THE PHARISEES AND SADDUCEES

The Pharisees and Sadducees were the two major religious groups in Israel at the time of Christ. The Pharisees were more religiously minded while the Sadducees were more politically minded. Although the groups disliked and distrusted each other, they became allies in their common hatred of Jesus.

PHARISEES

Positive Characteristics

- Were committed to obeying all of God's word
- Were admired by the common people for their apparent piety
- Believed in a bodily resurrection and eternal life
- Believed in angels and demons

Negative Characteristics

- Behaved as though their own religious rules were just as important as God's rules for living
- Were often hypocritical, forcing others to try to live up to standards they themselves could not live up to
- Believed that salvation came from perfect obedience to the law and was not based on forgiveness of sins
- Became so obsessed with obeying their legal interpretations in every detail that they completely ignored God's message of mercy and grace
- Were more concerned with appearing to be good than with obeying God

SADDUCEES

Positive Characteristics

- Believed God's word was limited to the first five books of the Bible: Genesis to Deuteronomy
- Were more practically minded than the Pharisees

Negative Characteristics

- Relied on logic while placing little importance on faith
- Did not believe all the Old Testament was God's word
- Did not believe in a bodily resurrection or eternal life
- Did not believe in angels or demons
- Were often willing to compromise their values with the Romans and others in order to maintain their status and influential positions

---

CHAPTER 3 JOHN THE BAPTIST PREACHES.
While they were living in Nazareth, John the Baptist began preaching out in the Judean wilderness. His constant theme was, ²"Turn from your sins . . . turn to God . . . for the Kingdom of Heaven is coming soon." ³Isaiah the prophet had told about John's ministry centuries before! He had written,

"I hear a shout from the wilderness, 'Prepare a road for the Lord— straighten out the path where he will walk.'"

⁴John's clothing was woven from camel's hair and he wore a leather belt; his food was locusts and wild honey. ⁵People from Jerusalem and from all over the Jordan Valley, and, in fact, from every section of Judea went out to the wilderness to hear him preach, ⁶and when they confessed their sins, he baptized them in the Jordan River.

⁷But when he saw many Pharisees and Sadducees coming to be baptized, he denounced them.

"You sons of snakes!" he warned. "Who said that you could escape the coming wrath of God?

⁸Before being baptized, prove that you have turned from sin by doing worthy deeds. ⁹Don't try to get by as you are, thinking, 'We are safe for we are Jews—descendants of Abraham.' That proves nothing. God can change these stones here into Jews!

¹⁰"And even now the axe of God's judgment is poised to chop down every unproductive tree. They will be chopped and burned.

¹¹"With water I baptize those who repent of their sins; but someone else is coming, far greater than I am, so great that I am not worthy to carry his shoes! He shall baptize you with the Holy Spirit and with fire. ¹²He will separate the chaff from the grain, burning the chaff with never-ending fire and storing away the grain."

¹³Then Jesus went from Galilee to the Jordan River to be baptized there by John. ¹⁴John didn't want to do it.

"This isn't proper," he said. "I am the one who needs to be baptized by you."

ACTIONS

3:8 John the Baptist called people to more than words or ritual; he told them to change their lives. God looks beyond our words and religious activities to see if our lives back up our words, and he judges our words by the actions that accompany them. Do your actions agree with your words?

INTEGRITY

3:15 Put yourself in John's shoes. Your work is going well; people are taking notice. But you know your work is to prepare people's hearts for Jesus (3:11; John 1:36). Now Jesus has arrived, and with him, the real test of your integrity. Will you be able to turn your followers over to him? John passed the test by publicly baptizing Jesus. Soon he would say, "He must become greater . . . and I must become less and less" (John 3:30). Can we put our egos and profitable work aside to point others to Jesus? Will we give up status so that everyone will benefit?

[15]But Jesus said, "Please do it, for I must do all that is right." So then John baptized him.

[16]After his baptism, as soon as Jesus came up out of the water, the heavens were opened to him and he saw the Spirit of God coming down in the form of a dove. [17]And a voice from heaven said, "This is my beloved Son, and I am wonderfully pleased with him."

CHAPTER **4** **JESUS IS TEMPTED.** Then Jesus was led out into the wilderness by the Holy Spirit, to be tempted there by Satan. [2]For forty days and forty nights he ate nothing and became very hungry. [3]Then Satan tempted him to get food by changing stones into loaves of bread.

"It will prove you are the Son of God," he said. [4]But Jesus told him, "No! For the Scriptures tell us that bread won't feed men's souls: obedience to every word of God is what we need."

[5]Then Satan took him to Jerusalem to the roof of the Temple. [6]"Jump off," he said, "and prove you are the Son of God; for the Scriptures declare, 'God will send his angels to keep you from harm,' . . . they will prevent you from smashing on the rocks below."

[7]Jesus retorted, "It also says not to put the Lord your God to a foolish test!"

[8]Next Satan took him to the peak of a very high mountain and showed him the nations of the world and all their glory. [9]"I'll give it all to you," he said, "if you will only kneel and worship me."

[10]"Get out of here, Satan," Jesus told him. "The Scriptures say, 'Worship only the Lord God. Obey only him.'"

[11]Then Satan went away, and angels came and cared for Jesus.

[12,13]When Jesus heard that John had been arrested, he left Judea and returned home to Nazareth in Galilee; but soon he moved to Capernaum, beside the Lake of Galilee, close to Zebulun and Naphtali. [14]This fulfilled Isaiah's prophecy:

[15,16]"The land of Zebulun and the land of Naphtali, beside the Lake, and the country-side beyond the Jordan River, and Upper Galilee where so many foreigners live—there the people who sat in darkness have seen a great Light; they sat in the land of death, and the Light broke through upon them."

[17]From then on, Jesus began to preach, "Turn from sin and turn to God, for the Kingdom of Heaven is near."

[18]One day as he was walking along the beach beside the Lake of Galilee, he saw two brothers—Simon, also called Peter, and Andrew—out in a boat fishing with a net, for they were commercial fishermen.

[19]Jesus called out, "Come along with me and I will show you how to fish for the souls of men!" [20]And they left their nets at once and went with him.

[21]A little farther up the beach he saw two other brothers, James and John, sitting in a boat with

I WONDER . . .

I'm trying to understand how the Old and New Testaments relate to each other. Which one is more important?

It's not that one is more important than the other. Instead, it's a question of timing.

Imagine being seven years old and your parents sitting you down and telling you all of the rules about driving a car. Not only would you have tuned them out after about two minutes, but ten years later, when it came time to drive, you wouldn't have remembered anything they said.

Timing is everything. Wise parents have figured this out; that's why they didn't give you all their rules as soon as you could talk. They waited until you were ready so that you would want to listen, the rules would make sense to you, and you would remember what they said.

The Old Testament was given to us for several reasons. After explaining Creation, its main purpose was to point the way to God's solution for the problem of mankind's sin. In Matthew 5:21-46, we see Jesus contrasting the Old and New Testament. Romans 7:7 tells us that the Old Testament Law was good because it showed us what sin was, and thus, showed us our need for a Savior.

The Old Testament points directly to Christ as the Savior that we needed. There are dozens of verses that tell the exact place of Jesus' birth, his sinless life, his death on a cross, his resurrection, and his return. Though the Old Testament was written from about 1450–430 B.C., it predicted minute details about the life of Jesus! This also serves to prove the authority of the Scriptures.

Also, the Old Testament is what helps the New Testament make sense. In Matthew 5, the beginning of the Sermon on the Mount, Jesus points to something that people had never heard before.

The Old Testament speaks of sacrifices (picturing Jesus as the ultimate sacrifice) and having faith in God's promise. This was how God prepared the way for Christ.

their father, Zebedee, mending their nets; and he called to them to come too. [22]At once they stopped their work and, leaving their father behind, went with him.

[23]Jesus traveled all through Galilee teaching in the Jewish synagogues, everywhere preaching the Good News about the Kingdom of Heaven. And he healed every kind of sickness and disease. [24]The report of his miracles spread far beyond the borders of Galilee so that sick folk were soon coming to be healed from as far away as Syria. And whatever their illness and pain, or if they were possessed by demons, or were insane, or paralyzed—he healed

them all. [25]Enormous crowds followed him wherever he went—people from Galilee, and the Ten Cities, and Jerusalem, and from all over Judea, and even from across the Jordan River.

CHAPTER 5 THE SERMON ON THE MOUNT. One day as the crowds were gathering, he went up the hillside with his disciples and sat down and taught them there.

[3]"Humble men are very fortunate!" he told them, "for the Kingdom of Heaven is given to them. [4]Those who mourn are fortunate! for they shall be comforted. [5]The meek and lowly are fortunate! for the whole wide world belongs to them.

[6]"Happy are those who long to be just and good, for they shall be completely satisfied. [7]Happy are the kind and merciful, for they shall be shown mercy. [8]Happy are those whose hearts are pure, for they shall see God. [9]Happy are those who strive for peace—they shall be called the sons of God. [10]Happy are those who are persecuted because they are good, for the Kingdom of Heaven is theirs.

[11]"When you are reviled and persecuted and lied about because you are my followers—wonderful! [12]Be *happy* about it! Be *very glad!* for a *tremendous reward* awaits you up in heaven. And remember, the ancient prophets were persecuted too.

[13]"You are the world's seasoning, to make it tolerable. If you lose your flavor, what will happen to the world? And you yourselves will be thrown out and trampled underfoot as worthless. [14]You are the world's light—a city on a hill, glowing in the night for all to see. [15,16]Don't hide your light! Let it shine for all; let your good deeds glow for all to see, so that they will praise your heavenly Father.

[17]"Don't misunderstand why I have come—it isn't to cancel the laws of Moses and the warnings of the prophets. No, I came to fulfill them and to make them all come true. [18]With all the earnestness I have I say: Every law in the Book will continue until its purpose is achieved. [19]And so if anyone breaks the least commandment and teaches others to, he shall

STRANGE

5:3-12 Jesus began his sermon with words that seem to contradict each other. But God's way of living usually contradicts the world's. If you want to live for God, you must be ready to say and do what seems strange to the world. You must be willing to give when others take, to love when others hate, to help when others abuse. In doing this, you will one day receive everything, while the others will end up with nothing.

DANGEROUS

5:21-22 Killing is a terrible sin, but *anger* is a great sin too because it also violates God's command to love. Anger in this case refers to a seething, brooding bitterness against someone. It is a dangerous emotion that always threatens to leap out of control and lead to violence, emotional hurt, increased mental stress, and other destructive results. There is spiritual damage as well. Anger keeps us from developing a spirit pleasing to God. Have you ever been proud that you didn't strike out and say what was really on your mind? Self-control is good, but Christ wants us to practice thought-control as well. Jesus said we will be held accountable even for our attitudes.

SEVEN REASONS NOT TO WORRY

1 The same God who created life in you can be trusted with the details of your life. 6:25

2 Worrying about the future hampers your efforts for today. 6:26

3 Worrying is more harmful than helpful. 6:27

4 God does not ignore those who depend on him. 6:28-30

5 Worry shows a lack of faith and of understanding of God. 6:32

6 There are real challenges God wants us to pursue, and worrying keeps us from them. 6:33

7 Living one day at a time keeps us from being consumed with worry. 6:34

be the least in the Kingdom of Heaven. But those who teach God's laws *and obey them* shall be great in the Kingdom of Heaven.

²⁰"But I warn you—unless your goodness is greater than that of the Pharisees and other Jewish leaders, you can't get into the Kingdom of Heaven at all!

²¹"Under the laws of Moses the rule was, 'If you murder, you must die.' ²²But I have added to that rule and tell you that if you are only *angry,* even in your own home, you are in danger of judgment! If you call your friend an idiot, you are in danger of being brought before the court. And if you curse him, you are in danger of the fires of hell.

²³"So if you are standing before the altar in the Temple, offering a sacrifice to God, and suddenly remember that a friend has something against you, ²⁴leave your sacrifice there beside the altar and go and apologize and be reconciled to him, and then come and offer your sacrifice to God. ²⁵Come to terms quickly with your enemy before it is too late and he drags you into court and you are thrown into a debtor's cell, ²⁶for you will stay there until you have paid the last penny.

²⁷"The laws of Moses said, 'You shall not commit adultery.' ²⁸But I say: Anyone who even looks at a woman with lust in his eye has already committed adultery with her in his heart. ²⁹So if your eye—even if it is your best eye! —causes you to lust, gouge it out and throw it away. Better for part of you to be destroyed than for all of you to be cast into hell. ³⁰And if your hand—even your right hand—causes you to sin, cut it off and throw it away. Better that than find yourself in hell.

³¹"The law of Moses says, 'If anyone wants to be rid of his wife, he can divorce her merely by giving her a letter of dismissal.' ³²But I say that a man who divorces his wife, except for fornication, causes her to commit adultery if she marries again. And he who marries her commits adultery.

³³"Again, the law of Moses says, 'You shall not break your vows to God but must fulfill them all.' ³⁴But I say: Don't make any vows! And even to say 'By heavens!' is a sacred vow to God, for the heavens are God's throne. ³⁵And if you say 'By the earth!' it is a sacred vow, for the earth is his foot-

stool. And don't swear 'By Jerusalem!' for Jerusalem is the capital of the great King. ³⁶Don't even swear 'By my head!' for you can't turn one hair white or black. ³⁷Say just a simple 'Yes, I will' or 'No, I won't.' Your word is enough. To strengthen your promise with a vow shows that something is wrong.

³⁸"The law of Moses says, 'If a man gouges out another's eye, he must pay with his own eye. If a tooth gets knocked out, knock out the tooth of the one who did it.' ³⁹But I say: Don't resist violence! If you are slapped on one cheek, turn the other too. ⁴⁰If you are ordered to court, and your shirt is taken

"Here's what I did..."

It was during a soccer game that I got to apply Matthew 5:39, about "turning the other cheek," in a very real way.

I was captain of our soccer team. The other team was out for blood—they took cheap shots every chance they got. The refs never saw any of it; I guess people don't realize how dirty girls can play. My team started taking matters into their own hands.

One time I was passed the ball and managed to have a clear break—only one person standing in my way. But she took a cheap shot, and instead of scoring, I was injured and taken out of the game. I was angry, but I started praying about it.

By halftime the other girls on my team were really down. But I told them not to seek revenge—not to take the attitude of "an eye for an eye," but to turn the other cheek, to play fair. I told them that's what I planned to do.

I went back into the game and made sure I played clean. My team followed my example. I scored two goals late in the game and our team tied, 2–2.

The most important thing to me wasn't the score of that game, though. It was the fact that playing clean really was better. Neither resisting nor returning violence was the better way—it really is best to play clean and fair so you can hold your head high. I think the whole team learned something that day. I know I did.

Susan

AGE 16

from you, give your coat too. ⁴¹If the military demand that you carry their gear for a mile, carry it two. ⁴²Give to those who ask, and don't turn away from those who want to borrow.

⁴³"There is a saying, 'Love your *friends* and hate your enemies.' ⁴⁴But I say: Love your *enemies!* Pray for those who *persecute* you! ⁴⁵In that way you will be acting as true sons of your Father in heaven. For he gives his sunlight to both the evil and the good, and sends rain on the just and on the unjust too. ⁴⁶If you love only those who love you, what good is that? Even scoundrels do

that much. [47]If you are friendly only to your friends, how are you different from anyone else? Even the heathen do that. [48]But you are to be perfect, even as your Father in heaven is perfect.

CHAPTER 6 HELP OTHERS WITHOUT BRAGGING.

"Take care! Don't do your good deeds publicly, to be admired, for then you will lose the reward from your Father in heaven. [2]When you give a gift to a beggar, don't shout about it as the hypocrites do—blowing trumpets in the synagogues and streets to call attention to their acts of charity! I tell you in all earnestness, they have received all the reward they will ever get. [3]But when you do a kindness to someone, do it secretly—don't tell your left hand what your right hand is doing. [4]And your Father, who knows all secrets, will reward you.

[5]"And now about prayer. When you pray, don't be like the hypocrites who pretend piety by praying publicly on street corners and in the synagogues where everyone can see them. Truly, that is all the reward they will ever get. [6]But when you pray, go away by yourself, all alone, and shut the door behind you and pray to your Father secretly, and your Father, who knows your secrets, will reward you.

[7,8]"Don't recite the same prayer over and over as the heathen do, who think prayers are answered only by repeating them again and again. Remember, your Father knows exactly what you need even before you ask him!

[9]"Pray along these lines: 'Our Father in heaven, we honor your holy name. [10]We ask that your kingdom will come now. May your will be done here on earth, just as it is in heaven. [11]Give us our food again today, as usual, [12]and forgive us our sins, just as we have forgiven those who have sinned against us. [13]Don't bring us into temptation, but deliver us from the Evil One. Amen.' [14,15]Your heavenly Father will forgive you if you forgive those who sin against you; but if *you* refuse to forgive *them, he* will not forgive *you.*

[16]"And now about fasting. When you fast, declining your food for a spiritual purpose, don't do it publicly, as the hypocrites do, who try to look wan and disheveled so people will feel sorry for them. Truly, that is the only reward they will ever get. [17]But when you fast, put on festive clothing, [18]so that no one will suspect you are hungry, except

your Father who knows every secret. And he will reward you.

[19]"Don't store up treasures here on earth where they can erode away or may be stolen. [20]Store them in heaven where they will never lose their value and are safe from thieves. [21]If your profits are in heaven, your heart will be there too.

[22]"If your eye is pure, there will be sunshine in your soul. [23]But if your eye is clouded with evil thoughts and desires, you are in deep spiritual darkness. And oh, how deep that darkness can be!

[24]"You cannot serve two masters: God and money. For you will hate one and love the other, or else the other way around.

[25]"So my counsel is: Don't worry about *things*—food, drink, and clothes. For you already have life and a body—and they are far more important than what to eat and wear. [26]Look at the birds! They don't worry about what to eat—they don't need to sow or reap or store up food—for your heavenly Father feeds them. And you are far more valuable to him than they are. [27]Will all your worries add a single moment to your life?

INCANTATION

6:7-8 Some people think that repeating the same words over and over—like a magic incantation—will ensure that God will hear them. It's not wrong to come to God with the same requests—Jesus encourages *persistent* prayer. But he condemns the shallow repetition of words that are not offered with a sincere heart. We can never pray too much if our prayers are honest and sincere. Before you start to pray, make sure you mean what you say.

SUBTLE

6:13 Jesus is not implying that God leads us into temptation. He is simply asking for deliverance from Satan and his deceit. All Christians struggle with temptation. Sometimes it is so subtle that we don't even realize what is happening to us. God has promised that he won't allow us to be tempted beyond our endurance (1 Corinthians 10:13). Ask God to help you recognize temptation and to be strong enough to overcome it and choose God's way.

ALL WHO LISTEN TO MY INSTRUCTIONS AND FOLLOW THEM ARE WISE, LIKE A MAN WHO BUILDS HIS HOUSE ON SOLID ROCK

MATTHEW 7:24

²⁸"And why worry about your clothes? Look at the field lilies! They don't worry about theirs. ²⁹Yet King Solomon in all his glory was not clothed as beautifully as they. ³⁰And if God cares so wonderfully for flowers that are here today and gone tomorrow, won't he more surely care for you, O men of little faith?

³¹,³²"So don't worry at all about having enough food and clothing. Why be like the heathen? For they take pride in all these things and are deeply concerned about them. But your heavenly Father already knows perfectly well that you need them, ³³and he will give them to you if you give him first place in your life and live as he wants you to.

³⁴"So don't be anxious about tomorrow. God will take care of your tomorrow too. Live one day at a time.

CHAPTER 7 DON'T CRITICIZE OTHERS. "Don't criticize, and then you won't be criticized. ²For others will treat you as you treat them. ³And why worry about a speck in the eye of a brother when you have a board in your own? ⁴Should you say, 'Friend, let me help you get that speck out of your eye,' when you can't even see because of the board in your own? ⁵Hypocrite! First get rid of the board. Then you can see to help your brother.

⁶"Don't give holy things to depraved men. Don't give pearls to swine! They will trample the pearls and turn and attack you.

⁷"Ask, and you will be given what you ask for. Seek, and you will find. Knock, and the door will be opened. ⁸For everyone who asks, receives. Anyone who seeks, finds. If only you will knock, the door will open. ⁹If a child asks his father for a loaf of bread, will he be given a stone instead? ¹⁰If he asks for fish, will he be given a poisonous snake? Of course not! ¹¹And if you hardhearted, sinful men know how to give good gifts to your children, won't your Father in heaven even more certainly give good gifts to those who ask him for them?

¹²"Do for others what you want them to do for you. This is the teaching of the laws of Moses in a nutshell.

¹³"Heaven can be entered only through the narrow gate! The highway to hell is broad, and its gate is wide enough for all the multitudes who choose its easy way. ¹⁴But the Gateway to Life is small, and the road is narrow, and only a few ever find it.

¹⁵"Beware of false teachers who come disguised as harmless sheep, but are wolves and will tear you apart. ¹⁶You can detect them by the way they act, just as you can identify a tree by its fruit. You need never confuse grapevines with thorn bushes or figs with thistles. ¹⁷Different kinds of fruit trees can quickly be identified by examining their fruit. ¹⁸A variety that produces delicious fruit never produces an inedible kind. And a tree producing an inedible kind can't produce what is good. ¹⁹So the trees having the inedible fruit are chopped down and thrown on the fire. ²⁰Yes, the way to identify a tree or a person is by the kind of fruit produced.

For over six months I've been praying that my dad would become a Christian. Why hasn't God answered my prayer?

I WONDER . . .

You have certainly been persistent.
And you're doing exactly what Matthew 7:7-11 is talking about. You're "asking, seeking, and knocking."

God answers our prayers in three different ways: "Yes," "No," or "Wait." In our instant society, where everything happens when we want it, "Wait" answers are not the ones we're accustomed to hearing. Especially when it seems like the prayer is not being answered. Or is it?

God, in his perfect wisdom, knows the perfect time for people to respond to his call, turn from their sin, and come into a right relationship with him. If we try to manipulate circumstances apart from God's will, perhaps these people will say no instead of yes.

Perhaps there's no one in your dad's life right now who could help him grow. Maybe there are important questions still unanswered that would cause him to respond out of emotion, rather than with his will. Perhaps there are hurts or misconceptions about God and the church that still need to be worked through before he can begin to examine God's love for him.

Whatever the reason, the best thing you can do is to keep praying for him. Also, ask a Christian friend if his or her father would be able to start a friendship with your dad.

Even persistence in prayer will not always change the heart that is hard toward God. People have a will that can say no to any openings God's love may try to penetrate. Just continue your persistent prayer. Never give up.

²¹"Not all who sound religious are really godly people. They may refer to me as 'Lord,' but still won't get to heaven. For the decisive question is whether they obey my Father in heaven. ²²At the Judgment many will tell me, 'Lord, Lord, we told others about you and used your name to cast out demons and to do many other great miracles.' ²³But I will reply, 'You have never been mine. Go away, for your deeds are evil.'

²⁴"All who listen to my instructions and follow them are wise, like a man who builds his house on solid rock. ²⁵Though the rain comes in torrents, and the floods rise and the storm winds beat against his house, it won't collapse, for it is built on rock.

²⁶"But those who hear my instructions and ignore them are foolish, like a man who builds his

house on sand. [27]For when the rains and floods come, and storm winds beat against his house, it will fall with a mighty crash." [28]The crowds were amazed at Jesus' sermons, [29]for he taught as one who had great authority, and not as their Jewish leaders.

CHAPTER 8 TWO MEN BELIEVE AND ARE HEALED.

Large crowds followed Jesus as he came down the hillside.

[2]*Look! A leper is approaching. He kneels before him, worshiping. "Sir," the leper pleads, "if you want to, you can heal me."*

[3]*Jesus touches the man. "I want to," he says. "Be healed." And instantly the leprosy disappears.*

[4]*Then Jesus says to him, "Don't stop to talk to anyone; go right over to the priest to be examined; and take with you the offering required by Moses' law for lepers who are healed—a public testimony of your cure."*

[5,6]When Jesus arrived in Capernaum, a Roman army captain came and pled with him to come to his home and heal his servant boy who was in bed paralyzed and racked with pain.

[7]"Yes," Jesus said, "I will come and heal him."

[8,9]Then the officer said, "Sir, I am not worthy to have you in my home; [and it isn't necessary for you to come]. If you will only stand here and say, 'Be healed,' my servant will get well! I know, because I am under the authority of my superior officers and I have authority over my soldiers, and I say to one, 'Go,' and he goes, and to another, 'Come,' and he comes, and to my slave boy, 'Do this or that,' and he does it. And I know you have authority to tell his sickness to go—and it will go!"

[10]Jesus stood there amazed! Turning to the crowd he said, "I haven't seen faith like this in all the land of Israel! [11]And I tell you this, that many Gentiles [like this Roman officer], shall come from all over the world and sit down in the Kingdom of Heaven with Abraham, Isaac, and Jacob. [12]And many an Israelite—those for whom the Kingdom was prepared—shall be cast into outer darkness, into the place of weeping and torment."

[13]Then Jesus said to the Roman officer, "Go on home. What you have believed has happened!" And the boy was healed that same hour!

[14]When Jesus arrived at Peter's house, Peter's mother-in-law was in bed with a high fever. [15]But when Jesus touched her hand, the fever left her; and she got up and prepared a meal for them!

[16]That evening several demon-possessed people were brought to Jesus; and when he spoke a single word, all the demons fled; and all the sick were healed. [17]This fulfilled the prophecy of Isaiah, "He took our sicknesses and bore our diseases."

[18]When Jesus noticed how large the crowd was growing, he instructed his disciples to get ready to cross to the other side of the lake.

[19]Just then one of the Jewish religious teachers said to him, "Teacher, I will follow you no matter where you go!"

[20]But Jesus said, "Foxes have dens and birds have nests, but I, the Messiah, have no home of my own—no place to lay my head."

[21]Another of his disciples said, "Sir, when my father is dead, then I will follow you."

[22]But Jesus told him, "Follow me *now!* Let those who are spiritually dead care for their own dead."

[23]Then he got into a boat and started across the lake with his disciples. [24]Suddenly a terrible storm came up, with waves higher than the boat. But Jesus was asleep.

[25]The disciples went to him and wakened him, shouting, "Lord, save us! We're sinking!"

[26]But Jesus answered, "O you men of little faith! Why are you so frightened?" Then he stood up and rebuked the wind and waves, and the storm subsided and all was calm. [27]The disciples just sat there, awed! "Who is this," they asked themselves, "that even the winds and the sea obey him?"

[28]When they arrived on the other side of the lake, in the country of the Gadarenes, two men with demons in them met him. They lived in a cemetery and were so dangerous that no one could go through that area.

[29]They began screaming at him, "What do you want with us, O Son of God? You have no right to torment us yet."

[30]A herd of pigs was feeding in the distance, [31]so the demons begged, "If you cast us out, send us into that herd of pigs."

[32]"All right," Jesus told them. "Begone."

And they came out of the men and entered the pigs, and the whole herd rushed over a cliff and drowned in the water below. [33]The herdsmen fled

HABITS

8:10-12 Jesus told the crowd that many religious Jews who should be in the Kingdom would be excluded because of their lack of faith. They were so entrenched in their religious traditions that they could not accept Christ and his new message. We must be careful not to become so set in our religious habits that we expect God to work only in specified ways.

ROUGH ROAD

8:19-20 Following Jesus is not always an easy or comfortable road. Often it means great cost and sacrifice, with no earthly rewards or security. Jesus didn't have a place to call home. You may find that following Christ costs you popularity, friendships, leisure time, or treasured habits. But while the costs of following Christ may be high, the value of being Christ's disciple is an investment that lasts for eternity and yields incredible rewards.

to the nearest city with the story of what had happened, [34] and the entire population came rushing out to see Jesus and begged him to go away and leave them alone.

CHAPTER 9 JESUS HEALS A PARALYZED MAN. So Jesus climbed into a boat and went across the lake to Capernaum, his hometown.

[2] Soon some men brought him a paralyzed boy on a mat. When Jesus saw their faith, he said to the sick boy, "Cheer up, son! For I have forgiven your sins!"

[3] "Blasphemy! This man is saying he is God!" exclaimed some of the religious leaders to themselves.

[4] Jesus knew what they were thinking and asked them, "Why are you thinking such evil thoughts? [5,6] I, the Messiah, have the authority on earth to forgive sins. But talk is cheap—anybody could say that. So I'll prove it to you by healing this man." Then, turning to the paralyzed man, he commanded, "Pick up your stretcher and go on home, for you are healed."

[7] And the boy jumped up and left!

[8] A chill of fear swept through the crowd as they saw this happen right before their eyes. How they praised God for giving such authority to a man!

[9] As Jesus was going on down the road, he saw a tax collector, Matthew, sitting at a tax collection booth. "Come and be my disciple," Jesus said to him, and Matthew jumped up and went along with him.

[10] Later, as Jesus and his disciples were eating dinner [at Matthew's house], there were many notorious swindlers there as guests!

[11] The Pharisees were indignant. "Why does your teacher associate with men like that?"

[12] "Because people who are well don't need a doctor! It's the sick people who do!" was Jesus' reply. [13] Then he added, "Now go away and learn the meaning of this verse of Scripture,

'It isn't your sacrifices and your gifts I want—I want you to be merciful.'

For I have come to urge sinners, not the self-righteous, back to God."

[14] One day the disciples of John the Baptist came to Jesus and asked him, "Why don't your disciples fast as we do and as the Pharisees do?"

[15] "Should the bridegroom's friends mourn and go without food while he is with them?" Jesus asked. "But the time is coming when I will be taken from them. Time enough then for them to refuse to eat.

[16] "And who would patch an old garment with unshrunk cloth? For the patch would tear away and make the hole worse. [17] And who would use old wineskins to store new wine? For the old skins would burst with the pressure, and the wine would be spilled and skins ruined. Only new wineskins are used to store new wine. That way both are preserved."

[18] As he was saying this, the rabbi of the local synagogue came and worshiped him. "My little daughter has just died," he said, "but you can bring her back to life again if you will only come and touch her."

[19] As Jesus and the disciples were going to the rabbi's home, [20] a woman who had been sick for twelve years with internal bleeding came up behind him and touched a tassel of his robe, [21] for she thought, "If I only touch him, I will be healed."

[22] Jesus turned around and spoke to her. "Daughter," he said, "all is well! Your faith has healed you." And the woman was well from that moment.

[23] When Jesus arrived at the rabbi's home and

LOW LIFE

9:11-12 The Pharisees constantly tried to trap Jesus, and they thought his association with these "low lifes" was the perfect opportunity. They were more concerned with criticism than encouragement, with their own appearance of holiness than in helping people, with outward respectability than practical help. But God is concerned for all people, including the sinful and hurting ones. The Christian life is not a popularity contest! We need to follow Jesus' example and share the Good News with the poor, lonely, and outcast—not just the good, talented, and popular.

"Here's what I did..."

I used to struggle a lot with doubt. Was God real? Did he really care about what happens to me? Is the Bible relevant? Then someone challenged me to actively try to apply a passage from the Bible every day for two weeks and see if that made any difference. I did. I read some of the Psalms and found that they were wonderfully relevant. When I felt lonely and had no one to turn to, I found that David's words perfectly expressed my feelings. Another passage I came across reminded me that God has promised never to leave us. Then when I came across Jesus' words in Matthew 7:24-27, I realized that it's only through obeying and applying God's Word that we know he's real. His Word is the only solid thing we have to build our lives on. The Matthew passage, and my two-week experiment, motivated me to try to live out what I read more and more every day.

Laura

AGE 17

9:27-30 Jesus didn't respond immediately to the blind men's pleas. He waited to see how earnest they were. Not everyone who says he or she wants help really wants it badly enough to do something about it. Jesus may have waited and questioned these men to make their desire and faith stronger. If, in your prayers, it seems as if God is too slow in giving his answer, maybe he is testing you as he did the blind men. Do you believe God can help you? Do you *really* want his help?

saw the noisy crowds and heard the funeral music, ²⁴he said, "Get them out, for the little girl isn't dead; she is only sleeping!" Then how they all scoffed and sneered at him!

²⁵When the crowd was finally outside, Jesus went in where the little girl was lying and took her by the hand, and she jumped up and was all right again! ²⁶The report of this wonderful miracle swept the entire countryside.

²⁷As Jesus was leaving her home, two blind men followed along behind, shouting, "O Son of King David, have mercy on us."

²⁸They went right into the house where he was staying, and Jesus asked them, "Do you believe I can make you see?"

"Yes, Lord," they told him, "we do."

²⁹Then he touched their eyes and said, "Because of your faith it will happen."

³⁰And suddenly they could see! Jesus sternly warned them not to tell anyone about it, ³¹but instead they spread his fame all over the town.

³²Leaving that place, Jesus met a man who couldn't speak because a demon was inside him. ³³So Jesus cast out the demon, and instantly the man could talk. How the crowds marveled! "Never in all our lives have we seen anything like this," they exclaimed.

³⁴But the Pharisees said, "The reason he can cast out demons is that he is demon-possessed himself—possessed by Satan, the demon king!"

³⁵Jesus traveled around through all the cities and villages of that area, teaching in the Jewish synagogues and announcing the Good News about the Kingdom. And wherever he went he healed people of every sort of illness. ³⁶And what pity he felt for the crowds that came, because their problems were so great and they didn't know what to do or where to go for help. They were like sheep without a shepherd.

³⁷"The harvest is so great, and the workers are so few," he told his disciples. ³⁸"So pray to the one in charge of the harvesting, and ask him to recruit more workers for his harvest fields."

CHAPTER 10 JESUS SENDS OUT THE DISCIPLES. Jesus called his twelve disciples to him and gave them authority to cast out evil spirits and to heal every kind of sickness and disease.

²⁻⁴Here are the names of his twelve disciples:

Simon (also called Peter), Andrew (Peter's brother), James (Zebedee's son), John (James' brother), Philip, Bartholomew, Thomas, Matthew (the tax collector), James (Alphaeus' son), Thaddaeus, Simon (a member of "The Zealots," a subversive political party), Judas Iscariot (the one who betrayed him).

⁵Jesus sent them out with these instructions: "Don't go to the Gentiles or the Samaritans, ⁶but only to the people of Israel—God's lost sheep. ⁷Go and announce to them that the Kingdom of Heaven is near. ⁸Heal the sick, raise the dead, cure the lepers, and cast out demons. Give as freely as you have received!

⁹"Don't take any money with you; ¹⁰don't even carry a duffle bag with extra clothes and shoes, or even a walking stick; for those you help should feed and care for you. ¹¹Whenever you enter a city or village, search for a godly man and stay in his home until you leave for the next town. ¹²When you ask permission to stay, be friendly, ¹³and if it turns out to be a godly home, give it your blessing; if not, keep the blessing. ¹⁴Any city or home that doesn't welcome you—shake off the dust of that place from your feet as you leave. ¹⁵Truly, the wicked cities of Sodom and Gomorrah will be better off at Judgment Day than they.

¹⁶"I am sending you out as sheep among wolves. Be as wary as serpents and harmless as doves. ¹⁷But beware! For you will be arrested and tried, and whipped in the synagogues. ¹⁸Yes, and you must stand trial before governors and kings for my sake. This will give you the opportunity to tell them about me, yes, to witness to the world.

¹⁹"When you are arrested, don't worry about what to say at your trial, for you will be given the right words at the right time. ²⁰For it won't be you doing the talking—it will be the Spirit of your heavenly Father speaking through you!

²¹"Brother shall betray brother to death, and fathers shall betray their own children. And children shall rise against their parents and cause their deaths. ²²Everyone shall hate you because you belong to me. But all of you who endure to the end shall be saved.

²³"When you are persecuted in one city, flee to

10:29-31 Jesus said that God cares for the sparrows' every need. We are far more valuable to God than these little birds, so valuable that God sent his only Son to die for us (John 3:16). You are of great worth to God. Because he places such value on you, you need never fear personal threats or difficult trials.

But don't think that because you are valuable to God he will take away all your troubles (see 10:16). The real test of value is how well something holds up under the wear, tear, and abuse of everyday life. Those who stand up for Christ in spite of their troubles truly have lasting value and will receive great rewards (see 5:11-12).

the next! I will return before you have reached them all!

²⁴"A student is not greater than his teacher. A servant is not above his master. ²⁵The student shares his teacher's fate. The servant shares his master's! And since I, the master of the household, have been called 'Satan,' how much more will you! ²⁶But don't be afraid of those who threaten you. For the time is coming when the truth will be revealed: their secret plots will become public information.

²⁷"What I tell you now in the gloom, shout abroad when daybreak comes. What I whisper in your ears, proclaim from the housetops!

²⁸"Don't be afraid of those who can kill only your bodies—but can't touch your souls! Fear only God who can destroy both soul and body in hell. ²⁹Not one sparrow (What do they cost? Two for a penny?) can fall to the ground without your Father knowing it. ³⁰And the very hairs of your head are all numbered. ³¹So don't worry! You are more valuable to him than many sparrows.

³²"If anyone publicly acknowledges me as his friend, I will openly acknowledge him as my friend before my Father in heaven. ³³But if anyone publicly denies me, I will openly deny him before my Father in heaven.

³⁴"Don't imagine that I came to bring peace to the earth! No, rather, a sword. ³⁵I have come to set a man against his father, and a daughter against her mother, and a daughter-in-law against her mother-in-law— ³⁶a man's worst enemies will be right in his own home! ³⁷If you love your father and mother more than you love me, you are not worthy of being mine; or if you love your son or daughter more than me, you are not worthy of being mine. ³⁸If you refuse to take up your cross and follow me, you are not worthy of being mine.

³⁹"If you cling to your life, you will lose it; but if you give it up for me, you will save it.

⁴⁰"Those who welcome you are welcoming me. And when they welcome me they are welcoming God who sent me. ⁴¹If you welcome a prophet because he is a man of God, you will be given the same reward a prophet gets. And if you welcome good and godly men because of their godliness, you will be given a reward like theirs.

⁴²"And if, as my representatives, you give even a cup of cold water to a little child, you will surely be rewarded."

CHAPTER 11 JOHN'S QUESTIONS ABOUT JESUS.
When Jesus had finished giving these instructions to his twelve disciples, he went off preaching in the cities where they were scheduled to go.

²John the Baptist, who was now in prison, heard about all the miracles the Messiah was doing, so he sent his disciples to ask Jesus, ³"Are you really the one we are waiting for, or shall we keep on looking?"

⁴Jesus told them, "Go back to John and tell him about the miracles you've seen me do— ⁵the blind people I've healed, and the lame people now walking without help, and the cured lepers, and the deaf

---

My parents are quietly putting up with my new faith. Mom thinks it's "nice" and Dad won't talk to me about it. How do I make them see Jesus is a real person?

I WONDER . . .

There are many difficult sayings of Jesus' in the New Testament. Matthew 10:34-39 is one of the toughest. What does Jesus mean when he says "a man's worst enemies will be right in his own home"?

If you have faced pressure and opposition from friends because of your new faith, you realize that your decision for Christ causes people to make decisions about you. Some will stay with you and support your decision because they are your true friends. Others will leave because they don't understand or because your values no longer encourage their life-style.

We also may find opposition at home. In these verses, Jesus is not telling us to be disobedient to our parents or to try to cause problems at home. He is just stating the fact that a person with different goals, values, purposes, perhaps even morals, may cause division. This is more than a fact, it is a promise! Rarely will the only Christian in a household go unchallenged.

Though it is uncommon for parents to be openly hostile toward someone in their home, it does happen. Put-downs can really hurt, especially if they come from someone you love.

The best course of action is to not try to make your parents see anything. Instead, just live your life in obedience to them as the Bible commands: "Children, obey your parents; this is the right thing to do because God has placed them in authority over you. Honor your father and mother. This is the first of God's Ten Commandments that ends with a promise. And this is the promise: that if you honor your father and mother, yours will be a long life, full of blessing" (Ephesians 6:1-3).

It is not your role or responsibility to make them change. That is the job of the Holy Spirit: "And when he has come he will convince the world of its sin, and of the availability of God's goodness, and of deliverance from judgment" (John 16:8). You are to be God's representative in your home, hopefully to be a part of bringing your family to Christ.

Don't neglect your family because it does not yet accept your faith. But don't neglect the higher mission of keeping God as your number-one priority either.

Find some Christian friends who will pray for you and pray with you about your situation. Go to them for encouragement and when you need advice on how to respond as each difficult situation arises.

who hear, and the dead raised to life; and tell him about my preaching the Good News to the poor. [6]Then give him this message, 'Blessed are those who don't doubt me.'"

[7]When John's disciples had gone, Jesus began talking about him to the crowds. "When you went out into the barren wilderness to see John, what did you expect him to be like? Grass blowing in the wind? [8]Or were you expecting to see a man dressed as a prince in a palace? [9]Or a prophet of God? Yes, and he is more than just a prophet. [10]For John is the man mentioned in the Scriptures—a messenger to precede me, to announce my coming, and prepare people to receive me.

[11]"Truly, of all men ever born, none shines more brightly than John the Baptist. And yet, even the lesser lights in the Kingdom of Heaven will be greater than he is! [12]And from the time John the Baptist began preaching and baptizing until now, ardent multitudes have been crowding toward the Kingdom of Heaven, [13]for all the laws and prophets looked forward [to the Messiah]. Then John appeared, [14]and if you are willing to understand what I mean, he is Elijah, the one the prophets said would come [at the time the Kingdom begins]. [15]If ever you were willing to listen, listen now!

[16]"What shall I say about this nation? These people are like children playing, who say to their little friends, [17]'We played wedding and you weren't happy, so we played funeral but you weren't sad.' [18]For John the Baptist doesn't even drink wine and often goes without food, and you say, 'He's crazy.' [19]And I, the Mes-

siah, feast and drink, and you complain that I am 'a glutton and a drinking man, and hang around with the worst sort of sinners!' But brilliant men like you can justify your every inconsistency!"

[20]Then he began to pour out his denunciations against the cities where he had done most of his miracles, because they hadn't turned to God.

[21]"Woe to you, Chorazin, and woe to you, Bethsaida! For if the miracles I did in your streets had been done in wicked Tyre and Sidon their people would have repented long ago in shame and humility. [22]Truly, Tyre and Sidon will be better off on the Judgment Day than you! [23]And Capernaum, though highly honored, shall go down to hell! For if the marvelous miracles I did in you had been done in Sodom, it would still be here today. [24]Truly, Sodom will be better off at the Judgment Day than you."

[25]And Jesus prayed this prayer: "O Father, Lord of heaven and earth, thank you for hiding the truth from those who think themselves so wise, and for revealing it to little children. [26]Yes, Father, for it pleased you to do it this way! . . .

[27]"Everything has been entrusted to me by my Father. Only the Father knows the Son, and the Father is known only by the Son and by those to whom the Son reveals him. [28]Come to me and I will give you rest—all of you who work so hard beneath a heavy yoke. [29,30]Wear my yoke—for it fits perfectly—and let me teach you; for I am gentle and humble, and you shall find rest for your souls; for I give you only light burdens."

CHAPTER **12** JESUS TALKS ABOUT THE SABBATH. About that time, Jesus was walking one day through some grainfields with his disciples. It was on the Sabbath, the Jewish day of worship, and his disciples were hungry; so they began breaking off heads of wheat and eating the grain.

[2]But some Pharisees saw them do it and protested, "Your disciples are breaking the law. They are harvesting on the Sabbath."

[3]But Jesus said to them, "Haven't you ever read what King David did when he and his friends were hungry? [4]He went into the Temple and they ate the

MOUTH

Mrs. Rogers puts the groceries in the trunk, buckles four-year-old Richie in his seat, and heads for home.

Soon Richie is holding his plastic airplane out the open window, watching its propeller spin. Mrs. Rogers notices what Richie is up to. "Don't do that. Keep your hands—and your toys—inside the car!" Richie smiles and slowly obeys.

But soon the hand-held plane banks to the right—back out the window.

"Richie!" Mrs. Rogers screams. "I told you, 'No!'"

Startled, the little boy drops the plane and lets fly with a word that four-year-old boys have no business knowing. Mrs. Rogers is shocked. "Richie! Where did you learn that word?"

"From Christi."

"What other words have you heard her say?"

Richie rolls off words that would make a sailor blush.

When Mrs. Rogers gets home, she marches into her 16-year-old daughter's bedroom. "Christie, Richie used some horrible language in the car today . . . and he said he learned it from you. You want to explain?"

"Gee, Mom," Christi responds nervously. "No way. Not me. I don't know why he would say something like that."

Obviously Christi is caught up in lying as well as profanity. She needs to read Matthew 12:33-37.

DOUBTS

11:4-6 As John sat in prison, he felt some doubts about whether Jesus really was the Messiah. If John's purpose was to prepare people for the coming Messiah (3:3), and if Jesus really was that Messiah, then why was John in prison instead of preaching to the crowds, preparing their hearts?

Jesus answered John's doubts by pointing to his acts of healing, his curing the lepers, raising the dead, and preaching the Good News. With so much evidence, Jesus' identity was obvious. If you sometimes doubt your salvation, the forgiveness of your sins, or God's work in your life, look at the evidence in Scripture and in your life. When you doubt, don't turn away from Christ, turn *to* him.

special bread permitted to the priests alone. That was breaking the law too. ⁵And haven't you ever read in the law of Moses how the priests on duty in the Temple may work on the Sabbath? ⁶And truly, one is here who is greater than the Temple! ⁷But if you had known the meaning of this Scripture verse, 'I want you to be merciful more than I want your offerings,' you would not have condemned those who aren't guilty! ⁸For I, the Messiah, am master even of the Sabbath."

⁹Then he went over to the synagogue ¹⁰and noticed there a man with a deformed hand. The Pharisees asked Jesus, "Is it legal to work by healing on the Sabbath day?" (They were, of course, hoping he would say yes, so they could arrest him!) ¹¹This was his answer: "If you had just one sheep, and it fell into a well on the Sabbath, would you work to rescue it that day? Of course you would. ¹²And how much more valuable is a person than a sheep! Yes, it is right to do good on the Sabbath." ¹³Then he said to the man, "Stretch out your arm." And as he did, his hand became normal, just like the other one!

¹⁴Then the Pharisees called a meeting to plot Jesus' arrest and death.

¹⁵But he knew what they were planning and left the synagogue, with many following him. He healed all the sick among them, ¹⁶but he cautioned them against spreading the news about his miracles. ¹⁷This fulfilled the prophecy of Isaiah concerning him:

¹⁸"Look at my Servant.
See my Chosen One.
He is my Beloved, in whom my soul
      delights.
I will put my Spirit upon him,
And he will judge the nations.
¹⁹He does not fight nor shout;
He does not raise his voice!
²⁰He does not crush the weak,
Or quench the smallest hope;
He will end all conflict with his final
      victory,
²¹And his name shall be the hope
Of all the world."

²²Then a demon-possessed man—he was both blind and unable to talk—was brought to Jesus, and Jesus healed him so that he could both speak and see. ²³The crowd was amazed. "Maybe Jesus is the Messiah!" they exclaimed.

²⁴But when the Pharisees heard about the miracle they said, "He can cast out demons because he is Satan, king of devils."

²⁵Jesus knew their thoughts and replied, "A divided kingdom ends in ruin. A city or home divided against itself cannot stand. ²⁶And if Satan is casting out Satan, he is fighting himself and destroying his own kingdom. ²⁷And if, as you claim, I am casting out demons by invoking the powers of Satan, then what power do your own people use when they cast them out? Let them answer your accusation! ²⁸But if I am casting out demons by the Spirit of God, then the Kingdom of God has arrived among you. ²⁹One cannot rob Satan's kingdom without first binding Satan. Only then can his demons be cast out! ³⁰Anyone who isn't helping me is harming me.

³¹,³²"Even blasphemy against me or any other sin can be forgiven—all except one: speaking against the Holy Spirit shall never be forgiven, either in this world or in the world to come.

³³"A tree is identified by its fruit. A tree from a select variety produces good fruit; poor varieties don't. ³⁴You brood of snakes! How could evil men like you speak what is good and right? For a man's heart determines his speech. ³⁵A good man's speech reveals the rich treasures within him. An evil-hearted man is filled with venom, and his speech reveals it. ³⁶And I tell you this, that you must give account on Judgment Day for every idle word you speak. ³⁷Your words now reflect your fate then: either you will be justified by them or you will be condemned."

³⁸One day some of the Jewish leaders, including some Pharisees, came to Jesus asking him to show them a miracle.

³⁹,⁴⁰But Jesus replied, "Only an evil, faithless nation would ask for further proof; and none will be given except what happened to Jonah the prophet! For as Jonah was in the great fish for three days and three nights, so I, the Messiah, shall be in the heart of the earth three days and three nights. ⁴¹The men of Nineveh shall arise against this nation at the judgment and condemn you. For when Jonah preached to them, they repented and turned to God from all their evil ways. And now a greater than Jonah is here—and you refuse to believe him. ⁴²The Queen of Sheba shall rise against this nation in the judgment and condemn it; for she came from a distant land to hear the wisdom of Solomon; and now a greater than Solomon

EVIDENCE

12:38-40 The Pharisees were asking for another miracle, but they were not sincerely seeking to know Jesus. Jesus knew that they had already seen enough miracles to prove he was the Messiah. They just had to open their hearts. But the Pharisees had already decided not to believe in Jesus; more miracles would not change that.

Many people have thought, *If I could just see a real miracle, then I could really believe in God.* But Jesus' response to the Pharisees applies to us also. We have plenty of evidence—Jesus' death, resurrection, and ascension, plus centuries of his work in the lives of believers around the world. Instead of looking for additional evidence or miracles, accept what God has already given and move forward. He may use your life as evidence to reach another person.

SOWING

13:8 This parable should encourage spiritual "farmers"—those who teach, preach, and lead others. The farmer sowed good seed, but not all of his sowing brought high yield. Some seed did not sprout, and even the plants that grew had varying yields. Don't be discouraged if no one seems to be listening to you as you faithfully teach the Word. Belief cannot be forced to follow a mathematical formula. Rather, it is a miracle of God's Holy Spirit as he uses your words to move others to come to him.

is here—and you refuse to believe him.

43-45"This evil nation is like a man possessed by a demon. For if the demon leaves, it goes into the deserts for a while, seeking rest but finding none. Then it says, 'I will return to the man I came from.' So it returns and finds the man's heart clean but empty! Then the demon finds seven other spirits more evil than itself, and all enter the man and live in him. And so he is worse off than before."

46,47As Jesus was speaking in a crowded house his mother and brothers were outside, wanting to talk with him. When someone told him they were there, 48he remarked, "Who is my mother? Who are my brothers?" 49He pointed to his disciples. "Look!" he said, "these are my mother and brothers." 50Then he added, "Anyone who obeys my Father in heaven is my brother, sister, and mother!"

CHAPTER 13 A STORY ABOUT A FARMER. Later

that same day, Jesus left the house and went down to the shore, 2,3where an immense crowd soon gathered. He got into a boat and taught from it while the people listened on the beach. He used many illustrations such as this one in his sermon:

"A farmer was sowing grain in his fields. 4As he scattered the seed across the ground, some fell beside a path, and the birds came and ate it. 5And some fell on rocky soil where there was little depth of earth; the plants sprang up quickly enough in the shallow soil, 6but the hot sun soon scorched them and they withered and died, for they had so little root. 7Other seeds fell among thorns, and the thorns choked out the tender blades. 8But some fell on good soil and produced a crop that was thirty, sixty, and even a hundred times as much as he had planted. 9If you have ears, listen!"

10His disciples came and asked him, "Why do you always use these hard-to-understand illustrations?"

11Then he explained to them that only they were permitted to understand about the Kingdom of Heaven, and others were not.

12,13"For to him who has will more be given," he told them, "and he will have great plenty; but from him who has not, even the little he has will be taken away. That is why I use these illustrations, so people will hear and see but not understand.

14"This fulfills the prophecy of Isaiah:

'They hear, but don't understand; they look, but don't see! 15For their hearts are fat and heavy, and their ears are dull, and they have closed their eyes in sleep, 16so they won't see and hear and understand and turn to God again, and let me heal them.'

But blessed are your eyes, for they see; and your ears, for they hear. 17Many a prophet and godly man has longed to see what you have seen and hear what you have heard, but couldn't.

18"Now here is the explanation of the story I told about the farmer planting grain: 19The hard path where some of the seeds fell represents the heart of a person who hears the Good News about the Kingdom and doesn't understand it; then Satan comes and snatches away the seeds from his heart. 20The shallow, rocky soil represents the heart of a man who hears the message and receives it with real joy, 21but he doesn't have much depth in his life, and the seeds don't root very deeply, and after a while when trouble comes, or persecution begins because of his beliefs, his enthusiasm fades, and he drops out. 22The ground covered with thistles represents a man who hears the message, but the cares of this life and his longing for money choke out God's Word, and he does less and less for God. 23The good ground represents the heart of a man who listens to the message and understands it and goes out and brings thirty, sixty, or even a hundred others into the Kingdom."

24Here is another illustration Jesus used: "The Kingdom of Heaven is like a farmer sowing good seed in his field; 25but one night as he slept, his enemy came and sowed thistles among the wheat. 26When the crop began to grow, the thistles grew too.

27"The farmer's men came and told him, 'Sir, the field where you planted that choice seed is full of thistles!'

28"'An enemy has done it,' he exclaimed.

"'Shall we pull out the thistles?' they asked.

29"'No,' he replied. 'You'll hurt the wheat if you do. 30Let both grow together until the harvest, and I will tell the reapers to sort out the thistles and burn them, and put the wheat in the barn.'"

31,32Here is another of his illustrations: "The Kingdom of Heaven is like a tiny mustard seed planted in a field. It is the smallest of all seeds but becomes the largest of plants, and grows into a tree where birds can come and find shelter."

SOILS

13:23 The four types of soil represent the different responses we can have to God's message. We respond differently because we are in different states of readiness. Some people are hardened, others are shallow, others are contaminated by distracting cares, and some are receptive. How has God's Word taken root in your life? What kind of soil are you?

³³He also used this example:

"The Kingdom of Heaven can be compared to a woman making bread. She takes a measure of flour and mixes in the yeast until it permeates every part of the dough."

^{34,35}Jesus constantly used these illustrations when speaking to the crowds. In fact, because the prophets said that he would use so many, he never spoke to them without at least one illustration. For it had been prophesied, "I will talk in parables; I will explain mysteries hidden since the beginning of time."

³⁶Then, leaving the crowds outside, he went into the house. His disciples asked him to explain to them the illustration of the thistles and the wheat.

³⁷"All right," he said, "I am the farmer who sows the choice seed. ³⁸The field is the world, and the seed represents the people of the Kingdom; the thistles are the people belonging to Satan. ³⁹The enemy who sowed the thistles among the wheat is the devil; the harvest is the end of the world, and the reapers are the angels.

⁴⁰"Just as in this story the thistles are separated and burned, so shall it be at the end of the world: ⁴¹I will send my angels, and they will separate out of the Kingdom every temptation and all who are evil, ⁴²and throw them into the furnace and burn them. There shall be weeping and gnashing of teeth. ⁴³Then the godly shall shine as the sun in their Father's Kingdom. Let those with ears, listen!

⁴⁴"The Kingdom of Heaven is like a treasure a man discovered in a field. In his excitement, he sold everything he owned to get enough money to buy the field—and get the treasure, too!

⁴⁵"Again, the Kingdom of Heaven is like a pearl merchant on the lookout for choice pearls. ⁴⁶He discovered a real bargain—a pearl of great value—and sold everything he owned to purchase it!

^{47,48}"Again, the Kingdom of Heaven can be illustrated by a fisherman—he casts a net into the water and gathers in fish of every kind, valuable and worthless. When the net is full, he drags it up onto the beach and sits down and sorts out the edible ones into crates and throws the others away. ⁴⁹That is the way it will be at the end of the world—the angels will come and separate the wicked people from the godly, ⁵⁰casting the wicked into the fire; there shall be weeping and gnashing of teeth. ⁵¹Do you understand?"

"Yes," they said, "we do."

⁵²Then he added, "Those experts in Jewish law who are now my disciples have double treasures—from the Old Testament as well as from the New!"

^{53,54}When Jesus had finished giving these illustrations, he returned to his hometown, Nazareth in Galilee, and taught there in the synagogue and astonished everyone with his wisdom and his miracles.

⁵⁵"How is this possible?" the people exclaimed.

"He's just a carpenter's son, and we know Mary his mother and his brothers—James, Joseph, Simon, and Judas. ⁵⁶And his sisters—they all live here. How can he be so great?" ⁵⁷And they became angry with him!

Then Jesus told them, "A prophet is honored everywhere except in his own country, and among his own people!" ⁵⁸And so he did only a few great miracles there, because of their unbelief.

CHAPTER 14   HEROD KILLS JOHN THE BAPTIST.

When King Herod heard about Jesus, ²he said to his men, "This must be John the Baptist, come back to life again. That is why he can do these miracles." ³For Herod had arrested John and chained him in prison at the demand of his wife Herodias, his brother Philip's ex-wife, ⁴because John had told him it was wrong for him to marry her. ⁵He would have killed John but was afraid of a riot, for all the people believed John was a prophet.

⁶But at a birthday party for Herod, Herodias' daughter performed a dance that greatly pleased him, ⁷so he vowed to give her anything she wanted. ⁸Consequently, at her mother's urging, the girl asked for John the Baptist's head on a tray.

⁹The king was grieved, but because of his oath, and because he didn't want to back down in front of his guests, he issued the necessary orders.

¹⁰So John was beheaded in the prison, ¹¹and his head was brought on a tray and given to the girl, who took it to her mother.

¹²Then John's disciples came for his body and buried it, and came to tell Jesus what had happened.

¹³As soon as Jesus heard the news, he went off by himself in a boat to a remote area to be alone. But the crowds saw where he was headed and followed by land from many villages.

¹⁴So when Jesus came out of the wilderness, a vast crowd was waiting for him, and he pitied them and healed their sick.

¹⁵That evening the disciples came to him and said, "It is already past time for supper, and there is nothing to eat here in the desert; send the crowds away so they can go to the villages and buy some food."

¹⁶But Jesus replied, "That isn't necessary—you feed them!"

¹⁷"What!" they exclaimed. "We have exactly five small loaves of bread and two fish!"

¹⁸"Bring them here," he said.

GIVING IN

14:9 Herod did not want to kill John the Baptist, but he gave the order so he wouldn't be embarrassed in front of his guests. How easy it is to give in to crowd pressure, to let ourselves be coerced into doing wrong. Don't place yourself in a position where it is too embarrassing to do what is right. Do what is right no matter how embarrassing or painful it may be.

EYES

14:28 Peter was not testing Jesus, something we are told not to do (4:7). Instead he was the only one in the boat to react in faith. His impulsive request led him to experience a rather unusual demonstration of God's power. Peter started to sink because he took his eyes off Jesus and focused on the high waves around him. His faith wavered when he realized what he was doing. We may not walk on water, but we do walk through tough situations. If we focus on the waves of difficult circumstances around us without looking to Christ for help, we too may despair and sink. To maintain your faith in the midst of difficult situations, keep your eyes on Christ's power rather than on your inadequacies.

[19]Then he told the people to sit down on the grass; and he took the five loaves and two fish, looked up into the sky, and asked God's blessing on the meal, then broke the loaves apart and gave them to the disciples to place before the people. [20]And everyone ate until full! And when the scraps were picked up afterwards, there were twelve basketfuls left over! [21](About five thousand men were in the crowd that day, besides all the women and children.)

[22]Immediately after this, Jesus told his disciples to get into their boat and cross to the other side of the lake while he stayed to get the people started home.

[23,24]Then afterwards he went up into the hills to pray. Night fell, and out on the lake the disciples were in trouble. For the wind had risen and they were fighting heavy seas.

[25]About four o'clock in the morning Jesus came to them, walking on the water! [26]They screamed in terror, for they thought he was a ghost.

[27]But Jesus immediately spoke to them, reassuring them. "Don't be afraid!" he said.

[28]Then Peter called to him: "Sir, if it is really you, tell me to come over to you, walking on the water."

[29]"All right," the Lord said, "come along!"

So Peter went over the side of the boat and walked on the water toward Jesus. [30]But when he looked around at the high waves, he was terrified and began to sink. "Save me, Lord!" he shouted.

[31]Instantly Jesus reached out his hand and rescued him. "O man of little faith," Jesus said. "Why did you doubt me?" [32]And when they had climbed back into the boat, the wind stopped.

[33]The others sat there, awestruck. "You really are the Son of God!" they exclaimed.

[34]They landed at Gennesaret. [35]The news of their arrival spread quickly throughout the city, and soon people were rushing around, telling everyone to bring in their sick to be healed. [36]The sick begged him to let them touch even the tassel of his robe, and all who did were healed.

CHAPTER 15 THE RULES THAT COUNT. Some Pharisees and other Jewish leaders now arrived from Jerusalem to interview Jesus.

[2]"Why do your disciples disobey the ancient Jewish traditions?" they demanded. "For they ignore our ritual of ceremonial handwashing before they eat." [3]He replied, "And why do your traditions violate the direct commandments of God? [4]For instance, God's law is 'Honor your father and mother; anyone who reviles his parents must die.' [5,6]But you say, 'Even if your parents are in need, you may give their support money to the church instead.' And so, by your man-made rule, you nullify the direct command of God to honor and care for your parents. [7]You hypocrites! Well did Isaiah prophesy of you, [8]'These people say they honor me, but their hearts are far away. [9]Their worship is worthless, for they teach their man-made laws instead of those from God.'"

[10]Then Jesus called to the crowds and said, "Listen to what I say and try to understand: [11]You aren't made unholy by eating nonkosher food! It is what you *say* and *think* that makes you unclean."

[12]Then the disciples came and told him, "You offended the Pharisees by that remark."

[13,14]Jesus replied, "Every plant not planted by my Father shall be rooted up, so ignore them. They are blind guides leading the blind, and both will fall into a ditch."

[15]Then Peter asked Jesus to explain what he meant when he said that people are not defiled by nonkosher food.

[16]"Don't you understand?" Jesus asked him. [17]"Don't you see that anything you eat passes through the digestive tract and out again? [18]But evil words come from an evil heart and defile the man who says them. [19]For from the heart come evil thoughts, murder, adultery, fornication, theft, lying, and slander. [20]These are what defile; but there is no spiritual defilement from eating without first going through the ritual of ceremonial handwashing!"

[21]Jesus then left that part of the country and walked the fifty miles to Tyre and Sidon.

[22]A woman from Canaan who was living there came to him, pleading, "Have mercy on me, O Lord, King David's Son! For my daughter has a demon within her, and it torments her constantly."

[23]But Jesus gave her no reply—not even a word. Then his disciples urged him to send her away. "Tell her to get going," they said, "for she is bothering us with all her begging."

DON'T MISS

15:23 The disciples asked Jesus to get rid of the woman because she was bothering them with her begging. They showed no compassion for her or sensitivity to her needs. It is possible to become so occupied with spiritual matters that we miss real spiritual needs right around us, whether out of prejudice or simply because of the inconvenience they cause. Instead of being bothered, be aware of the opportunities that surround you. Be open to the beauty of God's message for all people, and make an effort not to shut out those who are different from you.

²⁴Then he said to the woman, "I was sent to help the Jews—the lost sheep of Israel—not the Gentiles."

²⁵But she came and worshiped him and pled again, "Sir, help me!"

²⁶"It doesn't seem right to take bread from the children and throw it to the dogs," he said.

²⁷"Yes, it is!" she replied, "for even the puppies beneath the table are permitted to eat the crumbs that fall."

²⁸"Woman," Jesus told her, "your faith is large, and your request is granted." And her daughter was healed right then.

²⁹Jesus now returned to the Sea of Galilee and climbed a hill and sat there. ³⁰And a vast crowd brought him their lame, blind, maimed, and those who couldn't speak, and many others, and laid them before Jesus, and he healed them all. ³¹What a spectacle it was! Those who hadn't been able to say a word before were talking excitedly, and those with missing arms and legs had new ones; the crippled were walking and jumping around, and those who had been blind were gazing about them! The crowds just marveled, and praised the God of Israel.

³²Then Jesus called his disciples to him and said, "I pity these people—they've been here with me for three days now and have nothing left to eat; I don't want to send them away hungry or they will faint along the road."

³³The disciples replied, "And where would we get enough here in the desert for all this mob to eat?"

³⁴Jesus asked them, "How much food do you have?" And they replied, "Seven loaves of bread and a few small fish!"

³⁵Then Jesus told all of the people to sit down on the ground, ³⁶and he took the seven loaves and the fish, and gave thanks to God for them, and divided them into pieces, and gave them to the disciples who presented them to the crowd. ³⁷,³⁸And everyone ate until full—four thousand men besides the women and children! And afterwards, when the scraps were picked up, there were seven basketfuls left over!

³⁹Then Jesus sent the people home and got into the boat and crossed to Magadan.

CHAPTER **16** THE LEADERS WANT A MIRACLE.

One day the Pharisees and Sadducees came to test Jesus' claim of being the Messiah by asking him to show them some great demonstrations in the skies.

²,³He replied, "You are good at reading the weather signs of the skies—red sky tonight means fair weather tomorrow; red sky in the morning means foul weather all day—but you can't read the obvious signs of the times! ⁴This evil, unbelieving nation is asking for some strange sign in the heavens, but no further proof will be given except the miracle that happened to Jonah." Then Jesus walked out on them.

⁵Arriving across the lake, the disciples discovered they had forgotten to bring any food.

⁶"Watch out!" Jesus warned them; "beware of the yeast of the Pharisees and Sadducees."

⁷They thought he was saying this because they had forgotten to bring bread.

⁸Jesus knew what they were thinking and told them, "O men of little faith! Why are you so worried about having no food? ⁹Won't you ever understand? Don't you remember at all the five thousand I fed with five loaves, and the basketfuls left over? ¹⁰Don't you remember the four thousand I fed, and all that was left? ¹¹How could you even think I was talking about food? But again I say, 'Beware of the yeast of the Pharisees and Sadducees.'"

¹²Then at last they understood that by *yeast* he meant the *wrong teaching* of the Pharisees and Sadducees.

¹³When Jesus came to Caesarea Philippi, he asked his disciples, "Who are the people saying I am?"

¹⁴"Well," they replied, "some say John the Baptist; some, Elijah; some, Jeremiah or one of the other prophets."

¹⁵Then he asked them, "Who do *you* think I am?"

¹⁶Simon Peter answered, "The Christ, the Messiah, the Son of the living God."

¹⁷"God has blessed you, Simon, son of Jonah," Jesus said, "for my Father in heaven has personally revealed this to you—this is not from any human source. ¹⁸You are Peter, a stone; and upon this rock I will build my church; and all the powers of hell shall not prevail against it. ¹⁹And I will give you the keys of the Kingdom of Heaven; whatever doors you lock on earth shall be locked in heaven; and whatever doors you open on earth shall be open in heaven!"

²⁰Then he warned the disciples against telling others that he was the Messiah.

²¹From then on Jesus began to speak plainly to his disciples about going to Jerusalem, and what would happen to him there—that he would suffer at the hands of the Jewish leaders, that he would be killed, and that three days later he would be raised to life again.

²²But Peter took him aside to remonstrate with him. "Heaven forbid, sir," he said. "This is not

PROTECT

16:21-22 Peter, Jesus' friend and devoted follower who had just eloquently proclaimed his Lord's true identity as the Christ, sought to protect him from the suffering he prophesied. Great temptations can come from those who love us and seek to protect us from something we must experience. Be cautious of advice from a friend who says, "Surely God doesn't want you to face this."

THE CHURCH

Please check the appropriate box: **T**he church is: ☐ a building where religious people go on Sunday. ☐ a place where you're told all the things you should not do. ☐ where a nice, respectable person tells a bunch of nice, respectable people to be nicer and more respectable (with apologies to Mark Twain). **O**K, you ☐ the people of God all over the world; those who follow Jesus and proclaim him as Lord. **O**K, you probably figured out that the last response is the best. But most of us probably feel there is some truth to the other statements as well. Here in Matthew 16:18 we have the first biblical use of the term *church*. There are a lot of misconceptions about what the church is; here is an attempt to clear up at least a few. **M**ISCONCEPTION #1: *The church is a building.* While most local churches in America own buildings, they should not be confused as one and the same. The church is people—God's covenant people called to follow him in faith and action—not the structures where they meet. When we say, "I'm going to church," we're not simply talking about driving to, entering, and sitting down in a building. We mean we are meeting together as God's people, gathered in one place for the purposes of worship, fellowship, instruction, etc. **I**n many parts of the world, congregations often do not own property. They meet in homes, stores, schools, prisons, and other creative locations. (Even today in some places it's dangerous to be a follower of Jesus.) But it's not where the meeting is held, it's who holds it. Wherever Christians gather, there is the church. **M**ISCONCEPTION #2: *The church is where good people go to do religious things.* Let's make it very plain: There are no "good" people. (If you're unclear on this concept, read Romans, particularly chapter 3.) There are simply sinners who are forgiven and sinners who are not forgiven. If we could be good, Jesus would never have had to die on a cross for us. So the church isn't for "good" people; it's for sinners who know they've been forgiven and who come together regularly to celebrate God and the unbelievable love he has for us. Someone has put it this way: The church is not a showcase for saints; it's a hospital for sinners. **W**hen we come together, it isn't just because that's what religious people do on Sunday mornings and Wednesday nights. We come together to praise and worship our God, to thank him for all he has done for us. We thank and honor him for who he is—God and Creator of all, the One who loved us enough to let his Son die for our sins. We praise God with our attendance, our prayers, our music, the preaching of the Word, our money, our fellowship, and countless other ways. Worship is not primarily for us; it is first and foremost for God. **M**ISCONCEPTION #3: *The church is a human institution.* The way many Christians behave, it sometimes is difficult to see any difference between the church and other organizations. But the church is God's own institution, called into being as his instrument on this planet. It is the church that proclaims the Good News (gospel) of Jesus Christ; seeks justice for the poor and rejected and suffering; tries to influence society for the good of man and the glory of God; and lifts up the name of God the Father, God the Son, and God the Holy Spirit before an unbelieving world. In other words, we exist for God's pleasure and purposes before our own. As Psalm 100 says, "Try to realize what this means—the Lord is God! He made us—we are his people, the sheep of his pasture." **N**o, there are no perfect churches. Made up of sinful humans, how could any church be perfect? But the church is made up of God's people, called into existence by Jesus himself, and built on the rock-solid foundation of his promise that "all the powers of hell shall not prevail against it."

going to happen to you!"

²³Jesus turned on Peter and said, "Get away from me, you Satan! You are a dangerous trap to me. You are thinking merely from a human point of view, and not from God's."

²⁴Then Jesus said to the disciples, "If anyone wants to be a follower of mine, let him deny himself and take up his cross and follow me. ²⁵For anyone who keeps his life for himself shall lose it; and anyone who loses his life for me shall find it again. ²⁶What profit is there if you gain the whole world—and lose eternal life? What can be compared with the value of eternal life? ²⁷For I, the Son of Mankind, shall come with my angels in the glory of my Father and judge each person according to his deeds. ²⁸And some of you standing right here now will certainly live to see me coming in my Kingdom."

CHAPTER 17 JESUS SHINES LIKE THE SUN.
Six days later Jesus took Peter, James, and his brother John to the top of a high and lonely hill, ²and as they watched, his appearance changed so that his face shone like the sun and his clothing became dazzling white.

³Suddenly Moses and Elijah appeared and were talking with him. ⁴Peter blurted out, "Sir, it's wonderful that we can be here! If you want me to, I'll make three shelters, one for you and one for Moses and one for Elijah."

⁵But even as he said it, a bright cloud came over them, and a voice from the cloud said, *"This* is my beloved Son, and I am wonderfully pleased with him. Obey *him."*

⁶At this the disciples fell face downward to the ground, terribly frightened. ⁷Jesus came over and touched them. "Get up," he said, "don't be afraid."

⁸And when they looked, only Jesus was with them.

⁹As they were going down the mountain, Jesus commanded them not to tell anyone what they had seen until after he had risen from the dead.

¹⁰His disciples asked, "Why do the Jewish leaders insist Elijah must return before the Messiah comes?"

¹¹Jesus replied, "They are right. Elijah must come and set everything in order. ¹²And, in fact, he has already come, but he wasn't recognized, and was badly mistreated by many. And I, the Messiah, shall also suffer at their hands."

¹³Then the disciples realized he was speaking of John the Baptist.

¹⁴When they arrived at the bottom of the hill, a huge crowd was waiting for them. A man came and knelt before Jesus and said, ¹⁵"Sir, have mercy on my son, for he is mentally deranged and in great trouble, for he often falls into the fire or into the water; ¹⁶so I brought him to your disciples, but they couldn't cure him."

¹⁷Jesus replied, "Oh, you stubborn, faithless people! How long shall I bear with you? Bring him here to me." ¹⁸Then Jesus rebuked the demon in the boy and it left him, and from that moment the boy was well.

¹⁹Afterwards the disciples asked Jesus privately, "Why couldn't we cast that demon out?"

²⁰"Because of your little faith," Jesus told them. "For if you had faith even as small as a tiny mustard seed you could say to this mountain, 'Move!' and it would go far away. Nothing would be impossible. ²¹But this kind of demon won't leave unless you have prayed and gone without food."

²²,²³One day while they were still in Galilee, Jesus told them, "I am going to be betrayed into the power of those who will kill me, and on the third day afterwards I will be brought back to life again." And the disciples' hearts were filled with sorrow and dread.

²⁴On their arrival in Capernaum, the Temple tax collectors came to Peter and asked him, "Doesn't your master pay taxes?"

²⁵"Of course he does," Peter replied.

Then he went into the house to talk to Jesus about it, but before he had a chance to speak, Jesus asked him, "What do you think, Peter? Do kings levy assessments against their own people or against conquered foreigners?"

²⁶,²⁷"Against the foreigners," Peter replied.

"Well, then," Jesus said, "the citizens are free! However, we don't want to offend them, so go down to the shore and throw in a line, and open the mouth of the first fish you catch. You will find a coin to cover the taxes for both of us; take it and pay them."

CHAPTER 18 WHO IS THE GREATEST?
About that time the disciples came to Jesus to ask which of them would be greatest in the Kingdom of Heaven!

²Jesus called a small child over to him and set the little fellow down among them, ³and said, "Unless you turn to God from your sins and become as little children, you will never get into the Kingdom

BELIEVE

17:22-23 Again Jesus predicted his death; but more important, he told of his resurrection. Unfortunately, the disciples heard only the first part and became discouraged. They couldn't understand why Jesus wanted to go back to Jerusalem and the trouble he'd find there.

The disciples didn't fully comprehend the purpose of Jesus' death and resurrection until Pentecost (Acts 2). Don't get upset at yourself if you are slow to understand everything about Jesus. After all, the disciples were with him, saw his miracles, and heard his words—and they still had difficulty understanding. Despite their questions and doubts, however, they believed. We can do no less.

Jesus forgave

the paralyzed man lowered on a stretcher through the roof ... Matthew 9:2-8

the woman caught in adultery ... John 8:3-11

the woman who anointed his feet with oil ... Luke 7:47-50

Peter, for denying he knew Jesus ... John 18:15-18, 25-27; 21:15-19

the thief on the cross ... Luke 23:39-43

the people who crucified him ... Luke 23:34

Jesus not only taught frequently about forgiveness, he also demonstrated his own willingness to forgive. Here are several examples that should help us recognize his willingness to forgive us also.

---

of Heaven. [4]Therefore anyone who humbles himself as this little child is the greatest in the Kingdom of Heaven. [5]And any of you who welcomes a little child like this because you are mine is welcoming me and caring for me. [6]But if any of you causes one of these little ones who trusts in me to lose his faith, it would be better for you to have a rock tied to your neck and be thrown into the sea.

[7]"Woe upon the world for all its evils. Temptation to do wrong is inevitable, but woe to the man who does the tempting. [8]So if your hand or foot causes you to sin, cut it off and throw it away. Better to enter heaven crippled than to be in hell with both of your hands and feet. [9]And if your eye causes you to sin, gouge it out and throw it away. Better to enter heaven with one eye than to be in hell with two.

[10]"Beware that you don't look down upon a single one of these little children. For I tell you that in heaven their angels have constant access to my Father. [11]And I, the Messiah, came to save the lost. [12]"If a man has a hundred sheep, and one wanders away and is lost, what will he do? Won't he leave the ninety-nine others and go out into the hills to search for the lost one? [13]And if he finds it,

CHILDREN

18:6 Children are trusting by nature. They trust adults, which helps them learn about trusting God. Parents and others who influence young children are held accountable by God for how they affect these little ones' ability to trust. Jesus warned that anyone who turns little children away from faith will receive severe punishment.

he will rejoice over it more than over the ninety-nine others safe at home! [14]Just so, it is not my Father's will that even one of these little ones should perish.

[15]"If a brother sins against you, go to him privately and confront him with his fault. If he listens and confesses it, you have won back a brother. [16]But if not, then take one or two others with you and go back to him again, proving everything you say by these witnesses. [17]If he still refuses to listen, then take your case to the church, and if the church's verdict favors you, but he won't accept it, then the church should excommunicate him. [18]And I tell you this—whatever you bind on earth is bound in heaven, and whatever you free on earth will be freed in heaven.

[19]"I also tell you this—if two of you agree down here on earth concerning anything you ask for, my Father in heaven will do it for you. [20]For where two or three gather together because they are mine, I will be right there among them."

[21]Then Peter came to him and asked, "Sir, how often should I forgive a brother who sins against me? Seven times?"

KEEP TRACK

18:22 The rabbis taught that Jews should forgive three times those who offend them. Peter, in trying to be especially generous, asked Jesus if seven (the "perfect" number) was enough times to forgive someone. But Jesus answered, "Seventy times seven," meaning that we shouldn't even keep track of how many times we forgive someone. We should always forgive those who are truly repentant, no matter how many times they ask.

²²"No!" Jesus replied, "seventy times seven!

²³"The Kingdom of Heaven can be compared to a king who decided to bring his accounts up to date. ²⁴In the process, one of his debtors was brought in who owed him $10 million! ²⁵He couldn't pay, so the king ordered him sold for the debt, also his wife and children and everything he had.

²⁶"But the man fell down before the king, his face in the dust, and said, 'Oh, sir, be patient with me and I will pay it all.'

²⁷"Then the king was filled with pity for him and released him and forgave his debt.

²⁸"But when the man left the king, he went to a man who owed him $2,000 and grabbed him by the throat and demanded instant payment.

²⁹"The man fell down before him and begged him to give him a little time. 'Be patient and I will pay it,' he pled.

³⁰"But his creditor wouldn't wait. He had the man arrested and jailed until the debt would be paid in full.

³¹"Then the man's friends went to the king and told him what had happened. ³²And the king called before him the man he had forgiven and said, 'You evil-hearted wretch! Here I forgave you all that tremendous debt, just because you asked me to—³³shouldn't you have mercy on others, just as I had mercy on you?'

³⁴"Then the angry king sent the man to the torture chamber until he had paid every last penny due. ³⁵So shall my heavenly Father do to you if you refuse to truly forgive your brothers."

CHAPTER **19** **MARRIAGE AND DIVORCE.** After Jesus had finished this address, he left Galilee and circled back to Judea from across the Jordan River. ²Vast crowds followed him, and he healed their sick. ³Some Pharisees came to interview him and tried to trap him into saying something that would ruin him.

"Do you permit divorce?" they asked.

⁴"Don't you read the Scriptures?" he replied. "In them it is written that at the beginning God created man and woman, ⁵,⁶and that a man should leave his father and mother, and be forever united to his wife. The two shall become one—no longer two, but one! And no man may divorce what God has joined together."

⁷"Then, why," they asked, "did Moses say a man may divorce his wife by merely writing her a letter of dismissal?"

⁸Jesus replied, "Moses did that in recognition of your hard and evil hearts, but it was not what God had originally intended. ⁹And I tell you this, that anyone who divorces his wife, except for fornication, and marries another, commits adultery."

¹⁰Jesus' disciples then said to him, "If that is how it is, it is better not to marry!"

¹¹"Not everyone can accept this statement," Jesus said. "Only those whom God helps. ¹²Some are born without the ability to marry, and some are

---

Is temptation a sin? If it is, I'm sinning all the time. It seems like thoughts are always coming into my mind to do things that are wrong.

I WONDER . . .

If temptation were a sin, then Jesus was a sinner (see Matthew 4:1-11 for the story of when Satan tempted Jesus in the wilderness). Temptation is not a sin. According to Matthew 18:7-9, it's the natural consequence of living in this world.

What leads to sin is following the path temptation wants us to take. If taken far enough, the path will cause us to think and do what is wrong.

Though temptation always will be present, we do not have to wave the white flag and admit defeat. We have the power to resist, because the Holy Spirit lives in us.

God's Word also reminds us how to overcome temptation. First Corinthians 10:13 says "But remember this—the wrong desires that come into your life aren't anything new and different. Many others have faced exactly the same problems before you. And no temptation is irresistible. You can trust God to keep the temptation from becoming so strong that you can't stand up against it, for he has promised this and will do what he says. He will show you how to escape temptation's power so that you can bear up patiently against it."

Find the way of escape in this story:

At school a friend asks if you want to spend the night with some friends and watch videos. You check with your folks, assuring them there will be no R-rated videos. They give the OK. Everything is cool, so far.

Once you arrive, you look at the stack of videos and notice that half of them are R-rated. You get your friend alone and ask him what the deal is. He says the other guys picked out the videos. Besides, everyone (but you) has seen them before, so he didn't think you'd mind.

Do you stay and go against what your parents want, or do you go along with the group?

Let's say you stay. The next day Dad asks what movies you watched. Now you have to lie to stay out of trouble. So you lie. Unfortunately, your mom spoke with the mom of one of your friends on the phone and found out there were R-rated movies at the sleep-over. Now you're grounded until age 27!

Where were the escape hatches to the temptation to disobey your parents? When you found out that R-rated movies would be shown, you had two choices. You could have apologized to your friends, called your dad, and had him pick you up. Or you could have gone to a different part of the house and done something else.

God always provides a way of escape in every circumstance. We choose whether to take his way out or to do things we know are wrong.

If we stay close to God, we'll be more likely to resist and do what is right. We don't have to give in.

disabled by men, and some refuse to marry for the sake of the Kingdom of Heaven. Let anyone who can, accept my statement."

[13]Little children were brought for Jesus to lay his hands on them and pray. But the disciples scolded those who brought them. "Don't bother him," they said.

[14]But Jesus said, "Let the little children come to me, and don't prevent them. For of such is the Kingdom of Heaven." [15]And he put his hands on their heads and blessed them before he left.

[16]Someone came to Jesus with this question: "Good master, what must I do to have eternal life?"

[17]"When you call me good you are calling me God," Jesus replied, "for God alone is truly good. But to answer your question, you can get to heaven if you keep the commandments."

[18]"Which ones?" the man asked.

And Jesus replied, "Don't kill, don't commit adultery, don't steal, don't lie, [19]honor your father and mother, and love your neighbor as yourself!"

[20]"I've always obeyed every one of them," the youth replied. "What else must I do?"

[21]Jesus told him, "If you want to be perfect, go and sell everything you have and give the money to the poor, and you will have treasure in heaven; and come, follow me." [22]But when the young man heard this, he went away sadly, for he was very rich.

[23]Then Jesus said to his disciples, "It is almost impossible for a rich man to get into the Kingdom of Heaven. [24]I say it again—it is easier for a camel to go through the eye of a needle than for a rich man to enter the Kingdom of God!"

[25]This remark confounded the disciples. "Then who in the world can be saved?" they asked.

[26]Jesus looked at them intently and said, "Humanly speaking, no one. But with God, everything is possible."

[27]Then Peter said to him, "We left everything to follow you. What will we get out of it?"

[28]And Jesus replied, "When I, the Messiah, shall sit upon my glorious throne in the Kingdom, you my disciples shall certainly sit on twelve thrones judging the twelve tribes of Israel. [29]And anyone who gives up his home, brothers, sisters, father, mother, wife, children, or property, to follow me, shall receive a hundred times as much in return, and shall have eternal life. [30]But many who are first now will be last then; and some who are last now will be first then."

CHAPTER 20 A STORY ABOUT A VINEYARD.

Here is another illustration of the Kingdom of Heaven. "The owner of an estate went out early one morning to hire workers for his harvest field. [2]He agreed to pay them $20 a day and sent them out to work.

[3]"A couple of hours later he was passing a hiring hall and saw some men standing around waiting for jobs, [4]so he sent them also into his fields, telling them he would pay them whatever was right at the end of the day. [5]At noon and again around three o'clock in the afternoon he did the same thing.

[6]"At five o'clock that evening he was in town again and saw some more men standing around and asked them, 'Why haven't you been working today?'

[7]"'Because no one hired us,' they replied.

"'Then go on out and join the others in my fields,' he told them.

[8]"That evening he told the paymaster to call the men in and pay them, beginning with the last men first. [9]When the men hired at five o'clock were paid, each received $20. [10]So when the men hired earlier came to get theirs, they assumed they would receive much more. But they, too, were paid $20.

[11,12]"They protested, 'Those fellows worked only one hour, and yet you've paid

them just as much as those of us who worked all day in the scorching heat.'

[13]"'Friend,' he answered one of them, 'I did you no wrong! Didn't you agree to work all day for $20? [14]Take it and go. It is my desire to pay all the same; [15]is it against the law to give away my money if I want to? Should you be angry because I am kind?' [16]And so it is that the last shall be first, and the first, last."

[17]As Jesus was on the way to Jerusalem, he took the twelve disciples aside [18]and talked to them about what would happen to him when they arrived.

"I will be betrayed to the chief priests and other Jewish leaders, and they will condemn me to die. [19]And they will hand me over to the Roman government, and I will be mocked and crucified, and the third day I will rise to life again."

[20]Then the mother of James and John, the sons of Zebedee, brought them to Jesus and respectfully asked a favor.

[21]"What is your request?" he asked. She replied, "In your Kingdom, will you let my two sons sit on two thrones next to yours?"

[22]But Jesus told her, "You don't know what you are asking!" Then he turned to James and John and asked them, "Are you able to drink from the terrible cup I am about to drink from?"

"Yes," they replied, "we are able!"

[23]"You shall indeed drink from it," he told them. "But I have no right to say who will sit on the thrones next to mine. Those places are reserved for the persons my Father selects."

[24]The other ten disciples were indignant when they heard what James and John had asked for. [25]But Jesus called them together and said, "Among the heathen, kings are tyrants and each minor official lords it over those beneath him. [26]But among you it is quite different. Anyone wanting to be a leader among you must be your servant. [27]And if you want to be right at the top, you must serve like a slave. [28]Your attitude must be like my own, for I, the Messiah, did not come to be served, but to serve, and to give my life as a ransom for many."

[29]As Jesus and the disciples left the city of Jericho, a vast crowd surged along behind.

[30]Two blind men were sitting beside the road, and when they heard that Jesus was coming that way, they began shouting, "Sir, King David's Son, have mercy on us!"

[31]The crowd told them to be quiet, but they only yelled the louder.

[32,33]When Jesus came to the place where they were, he stopped in the road and called, "What do you want me to do for you?"

"Sir," they said, "we want to see!"

[34]Jesus was moved with pity for them and touched their eyes. And instantly they could see, and followed him.

CHAPTER **21** **JESUS RIDES INTO JERUSALEM.** As Jesus and the disciples approached Jerusalem, and were near the town of Bethphage on the Mount of Olives, Jesus sent two of them into the village ahead.

[2]"Just as you enter," he said, "you will see a donkey tied there, with its colt beside it. Untie them and bring them here. [3]If anyone asks you what you are doing, just say, 'The Master needs them,' and there will be no trouble."

[4]This was done to fulfill the ancient prophecy, [5]"Tell Jerusalem her King is coming to her, riding humbly on a donkey's colt!"

[6]The two disciples did as Jesus said, [7]and brought the animals to him and threw their garments over the colt for him to ride on. [8]And some in the crowd threw down their coats along the road ahead of him, and others cut branches from the trees and spread them out before him.

[9]Then the crowds surged on ahead and pressed along behind, shouting, "God bless King David's Son!" . . . "God's Man is here!". . . Bless him, Lord!" . . . "Praise God in highest heaven!"

[10]The entire city of Jerusalem was stirred as he entered. "Who is this?" they asked.

[11]And the crowds replied, "It's Jesus, the prophet from Nazareth up in Galilee."

[12]Jesus went into the Temple, drove out the merchants, and knocked over the moneychangers' tables and the stalls of those selling doves. [13]"The Scriptures say my Temple is a place of prayer," he declared, "but you have turned it into a den of thieves."

[14]And now the blind and crippled came to him, and he healed them there in the Temple. [15]But when the chief priests and other Jewish leaders saw these wonderful miracles and heard even the little children in the Temple shouting, "God bless the Son of David," they were disturbed and indignant and asked him, "Do you hear what these children are saying?"

[16]"Yes," Jesus replied. "Didn't you ever read the Scriptures? For they say, 'Even little babies shall praise him!'"

[17]Then he returned to Bethany, where he stayed overnight.

[18]In the morning, as he was returning to Jerusalem, he was hungry [19]and noticed a fig tree beside the road. He went over to see if there were any figs, but there were only leaves. Then he said to it, "Never bear fruit again!" And soon the fig tree withered up.

LEADERSHIP

20:27 Jesus' description of leadership: serve people, don't use them. Jesus served others and gave his life away. A real leader appreciates others and realizes he's not above any job. Does something need to be done? Take the initiative and do it like a faithful servant.

²⁰The disciples were utterly amazed and asked, "How did the fig tree wither so quickly?"

²¹Then Jesus told them, "Truly, if you have faith and don't doubt, you can do things like this and much more. You can even say to this Mount of Olives, 'Move over into the ocean,' and it will. ²²You can get anything—*anything* you ask for in prayer—if you believe."

²³When he had returned to the Temple and was teaching, the chief priests and other Jewish leaders came up to him and demanded to know by whose authority he had thrown out the merchants the day before.

²⁴"I'll tell you if you answer one question first," Jesus replied. ²⁵"Was John the Baptist sent from God or not?"

They talked it over among themselves. "If we say, 'From God,'" they said, "then he will ask why we didn't believe what John said. ²⁶And if we deny that God sent him, we'll be mobbed, for the crowd all think he was a prophet." ²⁷So they finally replied, "We don't know!"

And Jesus said, "Then I won't answer your question either.

²⁸"But what do you think about this? A man with two sons told the older boy, 'Son, go out and work on the farm today.' ²⁹'I won't,' he answered, but later he changed his mind and went. ³⁰Then the father told the youngest, 'You go!' and he said, 'Yes, sir, I will.' But he didn't. ³¹Which of the two was obeying his father?"

They replied, "The first, of course."

Then Jesus explained his meaning: "Surely evil men and prostitutes will get into the Kingdom before you do. ³²For John the Baptist told you to repent and turn to God, and you wouldn't, while very evil men and prostitutes did. And even when you saw this happening, you refused to repent, and so you couldn't believe.

³³"Now listen to this story: A certain landowner planted a vineyard with a hedge around it, and built a platform for the watchman, then leased the vineyard to some farmers on a sharecrop basis, and went away to live in another country.

³⁴"At the time of the grape harvest he sent his agents to the farmers to collect his share. ³⁵But the farmers attacked his men, beat one, killed one, and stoned another.

³⁶"Then he sent a larger group of his men to collect for him, but the results were the same. ³⁷Finally the owner sent his son, thinking they would surely respect him.

BLANK CHECK

21:22 This is not a guarantee that we can get anything we want simply by asking Jesus. God does not grant requests that would hurt us or others, or that violate his own nature or will. Jesus' statement is not a blank check—our prayers must focus on the work of God's Kingdom. Then we may go to him in peace and confidence, knowing he will respond to us in his love and wisdom.

³⁸"But when these farmers saw the son coming they said among themselves, 'Here comes the heir to this estate; come on, let's kill him and get it for ourselves!' ³⁹So they dragged him out of the vineyard and killed him.

⁴⁰"When the owner returns, what do you think he will do to those farmers?"

⁴¹The Jewish leaders replied, "He will put the wicked men to a horrible death and lease the vineyard to others who will pay him promptly."

⁴²Then Jesus asked them, "Didn't you ever read in the Scriptures: 'The stone rejected by the builders has been made the honored cornerstone; how remarkable! what an amazing thing the Lord has done'?

⁴³"What I mean is that the Kingdom of God shall be taken away from you, and given to a nation that will give God his share of the crop. ⁴⁴All who stumble on this rock of truth shall be broken, but those it falls on will be scattered as dust."

⁴⁵When the chief priests and other Jewish leaders realized that Jesus was talking about them—that they were the farmers in his story—⁴⁶they wanted to get rid of him but were afraid to try because of the crowds, for they accepted Jesus as a prophet.

CHAPTER 22 A STORY ABOUT A WEDDING.

Jesus told several other stories to show what the Kingdom of Heaven is like.

"For instance," he said, "it can be illustrated by the story of a king who prepared a great wedding dinner for his son. ³Many guests were invited, and when the banquet was ready he sent messengers to notify everyone that it was time to come. But all refused! ⁴So he sent other servants to tell them, 'Everything is ready and the roast is in the oven. Hurry!'

⁵"But the guests he had invited merely laughed and went on about their business, one to his farm, another to his store; ⁶others beat up his messengers and treated them shamefully, even killing some of them.

⁷"Then the angry king sent out his army and destroyed the murderers and burned their

PRETEND

21:30 The son who said he would obey and then didn't represented the nation of Israel in Jesus' day. They said they wanted to do God's will, but they constantly disobeyed. It is dangerous to pretend to obey God when our hearts are far from him, because God knows the intentions of our hearts. God isn't fooled. He knows when our actions don't match our words.

INVITED

22:1-14 In this culture, two invitations were expected when banquets were given. The first invitation asked the guests to attend; the second announced that all was ready. Here the king, God, invited his guests three times—and each time they refused to come. God wants us to join him at his banquet, which will last for eternity. That's why he sends us invitations again and again. Have you accepted his invitation?

city. [8]And he said to his servants, 'The wedding feast is ready, and the guests I invited aren't worthy of the honor. [9]Now go out to the street corners and invite everyone you see.'

[10]"So the servants did, and brought in all they could find, good and bad alike; and the banquet hall was filled with guests. [11]But when the king came in to meet the guests, he noticed a man who wasn't wearing the wedding robe [provided for him].

[12]"'Friend,' he asked, 'how does it happen that you are here without a wedding robe?' And the man had no reply.

[13]"Then the king said to his aides, 'Bind him hand and foot and throw him out into the outer darkness where there is weeping and gnashing of teeth.' [14]For many are called, but few are chosen."

[15]Then the Pharisees met together to try to think of some way to trap Jesus into saying something for which they could arrest him. [16]They decided to send some of their men along with the Herodians to ask him this question: "Sir, we know you are very honest and teach the truth regardless of the consequences, without fear or favor. [17]Now tell us, is it right to pay taxes to the Roman government or not?"

[18]But Jesus saw what they were after. "You hypocrites!" he exclaimed. "Who are you trying to fool with your trick questions? [19]Here, show me a coin." And they handed him a penny.

[20]"Whose picture is stamped on it?" he asked them. "And whose name is this beneath the picture?"

[21]"Caesar's," they replied.

"Well, then," he said, "give it to Caesar if it is his, and give God everything that belongs to God."

[22]His reply surprised and baffled them, and they went away.

[23]But that same day some of the Sadducees, who say there is no resurrection after death, came to him and asked, [24]"Sir, Moses said that if a man died without children, his brother should marry the widow and their children would get all the dead man's property. [25]Well, we had among us a family of seven brothers. The first of these men married and then died, without children, so his widow became the second brother's wife. [26]This brother also died without children, and the wife was passed to the next brother, and so on until she had been the wife of each of them. [27]And then she also died. [28]So whose wife will she be in the resurrection? For she was the wife of all seven of them!"

[29]But Jesus said, "Your error is caused by your ignorance of the Scriptures and of God's power! [30]For in the resurrection there is no marriage; everyone is as the angels in heaven. [31]But now, as to whether there is a resurrection of the dead—don't you ever read the Scriptures? Don't you realize that God was speaking directly to you when he said, [32]'I *am* the God of Abraham, Isaac, and Jacob'? So God is not the God of the dead, but of the *living.*"

[33]The crowds were profoundly impressed by his answers—[34,35]but not the Pharisees! When they heard that he had routed the Sadducees with his reply, they thought up a fresh question of their own to ask him. One of them, a lawyer, spoke up: [36]"Sir, which is the most important command in the laws of Moses?"

[37]Jesus replied, "'Love the Lord your God with all your heart, soul, and mind.' [38,39]This is the first and greatest commandment. The second most important is similar: 'Love your neighbor as much as you love yourself.' [40]All the other commandments and all the demands of the prophets stem from these two laws and are fulfilled if you obey them. Keep only these and you will find that you are obeying all the others."

[41]Then, surrounded by the Pharisees, he asked them a question: [42]"What about the Messiah? Whose son is he?"

"The son of David," they replied.

[43]"Then why does David, speaking under the inspiration of the Holy Spirit, call him 'Lord'?" Jesus asked. "For David said,

[44]'God said to my Lord, Sit at my right hand until I put your enemies beneath your feet.'

[45]Since David called him 'Lord,' how can he be merely his son?"

[46]They had no answer. And after that no one dared ask him any more questions.

HEAVEN

22:29 The Sadducees asked Jesus what marriage would be like in eternity. Jesus said it was more important to understand God's power than know what heaven will be like. In every generation and culture, views about heaven or eternal life tend to be based upon images and experiences of present life. Jesus said these faulty views are caused by ignorance of God's Word. We must not make up our own ideas about eternity by trying to put it and God into human terms. We should concentrate more on our relationship with God than about what heaven will look like. Eventually we will find out, and it will be far beyond our greatest expectations.

CHAPTER **23** **JESUS WARNS THE PEOPLE.** Then Jesus said to the crowds, and to his disciples, [2]"You would think these Jewish leaders and these Pharisees were Moses, the way they keep making up so many laws! [3]And of course you should obey their every whim! It may be all right to do what they say, but above anything else, *don't follow their example.* For they don't do what they tell you to do. [4]They load you with impossible demands that they themselves don't even try to keep.

[5]"Everything they do is done for show. They act holy by wearing on their arms little prayer

boxes with Scripture verses inside, and by lengthening the memorial fringes of their robes. [6]And how they love to sit at the head table at banquets and in the reserved pews in the synagogue! [7]How they enjoy the deference paid them on the streets and to be called 'Rabbi' and 'Master'! [8]Don't ever let anyone call you that. For only God is your Rabbi and all of you are on the same level, as brothers. [9]And don't address anyone here on earth as 'Father,' for only God in heaven should be addressed like that. [10]And don't be called 'Master,' for only one is your master, even the Messiah.

[11]"The more lowly your service to others, the greater you are. To be the greatest, be a servant. [12]But those who think themselves great shall be disappointed and humbled; and those who humble themselves shall be exalted.

[13,14]"Woe to you, Pharisees, and you other religious leaders. Hypocrites! For you won't let others enter the Kingdom of Heaven and won't go in yourselves. And you pretend to be holy, with all your long, public prayers in the streets, while you are evicting widows from their homes. Hypocrites! [15]Yes, woe upon you hypocrites. For you go to all lengths to make one convert, and then turn him into twice the son of hell you are yourselves. [16]Blind guides! Woe upon you! For your rule is that to swear 'By God's Temple' means nothing—you can break that oath, but to swear 'By the gold in the Temple' is binding! [17]Blind fools! Which is greater, the gold, or the Temple that sanctifies the gold? [18]And you say that to take an oath 'By the altar' can be broken, but to swear 'By the gifts on the altar' is binding! [19]Blind! For which is greater, the gift on the altar, or the altar itself that sanctifies the gift? [20]When you swear 'By the altar' you are swearing by it and everything on it, [21]and when you swear 'By the Temple' you are swearing by it and by God who lives in it. [22]And when you swear 'By heavens' you are swearing by the Throne of God and by God himself.

[23]"Yes, woe upon you, Pharisees, and you other religious leaders—hypocrites! For you tithe down to the last mint leaf in your garden, but ignore the important things—justice and mercy and faith. Yes, you should tithe, but you shouldn't leave the more important things undone. [24]Blind guides! You strain out a gnat and swallow a camel.

[25]"Woe to you, Pharisees, and you religious leaders—hypocrites! You are so careful to polish the outside of the cup, but the inside is foul with extortion and greed. [26]Blind Pharisees! First cleanse the inside of the cup, and then the whole cup will be clean.

[27]"Woe to you, Pharisees, and you religious leaders! You are like beautiful mausoleums—full of dead men's bones, and of foulness and corruption. [28]You try to look like saintly men, but underneath those pious robes of yours are hearts besmirched with every sort of hypocrisy and sin.

[29,30]"Yes, woe to you, Pharisees, and you religious leaders—hypocrites! For you build monuments to the prophets killed by your fathers and lay flowers on the graves of the godly men they destroyed, and say, 'We certainly would never have acted as our fathers did.'

[31]"In saying that, you are accusing yourselves of being the sons of wicked men. [32]And you are following in their steps, filling up the full measure of their evil. [33]Snakes! Sons of vipers! How shall you escape the judgment of hell?

[34]"I will send you prophets, and wise men, and inspired writers, and you will kill some by crucifixion, and rip open the backs of others with whips in your synagogues, and hound them from city to city, [35]so that you will become guilty of all the blood of murdered godly men from righteous Abel to Zechariah (son of Barachiah), slain by you in the Temple between the altar and the sanctuary. [36]Yes, all the accumulated judgment of the centuries shall break upon the heads of this very generation.

[37]"O Jerusalem, Jerusalem, the city that kills the prophets and stones all those God sends to her! How often I have wanted to gather your children together as a hen gathers her chicks beneath her wings, but you wouldn't let me. [38]And now your house is left to you, desolate. [39]For I tell you this, you will never see me again until you are ready to welcome the one sent to you from God."

CHAPTER 24 JESUS TELLS ABOUT THE FUTURE.

As Jesus was leaving the Temple grounds, his disciples came along and wanted to take him on a tour of the various Temple buildings.

[2]But he told them, "All these buildings will be knocked down, with not one stone left on top of another!"

[3]"When will this happen?" the disciples asked him later, as he sat on the slopes of the Mount of Olives. "What events will signal your return and the end of the world?"

[4]Jesus told them, "Don't let anyone fool you. [5]For many will come claiming to be the Messiah and will lead many astray. [6]When you hear of wars beginning, this does not signal my return; these must come, but the end is not yet. [7]The nations and kingdoms of the earth will rise against each other, and there will be famines and earthquakes in many

INSIDE

23:25-28 Jesus condemned the Pharisees and religious leaders for appearing saintly and holy but remaining full of corruption and greed on the inside. Living our Christianity merely as a show for others is like washing a cup on the outside only. When we are clean on the inside, our cleanliness on the outside won't be phony.

places. [8]But all this will be only the beginning of the horrors to come.

[9]"Then you will be tortured and killed and hated all over the world because you are mine, [10]and many of you shall fall back into sin and betray and hate each other. [11]And many false prophets will appear and lead many astray. [12]Sin will be rampant everywhere and will cool the love of many. [13]But those enduring to the end shall be saved.

[14]"And the Good News about the Kingdom will be preached throughout the whole world, so that all nations will hear it, and then, finally, the end will come.

[15]"So, when you see the horrible thing (told about by Daniel the prophet) standing in a holy place (Note to the reader: You know what is meant!), [16]then those in Judea must flee into the Judean hills. [17]Those on their porches must not even go inside to pack before they flee. [18]Those in the fields should not return to their homes for their clothes.

[19]"And woe to pregnant women and to those with babies in those days. [20]And pray that your flight will not be in winter, or on the Sabbath. [21]For there will be persecution such as the world has never before seen in all its history and will never see again.

[22]"In fact, unless those days are shortened, all mankind will perish. But they will be shortened for the sake of God's chosen people.

[23]"Then if anyone tells you, 'The Messiah has arrived at such and such a place, or has appeared here or there,' don't believe it. [24]For false Christs shall arise, and false prophets, and will do wonderful miracles so that if it were possible, even God's chosen ones would be deceived. [25]See, I have warned you.

[26]"So if someone tells you the Messiah has returned and is out in the desert, don't bother to go and look. Or, that he is hiding at a certain place, don't believe it! [27]For as the lightning flashes across the sky from east to west, so shall my coming be, when I, the Messiah, return. [28]And wherever the carcass is, there the vultures will gather.

[29]"Immediately after the persecution of those days the sun will be darkened, and the moon will not give light, and the stars will seem to fall from the heavens, and the powers overshadowing the earth will be convulsed.

[30]"And then at last the signal of my coming will appear in the heavens, and there will be deep mourning all around the earth. And the nations of the world will see me arrive in the clouds of heaven, with power and great glory. [31]And I shall send forth my angels with the sound of a mighty trumpet blast, and they shall gather my chosen ones from the farthest ends of the earth and heaven.

[32]"Now learn a lesson from the fig tree. When her branch is tender and the leaves begin to sprout, you know that summer is almost here. [33]Just so, when you see all these things beginning to happen, you can know that my return is near, even at the doors. [34]Then at last this age will come to its close.

[35]"Heaven and earth will disappear, but my words remain forever. [36]But no one knows the date and hour when the end will be—not even the angels. No, nor even God's Son. Only the Father knows.

[37,38]"The world will be at ease—banquets and parties and weddings—just as it was in Noah's time before the sudden coming of the flood; [39]people wouldn't believe what was going to happen until the flood actually arrived and took them all away. So shall my coming be.

[40]"Two men will be working together in the fields, and one will be taken, the other left. [41]Two women will be going about their household tasks; one will be taken, the other left.

[42]"So be prepared, for you don't know what day your Lord is coming.

[43]"Just as a man can prevent trouble from thieves by keeping watch for them, [44]so you can avoid trouble by always being ready for my unannounced return.

[45]"Are you a wise and faithful servant of the Lord? Have I given you the task of managing my household, to feed my children day by day? [46]Blessings on you if I return and find you faithfully doing your work. [47]I will put such faithful ones in charge of everything I own!

[48]"But if you are evil and say to yourself, 'My Lord won't be coming for a while,' [49]and begin oppressing your fellow servants, partying and getting drunk, [50]your Lord will arrive unannounced and unexpected, [51]and severely whip you and send you off to the judgment of the hypocrites; there will be weeping and gnashing of teeth.

FAKES

24:11 The Old Testament frequently mentions false prophets (2 Kings 3:13; Isaiah 44:25; Jeremiah 23:16; Ezekiel 13:2-3; Micah 3:5; Zechariah 13:2). False prophets were people who claimed to receive messages from God but preached a "health and wealth" message. They told the people what they wanted to hear, even when the nation was not following God as it should. We have false prophets today, too—popular leaders who spout a false gospel, telling people what they want to hear: "God wants you to be rich." "Do whatever your desires tell you." Or, "There is no such thing as sin or hell." Jesus said false teachers would come, and he warned his disciples—as he warns us—not to listen to their dangerous words.

CHAPTER **25** **A STORY ABOUT TEN BRIDESMAIDS.**
"The Kingdom of Heaven can be illustrated by the story of ten bridesmaids who took their lamps and went to meet the bridegroom. [2-4]But only five of

INVEST

25:15 The master divided the money up among his servants according to their abilities—no one received more or less money than he could handle. If he failed in his master's assignment, his excuse could not be that he was overwhelmed. Failure could come only from laziness or hatred for the master. Money, as used here, represents any kind of resource we are given. God gives us time, abilities, talents, and other resources that he expects us to invest wisely until he returns. We are responsible to use well what God has given us. The issue is not how much we have, but what we do with what we have.

them were wise enough to fill their lamps with oil, while the other five were foolish and forgot.

5,6"So, when the bridegroom was delayed, they lay down to rest until midnight, when they were roused by the shout, 'The bridegroom is coming! Come out and welcome him!'

7,8"All the girls jumped up and trimmed their lamps. Then the five who hadn't any oil begged the others to share with them, for their lamps were going out.

9"But the others replied, 'We haven't enough. Go instead to the shops and buy some for yourselves.'

10"But while they were gone, the bridegroom came, and those who were ready went in with him to the marriage feast, and the door was locked.

11"Later, when the other five returned, they stood outside, calling, 'Sir, open the door for us!'

12"But he called back, 'Go away! It is too late!'

13"So stay awake and be prepared, for you do not know the date or moment of my return.

14"Again, the Kingdom of Heaven can be illustrated by the story of a man going into another country, who called together his servants and loaned them money to invest for him while he was gone.

15"He gave $5,000 to one, $2,000 to another, and $1,000 to the last—dividing it in proportion to their abilities—and then left on his trip. 16The man who received the $5,000 began immediately to buy and sell with it and soon earned another $5,000. 17The man with $2,000 went right to work, too, and earned another $2,000.

18"But the man who received the $1,000 dug a hole in the ground and hid the money for safekeeping.

19"After a long time their master returned from his trip and called them to him to account for his money. 20The man to whom he had entrusted the $5,000 brought him $10,000.

21"His master praised him for good work. 'You have been faithful in handling this small amount,' he told him, 'so now I will give you many more responsibilities. Begin the joyous tasks I have assigned to you.'

22"Next came the man who had received the $2,000, with the report, 'Sir, you gave me $2,000 to use, and I have doubled it.'

23"'Good work,' his master said. 'You are a good and faithful servant. You have been faithful over this small amount, so now I will give you much more.'

24,25"Then the man with the $1,000 came and said, 'Sir, I knew you were a hard man, and I was afraid you would rob me of what I earned, so I hid your money in the earth and here it is!'

26"But his master replied, 'Wicked man! Lazy slave! Since you knew I would demand your profit, 27you should at least have put my money into the bank so I could have some interest. 28Take the money from this man and give it to the man with the $10,000. 29For the man who uses well what he is given shall be given more, and he shall have abundance. But from the man who is unfaithful, even what little responsibility he has shall be taken from him. 30And throw the useless servant out into outer darkness: there shall be weeping and gnashing of teeth.'

31"But when I, the Messiah, shall come in my glory, and all the angels with me, then I shall sit upon my throne of glory. 32And all the nations shall be gathered before me. And I will separate the people as a shepherd separates the sheep from the goats, 33and place the sheep at my right hand, and the goats at my left.

34"Then I, the King, shall say to those at my right, 'Come, blessed of my Father, into the Kingdom prepared for you from the founding of the world. 35For I was hungry and you fed me; I was thirsty and you gave me water; I was a stranger and you invited me into your homes; 36naked and you clothed me; sick and in prison, and you visited me.'

37"Then these righteous ones will reply, 'Sir, when did we ever see you hungry and feed you? Or thirsty and give you anything to drink? 38Or a stranger, and help you? Or naked, and clothe you? 39When did we ever see you sick or in prison, and visit you?'

40"And I, the King, will tell them, 'When you did it to these my brothers you were doing it to me!' 41Then I will turn to those on my left and say, 'Away with you, you cursed ones, into the eternal fire prepared for the devil and his demons. 42For I was hungry and you wouldn't feed me; thirsty, and you wouldn't give me anything to drink; 43a stranger, and you refused me hospitality; naked, and you wouldn't clothe me; sick, and in prison, and you didn't visit me.'

44"Then they will reply, 'Lord, when did we ever see

TOUGH TASK

25:31-46 God will separate his obedient followers from pretenders and unbelievers. The real evidence of our belief is the way we act. To treat all persons we encounter as if they are Jesus is no easy task. What we do for others demonstrates what we really think about Jesus' words to us—feed the hungry, give the homeless a place to stay, visit the sick. How well do your actions separate you from pretenders and unbelievers?

you hungry or thirsty or a stranger or naked or sick or in prison, and not help you?'

⁴⁵"And I will answer, 'When you refused to help the least of these my brothers, you were refusing help to me.'

⁴⁶"And they shall go away into eternal punishment; but the righteous into everlasting life."

CHAPTER 26 A STORY ABOUT TALENTS. When

Jesus had finished this talk with his disciples, he told them,

²"As you know, the Passover celebration begins in two days, and I shall be betrayed and crucified."

³At that very moment the chief priests and other Jewish officials were meeting at the residence of Caiaphas the High Priest, ⁴to discuss ways of capturing Jesus quietly and killing him. ⁵"But not during the Passover celebration," they agreed, "for there would be a riot."

⁶Jesus now proceeded to Bethany, to the home of Simon the leper. ⁷While he was eating, a woman came in with a bottle of very expensive perfume and poured it over his head.

⁸,⁹The disciples were indignant. "What a waste of good money," they said. "Why, she could have sold it for a fortune and given it to the poor."

¹⁰Jesus knew what they were thinking and said, "Why are you criticizing her? For she has done a good thing to me. ¹¹You will always have the poor among you, but you won't always have me. ¹²She has poured this perfume on me to prepare my body for burial. ¹³And she will always be remembered for this deed. The story of what she has done will be told throughout the whole world, wher-

ever the Good News is preached."

¹⁴Then Judas Iscariot, one of the twelve apostles, went to the chief priests ¹⁵and asked, "How much will you pay me to get Jesus into your hands?" And they gave him thirty silver coins. ¹⁶From that time on, Judas watched for an opportunity to betray Jesus to them.

MATTHEW

More than any other disciple, Matthew had a clear idea of how much it would cost to follow Jesus, yet he did not hesitate a moment. When he left his tax-collecting booth, he guaranteed himself unemployment. For several of the other disciples, there was always fishing to return to, but for Matthew, there was no turning back.

Two changes happened to Matthew when he decided to follow Jesus. First, Jesus gave him a new life. He not only belonged to a new group; he belonged to the Son of God. He was not just accepting a different way of life; he was now an accepted person. For a despised tax collector, that change must have been wonderful! Second, Jesus gave Matthew a new purpose for his skills. When he followed Jesus, the only tool from his past job that he carried with him was his pen. From the beginning, God had made him a record-keeper. Jesus' call eventually allowed him to put his skills to their finest work. Matthew was a keen observer, and he must have mentally recorded what he saw going on around him. The Gospel that bears his name came as a result.

Matthew's experience points out that each of us, from the beginning, is one of God's works in progress. Much of what God has for us he gives long before we are able to consciously respond to him. He trusts us with skills and abilities ahead of schedule. He has made us each capable of being his servant. When we trust him with what he has given us, we begin a life of real adventure. Matthew couldn't have known that God would use the very skills he had sharpened as a tax collector to record the greatest story ever lived. And God has no less meaningful a purpose for each of us. Have you recognized Jesus saying to you, "Come be my disciple"? What has been your response?

LESSONS: Jesus consistently accepted people from every level of society

Matthew was given a new life, and his God-given skills of record-keeping and attention to detail were given new purpose

Having been accepted by Jesus, Matthew immediately tried to bring others into contact with Jesus.

KEY VERSE: "As he was walking up the beach he saw Levi, the son of Alphaeus, sitting at his tax collection booth. 'Come with me,' Jesus told him. 'Come be my disciple.' And Levi jumped to his feet and went along" (Mark 2:14).

Matthew's story is told in the Gospels. He is also mentioned in Acts 1:14.

UPS:
- Was one of Jesus' 12 disciples
- Responded immediately to Jesus' call
- Invited many friends to his home to meet Jesus
- Compiled the Gospel of Matthew
- Clarified for his Jewish audience Jesus' fulfillment of Old Testament prophecies

STATS:
- Where: Capernaum
- Occupation: Tax collector, disciple of Jesus
- Relatives: Father: Alphaeus
- Contemporaries: Jesus, Pilate, Herod, other disciples

[17]On the first day of the Passover ceremonies, when bread made with yeast was purged from every Jewish home, the disciples came to Jesus and asked, "Where shall we plan to eat the Passover?"

[18]He replied, "Go into the city and see Mr. So-and-So, and tell him, 'Our Master says, my time has come, and I will eat the Passover meal with my disciples at your house.'" [19]So the disciples did as he told them and prepared the supper there.

[20,21]That evening as he sat eating with the Twelve, he said, "One of you will betray me."

[22]Sorrow chilled their hearts, and each one asked, "Am I the one?"

[23]He replied, "It is the one I served first. [24]For I must die just as was prophesied, but woe to the man by whom I am betrayed. Far better for that one if he had never been born."

[25]Judas, too, had asked him, "Rabbi, am I the one?" And Jesus had told him, "Yes."

[26]As they were eating, Jesus took a small loaf of bread and blessed it and broke it apart and gave it to the disciples and said, "Take it and eat it, for this is my body."

[27]And he took a cup of wine and gave thanks for it and gave it to them and said, "Each one drink from it, [28]for this is my blood, sealing the New Covenant. It is poured out to forgive the sins of multitudes. [29]Mark my words—I will not drink this wine again until the day I drink it new with you in my Father's Kingdom."

[30]And when they had sung a hymn, they went out to the Mount of Olives.

[31]Then Jesus said to them, "Tonight you will all desert me. For it is written in the Scriptures that God will smite the Shepherd, and the sheep of the flock will be scattered. [32]But after I have been brought back to life again, I will go to Galilee and meet you there."

[33]Peter declared, "If everyone else deserts you, I won't."

[34]Jesus told him, "The truth is that this very night, before the cock crows at dawn, you will deny me three times!"

[35]"I would die first!" Peter insisted. And all the other disciples said the same thing.

[36]Then Jesus brought them to a garden grove, Gethsemane, and told them to sit down and wait while he went on ahead to pray. [37]He took Peter with him and Zebedee's two sons James and John, and began to be filled with anguish and despair.

[38]Then he told them, "My soul is crushed with horror and sadness to the point of death . . . stay here . . . stay awake with me."

[39]He went forward a little, and fell face downward on the ground, and prayed, "My Father! If it is possible, let this cup be taken away from me. But I want your will, not mine."

[40]Then he returned to the three disciples and found them asleep. "Peter," he called, "couldn't you even stay awake with me one hour? [41]Keep alert and pray. Otherwise temptation will overpower you. For the spirit indeed is willing, but how weak the body is!"

[42]Again he left them and prayed, "My Father! If this cup cannot go away until I drink it all, your will be done."

[43]He returned to them again and found them sleeping, for their eyes were heavy, [44]so he went back to prayer the third time, saying the same things again.

[45]Then he came to the disciples and said, "Sleep on now and take your rest . . . but no! The time has come! I am betrayed into the hands of evil men! [46]Up! Let's be going! Look! Here comes the man who is betraying me!"

[47]At that very moment while he was still speaking, Judas, one of the Twelve, arrived with a great crowd armed with swords and clubs, sent by the Jewish leaders. [48]Judas had told them to arrest the man he greeted, for that would be the one they were after. [49]So now Judas came straight to Jesus and said, "Hello, Master!" and embraced him in friendly fashion.

[50]Jesus said, "My friend, go ahead and do what you have come for." Then the others grabbed him.

[51]One of the men with Jesus pulled out a sword and slashed off the ear of the High Priest's servant.

[52]"Put away your sword," Jesus told him. "Those using swords will get killed. [53]Don't you realize that I could ask my Father for thousands of angels to protect us, and he would send them instantly? [54]But if I did, how would the Scriptures be fulfilled that describe what is happening now?" [55]Then Jesus spoke to the crowd. "Am I some dangerous criminal," he asked, "that you had to

ALERT

26:40 Jesus used Peter's drowsiness to warn him about the kinds of temptation he would soon face. The way to overcome temptation is to be alert to it and pray. Being alert involves being aware of the possibilities of temptation, sensitive to the subtleties, and spiritually equipped to fight it. Because temptation strikes where we are most vulnerable, we can't resist it alone. Prayer is essential because God's strength can shore up our defenses and defeat Satan's power.

DENIAL

26:69ff There were three stages to Peter's denial. First, he acted confused and said he didn't know what the girl was talking about. Second, he vehemently denied Jesus. Third, he denied Jesus with an oath. Believers who deny Christ often begin doing so subtly by pretending not to know him. When opportunities to discuss religious issues come up, they walk away or pretend they don't know the answers. With only a little more pressure, they can be induced to flatly deny their relationship with Christ. If you find yourself subtly avoiding occasions to talk about Christ, watch out. You may be on the road to denying him.

arm yourselves with swords and clubs before you could arrest me? I was with you teaching daily in the Temple and you didn't stop me then. [56]But this is all happening to fulfill the words of the prophets as recorded in the Scriptures."

At that point, all the disciples deserted him and fled.

[57]Then the mob led him to the home of Caiaphas, the High Priest, where all the Jewish leaders were gathering. [58]Meanwhile, Peter was following far to the rear, and came to the courtyard of the High Priest's house and went in and sat with the soldiers, and waited to see what was going to be done to Jesus.

[59]The chief priests and, in fact, the entire Jewish Supreme Court assembled there and looked for witnesses who would lie about Jesus, in order to build a case against him that would result in a death sentence. [60,61]But even though they found many who agreed to be false witnesses, these always contradicted each other.

Finally two men were found who declared, "This man said, 'I am able to destroy the Temple of God and rebuild it in three days.'"

[62]Then the High Priest stood up and said to Jesus, "Well, what about it? Did you say that, or didn't you?" [63]But Jesus remained silent.

Then the High Priest said to him, "I demand in the name of the living God that you tell us whether you claim to be the Messiah, the Son of God."

[64]"Yes," Jesus said, "I am. And in the future you will see me, the Messiah, sitting at the right hand of God and returning on the clouds of heaven."

[65,66]Then the High Priest tore at his own clothing, shouting, "Blasphemy! What need have we for other witnesses? You have all heard him say it! What is your verdict?"

They shouted, "Death!—Death!—Death!"

[67]Then they spat in his face and struck him and some slapped him, [68]saying, "Prophesy to us, you Messiah! Who struck you that time?"

[69]Meanwhile, as Peter was sitting in the courtyard, a girl came over and said to him, "You were with Jesus, for both of you are from Galilee."

[70]But Peter denied it loudly. "I don't even know what you are talking about," he angrily declared.

[71]Later, out by the gate, another girl noticed him and said to those standing around, "This man was with Jesus—from Nazareth."

[72]Again Peter denied it, this time with an oath. "I don't even know the man," he said.

[73]But after a while the men who had been standing there came over to him and said, "We know you are one of his disciples, for we can tell by your Galilean accent."

[74]Peter began to curse and swear. "I don't even know the man," he said.

And immediately the cock crowed. [75]Then Peter remembered what Jesus had said, "Before the cock crows, you will deny me three times." And he went away, crying bitterly.

CHAPTER **27** JUDAS HANGS HIMSELF. When it was morning, the chief priests and Jewish leaders met again to discuss how to induce the Roman government to sentence Jesus to death. [2]Then they sent him in chains to Pilate, the Roman governor.

[3]About that time Judas, who betrayed him, when he saw that Jesus had been condemned to die, changed his mind and deeply regretted what he had done, and brought back the money to the chief priests and other Jewish leaders.

[4]"I have sinned," he declared, "for I have betrayed an innocent man."

"That's your problem," they retorted.

[5]Then he threw the money onto the floor of the Temple and went out and hanged himself. [6]The chief priests picked the money up. "We can't put it in the collection," they said, "since it's against our laws to accept money paid for murder."

[7]They talked it over and finally decided to buy a certain field where the clay was used by potters, and to make it into a cemetery for foreigners who died in Jerusalem. [8]That is why the cemetery is still called "The Field of Blood."

[9]This fulfilled the prophecy of Jeremiah which says,

"They took the thirty pieces of silver—the price at which he was valued by the people of Israel—[10]and purchased a field from the potters as the Lord directed me."

[11]Now Jesus was standing before Pilate, the Roman governor. "Are you the Jews' Messiah?" the governor asked him.

"Yes," Jesus replied.

[12]But when the chief priests and other Jewish leaders made their many accusations against him, Jesus remained silent.

[13]"Don't you hear what they are saying?" Pilate demanded.

[14]But Jesus said nothing, much to the governor's surprise.

[15]Now the governor's custom was to release one Jewish prisoner each year during the Passover celebration—anyone they wanted. [16]This year there was a particularly notorious criminal in jail named Barabbas, [17]and as the crowds gathered before Pilate's house that

REGRETS

27:3-4 Jesus' formal accuser wanted to drop his charges, but the religious leaders refused to halt the trial. When Judas first betrayed Jesus, perhaps he was trying to force Jesus' hand to get him to lead a revolt against Rome. This did not work, of course. Whatever his reason, Judas changed his mind, but it was too late. Many of the plans we set into motion cannot be reversed. It is best to think of the potential consequences before we launch into an action we may later regret.

THE RESURRECTION

August 2, 1492, was a dark day for the Jewish people in Spain. For political and social reasons, they were expelled from the country. Setting sail from Cadiz, they were scattered all over the area of Europe known as the Levant. The Jews, or part of them, were once again in exile. However, something was to happen the day after they set sail that would change the course of the Jewish nation and, for that matter, the course of history. On August 3, 1492, Christopher Columbus and his men set sail for the West, not knowing what they would find. They hoped to establish a new trade route to the Far East; instead, they discovered the New World! This New World would give birth to dozens of new nations. One of them, the United States of America, would become the promised land for persecuted and oppressed people from all over the planet—including millions of Jews. Often, when life seems bleak and hopeless, something happens that puts things in a new perspective. It happened with the Jews, and it happened at the death of Jesus of Nazareth. Imagine what must have been going through the disciples' minds as they witnessed (or heard about) the crucifixion of their Master. All their hopes and expectations—lifeless as the corpse that Joseph of Arimathea took away and laid in his tomb. Dead! Broken and crushed . . . along with the dreams of the Twelve and many others who had truly believed that Jesus was the Messiah who would lead Israel to freedom. And now he lay rotting in a tomb. If that were the end of the story, you would never have heard of Jesus or Christianity. Jesus' followers would have disappeared like the followers of dozens of other would-be Messiahs. If that were the end, you wouldn't be holding this book in your hands, reading it as countless millions of others have, basing your life on its principles. There would be no churches; no trace of what has been the founding faith of the New World that Columbus discovered. You probably are familiar with the story of the Resurrection. The bare facts are that Jesus was put to death by crucifixion; that his body was placed in a borrowed tomb; that Jesus' followers were scattered and dejected. But, as Matthew 28 tells us, Jesus didn't stay dead. On the Sunday morning following his death, some strange events took place around his grave. The strangest of all is that Jesus rose from the dead! We have a tendency to take the Resurrection story for granted—after all, we may have heard it dozens or even hundreds of times. But we need to remember that people didn't vacate their graveyards 2,000 years ago in Palestine any more than they do today. Dead people stayed dead back then, just like they do now. With one major exception. And that exception, the resurrection of Jesus, has made all the difference in eternity for countless Christians. When the early Christians, including the disciples, were called upon to defend their faith in Jesus as Messiah, they didn't point to his great moral teachings and ethical principles. They didn't even refer to his miracles. They pointed to one rock-solid proof: his death and resurrection. If anyone had ever shown that it was science fiction—perhaps by getting one of the disciples to confess that it was a lie, or going to the tomb and showing that Jesus' body was still there—Christianity would have fizzled out on the spot. It hasn't fizzled out yet, and it never will, for the same reason: Jesus Christ rose from the dead. Jesus himself pointed to his resurrection as his calling card, as proof that he was who he said he was. If it hadn't taken place, we would have reason to doubt the rest of his claims. Because Jesus really came back from death, it stands to reason that the rest of what he told us is true: that he is the way to the Father, that anyone who puts his or her faith in Christ can live forever with him in heaven; and that no matter how dark it looks right now, he will conduct us safely to the Promised Land.

morning he asked them, "Which shall I release to you—Barabbas, or Jesus your Messiah?" [18]For he knew very well that the Jewish leaders had arrested Jesus out of envy because of his popularity with the people.

[19]Just then, as he was presiding over the court, Pilate's wife sent him this message: "Leave that good man alone; for I had a terrible nightmare concerning him last night."

[20]Meanwhile the chief priests and Jewish officials persuaded the crowds to ask for Barabbas' release, and for Jesus' death. [21]So when the governor asked again, "Which of these two shall I release to you?" the crowd shouted back their reply: "Barabbas!"

[22]"Then what shall I do with Jesus, your Messiah?" Pilate asked.

And they shouted, "Crucify him!"

[23]"Why?" Pilate demanded. "What has he done wrong?" But they kept shouting, "Crucify! Crucify!"

[24]When Pilate saw that he wasn't getting anywhere and that a riot was developing, he sent for a bowl of water and washed his hands before the crowd, saying, "I am innocent of the blood of this good man. The responsibility is yours!"

[25]And the mob yelled back, "His blood be on us and on our children!"

[26]Then Pilate released Barabbas to them. And after he had whipped Jesus, he gave him to the Roman soldiers to take away and crucify.

[27]But first they took him into the armory and called out the entire contingent. [28]They stripped him and put a scarlet robe on him, [29]and made a crown from long thorns and put it on his head, and placed a stick in his right hand as a scepter and knelt before him in mockery. "Hail, King of the Jews," they yelled. [30]And they spat on him and grabbed the stick and beat him on the head with it.

[31]After the mockery, they took off the robe and put his own garment on him again, and took him out to crucify him.

[32]As they were on the way to the execution grounds they came across a man from Cyrene, in Africa—Simon was his name—and forced him to carry Jesus' cross. [33]Then they went out to an area known as Golgotha, that is, "Skull Hill," [34]where the soldiers gave him drugged wine to drink; but when he had tasted it, he refused.

[35]After the crucifixion, the soldiers threw dice to divide up his clothes among themselves. [36]Then they sat around and watched him as he hung there. [37]And they put a sign above his head, "This is Jesus, the King of the Jews."

[38]Two robbers were also crucified there that morning, one on either side of him. [39]And the people passing by hurled abuse, shaking their heads at him and saying, [40]"So! You can destroy the Temple and build it again in three days, can you? Well, then, come on down from the cross if you are the Son of God!"

[41-43]And the chief priests and Jewish leaders also mocked him. "He saved others," they scoffed, "but he can't save himself! So you are the King of Israel, are you? Come down from the cross and we'll believe you! He trusted God—let God show his approval by delivering him! Didn't he say, 'I am God's Son'?"

[44]And the robbers also threw the same in his teeth.

[45]That afternoon, the whole earth was covered with darkness for three hours, from noon until three o'clock.

[46]About three o'clock, Jesus shouted, "Eli, Eli, lama sabachthani?" which means, "My God, my God, why have you forsaken me?"

[47]Some of the bystanders misunderstood and thought he was calling for Elijah. [48]One of them ran and filled a sponge with sour wine and put it on a stick and held it up to him to drink. [49]But the rest said, "Leave him alone. Let's see whether Elijah will come and save him."

[50]Then Jesus shouted out again, dismissed his spirit, and died.

[51]And look! The curtain secluding the Holiest Place in the Temple was split apart from top to bottom; and the earth shook, and rocks broke, [52]and tombs opened, and many godly men and women who had died came back to life again. [53]After Jesus' resurrection, they left the cemetery and went into Jerusalem, and appeared to many people there.

[54]The soldiers at the crucifixion and their sergeant were terribly frightened by the earthquake and all that happened. They exclaimed, "Surely this was God's Son."

[55]And many women who had come down from Galilee with Jesus to care for him were watching from a distance. [56]Among them were Mary Magdalene and Mary the mother of James and Joseph, and the mother of James and John (the sons of Zebedee).

[57]When evening came, a rich man from Arimathea named Joseph, one of Jesus' followers, [58]went to Pilate and

HASSLE

27:29 People still hassle Christians for their faith, but believers can take courage that Jesus himself was mocked terribly. Taunting may hurt our feelings, but we should never let it change our faith (see 5:11-12).

AGONY

27:46 Jesus was not questioning God; he was quoting the first line of Psalm 22—a deep expression of the anguish he felt when he took on the sins of the world and thus was separated from his Father. *This* was what Jesus dreaded as he prayed to God in the garden to take the cup from him (26:39). The physical agony was horrible, but even worse was the period of spiritual separation from God. Jesus suffered this double death so that we would never have to experience eternal separation from God.

CHOICES

28:11-15 Jesus' resurrection was already causing a great stir in Jerusalem. A group of women was moving quickly through the streets, looking for the disciples to tell them the amazing news that Jesus was alive. At the same time, a group of religious leaders was plotting how to cover up the Resurrection.

Today there is still a great stir over the Resurrection, and there are still only two choices—to believe that Jesus rose from the dead, or to be closed to the truth, denying it, ignoring it, or rationalizing it away.

asked for Jesus' body. And Pilate issued an order to release it to him. [59]Joseph took the body and wrapped it in a clean linen cloth, [60]and placed it in his own new rock-hewn tomb, and rolled a great stone across the entrance as he left. [61]Both Mary Magdalene and the other Mary were sitting nearby watching.

[62]The next day—at the close of the first day of the Passover ceremonies—the chief priests and Pharisees went to Pilate, [63]and told him, "Sir, that liar once said, 'After three days I will come back to life again.' [64]So we request an order from you sealing the tomb until the third day, to prevent his disciples from coming and stealing his body and then telling everyone he came back to life! If that happens, we'll be worse off than we were at first."

[65]"Use your own Temple police," Pilate told them. "They can guard it safely enough."

[66]So they sealed the stone and posted guards to protect it from intrusion.

CHAPTER 28 JESUS COMES BACK TO LIFE!

Early on Sunday morning, as the new day was dawning, Mary Magdalene and the other Mary went out to the tomb.

[2]Suddenly there was a great earthquake; for an angel of the Lord came down from heaven and rolled aside the stone and sat on it. [3]His face shone like lightning and his clothing was a brilliant white. [4]The guards shook with fear when they saw him, and fell into a dead faint.

[5]Then the angel spoke to the women. "Don't be frightened!" he said. "I know you are looking for Jesus, who was crucified, [6]but he isn't here! For he has come back to life again, just as he said he would. Come in and see where his body was lying. . . . [7]And now, go quickly and tell his disciples that he has risen from the dead, and that he is going to Galilee to meet them there. That is my message to them."

[8]The women ran from the tomb, badly frightened, but also filled with joy, and rushed to find the disciples to give them the angel's message. [9]And as they were running, suddenly Jesus was there in front of them!

"Good morning!" he said. And they fell to the ground before him, holding his feet and worshiping him.

[10]Then Jesus said to them, "Don't be frightened! Go tell my brothers to leave at once for Galilee, to meet me there."

[11]As the women were on the way into the city, some of the Temple police who had been guarding the tomb went to the chief priests and told them what had happened. [12,13]A meeting of all the Jewish leaders was called, and it was decided to bribe the police to say they had all been asleep when Jesus' disciples came during the night and stole his body.

[14]"If the governor hears about it," the Council promised, "we'll stand up for you and everything will be all right."

[15]So the police accepted the bribe and said what they were told to. Their story spread widely among the Jews and is still believed by them to this very day.

[16]Then the eleven disciples left for Galilee, going to the mountain where Jesus had said they would find him. [17]There they met him and worshiped him—but some of them weren't sure it really was Jesus!

[18]He told his disciples, "I have been given all authority in heaven and earth. [19]Therefore go and make disciples in all the nations, baptizing them into the name of the Father and of the Son and of the Holy Spirit, [20]and then teach these new disciples to obey all the commands I have given you; and be sure of this—that I am with you always, even to the end of the world."

LAST WORDS

28:18-20 When someone is dying or leaving us, his last words are very important. Jesus left the disciples with these last words of instruction: they were under his authority; they were to make more disciples; they were to baptize and teach them to obey him; he would be with them always. Whereas in previous missions Jesus had sent his disciples only to the Jews (10:5-6), their mission from now on would be worldwide. Jesus is Lord of the earth, and he died for the sins of all those who trust him, everywhere.

We are to go—whether it is next door or to another country—and make disciples. It is not an option, but a command to all who call Jesus Lord. All of us are not evangelists, but we have all received gifts that we can use in helping to fulfill the Great Commission. As we obey, we have comfort in the knowledge that Jesus is always with us.

MEGA *Themes*

JESUS CHRIST, THE KING Jesus is revealed as the King of kings. His miraculous birth, his life and teaching, his miracles, and his triumph over death show us who he really is.

Jesus cannot be compared with any other person or power. He is the supreme ruler of time and eternity, heaven and earth, men and angels. We should give him his rightful place as King and Lord in our life.

1. In what ways is Jesus revealed as King in the book of Matthew?
2. In what ways did Jesus, though the King of kings, display humility in the book of Matthew?
3. What do you learn about the personal qualities of Jesus from these two lists? Why did so many people reject Jesus as King?
4. How does Jesus reign in the world today? What does it mean in terms of daily living for Jesus to be "the Lord" of your life?

THE MESSIAH Jesus was the Messiah, the One for whom the Jews had waited, who was to deliver them from Roman oppression. Yet, tragically, they didn't recognize him when he came. They were not ready to accept his kingship because it was not what they expected. They didn't understand that the true purpose of God's anointed deliverer was to die for all people, to free them from sin.

Because Jesus was sent by God, we can trust him with our life. It is worth everything we have to accept Christ and give ourselves to him because he came to be our Messiah, our Savior.

1. In what ways did Jesus fulfill the prophecy of a coming Savior who would rescue the people?
2. How was Jesus' plan of deliverance different from what the people had anticipated? How was Jesus' deliverance actually greater than they could have imagined?
3. In what ways has Jesus delivered you?
4. Based on the fact that Jesus, the Messiah, has rescued you, what will you do to live for him?

KINGDOM OF GOD Jesus came to earth to begin his Kingdom. His full Kingdom will be realized at his return and will be made up of all those who have faithfully followed him.

The way to enter God's Kingdom is by faith—by believing in Christ to save us from sin and change our lives. Then we must do the work of his Kingdom, helping prepare it for his return.

1. Matthew 5–7, known as the "Sermon on the Mount," introduces the values of Christ's Kingdom. In accordance with these chapters, make a list of at least ten guidelines Jesus gave showing how he wants those who belong to the Kingdom to live.
2. What would it mean for a person in your school to live by these Kingdom guidelines?
3. Chapter 13 is filled with parables that Jesus used when teaching to help describe his Kingdom. What do you learn about the Kingdom of God from these parables? What is the importance of the Kingdom of God?
4. In what ways are you living out the Kingdom guidelines or values? In what areas do you need to become more obedient to Christ's call to Kingdom values?

TEACHINGS Jesus taught the people using sermons, illustrations, and parables. He showed the true ingredients of faith and how to guard against an ineffective and hypocritical life.

Jesus' teachings show us how to prepare for life in his Kingdom by living properly right now. His life was an example of his teachings, as our lives should be.

1. What were the main purposes of Jesus' teachings?
2. How did different individuals and groups of people react to his teachings?
3. What seems to have caused some people to accept Jesus' teachings and others to reject them?
4. Describe the ways, both positive and negative, that people today respond to Jesus' teachings.
5. How are Jesus' teachings to be your authority in life? In what ways does this authority influence your decisions in your present life-style?

RESURRECTION When Jesus rose from the dead, he rose in power as the true King. In his victory over death, he established his credentials as King and his power and authority over evil.

The Resurrection shows that Jesus is all-powerful—that not even death could stop his plan of offering eternal life. People who believe in Jesus can hope for a resurrection like his. Our role is to live in that victory and share the message of his victory with those who do not yet know that "Jesus is alive!"

1. What difference does it make whether or not Jesus was resurrected?
2. What impact did Jesus' resurrection have on his disciples?
3. What impact has Jesus' resurrection made on mankind as a whole? On you specifically?

*H*as this ever happened to you? ■ Friends invite you to a just-released, critically-acclaimed movie. ■ "It's supposed to be great," they insist. "You'll like it. Trust us." ■ So you go—with high expectations. Only the movie isn't great. It drags on and on. As far as excitement goes, this particular film ranks right up there with reading the phone book. ■ You keep thinking, *This has got to get better. Surely there's a car chase or a joke or some sort of surprise plot twist in the next scene.* But nothing happens— nothing at all. The most adventurous moment of the film comes at the end when two of the actors go to a fancy French restaurant and eat snails. It's gross, but at least they're finally doing something. ■ When the final credits roll, you leave the theater, vowing, "Never again!" ■ Guess what? You don't have to spend your time with stale stories, boring characters, or tedious plots! Instead, you can read one of the most exciting books in existence! And it's right here, on the next few pages. ■ You name it, and the Gospel of Mark has it—demons, death, and outrageous special effects (also called miracles), all served up in a swirling atmosphere of intrigue, jealousy, controversy, and murder. In short, this book is an action-packed biography of the most influential person in the history of the world. ■ Go for it! And when you're done, you will vow, "Never again . . . never again will I think of the Bible as a boring book!"

STATS

PURPOSE: To present Jesus' person, work, and teachings

AUTHOR: John Mark. He accompanied Paul on his first missionary journey (Acts 13:13).

TO WHOM WRITTEN: The Christians in Rome, where Mark wrote the Gospel, and believers everywhere.

DATE WRITTEN: Between A.D. 55 and 65

SETTING: The Roman Empire. The empire, with its common language and excellent transportation and communication systems, was ripe to hear Jesus' message.

KEY PEOPLE: Jesus, the twelve disciples, Pilate, the Jewish religious leaders

KEY PLACES: Capernaum, Nazareth, Caesarea Philippi, Jericho, Bethany, Mount of Olives, Jerusalem, Golgotha

SPECIAL FEATURES: Mark was the first Gospel written. The other Gospels quote all but 31 verses of Mark. Mark records more miracles than does any other Gospel.

Mark

CHAPTER 1 PREPARING THE WAY FOR JESUS.

Here begins the wonderful story of Jesus the Messiah, the Son of God.

[2]In the book written by the prophet Isaiah, God announced that he would send his Son to earth, and that a special messenger would arrive first to prepare the world for his coming.

[3]"This messenger will live out in the barren wilderness," Isaiah said, "and will proclaim that everyone must straighten out his life to be ready for the Lord's arrival."

[4]This messenger was John the Baptist. He lived in the wilderness and taught that all should be baptized as a public announcement of their decision to turn their backs on sin, so that God could forgive them. [5]People from Jerusalem and from all over Judea traveled out into the Judean wastelands to see and hear John, and when they confessed their sins he baptized them in the Jordan River. [6]His clothes were woven from camel's hair and he wore a leather belt; locusts and wild honey were his food. [7]Here is a sample of his preaching:

"Someone is coming soon who is far greater than I am, so much greater that I am not even worthy to be his slave. [8]I baptize you with water but he will baptize you with God's Holy Spirit!"

[9]Then one day Jesus came from Nazareth in Galilee, and was baptized by John there in the Jordan River. [10]The moment Jesus came up out of the water, he saw the heavens open and the Holy Spirit in the form of a dove descending on him, [11]and a voice from heaven said, "You are my beloved Son; you are my Delight."

[12,13]Immediately the Holy Spirit urged Jesus into the desert. There, for forty days, alone except for desert animals, he was subjected to Satan's temptations to sin. And afterwards the angels came and cared for him.

[14]Later on, after John was arrested by King Herod, Jesus went to Galilee to preach God's Good News.

THRILLS

1:1 When you experience the excitement of a big event, you naturally want to tell someone. Telling the story can bring back that original thrill as you relive the experience. As you read Mark's first words, you can sense his excitement. Picture yourself in the crowd as Jesus heals and teaches. Imagine yourself as one of the disciples. Respond to Jesus' words of love and encouragement—and remember that he came for us who live today as well as for those who lived two thousand years ago.

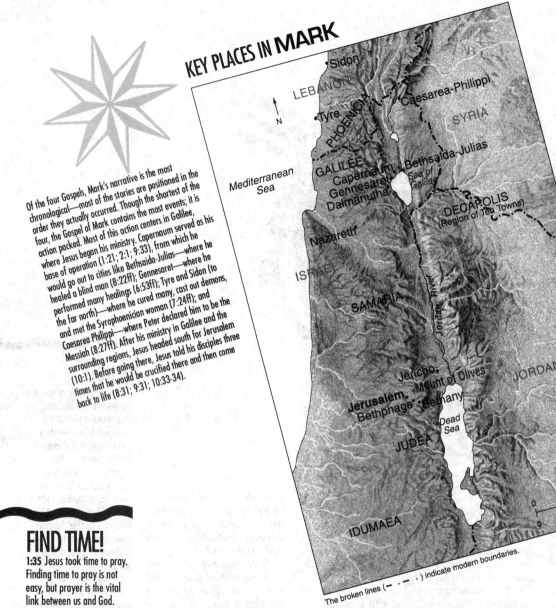

KEY PLACES IN MARK

Of the four Gospels, Mark's narrative is the most chronological—most of the stories are positioned in the order they actually occurred. Though the shortest of the four, the Gospel of Mark contains the most events; it is action packed. Most of this action centers in Galilee, where Jesus began his ministry. Capernaum served as his base of operation (1:21; 2:1; 9:33), from which he would go out to cities like Bethsaida-Julias—where he healed a blind man (8:22ff); Gennesaret—where he performed many healings (6:53ff); Tyre and Sidon (to the far north)—where he cured many, cast out demons, and met the Syrophoenician woman (7:24ff); and Caesarea Philippi—where Peter declared him to be the Messiah (8:27ff). After his ministry in Galilee and the surrounding regions, Jesus headed south for Jerusalem (10:1). Before going there, Jesus told his disciples three times that he would be crucified there and then come back to life (8:31; 9:31; 10:33-34).

The broken lines (— · — · · ·) indicate modern boundaries.

FIND TIME!

1:35 Jesus took time to pray. Finding time to pray is not easy, but prayer is the vital link between us and God. Like Jesus, we must find time away from others to talk with God, even if we have to get up before daybreak to do it!

¹⁵"At last the time has come!" he announced. "God's Kingdom is near! Turn from your sins and act on this glorious news!"

¹⁶One day as Jesus was walking along the shores of the Sea of Galilee, he saw Simon and his brother Andrew fishing with nets, for they were commercial fishermen.

¹⁷Jesus called out to them, "Come, follow me! And I will make you fishermen for the souls of men!" ¹⁸At once they left their nets and went along with him.

¹⁹A little farther up the beach, he saw Zebedee's sons, James and John, in a boat mending their nets. ²⁰He called them too, and immediately they left their father Zebedee in the boat with the hired men and went with him.

²¹Jesus and his companions now arrived at the town of Capernaum and on Saturday morning went into the Jewish place of worship—the synagogue—where he preached. ²²The congregation was surprised at his sermon because he spoke as an authority and didn't try to prove his points by quoting others—quite unlike what they were used to hearing!

²³A man possessed by a demon was present and began shouting, ²⁴"Why are you bothering us, Jesus

of Nazareth—have you come to destroy us demons? I know who you are—the holy Son of God!"

²⁵Jesus curtly commanded the demon to say no more and to come out of the man. ²⁶At that the evil spirit screamed and convulsed the man violently and left him. ²⁷Amazement gripped the audience and they began discussing what had happened.

"What sort of new religion is this?" they asked excitedly. "Why, even evil spirits obey his orders!"

²⁸The news of what he had done spread quickly through that entire area of Galilee.

²⁹,³⁰Then, leaving the synagogue, he and his disciples went over to Simon and Andrew's home, where they found Simon's mother-in-law sick in bed with a high fever. They told Jesus about her right away. ³¹He went to her bedside, and as he took her by the hand and helped her to sit up, the fever suddenly left, and she got up and prepared dinner for them!

³²,³³By sunset the courtyard was filled with the sick and demon-possessed, brought to him for healing; and a huge crowd of people from all over the city of Capernaum gathered outside the door to watch. ³⁴So Jesus healed great numbers of sick folk that evening and ordered many demons to come out of their victims. (But he refused to allow the demons to speak, because they knew who he was.)

³⁵The next morning he was up long before daybreak and went out alone into the wilderness to pray.

³⁶,³⁷Later, Simon and the others went out to find him, and told him, "Everyone is asking for you."

³⁸But he replied, "We must go on to other towns as well, and give my message to them too, for that is why I came."

³⁹So he traveled throughout the province of Galilee, preaching in the synagogues and releasing many from the power of demons.

⁴⁰Once a leper came and knelt in front of him and begged to be healed. "If you want to, you can make me well again," he pled.

⁴¹And Jesus, moved with pity, touched him and said, "I want to! Be healed!" ⁴²Immediately the leprosy was gone—the man was healed!

⁴³,⁴⁴Jesus then told him sternly, "Go and be examined immediately by the Jewish priest. Don't stop to speak to anyone along the way. Take along the offering prescribed by Moses for a leper who is healed, so that everyone will have proof that you are well again."

⁴⁵But as the man went on his way he began to shout the good news that he was healed; as a result, such throngs soon surrounded Jesus that he couldn't publicly enter a city anywhere, but had to stay out in the barren wastelands. And people from everywhere came to him there.

CHAPTER **2** **A HOLE IN THE ROOF.** Several days later he returned to Capernaum, and the news of his arrival spread quickly through the city. ²Soon the house where he was staying was so packed with visitors that there wasn't room for a single person

I used to like to go to parties a lot before I became a Christian. Are parties bad?

I WONDER . . .

In answering this type of question, it's tough not to sound heavy handed. After all, teenage parties do not exactly have a great reputation.

The key word to remember is not *yes* or *no*, but *why?*—your motive is the key.

If you were honest, you'd have to agree that many of the reasons people party are pretty selfish. Most parties cater to the notion that it's a person's right to have a good time, especially if it's not hurting anyone else.

If someone is living apart from God, why would he or she think anything different? The Bible agrees that if this life doesn't matter then "eat, drink, and be merry. What's the difference? For tomorrow we die, and that ends everything!" (1 Corinthians 15:32).

The motive behind going to parties is what God is most concerned about. If it's to get drunk, take drugs, pick up the opposite sex, then God wouldn't want you at parties.

The motive might be to be seen with the "cool" people. Being with certain people sometimes may help you feel accepted and even popular, but God accepts you as you are—and his acceptance is more important than anyone else's.

Jesus isn't against parties. He went to parties, and was, in fact, the life of the party! But his motives were entirely different than the selfish ones described above. He went to show people that he accepted them, to communicate truth about the character of God, and to celebrate life (see Mark 2:13-17).

Should you do the same? Perhaps, but here are a few questions to consider:
- Have you grown sufficiently in your faith that you will not be tempted if there is pressure to drink (or whatever)?
- Do you know someone who will go with so you can encourage each other to stay clean?
- Are you going as a light or as a hammer? That is, do you genuinely want to help those in darkness, or do you want to pound on them to feel good about your "moral" life-style?
- Is there a chance that you could be found "guilty by association"? When others hear you were at the party, how will they know you didn't drink? Is it worth the hassle it may cause in making sure your reputation stays intact?
- What do your parents think about you attending that party? Would you have to not tell them in order to go?

Remember, motive is the key. But even with good motives, be cautious. The results of such activities, even with the best of motives, may be more than you can handle.

more, not even outside the door. And he preached the Word to them. [3]Four men arrived carrying a paralyzed man on a stretcher. [4]They couldn't get to Jesus through the crowd, so they dug through the clay roof above his head and lowered the sick man on his stretcher, right down in front of Jesus.

[5]When Jesus saw how strongly they believed that he would help, Jesus said to the sick man, "Son, your sins are forgiven!"

[6]But some of the Jewish religious leaders said to themselves as they sat there, [7]"What? This is blasphemy! Does he think he is God? For only God can forgive sins."

[8]Jesus could read their minds and said to them at once, "Why does this bother you? [9-11]I, the Messiah, have the authority on earth to forgive sins. But talk is cheap—anybody could say that. So I'll prove it to you by healing this man." Then, turning to the paralyzed man, he commanded, "Pick up your stretcher and go on home, for you are healed!"

[12]The man jumped up, took the stretcher, and pushed his way through the stunned onlookers! Then how they praised God. "We've never seen anything like this before!" they all exclaimed.

[13]Then Jesus went out to the seashore again and preached to the crowds that gathered around him. [14]As he was walking up the beach he saw Levi, the son of Alphaeus, sitting at his tax collection booth. "Come with me," Jesus told him. "Come be my disciple."

And Levi jumped to his feet and went along.

[15]That night Levi invited his fellow tax collectors and many other notorious sinners to be his dinner guests so that they could meet Jesus and his disciples. (There were many men of this type among the crowds that followed him.) [16]But when some of the Jewish religious leaders saw him eating with these men of ill repute, they said to his disciples, "How can he stand it, to eat with such scum?"

[17]When Jesus heard what they were saying, he told them, "Sick people need the doctor, not healthy ones! I haven't come to tell good people to repent, but the bad ones."

[18]John's disciples and the Jewish leaders sometimes fasted, that is, went without food as part of their religion. One day some people came to Jesus and asked why his disciples didn't do this too.

[19]Jesus replied, "Do friends of the bridegroom refuse to eat at the wedding feast? Should they be sad while he is with them? [20]But some day he will be taken away from them, and then they will mourn. [21][Besides, going without food is part of the old way of doing things.] It is like patching an old garment with unshrunk cloth! What happens? The patch pulls away and leaves the hole worse than before. [22]You know better than to put new wine into old wineskins. They would burst. The wine would be spilled out and the wineskins ruined. New wine needs fresh wineskins."

[23]Another time, on a Sabbath day as Jesus and his disciples were walking through the fields, the disciples were breaking off heads of wheat and eating the grain.

[24]Some of the Jewish religious leaders said to Jesus, "They shouldn't be doing that! It's against our laws to work by harvesting grain on the Sabbath."

[25,26]But Jesus replied, "Didn't you ever hear about the time King David and his companions were hungry, and he went into the house of God— Abiathar was High Priest then—and they ate the special bread only priests were allowed to eat? That was against the law too. [27]But the Sabbath was made to benefit man, and not man to benefit the Sabbath. [28]And I, the Messiah, have authority even to decide what men can do on Sabbath days!"

CHAPTER 3 JESUS HEALS A CRIPPLED HAND.

While in Capernaum Jesus went over to the synagogue again, and noticed a man there with a deformed hand.

[2]Since it was the Sabbath, Jesus' enemies watched him closely. Would he heal the man's hand? If he did, they planned to arrest him!

[3]Jesus asked the man to come and stand in front of the congregation. [4]Then turning to his enemies he asked, "Is it all right to do kind deeds on Sabbath days? Or is this a day for doing harm? Is it a day to save lives or to destroy them?" But they wouldn't answer him. [5]Looking around at them angrily, for he was deeply disturbed by their indifference to human need, he said to the man, "Reach out your hand." He did, and instantly his hand was healed!

[6]At once the Pharisees went away and met with the Herodians to discuss plans for killing Jesus.

[7,8]Meanwhile, Jesus and his disciples withdrew to the beach, followed by a huge crowd from all over Galilee, Judea, Jerusalem, Idumea,

DON'T WAIT

2:14-15 The day that Levi met Jesus, he held a meeting at his house to introduce others to Jesus. Levi didn't waste any time starting to witness! Some people feel that new believers should wait for time, maturity, or training before they start telling others about Christ. But, like Levi, new believers can tell others about their faith right away with whatever knowledge, skill, or experience they already have.

ANGER

3:5 Jesus was angry about the Pharisees' uncaring attitudes. Anger itself is not wrong. It depends on what makes us angry and what we do with our anger. Too often we express our anger in selfish and harmful ways. By contrast, Jesus expressed his anger by correcting a problem—healing the man's hand. Use your anger to find constructive solutions rather than to add to the problem by tearing people down.

from beyond the Jordan River, and even from as far away as Tyre and Sidon. For the news about his miracles had spread far and wide and vast numbers came to see him for themselves.

[9]He instructed his disciples to bring around a boat and to have it standing ready to rescue him in case he was crowded off the beach. [10]For there had been many healings that day and as a result great numbers of sick people were crowding around him, trying to touch him.

[11]And whenever those possessed by demons caught sight of him they would fall down before him shrieking, "You are the Son of God!" [12]But he strictly warned them not to make him known.

[13]Afterwards he went up into the hills and summoned certain ones he chose, inviting them to come and join him there; and they did.

[14,15]Then he selected twelve of them to be his regular companions and to go out to preach and to cast out demons. [16-19]These are the names of the twelve he chose: Simon (he renamed him "Peter"), James and John (the sons of Zebedee, but Jesus called them "Sons of Thunder"), Andrew, Philip, Bartholomew, Matthew, Thomas, James (the son of Alphaeus), Thaddaeus, Simon (a member of a political party advocating violent overthrow of the Roman government), Judas Iscariot (who later betrayed him).

[20]When he returned to the house where he was staying, the crowds began to gather again, and soon it was so full of visitors that he couldn't even find time to eat. [21]When his friends heard what was happening they came to try to take him home with them.

"He's out of his mind," they said.

[22]But the Jewish teachers of religion who had arrived from Jerusalem said, "His trouble is that he's possessed by Satan, king of demons. That's why demons obey him."

[23]Jesus summoned these men and asked them (using proverbs they all understood), "How can Satan cast out Satan? [24]A kingdom divided against itself will collapse. [25]A home filled with strife and division destroys itself. [26]And if Satan is fighting against himself, how can he accomplish anything? He would never survive. [27][Satan must be bound before his demons are cast out], just as a strong man must be tied up before his house can be ransacked and his property robbed.

JUDAS ISCARIOT

It is easy to forget that Jesus chose Judas to be his disciple. We may also miss the point that while Judas betrayed Jesus, all the disciples abandoned him. The disciples, including Judas, all had the wrong idea of Jesus' mission on earth. They expected Jesus to become a political leader. But when he kept talking about dying, they all felt a mixture of anger, fear, and disappointment. They couldn't understand why Jesus had asked them to follow him if his mission was going to fail.

We don't know exactly why Judas betrayed Jesus. But we can see that Judas let his own desires become so important that Satan was able to control him. He got paid to set up Jesus for the religious leaders.

He tried to undo the evil he had done by returning the money to the priests, but it was too late. How sad that Judas ended his life in despair without ever experiencing the gift of forgiveness God could give to even him through Jesus Christ.

In betraying Jesus, Judas made the greatest mistake in history. But just the fact that Jesus knew Judas would betray him doesn't mean that Judas was a puppet of God's will. Judas made the choice. God knew what that choice would be and made it part of the plan. Judas didn't lose his relationship with Jesus; rather, he had never found Jesus. He is called the "son of hell" (John 17:12) because he was never saved.

Judas's life can help us if he makes us think again about our commitment to God. Is God's Spirit in us? Are we true disciples and followers, or uncommitted pretenders? We can choose disobedience and death, or we can choose repentance, forgiveness, hope, and eternal life. Judas's betrayal sent Jesus to the cross to guarantee that second choice, our only chance. Will we accept Christ's free gift, or—like Judas—betray him?

LESSONS: Evil plans and motives leave us open to being used by Satan for even greater evil
The consequences of evil are so devastating that even small lies and little wrongdoings have serious results
God's plan and purposes are worked out even in the worst possible events

KEY VERSES: "Then Satan entered into Judas Iscariot, who was one of the twelve disciples, and he went over to the chief priests and captains of the Temple guards to discuss the best way to betray Jesus to them" (Luke 22:3-4).
Jesus's story is told in the Gospels. He is also mentioned in Acts 1:17-19.

UPS:
• He was chosen as one of the 12 disciples; the only non-Galilean
• He kept the money bag for the expenses of the group
• He was able to recognize the evil in his betrayal of Jesus

DOWNS:
• He was greedy (John 12:6)
• He betrayed Jesus
• He committed suicide instead of seeking forgiveness

STATS:
• Where: probably from the town of Kerioth
• Occupation: disciple of Jesus
• Relatives: Father: Simon
• Contemporaries: Jesus, Pilate, Herod, the other 11 disciples

²⁸"I solemnly declare that any sin of man can be forgiven, even blasphemy against me; ²⁹but blasphemy against the Holy Spirit can never be forgiven. It is an eternal sin."

³⁰He told them this because they were saying he did his miracles by Satan's power [instead of acknowledging it was by the Holy Spirit's power].

^{31,32}Now his mother and brothers arrived at the crowded house where he was teaching, and they sent word for him to come out and talk with them. "Your mother and brothers are outside and want to see you," he was told.

³³He replied, "Who is my mother? Who are my brothers?" ³⁴Looking at those around him he said, "These are my mother and brothers! ³⁵Anyone who does God's will is my brother, and my sister, and my mother."

CHAPTER 4 A STORY ABOUT FOUR KINDS OF SOIL.

Once again an immense crowd gathered around him on the beach as he was teaching, so he got into a boat and sat down and talked from there. ²His usual method of teaching was to tell the people stories. One of them went like this:

³"Listen! A farmer decided to sow some grain. As he scattered it across his field, ⁴some of it fell on a path, and the birds came and picked it off the hard ground and ate it. ^{5,6}Some fell on thin soil with underlying rock. It grew up quickly enough, but soon wilted beneath the hot sun and died because the roots had no nourishment in the shallow soil. ⁷Other seeds fell among thorns that shot up and crowded the young plants so that they produced no grain. ⁸But some of the seeds fell into good soil and yielded thirty times as much as he had planted— some of it even sixty or a hundred times as much! ⁹If you have ears, listen!"

¹⁰Afterwards, when he was alone with the twelve and with his other disciples, they asked him, "What does your story mean?"

^{11,12}He replied, "You are permitted to know some truths about the Kingdom of God that are hidden to those outside the Kingdom:

'Though they see and hear, they will not understand or turn to God, or be forgiven for their sins.'

¹³But if you can't understand *this* simple illustration, what will you do about all the others I am going to tell?

¹⁴"The farmer I talked about is anyone who brings God's message to others, trying to plant good seed within their lives. ¹⁵The hard pathway, where some of the seed fell, represents the hard hearts of some of those who hear God's message; Satan comes at once to try to make them forget it. ¹⁶The rocky soil represents the hearts of those who hear the message with joy, ¹⁷but, like young plants in such soil, their roots don't go very deep, and though at first they get along fine, as soon as persecution begins, they wilt.

¹⁸"The thorny ground represents the hearts of people who listen to the Good News and receive it, ¹⁹but all too quickly the attractions of this world and the delights of wealth, and the search for success and lure of nice things come in and crowd out God's message from their hearts, so that no crop is produced.

²⁰"But the good soil represents the hearts of those who truly accept God's message and produce a plentiful harvest for God—thirty, sixty, or even a hundred times as much as was planted in their hearts."

²¹Then he asked them, "When someone lights a lamp, does he put a box over it to shut out the light? Of course not! The light couldn't be seen or used. A lamp is placed on a stand to shine and be useful.

²²"All that is now hidden will someday come to light. ²³If you have ears, listen! ²⁴And be sure to put into practice what you hear. The more you do this, the more you will understand what I tell you. ²⁵To him who has shall be given; from him who has not shall be taken away even what he has.

²⁶"Here is another story illustrating what the Kingdom of God is like:

"A farmer sowed his field ²⁷and went away, and as the days went by, the seeds grew and grew without his help. ²⁸For the soil made the seeds grow. First a leaf-blade pushed through, and later the wheat-heads formed and finally the grain ripened, ²⁹and then the farmer came at once with his sickle and harvested it."

³⁰Jesus asked, "How can I describe the Kingdom of God? What story shall I use to illustrate it? ^{31,32}It is like a tiny mustard seed! Though this is one of the smallest of seeds, yet it grows to become one of the largest of plants, with long branches where

RESPONSES

4:14-20 The four soils represent four different ways people respond to God's Word. Usually we think Jesus was talking about four different kinds of people, but he may also have been talking about (1) different times or phases in a person's life, or (2) how we willingly receive God's message in some areas of our lives and resist it in others. For example, you may be open to God where your future is concerned, but closed concerning how you spend your money. You may respond like good soil to God's demand for worship, but like rocky soil to his demand to give to those in need. Strive to be like good soil in every area of your life.

birds can build their nests and be sheltered."

[33]He used many such illustrations to teach the people as much as they were ready to understand. [34]In fact, he taught only by illustrations in his public teaching, but afterwards, when he was alone with his disciples, he would explain his meaning to them.

[35]As evening fell, Jesus said to his disciples, "Let's cross to the other side of the lake." [36]So they took him just as he was and started out, leaving the crowds behind (though other boats followed). [37]But soon a terrible storm arose. High waves began to break into the boat until it was nearly full of water and about to sink. [38]Jesus was asleep at the back of the boat with his head on a cushion. Frantically they wakened him, shouting, "Teacher, don't you even care that we are all about to drown?"

[39]Then he rebuked the wind and said to the sea, "Quiet down!" And the wind fell, and there was a great calm!

[40]And he asked them, "Why were you so fearful? Don't you even yet have confidence in me?"

[41]And they were filled with awe and said among themselves, "Who is this man, that even the winds and seas obey him?"

CHAPTER 5 JESUS HEALS A MAN WITH DEMONS.

When they arrived at the other side of the lake, a demon-possessed man ran out from a graveyard, just as Jesus was climbing from the boat.

[3,4]This man lived among the gravestones and had such strength that whenever he was put into handcuffs and shackles—as he often was—he snapped the handcuffs from his wrists and smashed the shackles and walked away. No one was strong enough to control him. [5]All day long and through the night he would wander among the tombs and in the wild hills, screaming and cutting himself with sharp pieces of stone.

[6]When Jesus was still far out on the water, the man had seen him and had run to meet him, and fell down before him.

[7,8]Then Jesus spoke to the demon within the man and said, "Come out, you evil spirit."

It gave a terrible scream, shrieking, "What are you going to do to me, Jesus, Son of the Most High God? For God's sake, don't torture me!"

[9]"What is your name?" Jesus asked, and the demon replied, "Legion, for there are many of us here within this man."

[10]Then the demons begged him again and again not to send them to some distant land.

[11]Now as it happened there was a huge herd of hogs rooting around on the hill above the lake. [12]"Send us into those hogs," the demons begged.

[13]And Jesus gave them permission. Then the evil spirits came out of the man and entered the hogs, and the entire herd plunged down the steep hillside into the lake and drowned.

[14]The herdsmen fled to the nearby towns and countryside, spreading the news as they ran. Every-

---

Now that I am a Christian, how should I act around my friends and family who are not believers?

I WONDER . . .

The most important thing you have going for you in both sets of relationships is that you already have a "relational bridge." Your friends and family knew what your life was like before you met Christ. Now they will have the chance to see you afterward.

In Mark 5:1-20, Jesus recognized that this was the case with the man he had just cleansed from demon possession. So he sent him back to his home instead of asking him to leave those who knew him best.

Another passage calls us Christ's ambassadors to our world (2 Corinthians 5:17-20). This means we are his hand-picked representatives! If people want to know what God is like, all they have to do is look at us.

God does not expect you to be perfect, but he does expect your faith to grow (Romans 10:17), and he expects you to try to live more like Jesus Christ would (Romans 12:1-2).

The people around you will be able to relate to your progress, not to perfection. Progress may be slow at first, but eventually, as you give areas of your life to Christ's control, changes will become noticeable. When this happens, you may find others starting to ask questions about your new faith.

When this happens, don't worry—although you may "feel" inadequate answering some of their questions, your responsibility is only to share what God has done for you and what you have learned, not to be the Bible expert. Sharing and living your faith as a new Christian is just as important (and biblical!) as being more mature in the faith or a Bible scholar. God is not limited by our lack of knowledge.

Though new Christians sometimes face unique hardships, Jesus knows that, as with the Gaderene demoniac, your changed life may have a much greater impact on those with whom you have relational bridges already built than a stranger who may speak more eloquently!

---

one rushed out to see for themselves. [15]And a large crowd soon gathered where Jesus was; but as they saw the man sitting there, fully clothed and perfectly sane, they were frightened. [16]Those who saw what happened were telling everyone about it, [17]and the crowd began pleading with Jesus to go away and leave them alone! [18]So he got back into the boat. The man who had been possessed by the demons begged Jesus to let him go along. [19]But Jesus said no.

"Go home to your friends," he told him, "and tell them what wonderful things God has done for you; and how merciful he has been."

²⁰So the man started off to visit the Ten Towns of that region and began to tell everyone about the great things Jesus had done for him; and they were awestruck by his story.

²¹When Jesus had gone across by boat to the other side of the lake, a vast crowd gathered around him on the shore.

²²The leader of the local synagogue, whose name was Jairus, came and fell down before him, ²³pleading with him to heal his little daughter.

"She is at the point of death," he said in desperation. "Please come and place your hands on her and make her live."

²⁴Jesus went with him, and the crowd thronged behind. ²⁵In the crowd was a woman who had been sick for twelve years with a hemorrhage. ²⁶She had suffered much from many doctors through the years and had become poor from paying them, and was no better but, in fact, was worse. ²⁷She had heard all about the wonderful miracles Jesus did, and that is why she came up behind him through the crowd and touched his clothes.

²⁸For she thought to herself, "If I can just touch his clothing, I will be healed." ²⁹And sure enough, as soon as she had touched him, the bleeding stopped and she knew she was well!

³⁰Jesus realized at once that healing power had gone out from him, so he turned around in the crowd and asked, "Who touched my clothes?"

³¹His disciples said to him, "All this crowd pressing around you, and you ask who touched you?"

³²But he kept on looking around to see who it was who had done it. ³³Then the frightened woman, trembling at the realization of what had happened to her, came and fell at his feet and told him what she had done. ³⁴And he said to her, "Daughter, your faith has made you well; go in peace, healed of your disease."

³⁵While he was still talking to her, messengers arrived from Jairus' home with the news that it was too late—his daughter was dead and there was no point in Jesus' coming now. ³⁶But Jesus ignored their comments and said to Jairus, "Don't be afraid. Just trust me."

³⁷Then Jesus halted the crowd and wouldn't let anyone go on with him to Jairus' home except Peter and James and John. ³⁸When they arrived, Jesus saw that all was in great confusion, with unrestrained weeping and wailing. ³⁹He went inside and spoke to the people.

"Why all this weeping and commotion?" he asked. "The child isn't dead; she is only asleep!"

⁴⁰They laughed at him in bitter derision, but he told them all to leave, and taking the little girl's father and mother and his three disciples, he went into the room where she was lying.

⁴¹,⁴²Taking her by the hand he said to her, "Get up, little girl!" (She was twelve years old.) And she jumped up and walked around! Her parents just couldn't get over it. ⁴³Jesus instructed them very earnestly not to tell what had happened and told them to give her something to eat.

CHAPTER **6** **REJECTED IN HIS HOMETOWN.** Soon afterwards he left that section of the country and returned with his disciples to Nazareth, his hometown. ²,³The next Sabbath he went to the synagogue to teach, and the people were astonished at his wisdom and his miracles because he was just a local man like themselves.

"He's no better than we are," they said. "He's just a carpenter, Mary's boy, and a brother of James and Joseph, Judas and Simon. And his sisters live right here among us." And they were offended!

⁴Then Jesus told them, "A prophet is honored everywhere except in his hometown and among his relatives and by his own family." ⁵And because of their unbelief he couldn't do any mighty miracles among them except to place his hands on a few sick people and heal them. ⁶And he could hardly accept the fact that they wouldn't believe in him.

Then he went out among the villages, teaching.

⁷And he called his twelve disciples together and sent them out two by two, with power to cast out demons. ⁸,⁹He told them to take nothing with them except their walking sticks—no food, no knapsack, no money, not even an extra pair of shoes or a change of clothes.

¹⁰"Stay at one home in each village—don't shift around from house to house while you are there," he said. ¹¹"And whenever a village won't accept you or listen to you, shake off the dust from your

ENTHUSIASTIC

5:19-20 This man who had been demon possessed became a living example of Jesus' power. He wanted to go with Jesus, but Jesus told him to go home and share his story there. If you have experienced Jesus' power, you, too, are a living example. Are you, like this man, enthusiastic about sharing the good news with those around you? Just as we would tell others about a doctor who cured a physical disease, we should tell about Christ who cures our sin.

PREJUDICE

6:2-3 Jesus was teaching effectively and wisely, but the people of his hometown saw him as only a carpenter. "He's no better than we are—he's just a common laborer," they said. They were offended that others could be impressed by him and follow him. They rejected his authority because he was one of their peers. They thought they knew him, but their preconceived notions about who he was made it impossible for them to accept his message. Don't let prejudice blind you to truth. As you learn more about Jesus, try to see him for who he really is.

"Go home to your friends," JESUS told him, "and tell them WHAT WONDERFUL THINGS GOD has done for YOU; and HOW merciful merciful merciful HE has been."

feet as you leave; it is a sign that you have abandoned it to its fate."

[12]So the disciples went out, telling everyone they met to turn from sin. [13]And they cast out many demons and healed many sick people, anointing them with olive oil.

[14]King Herod soon heard about Jesus, for his miracles were talked about everywhere. The king thought Jesus was John the Baptist come back to life again. So the people were saying, "No wonder he can do such miracles." [15] Others thought Jesus was Elijah the ancient prophet, now returned to life again; still others claimed he was a new prophet like the great ones of the past.

[16]"No," Herod said, "it is John, the man I beheaded. He has come back from the dead."

[17,18]For Herod had sent soldiers to arrest and imprison John because he kept saying it was wrong for the king to marry Herodias, his brother Philip's wife. [19]Herodias wanted John killed in revenge, but without Herod's approval she was powerless. [20]And Herod respected John, knowing that he was a good and holy man, and so he kept him under his protection. Herod was disturbed whenever he talked with John, but even so he liked to listen to him.

[21]Herodias' chance finally came. It was Herod's birthday and he gave a stag party for his palace aides, army officers, and the leading citizens of Galilee. [22,23]Then Herodias' daughter came in and danced before them and greatly pleased them all.

"Ask me for anything you like," the king vowed, "even half of my kingdom, and I will give it to you!"

[24]She went out and consulted her mother, who told her, "Ask for John the Baptist's head!"

[25]So she hurried back to the king and told him, "I want the head of John the Baptist—right now—on a tray!"

[26]Then the king was sorry, but he was embarrassed to break his oath in front of his guests. [27]So he sent one of his bodyguards to the prison to cut off John's head and bring it to him. The soldier killed John in the prison, [28]and brought back his head on a tray, and gave it to the girl and she took it to her mother.

[29]When John's disciples heard what had happened, they came for his body and buried it in a tomb.

TEAMWORK

6:7 The disciples were sent out in pairs. Individually they could have reached more areas of the country, but this was not Christ's plan. One advantage in going out by twos was that they could strengthen and encourage each other, especially when they faced rejection. Our strength comes from God, but he meets many of our needs through others. As you serve Christ, don't try to go it alone.

[30]The apostles now returned to Jesus from their tour and told him all they had done and what they had said to the people they visited.

[31]Then Jesus suggested, "Let's get away from the crowds for a while and rest." For so many people were coming and going that they scarcely had time to eat. [32]So they left by boat for a quieter spot. [33]But many people saw them leaving and ran on ahead along the shore and met them as they landed. [34]So the usual vast crowd was there as he stepped from the boat; and he had pity on them because they were like sheep without a shepherd, and he taught them many things they needed to know.

[35,36]Late in the afternoon his disciples came to him and said, "Tell the people to go away to the nearby villages and farms and buy themselves some food, for there is nothing to eat here in this desolate spot, and it is getting late."

[37]But Jesus said, *"You* feed them."

"With what?" they asked. "It would take a fortune to buy food for all this crowd!"

[38]"How much food do we have?" he asked. "Go and find out."

They came back to report that there were five loaves of bread and two fish. ³⁹,⁴⁰Then Jesus told the crowd to sit down, and soon colorful groups of fifty or a hundred each were sitting on the green grass.

⁴¹He took the five loaves and two fish and looking up to heaven, gave thanks for the food. Breaking the loaves into pieces, he gave some of the bread and fish to each disciple to place before the people. ⁴²And the crowd ate until they could hold no more!

⁴³,⁴⁴There were about 5,000 men there for that meal, and afterwards twelve basketfuls of scraps were picked up off the grass!

⁴⁵Immediately after this Jesus instructed his disciples to get back into the boat and strike out across the lake to Bethsaida, where he would join them later. He himself would stay and tell the crowds good-bye and get them started home.

⁴⁶Afterwards he went up into the hills to pray. ⁴⁷During the night, as the disciples in their boat were out in the middle of the lake, and he was alone on land, ⁴⁸he saw that they were in serious trouble, rowing hard and struggling against the wind and waves.

About three o'clock in the morning he walked out to them on the water. He started past them, ⁴⁹but when they saw something walking along beside them they screamed in terror, thinking it was a ghost, ⁵⁰for they all saw him.

But he spoke to them at once. "It's all right," he said. "It is I! Don't be afraid." ⁵¹Then he climbed into the boat and the wind stopped!

They just sat there, unable to take it in! ⁵²For they still didn't realize who he was, even after the miracle the evening before! For they didn't want to believe!

⁵³When they arrived at Gennesaret on the other side of the lake, they moored the boat ⁵⁴and climbed out.

The people standing around there recognized him at once, ⁵⁵and ran throughout the whole area to spread the news of his arrival, and began carrying sick folks to him on mats and stretchers. ⁵⁶Wherever he went—in villages and cities, and out on the farms—they laid the sick in the market plazas and streets, and begged him to let them at least touch the fringes of his clothes; and as many as touched him were healed.

CHAPTER 7 A BUNCH OF HYPOCRITES. One day some Jewish religious leaders arrived from Jerusalem to investigate him, ²and noticed that some of his disciples failed to follow the usual Jewish rituals before eating. ³(For the Jews, especially the Pharisees, will never eat until they have sprinkled their arms to the elbows, as required by their ancient traditions. ⁴So when they come home from the market they must always sprinkle themselves in this way before touching any food. This is but one of many examples of laws and regulations they have clung to for centuries, and still follow, such as their ceremony of cleansing for pots, pans and dishes.)

⁵So the religious leaders asked him, "Why don't your disciples follow our age-old customs? For they eat without first performing the washing ceremony."

⁶,⁷Jesus replied, "You bunch of hypocrites! Isaiah the prophet described you very well when he said, 'These people speak very prettily about the Lord but they have no love for him at all. Their worship is a farce, for they claim that God commands the people to obey their petty rules.' How right Isaiah was! ⁸For you ignore God's specific orders and substitute your own traditions. ⁹You are simply rejecting God's laws and trampling them under your feet for the sake of tradition.

¹⁰For instance, Moses gave you this law from God: 'Honor your father and mother.' And he said that anyone who speaks against his father or mother must die. ¹¹But you say it is perfectly all

LEGALISM

Perhaps you know someone like seventeen-year-old Neal.

A very opinionated churchgoer, he's got the Christian life all figured out (so he thinks). For Neal, there are no "gray areas." Everything is black and white, cut and dry. Certain deeds are expected, and most other activities simply are not acceptable for believers. And if you don't see things his way, Neal treats you like your relationship with the Lord is defective. Just look at some of his recent pronouncements:

• "Anybody who goes dancing is not walking with God."

• "How a girl who wears an outfit like that could call herself a Christian is beyond me!"

• "Going to a movie theater is no different than going into a bar. Both places are evil."

• "If you guys are serious about God, you'll be at youth group Wednesday night."

Is it any wonder that this outspoken junior has been nicknamed "Negative Neal"?

Legalism is the crazy idea that we can earn God's acceptance by strenuously following a lot of dos and don'ts. Legalistic people almost always feel either prideful ("I'm better than the people who do these things") or frustrated ("I can never measure up").

Is that what the Christian life is all about? A long list of rules and regulations? Not at all! Even if you don't know anyone as extreme as Neal, and even if you don't think you struggle with legalism, see what Jesus said in Mark 7:1-23.

EXCUSES

7:10-11 The Pharisees used God as an excuse to avoid helping their families, especially their parents. They thought it was more important to put money in the Temple treasury than to help their needy parents, although God's Law specifically says to honor fathers and mothers (Exodus 20:12) and to care for those in need (Leviticus 25:35-43). We should give money and time to God, but we must never use God as an excuse to neglect our responsibilities. Helping those in need is one of the most important ways to honor God.

right for a man to disregard his needy parents, telling them, 'Sorry, I can't help you! For I have given to God what I could have given to you.' [12,13]And so you break the law of God in order to protect your man-made tradition. And this is only one example. There are many, many others."

[14]Then Jesus called to the crowd to come and hear. "All of you listen," he said, "and try to understand. [15,16]Your souls aren't harmed by what you eat, but by what you think and say!"

[17]Then he went into a house to get away from the crowds, and his disciples asked him what he meant by the statement he had just made.

[18]"Don't you understand either?" he asked. "Can't you see that what you eat won't harm your soul? [19]For food doesn't come in contact with your heart, but only passes through the digestive system." (By saying this he showed that every kind of food is kosher.)

[20]And then he added, "It is the thought-life that pollutes. [21]For from within, out of men's hearts, come evil thoughts of lust, theft, murder, adultery, [22]wanting what belongs to others, wickedness, deceit, lewdness, envy, slander, pride, and all other folly. [23]All these vile things come from within; they are what pollute you and make you unfit for God."

[24]Then he left Galilee and went to the region of Tyre and Sidon, and tried to keep it a secret that he was there, but couldn't. For as usual the news of his arrival spread fast.

[25]Right away a woman came to him whose little girl was possessed by a demon. She had heard about Jesus and now she came and fell at his feet, [26]and pled with him to release her child from the demon's control. (But she was Syrophoenician—a "despised Gentile!")

[27]Jesus told her, "First I should help my own family—the Jews. It isn't right to take the children's food and throw it to the dogs."

[28]She replied, "That's true, sir, but even the puppies under the table are given some scraps from the children's plates."

[29]"Good!" he said. "You have answered well—so well that I have healed your little girl. Go on home, for the demon has left her!"

[30]And when she arrived home, her little girl was lying quietly in bed, and the demon was gone.

[31]From Tyre he went to Sidon, then back to the Sea of Galilee by way of the Ten Towns. [32]A deaf man with a speech impediment was brought to him, and everyone begged Jesus to lay his hands on the man and heal him.

[33]Jesus led him away from the crowd and put his fingers into the man's ears, then spat and touched the man's tongue with the spittle. [34]Then, looking up to heaven, he sighed and commanded, "Open!" [35]Instantly the man could hear perfectly and speak plainly!

[36]Jesus told the crowd not to spread the news, but the more he forbade them, the more they made it known, [37]for they were overcome with utter amazement. Again and again they said, "Everything he does is wonderful; he even corrects deafness and stammering!"

CHAPTER **8** ANOTHER MEALTIME MIRACLE.

One day about this time as another great crowd gathered, the people ran out of food again. Jesus called his disciples to discuss the situation.

"I pity these people," he said, "for they have been here three days and have nothing left to eat. [3]And if I send them home without feeding them, they will faint along the road! For some of them have come a long distance."

[4]"Are we supposed to find food for them here in the desert?" his disciples scoffed.

[5]"How many loaves of bread do you have?" he asked.

"Seven," they replied. [6]So he told the crowd to sit down on the ground. Then he took the seven loaves, thanked God for them, broke them into pieces and passed them to his disciples; and the disciples placed them before the people. [7]A few small fish were found, too, so Jesus also blessed these and told the disciples to serve them.

[8,9]And the whole crowd ate until they were full, and afterwards he sent them home. There were about 4,000 people in the crowd that day and when the scraps were picked up after the meal, there were seven very large basketfuls left over!

[10]Immediately after this he got into a boat with his disciples and came to the region of Dalmanutha.

[11]When the local Jewish leaders learned of his arrival, they came to argue with him.

"Do a miracle for us," they said. "Make something happen in the sky. Then we will believe in you."

[12]He sighed deeply when he heard this and he said, "Certainly not. How many more miracles do you people need?"

[13]So he got back into the boat and left them, and crossed to the other side of the lake. [14]But the disciples had forgotten to stock up on food before they left and had only one loaf of bread in the boat.

HE KNOWS

8:1-3 Do you ever feel that God is so busy with important concerns that he can't possibly be aware of your needs? Just as Jesus was concerned about those people's need for food, he is concerned about our daily needs. At another time Jesus said, "Don't worry at all about having enough food and clothing. . . . Your heavenly Father already knows perfectly well that you need them" (Matthew 6:31-32). Do you have concerns that you think would not interest God? There is no concern too large for him to handle, and no need too small to escape his interest.

¹⁵As they were crossing, Jesus said to them very solemnly, "Beware of the yeast of King Herod and of the Pharisees."

¹⁶"What does he mean?" the disciples asked each other. They finally decided that he must be talking about their forgetting to bring bread.

¹⁷Jesus realized what they were discussing and said, "No, that isn't it at all! Can't you understand? Are your hearts too hard to take it in? ¹⁸Your eyes are to see with—why don't you look? Why don't you open your ears and listen?' Don't you remember anything at all? ¹⁹"What about the 5,000 men I fed with five loaves of bread? How many basketfuls of scraps did you pick up afterwards?"

"Twelve," they said.

²⁰"And when I fed the 4,000 with seven loaves, how much was left?"

"Seven basketfuls," they said.

²¹"And yet you think I'm worried that we have no bread?"

²²When they arrived at Bethsaida, some people brought a blind man to him and begged him to touch and heal him. ²³Jesus took the blind man by the hand and led him out of the village, and spat upon his eyes, and laid his hands over them.

"Can you see anything now?" Jesus asked him.

²⁴The man looked around. "Yes!" he said, "I see men! But I can't see them very clearly; they look like tree trunks walking around!"

²⁵Then Jesus placed his hands over the man's eyes again and as the man stared intently, his sight was completely restored, and he saw everything clearly, drinking in the sights around him.

²⁶Jesus sent him home to his family. "Don't even go back to the village first," he said.

²⁷Jesus and his disciples now left Galilee and went out to the villages of Caesarea Philippi. As they were walking along he asked them, "Who do the people think I am? What are they saying about me?"

²⁸"Some of them think you are John the Baptist," the disciples replied, "and others say you are Elijah or some other ancient prophet come back to life again."

²⁹Then he asked, "Who do you think I am?" Peter replied, "You are the Messiah." ³⁰But Jesus warned them not to tell anyone!

³¹Then he began to tell them about the terrible things he would suffer, and that he would be rejected by the elders and the Chief Priests and the other Jewish leaders—and be killed, and that he would rise again three days afterwards. ³²He talked about it quite frankly with them, so Peter took him aside and chided him. "You shouldn't say things like that," he told Jesus.

³³Jesus turned and looked at his disciples and then said to Peter very sternly, "Satan, get behind me! You are looking at this only from a human point of view and not from God's."

³⁴Then he called his disciples and the crowds to come over and listen. "If any of you wants to be my follower," he told them, "you must put aside your own pleasures and shoulder your cross, and follow me closely. ³⁵If you insist on saving your life, you will lose it. Only those who throw away their lives for my sake and for the sake of the Good News will ever know what it means to really live.

³⁶"And how does a man benefit if he gains the whole world and loses his soul in the process? ³⁷For is anything worth more than his soul? ³⁸And anyone who is ashamed of me and my message in these days of unbelief and sin, I, the Messiah, will be ashamed of him when I return in the glory of my Father, with the holy angels."

CHAPTER **9** **THE TRANSFIGURATION.** Jesus went on to say to his disciples, "Some of you who are standing here right now will live to see the Kingdom of God arrive in great power!"

²Six days later Jesus took Peter, James and John to the top of a mountain. No one else was there.

Suddenly his face began to shine with glory, ³and his clothing became dazzling white, far more glorious than any earthly process could ever make it! ⁴Then Elijah and Moses appeared and began talking with Jesus!

SUCCESS

You've heard of *A Tale of Two Cities?* Call this "A Tale of Two Sisters."

Karen, a senior, has a 4.0 grade-point average and is practically guaranteed a scholarship. She is president of her class, and is both captain and number one seed on the girl's tennis team. Tan and very pretty, Karen dates Mitchell. Together they were voted by their class as "most likely to succeed." Karen's ambition? To marry Mitchell and be a stockbroker on Wall street in New York City.

If Karen represents "the best of times," then to many, Alice, a sophomore, probably embodies "the worst of times." She struggles in school, making mostly Cs. She is not especially popular, nor is she very athletic. No, the truth is that Alice is painfully shy and average-looking. She has not been blessed with a boyfriend, voted into office, or had predictions of greatness bestowed upon her. Most of her free time goes to serving as a Big Sister to two youngsters at a local orphanage. Her goal in life? To be a secretary.

Do you know anyone like Karen? Like Alice? Which girl do you think is the most successful? By what standards does our society judge success and failure? What does Jesus say in Mark 9:33-37?

YOU

8:29 Jesus asked the disciples who others thought he was; then he focused on them: "Who do *you* think I am?" It is not enough to know what others say about Jesus: you must know, understand, and accept for yourself that he is the Messiah. You must move from curiosity to commitment and from admiration to adoration.

5"Teacher, this is wonderful!" Peter exclaimed. "We will make three shelters here, one for each of you. . . ."

6He said this just to be talking, for he didn't know what else to say and they were all terribly frightened.

7But while he was still speaking these words, a cloud covered them, blotting out the sun, and a voice from the cloud said, *"This* is my beloved Son. Listen to *him."*

8Then suddenly they looked around and Moses and Elijah were gone, and only Jesus was with them.

9As they descended the mountainside he told them never to mention what they had seen until after he had risen from the dead. 10So they kept it to themselves, but often talked about it, and wondered what he meant by "rising from the dead."

11Now they began asking him about something the Jewish religious leaders often spoke of, that Elijah must return [before the Messiah could come]. 12,13Jesus agreed that Elijah must come first and prepare the way—and that he had, in fact, already come! And that he had been terribly mistreated, just as the prophets had predicted. Then Jesus asked them what the prophets could have been talking about when they predicted that the Messiah would suffer and be treated with utter contempt.

14At the bottom of the mountain they found a great crowd surrounding the other nine disciples, as some Jewish leaders argued with them. 15The crowd watched Jesus in awe as he came toward them, and then ran to greet him. 16"What's all the argument about?" he asked.

17One of the men in the crowd spoke up and said, "Teacher, I brought my son for you to heal—he can't talk because he is possessed by a demon. 18And whenever the demon is in control of him it dashes him to the ground and makes him foam at the mouth and grind his teeth and become rigid. So I begged your disciples to cast out the demon, but they couldn't do it."

19Jesus said [to his disciples], "Oh, what tiny faith you have; how much longer must I be with you until you believe? How much longer must I be patient with you? Bring the boy to me."

20So they brought the boy, but when he saw Jesus the demon convulsed the child horribly, and he fell to the ground writhing and foaming at the mouth.

21"How long has he been this way?" Jesus asked the father.

And he replied, "Since he was very small, 22and the demon often makes him fall into the fire or into water to kill him. Oh, have mercy on us and do something if you can."

23"If I can?" Jesus asked. *"Anything* is possible if you have faith."

24The father instantly replied, "I *do* have faith; oh, help me to have *more!"*

25When Jesus saw the crowd was growing he rebuked the demon.

"O demon of deafness and dumbness," he said, "I command you to come out of this child and enter him no more!"

26Then the demon screamed terribly and convulsed the boy again and left him; and the boy lay there limp and motionless, to all appearance dead. A murmur ran through the crowd—"He is dead."

27But Jesus took him by the hand and helped him to his feet and he stood up and was all right! 28Afterwards, when Jesus was alone in the house with his disciples, they asked him, "Why couldn't we cast that demon out?"

29Jesus replied, "Cases like this require prayer."

30,31Leaving that region they traveled through Galilee where he tried to avoid all publicity in order to spend more time with his disciples, teaching them. He would say to them, "I, the Messiah, am going to be betrayed and killed and three days later I will return to life again."

32But they didn't understand and were afraid to ask him what he meant.

33And so they arrived at Capernaum. When they were settled in the house where they were to stay he asked them, "What were you discussing out on the road?"

34But they were ashamed to answer, for they had been arguing about which of them was the greatest!

35He sat down and called them around him and said, "Anyone wanting to be the greatest must be the least—the servant of all!"

36Then he placed a little child among them; and taking the child in his arms he said to them, 37"Anyone who welcomes a little child like this in my name is welcoming me, and anyone who welcomes me is welcoming my Father who sent me!"

38One of his disciples, John, told him one day, "Teacher, we saw a man using your name to cast out demons; but we told him not to, for he isn't one of our group."

39"Don't forbid him!" Jesus said. "For no one doing miracles in my name will quickly turn against me. 40Anyone who isn't against us is for us. 41If anyone so much as gives you a cup of water

POWER

9:23 These words of Jesus' do not mean that we can automatically obtain anything we want if we just think positively. Jesus meant that anything is *possible* with faith because nothing is too difficult for God. This is not a teaching on how to pray as much as a statement about God's power to overcome obstacles to his work. We cannot have everything we pray for as if by magic, but, with faith, we can have everything we need to serve God.

RUTHLESS

9:43ff Jesus used startling language to stress the importance of cutting sin out of our life. Painful discipline is required of his true followers. Giving up a relationship, job, or habit that is against God's will may seem just as painful as cutting off a hand. Our high goal, however, is worth any sacrifice; Christ is worth any possible loss. Nothing should stand in the way of faith. We must be ruthless in removing sins from our life now in order to avoid being stuck with them for eternity. Make your choices from an eternal perspective.

because you are Christ's—I say this solemnly—he won't lose his reward. [42]But if someone causes one of these little ones who believe in me to lose faith—it would be better for that man if a huge millstone were tied around his neck and he were thrown into the sea. [43,44]"If your hand does wrong, cut it off. Better live forever with one hand than be thrown into the unquenchable fires of hell with two! [45,46]If your foot carries you toward evil, cut it off! Better be lame and live forever than have two feet that carry you to hell.

[47]"And if your eye is sinful, gouge it out. Better enter the Kingdom of God half blind than have two eyes and see the fires of hell, [48]where the worm never dies, and the fire never goes out—[49]where all are salted with fire.

[50]"Good salt is worthless if it loses its saltiness; it can't season anything. So don't lose your flavor! Live in peace with each other."

CHAPTER 10 MARRIAGE AND DIVORCE. Then he left Capernaum and went southward to the Judean borders and into the area east of the Jordan River. And as always there were the crowds; and as usual he taught them.

[2]Some Pharisees came and asked him, "Do you permit divorce?" Of course they were trying to trap him.

[3]"What did Moses say about divorce?" Jesus asked them.

[4]"He said it was all right," they replied. "He said that all a man has to do is write his wife a letter of dismissal."

[5]"And why did he say that?" Jesus asked. "I'll tell you why—it was a concession to your hardhearted wickedness. [6,7]But it certainly isn't God's way. For from the very first he made man and woman to be joined together permanently in marriage; therefore a man is to leave his father and mother, [8]and he and his wife are united so that they are no longer two, but one. [9]And no man may separate what God has joined together."

[10]Later, when he was alone with his disciples in the house, they brought up the subject again.

[11]He told them, "When a man divorces his wife to marry someone else, he commits adultery against her. [12]And if a wife divorces her husband and remarries, she, too, commits adultery."

[13]Once when some mothers were bringing their children to Jesus to bless them, the disciples shooed them away, telling them not to bother him.

[14]But when Jesus saw what was happening he was very much displeased with his disciples and said to them, "Let the children come to me, for the Kingdom of God belongs to such as they. Don't send them away! [15]I tell you as seriously as I know how that anyone who refuses to come to God as a little child will never be allowed into his Kingdom."

[16]Then he took the children into his arms and placed his hands on their heads and he blessed them.

[17]As he was starting out on a trip, a man came running to him and knelt down and asked, "Good Teacher, what must I do to get to heaven?"

[18]"Why do you call me good?" Jesus asked. "Only God is truly good! [19]But as for your question—you know the commandments: don't kill, don't commit adultery, don't steal, don't lie, don't cheat, respect your father and mother."

[20]"Teacher," the man replied, "I've never once broken a single one of those laws."

[21]Jesus felt genuine love for this man as he looked at him. "You lack only one thing," he told him; "go and sell all you have and give the money to the poor—and you shall have treasure in heaven—and come, follow me."

[22]Then the man's face fell, and he went sadly away, for he was very rich.

[23]Jesus watched him go, then turned around and said to his disciples, "It's almost impossible for the rich to get into the Kingdom of God!"

[24]This amazed them. So Jesus said it again: "Dear children, how hard it is for those who trust in riches to enter the Kingdom of God. [25]It is easier for a camel to go through the eye of a needle than for a rich man to enter the Kingdom of God."

[26]The disciples were incredulous! "Then who in the world can be saved, if not a rich man?" they asked.

[27]Jesus looked at them intently, then said, "Without God, it is utterly impossible. But with God everything is possible."

[28]Then Peter began to mention all that he and

BARRIERS

10:17-23 This young man wanted to be sure he would get eternal life, so he asked what he could *do*. Jesus lovingly addressed him with a challenge that brought out his true motives: "Sell all you have and give to the poor." Here was the barrier that could keep this young man out of the Kingdom: his love of money. Money represented his pride of accomplishment and self-effort. Ironically, the young man's attitude kept him from keeping the first commandment, to let nothing be more important than God (Exodus 20:3). He could not meet the one requirement Jesus gave—to turn his whole heart and life over to God. The man came to Jesus wondering what he could do; he left seeing what he was unable to do. What barriers are keeping you from turning your life over to Christ?

the other disciples had left behind. "We've given up everything to follow you," he said.

[29]And Jesus replied, "Let me assure you that no one has ever given up anything—home, brothers, sisters, mother, father, children, or property—for love of me and to tell others the Good News, [30]who won't be given back, a hundred times over, homes, brothers, sisters, mothers, children, and land—with persecutions!

"All these will be his here on earth, and in the world to come he shall have eternal life. [31]But many people who seem to be important now will be the least important then; and many who are considered least here shall be greatest there."

[32]Now they were on the way to Jerusalem, and Jesus was walking along ahead; and as the disciples were following they were filled with terror and dread.

Taking them aside, Jesus once more began describing all that was going to happen to him when they arrived at Jerusalem.

[33]"When we get there," he told them, "I, the Messiah, will be arrested and taken before the chief priests and the Jewish leaders, who will sentence me to die and hand me over to the Romans to be killed. [34]They will mock me and spit on me and flog me with their whips and kill me; but after three days I will come back to life again."

[35]Then James and John, the sons of Zebedee, came over and spoke to him in a low voice. "Master," they said, "we want you to do us a favor."

[36]"What is it?" he asked.

[37]"We want to sit on the thrones next to yours in your Kingdom," they said, "one at your right and the other at your left!"

[38]But Jesus answered, "You don't know what you are asking! Are you able to drink from the bitter cup of sorrow I must drink from? Or to be baptized with the baptism of suffering I must be baptized with?"

[39]"Oh, yes," they said, "we are!"

And Jesus said, "You shall indeed drink from my cup and be baptized with my baptism, [40]but I do not have the right to place you on thrones next to mine. Those appointments have already been made."

[41]When the other disciples dis-covered what James and John had asked, they were very indignant. [42]So Jesus called them to him and said, "As you know, the kings and great men of the earth lord it over the people; [43]but among you it is different. Whoever wants to be great among you must be your servant. [44]And whoever wants to be greatest of all must be the slave of all. [45]For even I, the Messiah, am not here to be served, but to help others, and to give my life as a ransom for many."

[46]And so they reached Jericho. Later, as they left town, a great crowd was following. Now it happened that a blind beggar named Bartimaeus (the son of Timaeus) was sitting beside the road as Jesus was going by.

[47]When Bartimaeus heard that Jesus from Nazareth was near, he began to shout out, "Jesus, Son of David, have mercy on me!"

[48]"Shut up!" some of the people yelled at him.

But he only shouted the louder, again and again, "O Son of David, have mercy on me!"

[49]When Jesus heard him, he stopped there in the road and said, "Tell him to come here."

So they called the blind man. "You lucky fellow," they said, "come on, he's calling you!"

"Here's what I did..."

In my school, people are popular only if they have the right looks, the right clothes, live in a certain neighborhood, play on the football team or are a cheerleader, or date a football player or cheerleader. The lines are pretty clearly drawn. And I'm on the other side of every one of those lines.

For a while it really bothered me. But when I tried to break into one of the cliques I found myself acting phony, and I couldn't stand it. I couldn't seem to help it, though; I wanted people to like me. I wanted to be popular.

Then, slowly, my viewpoint changed. The change started when my youth group studied the book of Mark. I really related to the disciples in chapters 9 and 10. They were trying to see who was more popular with Jesus, who would be considered the greatest. And Jesus said, "If you want to be the greatest, you have to become the lowest, the servant of all." He also said that, in God's eyes, many who seem to be most important now are least important, and many who seem least important now are really most important (Mark 10:31).

I realized it didn't really matter whether kids in my school thought I was great; what matters is what God thinks of me. If I want him to think I'm great, I have to forget about the phoniness and just try to be friends with all kinds of people.

I've started doing that, and now I have lots of friends. I still wouldn't be considered one of the "popular" people, but that's OK now. I'm in touch with God, and because of that, I know I'm popular with one Person whose opinion really matters.

Marita

AGE 16

^{50}Bartimaeus yanked off his old coat and flung it aside, jumped up and came to Jesus.

^{51}"What do you want me to do for you?" Jesus asked.

"O Teacher," the blind man said, "I want to see!"

^{52}And Jesus said to him, "All right, it's done. Your faith has healed you."

And instantly the blind man could see and followed Jesus down the road!

CHAPTER 11 CROWDS WELCOME JESUS.

As they neared Bethphage and Bethany on the outskirts of Jerusalem and came to the Mount of Olives, Jesus sent two of his disciples on ahead.

^{2}"Go into that village over there," he told them, "and just as you enter you will see a colt tied up that has never been ridden. Untie him and bring him here. ^{3}And if anyone asks you what you are doing, just say, 'Our Master needs him and will return him soon.'"

^{4,5}Off went the two men and found the colt standing in the street, tied outside a house. As they were untying it, some who were standing there demanded, "What are you doing, untying that colt?"

^{6}So they said what Jesus had told them to, and then the men agreed.

^{7}So the colt was brought to Jesus, and the disciples threw their cloaks across its back for him to ride on. ^{8}Then many in the crowd spread out their coats along the road before him, while others threw down leafy branches from the fields.

^{9}He was in the center of the procession with crowds ahead and behind, and all of them shouting, "Hail to the King!" "Praise God for him who comes in the name of the Lord!" . . . ^{10}"Praise God for the return of our father David's kingdom . . . " "Hail to the King of the universe!"

^{11}And so he entered Jerusalem and went into the Temple. He looked around carefully at everything and then left—for now it was late in the afternoon—and went out to Bethany with the twelve disciples.

^{12}The next morning as they left Bethany, he felt hungry. ^{13}A little way off he noticed a fig tree in full leaf, so he went over to see if he could find any figs on it. But no, there were only leaves, for it was too early in the season for fruit.

^{14}Then Jesus said to the tree, "You shall never bear fruit again!" And the disciples heard him say it.

^{15}When they arrived back to Jerusalem he went to the Temple and began to drive out the merchants and their customers, and knocked over the tables of the moneychangers and the stalls of those selling doves, ^{16}and stopped everyone from bringing in loads of merchandise.

^{17}He told them, "It is written in the Scriptures, 'My Temple is to be a place of prayer for all nations,' but you have turned it into a den of robbers."

^{18}When the chief priests and other Jewish leaders heard what he had done, they began planning how best to get rid of him. Their problem was their fear of riots because the people were so enthusiastic about Jesus' teaching.

^{19}That evening as usual they left the city.

^{20}Next morning, as the disciples passed the fig tree he had cursed, they saw that it was withered from the roots! ^{21}Then Peter remembered what Jesus had said to the tree on the previous day and exclaimed, "Look, Teacher! The fig tree you cursed has withered!"

^{22,23}In reply Jesus said to the disciples, "If you only have faith in God—this is the absolute truth—you can say to this Mount of Olives, 'Rise up and fall into the Mediterranean,' and your command will be obeyed. All that's required is that you really believe and have no doubt! ^{24}Listen to me! You can pray for *anything,* and *if you believe, you have it;* it's yours! ^{25}But when you are praying, first forgive anyone you are holding a grudge against, so that your Father in heaven will forgive you your sins too."

$^{26-28}$ By this time they had arrived in Jerusalem again, and as he was walking through the Temple area, the chief priests and other Jewish leaders came up to him demanding, "What's going on here? Who gave you the authority to drive out the merchants?"

^{29}Jesus replied, "I'll tell you if you answer one question! ^{30}What about John the Baptist? Was he sent by God, or not? Answer me!"

^{31}They talked it over among themselves. "If we reply that God sent him, then he will say, 'All right, why didn't you accept him?' ^{32}But if we say God didn't send him, then the people will start a riot." (For the people all believed strongly that John was a prophet.)

UPSET

11:14-15 Jesus became angry, but he did not sin in his anger. There is a place for righteous indignation. Christians should be upset about sin and injustice and should take a stand against them. Unfortunately, believers often are passive about these important issues and get angry over personal insults and petty irritations. Direct your anger toward the right issues.

MOTIVATED

11:24 Jesus, our example for prayer, once prayed, "Everything is possible. . . . Yet I want your will, not mine" (Mark 14:36). Often when we pray, we are motivated by our own interests and desires. We like to hear that we can have anything. But Jesus prayed with God's interests in mind. When we pray, we are to express our desires, but we should want God's will above ours. Check yourself to see if your prayers are focusing on your interests or on God's.

[33]So they said, "We can't answer. We don't know."

To which Jesus replied, "Then I won't answer your question either!"

CHAPTER 12 A STORY ABOUT A FARM. Here are some of the story-illustrations Jesus gave to the people at that time:

"A man planted a vineyard and built a wall around it and dug a pit for pressing out the grape juice, and built a watchman's tower. Then he leased the farm to tenant farmers and moved to another country. [2]At grape-picking time he sent one of his men to collect his share of the crop. [3]But the farmers beat up the man and sent him back empty-handed.

[4]"The owner then sent another of his men, who received the same treatment, only worse, for his head was seriously injured. [5]The next man he sent was killed; and later, others were either beaten or killed, until [6]there was only one left—his only son. He finally sent him, thinking they would surely give him their full respect.

[7]"But when the farmers saw him coming they said, 'He will own the farm when his father dies. Come on, let's kill him—and then the farm will be ours!' [8]So they caught him and murdered him and threw his body out of the vineyard.

[9]"What do you suppose the owner will do when he hears what happened? He will come and kill them all, and lease the vineyard to others. [10]Don't you remember reading this verse in the Scriptures? 'The Rock the builders threw away became the cornerstone, the most honored stone in the building! [11]This is the Lord's doing and it is an amazing thing to see.'"

[12]The Jewish leaders wanted to arrest him then and there for using this illustration, for they knew he was pointing at them—they were the wicked farmers in his story. But they were afraid to touch

WHAT JESUS SAID ABOUT LOVE

In Mark 12:28, a teacher of religion asked Jesus which one of all the commandments was the most important to follow. Jesus mentioned two commandments, one from Deuteronomy 6:5, the other from Leviticus 19:18. Both had to do with love. Why is love so important? Jesus said that all of the commandments were given for two simple reasons—to help us love God and love others as we should.

What Else Did Jesus Say about Love?	Reference
God loves us.	John 3:16
We are to love God.	Matthew 22:37
Because God loves us, he cares for us.	Matthew 6:25-34
God wants everyone to know how much he loves them.	John 17:23
God loves even those who hate him; we are to do the same.	Matthew 5:43-47, Luke 6:35
God seeks out even those most alienated from him.	Luke 15
God must be your first love.	Matthew 6:24; 10:37
You love God when you obey him.	John 14:21; 15:10
God loves Jesus his Son.	John 5:20; 10:17
Jesus loves God.	John 14:31
Those who refuse Jesus don't have God's love.	John 5:41-44
Jesus loves us just as God loves Jesus.	John 15:9
Jesus proved his love for us by dying on the cross so that we could live eternally with him.	John 3:14-15; 15:13-14
The love between God and Jesus is the perfect example of how we are to love others.	John 17:21-26
We are to love one another (John 13:34-35) and demonstrate that love.	Matthew 5:40-41; 10:42
We are not to love the praise of men (John 12:43), selfish recognition (Matthew 23:6), earthly belongings (Luke 16:19-31), or anything more than God.	Luke 16:13
Jesus' love extends to each individual.	John 10:11-15; Mark 10:21
Jesus wants us to love him through the good and difficult times.	Matthew 26:31-35
Jesus wants our love to be genuine.	John 21:15-17

IMAGE

12:17 The Pharisees and Herodians thought they had the perfect question to trap Jesus. But Jesus answered wisely, once again exposing their self-interest and wrong motives. Jesus said that the coin bearing the emperor's image should be given to the emperor. But whatever bears God's image—our life—belongs to God. Are you giving God all that is rightfully his? Make sure your life is given to God—you bear his image.

him for fear of a mob. So they left him and went away.

[13]But they sent other religious and political leaders to talk with him and try to trap him into saying something he could be arrested for.

[14]"Teacher," these spies said, "we know you tell the truth no matter what! You aren't influenced by the opinions and desires of men, but sincerely teach the ways of God. Now tell us, is it right to pay taxes to Rome, or not?"

[15]Jesus saw their trick and said, "Show me a coin and I'll tell you."

[16]When they handed it to him he asked, "Whose picture and title is this on the coin?" They replied, "The emperor's."

[17]"All right," he said, "if it is his, give it to him. But everything that belongs to God must be given to God!" And they scratched their heads in bafflement at his reply.

[18]Then the Sadducees stepped forward—a group of men who say there is no resurrection. Here was their question:

[19]"Teacher, Moses gave us a law that when a man dies without children, the man's brother should marry his widow and have children in his brother's name. [20-22]Well, there were seven brothers and the oldest married and died, and left no children. So the second brother married the widow, but soon he died too and left no children. Then the next brother married her and died without children, and so on until all were dead, and still there were no children; and last of all, the woman died too.

[23]"What we want to know is this: In the resurrection, whose wife will she be, for she had been the wife of each of them?"

[24]Jesus replied, "Your trouble is that you don't know the Scriptures and don't know the power of God. [25]For when these seven brothers and the woman rise from the dead, they won't be married—they will be like the angels.

[26]"But now as to whether there will be a resurrection—have you never read in the book of Exodus about Moses and the burning bush? God said to Moses, 'I *am* the God of Abraham, and I *am* the God of Isaac, and I *am* the God of Jacob.'

[27]"God was telling Moses that these men, though dead for hundreds of years, were still very much alive, for he would not have said, 'I *am* God' of those who don't exist! You have made a serious error."

[28]One of the teachers of religion who was standing there listening to the discussion realized that

Jesus had answered well. So he asked, "Of all the commandments, which is the most important?"

[29]Jesus replied, "The one that says, 'Hear, O Israel! The Lord our God is the one and only God. [30]And you must love him with all your heart and soul and mind and strength.'

[31]"The second is: 'You must love others as much as yourself.' No other commandments are greater than these."

[32]The teacher of religion replied, "Sir, you have spoken a true word in saying that there is only one God and no other. [33]And I know it is far more important to love him with all my heart and understanding and strength, and to love others as myself, than to offer all kinds of sacrifices on the altar of the Temple."

[34]Realizing this man's understanding, Jesus said to him, "You are not far from the Kingdom of God." And after that, no one dared ask him any more questions.

[35]Later, as Jesus was teaching the people in the Temple area, he asked them this question:

"Why do your religious teachers claim that the Messiah must be a descendant of King David? [36]For David himself said—and the Holy Spirit was speaking through him when he said it—'God said to my Lord, sit at my right hand until I make your enemies your footstool.' [37]Since David called him his Lord, how can he be his *son?*"

(This sort of reasoning delighted the crowd and they listened to him with great interest.)

[38]Here are some of the other things he taught them at this time:

"Beware of the teachers of religion! For they love to wear the robes of the rich and scholarly, and to have everyone bow to them as they walk through the markets. [39]They love to sit in the best seats in the synagogues and at the places of honor at banquets—[40]but they shamelessly cheat widows out of their homes and then, to cover up the kind of men they really are, they pretend to be pious by praying long prayers in public. Because of this, their punishment will be the greater."

[41]Then he went over to the collection boxes in the Temple and sat and watched as the crowds dropped in their money. Some who were rich put in

SIMPLE

12:29-31 God's laws are not burdensome in number or detail. They can be reduced to two simple rules for life: love God, and love others. These commands are from the Old Testament (Leviticus 19:18; Deuteronomy 6:5). When you love God completely and care for others as you care for yourself, then you have fulfilled the intent of the Ten Commandments and the other Old Testament laws. According to Jesus, these two rules summarize all God's laws. Let them rule your thoughts, decisions, and actions. When you are uncertain about what to do, ask yourself which course of action best demonstrates love for God and love for others.

large amounts. [42]Then a poor widow came and dropped in two pennies.

[43,44]He called his disciples to him and remarked, "That poor widow has given more than all those rich men put together! For they gave a little of their extra fat, while she gave up her last penny."

CHAPTER 13 JESUS TELLS ABOUT THE FUTURE.

As he was leaving the Temple that day, one of his disciples said, "Teacher, what beautiful buildings these are! Look at the decorated stonework on the walls."

[2]Jesus replied, "Yes, look! For not one stone will be left upon another, except as ruins."

[3,4]And as he sat on the slopes of the Mount of Olives across the valley from Jerusalem, Peter, James, John, and Andrew got alone with him and asked him, "Just when is all this going to happen to the Temple? Will there be some warning ahead of time?"

[5]So Jesus launched into an extended reply. "Don't let anyone mislead you," he said, [6]"for many will come declaring themselves to be your Messiah and will lead many astray. [7]And wars will break out near and far, but this is not the signal of the end-time.

[8]"For nations and kingdoms will proclaim war against each other, and there will be earthquakes in many lands, and famines. These herald only the early stages of the anguish ahead. [9]But when these things begin to happen, watch out! For you will be in great danger. You will be dragged before the courts, and beaten in the synagogues, and accused before governors and kings of being my followers. This is your opportunity to tell them the Good News. [10]And the Good News must first be made known in every nation before the end-time finally comes. [11]But when you are arrested and stand trial, don't worry about what to say in your defense. Just say what God tells you to. Then you will not be speaking, but the Holy Spirit will.

[12]"Brothers will betray each other to death, fathers will betray their own children, and children will betray their parents to be killed. [13]And everyone will hate you because you are mine. But all who endure to the end without renouncing me shall be saved.

[14]"When you see the horrible thing standing in the Temple —reader, pay attention!—flee, if you can, to the Judean hills. [15,16]Hurry! If you are on your rooftop porch, don't even go back into the house. If you are out in the fields, don't even return for your money or clothes.

[17]"Woe to pregnant women in those days, and to mothers nursing their children. [18]And pray that your flight will not be in winter. [19]For those will be days of such horror as have never been since the beginning of God's creation, nor will ever be again. [20]And unless the Lord shortens that time of calamity, not a soul in all the earth will survive. But for the sake of his chosen ones he will limit those days.

[21]"And then if anyone tells you, 'This is the Messiah,' or, 'That one is,' don't pay any attention. [22]For there will be many false Messiahs and false prophets who will do wonderful miracles that would deceive, if possible, even God's own children. [23]Take care! I have warned you!

[24]"After the tribulation ends, then the sun will grow dim and the moon will not shine, [25]and the stars will fall—the heavens will convulse.

[26]"Then all mankind will see me, the Messiah, coming in the clouds with great power and glory. [27]And I will send out the angels to gather together my chosen ones from all over the world—from the farthest bounds of earth and heaven.

[28]"Now, here is a lesson from a fig tree. When its buds become tender and its leaves begin to sprout, you know that spring has come. [29]And when you see these things happening that I've described, you can be sure that my return is very near, that I am right at the door.

[30]"Yes, these are the events that will signal the end of the age. [31]Heaven and earth shall disappear, but my words stand sure forever.

[32]"However, no one, not even the angels in heaven, nor I myself, knows the day or hour when these things will happen; only the Father knows. [33]And since you don't know when it will happen, stay alert. Be on the watch [for my return].

[34]"My coming can be compared with that of a man who went on a trip to another country. He laid out his employees' work for them to do while he was gone and told the gatekeeper to watch for his return.

[35-37]"Keep a sharp lookout! For you do not know when I will come, at evening, at midnight, early dawn or late daybreak. Don't let me find you sleeping. *Watch for my return!* This is my message to you and to everyone else."

CHAPTER 14 A PLOT TO KILL JESUS. The Passover observance began two days later—an annual Jewish holiday when no bread made with yeast was

---

VISION

13:9-10 As the early church began to grow, most of the disciples experienced the kind of persecution Jesus was talking about. Since the time of Christ, Christians have been persecuted in their own lands and in foreign mission fields. Though you may be safe from persecution now, your vision of God's Kingdom must not be limited by what happens only to you. A quick look at a newspaper will show you that many Christians in other parts of the world daily face hardships. Persecutions are an opportunity for Christians to witness for Christ to those opposed to him. They serve God's desire that the Good News be made available to everyone.

Jesus and the disciples ate the traditional Passover meal in an upper room in the city and then went to the Mount of Olives into a garden called Gethsemane. In the cool of the evening, Jesus prayed for strength to face the trial and suffering ahead.

eaten. The chief priests and other Jewish leaders were still looking for an opportunity to arrest Jesus secretly and put him to death.

²"But we can't do it during the Passover," they said, "or there will be a riot."

³Meanwhile Jesus was in Bethany, at the home of Simon the leper; during supper a woman came in with a beautiful flask of expensive perfume. Then, breaking the seal, she poured it over his head.

⁴,⁵Some of those at the table were indignant among themselves about this "waste," as they called it.

"Why, she could have sold that perfume for a fortune and given the money to the poor!" they snarled.

⁶But Jesus said, "Let her alone; why berate her for doing a good thing? ⁷You always have the poor among you, and they badly need your help, and you can aid them whenever you want to; but I won't be here much longer.

⁸"She has done what she could and has anointed my body ahead of time for burial. ⁹And I tell you this in solemn truth, that wherever the Good News is preached throughout the world, this woman's deed will be remembered and praised."

¹⁰Then Judas Iscariot, one of his disciples, went to the chief priests to arrange to betray Jesus to them.

¹¹When the chief priests heard why he had come, they were excited and happy and promised him a reward. So he began looking for the right time and place to betray Jesus.

¹²On the first day of the Passover, the day the lambs were sacrificed, his disciples asked him where he wanted to go to eat the traditional Passover supper. ¹³He sent two of them into Jerusalem to make the arrangements.

"As you are walking along," he told them, "you will see a man coming toward you carrying a pot of water. Follow him. ¹⁴At the house he enters, tell the man in charge, 'Our Master sent us to see the room you have ready for us, where we will eat the Passover supper this evening!' ¹⁵He will take you upstairs to a large room all set up. Prepare our supper there."

¹⁶So the two disciples went on ahead into the city and found everything as Jesus had said, and prepared the Passover.

¹⁷In the evening Jesus arrived with the other disciples, ¹⁸and as they were sitting around the table eating, Jesus said, "I solemnly declare that one of you will betray me, one of you who is here eating with me."

¹⁹A great sadness swept over them, and one by one they asked him, "Am I the one?"

²⁰He replied, "It is one of you twelve eating with me now. ²¹I must die, as the prophets declared long ago; but, oh, the misery ahead for the man by whom I am betrayed. Oh, that he had never been born!"

²²As they were eating, Jesus took bread and asked God's blessing on it and broke it in pieces and gave it to them and said, "Eat it—this is my body."

²³Then he took a cup of wine and gave thanks to God for it and gave it to them; and they all drank from it. ²⁴And he said to them, "This is my blood,

WORSHIP

14:6 Jesus was not saying that we should neglect the poor, nor was he justifying indifference to them. He was praising Mary for her unselfish act of worship. The essence of worshiping Christ is to regard him with utmost love, respect, and devotion and to be willing to sacrifice to him what is most precious.

BETRAYED!

14:19 Judas, the very man who would betray Jesus, was at the table with the others. He had already determined to betray Jesus, but in cold-blooded hypocrisy he shared the fellowship of this meal. It is easy to become enraged or shocked by what Judas did, yet when we profess commitment to Christ and then deny him with our life we also betray him. We deny Christ's truth because he taught us how to live, and we live otherwise. We deny Christ's love by not obeying him, and we deny Christ's deity by rejecting his authority. Do your words and actions match? If not, consider a change of mind and heart that will protect you from making a terrible mistake.

poured out for many, sealing the new agreement between God and man. [25]I solemnly declare that I shall never again taste wine until the day I drink a different kind in the Kingdom of God."

[26]Then they sang a hymn and went out to the Mount of Olives.

[27]"All of you will desert me," Jesus told them, "for God has declared through the prophets, 'I will kill the Shepherd, and the sheep will scatter.' [28]But after I am raised to life again, I will go to Galilee and meet you there."

[29]Peter said to him, "I will never desert you no matter what the others do!"

[30]"Peter," Jesus said, "before the cock crows a second time tomorrow morning you will deny me three times."

[31]"No!" Peter exploded. "Not even if I have to die with you! I'll *never* deny you!" And all the others vowed the same.

[32]And now they came to an olive grove called the Garden of Gethsemane, and he instructed his disciples, "Sit here, while I go and pray."

[33]He took Peter, James, and John with him and began to be filled with horror and deepest distress. [34]And he said to them, "My soul is crushed by sorrow to the point of death; stay here and watch with me."

[35]He went on a little further and fell to the ground and prayed that if it were possible the awful hour awaiting him might never come.

[36]"Father, Father," he said, "everything is possible for you. Take away this cup from me. Yet I want your will, not mine."

[37]Then he returned to the three disciples and found them asleep.

"Simon!" he said. "Asleep? Couldn't you watch with me even one hour? [38]Watch with me and pray lest the Tempter overpower you. For though the spirit is willing enough, the body is weak."

[39]And he went away again and prayed, repeating his pleadings. [40]Again he returned to them and found them sleeping, for they were very tired. And they didn't know what to say.

[41]The third time when he returned to them he said, "Sleep on; get your rest! But no! The time for sleep has ended! Look! I am betrayed into the hands of wicked men. [42]Come! Get up! We must go! Look! My betrayer is here!"

[43]And immediately, while he was still speaking, Judas (one of his disciples) arrived with a mob equipped with swords and clubs, sent out by the chief priests and other Jewish leaders.

[44]Judas had told them, "You will know which one to arrest when I go over and greet him. Then you can take him easily."[45]So as soon as they arrived he walked up to Jesus. "Master!" he exclaimed, and embraced him with a great show of friendliness. [46]Then the mob arrested Jesus and held him fast. [47]But someone pulled a sword and slashed at the High Priest's servant, cutting off his ear.

[48]Jesus asked them, "Am I some dangerous robber, that you come like this, armed to the teeth to capture me? [49]Why didn't you arrest me in the Temple? I was there teaching every day. But these things are happening to fulfill the prophecies about me."

[50]Meanwhile, all his disciples had fled. [51,52]There was, however, a young man following along behind, clothed only in a linen nightshirt. When the mob tried to grab him, he escaped, though his clothes were torn off in the process, so that he ran away completely naked.

[53]Jesus was led to the High Priest's home where all of the chief priests and other Jewish leaders soon gathered. [54]Peter followed far behind and then slipped inside the gates of the High Priest's residence and crouched beside a fire among the servants.

[55]Inside, the chief priests and the whole Jewish Supreme Court were trying to find something against Jesus that would be sufficient to condemn him to death. But their efforts were in vain. [56]Many false witnesses volunteered, but they contradicted each other.

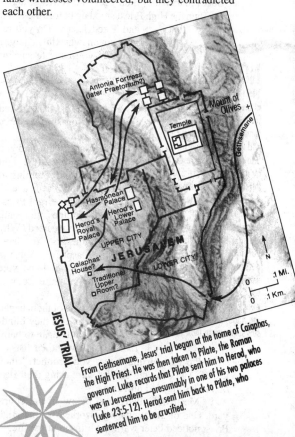

JESUS' TRIAL

From Gethsemane, Jesus' trial began at the home of Caiaphas, the High Priest. He was then taken to Pilate, the Roman governor. Luke records that Pilate sent him to Herod, who was in Jerusalem—presumably in one of his two palaces (Luke 23:5-12). Herod sent him back to Pilate, who sentenced him to be crucified.

WHY DID JESUS HAVE TO DIE?

The Problem	We have all done things that are wrong, and we have failed to obey God's law. Because of this, we have been separated from God our Creator and deserve death. By ourselves we can do nothing to become reunited with God.
Why Jesus Could Help	Jesus was not only a man, he was God's unique Son. Because Jesus never disobeyed God and never sinned, only he can bridge the gap between the sinless God and sinful mankind.
The Solution	Jesus freely offered his life for us, dying on the cross in our place, taking all our wrongdoing upon himself, and saving us from the consequences of sin—including God's judgment and death. God in his love and his justice sent Jesus to take our place.
The Results	Jesus took our past, present, and future sins upon himself so that we could have new life. Because all our wrongdoing is forgiven, we are reconciled to God. Furthermore, Jesus' resurrection from the dead is the proof that his sacrifice on the cross in our place was acceptable to God, and his resurrection has become the source of new life for those who believe that Jesus is the Son of God. All who believe in him may have new life and live it in union with him.

⁵⁷Finally some men stood up to lie about him and said, ⁵⁸"We heard him say, 'I will destroy this Temple made with human hands and in three days I will build another, made without human hands!'" ⁵⁹But even then they didn't get their stories straight!

⁶⁰Then the High Priest stood up before the Court and asked Jesus, "Do you refuse to answer this charge? What do you have to say for yourself?"

⁶¹To this Jesus made no reply.

Then the High Priest asked him. "Are you the Messiah, the Son of God?"

⁶²Jesus said, "I am, and you will see me sitting at the right hand of God, and returning to earth in the clouds of heaven."

^{63,64}Then the High Priest tore at his clothes and said, "What more do we need? Why wait for witnesses? You have heard his blasphemy. What is your verdict?" And the vote for the death sentence was unanimous.

⁶⁵Then some of them began to spit at him, and they blindfolded him and began to hammer his face with their fists.

"Who hit you that time, you prophet?" they jeered. And even the bailiffs were using their fists on him as they led him away.

^{66,67}Meanwhile Peter was below in the courtyard. One of the maids who worked for the High Priest noticed Peter warming himself at the fire.

She looked at him closely and then announced, "*You* were with Jesus, the Nazarene."

⁶⁸Peter denied it. "I don't know what you're talking about!" he said, and walked over to the edge of the courtyard.

Just then, a rooster crowed. ⁶⁹The maid saw him standing there and began telling the others, "There he is! There's that disciple of Jesus!"

⁷⁰Peter denied it again.

A little later others standing around the fire began saying to Peter, "You are, too, one of them, for you are from Galilee!"

⁷¹He began to curse and swear. "I don't even know this fellow you are talking about," he said.

⁷²And immediately the rooster crowed the second time. Suddenly Jesus' words flashed through Peter's mind: "Before the cock crows twice, you will deny me three times." And he began to cry.

CHAPTER 15 PILATE QUESTIONS JESUS. Early in the morning the chief priests, elders and teachers of religion—the entire Supreme Court—met to discuss their next steps. Their decision was to send Jesus under armed guard to Pilate, the Roman governor.

²Pilate asked him, "Are you the King of the Jews?"

NO EXCUSES

14:71 It is easy to get angry at the Jewish Supreme Court for their injustice in condemning Jesus, but Peter and the rest of the disciples also contributed to Jesus' pain by deserting him (14:50). While most of us are not like the Jewish leaders, we are all like the disciples, for all of us have been guilty of denying Christ as Lord in vital areas of our life. We may pride ourselves that we have not committed certain sins, but we are all guilty of sin. Don't excuse yourself by pointing the finger at others whose sins seem worse than yours.

GUILTY

15:15 Who was guilty of Jesus' death? In reality, everyone was at fault. The disciples deserted him in fear. Peter denied that he even knew Jesus. Judas betrayed him. The crowds who had followed him stood by and did nothing. Pilate tried to blame the crowds. The religious leaders actively promoted Jesus' death. The Roman soldiers tortured him. If you were there watching these trials, what would your response have been?

"Yes," Jesus replied, "it is as you say."

[3,4]Then the chief priests accused him of many crimes, and Pilate asked him, "Why don't you say something? What about all these charges against you?"

[5]But Jesus said no more, much to Pilate's amazement.

[6]Now, it was Pilate's custom to release one Jewish prisoner each year at Passover time—any prisoner the people requested. [7]One of the prisoners at that time was Barabbas, convicted along with others for murder during an insurrection.

[8]Now a mob began to crowd in toward Pilate, asking him to release a prisoner as usual.

[9]"How about giving you the 'King of Jews'?" Pilate asked. "Is he the one you want released?" [10](For he realized by now that this was a frameup, backed by the chief priests because they envied Jesus' popularity.)

[11]But at this point the chief priests whipped up the mob to demand the release of Barabbas instead of Jesus.

[12]"But if I release Barabbas," Pilate asked them, "what shall I do with this man you call your king?"

[13]They shouted back, "Crucify him!"

[14]"But why?" Pilate demanded. "What has he done wrong?" They only roared the louder, "Crucify him!"

[15]Then Pilate, afraid of a riot and anxious to please the people, released Barabbas to them. And he ordered Jesus flogged with a leaded whip, and handed him over to be crucified.

[16,17]Then the Roman soldiers took him into the barracks of the palace, called out the entire palace guard, dressed him in a purple robe, and made a crown of long, sharp thorns and put it on his head. [18]Then they saluted, yelling, "Yea! King of the Jews!" [19]And they beat him on the head with a cane, and spat on him, and went down on their knees to "worship" him.

[20]When they finally tired of their sport, they took off the purple robe and put his own clothes on him again, and led him away to be crucified.

[21]Simon of Cyrene, who was coming in from the country just then, was pressed into service to carry Jesus' cross. (Simon is the father of Alexander and Rufus.)

[22]And they brought Jesus to a place called Golgotha. (Golgotha means skull.) [23]Wine drugged with bitter herbs was offered to him there, but he refused it. [24]And then they crucified him—and threw dice for his clothes.

[25]It was about nine o'clock in the morning when the crucifixion took place.

[26]A signboard was fastened to the cross above his head, announcing his crime. It read, "The King of the Jews."

[27]Two robbers were also crucified that morning, their crosses on either side of his. [28]And so the Scripture was fulfilled that said, "He was counted among evil men."

[29,30]The people jeered at him as they walked by, and wagged their heads in mockery.

"Ha! Look at you now!" they yelled at him. "Sure, you can destroy the Temple and rebuild it in three days! If you're so wonderful, save yourself and come down from the cross."

[31]The chief priests and religious leaders were also standing around joking about Jesus.

"He's quite clever at 'saving' others," they said, "but he can't save himself!"

[32]"Hey there, Messiah!" they yelled at him. "You 'King of Israel'! Come on down from the cross and we'll believe you!"

And even the two robbers dying with him, cursed him.

[33]About noon, darkness fell across the entire land, lasting until three o'clock that afternoon.

DO RIGHT

15:15 Although Jesus was innocent according to Roman law, Pilate caved in under political pressure. He abandoned what he knew was right. He tried to give a decision that would please everyone while keeping himself safe. When we ignore God's statements of right and wrong and make decisions based on our audience, we fall into compromise and lawlessness. God promises to honor those who do right; not those who make everyone happy.

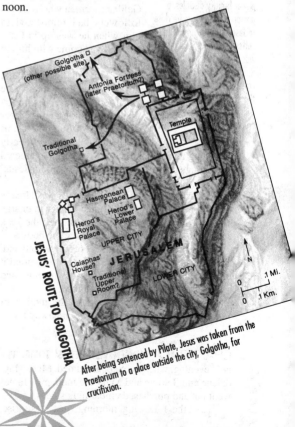

JESUS' ROUTE TO GOLGOTHA

After being sentenced by Pilate, Jesus was taken from the Praetorium to a place outside the city, Golgotha, for crucifixion.

³⁴Then Jesus called out with a loud voice, "Eli, Eli, lama sabachthani?" ("My God, my God, why have you deserted me?")

³⁵Some of the people standing there thought he was calling for the prophet Elijah. ³⁶So one man ran and got a sponge and filled it with sour wine and held it up to him on a stick.

"Let's see if Elijah will come and take him down!" he said.

³⁷Then Jesus uttered another loud cry and dismissed his spirit.

³⁸And the curtain in the Temple was split apart from top to bottom.

³⁹When the Roman officer standing beside his cross saw how he dismissed his spirit, he exclaimed, "Truly, this was the Son of God!"

⁴⁰Some women were there watching from a distance—Mary Magdalene, Mary (the mother of James the Younger and of Joses), Salome, and others. ⁴¹They and many other Galilean women who were his followers had ministered to him when he was up in Galilee, and had come with him to Jerusalem.

⁴²'⁴³This all happened the day before the Sabbath. Late that afternoon Joseph from Arimathea, an honored member of the Jewish Supreme Court (who personally was eagerly expecting the arrival of God's Kingdom), gathered his courage and went to Pilate and asked for Jesus' body.

⁴⁴Pilate couldn't believe that Jesus was already dead so he called for the Roman officer in charge and asked him. ⁴⁵The officer confirmed the fact, and Pilate told Joseph he could have the body.

⁴⁶Joseph bought a long sheet of linen cloth and, taking Jesus' body down from the cross, wound it in the cloth and laid it in a rock-hewn tomb, and rolled a stone in front of the entrance.

⁴⁷(Mary Magdalene and Mary the mother of Joses were watching as Jesus was laid away.)

CHAPTER **16** WOMEN VISIT JESUS' TOMB. The next evening, when the Sabbath ended, Mary Magdalene and Salome and Mary the mother of James went out and purchased embalming spices.

Early the following morning, just at sunrise,

they carried them out to the tomb. ³On the way they were discussing how they could ever roll aside the huge stone from the entrance.

⁴But when they arrived they looked up and saw that the stone—a *very* heavy one—was already moved away and the entrance was open! ⁵So they entered the tomb—and there on the right sat a young man clothed in white. The women were startled, ⁶but the angel said, "Don't be so surprised. Aren't you looking for Jesus, the Nazarene who was crucified? He isn't here! He has come back to life! Look, that's where his body was lying. ⁷Now go and give this message to his disciples including Peter:

"'Jesus is going ahead of you to Galilee. You will see him there, just as he told you before he died!'"

⁸The women fled from the tomb, trembling and bewildered, too frightened to talk.

⁹ It was early on Sunday morning when Jesus came back to life, and the first person who saw him was Mary Magdalene—the woman from whom he had cast out seven demons. ¹⁰'¹¹She found the disciples wet-eyed with grief and exclaimed that she had seen Jesus, and he was alive! But they didn't believe her!

¹²Later that dayhe appeared to two who were walking from Jerusalem into the country, but they didn't recognize him at first because he had changed his appearance. ¹³When they finally realized who he was, they rushed back to Jerusalem to tell the others, but no one believed them.

¹⁴Still later he appeared to the eleven disciples as they were eating together. He rebuked them for their unbelief—their stubborn refusal to believe those who had seen him alive from the dead.

¹⁵And then he told them, "You are to go into all the

CRIMINALS

15:32-37 When James and John asked Jesus for the places of honor next to him in his Kingdom, he told them they didn't know what they were asking (10:35-39). Here, where Jesus was preparing to inaugurate his Kingdom through his death, the places on his right and on his left were taken by dying men—criminals. This illustrates that Jesus' death is for *all* people. As Jesus explained to his two power-hungry disciples, a person who wants to be close to Jesus must be prepared to suffer and die as he himself was doing. The way to the Kingdom is the way of the cross. If we want the glory of the Kingdom, we must be willing to be united with the crucified Christ.

REMEMBERED

15:42-43 After Jesus died on the cross, Joseph of Arimathea asked for his body and then sealed it in a new tomb. Although an honored member of the Jewish Supreme Court, Joseph was a secret disciple of Jesus. Not all the religious leaders hated Jesus. Joseph risked his reputation as a religious leader to give a proper burial to the One he followed. It is frightening to risk one's reputation even for what is right. If your Christian witness endangers your reputation, consider Joseph. Today he is well known in the Christian church. How many of the other members of the Jewish Supreme Court can you name?

USED

15:47 These women could do very little—they couldn't speak before the Sanhedrin in Jesus' defense; they couldn't appeal to Pilate; they couldn't stand against the crowds; they couldn't overpower the Roman guards. But they did what they could. They stayed at the cross when the disciples had fled; they followed Jesus' body to its tomb; and they prepared spices for his body. Because they used the opportunities they had, they were the first to witness the Resurrection. God blessed their devotion and diligence. As believers, we should take advantage of the opportunities we have and do what we *can* for Christ, instead of worrying about what we *cannot* do.

EVIDENCE THAT JESUS ACTUALLY DIED AND AROSE

This evidence demonstrates Jesus' uniqueness in history and proves that he is God's Son. No one else was able to predict his own resurrection and then accomplish it.

Proposed Explanations for Empty Tomb	Evidence against These Explanations	References
Jesus was only unconscious and later revived.	A Roman soldier told Pilate Jesus was dead.	Mark 15:44-45
	The Roman soldiers did not break Jesus' legs because he had already died, and one of them pierced Jesus' side with a spear.	John 19:32-34
	Joseph of Arimathea and Nicodemus wrapped Jesus' body and placed it in the tomb.	John 19:38-40
The women made a mistake and went to the wrong tomb.	Mary Magdalene and Mary the mother of Jesus saw Jesus placed in the tomb.	Matthew 27:59-61 Mark 15:47 Luke 23:55
	On Sunday morning, Peter and John also went to the same tomb.	John 20:3-9
Unknown thieves stole Jesus' body.	The tomb was sealed and guarded by the Temple police, and probably Roman soldiers, too.	Matthew 27:65-66
The disciples stole Jesus' body	The disciples were ready to die for their faith. Stealing Jesus' body would have been admitting their faith was meaningless.	Acts 12:2
	The tomb was guarded and sealed.	Matthew 27:65-66
The religious leaders stole Jesus' body to secure it.	If the religious leaders had taken Jesus' body, they would have produced it to stop the rumors of his resurrection.	None

world and preach the Good News to everyone, everywhere. [16]Those who believe and are baptized will be saved. But those who refuse to believe will be condemned.

[17]"And those who believe shall use my authority to cast out demons, and they shall speak new languages. [18]They will be able even to handle snakes with safety, and if they drink anything poisonous, it won't hurt them; and they will be able to place their hands on the sick and heal them."

[19]When the Lord Jesus had finished talking with them, he was taken up into heaven and sat down at God's right hand.

[20]And the disciples went everywhere preaching, and the Lord was with them and confirmed what they said by the miracles that followed their messages.

MEGA Themes

JESUS CHRIST Jesus Christ alone is the Son of God. In Mark, Jesus demonstrates his divinity by overcoming disease, demons, and death. Although he had the power to be king of the earth, Jesus chose to obey the Father and die for us. Thus we see him in Mark as both Son of God and servant to man.

When Jesus rose from the dead, he proved that he was God, that he could forgive sin, and that he has the power to change our life. By trusting in Christ for forgiveness, we can begin a new life with him. As our guide, Jesus calls us to follow his example of obedience and service.

1. Which of Jesus' qualities do you see demonstrated in the Gospel of Mark?
2. Which of these qualities have you seen demonstrated in your church? Your youth group?
3. Which of these qualities have you experienced personally?
4. Which of Jesus' qualities do your non-Christian friends find it difficult to understand?
5. What could you do to be a living testimony of the gospel so that your friends could "read" your life to know Jesus?

SERVANT As the "Messiah," Jesus fulfilled the prophecies of the Old Testament by coming to earth. He did not come as a conquering king; he came as a servant. Jesus helped humankind by telling about God, showing compassion, and healing. But his ultimate act of service was giving his life as the sacrifice for sin.

Because of Jesus' example, we should be willing to serve God and others. Real greatness in Christ's Kingdom is shown by love and sacrifice. We should not be motivated by ambition, love of power, or position. Instead, we should do God's work because we love him.

1. Read 10:45. How do you feel toward Jesus when you read this verse?
2. In what ways did Jesus display his servanthood in Mark? What do you learn about being a servant from the life of Jesus?

3. How do you feel about being a servant to others? What can you do to deal with any negative feelings you may have about being a servant?
4. What specific actions could you perform that would serve your family members? Your friends at school? Your friends at church? Someone in your community who is needy? A non-Christian who has not known Jesus' love?
5. From your list above, identify two specific actions you will choose to do in order to be a servant for Jesus' love.

MIRACLES Mark records more of Jesus' miracles than his sermons. Jesus was clearly a man of power and action, not just words. Jesus did miracles to confirm his message to the people and to teach the disciples his true identity as God.

The more convinced we become that Jesus is God, the more we will see his power and his love. Jesus' mighty works show us that he is able to save anyone, regardless of his or her past. His miracles of forgiveness bring healing, wholeness, and changed lives to those who trust him.

1. Why were miracles such an important part of Jesus' ministry?
2. What do you learn about Jesus from Mark's record of his miracles?
3. What displays of Jesus' power do you see today?
4. What testimony could you give to Jesus' ability to change lives through his miraculous power?
5. Are there situations in your life, or in the lives of your friends or family, that need Jesus' healing touch? Choose one or two, and ask God to bring his power into those situations.

SPREADING THE GOSPEL Jesus directed his public ministry to the Jews first. When the Jewish leaders opposed him, Jesus also went to the non-Jewish world, healing and preaching. Roman soldiers, Syrians, and other Gentiles heard the Good News. Many believed in Jesus and followed him. Jesus' final message to his disciples challenged them to go into all the world and preach the gospel of salvation.

Jesus crossed national, racial, and economic barriers to spread his Good News. Jesus' message of faith and forgiveness is for the whole world and not just for our church, neighborhood, or nation. We must reach out beyond our own people and needs to fulfill the worldwide vision of Jesus Christ so that people everywhere might hear this great message and be saved from sin and death.

1. How did Jesus show that God's love and grace are available to all types of people?

2. The book of Mark literally pivots on 8:29. Read 8:27-30 and consider these questions:

   a. What would people today say if they were asked about Jesus?

   b. How would you answer Jesus' question, "Who do you say that I am?"

   c. What does your life say about who Jesus is?

3. What key truth do people need to know about Jesus?

4. Which of your friends need to know this truth? What could you do and say to give them the Good News?

5. Choose one friend and identify two specific ways you will share the Good news with him or her.

*T*hey were two kids in love. In fact, they were *engaged.* As in "headed for the altar," "marital bliss." And M. & J. had big plans, and even bigger dreams. Then the roof caved in. M. found out she was pregnant. ■ J. was hurt, confused, and ticked—he knew he wasn't the father. There was only one thing to do: call off the wedding. ■ But weird things started happening. M. claimed she'd been visited by a real-life angel, and that she'd been made pregnant by the Spirit of God! J. had heard some wild stories before, but *angels? Divine fertilization?* Come on! ■ Then J. started seeing angels! Surely it was all a dream . . . until the angel said (in a serious tone and with a straight face), "Hey, J., don't break off the engagement! The child inside M. really *is* the Savior of the world." J. gulped and mumbled, "Um, yeah . . . whatever you say." ■ Soon M. could no longer hide her pregnancy. People stared. Rumors flew. M. and J. purposely kept a low profile. Together they wondered what it would be like to be parents—especially of such a special child. ■ Did M. realize that her little baby would incite a king to slaughter thousands of newborn infants? Did J. know that the child would one day speak such profound words or perform astounding miracles? Did these two realize their precious boy would die in a brutal manner? ■ Even if they *were* able to grasp any of that, did they truly believe that their murdered son would come back to life? ■ Read about M. & J. and their son—mainly about their son—in the following pages. The story is the Gospel of Luke. It's one you won't forget.

STATS

PURPOSE: To present an accurate account of the life of Christ and to present Christ as the perfect man and Savior.

AUTHOR: Luke—a doctor (Colossians 4:14), a Greek and Gentile Christian. He is the only known Gentile author in the New Testament. He was a close friend and companion of Paul. He also wrote Acts, and the two books go together.

TO WHOM WRITTEN: Theophilus ("lover of God"), Gentiles, and people everywhere

DATE WRITTEN: About A.D. 60

SETTING: Luke wrote from Caesarea or from Rome.

KEY PEOPLE: Jesus, Elizabeth, Zacharias, John the Baptist, Mary, the disciples, Herod the Great, Pilate, Mary Magdalene

KEY PLACES: Bethlehem, Galilee, Judea, Jerusalem

Luke

HISTORY

1:3 As a medical doctor, Luke knew the importance of a thorough checkup. He used his skills in observation and analysis to do a complete investigation of the stories about Jesus. His diagnosis? The gospel of Jesus Christ is true! You can read Luke's account of Jesus' life with confidence that it was written by a clear thinker and a thoughtful researcher. Because the gospel is founded on historical truth, our spiritual growth must involve careful, disciplined, thorough investigation of God's Word. If this kind of study is not part of your life, find a pastor, teacher, or book to help you get started and to guide you in this important part of Christian growth.

CHAPTER 1 **AN ANGEL VISITS ZACHARIAS.** Dear friend who loves God:

¹,²Several biographies of Christ have already been written using as their source material the reports circulating among us from the early disciples and other eyewitnesses. ³However, it occurred to me that it would be well to recheck all these accounts from first to last and after thorough investigation to pass this summary on to you, ⁴to reassure you of the truth of all you were taught.

⁵My story begins with a Jewish priest, Zacharias, who lived when Herod was king of Judea. Zacharias was a member of the Abijah division of the Temple service corps. (His wife, Elizabeth, was, like himself, a member of the priest tribe of the Jews, a descendant of Aaron.) ⁶Zacharias and Elizabeth were godly folk, careful to obey all of God's laws in spirit as well as in letter. ⁷But they had no children, for Elizabeth was barren; and now they were both very old.

⁸,⁹One day as Zacharias was going about his work in the Temple—for his division was on duty that week—the honor fell to him by lot to enter the inner sanctuary and burn incense before the Lord. ¹⁰Meanwhile, a great crowd stood outside in the Temple court, praying as they always did during that part of the service when the incense was being burned.

¹¹,¹²Zacharias was in the sanctuary when suddenly an angel appeared, standing to the right of the altar of incense! Zacharias was startled and terrified.

¹³But the angel said, "Don't be afraid, Zacharias! For I have come to tell you that God has heard your prayer, and your wife, Elizabeth, will bear you a son! And you are to name him John.

Luke begins his account in the Temple in Jerusalem, giving us the background for the birth of John the Baptist, and then moves on to the city of Nazareth and the story of Mary, chosen to be Jesus' mother (1:26ff). As a result of Caesar's call for a census, Mary and Joseph had to travel to Bethlehem, where Jesus was born in fulfillment of prophecy (2:1ff). Jesus grew up in Nazareth and began his earthly ministry by being baptized by John (3:21-22) and tempted by Satan (4:1ff). Much of his ministry focused on Galilee—he set up his "home" in Capernaum (4:31ff), and from there he taught throughout the region (8:1ff). Later he visited the Gerasene country where he healed a demon-possessed man from Gadara (8:36ff). He fed more than 5,000 people with one lunch on the shores of the Sea of Galilee near Bethsaida-Julias (9:10ff). Jesus always traveled to Jerusalem for the major festivals and enjoyed visiting friends in nearby Bethany (10:38ff). He healed 10 lepers on the border between Galilee and Samaria (17:11) and helped a dishonest tax collector in Jericho turn his life around (19:1ff). The little villages of Bethphage and Bethany on the Mount of Olives were Jesus' resting places during his last days on earth. He was crucified outside Jerusalem's walls, but he would rise again. Two people on the road leading to Emmaus were among the first to see the resurrected Christ (24:13ff).

Mediterranean Sea

Sidon
ITUREA
LEBANON
TRACHONITIS
SYRIA
Tyre
PHOENICIA
GALILEE
Chorazin
Bethsaida-Julias
Bethsaida
Capernaum
Sea of Galilee
DECAPOLIS
(Region of Ten Towns)
Gadara
Nazareth
Nain
ISRAEL
SAMARIA
Jordan River
PEREA
Arimathea
JORDAN
Jericho
Mount of Olives
Emmaus
Jerusalem
Bethphage
Bethany
Bethlehem
Dead Sea
JUDEA
IDUMEA

The broken lines (— - — - —) indicate modern boundaries.

[14]You will both have great joy and gladness at his birth, and many will rejoice with you. [15]For he will be one of the Lord's great men. He must never touch wine or hard liquor—and he will be filled with the Holy Spirit, even from before his birth! [16]And he will persuade many a Jew to turn to the Lord his God. [17]He will be a man of rugged spirit and power like Elijah, the prophet of old; and he will precede the coming of the Messiah, preparing the people for his arrival. He will soften adult hearts to become like little children's, and will change disobedient minds to the wisdom of faith."

[18]Zacharias said to the angel, "But this is impos-

sible! I'm an old man now, and my wife is also well along in years."

[19]Then the angel said, "I am Gabriel! I stand in the very presence of God. It was he who sent me to you with this good news! [20]And now, because you haven't believed me, you are to be stricken silent, unable to speak until the child is born. For my words will certainly come true at the proper time."

[21]Meanwhile the crowds outside were waiting for Zacharias to appear and wondered why he was taking so long. [22]When he finally came out, he couldn't speak to them, and they realized from his gestures that he must have seen a vision in the

Temple. ²³He stayed on at the Temple for the remaining days of his Temple duties and then returned home. ²⁴Soon afterwards Elizabeth his wife became pregnant and went into seclusion for five months.

²⁵"How kind the Lord is," she exclaimed, "to take away my disgrace of having no children!"

²⁶The following month God sent the angel Gabriel to Nazareth, a village in Galilee, ²⁷to a virgin, Mary, engaged to be married to a man named Joseph, a descendant of King David.

²⁸Gabriel appeared to her and said, "Congratulations, favored lady! The Lord is with you!"

²⁹Confused and disturbed, Mary tried to think what the angel could mean.

³⁰"Don't be frightened, Mary," the angel told her, "for God has decided to wonderfully bless you! ³¹Very soon now, you will become pregnant and have a baby boy, and you are to name him 'Jesus.' ³²He shall be very great and shall be called the Son of God. And the Lord God shall give him the throne of his ancestor David. ³³And he shall reign over Israel forever; his Kingdom shall never end!"

³⁴Mary asked the angel, "But how can I have a baby? I am a virgin."

³⁵The angel replied, "The Holy Spirit shall come upon you, and the power of God shall overshadow you; so the baby born to you will be utterly holy—the Son of God. ³⁶Furthermore, six months ago your Aunt Elizabeth—'the barren one,' they called her—became pregnant in her old age! ³⁷For every promise from God shall surely come true."

³⁸Mary said, "I am the Lord's servant, and I am willing to do whatever he wants. May everything you said come true." And then the angel disappeared.

³⁹,⁴⁰A few days later Mary hurried to the highlands of Judea to the town where Zacharias lived, to visit Elizabeth.

⁴¹At the sound of Mary's greeting, Elizabeth's child leaped within her and she was filled with the Holy Spirit.

⁴²She gave a glad cry and exclaimed to Mary, "You are favored by God above all other women, and your child is destined for God's mightiest

MARY

, Jesus' mother. Motherhood is a painful privilege. Young Mary of Nazareth had the unique role of being mother to the Son of God. Yet the pains and pleasures of her motherhood are understood by mothers everywhere. Mary was the only human present at Jesus' birth who also witnessed his death. She saw Jesus arrive as her baby son, and she watched him die as her Savior.

Until Gabriel's surprise visit, Mary's life was going well. She had recently become engaged to a local carpenter, Joseph, and was anticipating married life. But God had other plans for her.

Angels don't usually make appointments before visiting. The angel greeted Mary as if she were the winner of a contest she had never entered; she found the angel's greeting puzzling and his presence frightening. What she heard next was the news almost every woman in Israel hoped to hear—that her child would be the Messiah, God's promised Savior. Mary did not doubt the message, but she wondered how she could be God's pregnant. Gabriel told her that the baby would be God's Son.

Mary's answer was one that God waits to hear from every person: "I am the Lord's servant, and I am willing to do whatever he wants" (Luke 1:38). Later, her song of joy to Elizabeth shows us how well Mary knew God—her thoughts were filled with his words from the Old Testament.

Just days after his birth, Jesus was taken to the Temple to be dedicated to God. There Joseph and Mary were met by two prophets, Simeon and Anna, who recognized the child as the Messiah and praised God. Simeon added some words for Mary that she must have remembered many times in the years that followed: "A sword shall pierce your soul" (Luke 2:34).

We can imagine that even if she had known all she would suffer as Jesus' mother, Mary would have given the same response. Is your life as available to be used by God as Mary's was?

LESSONS: God's best servants are often plain people available to him

God's plans involve extraordinary events in the lives of ordinary people

A person's character is revealed by his or her response to the unexpected

KEY VERSE: "I am the Lord's servant, and I am willing to do whatever he wants. May everything you said come true" (Luke 1:38).

Mary's story is told throughout the Gospels. She is also mentioned in Acts 1:14.

UPS:
• The mother of Jesus, the Messiah
• The one human who was with Jesus from birth to death
• Willing to be available to God
• Knew and applied God's Word

STATS:
• Where: Nazareth, Bethlehem
• Occupation: Homemaker
• Relatives: Husband: Joseph. Uncle and Aunt: Zacharias and Elizabeth. Children: Jesus, James, Joseph, Judas, and Simon, plus daughters.

praise. ⁴³What an honor this is, that the mother of my Lord should visit me! ⁴⁴When you came in and greeted me, the instant I heard your voice, my baby moved in me for joy! ⁴⁵You believed that God would do what he said; that is why he has given you this wonderful blessing."

⁴⁶Mary responded, "Oh, how I praise the Lord. ⁴⁷How I rejoice in God my Savior! ⁴⁸For he took notice of his lowly servant girl, and now generation after generation forever shall call me blest of God. ⁴⁹For he, the mighty Holy One, has done great things to me. ⁵⁰His mercy goes on from generation to generation, to all who reverence him.

⁵¹"How powerful is his mighty arm! How he scatters the proud and haughty ones! ⁵²He has torn princes from their thrones and exalted the lowly. ⁵³He has satisfied the hungry hearts and sent the rich away with empty hands. ⁵⁴And how he has helped his servant Israel! He has not forgotten his promise to be merciful. ⁵⁵For he promised our fathers—Abraham and his children—to be merciful to them forever."

⁵⁶Mary stayed with Elizabeth about three months and then went back to her own home.

⁵⁷By now Elizabeth's waiting was over, for the time had come for the baby to be born—and it was a boy. ⁵⁸The word spread quickly to her neighbors and relatives of how kind the Lord had been to her, and everyone rejoiced.

⁵⁹When the baby was eight days old, all the relatives and friends came for the circumcision ceremony. They all assumed the baby's name would be Zacharias, after his father. ⁶⁰But Elizabeth said, "No! He must be named John!"

⁶¹"What?" they exclaimed. "There is no one in all your family by that name." ⁶²So they asked the baby's father, talking to him by gestures.

⁶³He motioned for a piece of paper and to everyone's surprise wrote, "His name is *John!*" ⁶⁴Instantly Zacharias could speak again, and he began praising God.

⁶⁵Wonder fell upon the whole neighborhood, and the news of what had happened spread through the Judean hills. ⁶⁶And everyone who heard about it thought long thoughts and asked, "I wonder what this child will turn out to be? For the hand of the Lord is surely upon him in some special way."

⁶⁷Then his father, Zacharias, was filled with the Holy Spirit and gave this prophecy:

⁶⁸"Praise the Lord, the God of Israel, for he has come to visit his people and has redeemed them. ⁶⁹He is sending us a Mighty Savior from the royal line of his servant David, ⁷⁰just as he promised through his holy prophets long ago— ⁷¹someone to save us from our enemies, from all who hate us.

⁷²,⁷³"He has been merciful to our ancestors, yes, to Abraham himself, by remembering his sacred promise to him, ⁷⁴and by granting us the privilege of serving God fearlessly, freed from our enemies, ⁷⁵and by making us holy and acceptable, ready to stand in his presence forever.

⁷⁶"And you, my little son, shall be called the prophet of the glorious God, for you will prepare the way for the Messiah. ⁷⁷You will tell his people how to find salvation through forgiveness of their sins. ⁷⁸All this will be because the mercy of our God is very tender, and heaven's dawn is about to break upon us, ⁷⁹to give light to those who sit in darkness and death's shadow, and to guide us to the path of peace."

⁸⁰The little boy greatly loved God and when he grew up he lived out in the lonely wilderness until he began his public ministry to Israel.

CHAPTER **2** **JESUS IS BORN.** About this time Caesar Augustus, the Roman emperor, decreed that a census should be taken throughout the nation. ²(This census was taken when Quirinius was governor of Syria.)

³Everyone was required to return to his ancestral home for this registration. ⁴And because Joseph was a member of the royal line, he had to go to Bethlehem in Judea, King David's ancient home—journeying there from the Galilean village of Nazareth. ⁵He took with him Mary, his fiancée, who was obviously pregnant by this time.

⁶And while they were there, the time came for her baby to be born; ⁷and she gave birth to her first child, a son. She wrapped him in a blanket and laid him in a manger, because there was no room for them in the village inn.

⁸That night some shepherds were in the fields outside the village, guarding their flocks of sheep. ⁹Suddenly an angel appeared among them, and the landscape shone bright with the glory of the Lord. They were badly frightened, ¹⁰but the angel reassured them.

"Don't be afraid!" he said. "I bring you the most

UNLIKELY

1:46-55 Mary was young, poor, and female—all characteristics that, to the people of her day, would make her seem useless to God for any major task. But God chose Mary for one of the most important acts of obedience he has ever demanded of anyone. You may feel that your situation in life makes you an unlikely candidate for God's service. Don't limit God's choices. He can use you if you trust him.

GROW UP

2:7 Although our first impression of Jesus is as a baby in a manger, it must not be our last. The Christ child in the manger makes a beautiful Christmas scene, but we cannot leave him there. This tiny, helpless baby lived an amazing life, died for us, ascended to heaven, and will return to earth as King of kings. He will rule the world and judge all people according to their decisions about him. Do you still picture Jesus as a baby in a manger—or is he your Lord? Make sure you don't underestimate Jesus. Let him grow up in your life.

joyful news ever announced, and it is for everyone! [11]The Savior—yes, the Messiah, the Lord—has been born tonight in Bethlehem! [12]How will you recognize him? You will find a baby wrapped in a blanket, lying in a manger!"

[13]Suddenly, the angel was joined by a vast host of others—the armies of heaven—praising God: [14]"Glory to God in the highest heaven," they sang, "and peace on earth for all those pleasing him."

[15]When this great army of angels had returned again to heaven, the shepherds said to each other, "Come on! Let's go to Bethlehem! Let's see this wonderful thing that has happened, which the Lord has told us about."

[16]They ran to the village and found their way to Mary and Joseph. And there was the baby, lying in the manger. [17]The shepherds told everyone what had happened and what the angel had said to them about this child. [18]All who heard the shepherds' story expressed astonishment, [19]but Mary quietly treasured these things in her heart and often thought about them.

[20]Then the shepherds went back again to their fields and flocks, praising God for the visit of the angels, and because they had seen the child, just as the angel had told them.

[21]Eight days later, at the baby's circumcision ceremony, he was named Jesus, the name given him by the angel before he was even conceived.

[22]When the time came for Mary's purification offering at the Temple, as required by the laws of Moses after the birth of a child, his parents took him to Jerusalem to present him to the Lord; [23]for in these laws God had said, "If a woman's first child is a boy, he shall be dedicated to the Lord."

[24]At that time Jesus' parents also offered their sacrifice for purification—"either a pair of turtledoves or two young pigeons" was the legal requirement. [25]That day a man named Simeon, a Jerusalem resident, was in the Temple. He was a good man, very devout, filled with the Holy Spirit and constantly expecting the Messiah to come soon. [26]For the Holy Spirit had revealed to him that he would not die until he had seen him—God's anointed King. [27]The Holy Spirit had impelled him to go to the Temple that day; and so, when Mary and Joseph arrived to present the baby Jesus to the Lord in obedience to the law, [28]Simeon was there and took the child in his arms, praising God.

[29-31]"Lord," he said, "now I can die content! For I have seen him as you promised me I would. I have seen the Savior you have given to the world. [32]He is the Light that will shine upon the nations, and he will be the glory of your people Israel!"

[33]Joseph and Mary just stood there, marveling at what was being said about Jesus. [34,35]Simeon blessed them but then said to Mary,

"A sword shall pierce your soul, for this child shall be rejected by many in Israel, and this to their undoing. But he will be the greatest joy of many others. And the deepest thoughts of many hearts shall be revealed."

[36,37]Anna, a prophetess, was also there in the Temple that day. She was the daughter of Phanuel, of the Jewish tribe of Asher, and was very old, for she had been a widow for eighty-four years following seven years of marriage. She never left the Temple but stayed there night and day, worshiping God by praying and often fasting.

[38]She came along just as Simeon was talking with Mary and Joseph, and she also began thanking God and telling everyone in Jerusalem who had been awaiting the coming of the Savior that the Messiah had finally arrived.

[39]When Jesus' parents had fulfilled all the requirements of the Law of God they returned home to Nazareth in Galilee. [40]There the child became a strong, robust lad, and was known for wisdom beyond his years; and God poured out his blessings on him.

[41,42]When Jesus was twelve years old he accompanied his parents to Jerusalem for the annual Passover Festival, which they attended each year. [43]After the celebration was over they started home to Nazareth, but Jesus stayed behind in Jerusalem. His parents didn't miss him the first day, [44]for they assumed he was with friends among the other travelers. But when he didn't show up that evening, they started to look for him among their relatives and friends; [45]and when they couldn't find him, they went back to Jerusalem to search for him there.

[46,47]Three days later they finally discovered him. He was in the Temple, sitting among the teachers of Law, discussing deep questions with them and amazing everyone with his understanding and answers.

WISDOM

2:36 Although Simeon and Anna were very old, they still hoped to see the Messiah. Led by the Holy Spirit, they were among the first to bear witness to Jesus. In the Jewish culture, elders were respected, so Simeon's and Anna's prophecies carried extra weight. Our society, however, values youthfulness over wisdom, and potential contributions by the elderly often are ignored. As Christians, we should reverse those values wherever we can. Encourage older people to share their wisdom and experience. Listen carefully when they speak. Offer them your friendship and help them find ways to continue to serve God.

PARENTS

2:46-52 This is the first hint that Jesus realized he was God's Son. Even though Jesus knew his real Father, he did not reject his earthly parents. Jesus went back to Nazareth with them and lived under their authority for another 18 years. God's people do not despise human relationships or family responsibilities. If the Son of God obeyed his human parents, how much more should we honor our family members!

⁴⁸His parents didn't know what to think. "Son!" his mother said to him. "Why have you done this to us? Your father and I have been frantic, searching for you everywhere."

⁴⁹"But why did you need to search?" he asked. "Didn't you realize that I would be here at the Temple, in my Father's House?" ⁵⁰But they didn't understand what he meant.

⁵¹Then he returned to Nazareth with them and was obedient to them; and his mother stored away all these things in her heart. ⁵²So Jesus grew both tall and wise, and was loved by God and man.

CHAPTER **3** **JOHN THE BAPTIST PREACHES.** In the fifteenth year of the reign of Emperor Tiberius Caesar, a message came from God to John (the son of Zacharias), as he was living out in the deserts. (Pilate was governor over Judea at that time; Herod, over Galilee; his brother Philip, over Iturea and Trachonitis; Lysanias, over Abilene; and Annas and Caiaphas were High Priests.) ³Then John went from place to place on both sides of the Jordan River, preaching that people should be baptized to show that they had turned to God and away from their sins, in order to be forgiven.

⁴In the words of Isaiah the prophet, John was "a voice shouting from the barren wilderness, 'Prepare a road for the Lord to travel on! Widen the pathway before him! ⁵Level the mountains! Fill up the valleys! Straighten the curves! Smooth out the ruts! ⁶And then all mankind shall see the Savior sent from God.'"

⁷Here is a sample of John's preaching to the crowds that came for baptism: "You brood of snakes! You are trying to escape hell without truly turning to God! That is why you want to be baptized! ⁸First go and prove by the way you live that you really have repented. And don't think you are safe because you are descendants of Abraham. That isn't enough. God can produce children of Abraham from these desert stones! ⁹The axe of his judgment is poised over you, ready to sever your roots and cut you down. Yes, every tree that does not produce good fruit will be chopped down and thrown into the fire."

¹⁰The crowd replied, "What do you want us to do?"

FAITH

3:8 Many of John's hearers were shocked when he said that being Abraham's descendants was not enough. The religious leaders relied more on their family line than on their faith for their standing with God. For them, religion was inherited. But a relationship with God is not handed down from parents to children. Everyone has to find it on his or her own. Don't rely on someone else for your salvation. Put your faith in Jesus, and then exercise your faith by acting on it every day.

¹¹"If you have two coats," he replied, "give one to the poor. If you have extra food, give it away to those who are hungry."

¹²Even tax collectors—notorious for their corruption—came to be baptized and asked, "How shall we prove to you that we have abandoned our sins?"

¹³"By your honesty," he replied. "Make sure you collect no more taxes than the Roman government requires you to."

¹⁴"And us," asked some soldiers, "what about us?"

John replied, "Don't extort money by threats and violence; don't accuse anyone of what you know he didn't do; and be content with your pay!"

¹⁵Everyone was expecting the Messiah to come soon, and eager to know whether or not John was he. This was the question of the hour and was being discussed everywhere.

¹⁶John answered the question by saying, "I baptize only with water; but someone is coming soon who has far higher authority than mine; in fact, I am not even worthy of being his slave. He will baptize you with fire—with the Holy Spirit. ¹⁷He will separate chaff from grain, and burn up the chaff with eternal fire and store away the grain." ¹⁸He used many such warnings as he announced the Good News to the people.

^{19,20}(But after John had publicly criticized Herod, governor of Galilee, for marrying Herodias, his brother's wife, and for many other wrongs he had done, Herod put John in prison, thus adding this sin to all his many others.)

²¹Then one day, after the crowds had been baptized, Jesus himself was baptized; and as he was praying, the heavens opened, ²²and the Holy Spirit in the form of a dove settled upon him, and a voice from heaven said, "You are my much loved Son, yes, my delight."

²³⁻³⁸Jesus was about thirty years old when he began his public ministry.

Jesus was known as the son of Joseph. Joseph's father was Heli; Heli's father was Matthat; Matthat's father was Levi; Levi's father was Melchi; Melchi's father was Jannai; Jannai's father was Joseph; Joseph's father was Matthias; Matthias' father was Amos; Amos' father was Nahum; Nahum's father was Esli; Esli's father was Naggai; Naggai's father was Maath; Maath's father was Mattathias; Mattathias' father was Semein; Semein's

TIMING

3:23 Imagine the Savoir of the world driving nails in some small-town carpenter's shop until he was 30 years old! Jesus patiently trusted the Father's timing for his life and ministry. Are you waiting and wondering what your next step should be? Don't jump ahead. Instead, like Jesus, trust God's timing and guidance.

THE SPIRIT OF THE LORD IS UPON

HE *has appointed* ME

to preach
preach *Good News*
preach
to
the poor

ME

HE *has sent me to heal the brokenhearted*

and to ANNOUNCE

that captives *shall be* RELEASED

and the BLIND *shall* see

that the downtrodden *shall be* FREED

and that GOD IS READY *to give* BLESSINGS BLESSINGS BLESSINGS BLESSINGS

to ALL
w h o *come* to HIM.

LUKE 4:18-19

father was Josech; Josech's father was Joda; Joda's father was Joanan; Joanan's father was Rhesa; Rhesa's father was Zerubbabel; Zerubbabel's father was Shealtiel; Shealtiel's father was Neri; Neri's father was Melchi; Melchi's father was Addi; Addi's father was Cosam; Cosam's father was Elmadam; Elmadam's father was Er; Er's father was Joshua; Joshua's father was Eliezer; Eliezer's father was Jorim; Jorim's father was Matthat; Matthat's father was Levi; Levi's father was Simeon; Simeon's father was Judah; Judah's father was Joseph; Joseph's father was Jonam; Jonam's father was Eliakim; Eliakim's father was Melea; Melea's father was Menna; Menna's father was Mattatha; Mattatha's father was Nathan; Nathan's father was David; David's father was Jesse; Jesse's father was Obed; Obed's father was Boaz; Boaz' father was Salmon; Salmon's father was Nahshon; Nahshon's father was Amminadab; Amminadab's father was Admin; Admin's father was Arni; Arni's father was Hezron; Hezron's father was Perez; Perez' father was Judah; Judah's father was Jacob; Jacob's father was Isaac; Isaac's father was Abraham; Abraham's father was Terah; Terah's father was Nahor; Nahor's father was Serug; Serug's father was Reu; Reu's father was Peleg; Peleg's father was Eber; Eber's father was Shelah; Shelah's father was Cainan; Cainan's father was Arphaxad; Arphaxad's father was Shem; Shem's father was Noah; Noah's father

father was Methuselah; Methuselah's father was Enoch; Enoch's father was Jared; Jared's father was Mahalaleel; Mahalaleel's father was Cainan; Cainan's father was Enos; Enos' father was Seth; Seth's father was Adam; Adam's father was God.

CHAPTER 4 JESUS RESISTS TEMPTATION.

Then Jesus, full of the Holy Spirit, left the Jordan River, being urged by the Spirit out into the barren wastelands of Judea, where Satan tempted him for forty days. He ate nothing all that time and was very hungry.

[3]Satan said, "If you are God's Son, tell this stone to become a loaf of bread."

[4]But Jesus replied, "It is written in the Scriptures, 'Other things in life are much more important than bread!'"

[5]Then Satan took him up and revealed to him all the kingdoms of the world in a moment of time; [6,7]and the devil told him, "I will give you all these splendid kingdoms and their glory—for they are mine to give to anyone I wish—if you will only get down on your knees and worship me."

[8]Jesus replied, "We must worship God, and him alone. So it is written in the Scriptures."

[9-11]Then Satan took him to Jerusalem to a high roof of the Temple and said, "If you are the Son of God, jump off! For the Scriptures say that God will send his angels to guard you and to keep you from crashing to the pavement below!"

[12]Jesus replied, "The Scriptures also say, 'Do not put the Lord your God to a foolish test.'"

VULNERABLE

4:13 Christ's defeat of Satan was decisive but not final. Throughout his ministry, Jesus would confront Satan in many forms. Too often we see temptation as a once-and-for-all proposition. In reality, we need to be constantly on guard against the devil's ongoing attacks. Where are you most susceptible to temptation right now? How are you preparing to withstand it?

[13]When the devil had ended all the temptations, he left Jesus for a while and went away.

[14]Then Jesus returned to Galilee, full of the Holy Spirit's power. Soon he became well known throughout all that region [15]for his sermons in the synagogues; everyone praised him.

[16]When he came to the village of Nazareth, his boyhood home, he went as usual to the synagogue on Saturday, and stood up to read the Scriptures. [17]The book of Isaiah the prophet was handed to him, and he opened it to the place where it says:

[18,19]"The Spirit of the Lord is upon me; he has appointed me to preach Good News to the poor; he has sent me to heal the brokenhearted and to announce that captives shall be released and the blind shall see, that the downtrodden shall be freed from their oppressors, and that God is ready to give blessings to all who come to him."

[20]He closed the book and handed it back to the attendant and sat down, while everyone in the synagogue gazed at him intently. [21]Then he added, "These Scriptures came true today!"

[22]All who were there spoke well of him and were amazed by the beautiful words that fell from his lips. "How can this be?" they asked. "Isn't this Joseph's son?"

[23]Then he said, "Probably you will quote me that proverb, 'Physician, heal yourself'—meaning, 'Why don't you do miracles here in your hometown like those you did in Capernaum?' [24]But I solemnly declare to you that no prophet is accepted in his own hometown! [25,26]For example, remember how Elijah the prophet used a miracle to help the widow of Zarephath—a foreigner from the land of Sidon. There were many Jewish widows needing help in those days of famine, for there had been no rain for three and a half years, and hunger stalked the land; yet Elijah was not sent to them. [27]Or think of the prophet Elisha, who healed Naaman, a Syrian, rather than the many Jewish lepers needing help."

[28]These remarks stung them to fury; [29]and jumping up, they mobbed him and took him to the edge of the hill on which the city was built, to push him over the cliff. [30]But he walked away through the crowd and left them.

[31]Then he returned to Capernaum, a city in Galilee, and preached there in the synagogue every Saturday. [32]Here, too, the people were amazed at the things he said. For he spoke as one who knew the truth, instead of merely quoting the opinions of others as his authority.

[33]Once as he was teaching in the synagogue, a man possessed by a demon began shouting at Jesus, [34]"Go away! We want nothing to do with you, Jesus from Nazareth. You have come to destroy us. I know who you are—the Holy Son of God."

[35]Jesus cut him short. "Be silent!" he told the demon. "Come out!" The demon threw the man to the floor as the crowd watched, and then left him without hurting him further.

[36]Amazed, the people asked, "What is in this man's words that even demons obey him?"

CHURCH

4:16 Jesus went to the synagogue "as usual." Even though he was the perfect Son of God, and his local synagogue left much to be desired, he attended services every week. Jesus' example makes most excuses for not attending church sound weak and self-serving. Make regular worship a part of your life.

³⁷The story of what he had done spread like wildfire throughout the whole region.

³⁸After leaving the synagogue that day, he went to Simon's home where he found Simon's mother-in-law very sick with a high fever. "Please heal her," everyone begged.

³⁹Standing at her bedside he spoke to the fever, rebuking it, and immediately her temperature returned to normal, and she got up and prepared a meal for them!

⁴⁰As the sun went down that evening, all the villagers who had any sick people in their homes, no matter what their diseases were, brought them to Jesus; and the touch of his hands healed every one! ⁴¹Some were possessed by demons; and the demons came out at his command, shouting, "You are the Son of God." But because they knew he was the Christ, he stopped them and told them to be silent.

⁴²Early the next morning he went out into the desert. The crowds searched everywhere for him, and when they finally found him, they begged him not to leave them but to stay at Capernaum. ⁴³But he replied, "I must preach the Good News of the kingdom of God in other places too, for that is why I was sent." ⁴⁴So he continued to travel around preaching in synagogues throughout Judea.

CHAPTER 5 FISHING WITH JESUS.

One day as he was preaching on the shore of Lake Gennesaret, great crowds pressed in on him to listen to the Word of God. ²He noticed two empty boats standing at the water's edge while the fishermen washed their nets. ³Stepping into one of the boats, Jesus asked Simon, its owner,

to push out a little into the water, so that he could sit in the boat and speak to the crowds from there.

⁴When he had finished speaking, he said to Simon, "Now go out where it is deeper and let down your nets and you will catch a lot of fish!"

⁵"Sir," Simon replied, "we worked hard all last night and didn't catch a thing. But if you say so, we'll try again."

⁶And this time their nets were so full that they began to tear! ⁷A shout for help brought

JAMES

James, his brother John, and Peter made up this inner circle. Later, each played a key role among the first Christians. Peter became a great speaker; John became a great writer; James became the first of the 12 disciples to die for the faith.

James was older than his brother John. Zebedee, their father, owned a fishing business where they worked along with Peter and Andrew, who also became disciples of Jesus. While Peter, Andrew, and John spent some time with John the Baptist, James stayed with the boats and nets. Later, when Jesus called them all, James was as eager as his partners to follow.

James liked the idea of being chosen as one of Jesus' disciples, but he misunderstood Jesus' purpose. He and his brother even tried asking Jesus for special positions in the Kingdom they expected him to set up. Like all the disciples, James had a limited view of what Jesus was doing on earth. He hoped Jesus would start an earthly kingdom that would overthrow Rome and restore the nation of Israel. More than anything, James wanted to be with Jesus. He didn't understand his leader, but he understood that Jesus was worth following. But when Jesus died and rose from the grave, James finally understood.

James was the first of many to die for the gospel. He was willing to die because he knew Jesus had conquered death. And he realized that death was only the doorway to eternal life. Our lives will be affected by what we think about death. Jesus promised eternal life to those willing to trust him. If we believe this promise, he will give us the courage to stand for him even during dangerous times.

LESSON: Many of Jesus' followers do not consider the loss of life too heavy a price to pay for following him

KEY VERSES: "Then James and John, the sons of Zebedee, came over and spoke to him in a low voice. 'Master,' they said, 'we want you to do us a favor.' 'What is it?' he asked. 'We want to sit on the thrones next to yours in your Kingdom,' they said, 'one at your right and the other at your left!'" (Mark 10:35-37).

James's story is told in the Gospels. He is also mentioned in Acts 1:14 and 12:2.

UPS:
• One of the 12 disciples
• One of a special inner circle of three with Peter and John
• First of the 12 disciples to be killed for his faith

DOWN:
• There are two outbursts from James that indicate struggles with temper (Luke 9:54) and selfishness (Mark 10:37). Both times, he and his brother, John, spoke as one.

STATS:
• Where: Galilee
• Occupation: Fisherman, disciple
• Relatives: Father: Zebedee. Mother: Salome. Brother: John.
• Contemporaries: Jesus, Pilate, Herod Agrippa

their partners in the other boat, and soon both boats were filled with fish and on the verge of sinking.

[8]When Simon Peter realized what had happened, he fell to his knees before Jesus and said, "Oh, sir, please leave us—I'm too much of a sinner for you to have around." [9]For he was awestruck by the size of their catch, as were the others with him, [10]and his partners too—James and John, the sons of Zebedee. Jesus replied, "Don't be afraid! From now on you'll be fishing for the souls of men!"

[11]And as soon as they landed, they left everything and went with him.

[12]One day in a certain village he was visiting, there was a man with an advanced case of leprosy. When he saw Jesus he fell to the ground before him, face downward in the dust, begging to be healed.

"Sir," he said, "if you only will, you can clear me of every trace of my disease."

[13]Jesus reached out and touched the man and said, "Of course I will. Be healed." And the leprosy left him instantly! [14]Then Jesus instructed him to go at once without telling anyone what had happened and be examined by the Jewish priest. "Offer the sacrifice Moses' law requires for lepers who are healed," he said. "This will prove to everyone that you are well."

[15]Now the report of his power spread even faster and vast crowds came to hear him preach and to be healed of their diseases. [16]But he often withdrew to the wilderness for prayer.

[17]One day while he was teaching, some Jewish religious leaders and teachers of the Law were sitting nearby. (It seemed that these men showed up from every village in all Galilee and Judea, as well as from Jerusalem.) And the Lord's healing power was upon him.

[18,19]Then—look! Some men came carrying a paralyzed man on a sleeping mat. They tried to push through the crowd to Jesus but couldn't reach him. So they went up on the roof above him, took off some tiles and lowered the sick man down into the crowd, still on his sleeping mat, right in front of Jesus.

[20]Seeing their faith, Jesus said to the man, "My friend, your sins are forgiven!"

[21]"Who does this fellow think he is?" the Pharisees and teachers of the Law exclaimed among themselves. "This is blasphemy! Who but God can forgive sins?"

[22]Jesus knew what they were thinking, and he replied, "Why is it blasphemy? [23,24]I, the Messiah, have the authority on earth to forgive sins. But talk is cheap—anybody could say that. So I'll prove it to you by healing this man." Then, turning to the paralyzed man, he commanded, "Pick up your stretcher and go on home, for you are healed!"

[25]And immediately, as everyone watched, the man jumped to his feet, picked up his mat and went home praising God! [26]Everyone present was gripped with awe and fear. And they praised God, remarking over and over again, "We have seen strange things today."

[27]Later on as Jesus left the town he saw a tax collector—with the usual reputation for cheating—sitting at a tax collection booth. The man's name was Levi. Jesus said to him, "Come and be one of my disciples!" [28]So Levi left everything, sprang up and went with him.

[29]Soon Levi held a reception in his home with Jesus as the guest of honor. Many of Levi's fellow tax collectors and other guests were there.

[30]But the Pharisees and teachers of the Law complained bitterly to Jesus' disciples about his eating with such notorious sinners.

[31]Jesus answered them, "It is the sick who need a doctor, not those in good health. [32]My purpose is to invite sinners to turn from their sins, not to spend my time with those who think themselves already good enough."

[33]Their next complaint was that Jesus' disciples were feasting instead of fasting. "John the Baptist's disciples are constantly going without food and praying," they declared, "and so do the disciples of the Pharisees. Why are yours wining and dining?"

[34]Jesus asked, "Do happy men fast? Do wedding guests go hungry while celebrating with the groom? [35]But the time will come when the bridegroom will be killed; then they won't want to eat."

[36]Then Jesus used this illustration: "No one tears off a piece of a new garment to make a patch for an old one. Not only will the new garment be ruined, but the old garment will look worse with a new patch on it! [37]And no one puts new wine into old wineskins, for the new wine bursts the old skins, ruining the skins and spilling the wine. [38]New wine must be put into new wineskins. [39]But no one after drinking the old wine seems to want the fresh and the new. 'The old ways are best,' they say."

TRY IT!

5:18-20 It wasn't the sick man's faith that impressed Jesus, but the faith of his friends. Jesus responded to their faith and healed the man. For better or worse, our faith affects others. We cannot make another person a Christian, but we can do much through our words, actions, and love to give him or her a chance to respond. Look for opportunities to bring your friends to the living Christ.

QUALIFIED

6:13-16 Jesus picked ordinary men as his disciples. Today, God calls "ordinary" people to build his church, teach salvation, and serve others. Alone we may feel unqualified to serve Christ well. Together we are strong enough to serve God in any way. Ask for patience to accept differences and to build on the variety of strengths in your group.

CHAPTER 6 PICKING WHEAT ON THE SABBATH.

One Sabbath as Jesus and his disciples were walking through some grainfields, they were breaking off the heads of wheat, rubbing off the husks in their hands and eating the grains.

²But some Pharisees said, "That's illegal! Your disciples are harvesting grain, and it's against the Jewish law to work on the Sabbath."

³Jesus replied, "Don't you read the Scriptures? Haven't you ever read what King David did when he and his men were hungry? ⁴He went into the Temple and took the shewbread, the special bread that was placed before the Lord, and ate it—illegal as this was—and shared it with others." ⁵And Jesus added, "I am master even of the Sabbath."

⁶On another Sabbath he was in the synagogue teaching, and a man was present whose right hand was deformed. ⁷The teachers of the Law and the Pharisees watched closely to see whether he would heal the man that day, since it was the Sabbath. For they were eager to find some charge to bring against him.

⁸How well he knew their thoughts! But he said to the man with the deformed hand, "Come and stand here where everyone can see." So he did.

⁹Then Jesus said to the Pharisees and teachers of the Law, "I have a question for you. Is it right to do good on the Sabbath day, or to do harm? To save life, or to destroy it?"

¹⁰He looked around at them one by one and then said to the man, "Reach out your hand." And as he did, it became completely normal again. ¹¹At this, the enemies of Jesus were wild with rage and began to plot his murder.

¹²One day soon afterwards he went out into the mountains to pray, and prayed all night. ¹³At daybreak he called together his followers and chose twelve of them to be the inner circle of his disciples. (They were appointed as his "apostles," or "missionaries.") ¹⁴⁻¹⁶Here are their names:

Simon (he also called him Peter), Andrew (Simon's brother), James, John, Philip, Bartholomew, Matthew, Thomas, James (the son of Alphaeus), Simon (a member of the Zealots, a subversive political party), Judas (son of

"Here's what I did..."

Even before I became a Christian, the Bible amazed me. I remember being floored the first time I read Luke 6:27-38. That's the passage about loving and doing good to your enemies. *How could anyone act like that?*

A year later, just before my freshman year in high school, I became a Christian. And that year I had the chance to find out firsthand how someone can follow Jesus' words.

I did well in shop class, so I decided to make a small bookcase for my mother for Christmas. I designed it myself. I worked on it a lot in my spare time, finally getting to the point where I put final touches on it and left it in the finishing room, which was always locked.

After school, when I went back to get the bookcase, it was gone. The shop teacher did some investigating and finally discovered that a student named Andy had stolen it. "We've had problems with Andy before," Mr. Petrako said. "Andy needs to learn a lesson. I've arranged to have him meet you after school to return your bookshelf." That's all he said, but I knew what he meant.

I didn't need any encouragement to "teach Andy a lesson." I was furious. And since I was a football player, big for my age, I wouldn't have any trouble beating someone up.

I waited for Andy, psyching myself up to face my enemy. Finally he walked in.

Something happened to me when I saw him. I had expected a hoodlum, but what I saw was just a boy, smaller and younger than me, who was obviously afraid to face the person he had hurt. When I saw Andy's scared face, all the hate just leaked out of me. Andy said, "Here's your bookshelf. I'm sorry." I had no words for him. I growled something, took the bookcase, and fled.

That night I felt very confused. *What happened? What took away my hate?* As I thought about these things, I remembered the passage in Luke. I read it again: "Love your enemies. . . . When things are taken away from you, don't worry about getting them back."

Father God, I thought, *am I supposed to give the bookcase back to him? I can't! I made it for my mom!* I felt like God was asking me to respond to what I was reading. But how? Suddenly I knew. The next morning I went to school early, and started work on an identical bookcase. For four days straight I stayed as long as shop was open.

When the bookcase was finished, I had Andy meet me after school in an empty shop class. I said, "Andy, I want to give you this. It's a gift from me to you, and from me to Jesus. I'd never be able to do this if it weren't for Jesus."

That's all I could say then. I didn't know how to share my faith. All I knew was that Jesus had touched my life and I wanted to share it.

Well, after that I got to know Andy. Seeing his family situation, I understood him better. I invited him to youth group on Thursday afternoons. When there was a retreat and Andy couldn't afford to go, my friends and I scraped up enough money for him. And at that retreat, Andy became a Christian.

It's hard to know who was more excited about God right then, me or Andy.

David AGE 17

TOUGH LOVE

6:27 The Jews despised the Romans because they oppressed God's people, but Jesus told them to love these enemies. Such words turned many away from Christ. But Jesus wasn't talking about having affection for enemies; he was talking about an act of the will. You can't "fall into" this kind of love—it takes conscious effort. Loving our enemies means acting in their best interests. We can pray for them and we can think of ways to help them. Jesus loved the whole world, even though the world was in rebellion against God. He asks us to follow his example by loving our enemies.

James), Judas Iscariot (who later betrayed him).

¹⁷,¹⁸When they came down the slopes of the mountain, they stood with Jesus on a large, level area, surrounded by many of his followers who, in turn, were surrounded by the crowds. For people from all over Judea and from Jerusalem and from as far north as the seacoasts of Tyre and Sidon had come to hear him or to be healed. And he cast out many demons. ¹⁹Everyone was trying to touch him, for when they did, healing power went out from him and they were cured.

²⁰Then he turned to his disciples and said, "What happiness there is for you who are poor, for the Kingdom of God is yours! ²¹What happiness there is for you who are now hungry, for you are going to be satisfied! What happiness there is for you who weep, for the time will come when you shall laugh with joy! ²²What happiness it is when others hate you and exclude you and insult you and smear your name because you are mine! ²³When that happens, rejoice! Yes, leap for joy! For you will have a great reward awaiting you in heaven. And you will be in good company—the ancient prophets were treated that way too!

²⁴"But, oh, the sorrows that await the rich. For they have their only happiness down here. ²⁵They are fat and prosperous now, but a time of awful hunger is before them. Their careless laughter now means sorrow then. ²⁶And what sadness is ahead for those praised by the crowds—for *false* prophets have *always* been praised.

²⁷"Listen, all of you. Love your *enemies*. Do *good* to those who *hate* you. ²⁸Pray for the happiness of those who *curse* you; implore God's blessing on those who *hurt* you.

²⁹"If someone slaps you on one cheek, let him slap the other too! If someone demands your coat, give him your shirt besides. ³⁰Give what you have to anyone who asks you for it; and when things are taken away from you, don't worry about getting them back. ³¹Treat others as you want them to treat you.

³²"Do you think you deserve credit for merely loving those who love you? Even the godless do that! ³³And if you do good only to those who do you good—is that so wonderful? Even sinners do that much! ³⁴And if you lend money only to those who

can repay you, what good is that? Even the most wicked will lend to their own kind for full return!

³⁵"Love your *enemies!* Do good to *them!* Lend to *them!* And don't be concerned about the fact that they won't repay. Then your reward from heaven will be very great, and you will truly be acting as sons of God: for he is kind to the *unthankful* and to those who are *very wicked.*

³⁶"Try to show as much compassion as your Father does.

³⁷"Never criticize or condemn—or it will all come back on you. Go easy on others; then they will do the same for you. ³⁸For if you give, you will get! Your gift will return to you in full and overflowing measure, pressed down, shaken together to make room for more, and running over. Whatever measure you use to give—large or small—will be used to measure what is given back to you."

³⁹Here are some of the story-illustrations Jesus used in his sermons: "What good is it for one blind man to lead another? He will fall into a ditch and pull the other down with him. ⁴⁰How can a student know more than his teacher? But if he works hard, he may learn as much.

⁴¹"And why quibble about the speck in someone else's eye—his little fault—when a board is in your own? ⁴²How can you think of saying to him, 'Brother, let me help you get rid of that speck in your eye,' when you can't see past the board in yours? Hypocrite! First get rid of the board, and then perhaps you can see well enough to deal with his speck!

⁴³"A tree from good stock doesn't produce scrub fruit nor do trees from poor stock produce choice fruit. ⁴⁴A tree is identified by the kind of fruit it produces. Figs never grow on thorns, or grapes on bramble bushes. ⁴⁵A good man produces good deeds from a good heart. And an evil man produces evil deeds from his hidden wickedness. Whatever is in the heart overflows into speech.

⁴⁶"So why do you call me 'Lord' when you won't obey me? ⁴⁷,⁴⁸But all those who come and listen and obey me are like a man who builds a house on a strong foundation laid upon the underlying rock. When the floodwaters rise and break against the house, it stands firm, for it is strongly built.

⁴⁹"But those who listen and don't obey are like a man who builds a house without a foundation. When the floods sweep down against that house, it crumbles into a heap of ruins."

NO POINTING

6:41 Jesus doesn't mean we should ignore wrongdoing, but we are not to be so worried about others' sins that we overlook our own. We often rationalize our sins by pointing out the same mistakes in others. What kinds of specks in others' eyes are the easiest for you to criticize? Remember your own boards when you feel like criticizing, and you may find you have less to say.

CHAPTER **7** **A MAN IS HEALED FAR AWAY.** When Jesus had finished his sermon he went back into the city of Capernaum.

²Just at that time the highly prized slave of a Roman army captain was sick and near death. ³When the captain heard about Jesus, he sent some respected Jewish elders to ask him to come and heal his slave. ⁴So they began pleading earnestly with Jesus to come with them and help the man. They told him what a wonderful person the captain was.

"If anyone deserves your help, it is he," they said, ⁵"for he loves the Jews and even paid personally to build us a synagogue!"

⁶⁻⁸Jesus went with them; but just before arriving at the house, the captain sent some friends to say, "Sir, don't inconvenience yourself by coming to my home, for I am not worthy of any such honor or even to come and meet you. Just speak a word from where you are, and my servant boy will be healed! I know, because I am under the authority of my superior officers, and I have authority over my men. I only need to say 'Go!' and they go; or 'Come!' and they come; and to my slave, 'Do this or that,' and he does it. So just say, 'Be healed!' and my servant will be well again!"

⁹Jesus was amazed. Turning to the crowd he said, "Never among all the Jews in Israel have I met a man with faith like this."

¹⁰And when the captain's friends returned to his house, they found the slave completely healed.

¹¹Not long afterwards Jesus went with his disciples to the village of Nain, with the usual great crowd at his heels. ¹²A funeral procession was coming out as he approached the village gate. The boy who had died was the only son of his widowed mother, and many mourners from the village were with her.

¹³When the Lord saw her, his heart overflowed with sympathy. "Don't cry!" he said. ¹⁴Then he walked over to the coffin and touched it, and the bearers stopped. "Laddie," he said, "come back to life again."

¹⁵Then the boy sat up and began to talk to those around him! And Jesus gave him back to his mother.

¹⁶A great fear swept the crowd, and they exclaimed with praises to God, "A mighty prophet has risen among us," and, "We have seen the hand of God at work today."

¹⁷The report of what he did that day raced from end to end of Judea and even out across the borders.

¹⁸The disciples of John the Baptist soon heard of all that Jesus was doing. When they told John about it, ¹⁹he sent two of his disciples to Jesus to ask him, "Are you really the Messiah? Or shall we keep on looking for him?"

²⁰⁻²²The two disciples found Jesus while he was curing many sick people of their various diseases—healing the lame and the blind and casting out evil spirits. When they asked him John's question, this was his reply: "Go back to John and tell him all you have seen and heard here today: how those who were blind can see. The lame are walk-

---

There are so many things in my life that could pull me away from God. How can I make sure I will always be "good soil"?

I WONDER...

Skyscrapers must be carefully planned in order for them not to topple when a stiff wind hits. First, a huge hole is dug deep in the ground. Thousands of tons of concrete are poured, steel girders are welded into place, and everything is made to fit according to exact specifications. If the foundation is strong and straight, a strong building can be built on it.

The rest of the structure, however, must also be built strong, with the right materials fitted together in the right way, at the right time.

In Luke 8:9-18, Jesus tells a parable about the Word of God. He compares it to a seed being planted. Like the skyscraper, seeds need to be planted in the right kind of soil, at the right time. So it is with the Word of God. Only God knows when and how to plant his Spirit and life within each of us.

The first phase in your new life began when you accepted Christ's forgiveness and became a Christian: "And no one can ever lay any other real foundation than that one we already have—Jesus Christ" (1 Corinthians 3:11).

The second phase starts with the Word of God. If you study the Bible and have other Christians help you understand and apply it, your life in Christ will be strong. "There are various kinds of materials that can be used to build on that foundation. Some use gold and silver and jewels; and some build with sticks and hay or even straw!" (1 Corinthians 3:12). If you are exposed to teaching that downplays God's Word, it is like building your life with sticks, hay, and straw. It will collapse when problems or persecution from friends and family arise (see Matthew 7:21-28).

To build a solid Christian life, you should make sure that all you're hearing is lining up with what the Bible really says. You can do this by praying for direction, asking questions, and finding people who believe as you do that the Bible is God's blueprint for building a strong life.

---

ing without a limp. The lepers are completely healed. The deaf can hear again. The dead come back to life. And the poor are hearing the Good News. ²³And tell him, 'Blessed is the one who does not lose his faith in me.'"

²⁴After they left, Jesus talked to the crowd about John. "Who is this man you went out into the Judean wilderness to see?" he asked. "Did you find

him weak as grass, moved by every breath of wind? ²⁵Did you find him dressed in expensive clothes? No! Men who live in luxury are found in palaces, not out in the wilderness. ²⁶But did you find a prophet? Yes! And more than a prophet. ²⁷He is the one to whom the Scriptures refer when they say, 'Look! I am sending my messenger ahead of you, to prepare the way before you.' ²⁸In all humanity there is no one greater than John. And yet the least citizen of the Kingdom of God is greater than he."

²⁹And all who heard John preach—even the most wicked of them—agreed that God's requirements were right, and they were baptized by him. ³⁰All, that is, except the Pharisees and teachers of Moses' Law. They rejected God's plan for them and refused John's baptism.

³¹"What can I say about such men?" Jesus asked. "With what shall I compare them? ³²They are like a group of children who complain to their friends, 'You don't like it if we play "wedding" and you don't like it if we play "funeral"'! ³³For John the Baptist used to go without food and never took a drop of liquor all his life, and you said, 'He must be crazy!' ³⁴But I eat my food and drink my wine, and you say, 'What a glutton Jesus is! And he drinks! And has the lowest sort of friends!' ³⁵But I am sure you can always justify your inconsistencies."

³⁶One of the Pharisees asked Jesus to come to his home for lunch and Jesus accepted the invitation. As they sat down to eat, ³⁷a woman of the streets—a prostitute—heard he was there and brought an exquisite flask filled with expensive perfume. ³⁸Going in, she knelt behind him at his feet, weeping, with her tears falling down upon his feet; and she wiped them off with her hair and kissed them and poured the perfume on them.

³⁹When Jesus' host, a Pharisee, saw what was happening and who the woman was, he said to himself, "This proves that Jesus is no prophet, for if God had really sent him, he would know what kind of woman this one is!"

⁴⁰Then Jesus spoke up and answered his thoughts. "Simon," he said to the Pharisee, "I have something to say to you."

"All right, Teacher," Simon replied, "go ahead."

⁴¹Then Jesus told him this story: "A man loaned money to two people—$5,000 to one and $500 to the other. ⁴²But neither of them could pay him back, so he kindly forgave them both, letting them keep the money! Which do you suppose loved him most after that?"

⁴³"I suppose the one who had owed him the most," Simon answered.

"Correct," Jesus agreed.

⁴⁴Then he turned to the woman and said to Simon, "Look! See this woman kneeling here! When I entered your home, you didn't bother to offer me water to wash the dust from my feet, but she has washed them with her tears and wiped them with her hair. ⁴⁵You refused me the customary kiss of greeting, but she has kissed my feet again and again from the time I first came in. ⁴⁶You neglected the usual courtesy of olive oil to anoint my head, but she has covered my feet with rare perfume. ⁴⁷Therefore her sins—and they are many—are forgiven, for she loved me much; but one who is forgiven little, shows little love."

⁴⁸And he said to her, "Your sins are forgiven."

⁴⁹Then the men at the table said to themselves, "Who does this man think he is, going around forgiving sins?"

⁵⁰And Jesus said to the woman, "Your faith has saved you; go in peace."

CHAPTER **8** **WOMEN GO WITH JESUS.** Not long afterwards he began a tour of the cities and villages of Galilee to announce the coming of the Kingdom of God, and took his twelve disciples with him. ²Some women went along, from whom he had cast out demons or whom he had healed; among them were Mary Magdalene (Jesus had cast out seven demons from her), ³Joanna, Chuza's wife (Chuza was King Herod's business manager and was in charge of his palace and domestic affairs), Susanna, and many others who were contributing from their private means to the support of Jesus and his disciples.

⁴One day he gave this illustration to a large crowd that was gathering to hear him—while many others were still on the way, coming from other towns.

⁵"A farmer went out to his field to sow grain. As he scattered the seed on the ground, some of it fell on a footpath and was trampled on; and the birds came and ate it as it lay exposed. ⁶Other seed fell on shallow soil with rock beneath. This seed began

QUESTIONS

7:18-28 John was confused because the reports he received about Jesus were unexpected and incomplete. John's doubts were natural, and Jesus didn't rebuke him for them. Instead, Jesus responded in a way that John would understand by explaining that he had in fact accomplished the things the Messiah was supposed to accomplish. God also can handle our doubts, and he welcomes our questions. Do you have questions about Jesus—about who he is or what he expects of you? Admit them to yourself and to God, and begin looking for answers. Only as you admit your doubts can you begin to resolve them.

DISCOVER

7:29-30 The wicked people heard John's message and repented. In contrast, the religious leaders rejected his words. Wanting to live their own way, they refused to listen to other ideas. Rather than trying to force your plans on God, try to discover his plan for you.

to grow, but soon withered and died for lack of moisture. [7]Other seed landed in thistle patches, and the young grain stalks were soon choked out. [8]Still other fell on fertile soil; this seed grew and produced a crop one hundred times as large as he had planted." (As he was giving this illustration he said, "If anyone has listening ears, use them now!")

[9]His apostles asked him what the story meant.

[10]He replied, "God has granted you to know the meaning of these parables, for they tell a great deal about the Kingdom of God. But these crowds hear the words and do not understand, just as the ancient prophets predicted.

[11]"This is its meaning: The seed is God's message to men. [12]The hard path where some seed fell represents the hard hearts of those who hear the words of God, but then the devil comes and steals the words away and prevents people from believing and being saved. [13]The stony ground represents those who enjoy listening to sermons, but somehow the message never really gets through to them and doesn't take root and grow. They know the message is true, and sort of believe for awhile; but when the hot winds of persecution blow, they lose interest. [14]The seed among the thorns represents those who listen and believe God's words but whose faith afterwards is choked out by worry and riches and the responsibilities and pleasures of life. And so they are never able to help anyone else to believe the Good News.

[15]"But the good soil represents honest, goodhearted people. They listen to God's words and cling to them and steadily spread them to others who also soon believe."

[16][Another time he asked,] "Who ever heard of someone lighting a lamp and then covering it up to keep it from shining? No, lamps are mounted in the open where they can be seen. [17]This illustrates the fact that someday everything [in men's hearts] shall be brought to light and made plain to all. [18]So be careful how you listen; for whoever has, to him shall be given more; and whoever does not have, even what he thinks he has shall be taken away from him."

[19]Once when his mother and brothers came to see him, they couldn't get into the house where he was teaching because of the crowds. [20]When Jesus heard they were standing outside and wanted to see him, [21]he remarked, "My mother and my brothers are all those who hear the message of God and obey it."

[22]One day about that time, as he and his disciples were out in a boat, he suggested that they cross to the other side of the lake. [23]On the way across he lay down for a nap, and while he was sleeping the wind began to rise. A fierce storm developed that threatened to swamp them, and they were in real danger.

[24]They rushed over and woke him up. "Master, Master, we are sinking!" they screamed.

So he spoke to the storm: "Quiet down," he said, and the wind and waves subsided and all was calm! [25]Then he asked them, "Where is your faith?"

And they were filled with awe and fear of him and said to one another, "Who is this man, that even the winds and waves obey him?"

[26]So they arrived at the other side, in the Gerasene country across the lake from Galilee. [27]As he was climbing out of the boat a man from the city of Gadara came to meet him, a man who had been demon-possessed for a long time. Homeless and naked, he lived in a cemetery among the tombs. [28]As soon as he saw Jesus he shrieked and fell to the ground before him, screaming, "What do you want with me, Jesus, Son of God Most High? Please, I beg you, oh, don't torment me!"

[29]For Jesus was already commanding the demon to leave him. This demon had often taken control of the man so that even when shackled with chains he simply broke them and rushed out into the desert, completely under the demon's power. [30]"What is your name?" Jesus asked the demon. "Legion," they replied— for the man was filled with thousands of them! [31]They kept begging Jesus not to order them into the Bottomless Pit.

[32]A herd of pigs was feeding on the mountainside nearby, and the demons pled with him to let them enter into the pigs. And Jesus said they could. [33]So they left the man and went into the pigs, and immediately the whole herd rushed down the mountainside and fell over a cliff into the lake below, where they drowned. [34]The herdsmen rushed away to the nearby city, spreading the news as they ran.

[35]Soon a crowd came out to see for themselves what had happened and saw the man who had been demon-possessed sitting quietly at Jesus' feet, clothed and sane! And the whole crowd was badly frightened. [36]Then those who had seen it happen told how the demon-possessed man had been healed. [37]And everyone begged Jesus to go away

PIGS

8:33 The demons destroyed the pigs and hurt the herdsmen's finances. But can pigs and money compare with a human life? A man had been freed from the devil's power, but the villagers thought only about their pocketbooks. People have always tended to value personal gain over other people. Throughout history many wars have been fought to protect economic interests. Much injustice and oppression, both at home and abroad, is the direct result of some individual's or company's urge to get rich. People continually are being sacrificed to money. Don't think more highly of "pigs" than of people. Think carefully about how your decisions will affect other human beings, and be willing to choose a simpler life-style if it would keep other people from being harmed.

Gorillas are amazingly bright animals. Researchers have even been able to teach some gorillas to communicate by using sign language. Koko, one of the best ape "students" ever trained, has an impressive sign vocabulary through which she is able to communicate a number of surprisingly complicated concepts. But she was unprepared for the day an earthquake shook the ground underneath her. After it was over, one of her trainers asked Koko to describe what she had just experienced. Having no word in her vocabulary for "earthquake," Koko described it as best she could. Using sign language, she said, "Darn floor—big bite."

It's not entirely clear what she was trying to communicate with those words; perhaps the fear that the floor might open up and swallow her. She was trying to express something beyond her limited ability the only way she knew how. People have struggled throughout history in a similar way with a different—and much more significant—problem: how to describe who God is and what he's like. God communicated with humans in many ways in the past: talking freely with Adam and Eve, through the covenant sign of the rainbow, through a burning bush and columns of fire and smoke, through his Law, and through miracles and visions. Still, people who witnessed those signs must have felt like Koko—overwhelmed by the reality behind them. The people powerful and meaningful as all those were, they were only a hint of what they'd experienced but with no adequate way to express their feelings. But God had one more ultimate revelation to make: he came to our planet and became one of us. We refer to this revelation as "Jesus of Nazareth." Understandably, the coming of Jesus was an explosive event. Nothing like it had ever happened before, nor has it happened since. God—in human form—walking the same ground with us! Breathing our air, sharing our pain, laughing and bleeding just like we do, entering into all the exhilaration—and the anguish—of being human. Before this revelation, God had given us hints, glimpses, and whispers of who he was. Then he came in all his fullness.

But Jesus was not what people expected. Even the Jewish authorities—the people who knew more about God than anyone—were totally unprepared for the way God came. They expected a strong political and military Messiah, one who would free his people from Rome. Instead, the Messiah came as a "suffering servant," proclaiming a Kingdom that was "not of this world." Like so many others, the Jews were very confused to who Jesus really was. Jesus himself knew that even his closest followers felt that uncertainty. He asked them point-blank: "Who do you think I am?" Peter's response to this question, given here in Luke, was simple, direct, and tremendously powerful: "The Messiah—the Christ of God!" Peter's answer, simple though it was, set off shock waves that have rippled down through history. If Jesus was—and is—indeed the Messiah, the Son of the living God, then God had entered into human history in a way he had never done before, and life on this planet could never be the same again. Countless millions of lives since then give testimony that that is exactly what has happened. Jesus of Nazareth was, and is, the unique Son of God: fully God, fully human, Lord of lords and King of kings. That same question Jesus asked his disciples confronts each of us today: Who do you say Jesus is? Be careful how you answer. It makes all the difference in eternity.

and leave them alone (for a deep wave of fear had swept over them). So he returned to the boat and left, crossing back to the other side of the lake.

³⁸The man who had been demon-possessed begged to go too, but Jesus said no.

³⁹"Go back to your family," he told him, "and tell them what a wonderful thing God has done for you."

So he went all through the city telling everyone about Jesus' mighty miracle.

⁴⁰On the other side of the lake the crowds received him with open arms, for they had been waiting for him.

⁴¹And now a man named Jairus, a leader of a Jewish synagogue, came and fell down at Jesus' feet and begged him to come home with him, ⁴²for his only child was dying, a little girl twelve years old. Jesus went with him, pushing through the crowds.

^{43,44}As they went a woman who wanted to be healed came up behind and touched him, for she had been slowly bleeding for twelve years, and could find no cure (though she had spent everything she had on doctors). But the instant she touched the edge of his robe, the bleeding stopped.

⁴⁵"Who touched me?" Jesus asked.

Everyone denied it, and Peter said, "Master, so many are crowding against you. . . . "

⁴⁶But Jesus told him, "No, it was someone who deliberately touched me, for I felt healing power go out from me."

⁴⁷When the woman realized that Jesus knew, she began to tremble and fell to her knees before him and told why she had touched him and that now she was well.

⁴⁸"Daughter," he said to her, "your faith has healed you. Go in peace."

⁴⁹While he was still speaking to her, a messenger arrived from the Jairus' home with the news that the little girl was dead. "She's gone," he told her father; "there's no use troubling the Teacher now."

⁵⁰But when Jesus heard what had happened, he said to the father, "Don't be afraid! Just trust me, and she'll be all right."

⁵¹When they arrived at the house, Jesus wouldn't let anyone into the room except Peter, James, John, and the little girl's father and mother. ⁵²The home was filled with mourning people, but he said, "Stop the weeping! She isn't dead; she is only asleep!" ⁵³This brought scoffing and laughter, for they all knew she was dead.

⁵⁴Then he took her by the hand and called, "Get up, little girl!" ⁵⁵And at that moment her life returned and she jumped up! "Give her something to eat!" he said. ⁵⁶Her parents were overcome with happiness, but Jesus insisted that they not tell anyone the details of what had happened.

CHAPTER 9 AN ASSIGNMENT FOR THE DISCIPLES.
One day Jesus called together his twelve apostles and gave them authority over all demons—power to cast them out—and to heal all diseases. ²Then he sent them away to tell everyone about the coming of the Kingdom of God and to heal the sick.

³"Don't even take along a walking stick," he instructed them, "nor a beggar's bag, nor food, nor money. Not even an extra coat. ⁴Be a guest in only one home at each village.

⁵"If the people of a town won't listen to you when you enter it, turn around and leave, demonstrating God's anger against it by shaking its dust from your feet as you go."

⁶So they began their circuit of the villages, preaching the Good News and healing the sick.

⁷When reports of Jesus' miracles reached Herod, the governor, he was worried and puzzled, for some were saying, "This is John the Baptist come back to life again"; ⁸and others, "It is Elijah or some other ancient prophet risen from the dead." These rumors were circulating all over the land.

⁹"I beheaded John," Herod said, "so who is this man about whom I hear such strange stories?" And he tried to see him.

¹⁰After the apostles returned to Jesus and reported what they had done, he slipped quietly away with them toward the city of Bethsaida. ¹¹But the crowds found out where he was going and followed. And he welcomed them, teaching them again about the Kingdom of God and curing those who were ill.

¹²Late in the afternoon all twelve of the disciples came and urged him to send the people away to the nearby villages and farms, to find food and lodging for the night. "For there is nothing to eat here in this deserted spot," they said.

¹³But Jesus replied, *"You feed them!"*

"Why, we have only five loaves of bread and two fish among the lot of us," they protested; "or are you expecting us to go and buy enough for

JESUS

9:7 People couldn't accept Jesus for who he was, so they tried to come up with other solutions. Many thought he was John the Baptist or another prophet come back to life. Some suggested he was Elijah, the great prophet who did not die but was taken to heaven in a whirlwind (2 Kings 2:1-11). Few found the correct answer, as Peter did (9:20). Many today find it no easier to accept Jesus as the fully human yet fully divine Son of God—they still are trying to find alternate explanations: he was a great prophet, a radical political leader, a self-deceived rabble-rouser. None of these explanations can account for Jesus' miracles or, especially, his glorious resurrection. In the end, the attempts to explain Jesus away are far more difficult to believe than the truth.

this whole mob?" [14]For there were about 5,000 men there!

"Just tell them to sit down on the ground in groups of about fifty each," Jesus replied. [15]So they did.

[16]Jesus took the five loaves and two fish and looked up into the sky and gave thanks; then he broke off pieces for his disciples to set before the crowd. [17]And everyone ate and ate; still, twelve basketfuls of scraps were picked up afterwards!

[18]One day as he was alone, praying, with his disciples nearby, he came over and asked them, "Who are the people saying I am?"

[19]"John the Baptist," they told him, "or perhaps Elijah or one of the other ancient prophets risen from the dead."

[20]Then he asked them, "Who do you think I am?"

Peter replied, "The Messiah—the Christ of God!"

[21]He gave them strict orders not to speak of this to anyone. [22]"For I, the Messiah, must suffer much," he said, "and be rejected by the Jewish leaders—the elders, chief priests, and teachers of the Law—and be killed; and three days later I will come back to life again!"

[23]Then he said to all, "Anyone who wants to follow me must put aside his own desires and conveniences and carry his cross with him every day and *keep close to me!* [24]Whoever loses his life for my sake will save it, but whoever insists on keeping his life will lose it; [25]and what profit is there in gaining the whole world when it means forfeiting one's self?

[26]"When I, the Messiah, come in my glory and in the glory of the Father and the holy angels, I will be ashamed then of all who are ashamed of me and of my words now. [27]But this is the simple truth—some of you who are standing here right now will not die until you have seen the Kingdom of God."

[28]Eight days later he took Peter, James, and John with him into the hills to pray. [29]And as he was praying, his face began to shine, and his clothes became dazzling white and blazed with light. [30]Then two men appeared and began talking with him—Moses and Elijah! [31]They were splendid in appearance, glorious to see; and they were speaking of his death at Jerusalem, to be carried out in accordance with God's plan.

[32]Peter and the others had been very drowsy and had fallen asleep. Now they woke up and saw Jesus covered with brightness and glory, and the two men standing with him. [33]As Moses and Elijah were starting to leave, Peter, all confused and not even knowing what he was saying, blurted out, "Master, this is wonderful! We'll put up three shelters—one for you and one for Moses and one for Elijah!"

[34]But even as he was saying this, a bright cloud formed above them; and terror gripped them as it covered them. [35]And a voice from the cloud said, *"This* is my Son, my Chosen One; listen to *him."*

[36]Then, as the voice died away, Jesus was there alone with his disciples. They didn't tell anyone what they had seen until long afterwards.

[37]The next day as they descended from the hill, a huge crowd met him, [38]and a man in the crowd called out to him, "Teacher, this boy here is my only son, [39]and a demon keeps seizing him, making him scream; and it throws him into convulsions so that he foams at the mouth; it is always hitting him and hardly ever leaves him alone. [40]I begged your disciples to cast the demon out, but they couldn't."

[41]"O you stubborn faithless people," Jesus said [to his disciples], "how long should I put up with you? Bring him here."

[42]As the boy was coming the demon knocked him to the ground and threw him into a violent convulsion. But Jesus ordered the demon to come out, and healed the boy and handed him over to his father.

[43]Awe gripped the people as they saw this display of the power of God.

Meanwhile, as they were exclaiming over all the wonderful things he was doing, Jesus said to his disciples, [44]"Listen to me and remember what I say. I, the Messiah, am going to be betrayed." [45]But the disciples didn't know what he meant, for their minds had been sealed and they were afraid to ask him.

[46]Now came an argument among them as to which of them would be greatest [in the coming Kingdom]! [47]But Jesus knew their thoughts, so he stood a little child beside him [48]and said to them, "Any-

ENDANGERED

9:24-25 If this life is most important to you, you will do everything you can to protect it. You will not want to do anything that might endanger your safety, health, or comfort. By contrast, if following Jesus is most important, you may find yourself in some very unsafe, unhealthy, and uncomfortable places. You will risk death, but you will not fear it because you know Jesus will raise you to eternal life. The person who is concerned only with this life has no such assurance. His earthly life may be longer, but it will most likely be marred by feelings of boredom and worthlessness.

MOUNTAINS

9:33 Peter, James, and John experienced a wonderful moment on the mountain, and they didn't want to leave. Sometimes we, too, have such an exciting experience we want to stay where we are—away from the reality and problems of our daily life. Knowing that struggles await us encourages us to retreat from reality. Yet staying on top of a mountain does not allow us to minister to others. Instead of becoming spiritual giants, we would soon become giants of self-centeredness. We need times of retreat and renewal, but only so we can return to minister to the world. Our faith must make sense off the mountain as well as on it.

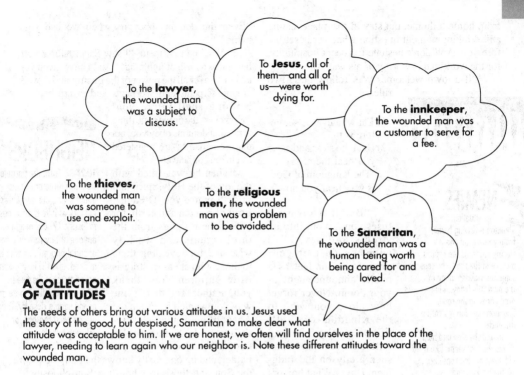

To the **lawyer**, the wounded man was a subject to discuss.

To **Jesus**, all of them—and all of us—were worth dying for.

To the **innkeeper**, the wounded man was a customer to serve for a fee.

To the **thieves**, the wounded man was someone to use and exploit.

To the **religious men**, the wounded man was a problem to be avoided.

To the **Samaritan**, the wounded man was a human being worth being cared for and loved.

A COLLECTION OF ATTITUDES

The needs of others bring out various attitudes in us. Jesus used the story of the good, but despised, Samaritan to make clear what attitude was acceptable to him. If we are honest, we often will find ourselves in the place of the lawyer, needing to learn again who our neighbor is. Note these different attitudes toward the wounded man.

---

one who takes care of a little child like this is caring for me! And whoever cares for me is caring for God who sent me. Your care for others is the measure of your greatness." ⁴⁹His disciple John came to him and said, "Master, we saw someone using your name to cast out demons. And we told him not to. After all, he isn't in our group."

⁵⁰But Jesus said, "You shouldn't have done that! For anyone who is not against you is for you."

⁵¹As the time drew near for his return to heaven, he moved steadily onward toward Jerusalem with an iron will.

⁵²One day he sent messengers ahead to reserve rooms for them in a Samaritan village. ⁵³But they were turned away! The people of the village refused to have anything to do with them because they were headed for Jerusalem.

⁵⁴When word came back of what had happened, James and John said to Jesus, "Master, shall we order fire down from heaven to burn them up?" ⁵⁵But Jesus turned and rebuked them, ⁵⁶and they went on to another village.

⁵⁷As they were walking along someone said to Jesus, "I will always follow you no matter where you go."

⁵⁸But Jesus replied, "Remember, I don't even own a place to lay my head. Foxes have dens to live in, and birds have nests, but I, the Messiah, have no earthly home at all."

⁵⁹Another time, when he invited a man to come with him and to be his disciple, the man agreed— but wanted to wait until his father's death.

⁶⁰Jesus replied, "Let those without eternal life concern themselves with things like that. Your duty is to come and preach the coming of the Kingdom of God to all the world."

⁶¹Another said, "Yes, Lord, I will come, but first let me ask permission of those at home."

⁶²But Jesus told him, "Anyone who lets himself be distracted from the work I plan for him is not fit for the Kingdom of God."

CHAPTER **10** **JESUS SENDS OUT 70 MESSENGERS.** The Lord now chose seventy other disciples and sent them on ahead in pairs to all the towns and villages he planned to visit later.

²These were his instructions to them: "Plead with the Lord of the harvest to send out more laborers to help you, for the harvest is so plentiful and the workers so few. ³Go now, and remember that I am sending you out as lambs among wolves. ⁴Don't take any money with you, or a beggar's bag, or even an extra pair of shoes. And don't waste time along the way.

⁵"Whenever you enter a home, give it your blessing. ⁶If it is worthy of the blessing, the blessing will stand; if not, the blessing will return to you.

⁷"When you enter a village, don't shift around

from home to home, but stay in one place, eating and drinking without question whatever is set before you. And don't hesitate to accept hospitality, for the workman is worthy of his wages!

8,9"If a town welcomes you, follow these two rules:

(1) Eat whatever is set before you.
(2) Heal the sick; and as you heal them, say, 'The Kingdom of God is very near you now.'

10"But if a town refuses you, go out into its streets and say, 11"We wipe the dust of your town from our feet as a public announcement of your doom. Never forget how close you were to the Kingdom of God!' 12Even wicked Sodom will be better off than such a city on the Judgment Day. 13What horrors await you, you cities of Chorazin and Bethsaida! For if the miracles I did for you had been done in the cities of Tyre and Sidon, their people would have sat in deep repentance long ago, clothed in sackcloth and throwing ashes on their heads to show their remorse. 14Yes, Tyre and Sidon will receive less punishment on the Judgment Day than you. 15And you people of Capernaum, what shall I say about you? Will you be exalted to heaven? No, you shall be brought down to hell."

16Then he said to the disciples, "Those who welcome you are welcoming me. And those who reject you are rejecting me. And those who reject me are rejecting God who sent me."

17When the seventy disciples returned, they joyfully reported to him, "Even the demons obey us when we use your name."

18"Yes," he told them, "I saw Satan falling from heaven as a flash of lightning! 19And I have given you authority over all the power of the Enemy, and to walk among serpents and scorpions and to crush them. Nothing shall injure you! 20However, the important thing is not that demons obey you, but that your names are registered as citizens of heaven."

21Then he was filled with the joy of the Holy Spirit and said, "I praise you, O Father, Lord of heaven and earth, for hiding these things from the intellectuals and worldly wise and for revealing them to those who are as trusting as little children. Yes, thank you, Father, for that is the way you wanted it. 22I am the Agent of my Father in everything; and no one really knows the Son except the Father, and no one really knows the Father except the Son and those to whom the Son chooses to reveal him."

23Then, turning to the twelve disciples, he said quietly, "How privileged you are to see what you have seen. 24Many a prophet and king of old has longed for these days, to see and hear what you have seen and heard!"

25One day an expert on Moses' laws came to test Jesus' orthodoxy by asking him this question: "Teacher, what does a man need to do to live forever in heaven?"

26Jesus replied, "What does Moses' law say about it?"

27"It says," he replied, "that you must love the Lord your God with all your heart, and with all your soul, and with all your strength, and with all your mind. And you must love your neighbor just as much as you love yourself."

28"Right!" Jesus told him. "*Do* this and *you* shall live!"

29The man wanted to justify (his lack of love for some kinds of people), so he asked, "Which neighbors?"

30Jesus replied with an illustration: "A Jew going on a trip from Jerusalem to Jericho was attacked by bandits. They stripped him of his clothes and money, and beat him up and left him lying half dead beside the road.

31"By chance a Jewish priest came along; and when he saw the man lying there, he crossed to the other side of the road and passed him by. 32A Jewish Temple-assistant walked

ENEMIES

The situation:
Shannon is driving home from youth group on a stormy night. As she rounds a curve in the road, she sees someone walking along in the mud. It's Jenny. A hundred yards up the road, Shannon sees Jenny's car in the ditch.

Should she stop and help?

Maybe that seems like a stupid question, but consider . . .

The background:
Jenny's life is like a fairy tale . . . no exaggeration:
—Her family has some major bucks.
—She drives a brand new BMW convertible.
—She always looks like she just stepped off the cover of a fashion magazine.
—She dates a really handsome college sophomore.
—She makes straight A's.
—She has traveled all over the world.

As you might imagine, many people are jealous of Jenny's good fortune. Shannon is right there among them. But Shannon's feelings go beyond envy to include, shall we say, extreme dislike.

See, last year, Jenny made some really rude remarks about Shannon—behind her back. Then, two weeks later, she absolutely humiliated her at a big party—right in front of everyone! The two haven't spoken since, and when they're in the same room, everyone can feel the tension.

The solution:
Read Luke 10:25-37.

NEIGHBORS

10:27-37 From the parable we learn three principles about loving our neighbors: (1) lack of love is often easy to justify; (2) our neighbor is anyone of any race or creed or social background who is in need; and (3) love means acting to meet the need. Wherever you live, there are needy people close by. There are no good reasons for refusing to help.

over and looked at him lying there, but then went on.

³³"But a despised Samaritan came along, and when he saw him, he felt deep pity. ³⁴Kneeling beside him the Samaritan soothed his wounds with medicine and bandaged them. Then he put the man on his donkey and walked along beside him till they came to an inn, where he nursed him through the night. ³⁵The next day he handed the innkeeper two twenty-dollar bills and told him to take care of the man. 'If his bill runs higher than that,' he said, 'I'll pay the difference the next time I am here.'

³⁶"Now which of these three would you say was a neighbor to the bandits' victim?"

³⁷The man replied, "The one who showed him some pity."

Then Jesus said, "Yes, now go and do the same."

³⁸As Jesus and the disciples continued on their way to Jerusalem they came to a village where a woman named Martha welcomed them into her home. ³⁹Her sister Mary sat on the floor, listening to Jesus as he talked.

⁴⁰But Martha was the jittery type and was worrying over the big dinner she was preparing.

She came to Jesus and said, "Sir, doesn't it seem unfair to you that my sister just sits here while I do all the work? Tell her to come and help me."

⁴¹But the Lord said to her, "Martha, dear friend, you are so upset over all these details!⁴²There is really only one thing worth being concerned about. Mary has discovered it—and I won't take it away from her!"

CHAPTER 11 JESUS TEACHES ABOUT PRAYER.

Once when Jesus had been out praying, one of his disciples came to him as he finished and said, "Lord, teach us a prayer to recite just as John taught one to his disciples."

²And this is the prayer he taught them: "Father, may your name be honored for its holiness; send your Kingdom soon. ³Give us our food day by day. ⁴And forgive our sins—for we have forgiven those who sinned against us. And don't allow us to be tempted."

⁵,⁶Then, teaching them more about prayer, he used this illustration: "Suppose you went to a friend's house at midnight, wanting to borrow three loaves of bread. You would shout up to him, 'A friend of mine has just arrived for a visit and I've nothing to give him to eat.' ⁷He would call down from his bedroom, 'Please don't ask me to get up. The door is locked for the night and we are all in bed. I just can't help you this time.'

⁸"But I'll tell you this—though he won't do it as a friend, if you keep knocking long enough, he will get up and give you everything you want—just because of your persistence. ⁹And so it is with prayer—keep on asking and you will keep on getting; keep on looking and you will keep on finding; knock and the door will be opened. ¹⁰Everyone who asks, receives; all who seek, find; and the door is opened to everyone who knocks.

¹¹"You men who are fathers—if your boy asks for bread, do you give him a stone? If he asks for fish, do you give him a snake? ¹²If he asks for an egg, do you give him a scorpion? [Of course not!]

¹³"And if even sinful persons like yourselves give children what they need, don't you realize that your heavenly Father will do at least as much, and give the Holy Spirit to those who ask for him?"

¹⁴Once, when Jesus cast out a demon from a man who couldn't speak, his voice returned to him. The crowd was excited and enthusiastic, ¹⁵but some said, "No wonder he can cast them out. He gets his power from Satan, the king of demons!" ¹⁶Others asked for something to happen in the sky to prove his claim of being the Messiah.

¹⁷He knew the thoughts of each of them, so he said, "Any kingdom filled with civil war is doomed; so is a home filled with argument and strife. ¹⁸Therefore, if what you say is true, that Satan is fighting against himself by empowering me to cast out his demons, how can his kingdom survive? ¹⁹And if I am empowered by Satan, what about your own followers? For they cast out demons! Do you think this proves they

PRAISE

11:1-4 Notice the order in this prayer. First Jesus praised God; then he made his requests. Praising God first puts us in the right frame of mind to tell him about our needs. Too often our prayers are more like shopping lists than conversations.

PRO JESUS

11:23 Jesus says, "Anyone who is not for me is against me," while earlier he stated, "Anyone who is not against you is for you." People who are neutral toward Christians are actually helping them more than hurting them because they are not setting up barriers. But while people can be neutral toward Christians, they cannot be neutral in their relationship with Jesus, or in the battle between Jesus and Satan. You can't be aloof or non-committal, because there are only two sides. Since God has already won the battle, why be on the losing side? If you aren't actively for Christ, you are against him.

are possessed by Satan? Ask *them* if you are right! [20]But if I am casting out demons because of power from God, it proves that the Kingdom of God has arrived.

[21]"For when Satan, strong and fully armed, guards his palace, it is safe—[22]until someone stronger and better-armed attacks and overcomes him and strips him of his weapons and carries off his belongings.

[23]"Anyone who is not for me is against me; if he isn't helping me, he is hurting my cause.

[24]"When a demon is cast out of a man, it goes to the deserts, searching there for rest; but finding none, it returns to the person it left, [25]and finds that its former home is all swept and clean. [26]Then it goes and gets seven other demons more evil than itself, and they all enter the man. And so the poor fellow is seven times worse off than he was before."

[27]As he was speaking, a woman in the crowd called out, "God bless your mother—the womb from which you came, and the breasts that gave you suck!"

[28]He replied, "Yes, but even more blessed are all who hear the Word of God and put it into practice."

[29,30]As the crowd pressed in upon him, he preached them this sermon: "These are evil times, with evil people. They keep asking for some strange happening in the skies [to prove I am the Messiah], but the only proof I will give them is a miracle like that of Jonah, whose experiences proved to the people of Nineveh that God had sent him. My similar experience will prove that God has sent me to these people.

[31]"And at the Judgment Day the Queen of Sheba shall arise and point her finger at this generation, condemning it, for she went on a long, hard journey to listen to the wisdom of Solomon; but one far greater than Solomon is here [and few pay any attention].

[32]"The men of Nineveh, too, shall arise and condemn this nation, for they repented at the preaching of Jonah; and someone far greater than Jonah is here [but this nation won't listen].

[33]"No one lights a lamp and hides it! Instead, he puts it on a lampstand to give light to all who enter the room. [34]Your eyes light up your inward being. A pure eye lets sunshine into your soul. A lustful

eye shuts out the light and plunges you into darkness. [35]So watch out that the sunshine isn't blotted out. [36]If you are filled with light within, with no dark corners, then your face will be radiant too, as though a floodlight is beamed upon you."

[37,38]As he was speaking, one of the Pharisees asked him home for a meal. When Jesus arrived, he sat down to eat without first performing the ceremonial washing required by Jewish custom. This greatly surprised his host.

[39]Then Jesus said to him, "You Pharisees wash the outside, but inside you are still dirty—full of greed and wickedness! [40]Fools! Didn't God make the inside as well as the outside? [41]Purity is best demonstrated by generosity.

[42]"But woe to you Pharisees! For though you are careful to tithe even the smallest part of your income, you completely forget about justice and the love of God. You should tithe, yes, but you should not leave these other things undone.

[43]"Woe to you Pharisees! For how you love the seats of honor in the synagogues and the respectful greetings from everyone as you walk through the markets! [44]Yes, awesome judgment is awaiting you. For you are like hidden graves in a field. Men go by you with no knowledge of the corruption they are passing."

[45]"Sir," said an expert in religious law who was standing there, "you have insulted my profession, too, in what you just said."

[46]"Yes," said Jesus, "the same horrors await you! For you crush men beneath impossible religious demands—demands that you yourselves would never think of trying to keep. [47]Woe to you! For you are exactly like your ancestors who killed the prophets long ago. [48]Murderers! You agree with your fathers that what they did was right—you would have done the same yourselves.

[49]"This is what God says about you: 'I will send prophets and apostles to you, and you will kill some of them and chase away the others.'

[50]"And you of this generation will be held responsible for the murder of God's servants from the founding of the world— [51]from the murder of Abel to the murder of Zechariah who perished between the altar and the sanctuary. Yes, it will surely be charged against you.

MOTIVES

11:52 Jesus criticized the Pharisees harshly because they (1) washed their hands but not their hearts, (2) remembered to tithe but forgot justice, (3) loved people's praise, (4) made impossible religious demands, and (5) didn't accept the truth about Jesus and prevented others from believing it, too. They wrongly focused on outward appearances and ignored the condition of their hearts. We do the same when our service is motivated by a desire to be seen rather than from a pure heart and love for others. Others may be fooled, but God isn't. Don't be a Christian on the outside only. Bring your inner life under God's control; then your outer life will naturally reflect him.

⁵²"Woe to you experts in religion! For you hide the truth from the people. You won't accept it for yourselves, and you prevent others from having a chance to believe it."

⁵³,⁵⁴The Pharisees and legal experts were furious; and from that time on they plied him fiercely with a host of questions, trying to trap him into saying something for which they could have him arrested.

CHAPTER **12** JESUS WARNS AGAINST HYPOCRISY.

Meanwhile the crowds grew until thousands upon thousands were milling about and crushing each other. He turned now to his disciples and warned them, "More than anything else, beware of these Pharisees and the way they pretend to be good when they aren't. But such hypocrisy cannot be hidden forever. ²It will become as evident as yeast in dough. ³Whatever they have said in the dark shall be heard in the light, and what you have whispered in the inner rooms shall be broadcast from the housetops for all to hear!

⁴"Dear friends, don't be afraid of these who want to murder you. They can only kill the body; they have no power over your souls. ⁵But I'll tell you whom to fear—fear God who has the power to kill and then cast into hell.

⁶"What is the price of five sparrows? A couple of pennies? Not much more than that. Yet God does not forget a single one of them. ⁷And he knows the number of hairs on your head! Never fear, you are far more valuable to him than a whole flock of sparrows.

⁸"And I assure you of this: I, the Messiah, will publicly honor you in the presence of God's angels if you publicly acknowledge me here on earth as your Friend. ⁹But I will deny before the angels those who deny me here among men. ¹⁰(Yet those who speak against me may be forgiven—while those who speak against the Holy Spirit shall never be forgiven.)

¹¹"And when you are brought to trial before these Jewish rulers and authorities in the synagogues, don't be concerned about what to say in your defense, ¹²for the Holy Spirit will give you the right words even as you are standing there."

¹³Then someone called from the crowd, "Sir, please tell my brother to divide my father's estate with me."

¹⁴But Jesus replied, "Man, who made me a judge over you to decide such things as that? ¹⁵Beware! Don't always be wishing for what you don't have. For real life and real living are not related to how rich we are."

¹⁶Then he gave an illustration: "A rich man had a fertile farm that produced fine crops. ¹⁷In fact, his barns were full to overflowing—he couldn't get everything in. He thought about his problem, ¹⁸and finally exclaimed, 'I know—I'll tear down my barns and build bigger ones! Then I'll have room enough. ¹⁹And I'll sit back and say to myself, "Friend, you have enough stored away for years to come. Now take it easy! Wine, women, and song for you!"'

²⁰"But God said to him, 'Fool! Tonight you die. Then who will get it all?'

²¹"Yes, every man is a fool who gets rich on earth but not in heaven."

²²Then turning to his disciples he said, "Don't worry about whether you have enough food to eat or clothes to wear. ²³For life consists of far more than food and clothes. ²⁴Look at the ravens—they don't plant or harvest or have barns to store away their food, and yet they get along all right—for God feeds them. And you are far more valuable to him than any birds!

²⁵"And besides, what's the use of worrying? What good does it do? Will it add a single day to your life? Of course not! ²⁶And if worry can't even do such little things as that, what's the use of worrying over bigger things?

²⁷"Look at the lilies! They don't toil and spin, and yet Solomon in all his glory was not robed as well as they are. ²⁸And if God provides clothing for the flowers that are here today and gone tomorrow, don't you suppose that he will provide clothing for you, you doubters? ²⁹And don't worry about food—what to eat and drink; don't worry at all that God will provide it for you. ³⁰All mankind scratches for its daily bread, but your heavenly Father knows your needs. ³¹He will always give you all you need from day to day if you will make the Kingdom of God your primary concern.

³²"So don't be afraid, little flock. For it gives your Father great happiness to give you the Kingdom. ³³Sell what you have and give to those in need. This will fatten your purses in heaven! And the purses of heaven have no rips or holes in them. Your treasures there will never disappear; no thief can steal them; no moth can destroy them. ³⁴Wherever your treasure is, there your heart and thoughts will also be.

³⁵"Be prepared—all dressed and ready— ³⁶for your Lord's return from the wedding feast. Then you will be ready to open the door and let him in the moment he arrives and knocks. ³⁷There will be great joy for those who are ready and waiting for his return. He himself will seat them and put on a waiter's uniform and serve them as they sit and eat!

VALUE

12:7 Our true value is God's estimate of our worth, not our peers'. Other people evaluate and categorize us according to how we perform, what we achieve, and how we look. But God's love gives us the real basis for our worth—we belong to him.

³⁸He may come at nine o'clock at night—or even at midnight. But whenever he comes, there will be joy for his servants who are ready!

³⁹"Everyone would be ready for him if they knew the exact hour of his return—just as they would be ready for a thief if they knew when he was coming. ⁴⁰So be ready all the time. For I, the Messiah, will come when least expected."

⁴¹Peter asked, "Lord, are you talking just to us or to everyone?"

⁴²⁻⁴⁴And the Lord replied, "I'm talking to any faithful, sensible man whose master gives him the responsibility of feeding the other servants. If his master returns and finds that he has done a good job, there will be a reward—his master will put him in charge of all he owns.

⁴⁵"But if the man begins to think, 'My Lord won't be back for a long time,' and begins to whip the men and women he is supposed to protect, and to spend his time at drinking parties and in drunkenness— ⁴⁶well, his master will return without notice and remove him from his position of trust and assign him to the place of the unfaithful. ⁴⁷He will be severely punished, for though he knew his duty he refused to do it.

⁴⁸"But anyone who is not aware that he is doing wrong will be punished only lightly. Much is required from those to whom much is given, for their responsibility is greater.

⁴⁹"I have come to bring fire to the earth, and, oh, that my task were completed! ⁵⁰There is a terrible baptism ahead of me, and how I am pent up until it is accomplished!

⁵¹"Do you think I have come to give peace to the earth? *No!* Rather, strife and division! ⁵²From now on families will be split apart, three in favor of me, and two against—or perhaps the other way around. ⁵³A father will decide one way about me; his son, the other; mother and daughter will disagree; and the decision of an honored mother-in-law will be spurned by her daughter-in-law."

⁵⁴Then he turned to the crowd and said, "When you see clouds beginning to form in the west, you say, 'Here comes a shower.' And you are right.

⁵⁵"When the south wind blows you say, 'Today will be a scorcher.' And it is. ⁵⁶Hypocrites! You interpret the sky well enough, but you refuse to notice the warnings all around you about the crisis ahead. ⁵⁷Why do you refuse to see for yourselves what is right?

CONFLICT

12:51-53 In these strange and unsettling words, Jesus revealed that his coming often results in conflict. He demands a response, and close groups can be torn apart when some choose to follow him and others refuse to do so. There is no middle ground with Jesus. Loyalties must be declared and commitments made, sometimes to the severing of other relationships. Life is easiest when a family believes together in Christ, but this often does not happen. Are you willing to risk your family's disapproval to gain eternal life?

⁵⁸"If you meet your accuser on the way to court, try to settle the matter before it reaches the judge, lest he sentence you to jail; ⁵⁹for if that happens, you won't be free again until the last penny is paid in full."

CHAPTER 13 JESUS TELLS THE PEOPLE TO REPENT.

About this time he was informed that Pilate had butchered some Jews from Galilee as they were sacrificing at the Temple in Jerusalem.

²"Do you think they were worse sinners than other men from Galilee?" he asked. "Is that why they suffered? ³Not at all! And don't you realize that you also will perish unless you leave your evil ways and turn to God?

⁴"And what about the eighteen men who died when the Tower of Siloam fell on them? Were they the worst sinners in Jerusalem? ⁵Not at all! And you, too, will perish unless you repent."

⁶Then he used this illustration: "A man planted a fig tree in his garden and came again and again to see if he could find any fruit on it, but he was always disappointed. ⁷Finally he told his gardener to cut it down. 'I've waited three years and there hasn't been a single fig!' he said. 'Why bother with it any longer? It's taking up space we can use for something else.'

⁸"'Give it one more chance,' the gardener answered. 'Leave it another year, and I'll give it special attention and plenty of fertilizer. ⁹If we get figs next year, fine; if not, I'll cut it down.'"

¹⁰One Sabbath as he was teaching in a synagogue, ¹¹he saw a seriously handicapped woman who had been bent double for eighteen years and was unable to straighten herself.

¹²Calling her over to him Jesus said, "Woman, you are healed of your sickness!" ¹³He touched her, and instantly she could stand straight. How she praised and thanked God!

¹⁴But the local Jewish leader in charge of the synagogue was very angry about it because Jesus had healed her on the Sabbath day. "There are six days of the week to work," he shouted to the crowd. "Those are the days to come for healing, not on the Sabbath!"

¹⁵But the Lord replied, "You hypocrite! You work on the Sabbath! Don't you untie your cattle from their stalls on the Sabbath and lead them out for water? ¹⁶And is it wrong for me, just because it is the Sabbath day, to free this Jewish woman from the bondage in which Satan has held her for eighteen years?"

SAVED

13:27 The people were eager to know who would be saved. Jesus explained that although many people know something about God, only a few have accepted his forgiveness. Just listening to his words or admiring his miracles is not enough—it is vital to turn from sin and trust in God to save us.

[17]This shamed his enemies. And all the people rejoiced at the wonderful things he did.

[18]Now he began teaching them again about the Kingdom of God: "What is the Kingdom like?" he asked. "How can I illustrate it? [19]It is like a tiny mustard seed planted in a garden; soon it grows into a tall bush and the birds live among its branches.

[20,21]"It is like yeast kneaded into dough, which works unseen until it has risen high and light."

[22]He went from city to city and village to village, teaching as he went, always pressing onward toward Jerusalem.

[23]Someone asked him, "Will only a few be saved?"

And he replied, [24,25]"The door to heaven is narrow. Work hard to get in, for the truth is that many will try to enter but when the head of the house has locked the door, it will be too late. Then if you stand outside knocking, and pleading, 'Lord, open the door for us,' he will reply, 'I do not know you.'

[26]"But we ate with you, and you taught in our streets,' you will say.

[27]"And he will reply, 'I tell you, I don't know you. You can't come in here, guilty as you are. Go away.'

[28]"And there will be great weeping and gnashing of teeth as you stand outside and see Abraham, Isaac, Jacob, and all the prophets within the Kingdom of God— [29]for people will come from all over the world to take their places there. [30]And note this: some who are despised now will be greatly honored then; and some who are highly thought of now will be least important then."

[31]A few minutes later some Pharisees said to him, "Get out of here if you want to live, for King Herod is after you!"

[32]Jesus replied, "Go tell that fox that I will keep on casting out demons and doing miracles of healing today and tomorrow; and the third day I will reach my destination. [33]Yes, today, tomorrow, and the next day! For it wouldn't do for a prophet of God to be killed except in Jerusalem!

[34]"O Jerusalem, Jerusalem! The city that murders the prophets. The city that stones those sent to help her. How often I have wanted to gather your children together even as a hen protects her brood under her wings, but you wouldn't let me. [35]And now—now your house is left desolate. And you will never again see me until you say, 'Welcome to him who comes in the name of the Lord.'"

CHAPTER 14 HEALING ON THE SABBATH. One Sabbath as he was in the home of a member of the Jewish Council, the Pharisees were watching him like hawks to see if he would heal a man who was present who was suffering from dropsy.

[3]Jesus said to the Pharisees and legal experts standing around, "Well, is it within the Law to heal a man on the Sabbath day, or not?"

[4]And when they refused to answer, Jesus took the sick man by the hand and healed him and sent him away.

[5]Then he turned to them: "Which of you doesn't work on the Sabbath?" he asked. "If your cow falls into a pit, don't you proceed at once to get it out?"

[6]Again they had no answer.

[7]When he noticed that all who came to the dinner were trying to sit near the head of the table, he gave them this advice: [8]"If you are invited to a wedding feast, don't always head for the best seat. For if someone more respected than you shows up, [9]the host will bring him over to where you are sitting and say, 'Let this man sit here instead.' And you, embarrassed, will have to take whatever seat is left at the foot of the table!

[10]"Do this instead—start at the foot; and when your host sees you he will come and say, 'Friend, we have a better place than this for you!' Thus you will be honored in front of all the other guests. [11]For everyone who tries to honor himself shall be humbled; and he who humbles himself shall be honored." [12]Then he turned to his host. "When you put on a dinner," he said, "don't invite friends, brothers, relatives, and rich neighbors! For they will return the invitation. [13]Instead, invite the poor, the crippled, the lame, and the blind. [14]Then at the resurrection of the godly, God will reward you for inviting those who can't repay you."

[15]Hearing this, a man sitting at the table with Jesus exclaimed, "What a privilege it would be to get into the Kingdom of God!"

[16]Jesus replied with this illustration: "A man prepared a great feast and sent out many invitations. [17]When all was ready, he sent his servant around to notify the guests that it was time for them to arrive. [18]But they all began making excuses. One said he had just bought a field and wanted to inspect it, and asked to be excused. [19]Another said he had just bought five pair of oxen and wanted to try them out. [20]Another had just been married and for that reason couldn't come.

[21]"The servant returned and reported to his master what they had said. His master was angry and told him to go quickly into the streets and alleys of the city and

ON TOP

14:7-11 Jesus advised people not to rush for the best seats at a feast. People today are just as eager to raise their social status, whether by being with the right people, dressing for success, or driving the right car. Wanting a nice car or hoping to be successful in your career is not wrong in itself—it is wrong only when you want these things just to impress others. Whom do you try to impress? Don't aim for prestige; look for a place to serve. If God wants you to serve on a wider scale, he will invite you to take a higher place.

SALTY

14:34 Salt can lose its flavor. When it gets wet and then dries, nothing is left but a tasteless residue. Many Christians blend into the world to avoid the cost of standing for Christ. Jesus says if Christians lose their distinctive saltiness, they become worthless. Just as salt flavors and preserves food, we are to preserve the good in the world, keep it from spoiling, and bring new flavor to life. This requires planning, willing sacrifice, and unswerving commitment to Christ's Kingdom. Being "salty" is not easy, but if a Christian fails in this function, he or she fails to represent Christ in the world. How salty are you?

to invite the beggars, crippled, lame, and blind. ²²But even then, there was still room.

²³"'Well, then,' said his master, 'go out into the country lanes and out behind the hedges and urge anyone you find to come, so that the house will be full. ²⁴For none of those I invited first will get even the smallest taste of what I had prepared for them.'"

²⁵Great crowds were following him. He turned around and addressed them as follows: ²⁶"Anyone who wants to be my follower must love me far more than he does his own father, mother, wife, children, brothers, or sisters—yes, more than his own life—otherwise he cannot be my disciple. ²⁷And no one can be my disciple who does not carry his own cross and follow me.

²⁸"But don't begin until you count the cost. For who would begin construction of a building without first getting estimates and then checking to see if he has enough money to pay the bills? ²⁹Otherwise he might complete only the foundation before running out of funds. And then how everyone would laugh!

³⁰"'See that fellow there?' they would mock. 'He started that building and ran out of money before it was finished!'

³¹"Or what king would ever dream of going to war without first sitting down with his counselors and discussing whether his army of 10,000 is strong enough to defeat the 20,000 men who are marching against him?

³²"If the decision is negative, then while the enemy troops are still far away, he will send a truce team to discuss terms of peace. ³³So no one can become my disciple unless he first sits down and counts his blessings—and then renounces them all for me.

³⁴"What good is salt that has lost its saltiness? ³⁵Flavorless salt is fit for nothing—not even for fertilizer. It is worthless and must be thrown out. Listen well if you would understand my meaning."

CHAPTER 15 A STORY ABOUT A LOST SHEEP.

Dishonest tax collectors and other notorious sinners often came to listen to Jesus' sermons; ²but this caused complaints from the Jewish religious leaders and the experts on Jewish law because he was associating with such despicable people—even eating with them!

³,⁴So Jesus used this illustration: "If you had a hundred sheep and one of them strayed away and was lost in the wilderness, wouldn't you leave the ninety-nine others to go and search for the lost one until you found it? ⁵And then you would joyfully carry it home on your shoulders. ⁶When you arrived you would call together your friends and neighbors to rejoice with you because your lost sheep was found.

⁷"Well, in the same way heaven will be happier over one lost sinner who returns to God than over ninety-nine others who haven't strayed away!

⁸"Or take another illustration: A woman has ten valuable silver coins and loses one. Won't she light a lamp and look in every corner of the house and sweep every nook and cranny until she finds it? ⁹And then won't she call in her friends and neighbors to rejoice with her? ¹⁰In the same way there is joy in the presence of the angels of God when one sinner repents."

¹¹To further illustrate the point, he told them this story: "A man had two sons. ¹²When the younger told his father, 'I want my share of your estate now, instead of waiting until you die!' his father agreed to divide his wealth between his sons.

¹³"A few days later this younger son packed all his belongings and took a trip to a distant land, and there wasted all his money on parties and prostitutes. ¹⁴About the time his money was gone a great famine swept over the land, and he began to starve. ¹⁵He persuaded a local farmer to hire him to feed his pigs. ¹⁶The boy became so hungry that even the pods he was feeding the swine looked good to him. And no one gave him anything.

¹⁷"When he finally came to his senses, he said to himself, 'At home even the hired men have food enough and to spare, and here I am, dying of hunger! ¹⁸I will go home to my father and say, "Father, I have sinned against both heaven and you, ¹⁹and am no longer worthy of being called your son. Please take me on as a hired man."'

²⁰"So he returned home to his father. And while he was still a long distance away, his father saw him coming, and was filled with loving pity and ran and embraced him and kissed him.

²¹"His son said to him, 'Father, I have sinned against heaven and you, and am not worthy of being called your son—'

OPPORTUNITY

15:30 In the story of the Prodigal Son, there is a contrast between the father's response and the older brother's reaction. The father was forgiving and overjoyed. The brother was unforgiving and bitter. The father forgave because he was joyful, and the son refused to forgive because he was bitter. The difference between bitterness and joy is our capacity to forgive. If you are refusing to forgive people, you are missing a wonderful opportunity of experiencing joy and sharing it with them.

[22]"But his father said to the slaves, 'Quick! Bring the finest robe in the house and put it on him. And a jeweled ring for his finger; and shoes! [23]And kill the calf we have in the fattening pen. We must celebrate with a feast, [24]for this son of mine was dead and has returned to life. He was lost and is found.' So the party began.

[25]"Meanwhile, the older son was in the fields working; when he returned home, he heard dance music coming from the house, [26]and he asked one of the servants what was going on.

[27]"'Your brother is back,' he was told, 'and your father has killed the calf we were fattening and has prepared a great feast to celebrate his coming home again unharmed.'

[28]"The older brother was angry and wouldn't go in. His father came out and begged him, [29]but he replied, 'All these years I've worked hard for you and never once refused to do a single thing you told me to; and in all that time you never gave me even one young goat for a feast with my friends. [30]Yet when this son of yours comes back after spending your money on prostitutes, you celebrate by killing the finest calf we have on the place.'

[31]"'Look, dear son,' his father said to him, 'you and I are very close, and everything I have is yours. [32]But it is right to celebrate. For he is your brother; and he was dead and has come back to life! He was lost and is found!'"

CHAPTER **16** A SHREWD ACCOUNTANT. Jesus now told this story to his disciples: "A rich man hired an accountant to handle his affairs, but soon a rumor went around that the accountant was thoroughly dishonest.

[2]"So his employer called him in and said, 'What's this I hear about your stealing from me? Get your report in order, for you are to be dismissed.'

[3]"The accountant thought to himself, 'Now what? I'm through here, and I haven't the strength to go out and dig ditches, and I'm too proud to beg. [4]I know just the thing! And then I'll have plenty of friends to take care of me when I leave!'

[5,6]"So he invited each one who owed money to his employer to come and discuss the situation. He asked the first one, 'How much do you owe him?' 'My debt is 850 gallons of olive oil,' the man replied. 'Yes, here is the contract you signed,' the

"Here's what I did..."

My mother and I had difficulty getting along. Often we would argue, sometimes over the stupidest things. After our fights, I'd feel real bad, but I didn't know what to do about it. I felt it was all her fault; she just didn't understand me; she was being totally unreasonable; etc.

Then I read the parable about the lost son. And I began to realize that the younger son felt he had every right to take his inheritance and go off on his own. But it didn't get him anywhere, and finally he decided to go back home. His father gave him a big welcome and didn't say "I told you so" or anything like that.

I got to thinking about my own attitude with my mom. And I had to admit that I probably was at fault at least some of the time. Hard as it was, I had to apologize when I was wrong and ask forgiveness. (It was probably really hard for the lost son, too.)

I sat down and went over the past several arguments that weren't really resolved, and wrote down the specifics on where I was wrong. Then I prayed hard that I could swallow my pride, and go and ask my mom to forgive me.

I finally did. And my mom reacted very much like the father in the story; she was very forgiving. Since then, I've tried to concentrate more on my own attitude than on my mom's. And, amazingly, we're arguing less. But even when we do argue, and I fall into the old patterns, I know that God will forgive me when I ask for it. (So does Mom—usually.)

Tracy

AGE 16

accountant told him. 'Tear it up and write another one for half that much!'

[7]"'And how much do you owe him?' he asked the next man. 'A thousand bushels of wheat,' was the reply. 'Here,' the accountant said, 'take your note and replace it with one for only 800 bushels!'

[8]"The rich man had to admire the rascal for being so shrewd. And it is true that the citizens of this world are more clever [in dishonesty!] than the godly are. [9]But shall I tell *you* to act that way, to buy friendship through cheating? Will this ensure your entry into an everlasting home in heaven? [10]*No!* For unless you are honest in small matters, you won't be in large ones. If you cheat even a little, you won't be honest with greater responsibilities. [11]And if you are untrustworthy about worldly wealth, who will trust you with the true riches of heaven? [12]And if you are not faithful with other people's money, why should you be entrusted with money of your own?

[13]"For neither you nor anyone else can serve two masters. You will hate one and show loyalty to the other, or else the other way around—you will be enthusiastic about one and despise the other. You cannot serve both God and money."

[14]The Pharisees, who dearly loved their money, naturally scoffed at all this.

[15]Then he said to them, "You wear a noble, pious expression in public, but God knows your evil hearts. Your pretense brings you honor from the people, but it is an abomination in the sight of God. [16]Until John the Baptist began to preach, the laws of Moses and the messages of the prophets were your guides. But John introduced the Good News that the Kingdom of God would come soon. And now eager multitudes are pressing in. [17]But that doesn't mean that the Law has lost its force in even the smallest point. It is as strong and unshakable as heaven and earth.

[18]"So anyone who divorces his wife and marries someone else commits adultery, and anyone who marries a divorced woman commits adultery."

[19]"There was a certain rich man," Jesus said, "who was splendidly clothed and lived each day in mirth and luxury. [20]One day Lazarus, a diseased beggar, was laid at his door. [21]As he lay there longing for scraps from the rich man's table, the dogs would come and lick his open sores. [22]Finally the beggar died and was carried by the angels to be with Abraham in the place of the righteous dead. The rich man also died and was buried, [23]and his soul went into hell. There, in torment, he saw Lazarus in the far distance with Abraham.

[24]"'Father Abraham,' he shouted, 'have some pity! Send Lazarus over here if only to dip the tip of his finger in water and cool my tongue, for I am in anguish in these flames.'

[25]"But Abraham said to him, 'Son, remember that during your lifetime you had everything you wanted, and Lazarus had nothing. So now he is here being comforted and you are in anguish. [26]And besides, there is a great chasm separating us, and anyone wanting to come to you from here is stopped at its edge; and no one over there can cross to us.'

[27]"Then the rich man said, 'O Father Abraham, then please send him to my father's home— [28]for I have five brothers—to warn them about this place

of torment lest they come here when they die.'

[29]"But Abraham said, 'The Scriptures have warned them again and again. Your brothers can read them any time they want to.'

[30]"The rich man replied, 'No, Father Abraham, they won't bother to read them. But if someone is sent to them from the dead, then they will turn from their sins.'

[31]"But Abraham said, 'If they won't listen to Moses and the prophets, they won't listen even though someone rises from the dead.'"

CHAPTER 17 A STORY ABOUT A SERVANT.

"There will always be temptations to sin," Jesus said one day to his disciples, "but woe to the man who does the tempting. [2,3]If he were thrown into the sea with a huge rock tied to his neck, he would be far better off than facing the punishment in store for those who harm these little children's souls. I am warning you!

"Rebuke your brother if he sins, and forgive him if he is sorry. [4]Even if he wrongs you seven times a day and each time turns again and asks forgiveness, forgive him."

[5]One day the apostles said to the Lord, "We need more faith; tell us how to get it."

[6]"If your faith were only the size of a mustard seed," Jesus answered, "it would be large enough to uproot that mulberry tree over there and send it hurtling into the sea! Your command would bring immediate results! [7-9]When a servant comes in from plowing or taking care of sheep, he doesn't just sit down and eat, but first prepares his master's meal and serves him his supper before he eats his own. And he is not even thanked, for he is merely doing what he is supposed to do. [10]Just so, if you merely obey me, you should not consider yourselves worthy of praise. For you have simply done your duty!"

[11]As they continued onward toward Jerusalem, they reached the border between Galilee and Samaria, [12]and as they entered a village there, ten lepers stood at a distance, [13]crying out, "Jesus, sir, have mercy on us!"

[14]He looked at them and said, "Go to the Jewish priest and show him that you are healed!" And as they were going, their leprosy disappeared.

[15]One of them came back to Jesus, shouting, "Glory to God, I'm healed!" [16]He fell flat on the ground in front of Jesus, face downward in the dust,

---

DIVORCE

16:18 Most religious leaders of Jesus' day permitted a man to divorce his wife for nearly any reason. Jesus' words about divorce went beyond Moses' (Deuteronomy 24:1-4). Stricter than any of the then-current schools of thought, they shocked his hearers (see Matthew 19:10) just as they shake today's readers. Jesus says in unmistakable terms that marriage is a lifetime commitment. As you think about marriage, remember that God intends it to be a permanent commitment.

FACE IT

17:3-4 To rebuke does not mean to point out every sin we see; it means to bring sin to a person's attention with the purpose of restoring him or her to God and to fellow humans. When you feel you must rebuke another Christian for a sin, check your attitudes before opening your mouth. Do you love the person? Are you willing to forgive? Unless rebuke is tied to forgiveness, it will not help the sinning person.

thanking him for what he had done. This man was a despised Samaritan.

[17]Jesus asked, "Didn't I heal ten men? Where are the nine? [18]Does only this foreigner return to give glory to God?"

[19]And Jesus said to the man, "Stand up and go; your faith has made you well."

[20]One day the Pharisees asked Jesus, "When will the Kingdom of God begin?" Jesus replied, "The Kingdom of God isn't ushered in with visible signs. [21]You won't be able to say, 'It has begun here in this place or there in that part of the country.' For the Kingdom of God is within you."

[22]Later he talked again about this with his disciples. "The time is coming when you will long for me to be with you even for a single day, but I won't be here," he said. [23]"Reports will reach you that I have returned and that I am in this place or that; don't believe it or go out to look for me. [24]For when I return, you will know it beyond all doubt. It will be as evident as the lightning that flashes across the skies. [25]But first I must suffer terribly and be rejected by this whole nation.

[26]"[When I return] the world will be [as indifferent to the things of God] as the people were in Noah's day. [27]They ate and drank and married— everything just as usual right up to the day when Noah went into the ark and the flood came and destroyed them all.

[28]"And the world will be as it was in the days of Lot: people went about their daily business—eating and drinking, buying and selling, farming and building— [29]until the morning Lot left Sodom. Then fire and brimstone rained down from heaven and destroyed them all. [30]Yes, it will be 'business as usual' right up to the hour of my return.

[31]"Those away from home that day must not return to pack; those in the fields must not return to town— [32]remember what happened to Lot's wife! [33]Whoever clings to his life shall lose it, and whoever loses his life shall save it. [34]That night two men will be asleep in the same room, and one will be taken away, the other left. [35,36]Two women will be working together at household tasks; one will be taken, the other left; and so it will be with men working side by side in the fields."

[37]"Lord, where will they be taken?" the disciples asked.

Jesus replied, "Where the body is, the vultures gather!"

CHAPTER **18** A STORY ABOUT A PERSISTENT WIDOW.

One day Jesus told his disciples a story to illustrate their need for constant prayer and to show them that they must keep praying until the answer comes.

[2]"There was a city judge," he said, "a very godless man who had great contempt for everyone. [3]A widow of that city came to him frequently to appeal for justice against a man who had harmed her. [4,5]The judge ignored her for a while, but eventually she got on his nerves.

"'I fear neither God nor man,' he said to himself, 'but this woman bothers me. I'm going to see that she gets justice, for she is wearing me out with her constant coming!'"

[6]Then the Lord said, "If even an evil judge can be worn down like that, [7]don't you think that God will surely give justice to his people who plead with him day and night? [8]Yes! He will answer them quickly! But the question is: When I, the Messiah, return, how many will I find who have faith [and are praying]?"

I've always been taught to be independent and self-sufficient. My youth leader says this isn't right. What's wrong about being proud about doing your best?

I WONDER . . .

Have you ever known someone who thought he was so good in sports that he rarely listened to the coach? Although all coaches love to have players with great natural ability, most would settle for those with a few skills who are teachable. An athlete is much easier to mold than to motivate.

Being totally self-reliant is sort of like an athlete allowing the coach to give him advice only when he wants it. Before too long the athlete will start to deteriorate in talent, and in the eyes of the coach. In the same way, we need to depend on God to lead us. And we should do what he says.

God wants us always to try to do our best. We should never do anything halfway. But there's a difference between doing our best and allowing God to do his best through us.

Taking the credit for everything we do is called pride—it's a dangerous thing. There is a good type of pride that comes from doing something well. Perhaps we've worked hard at something and everything has come out great. We feel good about ourselves, and that's OK. The problem comes when we take all the credit. That's the wrong kind of pride.

God wants us to recognize that he gave us our life and our talents. This shows humility and a deep respect for God.

The Pharisee in Luke 18:9-14 is a perfect example of someone with "bad pride." He was proud of his "holy" life. Although he acted like he was talking to God, he was really just talking to himself.

On the flip side is the tax collector. He had nothing to be proud of, especially as it related to his relationship with God. In humility, he asked God for mercy.

If we go through life with an I-can-make-it-OK-by-myself attitude, we're really saying to God, "I don't really need you after all." But God wants us to depend on him.

9Then he told this story to some who boasted of their virtue and scorned everyone else:

10"Two men went to the Temple to pray. One was a proud, self-righteous Pharisee, and the other a cheating tax collector. 11The proud Pharisee 'prayed' this prayer: 'Thank God, I am not a sinner like everyone else, especially like that tax collector over there! For I never cheat, I don't commit adultery, 12I go without food twice a week, and I give to God a tenth of everything I earn.'

13"But the corrupt tax collector stood at a distance and dared not even lift his eyes to heaven as he prayed, but beat upon his chest in sorrow, exclaiming, 'God, be merciful to me, a sinner.' 14I tell you, this sinner, not the Pharisee, returned home forgiven! For the proud shall be humbled, but the humble shall be honored."

15One day some mothers brought their babies to him to touch and bless. But the disciples told them to go away.

16,17Then Jesus called the children over to him and said to the disciples, "Let the little children come to me! Never send them away! For the Kingdom of God belongs to men who have hearts as trusting as these little children's. And anyone who doesn't have their kind of faith will never get within the Kingdom's gates."

18Once a Jewish religious leader asked him this question: "Good sir, what shall I do to get to heaven?"

19"Do you realize what you are saying when you call me 'good'?" Jesus asked him. "Only God is truly good, and no one else.

20"But as to your question, you know what the Ten Commandments say—don't commit adultery, don't murder, don't steal, don't lie, honor your parents, and so on." 21The man replied, "I've obeyed every one of these laws since I was a small child."

22"There is still one thing you lack," Jesus said. "Sell all you have and give the money to the poor—it will become treasure for you in heaven—and come, follow me."

23But when the man heard this he went sadly away, for he was very rich.

24Jesus watched him go and then said to his disciples, "How hard it is for the rich to enter the Kingdom of God! 25It is easier for a camel to go through the eye of a needle than for a rich man to enter the Kingdom of God."

26Those who heard him say this exclaimed, "If it is that hard, how can *anyone* be saved?"

27He replied, "God can do what men can't!"

28And Peter said, "We have left our homes and followed you."

29"Yes," Jesus replied, "and everyone who has done as you have, leaving home, wife, brothers, parents, or children for the sake of the Kingdom of God, 30will be repaid many times over now, as well as receiving eternal life in the world to come."

31Gathering the Twelve around him he told them, "As you know, we are going to Jerusalem. And when we get there, all the predictions of the ancient prophets concerning me will come true. 32I will be handed over to the Gentiles to be mocked and treated shamefully and spat upon, 33and lashed and killed. And the third day I will rise again."

34But they didn't understand a thing he said. He seemed to be talking in riddles.

35As they approached Jericho, a blind man was sitting beside the road, begging from travelers. 36When he heard the noise of a crowd going past, he asked what was happening. 37He was told that Jesus from Nazareth was going by, 38so he began shouting, "Jesus, Son of David, have mercy on me!"

39The crowds ahead of Jesus tried to hush the man, but he only yelled the louder, "Son of David, have mercy on me!"

40When Jesus arrived at the spot, he stopped. "Bring the blind man over here," he said. 41Then Jesus asked the man, "What do you want?"

"Lord," he pleaded, "I want to see!"

42And Jesus said, "All right, begin seeing! Your faith has healed you."

43And instantly the man could see and followed Jesus, praising God. And all who saw it happen praised God too.

CHAPTER **19** JESUS GIVES ZACCHAEUS A NEW LIFE. As Jesus was passing through Jericho, a man named Zacchaeus, one of the most influential Jews in the Roman tax-collecting business (and, of course, a very rich man), 3tried to get a look at Jesus, but he was too short to see over the crowds.

CHILDREN

18:15-17 It was customary for a mother to bring her children to a rabbi for a blessing, and that is why these mothers gathered about Jesus. The disciples, however, thought the children were unworthy of the Master's time—less important than whatever else he was doing. But Jesus welcomed them because little children have the kind of faith and trust needed to enter God's Kingdom. It is important to approach God with childlike attitudes of acceptance, faith, and trust.

GIVE UP

18:26-30 Peter and the other disciples had paid a high price—leaving their homes and jobs—to follow Jesus. But Jesus reminded Peter that following him has its benefits as well as its sacrifices. Any believer who has had to give up something to follow Christ will be paid back in this life as well as in the next. If you give up friends, you will find that God offers a secure relationship with himself now and forever. If you give up your family's approval, you will gain the love of the family of God. Don't dwell on what you have given up; think about what you have gained and give thanks for it. You can never outgive God.

[4]So he ran ahead and climbed into a sycamore tree beside the road, to watch from there.

[5]When Jesus came by, he looked up at Zacchaeus and called him by name! "Zacchaeus!" he said. "Quick! Come down! For I am going to be a guest in your home today!"

[6]Zacchaeus hurriedly climbed down and took Jesus to his house in great excitement and joy.

[7]But the crowds were displeased. "He has gone to be the guest of a notorious sinner," they grumbled.

[8]Meanwhile, Zacchaeus stood before the Lord and said, "Sir, from now on I will give half my wealth to the poor, and if I find I have overcharged anyone on his taxes, I will penalize myself by giving him back four times as much!"

[9,10]Jesus told him, "This shows that salvation has come to this home today. This man was one of the lost sons of Abraham, and I, the Messiah, have come to search for and to save such souls as his."

[11]And because Jesus was nearing Jerusalem, he told a story to correct the impression that the Kingdom of God would begin right away.

[12]"A nobleman living in a certain province was called away to the distant capital of the empire to be crowned king of his province. [13]Before he left he called together ten assistants and gave them each $2,000 to invest while he was gone. [14]But some of his people hated him and sent him their declaration of independence, stating that they had rebelled and would not acknowledge him as their king.

[15]"Upon his return he called in the men to whom he had given the money, to find out what they had done with it, and what their profits were.

[16]"The first man reported a tremendous gain—ten times as much as the original amount!

[17]"'Fine!' the king exclaimed. 'You are a good man. You have been faithful with the little I entrusted to you, and as your reward, you shall be governor of ten cities.'

[18]"The next man also reported a splendid gain—five times the original amount.

[19]"'All right!' his master said. 'You can be governor over five cities.'

[20]"But the third man brought back only the money he had started with. 'I've kept it safe,' he said, [21]'because I was afraid [you would demand my profits], for you are a hard man to deal with, taking what isn't yours and even confiscating the crops that others plant.' [22]'You vile and wicked slave,' the king roared. 'Hard, am I? That's exactly how I'll be toward you! If you knew so much about me and how tough I am, [23]then why didn't you deposit the money in the bank so that I could at least get some interest on it?'

[24]"Then turning to the others standing by he ordered, 'Take the money away from him and give it to the man who earned the most.'

[25]"'But, sir,' they said, 'he has enough already!'

[26]"'Yes,' the king replied, 'but it is always true that those who have, get more, and those who have little, soon lose even that. [27]And now about these enemies of mine who revolted—bring them in and execute them before me.'"

[28]After telling this story, Jesus went on toward Jerusalem, walking along ahead of his disciples. [29]As they came to the towns of Bethphage and Bethany, on the Mount of Olives, he sent two disciples ahead, [30]with instructions to go to the next village, and as they entered they were to look for a donkey tied beside the road. It would be a colt, not yet broken for riding.

"Untie him," Jesus said, "and bring him here. [31]And if anyone asks you what you are doing, just say, 'The Lord needs him.'"

[32]They found the colt as Jesus said, [33]and sure enough, as they were untying it, the owners demanded an explanation.

"What are you doing?" they asked. "Why are you untying our colt?"

[34]And the disciples simply replied, "The Lord needs him!" [35]So they brought the colt to Jesus and threw some of their clothing across its back for Jesus to sit on.

[36,37]Then the crowds spread out their robes along the road ahead of him, and as they reached the place where the road started down from the Mount of Olives, the whole procession began to shout and sing as they walked along, praising God for all the wonderful miracles Jesus had done.

[38]"God has given us a King!" they exulted. "Long live the King! Let all heaven rejoice! Glory to God in the highest heavens!"

[39]But some of the Pharisees among the crowd said, "Sir, rebuke your followers for saying things like that!"

[40]He replied, "If they keep quiet, the stones along the road will burst into cheers!"

[41]But as they came closer to Jerusalem and he saw the city ahead, he began to cry. [42]"Eternal peace was within your reach and you turned it down," he wept, "and now it is too late. [43]Your enemies will pile up earth against your walls and encircle you and close in on you, [44]and crush you to the ground, and your

UNPOPULAR

19:1-10 Tax collectors were among the most unpopular people in Israel. Jews by birth who chose to work for Rome were considered traitors. Besides, it was common knowledge that tax collectors made themselves rich by gouging their fellow Jews. No wonder the crowds were displeased when Jesus went home with the tax collector Zacchaeus. But despite the fact that Zacchaeus was both dishonest and a turncoat, Jesus loved him—and in response, the little tax collector was converted. In every society, certain groups of people are considered "untouchable" because of their politics, immoral behavior, or life-style. We should not avoid these people. Jesus loves them, and they need to hear his Good News.

children within you; your enemies will not leave one stone upon another—for you have rejected the opportunity God offered you."

⁴⁵Then he entered the Temple and began to drive out the merchants from their stalls, ⁴⁶saying to them, "The Scriptures declare, 'My Temple is a place of prayer; but you have turned it into a den of thieves.'"

⁴⁷After that he taught daily in the Temple, but the chief priests and other religious leaders and the business community were trying to find some way to get rid of him. ⁴⁸But they could think of nothing, for he was a hero to the people—they hung on every word he said.

CHAPTER 20 LEADERS CHALLENGE JESUS' AUTHORITY.

On one of those days when he was teaching and preaching the Good News in the Temple, he was confronted by the chief priests and other religious leaders and councilmen. ²They demanded to know by what authority he had driven out the merchants from the Temple.

³"I'll ask you a question before I answer," he replied. ⁴"Was John sent by God, or was he merely acting under his own authority?"

⁵They talked it over among themselves. "If we say his message was from heaven, then we are trapped because he will ask, 'Then why didn't you believe him?' ⁶But if we say John was not sent from God, the people will mob us, for they are convinced that he was a prophet." ⁷Finally they replied, "We don't know!"

⁸And Jesus responded, "Then I won't answer your question either."

⁹Now he turned to the people again and told them this story: "A man planted a vineyard and rented it out to some farmers, and went away to a distant land to live for several years. ¹⁰When harvest time came, he sent one of his men to the farm to collect his share of the crops. But the tenants beat him up and sent him back empty-handed. ¹¹Then he sent another, but the same thing happened; he was beaten up and insulted and sent away without collecting. ¹²A third man was sent and the same thing happened. He, too, was wounded and chased away.

¹³"'What shall I do?' the owner asked himself. 'I know! I'll send my cherished son. Surely they will show respect for him.'

¹⁴"But when the tenants saw his son, they said, 'This is our chance! This fellow will inherit all the land when his father dies. Come on. Let's kill him, and then it will be ours.' ¹⁵So they dragged him out of the vineyard and killed him.

"What do you think the owner will do? ¹⁶I'll tell you—he will come and kill them and rent the vineyard to others."

"But they would never do a thing like that," his listeners protested.

¹⁷Jesus looked at them and said, "Then what does the Scripture mean where it says, 'The Stone rejected by the builders was made the cornerstone'?" ¹⁸And he added, "Whoever stumbles over that Stone shall be broken; and those on whom it falls will be crushed to dust."

¹⁹When the chief priests and religious leaders heard about this story he had told, they wanted him arrested immediately, for they realized that he was talking about them. They were the wicked tenants in his illustration. But they were afraid that if they themselves arrested him, there would be a riot. So they tried to get him to say something that could be reported to the Roman governor as reason for arrest by him.

²⁰Watching their opportunity, they sent secret agents pretending to be honest men. ²¹They said to Jesus, "Sir, we know what an honest teacher you are. You always tell the truth and don't budge an inch in the face of what others think, but teach the ways of God. ²²Now tell us—is it right to pay taxes to the Roman government or not?"

²³He saw through their trickery and said, ²⁴"Show me a coin. Whose portrait is this on it? And whose name?"

They replied, "Caesar's—the Roman emperor's."

²⁵He said, "Then give the emperor all that is his—and give to God all that is his!"

²⁶Thus their attempt to outwit him before the

GIVING

The hot topic at school is what Kyla Whitfield will do with the huge inheritance she's getting as a result of her grandfather's death last week.

"How much do you think she'll end up getting?"

"Well, everyone says old man Whitfield was worth at least nine million dollars."

"Kyla gets it all?"

"No, I think they have to split it four ways."

"Oh my gosh! That's over two million dollars!"

"Well, she'll have to pay inheritance taxes on it first."

"But she'll still be a millionaire!"

"That's right."

"Oh, man! What I would do if I had a million dollars!"

"What would you do?"

"Spend most of it."

"On what?"

"I don't know . . . cars, a ski boat, whatever I wanted."

"What about giving?"

"What about it?"

"Would you give any of it away? You know, to other people, to your church, to charity?"

"Are you serious?"

That's a common response to the suggestion of giving. Unfortunately, even many Christians are that way.

What about you? Do you regularly give part of your money back to God? If not, why not? (By the way: "I will when I'm rich like Kyla" is a lousy excuse! See Luke 21:1-4.)

DUTY

20:20-26 Jesus turned his enemies' attempt to trap him into a powerful lesson: God's followers have legitimate obligations to both God and the government. But what is important is to keep our priorities straight. When the two authorities conflict, our duty to God always comes before our duty to the government.

people failed; and marveling at his answer, they were silent.

²⁷Then some Sadducees—men who believed that death is the end of existence, that there is no resurrection—²⁸came to Jesus with this:

"The laws of Moses state that if a man dies without children, the man's brother shall marry the widow, and their children will legally belong to the dead man, to carry on his name. ²⁹We know of a family of seven brothers. The oldest married and then died without any children. ³⁰His brother married the widow and he, too, died. Still no children. ³¹And so it went, one after the other, until each of the seven had married her and died, leaving no children. ³²Finally the woman died also. ³³Now here is our question: Whose wife will she be in the resurrection? For all of them were married to her!"

³⁴,³⁵Jesus replied, "Marriage is for people here on earth, but when those who are counted worthy of being raised from the dead get to heaven, they do not marry. ³⁶And they never die again; in these respects they are like angels, and are sons of God, for they are raised up in new life from the dead.

³⁷,³⁸"But as to your real question—whether or not there is a resurrection—why, even the writings of Moses himself prove this. For when he describes how God appeared to him in the burning bush, he speaks of God as 'the God of Abraham, the God of Isaac, and the God of Jacob.' To say that the Lord *is* some person's God means that person is *alive,* not dead! So from God's point of view, all men are living."

³⁹"Well said, sir!" remarked some of the experts in the Jewish law who were standing there. ⁴⁰And that ended their questions, for they dared ask no more!

⁴¹Then he presented *them* with a question. "Why is it," he asked, "that Christ, the Messiah, is said to be a descendant of King David? ⁴²,⁴³For David himself wrote in the book of Psalms: 'God said to my Lord, the Messiah, "Sit at my right hand until I place your enemies beneath your feet."' ⁴⁴How can the Messiah be both David's son and David's God at the same time?"

⁴⁵Then, with the crowds listening, he turned to his disciples and said, ⁴⁶"Beware of these experts in religion, for they love to parade in dignified robes and to be bowed to by the people as they walk along the street. And how they love the seats of honor in the synagogues and at religious festivals! ⁴⁷But even while they are praying long prayers with great outward piety, they are planning schemes to cheat widows out of their property. Therefore God's heaviest sentence awaits these men."

THE TEMPLE

21:5 The Temple the disciples were admiring was not Solomon's Temple. That was destroyed by the Babylonians in the sixth century B.C. This Temple was built by Ezra after the return from exile in the sixth century B.C. (see "The Temple in Jesus' Day"). It was a beautiful, imposing structure with a significant history, but Jesus said it would be completely destroyed. This happened in A.D. 70, when a Roman army burned Jerusalem. Now, as then, we can be sure of this: if God says something will happen, it will indeed take place!

CHAPTER 21 **THE WIDOW'S SMALL COINS.** As he stood in the Temple, he was watching the rich tossing their gifts into the collection box. ²Then a poor widow came by and dropped in two small copper coins.

³"Really," he remarked, "this poor widow has given more than all the rest of them combined. ⁴For they have given a little of what they didn't need, but she, poor as she is, has given everything she has."

⁵Some of his disciples began talking about the beautiful stonework of the Temple and the memorial decorations on the walls.

⁶But Jesus said, "The time is coming when all these things you are admiring will be knocked down, and not one stone will be left on top of another; all will become one vast heap of rubble."

⁷"Master!" they exclaimed. "When? And will there be any warning ahead of time?"

⁸He replied, "Don't let anyone mislead you. For

THE TEMPLE IN JESUS' DAY

to Jerusalem

Slaughtering places

COURT OF ISRAEL   to Mount of Olives

Holy of Holies   Barrier

Steps

SOLOMON'S PORCH

Altar   COURT OF
Holy Place   THE WOMEN   Storage areas
for wood, tools,
oil, grain

COURT OF THE PRIESTS

COURT OF THE GENTILES

ROYAL PORCH

BETRAYED

21:14-19 Jesus warned that in the coming persecutions his followers would be betrayed by their family members and friends. Christians of every age have had to face this possibility. It is reassuring to know that even when we feel completely abandoned, the Holy Spirit stays with us. He will comfort us, protect us, and give us the words we need. This assurance can give us the courage and hope to stand firm for Christ through all the difficult situations we face.

many will come announcing themselves as the Messiah, and saying, 'The time has come.' But don't believe them! [9]And when you hear of wars and insurrections beginning, don't panic. True, wars must come, but the end won't follow immediately—[10]for nation shall rise against nation and kingdom against kingdom, [11]and there will be great earthquakes, and famines in many lands, and epidemics, and terrifying things happening in the heavens.

[12]"But before all this occurs, there will be a time of special persecution, and you will be dragged into synagogues and prisons and before kings and governors for my name's sake. [13]But as a result, the Messiah will be widely known and honored. [14]Therefore, don't be concerned about how to answer the charges against you, [15]for I will give you the right words and such logic that none of your opponents will be able to reply! [16]Even those closest to you—your parents, brothers, relatives, and friends will betray you and have you arrested; and some of you will be killed. [17]And everyone will hate you because you are mine and are called by my name. [18]But not a hair of your head will perish! [19]For if you stand firm, you will win your souls.

[20]"But when you see Jerusalem surrounded by armies, then you will know that the time of its destruction has arrived. [21]Then let the people of Judea flee to the hills. Let those in Jerusalem try to escape, and those outside the city must not attempt to return. [22]For those will be days of God's judgment, and the words of the ancient Scriptures written by the prophets will be abundantly fulfilled. [23]Woe to expectant mothers in those days, and those with tiny babies. For there will be great distress upon this nation and wrath upon this people. [24]They will be brutally killed by enemy weapons, or sent away as exiles and captives to all the nations of the world; and Jerusalem shall be conquered and trampled down by the Gentiles until the period of Gentile triumph ends in God's good time.

[25]"Then there will be strange events in the skies—warnings, evil omens and portents in the sun, moon and stars; and down here on earth the nations will be in turmoil, perplexed by the roaring seas and strange tides. [26]The courage of many people will falter because of the fearful fate they see coming upon the earth, for the stability of the very heavens will be broken up. [27]Then the peoples of the earth shall see me, the Messiah, coming in a cloud with power and great glory. [28]So when all these things begin to happen, stand straight and look up! For your salvation is near."

[29]Then he gave them this illustration: "Notice the fig tree, or any other tree. [30]When the leaves come out, you know without being told that summer is near. [31]In the same way, when you see the events taking place that I've described you can be just as sure that the Kingdom of God is near.

[32]"I solemnly declare to you that when these things happen, the end of this age has come. [33]And though all heaven and earth shall pass away, yet my words remain forever true.

[34,35]"Watch out! Don't let my sudden coming catch you unawares; don't let me find you living in careless ease, carousing and drinking, and occupied with the problems of this life, like all the rest of the world. [36]Keep a constant watch. And pray that if possible you may arrive in my presence without having to experience these horrors."

[37,38]Every day Jesus went to the Temple to teach, and the crowds began gathering early in the morning to hear him. And each evening he returned to spend the night on the Mount of Olives.

CHAPTER 22 A PLAN TO KILL JESUS.

And now the Passover celebration was drawing near—the Jewish festival when only bread made without yeast was used. [2]The chief priests and other religious leaders were actively plotting Jesus' murder, trying to find a way to kill him without starting a riot—a possibility they greatly feared.

[3]Then Satan entered into Judas Iscariot, who was one of the twelve disciples, [4]and he went over to the chief priests and captains of the Temple guards to discuss the best way to betray Jesus to them. [5]They were, of course, delighted to know that he was ready to help them and promised him a reward. [6]So he began to look for an opportunity for them to arrest Jesus quietly when the crowds weren't around.

[7]Now the day of the Passover celebration arrived, when the Passover lamb was killed and eaten with the unleavened bread. [8]Jesus sent Peter and John ahead to find a place to prepare their Passover meal.

[9]"Where do you want us to go?" they asked.

WRAPPED UP

22:24 The most important event in human history was about to take place, but the disciples were still arguing about their prestige in the Kingdom! Looking back, we say, "This was no time to worry about status." But the disciples, wrapped up in their own concerns, did not perceive what Jesus had been trying to tell them about his approaching death and resurrection. What are your major concerns today? Twenty years from now will these worries look petty and inappropriate? Get your eyes off yourself and look for signs of the Kingdom of God that is about to break into human history for the second time.

¹⁰And he replied, "As soon as you enter Jerusalem, you will see a man walking along carrying a pitcher of water. Follow him into the house he enters, ¹¹and say to the man who lives there, 'Our Teacher says for you to show us the guest room where he can eat the Passover meal with his disciples.' ¹²He will take you upstairs to a large room all ready for us. That is the place. Go ahead and prepare the meal there."

¹³They went off to the city and found everything just as Jesus had said, and prepared the Passover supper.

¹⁴Then Jesus and the others arrived, and at the proper time all sat down together at the table; ¹⁵and he said, "I have looked forward to this hour with deep longing, anxious to eat this Passover meal with you before my suffering begins. ¹⁶For I tell you now that I won't eat it again until what it represents has occurred in the Kingdom of God."

¹⁷Then he took a glass of wine, and when he had given thanks for it, he said, "Take this and share it among yourselves. ¹⁸For I will not drink wine again until the Kingdom of God has come."

¹⁹Then he took a loaf of bread; and when he had thanked God for it, he broke it apart and gave it to them, saying, "This is my body, given for you. Eat it in remembrance of me."

²⁰After supper he gave them another glass of wine, saying, "This wine is the token of God's new agreement to save you—an agreement sealed with the blood I shall pour out to purchase back your souls. ²¹But here at this table, sitting among us as a friend, is the man who will betray me. ²²I must die. It is part of God's plan. But, oh, the horror awaiting that man who betrays me."

²³Then the disciples wondered among themselves which of them would ever do such a thing.

²⁴And they began to argue among themselves as to who would have the highest rank [in the coming Kingdom].

²⁵Jesus told them, "In this world the kings and great men order their slaves around, and the slaves have no choice but to like it! ²⁶But among you, the one who serves you best will be your leader. ²⁷Out in the world the master sits at the table and is served by his servants. But not here! For I am your servant. ²⁸Nevertheless, because you have stood true to me in these terrible days, ²⁹and because my Father has granted me a Kingdom, I, here and now, grant you the right ³⁰to eat and drink at my table in that Kingdom; and you will sit on thrones judging the twelve tribes of Israel.

³¹"Simon, Simon, Satan has asked to have you, to sift you like wheat, ³²but I have pleaded in prayer for you that your faith should not completely fail. So when you have repented and turned to me again, strengthen and build up the faith of your brothers."

³³Simon said, "Lord, I am ready to go to jail with you, and even to die with you."

³⁴But Jesus said, "Peter, let me tell you something. Between now and tomorrow morning when the rooster crows, you will deny me three times, declaring that you don't even know me."

³⁵Then Jesus asked them, "When I sent you out to preach the Good News and you were without money, duffle bag, or extra clothing, how did you get along?"

"Fine," they replied.

There aren't very many Christians at my school, and I'm kind of embarrassed about admitting I am one. Do I have to come out and let the whole world know I've become a Christian?

I WONDER . . .

High school guys and girls wear letter jackets that tell the world they're athletes. Most people wear such jackets with pride. They have accomplished something, and they want other people to know it.

Identifying yourself as a Christian, however, is not always real popular. Peter found that out when he was confronted by the people who were trying to get warm around the fire (see Luke 22:54-62). Although he had been with Jesus for three years and was one of his best friends, Peter denied even knowing who Jesus was! He was afraid and embarrassed. But something happened during the next two months that convinced him he would never be ashamed of Jesus again (read about Peter in the first four chapters of the book of Acts).

As a new Christian, it is hard to identify yourself with Christ because you don't know him very well. It's like striking up a friendship with the new kid at school. You want to be his friend, but you hold back because you aren't sure how popular he's going to be.

Jesus understands our fears. It can be tough to admit we're his followers. He will patiently wait until we are confident in our relationship with him before we begin to speak out for him. But I can imagine he is kind of disappointed, too.

It takes most new Christians some time before they aren't embarrassed about admitting they're Christians. But at some point, something clicks that convinces them that Jesus Christ *is* alive. It could be the feeling of being forgiven, a miraculous answer to prayer, or a quiet realization that the Bible is accurate and everything Jesus said about himself is true!

However it happens, God doesn't expect you to get on the P.A. at school and make the "big announcement." He just expects you to be ready in case anyone asks you about your faith: "Quietly trust yourself to Christ your Lord, and if anybody asks why you believe as you do, be ready to tell him, and do it in a gentle and respectful way" (1 Peter 3:15).

WHY THE CROSS?

A youth pastor was talking to a group of junior highers about the cross of Christ, explaining how Jesus' death had provided for their individual forgiveness and salvation. He died for you. "It's personal," he said. "Jesus didn't just die for people in general. He died for you." He paused to let the impact of the statement sink in. Suddenly one seventh-grade girl blurted out: "So?" **"So?"** As irreverent and inappropriate as that question seems, that seventh grader's response is sadly representative of how people think today. We know Jesus died on a cross for us; we just don't see the connection between that event 2,000 years ago and our lives today.

What is the cross about? Why did Jesus have to die in such a horrible death? The cross has inspired endless debates, wars, books, songs, and lives through the centuries. I hope this short note may help you gain some insight into why Jesus had to die, and why he died in such a gruesome way. **F**irst, there's humanity's problem. All humans are sinners. We've broken God's laws, so we stand guilty before God and deserving of punishment. Sin has warped every aspect of human life; it has had such a radical effect on us that we stand in open rebellion and defiance of the God who made us and loves us. Think this is overstating the case? Consider this: God made himself vulnerable to human beings one time, and we murdered him. **B**ecause of our sinful nature, we are incapable of pleasing God or doing anything on our own to change the situation. We are, as Paul writes in Ephesians 2:5 and Colossians 2:13, dead in our sins—and dead people can't exactly help themselves. We desperately need help from someone who can please God, who can do something about the desperate state of human souls. Jesus, by virtue of his sinless life, is that Someone. But helping us is a terribly expensive process. **A**gain, we are guilty before God—we deserve his anger and punishment. But God took the wrath we deserve and poured it out on Jesus, on the cross. In some ways, it is beyond human understanding. Jesus took upon himself our sins—every mean, dishonest, disgusting thought or action—and was transformed from the perfect, holy, righteous Person he was into utter sin itself. Second Corinthians 5:21 tells us, "For God took the sinless Christ and poured into him our sins. Then, in exchange, he poured God's goodness into us!" On the cross Jesus received the punishment our sins deserve. As the perfect God-man, he alone was in a position to do that. Jesus stood in the chasm between God and man, which was created by our sins, and brought us back together by his blood. As horrible as the physical agony must have been, the spiritual agony of this transformation and punishment was worse. No wonder he screamed out, "My God, my God, why have you deserted me?" Jesus was deserted by God so that you and I never have to be. **T**hat's the second fact you need to know. Jesus took your place on the cross and bore the terrible brunt of the sentence God could have imposed on you. He died for you. Take it personally. **I**t's still a mystery how the death of one righteous Man—the only righteous Man—pays for the sins of the world. Still, though we may not understand it, we can depend upon it for our salvation. It is the only way to peace with God and eternal life. It's fitting that God took the cross of Christ—the single darkest hour in the history of humanity—and turned it into the way of redemption for all people everywhere. That's the kind of God the Bible talks about. A God who loves you so much he would even die on a cross for you.

³⁶"But now," he said, "take a duffle bag if you have one and your money. And if you don't have a sword, better sell your clothes and buy one! ³⁷For the time has come for this prophecy about me to come true: 'He will be condemned as a criminal!' Yes, everything written about me by the prophets will come true."

³⁸"Master," they replied, "we have two swords among us."

"Enough!" he said.

³⁹Then, accompanied by the disciples, he left the upstairs room and went as usual to the Mount of Olives. ⁴⁰There he told them, "Pray God that you will not be overcome by temptation."

⁴¹,⁴²He walked away, perhaps a stone's throw, and knelt down and prayed this prayer: "Father, if you are willing, please take away this cup of horror from me. But I want your will, not mine." ⁴³Then an angel from heaven appeared and strengthened him, ⁴⁴for he was in such agony of spirit that he broke into a sweat of blood, with great drops falling to the ground as he prayed more and more earnestly. ⁴⁵At last he stood up again and returned to the disciples—only to find them asleep, exhausted from grief.

⁴⁶"Asleep!" he said. "Get up! Pray God that you will not fall when you are tempted."

⁴⁷But even as he said this, a mob approached, led by Judas, one of his twelve disciples. Judas walked over to Jesus and kissed him on the cheek in friendly greeting.

⁴⁸But Jesus said, "Judas, how can you do this—betray the Messiah with a kiss?"

⁴⁹When the other disciples saw what was about to happen, they exclaimed, "Master, shall we fight? We brought along the swords!" ⁵⁰And one of them slashed at the High Priest's servant and cut off his right ear.

⁵¹But Jesus said, "Don't resist any more." And he touched the place where the man's ear had been and restored it. ⁵²Then Jesus addressed the chief priests and captains of the Temple guards and the religious leaders who headed the mob. "Am I a robber," he asked, "that you have come armed with swords and clubs to get me? ⁵³Why didn't you arrest me in the Temple? I was there every day. But this is your moment—the time when Satan's power reigns supreme."

⁵⁴So they seized him and led him to the High Priest's residence, and Peter followed at a distance. ⁵⁵The soldiers lit a fire in the courtyard and sat around it for warmth, and Peter joined them there.

⁵⁶A servant girl noticed him in the firelight and began staring at him. Finally she spoke: "This man was with Jesus!"

⁵⁷Peter denied it. "Woman," he said, "I don't even know the man!"

⁵⁸After a while someone else looked at him and said, "You must be one of them!"

"No sir, I am not!" Peter replied.

⁵⁹About an hour later someone else flatly stated, "I know this fellow is one of Jesus' disciples, for both are from Galilee."

⁶⁰But Peter said, "Man, I don't know what you are talking about." And as he said the words, a rooster crowed.

⁶¹At that moment Jesus turned and looked at Peter. Then Peter remembered what he had said—"Before the rooster crows tomorrow morning, you will deny me three times." ⁶²And Peter walked out of the courtyard, crying bitterly.

⁶³,⁶⁴Now the guards in charge of Jesus began mocking him. They blindfolded him and hit him with their fists and asked, "Who hit you that time, prophet?" ⁶⁵And they threw all sorts of other insults at him.

⁶⁶Early the next morning at daybreak the Jewish Supreme Court assembled, including the chief priests and all the top religious authorities of the nation. Jesus was led before this Council ⁶⁷,⁶⁸and instructed to state whether or not he claimed to be the Messiah.

But he replied, "If I tell you, you won't believe me or let me present my case. ⁶⁹But the time is soon coming when I, the Messiah, shall be enthroned beside Almighty God."

⁷⁰They all shouted, "Then you claim you are the Son of God?"

And he replied, "Yes, I am."

⁷¹"What need do we have for other witnesses?" they shouted. "For we ourselves have heard him say it."

BITTER TEARS

22:62 Peter wept bitterly because he realized he had denied his Lord and because he had turned away from a dear friend who had loved and taught him for three years. Peter had said he would *never* deny Christ, but he went against all he had boldly promised. Unable to stand up for his Lord for even 12 hours, he had failed as a disciple and as a friend. We need to be aware of our own breaking points and not become overconfident or self-sufficient. When we fail, we must remember that Christ can use those who recognize their failure. From this humiliating experience Peter learned much that would help him in the leadership responsibilities he soon would assume.

CHAPTER **23** JESUS STANDS BEFORE PILATE.
Then the entire Council took Jesus over to Pilate, the governor. ²They began at once accusing him: "This fellow has been leading our people to ruin by telling them not to pay their taxes to the Roman government and by claiming he is our Messiah—a King."

³So Pilate asked him, "Are you their Messiah—their King?"

"Yes," Jesus replied, "it is as you say."

⁴Then Pilate turned to the chief priests and to the mob and said, "So? That isn't a crime!"

⁵Then they became desperate. "But he is causing riots against the government everywhere he goes, all over Judea, from Galilee to Jerusalem!"

⁶"Is he then a Galilean?" Pilate asked.

⁷When they told him yes, Pilate said to take him to King Herod, for Galilee was under Herod's jurisdiction; and Herod happened to be in Jerusalem at the time. ⁸Herod was delighted at the opportunity to see Jesus, for he had heard a lot about him and had been hoping to see him perform a miracle.

⁹He asked Jesus question after question, but there was no reply. ¹⁰Meanwhile, the chief priests and the other religious leaders stood there shouting their accusations.

¹¹Now Herod and his soldiers began mocking and ridiculing Jesus; and putting a kingly robe on him, they sent him back to Pilate. ¹²That day Herod and Pilate—enemies before—became fast friends.

¹³Then Pilate called together the chief priests and other Jewish leaders, along with the people, ¹⁴and announced his verdict:

"You brought this man to me, accusing him of leading a revolt against the Roman government. I have examined him thoroughly on this point and find him innocent. ¹⁵Herod came to the same conclusion and sent him back to us—nothing this man has done calls for the death penalty. ¹⁶I will therefore have him scourged with leaded thongs and release him."

¹⁷,¹⁸ But now a mighty roar rose from the crowd as with one voice they shouted. "Kill him, and release Barabbas to us!" ¹⁹(Barabbas was in prison for starting an insurrection in Jerusalem against the government, and for murder.) ²⁰Pilate argued with them, for he wanted to release Jesus. ²¹But they shouted, "Crucify him! Crucify him!"

²²Once more, for the third time, he demanded, "Why? What crime has he committed? I have found no reason to sentence him to death. I will therefore scourge him and let him go." ²³But they shouted louder and louder for Jesus' death, and their voices prevailed.

²⁴So Pilate sentenced Jesus to die as they demanded. ²⁵And he released Barabbas, the man in prison for insurrection and murder, at their request.

But he delivered Jesus over to them to do with as they would.

²⁶As the crowd led Jesus away to his death, Simon of Cyrene, who was just coming into Jerusalem from the country, was forced to follow, carrying Jesus' cross. ²⁷Great crowds trailed along behind, and many grief-stricken women.

²⁸But Jesus turned and said to them, "Daughters of Jerusalem, don't weep for me, but for yourselves and for your children. ²⁹For the days are coming when the women who have no children will be counted fortunate indeed. ³⁰Mankind will beg the mountains to fall on them and crush them, and the hills to bury them. ³¹For if such things as this are done to me, the Living Tree, what will they do to you?"

³²,³³Two others, criminals, were led out to be executed with him at a place called "The Skull." There all three were crucified—Jesus on the center cross, and the two criminals on either side.

³⁴"Father, forgive these people," Jesus said, "for they don't know what they are doing."

And the soldiers gambled for his clothing, throwing dice for each piece. ³⁵The crowd watched. And the Jewish leaders laughed and scoffed. "He was so good at helping others," they said, "let's see him save himself if he is really God's Chosen One, the Messiah."

³⁶The soldiers mocked him, too, by offering him a drink—of sour wine. ³⁷And they called to him, "If you are the King of the Jews, save yourself!"

³⁸A signboard was nailed to the cross above him with these words: "This is the King of the Jews."

³⁹One of the criminals hanging beside him scoffed, "So you're the Messiah, are you? Prove it by saving yourself—and us, too, while you're at it!"

⁴⁰,⁴¹But the other criminal protested. "Don't you even fear God when you are dying? We deserve to die for our evil deeds, but this man hasn't done one thing wrong." ⁴²Then he said, "Jesus, remember me when you come into your Kingdom."

⁴³And Jesus replied, "Today you will be with me in Paradise. This is a solemn promise."

⁴⁴By now it was noon, and darkness fell across the whole land for three hours, until three o'clock. ⁴⁵The light from the sun was gone—and suddenly the thick veil hanging in the Temple split apart.

⁴⁶Then Jesus shouted, "Father, I commit my spirit to you," and with those words he died.

⁴⁷When the captain of the Roman military unit

NEW LIFE

23:34 Jesus asked God to forgive the people who were putting him to death—Jewish leaders, Roman politicians and soldiers, bystanders—and God answered that prayer by opening up the way of salvation even to Jesus' murderers. The Roman officer and soldiers who witnessed the crucifixion said, "Surely this was God's Son" (Matthew 27:54). Soon many priests were converted to the Christian faith (Acts 6:7). Since we are all sinners, we all played a part in putting Jesus to death. The Good News is that God is gracious. He will forgive us and give us new life through his Son.

MERCY

23:39-43 As this man was about to die, he turned to Christ for forgiveness, and Christ accepted him. This shows that our works don't save us—our faith in Christ does. It is never too late to turn to God. Even in his misery, Jesus had mercy on this criminal who decided to believe in him. Our lives are much more useful and fulfilling if we turn to God early, but even those who repent at the very last moment will be with God in his Kingdom.

handling the executions saw what had happened, he was stricken with awe before God and said, "Surely this man was innocent."

⁴⁸And when the crowd that came to see the crucifixion saw that Jesus was dead they went home in deep sorrow. ⁴⁹Meanwhile, Jesus' friends, including the women who had followed him down from Galilee, stood in the distance watching.

⁵⁰⁻⁵²Then a man named Joseph, a member of the Jewish Supreme Court, from the city of Arimathea in Judea, went to Pilate and asked for the body of Jesus. He was a godly man who had been expecting the Messiah's coming and had not agreed with the decision and actions of the other Jewish leaders. ⁵³So he took down Jesus' body and wrapped it in a long linen cloth and laid it in a new, unused tomb hewn into the rock [at the side of a hill]. ⁵⁴This was done late on Friday afternoon, the day of preparation for the Sabbath.

⁵⁵As the body was taken away, the women from Galilee followed and saw it carried into the tomb. ⁵⁶Then they went home and prepared spices and ointments to embalm him; but by the time they were finished it was the Sabbath, so they rested all that day as required by the Jewish law.

CHAPTER **24** JESUS IS ALIVE! But very early on Sunday morning they took the ointments to the tomb—²and found that the huge stone covering the entrance had been rolled aside. ³So they went in—but the Lord Jesus' body was gone.

⁴They stood there puzzled, trying to think what could have happened to it. Suddenly two men appeared before them, clothed in shining robes so bright their eyes were dazzled. ⁵The women were terrified and bowed low before them.

Then the men asked, "Why are you looking in a tomb for someone who is alive? ⁶,⁷He isn't here! He has come back to life again! Don't you remember what he told you back in Galilee—that the Messiah must be betrayed into the power of evil men and be crucified and that he would rise again the third day?"

⁸Then they remembered ⁹and rushed back to Jerusalem to tell his eleven disciples—and everyone else—what had happened. ¹⁰(The women who went to the tomb were Mary Magdalene and Joanna and Mary the mother of James, and several others.) ¹¹But the story sounded like a fairy tale to the men—they didn't believe it.

¹²However, Peter ran to the tomb to look. Stooping, he peered in and saw the empty linen wrappings; and then he went back home again, wondering what had happened.

¹³That same day, Sunday, two of Jesus' followers were walking to the village of Emmaus, seven miles out of Jerusalem. ¹⁴As they walked along they were talking of Jesus' death, ¹⁵when suddenly Jesus himself came along and joined them and began walking beside them. ¹⁶But they didn't recognize him, for God kept them from it.

¹⁷"You seem to be in a deep discussion about something," he said. "What are you so concerned about?" They stopped short, sadness written across their faces. ¹⁸And one of them, Cleopas, replied, "You must be the only person in Jerusalem who hasn't heard about the terrible things that happened there last week."

¹⁹"What things?" Jesus asked.

"The things that happened to Jesus, the Man from Nazareth," they said. "He was a Prophet who did incredible miracles and was a mighty Teacher, highly regarded by both God and man. ²⁰But the chief priests and our religious leaders arrested him and handed him over to the Roman government to

My church regularly does something called "Communion." What is it supposed to do for me?

I WONDER . . .

Have you ever saved something from a special event because you wanted to remember how great that moment was? Odds are you have. And if you ask your parents to take you through their "nostalgia boxes" sometime, they'll probably say things like: "This is the varsity letter I won my senior year for swimming." Or, "Here is the ring box from the ring your father gave me the day he proposed."

Certain items help us remember special moments in our lives.

When Jesus was about to die, be resurrected, and return to heaven, he wanted to leave his followers something tangible to remember him by. He could have left a physical item like a robe or a cup. But people probably would begin to worship the object instead of God, and the object would be seen by just a few. So instead, he left an "act," something we could do.

Communion (The Lord's Supper, Eucharist) is that act—a word picture of what Jesus did on the cross. There, his body was broken and his blood was shed . . . for us. Luke 24:13-35 says that Jesus was recognized as "he was breaking the bread" (verse 35). Communion helps us recognize who Jesus is and that he is with us as we worship.

Because Communion is celebrated by believers throughout the world, it is a unifying act. And because we retell the message of Christ's death, we are reminded that he is going to return someday to take us to heaven. (See also 1 Corinthians 11:23-26).

Christian's will always need those reminders. There are too many distractions that cause us to lose our focus on what really matters in this life. Communion briefly reminds us that real *life* revolves not around us, but around one incredible act of love at a certain time in history. "This is my body. . . . This is my blood . . . do this in remembrance of me."

be condemned to death, and they crucified him. [21]We had thought he was the glorious Messiah and that he had come to rescue Israel.

"And now, besides all this—which happened three days ago— [22,23]some women from our group of his followers were at his tomb early this morning and came back with an amazing report that his body was missing, and that they had seen some angels there who told them Jesus is alive! [24]Some of our men ran out to see, and sure enough, Jesus' body was gone, just as the women had said."

[25]Then Jesus said to them, "You are such foolish, foolish people! You find it so hard to believe all that the prophets wrote in the Scriptures! [26]Wasn't it clearly predicted by the prophets that the Messiah would have to suffer all these things before entering his time of glory?"

[27]Then Jesus quoted them passage after passage from the writings of the prophets, beginning with the book of Genesis and going right on through the Scriptures, explaining what the passages meant and what they said about himself.

[28]By this time they were nearing Emmaus and the end of their journey. Jesus would have gone on, [29]but they begged him to stay the night with them, as it was getting late. So he went home with them. [30]As they sat down to eat, he asked God's blessing on the food and then took a small loaf of bread and broke it and was passing it over to them, [31]when suddenly—it was as though their eyes were opened—they recognized him! And at that moment he disappeared!

[32]They began telling each other how their hearts had felt strangely warm as he talked with them and explained the Scriptures during the walk down the road. [33,34]Within the hour they were on their way back to Jerusalem, where the eleven disciples and the other followers of Jesus greeted them with these words, "The Lord has really risen! He appeared to Peter!"

[35]Then the two from Emmaus told their story of how Jesus had appeared to them as they were walking along the road and how they had recognized him as he was breaking the bread.

[36]And just as they were telling about it, Jesus himself was suddenly standing there among them, and greeted them. [37]But the whole group was terribly frightened, thinking they were seeing a ghost!

[38]"Why are you frightened?" he asked. "Why do you doubt that it is really I? [39]Look at my hands! Look at my feet! You can see that it is I, myself! Touch me and make sure that I am not a ghost! For ghosts don't have bodies, as you see that I do!" [40]As he spoke, he held out his hands for them to see [the marks of the nails], and showed them [the wounds in] his feet.

[41]Still they stood there undecided, filled with joy and doubt.

Then he asked them, "Do you have anything here to eat?"

[42]They gave him a piece of broiled fish, [43]and he ate it as they watched!

[44]Then he said, "When I was with you before, don't you remember my telling you that everything written about me by Moses and the prophets and in the Psalms must all come true?" [45]Then he opened their minds to understand at last these many Scriptures! [46]And he said, "Yes, it was written long ago that the Messiah must suffer and die and rise again from the dead on the third day; [47]and that this message of salvation should be taken from Jerusalem to all the nations: *There is forgiveness of sins*

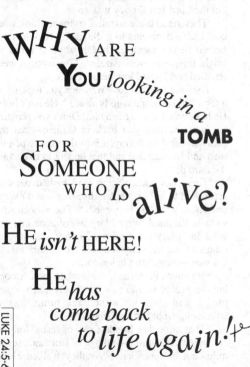

WHY ARE YOU looking in a TOMB FOR SOMEONE WHO IS alive? HE isn't HERE! HE has come back to life again! †

for all who turn to me. ⁴⁸You have seen these prophecies come true.

⁴⁹"And now I will send the Holy Spirit upon you, just as my Father promised. Don't begin telling others yet—stay here in the city until the Holy Spirit comes and fills you with power from heaven."

⁵⁰Then Jesus led them out along the road to Bethany, and lifting his hands to heaven, he blessed them, ⁵¹and then began rising into the sky, and went on to heaven. ⁵²And they worshiped him, and returned to Jerusalem filled with mighty joy, ⁵³and were continually in the Temple, praising God.

MEGA *Themes*

JESUS CHRIST, THE SAVIOR Luke describes how God's Son entered human history. Jesus lived as the perfect man. After a perfect ministry, he provided a perfect sacrifice for our sin so we could be saved.

Jesus is our perfect leader and Savior. He offers forgiveness to all who believe that what he says is true and accept him as Lord of their life.

1. How do you think Luke would answer this question: "What was Jesus like?"
2. What do you learn about Jesus in Luke 2:41-52?
3. Why is it so important that Jesus shared our human experiences, including all types of temptations?
4. Based on your responses to these questions, how would you describe Jesus to someone who had never heard of him?
5. What impact does this have on the person you are today? This is your testimony of who Jesus is in your life. Who do you know that needs to hear and understand your testimony?

HISTORY Luke was a medical doctor and historian. He put great emphasis on dates and details, connecting Jesus to events and people in history.

Luke's devotion to accuracy gives us confidence in the reliability of the history of Jesus' life. Even more important, we can believe with certainty that Jesus is God.

1. What difference does it make whether or not Luke is historically accurate?
2. Why is it so important that Jesus actually lived, died, and rose again as opposed to this just being an allegory (symbolic story) that someone used to describe how much God loves us?
3. What historical facts clearly reveal that Jesus was both man and God?
4. How does the fact that Jesus was both man and God affect your relationship with him? How does it affect your life?

CARING FOR PEOPLE Jesus was deeply interested in people and relationships. He showed warm concern for his followers and friends—men, women, and children.

Jesus' love for people is good news for everyone. His message is for all people in every nation. Each of us has an opportunity to respond to him in faith.

1. Jesus built his earthly ministry through personal relationships. What does this imply for how he wants you to minister to others?
2. What does it take for you to feel loved by someone? To trust that the person truly cares for you?
3. How would a person have to act to touch the people in your school with Christ's love?
4. What can you do to show Christ's love to the kids at your school?

HOLY SPIRIT The Holy Spirit was present at Jesus' birth, baptism, ministry, and resurrection. As a perfect example for us, Jesus lived in dependence on the Holy Spirit.

The Holy Spirit was sent by God as confirmation of Jesus' authority. The Holy Spirit is given to enable people to live for Christ. By faith we can have the Holy Spirit's presence and power to witness and to serve.

1. In 4:1-20, what role did the Holy Spirit play in Jesus' life?
2. In what ways does the Spirit work in you during times of temptation or weariness, and during opportunities to do his ministry?
3. What do you think it means to be "full of the Spirit"?
4. How can you keep yourself daily filled with his Spirit?
5. What do you want to see the Holy Spirit do in your life? What will you do to keep yourself reliant on God's Spirit so that this will be accomplished?

Questions. Life is jam-packed with them. ■ *Dumb* questions: •"If the plural of goose is geese, shouldn't the plural of moose be meese?" •"Um, if God can do anything, can he make a rock so big that even he couldn't lift it?" ■ *Mysterious* questions: •"Gentlemen, we know that buttered bread usually falls butter-side-down and cats generally land feet-first. Now we will discover what happens when a piece of buttered bread is strapped to the back of a cat and both are tossed off a two-story building." ■ *Serious* questions: •"What will bring me long-lasting fulfillment?" •"How can I have a rich and satisfying life?" ■ Even people who don't (or won't) openly discuss serious issues have ideas about where to find happiness. Ray's formula for fulfillment includes partying and an active sex life. Anne thinks she'll find it in a 4.0 grade point average and a college scholarship. Kevin is banking on his athletic ability to do the trick. Sherry's relying on beauty and bucks. ■ *Nagging* questions: •"If happiness really *is* found in the things mentioned above, why are there people with 'awesome' sex lives, staggering IQs, truckloads of trophies, 'drop-dead' good looks, or bulging bank accounts who are unhappy?" •"Why don't more people consider what Jesus had to say about happiness and fulfillment?" ■ *Personal* questions: •"Have *you* ever really looked at and pondered Jesus' teachings in the Gospel of John?" •"What are you waiting for?"

STATS

PURPOSE: To prove conclusively that Jesus is the Son of God and that all who believe in him will have eternal life

AUTHOR: John, the apostle, son of Zebedee, brother of James, called a "Son of Thunder"

TO WHOM WRITTEN: New Christians and searching non-Christians

DATE WRITTEN: Probably A.D. 85–90

SETTING: Written after the destruction of Jerusalem in A.D. 70 and before John's exile to the island of Patmos

KEY PEOPLE: Jesus, John the Baptist, the disciples, Mary, Martha, Lazarus, Jesus' mother, Pilate, Mary Magdalene

KEY PLACES: Judean countryside, Samaria, Galilee, Bethany, Jerusalem

John

CHAPTER 1 GOD BECOMES A HUMAN. Before anything else existed, there was Christ, with God. He has always been alive and is himself God. ³He created everything there is—nothing exists that he didn't make. ⁴Eternal life is in him, and this life gives light to all mankind. ⁵His life is the light that shines through the darkness—and the darkness can never extinguish it.

⁶,⁷God sent John the Baptist as a witness to the fact that Jesus Christ is the true Light. ⁸John himself was not the Light; he was only a witness to identify it.

⁹Later on, the one who is the true Light arrived to shine on everyone coming into the world.

¹⁰But although he made the world, the world didn't recognize him when he came. ¹¹,¹²Even in his own land and among his own people, the Jews, he was not accepted. Only a few would welcome and receive him. But to all who received him, he gave the right to become children of God. All they needed to do was to trust him to save them. ¹³All those who believe this are reborn!—not a physical rebirth resulting from human passion or plan—but from the will of God.

¹⁴And Christ became a human being and lived here on earth among us and was full of loving forgiveness and truth. And some of us have seen his glory—the glory of the only Son of the heavenly Father!

¹⁵John pointed him out to the people, telling the crowds, "This is the one I was talking about when I said, 'Someone is coming who is greater by far than I am—for he existed long before I did!'" ¹⁶We have all benefited from the rich blessings he brought to us—blessing upon blessing heaped upon us! ¹⁷For Moses gave us only the Law with its rigid demands and merciless justice, while Jesus Christ brought us loving forgiveness as well. ¹⁸No one has ever actually seen God, but, of course, his only Son has, for he is the companion of the Father and has told us all about him.

COMPLEX

1:3-5 Do you ever feel as though your life is so complex that God would never understand? Remember, God created the entire universe—nothing is too complex for him to understand. He created you, he is alive today, and his love is bigger than any problem you may face.

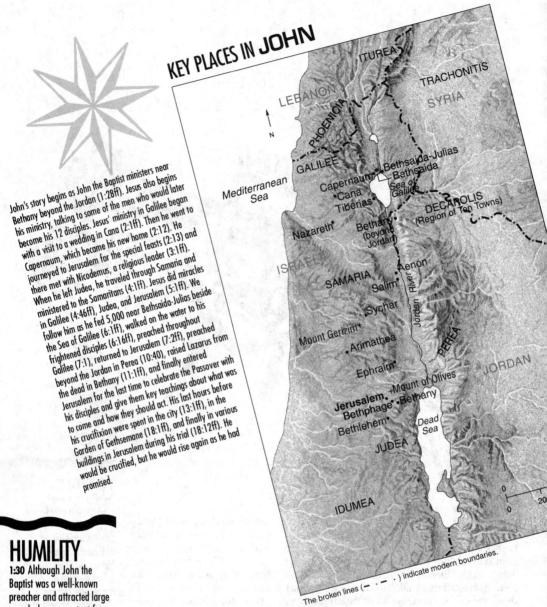

KEY PLACES IN JOHN

John's story begins as John the Baptist ministers near Bethany beyond the Jordan (1:28ff). Jesus also begins his ministry, talking to some of the men who would later become his 12 disciples. Jesus' ministry in Galilee began with a visit to a wedding in Cana (2:1ff). Then he went to Capernaum, which became his new home (2:12). He journeyed to Jerusalem for the special feasts (3:1ff). There he met with Nicodemus, a religious leader (3:1ff). When he left Judea, he traveled through Samaria and ministered to the Samaritans (4:1ff). Jesus did miracles in Galilee (4:46ff), Judea, and Jerusalem (5:1ff). We follow him as he fed 5,000 near Bethsaida-Julias beside the Sea of Galilee (6:1ff), walked on the water to his frightened disciples (6:16ff), preached throughout Galilee (7:1), returned to Jerusalem (7:2ff), preached beyond the Jordan in Perea (10:40), raised Lazarus from the dead in Bethany (11:1ff), and finally entered Jerusalem for the last time to celebrate the Passover with his disciples and give them key teachings about what was to come and how they should act. His last hours before his crucifixion were spent in the city (13:1ff), in the Garden of Gethsemane (18:1ff), and finally in various buildings in Jerusalem during his trial (18:12ff). He would be crucified, but he would rise again as he had promised.

The broken lines (— · — · —) indicate modern boundaries.

HUMILITY

1:30 Although John the Baptist was a well-known preacher and attracted large crowds, he was content for Jesus to take the higher place. This is true humility, the basis for greatness in preaching, teaching, or any other work we do for Christ. When you are content to do what God wants you to do and let Jesus Christ be honored for it, God will do great things through you.

[19]The Jewish leaders sent priests and assistant priests from Jerusalem to ask John whether he claimed to be the Messiah.

[20]He denied it flatly. "I am not the Christ," he said.

[21]"Well then, who are you?" they asked. "Are you Elijah?"

"No," he replied.

"Are you the Prophet?"

"No."

[22]"Then who are you? Tell us, so we can give an answer to those who sent us. What do you have to say for yourself?"

[23]He replied, "I am a voice from the barren wilderness, shouting as Isaiah prophesied, 'Get ready for the coming of the Lord!'"

[24,25]Then those who were sent by the Pharisees asked him, "If you aren't the Messiah or Elijah or the Prophet, what right do you have to baptize?"

[26]John told them, "I merely baptize with water, but right here in the crowd is someone you have never met, [27]who will soon begin his ministry among you, and I am not even fit to be his slave."

[28]This incident took place at Bethany, a village

on the other side of the Jordan River where John was baptizing.

²⁹The next day John saw Jesus coming toward him and said, "Look! There is the Lamb of God who takes away the world's sin! ³⁰He is the one I was talking about when I said, 'Soon a man far greater than I am is coming, who existed long before me!' ³¹I didn't know he was the one, but I am here baptizing with water in order to point him out to the nation of Israel."

³²Then John told about seeing the Holy Spirit in the form of a dove descending from heaven and resting upon Jesus.

³³"I didn't know he was the one," John said again, "but at the time God sent me to baptize he told me, 'When you see the Holy Spirit descending and resting upon someone—he is the one you are looking for. He is the one who baptizes with the Holy Spirit.' ³⁴I saw it happen to this man, and I therefore testify that he is the Son of God."

³⁵The following day as John was standing with two of his disciples, ³⁶Jesus walked by. John looked at him intently and then declared, "See! There is the Lamb of God!"

³⁷Then John's two disciples turned and followed Jesus.

³⁸Jesus looked around and saw them following. "What do you want?" he asked them.

"Sir," they replied, "where do you live?"

³⁹"Come and see," he said. So they went with him to the place where he was staying and were with him from about four o'clock that afternoon until the evening. ⁴⁰(One of these men was Andrew, Simon Peter's brother.)

⁴¹Andrew then went to find his brother Peter and told him, "We have found the Messiah!" ⁴²And he brought Peter to meet Jesus.

Jesus looked intently at Peter for a moment and then said, "You are Simon, John's son—but you shall be called Peter, the rock!"

⁴³The next day Jesus decided to go to Galilee. He found Philip and told him, "Come with me." ⁴⁴(Philip was from Bethsaida, Andrew and Peter's hometown.)

⁴⁵Philip now went off to look for Nathanael and told him, "We have found the Messiah!— the very person Moses and the prophets told about! His name is Jesus, the son of Joseph from Nazareth!"

⁴⁶"Nazareth!" exclaimed Nathanael. "Can anything good come from there?"

"Just come and see for yourself," Philip declared.

⁴⁷As they approached, Jesus said, "Here comes an honest man—a true son of Israel."

⁴⁸"How do you know what I am like?" Nathanael demanded.

And Jesus replied, "I could see you under the fig tree before Philip found you."

⁴⁹Nathanael replied, "Sir, you are the Son of God—the King of Israel!"

⁵⁰Jesus asked him, "Do you believe all this just because I told you I had seen you under the fig tree? You will see greater proofs than this. ⁵¹You will even see heaven open and the angels of God coming back and forth to me, the Messiah."

CHAPTER 2 JESUS TURNS WATER INTO WINE.

Two days later Jesus' mother was a guest at a wedding in the village of Cana in Galilee, ²and Jesus and his disciples were invited too. ³The wine supply ran out during the festivities, and Jesus' mother came to him with the problem.

⁴"I can't help you now," he said. "It isn't yet my time for miracles."

⁵But his mother told the servants, "Do whatever he tells you to."

"Here's what I did..."

It was an incredible weekend. A twister hit my town, and suddenly our house was ruined, my wrist was broken, and I lost my best friend.

I didn't know what to do, where to turn. It was too much to take in all at once. I felt depressed. Then I was angry; I felt ripped off. In all the confusion of adjusting to these disasters, I finally decided to open the Bible.

I started reading the Gospel of John. And as I thought about Jesus and all he gave up to come down to earth and live among us, my attitude started to change. I thought about verses 10-12 in the first chapter, how Jesus wasn't respected by the very people he came to help. If anybody had the right to feel self-pity, he did! But Jesus did it all for love, all for us.

The first 27 verses of chapter one opened my eyes to God's faithfulness and love. They made me realize that God would stand by me through everything, even this terrible time. I turned everything over to God, and discovered a joy that was as incredible as everything that had happened to me in that one terrible weekend. I began to live the kind of Christian life I'd been missing so long when I was just going my own way. The following weeks were the happiest I'd ever felt, even though I still had to deal with the sorrow over losing my friend and our home. I found that the love of God was so much more real, and it gave me strength.

Barbara

AGE 15

ANGER

2:15-16 Jesus was obviously angry at the merchants who exploited those who had come to God's house to worship. There is a difference between uncontrolled rage and righteous indignation—yet both are called anger. We must be very careful how we use the powerful emotion of anger. It is right to be angry about injustice and sin; it is wrong to be angry over small, personal offenses.

[6]Six stone waterpots were standing there; they were used for Jewish ceremonial purposes and held perhaps twenty to thirty gallons each. [7,8]Then Jesus told the servants to fill them to the brim with water. When this was done he said, "Dip some out and take it to the master of ceremonies."

[9]When the master of ceremonies tasted the water that was now wine, not knowing where it had come from (though, of course, the servants did), he called the bridegroom over.

[10]"This is wonderful stuff!" he said. "You're different from most. Usually a host uses the best wine first, and afterwards, when everyone is full and doesn't care, then he brings out the less expensive brands. But you have kept the best for the last!"

[11]This miracle at Cana in Galilee was Jesus' first public demonstration of his heaven-sent power. And his disciples believed that he really was the Messiah.

[12]After the wedding he left for Capernaum for a few days with his mother, brothers, and disciples.

[13]Then it was time for the annual Jewish Passover celebration, and Jesus went to Jerusalem.

[14]In the Temple area he saw merchants selling cattle, sheep, and doves for sacrifices, and moneychangers behind their counters. [15]Jesus made a whip from some ropes and chased them all out, and drove out the sheep and oxen, scattering the moneychangers' coins over the floor and turning over their tables! [16]Then, going over to the men selling doves, he told them, "Get these things out of here. Don't turn my Father's House into a market!"

[17]Then his disciples remembered this prophecy from the Scriptures: "Concern for God's House will be my undoing."

[18]"What right have you to order them out?" the Jewish leaders demanded. "If you have this authority from God, show us a miracle to prove it."

[19]"All right," Jesus replied, "this is the miracle I will do for you: Destroy this sanctuary and in three days I will raise it up!"

[20]"What!" they exclaimed. "It took forty-six years to build this Temple, and you can do it in three days?" [21]But by "this sanctuary" he meant his body. [22]After he came back to life again, the disciples remembered his saying this and realized that what he had quoted from the Scriptures really did refer to him, and had all come true!

[23]Because of the miracles he did in Jerusalem at the Passover celebration, many people were convinced that he was indeed the Messiah. [24,25]But Jesus didn't trust them, for he knew mankind to the core. No one needed to tell him how changeable human nature is!

For GOD loved THE WORLD so much that He gave HIS ONLY SON so that Any One who believes in HIM shall not Perish BUT HAVE ETERNAL ETERNAL ETERNAL LIFE LIFE

NEW LIFE

3:6 Jesus says that the Holy Spirit gives new life from heaven. Who is the Holy Spirit? God is three persons in one—the Father, the Son, and the Holy Spirit. God became a man in Jesus so that Jesus could die for our sins. Jesus rose from the dead to offer salvation to all people through spiritual renewal and rebirth. When Jesus ascended into heaven, his physical presence left the earth, but he promised to send the Holy Spirit so that his spiritual presence would still be among mankind (see Luke 24:49). In Old Testament days, the Holy Spirit empowered specific individuals for specific purposes. Then came Pentecost (Acts 2), and now all believers have the power of the Holy Spirit available to them. For more on the Holy Spirit, read 14:16-28; Romans 8:9; 1 Corinthians 12:13; and 2 Corinthians 1:22.

CHAPTER 3 JESUS TALKS WITH NICODEMUS.

After dark one night a Jewish religious leader named Nicodemus, a member of the sect of the Pharisees, came for an interview with Jesus. "Sir," he said, "we all know that God has sent you to teach us. Your miracles are proof enough of this."

³Jesus replied, "With all the earnestness I possess I tell you this: Unless you are born again, you can never get into the Kingdom of God."

⁴"Born again!" exclaimed Nicodemus. "What do you mean? How can an old man go back into his mother's womb and be born again?"

⁵Jesus replied, "What I am telling you so earnestly is this: Unless one is born of water and the Spirit, he cannot enter the Kingdom of God. ⁶Men can only reproduce human life, but the Holy Spirit gives new life from heaven; ⁷so don't be surprised at my statement that you must be born again! ⁸Just as you can hear the wind but can't tell where it comes from or where it will go next, so it is with the Spirit. We do not know on whom he will next bestow this life from heaven."

⁹"What do you mean?" Nicodemus asked.

¹⁰,¹¹Jesus replied, "You, a respected Jewish teacher, and yet you don't understand these things? I am telling you what I know and have seen—and yet you won't believe me. ¹²But if you don't even believe me when I tell you about such things as these that happen here among men, how can you possibly believe if I tell you what is going on in heaven? ¹³For only I, the Messiah, have come to earth and will return to heaven again. ¹⁴And as Moses in the wilderness lifted up the bronze image of a serpent on a pole, even so I must be lifted up upon a pole, ¹⁵so that anyone who believes in me will have eternal life. ¹⁶For God loved the world so much that he gave his only Son so that anyone who believes in him shall not perish but have eternal life. ¹⁷God did not send his Son into the world to condemn it, but to save it.

¹⁸"There is no eternal doom awaiting those who trust him to save them. But those who don't trust him have already been tried and condemned for not believing in the only Son of God. ¹⁹Their sentence is based on this fact: that the Light from heaven came into the world, but they loved the darkness more than the Light, for their deeds were evil. ²⁰They hated the heavenly Light because they wanted to sin in the darkness. They stayed away from that Light for fear their sins would be exposed and they would be punished.

JOHN THE BAPTIST

In almost any crowd, John the Baptist would be called unique. He wore odd clothes, ate strange food, and preached an unusual message. He would not have agreed with our habit of evaluating people by how they dress—or by how they act. He would have insisted that we listen to what he had to say.

John really wasn't interested in being unique. What he wanted to do more than anything was to obey God. And he wasn't afraid to ask others to do the same. John realized that he had a special role to play in the world. His job was to tell the world that the Savior was about to arrive. John was totally committed to his purpose.

This wild-looking man stood face-to-face with people and told them to repent. He told them the best way to get ready for the Savior was to be deeply sorry for their sins. Although John was preparing people to receive Jesus when he physically came to the world, John's message still applies today when we realize that Jesus wants to come into our life, too. We can't receive the Savior until we know we need him. We won't know we need him until we realize we are sinners.

Today, we still need to hear John's favorite word—repent! If you don't know what it means, you may not have done it. Repenting means that you are not only deeply sorry for your sinfulness but are also serious in wanting God's help to live his way. Until you have repented, you won't experience God's forgiveness or the strength he offers to live a life of obedience. Repentance may be the most important thing you think about today.

LESSONS: God does not guarantee an easy or safe life to those who serve him

Doing what God desires is the greatest possible life-investment

Standing for the truth is more important than life itself

KEY VERSE: "'Truly, of all men ever born, none shines more brightly than John the Baptist. And yet, even the lesser lights in the Kingdom of Heaven will be greater than he is!'" (Matthew 11:11).

John's story is told in all four Gospels. His coming was predicted in Isaiah 40:3 and Malachi 4:5ff; and he is mentioned in Acts 1:5,22; 10:37; 11:16; 13:24-25; 18:25; 19:3-4.

UPS:
- The God-appointed messenger to announce the arrival of Jesus
- A preacher whose theme was repentance
- A fearless confronter
- Known for his remarkable life-style
- Uncompromising

DOWN:
- Momentary doubt about Jesus' identity

STATS:
- Where: Judea
- Occupation: Prophet
- Relatives: Father: Zacharias. Mother: Elizabeth. Distant cousin: Jesus.
- Contemporaries: Herod, Herodias

²¹But those doing right come gladly to the Light to let everyone see that they are doing what God wants them to."

²²Afterwards Jesus and his disciples left Jerusalem and stayed for a while in Judea and baptized there.

PREJUDICE

It may be the nineties, but some people's attitudes show they are still living in the past.

Here's the story: Randy C. and Darnell T. are close friends. Randy is white; Darnell is black. When Darnell's parents went cross-country to a funeral, Darnell stayed for the week with Randy. No big deal, right?

Wrong. The first afternoon, Randy took Darnell to the neighborhood pool. Everyone glared at them, most started whispering, and some actually got out of the pool and left.

The second night of Darnell's stay, someone shattered the rear window in Mr. C.'s car. The third night, someone (or some ones) scrawled racial slurs on the C.'s garage door.

When school started, Randy's white friends avoided him. Randy finally confronted Keith, asked what his problem was, and got this reply: "Hey, look, Randy—you changed, not us. You're the one who's trying to be Mr. Civil Rights, OK?"

Randy was (and is) shocked. Even at church, people are treating him weirdly. Says Randy, "What is going on?! I invited a friend to stay with me while his parents were gone. Would someone please tell me what in the world is wrong with that? So what if his skin is a different color? I don't understand why so many people are so full of hate."

Which person are you most like? Randy, Darnell, or Keith? Consider how Jesus treated people who were different from himself. (See John 4:1-42.)

²³,²⁴At this time John the Baptist was not yet in prison. He was baptizing at Aenon, near Salim, because there was plenty of water there. ²⁵One day someone began an argument with John's disciples, telling them that Jesus' baptism was best. ²⁶So they came to John and said, "Master, the man you met on the other side of the Jordan River—the one you said was the Messiah—he is baptizing too, and everybody is going over there instead of coming here to us."

²⁷John replied, "God in heaven appoints each man's work. ²⁸My work is to prepare the way for that man so that everyone will go to him. You yourselves know how plainly I told you that I am not the Messiah. I am here to prepare the way for him—that is all. ²⁹The crowds will naturally go to the main attraction—the bride will go where the bridegroom is! A bridegroom's friends rejoice with him. I am the Bridegroom's friend, and I am filled with joy at his success. ³⁰He must become greater and greater, and I must become less and less.

³¹"He has come from heaven and is greater than anyone else. I am of the earth, and my understanding is limited to the things of earth. ³²He tells what he has seen and heard, but how few believe what he tells them! ³³,³⁴Those who believe him discover that God is a fountain of truth. For this one—sent by

God—speaks God's words, for God's Spirit is upon him without measure or limit. ³⁵The Father loves this man because he is his Son, and God has given him everything there is. ³⁶And all who trust him—God's Son—to save them have eternal life; those who don't believe and obey him shall never see heaven, but the wrath of God remains upon them."

CHAPTER 4 JESUS AND THE WOMAN AT A WELL.

When the Lord knew that the Pharisees had heard about the greater crowds coming to him than to John to be baptized and to become his disciples—(though Jesus himself didn't baptize them, but his disciples did)— ³he left Judea and returned to the province of Galilee.

⁴He had to go through Samaria on the way, ⁵,⁶and around noon as he approached the village of Sychar, he came to Jacob's Well, located on the parcel of ground Jacob gave to his son Joseph. Jesus was tired from the long walk in the hot sun and sat wearily beside the well.

⁷Soon a Samaritan woman came to draw water, and Jesus asked her for a drink. ⁸He was alone at the time as his disciples had gone into the village to buy some food. ⁹The woman was surprised that a Jew would ask a "despised Samaritan" for anything—usually they wouldn't even speak to them!—and she remarked about this to Jesus.

¹⁰He replied, "If you only knew what a wonderful gift God has for you, and who I am, you would ask me for some *living* water!"

¹¹"But you don't have a rope or a bucket," she said, "and this is a very deep well! Where would you get this living water? ¹²And besides, are you greater than our ancestor Jacob? How can you offer better water than this which he and his sons and cattle enjoyed?"

¹³Jesus replied that people soon became thirsty again after drinking this water. ¹⁴"But the water I give them," he said, "becomes a perpetual spring within them, watering them forever with eternal life."

¹⁵"Please, sir," the woman said, "give me some of that water! Then I'll never be thirsty again and won't have to make this long trip out here every day."

¹⁶"Go and get your husband," Jesus told her.

¹⁷,¹⁸"But I'm not married," the woman replied.

NO LESS

4:7-9 This woman (1) was a Samaritan, a member of the hated mixed race; (2) had a bad reputation; and (3) was in a public place. No respectable Jewish man would talk to a woman under such circumstances. But Jesus did. The gospel is for every person, no matter what his or her race, social position, or past sins. We must be prepared to share this gospel at any time in any place. Jesus crossed all barriers to share the Good News; we who follow him must do no less.

"All too true!" Jesus said. "For you have had five husbands, and you aren't even married to the man you're living with now."

[19]"Sir," the woman said, "you must be a prophet. [20]But say, tell me, why is it that you Jews insist that Jerusalem is the only place of worship, while we Samaritans claim it is here [at Mount Gerizim], where our ancestors worshiped?"

[21-24]Jesus replied, "The time is coming, ma'am, when we will no longer be concerned about whether to worship the Father here or in Jerusalem. For it's not *where* we worship that counts, but *how* we worship—is our worship spiritual and real? Do we have the Holy Spirit's help? For God is Spirit, and we must have his help to worship as we should. The Father wants this kind of worship from us. But you Samaritans know so little about him, worshiping blindly, while we Jews know all about him, for salvation comes to the world through the Jews."

[25]The woman said, "Well, at least I know that the Messiah will come—the one they call Christ—and when he does, he will explain everything to us."

[26]Then Jesus told her, "I am the Messiah!"

[27]Just then his disciples arrived. They were surprised to find him talking to a woman, but none of them asked him why, or what they had been discussing.

[28,29]Then the woman left her waterpot beside the well and went back to the village and told everyone, "Come and meet a man who told me everything I ever did! Can this be the Messiah?" [30]So the people came streaming from the village to see him.

[31]Meanwhile, the disciples were urging Jesus to eat. [32]"No," he said, "I have some food you don't know about."

[33]"Who brought it to him?" the disciples asked each other.

[34]Then Jesus explained: "My nourishment comes from doing the will of God who sent me, and from finishing his work. [35]Do you think the work of harvesting will not begin until the summer ends four months from now? Look around you! Vast fields of human souls are ripening all around us, and are ready now for reaping. [36]The reapers will be paid good wages and will be gathering eternal souls into the granaries of heaven! What joys await the sower and the reaper, both together! [37]For it is true that one sows and someone else reaps. [38]I sent you to reap where you didn't sow; others did the work, and you received the harvest."

[39]Many from the Samaritan village believed he was the Messiah because of the woman's report: "He told me everything I ever did!" [40,41]When they came out to see him at the well, they begged him to stay at their village; and he did, for two days, long enough for many of them to believe in him after hearing him. [42]Then they said to the woman, "Now we believe because we have heard him ourselves, not just because of what you told us. He is indeed the Savior of the world."

[43,44]At the end of the two days' stay he went on into Galilee. Jesus used to say, "A prophet is honored everywhere except in his own country!" [45]But the Galileans welcomed him with open arms, for they had been in Jerusalem at the Passover celebration and had seen some of his miracles.

[46,47]In the course of his journey through Galilee he arrived at the town of Cana, where he had turned the water into wine. While he was there, a man in the city of Capernaum, a government official, whose son was very sick, heard that Jesus had come from Judea and was traveling in Galilee. This man went over to Cana, found Jesus, and begged him to come to Capernaum with him and heal his son, who was now at death's door.

[48]Jesus asked, "Won't any of you believe in me unless I do more and more miracles?"

[49]The official pled, "Sir, please come now before my child dies."

[50]Then Jesus told him, "Go back home. Your son is healed!" And the man believed Jesus and started home. [51]While he was on his way, some of his servants met him with the news that all was well—his son had recovered. [52]He asked them when the lad had begun to feel better, and they replied, "Yesterday afternoon at about one o'clock his fever suddenly disappeared!" [53]Then the father realized it was the same moment that Jesus had told him, "Your son is healed." And the officer and his entire household believed that Jesus was the Messiah.

[54]This was Jesus' second miracle in Galilee after coming from Judea.

READY

4:35 Sometimes Christians excuse themselves from witnessing by saying their family or friends aren't ready to believe. Jesus, however, makes it clear that around us a continual harvest waits to be reaped. Don't let Jesus find you making excuses. Look around. You will find people ready to hear God's Word.

BELIEVE IT!

4:50 This government official not only believed that Jesus could heal, he also obeyed Jesus by returning home and thus demonstrating his faith. It isn't enough for us to say we believe that Jesus can take care of our problems. We need to act as if he can. When you pray about a need or problem, live as though you believe Jesus can do what he says.

CHAPTER 5 JESUS HEALS A SICK MAN. Afterwards Jesus returned to Jerusalem for one of the Jewish religious holidays. [2]Inside the city, near the Sheep Gate, was Bethesda Pool, with five covered platforms or porches surrounding it. [3]Crowds of sick folks—lame, blind, or with paralyzed limbs—lay on the platforms (waiting for a certain movement of the water, [4]for an angel of the Lord came from time to time and disturbed the water, and the first person to step down into it afterwards was healed).

[5]One of the men lying there had been sick for thirty-eight years. [6]When Jesus saw him and knew how long he had been ill, he asked him, "Would you like to get well?"

[7]"I can't," the sick man said, "for I have no one to help me into the pool at the movement of the water. While I am trying to get there, someone else always gets in ahead of me."

[8]Jesus told him, "Stand up, roll up your sleeping mat and go on home!"

[9]Instantly, the man was healed! He rolled up the mat and began walking!

But it was on the Sabbath when this miracle was done. [10]So the Jewish leaders objected. They said to the man who was cured, "You can't work on the Sabbath! It's illegal to carry that sleeping mat!"

[11]"The man who healed me told me to," was his reply.

[12]"Who said such a thing as that?" they demanded.

[13]The man didn't know, and Jesus had disappeared into the crowd. [14]But afterwards Jesus found him in the Temple and told him, "Now you are well; don't sin as you did before, or something even worse may happen to you."

[15]Then the man went to find the Jewish leaders and told them it was Jesus who had healed him.

[16]So they began harassing Jesus as a Sabbath breaker.

[17]But Jesus replied, "My Father constantly does good, and I'm following his example."

[18]Then the Jewish leaders were all the more eager to kill him because in addition to disobeying their Sabbath laws, he had spoken of God as his Father, thereby making himself equal with God.

[19]Jesus replied, "The Son can do nothing by himself. He does only what he sees the Father doing, and in the same way. [20]For the Father loves the Son, and tells him everything he is doing; and the Son will do far more awesome miracles than this man's healing. [21]He will even raise from the dead anyone he wants to, just as the Father does. [22]And the Father leaves all judgment of sin to his

Son, [23]so that everyone will honor the Son, just as they honor the Father. But if you refuse to honor God's Son, whom he sent to you, then you are certainly not honoring the Father.

[24]"I say emphatically that anyone who listens to my message and believes in God who sent me has eternal life, and will never be damned for his sins, but has already passed out of death into life.

[25]"And I solemnly declare that the time is coming, in fact, it is here, when the dead shall hear my voice—the voice of the Son of God—and those who listen shall live. [26]The Father has life in himself, and has granted his Son to have life in himself, [27]and to judge the sins of all mankind because he is the Son of Man. [28]Don't be so surprised! Indeed the time is coming when all the dead in their graves shall hear the voice of God's Son, [29]and shall rise again—those who have done good, to eternal life; and those who have continued in evil, to judgment.

[30]"But I pass no judgment without consulting the Father. I judge as I am told. And my judgment is absolutely fair and just, for it is according to the will of God who sent me and is not merely my own.

[31]"When I make claims about myself they aren't believed, [32,33]but someone else, yes, John the Baptist, is making these claims for me too. You have gone out to listen to his preaching, and I can assure you that all he says about me is true! [34]But the truest witness I have is not from a man, though I have reminded you about John's witness so that you will believe in me and be saved. [35]John shone brightly for a while, and you benefited and rejoiced, [36]but I have a greater witness than John. I refer to the miracles I do; these have been assigned me by the Father, and they prove that the Father has sent me. [37]And the Father himself has also testified about me, though not appearing to you personally, or speaking to you directly. [38]But you are not listening to him, for you refuse to believe me—the one sent to you with God's message.

[39]"You search the Scriptures, for you believe they give you eternal life. And the Scriptures point to me! [40]Yet you won't come to me so that I can give you this life eternal!

[41,42]"Your approval or disapproval means nothing to me, for as I know so well, you don't have God's love within you. [43]I know, because I have come to you representing my Father and you refuse to welcome me, though you readily enough receive those who aren't sent from him, but represent only themselves! [44]No wonder you can't believe! For

TRAPPED

5:6 Jesus appropriately asked, "Would you like to get well?" After 38 years, this man's problem had become a way of life. No one had ever helped him. He had no hope of ever being healed and no desire to help himself. No matter how trapped you feel in your infirmities, God can minister to your deepest needs. Don't let a problem or hardship cause you to lose hope. God may have special work for you to do in spite of your condition, or even because of it. Many have ministered effectively to hurting people because they have triumphed, with God's help, over their own hurts.

CHOICES

5:19-23 Because of his unity with God, Jesus lived as God wanted him to live. Because of our identification with Jesus, we must live as he wants us to live. The questions "What would Jesus do?" and "What would Jesus have me do?" may help us make the right choices.

you gladly honor each other, but you don't care about the honor that comes from the only God!

[45]"Yet it is not I who will accuse you of this to the Father—Moses will! Moses, on whose laws you set your hopes of heaven. [46]For you have refused to believe Moses. He wrote about me, but you refuse to believe him, so you refuse to believe in me. [47]And since you don't believe what he wrote, no wonder you don't believe me either."

CHAPTER 6 JESUS FEEDS 5,000 PEOPLE.

After this, Jesus crossed over the Sea of Galilee, also known as the Sea of Tiberias. [2-5]And a huge crowd, many of them pilgrims on their way to Jerusalem for the annual Passover celebration, were following him wherever he went, to watch him heal the sick. So when Jesus went up into the hills and sat down with his disciples around him, he soon saw a great multitude of people climbing the hill, looking for him.

Turning to Philip he asked, "Philip, where can we buy bread to feed all these people?" [6](He was testing Philip, for he already knew what he was going to do.)

[7]Philip replied, "It would take a fortune to begin to do it!"

[8,9]Then Andrew, Simon Peter's brother, spoke up. "There's a youngster here with five barley loaves and a couple of fish! But what good is that with all this mob?"

[10]"Tell everyone to sit down," Jesus ordered. And all of them—the approximate count of the men only was five thousand—sat down on the grassy slopes. [11]Then Jesus took the loaves and gave thanks to God and passed them out to the people. Afterwards he did the same with the fish. And everyone ate until full!

[12]"Now gather the scraps," Jesus told his disciples, "so that nothing is wasted." [13]And twelve baskets were filled with the leftovers!

[14]When the people realized what a great miracle had happened, they exclaimed, "Surely, he is the Prophet we have been expecting!"

[15]Jesus saw that they were ready to take him by force and make him their king, so he went higher into the mountains alone.

[16]That evening his disciples went down to the shore to wait for him. [17]But as darkness fell and Jesus still hadn't come back, they got into the boat and headed out across the lake toward Capernaum. [18,19]But soon a gale swept down upon them as they rowed, and the sea grew very rough. They were three or four miles out when suddenly they saw Jesus walking toward the boat! They were terrified, [20]but he called out to them and told them not to be afraid. [21]Then they were willing to let him in, and immediately the boat was where they were going!

[22,23]The next morning, back across the lake, crowds began gathering on the shore [waiting to see Jesus]. For they knew that he and his disciples had come over together and that the disciples had gone off in their boat, leaving him behind. Several small boats from Tiberias were nearby, [24]so when the people saw that Jesus wasn't there, nor his disciples, they got into the boats and went across to Capernaum to look for him.

[25]When they arrived and found him, they said, "Sir, how did you get here?" [26]Jesus replied, "The truth of the matter is that you want to be with me because I fed you, not because you believe in me. [27]But you shouldn't be so concerned about perishable things like food. No, spend your energy seeking the eternal life that I, the Messiah, can give you. For God the Father has sent me for this very purpose."

[28]They replied, "What should we do to satisfy God?"

[29]Jesus told them, "This is the will of God, that you believe in the one he has sent."

[30,31]They replied, "You must show us more miracles if you want us to believe you are the Messiah. Give us free bread every day, like our fathers had while they journeyed through the wilderness! As the Scriptures say, 'Moses gave them bread from heaven.'"

[32]Jesus said, "Moses didn't give it to them. My Father did. And now he offers you true Bread from heaven. [33]The true Bread is a Person—the one sent by God from heaven, and he gives life to the world."

[34]"Sir," they said, "give us that bread every day of our lives!"

[35]Jesus replied, "I am the Bread of Life. No one coming to me will ever be hungry again. Those believing in me will never thirst. [36]But the trouble is, as I have told you before, you haven't believed even though you have seen me. [37]But some will come to me—those the Father has given me—and I will never, never reject them. [38]For I have come here from heaven to do the will of God who sent me, not to have my own way.

ALL

6:8-9 The disciples are contrasted with the youngster who brought what he had. They certainly had more resources than he did, but they knew they didn't have enough, so they didn't give anything at all. The youngster gave what little he had and it made all the difference. If we offer nothing to God, he will have nothing to use. But he can take what little we have and turn it into something great.

THE WAY

6:26 Jesus criticized the people who followed him only for the physical and temporal benefits, not because they were spiritually hungry. We should follow Christ because we need the truth. Many people use religion to gain prestige, comfort, friends, or votes. But those are self-centered motives. True believers follow Jesus simply because they know his way is the way to live.

³⁹And this is the will of God, that I should not lose even one of all those he has given me, but that I should raise them to eternal life at the Last Day. ⁴⁰For it is my Father's will that everyone who sees his Son and believes on him should have eternal life—that I should raise him at the Last Day."

⁴¹Then the Jews began to murmur against him because he claimed to be the Bread from heaven.

⁴²"What?" they exclaimed. "Why, he is merely Jesus the son of Joseph, whose father and mother we know. What is this he is saying, that he came down from heaven?"

⁴³But Jesus replied, "Don't murmur among yourselves about my saying that. ⁴⁴For no one can come to me unless the Father who sent me draws him to me, and at the Last Day I will cause all such to rise again from the dead. ⁴⁵As it is written in the Scriptures, 'They shall all be taught of God.' Those the Father speaks to, who learn the truth from him, will be attracted to me. ⁴⁶(Not that anyone actually sees the Father, for only I have seen him.)

⁴⁷"How earnestly I tell you this—anyone who believes in me already has eternal life! ⁴⁸⁻⁵¹Yes, I am the Bread of Life! When your fathers in the wilderness ate bread from the skies, they all died. But the Bread from heaven gives eternal life to everyone who eats it. I am that Living Bread that came down out of heaven. Anyone eating this Bread shall live forever; this Bread is my flesh given to redeem humanity."

⁵²Then the Jews began arguing with each other about what he meant. "How can this man give us his flesh to eat?" they asked.

⁵³So Jesus said it again, "With all the earnestness I possess I tell you this: Unless you eat the flesh of the Messiah and drink his blood, you cannot have eternal life within you. ⁵⁴But anyone who does eat my flesh and drink my blood has eternal life, and I will raise him at the Last Day. ⁵⁵For my flesh is the true food, and my blood is the true drink. ⁵⁶Everyone who eats my flesh and drinks my blood is in me, and I in him. ⁵⁷I live by the power of the living Father who sent me, and in the same way those who partake of me shall live because of me! ⁵⁸I am the true Bread from heaven; and anyone who eats this Bread shall live forever, and not die as your fathers did—though they ate bread from heaven." ⁵⁹(He preached this sermon in the synagogue in Capernaum.)

⁶⁰Even his disciples said, "This is very hard to understand. Who can tell what he means?"

⁶¹Jesus knew within himself that his disciples were complaining and said to them, "Does *this* offend you? ⁶²Then what will you think if you see me, the Messiah, return to heaven again? ⁶³Only the Holy Spirit gives eternal life. Those born only once, with physical birth, will never receive this gift. But now I have told you how to get this true spiritual life. ⁶⁴But some of you don't believe me." (For Jesus knew from the beginning who didn't believe and knew the one who would betray him.)

⁶⁵And he remarked, "That is what I meant when I said that no one can come to me unless the Father attracts him to me."

⁶⁶At this point many of his disciples turned away and deserted him.

⁶⁷Then Jesus turned to the Twelve and asked, "Are you going too?"

⁶⁸Simon Peter replied, "Master, to whom shall we go? You alone have the words that give eternal life, ⁶⁹and we believe them and know you are the holy Son of God."

⁷⁰Then Jesus said, "I chose the twelve of you, and one is a devil." ⁷¹He was speaking of Judas, son of Simon Iscariot, one of the Twelve, who would betray him.

CHAPTER 7 JESUS' BROTHERS MAKE FUN OF HIM.

After this, Jesus went to Galilee, going from village to village, for he wanted to stay out of Judea where the Jewish leaders were plotting his death. ²But soon it was time for the Tabernacle Ceremonies, one of the annual Jewish holidays, ³and Jesus' brothers urged him to go to Judea for the celebration.

"Go where more people can see your miracles!" they scoffed. ⁴"You can't be famous when you hide like this! If you're so great, prove it to the world!" ⁵For even his brothers didn't believe in him.

⁶Jesus replied, "It is not the right time for me to go now. But you can go anytime and it will make no difference, ⁷for the world can't hate you; but it does hate me, because I accuse it of sin and evil. ⁸You go on, and I'll come later when it is the right time." ⁹So he remained in Galilee.

¹⁰But after his brothers had left for the celebration, then he went too, though secretly, staying out of the public eye. ¹¹The Jewish leaders tried to find him at the celebration and kept asking if anyone had seen him. ¹²There was a lot of discussion about him among the crowds. Some said, "He's a

wonderful man," while others said, "No, he's duping the public." [13]But no one had the courage to speak out for him in public for fear of reprisals from the Jewish leaders.

[14]Then, midway through the festival, Jesus went up to the Temple and preached openly. [15]The Jewish leaders were surprised when they heard him. "How can he know so much when he's never been to our schools?" they asked.

[16]So Jesus told them, "I'm not teaching you my own thoughts, but those of God who sent me. [17]If any of you really determines to do God's will, then you will certainly know whether my teaching is from God or is merely my own. [18]Anyone presenting his own ideas is looking for praise for himself, but anyone seeking to honor the one who sent him is a good and true person. [19]None of *you* obeys the laws of Moses! So why pick on *me* for breaking them? Why kill *me* for this?"

[20]The crowd replied, "You're out of your mind! Who's trying to kill you?"

[21-23]Jesus replied, "I worked on the Sabbath by healing a man, and you were surprised. But you work on the Sabbath, too, whenever you obey Moses' law of circumcision (actually, however, this tradition of circumcision is older than the Mosaic law); for if the correct time for circumcising your children falls on the Sabbath, you go ahead and do it, as you should. So why should I be condemned for making a man completely well on the Sabbath? [24]Think this through and you will see that I am right."

[25]Some of the people who lived there in Jerusalem said among themselves, "Isn't this the man they are trying to kill? [26]But here he is preaching in public, and they say nothing to him. Can it be that our leaders have learned, after all, that he really is the Messiah? [27]But how could he be? For we know where this man was born; when Christ comes, he will just appear and no one will know where he comes from."

[28]So Jesus, in a sermon in the Temple, called out, "Yes, you know me and where I was born and raised, but I am the representative of one you don't know, and he is Truth. [29]I know him because I was with him, and he sent me to you."

[30]Then the Jewish leaders sought to arrest him; but no hand was laid on him, for God's time had not yet come.

[31]Many among the crowds at the Temple believed on him. "After all," they said, "what miracles do you expect the Messiah to do that this man hasn't done?"

[32]When the Pharisees heard that the crowds were in this mood, they and the chief priests sent officers to arrest Jesus. [33]But Jesus told them, "[Not yet!] I am to be here a little longer. Then I shall return to the one who sent me. [34]You will search for me but not find me.

And you won't be able to come where I am!"

[35]The Jewish leaders were puzzled by this statement. "Where is he planning to go?" they asked. "Maybe he is thinking of leaving the country and going as a missionary among the Jews in other lands, or maybe even to the Gentiles! [36]What does he mean about our looking for him and not being able to find him, and, 'You won't be able to come where I am'?"

[37]On the last day, the climax of the holidays, Jesus shouted to the crowds, "If anyone is thirsty, let him come to me and drink. [38]For the Scriptures declare that rivers of living water shall flow from the inmost being of anyone who believes in me." [39](He was speaking of the Holy Spirit, who would be given to everyone believing in him; but the Spirit had not yet been given, because Jesus had not yet returned to his glory in heaven.)

[40]When the crowds heard him say this, some of them declared, "This man surely is the prophet who will come just before the Messiah." [41,42]Others said, "He *is* the Messiah." Still others, "But he *can't* be! Will the Messiah come from *Galilee?* For the Scriptures clearly state that the Messiah will be born of the royal line of David, in *Bethlehem,* the village where David was born." [43]So the crowd was divided about him. [44]And some wanted him arrested, but no one touched him.

[45]The Temple police who had been sent to arrest him returned to the chief priests and Pharisees. "Why didn't you bring him in?" they demanded.

[46]"He says such wonderful things!" they mumbled. "We've never heard anything like it."

[47]"So you also have been led astray?" the Pharisees mocked. [48]"Is there a single one of us Jewish rulers or Pharisees who believes he is the Messiah? [49]These stupid crowds do, yes; but what do they know about it? A curse upon them anyway!"

[50]Then Nicodemus spoke up. (Remember him? He was the Jewish leader who came secretly to interview Jesus.) [51]"Is it legal to convict a man before he is even tried?" he asked.

[52]They replied, "Are you a wretched Galilean too? Search the Scriptures and see for yourself—no prophets will come from Galilee!"

[53] Then the meeting broke up and everybody went home.

DON'T JUMP

7:40-43 The crowd was asking questions about Jesus. As a result, some believed, others were hostile, and others disqualified Jesus as the Messiah because he was from Nazareth, not Bethlehem (Micah 5:2). But he *was* born in Bethlehem (Luke 2:1-7), although he grew up in Nazareth. If they had looked more carefully, they would not have jumped to the wrong conclusions. When you search for God's truth, make sure you look carefully and thoughtfully at the Bible with an open heart and mind. Don't jump to conclusions before knowing more of what the Bible says.

CHAPTER 8   JESUS FORGIVES A GUILTY WOMAN.

Jesus returned to the Mount of Olives, ²but early the next morning he was back again at the Temple. A crowd soon gathered, and he sat down and talked to them. ³As he was speaking, the Jewish leaders and Pharisees brought a woman caught in adultery and placed her out in front of the staring crowd.

⁴"Teacher," they said to Jesus, "this woman was caught in the very act of adultery. ⁵Moses' law says to kill her. What about it?"

⁶They were trying to trap him into saying something they could use against him, but Jesus stooped down and wrote in the dust with his finger. ⁷They kept demanding an answer, so he stood up again and said, "All right, hurl the stones at her until she dies. But only he who never sinned may throw the first!"

⁸Then he stooped down again and wrote some more in the dust. ⁹And the Jewish leaders slipped away one by one, beginning with the eldest, until only Jesus was left in front of the crowd with the woman.

¹⁰Then Jesus stood up again and said to her, "Where are your accusers? Didn't even one of them condemn you?"

¹¹"No, sir," she said.

And Jesus said, "Neither do I. Go and sin no more."

¹²Later, in one of his talks, Jesus said to the people, "I am the Light of the world. So if you follow me, you won't be stumbling through the darkness, for living light will flood your path."

¹³The Pharisees replied, "You are boasting—and lying!"

¹⁴Jesus told them, "These claims are true even though I make them concerning myself. For I know where I came from and where I am going, but you don't know this about me. ¹⁵You pass judgment on me without knowing the facts. I am not judging you now; ¹⁶but if I were, it would be an absolutely correct judgment in every respect, for I have with me the Father who sent me. ¹⁷Your laws say that if two men agree on something that has happened, their witness is accepted as fact. ¹⁸Well, I am one witness, and my Father who sent me is the other."

¹⁹"Where is your father?" they asked.

Jesus answered, "You don't know who I am, so you don't know who my Father is. If you knew me, then you would know him too."

²⁰Jesus made these statements while in the section of the Temple known as the Treasury. But he was not arrested, for his time had not yet run out.

²¹Later he said to them again, "I am going away; and you will search for me, and die in your sins. And you cannot come where I am going."

²²The Jews asked, "Is he planning suicide? What does he mean, 'You cannot come where I am going'?"

²³Then he said to them, "You are from below; I am from above. You are of this world; I am not. ²⁴That is why I said that you will die in your sins; for unless you believe that I am the Messiah, the Son of God, you will die in your sins."

²⁵"Tell us who you are," they demanded.

He replied, "I am the one I have always claimed to be. ²⁶I could condemn you for much and teach you much, but I won't, for I say only what I am told to by the one who sent me; and he is Truth." ²⁷But they still didn't understand that he was talking to them about God.

²⁸So Jesus said, "When you have killed the Messiah, then you will realize that I am he and that I have not been telling you my own ideas, but have spoken what the Father taught me. ²⁹And he who sent me is with me—he has not deserted me—for I always do those things that are pleasing to him."

³⁰,³¹Then many of the Jewish leaders who heard him say these things began believing him to be the Messiah.

Jesus said to them, "You are truly my disciples if you live as I tell you to, ³²and you will know the truth, and the truth will set you free."

³³"But we are descendants of Abraham," they said, "and have never been slaves to any man on earth! What do you mean, 'set free'?"

³⁴Jesus replied, "You are slaves of sin, every one of you. ³⁵And slaves don't have rights, but the Son has every right there is! ³⁶So if the Son sets you free, you will indeed be free—³⁷(Yes, I realize that you are descendants of Abraham!) And yet some of you are trying to kill me because my message does not find a home within your hearts. ³⁸I am telling you what I saw when I was with my Father. But you are following the advice of *your* father."

³⁹"Our father is Abraham," they declared.

"No!" Jesus replied, "for if he were, you would follow his good example. ⁴⁰But instead you are trying to kill me—and all because I told you the truth I heard from God. Abraham wouldn't do a thing like that! ⁴¹No, you are obeying your *real* father when you act that way."

They replied, "We were not born out of wedlock—our true Father is God himself."

STONED

8:9 When Jesus said that only those who had not sinned should throw the first stone, the leaders slipped away, the eldest to the youngest. Evidently the older men were more aware of their sins than the younger. Age and experience temper youthful idealism and self-righteousness. Whatever your age, take an honest look at your life, recognize your sinful nature, and spend more time looking for ways to help others rather than hurt them.

FREE

8:34-35 Sin has a way of enslaving us, controlling us, dominating us, and dictating our actions. Jesus can free you from this slavery that keeps you from becoming the person that God created you to be. If sin is restraining, mastering, or enslaving you, Jesus can break its power over your life.

[42]Jesus told them, "If that were so, then you would love me, for I have come to you from God. I am not here on my own, but he sent me. [43]Why can't you understand what I am saying? It is because you are prevented from doing so! [44]For you are the children of your father the devil and you love to do the evil things he does. He was a murderer from the beginning and a hater of truth—there is not an iota of truth in him. When he lies, it is perfectly normal; for he is the father of liars. [45]And so when I tell the truth, you just naturally don't believe it!

[46]"Which of you can truthfully accuse me of one single sin? [No one!] And since I am telling you the truth, why don't you believe me? [47]Anyone whose Father is God listens gladly to the words of God. Since you don't, it proves you aren't his children."

[48]"You Samaritan! Foreigner! Devil!" the Jewish leaders snarled. "Didn't we say all along you were possessed by a demon?"

[49]"No," Jesus said, "I have no demon in me. For I honor my Father—and you dishonor me. [50]And though I have no wish to make myself great, God wants this for me and judges [those who reject me]. [51]With all the earnestness I have I tell you this—no one who obeys me shall ever die!"

[52]The leaders of the Jews said, "Now we know you are possessed by a demon. Even Abraham and the mightiest prophets died, and yet you say that obeying you will keep a man from dying! [53]So you are greater than our father Abraham, who died? And greater than the prophets, who died? Who do you think you are?" [54]Then Jesus told them this: "If I am merely boasting about myself, it doesn't count. But it is my Father—and you claim him as your God—who is saying these glorious things about me. [55]But you do not even know him. I do. If I said otherwise, I would be as great a liar as you! But it is true—I know him and fully obey him. [56]Your father Abraham rejoiced to see my day. He knew I was coming and was glad."

[57]*The Jewish leaders:* "You aren't even fifty years old—sure, you've seen Abraham!"

[58]*Jesus:* "The absolute truth is that I was in existence before Abraham was ever born!"

[59]At that point the Jewish leaders picked up stones to kill him. But Jesus was hidden from them, and walked past them and left the Temple.

CHAPTER **9** JESUS HEALS A BLIND MAN. As he was walking along, he saw a man blind from birth.

[2]"Master," his disciples asked him, "why was this man born blind? Was it a result of his own sins or those of his parents?"

[3]"Neither," Jesus answered. "But to demonstrate the power of God. [4]All of us must quickly carry out the tasks assigned us by the one who sent me, for there is little time left before the night falls and all work comes to an end. [5]But while I am still here in the world, I give it my light."

[6]Then he spat on the ground and made mud from the spittle and smoothed the mud over the blind man's eyes, [7]and told him, "Go and wash in the Pool of Siloam" (the word *Siloam* means "Sent"). So the man went where he was sent and washed and came back seeing!

[8]His neighbors and others who knew him as a blind beggar asked each other, "Is this the same fellow—that beggar?"

[9]Some said yes, and some said no. "It can't be the same man," they thought, "but he surely looks like him!"

And the beggar said, "I *am* the same man!"

[10]Then they asked him how in the world he could see. What had happened?

[11]And he told them, "A man they call Jesus made mud and smoothed it over my eyes and told me to go to the Pool of Siloam and wash off the mud. I did, and I can see!"

[12]"Where is he now?" they asked.

"I don't know," he replied.

[13]Then they took the man to the Pharisees. [14]Now as it happened, this all occurred on a Sabbath. [15]Then the Pharisees asked him all about it. So he told them how Jesus had smoothed the mud over his eyes, and when it was washed away, he could see!

[16]Some of them said, "Then this fellow Jesus is not from God because he is working on the Sabbath."

Others said, "But how could an ordinary sinner do such miracles?" So there was a deep division of opinion among them.

[17]Then the Pharisees turned on the man who had been blind and demanded, "This man who opened your eyes—who do you say he is?"

"I think he must be a prophet sent from God," the man replied.

[18]The Jewish leaders wouldn't believe he had been blind, until they called in his parents [19]and asked them, "Is this your son? Was he born blind? If so, how can he see?"

[20]His parents replied, "We know this is our son

STRENGTH

9:2-3 A common belief in Jewish culture was that calamity or suffering was the result of some great sin. But Christ used this man's suffering to teach about faith and to glorify God. We live in a sinful world where good behavior is not always rewarded and bad behavior is not always punished. Therefore, innocent people sometimes suffer. If God took suffering away whenever we asked, we would follow him for comfort and convenience, not out of love and devotion. Regardless of the reasons for our suffering, Jesus has the power to help us deal with it. When you suffer from a disease, tragedy, or handicap, try not to ask, "Why did this happen to me?" or "What did I do wrong?" Instead, ask God to give you strength through the trial and offer you a deeper perspective on what is happening.

and that he was born blind, [21]but we don't know what happened to make him see, or who did it. He is old enough to speak for himself. Ask him."

[22,23]They said this in fear of the Jewish leaders who had announced that anyone saying Jesus was the Messiah would be excommunicated.

[24]So for the second time they called in the man who had been blind and told him, "Give the glory to God, not to Jesus, for we know Jesus is an evil person."

[25]"I don't know whether he is good or bad," the man replied, "but I know this: *I was blind, and now I see!*"

[26]"But what did he do?" they asked. "How did he heal you?"

[27]"Look!" the man exclaimed. "I told you once; didn't you listen? Why do you want to hear it again? Do you want to become his disciples too?"

[28]Then they cursed him and said, "You are his disciple, but we are disciples of Moses. [29]We know God has spoken to Moses, but as for this fellow, we don't know anything about him."

[30]"Why, that's very strange!" the man replied. "He can heal blind men, and yet you don't know anything about him! [31]Well, God doesn't listen to evil men, but he has open ears to those who worship him and do his will. [32]Since the world began there has never been anyone who could open the eyes of someone born blind. [33]If this man were not from God, he couldn't do it."

[34]"You illegitimate bastard, you!" they shouted. "Are you trying to teach *us?*" And they threw him out.

[35]When Jesus heard what had happened, he found the man and said, "Do you believe in the Messiah?"

[36]The man answered, "Who is he, sir, for I want to."

[37]"You have seen him," Jesus said, "and he is speaking to you!"

[38]"Yes, Lord," the man said, "I believe!" And he worshiped Jesus.

[39]Then Jesus told him, "I have come into the world to give sight to those who are spiritually blind and to show those who think they see that they are blind."

[40]The Pharisees who were standing there asked, "Are you saying we are blind?"

[41]"If you were blind, you wouldn't be guilty," Jesus replied. "But your guilt remains because you claim to know what you are doing.

NEW FAITH

9:28,34 The man's new faith was severely tested by some of the authorities. He was cursed and evicted from the Temple. You also may expect persecution when you follow Jesus. You may lose friends; you may even lose your life. But no one can ever take away the eternal life you have been given by Jesus.

CHAPTER 10 JESUS: THE GOOD SHEPHERD.

"Anyone refusing to walk through the gate into a sheepfold, who sneaks over the wall, must surely be a thief! [2]For a shepherd comes through the gate. [3]The gatekeeper opens the gate for him, and the sheep hear his voice and come to him; and he calls his own sheep by name and leads them out. [4]He walks ahead of them; and they follow him, for they recognize his voice. [5]They won't follow a stranger but will run from him, for they don't recognize his voice."

[6]Those who heard Jesus use this illustration didn't understand what he meant, [7]so he explained it to them.

"I am the Gate for the sheep," he said. [8]"All others who came before me were thieves and robbers. But the true sheep did not listen to them. [9]Yes, I am the Gate. Those who come in by way of the Gate will be saved and will go in and out and find green pastures. [10]The thief's purpose is to steal, kill and destroy. My purpose is to give life in all its fullness.

[11]"I am the Good Shepherd. The Good Shepherd lays down his life for the sheep. [12]A hired man will run when he sees a wolf coming and will leave the sheep, for they aren't his and he isn't their shepherd. And so the wolf leaps on them and scatters the flock. [13]The hired man runs because he is hired and has no real concern for the sheep.

[14]"I am the Good Shepherd and know my own sheep, and they know me, [15]just as my Father knows me and I know the Father; and I lay down my life for the sheep. [16]I have other sheep, too, in another fold. I must bring them also, and they will heed my voice; and there will be one flock with one Shepherd.

[17]"The Father loves me because I lay down my life that I may have it back again. [18]No one can kill me without my consent—I lay down my life voluntarily. For I have the right and power to lay it down when I want to and also the right and power to take it again. For the Father has given me this right."

[19]When he said these things, the Jewish leaders were again divided in their opinions about him. [20]Some of them said, "He has a demon or else is crazy. Why listen to a man like that?"

[21]Others said, "This doesn't sound to us like a man possessed by a demon! Can a demon open the eyes of blind men?"

BLIND

10:24 These leaders were waiting for the signs and answers *they* thought would convince them of Jesus' identity. Thus they couldn't hear the truth Jesus was giving them. Jesus tried to correct their mistaken ideas, but they clung to the wrong idea of what kind of Messiah God would send. Such blindness still keeps people away from Jesus. They want him on their own terms; they do not want him if it means changing their whole life.

22,23It was winter, and Jesus was in Jerusalem at the time of the Dedication Celebration. He was at the Temple, walking through the section known as Solomon's Hall. 24The Jewish leaders surrounded him and asked, "How long are you going to keep us in suspense? If you are the Messiah, tell us plainly."

25"I have already told you, and you don't believe me," Jesus replied. "The proof is in the miracles I do in the name of my Father. 26But you don't believe me because you are not part of my flock. 27My sheep recognize my voice, and I know them, and they follow me. 28I give them eternal life and they shall never perish. No one shall snatch them away from me, 29for my Father has given them to me, and he is more powerful than anyone else, so no one can kidnap them from me. 30I and the Father are one."

31Then again the Jewish leaders picked up stones to kill him.

32Jesus said, "At God's direction I have done many a miracle to help the people. For which one are you killing me?"

33They replied, "Not for any good work, but for blasphemy; you, a mere man, have declared yourself to be God."

34-36"In your own Law it says that men are gods!" he replied. "So if the Scripture, which cannot be untrue, speaks of those as gods to whom the message of God came, do you call it blasphemy when the one sanctified and sent into the world by the Father says, 'I am the Son of God'? 37Don't believe me unless I do miracles of God. 38But if I do, believe them even if you don't believe me. Then you will become convinced that the Father is in me, and I in the Father."

39Once again they started to arrest him. But he walked away and left them, 40and went beyond the Jordan River to stay near the place where John was first baptizing. 41And many followed him.

"John didn't do miracles," they remarked to one another, "but all his predictions concerning this man have come true." 42And many came to the decision that he was the Messiah.

CHAPTER **11** JESUS BRINGS LAZARUS TO LIFE. Do you remember Mary, who poured the costly perfume on Jesus' feet and wiped them with her hair? Well, her brother Lazarus, who lived in Bethany with Mary and her sister Martha, was sick. 3So the two sisters sent a message to Jesus telling him, "Sir, your good friend is very, very sick."

4But when Jesus heard about it he said, "The purpose of his illness is not death, but for the glory of God. I, the Son of God, will receive glory from this situation."

5Although Jesus was very fond of Martha, Mary, and Lazarus, 6he stayed where he was for the next two days and made no move to go to them.

Bad things seem to happen all the time. Does God care about what is happening in the world?

There are bad things that happen, and then there are tragedies. At some time in life everyone will experience both of these. Let's cover them one at a time.

I WONDER . . .

The person who flunks a math test had something bad happen to him. Did he learn that it is important to keep up with assignments and study before a test? Hopefully.

A 10-year-old boy races out from behind a parked car and is almost hit by a car. He is scared to death, realizing that he could have been killed! Did he learn a lesson about not darting into the street? He better have; he may not get another chance!

In each case the person probably was not happy about what happened. But each situation in life, good and bad, is a learning experience.

Does God care that we learn important lessons about studying and safety? He cares very much!

Ask your folks about the five worst things that have happened to them. Then ask what they learned from these bad experiences. Finally, ask them if they were thankful that these occurred.

Going through tough times is bad only when you don't learn something when it's over.

Now let's discuss tragedy.

Unfortunately, no one is immune from what we believe is the ultimate tragedy—death. Even Jesus went through the loss and grief of someone he loved (see John 11). It is the timing of death (especially when someone dies young), and how it occurs (like an innocent victim killed by a drunk driver), that makes us wonder if God really cares.

When Adam and Eve disobeyed God in the Garden of Eden, their punishment was separation from God. This incident also set in motion the life cycle, ending in death. But the good news is that Jesus Christ's death on the cross killed death! Not physical death, but spiritual death for all those who receive his gift of forgiveness.

The curse brought on the human race by Adam was physical death. Since that time man has discovered ways to make death happen in some pretty ugly ways (nuclear bombs, lung cancer, AIDS, and many others).

Still, as terrible as those may be, God knows that spiritual death is far worse than physical death. That's why he focused his attention on taking care of the real penalty for our sin—spiritual death! (See Romans 6:23.) God also knows how tragedy can point us to him and his purposes: "And we know that all that happens to us is working for our good if we love God and are fitting into his plans" (Romans 8:28).

Although God is not in heaven pushing buttons to make people die young, he can use any situation for good. And remember, whatever happens to you, God cares. He loves you and wants to work out his purposes in your life.

TIMING

11:5-7 Jesus loved this family and often stayed with them. He knew their pain but did not respond immediately. His delay had a specific purpose. God's timing, especially his delays, may make us think he is not answering or is not answering the way we want. But he will meet all our needs according to his perfect schedule and purpose. Patiently await his timing.

[7]Finally, after the two days, he said to his disciples, "Let's go to Judea."

[8]But his disciples objected. "Master," they said, "only a few days ago the Jewish leaders in Judea were trying to kill you. Are you going there again?"

[9]Jesus replied, "There are twelve hours of daylight every day, and during every hour of it a man can walk safely and not stumble. [10]Only at night is there danger of a wrong step, because of the dark." [11]Then he said, "Our friend Lazarus has gone to sleep, but now I will go and waken him!"

[12,13]The disciples, thinking Jesus meant Lazarus was having a good night's rest, said, "That means he is getting better!" But Jesus meant Lazarus had died.

[14]Then he told them plainly, "Lazarus is dead. [15]And for your sake, I am glad I wasn't there, for this will give you another opportunity to believe in me. Come, let's go to him."

[16]Thomas, nicknamed "The Twin," said to his fellow disciples, "Let's go too—and die with him."

[17]When they arrived at Bethany, they were told that Lazarus had already been in his tomb for four days. [18]Bethany was only a couple of miles down the road from Jerusalem, [19]and many of the Jewish leaders had come to pay their respects and to console Martha and Mary on their loss. [20]When Martha got word that Jesus was coming, she went to meet him. But Mary stayed at home.

[21]Martha said to Jesus, "Sir, if you had been here, my brother wouldn't have died. [22]And even now it's not too late, for I know that God will bring my brother back to life again, if you will only ask him to."

[23]Jesus told her, "Your brother will come back to life again."

[24]"Yes," Martha said, "when everyone else does, on Resurrection Day."

[25]Jesus told her, "I am the one who raises the dead and gives them life again. Anyone who believes in me, even though he dies like anyone else, shall live again. [26]He is given eternal life for believing in me and shall never perish. Do you believe this, Martha?"

[27]"Yes, Master," she told him. "I believe you are the Messiah, the Son of God, the one we have so long awaited."

[28]Then she left him and returned to Mary and, calling her aside from the mourners, told her, "He is here and wants to see you." [29]So Mary went to him at once.

[30]Now Jesus had stayed outside the village, at the place where Martha met him. [31]When the Jewish leaders who were at the house trying to console Mary saw her leave so hastily, they assumed she was going to Lazarus' tomb to weep; so they followed her.

[32]When Mary arrived where Jesus was, she fell down at his feet, saying, "Sir, if you had been here, my brother would still be alive."

[33]When Jesus saw her weeping and the Jewish leaders wailing with her, he was moved with indignation and deeply troubled. [34]"Where is he buried?" he asked them.

They told him, "Come and see." [35]Tears came to Jesus' eyes.

[36]"They were close friends," the Jewish leaders said. "See how much he loved him."

[37,38]But some said, "This fellow healed a blind man—why couldn't he keep Lazarus from dying?"

And again Jesus was moved with deep anger. Then they came to the tomb. It was a cave with a heavy stone rolled across its door.

[39]"Roll the stone aside," Jesus told them.

But Martha, the dead man's sister, said, "By now the smell will be terrible, for he has been dead four days."

[40]"But didn't I tell you that you will see a wonderful miracle from God if you believe?" Jesus asked her.

[41]So they rolled the stone aside. Then Jesus looked up to heaven and said, "Father, thank you for hearing me. [42](You always hear me, of course, but I said it because of all these people standing here, so that they will believe you sent me.)" [43]Then he shouted, "Lazarus, come out!"

[44]And Lazarus came—bound up in the gravecloth, his face muffled in a head swath. Jesus told them, "Unwrap him and let him go!"

[45]And so at last many of the Jewish leaders who were with Mary and saw it happen, finally believed on him. [46]But some went away to the Pharisees and reported it to them.

[47]Then the chief priests and Pharisees convened a council to discuss the situation.

"What are we going to do?" they asked each other. "For this man certainly does miracles. [48]If we let him alone the whole nation will follow him—and then the Roman army will come and kill us and take over the Jewish government."

HE CARES

11:33-38 John stresses that we have a God who cares. This contrasts with the Greek concept of God that was popular in his day—a God with no emotions and no messy involvement with humans. Here we see many of Jesus' emotions—compassion, indignation, sorrow, even frustration. Jesus often expressed deep emotion, and we must never be afraid to reveal our true feelings to him. He understands what we feel because he experienced emotions, too. Be honest, and don't try to hide anything from your Savior. He cares.

[49]And one of them, Caiaphas, who was High Priest that year, said, "You stupid idiots— [50]let this one man die for the people—why should the whole nation perish?"

[51]This prophecy that Jesus should die for the entire nation came from Caiaphas in his position as High Priest—he didn't think of it by himself, but was inspired to say it. [52]It was a prediction that Jesus' death would not be for Israel only, but for all the children of God scattered around the world. [53]So from that time on the Jewish leaders began plotting Jesus' death.

[54]Jesus now stopped his public ministry and left Jerusalem; he went to the edge of the desert, to the village of Ephraim, and stayed there with his disciples.

[55]The Passover, a Jewish holy day, was near, and many country people arrived in Jerusalem several days early so that they could go through the cleansing ceremony before the Passover began. [56]They wanted to see Jesus, and as they gossiped in the Temple, they asked each other, "What do you think? Will he come for the Passover?" [57]Meanwhile the chief priests and Pharisees had publicly announced that anyone seeing Jesus must report him immediately so that they could arrest him.

CHAPTER 12
MARY ANOINTS JESUS' FEET. Six days before the Passover ceremonies began, Jesus arrived in Bethany where Lazarus was—the man he had brought back to life. [2]A banquet was prepared in Jesus' honor. Martha served, and Lazarus sat at the table with him. [3]Then Mary took a jar of costly perfume made from essence of nard, and anointed Jesus' feet with it and wiped them with her hair. And the house was filled with fragrance.

[4]But Judas Iscariot, one of his disciples—the one who would betray him— said, [5]"That perfume was worth a fortune. It should have been sold and the money given to the poor." [6]Not that he cared for the poor, but he was in charge of the disciples' funds and often dipped into them for his own use!

[7]Jesus replied, "Let her alone. She did it in preparation for my burial. [8]You can always help the poor, but I won't be with you very long."

[9]When the ordinary people of Jerusalem heard of his arrival, they flocked to see him and also to see Lazarus—the man who had come back to life again. [10]Then the chief priests decided to kill Lazarus too, [11]for it was because of him that many of the Jewish leaders had deserted

MARY & MARTHA

Hospitality is an art. Making sure a guest is welcomed, warmed, and well fed requires creativity, organization, and teamwork. Mary and Martha's ability to accomplish these makes them the best sister hospitality team in the Bible. Jesus often stayed in their home.

For Mary, hospitality meant giving more attention to the guest himself than to his needs. She was more interested in her guest's words than in the cleanliness of her home or the timeliness of her meals. She let her sister Martha take care of those details. Mary was mainly a "responder." She did little preparation and lots of participation. She needed to learn that action often is appropriate and necessary.

Unlike her sister, Martha worried about details. She wished to please, to serve, to do the right thing—but she often succeeded in making everyone around her feel uncomfortable. Perhaps she was the oldest and felt specially responsible. So she tried too hard to have everything perfect. Mary's lack of cooperation bothered Martha so much that she finally asked Jesus to tell Mary to help. Jesus gently pointed out that Mary was actually doing her part.

Each sister had her own lesson to learn. Mary learned that worship sometimes involves service. Do people in your life know you care about them? Martha learned that obedient service often goes unnoticed. The last time she appears in the Gospels she is again serving a meal to Jesus and the disciples—this time without complaint. When was the last time you gladly served someone without being noticed?

LESSONS: Getting caught up in details can make us forget the main reasons for our actions

There is a proper time to listen to Jesus and a proper time to work for him

KEY VERSE: "But Martha was the jittery type and was worrying over the big dinner she was preparing. She came to Jesus and said, 'Sir, doesn't it seem unfair to you that my sister just sits here while I do all the work? Tell her to come and help me'" (Luke 10:40).

Mary and Martha's story is told in Luke 10:38-42 and John 11:17-45.

UPS:
- Known as hospitable homeowners
- Friends of Jesus, they believed in him with growing faith
- Martha had a strong desire to do everything exactly right
- Mary had a deep concern for people's feelings

DOWNS:
- Martha expected others to agree with her priorities and was overly concerned with details
- Martha tended to feel sorry for herself when her efforts were not recognized
- Mary would let others do the work
- Mary tended to respond, not prepare

STATS:
- Where: Bethany
- Relative: Brother: Lazarus

and believed in Jesus as their Messiah.

[12]The next day, the news that Jesus was on the way to Jerusalem swept through the city, and a huge crowd of Passover visitors [13]took palm branches and went down the road to meet him, shouting, "The Savior! God bless the King of Israel! Hail to God's Ambassador!"

[14]Jesus rode along on a young donkey, fulfilling the prophecy that said: [15]"Don't be afraid of your King, people of Israel, for he will come to you meekly, sitting on a donkey's colt!"

[16](His disciples didn't realize at the time that this was a fulfillment of prophecy; but after Jesus returned to his glory in heaven, then they noticed how many prophecies of Scripture had come true before their eyes.)

[17]And those in the crowd who had seen Jesus call Lazarus back to life were telling all about it. [18]That was the main reason why so many went out to meet him—because they had heard about this mighty miracle.

[19]Then the Pharisees said to each other, "We've lost. Look—the whole world has gone after him!"

[20]Some Greeks who had come to Jerusalem to attend the Passover [21]paid a visit to Philip, who was from Bethsaida, and said, "Sir, we want to meet Jesus." [22]Philip told Andrew about it, and they went together to ask Jesus.

[23,24]Jesus replied that the time had come for him to return to his glory in heaven, and that "I must fall and die like a kernel of wheat that falls into the furrows of the earth. Unless I die I will be alone—a single seed. But my death will produce many new wheat kernels—a plentiful harvest of new lives. [25]If you love your life down here—you will lose it. If you despise your life down here—you will exchange it for eternal glory.

[26]"If these Greeks want to be my disciples, tell them to come and follow me, for my servants must be where I am. And if they follow me, the Father will honor them. [27]Now my soul is deeply troubled. Shall I pray, 'Father, save me from what lies ahead'? But that is the very reason why I came! [28]Father, bring glory and honor to your name."

Then a voice spoke from heaven saying, "I have already done this, and I will do it again." [29]When the crowd heard the voice, some of them thought it was thunder, while others declared an angel had spoken to him.

[30]Then Jesus told them, "The voice was for your benefit, not mine. [31]The time of judgment for the world has come—and the time when Satan, the prince of this world, shall be cast out. [32]And when I am lifted up [on the cross], I will draw everyone to me." [33]He said this to indicate how he was going to die.

[34]"Die?" asked the crowd. "We understood that the Messiah would live forever and never die. Why are you saying he will die? What Messiah are you talking about?"

[35]Jesus replied, "My light will shine out for you just a little while longer. Walk in it while you can, and go where you want to go before the darkness falls, for then it will be too late for you to find your way. [36]Make use of the Light while there is still time; then you will become light bearers."

After saying these things, Jesus went away and was hidden from them.

[37]But despite all the miracles he had done, most of the people would not believe he was the Messiah. [38]This is exactly what Isaiah the prophet had predicted: "Lord, who will believe us? Who will accept God's mighty miracles as proof?" [39]But they couldn't believe, for as Isaiah also said: [40]"God has blinded their eyes and hardened their hearts so that they can neither see nor understand nor turn to me to heal them." [41]Isaiah was referring to Jesus when he made this prediction, for he had seen a vision of the Messiah's glory.

[42]However, even many of the Jewish leaders believed him to be the Messiah but wouldn't admit it to anyone because of their fear that the Pharisees would excommunicate them from the synagogue; [43]for they loved the praise of men more than the praise of God.

[44]Jesus shouted to the crowds, "If you trust me, you are really trusting God. [45]For when you see me, you are seeing the one who sent me. [46]I have come as a Light to shine in this dark world, so that all who put their trust in me will no longer wander in the darkness. [47]If anyone hears me and doesn't obey me, I am not his judge—for I have come to save the world and not to judge it. [48]But all who reject me and my message will be judged at the Day of Judgment by the truths I have spoken. [49]For these are not my own ideas, but I have told you what the Father said to tell you. [50]And I know his instructions lead to eternal life; so whatever he tells me to say, I say!"

LOOK BACK

12:16 After Jesus' resurrection, the disciples understood many of the prophecies they had missed along the way. Jesus' words and actions took on new meaning and made more sense. In retrospect, they saw how Jesus had led them into a deeper and better understanding of his truth. Stop now and think about the events in your life leading up to where you are now. How has God led you to this point? As you grow older, you will look back and see God's involvement more clearly than you do now. Let this truth encourage you to live a life of faith today.

REACH OUT

12:37-38 Jesus had performed many miracles, but most people still didn't believe in him. Likewise, many today won't believe despite all God does. Don't be discouraged if your witness for Christ doesn't turn as many to him as you'd like. Your job is to continue as a faithful witness. You are not responsible for the decisions of others, but simply to reach out to others.

CHAPTER 13 JESUS WASHES HIS DISCIPLES FEET.

Jesus knew on the evening of Passover Day that it would be his last night on earth before returning to his Father. During supper the devil had already suggested to Judas Iscariot, Simon's son, that this was the night to carry out his plan to betray Jesus. Jesus knew that the Father had given him everything and that he had come from God and would return to God. And how he loved his disciples! ⁴So he got up from the supper table, took off his robe, wrapped a towel around his loins, ⁵poured water into a basin, and began to wash the disciples' feet and to wipe them with the towel he had around him.

⁶When he came to Simon Peter, Peter said to him, "Master, you shouldn't be washing our feet like this!"

⁷Jesus replied, "You don't understand now why I am doing it; some day you will."

⁸"No," Peter protested, "you shall never wash my feet!"

"But if I don't, you can't be my partner," Jesus replied.

⁹Simon Peter exclaimed, "Then wash my hands and head as well—not just my feet!"

¹⁰Jesus replied, "One who has bathed all over needs only to have his feet washed to be entirely clean. Now you are clean—but that isn't true of everyone here." ¹¹For Jesus knew who would betray him. That is what he meant when he said, "Not all of you are clean."

¹²After washing their feet he put on his robe again and sat down and asked, "Do you understand what I was doing? ¹³You call me 'Master' and 'Lord,' and you do well to say it, for it is true. ¹⁴And since I, the Lord and Teacher, have washed your feet, you ought to wash each other's feet. ¹⁵I have given you an example to follow: do as I have done to you. ¹⁶How true it is that a servant is not greater than his master. Nor is the messenger more important than the one who sends him. ¹⁷You know these things—now do them! That is the path of blessing.

¹⁸"I am not saying these things to all of you; I know so well each one of you I chose. The Scripture declares, 'One who eats supper with me will betray me,' and this will soon come true. ¹⁹I tell you this now so that when it happens, you will believe on me.

²⁰"Truly, anyone welcoming my messenger is welcoming me. And to welcome me is to welcome the Father who sent me."

²¹Now Jesus was in great anguish of spirit and exclaimed, "Yes, it is true—one of you will betray me." ²²The disciples looked at each other, wondering whom he could mean. ²³Since I was sitting next to Jesus at the table, being his closest friend, ²⁴Simon Peter motioned to me to ask him who it was who would do this terrible deed.

²⁵So I turned and asked him, "Lord, who is it?"

²⁶He told me, "It is the one I honor by giving the bread dipped in the sauce."

And when he had dipped it, he gave it to Judas, son of Simon Iscariot.

²⁷As soon as Judas had eaten it, Satan entered into him. Then Jesus told him, "Hurry—do it now."

²⁸None of the others at the table knew what Jesus meant. ²⁹Some thought that since Judas was their treasurer, Jesus was telling him to go and pay for the food or to give some money to the poor. ³⁰Judas left at once, going out into the night.

³¹As soon as Judas left the room, Jesus said, "My time has come; the glory of God will soon surround me—and God shall receive great praise because of all that happens to me. ³²And God shall give me his own glory, and this so very soon. ³³Dear, dear children, how brief are these moments before I must go away and leave you! Then, though you search for me, you cannot come to me—just as I told the Jewish leaders.

³⁴"And so I am giving a new commandment to you now—love each other just as much as I love you. ³⁵Your strong love for each other will prove to the world that you are my disciples."

³⁶Simon Peter said, "Master, where are you going?"

And Jesus replied, "You can't go with me now; but you will follow me later."

³⁷"But why can't I come now?" he asked, "for I am ready to die for you."

³⁸Jesus answered, "Die for me? No—three times before the cock crows tomorrow morning, you will deny that you even know me!

ACTIVE LOVE

13:35 Love is not simply warm feelings; instead it is an attitude that reveals itself in action. How can we love others as Christ loves us? By helping when it's not convenient, by giving when it hurts, by devoting energy to others' welfare rather than our own, by absorbing hurts from others without complaining or fighting back. This kind of loving is hard to do. That is why people will notice when you do it and will know you are empowered by a supernatural source. The Bible has another beautiful description of love in 1 Corinthians 13.

CHAPTER 14 JESUS: THE WAY, TRUTH, AND LIFE.

"Let not your heart be troubled. You are trusting God, now trust in me. ²·³There are many homes up there where my Father lives, and I am going to prepare them for your coming. When everything is ready, then I will come and get you, so that you can always be with me where I am. If this weren't so, I would tell you plainly. ⁴And you know where I am going and how to get there."

⁵"No, we don't," Thomas said. "We haven't any idea where you are going, so how can we know the way?"

JESUS *told him,* "I AM THE **WAY**— YES, AND THE **TRUTH** AND THE **LIFE.** NO ONE CAN GET TO THE FATHER EXCEPT BY MEANS OF ME.

JOHN 14:6

⁶Jesus told him, "I am the Way—yes, and the Truth and the Life. No one can get to the Father except by means of me. ⁷If you had known who I am, then you would have known who my Father is. From now on you know him—and have seen him!"

⁸Philip said, "Sir, show us the Father and we will be satisfied."

⁹Jesus replied, "Don't you even yet know who I am, Philip, even after all this time I have been with you? Anyone who has seen me has seen the Father! So why are you asking to see him? ¹⁰Don't you believe that I am in the Father and the Father is in me? The words I say are not my own but are from my Father who lives in me. And he does his work through me. ¹¹Just believe it—that I am in the Father and the Father is in me. Or else believe it because of the mighty miracles you have seen me do.

¹²,¹³⁴"In solemn truth I tell you, anyone believing in me shall do the same miracles I have done, and even greater ones, because I am going to be with the Father. You can ask him for *anything,* using my name, and I will do it, for this will bring praise to the Father because of what I, the Son, will do for you. ¹⁴Yes, ask *anything,* using my name, and I will do it!

¹⁵,¹⁶"If you love me, obey me; and I will ask the Father and he will give you another Comforter, and he will never leave you. ¹⁷He is the Holy Spirit, the Spirit who leads into all truth. The world at large cannot receive him, for it isn't looking for him and doesn't recognize him. But you do, for he lives with you now and some day shall be in you. ¹⁸No, I will not abandon you or leave you as orphans in the storm—I will come to you. ¹⁹In just a little while I will be gone from the world, but I will still be present with you. For I will live again—and you will too. ²⁰When I come back to life again, you will know that I am in my Father, and you in me, and I in you. ²¹The one who obeys me is the one who loves me; and because he loves me, my Father will love him; and I will too, and I will reveal myself to him."

²²Judas (not Judas Iscariot, but his other disciple with that name) said to him, "Sir, why are you going to reveal yourself only to us disciples and not to the world at large?"

²³Jesus replied, "Because I will only reveal myself to those who love me and obey me. The Father will love them too, and we will come to them and live with them. ²⁴Anyone who doesn't obey me doesn't love me. And remember, I am not making up this answer to your question! It is the answer given by the Father who sent me.

²⁵"I am telling you these things now while I am still with you. ²⁶But when the Father sends the Comforter instead of me—and by the Comforter I mean the Holy Spirit—he will teach you much, as well as remind you of everything I myself have told you.

²⁷"I am leaving you with a gift—peace of mind and heart! And the peace I give isn't fragile like the peace the world gives. So don't be troubled or afraid. ²⁸Remember what I told you—I am going away, but I will come back to you again. If you really love me, you will be very happy for me, for now I can go to the Father, who is greater than I am. ²⁹I have told you these things before they happen so that when they do, you will believe [in me].

³⁰"I don't have much more time to talk to you, for the evil prince of this world approaches. He has no power over me, ³¹but I will freely do what the Father requires of me so that the world will know that I love the Father. Come, let's be going.

THE WAY

14:6 Jesus says he is the *only* way to God the Father. Some people may argue that this is too narrow. In reality, it is wide enough for the whole world if the world chooses to accept it. Instead of worrying about how limited it sounds to have only one way, we should be saying, "Thank you God, for providing a sure way to get to you!"

ACCURATE

14:26 Jesus promised the disciples that the Holy Spirit would help them remember what he had been teaching them. This promise underscores the validity of the New Testament. The disciples were eyewitnesses of Jesus' life and teachings, and the Holy Spirit helped them remember without taking away their individual perspective. We can be confident that the Gospels are accurate records of what Jesus taught and did (see 1 Corinthians 2:10-14).

CHAPTER 15 **THE VINE AND THE BRANCHES.** "I am the true Vine, and my Father is the Gardener. ²He lops off every branch that doesn't produce. And he prunes those branches that bear fruit for even larger crops. ³He has already tended you by pruning you back for greater strength and usefulness by means of the commands I gave you. ⁴Take care to live in me, and let me live in you. For a branch can't produce fruit when severed from the vine. Nor can you be fruitful apart from me.

⁵"Yes, I am the Vine; you are the branches. Whoever lives in me and I in him shall produce a large crop of fruit. For apart from me you can't do a thing. ⁶If anyone separates from me, he is thrown away like a useless branch, withers, and is gathered into a pile with all the others and burned. ⁷But if you stay in me and obey my commands, you may ask any request you like, and it will be granted! ⁸My true disciples produce bountiful harvests. This brings great glory to my Father.

⁹"I have loved you even as the Father has loved me. Live within my love. ¹⁰When you obey me you are living in my love, just as I obey my Father and live in his love. ¹¹I have told you this so that you will be filled with my joy. Yes, your cup of joy will overflow! ¹²I demand that you love each other as much as I love you. ¹³And here is how to measure it—the greatest love is shown when a person lays down his life for his friends; ¹⁴and you are my friends if you obey me. ¹⁵I no longer call you slaves, for a master doesn't confide in his slaves; now you are my friends, proved by the fact that I have told you everything the Father told me.

¹⁶"You didn't choose me! I chose you! I appointed you to go and produce lovely fruit always, so that no matter what you ask for from the Father, using my name, he will give it to you. ¹⁷I demand that you love each other, ¹⁸for you get enough hate from the world! But then, it hated me before it hated you. ¹⁹The world would love you if you belonged to it; but you don't— for I chose you to come out of the world, and so it hates you. ²⁰Do you remember what I told you? 'A slave isn't greater than his master!' So since they persecuted me, naturally they will persecute you. And if they had listened to me, they would listen to you! ²¹The people of the world will persecute you because you belong to me, for they don't know God who sent me.

²²"They would not be guilty if I had not come and spoken to them. But now they have no excuse for their sin. ²³Anyone hating me is also hating my Father. ²⁴If I hadn't done such mighty miracles among them they would not be counted guilty. But as it is, they saw these miracles and yet they hated both of us—me and my Father. ²⁵This has fulfilled what the prophets said concerning the Messiah, 'They hated me without reason.'

²⁶"But I will send you the Comforter—the Holy Spirit, the source of all truth. He will come to you from the Father and will tell you all about me. ²⁷And you also must tell everyone about me because you have been with me from the beginning.

CHAPTER 16 **THE HOLY SPIRIT.** "I have told you these things so that you won't be staggered [by all that lies ahead.] ²For you will be excommunicated from the synagogues, and indeed the time is coming when those who kill you will think they are doing God a service. ³This is because they have never known the Father or me. ⁴Yes, I'm telling you these things now so that when they happen you will remember I warned you. I didn't tell you earlier because I was going to be with you for a while longer.

⁵"But now I am going away to the one who sent me; and none of you seems interested in the purpose of my going; none wonders why. ⁶Instead you are only filled with sorrow. ⁷But the fact of the matter is that it is best for you that I go away, for if

"Here's what I did..."

One day I came home from school only to find a note saying that my mother had been rushed to the hospital! I called the hospital and discovered that she had a blood clot in her upper leg and would have to be hospitalized for a while.

Suddenly our household was thrown into chaos. Nothing seemed normal without Mom. Plus I was worried that this could be something serious, or lead to something serious.

Through this time, I read the Bible a lot. I memorized John 14:27: "I am leaving you with a gift—peace of mind and heart! And the peace I give isn't fragile like the peace the world gives. So don't be troubled or afraid." These words of Jesus' helped me not to freak out. Instead I gave the situation to God and trusted him to see me through it. Every time I started to worry, I repeated this verse to myself and felt calmer. Jesus understood what I was going through—and he was in control! The more I concentrated on this, the more peace I felt. It was strange to feel so peaceful even when there was plenty I could worry about. But I just kept reminding myself of this verse, and it helped me get through that difficult time.

Kris
AGE 15

I don't, the Comforter won't come. If I do, he will—for I will send him to you.

[8]"And when he has come he will convince the world of its sin, and of the availability of God's goodness, and of deliverance from judgment. [9]The world's sin is unbelief in me; [10]there is righteousness available because I go to the Father and you shall see me no more; [11]there is deliverance from judgment because the prince of this world has already been judged.

[12]"Oh, there is so much more I want to tell you, but you can't understand it now. [13]When the Holy Spirit, who is truth, comes, he shall guide you into all truth, for he will not be presenting his own ideas, but will be passing on to you what he has heard. He will tell you about the future. [14]He shall praise me and bring me great honor by showing you my glory. [15]All the Father's glory is mine; this is what I mean when I say that he will show you my glory.

[16]"In just a little while I will be gone, and you will see me no more; but just a little while after that, and you will see me again!"

[17,18]"Whatever is he saying?" some of his disciples asked. "What is this about 'going to the Father'? We don't know what he means."

[19]Jesus realized they wanted to ask him so he said, "Are you asking yourselves what I mean? [20]The world will greatly rejoice over what is going to happen to me, and you will weep. But your weeping shall suddenly be turned to wonderful joy [when you see me again]. [21]It will be the same joy as that of a woman in labor when her child is born—her anguish gives place to rapturous joy and the pain is forgotten. [22]You have sorrow now, but I will see you again and then you will rejoice; and no one can rob you of that joy. [23]At that time you won't need to ask me for anything, for you can go directly to the Father and ask him, and he will give you what you ask for because you use my name. [24]You haven't tried this before, [but begin now]. Ask, using my name, and you will receive, and your cup of joy will overflow.

[25]"I have spoken of these matters very guardedly, but the time will come when this will not be necessary and I will tell you plainly all about the Father. [26]Then you will present your petitions over my signature! And I won't need to ask the Father to grant you these requests, [27]for the Father himself

WARNINGS

16:1-16 In his last moments with his disciples, Jesus (1) warned them about further persecution, (2) told them where he was going, when he was leaving, and why, and (3) assured them they would not be left alone, but that the Spirit would come. He knew what lay ahead, and he did not want their faith shaken or destroyed. God wants you to know that you are not alone in the world. You have the Holy Spirit to comfort you, teach you truth, and help you.

loves you dearly because you love me and believe that I came from the Father. [28]Yes, I came from the Father into the world and will leave the world and return to the Father."

[29]"At last you are speaking plainly," his disciples said, "and not in riddles. [30]Now we understand that you know everything and don't need anyone to tell you anything. From this we believe that you came from God."

[31]"Do you finally believe this?" Jesus asked. [32]"But the time is coming—in fact, it is here—when you will be scattered, each one returning to his own home, leaving me alone. Yet I will not be alone, for the Father is with me. [33]I have told you all this so that you will have peace of heart and mind. Here on earth you will have many trials and sorrows; but cheer up, for I have overcome the world."

CHAPTER **17** **JESUS PRAYS FOR HIMSELF.** When Jesus had finished saying all these things he looked up to heaven and said, "Father, the time has come. Reveal the glory of your Son so that he can give the glory back to you. [2]For you have given him authority over every man and woman in all the earth. He gives eternal life to each one you have given him. [3]And this is the way to have eternal life—by knowing you, the only true God, and Jesus Christ, the one you sent to earth! [4]I brought glory to you here on earth by doing everything you told me to. [5]And now, Father, reveal my glory as I stand in your presence, the glory we shared before the world began.

[6]"I have told these men all about you. They were in the world, but then you gave them to me. Actually, they were always yours, and you gave them to me; and they have obeyed you. [7]Now they know that everything I have is a gift from you, [8]for I have passed on to them the commands you gave me; and they accepted them and know of a certainty that I came down to earth from you, and they believe you sent me.

[9]"My plea is not for the world but for those you have given me because they belong to you. [10]And all of them, since they are mine, belong to you; and you have given them back to me with everything else of yours, and so *they are my glory!* [11]Now I am leaving the world, and leaving them behind, and coming to you. Holy Father, keep them in your own care—all those you have given me—so that they will be united just as we are, with none missing.

IN THE WORLD

17:18 Jesus didn't ask God to take believers *out* of the world, but instead to use them *in* the world. Because Jesus sends us into the world, we should not try to escape from the world or avoid all relationships with non-Christians. We are called to be salt and light (Matthew 5:13-16), and we are to do the work God sent us to do.

¹²During my time here I have kept safe within your family all of these you gave me. I guarded them so that not one perished, except the son of hell, as the Scriptures foretold.

¹³"And now I am coming to you. I have told them many things while I was with them so that they would be filled with my joy. ¹⁴I have given them your commands. And the world hates them because they don't fit in with it, just as I don't. ¹⁵I'm not asking you to take them out of the world, but to keep them safe from Satan's power. ¹⁶They are not part of this world any more than I am. ¹⁷Make them pure and holy through teaching them your words of truth. ¹⁸As you sent me into the world, I am sending them into the world, ¹⁹and I consecrate myself to meet their need for growth in truth and holiness.

²⁰"I am not praying for these alone but also for the future believers who will come to me because of the testimony of these. ²¹My prayer for all of them is that they will be of one heart and mind, just as you and I are, Father—that just as you are in me and I am in you, so they will be in us, and the world will believe you sent me.

²²"I have given them the glory you gave me—the glorious unity of being one, as we are—²³I in them and you in me, all being perfected into one—so that the world will know you sent me and will understand that you love them as much as you love me. ²⁴Father, I want them with me—these you've given me—so that they can see my glory. You gave me the glory because you loved me before the world began!

²⁵"O righteous Father, the world doesn't know you, but I do; and these disciples know you sent me. ²⁶And I have revealed you to them and will keep on revealing you so that the mighty love you have for me may be in them, and I in them."

CHAPTER **18** **JESUS IS ARRESTED.** After saying these things Jesus crossed the Kidron ravine with his disciples and entered a grove of olive trees. ²Judas, the betrayer, knew this place, for Jesus had gone there many times with his disciples.

³The chief priests and Pharisees had given Judas a squad of soldiers and police to accompany him. Now with blazing torches, lanterns, and weapons they arrived at the olive grove.

⁴,⁵Jesus fully realized all that was going to happen to him. Stepping forward to meet them he asked, "Whom are you looking for?"

"Jesus of Nazareth," they replied.

"I am he," Jesus said. ⁶And as he said it, they all fell backwards to the ground!

⁷Once more he asked them, "Whom are you searching for?"

And again they replied, "Jesus of Nazareth."

⁸"I told you I am he," Jesus said; "and since I am the one you are after, let these others go." ⁹He did this to carry out the prophecy he had just made, "I have not lost a single one of those you gave me. . . ."

¹⁰Then Simon Peter drew a sword and slashed off the right ear of Malchus, the High Priest's servant.

¹¹But Jesus said to Peter, "Put your sword away. Shall I not drink from the cup the Father has given me?"

¹²So the Jewish police, with the soldiers and their lieutenant, arrested Jesus and tied him. ¹³First they took him to Annas, the father-in-law of Caiaphas, the High Priest that year. ¹⁴Caiaphas was the one who told the other Jewish leaders, "Better that one should die for all."

¹⁵Simon Peter followed along behind, as did another of the disciples who was acquainted with the High Priest. So that other disciple was permitted into the courtyard along with Jesus, ¹⁶while Peter stood outside the gate. Then the other disciple spoke to the girl watching at the gate, and she let Peter in. ¹⁷The girl asked Peter, "Aren't you one of Jesus' disciples?"

"No," he said, "I am not!"

¹⁸The police and the household servants were standing around a fire they had made, for it was cold. And Peter stood there with them, warming himself.

¹⁹Inside, the High Priest began asking Jesus about his followers and what he had been teaching them.

²⁰Jesus replied, "What I teach is widely known, for I have preached regularly in the synagogue and Temple; I have been heard by all the Jewish leaders and teach nothing in private that I have not said in public. ²¹Why are you asking me this question? Ask those who heard me. You have some of them here. They know what I said."

²²One of the soldiers standing there struck Jesus with his fist. "Is that the way to answer the High Priest?" he demanded.

²³"If I lied, prove it," Jesus replied. "Should you hit a man for telling the truth?"

²⁴Then Annas sent Jesus, bound, to Caiaphas the High Priest.

²⁵Meanwhile, as Simon Peter was standing by the fire, he was asked again, "Aren't you one of his disciples?"

"Of course not," he replied.

²⁶But one of the household slaves of the High Priest—a relative of the man whose ear Peter had cut off—asked, "Didn't I see you out there in the olive grove with Jesus?"

COME

18:22-27 We can easily get angry at the Jewish Supreme Court for their injustice in condemning Jesus, but Peter and the rest of the disciples also contributed to Jesus' pain by deserting and denying him (Matthew 26:56). While most of us are not like the religious leaders, we all are like the disciples, for all of us have been guilty of denying Christ as Lord in vital areas of our life. Don't excuse yourself by pointing at others whose sins seem worse than yours. Instead, come to Jesus for forgiveness and healing.

²⁷Again Peter denied it. And immediately a rooster crowed.

²⁸Jesus' trial before Caiaphas ended in the early hours of the morning. Next he was taken to the palace of the Roman governor. His accusers wouldn't go in themselves for that would "defile" them, they said, and they wouldn't be allowed to eat the Passover lamb. ²⁹So Pilate, the governor, went out to them and asked, "What is your charge against this man? What are you accusing him of doing?"

³⁰"We wouldn't have arrested him if he weren't a criminal!" they retorted.

³¹"Then take him away and judge him yourselves by your own laws," Pilate told them.

"But we want him crucified," they demanded, "and your approval is required." ³²This fulfilled Jesus' prediction concerning the method of his execution.

³³Then Pilate went back into the palace and called for Jesus to be brought to him. "Are you the King of the Jews?" he asked him.

³⁴"'King' as *you* use the word or as the *Jews* use it?" Jesus asked.

³⁵"Am I a Jew?" Pilate retorted. "Your own people and their chief priests brought you here. Why? What have you done?"

³⁶Then Jesus answered, "I am not an earthly king. If I were, my followers would have fought when I was arrested by the Jewish leaders. But my Kingdom is not of the world."

³⁷Pilate replied, "But you are a king then?"

"Yes," Jesus said. "I was born for that purpose. And I came to bring truth to the world. All who love the truth are my followers."

³⁸"What is truth?" Pilate exclaimed. Then he went out again to the people and told them, "He is not guilty of any crime. ³⁹But you have a custom of asking me to release someone from prison each year at Passover. So if you want me to, I'll release the 'King of the Jews.'"

⁴⁰But they screamed back. "No! Not this man, but Barabbas!" Barabbas was a robber.

CHAPTER 19 PILATE JUDGES JESUS. Then Pilate laid open Jesus' back with a leaded whip, ²and the soldiers made a crown of thorns and placed it on his head and robed him in royal purple. ³"Hail, 'King of the Jews!'" they mocked, and struck him with their fists.

⁴Pilate went outside again and said to the Jews, "I am going to bring him out to you now, but understand clearly that I find him *not guilty.*"

⁵Then Jesus came out wearing the crown of thorns and the purple robe. And Pilate said, "Behold the man!"

⁶At sight of him the chief priests and Jewish officials began yelling, "Crucify! Crucify!"

"*You* crucify him," Pilate said. "I find him *not guilty.*"

⁷They replied, "By our laws he ought to die because he called himself the Son of God."

⁸When Pilate heard this, he was more frightened than ever. ⁹He took Jesus back into the palace again and asked him, "Where are you from?" but Jesus gave no answer.

¹⁰"You won't talk to me?" Pilate demanded. "Don't you realize that I have the power to release you or to crucify you?"

¹¹Then Jesus said, "You would have no power at all over me unless it were given to you from above. So those who brought me to you have the greater sin."

¹²Then Pilate tried to release him, but the Jewish leaders told him, "If you release this man, you are no friend of Caesar's. Anyone who declares himself a king is a rebel against Caesar."

¹³At these words Pilate brought Jesus out to them again and sat down at the judgment bench on the stone-paved platform. ¹⁴It was now about noon of the day before Passover.

And Pilate said to the Jews, "Here is your king!"

¹⁵"Away with him," they yelled. "Away with him—crucify him!"

"What? Crucify your king?" Pilate asked.

"We have no king but Caesar," the chief priests shouted back.

¹⁶Then Pilate gave Jesus to them to be crucified.

¹⁷So they had him at last, and he was taken out of the city, carrying his cross to the place known as "The Skull," in Hebrew, "Golgotha." ¹⁸There they crucified him and two others with him, one on either side, with Jesus between them. ¹⁹And Pilate posted a sign over him reading, "Jesus of Nazareth, the King of the Jews." ²⁰The place where Jesus was crucified was near the city; and the signboard was written in Hebrew, Latin, and Greek, so that many people read it.

²¹Then the chief priests said to Pilate, "Change it from 'The King of the Jews' to 'He said, I am King of the Jews.'"

TRAGEDY

18:36-37 Pilate asked Jesus a straightforward question and Jesus answered clearly. He is a King, but one whose Kingdom is not of this world. There seems to have been no question in Pilate's mind that Jesus spoke the truth and was innocent of any crime. It also seems apparent that while recognizing the truth, Pilate chose to reject it. It is a tragedy when we fail to recognize the truth. It is a greater tragedy when we recognize the truth but fail to heed it.

FAMILY

19:25-27 Even while dying on the cross, Jesus was concerned about his family. He instructed John to care for Mary, his mother. Our families are precious gifts from God, and we should value and care for them under all circumstances. What can you do today to show your love to your family?

[22]Pilate replied, "What I have written, I have written. It stays exactly as it is."

[23,24]When the soldiers had crucified Jesus, they put his garments into four piles, one for each of them. But they said, "Let's not tear up his robe," for it was seamless. "Let's throw dice to see who gets it." This fulfilled the Scripture that says,

"They divided my clothes among them and cast lots for my robe."

[25]So that is what they did.

Standing near the cross were Jesus' mother, Mary, his aunt, the wife of Cleopas, and Mary Magdalene. [26]When Jesus saw his mother standing there beside me, his close friend, he said to her, "He is your son."

[27]And to me he said, "She is your mother!" And from then on I took her into my home.

[28]Jesus knew that everything was now finished, and to fulfill the Scriptures said, "I'm thirsty." [29]A jar of sour wine was sitting there, so a sponge was soaked in it and put on a hyssop branch and held up to his lips.

[30]When Jesus had tasted it, he said, "It is finished," and bowed his head and dismissed his spirit.

[31]The Jewish leaders didn't want the victims hanging there the next day, which was the Sabbath (and a very special Sabbath at that, for it was the Passover), so they asked Pilate to order the legs of the men broken to hasten death; then their bodies could be taken down. [32]So the soldiers came and broke the legs of the two men crucified with Jesus; [33]but when they came to him, they saw that he was dead already, so they didn't break his. [34]However, one of the soldiers pierced his side with a spear, and blood and water flowed out. [35]I saw all this myself and have given

an accurate report so that you also can believe. [36,37]The soldiers did this in fulfillment of the Scripture that says, "Not one of his bones shall be broken," and, "They shall look on him whom they pierced."

[38]Afterwards Joseph of Arimathea, who had been a secret disciple of Jesus for fear of the Jewish leaders, boldly asked Pilate for permission to take Jesus' body down; and Pilate told him to go ahead. So he came and took it away.

THOMAS

Even though some of Thomas's attitudes earned him the nickname "Doubter," we also need to respect his faith. Thomas expressed his doubts because he wanted to know the truth. He didn't hang on to his doubts but humbly believed when they were answered. Expressing doubts is a good way to clarify the truth.

The Bible doesn't tell us a lot about Thomas, but the brief glimpses are consistent. He tried hard to be faithful to what he knew, even though he didn't always feel like it. At one point, when it was clear to everyone that Jesus' life was in danger, only Thomas put into words what most were feeling: "Let's go too—and die with him" (John 11:16). He didn't hesitate to follow Jesus. Sometimes we have to go against our feelings in order to obey Christ.

We don't know why Thomas was missing the first time Jesus appeared to the disciples after the Resurrection. Whatever the reason, Thomas was reluctant to believe their story that Jesus was alive. Not even 10 friends could change his mind! But, because Thomas's doubt was honest, God didn't leave him in doubt.

We can doubt without having to live a doubting way of life. Doubt helps us clarify what we believe. Doubt works better at sharpening our mind than changing it. Doubts can help us ask good questions, seek for answers, push for decisions. But doubt was never meant to be a permanent condition. Doubt is one foot lifted, poised to step forward or back. There is no motion until the foot comes down.

When you experience doubt, take encouragement from Thomas. He didn't stay in his doubt but allowed Jesus to bring him to belief. Take encouragement also from the fact that countless other followers of Christ have struggled with doubts. The answers God gave them may be of great help. Don't settle into doubt, but move beyond it to decision and belief. Find another Christian with whom you can share your doubts. Silent doubts rarely find answers.

LESSONS: Jesus does not reject doubts that are honest and directed toward belief Better to doubt out loud than to disbelieve in silence

KEY VERSES: "Then [Jesus] said to Thomas, 'Put your finger into my hands. Put your hand into my side. Don't be faithless any longer. Believe!' 'My Lord and my God!' Thomas said" (John 20:27-28). Thomas's story is told in the Gospels. He also is mentioned in Acts 1:14.

UPS:
• One of Jesus' 12 disciples
• Had a great capacity for intensity, both in doubt and belief
• Was a loyal and honest man

DOWNS:
• Along with the others, abandoned Jesus at his arrest
• Refused to believe the others' claims to have seen Christ and demanded proof
• Struggled with a pessimistic outlook

STATS:
• Where: Galilee, Judea, Samaria
• Occupation: Disciple of Jesus
• Contemporaries: Jesus, other disciples, Herod, Pilate

JESUS' APPEARANCES AFTER HIS RESURRECTION

The truth of Christianity rests heavily on the Resurrection. If Jesus rose from the grave, who saw him? How trustworthy were the witnesses? Those who claimed to have seen the risen Jesus went on to turn the world upside down. Most of them also died for being followers of Christ. People rarely die for half-hearted belief. These are people who saw Jesus risen from the grave:

Mary Magdalene	Mark 16:9-11; John 20:10-18
The other women at the tomb	Matthew 28:8-10
Peter in Jerusalem	Luke 24:34; 1 Corinthians 15:5
The two travelers on the road	Mark 16:12-13; Luke 24:13-35
Ten disciples behind closed doors	Mark 16:14; Luke 24:36-43; John 20:19-25
All the disciples, with Thomas (excluding Judas Iscariot)	John 20:26-31; 1 Corinthians 15:5
Seven disciples while fishing	John 21:1-14
Eleven disciples on the mountain	Matthew 28:16-20
A crowd of more than 500	1 Corinthians 15:6
His brother James	1 Corinthians 15:7
Those who watched him ascend into heaven	Luke 24:44-49; Acts 1:3-8

[39]Nicodemus, the man who had come to Jesus at night, came too, bringing a hundred pounds of embalming ointment made from myrrh and aloes. [40]Together they wrapped Jesus' body in a long linen cloth saturated with the spices, as is the Jewish custom of burial. [41]The place of crucifixion was near a grove of trees, where there was a new tomb, never used before. [42]And so, because of the need for haste before the Sabbath, and because the tomb was close at hand, they laid him there.

CHAPTER 20 PETER AND JOHN AT JESUS' TOMB.

Early Sunday morning, while it was still dark, Mary Magdalene came to the tomb and found that the stone was rolled aside from the entrance.

[2]She ran and found Simon Peter and me and said, "They have taken the Lord's body out of the tomb, and I don't know where they have put him!"

[3,4]We ran to the tomb to see; I outran Peter and got there first, [5]and stooped and looked in and saw the linen cloth lying there, but I didn't go in. [6]Then Simon Peter arrived and went on inside. He also noticed the cloth lying there, [7]while the swath that had covered Jesus' head was rolled up in a bundle and was lying at the side. [8]Then I went in too, and

saw, and believed [that he had risen]—[9]for until then we hadn't realized that the Scriptures said he would come to life again!

[10]We went on home, [11]and by that time Mary had returned to the tomb and was standing outside crying. And as she wept, she stooped and looked in [12]and saw two white-robed angels sitting at the head and foot of the place where the body of Jesus had been lying.

[13]"Why are you crying?" the angels asked her.

"Because they have taken away my Lord," she replied, "and I don't know where they have put him."

[14]She glanced over her shoulder and saw someone standing behind her. It was Jesus, but she didn't recognize him!

[15]"Why are you crying?" he asked her. "Whom are you looking for?"

She thought he was the gardener. "Sir," she said, "if you have taken him away, tell

PROOF

20:29 Some people think they would believe in Jesus if they could see a definite sign or miracle. But Jesus says we are blessed if we can believe without seeing. We have all the proof we need in the words of the Bible and the testimony of believers. A physical appearance would not make Jesus any more real to us than he is while living within us.

me where you have put him, and I will go and get him."

[16]"Mary!" Jesus said. She turned toward him. "Master!" she exclaimed.

[17]"Don't touch me," he cautioned, "for I haven't yet ascended to the Father. But go find my brothers and tell them that I ascend to my Father and your Father, my God and your God."

[18]Mary Magdalene found the disciples and told them, "I have seen the Lord!" Then she gave them his message.

[19]That evening the disciples were meeting behind locked doors, in fear of the Jewish leaders, when suddenly Jesus was standing there among them! After greeting them, [20]he showed them his hands and side. And how wonderful was their joy as they saw their Lord!

[21]He spoke to them again and said, "As the Father has sent me, even so I am sending you." [22]Then he breathed on them and told them, "Receive the Holy Spirit. [23]If you forgive anyone's sins, they are forgiven. If you refuse to forgive them, they are unforgiven."

[24]One of the disciples, Thomas, "The Twin," was not there at the time with the others. [25]When they kept telling him, "We have seen the Lord," he replied, "I won't believe it unless I see the nail wounds in his hands—and put my fingers into them—and place my hand into his side."

[26]Eight days later the disciples were together again, and this time Thomas was with them. The doors were locked; but suddenly, as before, Jesus was standing among them and greeting them.

[27]Then he said to Thomas, "Put your finger into my hands. Put your hand into my side. Don't be faithless any longer. Believe!"

[28]"My Lord and my God!" Thomas said.

[29]Then Jesus told him, "You believe because you have seen me. But blessed are those who haven't seen me and believe anyway."

[30,31]Jesus' disciples saw him do many other miracles besides the ones told about in this book, but these are recorded so that you will believe that he is the Messiah, the Son of God, and that believing in him you will have life.

CHAPTER **21** JESUS HELPS CATCH FISH. Later Jesus appeared again to the disciples beside the Lake of Galilee. This is how it happened:

[2]A group of us were there—Simon Peter, Thomas, "The Twin," Nathanael from Cana in Galilee, my brother James and I and two other disciples.

[3]Simon Peter said, "I'm going fishing."

"We'll come too," we all said. We did, but caught nothing all night. [4]At dawn we saw a man standing on the beach but couldn't see who he was.

[5]He called, "Any fish, boys?"

"No," we replied.

[6]Then he said, "Throw out your net on the right-hand side of the boat, and you'll get plenty of them!" So we did, and couldn't draw in the net because of the weight of the fish, there were so many!

[7]Then I said to Peter, "It is the Lord!" At that, Simon Peter put on his tunic (for he was stripped to the waist) and jumped into the water [and swam ashore]. [8]The rest of us stayed in the boat and pulled the loaded net to the beach, about 300 feet away. [9]When we got there, we saw that a fire was kindled and fish were frying over it, and there was bread.

After I became a Christian I was told to start reading the Bible. But it is hard to understand and is bigger than any book I ever even attempted to read. Where do I start?

I WONDER . .

Unfortunately, at no place in the Bible does it say, "Start here," and then, "Read this next." Consequently, we need help.

When two people in love have to be separated for a while, they usually send streams of letters to each other. Webbed inside the boring facts about daily life is a story of love and devotion to the other person.

To find the "good stuff" you would have to wade through the details. If you wanted to find out how the relationship developed, you would need to go through those details.

Sometimes that's how it is with the Bible. The events that occurred so long ago don't seem to have any relevance to us today. But if your goal was to understand the relationship between God and his people, from Adam to Jesus, those details would become essential information.

New Christians usually want the "good stuff." Later, as they grow in their faith, they will be more interested in the details that will help them put God's whole plan together.

So for now, consider these suggestions:

• Get to know Jesus the Christ. Listen to his words. Try to understand what each story is saying and watch how Christ treats others. John tells us that he wrote his book "so that you will believe that [Jesus] is the Messiah, the Son of God, and that believing in him you will have life" (John 20:31). The first four books of the New Testament give four different perspectives on Jesus' life. Getting to know him should be your first priority.

• Next, start reading through some of the smaller letters that Paul, Peter, and John wrote (Paul's letters are everything between Romans and Philemon).

• Try Proverbs next. You can read one chapter a day and finish the book in a month.

• After this, read Psalms. This collection of poetry offers us comfort in times of distress, examples of how to praise God and what to praise him for, and a beautiful picture of God's loving character.

There is no short-cut to the Christian life. We must be disciplined enough to dig in the Bible to find all the buried treasure that God wants to give those who will dig deep enough. Have fun.

¹⁰"Bring some of the fish you've just caught," Jesus said. ¹¹So Simon Peter went out and dragged the net ashore. By his count there were 153 large fish; and yet the net hadn't torn.

¹²"Now come and have some breakfast!" Jesus said; and none of us dared ask him if he really was the Lord, for we were quite sure of it. ¹³Then Jesus went around serving us the bread and fish.

¹⁴This was the third time Jesus had appeared to us since his return from the dead.

¹⁵After breakfast Jesus said to Simon Peter, "Simon, son of John, do you love me more than these others?"

"Yes," Peter replied, "you know I am your friend."

"Then feed my lambs," Jesus told him.

¹⁶Jesus repeated the question: "Simon, son of John, do you *really* love me?"

"Yes, Lord," Peter said, "you know I am your friend."

"Then take care of my sheep," Jesus said.

¹⁷Once more he asked him, "Simon, son of John, are you even my friend?"

Peter was grieved at the way Jesus asked the question this third time. "Lord, you know my heart; you know I am," he said.

Jesus said, "Then feed my little sheep. ¹⁸When you were young, you were able to do as you liked and go wherever you wanted to; but when you are old, you will stretch out your hands and others will direct you and take you where you don't want to go." ¹⁹Jesus said this to let him know what kind of death he would die to glorify God. Then Jesus told him, "Follow me."

²⁰Peter turned around and saw the disciple Jesus loved following, the one who had leaned around at supper that time to ask Jesus, "Master, which of us will betray you?" ²¹Peter asked Jesus, "What about him, Lord? What sort of death will he die?"

²²Jesus replied, "If I want him to live until I return, what is that to you? *You* follow me."

²³So the rumor spread among the brotherhood that that disciple wouldn't die! But that isn't what Jesus said at all! He only said, "If I want him to live until I come, what is that to you?"

²⁴*I am that disciple!* I saw these events and have recorded them here. And we all know that my account of these things is accurate.

²⁵And I suppose that if all the other events in Jesus' life were written, the whole world could hardly contain the books!

MEGA *Themes*

JESUS CHRIST, SON OF GOD John shows us that Jesus is unique as God's special Son, yet he is fully God. Because Jesus is fully God, he is able to reveal God to us clearly and accurately.

Because Jesus is God's Son, we can perfectly trust what he says. By trusting him, we can gain an open mind to understand God's message and fulfill his purpose in our lives.

1. What are the key points that John emphasizes in John 1:1-18?
2. What do you learn about God by looking at Jesus?
3. In what ways has knowing Christ made a difference in your life?
4. Based on John's Gospel and your life, what would you say this statement means: "Jesus Christ is God's perfect revelation of himself"?

ETERNAL LIFE Because Jesus is God, he lives forever. Before the world began, Jesus lived with God, and he will reign forever with God. In John, we see Jesus revealed in power and magnificence even before his resurrection.

Jesus offers eternal life to us. We are invited to live in a personal, eternal relationship with him that begins now. Although we must eventually age and die, by trusting Christ, we can have a new life that lasts forever.

1. How does the idea of eternal life affect the way you view your earthly life?
2. What effect should the promise of eternal life in Jesus Christ have on the way you relate to non-Christians?
3. How can you be more faithful to the reality of eternal life in how you live your life now on earth?

BELIEVE John records eight specific signs or miracles that reveal the nature of Jesus' power and love. We see Christ's power over everything created, and we see his love for all people. These signs encourage us to believe in him.

Believing is active, living, and continuous trust in Jesus as God. When we believe in Jesus' life, words, death, and resurrection, and when we commit our life to him, he cleanses us from sin and empowers us to follow him. Jesus provides the cleansing and empowering; it is our role to respond in true belief.

1. What did John want to communicate about Jesus through the eight miracles he included in his book?
2. What did John want to communicate through the names or descriptions of Jesus?
3. What is the difference between knowing about Jesus and believing in him?
4. How did you come to believe in Jesus? What does it mean to you to be a "believer"?
5. What would you want to communicate about Jesus to your non-Christian friends? What could you do to begin to clearly communicate that message?

HOLY SPIRIT Jesus taught his disciples that after he went back to heaven, the Holy Spirit would come. Then the Holy Spirit would indwell, guide, counsel, and comfort all those who follow Jesus. Through the Holy Spirit, Christ's presence and power are multiplied in all who believe.

Through God's Holy Spirit we are drawn to him in faith. We must know the Holy Spirit to understand all that Jesus taught. We can experience Jesus' love and guidance as we allow the Holy Spirit to do his work in us.

1. In 14:15-31 and 16:5-16 Jesus teaches specifically about the Holy Spirit. List the key points of his teaching.
2. What resources are provided by the Holy Spirit?
3. Why do you think God gives his Holy Spirit to believers?
4. What can you do to develop a daily reliance on the Spirit so that you are able to enjoy his presence and blessings?

RESURRECTION On the third day after Jesus died, he rose from the dead. This was verified by his disciples and many eyewitnesses. This reality changed the disciples from frightened deserters to dynamic leaders in the new church. This fact is the foundation of the Christian faith.

We can be changed, as the disciples were, and have confidence that our bodies will one day be raised to live with Christ forever. The same power that raised Christ to life can give you the ability to follow Christ each day. God wants us to live in victory, not in fear or despair.

1. What makes the Resurrection so essential to Christian faith?
2. Describe how you might have felt if you had been one of the disciples who thought Jesus was dead and then saw him alive. What impact would this experience have had on your life?
3. What does it mean to live as a Christian who takes the Resurrection seriously?

*A*ssemble nine very different people: •The class cut-up who makes everything funny •The preppie rich kid with her very own BMW •The minority student from the not-so-nice part of town •The human computer who would rather do calculus problems than anything else •The mammoth football jock who loves to bash things—especially quarterbacks •The student whose recent "achievements" read like a sleazy novel •The school airhead who is not exactly headed for a career as a genetic scientist •The campus philosopher/political activist who *loves* to argue and *hates* shallow people •The quiet classmate who, for whatever reasons, never fits in ■ Now, give this diverse crowd a simple task to do . . . together. ■ Even if you could get them all in the same room, they'd *never* complete the assignment. What they'd most likely produce is nonstop arguing, bickering, and chaos! If they functioned as a team at all, it would be bumpy and very brief. ■ So, how do we explain the first-century church? How did *several hundred* radically different people accomplish the *complicated and time-consuming project* of taking Jesus' story all over the world? ■ How did they handle conflicts? What kept them going when hard times hit? What is it that those first Christians had that is lacking among believers today? ■ If you'd like the answers to those questions (and you'd like to see how you can help improve your own church), dive into the book of Acts.

STATS

PURPOSE: To give an accurate account of the birth and growth of the Christian church

AUTHOR: Luke

TO WHOM WRITTEN: Theophilus ("lover of God") and people everywhere

DATE WRITTEN: Between A.D. 63 and 70

SETTING: Acts is the link between Christ's life and the life of the church, between the Gospels and the Epistles

KEY PEOPLE: Peter, John, James, Stephen, Philip, Paul, Barnabas, Cornelius, James (Jesus' brother), Timothy, Lydia, Silas, Titus, Apollos, Agabus, Ananias, Felix, Festus, Agrippa, Luke

KEY PLACES: Jerusalem, Samaria, Lydda, Joppa, Antioch, Cyprus, Antioch in Pisidia, Iconium, Lystra, Derbe, Philippi, Thessalonica, Beroea, Athens, Corinth, Ephesus, Caesarea, Malta, Rome

Acts

CHANGED

1:3 Today there are still people who doubt Jesus' resurrection. But Jesus appeared to the apostles on many occasions after his resurrection, proving that he was alive. Look at the change the Resurrection made in the disciples' lives. At Jesus' death, they scattered. They were disillusioned and they feared for their lives. Then, after seeing the resurrected Christ, they grew fearless and risked everything to spread the Good News about him around the world. They faced imprisonment, beatings, rejection, and martyrdom, yet they never compromised their mission. These men would not have risked their lives for something they knew was a fraud. They knew Jesus was raised from the dead, and the early church was fired with their enthusiasm to tell others.

CHAPTER **1** **JESUS GOES UP TO HEAVEN.** Dear friend who loves God:

In my first letter I told you about Jesus' life and teachings and how he returned to heaven after giving his chosen apostles further instructions from the Holy Spirit. ³During the forty days after his crucifixion he appeared to the apostles from time to time, actually alive, and proved to them in many ways that it was really he himself they were seeing. And on these occasions he talked to them about the Kingdom of God.

⁴In one of these meetings he told them not to leave Jerusalem until the Holy Spirit came upon them in fulfillment of the Father's promise, a matter he had previously discussed with them.

⁵"John baptized you with water," he reminded them, "but you shall be baptized with the Holy Spirit in just a few days."

⁶And another time when he appeared to them, they asked him, "Lord, are you going to free Israel [from Rome] now and restore us as an independent nation?"

⁷"The Father sets those dates," he replied, "and they are not for you to know. ⁸But when the Holy Spirit has come upon you, you will receive power to testify about me with great effect, to the people in Jerusalem, throughout Judea, in Samaria, and to the ends of the earth, about my death and resurrection."

⁹It was not long afterwards that he rose into the sky and disappeared into a cloud, leaving them

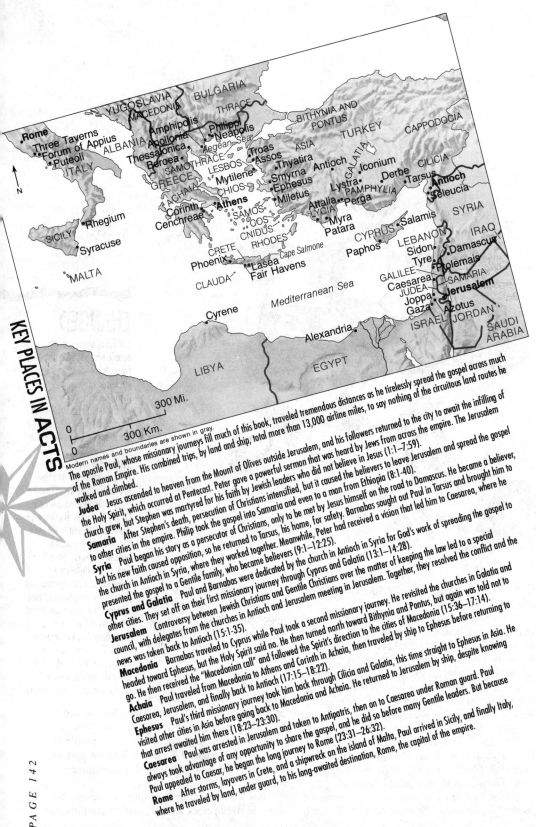

KEY PLACES IN ACTS

Modern names and boundaries are shown in gray.

The apostle Paul, whose missionary journeys fill much of this book, traveled tremendous distances as he tirelessly spread the gospel across much of the Roman Empire. His combined trips, by land and ship, total more than 13,000 airline miles, to say nothing of the circuitous land routes he walked and climbed.

Judea Jesus ascended to heaven from the Mount of Olives outside Jerusalem, and his followers returned to the city to await the infilling of the Holy Spirit, which occurred at Pentecost. Peter gave a powerful sermon that was heard by Jews from across the empire. The Jerusalem church grew, but Stephen was martyred for his faith by Jewish leaders who did not believe in Jesus (1:1–7:59).

Samaria After Stephen's death, persecution of Christians intensified, but it caused the believers to leave Jerusalem and spread the gospel to other cities in the empire. Philip took the gospel into Samaria and even to a man from Ethiopia (8:1-40).

Syria Paul began his story as a persecutor of Christians, only to be met by Jesus himself on the road to Damascus. He became a believer, but his new faith caused opposition, so he returned to Tarsus, his home, for safety. Barnabas sought out Paul in Tarsus and brought him to the church in Antioch in Syria, where they worked together. Meanwhile, Peter had received a vision that led him to Caesarea, where he presented the gospel to a Gentile family, who became believers by the church in Antioch in Syria for God's work of spreading the gospel (9:1–12:25).

Cyprus and Galatia Paul and Barnabas were dedicated by the church in Antioch and Galatia (13:1–14:28). other cities. They set off on their first missionary journey through Cyprus and Galatia (13:1–14:28).

Jerusalem Controversy between Jewish Christians and Gentile Christians over the matter of keeping the law led to a special council, with delegates from the churches in Antioch and Jerusalem meeting in Jerusalem. Together, they resolved the conflict and the news was taken back to Antioch (15:1-35).

Macedonia Barnabas traveled to Cyprus while Paul took a second missionary journey. He revisited the churches in Galatia and headed toward Ephesus, but the Holy Spirit said no. He then turned north toward Bithynia and Pontus, but again was told not to go. He then received the "Macedonian call" and followed the Spirit's direction to the cities of Macedonia (15:36–17:14).

Achaia Paul traveled from Macedonia to Athens and Corinth in Achaia, then traveled by ship to Ephesus before returning to Caesarea, Jerusalem, and finally back to Antioch (17:15–18:22).

Ephesus Paul's third missionary journey took him back through Cilicia and Galatia, this time straight to Ephesus in Asia. He visited other cities in Asia before going back to Macedonia and Achaia. He returned to Jerusalem by ship, despite knowing that arrest awaited him there (18:23–23:30).

Caesarea Paul was arrested in Jerusalem and taken to Antipatris, then on to Caesarea under Roman guard. Paul always took advantage of any opportunity to share the gospel, and he did so before many Gentile leaders. But because Paul appealed to Caesar, he began the long journey to Rome (23:31–26:32).

Rome After storms, layovers in Crete, and a shipwreck on the island of Malta, Paul arrived in Sicily, and finally Italy, where he traveled by land, under guard, to his long-awaited destination, Rome, the capital of the empire.

staring after him. [10]As they were straining their eyes for another glimpse, suddenly two white-robed men were standing there among them, [11]and said, "Men of Galilee, why are you standing here staring at the sky? Jesus has gone away to heaven, and some day, just as he went, he will return!"

[12]They were at the Mount of Olives when this happened, so now they walked the half mile back to Jerusalem [13]and held a prayer meeting in an upstairs room of the house where they were staying.

[14]Here is the list of those who were present at the meeting: Peter, John, James, Andrew, Philip, Thomas, Bartholomew, Matthew, James (son of Alphaeus), Simon (also called "The Zealot"), Judas (son of James), and the brothers of Jesus. Several women, including Jesus' mother, were also there.

[15]This prayer meeting went on for several days. During this time, on a day when about 120 people were present, Peter stood up and addressed them as follows:

[16]"Brothers, it was necessary for the Scriptures to come true concerning Judas, who betrayed Jesus by guiding the mob to him, for this was predicted long ago by the Holy Spirit, speaking through King David. [17]Judas was one of us, chosen to be an apostle just as we were. [18]He bought a field with the money he received for his treachery and falling headlong there, he burst open, spilling out his bowels. [19]The news of his death spread rapidly among all the people of Jerusalem, and they named the place 'The Field of Blood.' [20]King David's prediction of this appears in the Book of Psalms, where he says, 'Let his home become desolate with no one living in it.' And again, 'Let his work be given to someone else to do.'

[21,22]"So now we must choose someone else to take Judas' place and to join us as witnesses of Jesus' resurrection. Let us select someone who has been with us constantly from our first association with the Lord—from the time he was baptized by John until the day he was taken from us into heaven."

[23]The assembly nominated two men: Joseph Justus (also called Barsabbas) and Matthias. [24,25]Then they all prayed for the right man to be chosen. "O Lord," they said, "you know every heart; show us which of these men you have chosen as an apostle to replace Judas the traitor, who has gone on to his proper place."

[26]Then they drew straws, and in this manner Matthias was chosen and became an apostle with the other eleven.

CHOOSE WELL

1:21-22 The apostles had to choose a replacement for Judas Iscariot. They outlined specific criteria for making the choice. When the "finalists" had been chosen, the apostles prayed, asking God to guide the selection process. This gives us a good example of how to proceed when we are making important decisions. Set up criteria consistent with the Bible, examine the alternatives, and pray for wisdom and guidance to reach a wise decision.

CHAPTER **2** **THE HOLY SPIRIT COMES.** Seven weeks had gone by since Jesus' death and resurrection, and the Day of Pentecost had now arrived. As the believers met together that day, [2]suddenly there was a sound like the roaring of a mighty windstorm in the skies above them and it filled the house where they were meeting. [3]Then, what looked like flames or tongues of fire appeared and settled on their heads. [4]And everyone present was filled with the Holy Spirit and began speaking in languages they didn't know, for the Holy Spirit gave them this ability.

[5]Many godly Jews were in Jerusalem that day for the religious celebrations, having arrived from many nations. [6]And when they heard the roaring in the sky above the house, crowds came running to see what it was all about, and were stunned to hear their own languages being spoken by the disciples.

[7]"How can this be?" they exclaimed. "For these men are all from Galilee, [8]and yet we hear them speaking all the native languages of the lands where we were born! [9]Here we are—Parthians,

But when THE HOLY SPIRIT has come upon you, You will receive POWER to TESTIFY about ME with GREAT EFFECT

THE HOLY SPIRIT

Author Sheldon Vanauken has described a scene in which the characters in a drama sit around and discuss their play. The playwright's name is Smith. Some of the characters believe Smith exists; some don't. One of them recalls an earlier scene where a character named Smithson claimed that he was Smith, and that he had written himself into the play. After considerable debate over the likelihood of that happening, another character speaks: **"L**ook, do you know what's so impressive about all this? It's the idea of a sort of a trinity: Smith outside writing the play; and inside as a character; and inside each of us, too. I don't know whether it's true, but it's exactly the way it would be if it were. . . . This thing has the feel of something true. A sort of rightness." **N**o one can truly understand—much less explain—the Trinity, God in three persons. But Vanauken's analogy is a good attempt: an Author who writes characters into existence, then writes himself in as one of the players, and also is somehow in each of his characters. **H**istorically, Christians have believed that God exists in three persons, the Father, Son, and Holy Spirit. The least understood of these three, though, is the Holy Spirit. So just who is the Holy Spirit and what does he do?

- "He," not "it." The New Testament always refers to the Holy Spirit as "he," not "it." The Spirit is personal, not merely a "force" or instrument. Just as God the Father and God the Son represent distinct personalities within the Trinity, so does the Spirit. We don't have any real point of reference to help us understand this since we don't know anyone else who is pure spirit. Still, it is true: the Holy Spirit is a person with intellect, feelings, will, and other personal characteristics.
- Truly God. The Holy Spirit is not in any way less than or inferior to the Father or the Son. One of the clearest statements of this reality is found in Matthew 28:19, where Jesus tells the disciples: "Therefore go and make disciples in all the nations, baptizing them into the name of the Father and of the Son and of the Holy Spirit." (Also check out John 14:16-26 and 15:26-27; 2 Corinthians 3:17 and 13:14.) The classic description of the Trinity is "one in essence, three in persons." The Holy Spirit is the third person described here, and he is just as much God as are the Father and the Son.
- The Spirit's functions. We can do little more here than simply list the roles that the Holy Spirit fulfills: he anoints and serves alongside the Messiah (Isaiah 48:16, 61:1; Luke 4:18-19); he ushers in the "last days" (Joel 2:28-32; Acts 2:14-36); he unifies the body of Christ (1 Corinthians 12:4-11; Ephesians 4:1-16); he gives new life (John 3:5-8); he convicts us of sin and enables us to repent and come to faith in Christ (John 16:8); he testifies to Jesus as the Messiah (John 14:26 and 16:14); he guides us into truth (John 16:13); he bears fruit in our life (Galatians 5:22-25); he is present in all Christians (Romans 8:9-11; 1 Corinthians 12–14); he prays for us (Romans 8:26); he gives us supernatural gifts (1 Corinthians 6:19). Even from this very brief list you can begin to see how crucial the Spirit's role is in our life. Knowing this, it is understandable that Jesus calls the Holy Spirit the "Helper" or "Comforter" (John 15:26). **A**s characters in a divine drama, it is comforting for us to know that there is indeed an Author who knows and loves the people he created so much that he "wrote himself into the play." And that now, having left the visible stage, he remains behind in an unseen—but no less real—way, guiding and strengthening his people.

Medes, Elamites, men from Mesopotamia, Judea, Cappadocia, Pontus, Asia Minor, [10]Phrygia, Pamphylia, Egypt, the Cyrene language areas of Libya, visitors from Rome—both Jews and Jewish converts—[11]Cretans, and Arabians. And we all hear these men telling in our own languages about the mighty miracles of God!"

[12]They stood there amazed and perplexed. "What can this mean?" they asked each other.

[13]But others in the crowd were mocking. "They're drunk, that's all!" they said.

[14]Then Peter stepped forward with the eleven apostles and shouted to the crowd, "Listen, all of you, visitors and residents of Jerusalem alike! [15]Some of you are saying these men are drunk! It isn't true! It's much too early for that! People don't get drunk by 9:00 A.M.! [16]No! What you see this morning was predicted centuries ago by the prophet Joel—[17]'In the last days,' God said, 'I will pour out my Holy Spirit upon all mankind, and your sons and daughters shall prophesy, and your young men shall see visions, and your old men dream dreams. [18]Yes, the Holy Spirit shall come upon all my servants, men and women alike, and they shall prophesy. [19]And I will cause strange demonstrations in the heavens and on the earth—blood and fire and clouds of smoke; [20]the sun shall turn black and the moon blood-red before that awesome Day of the Lord arrives. [21]But anyone who asks for mercy from the Lord shall have it and shall be saved.'

[22]"O men of Israel, listen! God publicly endorsed Jesus of Nazareth by doing tremendous miracles through him, as you well know. [23]But God, following his prearranged plan, let you use the Roman government to nail him to the cross and murder him. [24]Then God released him from the horrors of death and brought him back to life again, for death could not keep this man within its grip.

[25]"King David quoted Jesus as saying:

'I know the Lord is always with me. He is helping me. God's mighty power supports me.

[26]'No wonder my heart is filled with joy and my tongue shouts his praises! For I know all will be well with me in death—

[27]'You will not leave my soul in hell or let the body of your Holy Son decay.

[28]'You will give me back my life and give me wonderful joy in your presence.'

[29]"Dear brothers, think! David wasn't referring to himself when he spoke these words I have quoted, for he died and was buried, and his tomb is still here among us. [30]But he was a prophet, and knew God had promised with an unbreakable oath that one of David's own descendants would [be the Messiah and] sit on David's throne. [31]David was looking far into the future and predicting the Messiah's resurrection, and saying that the Messiah's soul would not be left in hell and his body would not decay. [32]He was speaking of Jesus, and we all are witnesses that Jesus rose from the dead.

My mom has said some pretty bad things to me over the years. Now that I'm a Christian, I know I should forgive her, but I can't. What should I do?

I WONDER . . .

The gap between knowing you need to forgive someone and actually being able to do it often seems like a vast canyon. You can see the other side, but getting there seems impossible.

Ever seen a shower drain plugged up with a two-month accumulation of hair? The water slowly seeps through the molding mass of greasy, soapy yuk. No amount of plunging can bring the glob up because it's too deep.

The next solution usually is to burn away the clog by applying something like Drāno. Sometimes this works if the buildup is not too severe. The last resort, of course, is to call a plumber. He'll come in with a narrow, hard, yet flexible piece of metal called a snake and drill through the clog until the water is flowing freely.

Unforgiveness is like a clogged drain. Sometimes it is fairly easy to unclog. Someone hurts us, we let them know they hurt us, they say they're sorry, we forgive them, and the whole episode is forgotten. But when unforgiveness collects from years of hurt it becomes similar to what a drain would look like after years of bathing your cat in the sink without cleaning out the drain! You might as well buy a new sink.

Likewise, our sin can collect and becomes a gross, yucky mass that eventually clogs our relationship with God. Until it is removed, we can't really receive anything meaningful from him. Jesus came to "unclog our pipes" so God's love and forgiveness could flow to us freely. He did nothing wrong—we were the transgressors—yet he died to open the way for that flow of love.

From what you wrote, your mom's sin against you has clogged your relationship. You may have every right not to forgive your mom, but you must put aside that right for a greater goal—you must "die" and open yourself to learning how you and your mom can love each other. Otherwise the clog will only get worse.

God took the initiative with us by humbling himself and forgiving all of our sin (to see the comparison of how much God has forgiven us and how much we must forgive others, see Matthew 18:21-34). You must do the same with the person who has wronged you.

The forgiveness must be from your heart and must not be dependent upon whether she feels sorry for what she has done. Forgiving someone is a gift only you can offer. You can't make someone take a free gift, they must reach out and receive it. Though the canyon looks deep and treacherous, the reward on the other side is a clear conscience, times of wonderful refreshment (see Acts 3:19), and—hopefully—a renewed relationship.

³³"And now he sits on the throne of highest honor in heaven, next to God. And just as promised, the Father gave him the authority to send the Holy Spirit—with the results you are seeing and hearing today.

³⁴"[No, David was not speaking of himself in these words of his I have quoted], for he never ascended into the skies. Moreover, he further stated, 'God spoke to my Lord, the Messiah, and said to him, Sit here in honor beside me ³⁵until I bring your enemies into complete subjection.'

³⁶"Therefore I clearly state to everyone in Israel that God has made this Jesus you crucified to be the Lord, the Messiah!"

³⁷These words of Peter's moved them deeply, and they said to him and to the other apostles, "Brothers, what should we do?"

³⁸And Peter replied, "Each one of you must turn from sin, return to God, and be baptized in the name of Jesus Christ for the forgiveness of your sins; then you also shall receive this gift, the Holy Spirit. ³⁹For Christ promised him to each one of you who has been called by the Lord our God, and to your children and even to those in distant lands!"

⁴⁰Then Peter preached a long sermon, telling about Jesus and strongly urging all his listeners to save themselves from the evils of their nation. ⁴¹And those who believed Peter were baptized—about three thousand in all! ⁴²They joined with the other believers in regular attendance at the apostles' teaching sessions and at the Communion services and prayer meetings.

⁴³A deep sense of awe was on them all, and the apostles did many miracles. ⁴⁴And all the believers met together constantly and shared everything with each other, ⁴⁵selling their possessions and dividing with those in need. ⁴⁶They worshiped together regularly at the Temple each day, met in small groups in homes for Communion, and shared their meals with great joy and thankfulness, ⁴⁷praising God. The whole city was favorable to them, and each day God added to them all who were being saved.

CHAPTER **3** PETER AND JOHN HEAL A MAN. Peter and John went to the Temple one afternoon to take part in the three o'clock daily prayer meeting. ²As they approached the Temple, they saw a man lame from birth carried along the street and laid beside the Temple gate—the one called The Beautiful Gate—as was his custom every day. ³As Peter and John were passing by, he asked them for some money.

⁴They looked at him intently, and then Peter said, "Look here!"

⁵The lame man looked at them eagerly, expecting a gift.

⁶But Peter said, "We don't have any money for you! But I'll give you something else! I command you in the name of Jesus Christ of Nazareth, *walk!* "

^{7,8}Then Peter took the lame man by the hand and pulled him to his feet. And as he did, the man's feet and ankle-bones were healed and strengthened so that he came up with a leap, stood there a moment and began walking! Then, walking, leaping, and praising God, he went into the Temple with them.

⁹When the people inside saw him walking and heard him praising God, ¹⁰and realized he was the lame beggar they had seen so often at The Beautiful Gate, they were inexpressibly surprised! ¹¹They all rushed out to Solomon's Hall, where he was holding tightly to Peter and John! Everyone stood there awed by the wonderful thing that had happened.

¹²Peter saw his opportunity and addressed the crowd. "Men of Israel," he said, "what is so surprising about this? And why look at us as though we by our own power and godliness had made this man walk? ¹³For it is the God of Abraham, Isaac, Jacob and of all our ancestors who has brought glory to his servant Jesus by doing this. I refer to the Jesus whom you rejected before Pilate, despite Pilate's determination to release him. ¹⁴You didn't want him freed—this holy, righteous one. Instead you demanded the release of a murderer. ¹⁵And you killed the Author of Life; but God brought him back to life again. And John and I are witnesses of this fact, for after you killed him we saw him alive!

¹⁶"Jesus' name has healed this man—and you know how lame he was before. Faith in Jesus'

TOGETHER

2:44 Recognizing the other believers as brothers and sisters in the family of God, the Christians in Jerusalem shared all they had so that all could benefit from God's blessings. It is tempting—especially if we have material wealth—to cut ourselves off from one another, each taking care of, providing for, and enjoying his own little piece of the world. But as part of God's spiritual family, we have a responsibility to help one another in every way possible. God's family works best when its members work together.

BETTER

3:6 The lame beggar asked for money, but Peter gave him something much better—the use of his legs. We often ask God to solve a small problem, but he wants to give us a new life and help for *all* our problems. When we ask God for help, he may say, "I've got something even better for you." Ask God for what you want, but don't be surprised when he gives you what you really *need*.

REFRESHED

3:19 When we repent, God promises not only to wipe away our sin, but also to bring spiritual refreshment. Repentance may seem painful at first because it is hard to give up certain sins. But God will give you a better way. As Hosea promised, "Let us press on to know him, and he will respond to us as surely as the coming of dawn or the rain of early spring" (Hosea 6:3). Do you feel a need to be refreshed?

name—faith given us from God—has caused this perfect healing.

[17]"Dear brothers, I realize that what you did to Jesus was done in ignorance; and the same can be said of your leaders. [18]But God was fulfilling the prophecies that the Messiah must suffer all these things. [19]Now change your mind and attitude to God and turn to him so he can cleanse away your sins and send you wonderful times of refreshment from the presence of the Lord [20]and send Jesus your Messiah back to you again. [21,22]For he must remain in heaven until the final recovery of all things from sin, as prophesied from ancient times. Moses, for instance, said long ago, 'The Lord God will raise up a Prophet among you, who will resemble me! Listen carefully to everything he tells you. [23]Anyone who will not listen to him shall be utterly destroyed.'

[24]"Samuel and every prophet since have all spoken about what is going on today. [25]You are the children of those prophets; and you are included in God's promise to your ancestors to bless the entire world through the Jewish race—that is the promise God gave to Abraham. [26]And as soon as God had brought his servant to life again, he sent him first of all to you men of Israel, to bless you by turning you back from your sins."

CHAPTER 4 PETER AND JOHN'S COURAGE.

While they were talking to the people, the chief priests, the captain of the Temple police, and some of the Sadducees came over to them, [2]very disturbed that Peter and John were claiming that Jesus had risen from the dead. [3]They arrested them and since it was already evening, jailed them overnight. [4]But many of the people who heard their message believed it, so that the number of believers now reached a new high of about five thousand men!

[5]The next day it happened that the Council of all the Jewish leaders was in session in Jerusalem— [6]Annas the High Priest was there, and Caiaphas, John, Alexander, and others of the High Priest's relatives. [7]So the two disciples were brought in before them.

"By what power, or by whose authority have you done this?" the Council demanded.

[8]Then Peter, filled with the Holy Spirit, said to them, "Honorable leaders and elders of our nation, [9]if you mean the good deed done to the cripple, and how he was healed, [10]let me clearly state to you and

to all the people of Israel that it was done in the name and power of Jesus from Nazareth, the Messiah, the man you crucified—but God raised back to life again. It is by his authority that this man stands here healed! [11]For Jesus the Messiah is (the one referred to in the Scriptures when they speak of) a 'stone discarded by the builders which be-

came the capstone of the arch.' [12]There is salvation in no one else! Under all heaven there is no other name for men to call upon to save them."

[13]When the Council saw the boldness of Peter and John and could see that they were obviously uneducated non-professionals, they were amazed and realized what being with Jesus had done for them! [14]And the Council could hardly discredit the healing when the man they had healed was standing right there beside them! [15]So they sent them out of the Council chamber and conferred among themselves.

[16]"What shall we do with these men?" they asked each other. "We can't deny that they have done a tremendous miracle, and everybody in Jerusalem knows about it. [17]But perhaps we can stop them from spreading their propaganda. We'll tell them that if they do it again we'll really throw the book at them." [18]So they called them back in, and told them never again to speak about Jesus.

[19]But Peter and John replied, "You decide whether God wants us to obey you instead of him! [20]We cannot stop telling about the wonderful things we saw Jesus do and heard him say."

[21]The Council then threatened them further and finally let them go because they didn't know how to punish them without starting a riot. For everyone was praising God for this wonderful miracle— [22]the healing of a man who had been lame for forty years.

²³As soon as they were freed, Peter and John found the other disciples and told them what the Council had said.

²⁴Then all the believers united in this prayer:

"O Lord, Creator of heaven and earth and of the sea and everything in them— ^{25,26}you spoke long ago by the Holy Spirit through our ancestor King David, your servant, saying, 'Why do the heathen rage against the Lord, and the foolish nations plan their little plots against Almighty God? The kings of the earth unite to fight against him and against the anointed Son of God!'

²⁷"That is what is happening here in this city today! For Herod the king, and Pontius Pilate the governor, and all the Romans—as well as the people of Israel—are united against Jesus, your anointed Son, your holy servant. ²⁸They won't stop at anything that you in your wise power will let them do. ²⁹And now, O Lord, hear their threats, and grant to your servants great boldness in their preaching, ³⁰and send your healing power, and may miracles and wonders be done by the name of your holy servant Jesus."

³¹After this prayer, the building where they were meeting shook, and they were all filled with the Holy Spirit and boldly preached God's message.

³²All the believers were of one heart and mind, and no one felt that what he owned was his own; everyone was sharing. ³³And the apostles preached powerful sermons about the resurrection of the Lord Jesus, and there was warm fellowship among all the believers, ^{34,35}and no poverty—for all who owned land or houses sold them and brought the money to the apostles to give to others in need.

³⁶For instance, there was Joseph (the one the apostles nicknamed "Barnabas, the encourager." He was of the tribe of Levi, from the island of Cyprus). ³⁷He was one of those who sold a field he owned and brought the money to the apostles for distribution to those in need.

CHAPTER 5 ANANIAS AND SAPPHIRA LIE TO GOD.

But there was a man named Ananias (with his wife Sapphira) who sold some property ²and brought only part of the money, claiming it was the full price. (His wife had agreed to this deception.)

STRENGTH

4:24-30 Notice how the believers prayed. First they praised God, then they told God their specific problem and asked for his help. They did not ask God to remove the problem, but to help them deal with it. This is a model for us to follow when we pray. We may ask God to remove our problems, and he may choose to do so, but we must recognize that often God will leave the problem in place and give us the strength to deal with it.

³But Peter said, "Ananias, Satan has filled your heart. When you claimed this was the full price, you were lying to the Holy Spirit. ⁴The property was yours to sell or not, as you wished. And after selling it, it was yours to decide how much to give. How could you do a thing like this? You weren't lying to us, but to God."

⁵As soon as Ananias heard these words, he fell to the floor, dead! Everyone was terrified, ⁶and the younger men covered him with a sheet and took him out and buried him.

⁷About three hours later his wife came in, not knowing what had happened. ⁸Peter asked her, "Did you people sell your land for such and such a price?"

"Yes," she replied, "we did."

⁹And Peter said, "How could you and your husband even think of doing a thing like this—conspiring together to test the Spirit of God's ability to know what is going on? Just outside that door are the young men who buried your husband, and they will carry you out too."

¹⁰Instantly she fell to the floor, dead, and the young men came in and, seeing that she was dead, carried her out and buried her beside her husband. ¹¹Terror gripped the entire church and all others who heard what had happened.

¹²Meanwhile, the apostles were meeting regularly at the Temple in the area known as Solomon's Hall, and they did many remarkable miracles among the people. ¹³The other believers didn't dare join them, though, but all had the highest regard for them. ¹⁴And more and more believers were added to the Lord, crowds both of men and women. ¹⁵Sick people were brought out into the streets on beds and mats so that at least Peter's shadow would fall across some of them as he went by! ¹⁶And crowds came in from the Jerusalem suburbs, bringing their sick

ATTRACTIVE

5:14 What makes Christianity attractive? It is easy to be drawn to churches because of exciting programs, good speakers, beautiful facilities, or friendly people. Believers were attracted to the early church by God's power and miracles; the generosity, sincerity, honesty, and unity of the members; and the character of the leaders. We must be careful that our standards don't slip. God wants to add to his *church*, not just to programs or congregations.

REACTIONS

5:17-18 The apostles had power to do miracles, great boldness in preaching, and God's presence in their lives—yet they were not free from hatred and persecution. They were arrested and put in jail, beaten with rods and whips, and slandered by community leaders. Faith in God does not make troubles disappear; it makes troubles appear less fearsome because it puts them in the right perspective. You cannot expect everyone to react favorably when you share something as dynamic as your faith in Christ. Some will be jealous of you, frightened, or threatened. Expect some negative reactions. But remember that you must be more concerned about God's reactions than people's reaction.

folk and those possessed by demons; and every one of them was healed.

¹⁷The High Priest and his relatives and friends among the Sadducees reacted with violent jealousy ¹⁸and arrested the apostles, and put them in the public jail.

¹⁹But an angel of the Lord came at night, opened the gates of the jail and brought them out. Then he told them, ²⁰"Go over to the Temple and preach about this Life!"

²¹They arrived at the Temple about daybreak and immediately began preaching! Later that morning the High Priest and his courtiers arrived at the Temple, and, convening the Jewish Council and the entire Senate, they sent for the apostles to be brought for trial. ²²But when the police arrived at the jail, the men weren't there, so they returned to the Council and reported, ²³"The jail doors were locked, and the guards were standing outside, but when we opened the gates, no one was there!"

²⁴When the police captain and the chief priests heard this, they were frantic, wondering what would happen next and where all this would end! ²⁵Then someone arrived with the news that the men they had jailed were out in the Temple, preaching to the people!

²⁶,²⁷The police captain went with his officers and arrested them (without violence, for they were afraid the people would kill them if they roughed up the disciples) and brought them in before the Council.

²⁸"Didn't we tell you never again to preach about this Jesus?" the High Priest demanded. "And instead you have filled all Jerusalem with your teaching and intend to bring the blame for this man's death on us!"

²⁹But Peter and the apostles replied, "We must obey God rather than men. ³⁰The God of our ancestors brought Jesus back to life again after you had killed him by hanging him on a cross. ³¹Then, with mighty power, God exalted him to be a Prince and Savior, so that the people of Israel would have an opportunity for repentance, and for their sins to be forgiven. ³²And we are witnesses of these things and so is the Holy Spirit, who is given by God to all who obey him."

³³At this, the Council was furious and decided to kill them. ³⁴But one of their members, a Pharisee named Gamaliel (an expert on religious law and very popular with the people), stood up and requested that the apostles be sent outside the Council chamber while he talked.

³⁵Then he addressed his colleagues as follows: "Men of Israel, take care what you are planning to do to these men! ³⁶Some time ago there was that fellow Theudas, who pretended to be someone great. About four hundred others joined him, but he was killed, and his followers were harmlessly dispersed.

³⁷"After him, at the time of the taxation, there was Judas of Galilee. He drew away some people as disciples, but he also died, and his followers scattered.

³⁸"And so my advice is, leave these men alone. If what they teach and do is merely on their own, it will soon be overthrown. ³⁹But if it is of God, you will not be able to stop them, lest you find yourselves fighting even against God."

⁴⁰The Council accepted his advice, called in the apostles, had them beaten, and then told them never again to speak in the name of Jesus, and finally let them go. ⁴¹They left the Council chamber rejoicing that God had counted them worthy to suffer dishonor for his name. ⁴²And every day, in the Temple and in their home Bible classes, they continued to teach and preach that Jesus is the Messiah.

CHAPTER 6 SEVEN MEN WITH SPECIAL WORK.

But with the believers multiplying rapidly, there were rumblings of discontent. Those who spoke only Greek complained that their widows were being discriminated against, that they were not being given as much food in the daily distribution as the widows who spoke Hebrew. ²So the Twelve called a meeting of all the believers.

"We should spend our time preaching, not administering a feeding program," they said. ³"Now look around among yourselves, dear brothers, and select seven men, wise and full of the Holy Spirit, who are well thought of by everyone; and we will put them in charge of this business. ⁴Then we can spend our time in prayer, preaching, and teaching."

⁵This sounded reasonable to the whole assembly, and they elected the following: Stephen (a man unusually full of faith and the Holy Spirit), Philip, Prochorus, Nicanor, Timon, Parmenas, Nicolaus of Antioch (a Gentile convert to the Jewish faith, who had become a Christian).

⁶These seven were presented to the apostles, who prayed for them and laid their hands on them in blessing.

⁷God's message was preached in ever-widening circles, and the number of disciples increased vastly in Jerusalem; and many of the Jewish priests were converted too.

THE WAVE

6:7 The gospel spread in "ever-widening circles" like ripples on a pond where, from a single center, each wave touches the next, spreading wider and farther. The gospel still spreads this way today. You don't have to change the world single-handedly—it is enough just to be part of the wave, touching those around you, who in turn will touch others until all have felt the movement. Don't ever feel that your part is insignificant or unimportant.

ACCUSED

7:2ff Stephen wasn't really defending himself. Instead he took the offensive, seizing the opportunity to summarize his teaching about Jesus. Stephen was accusing these religious leaders of failing to obey God's laws—the laws they prided themselves in following so meticulously. This was the same accusation that Jesus had leveled against them. When we witness for Jesus, we don't need to be on the defensive. Instead we should simply share our faith.

[8]Stephen, the man so full of faith and the Holy Spirit's power, did spectacular miracles among the people.

[9]But one day some of the men from the Jewish cult of "The Freedmen" started an argument with him, and they were soon joined by Jews from Cyrene, Alexandria in Egypt, and the Turkish provinces of Cilicia, and Asia Minor. [10]But none of them was able to stand against Stephen's wisdom and spirit.

[11]So they brought in some men to lie about him, claiming they had heard Stephen curse Moses, and even God.

[12]This accusation roused the crowds to fury against Stephen, and the Jewish leaders arrested him and brought him before the Council. [13]The lying witnesses testified again that Stephen was constantly speaking against the Temple and against the laws of Moses.

[14]They declared, "We have heard him say that this fellow Jesus of Nazareth will destroy the Temple and throw out all of Moses' laws." [15]At this point everyone in the Council chamber saw Stephen's face become as radiant as an angel's!

CHAPTER 7 STEPHEN IS EXECUTED.

Then the High Priest asked him, "Are these accusations true?"

[2]This was Stephen's lengthy reply: "The glorious God appeared to our ancestor Abraham in Iraq before he moved to Syria, [3]and told him to leave his native land, to say good-bye to his relatives and to start out for a country that God would direct him to. [4]So he left the land of the Chaldeans and lived in Haran, in Syria, until his father died. Then God brought him here to the land of Israel, [5]but gave him no property of his own, not one little tract of land.

"However, God promised that eventually the whole country would belong to him and his descendants—though as yet he had no children! [6]But God also told him that these descendants of his would leave the land and live in a foreign country and there become slaves for 400 years. [7]'But I will punish the nation that enslaves them,' God told him, 'and afterwards my people will return to this land of Israel and worship me here.'

[8]"God also gave Abraham the ceremony of circumcision at that time, as evidence of the covenant between God and the people of Abraham. And so Isaac, Abraham's son, was circumcised when he was eight days old. Isaac became the father of Jacob, and Jacob was the father of the twelve patriarchs of the Jewish nation. [9]These men were very jealous of Joseph and sold him to be a slave in Egypt. But God was with him, [10]and delivered him out of all of his anguish, and gave him favor before Pharaoh, king of Egypt. God also gave Joseph unusual wisdom so that Pharaoh appointed him governor over all Egypt, as well as putting him in charge of all the affairs of the palace.

[11]"But a famine developed in Egypt and Canaan, and there was great misery for our ancestors. When their food was gone, [12]Jacob heard that there was still grain in Egypt, so he sent his sons to buy some. [13]The second time they went, Joseph revealed his identity to his brothers, and they were introduced to Pharaoh. [14]Then Joseph sent for his father Jacob and all his brothers' families to come to Egypt, seventy-five persons in all. [15]So Jacob came to Egypt, where he died, and all his sons. [16]All of them were taken to Shechem and buried in the tomb Abraham bought from the sons of Hamor, Shechem's father.

[17,18]"As the time drew near when God would fulfill his promise to Abraham to free his descendants from slavery, the Jewish people greatly multiplied in Egypt; but then a king was crowned who had no respect for Joseph's memory. [19]This king plotted against our race, forcing parents to abandon their children in the fields.

[20]"About that time Moses was born—a child of divine beauty. His parents hid him at home for three months, [21]and when at last they could no longer keep him hidden and had to abandon him, Pharaoh's daughter found him and adopted him as her own son, [22]and taught him all the wisdom of the Egyptians, and he became a mighty prince and orator.

[23]"One day as he was nearing his fortieth birthday, it came into his mind to visit his brothers, the people of Israel. [24]During this visit he saw an Egyptian mistreating a man of Israel. So Moses killed the Egyptian. [25]Moses supposed his brothers would realize that God had sent him to help them, but they didn't.

[26]"The next day he visited them again and saw two men of Israel fighting. He tried to be a peacemaker. 'Gentlemen,' he said, 'you are brothers and shouldn't be fighting like this! It is wrong!'

[27]"But the man in the wrong told Moses to mind his own business. 'Who made *you* a ruler and judge over us?' he asked. [28]'Are you going to kill me as you killed that Egyptian yesterday?'

[29]"At this, Moses fled the country and lived in the land of Midian, where his two sons were born.

[30]"Forty years later, in the desert near Mount Sinai, an Angel appeared to him in a flame of fire in a bush. [31]Moses saw it and wondered what it was, and as he ran to see, the voice of the Lord called out

to him, [32]'I am the God of your ancestors—of Abraham, Isaac and Jacob.' Moses shook with terror and dared not look.

[33]"And the Lord said to him, 'Take off your shoes, for you are standing on holy ground. [34]I have seen the anguish of my people in Egypt and have heard their cries. I have come down to deliver them. Come, I will send you to Egypt.' [35]And so God sent back the same man his people had previously rejected by demanding, 'Who made *you* a ruler and judge over us?' Moses was sent to be their ruler and savior. [36]And by means of many remarkable miracles he led them out of Egypt and through the Red Sea, and back and forth through the wilderness for forty years.

[37]"Moses himself told the people of Israel, 'God will raise up a Prophet much like me from among your brothers.' [38]How true this proved to be, for in the wilderness, Moses was the go-between—the mediator between the people of Israel and the Angel who gave them the Law of God—the Living Word—on Mount Sinai.

[39]"But our fathers rejected Moses and wanted to return to Egypt. [40]They told Aaron, 'Make idols for us, so that we will have gods to lead us back; for we don't know what has become of this Moses, who brought us out of Egypt.' [41]So they made a calf idol and sacrificed to it, and rejoiced in this thing they had made.

[42]"Then God turned away from them and gave them up, and let them serve the sun, moon, and stars as their gods! In the book of Amos' prophecies the Lord God asks, 'Was it to me you were sacrificing during those forty years in the desert, Israel? [43]No, your real interest was in your heathen gods—Sakkuth, and the star god Kaiway, and in all the images you made. So I will send you into captivity far away beyond Babylon.'

[44]"Our ancestors carried along with them a portable Temple, or Tabernacle, through the wilderness. In it they kept the stone tablets with the Ten Commandments written on them. This building was constructed in exact accordance with the plan shown to Moses by the Angel. [45]Years later, when Joshua led the battles against the Gentile nations, this Tabernacle was taken with them into their new territory, and used until the time of King David.

[46]"God blessed David greatly, and

STEPHEN

UPS:
- One of seven leaders chosen to supervise food distribution to the needy in the early church
- Known for his spiritual qualities of faith, wisdom, grace, and power, and for the Spirit's presence in his life
- Outstanding leader, teacher, and debater
- First to give his life for the gospel

STATS:
- Church responsibilities: Deacon—distributing food to the needy
- Contemporaries: Paul, Caiaphas, Gamaliel, the apostles

The book you hold in your hand is there today because thousands of Christians throughout history have given their lives to carry the gospel around the world. They died for the Good News. It is important for us to remember, though, that a person cannot give his life for the gospel until he has learned to live his life for the gospel. Stephen was just that kind of person.

One way God trains his servants is to have them do jobs that don't seem very important or glamorous. We meet Stephen in the New Testament when he is appointed with others to manage the distribution of food among Christians in Jerusalem. Because many people lost jobs and belongings when they became Christians, it became necessary for all Christians to share what they had with each other. Stephen and others were asked to make sure that the available food was handed out fairly. It was probably a job with more headaches than thank-yous.

Stephen also proved himself as a powerful speaker. When he was harassed about his faith, he responded calmly and clearly. His logic devastated their arguments. Stephen was hauled before the official religious court where he used a summary of the Jews' own history to show that Jesus was the Savior. The court was unable to answer him, so they decided to silence him. They stoned him to death while he prayed for their forgiveness. Stephen's final words show how much he had become like Jesus in a short time. His death had a lasting effect on a young Paul, who would later change from fiercely destroying the faith to radically defending it.

Stephen's life is a continual challenge to Christians. Because he was the first to die for the faith, his sacrifice raises questions: How many risks do we take in being Jesus' followers? Would we be willing to die for him? Are we really willing to live for him?

LESSONS: Striving for excellence in small assignments prepares a person for greater responsibilities

Real understanding of God always leads to practical and compassionate actions toward people

KEY VERSES: "And as the murderous stones came hurling at him, Stephen prayed, 'Lord Jesus, receive my spirit.' And he fell to his knees, shouting, 'Lord, don't charge them with this sin!' and with that, he died" (Acts 7:59-60).

Stephen's story is told in Acts 6:3–8:2. He also is mentioned in Acts 11:19; 22:20.

PREPARING

8:4 Persecution forced the believers out of their homes in Jerusalem, but with them went the gospel. Often we have to become uncomfortable before we'll move. Discomfort may be unwanted, but it is not unproductive, for out of our hurting God works his purposes. The next time you are tempted to complain about uncomfortable or painful circumstances, stop and ask if God may be preparing you for a special task.

David asked for the privilege of building a permanent Temple for the God of Jacob. [47]But it was Solomon who actually built it. [48,49]However, God doesn't live in temples made by human hands. 'The heaven is my throne,' says the Lord through his prophets, 'and earth is my footstool. What kind of home could you build?' asks the Lord. 'Would I stay in it? [50]Didn't I make both heaven and earth?'

[51]"You stiff-necked heathen! Must you forever resist the Holy Spirit? But your fathers did, and so do you! [52]Name one prophet your ancestors didn't persecute! They even killed the ones who predicted the coming of the Righteous One—the Messiah whom you betrayed and murdered. [53]Yes, and you deliberately destroyed God's laws, though you received them from the hands of angels."

[54]The Jewish leaders were stung to fury by Stephen's accusation and ground their teeth in rage. [55]But Stephen, full of the Holy Spirit, gazed steadily upward into heaven and saw the glory of God and Jesus standing at God's right hand. [56]And he told them, "Look, I see the heavens opened and Jesus the Messiah standing beside God, at his right hand!"

[57]Then they mobbed him, putting their hands over their ears, and drowning out his voice with their shouts, [58]and dragged him out of the city to stone him. The official witnesses—the executioners—took off their coats and laid them at the feet of a young man named Paul.

[59]And as the murderous stones came hurtling at him, Stephen prayed, "Lord Jesus, receive my spirit." [60]And he fell to his knees, shouting, "Lord, don't charge them with this sin!" and with that, he died.

CHAPTER **8** **PHILIP AND AN ETHIOPIAN.** Paul was in complete agreement with the killing of Stephen.

And a great wave of persecution of the believers began that day, sweeping over the church in Jerusalem, and everyone except the apostles fled into Judea and Samaria. [2](But some godly Jews came and with great sorrow buried Stephen.) [3]Paul was like a wild man, going everywhere to devastate the believers, even entering private homes and dragging out men and women alike and jailing them.

[4]But the believers who had fled Jerusalem went everywhere preaching the Good News about Jesus! [5]Philip, for instance, went to the city of Samaria and told the people there about Christ. [6]Crowds listened intently to what he had to say because of the miracles he did. [7]Many evil spirits were cast out, screaming as they left their victims, and many who were paralyzed or lame were healed, [8]so there was much joy in that city!

[9-11]A man named Simon had formerly been a sorcerer there for many years; he was a very influential, proud man because of the amazing things he could do—in fact, the Samaritan people often spoke of him as the Messiah. [12]But now they believed Philip's message that Jesus was the Messiah, and his words concerning the Kingdom of God; and many men and women were baptized. [13]Then Simon himself believed and was baptized and began following Philip wherever he went, and was amazed by the miracles he did.

[14]When the apostles back in Jerusalem heard that the people of Samaria had accepted God's message, they sent down Peter and John. [15]As soon as they arrived, they began praying for these new Christians to receive the Holy Spirit, [16]for as yet he had not come upon any of them. For they had only been baptized in the name of the Lord Jesus. [17]Then Peter and John laid their hands upon these believers, and they received the Holy Spirit.

[18]When Simon saw this—that the Holy Spirit was given when the apostles placed their hands upon people's heads—he offered money to buy this power.

[19]"Let me have this power too," he exclaimed, "so that when I lay my hands on people, they will receive the Holy Spirit!"

[20]But Peter replied, "Your money perish with you for thinking God's gift can be bought! [21]You can have no part in this, for your heart is not right before God. [22]Turn from this great wickedness and pray. Perhaps God will yet forgive your evil thoughts— [23]for I can see that there is jealousy and sin in your heart."

[24]"Pray for me," Simon exclaimed, "that these terrible things won't happen to me."

[25]After testifying and preaching in Samaria, Peter and John returned to Jerusalem, stopping at several Samaritan villages along the way to preach the Good News to them too.

[26]But as for Philip, an angel of the Lord said to him, "Go over to the road that runs from Jerusalem through the Gaza Desert, arriving around noon." [27]So he did, and who should be coming down the road but the

CRITICISM

8:24 Do you remember the last time a parent or friend strongly criticized you? Were you hurt? Angry? Defensive? Learn a lesson from Simon and his reaction to Peter's words. Simon exclaimed, "Pray for me!" When you are rebuked for a serious mistake, it is for your good. Admit your error and ask for prayer.

Treasurer of Ethiopia, a eunuch of great authority under Candace the queen. He had gone to Jerusalem to worship ²⁸and was now returning in his chariot, reading aloud from the book of the prophet Isaiah.

²⁹The Holy Spirit said to Philip, "Go over and walk along beside the chariot."

³⁰Philip ran over and heard what he was reading and asked, "Do you understand it?"

³¹"Of course not!" the man replied. "How can I when there is no one to instruct me?" And he begged Philip to come up into the chariot and sit with him.

³²The passage of Scripture he had been reading from was this:

"He was led as a sheep to the slaughter, and as a lamb is silent before the shearers, so he opened not his mouth; ³³in his humiliation, justice was denied him; and who can express the wickedness of the people of his generation? For his life is taken from the earth."

³⁴The eunuch asked Philip, "Was Isaiah talking about himself or someone else?"

³⁵So Philip began with this same Scripture and then used many others to tell him about Jesus.

³⁶As they rode along, they came to a small body of water, and the eunuch said, "Look! Water! Why can't I be baptized?"

³⁷ "You can," Philip answered, "if you believe with all your heart."

And the eunuch replied, "I believe that Jesus Christ is the Son of God."

³⁸He stopped the chariot, and they went down into the water and Philip baptized him. ³⁹And when they came up out of the water, the Spirit of the Lord caught away Philip, and the eunuch never saw him again, but went on his way rejoicing. ⁴⁰Meanwhile, Philip found himself at Azotus! He preached the Good News there and in every city along the way, as he traveled to Caesarea.

CHAPTER **9** **PAUL MEETS JESUS.** But Paul, threatening with every breath and eager to destroy every Christian, went to the High Priest in Jerusalem. ²He requested a letter addressed to synagogues in Damascus, requiring their cooperation in the persecution of any believers he found there, both men and women, so that he could bring them in chains to Jerusalem.

³As he was nearing Damascus on this mission, suddenly a brilliant light from heaven spotted down upon him! ⁴He fell to the ground and heard a voice saying to him, "Paul! Paul! Why are you persecuting me?"

⁵"Who is speaking, sir?" Paul asked.

And the voice replied, "I am Jesus, the one you are persecuting! ⁶Now get up and go into the city

and await my further instructions."

⁷The men with Paul stood speechless with surprise, for they heard the sound of someone's voice but saw no one! ⁸·⁹As Paul picked himself up off the ground, he found that he was blind. He had to be

> **Some kids at school (and even some teachers) give Christians a pretty tough time. This makes me not want to let anyone know I'm a believer. What should I do?** *I WONDER . . .*
>
> Rejection comes with being a Christian, because our life and beliefs go against the flow of the rest of the world. Growing closer to God will naturally make you grow further away from the world.
>
> Read Acts 7:54-59. Stephen took a stand for Christ that cost him much more than rejection from a few friends. It cost him his life. Read further, and in Acts 8 and 9 you will see what the results of a fearless faith can be.
>
> Imagine being able to see all of history from beginning to end. You would understand so much more because you could see the whole picture. But only God can do that—so we have to trust him. We have to live on this earth without being able to see the future.
>
> If Stephen had known what his death would accomplish, he would have died smiling. A man named Paul was one of the foremost persecutors of Christians. But Paul's life was turned around, and he became a follower of Christ. Paul had heard Stephen speak—and he had watched him die.
>
> Paul didn't just become a church-only, pew-sitter type of follower. He traveled throughout the world, sharing the Good News about Christ. He also wrote nearly half of the books of the New Testament! Stephen's rejection helped bring Paul to Christ.
>
> People are watching you and other Christians at school. They are seeing how you respond to rejection and verbal abuse. Within those crowded halls are people who want to believe in something true, something worth living for no matter what the cost. And when they find it, they may make an incredible impact in their world for Christ.
>
> What do they learn from watching you?

led into Damascus and was there three days, blind, going without food and water all that time.

¹⁰Now there was in Damascus a believer named Ananias. The Lord spoke to him in a vision, calling, "Ananias!"

"Yes, Lord!" he replied.

¹¹And the Lord said, "Go over to Straight Street and find the house of a man named Judas and ask there for Paul of Tarsus. He is praying to me right now, for ¹²I have shown him a vision of a man named Ananias coming in and laying his hands on him so that he can see again!"

¹³"But Lord," exclaimed Ananias, "I have heard about the terrible things this man has done to the

DON'T WAIT

9:20 Immediately after receiving his sight, Paul went to the synagogue to tell the Jews about Jesus Christ. Some Christians counsel new believers to wait until they are thoroughly grounded in their faith before attempting to share the gospel. Paul took time alone to learn about Jesus before beginning his worldwide ministry, but he did not wait to witness. Although we should not rush into a ministry unprepared, we do not need to wait before telling others what has happened to us.

believers in Jerusalem! [14]And we hear that he has arrest warrants with him from the chief priests, authorizing him to arrest every believer in Damascus!"

[15]But the Lord said, "Go and do what I say. For Paul is my chosen instrument to take my message to the nations and before kings, as well as to the people of Israel. [16]And I will show him how much he must suffer for me."

[17]So Ananias went over and found Paul and laid his hands on him and said, "Brother Paul, the Lord Jesus, who appeared to you on the road, has sent me so that you may be filled with the Holy Spirit and get your sight back."

[18]Instantly (it was as though scales fell from his eyes) Paul could see and was immediately baptized. [19]Then he ate and was strengthened.

He stayed with the believers in Damascus for a few days [20]and went at once to the synagogue to tell everyone there the Good News about Jesus—that he is indeed the Son of God!

[21]All who heard him were amazed. "Isn't this the same man who persecuted Jesus' followers so bitterly in Jerusalem?" they asked. "And we understand that he came here to arrest them all and take them in chains to the chief priests."

[22]Paul became more and more fervent in his preaching, and the Damascus Jews couldn't withstand his proofs that Jesus was indeed the Christ.

[23]After a while the Jewish leaders determined to kill him. [24]But Paul was told about their plans, that they were watching the gates of the city day and night prepared to murder him. [25]So during the night some of his converts let him down in a basket through an opening in the city wall!

[26]Upon arrival in Jerusalem he tried to meet with the believers, but they were all afraid of him. They thought he was faking! [27]Then Barnabas brought him to the apostles and told them how Paul had seen the Lord on the way to Damascus, what the Lord had said to him, and all about his powerful preaching in the name of Jesus. [28]Then they accepted him, and after that he was constantly with the believers [29]and preached boldly in the name of the Lord. But then some Greek-speaking Jews with whom he had argued plotted to murder him. [30]However, when the other believers heard about his danger, they took him to Caesarea and then sent him to his home in Tarsus.

[31]Meanwhile, the church had peace throughout Judea, Galilee and Samaria, and grew in strength and numbers. The believers learned how to walk in the fear of the Lord and in the comfort of the Holy Spirit.

[32]Peter traveled from place to place to visit them, and in his travels came to the believers in the town of Lydda. [33]There he met a man named Aeneas, paralyzed and bedridden for eight years.

[34]Peter said to him, "Aeneas! Jesus Christ has healed you! Get up and make your bed." And he was healed instantly. [35]Then the whole population of Lydda and Sharon turned to the Lord when they saw Aeneas walking around.

[36]In the city of Joppa there was a woman named Dorcas ("Gazelle"), a believer who was always doing kind things for others, especially for the poor. [37]About this time she became ill and died. Her friends prepared her for burial and laid her in an upstairs room. [38]But when they learned that Peter was nearby at Lydda, they sent two men to beg him to return with them to Joppa. [39]This he did; as soon as he arrived, they took him upstairs where Dorcas lay. The room was filled with weeping widows who were showing one another the coats and other garments Dorcas had made for them. [40]But Peter asked them all to leave the room; then he knelt and prayed. Turning to the body he said, "Get up, Dorcas," and she opened her eyes! And when she saw Peter, she sat up! [41]He gave her his hand and helped her up and called in the believers and widows, presenting her to them.

[42]The news raced through the town, and many believed in the Lord. [43]And Peter stayed a long time in Joppa, living with Simon, the tanner.

IMPACT

9:36-42 Dorcas had an enormous impact on her community by "always doing kind things for others, especially for the poor." When she died, the room was filled with mourners, people she had helped. When she was brought back to life, the news raced through the town. God uses great preachers like Peter and Paul, but he also uses those who have other gifts, like kindness. Make good use of the gifts God has given you.

CHAPTER 10 A ROMAN CAPTAIN CALLS FOR PETER.

In Caesarea there lived a Roman army officer, Cornelius, a captain of an Italian regiment. [2]He was a godly man, deeply reverent, as was his entire household. He gave generously to charity and was a man of prayer. [3]While wide awake one afternoon he had a vision—it was about three o'clock—and in this vision he saw an angel of God coming toward him.

"Cornelius!" the angel said.

[4]Cornelius stared at him in terror. "What do you want, sir?" he asked the angel.

And the angel replied, "Your prayers and charities have not gone unnoticed by God! [5,6]Now send some men to Joppa to find a man named Simon Peter, who is staying with Simon, the tanner, down by the shore, and ask him to come and visit you."

[7]As soon as the angel was gone, Cornelius called two of his household servants and a godly soldier, one of his personal bodyguard, [8]and told them what had happened and sent them off to Joppa.

[9,10]The next day as they were nearing the city, Peter went up on the flat roof of his house to pray. It was noon and he was hungry, but while lunch was being prepared, he fell into a trance. [11]He saw the sky open and a great canvas sheet, suspended by its four corners, settle to the ground. [12]In the sheet were all sorts of animals, snakes, and birds [forbidden to the Jews for food].

[13]Then a voice said to him, "Go kill and eat any of them you wish."

[14]"Never, Lord," Peter declared, "I have never in all my life eaten such creatures, for they are forbidden by our Jewish laws."

[15]The voice spoke again, "Don't contradict God! If he says something is kosher, then it is."

[16]The same vision was repeated three times. Then the sheet was pulled up again to heaven.

[17]Peter was very perplexed. What could the vision mean? What was he supposed to do?

Just then the men sent by Cornelius had found the house and were standing outside at the gate, [18]inquiring whether this was the place where Simon Peter lived!

[19]Meanwhile, as Peter was puzzling over the vision, the Holy Spirit said to him, "Three men have come to see you. [20]Go down and meet them and go with them. All is well, I have sent them."

[21]So Peter went down. "I'm the man you're looking for," he said. "Now what is it you want?"

[22]Then they told him about Cornelius the Roman officer, a good and godly man, well thought of by the Jews, and how an angel had instructed him to send for Peter to come and tell him what God wanted him to do.

[23]So Peter invited them in and lodged them overnight.

The next day he went with them, accompanied by some other believers from Joppa.

[24]They arrived in

PAUL

No person, apart from Jesus himself, shaped the history of Christianity as much as the apostle Paul. Paul was a leader in the frenzied persecution of Christians following Stephen's death. Eventually, Paul met Christ personally and his life was changed. However, Paul never lost his energy or intensity—it was redirected so that it was dedicated to Christ.

Paul was brought up in a very religious home. His training was the best available. He was an expert in the Jewish Bible, the Old Testament. Convinced that the Christian movement was dangerous to Judaism, Paul hated the Christian faith and persecuted Christians without mercy. At one point, Paul got permission to travel to Damascus to arrest Christians and bring them back to Jerusalem. His plans—but God had other plans. Paul was met on the road to Damascus by Jesus Christ . . . and Paul's life was never the same. Paul became God's key tool in taking the gospel to non-Jewish people. Until Paul was converted, little had been done to carry Christ's message eventually carried the gospel and his missionary teams across the entire Roman Empire.

Paul worked hard to convince the Jews that Gentiles were acceptable to God, but he spent even more time convincing Gentiles themselves that they were acceptable to God. People's lives were changed and challenged by meeting Christ through Paul. God did not waste any part of Paul—his background, his training, his citizenship, his mind, or even his weaknesses. He used them all. Are you willing to let God do the same for you? You will never know what he can do with you until you allow him to have all that you are!

LESSONS: The Good News is that forgiveness and eternal life are a gift of God's grace received by faith in Christ and available to all people. Obedience results from a relationship with God, but obedience will never create or earn that relationship.

God will use our past and present so that we may serve him with our future

KEY VERSES: "For to me, living means opportunities for Christ, and dying—well, that's better yet! But if living will give me more opportunities to win people to Christ, then I really don't know which is better, to live or die!" (Philippians 1:21-22).

Paul's story is told in Acts 7:58–28:31 and throughout his New Testament letters.

UPS:
- Transformed by God from a persecutor of Christians to a preacher for Christ
- Preached for Christ throughout the Roman Empire on three missionary journeys
- Wrote letters, which became part of the New Testament, to various churches
- Was never afraid to face an issue head-on and deal with it
- Was sensitive to God's leading and, despite his strong personality, always did as God directed
- Often is called the apostle to the Gentiles

DOWNS:
- Witnessed and approved of Stephen's stoning
- Set out to destroy Christianity by persecuting Christians

STATS:
- Where: Born in Tarsus but became a world traveler for Christ
- Occupations: Trained as a Pharisee, learned the tentmaking trade, served as a missionary
- Contemporaries: Gamaliel, Stephen, the apostles, Luke, Barnabas, Timothy

Caesarea the following day, and Cornelius was waiting for him and had called together his relatives and close friends to meet Peter. ²⁵As Peter entered his home, Cornelius fell to the floor before him in worship.

²⁶But Peter said, "Stand up! I'm not a god!"

²⁷So he got up, and they talked together for a while and then went in where the others were assembled.

²⁸Peter told them, "You know it is against the Jewish laws for me to come into a Gentile home like this. But God has shown me in a vision that I should never think of anyone as inferior. ²⁹So I came as soon as I was sent for. Now tell me what you want."

³⁰Cornelius replied, "Four days ago I was praying as usual at this time of the afternoon, when suddenly a man was standing before me clothed in a radiant robe! ³¹He told me, 'Cornelius, your prayers are heard and your charities have been noticed by God! ³²Now send some men to Joppa and summon Simon Peter, who is staying in the home of Simon, a tanner, down by the shore.' ³³So I sent for you at once, and you have done well to come so soon. Now here we are, waiting before the Lord, anxious to hear what he has told you to tell us!"

³⁴Then Peter replied, "I see very clearly that the Jews are not God's only favorites! ³⁵In every nation he has those who worship him and do good deeds and are acceptable to him. ³⁶,³⁷I'm sure you have heard about the Good News for the people of Israel—that there is peace with God through Jesus, the Messiah, who is Lord of all creation. This message has spread all through Judea, beginning with John the Baptist in Galilee. ³⁸And you no doubt know that Jesus of Nazareth was anointed by God with the Holy Spirit and with power, and he went around doing good and healing all who were possessed by demons, for God was with him.

³⁹"And we apostles are witnesses of all he did throughout Israel and in Jerusalem, where he was murdered on a cross. ⁴⁰,⁴¹But God brought him back to life again three days later and showed him to certain witnesses God had selected beforehand—not to the general public, but to us who ate and drank with him after he rose from the dead. ⁴²And he sent us to preach the Good News everywhere and to testify that Jesus is ordained of God to be the Judge of all—living and dead. ⁴³And all the prophets have written about him, saying that everyone

who believes in him will have their sins forgiven through his name."

⁴⁴Even as Peter was saying these things, the Holy Spirit fell upon all those listening! ⁴⁵The Jews who came with Peter were amazed that the gift of the Holy Spirit would be given to Gentiles too! ⁴⁶,⁴⁷But there could be no doubt about it, for they heard them speaking in tongues and praising God.

Peter asked, "Can anyone object to my baptizing them, now that they have received the Holy Spirit just as we did?" ⁴⁸So he did, baptizing them in the name of Jesus, the Messiah. Afterwards Cornelius begged him to stay with them for several days.

CHAPTER 11 WHY PETER PREACHES TO GENTILES.

Soon the news reached the apostles and other brothers in Judea that Gentiles also were being converted! ²But when Peter arrived back in Jerusalem, the Jewish believers argued with him.

³"You fellowshiped with Gentiles and even ate with them," they accused.

⁴Then Peter told them the whole story. ⁵"One day in Joppa," he said, "while I was praying, I saw a vision—a huge sheet, let down by its four corners from the sky. ⁶Inside the sheet were all sorts of animals, reptiles, and birds [which we are not to eat]. ⁷And I heard a voice say, 'Kill and eat whatever you wish.'

⁸"'Never, Lord,' I replied. 'For I have never yet eaten anything forbidden by our Jewish laws!'

⁹"But the voice came again, 'Don't say it isn't right when God declares it is!'

¹⁰"This happened *three times* before the sheet and all it contained disappeared into heaven. ¹¹Just then three men who had come to take me with them to Caesarea arrived at the house where I was staying! ¹²The Holy Spirit told me to go with them and not to worry about their being Gentiles! These six brothers here accompanied me, and we soon arrived at the home of the man who had sent the messengers. ¹³He told us how an angel had appeared to him and told him to send messengers to Joppa to find Simon Peter! ¹⁴'He will tell you how you and all your household can be saved!' the angel had told him.

¹⁵"Well, I began telling them the Good News, but just as I was getting started with my sermon, the

STAY

10:48 Cornelius wanted Peter to stay with him for several days. As a new believer, Cornelius realized his need for teaching and fellowship. Are you that eager to learn more about Christ? Recognize your need to be with more mature Christians, and then learn from them.

SHOCKED

11:2-18 When Peter brought the news of Cornelius's conversion back to Jerusalem, the believers were shocked that he had eaten with Gentiles. After they heard the whole story, however, they began praising God (11:18). Their reactions teach us how to handle disagreements with other Christians. Before judging the behavior of fellow believers, it is important to hear them out. The Holy Spirit may be using them to teach us something important.

Holy Spirit fell on them, just as he fell on us at the beginning! [16]Then I thought of the Lord's words when he said, 'Yes, John baptized with water, but you shall be baptized with the Holy Spirit.' [17]And since it was *God* who gave these Gentiles the same gift he gave us when we believed on the Lord Jesus Christ, who was I to argue?"

[18]When the others heard this, all their objections were answered and they began praising God! "Yes," they said, "God has given to the Gentiles, too, the privilege of turning to him and receiving eternal life!"

[19]Meanwhile, the believers who fled from Jerusalem during the persecution after Stephen's death traveled as far as Phoenicia, Cyprus, and Antioch, scattering the Good News, but only to Jews. [20]However, some of the believers who went to Antioch from Cyprus and Cyrene also gave their message about the Lord Jesus to some Greeks. [21]And the Lord honored this effort so that large numbers of these Gentiles became believers.

[22]When the church at Jerusalem heard what had happened, they sent Barnabas to Antioch to help the new converts. [23]When he arrived and saw the wonderful things God was doing, he was filled with excitement and joy, and encouraged the believers to stay close to the Lord, whatever the cost. [24]Barnabas was a kindly person, full of the Holy Spirit and strong in faith. As a result, large numbers of people were added to the Lord.

[25]Then Barnabas went on to Tarsus to hunt for Paul. [26]When he found him, he brought him back to Antioch; and both of them stayed there for a full year teaching the many new converts. (It was there at Antioch that the believers were first called "Christians.")

[27]During this time some prophets came down from Jerusalem to Antioch, [28]and one of them, named Agabus, stood up in one of the meetings to predict by the Spirit that a great famine was coming upon the land of Israel. (This was fulfilled during the reign of Claudius.) [29]So the believers decided to send relief to the Christians in Judea, each giving as much as he could. [30]This they did, consigning their gifts to Barnabas and Paul to take to the elders of the church in Jerusalem.

JOHN MARK

What did you learn from your last mistake? Mistakes can be effective teachers because the consequences have a way of making lessons painfully clear. But those who learn from their mistakes gain wisdom. John Mark, with the help of some time and encouragement, became a wise learner.

Mark was eager to do the right thing, but he had trouble staying with a task. In his Gospel, Mark mentions a young man (probably referring to himself) who fled in such fear during Jesus' arrest that he left his clothes behind. Mark's tendency to run showed up later when Paul and Barnabas took him as their assistant on their first missionary journey. Early in the trip, Mark left them and returned to Jerusalem. Paul didn't appreciate Mark's quitting. Two years later, Paul would not consider letting Mark try again. As a result, the team split up. Barnabas took Mark with him, and Paul chose Silas. Barnabas was patient with Mark, and the young man turned out to be a good investment. In fact, Paul and Mark were later reunited and the older apostle became a close friend of the young disciple.

Mark was able to watch closely the lives of three Christian leaders—Barnabas, Paul, and Peter. The material in Mark's Gospel seems to have come mostly from Peter. As his helper, Mark had a chance to hear Peter's stories of the years with Jesus over and over. Mark became one of the first to put Jesus' life into writing. He had someone who encouraged him to learn from his mistakes.

Barnabas played a key role in Mark's life. He stood beside the young man in his failure, giving him patient encouragement. Mark's experience can remind us to learn from our mistakes and to appreciate the patience of others. Is there a Barnabas in your life whom you need to thank for his or her encouragement to you?

LESSONS: Personal maturity usually comes from a combination of time and mistakes. Effective living is not measured by what we accomplish so much as by what we overcome in order to accomplish a person's life. Encouragement can change a person's life

KEY VERSE: "Only Luke is with me. Bring Mark with you when you come, for I need him" (Paul writing to Timothy, 2 Timothy 4:11).

John Mark's story is told in Acts 12:25–13:13 and 15:36-39. He is also mentioned in Colossians 4:10; 2 Timothy 4:11; Philemon 1:24; 1 Peter 5:13.

UPS:
- Wrote the Gospel of Mark
- He and his mother provided their home as one of the main meeting places for the Christians in Jerusalem
- Persistent beyond his youthful mistakes
- Was an assistant and traveling companion to three of the greatest early missionaries

DOWNS:
- Probably the nameless young man described in the Gospel of Mark who fled in panic when Jesus was arrested
- Left Paul and Barnabas during the first missionary journey

STATS:
- Where: Jerusalem
- Occupation: Missionary-in-training, Gospel writer, traveling companion
- Relatives: Mother: Mary. Uncle: Barnabas.
- Contemporaries: Paul, Peter, Timothy, Luke, Silas

CHAPTER 12 AN ANGEL LETS PETER OUT OF PRISON.

About that time King Herod moved against some of the believers [2]and killed the apostle James (John's brother). [3]When Herod saw how much this pleased the Jewish leaders, he arrested Peter during the Passover celebration [4]and imprisoned him, placing him under the guard of sixteen soldiers. Herod's intention was to deliver Peter to the Jews for execution after the Passover. [5]But earnest prayer was going up to God from the church for his safety all the time he was in prison.

[6]The night before he was to be executed, he was asleep, double-chained between two soldiers with others standing guard before the prison gate, [7]when suddenly there was a light in the cell and an angel of the Lord stood beside Peter! The angel slapped him on the side to awaken him and said, "Quick! Get up!" And the chains fell off his wrists! [8]Then the angel told him, "Get dressed and put on your shoes." And he did. "Now put on your coat and follow me!" the angel ordered.

[9]So Peter left the cell, following the angel. But all the time he thought it was a dream or vision and didn't believe it was really happening. [10]They passed the first and second cell blocks and came to the iron gate to the street, and this opened to them of its own accord! So they passed through and walked along together for a block, and then the angel left him.

[11]Peter finally realized what had happened! "It's really true!" he said to himself. "The Lord has sent his angel and saved me from Herod and from what the Jews were hoping to do to me!"

[12]After a little thought he went to the home of Mary, mother of John Mark, where many were gathered for a prayer meeting.

[13]He knocked at the door in the gate, and a girl named Rhoda came to open it. [14]When she recognized Peter's voice, she was so overjoyed that she ran back inside to tell everyone that Peter was standing outside in the street. [15]They didn't believe her. "You're out of your mind," they said. When she insisted they decided, "It must be his angel. [They must have killed him.]"

[16]Meanwhile Peter continued knocking. When they finally went out and opened the door, their surprise knew no bounds. [17]He motioned for them to quiet down and told them what had happened and how the Lord had brought him out of jail. "Tell James and the others what happened," he said—and left for safer quarters.

[18]At dawn, the jail was in great commotion. What had happened to Peter? [19]When Herod sent for him and found that he wasn't there, he had the sixteen guards arrested, court-martialed and sentenced to death. Afterwards he left to live in Caesarea for a while.

[20]While he was in Caesarea, a delegation from Tyre and Sidon arrived to see him. He was highly displeased with the people of those two cities, but the delegates made friends with Blastus, the royal secretary, and asked for peace, for their cities were economically dependent upon trade with Herod's country. [21]An appointment with Herod was granted, and when the day arrived he put on his royal robes, sat on his throne, and made a speech to them. [22]At its conclusion the people gave him a great ovation, shouting, "It is the voice of a god and not of a man!"

[23]Instantly, an angel of the Lord struck Herod with a sickness so that he was filled with maggots and died—because he accepted the people's worship instead of giving the glory to God.

[24]God's Good News was spreading rapidly and there were many new believers.

[25]Barnabas and Paul now visited Jerusalem and as soon as they had finished their business, returned to Antioch, taking John Mark with them.

PRIDE

Seventeen-year-old Leslie loves music and has always wanted to be a singer. Not just a member of the youth choir. No, Leslie wants to be big-time, performing in front of a packed auditorium of cheering fans.

Leslie is talented, she practices a lot, and every now and then she gets to do solos at church. But last night, she finally got the big break she's been hoping for. She sang three songs at a huge youth rally in a city 250 miles away. Over 2,000 young people. A big stage. Lights. Professional sound equipment. Top-notch technicians. A $300 honorarium. We're talking "big time!"

Well, it went great. The audience loved her. Afterward, a handful of youth pastors asked her, "How can I book you to sing for my group?" People complimented her like crazy, tossing around words and phrases like "wonderful," "beautiful," and "going places." Some even asked when her first album would be out. The killer was the group of younger kids who asked Leslie to autograph their Bibles!

The day after, Leslie is still basking in her sudden success.

The day after, Leslie is a victim of pride.

Why is success and/or adulation so difficult to handle? Where do our talents come from? What happens if we forget God and get a big head? See Acts 12:19-23.

ANSWERS

12:13-15 The prayers of the little group of believers were answered, even as they prayed. But when the answer arrived at the door, they didn't believe it. We should be people of faith who believe that God answers the prayers of those who seek his will. When you pray, believe you'll get an answer—and when the answer comes, don't be surprised!

THREAD

13:1 What variety there is in the church! The only common thread among these five men was their deep faith in Christ. We must never exclude anyone whom Christ has called to follow him.

CHAPTER 13 PAUL'S FIRST MISSIONARY JOURNEY.

Among the prophets and teachers of the church at Antioch were Barnabas and Symeon (also called "The Black Man"), Lucius (from Cyrene), Manaen (the foster-brother of King Herod), and Paul. [2]One day as these men were worshiping and fasting the Holy Spirit said, "Dedicate Barnabas and Paul for a special job I have for them." [3]So after more fasting and prayer, the men laid their hands on them—and sent them on their way.

[4]Directed by the Holy Spirit they went to Seleucia and then sailed for Cyprus. [5]There, in the town of Salamis, they went to the Jewish synagogue and preached. (John Mark went with them as their assistant.)

[6,7]Afterwards they preached from town to town across the entire island until finally they reached Paphos where they met a Jewish sorcerer, a fake prophet named Bar-Jesus. He had attached himself to the governor, Sergius Paulus, a man of considerable insight and understanding. The governor invited Barnabas and Paul to visit him, for he wanted to hear their message from God. [8]But the sorcerer, Elymas (his name in Greek), interfered and urged the governor to pay no attention to what Paul and Barnabas said, trying to keep him from trusting the Lord.

[9]Then Paul, filled with the Holy Spirit, glared angrily at the sorcerer and said, [10]"You son of the devil, full of every sort of trickery and villainy, enemy of all that is good, will you never end your opposition to the Lord? [11]And now God has laid his hand of punishment upon you, and you will be stricken awhile with blindness."

Instantly mist and darkness fell upon him, and he began wandering around begging for someone to take his hand and lead him. [12]When the governor saw what happened, he believed and was astonished at the power of God's message.

[13]Now Paul and those with him left Paphos by ship for Turkey, landing at the port town of Perga. There John deserted them and returned to Jerusalem. [14]But Barnabas and Paul went on to Antioch, a city in the province of Pisidia.

On the Sabbath they went into the synagogue for the services. [15]After the usual readings from the Books of Moses and from the Prophets, those in charge of the service sent them this message: "Brothers, if you have any word of instruction for us come and give it!"

[16]So Paul stood, waved a greeting to them and began. "Men of Israel," he said, "and all others here who reverence God, [let me begin my remarks with a bit of history].

[17]"The God of this

BARNABAS

Think about the people who really matter in your life. Odds are that many of them are encouragers who have found ways to help you keep going. Good friends can tell when you are doing well and when you need to try harder. Mostly, they never give up on you! Everyone needs that kind of encouragement.

Among the first Christians, a man named Joseph was such an encourager that other believers nicknamed him "son of encouragement," or "Barnabas." Barnabas had an unusual ability to find people he could help. Whenever Barnabas encouraged Christians, the result was that others became believers!

Barnabas's actions were crucial to the early church. In a way, we can thank him for most of the New Testament. God used Barnabas's relationship with Paul at one point and with Mark at another to help these two men when either might have failed. Barnabas did wonders with encouragement.

We are surrounded by people we can encourage. Instead, we usually criticize. It may be important at times to show people where they are wrong, but we will be of greater help in the long run if we encourage people. They will accept our honest criticism if they know we want the best for them. Be prepared to encourage people today.

LESSONS: Encouragement is one of the most effective ways to help others

Sooner or later, true obedience to God will involve risk

There always is someone who needs encouragement

KEY VERSES: "When he arrived and saw the wonderful things God was doing, he was filled with excitement and joy, and encouraged the believers to stay close to the Lord, whatever the cost. Barnabas was a kindly person, full of the Holy Spirit and strong in faith. As a result, large numbers of people were added to the Lord" (Acts 11:23-24).

Barnabas's story is told in Acts 9:27–15:39. He also is mentioned in 1 Corinthians 9:6; Galatians 2:1,9,13; Colossians 4:10.

UPS:
- One of the first to sell possessions to help the Christians in Jerusalem
- First to travel with Paul as a missionary team
- Was an encourager, as his nickname shows, and thus one of the most quietly influential people in the early days of Christianity
- Called an apostle, although not one of the original Twelve

DOWN:
- Temporarily stayed aloof from Gentile believers until Paul corrected him

STATS:
- Where: Cyprus, Jerusalem, Antioch
- Occupation: Missionary, teacher
- Relatives: Sister: Mary. Nephew: John Mark.
- Contemporaries: Peter, Silas, Paul, Herod Agrippa I

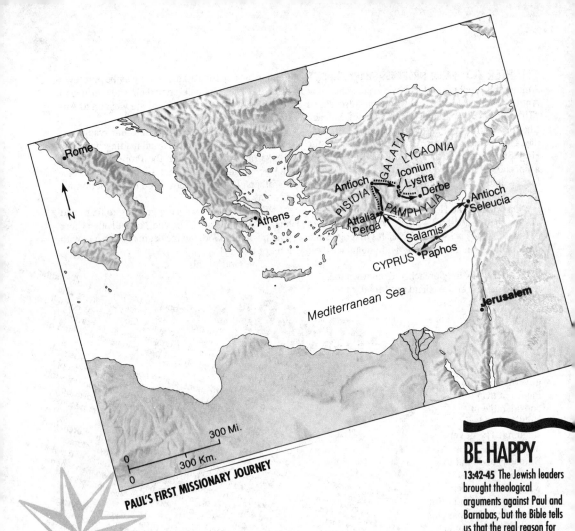

PAUL'S FIRST MISSIONARY JOURNEY

Map labels: Rome, Athens, Antioch, PISIDIA, GALATIA, LYCAONIA, Iconium, Lystra, Derbe, PAMPHYLIA, Attalia, Perga, Salamis, CYPRUS, Paphos, Antioch, Seleucia, Jerusalem, Mediterranean Sea, N, 300 Mi., 300 Km., 0

nation Israel chose our ancestors and honored them in Egypt by gloriously leading them out of their slavery. ¹⁸And he nursed them through forty years of wandering around in the wilderness. ¹⁹,²⁰Then he destroyed seven nations in Canaan and gave Israel their land as an inheritance. Judges ruled for about four hundred and fifty years and were followed by Samuel the prophet.

²¹"Then the people begged for a king, and God gave them Saul (son of Kish), a man of the tribe of Benjamin, who reigned for forty years. ²²But God removed him and replaced him with David as king, a man about whom God said, 'David (son of Jesse) is a man after my own heart, for he will obey me.' ²³And it is one of King David's descendants, Jesus, who is God's promised Savior of Israel!

²⁴"But before he came, John the Baptist preached the need for everyone in Israel to turn from sin to God. ²⁵As John was finishing his work he asked, 'Do you think I am the Messiah? No! But he is coming soon—and in comparison with him, I am utterly worthless.'

²⁶"Brothers—you sons of Abraham, and also all of you Gentiles here who reverence God—this salvation is for all of us! ²⁷The Jews in Jerusalem and their leaders fulfilled prophecy by killing Jesus; for they didn't recognize him or realize that he is the one the prophets had written about, though they heard the prophets' words read every Sabbath. ²⁸They found no just cause to execute him, but asked Pilate to have him killed anyway. ²⁹When they had fulfilled all the prophecies concerning his death, he was taken from the cross and placed in a tomb.

³⁰"But God brought him back to life again! ³¹And he was seen many times during the next few days by the men who had accompanied him to Jerusalem from Galilee—these men have constantly testified to this in public witness.

³²,³³"And now Barnabas and I are here to bring

BE HAPPY

13:42-45 The Jewish leaders brought theological arguments against Paul and Barnabas, but the Bible tells us that the real reason for their denunciation was jealousy (5:17). When we see others succeeding where we haven't or receiving the glory that we want, it is hard to be happy for them. Jealousy is our natural reaction. But it is tragic when our own jealous feelings make us try to stop God's work. If a work is God's work, rejoice in it—no matter who is doing it.

you this Good News—that God's promise to our ancestors has come true in our own time, in that God brought Jesus back to life again. This is what the second Psalm is talking about when it says concerning Jesus, 'Today I have honored you as my Son.'

34"For God had promised to bring him back to life again, no more to die. This is stated in the Scripture that says, 'I will do for you the wonderful thing I promised David.' 35In another Psalm he explained more fully, saying, 'God will not let his Holy One decay.' 36This was not a reference to David, for after David had served his generation according to the will of God, he died and was buried, and his body decayed. 37[No, it was a reference to another]—someone God brought back to life, whose body was not touched at all by the ravages of death.

38"Brothers! Listen! In this man Jesus there is forgiveness for your sins! 39Everyone who trusts in him is freed from all guilt and declared righteous—something the Jewish law could never do. 40Oh, be careful! Don't let the prophets' words apply to you. For they said, 41'Look and perish, you despisers [of the truth], for I am doing something in your day—something that you won't believe when you hear it announced.'"

42As the people left the synagogue that day, they asked Paul to return and speak to them again the next week. 43And many Jews and godly Gentiles who worshiped at the synagogue followed Paul and Barnabas down the street as the two men urged them to accept the mercies God was offering. 44The following week almost the entire city turned out to hear them preach the Word of God.

45But when the Jewish leaders saw the crowds, they were jealous, and cursed and argued against whatever Paul said.

46Then Paul and Barnabas spoke out boldly and declared, "It was necessary that this Good News from God should be given first to you Jews. But since you have rejected it and shown yourselves unworthy of eternal life—well, we will offer it to Gentiles. 47For this is as the Lord commanded when he said, 'I have made you a light to the Gentiles, to lead them from the farthest corners of the earth to my salvation.'"

48When the Gentiles heard this, they were very glad and rejoiced in Paul's message; and as many as wanted eternal life, believed. 49So God's message spread all through that region.

50Then the Jewish leaders stirred up both the godly women and the civic leaders of the city and incited a mob against Paul and Barnabas, and ran them out of town. 51But they shook off the dust of their feet against the town and went on to the city of Iconium. 52And their converts were filled with joy and with the Holy Spirit.

CHAPTER 14   PAUL AND BARNABAS SEEN AS GODS.

At Iconium, Paul and Barnabas went together to the synagogue and preached with such power that many—both Jews and Gentiles—believed.

2But the Jews who spurned God's message stirred up distrust among the Gentiles against Paul and Barnabas, saying all sorts of evil things about them. 3Nevertheless, they stayed there a long time, preaching boldly, and the Lord proved their message was from him by giving them power to do great miracles. 4But the people of the city were divided in their opinion about them. Some agreed with the Jewish leaders, and some backed the apostles.

5,6When Paul and Barnabas learned of a plot to incite a mob of Gentiles, Jews, and Jewish leaders to attack and stone them, they fled for their lives, going to the cities of Lycaonia, Lystra, Derbe, and the surrounding area, 7and preaching the Good News there.

8While they were at Lystra, they came upon a man with crippled feet who had been that way from birth, so he had never walked. 9He was listening as Paul preached, and Paul noticed him and realized he had faith to be healed. 10So Paul called to him, "Stand up!" and the man leaped to his feet and started walking!

11When the listening crowd saw what Paul had done, they shouted (in their local dialect, of course), "These men are gods in human bodies!" 12They decided that Barnabas was the Greek god Jupiter, and that Paul, because he was the chief speaker, was Mercury! 13The local priest of the Temple of Jupiter, located on the outskirts of the city, brought them cartloads of flowers and prepared to sacrifice oxen to them at the city gates before the crowds.

14But when Barnabas and Paul saw what was happening, they ripped at their clothing in dismay and ran out among the people, shouting, 15"Men! What are you doing? We are merely human beings like yourselves! We have come to bring you the Good News that you are invited to turn from the worship of these foolish things and to pray instead to the living God, who made heaven and earth and sea and everything in them. 16In bygone days he permitted the nations to go their own ways, 17but he never left himself without a witness; there were always his reminders—the kind things he did such

EVIDENCE

14:15-18 Responding to the people of Lystra, Paul and Barnabas reminded them that God never leaves himself "without a witness." Rain and crops, for example, demonstrate God's goodness. As did the health and gladness people enjoyed because they had the food they needed. Later Paul wrote that this evidence in nature and in people's lives leaves people without an excuse for unbelief (Romans 1:20). When in doubt about God, look around and you will see plenty of evidence that he is at work in our world.

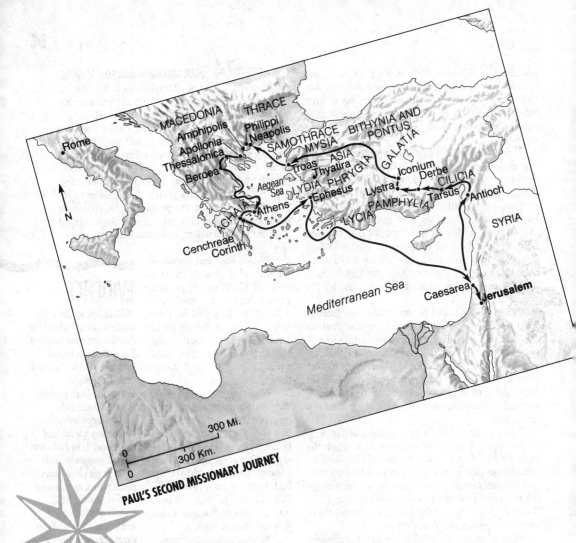

PAUL'S SECOND MISSIONARY JOURNEY

as sending you rain and good crops and giving you food and gladness."

¹⁸But even so, Paul and Barnabas could scarcely restrain the people from sacrificing to them!

¹⁹Yet only a few days later, some Jews arrived from Antioch and Iconium and turned the crowds into a murderous mob that stoned Paul and dragged him out of the city, apparently dead. ²⁰But as the believers stood around him, he got up and went back into the city!

The next day he left with Barnabas for Derbe. ²¹After preaching the Good News there and making many disciples, they returned again to Lystra, Iconium and Antioch, ²²where they helped the believers to grow in love for God and each other. They encouraged them to continue in the faith in spite of all the persecution, reminding them that they must enter into the Kingdom of God through many tribulations. ²³Paul and Barnabas also appointed elders in every church and prayed for them with fasting, turning them over to the care of the Lord in whom they trusted.

²⁴Then they traveled back through Pisidia to Pamphylia, ²⁵preached again in Perga, and went on to Attalia.

²⁶Finally they returned by ship to Antioch, where their journey had begun and where they had been committed to God for the work now completed.

²⁷Upon arrival they called together the believers and reported on their trip, telling how God had opened the door of faith to the Gentiles too. ²⁸And they stayed there with the believers at Antioch for a long while.

CHAPTER **15** A CHURCH CONFLICT. While Paul and Barnabas were at Antioch, some men from Judea arrived and began to teach the believers that unless they adhered to the ancient Jewish custom of circumcision, they could not be saved. ²Paul and Barnabas argued and discussed this with them at length, and finally the believers sent them to Jerusalem, accompanied by some local men, to talk to the apostles and elders there about this question. [3]After the entire congregation had escorted them out of the city, the delegates went on to Jerusalem, stopping along the way in the cities of Phoenicia and Samaria to visit the believers, telling them—much to everyone's joy—that the Gentiles, too, were being converted.

[4]Arriving in Jerusalem, they met with the church leaders—all the apostles and elders were present—and Paul and Barnabas reported on what God had been doing through their ministry. [5]But then some of the men who had been Pharisees before their conversion stood to their feet and declared that all Gentile converts must be circumcised and required to follow all the Jewish customs and ceremonies.

[6]So the apostles and church elders set a further meeting to decide this question.

[7]At the meeting, after long discussion, Peter stood and addressed them as follows: "Brothers, you all know that God chose me from among you long ago to preach the Good News to the Gentiles so that they also could believe. [8]God, who knows men's hearts, confirmed the fact that he accepts Gentiles by giving them the Holy Spirit, just as he gave him to us. [9]He made no distinction between them and us, for he cleansed their lives through faith, just as he did ours. [10]And now are you going to correct God by burdening the Gentiles with a yoke that neither we nor our fathers were able to bear? [11]Don't you believe that all are saved the same way, by the free gift of the Lord Jesus?"

[12]There was no further discussion, and everyone now listened as Barnabas and Paul told about the miracles God had done through them among the Gentiles.

[13]When they had finished, James took the floor. "Brothers," he said, "listen to me. [14]Peter has told you about the time God first visited the Gentiles to take from them a people to bring honor to his name. [15]And this fact of Gentile conversion agrees with what the prophets predicted. For instance, listen to this passage from the prophet Amos:

[16]'Afterwards' [says the Lord], 'I will return and renew the broken contract with David, [17]so that Gentiles, too, will find the Lord—all those marked with my name.'

[18]That is what the Lord says, who reveals his plans made from the beginning.

[19]"And so my judgment is that we should not insist that the Gentiles who turn to God must obey our Jewish laws, [20]except that we should write to them to refrain from eating meat sacrificed to idols, from all fornication, and also from eating unbled meat of strangled animals. [21]For these things have been preached against in Jewish synagogues in every city on every Sabbath for many generations."

[22]Then the apostles and elders and the whole congregation voted to send delegates to Antioch with Paul and Barnabas, to report on this decision. The men chosen were two of the church leaders—Judas (also called Barsabbas) and Silas.

[23]This is the letter they took along with them:

"*From:* The apostles, elders and brothers at Jerusalem.

"*To:* The Gentile brothers in Antioch, Syria and Cilicia. Greetings!

[24]"We understand that some believers from here have upset you and questioned your salvation, but they had no such instructions from us. [25]So it seemed wise to us, having unanimously agreed on our decision, to send to you these two official representatives, along with our beloved Barnabas and Paul. [26]These men—Judas and Silas, who have risked their lives for the sake of our Lord Jesus Christ—will confirm orally what we have decided concerning your question.

[27-29]"For it seemed good to the Holy Spirit and to us to lay no greater burden of Jewish laws on you than to abstain from eating food offered to idols and from unbled meat of strangled animals, and, of course, from fornication. If you do this, it is enough. Farewell."

[30]The four messengers went at once to Antioch, where they called a general meeting of the Christians and gave them the letter. [31]And there was great joy throughout the church that day as they read it.

[32]Then Judas and Silas, both being gifted speakers, preached long sermons to the believers, strengthening their faith. [33]They stayed several days, and then Judas and Silas returned to Jerusalem taking greetings and appreciation to those who had sent them. [34,35]Paul and Barnabas stayed on at Antioch to assist several others who were preaching and teaching there.

[36]Several days later Paul suggested to Barnabas that they return again to Turkey and visit each city where they had preached before, to see how the new converts were getting along. [37]Barnabas agreed and wanted to take along John Mark. [38]But Paul didn't like that idea at all, since John had deserted them in Pamphylia. [39]Their disagreement over this was so sharp that they separated. Barnabas took Mark with him and sailed for Cyprus, [40,41]while Paul chose Silas and, with the blessing of the believers, left for Syria and Cilicia to encourage the churches there.

ATTITUDE

15:23-29 This letter answered their questions and brought great joy to the Gentile Christians in Antioch (15:31). Beautifully written, it appeals to the Holy Spirit's guidance and explains what should be done as though the readers already knew it. It is helpful when people learn to be careful not only in what they say, but also in how they say it. We may be correct in our content, but we can lose our audience by our tone of voice or attitude.

CHAPTER 16 TIMOTHY IS PAUL'S HELPER. Paul and Silas went first to Derbe and then on to Lystra where they met Timothy, a believer whose mother was a Christian Jewess, but his father a Greek. [2]Timothy was well thought of by the brothers in Lystra and Iconium, [3]so Paul asked him to join them on their journey. In deference to the Jews of the area, he circumcised Timothy before they left, for everyone knew that his father was a Greek [and hadn't permitted this before]. [4]Then they went from city to city, making known the decision concerning the Gentiles, as decided by the apostles and elders in Jerusalem. [5]So the church grew daily in faith and numbers.

[6]Next they traveled through Phrygia and Galatia because the Holy Spirit had told them not to go into the Turkish province of Asia Minor at that time. [7]Then going along the borders of Mysia they headed north for the province of Bithynia, but again the Spirit of Jesus said no. [8]So instead they went on through Mysia province to the city of Troas.

[9]That night Paul had a vision. In his dream he saw a man over in Macedonia, Greece, pleading with him, "Come over here and help us." [10]Well, that settled it. We would go to Macedonia, for we could only conclude that God was sending us to preach the Good News there.

[11]We went aboard a boat at Troas, and sailed straight across to Samothrace, and the next day on to Neapolis, [12]and finally reached Philippi, a Roman colony just inside the Macedonian border, and stayed there several days. [13]On the Sabbath we went a little way outside the city to a riverbank where we understood some people met for prayer; and we taught the Scriptures to some women who came. [14]One of them was Lydia, a saleswoman from Thyatira, a merchant of purple cloth. She was already a worshiper of God and as she listened to us, the Lord opened her heart and she accepted all that Paul was saying. [15]She was baptized along with all her household and asked us to be her guests. "If you agree that I am faithful to the Lord," she said, "come and stay at my home." And she urged us until we did.

[16]One day as we were going down to the place of prayer beside the river, we met a demon-possessed slave girl, who was a fortune-teller and earned much money for her masters. [17]She followed along behind us shouting, "These men are servants of God, and they have come to tell you how to have your sins forgiven."

[18]This went on day after day until Paul, in great distress, turned and spoke to the demon within her. "I command you in the name of Jesus Christ to come out of her," he said. And instantly it left her.

[19]Her masters' hopes of wealth were now shattered; they grabbed Paul and Silas and dragged them before the judges at the marketplace. [20,21]"These Jews are corrupting our city," they shouted. "They are teaching the people to do things that are against the Roman laws."

[22]A mob was quickly formed against Paul and Silas, and the judges ordered them stripped and beaten with wooden whips. [23]Again and again the rods slashed down across their bared backs; and afterwards they were thrown into prison. The jailer was threatened with death if they escaped, [24]so he took no chances, but put them into the inner dungeon and clamped their feet into the stocks.

[25]Around midnight, as Paul and Silas were praying and singing hymns to the Lord—and the other prisoners were listening— [26]suddenly there was a great earthquake; the prison was shaken to its foundations, all the doors flew open—and the chains of every prisoner fell off! [27]The jailer wakened to see the prison doors wide open, and assuming the prisoners had escaped, he drew his sword to kill himself.

[28]But Paul yelled to him, "Don't do it! We are all here!"

[29]Trembling with fear, the jailer called for lights and ran to the dungeon and fell down before Paul and Silas. [30]He brought them out and begged them, "Sirs, what must I do to be saved?"

[31]They replied, "Believe on the Lord Jesus and you will be saved, and your entire household."

[32]Then they told him and all his household the Good News from the Lord. [33]That

BARRIERS

16:2-3 Timothy and his mother, Eunice, were from Lystra. Eunice had probably heard Paul's preaching during his first missionary journey (Acts 14:5-6). Timothy was the son of a Jewish mother and a Greek father—to the Jews, he was a half-breed, like a Samaritan. So Paul asked Timothy to be circumcised to erase some of the stigma he had with Jewish believers. Timothy was not required to be circumcised (the Jerusalem Council had decided that—chapter 15), but he voluntarily did so to overcome barriers to his witness for Christ. Sometimes we must go beyond minimum requirements to help our audience receive our testimony.

GOD'S WILL

16:6 We don't know how the Holy Spirit told Paul that he and his men were not to go into Asia. It may have been through a prophet, a vision, an inner conviction, or some other circumstance. To know God's will does not mean we must hear his voice. He leads in many ways. When seeking God's will: (1) make sure your plan is in harmony with God's word; (2) ask mature Christians for their advice; (3) check your own motives (are you doing what you want or what you think God wants?); and (4) ask God to open and close doors of circumstances.

PRAISE

16:22-25 Paul and Silas were stripped, beaten, whipped, and placed in stocks in the inner dungeon. Despite this dismal situation, they praised God, praying and singing as the other prisoners listened. No matter what our circumstances, we should praise God. Others may come to Christ because of our example.

same hour he washed their stripes, and he and all his family were baptized. [34]Then he brought them up into his house and set a meal before them. How he and his household rejoiced because all were now believers! [35]The next morning the judges sent police officers over to tell the jailer, "Let those men go!" [36]So the jailer told Paul they were free to leave.

[37]But Paul replied, "Oh no they don't! They have publicly beaten us without trial and jailed us—and we are Roman citizens! So now they want us to leave secretly? Never! Let them come themselves and release us!"

[38]The police officers reported to the judges, who feared for their lives when they heard Paul and Silas were Roman citizens. [39]So they came to the jail and begged them to go, and brought them out and pled with them to leave the city. [40]Paul and Silas then returned to the home of Lydia, where they met with the believers and preached to them once more before leaving town.

CHAPTER 17
PAUL VISITS TWO TOWNS.

Now they traveled through the cities of Amphipolis and Apollonia and came to Thessalonica, where there was a Jewish synagogue. [2]As was Paul's custom, he went there to preach, and for three Sabbaths in a row he opened the Scriptures to the people, [3]explaining the prophecies about the sufferings of the Messiah and his coming back to life, and proving that Jesus is the Messiah. [4]Some who listened were persuaded and became converts—including a large number of godly Greek men and also many important women of the city.

[5]But the Jewish leaders were jealous and incited some worthless fellows from the streets to form a mob and start a riot. They attacked the home of Jason, planning to take Paul and Silas to the City Council for punishment. [6]Not finding them there, they dragged out Jason and some of the other believers, and took them before the Council instead. "Paul and Silas have turned the rest of the world upside down, and now they are here disturbing our city," they shouted, [7]"and Jason has let them into his home. They are all guilty of treason, for they claim another king, Jesus, instead of Caesar."

[8,9]The people of the city, as well as the judges, were concerned at these reports and let them go only after they had posted bail.

[10]That night the Christians hurried Paul and Silas to Beroea, and, as usual, they went to the synagogue to preach. [11]But the people of Beroea were more

SILAS

One word that doesn't fit in the lives of the first Christians is boring. There were just too many exciting things happening. Hundreds of people who had never heard of Jesus before were trusting him with their lives. Christian missionaries were taking hazardous journeys over land and sea. Even preaching the gospel was sometimes dangerous, since there was often resistance and hatred of the message. Right in the middle of all the excitement was a young man named Silas.

We first meet Silas when he is sent as a representative from Jerusalem, with Paul and Barnabas, to spread the official news that people did not have to become Jews before they became Christians. It was an important mission. Later, Silas joined Paul and Timothy as an effective traveling ministry team. Life continued to be exciting. Paul and Silas spent a night singing in a Philippian prison after being severely beaten. Another time, they were almost beaten in Thessalonica but were able to pull off a daring escape in the night. Then Paul left Silas and Timothy in Beroea while he traveled on to Athens. Their job was to encourage the young believers in that new church. The team was reunited in Corinth. In each place they visited, they left behind a small group of Christians.

We don't know what eventually happened to Silas. He spent some time with Peter and is mentioned as the coauthor of 1 Peter. He continued to live the same faithful life that had made him a good choice to represent the church in Jerusalem. He was a helpful and encouraging member of Paul's team. Though he was never in the spotlight, his consistent life is a good model for us.

LESSONS: Partnership is a significant part of effective ministry

God never guarantees that his servants will not suffer

Obedience to God may mean giving up what makes us feel secure

KEY VERSE: "These men—Judas and Silas, who have risked their lives for the sake of our Lord Jesus Christ—will confirm orally what we have decided concerning your question" (Acts 15:26).

Silas's story is told in Acts 15:22–19:10. He is also mentioned in 2 Corinthians 1:19; 1 Thessalonians 1:1; 2 Thessalonians 1:1; 1 Peter 5:12.

UPS:
- A leader in the Jerusalem church
- Represented the church in carrying the "acceptance letter" prepared by the Jerusalem Council to the Gentile believers in Antioch
- Was closely associated with Paul from the second missionary journey on
- When imprisoned with Paul in Philippi, sang songs of praise to God
- Worked as a secretary for both Paul and Peter, using "Silvanus" as his pen name

STATS:
- Where: Roman citizen living in Jerusalem
- Occupation: One of the first career missionaries
- Contemporaries: Paul, Timothy, Peter, Mark, Barnabas

PAUL'S THIRD MISSIONARY JOURNEY

open-minded than those in Thessalonica, and gladly listened to the message. They searched the Scriptures day by day to check up on Paul and Silas' statements to see if they were really so. ¹²As a result, many of them believed, including several prominent Greek women and many men also.

¹³But when the Jews in Thessalonica learned that Paul was preaching in Beroea, they went over and stirred up trouble. ¹⁴The believers acted at once, sending Paul on to the coast, while Silas and Timothy remained behind. ¹⁵Those accompanying Paul went on with him to Athens and then returned to Beroea with a message for Silas and Timothy to hurry and join him.

¹⁶While Paul was waiting for them in Athens, he was deeply troubled by all the idols he saw everywhere throughout the city. ¹⁷He went to the synagogue for discussions with the Jews and the devout Gentiles, and spoke daily in the public square to all who happened to be there.

¹⁸He also had an encounter with some of the Epicurean and Stoic philosophers. Their reaction, when he told them about Jesus and his resurrection, was, "He's a dreamer," or, "He's pushing some foreign religion."

¹⁹But they invited him to the forum at Mars Hill. "Come and tell us more about this new religion," they said, ²⁰"for you are saying some rather startling things and we want to hear more." ²¹(I should explain that all the Athenians as well as the foreigners in Athens seemed to spend all their time discussing the latest new ideas!)

²²So Paul, standing before them at the Mars Hill forum, addressed them as follows:

"Men of Athens, I notice that you are very religious, ²³for as I was out walking I saw your many altars, and one of them had this inscription on it—'To the Unknown God.' You have been worshiping him without knowing who he is, and

COMPARE

17:11 How do you evaluate sermons and teachings? The people in Beroea opened the Scriptures for themselves and searched for truths to verify or disprove the message they heard. Always compare what you hear with what the Bible says. A preacher or teacher who gives God's true message will never contradict or explain away anything in God's word.

now I wish to tell you about him.

[24]"He made the world and everything in it, and since he is Lord of heaven and earth, he doesn't live in man-made temples; [25]and human hands can't minister to his needs—for he has no needs! He himself gives life and breath to everything, and satisfies every need there is. [26]He created all the people of the world from one man, Adam, and scattered the nations across the face of the earth. He decided beforehand which should rise and fall, and when. He determined their boundaries.

[27]"His purpose in all of this is that they should seek after God, and perhaps feel their way toward him and find him—though he is not far from any one of us. [28]For in him we live and move and are! As one of your own poets says it, 'We are the sons of God.' [29]If this is true, we shouldn't think of God as an idol made by men from gold or silver or chipped from stone. [30]God tolerated man's past ignorance about these things, but now he commands everyone to put away idols and worship only him. [31]For he has set a day for justly judging the world by the man he has appointed, and has pointed him out by bringing him back to life again."

[32]When they heard Paul speak of the resurrection of a person who had been dead, some laughed, but others said, "We want to hear more about this later." [33]That ended Paul's discussion with them, [34]but a few joined him and became believers. Among them was Dionysius, a member of the City Council, and a woman named Damaris, and others.

CHAPTER **18** PAUL WITH PRISCILLA AND AQUILA.

Then Paul left Athens and went to Corinth. [2,3]There he became acquainted with a Jew named Aquila, born in Pontus, who had recently arrived from Italy with his wife, Priscilla. They had been expelled from Italy as a result of Claudius Caesar's order to deport all Jews from Rome. Paul lived and worked with them, for they were tentmakers just as he was.

[4]Each Sabbath found Paul at the synagogue, trying to convince the Jews and Greeks alike. [5]And after the arrival of Silas and Timothy from Macedonia, Paul spent his full time preaching and testifying to the Jews that Jesus is the Messiah. [6]But when the Jews opposed him and blasphemed, hurling abuse at Jesus, Paul shook off the dust from his robe and said, "Your blood be upon your own heads—I am innocent—from now on I will preach to the Gentiles."

[7]After that he stayed with Titus Justus, a Gentile who worshiped God and lived next door to the synagogue. [8]However, Crispus, the leader of the synagogue, and all his household believed in the Lord and were baptized—as were many others in Corinth.

[9]One night the Lord spoke to Paul in a vision and told him, "Don't be afraid! Speak out! Don't quit! [10]For I am with you and no one can harm you. Many people here in this city belong to me." [11]So Paul stayed there the next year and a half, teaching the truths of God.

I'm not the kind of person that can take everything at face value. I have to have more proof. Is it wrong to want to know the answers to questions I have about the Bible?

I WONDER . . .

The Christians in Beroea were complimented by Luke, the writer of Acts, because "they searched the Scriptures day by day to check up on Paul and Silas' statements to see if they were really so" (Acts 17:11).

Because being a Christian means accepting Christ's forgiveness by faith, some think we must believe everything just because another Christian said it. But getting your questions answered by studying the Bible is an important part of being a Christian. Although not every question about the Bible or the Christian life can be answered most of them can.

Some people are natural skeptics. They challenge everything in the Bible. But often they aren't looking for answers—just an argument. If, however, you have the prayerful heart of a seeker, God will help you unlock the secrets of his word. "Ask, and you will be given what you ask for. Seek, and you will find. Knock, and the door will be opened. For everyone who asks, receives. Anyone who seeks, finds. If only you will knock, the door will open" (Matthew 7:7-8).

[12]But when Gallio became governor of Achaia, the Jews rose in concerted action against Paul and brought him before the governor for judgment. [13]They accused Paul of "persuading men to worship God in ways that are contrary to Roman law." [14]But just as Paul started to make his defense, Gallio turned to his accusers and said, "Listen, you Jews, if this were a case involving some crime, I would be obliged to listen to you, [15]but since it is merely a bunch of questions of semantics and personalities and your silly Jewish laws, you take care of it. I'm not interested and I'm not touching it." [16]And he drove them out of the courtroom.

[17]Then the mob grabbed Sosthenes, the new leader of the synagogue, and beat him outside the courtroom. But Gallio couldn't have cared less.

WORTH IT

17:32-34 Paul's speech received a mixed reaction: some laughed, some kept searching for more information, and a few believed. Don't hesitate to tell others about Christ because you fear that some will not believe you. And don't expect a unanimously positive response to your witnessing. Even if only a few believe, it's worth the effort.

¹⁸Paul stayed in the city several days after that and then said good-bye to the Christians and sailed for the coast of Syria, taking Priscilla and Aquila with him. At Cenchreae Paul had his head shaved according to Jewish custom, for he had taken a vow. ¹⁹Arriving at the port of Ephesus, he left us aboard ship while he went over to the synagogue for a discussion with the Jews. ²⁰They asked him to stay for a few days, but he felt that he had no time to lose. ²¹"I must by all means be at Jerusalem for the holiday," he said. But he promised to return to Ephesus later if God permitted; and so he set sail again. ²²The next stop was at the port of Caesarea from where he visited the church [at Jerusalem] and then sailed on to Antioch. ²³After spending some time there, he left for Turkey again, going through Galatia and Phrygia visiting all the believers, encouraging them and helping them grow in the Lord.

²⁴As it happened, a Jew named Apollos, a wonderful Bible teacher and preacher, had just arrived in Ephesus from Alexandria in Egypt. ^{25,26}While he was in Egypt, someone had told him about John the Baptist and what John had said about Jesus, but that is all he knew. He had never heard the rest of the story! So he was preaching boldly and enthusiastically in the synagogue, "The Messiah is coming! Get ready to receive him!" Priscilla and Aquila were there and heard him—and it was a powerful sermon. Afterwards they met with him and explained what had happened to Jesus since the time of John, and all that it meant!

²⁷Apollos had been thinking about going to Greece, and the believers encouraged him in this. They wrote to their fellow-believers there, telling them to welcome him. And upon his arrival in Greece, he was greatly used of God to strengthen the church, ²⁸for he powerfully refuted all the Jewish arguments in public debate, showing by the Scriptures that Jesus is indeed the Messiah.

CHAPTER 19 GOD SENDS THE HOLY SPIRIT.

While Apollos was in Corinth, Paul traveled through Turkey and arrived in Ephesus, where he found several disciples. ²"Did you receive the Holy Spirit when you believed?" he asked them.

"No," they replied, "we don't know what you mean. What is the Holy Spirit?"

³"Then what beliefs did you acknowledge at your baptism?" he asked.

And they replied, "What John the Baptist taught."

⁴Then Paul pointed out to them that John's baptism was to demonstrate a desire to turn from sin to God and that those receiving his baptism must then go on to believe in Jesus, the one John said would come later.

⁵As soon as they heard this, they were baptized in the name of the Lord Jesus. ⁶Then, when Paul laid his hands upon their heads, the Holy Spirit came on them, and they spoke in other languages and prophesied. ⁷The men involved were about twelve in number.

⁸Then Paul went to the synagogue and preached boldly each Sabbath day for three months, telling what he believed and why, and persuading many to believe in Jesus. ⁹But some rejected his message and publicly spoke against Christ, so he left, refusing to preach to them again. Pulling out the believers, he began a separate meeting at the lecture hall of Tyrannus and preached there daily. ¹⁰This went on for the next two years, so that everyone in the Turkish province of Asia Minor—both Jews and Greeks—heard the Lord's message.

¹¹And God gave Paul the power to do unusual miracles, ¹²so that even when his handkerchiefs or parts of his clothing were placed upon sick people, they were healed, and any demons within them came out.

¹³A team of itinerant Jews who were traveling from town to town casting out demons planned to experiment by using the name of the Lord Jesus. The incantation they decided on was this: "I adjure you by Jesus, whom Paul preaches, to come out!" ¹⁴Seven sons of Sceva, a Jewish priest, were doing this. ¹⁵But when they tried it on a man possessed by a demon, the demon replied, "I know Jesus and I know Paul, but who are you?" ¹⁶And he leaped on two of them and beat them up, so that they fled out of his house naked and badly injured.

¹⁷The story of what happened spread quickly all through Ephesus, to Jews and Greeks alike; and a solemn fear descended on the city, and the name of the Lord Jesus was greatly honored. ^{18,19}Many of

DEBATABLE

18:27-28 Apollos was from Alexandria in Egypt, the second largest city in the Roman Empire, home of a great university. He was a scholar, orator, and debater. After his knowledge about Christ was more complete, God greatly used his gifts to strengthen and encourage the church. Reason is a powerful tool in the right hands and the right situation. Apollos used his reasoning ability to convince many in Greece of the truth of the gospel. You don't have to turn off your mind when you turn to Christ. You can use logic or debate to bring others to God.

POWER

19:13 Many Ephesians engaged in exorcism and occult practices for profit, even sending demons from people (see 19:18-19). The sons of Sceva were impressed by Paul's work, whose power to cast out demons came from God's Holy Spirit, not from witchcraft, and was obviously more powerful than theirs. They discovered, however, that no person can control or duplicate God's power. These men were calling upon the name without knowing the person. It is knowing Jesus, not reciting his name like a magic charm, that gives us the power to change people. Christ works his power only through those he chooses.

the believers who had been practicing black magic confessed their deeds and brought their incantation books and charms and burned them at a public bonfire. (Someone estimated the value of the books at $10,000.) [20]This indicates how deeply the whole area was stirred by God's message.

[21]Afterwards Paul felt impelled by the Holy Spirit to go across to Greece before returning to Jerusalem. "And after that," he said, "I must go on to Rome!" [22]He sent his two assistants, Timothy and Erastus, on ahead to Greece while he stayed awhile longer in Asia Minor.

[23]But about that time, a big blowup developed in Ephesus concerning the Christians. [24]It began with Demetrius, a silversmith who employed many craftsmen to manufacture silver shrines of the Greek goddess Diana. [25]He called a meeting of his men, together with others employed in related trades, and addressed them as follows:

"Gentlemen, this business is our income. [26]As you know so well from what you've seen and heard, this man Paul has persuaded many, many people that handmade gods aren't gods at all. As a result, our sales volume is going down! And this trend is evident not only here in Ephesus, but throughout the entire province! [27]Of course, I am not only talking about the business aspects of this situation and our loss of income, but also of the possibility that the temple of the great goddess Diana will lose its influence, and that Diana—this magnificent goddess worshiped not only throughout this part of Turkey but all around the world—will be forgotten!"

[28]At this their anger boiled and they began shouting, "Great is Diana of the Ephesians!"

[29]A crowd began to gather, and soon the city was filled with confusion. Everyone rushed to the amphitheater, dragging along Gaius and Aristarchus, Paul's traveling companions, for trial. [30]Paul wanted to go in, but the disciples wouldn't let him. [31]Some of the Roman officers of the province, friends of Paul, also sent a message to him, begging him not to risk his life by entering.

[32]Inside the people were all shouting, some one thing and some another—everything was in confusion. In fact, most of them didn't even know why they were there.

[33]Alexander was spotted among the crowd by some of the Jews and dragged forward. He motioned for silence and tried to speak. [34]But when the crowd realized he was a Jew, they started shouting again and kept it up for

AQUILA & PRISCILLA

Some couples know how to make the most of life. They fit together, let each do his best, and form an effective team. Their combined efforts affect those around them. Aquila and Priscilla were such a couple. They are never mentioned apart from one another in the Bible. Together, they loved God and people.

Priscilla and Aquila met Paul in Corinth while he was on his second missionary journey. They had just left Rome. Their home was as movable as the tents they made in their business. They invited Paul to stay with them, and he joined them in tentmaking. He helped them by sharing his wisdom about God.

Priscilla and Aquila made good use of what they learned from Paul. They listened and evaluated what they heard. For instance, when another preacher named Apollos came to town, they listened to what he had to say. They realized he was a good speaker, but that there were important things he needed to learn. Instead of correcting Apollos in public, they quietly took him home with them and shared with him what he needed to know. Apollos had been preaching John the Baptist's message of repentance. Priscilla and Aquila told Apollos about Jesus' life, death, and resurrection, and how God's Spirit wanted to live in us. Apollos then used his great ability to tell the whole story!

This couple continued to use their home as a place for training and worship. Later, back in Rome, one of the churches met in their house. (The first Christians did not meet in church buildings, but in the homes of believers.) It is easy to imagine that anywhere Aquila and Priscilla lived would be a real place of fellowship.

LESSONS: Couples can have an effective ministry together

The home is a valuable tool for evangelism

KEY VERSES: "Tell Priscilla and Aquila hello. They have been my fellow workers in the affairs of Christ Jesus. In fact, they risked their lives for me, and I am not the only one who is thankful to them; so are all the Gentile churches" (Romans 16:3-4). Their story is told in Acts 18. They are also mentioned in Romans 16:3-5; 1 Corinthians 16:19; 2 Timothy 4:19.

UPS:
- Outstanding husband-wife team who ministered in the early church
- Supported themselves by tentmaking while serving Christ
- Close friends of Paul
- Explained the full message of Christ to Apollos

STATS:
- Where: Originally from Rome; moved to Corinth, then Ephesus
- Occupation: Tentmakers
- Contemporaries: Emperor Claudius, Paul, Timothy, Apollos

PAUL'S VOYAGE TO ROME

two hours: "Great is Diana of the Ephesians! Great is Diana of the Ephesians!"

³⁵At last the mayor was able to quiet them down enough to speak. "Men of Ephesus," he said, "everyone knows that Ephesus is the center of the religion of the great Diana, whose image fell down to us from heaven. ³⁶Since this is an indisputable fact, you shouldn't be disturbed no matter what is said, and should do nothing rash. ³⁷Yet you have brought these men here who have stolen nothing from her temple and have not defamed her. ³⁸If Demetrius and the craftsmen have a case against them, the courts are currently in session and the judges can take the case at once. Let them go through legal channels. ³⁹And if there are complaints about other matters, they can be settled at the regular City Council meetings; ⁴⁰for we are in danger of being called to account by the Roman government for today's riot, since there is no cause for it. And if Rome demands an explanation, I won't know what to say."

⁴¹Then he dismissed them, and they dispersed.

CHAPTER 20 ON TO GREECE AND MACEDONIA.

When it was all over, Paul sent for the disciples, preached a farewell message to them, said goodbye and left for Macedonia, ²preaching to the believers along the way in all the cities he passed through. ³He was in Greece three months and was preparing to sail for Syria when he discovered a plot by the Jews against his life, so he decided to go north to Macedonia first.

⁴Several men were traveling with him, going as far as Turkey; they were Sopater of Beroea, the son of Pyrrhus; Aristarchus and Secundus, from Thessalonica; Gaius, from Derbe; and Timothy; and Tychicus and Trophimus, who were returning to their homes in Turkey, ⁵and had gone on ahead and were waiting for us at Troas. ⁶As

SUCCESS

20:24 We often feel that life is a failure unless we're getting a lot out of it: glory, fun, money, popularity. But Paul thought life was worth *nothing* unless he used it for God's work. What he put *into* life was far more important than what he got out. Which is more important to you—what you get out of life, or what you put into it?

soon as the Passover ceremonies ended, we boarded ship at Philippi in northern Greece and five days later arrived in Troas, Turkey, where we stayed a week.

[7]On Sunday we gathered for a Communion service, with Paul preaching. And since he was leaving the next day, he talked until midnight! [8]The upstairs room where we met was lighted with many flickering lamps; [9]and as Paul spoke on and on, a young man named Eutychus, sitting on the windowsill, went fast asleep and fell three stories to his death below. [10-12]Paul went down and took him into his arms. "Don't worry," he said, "he's all right!" And he was! What a wave of awesome joy swept through the crowd! They all went back upstairs and ate the Lord's Supper together; then Paul preached another long sermon—so it was dawn when he finally left them!

[13]Paul was going by land to Assos, and we went on ahead by ship. [14]He joined us there and we sailed together to Mitylene; [15]the next day we passed Chios; the next, we touched at Samos; and a day later we arrived at Miletus.

[16]Paul had decided against stopping at Ephesus this time, as he was hurrying to get to Jerusalem, if possible, for the celebration of Pentecost.

[17]But when we landed at Miletus, he sent a message to the elders of the church at Ephesus asking them to come down to the boat to meet him.

[18]When they arrived he told them, "You men know that from the day I set foot in Turkey until now [19]I have done the Lord's work humbly—yes, and with tears—and have faced grave danger from the plots of the Jews against my life. [20]Yet I never shrank from telling you the truth, either publicly or in your homes. [21]I have had one message for Jews and Gentiles alike—the necessity of turning from sin to God through faith in our Lord Jesus Christ.

[22]"And now I am going to Jerusalem, drawn there irresistibly by the Holy Spirit, not knowing what awaits me, [23]except that the Holy Spirit has told me in city after city that jail and suffering lie ahead. [24]But life is worth nothing unless I use it for doing the work assigned me by the Lord Jesus—the work of telling others the Good News about God's mighty kindness and love.

[25]"And now I know that none of you among whom I went about teaching the Kingdom will ever see me again. [26]Let me say plainly that no man's blood can be laid at my door, [27]for I didn't shrink from declaring all God's message to you.

[28]"And now beware! Be sure that you feed and shepherd God's flock—his church, purchased with his blood—for the Holy Spirit is holding you responsible as overseers. [29]I know full well that after I leave you, false teachers, like vicious wolves, will appear among you, not sparing the flock. [30]Some of you yourselves will distort the truth in order to draw a following. [31]Watch out! Remember the three years I was with you—my constant watchcare over you night and day and my many tears for you.

[32]"And now I entrust you to God and his care and to his wonderful words that are able to build your faith and give you all the inheritance of those who are set apart for himself.

[33]"I have never been hungry for money or fine clothing— [34]you know that these hands of mine worked to pay my own way and even to supply the needs of those who were with me. [35]And I was a constant example to you in helping the poor; for I remembered the words of the Lord Jesus, 'It is more blessed to give than to receive.'"

[36]When he had finished speaking, he knelt and prayed with them, [37]and they wept aloud as they embraced him in farewell, [38]sorrowing most of all because he said that he would never see them again. Then they accompanied him down to the ship.

FOCUS

20:33 Paul was satisfied with whatever he had, wherever he was, as long as he could do God's work. Examine your attitudes toward wealth and comfort. If you focus more on what you don't have than on what you do have, it's time to reexamine your priorities and put God's work back in first place.

"Here's what I did..."

At my high school we have a Christian Bible study group called Saints' Battalion. A few months ago, Satanists on our campus formed a group they call Young Satanists of America. Before their own group meetings, held on the same day we have ours, they come into our meetings and bother us in every way they can. I know that in their meetings they put down Christianity and exalt Satan as a "philosophy."

We cannot ban them from coming to our meetings because our group has to be open to all. They still remain a problem. Our group and my church continue to pray about this problem. A passage that has really encouraged us is Acts 19:13-20. It talks about the power in the name of Jesus to cast out demons, and about how lots of people who heard about Christ burned their witchcraft books and turned to God. We use this passage to claim the power of Jesus, and we pray that many of the Young Satanists who come to our meetings will hear God's word and turn to Christ.

Rick

AGE 16

CHAPTER 21 PAUL JOURNEYS TO JERUSALEM.

After parting from the Ephesian elders, we sailed straight to Cos. The next day we reached Rhodes and then went to Patara. [2]There we boarded a ship sailing for the Syrian province of Phoenicia. [3]We sighted the island of Cyprus, passed it on our left, and landed at the harbor of Tyre, in Syria, where the ship unloaded. [4]We went ashore, found the local believers, and stayed with them a week. These disciples warned Paul—the Holy Spirit prophesying through them—not to go on to Jerusalem. [5]At the end of the week when we returned to the ship, the entire congregation including wives and children walked down to the beach with us where we prayed and said our farewells. [6]Then we went aboard, and they returned home.

[7]The next stop after leaving Tyre was Ptolemais, where we greeted the believers but stayed only one day. [8]Then we went on to Caesarea and stayed at the home of Philip the Evangelist, one of the first seven deacons. [9]He had four unmarried daughters who had the gift of prophecy.

[10]During our stay of several days, a man named Agabus, who also had the gift of prophecy, arrived from Judea [11]and visited us. He took Paul's belt, bound his own feet and hands with it, and said, "The Holy Spirit declares, 'So shall the owner of this belt be bound by the Jews in Jerusalem and turned over to the Romans.'" [12]Hearing this, all of us—the local believers and his traveling companions—begged Paul not to go on to Jerusalem.

[13]But he said, "Why all this weeping? You are breaking my heart! For I am ready not only to be jailed at Jerusalem but also to die for the sake of the Lord Jesus." [14]When it was clear that he wouldn't be dissuaded, we gave up and said, "The will of the Lord be done."

[15]So shortly afterwards we packed our things and left for Jerusalem. [16]Some disciples from Caesarea accompanied us, and on arrival we were guests at the home of Mnason, originally from Cyprus, one of the early believers; [17]and all the believers at Jerusalem welcomed us cordially.

[18]The second day Paul took us with him to meet with James and the elders of the Jerusalem church. [19]After greetings were exchanged, Paul recounted the many things God had accomplished among the Gentiles through his work.

[20]They praised God but then said, "You know, dear brother, how many thousands of Jews have also believed, and they are all very insistent that Jewish believers must continue to follow the Jewish traditions and customs. [21]Our Jewish Christians here at Jerusalem have been told that you are against the laws of Moses, against our Jewish customs, and that you forbid the circumcision of their children. [22]Now what can be done? For they will certainly hear that you have come.

[23]"We suggest this: We have four men here who are preparing to shave their heads and take some vows. [24]Go with them to the Temple and have your head shaved too—and pay for theirs to be shaved.

"Then everyone will know that you approve of this custom for the Hebrew Christians and that you yourself obey the Jewish laws and are in line with our thinking in these matters.

[25]"As for the Gentile Christians, we aren't asking them to follow these Jewish customs at all—except for the ones we wrote to them about: not to eat food offered to idols, not to eat unbled meat from strangled animals, and not to commit fornication."

[26,27]So Paul agreed to their request and the next day went with the men to the Temple for the ceremony, thus publicizing his vow to offer a sacrifice seven days later with the others.

The seven days were almost ended when some Jews from Turkey saw him in the Temple and roused a mob against him. They grabbed him, [28]yelling, "Men of Israel! Help! Help! This is the man who preaches against our people and tells everybody to disobey the Jewish laws. He even talks against the Temple and defiles it by bringing Gentiles in!" [29](For down in the city earlier that day, they had seen him with Trophimus, a Gentile from Ephesus in Turkey, and assumed that Paul had taken him into the Temple.)

[30]The whole population of the city was electrified by these accusations and a great riot followed. Paul was dragged out of the Temple, and immediately the gates were closed behind him. [31]As they were killing him, word reached the commander of the Roman garrison that all Jerusalem was in an uproar. [32]He quickly ordered out his soldiers and officers and ran down among the crowd. When the mob saw the troops coming, they quit beating Paul. [33]The commander arrested him and ordered him bound with double chains. Then he asked the

HE HAD TO

21:13-14 Paul knew that he would be imprisoned in Jerusalem. His friends pleaded with him not to go there, but Paul knew God wanted him to. No one wants to face hardship or suffering, but a faithful disciple wants above all else to please God. When we really want to do God's will, we must accept all that comes with it—even the pain. Then we can say with Paul, "The will of the Lord be done."

IN COMMON

22:3 When Paul said "just as you have tried to do today," he acknowledged their sincere motives in trying to kill him and recognized that he would have done the same to Christian leaders a few years earlier. Paul always tried to find something he and his audience had in common before he launched into a full-scale defense of Christianity. When you witness for Christ, first identify yourself with your audience. They are much more likely to listen to you if they feel they have something in common with you.

crowd who he was and what he had done. ³⁴Some shouted one thing and some another. When he couldn't find out anything in all the uproar and confusion, he ordered Paul to be taken to the armory. ³⁵As they reached the stairs, the mob grew so violent that the soldiers lifted Paul to their shoulders to protect him, ³⁶and the crowd surged behind shouting, "Away with him, away with him!"

³⁷,³⁸As Paul was about to be taken inside, he said to the commander, "May I have a word with you?"

"Do you know Greek?" the commander asked, surprised. "Aren't you that Egyptian who led a rebellion a few years ago and took 4,000 members of the Assassins with him into the desert?"

³⁹"No," Paul replied, "I am a Jew from Tarsus in Cilicia which is no small town. I request permission to talk to these people."

⁴⁰The commander agreed, so Paul stood on the stairs and motioned to the people to be quiet; soon a deep silence enveloped the crowd, and he addressed them in Hebrew as follows:

CHAPTER **22** **PAUL IS ARRESTED.** "Brothers and fathers, listen to me as I offer my defense." ²(When they heard him speaking in Hebrew, the silence was even greater.) ³"I am a Jew," he said, "born in Tarsus, a city in Cilicia, but educated here in Jerusalem under Gamaliel, at whose feet I learned to follow our Jewish laws and customs very carefully. I became very anxious to honor God in everything I did, just as you have tried to do today. ⁴And I persecuted the Christians, hounding them to death, binding and delivering both men and women to prison. ⁵The High Priest or any member of the Council can testify that this is so. For I asked them for letters to the Jewish leaders in Damascus, with instructions to let me bring any Christians I found to Jerusalem in chains to be punished.

⁶"As I was on the road, nearing Damascus, suddenly about noon a very bright light from heaven shone around me. ⁷And I fell to the ground and heard a voice saying to me, 'Paul, Paul, why are you persecuting me?'

⁸"'Who is it speaking to me, sir?' I asked. And he replied, 'I am Jesus of Nazareth, the one you are persecuting.' ⁹The men with me saw the light but didn't understand what was said.

¹⁰"And I said, 'What shall I do, Lord?'

"And the Lord told me, 'Get up and go into Damascus, and there you will be told what awaits you in the years ahead.'

¹¹"I was blinded by the intense light and had to be led into Damascus by my companions. ¹²There a man named Ananias, as godly a man as you could find for obeying the law and well thought of by all the Jews of Damascus, ¹³came to me, and standing beside me said, 'Brother Paul, receive your sight!'

And that very hour I could see him!

¹⁴"Then he told me, 'The God of our fathers has chosen you to know his will and to see the Messiah and hear him speak. ¹⁵You are to take his message everywhere, telling what you have seen and heard. ¹⁶And now, why delay? Go and be baptized and be cleansed from your sins, calling on the name of the Lord.'

¹⁷,¹⁸"One day after my return to Jerusalem, while I was praying in the Temple, I fell into a trance and saw a vision of God saying to me, 'Hurry! Leave Jerusalem, for the people here won't believe you when you give them my message.'

¹⁹"'But Lord,' I argued, 'they certainly know that I imprisoned and beat those in every synagogue who believed on you. ²⁰And when your witness Stephen was killed, I was standing there agreeing—keeping the coats they laid aside as they stoned him.'

²¹"But God said to me, 'Leave Jerusalem, for I will send you far away to the *Gentiles!'*"

²²The crowd listened until Paul came to that word, then with one voice they shouted, "Away with such a fellow! Kill him! He isn't fit to live!" ²³They yelled and threw their coats in the air and tossed up handfuls of dust.

²⁴So the commander brought him inside and ordered him lashed with whips to make him confess his crime. He wanted to find out why the crowd had become so furious!

²⁵As they tied Paul down to lash him, Paul said to an officer standing there, "Is it legal for you to whip a Roman citizen who hasn't even been tried?"

²⁶The officer went to the commander and asked, "What are you doing? This man is a Roman citizen!"

²⁷So the commander went over and asked Paul, "Tell me, are you a Roman citizen?"

"Yes, I certainly am."

²⁸"I am too," the commander muttered, "and it cost me plenty!"

"But I am a citizen by birth!"

²⁹The soldiers standing ready to lash him, quickly disappeared when they heard Paul was a Roman citizen, and the commander was frightened because he had ordered him bound and whipped.

³⁰The next day the commander freed him from his chains and ordered the chief priests into session with the Jewish Council. He had Paul brought in before them to try to find out what the trouble was all about.

IN THE HEAT

22:30 God used Paul's persecution as an opportunity for him to witness. Here even his enemies were creating a platform for him to address the entire Jewish Council. If we are sensitive to the Holy Spirit's leading, we will notice increased opportunities to share our faith, even in the heat of opposition.

UNSUNG HEROES IN ACTS

When we think of the success of the early church, we often think of the work of the apostles. But the church could have died if it hadn't been for the "unsung" heroes, the men and women who through some small but committed act moved the church forward.

Hero	Reference	Heroic Action
LAME BEGGER	3:9-12	After his healing, he praised God. With the crowds gathering to see what happened, Peter used the opportunity to tell many about Jesus.
FIVE DEACONS	6:2-5	Everyone knows Stephen, and many people know Philip, but there were five other men chosen to be deacons. They not only laid the foundation for service in the church, but their hard work gave the apostles more time to preach the gospel.
ANANIAS	9:10-19	He had the responsibility of being the first to demonstrate Christ's love to Paul after his conversion.
CORNELIUS	10:34-35	His example showed Peter that the gospel was for all people, Jews and Gentiles.
RHODA	12:13-15	Her persistence brought Peter inside Mary's home, where he would be safe.
JAMES	15:13-21	He took command of the Jerusalem Council and had the courage and discernment to make a decision that would affect literally millions of Christians for many generations.
LYDIA	16:13-15	She opened her home in Philippi to Paul; there he led many to Christ and founded a church.
JASON	17:5-7	He risked his life for the gospel by allowing Paul to stay in his home. He stood up for what was true and right, even though he faced persecution for it.
PAUL'S NEPHEW	23:16-24	He saved Paul's life by telling officials of a plot to murder Paul.
JULIUS	27:43	He spared Paul's life when the other soldiers wanted to kill him.

CHAPTER 23 Gazing intently at the Council, Paul began:

"Brothers, I have always lived before God in all good conscience!"

²Instantly Ananias the High Priest commanded those close to Paul to slap him on the mouth.

³Paul said to him, "God shall slap you, you whitewashed pigpen. What kind of judge are you to break the law yourself by ordering me struck like that?"

⁴Those standing near Paul said to him, "Is that the way to talk to God's High Priest?"

⁵"I didn't realize he was the High Priest, brothers," Paul replied, "for the Scriptures say, 'Never speak evil of any of your rulers.'"

⁶Then Paul thought of something! Part of the Council were Sadducees, and part were Pharisees! So he shouted, "Brothers, I am a Pharisee, as were all my ancestors! And I am being tried here today because I believe in the resurrection of the dead!"

⁷This divided the Council right down the middle—the Pharisees against the Sadducees— ⁸for the Sadducees say there is no resurrection or angels or even eternal spirit within us, but the Pharisees believe in all of these.

⁹So a great clamor arose. Some of the Jewish leaders jumped up to argue that Paul was all right. "We see nothing wrong with him," they shouted. "Perhaps a spirit or angel spoke to him [there on the Damascus road]."

[10]The shouting grew louder and louder, and the men were tugging at Paul from both sides, pulling him this way and that. Finally the commander, fearing they would tear him apart, ordered his soldiers to take him away from them by force and bring him back to the armory.

[11]That night the Lord stood beside Paul and said, "Don't worry, Paul; just as you have told the people about me here in Jerusalem, so you must also in Rome."

[12,13]The next morning some forty or more of the Jews got together and bound themselves by a curse neither to eat nor drink until they had killed Paul! [14]Then they went to the chief priests and elders and told them what they had done. [15]"Ask the commander to bring Paul back to the Council again," they requested. "Pretend you want to ask a few more questions. We will kill him on the way."

[16]But Paul's nephew got wind of their plan and came to the armory and told Paul.

[17]Paul called one of the officers and said, "Take this boy to the commander. He has something important to tell him."

[18]So the officer did, explaining, "Paul, the prisoner, called me over and asked me to bring this young man to you to tell you something."

[19]The commander took the boy by the hand, and leading him aside asked, "What is it you want to tell me, lad?"

[20]"Tomorrow," he told him, "the Jews are going to ask you to bring Paul before the Council again, pretending they want to get some more information. [21]But don't do it! There are more than forty men hiding along the road ready to jump him and kill him. They have bound themselves under a curse to neither eat nor drink till he is dead. They are out there now, expecting you to agree to their request."

[22]"Don't let a soul know you told me this," the commander warned the boy as he left. [23,24]Then the commander called two of his officers and ordered, "Get 200 soldiers ready to leave for Caesarea at nine o'clock tonight! Take 200 spearmen and 70 mounted cavalry. Give Paul a horse to ride and get him safely to Governor Felix."

[25]Then he wrote this letter to the governor:

[26]*"From:* Claudius Lysias

"To: His Excellency, Governor Felix.

"Greetings!

[27]"This man was seized by the Jews, and they were killing him when I sent the soldiers to rescue him, for I learned that he was a Roman citizen. [28]Then I took him to their Council to try to find out what he had done. [29]I soon discovered it was something about their Jewish beliefs, certainly nothing worthy of imprisonment or death. [30]But when I was informed of a plot to kill him, I decided to send him on to you and will tell his accusers to bring their charges before you."

[31]So that night, as ordered, the soldiers took Paul to Antipatris. [32]They returned to the armory the next morning, leaving him with the cavalry to take him on to Caesarea.

[33]When they arrived in Caesarea, they presented Paul and the letter to the governor. [34]He read it and then asked Paul where he was from.

"Cilicia," Paul answered.

[35]"I will hear your case fully when your accusers arrive," the governor told him, and ordered him kept in the prison at King Herod's palace.

CHAPTER **24** PAUL BEFORE FELIX. Five days later Ananias the High Priest arrived with some of the Jewish leaders and the lawyer Tertullus, to make their accusations against Paul. [2]When Tertullus was called forward, he laid charges against Paul in the following address to the governor:

"Your Excellency, you have given quietness and peace to us Jews and have greatly reduced the discrimination against us. [3]And for this we are very, very grateful to you. [4]But lest I bore you, kindly give me your attention for only a moment as I briefly outline our case against this man. [5]For we have found him to be a troublemaker, a man who is constantly inciting the Jews throughout the entire world to riots and rebellions against the Roman government. He is a ringleader of the sect known as the Nazarenes. [6]Moreover, he was trying to defile the Temple when we arrested him.

"We would have given him what he justly deserves, [7]but Lysias, the commander of the garrison, came and took him violently away from us, [8]demanding that he be tried by Roman law. You can find out the truth of our accusations by examining him yourself."

[9]Then all the other Jews chimed in, declaring that everything Tertullus said was true.

[10]Now it was Paul's turn. The governor motioned for him to rise and speak.

Paul began: "I know, sir, that you have been a judge of Jewish affairs for many years, and this gives me confidence as I make my defense. [11]You can quickly discover that it was no more than twelve days ago that I arrived in Jerusalem to

AMAZING!

23:23-24 The Roman commander ordered Paul to be sent to Caesarea. Jerusalem was the seat of Jewish government, but Caesarea was the area's Roman headquarters. God works in amazing and amusing ways. He could have gotten Paul to Caesarea in many ways, but he chose to use the Roman army to deliver Paul from his enemies. God's ways are not ours—we are limited; he is not. Don't ask him to respond your way. When God intervenes, anything can happen—often much more and much better than you could ever anticipate.

24:25 Paul's talk with Felix became so personal that Felix felt convicted. Felix, like Herod Antipas (Mark 6:17-18), had taken another man's wife. Paul's words were interesting until they focused on "righteousness and self-control and the judgment to come." Many people are glad to discuss the gospel as long as it doesn't touch their lives too personally. When it does, some will resist or run away. But this is what the gospel is all about—God's power to change lives. The gospel must move from principles and doctrine into a life-changing dynamic.

worship at the Temple, [12]and you will discover that I have never incited a riot in any synagogue or on the streets of any city; [13]and these men certainly cannot prove the things they accuse me of doing.

[14]"But one thing I do confess, that I believe in the way of salvation, which they refer to as a sect; I follow that system of serving the God of our ancestors; I firmly believe in the Jewish law and everything written in the books of prophecy; [15]and I believe, just as these men do, that there will be a resurrection of both the righteous and ungodly. [16]Because of this, I try with all my strength to always maintain a clear conscience before God and man.

[17]"After several years away, I returned to Jerusalem with money to aid the Jews and to offer a sacrifice to God. [18]My accusers saw me in the Temple as I was presenting my thank offering. I had shaved my head as their laws required, and there was no crowd around me, and no rioting! But some Jews from Turkey were there [19](who ought to be here if they have anything against me)— [20]but look! Ask these men right here what wrongdoing their Council found in me, [21]except that I said one thing I shouldn't when I shouted out, 'I am here before the Council to defend myself for believing that the dead will rise again!'"

[22]Felix, who knew Christians didn't go around starting riots, told the Jews to wait for the arrival of Lysias, the garrison commander, and then he would decide the case. [23]He ordered Paul to prison but instructed the guards to treat him gently and not to forbid any of his friends from visiting him or bringing him gifts to make his stay more comfortable.

[24]A few days later Felix came with Drusilla, his legal wife, a Jewess. Sending for Paul, they listened as he told them about faith in Christ Jesus. [25]And as he reasoned with them about righteousness and self-control and the judgment to come, Felix was terrified.

"Go away for now," he replied, "and when I have a more convenient time, I'll call for you again."

[26]He also hoped that Paul would bribe him, so he sent for him from time to time and talked with him. [27]Two years went by in this way; then Felix was succeeded by Porcius Festus. And because Felix wanted to gain favor with the Jews, he left Paul in chains.

CHAPTER **25** **PAUL BEFORE FESTUS.** Three days after Festus arrived in Caesarea to take over his new responsibilities, he left for Jerusalem, [2]where the chief priests and other Jewish leaders got hold of him and gave him their story about Paul. [3]They begged him to bring Paul to Jerusalem at once. (Their plan was to waylay and kill him.) [4]But Festus replied that since Paul was at Caesarea and he himself was returning there soon, [5]those with authority in this affair should return with him for the trial.

[6]Eight or ten days later he returned to Caesarea and the following day opened Paul's trial.

[7]On Paul's arrival in court the Jews from Jerusalem gathered around, hurling many serious accusations which they couldn't prove. [8]Paul denied the charges: "I am not guilty," he said. "I have not opposed the Jewish laws or desecrated the Temple or rebelled against the Roman government."

[9]Then Festus, anxious to please the Jews, asked him, "Are you willing to go to Jerusalem and stand trial before me?"

[10,11]But Paul replied, "No! I demand my privilege of a hearing before the emperor himself. You know very well I am not guilty. If I have done something worthy of death, I don't refuse to die! But if I am innocent, neither you nor anyone else has a right to turn me over to these men to kill me. *I appeal to Caesar.*"

[12]Festus conferred with his advisors and then replied, "Very well! You have appealed to Caesar, and to Caesar you shall go!"

[13]A few days later King Agrippa arrived with Bernice for a visit with Festus. [14]During their stay of several days Festus discussed Paul's case with the king. "There is a prisoner here," he told him, "whose case was left for me by Felix. [15]When I was in Jerusalem, the chief priests and other Jewish leaders gave me their side of the story and asked me to have him killed. [16]Of course I quickly pointed out to them that Roman law does not convict a man before he is tried. He is given an opportunity to defend himself face to face with his accusers.

[17]"When they came here for the trial, I called the case the very next day and ordered Paul brought in. [18]But the accusations made against him weren't at all what I supposed they would be. [19]It was something about their religion and about someone called Jesus who died, but Paul insists is alive! [20]I was perplexed as to how to decide a case of this kind

AUDIENCE

25:23 Paul was in prison, but that didn't stop him from making the most of his situation. Military officers and prominent city leaders met in the palace room with Agrippa to hear this case. Paul saw this new audience as yet another opportunity to present the gospel. Rather than complain about your present situation, look for opportunities to serve God and share him with others. Problems may be opportunities in disguise.

and asked him whether he would be willing to stand trial on these charges in Jerusalem. [21]But Paul appealed to Caesar! So I ordered him back to jail until I could arrange to get him to the emperor."

[22]"I'd like to hear the man myself," Agrippa said.

And Festus replied, "You shall—tomorrow!"

[23]So the next day, after the king and Bernice had arrived at the courtroom with great pomp, accompanied by military officers and prominent men of the city, Festus ordered Paul brought in.

[24]Then Festus addressed the audience: "King Agrippa and all present," he said, "this is the man whose death is demanded both by the local Jews and by those in Jerusalem! [25]But in my opinion he has done nothing worthy of death. However, he appealed his case to Caesar, and I have no alternative but to send him. [26]But what shall I write the emperor? For there is no real charge against him! So I have brought him before you all, and especially you, King Agrippa, to examine him and then tell me what to write. [27]For it doesn't seem reasonable to send a prisoner to the emperor without any charges against him!"

CHAPTER **26** AGRIPPA WANTS TO HEAR PAUL.

Then Agrippa said to Paul, "Go ahead. Tell us your story."

So Paul, with many gestures, presented his defense:

[2]"I am fortunate, King Agrippa," he began, "to be able to present my answer before you, [3]for I know you are an expert on Jewish laws and customs. Now please listen patiently!

[4]"As the Jews are well aware, I was given a thorough Jewish training from my earliest childhood in Tarsus and later at Jerusalem, and I lived accordingly. [5]If they would admit it, they know that I have always been the strictest of Pharisees when it comes to obedience to Jewish laws and customs. [6]But the real reason behind their accusations is something else—it is because I am looking forward to the fulfillment of God's promise made to our ancestors. [7]The twelve tribes of Israel strive night and day to attain this same hope I have! Yet, O King, for me it is a crime, they say! [8]But is it a crime to believe in the resurrection of the dead? Does it seem incredible to you that God can bring men back to life again?

[9]"I used to believe that I ought to do many horrible things to the followers of Jesus of Nazareth. [10]I imprisoned many of the saints in Jerusalem, as authorized by the High Priests; and when they were condemned to death, I cast my vote against them. [11]I used torture to try to make Christians everywhere curse Christ. I was so violently opposed to them that I even hounded them in distant cities in foreign lands.

[12]"I was on such a mission to Damascus, armed with the authority and commission of the chief priests, [13]when one day about noon, sir, a light from heaven brighter than the sun shone down on me and my companions. [14]We all fell down, and I heard a voice speaking to me in Hebrew, 'Paul, Paul, why are you persecuting me? You are only hurting yourself.'

[15]"'Who are you, sir?' I asked.

"And the Lord replied, 'I am Jesus, the one you are persecuting. [16]Now stand up! For I have appeared to you to appoint you as my servant and my witness. You are to tell the world about this experience and about the many other occasions when I shall appear to you. [17]And I will protect you from both your own people and the Gentiles. Yes, I am going to send you to the Gentiles [18]to open their eyes to their true condition so that they may repent and live in the light of God instead of in Satan's darkness, so that they may receive forgiveness for their sins and God's inheritance along with all people everywhere whose sins are cleansed away, who are set apart by faith in me.'

[19]"And so, O King Agrippa, I was not disobedient to that vision from heaven! [20]I preached first to those in Damascus, then in Jerusalem and through Judea, and also to the Gentiles that all must forsake their sins and turn to God—and prove their repentance by doing good deeds. [21]The Jews arrested me in the Temple for preaching this and tried to kill me, [22]but God protected me so that I am still alive today to tell these facts to everyone, both great and small. I teach nothing except what the Prophets and Moses said— [23]that the Messiah would suffer and be the First to rise from the dead, to bring light to Jews and Gentiles alike."

[24]Suddenly Festus shouted, "Paul, you are insane. Your long studying has broken your mind!"

[25]But Paul replied, "I am not insane, Most Excellent Festus. I speak words of sober truth. [26]And King Agrippa knows about these things. I speak frankly for I am sure these events are all familiar to him, for they were not done in a corner! [27]King Agrippa, do you believe the Prophets? But I know you do—"

[28]Agrippa interrupted him. "With trivial proofs

FACTS

26:26 Paul was appealing to the *facts*—people were still alive who had heard Jesus and seen his miracles; the empty tomb could still be seen; and the Christian message was turning the world upside down (17:6). The history of Jesus' life and the early church are facts that are still open for us to examine. We can study eyewitness accounts of Jesus' life in the Bible as well as historical and archaeological records of the early church. Examine the events and facts as verified by many witnesses. Reconfirm your faith with the truth of these accounts.

like these, you expect me to become a Christian?"

29And Paul replied, "Would to God that whether my arguments are trivial or strong, both you and everyone here in this audience might become the same as I am, except for these chains."

30Then the king, the governor, Bernice, and all the others stood and left. 31As they talked it over afterwards they agreed, "This man hasn't done anything worthy of death or imprisonment."

32And Agrippa said to Festus, "He could be set free if he hadn't appealed to Caesar!"

CHAPTER **27** PAUL'S SHIP IS WRECKED. Arrangements were finally made to start us on our way to Rome by ship; so Paul and several other prisoners were placed in the custody of an officer named Julius, a member of the imperial guard. 2We left on a boat that was scheduled to make several stops along the Turkish coast. I should add that Aristarchus, a Greek from Thessalonica, was with us.

3The next day when we docked at Sidon, Julius was very kind to Paul and let him go ashore to visit with friends and receive their hospitality. 4Putting to sea from there, we encountered headwinds that made it difficult to keep the ship on course, so we sailed north of Cyprus between the island and the mainland 5and passed along the coast of the provinces of Cilicia and Pamphylia, landing at Myra, in the province of Lycia. 6There our officer found an Egyptian ship from Alexandria, bound for Italy, and put us aboard.

7,8We had several days of rough sailing, and finally neared Cnidus; but the winds had become too strong, so we ran across to Crete, passing the port of Salome. Beating into the wind with great difficulty and moving slowly along the southern coast, we arrived at Fair Havens, near the city of Lasea. 9There we stayed for several days. The weather was becoming dangerous for long voyages by then because it was late in the year, and Paul spoke to the ship's officers about it.

10"Sirs," he said, "I believe there is trouble ahead if we go on—perhaps shipwreck, loss of cargo, injuries, and death." 11But the officers in charge of the prisoners listened more to the ship's captain and the owner than to Paul. 12And since Fair Havens was an exposed harbor—a poor place to spend the winter—most of the crew advised trying to go further up the coast to Phoenix in order to winter there; Phoenix was a good harbor with only a northwest and southwest exposure.

13Just then a light wind began blowing from the south, and it looked like a perfect day for the trip; so they pulled up anchor and sailed along close to shore.

14,15But shortly afterwards the weather changed abruptly, and a heavy wind of typhoon strength (a "northeaster," they called it) caught the ship and blew it out to sea. They tried at first to face back to shore but couldn't, so they gave up and let the ship run before the gale.

16We finally sailed behind a small island named Clauda, where with great difficulty we hoisted aboard the lifeboat that was being towed behind us, 17and then banded the ship with ropes to strengthen the hull. The sailors were afraid of being driven across to the quicksands of the African coast, so they lowered the topsails and were thus driven before the wind.

18The next day as the seas grew higher, the crew began throwing the cargo overboard. 19The following day they threw out the tackle and anything else they could lay their hands on. 20The terrible storm raged unabated many days, until at last all hope was gone.

21No one had eaten for a long time, but finally Paul called the crew together and said, "Men, you should have listened to me in the first place and not left Fair Havens—you would have avoided all this injury and loss! 22But cheer up! Not one of us will lose our lives, even though the ship will go down.

23"For last night an angel of the God to whom I belong and whom I serve stood beside me 24and said, 'Don't be afraid, Paul—for you will surely stand trial before Caesar! What's more, God has granted your request and will save the lives of all those sailing with you.' 25So take courage! For I believe God! It will be just as he said! 26But we will be shipwrecked on an island."

27About midnight on the fourteenth night of the storm, as we were being driven to and fro on the Adriatic Sea, the sailors suspected land was near. 28They sounded and found 120 feet of water below them. A little later they sounded again and found only 90 feet. 29At this rate they knew they would soon be driven ashore; and fearing rocks along the coast, they threw out four anchors from the stern and prayed for daylight.

30Some of the sailors planned to abandon the ship and lowered the emergency boat as though they were going to put out anchors from the prow. 31But Paul said to the soldiers and commanding officer, "You will all die unless everyone stays aboard." 32So the soldiers cut the ropes and let the boat fall off.

33As the darkness gave way to the early morning light, Paul begged everyone to eat. "You haven't

EVEN BETTER

27:1—28:24 One of Paul's most important journeys was to Rome, but he didn't get there in quite the way he had expected. It turned out to be more of a legal journey than a missionary journey, thanks to a series of legal trials and transactions. These events resulted in Paul being delivered to Rome where he told his story of the gospel in the most amazing places, including the palace of the emperor! Sometimes we feel frustrated because our plans don't work out the way we wanted them to. But God is never out of control! He knows how to work things out so that the results are even better than we expected. Trusting God with your plans is a surefire plan for success!

touched food for two weeks," he said. ³⁴"Please eat something now for your own good! For not a hair of your heads shall perish!"

³⁵Then he took some hardtack and gave thanks to God before them all, and broke off a piece and ate it. ³⁶Suddenly everyone felt better and began eating, ³⁷all 276 of us—for that is the number we had aboard. ³⁸After eating, the crew lightened the ship further by throwing all the wheat overboard.

³⁹When it was day, they didn't recognize the coastline, but noticed a bay with a beach and wondered whether they could get between the rocks and be driven up onto the beach. ⁴⁰They finally decided to try. Cutting off the anchors and leaving them in the sea, they lowered the rudders, raised the foresail, and headed ashore. ⁴¹But the ship hit a sandbar and ran aground. The bow of the ship stuck fast, while the stern was exposed to the violence of the waves and began to break apart.

⁴²The soldiers advised their commanding officer to let them kill the prisoners lest any of them swim ashore and escape. ⁴³But Julius wanted to spare Paul, so he told them no. Then he ordered all who could swim to jump overboard and make for land, ⁴⁴and the rest to try for it on planks and debris from the broken ship. So everyone escaped safely ashore!

CHAPTER **28** PAUL IS SHIPWRECKED ON MALTA.

We soon learned that we were on the island of Malta. The people of the island were very kind to us, building a bonfire on the beach to welcome and warm us in the rain and cold.

³As Paul gathered an armful of sticks to lay on the fire, a poisonous snake, driven out by the heat, fastened itself onto his hand! ⁴The people of the island saw it hanging there and said to each other, "A murderer, no doubt! Though he escaped the sea, justice will not permit him to live!"

⁵But Paul shook off the snake into the fire and was unharmed. ⁶The people waited for him to begin swelling or suddenly fall dead; but when they had waited a long time and no harm came to him, they changed their minds and decided he was a god.

⁷Near the shore where we landed was an estate belonging to Publius, the governor of the island. He welcomed us courteously and fed us for three days. ⁸As it happened, Publius' father was ill with fever and dysentery. Paul went in and prayed for him, and laying his hands on him, healed him! ⁹Then all the other sick people in the island came and were cured. ¹⁰As a result we were showered with gifts, and when the time came to sail, people put on board all sorts of things we would need for the trip.

¹¹It was three months after the shipwreck before we set sail again, and this time it was in *The Twin Brothers* of Alexandria, a ship that had wintered at the island. ¹²Our first stop was Syracuse, where we stayed

three days. ¹³From there we circled around to Rhegium; a day later a south wind began blowing, so the following day we arrived at Puteoli, ¹⁴where we found some believers! They begged us to stay with them seven days. Then we went on to Rome.

¹⁵The brothers in Rome had heard we were coming and came to meet us at the Forum on the Appian Way. Others joined us at The Three Taverns. When Paul saw them, he thanked God and took courage.

¹⁶When we arrived in Rome, Paul was permitted to live wherever he wanted to, though guarded by a soldier.

¹⁷Three days after his arrival, he called together the local Jewish leaders and spoke to them as follows:

"Brothers, I was arrested by the Jews in Jerusalem and handed over to the Roman government for prosecution, even though I had harmed no one nor violated the customs of our ancestors. ¹⁸The Romans gave me a trial and wanted to release me, for they found no cause for the death sentence demanded by the Jewish leaders. ¹⁹But when the Jews protested the decision, I felt it necessary, with no malice against them, to appeal to Caesar. ²⁰I asked you to come here today so we could get acquainted and I could tell you that it is because I believe the Messiah has come that I am bound with this chain."

²¹They replied, "We have heard nothing against you! We have had no letters from Judea or reports from those arriving from Jerusalem. ²²But we want to hear what you believe, for the only thing we know about these Christians is that they are denounced everywhere!"

²³So a time was set, and on that day large numbers came to his house. He told them about the Kingdom of God and taught them about Jesus from the Scriptures—from the five books of Moses and the books of prophecy. He began lecturing in the morning and went on into the evening!

²⁴Some believed and some didn't. ²⁵But after they had argued back and forth among themselves, they left with this final word from Paul ringing in their ears: "The Holy Spirit was right when he said through Isaiah the prophet,

²⁶"'Say to the Jews, "You will hear and see but not understand, ²⁷for your hearts are too fat and your ears don't listen and you have closed your eyes against understanding, for you don't want to see and hear and understand and turn to me to heal you.'"

²⁸,²⁹ So I want you to realize that this salvation from God is available to the Gentiles too, and they will accept it."

³⁰Paul lived for the next two years in his rented house and welcomed all who visited him, ³¹telling them with all boldness about the Kingdom of God and about the Lord Jesus Christ; and no one tried to stop him.

WHAT ABOUT THOSE WHO'VE NEVER HEARD?

"What about the native in deep dark Africa? God wouldn't send him to hell for not accepting Christ when he's never even heard of him, would he? What about the millions of Hindus and Buddhists who are good, moral people, but have never heard the gospel—God couldn't possibly send them to hell, could he?" **If** you've been following Jesus for very long, you've probably had a couple of discussions that with questions like these. What does God do with those who've never heard of Jesus? **T**he Bible doesn't deal with that question directly. Instead, it talks about Jesus in rather exclusive terms. Take a look at Acts 4:12: "There is salvation in no one else [other than Jesus Christ]! Under all heaven there is no other name for men to call upon to save them." Because the Bible doesn't talk directly about the problem, we must proceed with humility and caution. Still, we aren't left totally in the dark. **F**irst, remember that God doesn't owe it to anybody to save him or her from hell and take that person to heaven for all eternity. He would be entirely justified in condemning everyone, for "all have sinned; all fall short of God's glorious ideal" (Romans 3:23). That's the nature of grace—we get what we don't deserve, instead of what we do deserve. Even if God arbitrarily chose whom to save and whom to condemn, he could not be accused of being unjust or unmerciful. **S**till, why would God condemn someone who has never heard of Christ for never claiming forgiveness through the cross of Christ? He wouldn't. Romans 1 (especially verses 18-20) makes it clear that God has created every one of us with the knowledge of our Creator. We have to try to suppress it. Psalm 19 begins, "The heavens are telling the glory of God. Without a sound or word, silent in the skies, their message reaches out to all the world." Every person ever born has a innate knowledge that there is a Creator, someone bigger, smarter, and more powerful than we are, who put us here in this universe. Those who do not hear the message about Jesus are responsible for how they respond to the knowledge they do have about God. **S**o, for anyone who has heard the Good News of Jesus—that God came to earth as a man named Jesus of Nazareth, and that he lived, died and rose again so that through him we could have forgiveness of sins and eternal life—salvation comes through faith in Jesus. For the person who's never heard of Jesus and his love for us, salvation comes based on the knowledge of our loving Creator, and responding to that knowledge with love, obedience, and worship. For all people, Christ is the only one who has opened the way for us to be restored to God. It is his act on the cross and his resurrection that enables any of us to approach our holy and all-righteous God. **W**e don't have all the answers to all the questions that confuse us about life and death, heaven and hell, and so on. But we can know the one who not only knows the truth, but is the Truth—and we know that he is loving, kind, and merciful. He will do what is right.

MEGA Themes

CHURCH BEGINNINGS Acts is the history of how Christianity was founded and organized and solved its problems. The community of believers began by faith in the risen Christ and in the power of the Holy Spirit, who enabled them to witness, love, and serve, and so reach their world for Christ.

New churches are continually being founded. By faith in Jesus Christ and in the power of the Holy Spirit, the church can be a vibrant agent for change. Acts gives important remedies for solving new problems we may face. God wants us to work together to bring his Good News to the world.

1. Read 2:42-47 and 4:32-37. Describe the relationships in these first gatherings.
2. What is similar and what is different about your church and these early gatherings?
3. What do you learn from 6:1-7 about how to deal with conflict in the church? What do you learn about the importance of servants in the church?
4. What can you do to help resolve a conflict or to serve in your church?

HOLY SPIRIT The church did not start or grow by its own power or enthusiasm. The disciples were empowered by God's Holy Spirit, the promised Comforter sent by Jesus when he went to heaven.

The Holy Spirit's work demonstrated that Christianity is supernatural. Thus the church became more Holy Spirit–conscious than problem-conscious. By faith, any believer can experience the Holy Spirit's power to do Christ's work.

1. Summarize the various acts God performed through his Holy Spirit in chapters 1–5. What was God's purpose in acting so dramatically?
2. What were the key results of the Holy Spirit's work in the early church?
3. In what ways do you need to rely upon the Holy Spirit?

CHURCH GROWTH Acts presents the history of a dynamic, growing community of believers from Jerusalem to Syria, Africa, Asia, and Europe. In the first century, it spread from believing Jews to non-Jews in 39 cities and 30 countries or provinces.

When the Holy Spirit works, there is movement, excitement, and growth. He gives us the motivation and ability to get the gospel to the whole world. You can be an important part of this great world movement. Begin in your neighborhood and

school to live for Christ and share the gospel with others.

1. How did the growth of the church in Acts accomplish Jesus' words in 1:8?
2. Look again at 1:8. What would be your Jerusalem? Judea? Samaria?
3. In what specific ways can you be used by God in each of the areas you listed above?

WITNESSING Peter, John, Philip, Paul, Barnabas, and thousands more told others about their new faith in Christ. By personal testimony, preaching, or defense before authorities, they shared the story with boldness and courage.

We are God's people, chosen to be part of his plan to reach the world. In love and by faith, we can have the Holy Spirit's help as we share the gospel. Witnessing also strengthens our faith.

1. In what ways did the early witnesses for Jesus share their message?
2. Looking back at your responses under church growth, what are some of the opportunities you have for being a witness for Christ?
3. What are you doing now to be a witness for Christ? What could you do to be more effective?

OPPOSITION Through imprisonment, beatings, plots, and riots, Christians were persecuted by both Jews and Gentiles. But the opposition became a catalyst, an energizer for the spread of Christianity. In the face of opposition it became evident that Christianity was not the work of humans, but of God.

God can work through any opposition. When you are treated harshly through ridicule, lies, or physical abuse from hostile unbelievers, realize that it is happening because of your faithful witness. Take every opportunity, even those that opposition brings, for communicating the Good News of Jesus Christ.

1. Describe how the various followers of Jesus responded to opposition and persecution.
2. How do you think these individuals felt when they were being threatened, ridiculed, beaten, even stoned? What motivated them to continue?
3. What potential opposition awaits you in your efforts to be a witness for Christ?
4. What are some possible responses that you might have when faced with this opposition?
5. How might God use the opposition you face to bring glory to himself and further his Kingdom?

*I*magine you're out on an evening run when you happen upon your dream car. As you admire its beauty, you notice a key in the ignition . . . and unlocked doors. The car seems to say, "Take me out for a quick spin." You glance around. The street is deserted. ■ "But that would be stealing!" your conscience protests. "No way!" another voice blurts in. "You're not going to *keep* it." For an agonizingly long moment the inner voices battle—then adventure wins out. Your heart pounds as you slide into the driver's seat and the engine hums to life. ■ "This is awesome!" you say, slipping the car into gear. You intend to make one slow trip around the block—but the speedometer goes up to 160 mph, and when will you *ever* get another chance like this? You head for the open road. ■ What happens next is a blur. You remember the exhilaration of 143 mph, then flashing blue lights, cold steel handcuffs, being in court, and the judge's gavel pounding out a guilty verdict. The sentence: $10,000 and six months incarceration. You deserve punishment, but that's a severe penalty! ■ Then the judge does something curious. He removes his robe, whips out his checkbook, and pays your fine! Next he announces he will serve your jail sentence. Then he looks you in the eyes and says, "I love you." ■ This analogy isn't perfect, but it *does* help explain how God deals with sinful humanity. The very penalty he demands (death for sin), he provided (the death of Christ on the cross). If you'd like an even better explanation of God's perfect justice and his intense love for you, read the book of Romans.

STATS

PURPOSE: To introduce Paul to the Romans and to give a sample of his message before he arrives in Rome

AUTHOR: Paul

TO WHOM WRITTEN: The Christians in Rome and believers everywhere

DATE WRITTEN: About A.D. 57, from Corinth, as Paul was preparing for his visit to Jerusalem

SETTING: Apparently Paul had finished his work in the east, and he planned to visit Rome on his way to Spain after first bringing a collection to Jerusalem for the poor Christians there (15:22-28). The Roman church was mostly Jewish but also contained many Gentiles.

KEY PEOPLE: Paul, Phoebe

KEY PLACE: Rome

Romans

CHAPTER 1 PAUL WRITES WITH GOOD NEWS.

Dear friends in Rome: [1]This letter is from Paul, Jesus Christ's slave, chosen to be a missionary, and sent out to preach God's Good News. [2]This Good News was promised long ago by God's prophets in the Old Testament. [3]It is the Good News about his Son, Jesus Christ our Lord, who came as a human baby, born into King David's royal family line; [4]and by being raised from the dead he was proved to be the mighty Son of God, with the holy nature of God himself.

[5]And now, through Christ, all the kindness of God has been poured out upon us undeserving sinners; and now he is sending us out around the world to tell all people everywhere the great things God has done for them, so that they, too, will believe and obey him.

[6,7]And you, dear friends in Rome, are among those he dearly loves; you, too, are invited by Jesus Christ to be God's very own—yes, his holy people. May all God's mercies and peace be yours from God our Father and from Jesus Christ our Lord.

[8]Let me say first of all that wherever I go I hear you being talked about! For your faith in God is becoming known around the world. How I thank God through Jesus Christ for this good report, and for each one of you. [9]God knows how often I pray for you. Day and night I bring you and your needs in prayer to the one I serve with all my might, telling others the Good News about his Son.

[10]And one of the things I keep on praying for is the opportunity, God willing, to come at last to see you and, if possible, that I will have a safe trip. [11,12]For I long to visit you so that I can impart to you the faith that will help your church grow strong in the Lord. Then, too, I need your help, for I want not only to share my faith with you but to be encouraged by yours: Each of us will be a blessing to the other.

GOOD NEWS

1:2-17 Paul was not ashamed because his message was *Good News.* It was powerful, it was for everyone, and it was part of God's revealed plan. When you are tempted to be ashamed, remember what the Good News is all about. If you focus on God and on what he is doing in the world rather than on your own inadequacy, your embarrassment will soon disappear.

¹³I want you to know, dear brothers, that I planned to come many times before (but was prevented) so that I could work among you and see good results, just as I have among the other Gentile churches. ¹⁴For I owe a great debt to you and to everyone else, both to civilized people and uncivilized alike; yes, to the educated and uneducated alike. ¹⁵So, to the fullest extent of my ability, I am ready to come also to you in Rome to preach God's Good News.

¹⁶For I am not ashamed of this Good News about Christ. It is God's powerful method of bringing all who believe it to heaven. This message was preached first to the Jews alone, but now everyone is invited to come to God in this same way. ¹⁷This Good News tells us that God makes us ready for heaven—makes us right in God's sight—when we put our faith and trust in Christ to save us. This is accomplished from start to finish by faith. As the Scripture says it, "The man who finds life will find it through trusting God."

¹⁸But God shows his anger from heaven against all sinful, evil men who push away the truth from them. ¹⁹For the truth about God is known to them instinctively; God has put this knowledge in their hearts. ²⁰Since earliest times men have seen the earth and sky and all God made, and have known of his existence and great eternal power. So they will have no excuse [when they stand before God at Judgment Day].

²¹Yes, they knew about him all right, but they wouldn't admit it or worship him or even thank him for all his daily care. And after awhile they began to think up silly ideas of what God was like and what he wanted them to do. The result was that their foolish minds became dark and confused. ²²Claiming themselves to be wise without God, they became utter fools instead. ²³And then, instead of worshiping the glorious, ever-living God, they took wood and stone and made idols for themselves, carving them to look like mere birds and animals and snakes and puny men.

²⁴So God let them go ahead into every sort of sex sin, and do whatever they wanted to—yes, vile and sinful things with each other's bodies. ²⁵Instead of believing what they knew was the truth about God, they deliberately chose to believe lies. So they prayed to the things God made, but wouldn't obey the blessed God who made these things.

²⁶That is why God let go of them and let them do all these evil things, so that even their women turned against God's natural plan for them and indulged in sex sin with each other. ²⁷And the men, instead of having normal sex relationships with women, burned with lust for each other, men doing shameful things with other men and, as a result, getting paid within their own souls with the penalty they so richly deserved.

²⁸So it was that when they gave God up and would not even acknowledge him, God gave them up to doing everything their evil minds could think of. ²⁹Their lives became full of every kind of wickedness and sin, of greed and hate, envy, murder, fighting, lying, bitterness, and gossip.

³⁰They were backbiters, haters of God, insolent, proud, braggarts, always thinking of new ways of sinning and continually being disobedient to their parents. ³¹They tried to misunderstand, broke their promises, and were heartless—without pity. ³²They were fully aware of God's death penalty for these crimes, yet they went right ahead and did them anyway and encouraged others to do them, too.

CHAPTER **2** **GOD WILL JUDGE US ALL.** "Well," you may be saying, "what terrible people you have been talking about!" But wait a minute! You are just as bad. When you say they are wicked and

ALTERNATIVES

James and Kristy are watching a popular afternoon talk show. Today's topic is "Should homosexual marriage be legalized?" Most of the guests, as well as members of the studio audience, are gay and lesbian activists who are "tired of being treated like second-class citizens."

Says the most outspoken member of the panel: "Why can't people just accept us as we are? We didn't choose to be homosexual. We were born this way. We don't condemn straight people for acting on their natural desires. Why condemn us for being the way God made us?"

With each statement like this, the talk show host nods approvingly and the audience cheers loudly.

All except the one guy on the panel who is a minister. He is trying patiently (and lovingly) to point out why homosexuality is not acceptable behavior, but the others keep interrupting him and describing him as "backwards," "narrow-minded," and a "religious extremist."

By the end of the show, James and Kristy feel a little bit differently. They aren't ready to accept everything about the homosexual lifestyle, but they do wonder if maybe they haven't been a bit intolerant in their views.

What do you think? Is homosexuality just "an alternative life-style"? Is it really OK? See what God says about it in Romans 1:24-28.

NO EXCUSE

1:18-20 Paul answers a common objection: How could a loving God send anyone to hell, especially someone who has never heard the Good News of Jesus? In fact, says Paul, God has revealed himself to *all* people. Everyone knows what God requires, but no one lives up to it. If people suppress God's truth in order to live their own way, they have no excuse. They know the truth, and they will have to endure the consequences of ignoring it.

should be punished, you are talking about yourselves, for you do these very same things. ²And we know that God, in justice, will punish anyone who does such things as these. ³Do you think that God will judge and condemn others for doing them and overlook you when you do them, too? ⁴Don't you realize how patient he is being with you? Or don't you care? Can't you see that he has been waiting all this time without punishing you, to give you time to turn from your sin? His kindness is meant to lead you to repentance.

⁵But no, you won't listen; and so you are saving up terrible punishment for yourselves because of your stubbornness in refusing to turn from your sin; for there is going to come a day of wrath when God will be the just Judge of all the world. ⁶He will give each one whatever his deeds deserve. ⁷He will give eternal life to those who patiently do the will of God, seeking for the unseen glory and honor and eternal life that he offers. ⁸But he will terribly punish those who fight against the truth of God and walk in evil ways—God's anger will be poured out upon them. ⁹There will be sorrow and suffering for Jews and Gentiles alike who keep on sinning. ¹⁰But there will be glory and honor and peace from God for all who obey him, whether they are Jews or Gentiles. ¹¹For God treats everyone the same.

¹²⁻¹⁵He will punish sin wherever it is found. He will punish the heathen when they sin, even though they never had God's written laws, for down in their hearts they know right from wrong. God's laws are written within them; their own conscience accuses them, or sometimes excuses them. And God will punish the Jews for sinning because they

THE GOSPEL GOES TO ROME

When Paul wrote his letter to the church in Rome he had not yet been there, but he had taken the gospel "all the way from Jerusalem clear over into Illyricum" (15:19). He planned to visit and preach in Rome one day, and hoped to continue to take the gospel farther west—even to Spain.

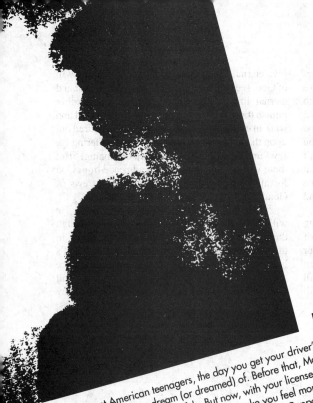

HOMOSEXUALITY

If you're like most American teenagers, the day you get your driver's license and can take the car out for a drive—alone—is a day you dream (or dreamed) of. Before that, Mom, Dad, or the driving teacher rode "shotgun" to make sure you drove safely. But now, with your license, you're on your own. The thrill of freedom and the increased sense of responsibility make you feel more like an adult. No one will tell you when to stop or remind you to use your turn signal. It's up to you. **S**uppose you decide that, contrary to everything you've been told up to now, you want to drive on the left-hand side of the road. (Remember, we're talking about the U.S., not England or Hong Kong.) You will quickly encounter serious opposition to your choice of driving style (like a head-on collision). You can either learn from your observations and experiences, or you can insist that you have the right to drive however you wish, and whatever happens, happens. **W**hen it comes to driving, it's pretty obvious what the wisest choice is. Here in Romans 1, Paul addresses an issue that seems equally clear-cut, and yet men and women have struggled with it since Adam and Eve were evicted from Eden. The issue is homosexuality. **P**aul argues that all people everywhere are without excuse in knowing that there is a God. Proclaiming that nature itself reveals its Creator, Paul then begins a scathing rebuke against people who deny God and his plan for creation. These people, he writes, go against God's design for human sexuality, and in so doing, will experience drastic consequences for their behavior. Like our fictional teenage driver, men and women who practice homosexuality experience tremendous opposition—socially, emotionally, physically, and spiritually. Yet they ignore all these warning signs. Sooner or later, though, they will crash and burn. **T**wo important messages need to be given on the subject of homosexuality. One is for our society, which has lost any meaningful idea of sin, righteousness, holiness and truth. That message is that all life-styles are not acceptable. Some life-styles—such as alcoholism, or materialism . . . or homosexuality— are wrong; they are sinful. Those who engage in such behaviors should come to God in confession and repentance and ask for his forgiveness and healing. **T**he second message is for the church (meaning all Christians). What they need to understand is that while homosexuality is sin, it is not the unforgivable sin. God loves homosexuals just as much as he loves other sinners. Jesus' death on the cross paid for the sin of homosexuality, just as it paid for the sins of lying, greed, lust, hate, and pride. It has been said—and it is true—that the church is a hospital for sinners, not a showcase for saints. It is a place where believers who have committed the sins of hatred, prejudice, and self-righteousness toward homosexuals need to go to ask the Lord for forgiveness and healing. **H**omosexuals, like all sinners, stand guilty before God. If that in the sin of homosexuality can come to be freed and forgiven. It is a place where those caught Bible—is that there is hope for sinners of all kinds through the life, death, and resurrection of Jesus were the whole story, there would be no hope. The great message of Romans—and of the entire Christ. He is the one who will set us free, regardless of our sin.

have his written laws but don't obey them. They know what is right but don't do it. After all, salvation is not given to those who know what to do, unless they do it. [16]The day will surely come when at God's command Jesus Christ will judge the secret lives of everyone, their inmost thoughts and motives; this is all part of God's great plan, which I proclaim.

[17]You Jews think all is well between yourselves and God because he gave his laws to you; you brag that you are his special friends. [18]Yes, you know what he wants; you know right from wrong and favor the right because you have been taught his laws from earliest youth. [19]You are so sure of the way to God that you could point it out to a blind man. You think of yourselves as beacon lights, directing men who are lost in darkness to God. [20]You think that you can guide the simple and teach even children the affairs of God, for you really know his laws, which are full of all knowledge and truth.

[21]Yes, you teach others—then why don't you teach yourselves? You tell others not to steal—do *you* steal? [22]You say it is wrong to commit adultery—do *you* do it? You say "Don't pray to idols" and then make money your god instead.

[23]You are so proud of knowing God's laws, *but you dishonor him by breaking them.* [24]No wonder the Scriptures say that the world speaks evil of God because of you.

[25]Being a Jew is worth something if you obey God's laws; but if you don't, then you are no better off than the heathen. [26]And if the heathen obey God's laws, won't God give them all the rights and honors he planned to give the Jews? [27]In fact, those heathen will be much better off than you Jews who know so much about God and have his promises but don't obey his laws.

[28]For you are not real Jews just because you were born of Jewish parents or because you have gone through the Jewish initiation ceremony of circumcision. [29]No, a real Jew is anyone whose heart is right with God. For God is not looking for those who cut their bodies in actual body circumcision, but he is looking for those with changed hearts and minds. Whoever has that kind of change in his life will get his praise from God, even if not from you.

CHAPTER **3** **GOD REMAINS FAITHFUL.** Then what's the use of being a Jew? Are there any special benefits for them from God? Is there any value in the Jewish circumcision ceremony? [2]Yes, being a Jew has many advantages.

First of all, God trusted them with his laws [so that they could know and do his will]. [3]True, some of them were unfaithful, but just because they broke their promises to God, does that mean God will break his promises? [4]Of course not! Though everyone else in the world is a liar, God is not. Do you remember what the book of Psalms says about this? That God's words will always prove true and right, no matter who questions them.

[5]"But," some say, "our breaking faith with God is good, our sins serve a good purpose, for people will notice how good God is when they see how bad we are. Is it fair, then, for him to punish us when our sins are helping him?" (That is the way some people talk.) [6]God forbid! Then what kind of God would he be, to overlook sin? How could he ever condemn anyone? [7]For he could not judge and condemn me as a sinner if my dishonesty brought

"Here's what I did..."

During my freshman and sophomore years in high school, I led something of a double life. At home and at church, I was a "good Christian kid." I read my Bible, helped with Sunday school, and went to youth group. I really wanted to live a committed Christian life, but at school I was embarrassed to make it known that I was a Christian. I guess I was afraid of what people would think of me if they knew. When people said, "Come on, let's party," I'd feel torn. I loved God and knew he didn't approve of their idea of "party," but too often I just couldn't stand up to these people. I'd give in, then feel bad about myself for compromising what I knew was right.

The summer before my junior year, I knew things would have to change. That's when I read Romans 2:6-8. Verse 6 says God will give to each person as his deeds deserve. I got to thinking about what my deeds deserve, and it scared me. I realized how self-seeking I was. I really did want to please God, not hurt him or get him mad at me. I decided right then to "patiently do the will of God, seeking for the unseen glory and honor and eternal life that he offers."

So I memorized that verse and decided to let people at school know I'm a Christian. It's made a big difference. For one thing, I met other Christians who were there all the time, but whom I hadn't bothered to get to know before. The last two years have been much better than the first two. I found that taking a stand against certain things didn't really cost me friends. In fact, because I've found other friends who know what friendship is about, I actually have more and better friends than before. But most of all I have a clear conscience; I know I'm trying to do God's will every day, at school as well as at church.

Lisa AGE 18

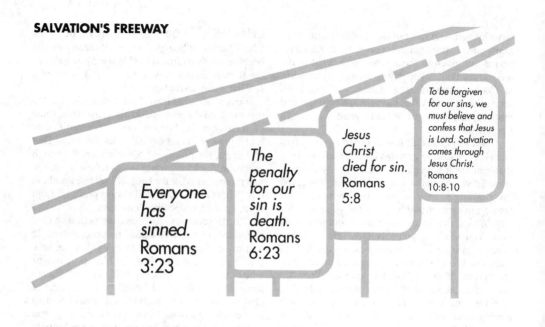

Everyone has sinned. Romans 3:23

The penalty for our sin is death. Romans 6:23

Jesus Christ died for sin. Romans 5:8

To be forgiven for our sins, we must believe and confess that Jesus is Lord. Salvation comes through Jesus Christ. Romans 10:8-10

him glory by pointing up his honesty in contrast to my lies. [8]If you follow through with that idea you come to this: the worse we are, the better God likes it! But the damnation of those who say such things is just. Yet some claim that this is what I preach!

[9]Well, then, are we Jews *better* than others? No, not at all, for we have already shown that all men alike are sinners, whether Jews or Gentiles. [10]As the Scriptures say,

"No one is good—no one in all the world is innocent."

[11]No one has ever really followed God's paths or even truly wanted to.

[12]Every one has turned away; all have gone wrong. No one anywhere has kept on doing what is right; not one.

[13]Their talk is foul and filthy like the stench from an open grave. Their tongues are loaded with lies. Everything they say has in it the sting and poison of deadly snakes.

[14]Their mouths are full of cursing and bitterness.

[15]They are quick to kill, hating anyone who disagrees with them.

[16]Wherever they go they leave misery and trouble behind them, [17]and they have never known what it is to feel secure or enjoy God's blessing.

[18]They care nothing about God nor what he thinks of them.

[19]So the judgment of God lies very heavily upon the Jews, for they are responsible to keep God's laws instead of doing all these evil things; not one of them has any excuse; in fact, all the world stands hushed and guilty before Almighty God.

[20]Now do you see it? No one can ever be made right in God's sight by doing what the law commands. For the more we know of God's laws, the clearer it becomes that we aren't obeying them; his laws serve only to make us see that we are sinners.

[21,22]But now God has shown us a different way to heaven—not by "being good enough" and trying to keep his laws, but by a new way (though not new, really, for the Scriptures told about it long ago). Now God says he will accept and acquit us—declare us "not guilty"— if we trust Jesus Christ to take away our sins. And we all can be saved in this same way, by coming to Christ, no matter who we are or what we have been like. [23]Yes, all have sinned; all fall short of God's glorious ideal; [24]yet now God declares us "not guilty" of offending him if we trust in Jesus Christ, who in his kindness freely takes away our sins.

[25]For God sent Christ Jesus to take the punishment for our sins and to end all God's anger against us. He used Christ's blood and our faith as the means of saving us from his wrath. In this way he was being entirely fair, even though he did not punish those who sinned in former times. For he was looking forward to the time when Christ would come

CUT OFF

3:23 Some sins seem bigger than others because their obvious consequences are much more serious. Murder, for example, seems much worse than hatred; adultery seems worse than lust. But this does not mean we can get away with some sins and not with others. All sin makes us sinners, and all sin cuts us off from our holy God. All sin, therefore, leads to death (because it disqualifies us from living with God), regardless of how great or small it seems. Don't minimize "little" sins or overrate "big" sins. All sins separate us from God—but they all can be forgiven.

and take away those sins. ²⁶And now in these days also he can receive sinners in this same way because Jesus took away their sins.

But isn't this unfair for God to let criminals go free, and say that they are innocent? No, for he does it on the basis of their trust in Jesus who took away their sins.

²⁷Then what can we boast about doing to earn our salvation? Nothing at all. Why? Because our acquittal is not based on our good deeds; it is based on what Christ has done and our faith in him. ²⁸So it is that we are saved by faith in Christ and not by the good things we do.

²⁹And does God save only the Jews in this way? No, the Gentiles, too, may come to him in this same manner. ³⁰God treats us all the same; all, whether Jews or Gentiles, are acquitted if they have faith. ³¹Well then, if we are saved by faith, does this mean that we no longer need obey God's laws? Just the opposite! In fact, only when we trust Jesus can we truly obey him.

CHAPTER **4** **ABRAHAM BELIEVED GOD.** Abraham was, humanly speaking, the founder of our Jewish nation. What were his experiences concerning this question of being saved by faith? Was it because of his good deeds that God accepted him? If so, then he would have something to boast about. But from God's point of view Abraham had no basis at all for pride. ³For the Scriptures tell us Abraham *believed God,* and that is why God canceled his sins and declared him "not guilty."

⁴⁵But didn't he earn his right to heaven by all the good things he did? No, for being saved is a gift; if a person could earn it by being good, then it wouldn't be free—but it is! It is *given* to those who do *not* work for it. For God declares sinners to be good in his sight if they have faith in Christ to save them from God's wrath.

⁶King David spoke of this, describing the happiness of an undeserving sinner who is declared "not guilty" by God. ⁷"Blessed and to be envied," he said, "are those whose sins are forgiven and put out of sight. ⁸Yes, what joy there is for anyone whose sins are no longer counted against him by the Lord."

⁹Now then, the question: Is this blessing given only to those who have faith in Christ but also keep the Jewish laws, or is the blessing also given to those who do not keep the Jewish rules but only trust in Christ? Well, what about Abraham? We say that he received these blessings through his faith. Was it by faith alone, or because he also kept the Jewish rules?

¹⁰For the answer to that question, answer this one: *When* did God give this blessing to Abraham? It was *before he became a Jew*—before he went through the Jewish initiation ceremony of circumcision.

¹¹It wasn't until later on, *after* God had promised to bless him *because of his faith,* that he was circum-

cised. The circumcision ceremony was a sign that Abraham already had faith and that God had already accepted him and declared him just and good in his sight—before the ceremony took place. So Abraham is the spiritual father of those who believe and are saved without obeying Jewish laws. We see, then, that those who do not keep these rules are justified by God through faith. ¹²And Abraham is also the spiritual father of those Jews who have been circumcised. They can see from his example that it is not this ceremony that saves them, for Abraham found favor with God by faith alone *before he was circumcised.*

¹³It is clear, then, that God's promise to give the whole earth to Abraham and his descendants was not because Abraham obeyed God's laws but because he trusted God to keep his promise. ¹⁴So if you still claim that God's blessings go to those who are "good enough," then you are saying that God's promises to those who have faith are meaningless, and faith is foolish. ¹⁵But the fact of the matter is this: when we try to gain God's blessing and salvation by keeping his laws we always end up under his anger, for we always fail to keep them. The only way we can keep from breaking laws is not to have any to break!

¹⁶So God's blessings are given to us by faith, as a free gift; we are certain to get them whether or not we follow Jewish customs if we have faith like Abraham's, for Abraham is the father of us all when it comes to these matters of faith. ¹⁷That is what the Scriptures mean when they say that God made Abraham the father of many nations. God will accept all people in every nation who trust God as Abraham did. And this promise is from God himself, who makes the dead live again and speaks of future events with as much certainty as though they were already past.

¹⁸So, when God told Abraham that he would give him a son who would have many descendants and become a great nation, Abraham believed God even though such a promise just couldn't come to pass! ¹⁹And because his faith was strong, he didn't worry about the fact that he was too old to be a father at the age of one hundred, and that Sarah his wife, at ninety, was also much too old to have a baby.

²⁰But Abraham never doubted. He believed God, for his faith and trust grew ever stronger, and

A GIFT

4:5 When some people learn we are saved through faith, they start to worry: "Do I have enough faith?" "Is my faith strong enough to save me?" These people miss the point. It is Jesus Christ who saves us, not *our* feelings or actions. He is strong enough to save us no matter how weak our faith is. Jesus offers us salvation as a gift because he loves us, not because we have earned it through our powerful faith. What, then, is the role of faith? Faith is believing and trusting in Jesus Christ, reaching out to accept his wonderful gift of salvation. Faith is effective whether it is great or small, timid or bold—because God loves us.

he praised God for this blessing even before it happened. [21]He was completely sure that God was well able to do anything he promised. [22]And because of Abraham's faith God forgave his sins and declared him "not guilty."

[23]Now this wonderful statement—that he was accepted and approved through his faith—wasn't just for Abraham's benefit. [24]It was for us, too, assuring us that God will accept us in the same way he accepted Abraham—when we believe the promises of God who brought back Jesus our Lord from the dead. [25]He died for our sins and rose again to make us right with God, filling us with God's goodness.

CHAPTER **5** **FINDING PEACE AND JOY.** So now, since we have been made right in God's sight by faith in his promises, we can have real peace with him because of what Jesus Christ our Lord has done for us. [2]For because of our faith, he has brought us into this place of highest privilege where we now stand, and we confidently and joyfully look forward to actually becoming all that God has had in mind for us to be.

[3]We can rejoice, too, when we run into problems and trials, for we know that they are good for us— they help us learn to be patient. [4]And patience develops strength of character in us and helps us trust God more each time we use it until finally our hope and faith are strong and steady. [5]Then, when that happens, we are able to hold our heads high no matter what happens and know that all is well, for we know how dearly God loves us, and we feel this warm love everywhere within us because God has given us the Holy Spirit to fill our hearts with his love.

[6]When we were utterly helpless, with no way of escape, Christ came at just the right time and died for us sinners who had no use for him. [7]Even if we were good, we really wouldn't expect anyone to die for us, though, of course, that might be barely possible. [8]But God showed his great love for us by sending Christ to die for us while we were still sinners. [9]And since by his blood he did all this for us as sinners, how much more will he do for us now that he has declared us not guilty? Now he will save us from all of God's wrath to come. [10]And since, when we were his enemies, we were brought back to God by the death of his Son, what blessings he must have for us now that we are his friends and he is living within us!

[11]Now we rejoice in our wonderful new relationship with God—all because of what our Lord Jesus Christ has done in dying for our sins—making us friends of God.

[12]When Adam sinned, sin entered the entire human race. His sin spread death throughout all the world, so everything began to grow old and die, for all sinned. [13][We know that it was Adam's sin that caused this] because although, of course, people were sinning from the time of Adam until Moses, God did not in those days judge them guilty of death for breaking his laws—because he had not yet given his laws to them nor told them what he wanted them to do. [14]So when their bodies died it was not for their own sins since they themselves had never disobeyed God's special law against eating the forbidden fruit, as Adam had.

What a contrast between Adam and Christ who was yet to come! [15]And what a difference between man's sin and God's forgiveness!

For this one man, Adam, brought death to many through his *sin*. But this one man, Jesus Christ, brought forgiveness to many through God's *mercy*. [16]Adam's *one* sin brought the penalty of death to many, while Christ freely takes away *many* sins and gives glorious life instead. [17]The sin of this one man, Adam, caused *death to be king over all*, but all who will take God's gift of forgiveness and acquittal are *kings of life* because of this one man, Jesus Christ. [18]Yes, Adam's *sin* brought *punishment* to all, but Christ's *righteousness* makes men *right with God*, so that they can live. [19]Adam caused many to be sinners because he *disobeyed* God, and Christ caused many to be made acceptable to God because he *obeyed*.

[20]The Ten Commandments were given so that all could see the extent of their failure to obey God's laws. But the more we see our sinfulness, the more we see God's abounding grace forgiving us. [21]Before, sin ruled over all men and brought them to death, but now God's kindness rules instead, giving us right standing with God and resulting in eternal life through Jesus Christ our Lord.

CHAPTER **6** **CHRIST BROKE SIN'S POWER.** Well then, shall we keep on sinning so that God can keep on showing us more and more kindness and forgiveness?

[2,3]Of course not! Should we keep on sinning when

OVERCOME

5:2-4 Paul tells us that in the future we will *become*, but until then we must *overcome*. This means we will experience difficulties that will help us grow. Problems we face will help develop our patience—which in turn will strengthen our character, deepen our trust in God, and give us greater confidence about the future. You probably find your patience tested in some way every day. Thank God for these opportunities to grow and deal with them in his strength (see also James 1:2-4; 1 Peter 1:6-7).

BEFORE

5:8 *While we were still sinners*—these are amazing words. God sent Jesus to die for us not because we were good enough, but because he loved us so much. Whenever you feel uncertain about God's love for you, remember that God loved you even before you turned to him.

we don't have to? For sin's power over us was broken when we became Christians and were baptized to become a part of Jesus Christ; through his death the power of your sinful nature was shattered. ⁴Your old sin-loving nature was buried with him by baptism when he died; and when God the Father, with glorious power, brought him back to life again, you were given his wonderful new life to enjoy.

⁵For you have become a part of him, and so you died with him, so to speak, when he died; and now you share his new life and shall rise as he did. ⁶Your old evil desires were nailed to the cross with him; that part of you that loves to sin was crushed and fatally wounded, so that your sin-loving body is no longer under sin's control, no longer needs to be a slave to sin; ⁷for when you are deadened to sin you are freed from all its allure and its power over you. ⁸And since your old sin-loving nature "died" with Christ, we know that you will share his new life. ⁹Christ rose from the dead and will never die again. Death no longer has any power over him. ¹⁰He died once for all to end sin's power, but now he lives forever in unbroken fellowship with God. ¹¹So look upon your old sin nature as dead and unresponsive to sin, and instead be alive to God, alert to him, through Jesus Christ our Lord.

¹²Do not let sin control your puny body any longer; do not give in to its sinful desires. ¹³Do not let any part of your bodies become tools of wickedness, to be used for sinning; but give yourselves completely to God—every part of you—for you are back from death and you want to be tools in the hands of God, to be used for his good purposes. ¹⁴Sin need never again be your master, for now you are no longer tied to the law where sin enslaves you, but you are free under God's favor and mercy.

¹⁵Does this mean that now we can go ahead and sin and not worry about it? (For our salvation does not depend on keeping the law but on receiving God's grace!) Of course not!

¹⁶Don't you realize that you can choose your own master? You can choose sin (with death) or else obedience (with acquittal). The one to whom you offer yourself—he will take you and be your master, and you will be his slave. ¹⁷Thank God that though you once chose to be slaves of sin, now you have obeyed with all your heart the teaching to which God has committed you. ¹⁸And now you are free from your old master, sin; and you have become slaves to your new master, righteousness.

¹⁹I speak this way, using the illustration of slaves and masters, because it is easy to understand: just as you used to be slaves to all kinds of sin, so now you must let yourselves be slaves to all that is right and holy.

²⁰In those days when you were slaves of sin you didn't bother much with goodness. ²¹And what was the result? Evidently not good, since you are ashamed now even to think about those things you used to do, for all of them end in eternal doom. ²²But now you are free from the power of sin and are slaves of God, and his benefits to you include holiness and everlasting life. ²³For the wages of sin is death, but the free gift of God is eternal life through Jesus Christ our Lord.

CHAPTER **7** **YOU CAN SERVE GOD.** Don't you understand yet, dear Jewish brothers in Christ, that when a person dies the law no longer holds him in its power?

²Let me illustrate: when a woman marries, the law binds her to her husband as long as he is alive. But if he dies, she is no longer bound to him; the laws of marriage no longer apply to her. ³Then she can marry someone else if she wants to. That would be wrong while he was alive, but it is perfectly all right after he dies.

⁴Your "husband," your master, used to be the Jewish law; but you "died," as it were, with Christ on the cross; and since you are "dead," you are no longer "married to the law," and it has no more control over you. Then you came back to life again when Christ did and are a new person. And now you are "married," so to speak, to the one who rose from the dead, so that you can produce good fruit, that is, good deeds for God. ⁵When your old nature was still active, sinful desires were at work within you, making you want to do whatever God said not to and producing sinful deeds, the rotting fruit of death. ⁶But now you need no longer worry about the Jewish laws and customs because you "died" while in their captivity, and now you can really serve God; not in the old way, mechanically obeying a set of rules, but in the new way, [with all of your hearts and minds].

⁷Well then, am I suggesting that these laws of God are evil? Of course not! No, the law is not sinful, but it was the law that showed me my sin. I would never have known the sin in my heart—the evil desires that are hidden there—if the law had not said, "You must not have evil desires in your heart." ⁸But sin used this law against evil desires by reminding me that such desires are wrong, and arousing all kinds of forbidden desires within me! Only if there were no laws to break would there be no sinning.

⁹That is why I felt fine so long as I did not understand what the law really demanded. But when I learned the truth, I

SHARKS

7:9-11 If people feel fine without the law, why did God give it? Because sin is real and dangerous. Imagine a sunny day at the beach. You have just plunged into the surf and you've never felt better. Suddenly you notice a sign on the pier: "No swimming: Sharks in water." Your day is ruined. Is it the sign's fault? Are you angry with the people who put it up? Of course not. The law is like the sign. It is essential, and we are grateful for it—but it doesn't get rid of the sharks.

realized that I had broken the law and was a sinner, doomed to die. ¹⁰So as far as I was concerned, the good law which was supposed to show me the way of life resulted instead in my being given the death penalty. ¹¹Sin fooled me by taking the good laws of God and using them to make me guilty of death. ¹²But still, you see, the law itself was wholly right and good.

¹³But how can that be? Didn't the law cause my doom? How then can it be good? No, it was sin, devilish stuff that it is, that used what was good to bring about my condemnation. So you can see how cunning and deadly and damnable it is. For it uses God's good laws for its own evil purposes.

¹⁴The law is good, then, and the trouble is not there but with *me* because I am sold into slavery with Sin as my owner. ¹⁵I don't understand myself at all, for I really want to do what is right, but I can't. I do what I don't want to—what I hate. ¹⁶I know perfectly well that what I am doing is wrong, and my bad conscience proves that I agree with these laws I am breaking. ¹⁷But I can't help myself because I'm no longer doing it. It is sin inside me that is stronger than I am that makes me do these evil things.

¹⁸I know I am rotten through and through so far as my old sinful nature is concerned. No matter which way I turn I can't make myself do right. I want to but I can't. ¹⁹When I want to do good, I don't; and when I try not to do wrong, I do it anyway. ²⁰Now if I am doing what I don't want to, it is plain where the trouble is: sin still has me in its evil grasp.

²¹It seems to be a fact of life that when I want to do what is right, I inevitably do what is wrong. ²²I love to do God's will so far as my new nature is concerned; ²³⁻²⁵but there is something else deep within me, in my lower nature, that is at war with my mind and wins the fight and makes me a slave to the sin that is still within me. In my mind I want to be God's willing servant, but instead I find myself still enslaved to sin.

So you see how it is: my new life tells me to do right, but the old nature that is still inside me loves to sin. Oh, what a terrible predicament I'm in! Who will free me from my slavery to this deadly lower nature? Thank God! It has been done by Jesus Christ our Lord. He has set me free.

STRUGGLE

7:15 This is more than the cry of one desperate man—it describes the experience of any Christian struggling against sin. We must never underestimate the power of sin. Satan is a crafty tempter, and we have a great ability to make excuses. Instead of trying to overcome sin with human willpower, we must take hold of the tremendous power of Christ that is available to us. This is God's provision for victory over sin; he sends the Holy Spirit to live in us and give us power. And when we fall, he lovingly reaches out to us and helps us get up again.

CHAPTER 8 THE HOLY SPIRIT FREES US FROM SIN.

So there is now no condemnation awaiting those who belong to Christ Jesus. ²For the power of the life-giving Spirit—and this power is mine through Christ Jesus—has freed me from the vicious circle of sin and death. ³We aren't saved from sin's grasp by knowing the commandments of God because we can't and don't keep them, but God put into effect a different plan to save us. He sent his own Son in a human body like ours—except that ours are sinful—and destroyed sin's control over us by giving himself as a sacrifice for our sins. ⁴So now we can obey God's laws if we follow after the Holy Spirit and no longer obey the old evil nature within us.

⁵Those who let themselves be controlled by their lower natures live only to please themselves, but those who follow after the Holy Spirit find themselves doing those things that please God. ⁶Following after the Holy Spirit leads to life and peace, but following after the old nature leads to death ⁷because the old sinful nature within us is against God. It never did obey God's laws and it never will. ⁸That's why those who are still under the control of their old sinful selves, bent on following their old evil desires, can never please God.

⁹But you are not like that. You are controlled by your new nature if you have the Spirit of God living in you. (And remember that if anyone doesn't have the Spirit of Christ living in him, he is not a Christian at all.) ¹⁰Yet, even though Christ lives within you, your body will die because of sin; but your spirit will live, for Christ has pardoned it. ¹¹And if the Spirit of God, who raised up Jesus from the dead, lives in you, he will make your dying bodies live again after you die, by means of this same Holy Spirit living within you.

¹²So, dear brothers, you have no obligations whatever to your old sinful nature to do what it begs you to do. ¹³For if you keep on following it you are lost and will perish, but if through the power of the Holy Spirit you crush it and its evil deeds, you shall live. ¹⁴For all who are led by the Spirit of God are sons of God.

¹⁵And so we should not be like cringing, fearful slaves, but we should behave like God's very own children, adopted into the bosom of his

GOOD

8:28 God works out all things—not just isolated incidents—for our good. This does not mean that all that happens to us is good. Evil is prevalent in our fallen world, but God is able to turn it around for our long-range good. Note that God is not working to make us happy, but to fulfill his purpose. Note also that this promise is not for everybody. It can be claimed only by those who love God and are fitting into his plans. Such people have a new perspective, a new mind-set. They trust in God, not life's treasures; they look to their security in heaven, not on earth; they learn to accept pain and persecution rather than resent it, because it brings them closer to God.

family, and calling to him, "Father, Father." [16]For his Holy Spirit speaks to us deep in our hearts and tells us that we really are God's children. [17]And since we are his children, we will share his treasures—for all God gives to his Son Jesus is now ours too. But if we are to share his glory, we must also share his suffering.

[18]Yet what we suffer now is nothing compared to the glory he will give us later. [19]For all creation is waiting patiently and hopefully for that future day when God will resurrect his children. [20,21]For on that day thorns and thistles, sin, death, and decay—the things that overcame the world against its will at God's command—will all disappear, and the world around us will share in the glorious freedom from sin which God's children enjoy.

[22]For we know that even the things of nature, like animals and plants, suffer in sickness and death as they await this great event. [23]And even we Christians, although we have the Holy Spirit within us as a foretaste of future glory, also groan to be released from pain and suffering. We, too, wait anxiously for that day when God will give us our full rights as his children, including the new bodies he has promised us—bodies that will never be sick again and will never die.

[24]We are saved by trusting. And trusting means looking forward to getting something we don't yet have—for a man who already has something doesn't need to hope and trust that he will get it. [25]But if we must keep trusting God for something that hasn't happened yet, it teaches us to wait patiently and confidently.

[26]And in the same way—by our faith—the Holy Spirit helps us with our daily problems and in our praying. For we don't even know what we should pray for nor how to pray as we should, but the Holy Spirit prays for us with such feeling that it cannot be expressed in words. [27]And the Father who knows all hearts knows, of course, what the Spirit is saying as he pleads for us in harmony with God's own will. [28]And we know that all that happens to us is working for our good if we love God and are fitting into his plans.

[29]For from the very beginning God decided that those who came to him—and all along he knew who would—should become like his Son, so that his Son would be the First, with many brothers. [30]And having chosen us, he called us to come to him; and when we came, he declared us "not guilty," filled us with Christ's goodness, gave us right standing with himself, and promised us his glory.

[31]What can we ever say to such wonderful things as these? If God is on our side, who can ever be against us? [32]Since he did not spare even his own Son for us but gave him up for us all, won't he also surely give us everything else?

[33]Who dares accuse us whom God has chosen for his own? Will God? No! He is the one who has forgiven us and given us right standing with himself.

[34]Who then will condemn us? Will Christ? *No!* For he is the one who died for us and came back to

---

Since becoming a Christian, it seems like I am always fighting against certain thoughts and habits that I used to never give a second thought about. Why is this happening?

I WONDER...

Picture your life as a door. Before you became a Christian, your sins were like nails being pounded into the door and left there. When you asked Christ to forgive you, all of the nails you had collected were removed! Unfortunately, what was left was a door full of holes, not very pleasant to look at and not very useful.

But God began patching up the holes! More accurately, he began to heal the scars left by sin, making your life into a door that will look unscarred after years of constant pounding. We truly can become a new creation (see 2 Corinthians 5:17).

That is why it is so important for people to come to know Christ's forgiveness early in life. Because we inherited a sinful nature from Adam (Romans 5:12), time and wrong choices can pound some pretty large nails into our lives. And those scars may take longer to heal. Paul knew this all too well, as you can see if you read his words in Romans 7:15–8:2. Like him, we all experience the tug to give in again to our sin nature, but our new nature moves us to resist.

So what you are experiencing is a new sensitivity to sin. Since sin wants to "drive a hole" in you and Christ wants to keep you unscarred by the effects of sin, it is no longer comfortable to ignore the constant pounding. Confessing your sin will always remove the nail.

This new sensitivity to sin means two things. First, it is a definite sign that God's Holy Spirit has truly entered your life (Romans 8:9). It is likely you would still be numb to the nails (sin) if you had rejected Christ's forgiveness. Second, it means that God is reminding you of his great love for you (Romans 8:38-39). Now your conscience advises you where you could stray off-course. He does not want you to be left scarred by the consequences of your sin, so he begins at the source of it—your thought life.

---

life again for us and is sitting at the place of highest honor next to God, pleading for us there in heaven.

[35]Who then can ever keep Christ's love from us? When we have trouble or calamity, when we are hunted down or destroyed, is it because he doesn't love us anymore? And if we are hungry or penniless or in danger or threatened with death, has God deserted us?

[36]No, for the Scriptures tell us that for his sake we must be ready to face death at every moment of

What can we ever say to *such wonderful things* as these?

If GOD IS ON OUR SIDE, who can ever be against us?

ROMANS 8:31

the day—we are like sheep awaiting slaughter; [37]but despite all this, overwhelming victory is ours through Christ who loved us enough to die for us. [38]For I am convinced that nothing can ever separate us from his love. Death can't, and life can't. The angels won't, and all the powers of hell itself cannot keep God's love away. Our fears for today, our worries about tomorrow, [39]or where we are—high above the sky, or in the deepest ocean—nothing will ever be able to separate us from the love of God demonstrated by our Lord Jesus Christ when he died for us.

CHAPTER 9 GOD IS SOVEREIGN. O Israel, my people! O my Jewish brothers! How I long for you to come to Christ. My heart is heavy within me, and I grieve bitterly day and night because of you. Christ knows and the Holy Spirit knows that it is no mere pretense when I say that I would be willing to be forever damned if that would save you. [4]God has given you so much, but still you will not listen to him. He took you as his own special, chosen people and led you along with a bright cloud of glory and told you how very much he wanted to bless you. He gave you his rules for daily life so you would know what he wanted you to do. He let

you worship him and gave you mighty promises. [5]Great men of God were your fathers, and Christ himself was one of you, a Jew so far as his human nature is concerned, he who now rules over all things. Praise God forever!

[6]Well then, has God failed to fulfill his promises to the Jews? No! [For these promises are only to those who are truly Jews.] And not everyone born into a Jewish family is truly a Jew! [7]Just the fact that they come from Abraham doesn't make them truly Abraham's children. For the Scriptures say that the promises apply only to Abraham's son Isaac and Isaac's descendants, though Abraham had other children too. [8]This means that not all of Abraham's children are children of God, but only those who believe the promise of salvation which he made to Abraham.

[9]For God had promised, "Next year I will give you and Sarah a son." [10-13]And years later, when this son Isaac was grown up and married and Rebecca his wife was about to bear him twin children, God told her that Esau, the child born first, would be a servant to Jacob, his twin brother. In the words of the Scripture, "I chose to bless Jacob but not Esau." And God said this before the children were even born, before they had done anything either good or bad. This proves that God was doing what he had decided from the beginning; it was not because of what the children did but because of what God wanted and chose.

[14]Was God being unfair? Of course not. [15]For God had said to Moses, "If I want to be kind to someone, I will. And I will take pity on anyone I want to." [16]And so God's blessings are not given just because someone decides to have them or works hard to get them. They are given because God takes pity on those he wants to.

[17]Pharaoh, king of Egypt, was an example of this fact. For God told him he had given him the kingdom of Egypt for the very purpose of displaying the awesome power of God against him, so that all the world would hear about God's glorious name. [18]So you see, God is kind to some just because he wants to be, and he makes some refuse to listen.

[19]Well then, why does God blame them for not listening? Haven't they done what he made them do?

TRYING

9:31-33 Sometimes we are like these people, trying "hard to get right with God by keeping his laws." We may think church attendance, church work, giving offerings, and being nice will be enough. After all, we've played by the rules, haven't we? But Paul's words sting—this approach never succeeds. Paul explains that God's plan is not for those who try to earn his favor by being good; it is for those who realize they can never be good enough and so must depend on Christ. Only by putting our faith in what Jesus Christ has done will we be saved. If we do that, we will "never be disappointed."

[20]No, don't say that. Who are you to criticize God? Should the thing made say to the one who made it, "Why have you made me like this?" [21]When a man makes a jar out of clay, doesn't he have a right to use the same lump of clay to make one jar beautiful, to be used for holding flowers, and another to throw garbage into? [22]Does not God have a perfect right to show his fury and power against those who are fit only for destruction, those he has been patient with for all this time? [23,24]And he has a right to take others such as ourselves, who have been made for pouring the riches of his glory into, whether we are Jews or Gentiles, and to be kind to us so that everyone can see how very great his glory is.

[25]Remember what the prophecy of Hosea says? There God says that he will find other children for himself (who are not from his Jewish family) and will love them, though no one had ever loved them before. [26]And the heathen, of whom it once was said, "You are not my people," shall be called "sons of the Living God."

[27]Isaiah the prophet cried out concerning the Jews that though there would be millions of them, only a small number would ever be saved. [28]"For the Lord will execute his sentence upon the earth, quickly ending his dealings, justly cutting them short."

[29]And Isaiah says in another place that except for God's mercy all the Jews would be destroyed—all of them—just as everyone in the cities of Sodom and Gomorrah perished.

[30]Well then, what shall we say about these things? Just this, that God has given the Gentiles the opportunity to be acquitted by faith, even though they had not been really seeking God. [31]But the Jews, who tried so hard to get right with God by keeping his laws, never succeeded. [32]Why not? Because they were trying to be saved by keeping the law and being good instead of by depending on faith. They have stumbled over the great stumbling stone. [33]God warned them of this in the Scriptures when he said, "I have put a Rock in the path of the Jews, and many will stumble over him (Jesus). Those who believe in him will never be disappointed."

CHAPTER **10** SOME DON'T UNDERSTAND. Dear brothers, the longing of my heart and my prayer is that the Jewish people might be saved. [2]I know what enthusiasm they have for the honor of God, but it is misdirected zeal. [3]For they don't understand that Christ has died to make them right with God. Instead they are trying to make themselves good enough to gain God's favor by keeping the Jewish laws and customs, but that is not God's way of salvation. [4]They don't understand that Christ

gives to those who trust in him everything they are trying to get by keeping his laws. He ends all of that.

[5]For Moses wrote that if a person could be perfectly good and hold out against temptation all his life and never sin once, only then could he be pardoned and saved. [6]But the salvation that comes through faith says, "You don't need to search the heavens to find Christ and bring him down to help you," and, [7]"You don't need to go among the dead to bring Christ back to life again."

[8]For salvation that comes from trusting Christ—which is what we preach—is already within easy reach of each of us; in fact, it is as near as our own hearts and mouths. [9]For if you tell others with your own mouth that Jesus Christ is your Lord and believe in your own heart that God has raised him from the dead, you will be saved. [10]For it is by believing in his heart that a man becomes right with God; and with his mouth he tells others of his faith, confirming his salvation.

[11]For the Scriptures tell us that no one who believes in Christ will ever be disappointed. [12]Jew and Gentile are the same in this respect: they all have the same Lord who generously gives his riches to all those who ask him for them. [13]Anyone who calls upon the name of the Lord will be saved.

[14]But how shall they ask him to save them unless they believe in him? And how can they believe in him if they have never heard about him? And how can they hear about him unless someone tells them? [15]And how will anyone go and tell them unless someone sends him? That is what the Scriptures are talking about when they say, "How beautiful are the feet of those who preach the Gospel of peace with God and bring glad tidings of good things." In other words, how welcome are those who come preaching God's Good News!

[16]But not everyone who hears the Good News has welcomed it, for Isaiah the prophet said, "Lord, who has believed me when I told them?" [17]Yet faith comes from listening to this Good News—the Good News about Christ.

[18]But what about the Jews? Have they heard God's Word? Yes, for it has gone wherever they are; the Good News has been told to the ends of the earth. [19]And did they understand [that God would give his salvation to others if they refused to take it]? Yes, for even back in the time of Moses, God had said that he would make his people jealous and

CLOSE

10:8-12 Have you ever been asked, "How do I become a Christian?" These verses give you the beautiful answer—salvation is as close as your own heart and mouth. People think it must be a complicated process, but it isn't. If they believe in their hearts and say with their mouths that Christ is the risen Lord, they will be saved.

try to wake them up by giving his salvation to the foolish heathen nations. [20]And later on Isaiah said boldly that God would be found by people who weren't even looking for him. [21]In the meantime, he keeps on reaching out his hands to the Jews, but they keep arguing and refusing to come.

CHAPTER 11 GOD'S KINDNESS FOR ISRAEL.

I ask then, has God rejected and deserted his people the Jews? Oh no, not at all. Remember that I myself am a Jew, a descendant of Abraham and a member of Benjamin's family.

[2,3]No, God has not discarded his own people whom he chose from the very beginning. Do you remember what the Scriptures say about this? Elijah the prophet was complaining to God about the Jews, telling God how they had killed the prophets and torn down God's altars; Elijah claimed that he was the only one left in all the land who still loved God, and now they were trying to kill him too.

[4]And do you remember how God replied? God said, "No, you are not the only one left. I have seven thousand others besides you who still love me and have not bowed down to idols!"

[5]It is the same today. Not all the Jews have turned away from God; there are a few being saved as a result of God's kindness in choosing them. [6]And if it is by God's kindness, then it is not by their being good enough. For in that case the free gift would no longer be free—it isn't free when it is earned.

[7]So this is the situation: Most of the Jews have not found the favor of God they are looking for. A few have—the ones God has picked out—but the eyes of the others have been blinded. [8]This is what our Scriptures refer to when they say that God has put them to sleep, shutting their eyes and ears so that they do not understand what we are talking about when we tell them of Christ. And so it is to this very day.

[9]King David spoke of this same thing when he said, "Let their good food and other blessings trap them into thinking all is well between themselves and God. Let these good things boomerang on them and fall back upon their heads to justly crush them. [10]Let their eyes be dim," he said, "so that they cannot see, and let them walk bent-backed forever with a heavy load."

[11]Does this mean that God has rejected his Jewish people forever? Of course not! His purpose was to make his salvation available to the Gentiles, and then the Jews would be jealous and begin to want God's salvation for themselves. [12]Now if the whole world became rich as a result of God's offer of salvation, when the Jews stumbled over it and turned it down, think how much greater a blessing the world will share in later on when the Jews, too, come to Christ.

[13]As you know, God has appointed me as a special messenger to you Gentiles. I lay great stress on this and remind the Jews about it as often as I can, [14]so that if possible I can make them want what you Gentiles have and in that way save some of them. [15]And how wonderful it will be when they become Christians! When God turned away from them it meant that he turned to the rest of the world to offer his salvation; and now it is even more wonderful when the Jews come to Christ. It will be like dead people coming back to life. [16]And since Abraham and the prophets are God's people, their children will be too. For if the roots of the tree are holy, the branches will be too.

[17]But some of these branches from Abraham's tree, some of the Jews, have been broken off. And you Gentiles who were branches from, we might say, a wild olive tree, were grafted in. So now you, too, receive the blessing God has promised Abraham and his children, sharing in God's rich nourishment of his own special olive tree.

[18]But you must be careful not to brag about being put in to replace the branches that were broken off. Remember that you are important only because you are now a part of God's tree; you are just a branch, not a root.

[19]"Well," you may be saying, "those branches were broken off to make room for me, so I must be pretty good."

[20]Watch out! Remember that those branches, the Jews, were broken off because they didn't believe God, and you are there only because you do. Do not be proud; be humble and grateful—and careful. [21]For if God did not spare the branches he put there

FREE

11:6 This great truth can be hard to grasp. Do you think it's easier for God to love you when you're good? Do you secretly suspect God chose you because you deserved to be chosen? Do you think some people's behavior is so bad that God couldn't possibly save them? If you ever think this way, you don't entirely understand the Good News that salvation is a free gift. It cannot be earned, in whole or in part; it can only be accepted with thankfulness and praise.

BRAND NEW

12:2 "The behavior and customs of this world" are usually selfish and often corrupting, and many Christians wisely decide that much worldly behavior is off-limits for them. Our refusal to conform to the world, however, must go even deeper than the level of behavior and customs—it must be firmly founded in our minds. This verse is also translated, "Do not be conformed to this world, but be transformed by the renewal of your mind." It is possible to avoid most worldly customs and still be proud, covetous, selfish, stubborn, and arrogant. Only when our mind is renewed by the new attitude Christ gives us are we truly transformed. If our character is like Christ's, we can be sure our behavior will honor God.

in the first place, he won't spare you either.

²²Notice how God is both kind and severe. He is very hard on those who disobey, but very good to you if you continue to love and trust him. But if you don't, you too will be cut off. ²³On the other hand, if the Jews leave their unbelief behind them and come back to God, God will graft them back into the tree again. He has the power to do it.

²⁴For if God was willing to take you who were so far away from him—being part of a wild olive tree—and graft you into his own good tree—a very unusual thing to do—don't you see that he will be far more ready to put the Jews back again, who were there in the first place?

²⁵I want you to know about this truth from God, dear brothers, so that you will not feel proud and start bragging. Yes, it is true that some of the Jews have set themselves against the Gospel now, but this will last only until all of you Gentiles have come to Christ—those of you who will. ²⁶And then all Israel will be saved.

Do you remember what the prophets said about this? "There shall come out of Zion a Deliverer, and he shall turn the Jews from all ungodliness. ²⁷At that time I will take away their sins, just as I promised."

²⁸Now many of the Jews are enemies of the Gospel. They hate it. But this has been a benefit to you, for it has resulted in God's giving his gifts to you Gentiles. Yet the Jews are still beloved of God because of his promises to Abraham, Isaac, and Jacob. ²⁹For God's gifts and his call can never be withdrawn; he will never go back on his promises. ³⁰Once you were rebels against God, but when the Jews refused his gifts God was merciful to you instead. ³¹And now the Jews are the rebels, but some day they, too, will share in God's mercy upon you. ³²For God has given them all up to sin so that he could have mercy upon all alike.

³³Oh, what a wonderful God we have! How great are his wisdom and knowledge and riches! How impossible it is for us to understand his decisions and his methods! ³⁴For who among us can know the mind of the Lord? Who knows enough to be his counselor and guide? ³⁵And who could ever offer to the Lord enough to induce him to act? ³⁶For everything comes from God alone. Everything lives by his power, and everything is for his glory. To him be glory evermore.

CHAPTER **12** **GIVE YOUR LIFE TO GOD.** And so, dear brothers, I plead with you to give your bodies to God. Let them be a living sacrifice, holy—the kind he can accept. When you think of what he has done for you, is this too much to ask? ²Don't copy the behavior and customs of this world, but be a new and different person with a fresh newness in all you do and think. Then you will learn from your own experience how his ways will really satisfy you.

³As God's messenger I give each of you God's warning: Be honest in your estimate of yourselves, measuring your value by how much faith God has given you. ⁴,⁵Just as there are many parts to our bodies, so it is with Christ's body. We are all parts of it, and it takes every one of us to make it complete, for we each have different work to do. So we belong to each other, and each needs all the others.

⁶God has given each of us the ability to do certain things well. So if God has given you the ability to prophesy, then prophesy whenever you can—as often as your faith is strong enough to receive a message from God. ⁷If your gift is that of serving others, serve them well. If you are a teacher, do a good job of teaching. ⁸If you are a preacher, see to it that your sermons are strong and helpful. If God has given you money, be generous in helping others with it. If God has given you

GIFTS

12:4-8 God gives us gifts so we can build up his church. To use them effectively, we must (1) realize that all gifts and abilities come from God; (2) understand that not everyone has the same gifts; (3) know who we are and what we do best; (4) dedicate our gifts to God's service and not to our personal success; (5) be willing to spend our gifts generously, not holding back anything from God's service.

"Here's what I did..."

My boyfriend and I didn't have a very good relationship; we couldn't communicate much. I decided that it was time to break up. I tried to be as tactful as I could; I didn't want to hurt his feelings. His reaction was to call me a couple of names that were hurtful, demeaning, and completely untrue. Not only did he say these things to me, he said them to other people.

That enraged me. I thought of different ways to respond, to get even. But then I recalled a verse that tells us not to take revenge. I looked up Romans 12:19; it says, "Never avenge yourselves. Leave that to God, for he has said that he will repay those who deserve it." This helped me to remove any thoughts of revenge from my mind and to concentrate instead on forgiving him and praying for him. As I do this, concern for his spiritual life overshadows my feelings of anger and hurt.

Lavonne

AGE 16

administrative ability and put you in charge of the work of others, take the responsibility seriously. Those who offer comfort to the sorrowing should do so with Christian cheer.

[9]Don't just pretend that you love others: really love them. Hate what is wrong. Stand on the side of the good. [10]Love each other with brotherly affection and take delight in honoring each other. [11]Never be lazy in your work, but serve the Lord enthusiastically.

[12]Be glad for all God is planning for you. Be patient in trouble, and prayerful always. [13]When God's children are in need, you be the one to help them out. And get into the habit of inviting guests home for dinner or, if they need lodging, for the night.

[14]If someone mistreats you because you are a Christian, don't curse him; pray that God will bless him. [15]When others are happy, be happy with them. If they are sad, share their sorrow. [16]Work happily together. Don't try to act big. Don't try to get into the good graces of important people, but enjoy the company of ordinary folks. And don't think you know it all!

[17]Never pay back evil for evil. Do things in such a way that everyone can see you are honest clear through. [18]Don't quarrel with anyone. Be at peace with everyone, just as much as possible.

[19]Dear friends, never avenge yourselves. Leave that to God, for he has said that he will repay those who deserve it. [Don't take the law into your own hands.] [20]Instead, feed your enemy if he is hungry. If he is thirsty give him something to drink and you will be "heaping coals of fire

on his head." In other words, he will feel ashamed of himself for what he has done to you. [21]Don't let evil get the upper hand, but conquer evil by doing good.

CHAPTER 13 OBEY THE GOVERNMENT.

Obey the government, for God is the one who has put it there. There is no government anywhere that God has not placed in power. [2]So those who refuse to obey the laws of the land are refusing to obey God, and punishment will follow. [3]For the policeman does not frighten people who are doing right; but those doing evil will always fear him. So if you don't want to be afraid, keep the laws and you will get along well. [4]The policeman is sent by God to help you. But if you are doing something wrong, of course you should be afraid, for he will have you punished. He is sent by God for that very purpose. [5]Obey the laws, then, for two reasons: first, to keep from being punished, and second, just because you know you should.

[6]Pay your taxes too, for these same two reasons. For government workers need to be paid so that they can keep on doing God's work, serving you. [7]Pay everyone whatever he ought to have: pay your taxes and import duties gladly, obey those over you, and give honor and respect to all those to whom it is due.

[8]Pay all your debts except the debt of love for others—never finish paying that! For if you love them, you will be obeying all of God's laws, fulfilling all his requirements. [9]If you love your neighbor as much as you love yourself you will not want to harm or cheat him, or kill him or steal from him. And you won't sin with his wife or want what is his, or do anything else the Ten Commandments say is wrong. All ten are wrapped up in this one, to love your neighbor as you love yourself. [10]Love does no wrong to anyone. That's why it fully satisfies all of God's requirements. It is the only law you need.

[11]Another reason for right living is this: you know how late it is; time is running out. Wake up, for the coming of the Lord is nearer now than when we first believed. [12,13]The night is far gone, the day of his return will soon be here. So quit the evil deeds of darkness and put on the armor of right living, as we who live in the daylight should! Be decent and true in everything you do so that all can

approve your behavior. Don't spend your time in wild parties and getting drunk or in adultery and lust or fighting or jealousy. [14]But ask the Lord Jesus Christ to help you live as you should, and don't make plans to enjoy evil.

CHAPTER 14 DON'T CRITICIZE OTHER CHRISTIANS.

Give a warm welcome to any brother who wants to join you, even though his faith is weak. Don't criticize him for having different ideas from yours about what is right and wrong. [2]For instance, don't argue with him about whether or not to eat meat that has been offered to idols. You may believe there is no harm in this, but the faith of others is weaker; they think it is wrong and will go without any meat at all and eat vegetables rather than eat that kind of meat. [3]Those who think it is all right to eat such meat must not look down on those who won't. And if you are one of those who won't, don't find fault with those who do. For God has accepted them to be his children. [4]They are God's servants, not yours. They are responsible to him, not to you. Let him tell them whether they are right or wrong. And God is able to make them do as they should.

[5]Some think that Christians should observe the Jewish holidays as special days to worship God, but others say it is wrong and foolish to go to all that trouble, for every day alike belongs to God. On questions of this kind everyone must decide for himself. [6]If you have special days for worshiping the Lord, you are trying to honor him; you are doing a good thing. So is the person who eats meat that has been offered to idols; he is thankful to the Lord for it; he is doing right. And the person who won't touch such meat, he, too, is anxious to please the Lord, and is thankful. [7]We are not our own bosses to live or die as we ourselves might choose. [8]Living or dying we follow the Lord. Either way we are his. [9]Christ died and rose again for this very purpose, so that he can be our Lord both while we live and when we die.

[10]You have no right to criticize your brother or look down on him. Remember, each of us will stand personally before the Judgment Seat of God. [11]For it is written, "As I live," says the Lord, "every knee shall bow to me and every tongue confess to God." [12]Yes, each of us will give an account of himself to God.

[13]So don't criticize each other anymore. Try instead to live in such a way that you will never make your brother stumble by letting him see you doing something he thinks is wrong.

[14]As for myself, I am perfectly sure on the authority of the Lord Jesus that there is nothing really wrong with eating meat that has been offered to idols. But if someone believes it is wrong, then he shouldn't do it because for him it is wrong.

[15]And if your brother is bothered by what you eat, you are not acting in love if you go ahead and eat it. Don't let your eating ruin someone for whom Christ died. [16]Don't do anything that will cause criticism against yourself even though you know that what you do is right.

[17]For, after all, the important thing for us as Christians is not what we eat or drink but stirring up goodness and peace and joy from the Holy Spirit. [18]If you let Christ be Lord in these affairs, God will be glad; and so will others. [19]In this way aim for harmony in the church, and try to build each other up.

[20]Don't undo the work of God for a chunk of meat. Remember, there is nothing wrong with the meat, but it is wrong to eat it if it makes another stumble. [21]The right thing to do is to quit eating meat or drinking wine or doing anything else that offends your brother or makes him sin. [22]You may know that there is nothing wrong with what you do, even from God's point of view, but keep it to yourself; don't flaunt your faith in front of others who might be hurt by it. In this situation, happy is the man who does not sin by doing what he knows is right. [23]But anyone who believes that something he wants to do is wrong shouldn't do it. He sins if he does, for he thinks it is wrong, and so for him it *is* wrong. Anything that is done apart from what he feels is right is sin.

STRENGTH

14:1 Who is weak in faith and who is strong? We are all weak in some areas and strong in others. Our faith is strong in an area if we can survive contact with sin without falling into it. It is weak if we must avoid certain activities or places in order to protect our spiritual life. We need to take a self-inventory to find our weaknesses and strengths.

In areas of strength, we should not fear that we will be defiled by the world. Rather, from our position of strength we should lead the world. In areas of weakness, however, we need to play it safe. If we have a strong faith but shelter it, we are not doing Christ's work in the world. If we have a weak faith but expose it, we are being extremely foolish.

CHAPTER 15 THINK OF OTHERS FIRST.

Even if we believe that it makes no difference to the Lord whether we do these things, still we cannot just go ahead and do them to please ourselves; for we must bear the "burden" of being considerate of the doubts and fears of others—of those who feel these things are wrong. Let's please the other fellow, not ourselves, and do what is for his good and thus build him up in the Lord. [3]Christ didn't please himself. As the Psalmist said, "He came for the very purpose of suffering under the insults of those who were against the Lord." [4]These things that were written in the Scriptures so long ago are to teach us patience and to encourage us so that we will look forward expectantly to the time when

God will conquer sin and death.

[5]May God who gives patience, steadiness, and encouragement help you to live in complete harmony with each other—each with the attitude of Christ toward the other. [6]And then all of us can praise the Lord together with one voice, giving glory to God, the Father of our Lord Jesus Christ.

[7]So warmly welcome each other into the church, just as Christ has warmly welcomed you; then God will be glorified. [8]Remember that Jesus Christ came to show that God is true to his promises and to help the Jews. [9]And remember that he came also that the Gentiles might be saved and give glory to God for his mercies to them. That is what the psalmist meant when he wrote: "I will praise you among the Gentiles and sing to your name."

SILENT

14:23–15:6 We try to steer clear of actions forbidden by Scripture, of course. But when Scripture is silent, we should follow our conscience. When God shows us something is wrong for us, we should avoid it—but we should not look down on other Christians who exercise their freedom in those areas.

[10]And in another place, "Be glad, O you Gentiles, along with his people the Jews."

[11]And yet again, "Praise the Lord, O you Gentiles; let everyone praise him."

[12]And the prophet Isaiah said, "There shall be an Heir in the house of Jesse, and he will be King over the Gentiles; they will pin their hopes on him alone."

[13]So I pray for you Gentiles that God who gives you hope will keep you happy and full of peace as you believe in him. I pray that God will help you overflow with hope in him through the Holy Spirit's power within you.

[14]I know that you are wise and good, my brothers, and that you know these things so well that you are able to teach others all about them. [15,16]But even so I have been bold enough to emphasize some of these points, knowing that all you need is this reminder from me; for I am, by God's grace, a special messenger from Jesus Christ to you Gentiles, bringing you the Gospel and offering you up as a fragrant sacrifice to God; for you have been made pure and pleasing to him by the Holy Spirit. [17]So it is right for me to be a little proud of all Christ Jesus has done through me. [18]I dare not judge how effectively he has used others, but I know this: he has used me to win the Gentiles to God. [19]I have won them by my message and by the good way I have lived before them and by the miracles done through me as signs from God—all by the Holy Spirit's power. In this way I have preached the full Gospel of Christ all the way from Jerusalem clear over into Illyricum.

[20]But all the while my ambition has been to go still farther, preaching where the name of Christ has never yet been heard, rather than where a church has already been started by someone else. [21]I have been following the plan spoken of in the Scriptures where Isaiah says that those who have never heard the name of Christ before will see and understand. [22]In fact, that is the very reason I have been so long in coming to visit you.

[23]But now at last I am through with my work here, and I am ready to come after all these long years of waiting. [24]For I am planning to take a trip to Spain, and when I do, I will stop off there in Rome; and after we have had a good time together for a little while, you can send me on my way again.

[25]But before I come, I must go down to Jerusalem to take a gift to the Jewish Christians there. [26]For you see, the Christians in Macedonia and Achaia have taken up an offering for those in Jerusalem who are going through such hard times. [27]They were very glad to do this, for they feel that they owe a real debt to the Jerusalem Christians. Why? Because the news about Christ came to these Gentiles from the church in Jerusalem. And since they received this wonderful spiritual gift of the Gospel from there, they feel that the least they can do in return is to give some material aid. [28]As soon as I have delivered this money and completed this good deed of theirs, I will come to see you on my way to Spain. [29]And I am sure that when I come the Lord will give me a great blessing for you.

[30]Will you be my prayer partners? For the Lord Jesus Christ's sake and because of your love for me—given to you by the Holy Spirit—pray much with me for my work. [31]Pray that I will be protected in Jerusalem from those who are not Christians. Pray also that the Christians there will be willing to accept the money I am bringing them. [32]Then I will be able to come to you with a happy heart by the will of God, and we can refresh each other.

[33]And now may our God, who gives peace, be with you all. Amen.

CHAPTER 16 PAUL GREETS HIS FRIENDS.

Phoebe, a dear Christian woman from the town of Cenchreae, will be coming to see you soon. She has worked hard in the church there. Receive her as your sister in the Lord, giving her a warm Christian welcome. Help her in every way you can, for she has helped many in their needs, including me. [3]Tell Priscilla and Aquila hello. They have been my

GOD'S WORK

15:17 Paul was not proud of what he had done, but of what God had done through him. Being proud of God's work is not a sin—it is worship. If you are not sure whether your pride is selfish or holy, ask yourself this question: Are you just as proud of what God is doing through other people as of what he is doing through you?

fellow workers in the affairs of Christ Jesus. [4]In fact, they risked their lives for me, and I am not the only one who is thankful to them; so are all the Gentile churches.

[5]Please give my greetings to all those who meet to worship in their home. Greet my good friend Epaenetus. He was the very first person to become a Christian in Asia. [6]Remember me to Mary, too, who has worked so hard to help us. [7]Then there are Andronicus and Junias, my relatives who were in prison with me. They are respected by the apostles and became Christians before I did. Please give them my greetings. [8]Say hello to Ampliatus, whom I love as one of God's own children, [9]and Urbanus, our fellow worker, and beloved Stachys.

[10]Then there is Apelles, a good man whom the Lord approves; greet him for me. And give my best regards to those working at the house of Aristobulus. [11]Remember me to Herodion my relative. Remember me to the Christian slaves over at Narcissus House. [12]Say hello to Tryphaena and Tryphosa, the Lord's workers, and to dear Persis, who has worked so hard for the Lord. [13]Greet Rufus for me, whom the Lord picked out to be his very own; and also his dear mother who has been such a mother to me. [14]And please give my greetings to Asyncritus, Phlegon, Hermes, Patrobas, Hermas,

and the other brothers who are with them. [15]Give my love to Philologus, Julia, Nereus and his sister, and to Olympas, and all the Christians who are with them. [16]Shake hands warmly with each other. All the churches here send you their greetings.

[17]And now there is one more thing to say before I end this letter. Stay away from those who cause divisions and are upsetting people's faith, teaching things about Christ that are contrary to what you have been taught. [18]Such teachers are not working for our Lord Jesus but only want gain for themselves. They are good speakers, and simpleminded people are often fooled by them. [19]But everyone knows that you stand loyal and true. This makes me very happy. I want you always to remain very clear about what is right and to stay innocent of any wrong. [20]The God of peace will soon crush Satan under your feet. The blessings from our Lord Jesus Christ be upon you.

[21]Timothy my fellow worker, and Lucius and Jason and Sosipater, my relatives, send you their good wishes. [22]I, Tertius, the one who is writing this letter for Paul, send my greetings too, as a Christian brother. [23]Gaius says to say hello to you for him. I am his guest, and the church meets here in his home. Erastus, the city treasurer, sends you his greetings and so does Quartus, a Christian brother.

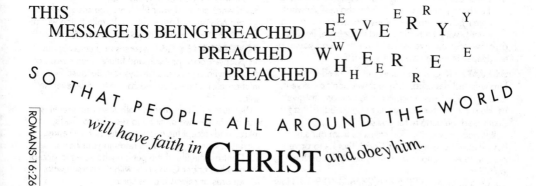

THIS IS GOD'S PLAN OF SALVATION FOR YOU GENTILES, kept secret from THE BEGINNING OF TIME But NOW as the prophets foretold and as GOD COMMANDS, THIS MESSAGE IS BEING PREACHED EVERY PREACHED WHERE PREACHED SO THAT PEOPLE ALL AROUND THE WORLD will have faith in CHRIST and obey him.

²⁴Good-bye. May the grace of our Lord Jesus Christ be with you all.

²⁵⁻²⁷I commit you to God, who is able to make you strong and steady in the Lord, just as the Gospel says, and just as I have told you. This is God's plan of salvation for you Gentiles, kept secret from the beginning of time. But now as the prophets foretold and as God commands, this message is being preached everywhere, so that people all around the world will have faith in Christ and obey him. To God, who alone is wise, be the glory forever through Jesus Christ our Lord. Amen.

Sincerely, Paul

MEGA *Themes*

SIN Sin means refusing to do God's will and failing to do all that God wants. Since Adam rebelled against God, it has become our nature to disobey God. Our sin cuts us off from God; sin causes us to want to live our own way rather than God's way. Because God is morally perfect, just, and fair, he is right to condemn sin.

Each person has sinned, either by rebelling against God or by ignoring his will. No matter what our background or how hard we try to live a good and moral life, we cannot earn salvation or remove our sin. Only Christ can save us.

1. Through Paul's writings to Rome, God reveals to us how destructive sin is in our world, how widespread it is in mankind, how fatal it is to individuals. Survey chapters 1, 3, and 5 and list the key teachings you find on the topic of sin.
2. What are some of the consequences of mankind's choices to rebel against God's will?
3. How does sin enslave a person?
4. Now read 7:14-25 to catch a glimpse of Paul's personal battle with sin. How does Paul overcome his weaknesses?
5. Check out your life in light of this study. What are the consequences of your sinful choices? At what points has sin enslaved you? Where can you identify with the feelings and thoughts of Paul?
6. How does an awareness of your sin lead you to a deeper reliance upon Jesus Christ?

SALVATION Our sin points out our need to be forgiven and cleansed. Although we don't deserve it, God in his kindness reaches out to love and forgive us. He provides the way for us to be saved. Christ's death paid the penalty for our sin.

It is good news that God saves us from our sin. But we must believe in Jesus Christ, that he forgave our sin, to enter into a wonderful new relationship with God.

1. Read Romans 3:23; 5:8; 6:23; and 10:9-10. How would you use these verses to explain what it means to receive salvation through Jesus Christ?
2. Describe your own personal response to the message of salvation. When did you first hear it? When did you first believe?
3. What difference has Christ's salvation made in your daily life?
4. How does knowing that God has forgiven your sins affect the way you live?

GROWTH By God's power, believers are made holy. This is known as "sanctification." It means we are set apart from sin, enabled to obey and to become more like Christ. When we are growing in our relationship with Christ, the Holy Spirit frees us from the demands of the law and from the fear of God's judgment.

Because we are free from sin's control, the law's demands, and fear of God's punishment, we can grow in our relationship with Christ. By trusting in the Holy Spirit and allowing him to help us, we can overcome sin and temptation. Without the Holy Spirit, we will be unable to conquer sin's power.

1. Rewrite 12:1-2 in your own words.
2. How has God transformed you?
3. In what areas of your life have you struggled—or are now struggling—with conformity to the world?
4. What should you do to submit more fully to God?

SOVEREIGNTY God oversees and cares about his people—past, present, and future. God's ways of dealing with people are always fair. Because God is in charge of all creation, he can save whomever he wills.

Because of God's mercy, both Jews and Gentiles can be saved—we all need to respond to God's mercy and accept his gracious offer of forgiveness. God is sovereign, so let him reign in your heart.

1. Contrast the life of the person who seeks to accept and live under God's rule with the person who ignores or rejects him as Lord.

2. Describe Jesus' lordship in your life. What does it mean to let him be Lord over your life?
3. What confidence do you have because of the sovereignty of God?

SERVICE When our purpose is to give credit to God for his love, power, and perfection in all we do, we can serve him properly. Serving God unifies all believers and enables them to be loving and sensitive to others.

None of us can be fully Christlike by himself or herself—it takes the entire body of Christ to fully express Christ. By actively and vigorously building up other believers, Christians can be a symphony of service to God.

1. Chapters 12–15 include various teachings on how to live with fellow believers as members of Christ's body. List a number of the ways we are to relate to each other to show that we are unified.
2. Who are the Christians with whom you are the closest? Why do you feel close to these people?
3. What Christians are hard for you to love? What could you do to get along better with them?
4. What acts of service could you do for those you listed in questions 2 and 3?

*F*ifteen-year-old Dicky just recently accepted Christ. Yesterday, he watched in total disbelief as two of the "leaders" of his church got into a shouting (and shoving!) match after Sunday services. Dicky quietly asks *you* why supposedly "mature" Christians act that way. What do you say? ■ Kim has discovered that a man and woman who are active in the church aren't really married, but are living together. "How can they do that? Why doesn't the preacher talk to them? Isn't that a sin?" Kim says, puzzled. What would you tell her? ■ Twelve-year-old Abby knows, as a Christian, that certain activities are wrong—drunkenness, premarital sex, lying, stealing, etc. But what about all those "gray areas" that God's word *doesn't* address? Is it OK to dance, go to certain parties, or buy expensive clothes? What about her favorite videos on MTV and songs on the radio? And how does God feel about the movies she's watched recently? "I want to do what's right," she tells you, "but sometimes it's hard to know. Aren't there some guidelines from the Bible that can help?" How do you answer? ■ These questions are far from new. Christians (and churches) have struggled with immaturity, division, and immorality since the first hymn was sung. Fortunately, the apostle Paul's first letter to the Corinthians has some real and practical answers. If you're looking to live a godly life in a godless culture, or if you want to help someone else do so, keep reading.

STATS

PURPOSE: To identify problems in the Corinthian church, to offer solutions, and to teach the believers how to live for Christ in a corrupt society

AUTHOR: Paul

TO WHOM WRITTEN: The church in Corinth

DATE WRITTEN: About A.D. 55, near the end of Paul's three-year ministry in Ephesus during his third missionary journey

SETTING: Corinth was a major cosmopolitan city, a seaport and major trade center—the most important city in Achaia. It was also filled with idolatry and immorality. The church was largely made up of Gentiles. Paul had established this church on his second missionary journey.

KEY PEOPLE: Paul, Timothy, members of Chloe's household

KEY PLACES: Worship meetings in Corinth

1 Corinthians

CHAPTER 1   PAUL: CHOSEN TO BE A MISSIONARY.

From: Paul, chosen by God to be Jesus Christ's missionary, and from brother Sosthenes.

²*To:* The Christians in Corinth, invited by God to be his people and made acceptable to him by Christ Jesus. *And to:* All Christians everywhere— whoever calls upon the name of Jesus Christ, our Lord and theirs.

³May God our Father and the Lord Jesus Christ give you all of his blessings, and great peace of heart and mind.

⁴I can never stop thanking God for all the wonderful gifts he has given you, now that you are Christ's: ⁵he has enriched your whole life. He has helped you speak out for him and has given you a full understanding of the truth; ⁶what I told you Christ could do for you has happened! ⁷Now you have every grace and blessing; every spiritual gift and power for doing his will are yours during this time of waiting for the return of our Lord Jesus Christ. ⁸And he guarantees right up to the end that you will be counted free from all sin and guilt on that day when he returns. ⁹God will surely do this

for you, for he always does just what he says, and he is the one who invited you into this wonderful friendship with his Son, even Christ our Lord.

¹⁰But, dear brothers, I beg you in the name of the Lord Jesus Christ to stop arguing among yourselves. Let there be real harmony so that there won't be splits in the church. I plead with you to be of one mind, united in thought and purpose. ¹¹For some of those who live at Chloe's house have told me of your arguments and quarrels, dear brothers. ¹²Some of you are saying, "I am a follower of Paul"; and others say that they are for Apollos or for Peter; and some that they alone are the true followers of Christ. ¹³And so, in effect, you have broken Christ into many pieces.

But did I, Paul, die for your sins? Were any of

USEFUL

1:1 Paul was specially selected by God to preach about Jesus Christ. Each Christian has a task to do. One task may seem more spectacular than another, but all are necessary to carry out God's greater plans for the world (12:12-27). Be useful to God by using your gifts in his service. As you discover what he wants, be ready to serve.

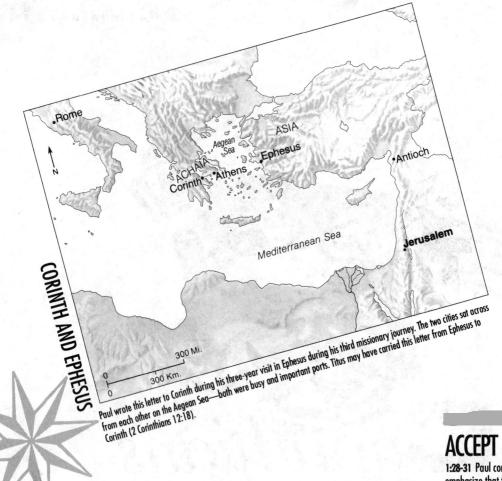

CORINTH AND EPHESUS

Paul wrote this letter to Corinth during his three-year visit in Ephesus during his third missionary journey. The two cities sat across from each other on the Aegean Sea—both were busy and important ports. Titus may have carried this letter from Ephesus to Corinth (2 Corinthians 12:18).

you baptized in my name? ¹⁴I am so thankful now that I didn't baptize any of you except Crispus and Gaius. ¹⁵For now no one can think that I have been trying to start something new, beginning a "Church of Paul." ¹⁶Oh, yes, and I baptized the family of Stephanas. I don't remember ever baptizing anyone else. ¹⁷For Christ didn't send me to baptize, but to preach the Gospel; and even my preaching sounds poor, for I do not fill my sermons with profound words and high sounding ideas, for fear of diluting the mighty power there is in the simple message of the cross of Christ.

¹⁸I know very well how foolish it sounds to those who are lost, when they hear that Jesus died to save them. But we who are saved recognize this message as the very power of God. ¹⁹For God says, "I will destroy all human plans of salvation no matter how wise they seem to be, and ignore the best ideas of men, even the most brilliant of them."

²⁰So what about these wise men, these scholars, these brilliant debaters of this world's great affairs? God has made them all look foolish and shown their wisdom to be useless nonsense. ²¹For God in his wisdom saw to it that the world would never find God through human brilliance, and then he stepped in and saved all those who believed his message, which the world calls foolish and silly. ²²It seems foolish to the Jews because they want a sign from heaven as proof that what is preached is true; and it is foolish to the Gentiles because they believe only what agrees with their philosophy and seems wise to them. ²³So when we preach about Christ dying to save them, the Jews are offended and the Gentiles say it's all nonsense. ²⁴But God has opened the eyes of those called to salvation, both Jews and Gentiles, to see that Christ is the mighty power of God to save them; Christ himself is the

ACCEPT

1:28-31 Paul continues to emphasize that the way to receive salvation is so ordinary and simple that *any* person who wants to can understand it. Skill does not get you into God's Kingdom—simple faith does. God planned it this way so no one could boast that his achievements helped him secure eternal life. Salvation is totally from God through Jesus' death, which allowed us to become perfect in God's eyes. There is *nothing* we can do to become acceptable to God; we need only accept what Jesus has already done for us. He has done the work.

center of God's wise plan for their salvation. ²⁵This so-called "foolish" plan of God is far wiser than the wisest plan of the wisest man, and God in his weakness—Christ dying on the cross—is far stronger than any man.

²⁶Notice among yourselves, dear brothers, that few of you who follow Christ have big names or power or wealth. ²⁷Instead, God has deliberately chosen to use ideas the world considers foolish and of little worth in order to shame those people considered by the world as wise and great. ²⁸He has chosen a plan despised by the world, counted as nothing at all, and used it to bring down to nothing those the world considers great, ²⁹so that no one anywhere can ever brag in the presence of God.

³⁰For it is from God alone that you have your life through Christ Jesus. He showed us God's plan of salvation; he was the one who made us acceptable to God; he made us pure and holy and gave himself to purchase our salvation. ³¹As it says in the Scriptures, "If anyone is going to boast, let him boast only of what the Lord has done."

CHAPTER 2 THE HOLY SPIRIT GIVES US WISDOM.

Dear brothers, even when I first came to you I didn't use lofty words and brilliant ideas to tell you God's message. ²For I decided that I would speak only of Jesus Christ and his death on the cross. ³I came to you in weakness—timid and trembling. ⁴And my preaching was very plain, not with a lot of oratory and human wisdom, but the Holy Spirit's power was in my words, proving to those who heard them that the message was from God. ⁵I did this because I wanted your faith to stand firmly upon God, not on man's great ideas.

⁶Yet when I am among mature Christians I do speak with words of great wisdom, but not the kind that comes from here on earth, and not the kind that appeals to the great men of this world, who are doomed to fall. ⁷Our words are wise because they are from God, telling of God's wise plan to bring us into the glories of heaven. This plan was hidden in former times, though it was made for our benefit before the world began. ⁸But the great men of the world have not understood it; if they

FUTURE

2:9 We cannot imagine all that God has in store for us both in this life and for eternity. He will create a new heaven and a new earth (Isaiah 65:17; Revelation 21:1), and we will live with him forever. Until then, his Holy Spirit comforts and guides us. Knowing the future that awaits us should give us hope and courage to press on in this life, to endure hardship, and to avoid giving in to temptation. This world is not all there is.

HIGHLIGHTS OF 1 CORINTHIANS

The Meaning of the Cross, 1:18–2:16. Be considerate of one another because of what Christ has done for us. There is no place for pride or a know-it-all attitude. We are to have the mind of Christ.

The Story of the Last Supper, 1:23-29. The Last Supper is a time of reflection on Christ's final words to his disciples before he died on the cross; we must celebrate this in an orderly and correct manner.

The Poem of Love, 13:1-13. Love is to guide all we do. We have different gifts, abilities, likes, dislikes—but we are called, without exception, to love.

The Christian's Destiny, 15:42-58. We are promised by Christ, who died for us, that just as he came back to life after death, our perishable body will be exchanged for a heavenly body. Then we will live and reign with Christ.

had, they never would have crucified the Lord of Glory.

[9]That is what is meant by the Scriptures which say that no mere man has ever seen, heard, or even imagined what wonderful things God has ready for those who love the Lord. [10]But we know about these things because God has sent his Spirit to tell us, and his Spirit searches out and shows us all of God's deepest secrets. [11]No one can really know what anyone else is thinking or what he is really like except that person himself. And no one can know God's thoughts except God's own Spirit. [12]And God has actually given us his Spirit (not the world's spirit) to tell us about the wonderful free gifts of grace and blessing that God has given us. [13]In telling you about these gifts we have even used the very words given to us by the Holy Spirit, not words that we as men might choose. So we use the Holy Spirit's words to explain the Holy Spirit's facts. [14]But the man who isn't a Christian can't understand and can't accept these thoughts from God, which the Holy Spirit teaches us. They sound foolish to him because only those who have the Holy Spirit within them can understand what the Holy Spirit means. Others just can't take it in. [15]But the spiritual man has insight into everything, and that bothers and baffles the man of the world, who can't understand him at all. [16]How could he? For certainly he has never been one to know the Lord's thoughts, or to discuss them with him, or to move the hands of God by prayer. But, strange as it seems, we Christians actually do have within us a portion of the very thoughts and mind of Christ.

CHAPTER **3** Dear brothers, I have been talking to you as though you were still just babies in the Christian life who are not following the Lord but your own desires; I cannot talk to you as I would to healthy Christians who are filled with the Spirit. [2]I have had to feed you with milk and not with solid food because you couldn't digest anything stronger. And even now you still have to be fed on milk. [3]For you are still only baby Christians, controlled by your own desires, not God's. When you are jealous of one another and divide up into quarreling groups, doesn't that prove you are still babies, wanting your own way? In fact, you are acting like people who don't belong to the Lord at all. [4]There you are, quarreling about whether I am

DESIRES

3:1-3 Paul called the Corinthians babies in the Christian life because they were not yet spiritually healthy and mature. The proof was that they quarreled like children. Baby Christians are controlled by their own desires; mature believers, by God's desires. How much influence do your own desires have on your life? Make it your goal to let God's desires be your own.

greater than Apollos, and dividing the church. Doesn't this show how little you have grown in the Lord?

[5]Who am I, and who is Apollos, that we should be the cause of a quarrel? Why, we're just God's servants, each of us with certain special abilities, and with our help you believed. [6]My work was to plant the seed in your hearts, and Apollos' work was to water it, but it was God, not we, who made the garden grow in your hearts. [7]The person who does the planting or watering isn't very important, but God is important because he is the one who makes things grow. [8]Apollos and I are working as a team, with the same aim, though each of us will be rewarded for his own hard work. [9]We are only God's coworkers. You are *God's* garden, not ours; you are *God's* building, not ours.

[10]God, in his kindness, has taught me how to be an expert builder. I have laid the foundation and Apollos has built on it. But he who builds on the foundation must be very careful. [11]And no one can ever lay any other real foundation than that one we already have—Jesus Christ. [12]But there are various kinds of materials that can be used to build on that foundation. Some use gold and silver and jewels; and some build with sticks and hay or even straw! [13]There is going to come a time of testing at Christ's Judgment Day to see what kind of material each builder has used. Everyone's work will be put through the fire so that all can see whether or not it keeps its value, and what was really accomplished. [14]Then every workman who has built on the foundation with the right materials, and whose work still stands, will get his pay. [15]But if the house he has built burns up, he will have a great loss. He himself will be saved, but like a man escaping through a wall of flames.

[16]Don't you realize that all of you together are the house of God, and that the Spirit of God lives among you in his house? [17]If anyone defiles and

WISDOM

3:18-19 Paul was not telling the Corinthian believers to neglect the pursuit of knowledge. He was saying that if you have to choose between earthly knowledge and heavenly wisdom, choose heavenly wisdom even though you might look foolish to the world. Worldly wisdom, if it holds you back from God, is not really wisdom. The Corinthians were using so-called worldly wisdom to evaluate their leaders and teachers. Their pride made them value the presentation of the message more than its content.

JUDGING

4:5 It is tempting to judge fellow Christians, evaluating whether or not they are good followers of Christ. But only God knows a person's heart, and he is the only one with the right to judge. Paul's warning to the Corinthians should also warn us. We should help those who are sinning (see 5:12-13), but we must not judge who is a better servant for Christ. When you judge someone, you automatically consider yourself better, and that is pride.

spoils God's home, God will destroy him. For God's home is holy and clean, and you are that home.

¹⁸Stop fooling yourselves. If you count yourself above average in intelligence, as judged by this world's standards, you had better put this all aside and be a fool rather than let it hold you back from the true wisdom from above. ¹⁹For the wisdom of this world is foolishness to God. As it says in the book of Job, God uses man's own brilliance to trap him; he stumbles over his own "wisdom" and falls. ²⁰And again, in the book of Psalms, we are told that the Lord knows full well how the human mind reasons and how foolish and futile it is.

²¹So don't be proud of following the wise men of this world. For God has already given you everything you need. ²²He has given you Paul and Apollos and Peter as your helpers. He has given you the whole world to use, and life and even death are your servants. He has given you all of the present and all of the future. All are yours, ²³and you belong to Christ, and Christ is God's.

CHAPTER **4** CLIQUES IN THE CHURCH. So Apollos and I should be looked upon as Christ's servants who distribute God's blessings by explaining God's secrets. ²Now the most important thing about a servant is that he does just what his master tells him to. ³What about me? Have I been a good servant? Well, I don't worry over what you think about this or what anyone else thinks. I don't even trust my own judgment on this point. ⁴My conscience is clear, but even that isn't final proof. It is the Lord himself who must examine me and decide.

⁵So be careful not to jump to conclusions before the Lord returns as to whether someone is a good servant or not. When the Lord comes, he will turn on the light so that everyone can see exactly what each one of us is really like, deep down in our hearts. Then everyone will know why we have been doing the Lord's work. At that time God will give to each one whatever praise is coming to him.

⁶I have used Apollos and myself as examples to illustrate what I have been saying: that you must not have favorites. You must not be proud of one of God's teachers more than another. ⁷What are you so puffed up about? What do you have that God hasn't given you? And if all you have is from God, why act as though you are so great, and as though you have accomplished something on your own?

⁸You seem to think you already have all the spiritual food you need. You are full and spiritually contented, rich kings on your thrones, leaving us far behind! I wish you really were already on your thrones, for when that time comes you can be sure that we will be there, too, reigning with you.

⁹Sometimes I think God has put us apostles at the very end of the line, like prisoners soon to be killed, put on display at the end of a victor's parade, to be stared at by men and angels alike.

¹⁰Religion has made us foolish, you say, but of

I hear a lot about the New Age movement. Some of my friends say they are in it. How is this different than what I believe as a Christian?

I WONDER...

The most convenient religion is one you create yourself, and that is what the New Age movement does for people. It allows them to create their own rules concerning God, their behavior, and how to make it to the next life.

Because of this, *New Age* is impossible to define! But, generally, here is what most New-Agers believe:

•They believe that God is everywhere and in everybody. Because we are humans, we all have a unity of spirit that allows us to be brothers no matter what. God is not good or bad. In fact, each person is a god. He or she is the center of the universe. Morality, therefore, isn't important (since God is not seen as either good or bad). But the mind and intellect are very important, because, supposedly, a person has to think deep thoughts to understand these concepts.

•They believe that "salvation" comes through reincarnation. This means coming back to life again in the form of someone or something else, again and again, until you get it right. (Reincarnation is a lie; the Bible is very clear on this point. See Hebrews 9:27.)

There are so many strains within the New Age movement that it's impossible to outline them all. But the key is believing that there is no personal God, that humans are not sinful, and that the next life is assured in some form, no matter what you have done. This is a very convenient religion if you just want to do your own thing.

But listen to God: "The Lord says: Cursed is the man who puts his trust in mortal man and turns his heart away from God" (Jeremiah 17:5). When people set their own beliefs and thoughts up as more important than what God thinks, they are actually being cursed by him!

Nearly every belief within the New Age movement allows you to become your own god. Eve was told by Satan that she would become like God if she ate of the fruit of the tree (Genesis 3:1-6). People are being told they can be god of their lives if they would just look away from the one, true God.

The Bible must be our authority on what we are to believe about God, ourselves, and what it takes to be saved from our sin. If it isn't, everyone can create a religion to suit his or her own desires. And that is a religion that will lead to destruction. Don't believe that? Just take a look at 1 Corinthians 1:19: "God says, 'I will destroy all human plans of salvation no matter how wise they seem to be, and ignore the best ideas of men, even the most brilliant of them.'"

There's only one place to find the real answers to who God is and what he's about: his holy Word, the Bible.

AIDS: WHAT WOULD JESUS DO?

There are few more explosive topics in America than that of AIDS. Conservatives believe AIDS is God's judgment on certain sinners. Gay rights groups and others scream just as loudly that this is a medical issue, not a moral one. Who's right? And how should Christians respond to this overwhelming problem? In one sense, AIDS (Acquired Immune Deficiency Syndrome) is primarily a medical issue. The AIDS virus attacks the body's immune system, making the body defenseless against the diseases a healthy person's immune system would destroy. AIDS is an "equal opportunity" nightmare: it affects everyone: young, old, male, female, gay, or straight. But this is only a part of the picture. Since the majority of people in our country infected with AIDS are homosexual men and IV drug abusers. Many Christians and churches have jumped on the special judgment on those homosexuals and junkies. Many people believe that AIDS must be a "judgment bandwagon," too, pointing to passages like Romans 1 (or 1 Corinthians 6:9) as evidence of God's special displeasure on the sin of homosexuality. Is this a reasonable belief? Did God get "fed up" with gays and junkies and punish them with AIDS? There are a number of problems with this belief. First, while male homosexuals make up the highest percentage of persons with AIDS in our culture, female homosexuals (lesbians) seldom contract it. Does this mean that God hates male gays, but female gays are OK? That is obviously inconsistent, and God is never inconsistent. As for drug abusers, those who inject drugs intravenously and share their needles with one another often contract the AIDS virus. Those who don't use or share needles don't get it nearly as frequently. So does God only hate those drug abusers who inject drugs and share needles? That's clearly illogical. If AIDS isn't a punishment from God, why has it hit the male gay community and IV drug abusers so hard? The answer is that gay men and IV drug abusers participate in activities that pass the virus from person to person very effectively. God hasn't singled out particular groups for special judgment; rather, those people engage in activities that are particularly risky as regards the transmission of AIDS. God created the universe to run in accordance with natural laws, like gravity, inertia, etc. When you try to defy those laws, you lose. You may not like the law of gravity, but jump off a building and you will—like it or not—encounter it. There are natural laws governing human behavior, too. One such law is that your body is not made for sexual promiscuity. Violate that law and you risk contracting AIDS or other diseases (syphilis, gonorrhea, herpes, etc.). Likewise, your body was not made to handle large amounts of drugs. Continually inject them into your veins and you probably will experience a lot of physical problems— one of which may be AIDS. So it's not that God is using AIDS to "get" certain kinds of people. AIDS simply is a natural—though terrifying—result of human behavior that goes against God's design for our lives. As the Psalmist wrote in Psalm 143:1-2, "Hear my prayer, O Lord; answer my plea because you are faithful to your promises. Don't bring me to trial! For as compared with you, no one is perfect [or righteous]." Since a cure for AIDS is many years away, the only reasonable, Christian response is to follow God's standards for sexual morality: sex is made for marriage only—to be kept in the context of a faithful, monogamous relationship between husband and wife. Anything else is unbiblical, sinful, and potentially fatal. Likewise, we must reaffirm God's ownership of our bodies by not abusing them with drugs. Paul writes in 1 Corinthians 6:19-20, ... "Haven't you yet learned that your body is the home of the Holy Spirit . . . and that he lives within you? because God has bought you with a great price. So use every part of your body to give glory back to God, because he owns it." Where we have failed to live up to this, we need to confess our sins, repent, and ask God's forgiveness. Many Christians also need to confess their judgmental attitudes toward persons with AIDS. There is no room in Christianity for feelings of superiority or self-righteousness. Jesus had strong words for those who were guilty of spiritual pride, of thinking they were better than others. Our response toward anyone with this terrible disease should be concern, compassion, and a hand reaching out to ease his or her pain and distress. Isn't that how Jesus deals with people, regardless of their sins?

course you are all such wise and sensible Christians! We are weak, but not you! You are well thought of, while we are laughed at. [11]To this very hour we have gone hungry and thirsty, without even enough clothes to keep us warm. We have been kicked around without homes of our own. [12]We have worked wearily with our hands to earn our living. We have blessed those who cursed us. We have been patient with those who injured us. [13]We have replied quietly when evil things have been said about us. Yet right up to the present moment we are like dirt underfoot, like garbage.

[14]I am not writing about these things to make you ashamed, but to warn and counsel you as beloved children. [15]For although you may have ten thousand others to teach you about Christ, remember that you have only me as your father. For I was the one who brought you to Christ when I preached the Gospel to you. [16]So I beg you to follow my example and do as I do.

[17]That is the very reason why I am sending Timothy—to help you do this. For he is one of those I won to Christ, a beloved and trustworthy child in the Lord. He will remind you of what I teach in all the churches wherever I go.

[18]I know that some of you will have become proud, thinking that I am afraid to come to deal with you. [19]But I will come, and soon, if the Lord will let me, and then I'll find out whether these proud men are just big talkers or whether they really have God's power. [20]The Kingdom of God is not just talking; it is living by God's power. [21]Which do you choose? Shall I come with punishment and scolding, or shall I come with quiet love and gentleness?

CHAPTER 5 **SIN IN THE CHURCH.** Everyone is talking about the terrible thing that has happened there among you, something so evil that even the heathen don't do it: you have a man in your church who is living in sin with his father's wife. [2]And are you still so conceited, so "spiritual"? Why aren't you mourning in sorrow and shame and seeing to it that this man is removed from your membership?

[3,4]Although I am not there with you, I have been thinking a lot about this, and in the name of the Lord Jesus Christ I have already decided what to do, just as though I were there. You are to call a meeting of the church—and the power of the Lord Jesus will be with you as you meet, and I will be there in spirit—[5]and cast out this man from the fellowship of the church and into Satan's hands, to punish him, in the hope that his soul will be saved when our Lord Jesus Christ returns.

[6]What a terrible thing it is that you are boasting about your purity and yet you let this sort of thing

go on. Don't you realize that if even one person is allowed to go on sinning, soon all will be affected? [7]Remove this evil cancer—this wicked person—from among you, so that you can stay pure. Christ, God's Lamb, has been slain for us. [8]So let us feast

---

My Christian friends are dragging me down. How am I supposed to grow as a Christian if these friends aren't really trying to do anything with their faith?

I WONDER...

Because God is the one who "invited you into this wonderful friendship with his Son" (1 Corinthians 1:9), it's his responsibility, not yours, to make sure you grow in your faith. He has no intention of abandoning you.

Many people have been touched by divorce in one way or another. Kids of divorced parents are often determined to make sure that their own marriage is a success. They seek out positive role models to observe, and they pour through numerous resources about having a quality marriage. But, the opposite also can be true. Kids who grow up without a good model of what a family is supposed to look like can easily repeat their parents' mistakes.

Because your friends are acting like they have "divorced God," you are faced with a choice. Will you learn from their mistakes and search out people and other resources to help you succeed in your relationship with Christ? Or will you follow their lead and turn your back on God as well? If you're serious about giving God every chance to make himself real in your life, consider these suggestions:

First, pray for your friends and for an opportunity to talk to them about the situation. Don't worry about how much you've blown it by participating in whatever they've done. It's more important to think about your future than to dwell on the past. Next, go to one of your Christian friends, perhaps the leader of the group, and say something like: "I really want to give God a shot, but you're not helping much. I need your help. Can I count on you?" If this person says yes, it worked! If not, go to another friend and tell him the same thing. If no one responds, wait a week or two and start the process again, trusting that God has been working in their hearts. Or find some new friends you can count on. Maybe that's the answer God has for you.

Remember, God is faithful. He knows that you need friends and a group to hang around with. The last thing you need are people who are heading in the wrong direction.

---

upon him and grow strong in the Christian life, leaving entirely behind us the cancerous old life with all its hatreds and wickedness. Let us feast instead upon the pure bread of honor and sincerity and truth.

[9]When I wrote to you before I said not to mix with evil people. [10]But when I said that I wasn't talking about unbelievers who live in sexual sin or are greedy cheats and thieves and idol worshipers.

For you can't live in this world without being with people like that. [11]What I meant was that you are not to keep company with anyone who claims to be a brother Christian but indulges in sexual sins, or is greedy, or is a swindler, or worships idols, or is a drunkard, or abusive. Don't even eat lunch with such a person.

[12]It isn't our job to judge outsiders. But it certainly is our job to judge and deal strongly with those who are members of the church and who are sinning in these ways. [13]God alone is the Judge of those on the outside. But you yourselves must deal with this man and put him out of your church.

CHAPTER 6 LAWSUITS.

How is it that when you have something against another Christian, you "go to law" and ask a heathen court to decide the matter instead of taking it to other Christians to decide which of you is right? [2]Don't you know that someday we Christians are going to judge and govern the world? So why can't you decide even these little things among yourselves? [3]Don't you realize that we Christians will judge and reward the very angels in heaven? So you should be able to decide your problems down here on earth easily enough. [4]Why then go to outside judges who are not even Christians? [5]I am trying to make you ashamed. Isn't there anyone in all the church who is wise enough to decide these arguments? [6]But, instead, one Christian sues another and accuses his Christian brother in front of unbelievers.

[7]To have such lawsuits at all is a real defeat for you as Christians. Why not just accept mistreatment and leave it at that? It would be far more honoring to the Lord to let yourselves be cheated. [8]But, instead, you yourselves are the ones who do wrong, cheating others, even your own brothers.

[9,10]Don't you know that those doing such things have no share in the Kingdom of God? Don't fool yourselves. Those who live immoral lives, who are idol worshipers, adulterers or homosexuals—will have no share in his Kingdom. Neither will thieves or greedy people, drunkards, slanderers, or robbers. [11]There was a time when some of you were just like that but now your sins are washed away, and you are set apart for God; and he has accepted you because of what the Lord Jesus Christ and the Spirit of our God have done for you.

[12]I can do anything I want to if Christ has not said no, but some of these things aren't good for me. Even if I am allowed to do them, I'll refuse to if I think they might get such a grip on me that I can't easily stop when I want to. [13]For instance, take the matter of eating. God has given us an appetite for food and stomachs to digest it. But that doesn't mean we should eat more than we need. Don't think of eating as important because someday God will do away with both stomachs and food.

But sexual sin is never right: our bodies were not made for that but for the Lord, and the Lord wants to fill our bodies with himself. [14]And God is going to raise our bodies from the dead by his power just as he raised up the Lord Jesus Christ. [15]Don't you realize that your bodies are actually parts and members of Christ? So should I take part of Christ and join him to a prostitute? Never! [16]And don't you know that if a man joins himself to a prostitute she becomes a part of him and he

DRUGS

Scene 1: Lyle is having a massive argument with his parents. (They've just discovered a small amount of marijuana in his coat pocket.)

"Lighten up, OK? It's no big deal! It's just a little grass."

"'No big deal'? Listen here, that grass is illegal! You could go to jail for that grass!"

"Lyle, how could you do this to your father and me?"

"What? I'm not doing anything to you! It's my life!"

"That's right. It's your life. But you're gonna cut it short if you fill your body with drugs."

"Aw, come off of it! I don't 'fill my body with drugs.' I smoke a little harmless grass."

Scene 2: Gary looks nervously over his shoulder. No one is watching, so he pulls a pill bottle—containing anabolic steroids—out of his locker.

Quickly he turns and heads for the gym. Time to pump some serious iron.

Scene 3: With her parents out for the evening, Staci and her friend Kimberly search the workshop and garage for gas, paint thinner, or anything else with the right kind of fumes to get them high.

Drugs (no matter what kind) damage the human body. If you're a Christian, your body doesn't belong to you. God owns it, and he tells you to take care of it.

For that reason alone, you must resist the temporary thrill of a chemical high. See 1 Corinthians 6:19-20.

SEX

6:13 Sexual sin is a temptation we cannot escape. In movies and on television, sex outside of marriage is treated as a normal—even desirable—part of life, while marriage is often shown as confining and joyless. We can even be looked down upon by others if suspected of being pure. But God does not forbid sexual sin just to be difficult. He knows its power to destroy us physically and spiritually. No one should underestimate the power of sexual sin. It has devastated countless lives and destroyed families, communities, and even nations. God wants to protect us from damaging ourselves and others, so he offers to fill us—our loneliness, our desires—with himself.

COUPLES

7:9 Sexual pressure is not the best motive for getting married, but it is better to marry the right person than to burn with lust. Many new believers in Corinth thought that all sex was wrong, so engaged couples were deciding not to get married. In this passage, Paul is telling couples who wanted to marry that they should not deny their normal sexual drives by avoiding marriage. This does not mean, however, that people who have trouble controlling their thoughts should marry the first person who comes along. It is better to deal with the pressure of desire than to deal with an unhappy marriage.

becomes a part of her? For God tells us in the Scripture that in his sight the two become one person. [17]But if you give yourself to the Lord, you and Christ are joined together as one person.

[18]That is why I say to run from sex sin. No other sin affects the body as this one does. When you sin this sin it is against your own body. [19]Haven't you yet learned that your body is the home of the Holy Spirit God gave you, and that he lives within you? Your own body does not belong to you. [20]For God has bought you with a great price. So use every part of your body to give glory back to God because he owns it.

CHAPTER **7** QUESTIONS ABOUT MARRIAGE.

Now about those questions you asked in your last letter: my answer is that if you do not marry, it is good. [2]But usually it is best to be married, each man having his own wife, and each woman having her own husband, because otherwise you might fall back into sin.

[3]The man should give his wife all that is her right as a married woman, and the wife should do the same for her husband: [4]for a girl who marries no longer has full right to her own body, for her husband then has his rights to it, too; and in the same way the husband no longer has full right to his own body, for it belongs also to his wife. [5]So do not refuse these rights to each other. The only exception to this rule would be the agreement of both husband and wife to refrain from the rights of marriage for a limited time, so that they can give themselves more completely to prayer. Afterwards, they should come together again so that Satan won't be able to tempt them because of their lack of self-control.

[6]I'm not saying you *must* marry, but you certainly *may* if you wish. [7]I wish everyone could get along without marrying, just as I do. But we are not all the same. God gives some the gift of a husband or wife, and others he gives the gift of being able to stay happily unmarried. [8]So I say to those who aren't married and to widows—better to stay unmarried if you can, just as I am. [9]But if you can't control yourselves, go ahead and marry. It is better to marry than to burn with lust.

[10]Now, for those who are married I have a command, not just a suggestion. And it is not a command from me, for this is what the Lord himself has said: A wife must not leave her husband. [11]But if she is separated from him, let her remain single or else go back to him. And the husband must not divorce his wife.

[12]Here I want to add some suggestions of my own. These are not direct commands from the Lord, but they seem right to me: If a Christian has a wife who is not a Christian, but she wants to stay with him anyway, he must not leave her or divorce her. [13]And if a Christian woman has a husband who isn't a Christian, and he wants her to stay with him, she must not leave him. [14]For perhaps the husband who isn't a Christian may become a Christian with the help of his Christian wife. And the wife who isn't a Christian may become a Christian with the help of her Christian husband. Otherwise, if the family separates, the children might never come to know the Lord; whereas a united family may, in God's plan, result in the children's salvation.

[15]But if the husband or wife who isn't a Christian is eager to leave, it is permitted. In such cases the Christian husband or wife should not insist that the other stay, for God wants his children to live in peace and harmony. [16]For, after all, there is no assurance to you wives that your husbands will be converted if they stay; and the same may be said to you husbands concerning your wives.

[17]But be sure in deciding these matters that you are living as God intended, marrying or not marrying in accordance with God's direction and help, and accepting whatever situation God has put you into. This is my rule for all the churches.

[18]For instance, a man who already has gone through the Jewish ceremony of circumcision before he became a Christian shouldn't worry about it; and if he hasn't been circumcised, he shouldn't do it now. [19]For it doesn't make any difference at all whether a Christian has gone through this ceremony or not. But it makes a lot of difference whether he is pleasing God and keeping God's commandments. That is the important thing.

[20]Usually a person should keep on with the work he was doing when God called him. [21]Are you a slave? Don't let that worry you—but of course, if you get a chance to be free, take it. [22]If the Lord calls you, and you are a slave, remember that Christ has set you free from the awful power of sin; and if he has called you and you are free, remember that you are now a slave of Christ. [23]You have been bought and paid for by Christ, so you belong to him—be free now from all these earthly prides and fears. [24]So, dear brothers, whatever situation a person is in when he becomes a Christian, let him stay there, for now the Lord is there to help him.

[25]Now I will try to answer your other question.

RIGHT HERE

7:20 Often we are so concerned about what we *could* be doing for God somewhere else that we miss great opportunities right where we are. Paul says that when someone becomes a Christian, he should usually continue with the work he previously has been doing—provided it isn't immoral or unethical. Every job can become Christian work when you realize that the purpose of your life is to honor, serve, and speak out for Christ. Because God has placed you where you are, look carefully for opportunities to serve him there.

What about girls who are not yet married? Should they be permitted to do so? In answer to this question, I have no special command for them from the Lord. But the Lord in his kindness has given me wisdom that can be trusted, and I will be glad to tell you what I think.

²⁶Here is the problem: We Christians are facing great dangers to our lives at present. In times like these I think it is best for a person to remain unmarried. ²⁷Of course, if you already are married, don't separate because of this. But if you aren't, don't rush into it at this time. ²⁸But if you men decide to go ahead anyway and get married now, it is all right; and if a girl gets married in times like these, it is no sin. However, marriage will bring extra problems that I wish you didn't have to face right now.

²⁹The important thing to remember is that our remaining time is very short, [and so are our opportunities for doing the Lord's work]. For that reason those who have wives should stay as free as possible for the Lord; ³⁰happiness or sadness or wealth should not keep anyone from doing God's work. ³¹Those in frequent contact with the exciting things the world offers should make good use of their opportunities without stopping to enjoy them; for the world in its present form will soon be gone.

³²In all you do, I want you to be free from worry. An unmarried man can spend his time doing the Lord's work and thinking how to please him. ³³But a married man can't do that so well; he has to think about his earthly responsibilities and how to please his wife. ³⁴His interests are divided. It is the same with a girl who marries. She faces the same problem. A girl who is not married is anxious to please the Lord in all she is and does. But a married woman must consider other things such as housekeeping and the likes and dislikes of her husband.

³⁵I am saying this to help you, not to try to keep you from marrying. I want you to do whatever will help you serve the Lord best, with as few other things as possible to distract your attention from him.

³⁶But if anyone feels he ought to marry because he has trouble controlling his passions, it is all right; it is not a sin; let him marry. ³⁷But if a man has the willpower not to marry and decides that he doesn't need to and won't, he has made a wise decision. ³⁸So the person who marries does well, and the person who doesn't marry does even better.

³⁹The wife is part of her husband as long as he lives; if her husband dies, then she may marry again, but only if she marries a Christian. ⁴⁰But in my opinion she will be happier if she doesn't marry again; and I think I am giving you counsel from God's Spirit when I say this.

CHAPTER 8 FOOD OFFERED TO IDOLS.

Next is your question about eating food that has been sacrificed to idols. On this question everyone feels that only his answer is the right one! But although being a "know-it-all" makes us feel important, what is really needed to build the church is love. ²If anyone thinks he knows all the answers, he is just showing his ignorance. ³But the person who truly loves God is the one who is open to God's knowledge.

⁴So now, what about it? Should we eat meat that has been sacrificed to idols? Well, we all know that an idol is not really a god, and that there is only one God, and no other. ⁵According to some people, there are a great many gods, both in heaven and on earth. ⁶But we know that there is only one God, the Father, who created all things and made us to be his own; and one Lord Jesus Christ, who made everything and gives us life.

⁷However, some Christians don't realize this. All their lives they have been used to thinking of idols as alive, and have believed that food offered to the idols is really being offered to actual gods. So when they eat such food it bothers them and hurts their tender consciences. ⁸Just remember that God doesn't care whether we eat it or not. We are no worse off if we don't eat it, and no better off if we do. ⁹But be careful not to use your freedom to eat it, lest you cause some Christian brother to sin whose conscience is weaker than yours.

¹⁰You see, this is what may happen: Someone who thinks it is wrong to eat this food will see you eating at a temple restaurant, for you know there is no harm in it. Then he will become bold enough to do it too, although all the time he still feels it is wrong. ¹¹So

NO PROBLEMS?

7:28 Many people think that finding the right boyfriend or girlfriend, and especially getting married, will solve all their problems. It does feel good to have someone special, someone who cares for you and whom you care for. But no relationship, even marriage, is a "cure for whatever ails you"! For example, here are a few of the problems even marriage won't solve: (1) loneliness, (2) sexual temptation, (3) satisfaction of one's deepest emotional needs, (4) elimination of life's difficulties. Marriage alone does not hold two people together, but commitment does—commitment to Christ and to each other despite conflicts and problems. Marriage can be great, but it isn't the solution to problems. There is only one reliable solution for anyone: trusting in Christ! Focus on Christ, not humans, to solve your problems.

FREEDOM

8:10-13 Christian freedom does not mean "anything goes." It means that our salvation is not determined by legalism, good works, or rules, but by the free gift of God (Ephesians 2:8-9). Christian freedom is tied to Christian responsibility. New believers are sensitive to what is right or wrong. Some actions may be perfectly all right for us to do, but may harm a Christian brother or sister who is still young in the faith. We must be careful not to offend a sensitive or younger Christian or, by our example, to cause him or her to sin.

because you "know it is all right to do it," you will be responsible for causing great spiritual damage to a brother with a tender conscience for whom Christ died. ¹²And it is a sin against Christ to sin against your brother by encouraging him to do something he thinks is wrong. ¹³So if eating meat offered to idols is going to make my brother sin, I'll not eat any of it as long as I live because I don't want to do this to him.

CHAPTER **9** **THE RIGHT OF AN APOSTLE.** I am an apostle, God's messenger, responsible to no mere man. I am one who has actually seen Jesus our Lord with my own eyes. And your changed lives are the result of my hard work for him. ²If in the opinion of others, I am not an apostle, I certainly am to you, for you have been won to Christ through me. ³This is my answer to those who question my rights.

⁴Or don't I have any rights at all? Can't I claim the same privilege the other apostles have of being a guest in your homes? ⁵If I had a wife, and if she were a believer, couldn't I bring her along on these trips just as the other disciples do, and as the Lord's brothers do, and as Peter does? ⁶And must Barnabas and I alone keep working for our living while you supply these others? ⁷What soldier in the army has to pay his own expenses? And have you ever heard of a farmer who harvests his crop and doesn't have the right to eat some of it? What shepherd takes care of a flock of sheep and goats and isn't allowed to drink some of the milk? ⁸And I'm not merely quoting the opinions of men as to what is right. I'm telling you what God's law says. ⁹For in the law God gave to Moses he said that you must not put a muzzle on an ox to keep it from eating when it is treading out the wheat. Do you suppose God was thinking only about oxen when he said this? ¹⁰Wasn't he also thinking about us? Of course he was. He said this to show us that Christian workers should be paid by those they help. Those who do the plowing and threshing should expect some share of the harvest.

MAKING CHOICES IN SENSITIVE ISSUES

All of us make hundreds of choices every day. Most choices have no right or wrong attached to them—like what you wear or what you eat. But we always face decisions that carry a little more weight. We don't want to do wrong, and we don't want to cause others to do wrong. So how can we make right decisions?

If I choose one course of action . . .

. . . am I motivated by a desire to help others to know Christ? (9:23; 10:33)

. . . will it help my witness for Christ? (9:19-22)

. . . will it help me do my best? (9:25)

. . . will it glorify God? (10:31)

. . . is it against a specific command in Scripture and thus will it cause me to sin? (10:12)

. . . will I be acting lovingly or selfishly? (10:28-31)

. . . will it be best and helpful? (10:23,33)

. . . will it encourage someone else to sin? (10:32)

. . . will I be thinking only of myself, or do I truly care about the other person? (10:24)

[11]We have planted good spiritual seed in your souls. Is it too much to ask, in return, for mere food and clothing? [12]You give them to others who preach to you, and you should. But shouldn't we have an even greater right to them? Yet we have *never* used this right but supply our own needs without your help. We have never demanded payment of any kind for fear that, if we did, you might be less interested in our message to you from Christ.

[13]Don't you realize that God told those working in his temple to take for their own needs some of the food brought there as gifts to him? And those who work at the altar of God get a share of the food that is brought by those offering it to the Lord. [14]In the same way the Lord has given orders that those who preach the Gospel should be supported by those who accept it.

[15]Yet I have never asked you for one penny. And I am not writing this to hint that I would like to start now. In fact, I would rather die of hunger than lose the satisfaction I get from preaching to you without charge. [16]For just preaching the Gospel isn't any special credit to me—I couldn't keep from preaching it if I wanted to. I would be utterly miserable. Woe unto me if I don't.

[17]If I were volunteering my services of my own free will, then the Lord would give me a special reward; but that is not the situation, for God has picked me out and given me this sacred trust, and I have no choice. [18]Under this circumstance, what is my pay? It is the special joy I get from preaching the Good News without expense to anyone, never demanding my rights.

[19]And this has a real advantage: I am not bound to obey anyone just because he pays my salary; yet I have freely and happily become a servant of any and all so that I can win them to Christ. [20]When I am with the Jews I seem as one of them so that they will listen to the Gospel and I can win them to Christ. When I am with Gentiles who follow Jewish customs and ceremonies I don't argue, even though I don't agree, because I want to help them. [21]When with the heathen I agree with them as much as I can, except of course that I must always do what is right as a Christian. And so, by agreeing, I can win their confidence and help them too.

[22]When I am with those whose consciences bother them easily, I don't act as though I know it all and don't say they are foolish; the result is that they are willing to let me help them. Yes, whatever a person is like, I try to find common ground with him so that he will let me tell him about Christ and let Christ save him. [23]I do this to get the Gospel to them and also for the blessing I myself receive when I see them come to Christ.

[24]In a race everyone runs, but only one person gets first prize. So run your race to win. [25]To win the contest you must deny yourselves many things that would keep you from doing your

TEMPTATION

10:13 In a culture filled with moral depravity and pressures, Paul gave strong encouragement to the Corinthians about temptation. He said: (1) wrong desires and temptations happen to everyone, so don't feel you've been singled out; (2) others have resisted temptation, and so can you; (3) any temptation can be resisted because God will help you resist it. God helps you resist temptation by helping you recognize people and situations that give you trouble. Run from anything you know is wrong, choose to do only what is right, pray for God's help, and seek friends who love God and can offer help in times of temptation. Running from a tempting situation is the first step to victory (see 2 Timothy 2:22).

best. An athlete goes to all this trouble just to win a blue ribbon or a silver cup, but we do it for a heavenly reward that never disappears. [26]So I run straight to the goal with purpose in every step. I fight to win. I'm not just shadow-boxing or playing around. [27]Like an athlete I punish my body, treating it roughly, training it to do what it should, not what it wants to. Otherwise I fear that after enlisting others for the race, I myself might be declared unfit and ordered to stand aside.

CHAPTER **10** LESSONS ABOUT IDOL WORSHIP.

For we must never forget, dear brothers, what happened to our people in the wilderness long ago. God guided them by sending a cloud that moved along ahead of them; and he brought them all safely through the waters of the Red Sea. [2]This might be called their "baptism"—baptized both in sea and cloud!—as followers of Moses—their commitment to him as their leader. [3,4]And by a miracle God sent them food to eat and water to drink there in the desert; they drank the water that Christ gave them. He was there with them as a mighty Rock of spiritual refreshment. [5]Yet after all this most of them did not obey God, and he destroyed them in the wilderness.

[6]From this lesson we are warned that we must not desire evil things as they did, [7]nor worship idols as they did. (The Scriptures tell us, "The people sat down to eat and drink and then got up to dance" in worship of the golden calf.)

[8]Another lesson for us is what happened when some of them sinned with other men's wives, and 23,000 fell dead in one day. [9]And don't try the Lord's patience—they did and died from snake bites. [10]And don't murmur against God and his dealings with you as some of them did, for that is why God sent his Angel to destroy them.

[11]All these things happened to them as examples—as object lessons to us—to warn us against doing the same things; they were written down so that we could read about them and learn from them in these last days as the world nears its end.

[12]So be careful. If you are thinking, "Oh, I would never behave like that"—let this be a warning to you. For you too may fall into sin. [13]But remember this—the wrong desires that come into your life aren't anything new and different. Many others have faced exactly the same problems before you. And no temptation is irresistible. You can trust God to keep the temptation from becoming so strong that you can't stand up against it, for he has promised this and will do what he says. He will show you how to escape temptation's power so that you can bear up patiently against it.

[14]So, dear friends, carefully avoid idol worship of every kind.

[15]You are intelligent people. Look now and see for yourselves whether what I am about to say is true. [16]When we ask the Lord's blessing upon our drinking from the cup of wine at the Lord's Table, this means, doesn't it, that all who drink it are sharing together the blessing of Christ's blood? And when we break off pieces of the bread from the loaf to eat there together, this shows that we are sharing together in the benefits of his body. [17]No matter how many of us there are, we all eat from the same loaf, showing that we are all parts of the one body of Christ. [18]And the Jewish people, all who eat the sacrifices, are united by that act.

[19]What am I trying to say? Am I saying that the idols to whom the heathen bring sacrifices are really alive and are real gods, and that these sacrifices are of some value? No, not at all. [20]What I am saying is that those who offer food to these idols are united together in sacrificing to demons, certainly not to God. And I don't want any of you to be partners with demons when you eat the same food, along with the heathen, that has been offered to

"Here's what I did..."

For many years I had a problem with gossiping. I knew it was wrong, but I kept giving in to temptation. I prayed about it a lot. Then the Lord gave me two Scriptures that have helped me begin to conquer it.

The first is 1 Corinthians 10:13. That verse says that God will always provide a way to escape temptation's power. So I reminded myself of this whenever the temptation to pass on some juicy bit of news came my way. It helped some, but I still gave in more often than I wanted to.

Then God gave me something that's helped me even more. It's Psalm 141:3: "Help me, Lord, to keep my mouth shut and my lips sealed." That's exactly the prayer I started praying whenever I was tempted to gossip. This prayer-verse became my way to escape the temptation; whenever I take the time to pray it, I find I can keep my mouth shut. But I have to take a moment to refocus my thoughts on the prayer rather than on the temptation to say something, or I find myself giving in to temptation.

This experience has shown me just how practical the Bible can be. With God's power I can conquer anything!

Brooke

AGE 18

these idols. [21]You cannot drink from the cup at the Lord's Table and at Satan's table, too. You cannot eat bread both at the Lord's Table and at Satan's table.

[22]What? Are you tempting the Lord to be angry with you? Are you stronger than he is?

[23]You are certainly free to eat food offered to idols if you want to; it's not against God's laws to eat such meat, but that doesn't mean that you should go ahead and do it. It may be perfectly legal, but it may not be best and helpful. [24]Don't think only of yourself. Try to think of the other fellow, too, and what is best for him.

[25]Here's what you should do. Take any meat you want that is sold at the market. Don't ask whether or not it was offered to idols, lest the answer hurt your conscience. [26]For the earth and every good thing in it belongs to the Lord and is yours to enjoy.

[27]If someone who isn't a Christian asks you out to dinner, go ahead; accept the invitation if you want to. Eat whatever is on the table and don't ask any questions about it. Then you won't know whether or not it has been used as a sacrifice to idols, and you won't risk having a bad conscience over eating it. [28]But if someone warns you that this meat has been offered to idols, then don't eat it for the sake of the man who told you, and of his conscience. [29]In this case *his* feeling about it is the important thing, not yours.

But why, you may ask, must I be guided and limited by what someone else thinks? [30]If I can thank God for the food and enjoy it, why let someone spoil everything just because he thinks I am wrong? [31]Well, I'll tell you why. It is because you must do everything for the glory of God, even your eating and drinking. [32]So don't be a stumbling block to anyone, whether they are Jews or Gentiles or Christians. [33]That is the plan I follow, too. I try to please everyone in everything I do, not doing what I like or what is best for me but what is best for them, so that they may be saved.

CHAPTER 11 HONOR AND RESPECT IN WORSHIP.

And you should follow my example, just as I follow Christ's.

[2]I am so glad, dear brothers, that you have been remembering and doing everything I taught you. [3]But there is one matter I want to remind you about: that a wife is responsible to her husband, her husband is responsible to Christ, and Christ is responsible to God. [4]That is why, if a man refuses to remove his hat while praying or preaching, he dishonors Christ. [5]And that is why a woman who publicly prays or prophesies without a covering on her head dishonors her husband [for her covering is a sign of her subjection to him]. [6]Yes, if she refuses to wear a head covering, then she should cut off all her hair. And if it is shameful for a woman to have her head shaved, then she should wear a covering. [7]But a man should not wear anything on his head [when worshiping, for his hat is a sign of subjection to men].

God's glory is man made in his image, and man's glory is the woman. [8]The first man didn't come from woman, but the first woman came out of man. [9]And Adam, the first man, was not made for Eve's benefit, but Eve was made for Adam. [10]So a woman should wear a covering on her head as a sign that she is under man's authority, a fact for all the angels to notice and rejoice in.

[11]But remember that in God's plan men and women need each other. [12]For although the first woman came out of man, all men have been born from women ever since, and both men and women come from God their Creator.

[13]What do you yourselves really think about this? Is it right for a woman to pray in public without covering her head? [14,15]Doesn't even instinct itself teach us that women's heads should be covered? For women are proud of their long hair, while a man with long hair tends to be ashamed. [16]But if anyone wants to argue about this, all I can say is that we never teach anything else than this— that a woman should wear a covering when prophesying or praying publicly in the church, and all the churches feel the same way about it.

[17]Next on my list of items to write you about is

THE BEST

10:33 Paul's criterion was not what he liked best, but what was best for those around him. There are several hurtful attitudes toward others: (1) being insensitive and doing what we want, no matter who is hurt by our actions; (2) being oversensitive and doing nothing, for fear that someone may be displeased; (3) being a "yes person" by going along with everything, trying to gain approval from people rather than from God. In this age of "me first" and "looking out for number one," Paul's startling statement is a good standard. When we make the good of others one of our primary goals, we develop a servant's heart.

EQUALS

11:3-4 Submission is a key element in the smooth functioning of any business, government, or family. God ordained submission in certain relationships to prevent chaos. We must understand, however, that submission is not surrender, withdrawal, or apathy. Nor does it mean inferiority. God created all people in his image; all have equal value. Submission is mutual commitment and cooperation.

Thus God calls for submission among *equals*. He did not make the man superior; he made a way for the man and woman to work together. Jesus Christ, although equal with God the Father, submitted to him to carry out the plan for salvation. Likewise, although equal to man under God, the wife should submit to her husband for the sake of their marriage and family. Submission between equals is submission by choice, not force. We serve God in these relationships by willing submission to others in our church, to our spouses, and to our government leaders.

something else I cannot agree with. For it sounds as if more harm than good is done when you meet together for your communion services. ¹⁸Everyone keeps telling me about the arguing that goes on in these meetings, and the divisions developing among you, and I can just about believe it. ¹⁹But I suppose you feel this is necessary so that you who are always right will become known and recognized!

²⁰When you come together to eat, it isn't the Lord's Supper you are eating, ²¹but your own. For I am told that everyone hastily gobbles all the food he can without waiting to share with the others, so that one doesn't get enough and goes hungry while another has too much to drink and gets drunk. ²²What? Is this really true? Can't you do your eating and drinking at home to avoid disgracing the church and shaming those who are poor and can bring no food? What am I supposed to say about these things? Do you want me to praise you? Well, I certainly do not!

²³For this is what the Lord himself has said about his Table, and I have passed it on to you before: That on the night when Judas betrayed him, the Lord Jesus took bread, ²⁴and when he had given thanks to God for it, he broke it and gave it to his disciples and said, "Take this and eat it. This is my body, which is given for you. Do this to remember me." ²⁵In the same way, he took the cup of wine after supper, saying, "This cup is the new agreement between God and you that has been established and set in motion by my blood. Do this in remembrance of me whenever you drink it." ²⁶For every time you eat this bread and drink this cup you are retelling the message of the Lord's death, that he has died for you. Do this until he comes again.

²⁷So if anyone eats this bread and drinks from this cup of the Lord in an unworthy manner, he is guilty of sin against the body and the blood of the Lord. ²⁸That is why a man should examine himself carefully before eating the bread and drinking from the cup. ²⁹For if he eats the bread and drinks from the cup unworthily, not thinking about the body of Christ and what it means, he is eating and drinking God's judgment upon himself; for he is trifling with the death of Christ. ³⁰That is why many of you are weak and sick, and some have even died.

³¹But if you carefully examine yourselves before eating you will not need to be judged and punished. ³²Yet, when we are judged and punished by the Lord, it is so that we will not be condemned with the rest of the world. ³³So, dear brothers, when you gather for the Lord's Supper—the communion service—wait for each other; ³⁴if anyone is really hungry he should eat at home so that he won't bring punishment upon himself when you meet together. I'll talk to you about the other matters after I arrive.

CHAPTER 12 EVERYONE HAS SPECIAL ABILITIES.

And now, brothers, I want to write about the special abilities the Holy Spirit gives to each of you, for I don't want any misunderstanding about them. ²You will remember that before you became Christians you went around from one idol to another, not one of which could speak a single word. ³But now you are meeting people who claim to speak messages from the Spirit of God. How can you know whether they are really inspired by God or whether they are fakes? Here is the test: no one speaking by the power of the Spirit of God can curse Jesus, and no one can say, "Jesus is Lord," and really mean it, unless the Holy Spirit is helping him.

⁴Now God gives us many kinds of special abilities, but it is the same Holy Spirit who is the source of them all. ⁵There are different kinds of service to God, but it is the same Lord we are serving. ⁶There are many ways in which God works in our lives, but it is the same God who does the work in and through all of us who are his. ⁷The Holy Spirit displays God's power through each of us as a means of helping the entire church.

⁸To one person the Spirit gives the ability to give wise advice; someone else may be especially good at studying and teaching, and this is his gift from the same Spirit. ⁹He gives special faith to another, and to someone else the power to heal the sick. ¹⁰He gives power for doing miracles to some, and to others power to prophesy and preach. He gives someone else the power to know whether evil spirits are speaking through those who claim to be giving God's messages—or whether it is really the Spirit of God who is speaking. Still another person is able to speak in languages he never learned; and others, who do not know the language either, are given power to understand what he is saying. ¹¹It is the same and only Holy Spirit who gives all these gifts and powers, deciding which each one of us should have.

¹²Our bodies have many parts, but the many parts make up only one body when they are all put together. So it is with the "body" of Christ. ¹³Each of us is a part of the one body of Christ. Some of us are Jews, some are Gentiles, some are slaves, and some are free. But the Holy Spirit has fitted us all together into one body. We have been baptized into Christ's body by the one Spirit, and have all been given that same Holy Spirit.

¹⁴Yes, the body has many parts, not just one part.

TEST THEM

12:3 Anyone can claim to speak for God, and the world is full of false teachers. Paul gives us a test to help us discern whether or not a messenger is really from God: does he or she confess Christ as Lord? Don't naively accept the words of all who claim to speak for God. Test their credentials by finding what they teach about Christ.

BODY LIFE

12:14-17 Using the analogy of the body, Paul emphasizes the importance of each church member. If a seemingly insignificant part is taken away, the whole body becomes less effective (12:22). Thinking that your gift is more important than someone else's is spiritual pride. We should not look down on those who seem unimportant, and we should not be jealous of others who have impressive gifts. Instead, we must use the gifts we have been given and encourage others to use theirs. If we don't, the body of believers will be less effective.

[15]If the foot says, "I am not a part of the body because I am not a hand," that does not make it any less a part of the body. [16]And what would you think if you heard an ear say, "I am not part of the body because I am only an ear and not an eye"? Would that make it any less a part of the body? [17]Suppose the whole body were an eye—then how would you hear? Or if your whole body were just one big ear, how could you smell anything?

[18]But that isn't the way God has made us. He has made many parts for our bodies and has put each part just where he wants it. [19]What a strange thing a body would be if it had only one part! [20]So he has made many parts, but still there is only one body.

[21]The eye can never say to the hand, "I don't need you." The head can't say to the feet, "I don't need you."

[22]And some of the parts that seem weakest and least important are really the most necessary. [23]Yes, we are especially glad to have some parts that seem rather odd! And we carefully protect from the eyes of others those parts that should not be seen, [24]while of course the parts that may be seen do not require this special care. So God has put the body together in such a way that extra honor and care are given to those parts that might otherwise seem less important. [25]This makes for happiness among the parts, so that the parts have the same care for each other that they do for themselves. [26]If one part suffers, all parts suffer with it, and if one part is honored, all the parts are glad.

[27]Now here is what I am trying to say: All of you together are the one body of Christ, and each one of you is a separate and necessary part of it. [28]Here is a list of some of the parts he has placed in his Church, which is his body:

Apostles,
Prophets—those who preach God's Word,
Teachers,
Those who do miracles,
Those who have the gift of healing;
Those who can help others,
Those who can get others to work together,
Those who speak in languages they have
never learned.

[29]Is everyone an apostle? Of course not. Is everyone a preacher? No. Are all teachers? Does everyone have the power to do miracles? [30]Can everyone heal the sick? Of course not. Does God give all of us the ability to speak in languages we've never learned? Can just anyone understand and translate what those are saying who have that gift of foreign speech? [31]No, but try your best to have the more important of these gifts.

First, however, let me tell you about something else that is better than any of them!

CHAPTER 13 **WHAT IS LOVE?** If I had the gift of being able to speak in other languages without learning them and could speak in every language there is in all of heaven and earth, but didn't love others, I would only be making noise. [2]If I had the gift of prophecy and knew all about what is going to happen in the future, knew everything about *everything*, but didn't love others, what good would it do? Even if I had the gift of faith so that I could speak to a mountain and make it move, I would still be worth nothing at all without love. [3]If I gave everything I have to poor people, and if I were burned alive for preaching the Gospel but didn't love others, it would be of no value whatever.

[4]Love is very patient and kind, never jealous or envious, never boastful or proud, [5]never haughty or selfish or rude. Love does not demand its own way. It is not irritable or touchy. It does not hold grudges and will hardly even notice when others do it wrong. [6]It is never glad about injustice, but rejoices whenever truth wins out. [7]If you love someone, you will be loyal to him no matter what the cost. You will always believe in him, always expect the best of him, and always stand your ground in defending him.

[8]All the special gifts and powers from God will someday come to an end, but love goes on forever. Someday prophecy and speaking in unknown languages and special knowledge—these gifts will disappear. [9]Now we know so little, even with our special gifts, and the preaching of those most gifted is still so poor. [10]But when we have been made perfect and complete, then the need for these inadequate special gifts will come to an end, and they will disappear.

[11]It's like this: when I was a child I spoke and thought and reasoned as a child does. But when I became a man my thoughts grew far beyond those of my childhood, and now I have put away the childish things. [12]In the same way, we can see and understand only a little about God now, as if we

LOVE

13:4-7 Our society confuses love and lust. Unlike lust, God's kind of love is directed outward toward others, not inward toward ourselves. It is utterly unselfish.

were peering at his reflection in a poor mirror; but someday we are going to see him in his completeness, face to face. Now all that I know is hazy and blurred, but then I will see everything clearly, just as clearly as God sees into my heart right now.

¹³There are three things that remain—faith, hope, and love—and the greatest of these is love.

CHAPTER **14** **PROPHECY AND TONGUES.** Let love be your greatest aim; nevertheless, ask also for the special abilities the Holy Spirit gives, and especially the gift of prophecy, being able to preach the messages of God.

²But if your gift is that of being able to "speak in tongues," that is, to speak in languages you haven't learned, you will be talking to God but not to others, since they won't be able to understand you. You will be speaking by the power of the Spirit, but it will all be a secret. ³But one who prophesies, preaching the messages of God, is helping others grow in the Lord, encouraging and comforting them. ⁴So a person "speaking in tongues" helps himself grow spiritually, but one who prophesies, preaching messages from God, helps the entire church grow in holiness and happiness.

⁵I wish you all had the gift of "speaking in tongues," but even more I wish you were all able to prophesy, preaching God's messages, for that is a greater and more useful power than to speak in unknown languages—unless, of course, you can tell everyone afterwards what you were saying, so that they can get some good out of it too.

⁶Dear friends, even if I myself should come to you talking in some language you don't understand, how would that help you? But if I speak plainly what God has revealed to me, and tell you the things I know, and what is going to happen, and the great truths of God's Word— that is what you need; that is what will help you. ⁷Even musical instruments—the flute, for instance, or the harp—are examples of the need for speaking in plain, simple English rather than in unknown languages. For no one will recognize the tune the flute is playing unless each note is sounded clearly. ⁸And if the army bugler doesn't play the right notes, how will the soldiers know that they are being called to battle? ⁹In the same way, if you talk to a person in some language he doesn't understand, how will he know what you mean?

You might as well be talking to an empty room.

¹⁰I suppose that there are hundreds of different languages in the world, and all are excellent for those who understand them, ¹¹but to me they mean nothing. A person talking to me in one of these languages will be a stranger to me and I will be a stranger to him. ¹²Since you are so anxious to have special gifts from the Holy Spirit, ask him for the very best, for those that will be of real help to the whole church.

¹³If someone is given the gift of speaking in unknown tongues, he should pray also for the gift of knowing what he has said, so that he can tell people afterwards plainly. ¹⁴For if I pray in a language I don't understand, my spirit is praying, but I don't know what I am saying.

¹⁵Well, then, what shall I do? I will do both. I will pray in unknown tongues and also in ordinary language that everyone understands. I will sing in unknown tongues and also in ordinary language so that I can understand the praise I am giving; ¹⁶for if you praise and thank God with the spirit alone, speaking in another language, how can those who don't understand you be praising God along with you? How can they join you in giving thanks when they don't know what you are saying? ¹⁷You will be giving thanks very nicely, no doubt, but the other people present won't be helped.

¹⁸I thank God that I "speak in tongues" privately more than any of the rest of you. ¹⁹But in public worship I would much rather speak five words that people can understand and be helped by than ten thousand words while "speaking in tongues" in an unknown language.

²⁰Dear brothers, don't be childish in your understanding of these things. Be innocent babies when

"Here's what I did..."

After a bad dating experience, I decided to find out what God wanted a dating relationship to be. I talked to my youth pastor and studied Scripture. This time, when I felt ready to date again, I made sure I went out with a Christian.

Jenny and I talked about God's will right from the beginning and adopted 1 Corinthians 13 as the basis for our relationship. Even though the romance didn't last forever, it was a very positive experience. We both tried to let verses 4-7 guide all our thoughts and actions toward each other, even when we broke up. I learned a lot from that. God's way really is so much better than any other way of running your life—or of having a relationship.

Sam AGE 16

it comes to planning evil, but be men of intelligence in understanding matters of this kind. [21]We are told in the ancient Scriptures that God would send men from other lands to speak in foreign languages to his people, but even then they would not listen. [22]So you see that being able to "speak in tongues" is not a sign to God's children concerning his power, but is a sign to the unsaved. However, prophecy (preaching the deep truths of God) is what the Christians need, and unbelievers aren't yet ready for it. [23]Even so, if an unsaved person, or someone who doesn't have these gifts, comes to church and hears you all talking in other languages, he is likely to think you are crazy. [24]But if you prophesy, preaching God's Word, [even though such preaching is mostly for believers] and an unsaved person or a new Christian comes in who does not understand about these things, all these sermons will convince him of the fact that he is a sinner, and his conscience will be pricked by everything he hears. [25]As he listens, his secret thoughts will be laid bare, and he will fall down on his knees and worship God, declaring that God is really there among you.

[26]Well, my brothers, let's add up what I am saying. When you meet together some will sing, another will teach, or tell some special information God has given him, or speak in an unknown language, or tell what someone else is saying who is speaking in the unknown language, but everything that is done must be useful to all, and build them up in the Lord. [27]No more than two or three should speak in an unknown language, and they must speak one at a time, and someone must be ready to interpret what they are saying. [28]But if no one is present who can interpret, they must not speak out loud. They must talk silently to themselves and to God in the unknown language but not publicly.

[29,30]Two or three may prophesy, one at a time, if they have the gift, while all the others listen. But if, while someone is prophesying, someone else receives a message or idea from the Lord, the one who is speaking should stop. [31]In this way all who have the gift of prophecy can speak, one after the other, and everyone will learn and be encouraged and helped. [32]Remember that a person who has a message from God has the power to stop himself or wait his turn. [33]God is not one who likes things to be disorderly and upset. He likes harmony, and he finds it in all the other churches.

REAL WORSHIP

14:26ff Everything done in worship services must be beneficial to the worshipers. This principle touches every aspect—singing, preaching, and the exercise of spiritual gifts. Those contributing to the service (singers, speakers, readers) must have love as their chief motivation, giving useful words or help that will strengthen the faith of other believers.

[34]Women should be silent during the church meetings. They are not to take part in the discussion, for they are subordinate to men as the Scriptures also declare. [35]If they have any questions to ask, let them ask their husbands at home, for it is improper for women to express their opinions in church meetings.

[36]You disagree? And do you think that the knowledge of God's will begins and ends with you Corinthians? Well, you are mistaken! [37]You who claim to have the gift of prophecy or any other special ability from the Holy Spirit should be the first to realize that what I am saying is a commandment from the Lord himself. [38]But if anyone still disagrees—well, we will leave him in his ignorance.

[39]So, my fellow believers, long to be prophets so that you can preach God's message plainly; and never say it is wrong to "speak in tongues"; [40]however, be sure that everything is done properly in a good and orderly way.

CHAPTER 15 CHRIST ROSE FROM THE DEAD.

Now let me remind you, brothers, of what the Gospel really is, for it has not changed—it is the same Good News I preached to you before. You welcomed it then and still do now, for your faith is squarely built upon this wonderful message; [2]and it is this Good News that saves you if you still firmly believe it, unless of course you never really believed it in the first place.

[3]I passed on to you right from the first what had been told to me, that Christ died for our sins just as the Scriptures said he would, [4]and that he was buried, and that three days afterwards he arose from the grave just as the prophets foretold. [5]He was seen by Peter and later by the rest of "the Twelve." [6]After that he was seen by more than five hundred Christian brothers at one time, most of whom are still alive, though some have died by now. [7]Then James saw him, and later all the apostles. [8]Last of all I saw him too, long after the others, as though I had been born almost too late for this. [9]For I am the least worthy of all the apostles, and I shouldn't even be called an apostle at all after the way I treated the church of God.

[10]But whatever I am now it is all because God poured out such kindness and grace upon me—and not without results: for I have worked harder than all the other apostles, yet actually I wasn't doing it, but God working in me, to bless me. [11]It makes no difference who worked the hardest, I or they; the important thing is that we preached the Gospel to you and you believed it.

[12]But tell me this! Since you believe what we preach, that *Christ* rose from the dead, why are some of you saying that dead people will never

come back to life again? [13]For if there is no resurrection of the dead, then Christ must still be dead. [14]And if he is still dead, then all our preaching is useless and your trust in God is empty, worthless, hopeless; [15]and we apostles are all liars because we have said that God raised Christ from the grave, and of course that isn't true if the dead do not come back to life again. [16]If they don't, then Christ is still dead, [17]and you are very foolish to keep on trusting God to save you, and you are still under condemnation for your sins; [18]in that case, all Christians who have died are lost! [19]And if being a Christian is of value to us only now in this life, we are the most miserable of creatures.

[20]But the fact is that Christ did actually rise from the dead and has become the first of millions who will come back to life again someday.

[21]Death came into the world because of what one man (Adam) did, and it is because of what this other man (Christ) has done that now there is the resurrection from the dead. [22]Everyone dies because all of us are related to Adam, being members of his sinful race, and wherever there is sin, death results. But all who are related to Christ will rise again. [23]Each, however, in his own turn: Christ rose first; then when Christ comes back, all his people will become alive again.

[24]After that the end will come when he will turn the Kingdom over to God the Father, having put down all enemies of every kind. [25]For Christ will be King until he has defeated all his enemies, [26]including the last enemy—death. This too must be defeated and ended. [27]For the rule and authority over all things has been given to Christ by his Father; except, of course, Christ does not rule over the Father himself, who gave him this power to rule. [28]When Christ has finally won the battle against all his enemies, then he, the Son of God, will put himself also under his Father's orders, so that God who has given him the victory over everything else will be utterly supreme.

[29]If the dead will not come back to life again, then what point is there in people being baptized for those who are gone? Why do it unless you believe that the dead will someday rise again? [30]And why should we ourselves be continually risking our lives, facing death hour by hour? [31]For it is a fact that I face death daily; that is as true as my pride in your growth in the Lord. [32]And what value was there in fighting wild beasts—those men of Ephesus—if it was only for what I gain in this life down here? If we will never live again after we die, then we might as well go and have ourselves a good time: let us eat, drink, and be merry. What's the difference? For tomorrow we die, and that ends everything!

[33]Don't be fooled by those who say such things. If you listen to them you will start acting like them.

[34]Get some sense and quit your sinning. For to your shame I say it; some of you are not even Christians at all and have never really known God.

[35]But someone may ask, "How will the dead be brought back to life again? What kind of bodies will they have?" [36]What a foolish question! You will find the answer in your own garden! When you put a seed into the ground it doesn't grow into a plant unless it "dies" first. [37]And when the green shoot comes up out of the seed, it is very different from the seed you first planted. For all you put into the ground is a dry little seed of wheat or whatever it is you are planting, [38]then God gives it a beautiful new body—just the kind he wants it to have; a different kind of plant grows from each kind of seed. [39]And just as there are different kinds of seeds and plants, so also there are different kinds of flesh. Humans, animals, fish, and birds are all different.

[40]The angels in heaven have bodies far different from ours, and the beauty and the glory of their bodies is different from the beauty and the glory of ours. [41]The sun has one kind of glory while the moon and stars have another kind. And the stars differ from each other in their beauty and brightness.

[42]In the same way, our earthly bodies which die and decay are different from the bodies we shall have when we come back to life again, for they will never die. [43]The bodies we have now embarrass us, for they become sick and die; but they will be full of glory when we come back to life again. Yes, they are weak, dying bodies now, but when we live again they will be full of strength. [44]They are just human bodies at death, but when they come back to life they will be superhuman bodies. For just as there are natural, human bodies, there are also supernatural, spiritual bodies.

[45]The Scriptures tell us that the first man, Adam, was given a natural, human body but Christ is more than that, for he was life-giving Spirit.

[46]First, then, we have these human bodies, and later on God gives us spiritual, heavenly bodies. [47]Adam was made from the dust of the earth, but Christ came from heaven above. [48]Every human being has a body just like Adam's, made of dust, but all who become Christ's will have the same kind of body as his—a body from heaven. [49]Just as each of us now has a body like Adam's, so we shall some day have a body like Christ's.

PROOF

15:5-8 There will always be people who will say that Jesus didn't rise from the dead. Paul assures us that many people saw Jesus after his resurrection, including more than 500 Christian believers. The resurrection is a historical fact. Don't be discouraged by doubters who deny the resurrection. Be filled with hope by the knowledge that one day you, and they, will stand before the living proof when Christ returns.

^{50}I tell you this, my brothers: an earthly body made of flesh and blood cannot get into God's Kingdom. These perishable bodies of ours are not the right kind to live forever.

^{51}But I am telling you this strange and wonderful secret: we shall not all die, but we shall all be given new bodies! ^{52}It will all happen in a moment, in the twinkling of an eye, when the last trumpet is blown. For there will be a trumpet blast from the sky, and all the Christians who have died will suddenly become alive, with new bodies that will never, never die; and then we who are still alive shall suddenly have new bodies too. ^{53}For our earthly bodies, the ones we have now that can die, must be transformed into heavenly bodies that cannot perish but will live forever.

^{54}When this happens, then at last this Scripture will come true—"Death is swallowed up in victory." ^{55,56}O death, where then your victory? Where then your sting? For sin—the sting that causes death—will all be gone; and the law, which reveals our sins, will no longer be our judge. ^{57}How we thank God for all of this! It is he who makes us victorious through Jesus Christ our Lord!

^{58}So, my dear brothers, since future victory is sure, be strong and steady, always abounding in the Lord's work, for you know that nothing you do for the Lord is ever wasted as it would be if there were no resurrection.

RESULTS

15:58 Paul said that because of the Resurrection, nothing we do is wasted. Sometimes we hesitate to do good because we don't see any results. But if we can maintain a heavenly perspective, we will understand that we don't often see the good that results from our efforts. Truly believing that Christ has won the ultimate victory will affect the way we live right now. Don't let discouragement over an apparent lack of results keep you from working. Do the good that you have opportunity to do, knowing that your work will have eternal results.

CHAPTER 16 GIVING AN OFFERING.

Now here are the directions about the money you are collecting to send to the Christians in Jerusalem; (and, by the way, these are the same directions I gave to the churches in Galatia). ^{2}On every Lord's Day each of you should put aside something from what you have earned during the week, and use it for this offering. The amount depends on how much the Lord has helped you earn. Don't wait until I get there and then try to collect it all at once. ^{3}When I come I will send your loving gift with a letter to Jerusalem, to be taken there by trustworthy messengers you yourselves will choose. ^{4}And if it seems wise for me to go along too, then we can travel together.

^{5}I am coming to visit you after I have been to Macedonia first, but I will be staying there only for a little while. ^{6}It could be that I will stay longer with you, perhaps all winter, and then you can send me on to my next destination. ^{7}This time I don't want to make just a passing visit and then go right on; I want to come and stay awhile, if the Lord will let me. ^{8}I will be staying here at Ephesus until the holiday of Pentecost, ^{9}for there is a wide open door for me to preach and teach here. So much is happening, but there are many enemies.

^{10}If Timothy comes make him feel at home, for he is doing the Lord's work just as I am. ^{11}Don't let anyone despise or ignore him [because he is young], but send him back to me happy with his time among you; I am looking forward to seeing him soon, along with the others who are returning.

^{12}I begged Apollos to visit you along with the others, but he thought that it was not at all God's will for him to go now; he will be seeing you later on when he has the opportunity.

^{13}Keep your eyes open for spiritual danger; stand true to the Lord; act like men; be strong; ^{14}and whatever you do, do it with kindness and love.

^{15}Do you remember Stephanas and his family? They were the first to become Christians in Greece, and they are spending their lives helping and serving Christians everywhere. ^{16}Please follow their instructions and do everything you can to help them as well as all others like them who work hard at your side with such real devotion. ^{17}I am so glad that Stephanas, Fortunatus, and Achaicus have arrived here for a visit. They have been making up for the help you aren't here to give me. ^{18}They have cheered me greatly and have been a wonderful encouragement to me, as I am sure they were to you, too. I hope you properly appreciate the work of such men as these.

^{19}The churches here in Asia send you their loving greetings. Aquila and Priscilla send you their love, and so do all the others who meet in their home for their church service. ^{20}All the friends here have asked me to say hello to you for them. And give each other a loving handshake when you meet.

^{21}I will write these final words of this letter with my own hand: ^{22}if anyone does not love the Lord, that person is cursed. Lord Jesus, come! ^{23}May the love and favor of the Lord Jesus Christ rest upon you. ^{24}My love to all of you, for we all belong to Christ Jesus.

Sincerely, Paul

RETURN

16:22 The Lord Jesus Christ is coming back to earth again. To Paul, this was a glad hope, the best he could look forward to. He was not afraid of seeing Christ—he could hardly wait! Do you share Paul's eager anticipation? Those who love Christ are looking forward to that wonderful time of his return (Titus 2:13).

MEGA Themes

LOYALTIES The Corinthians were rallying around various church leaders and teachers—Peter, Paul, and Apollos. These loyalties led to intellectual pride and divided the church.

Our loyalty to human leaders or human wisdom must never divide us into various groups. We must care for our fellow Christians, not fight with them. Your allegiance must be to Christ. Let him lead you.

1. How did Paul feel about the various groups who were giving their allegiance to him or Peter or Apollos?
2. What did Paul want to change about their attitude? Why?
3. Based on this passage, at what point does loyalty become a problem in the church?
4. Who are the key Christian leaders you respect? Describe the attitude you should have toward them.

IMMORALITY Paul received a report of uncorrected sexual sin in the church at Corinth. The people had grown indifferent to immorality. Others had misconceptions about marriage. We are to live morally because our bodies should be ready to serve God.

Christians must never compromise with sinful ideas and practices. You should not become just like those around you, even if everyone seems to disagree with your moral beliefs. You must live up to God's standard of morality and not go along with immoral behavior.

1. What specific immorality does Paul condemn in chapter 5?
2. Why is this type of immorality such an offense to God?
3. Why do you think the Corinthians were tolerating this behavior? How did Paul indicate that they should deal with this ongoing sin? How is this different than the way they should respond to someone who was sinning but was not claiming to be a Christian? (See 5:9-11.)
4. How can you make an impact on your world without allowing the world to influence you?

FREEDOM Paul taught freedom of choice on practices not expressly forbidden in Scripture. Some believers thought that certain actions—like buying the meat of animals used in pagan rituals—were wrong. Others believed they could do such things without sinning because they were free from the law.

We are free in Christ, yet we must not abuse our Christian freedom by being inconsiderate and insensitive to others. We must never encourage others to do wrong by anything we do. Love should guide our behavior.

1. In chapter 8, Paul instructs the Corinthians on their freedom in Christ. What key principles do you find in this passage for dealing with areas of conduct that are "grays," not black or white?
2. What are some of the "gray areas" that Christians have different opinions about?
3. How could you as a Christian misuse your freedom in Christ and hurt someone else in these "gray" areas?
4. Identify specific ways that you could apply the principles of chapter 8 to your freedom in Christ.

WORSHIP Paul addressed disorder in worship. People were taking the Lord's Supper without first confessing sin. There was misuse of spiritual gifts and confusion over the role of women in the church.

Worship must be carried out properly and orderly. Everything we do to worship God should be done in a manner worthy of his high honor.

1. What concerns did Paul have concerning worship in the Corinthian church? What does this teach you about Paul's view of worship?
2. What actions or attitudes sometimes disrupt true worship in your church?
3. What actions and attitudes encourage true worship in your church?
4. What can you do in your church to help people's worship remain true?

RESURRECTION Some people denied that Christ rose from the dead. Others believed that people would not be physically resurrected. Christ's resurrection assures us that we will have new, living bodies after we die. The fact of the Resurrection is the secret of Christian hope.

Because we will be raised again to life after we die, our life is not in vain. We must stay faithful to God in how we live and serve. And we should live today knowing that we will spend eternity with Christ. Eternal life has already begun!

1. Read chapter 15. According to Paul, what is the importance of the Resurrection?
2. What misconceptions did some of the Corinthians have regarding the Resurrection? How did Paul correct those wrong ideas?
3. What would be different about life if Jesus had not risen from the dead?
4. How would you respond if asked to describe the difference Christ's resurrection has made in your own life?

Ministry . . . or Madness?: A Quiz Just for You. ■ 1. At Bible club, it rains, a kid throws up on you, and one obnoxious six-year-old complains for *90 minutes* about watery punch. Do you: (a) Dump the watery punch on the obnoxious kid? (b) Wipe throw up *and* dump the punch on the obnoxious kid? (c) Retire from your Bible club career? (d) Pray (really hard!) for patience and kindness? ■ 2. Your youth group gives 400 hard-earned dollars to a family whose house just burned down. The family never even acknowledges the gift! Do you: (a) Break out your lecture on the importance of gratitude? (b) Think of all the ways *you* could have used the cash? (c) Ask for the money back? (d) Trust that God is in control? ■ 3. During a church mission trip, some older teens surround you and call you names, shove you, and make fun of the Christian message on your T-shirt. Do you: (a)"Do a Samson" (i.e., beat them up in the name of Jesus)? (b) Change your shirt? (c) Vow never to stand up for Christ again? (d) Consider it an honor to suffer for Christ? ■ 4. Second Corinthians discusses: (a) Living for the Lord when nothing seems to go right? (b) Why it *is* worth it (no matter what happens) to serve God and others? (c) The amazing truth that we can't outgive God? (d) The importance of telling others about Jesus Christ? (e) All of the above.

■ Being Christ's ambassador isn't crazy—it's the only way to find deep-down satisfaction! Tempted to give up? Second Corinthians is just what you need.

STATS

PURPOSE: To affirm Paul's own ministry, defend his authority as an apostle, and refute the false teachers in Corinth

AUTHOR: Paul

TO WHOM WRITTEN: The church in Corinth, and Christians everywhere

DATE WRITTEN: About A.D. 55–57, from Macedonia

SETTING: Paul had already written three letters to the Corinthians (two are now lost). In 1 Corinthians (the second of these letters), he used strong words to correct and teach. Most of the church had responded in the right spirit. There were, however, those who were denying Paul's authority and questioning his motives.

KEY PEOPLE: Paul, Timothy, Titus, false teachers

KEY PLACES: Corinth, Jerusalem

2Corinthians

COMFORT

1:3-4 Many think that when God comforts us, our hardships go away. If that were so, people would turn to God only to be relieved of pain and not out of love for him. Real comfort can also mean receiving strength, encouragement, and hope to deal with our hardships. The more we suffer, the more comfort God gives us (1:5). If you are feeling overwhelmed, allow God to comfort you. Remember, every trial you endure will later become an opportunity to minister to others suffering similar hardships.

CHAPTER 1 **PAUL: A MESSENGER OF GOD.** Dear friends: This letter is from me, Paul, appointed by God to be Jesus Christ's messenger; and from our dear brother Timothy. We are writing to all of you Christians there in Corinth and throughout Greece. [2]May God our Father and the Lord Jesus Christ mightily bless each one of you and give you peace.

[3,4]What a wonderful God we have—he is the Father of our Lord Jesus Christ, the source of every mercy, and the one who so wonderfully comforts and strengthens us in our hardships and trials. And why does he do this? So that when others are troubled, needing our sympathy and encouragement, we can pass on to them this same help and comfort God has given us. [5]You can be sure that the more we undergo sufferings for Christ, the more he will shower us with his comfort and encouragement. [6,7]We are in deep trouble for bringing you God's comfort and salvation. But in our trouble God has comforted us—and this, too, to help you: to show you from our personal experience how God will tenderly comfort you when you undergo these same sufferings. He will give you the strength to endure.

[8]I think you ought to know, dear brothers, about the hard time we went through in Asia. We were really crushed and overwhelmed, and feared we would never live through it. [9]We felt we were doomed to die and saw how powerless we were to help ourselves; but that was good, for then we put everything into the hands of God, who alone could save us, for he can

Paul had searched for Titus, hoping to meet him in Troas and receive news about the Corinthian church. When he did not find Titus in Troas, Paul went on to Macedonia (2:13), most likely to Philippi, where he found Titus.

even raise the dead. ¹⁰And he did help us and saved us from a terrible death; yes, and we expect him to do it again and again. ¹¹But you must help us too by praying for us. For much thanks and praise will go to God from you who see his wonderful answers to your prayers for our safety!

¹²We are so glad that we can say with utter honesty that in all our dealings we have been pure and sincere, quietly depending upon the Lord for his help and not on our own skills. And that is even more true, if possible, about the way we have acted toward you. ¹³,¹⁴My letters have been straightforward and sincere; nothing is written between the lines! And even though you don't know me very well (I hope someday you will), I want you to try to accept me and be proud of me as you already are to some extent; just as I shall be of you on that day when our Lord Jesus comes back again.

¹⁵,¹⁶It was because I was so sure of your understanding and trust that I planned to stop and see you on my way to Macedonia, as well as afterwards when I returned, so that I could be a double blessing to you and so that you could send me on my way to Judea.

¹⁷Then why, you may be asking, did I change my plan? Hadn't I really made up my mind yet? Or am I like a man of the world who says yes when he really means no? ¹⁸Never! As surely as God is true, I am not that sort of person. My yes means yes.

¹⁹Timothy and Silvanus and I have been telling you about Jesus Christ the Son of God. He isn't one to say yes when he means no. He always does exactly what he says. ²⁰He carries out and fulfills all of God's promises, no matter how many of them there are; and we have told everyone how faithful he is, giving glory to his name. ²¹It is this God who has made you and me into faithful Christians and commissioned us apostles to preach the Good News. ²²He has put his brand upon us—his mark of ownership—and given us his Holy Spirit in our hearts as guarantee that we belong to him and as the first installment of all that he is going to give us.

IDENTIFY

1:21-22 Paul mentions two gifts God gives us when we become believers: a "mark of ownership" to show who our master is and the Holy Spirit as a guarantee that we belong to him (Ephesians 1:13-14). With the privilege of belonging to God comes the responsibility of identifying ourselves as faithful representatives and servants of our master. Don't be ashamed to let others know you are his.

²³I call upon this God to witness against me if I am not telling the absolute truth: the reason I haven't come to visit you yet is that I don't want to sadden you with a severe rebuke. ²⁴When I come, although I can't do much to help your faith, for it is strong already, I want to be able to do something about your joy: I want to make you happy, not sad.

CHAPTER 2 FORGIVENESS AND ACCEPTANCE.

"No," I said to myself, "I won't do it. I'll not make them unhappy with another painful visit." ²For if I make you sad, who is going to make me happy? You are the ones to do it, and how can you if I cause you pain? ³That is why I wrote as I did in my last letter, so that you will get things straightened out before I come. Then, when I do come, I will not be made sad by the very ones who ought to give me greatest joy. I felt sure that your happiness was so bound up in mine that you would not be happy either unless I came with joy.

⁴Oh, how I hated to write that letter! It almost broke my heart, and I tell you honestly that I cried over it. I didn't want to hurt you, but I had to show you how very much I loved you and cared about what was happening to you.

⁵,⁶Remember that the man I wrote about, who caused all the trouble, has not caused sorrow to me as much as to all the rest of you—though I certainly have my share in it too. I don't want to be harder on him than I should. He has been punished enough by your united disapproval. ⁷Now it is time to forgive him and comfort him. Otherwise he may become so bitter and discouraged that he won't be able to recover. ⁸Please show him now that you still do love him very much.

⁹I wrote to you as I did so that I could find out how far you would go in obeying me. ¹⁰When you forgive anyone, I do too. And whatever I have forgiven (to the extent that this affected me too) has been by Christ's authority, and for your good. ¹¹A further reason for forgiveness is to keep from being outsmarted by Satan, for we know what he is trying to do.

¹²Well, when I got as far as the city of Troas, the Lord gave me tremendous opportunities to preach the Gospel. ¹³But Titus, my dear brother, wasn't there to meet me and I couldn't rest, wondering where he was and what had happened to him. So I said good-bye and went right on to Macedonia to try to find him.

¹⁴But thanks be to God! For through what Christ has done, he has triumphed over us so that now wherever we go he uses us to tell others about the Lord and to spread the Gospel like a sweet perfume. ¹⁵As far as God is concerned there is a sweet, wholesome fragrance in our lives. It is the fragrance of Christ within us, an aroma to both the saved and the unsaved all around us. ¹⁶To those who are not being saved, we seem a fearful smell of death and doom, while to those who know Christ we are a life-giving perfume. But who is adequate for such a task as this? ¹⁷Only those who, like ourselves, are men of integrity, sent by God, speaking with Christ's power, with God's eye upon us. We are not like those hucksters—and there are many of them—whose idea in getting out the Gospel is to make a good living out of it.

CHAPTER 3 OUR SUCCESS COMES FROM GOD.

Are we beginning to be like those false teachers of yours who must tell you all about themselves and bring long letters of recommendation with them? I think you hardly need someone's letter to tell you about us, do you? And we don't need a recommendation from you, either! ²The only letter I need is you yourselves! By looking at the good change in your hearts, everyone can see that we have done a good work among you. ³They can see that you are a letter from Christ, written by us. It is not a letter written with pen and ink, but by the Spirit of the living God; not one carved on stone, but in human hearts.

⁴We dare to say these good things about ourselves

"Here's what I did..."

Last year I went through a very difficult time for a whole month. It was one thing after another; I wasn't sure I could take it. God saw me through it, but I still had lots of unresolved questions about why those things had to happen to me.

Not long afterward my friend's sister had a leukemia relapse. When I found out, I prayed and cried for a while. Then I decided to write her a note of encouragement. Later that night, I read 2 Corinthians 1:3-7 and it felt like God was speaking tender words of comfort right to me. I realized that there was a reason for the pain I had gone through not long before; it was so that I could relate to the pain of other people and offer true encouragement.

I was not only able to offer my friend's sister some sincere encouragement, but also my nagging questions over why God let me go through my pain were answered. Since then, whenever something painful happens to me I find it much easier to believe that there's a good reason for it.

Linda AGE 17

only because of our great trust in God through Christ, that he will help us to be true to what we say, [5]and not because we think we can do anything of lasting value by ourselves. Our only power and success comes from God. [6]He is the one who has helped us tell others about his new agreement to save them. We do not tell them that they must obey every law of God or die; but we tell them there is life for them from the Holy Spirit. The old way, trying to be saved by keeping the Ten Commandments, ends in death; in the new way, the Holy Spirit gives them life.

[7]Yet that old system of law that led to death began with such glory that people could not bear to look at Moses' face. For as he gave them God's law to obey, his face shone out with the very glory of God—though the brightness was already fading away. [8]Shall we not expect far greater glory in these days when the Holy Spirit is giving life? [9]If the plan that leads to doom was glorious, much more glorious is the plan that makes men right with God. [10]In fact, that first glory as it shone from Moses' face is worth nothing at all in comparison with the overwhelming glory of the new agreement. [11]So if the old system that faded into nothing was full of heavenly glory, the glory of God's new plan for our salvation is certainly far greater, for it is eternal.

[12]Since we know that this new glory will never go away, we can preach with great boldness, [13]and not as Moses did, who put a veil over his face so that the Israelis could not see the glory fade away.

[14]Not only Moses' face was veiled, but his people's minds and understanding were veiled and blinded too. Even now when the Scripture is read it seems as though Jewish hearts and minds are covered by a thick veil, because they cannot see and understand the real meaning of the Scriptures. For this veil of misunderstanding can be removed only by believing in Christ. [15]Yes, even today when they read Moses' writings their hearts are blind and they think that obeying the Ten Commandments is the way to be saved.

[16]But whenever anyone turns to the Lord from his sins, then the veil is taken away. [17]The Lord is the Spirit who gives them life, and where he is there is freedom [from trying to be saved by keeping the laws of God]. [18]But we Christians have no veil over our faces; we can be mirrors that brightly reflect the glory of the Lord. And as the Spirit of the Lord works within us, we become more and more like him.

CHAPTER 4 SATAN BLINDS, BUT GOD GIVES LIGHT.

It is God himself, in his mercy, who has given us this wonderful work [of telling his Good News to others], and so we never give up. [2]We do not try to trick people into believing—we are not interested in fooling anyone. We never try to get anyone to believe that the Bible teaches what it doesn't. All such shameful methods we forego. We stand in the presence of God as we speak and so we tell the truth, as all who know us will agree.

[3]If the Good News we preach is hidden to anyone, it is hidden from the one who is on the road to eternal death. [4]Satan, who is the god of this evil world, has made him blind, unable to see the glorious light of the Gospel that is shining upon him or to understand the amazing message we preach about the glory of Christ, who is God. [5]We don't go around preaching about ourselves but about Christ Jesus as Lord. All we say of ourselves is that we are your slaves because of what Jesus has done for us. [6]For God, who said, "Let there be light in the darkness," has made us understand that it is the brightness of his glory that is seen in the face of Jesus Christ.

[7]But this precious treasure—this light and power that now shine within us—is held in a perishable container, that is, in our weak bodies. Everyone can see that the glorious power within must be from God and is not our own.

[8]We are pressed on every side by troubles, but not crushed and broken. We are perplexed because we don't know why things happen as they do, but we don't give up and quit. [9]We are hunted down, but God never abandons us. We get knocked down, but we get up again and keep going. [10]These bodies of ours are constantly facing death just as Jesus did; so it is clear to all that it is only the living Christ within [who keeps us safe].

[11]Yes, we live under constant danger to our lives because we serve the Lord, but this gives us constant opportunities to show forth the power of Jesus Christ within our dy-

ing bodies. [12]Because of our preaching we face death, but it has resulted in eternal life for you.

[13]We boldly say what we believe [trusting God to care for us], just as the psalm writer did when he said, "I believe and therefore I speak." [14]We know that the same God who brought the Lord Jesus back from death will also bring us back to life again with Jesus and present us to him along with you. [15]These sufferings of ours are for your benefit. And the more of you who are won to Christ, the more there are to thank him for his great kindness, and the more the Lord is glorified.

[16]That is why we never give up. Though our bodies are dying, our inner strength in the Lord is growing every day. [17]These troubles and sufferings of ours are, after all, quite small and won't last very long. Yet this short time of distress will result in God's richest blessing upon us forever and ever! [18]So we do not look at what we can see right now, the troubles all around us, but we look forward to the joys in heaven which we have not yet seen. The troubles will soon be over, but the joys to come will last forever.

CHAPTER 5 WE WILL HAVE NEW BODIES. For

we know that when this tent we live in now is taken down—when we die and leave these bodies—we will have wonderful new bodies in heaven, homes that will be ours forevermore, made for us by God himself and not by human hands. [2]How weary we grow of our present bodies. That is why we look forward eagerly to the day when we shall have heavenly bodies that we shall put on like new clothes. [3]For we shall not be merely spirits without bodies. [4]These earthly bodies make us groan and sigh, but we wouldn't like to think of dying and having no bodies at all. We want to slip into our new bodies so that these dying bodies will, as it were, be swallowed up by everlasting life. [5]This is what God has prepared for us, and as a guarantee he has given us his Holy Spirit.

[6]Now we look forward with confidence to our heavenly bodies, realizing that every moment we spend in these earthly bodies is time spent away from our eternal home in heaven with Jesus. [7]We know these things are true by believing, not by seeing. [8]And we are not afraid but are quite content to die, for then we will be at home with the Lord. [9]So our aim is to please him always in everything we do, whether we are here in this body or away from this body and with him in heaven. [10]For we must all stand before Christ to be judged and have our lives laid bare—before him. Each of us will receive whatever he deserves for the good or bad things he has done in his earthly body.

[11]It is because of this solemn fear of the Lord, which is ever present in our minds, that we work so hard to win others. God knows our hearts, that they are pure in this matter, and I hope that, deep within, you really know it too.

[12]Are we trying to pat ourselves on the back again? No, I am giving you some good ammunition! You can use this on those preachers of yours who brag about how well they look and preach but don't have true and honest hearts. You can boast about us that we, at least, are well intentioned and honest.

[13,14]Are we insane [to say such things about ourselves]? If so, it is to bring glory to God. And if we are in our right minds, it is for your benefit. Whatever we do, it is certainly not for our own profit but because Christ's love controls us now. Since we believe that Christ died for all of us, we should also believe that we have died to the old life we used to live. [15]He died for all so that all who live—having received eternal life from him—might live no longer for themselves, to please themselves, but to spend their lives pleasing Christ who died and rose again for them. [16]So stop evaluating Christians by what the world thinks about them or by what they seem to be like on the outside. Once I mistakenly thought of Christ that way, merely as a human being like myself. How differently I feel now!

MADE NEW

5:16-17 Christians are brand new people on the *inside*. The Holy Spirit gives them new life, and they are not the same any more. We are not reformed, rehabilitated, or reeducated—we are new creations, living in vital union with Christ (Colossians 2:6-7). We are not merely turning over a new leaf; we are beginning a new life under a new Master.

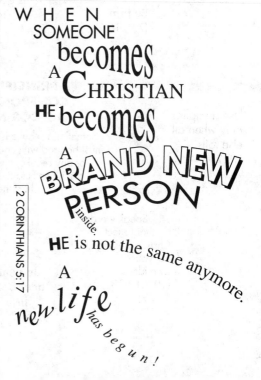

WHEN SOMEONE becomes A CHRISTIAN HE becomes A BRAND NEW PERSON *inside*. HE is not the same anymore. A new life has begun!

2 CORINTHIANS 5:17

AMBASSADOR

5:20 An ambassador is an official representative from one country to another. As believers, we are Christ's ambassadors, sent with his message of peace to the world. An ambassador of reconciliation has an important responsibility. We dare not take this responsibility lightly. How well are you fulfilling your commission as Christ's ambassador?

[17]When someone becomes a Christian, he becomes a brand new person inside. He is not the same anymore. A new life has begun!

[18]All these new things are from God who brought us back to himself through what Christ Jesus did. And God has given us the privilege of urging everyone to come into his favor and be reconciled to him. [19]For God was in Christ, restoring the world to himself, no longer counting men's sins against them but blotting them out. This is the wonderful message he has given us to tell others. [20]We are Christ's ambassadors. God is using us to speak to you: we beg you, as though Christ himself were here pleading with you, receive the love he offers you—be reconciled to God. [21]For God took the sinless Christ and poured into him our sins. Then, in exchange, he poured God's goodness into us!

CHAPTER 6 WHEN LIFE IS HARD, LEAN ON GOD.

As God's partners, we beg you not to toss aside this marvelous message of God's great kindness. [2]For God says, "Your cry came to me at a favorable time, when the doors of welcome were wide open. I helped you on a day when salvation was being offered." Right now God is ready to welcome you. Today he is ready to save you.

[3]We try to live in such a way that no one will ever be offended or kept back from finding the Lord by the way we act, so that no one can find fault with us and blame it on the Lord. [4]In fact, in everything we do we try to show that we are true ministers of God.

We patiently endure suffering and hardship and trouble of every kind. [5]We have been beaten, put in jail, faced angry mobs, worked to exhaustion, stayed awake through sleepless nights of watching, and gone without food. [6]We have proved ourselves to be what we claim by our wholesome lives and by our understanding of the Gospel and by our patience. We have been kind and truly loving and filled with the Holy Spirit. [7]We have been truthful,

PRINCIPLES OF CONFRONTATION IN 2 CORINTHIANS

Sometimes rebuke is necessary, but it must be used with caution. The purpose of any rebuke, confrontation, or discipline is to help people, not hurt them.

Affirm all you see that is good. (7:4)

Be firm. (7:9; 10:2)

Be accurate and honest. (7:14; 8:21)

Use discipline only when all else fails. (13:2)

Know the facts. (11:22-27)

Speak words that reflect Christ's message, not your own ideas. (10:3,12-13; 12:19)

Be gentle after being firm. (7:15; 13:11-13)

Follow up after the confrontation. (7:13; 12:14)

with God's power helping us in all we do. All of the godly man's arsenal—weapons of defense, and weapons of attack—have been ours.

⁸We stand true to the Lord whether others honor us or despise us, whether they criticize us or commend us. We are honest, but they call us liars.

⁹The world ignores us, but we are known to God; we live close to death, but here we are, still very much alive. We have been injured but kept from death. ¹⁰Our hearts ache, but at the same time we have the joy of the Lord. We are poor, but we give rich spiritual gifts to others. We own nothing, and yet we enjoy everything.

¹¹Oh, my dear Corinthian friends! I have told you all my feelings; I love you with all my heart. ¹²Any coldness still between us is not because of any lack of love on my part but because your love is too small and does not reach out to me and draw me in. ¹³I am talking to you now as if you truly were my very own children. Open your hearts to us! Return our love!

¹⁴Don't be teamed with those who do not love the Lord, for what do the people of God have in common with the people of sin? How can light live with darkness? ¹⁵And what harmony can there be between Christ and the devil? How can a Christian be a partner with one who doesn't believe? ¹⁶And what union can there be between God's temple and idols? For you are God's temple, the home of the living God, and God has said of you, "I will live in them and walk among them, and I will be their God and they shall be my people." ¹⁷That is why the Lord has said, "Leave them; separate yourselves from them; don't touch their filthy things, and I will welcome you ¹⁸and be a Father to you, and you will be my sons and daughters."

CHAPTER 7 PAUL IS PROUD OF THE CHRISTIANS.

Having such great promises as these, dear friends, let us turn away from everything wrong, whether of body or spirit, and purify ourselves, living in the wholesome fear of God, giving ourselves to him alone. ²Please open your hearts to us again, for not one of you has suffered any wrong from us. Not one of you was led astray. We have cheated no one nor taken advantage of anyone. ³I'm not saying this to scold or blame you, for, as I have said before, you are in my heart forever, and I live and die with you. ⁴I have the highest confidence in you, and my pride in you is great. You have greatly encouraged me; you have made me so happy in spite of all my suffering.

⁵When we arrived in Macedonia there was no rest for us; outside, trouble was on every hand and all around us; within us, our hearts were full of dread and fear. ⁶Then God who cheers those who are discouraged refreshed us by the arrival of Titus.

⁷Not only was his presence a joy, but also the news that he brought of the wonderful time he had with you. When he told me how much you were looking forward to my visit, and how sorry you were about what had happened, and about your loyalty and

I've been a Christian about nine months. Although I have made a lot of friends who are Christians, I still have quite a few who aren't. Should I still be hanging out with friends who aren't Christians?

I WONDER . .

Find a quarter and two pennies. Place the quarter on a table. Put the two pennies about five inches below the quarter, one inch apart.

Now, pretend God is the quarter, you are the penny on the left, and your friend is the penny on the right. As you grow closer to God (move your penny up an inch or two), what happens to the distance between you and your friend? It gets wider! When only one person in a friendship moves closer to God, that's what happens to the relationship automatically!

There are degrees in friendships and stages we go through to make them stronger. But all friendships take time. And our closest friends affect us. Think about the friends you used to hang around with. You probably did the same things, used the same slang, laughed at the same type of jokes, etc.

Hanging around with old friends who aren't Christians will probably not help you become a stronger Christian. That's what 2 Corinthians 6:14 is about. If you spend all of your deeper friendship time with unbelievers, you'll tend to become like them and not move closer to God.

However, God doesn't want you to be totally isolated from those who aren't Christians. In fact, if you get to the point where you don't have any non-Christian friends, you're probably doing something wrong. If you're going to be Christ's representative to those who don't know him (see 2 Corinthians 5:18-20), you have to be around them! Just be careful, and remember that your goal is to point them to Christ.

"Be with wise men and become wise. Be with evil men and become evil" (Proverbs 13:20). And, "If you are looking for advice, stay away from fools" (Proverbs 14:7).

Especially in the early stages of your Christian life, you need to be around people who will be your friends and help you grow spiritually at the same time.

warm love for me, well, I overflowed with joy!

⁸I am no longer sorry that I sent that letter to you, though I was very sorry for a time, realizing how painful it would be to you. But it hurt you only for a little while. ⁹Now I am glad I sent it, not because it hurt you but because the pain turned you to God. It was a good kind of sorrow you felt, the kind of sorrow God wants his people to have, so that I need not come to you with harshness. ¹⁰For God sometimes uses sorrow in our lives to help us turn away from sin and seek eternal life. We should

never regret his sending it. But the sorrow of the man who is not a Christian is not the sorrow of true repentance and does not prevent eternal death.

[11]Just see how much good this grief from the Lord did for you! You no longer shrugged your shoulders but became earnest and sincere and very anxious to get rid of the sin that I wrote you about. You became frightened about what had happened and longed for me to come and help. You went right to work on the problem and cleared it up [punishing the man who sinned]. You have done everything you could to make it right.

[12]I wrote as I did so the Lord could show how much you really do care for us. That was my purpose even more than to help the man who sinned or his father to whom he did the wrong.

[13]In addition to the encouragement you gave us by your love, we were made happier still by Titus' joy when you gave him such a fine welcome and set his mind at ease. [14]I told him how it would be—told him before he left me of my pride in you—and you didn't disappoint me. I have always told you the truth and now my boasting to Titus has also proved true! [15]He loves you more than ever when he remembers the way you listened to him so willingly and received him so anxiously and with such deep concern. [16]How happy this makes me, now that I am sure all is well between us again. Once again I can have perfect confidence in you.

CHAPTER 8 GENEROUS GIVING PLEASES GOD.

Now I want to tell you what God in his grace has done for the churches in Macedonia.

[2]Though they have been going through much trouble and hard times, they have mixed their wonderful joy with their deep poverty, and the result has been an overflow of giving to others. [3]They gave not only what they could afford but far more; and I can testify that they did it because they wanted to and not because of nagging on my part. [4]They begged us to take the money so they could share in the joy of helping the Christians in Jerusalem. [5]Best of all, they went beyond our highest hopes, for their first action was to dedicate themselves to the Lord and to us, for whatever directions God might give to them through us. [6]They were so enthusiastic about it that we have urged Titus, who encouraged your giving in the first place, to visit

you and encourage you to complete your share in this ministry of giving. [7]You people there are leaders in so many ways—you have so much faith, so many good preachers, so much learning, so much enthusiasm, so much love for us. Now I want you to be leaders also in the spirit of cheerful giving.

[8]I am not giving you an order; I am not saying you must do it, but others are eager for it. This is one way to prove that your love is real, that it goes beyond mere words.

[9]You know how full of love and kindness our Lord Jesus was: though he was so very rich, yet to help you he became so very poor, so that by being poor he could make you rich.

[10]I want to suggest that you finish what you started to do a year ago, for you were not only the first to propose this idea, but the first to begin doing something about it. [11]Having started the ball rolling so enthusiastically, you should carry this project through to completion just as gladly, giving whatever you can out of whatever you have. Let your enthusiastic idea at the start be equalled by your realistic action now. [12]If you are really eager to give, then it isn't important how much you have to give. God wants you to give what you have, not what you haven't.

[13]Of course, I don't mean that those who receive your gifts should have an easy time of it at your expense, [14]but you should divide with them. Right now you have plenty and can help them; then at some other time they can share with you when you need it. In this way, each will have as much as he needs. [15]Do you remember what the Scriptures say about this? "He that gathered much had nothing left over, and he that gathered little had enough." So you also should share with those in need.

[16]I am thankful to God that he has given Titus the same real concern for you that I have. [17]He is glad to follow my suggestion that he visit you again—but I think he would

have come anyway, for he is very eager to see you! [18]I am sending another well-known brother with him, who is highly praised as a preacher of the Good News in all the churches. [19]In fact, this man was elected by the churches to travel with me to take the gift to Jerusalem. This will glorify the Lord and show our eagerness to help each other. [20]By traveling together we will guard against any suspicion, for we are anxious that no one should find fault with the way we are handling this large gift. [21]God knows we are honest, but I want everyone else to know it too. That is why we have made this arrangement.

[22]And I am sending you still another brother, whom we know from experience to be an earnest Christian. He is especially interested as he looks forward to this trip because I have told him all about your eagerness to help.

[23]If anyone asks who Titus is, say that he is my partner, my helper in helping you, and you can also say that the other two brothers represent the assemblies here and are splendid examples of those who belong to the Lord.

[24]Please show your love for me to these men and do for them all that I have publicly boasted you would.

CHAPTER 9 GOD LIKES PEOPLE WHO GIVE HAPPILY.

I realize that I really don't even need to mention this to you, about helping God's people. [2]For I know how eager you are to do it, and I have boasted to the friends in Macedonia that you were ready to send an offering a year ago. In fact, it was this enthusiasm of yours that stirred up many of them to begin helping. [3]But I am sending these men just to be sure that you really are ready, as I told them you would be, with your money all collected; I don't want it to turn out that this time I was wrong in my boasting about you. [4]I would be very much ashamed—and so would you—if some of these Macedonian people come with me, only to find that you still aren't ready after all I have told them!

[5]So I have asked these other brothers to arrive ahead of me to see that the gift you promised is on hand and waiting. I want it to be a real gift and not look as if it were being given under pressure.

[6]But remember this—if you give little, you will get little. A farmer who plants just a few seeds will get only a small crop, but if he plants much, he will reap much. [7]Everyone must make up his own mind as to how much he should give. Don't force anyone to give more than he really wants to, for cheerful givers are the ones God prizes. [8]God is able to make it up to you by giving you everything you need and more so that there will not only be enough for your own needs but plenty left over to give joyfully to others. [9]It is as the Scriptures say: "The godly man

gives generously to the poor. His good deeds will be an honor to him forever."

[10]For God, who gives seed to the farmer to plant, and later on good crops to harvest and eat, will give you more and more seed to plant and will make it grow so that you can give away more and more fruit from your harvest.

[11]Yes, God will give you much so that you can give away much, and when we take your gifts to those who need them they will break out into thanksgiving and praise to God for your help. [12]So two good things happen as a result of your gifts—those in need are helped, and they overflow with thanks to God. [13]Those you help will be glad not only because of your generous gifts to themselves and to others, but they will praise God for this proof that your deeds are as good as your doctrine. [14]And they will pray for you with deep fervor and feeling because of the wonderful grace of God shown through you.

[15]Thank God for his Son—his Gift too wonderful for words.

CHAPTER 10 PAUL'S AUTHORITY. I plead with

you—yes, I, Paul—and I plead gently, as Christ himself would do. Yet some of you are saying, "Paul's letters are bold enough when he is far away, but when he gets here he will be afraid to raise his voice!"

[2]I hope I won't need to show you when I come how harsh and rough I can be. I don't want to carry out my present plans against some of you who seem to think my deeds and words are merely those of an ordinary man. [3]It is true that I am an ordinary, weak human being, but I don't use human plans and methods to win my battles. [4]I use God's mighty weapons, not those made by men, to knock down the devil's strongholds. [5]These weapons can break down every proud argument against God and every wall that can be built to keep men from finding him. With these weapons I can capture rebels and bring them back to God and change them into men whose hearts' desire is obedience to Christ. [6]I will use these weapons against every rebel who remains after I have first used them on you yourselves and you surrender to Christ.

[7]The trouble with you is that you look at me and I seem weak and powerless, but you don't look

WEAPONS

10:3-6 Christians must choose whose methods to use, God's or man's. Paul assures us that God's mighty weapons—prayer, faith, hope, love, God's Word, the Holy Spirit—are powerful and effective (see Ephesians 6:13-18)! When dealing with the pride that keeps people from a relationship with Christ, we may be tempted to use our own methods. But nothing can break down Satan's barriers like God's weapons.

beneath the surface. Yet if anyone can claim the power and authority of Christ, I certainly can. [8]I may seem to be boasting more than I should about my authority over you—authority to help you, not to hurt you—but I shall make good every claim. [9]I say this so that you will not think I am just blustering when I scold you in my letters.

[10]"Don't bother about his letters," some say. "He sounds big, but it's all noise. When he gets here you will see that there is nothing great about him, and you have never heard a worse preacher!" [11]This time my personal presence is going to be just as rough on you as my letters are!

[12]Oh, don't worry, I wouldn't dare say that I am as wonderful as these other men who tell you how good they are! Their trouble is that they are only comparing themselves with each other and measuring themselves against their own little ideas. What stupidity!

[13]But we will not boast of authority we do not have. Our goal is to measure up to God's plan for us, and this plan includes our working there with you. [14]We are not going too far when we claim authority over you, for we were the first to come to you with the Good News concerning Christ. [15]It is not as though we were trying to claim credit for the work someone else has done among you. Instead, we hope that your faith will grow and that, still within the limits set for us, our work among you will be greatly enlarged.

[16]After that, we will be able to preach the Good News to other cities that are far beyond you, where no one else is working; then there will be no question about being in someone else's field. [17]As the Scriptures say, "If anyone is going to boast, let him boast about what the Lord has done and not about himself." [18]When someone boasts about himself and how well he has done, it doesn't count for much. But when the Lord commends him, that's different!

CHAPTER 11 SMOOTH TALKERS & PHONY TEACHERS.

I hope you will be patient with me as I keep on talking like a fool. Do bear with me and let me say what is on my heart. [2]I am anxious for you with the deep concern of God himself—anxious that your love should be for Christ alone, just as a pure maiden saves her love for one man only, for the one who will be her husband. [3]But I am frightened, fearing that in some way you will be led away from your pure and simple devotion to our Lord, just as Eve was deceived by Satan in the Garden of Eden. [4]You seem so gullible: you believe whatever anyone tells you even if he is preaching about another Jesus than the one we preach, or a different spirit than the Holy Spirit you received, or shows you a different way to be saved. You swallow it all.

[5]Yet I don't feel that these marvelous "messengers from God," as they call themselves, are any better than I am. [6]If I am a poor speaker, at least I know what I am talking about, as I think you realize by now, for we have proved it again and again.

[7]Did I do wrong and cheapen myself and make you look down on me because I preached God's Good News to you without charging you anything? [8,9] Instead I "robbed" other churches by taking what they sent me and using it up while I was with you so that I could serve you without cost. And when that was gone and I was getting hungry, I still didn't ask you for anything, for the Christians from Macedonia brought me another gift. I have never yet asked you for one cent, and I never will. [10]I promise this with every ounce of truth I possess—that I will tell everyone in Greece about it! [11]Why? Because I don't love you? God knows I do. [12]But I will do it to cut out the ground from under the feet of those who boast that they are doing God's work in just the same way we are.

[13]God never sent those men at all; they are "phonies" who have fooled you into thinking they are Christ's apostles. [14]Yet I am not surprised! Satan can change himself into an angel of light, [15]so it is no wonder his servants can do it too, and seem like godly ministers. In the end they will get every bit of punishment their wicked deeds deserve.

[16]Again I plead, don't think that I have lost my wits to talk like this; but even if you do, listen to me anyway—a witless man, a fool—while I also boast a little as they do. [17]Such bragging isn't something the Lord commanded me to do, for I am acting like

SERVING GOD

"Tom, maybe you've got the dates mixed up," Jeff says.

"No way—the prison outreach is the same weekend."

"But what about Ben's ski party?"

"I guess I'll have to miss it."

"But, Tom, you can't! Everybody will be at Ben's—including every babe in the whole sophomore class! It's the party of the year!"

"Look, I wish I could go. But I promised to sing with the group at this prison thing."

"Can't you get out of it?"

Tom shakes his head. "Jeff, you just don't understand."

"Well, I say you're making a huge mistake. You'll regret it if you miss Ben's party."

Two weeks later "the" weekend has come and gone. Ben's party was every bit as fun as advertised. Great weather, great skiing—it was a certified blast!

And the prison outreach? Not quite so successful. Not only did the prisoners shower Tom's group with verbal abuse during the concert, but afterwards, during a meal stop on the way home, someone broke into the church van and stole the group's sound equipment!

Does it really pay to serve the Lord? Is the hardship encountered worth all the effort? Take it from the apostle Paul, a guy who should know. He endured unbelievable difficulties (2 Corinthians 4:8-10; 6:4-10; 11:23-28), and yet he was faithful to the end of his life.

Ask God to make you like that.

a brainless fool. [18]Yet those other men keep telling you how wonderful they are, so here I go: [19,20](You think you are so wise—yet you listen gladly to those fools; you don't mind at all when they make you their slaves and take everything you have, and take advantage of you, and put on airs, and slap you in the face. [21]I'm ashamed to say that I'm not strong and daring like that!

But whatever they can boast about—I'm talking like a fool again—I can boast about it, too.)

[22]They brag that they are Hebrews, do they? Well, so am I. And they say that they are Israelites, God's chosen people? So am I. And they are descendants of Abraham? Well, I am too.

[23]They say they serve Christ? But I have served him far more! (Have I gone mad to boast like this?) I have worked harder, been put in jail more often, been whipped times without number, and faced death again and again and again. [24]Five different times the Jews gave me their terrible thirty-nine lashes. [25]Three times I was beaten with rods. Once

I was stoned. Three times I was shipwrecked. Once I was in the open sea all night and the whole next day. [26]I have traveled many weary miles and have been often in great danger from flooded rivers and from robbers and from my own people, the Jews, as well as from the hands of the Gentiles. I have faced grave dangers from mobs in the cities and from death in the deserts and in the stormy seas and from men who claim to be brothers in Christ but are not. [27]I have lived with weariness and pain and sleepless nights. Often I have been hungry and thirsty and have gone without food; often I have shivered with cold, without enough clothing to keep me warm.

[28]Then, besides all this, I have the constant worry of how the churches are getting along: [29]Who makes a mistake and I do not feel his sadness? Who falls without my longing to help him? Who is spiritually hurt without my fury rising against the one who hurt him?

[30]But if I must brag, I would rather brag about the things that show how weak I am. [31]God, the Father of our Lord Jesus Christ, who is to be praised forever and ever, knows I tell the truth. [32]For instance, in Damascus the governor under King Aretas kept guards at the city gates to catch me; [33]but I was let down by rope and basket from a hole in the city wall, and so I got away! [What popularity!]

SMOOTH TALK

11:3-4 The Corinthian believers fell for smooth talk and messages that sounded good and seemed to make sense. Today there are many false teachings that seem to make sense. Don't believe anyone simply because he or she sounds like an authority or says things you like to hear. Search the Bible and check people's words against God's Word. The Bible should be your authoritative guide to all teaching.

GOD said, I AM WITH YOU That is all you need. MY POWER shows up BEST in weak people. NOW I AM GLAD to BOAST about HOW weak I AM; I AM GLAD to be A LIVING DEMONSTRATION OF CHRIST'S POWER instead of SHOWING OFF MY OWN POWER AND ABILITIES

CHAPTER 12 PAUL'S PHYSICAL PROBLEMS. This boasting is all so foolish, but let me go on. Let me tell about the visions I've had, and revelations from the Lord.

[2,3]Fourteen years ago I was taken up to heaven for a visit. Don't ask me whether my body was there or just my spirit, for I don't know; only God can answer that. But anyway, there I was in paradise, [4]and heard things so astounding that they are beyond a man's power to describe or put in words (and anyway I am not allowed to tell them to others). [5]That experience is something worth bragging about, but I am not going to do it. I am going to boast only about how weak I am and how great God is to use such weakness for his glory. [6]I have plenty to boast about and would be no fool in doing it, but I don't want anyone to think more highly of me than he should from what he can actually see in my life and my message.

[7]I will say this: because these experiences I had were so tremendous, God was afraid I might be puffed up by them; so I was given a physical condition which has been a thorn in my flesh, a messenger from Satan to hurt and bother me and prick my pride. [8]Three different times I begged God to make me well again.

[9]Each time he said, "No. But I am with you; that is all you need. My power shows up best in weak people." Now I am glad to boast about how weak I am; I am glad to be a living demonstration of Christ's power, instead of showing off my own power and abilities. [10]Since I know it is all for Christ's good, I am quite happy about "the thorn," and about insults and hardships, persecutions and difficulties; for when I am weak, then I am strong—the less I have, the more I depend on him.

[11]You have made me act like a fool—boasting like this—for you people ought to be writing about me and not making me write about myself. There isn't a single thing these other marvelous fellows have that I don't have too, even though I am really worth nothing at all. [12]When I was there I certainly gave you every proof that I was truly an apostle, sent to you by God himself, for I patiently did many wonders and signs and mighty works among you. [13]The only thing I didn't do for you, which I do everywhere else in all other churches, was to become a burden to you—I didn't ask you to give me food to eat and a place to stay. Please forgive me for this wrong!

[14]Now I am coming to you again, the third time; and it is still not going to cost you anything, for I don't want your money. I want *you!* And anyway, you are my children, and little children don't pay for their father's and mother's food—it's the other way around; parents supply food for their children. [15]I am glad to give you myself and all I have for your spiritual good, even though it seems that the more I love you, the less you love me.

[16]Some of you are saying, "It's true that his visits didn't seem to cost us anything, but he is a sneaky fellow, that Paul, and he fooled us. As sure as anything he must have made money from us some way."

[17]But how? Did any of the men I sent to you take advantage of you? [18]When I urged Titus to visit you and sent our other brother with him, did they make any profit? No, of course not. For we have the same Holy Spirit and walk in each other's steps, doing things the same way.

[19]I suppose you think I am saying all this to get back into your good graces. That isn't it at all. I tell you, with God listening as I say it, that I have said this to help *you,* dear friends—to build you up spiritually—and not to help myself. [20]For I am afraid that when I come to visit you I won't like what I find, and then you won't like the way I will

have to act. I am afraid that I will find you quarreling, and envying each other, and being angry with each other, and acting big, and saying wicked things about each other and whispering behind each other's backs, filled with conceit and disunity. [21]Yes, I am afraid that when I come God will humble me before you and I will be sad and mourn because many of you have sinned before and don't even care about the wicked, impure things you have done: your lust and immorality, and the taking of other men's wives.

CHAPTER **13**   **CHECK UP ON YOURSELVES.** This is the third time I am coming to visit you. The Scriptures tell us that if two or three have seen a wrong, it must be punished. [Well, this is my third warning as I come now for this visit.] [2]I have already warned those who had been sinning when I was there last; now I warn them again and all others, just as I did then, that this time I come ready to punish severely and I will not spare them.

[3]I will give you all the proof you want that Christ speaks through me. Christ is not weak in his dealings with you but is a mighty power within you. [4]His weak, human body died on the cross, but now he lives by the mighty power of God. We, too, are weak in our bodies, as he was, but now we live and are strong, as he is, and have all of God's power to use in dealing with you.

[5]Check up on yourselves. Are you really Christians? Do you pass the test? Do you feel Christ's presence and power more and more within you? Or are you just pretending to be Christians when actually you aren't at all? [6]I hope you can agree that I have stood that test and truly belong to the Lord.

[7]I pray that you will live good lives, not because that will be a feather in our caps, proving that what we teach is right; no, for we want you to do right even if we ourselves are despised. [8]Our responsibility is to encourage the right at all times, not to hope for evil. [9]We are glad to be weak and despised if you are really strong. Our greatest wish and prayer is that you will become mature Christians.

[10]I am writing this to you now in the hope that I won't need to scold and punish when I come; for I want to use the Lord's authority that he has given me, not to punish you but to make you strong.

[11]I close my letter with these last words: Be happy. Grow in Christ. Pay attention to what I have said. Live in harmony and peace. And may the God of love and peace be with you.

[12]Greet each other warmly in the Lord. [13]All the Christians here send you their best regards. [14]May the grace of our Lord Jesus Christ be with you all. May God's love and the Holy Spirit's friendship be yours.

Paul

MEGA *Themes*

TRIALS Paul experienced great suffering, persecution, and opposition in his ministry. He even struggled with a personal weakness—a "thorn in the flesh." Through it all, Paul affirmed God's faithfulness.

God is faithful. His strength is sufficient for any trial—and trials can keep us from becoming prideful and teach us dependence on God. We must look to God for comfort during trials. As he comforts us, we can learn to comfort others.

1. What are some of the feelings Paul expressed regarding his personal trial?
2. What truth had Paul learned from his suffering and persecution?
3. Based on Paul's example, what feelings can you expect when you encounter trials?
4. What attitude does God want you to have during trials? Why?
5. Describe a time when you encountered personal difficulty. How did you feel then? How do you feel about the experience now? What did you learn about God from that experience?

CHURCH DISCIPLINE Paul defends his role in church discipline. Neither immorality nor false teaching could be ignored. The church was to be neither too lax nor too severe in administering discipline. The church was to restore the corrected person when he or she repented.

The goal of discipline in the church should be correction, not vengeance. For churches to be effective, they must confront and solve problems, not ignore them. But in everything we must act in and on behalf of God's love.

1. In 2:5-11, we are given a glimpse into what church discipline should be about. What does this passage teach you about Paul?
2. What was Paul's motive for seeing the person disciplined?
3. What should the church's role be when dealing with members who refuse to repent of sin?
4. What does this teach you about how God wants you to deal with your personal sins?

HOPE Paul tried to encourage the Corinthians as they faced trials by reminding them that they would receive new bodies in heaven. This would be a great victory in contrast to their present suffering.

Knowing we will receive new bodies gives us hope. No matter what we face, we can keep going, for our faithful service will result in triumph.

1. Summarize the hope Paul gives to the Corinthians in 5:1-11.

2. Why did Paul use this part of his letter to communicate this hope to the Corinthians? (See 4:13-18.)
3. Under what circumstances would you most need to be reminded of your heavenly hope?
4. How should being reminded of that promise bring hope to you in your present circumstances?

GIVING Paul organized a collection of funds for the poor in the Jerusalem church. Many of the Asian churches gave money. Paul explains and defends his beliefs about giving, and he urges the Corinthians to follow through on their previous commitment.

We, too, should honor our financial commitments. Our giving must be generous, sacrificial, according to a plan, and based on need. Generosity helps the needy, enabling them to thank God. Giving is a part of our godliness.

1. What benefit had Paul received from the believers' giving? What benefit had the believers themselves received as a result of their giving?
2. What should Christians understand about giving money for God's work in the church? How could this be applied to giving other personal resources, such as time and service?
3. In what ways would God want you to continue what you are doing in your giving? How should you change what you are doing?

SOUND DOCTRINE False teachers were challenging Paul's ministry and authority as an apostle. Paul asserted his authority to preserve correct Christian doctrine. His sincerity, love for Christ, and concern for the people were his defense.

We should share Paul's concern for correct teaching in our churches. In so doing, we must also share his motivation—love for Christ and people—and we should be sincere.

1. Describe the common characteristics of those who were opposing Paul (chapters 10–11).
2. How was Paul responding to their opposition? Why do you think he was so concerned about their influence?
3. Contrast Paul's ministry with the actions of those who opposed him. What were the key differences?
4. How can you avoid being deceived by teachers of false doctrine?
5. We must not only know sound doctrine, but also live according to its truth. What areas of your daily life reflect sound doctrine?

*E*ver known a church like Matt's? Words like *different* and *strict* don't even begin to tell the story. Maybe Matt's best friend Randy gave the best description. He attended Matt's church for several months—then quit. Matt wanted to know why. ■ "I just don't like it, OK?" Randy finally said. "It's the 'don't church.' You guys have about fifty million rules—Don't date. Don't wear certain clothes. Don't go to the movies. Don't dance. Don't go to parties. Don't wear jewelry. Don't be friends with non-Christians. And the list just keeps going. I can't even *remember* all the rules, much less *follow* them! Besides, some people there act like they're *better* than people who go to other churches." ■ "But you said you *liked* our preacher—and the services." ■ "I guess I did—at first. But I came home feeling more and more guilty, and further away from God than ever. Sorry Matt, but if following all those rules is how I'm supposed to get close to God, I might as well forget it . . . . Hey, I want to be a good Christian—but I'll never be *that* good." ■ Almost 2,000 years ago there was another "don't church" of Christians trying to follow rules. In fact, a whole book of the Bible addresses trying to *earn* God's acceptance by doing "right" things. ■ Read Galatians. You'll find that anyone who thinks the Bible doesn't relate to modern times has never read it!

STATS

PURPOSE: To refute the Judaizers (who taught that Gentile believers must obey the Jewish law to be saved), and to call Christians to faith and freedom in Christ

AUTHOR: Paul

TO WHOM WRITTEN: The churches in southern Galatia founded on Paul's first missionary journey (including Iconium, Lystra, Derbe), and Christians everywhere

DATE WRITTEN: About A.D. 49, from Antioch, prior to the Jerusalem Council (A.D. 50)

SETTING: The most pressing controversy of the early church was the relationship of new believers, especially Gentiles, to the Jewish laws. When this problem hit the converts and young churches Paul founded on his first missionary journey, Paul wrote to correct it. Later, at the council in Jerusalem, the conflict was officially resolved by the church leaders.

KEY PEOPLE: Paul, Peter, Barnabas, Titus, Abraham

KEY PLACES: Galatia, Jerusalem

Galatians

CHAPTER 1 PAUL: CHRIST'S MISSIONARY.

From: Paul the missionary and all the other Christians here.

To: The churches of Galatia.

I was not called to be a missionary by any group or agency. My call is from Jesus Christ himself and from God the Father who raised him from the dead. ³May peace and blessing be yours from God the Father and from the Lord Jesus Christ. ⁴He died for our sins just as God our Father planned, and rescued us from this evil world in which we live. ⁵All glory to God through all the ages of eternity. Amen.

⁶I am amazed that you are turning away so soon from God who, in his love and mercy, invited you to share the eternal life he gives through Christ; you are already following a different "way to heaven," which really doesn't go to heaven at all. ⁷For there is no other way than the one we showed you; you are being fooled by those who twist and change the truth concerning Christ.

⁸Let God's curses fall on anyone, including myself, who preaches any other way to be saved than the one we told you about; yes, if an angel comes from heaven and preaches any other message, let him be forever cursed. ⁹I will say it again: if anyone preaches any other gospel than the one you welcomed, let God's curse fall upon him.

¹⁰You can see that I am not trying to please you by sweet talk and flattery; no, I am trying to please God. If I were still trying to please men I could not be Christ's servant.

TWISTED

1:7 Twisted truth is sometimes more difficult to spot than outright lies. The Judaizers were twisting the truth about Christ. They claimed to follow him, but they denied that Jesus' work on the cross was sufficient for salvation. There will always be people who twist the Good News. Either they do not understand what the Bible teaches, or they are uncomfortable with the truth as it stands. How can we tell when people are twisting the truth? Find out what they teach about Jesus Christ. If their teaching does not match the truth in God's Word, then it is twisted.

CITIES IN GALATIA

Paul visited several cities in Galatia on each of his three missionary journeys. On his first journey he went through Antioch in Pisidia, Iconium, Lystra, and Derbe, then retraced his steps. On his second journey he went by land from Antioch in Syria through the four cities in Galatia. On his third journey he also went through those cities on the main route to Ephesus.

CHANGED

1:24 Paul's changed life brought many comments from people who saw or heard of him. His new life astonished them, and they glorified God because only God could have turned this zealous persecutor of Christians into a Christian himself. We may not have had as dramatic a change as Paul had, but our new life should glorify our Savior. When people look at us, do they recognize that God has made changes in us? If not, perhaps we are not living as we should.

[11]Dear friends, I solemnly swear that the way to heaven that I preach is not based on some mere human whim or dream. [12]For my message comes from no less a person than Jesus Christ himself, who told me what to say. No one else has taught me.

[13]You know what I was like when I followed the Jewish religion—how I went after the Christians mercilessly, hunting them down and doing my best to get rid of them all. [14]I was one of the most religious Jews of my own age in the whole country and tried as hard as I possibly could to follow all the old, traditional rules of my religion.

[15]But then something happened! For even before I was born, God had chosen me to be his and called me—what kindness and grace—[16]to reveal his Son within me so that I could go to the Gentiles and show them the Good News about Jesus.

When all this happened to me I didn't go at once and talk it over with anyone else; [17]I didn't go up to Jerusalem to consult with those who were apostles before I was. No, I went away into the deserts of Arabia and then came back to the city of Damascus.[18]It was not until three years later that I finally went to Jerusalem for a visit with Peter and stayed there with him for fifteen days. [19]And the only other apostle I met at that time was James, our Lord's brother. [20](Listen to what I am saying, for I am telling you this in the very presence of God. This is exactly what happened—I am not lying to you.) [21]Then after this visit I went to Syria and Cilicia. [22]And still the Christians in Judea didn't even know what I looked like. [23]All they knew was what people were saying, that "our former enemy is now preaching the very faith he tried to wreck." [24]And they gave glory to God because of me.

CHAPTER 2 CHURCH LEADERS ACCEPTED PAUL.

Then fourteen years later I went back to Jerusalem again, this time with Barnabas; and Titus came along too. [2]I went there with definite orders from God to confer with the brothers there about the message I was preaching to the Gentiles. I talked privately to the leaders of the church so that they would all understand just what I had been teaching and, I hoped, agree that it was right. ³And they did agree; they did not even demand that Titus, my companion, should be circumcised, though he was a Gentile.

⁴Even that question wouldn't have come up except for some so-called "Christians" there—false ones, really—who came to spy on us and see what freedom we enjoyed in Christ Jesus, as to whether we obeyed the Jewish laws or not. They tried to get us all tied up in their rules, like slaves in chains. ⁵But we did not listen to them for a single moment, for we did not want to confuse you into thinking that salvation can be earned by being circumcised and by obeying Jewish laws.

⁶And the great leaders of the church who were there had nothing to add to what I was preaching. (By the way, their being great leaders made no difference to me, for all are the same to God.) ⁷⁻⁹In fact, when Peter, James, and John, who were known as the pillars of the church, saw how greatly God had used me in winning the Gentiles, just as Peter had been blessed so greatly in his preaching to the Jews—for the same God gave us each our special gifts—they shook hands with Barnabas and me and encouraged us to keep right on with our preaching to the Gentiles while they continued their work with the Jews. ¹⁰The only thing they did suggest was that we must always remember to help the poor, and I, too, was eager for that.

¹¹But when Peter came to Antioch I had to oppose him publicly, speaking strongly against what he was doing, for it was very wrong. ¹²For when he first arrived, he ate with the Gentile Christians [who don't bother with circumcision and the many other Jewish laws]. But afterwards, when some Jewish friends of James came, he wouldn't eat with the Gentiles anymore because he was afraid of what these Jewish legalists, who insisted that circumcision was necessary for salvation, would say; ¹³and then all the other Jewish Christians and even Barnabas became hypocrites too, following Peter's example, though they certainly knew better. ¹⁴When I saw what was happening and that they weren't being honest about what they really believed and weren't following the truth of the Gospel, I said to Peter in front of all the others, "Though you are a Jew by birth, you have long since discarded the Jewish laws; so why, all of a sudden, are you trying to make these Gentiles obey them? ¹⁵You and I are Jews by birth, not mere Gentile sinners, ¹⁶and yet we Jewish Christians know very well that we cannot become right with God by obeying our Jewish laws but only by faith in Jesus Christ to take away our sins. And so we, too, have trusted Jesus Christ, that we might be accepted by God because of faith—and not because we have obeyed the Jewish laws. For no one will ever be saved by obeying them."

¹⁷But what if we trust Christ to save us and then find that we are wrong and that we cannot be saved without being circumcised and obeying all the other Jewish laws? Wouldn't we need to say that faith in Christ had ruined us? God forbid that anyone should dare to think such things about our Lord. ¹⁸Rather, we are sinners if we start rebuilding the old systems I have been destroying of trying to be saved by keeping Jewish laws, ¹⁹for it was through reading the Scripture that I came to realize that I could never find God's favor by trying—and failing—to obey the laws. I came to realize that acceptance with God comes by believing in Christ.

²⁰I have been crucified with Christ: and I myself no longer live, but Christ lives in me. And the real life I now have within this body is a result of my trusting in the Son of God, who loved me and gave himself for me. ²¹I am not one of those who treats Christ's death as meaningless. For if we could be saved by keeping Jewish laws, then there was no need for Christ to die.

POOR

2:10 Here the apostles were referring to the poor people of Jerusalem. While many Gentile converts were financially comfortable, the Jerusalem church was suffering from a severe famine in Palestine (see Acts 11:28-30). Much of Paul's time was spent gathering funds for the Jewish Christians (Acts 24:17; Romans 15:25-29; 1 Corinthians 16:1-4; 2 Corinthians 8). Believers caring for the poor is a constant theme of Scripture, but often we do nothing about it. Both in your own city and across the oceans, there are people who need help. What can you do to show them God's love?

CHAPTER 3 JEWISH LAW AND FAITH IN CHRIST. Oh, foolish Galatians! What magician has hypnotized you and cast an evil spell upon you? For you used to see the meaning of Jesus Christ's death as clearly as though I had waved a placard before you with a picture on it of Christ dying on the cross. ²Let me ask you this one question: Did you receive the Holy Spirit by trying to keep the Jewish laws? Of course not, for the Holy Spirit came upon you only after you heard about Christ and trusted him to save you. ³Then have you gone completely crazy? For if trying to obey the Jewish laws never gave you spiritual life in the first place, why do you think that trying to obey them now will make you stronger Christians? ⁴You have suffered so much for the Gospel. Now are you going to just throw it all overboard? I can hardly believe it!

⁵I ask you again, does God give you the power of the Holy Spirit and work miracles among you as a result of your trying to obey the Jewish laws? No,

of course not. It is when you believe in Christ and fully trust him.

[6]Abraham had the same experience—God declared him fit for heaven only because he believed God's promises. [7]You can see from this that the real children of Abraham are all the men of faith who truly trust in God.

[8,9]What's more, the Scriptures looked forward to this time when God would save the Gentiles also, through their faith. God told Abraham about this long ago when he said, "I will bless those in every nation who trust in me as you do." And so it is: all who trust in Christ share the same blessing Abraham received.

[10]Yes, and those who depend on the Jewish laws to save them are under God's curse, for the Scriptures point out very clearly, "Cursed is everyone who at any time breaks a single one of these laws that are written in God's Book of the Law." [11]Consequently, it is clear that no one can ever win God's favor by trying to keep the Jewish laws because God has said that the only way we can be right in his sight is by faith. As the prophet Habakkuk says it, "The man who finds life will find it through trusting God." [12]How different from this way of faith is the way of law, which says that a man is saved by obeying every law of God, without one slip. [13]But Christ has bought us out from under the doom of that impossible system by taking the curse for our wrongdoing upon himself. For it is written in the Scripture, "Anyone who is hanged on a tree is cursed" [as Jesus was hung upon a wooden cross].

[14]Now God can bless the Gentiles, too, with this same blessing he promised to Abraham; and all of us as Christians can have the promised Holy Spirit through this faith.

[15]Dear brothers, even in everyday life a promise made by one man to another, if it is written down and signed, cannot be changed. He cannot decide afterward to do something else instead.

[16]Now, God gave some promises to Abraham and his Child. And notice that it doesn't say the promises were to his *children,* as it would if all his sons—all the Jews—were being spoken of, but to his *Child*—and that, of course, means Christ. [17]Here's what I am trying to say: God's promise to save through faith—and God wrote this promise down and signed it—could not be canceled or changed four hundred and thirty years later when God gave the Ten Commandments. [18]If *obeying those laws* could save us, then it is obvious that this would be a different way of gaining God's favor than Abraham's way, for he simply accepted God's promise.

[19]Well then, why were the laws given? They were added after the promise was given, to show men how guilty they are of breaking God's laws. But this system of law was to last only until the coming of Christ, the Child to whom God's promise was made. (And there is this further difference. God gave his laws to angels to give to Moses, who then gave them to the people; [20]but when God gave his promise to Abraham, he did it by himself alone, without angels or Moses as go-betweens.)

[21,22]Well then, are God's laws and God's promises against each other? Of course not! If we could be saved by his laws, then God would not have had to give us a different way to get out of the grip of sin—for the Scriptures insist we are all its prisoners. The only way out is through faith in Jesus Christ; the way of escape is open to all who believe him.

[23]Until Christ came we were guarded by the law, kept in protective custody, so to speak, until we could believe in the coming Savior.

[24]Let me put it another way. The Jewish laws were our teacher and guide until Christ came to give us right standing with God through our faith. [25]But now that Christ has come, we don't need those laws any longer to guard us and lead us to him. [26]For now we are all children of God through faith in Jesus Christ, [27]and we who have been baptized into union with Christ are enveloped by him.

FREEDOM

Cindi storms up upstairs, slams her bedroom door, and flings herself onto the bed. Burying her face in a pillow, she lets out a yell of disgust.

Rolling over, she stares at the ceiling and begins thinking:

Ooooh. I can't believe them! They're like the Gestapo! Why don't they just go ahead and put bars around my room? They don't let me do anything. They ask me six million questions about everything. They hate all my friends. They make me dress like a street person.

Cindi glances at the calendar above her desk.

Nine more months—then I can go to college and do whatever I want. I'll be totally free. If I don't want to go to church, I won't have to. If I want to trash my room and leave it that way the whole semester, I can. I'll be able to go out when I want and see who I want without them totally humiliating me.

Oh, gosh, that is gonna be so great! No more missing out on life. There'll be parties, tons of awesome guys, and . . .

Cindi's daydream is shattered by a voice yelling:

"Cindi! Come pick up your shoes from out of the middle of the living room floor—now!"

Cindi groans, and heads downstairs, mumbling, "Enjoy it now, Mom. Because in nine months, I'm out of here."

Is that freedom? Being able to do whatever you want? Or does real freedom have certain limits? See Galatians 5:16-25 to find out.

²⁸We are no longer Jews or Greeks or slaves or free men or even merely men or women, but we are all the same—we are Christians; we are one in Christ Jesus. ²⁹And now that we are Christ's we are the true descendants of Abraham, and all of God's promises to him belong to us.

CHAPTER 4 PAUL'S CONCERN FOR THE GALATIANS.

But remember this, that if a father dies and leaves great wealth for his little son, that child is not much better off than a slave until he grows up, even though he actually owns everything his father had. ²He has to do what his guardians and managers tell him to until he reaches whatever age his father set.

³And that is the way it was with us before Christ came. We were slaves to Jewish laws and rituals, for we thought they could save us. ⁴But when the right time came, the time God decided on, he sent his Son, born of a woman, born as a Jew, ⁵to buy freedom for us who were slaves to the law so that he could adopt us as his very own sons. ⁶And because we are his sons, God has sent the Spirit of his Son into our hearts, so now we can rightly speak of God as our dear Father. ⁷Now we are no longer slaves but God's own sons. And since we are his sons, everything he has belongs to us, for that is the way God planned.

⁸Before you Gentiles knew God you were slaves to so-called gods that did not even exist. ⁹And now so that you have found God (or I should say, now that God has found you), how can it be that you want to go back again and become slaves once more to another poor, weak, useless religion of trying to get to heaven by obeying God's laws? ¹⁰You are trying to find favor with God by what you do or don't do on certain days or months or seasons or years. ¹¹I fear for you. I am afraid that all my hard work for you was worth nothing.

¹²Dear brothers, please feel as I do about these things, for I am as free from these chains as you

---

Ceremonial Law
This kind of law relates specifically to Israel's worship. Its primary purpose was to point forward to Jesus Christ. Therefore, these laws were no longer necessary after Jesus' death and resurrection. While we are no longer bound by ceremonial laws, the principles behind them—to worship and love a holy God—still apply. The Jewish Christians often accused the Gentile Christians of violating the ceremonial law.

Civil Law
This type of law dictated Israel's daily living. Because modern society and culture are so radically different, some of these guidelines cannot be followed specifically. But the principles behind the commands should guide our conduct. At times, Paul asked Gentile Christians to follow some of these laws, not because they had to, but to promote unity.

Moral Law
This sort of law is the direct command of God—for example, the Ten Commandments (Exodus 20:1-17). It requires strict obedience. It reveals the nature and will of God, and it still applies to us today. We are to obey this moral law, not to obtain salvation, but to live in ways pleasing to God.

WHAT IS THE LAW?

Part of the Jewish law included those laws found in the Old Testament. In the Old Testament there were three categories of law: ceremonial laws, civil laws, and moral laws. When Paul says that non-Jews (Gentiles) are no longer bound by these laws, he is not saying that the Old Testament laws do not apply to us today. He is saying certain types of laws may not apply to us.

BUT when the
HOLY SPIRIT
CONTROLS
OUR LIVES
HE *will produce*
this kind of fruit in **U**s:

Love
JOY
PEACE
P A T I E N C E
kindness
Goodness
F A I T H F U L N E S S
gentleness
SELF-CONTROL.

used to be. You did not despise me then when I first preached to you, [13]even though I was sick when I first brought you the Good News of Christ. [14]But even though my sickness was revolting to you, you didn't reject me and turn me away. No, you took me in and cared for me as though I were an angel from God or even Jesus Christ himself.

[15]Where is that happy spirit that we felt together then? For in those days I know you would gladly have taken out your own eyes and given them to replace mine if that would have helped me.

[16]And now have I become your enemy because I tell you the truth?

[17]Those false teachers who are so anxious to win your favor are not doing it for your good. What they are trying to do is to shut you off from me so that you will pay more attention to them. [18]It is a fine thing when people are nice to you with good motives and sincere hearts, especially if they aren't doing it just when I am with you! [19]Oh, my children, how you are hurting me! I am once again suffering for you the pains of a mother waiting for her child to be born—longing for the time when you will finally be filled with Christ. [20]How I wish I could be there with you right now and not have to

reason with you like this, for at this distance I frankly don't know what to do.

[21]Listen to me, you friends who think you have to obey the Jewish laws to be saved: Why don't you find out what those laws really mean? [22]For it is written that Abraham had two sons, one from his slave-wife and one from his freeborn wife. [23]There was nothing unusual about the birth of the slave-wife's baby. But the baby of the freeborn wife was born only after God had especially promised he would come.

[24,25]Now this true story is an illustration of God's two ways of helping people. One way was by giving them his laws to obey. He did this on Mount Sinai, when he gave the Ten Commandments to Moses. Mount Sinai, by the way, is called "Mount Hagar" by the Arabs—and in my illustration, Abraham's slave-wife Hagar represents Jerusalem, the mother-city of the Jews, the center of that system of trying to please God by trying to obey the Commandments; and the Jews, who try to follow that system, are her slave children. [26]But our mother-city is the heavenly Jerusalem, and she is not a slave to Jewish laws.

[27]That is what Isaiah meant when he prophesied, "Now you can rejoice, O childless woman; you can shout with joy though you never before had a child. For I am going to give you many children—more children than the slave-wife has."

[28]You and I, dear brothers, are the children that God promised, just as Isaac was. [29]And so we who are born of the Holy Spirit are persecuted now by those who want us to keep the Jewish laws, just as Isaac, the child of promise, was persecuted by Ishmael, the slave-wife's son.

[30]But the Scriptures say that God told Abraham to send away the slave-wife and her son, for the slave-wife's son could not inherit Abraham's home and lands along with the free woman's son. [31]Dear brothers, we are not slave children, obligated to the Jewish laws, but children of the free woman, acceptable to God because of our faith.

BE OPEN

4:16 Paul did not gain great popularity when he criticized the Galatians for turning away from their first faith in Christ. Human nature hasn't changed much—we still get angry when we're scolded. But don't write off someone who challenges you. There may be truth in what he says. Receive his words with humility; carefully think them over. If you discover you need to change an attitude or action, take steps to do it.

LOVE

5:14-15 When we are not motivated by love, we become critical of others. We stop looking for good in them and see only their faults. Soon the unity of believers becomes broken. Have you talked behind someone's back? Have you focused on others' shortcomings instead of their strengths? Remind yourself of Jesus' command to love others as we love ourselves (Matthew 22:39). When you begin to feel critical of someone, make a list of that person's positive qualities. And don't say anything behind his back that you wouldn't say to his face.

CHAPTER **5** **FREEDOM: CHRIST'S SPECIAL GIFT.**
So Christ has made us free. Now make sure that you stay free, and don't get all tied up again in the chains of slavery to Jewish laws and ceremonies. [2]Listen to me, for this is serious: *if you are counting on circumcision and keeping the Jewish laws to make you right with God, then Christ cannot save you.* [3]I'll say it again. Anyone trying to find favor with God by being circumcised must always obey every other Jewish law or perish. [4]Christ is useless to you if you are counting on clearing your debt to God by keeping those laws; you are lost from God's grace.

[5]But we by the help of the Holy Spirit are counting on Christ's death to clear away our sins and make us right with God. [6]And we to whom Christ has given eternal life don't need to worry about whether we have been circumcised or not, or whether we are obeying the Jewish ceremonies or not; for all we need is faith working through love.

[7]You were getting along so well. Who has interfered with you to hold you back from following the truth? [8]It certainly isn't God who has done it, for he is the one who has called you to freedom in Christ. [9]But it takes only one wrong person among you to infect all the others.

[10]I am trusting the Lord to bring you back to believing as I do about these things. God will deal with that person, whoever he is, who has been troubling and confusing you.

[11]Some people even say that I myself am preaching that circumcision and Jewish laws are necessary to the plan of salvation. Well, if I preached that, I would be persecuted no more—for that message doesn't offend anyone. The fact that I am still being persecuted proves that I am still preaching salvation through faith in the cross of Christ alone.

[12]I only wish these teachers who want you to cut yourselves by being circumcised would cut themselves off from you and leave you alone!

[13]For, dear brothers, you have been given freedom: not freedom to do wrong, but freedom to love and serve each other. [14]For the whole Law can be summed up in this one command: "Love others as you love yourself." [15]But if instead of showing love among yourselves you are always critical and catty, watch out! Beware of ruining each other.

[16]I advise you to obey only the Holy Spirit's instructions. He will tell you where to go and what to do, and then you won't always be doing the wrong things your evil nature wants you to. [17]For we naturally love to do evil things that are just the opposite from the things that the Holy Spirit tells us to do; and the good things we want to do when the Spirit has his way with us are just the opposite of our natural desires. These two forces within us are constantly fighting each other to win control

over us, and our wishes are never free from their pressures. [18]When you are guided by the Holy Spirit, you need no longer force yourself to obey Jewish laws.

[19]But when you follow your own wrong inclina-

I know that taking drugs is wrong, but the Bible doesn't talk about them. What should I say to someone if they ask me about drugs?

I WONDER . . .

There are some areas where the Bible is silent. A good example is R-rated movies. The Bible doesn't specifically forbid attending movies that contain vulgar language, violence, or sex. In such cases, it is essential to seek the wisdom of those who know God's word well. By looking at a number of passages, it is obvious we should avoid those kind of movies.

Of course, there are many areas where the Bible is specific in its warnings. Homosexuality is a good example (see 1 Corinthians 6:9-10). Then there are areas that are "hidden" to a degree. Taking drugs falls into this category.

Originally the New Testament was written in Greek, a much more complicated language than English. Trying to translate a word from Greek to English often can only be done by a phrase.

In Galatians 5:20, Christians are warned against becoming involved in spiritism. The word *spiritism* (encouraging the activity of demons), actually comes from the Greek noun, *pharmakeia*, from which we get the word *pharmacy* (better known as a drug store!). When most of the Bible was translated, drug problems were not common, but there was "spiritism."

The connection is frightening. Spiritism (sorcery, witchcraft) actually happens when drugs are taken! These aren't the aspirin type of drugs, but the kinds that alter a person's emotions, reflexes, and brain waves.

To get even more specific, taking drugs is like opening your subconscious to demons! The connection between drugs and witchcraft is easily seen by going to the original Greek word.

Unknowingly, a person who takes drugs opens himself or herself to demonic influence. It's like an invitation to the spirit world to start influencing that person's life. That's why it's so dangerous.

Although many may laugh at this explanation, it's a message that must be given to those who are taking drugs.

Drugs also should be avoided because they harm our bodies. The Bible is very clear about our responsibility to take care of ourselves. See 1 Corinthians 6:19-20; Romans 12:1-2; and 3 John 1:2-3.

---

tions, your lives will produce these evil results: impure thoughts, eagerness for lustful pleasure, [20]idolatry, spiritism (that is, encouraging the activity of demons), hatred and fighting, jealousy and anger, constant effort to get the best for yourself, complaints and criticisms, the feeling that everyone else is wrong except those in your own little

FRUIT

5:22-23 The Spirit produces character traits, not specific actions. We can't go out and *do* these things, and we can't obtain them by trying to get them. If we want the fruit of the Spirit to develop in our life, we must recognize that all of these characteristics are found in Christ. The way to grow them is to know Christ, love him, remember him, imitate him (see John 15:4-5). The result will be that we will fulfill the intended purpose of the law—loving God and man. Which of these qualities most needs further development in your life?

group—and there will be wrong doctrine, [21]envy, murder, drunkenness, wild parties, and all that sort of thing. Let me tell you again, as I have before, that anyone living that sort of life will not inherit the Kingdom of God.

[22]But when the Holy Spirit controls our lives he will produce this kind of fruit in us: love, joy, peace, patience, kindness, goodness, faithfulness, [23] gentleness and self-control; and here there is no conflict with Jewish laws.

[24]Those who belong to Christ have nailed their natural evil desires to his cross and crucified them there.

[25]If we are living now by the Holy Spirit's power, let us follow the Holy Spirit's leading in every part of our lives. [26]Then we won't need to look for honors and popularity, which lead to jealousy and hard feelings.

CHAPTER 6 WE REAP WHAT WE SOW.

Dear brothers, if a Christian is overcome by some sin, you who are godly should gently and humbly help him back onto the right path, remembering that next time it might be one of you who is in the wrong. [2]Share each other's troubles and problems, and so obey our Lord's command. [3]If anyone thinks he is too great to stoop to this, he is fooling himself. He is really a nobody.

[4]Let everyone be sure that he is doing his very best, for then he will have the personal satisfaction of work well done and won't need to compare himself with someone else. [5]Each of us must bear some faults and burdens of his own. For none of us is perfect!

[6]Those who are taught the Word of God should help their teachers by paying them.

[7]Don't be misled; remember that you can't ignore God and get away with it: a man will always reap just the kind of crop he sows! [8]If he sows to please his own wrong desires, he will be planting seeds of evil and he will surely reap a harvest of spiritual decay and death; but if he plants the good things of the Spirit, he will reap the everlasting life that the Holy Spirit gives him. [9]And let us not get tired of doing what is right, for after a while we will reap a harvest of blessing if we don't get discouraged and give up. [10]That's why whenever we can we should always be kind to everyone, and especially to our Christian brothers.

[11]I will write these closing words in my own handwriting. See how large I have to make the letters! [12]Those teachers of yours who are trying to convince you to be circumcised are doing it for just one reason: so that they can be popular and avoid the persecution they would get if they admitted that the cross of Christ alone can save. [13]And even those teachers who submit to circumcision don't try to keep the other Jewish laws; but they want you to be circumcised in order that they can boast that you are their disciples.

[14]As for me, God forbid that I should boast about anything except the cross of our Lord Jesus Christ. Because of that cross, my interest in all the attractive things of the world was killed long ago, and the world's interest in me is also long dead. [15]It doesn't make any difference now whether we have been circumcised or not; what counts is whether we really have been changed into new and different people.

[16]May God's mercy and peace be upon all of you who live by this principle and upon those everywhere who are really God's own.

[17]From now on please don't argue with me about these things, for I carry on my body the scars of the whippings and wounds from Jesus' enemies that mark me as his slave.

[18]Dear brothers, may the grace of our Lord Jesus Christ be with you all.

Sincerely, Paul

EVERY PART

5:25 God is interested in every part of our life, not just the spiritual part. As we live by the Holy Spirit's power, we need to submit every aspect of our life to God—emotional, physical, social, intellectual, and vocational. Paul says, "You're saved, so live like it!" The Holy Spirit is the source of your new life, so walk with him. Don't let anything or anyone else determine your values and standards in any area of your life.

MEGA *Themes*

LAW A group of Jewish teachers were insisting that non-Jewish believers obey Jewish laws and traditions. These teachers believed that a person was saved by following the law of Moses (with emphasis on circumcision, the sign of the covenant) in addition to faith in Christ. Paul opposed them, showing that the law can't save anyone.

The law can't save us. It wasn't ever meant to be our salvation. It was intended to be a guide, to point out our need to be forgiven. Christ fulfilled the obligations of the law for us. We must turn to him to be saved. Christ alone can make us right with God. Then we should obey God in response to what he has done for us.

1. What error had the Jewish believers made concerning the role of the law?
2. What truth did Paul use to correct their error?
3. Based on Galatians, why are good works not enough to bring a person salvation?
4. How does the law point out our need for salvation?
5. How should you respond to the law now that you have been saved through Jesus Christ?

FAITH God's gracious gift to us saves us from God's judgment and the penalty for sin. We receive salvation by faith—trusting in Christ, not in anything else. Becoming a Christian is in no way based on our work, wise choices, or good character. We can only be right with God by believing in Christ.

Eternal life comes only through faith in Christ. You must never add to this truth or twist it. We are saved by faith and faith alone. Have you placed your whole trust and confidence in Christ? He alone can forgive you and bring you into relationship with God.

1. What does it mean to be saved by faith?
2. How would you answer a person who said: "I have been good, so I know God will let me into heaven"?
3. In spite of your sin, God gave you faith. What does this reveal to you about God?
4. How have you responded to God's offer of salvation?

5. During this past week, how have you lived your life by faith?

FREEDOM Galatians sets forth our freedom in Christ. We are not under the jurisdiction of Jewish laws and traditions, nor under the authority of Jerusalem. Faith in Christ brings true freedom from sin and from the futile attempt to be right with God by keeping the law.

We are free in Christ, free to serve him—but freedom is a privilege. Let us use our freedom to love and to serve, not to do wrong.

1. Finish these sentences:
   a) Christian freedom means _____
   b) Christian freedom does not mean _____
2. In what ways could your freedom in Christ be misused?
3. For what purpose has God given you freedom? How are you fulfilling that purpose in your life?

HOLY SPIRIT We become Christians through the work of the Holy Spirit. The Spirit brings new life, and even our faith is a gift from him. The Holy Spirit instructs us, guides us, leads us, and gives us power. He ends our bondage to evil desires; brings us love, joy and peace; and changes us into the image of Christ.

When the Holy Spirit controls us, he produces his fruit in us. Through faith, we can have the Holy Spirit within us, strengthening and guarding us and helping us grow spiritually.

1. According to chapter 3, how does a person receive the Holy Spirit?
2. According to 5:16-26, what difference does the Holy Spirit bring to a person's life? What difference has the Holy Spirit made in your life?
3. Why do you need the Holy Spirit to be at work in your life?
4. What can you do to continue to "walk in the Spirit"?

An argument with a friend •A hug from Mom •A drive with Dad •A note in your locker •A prayer before bedtime ■ Every event of every day underlines this fundamental fact: *Life is made up of relationships.* We relate in a "horizontal" way to other people; we relate in a "vertical" manner to our Creator. Pretty basic stuff, right? ■ But here's where things get profound: Our problems, individual and national, are due to *broken-down relationships.* It's because we fail to relate properly to God and to each other that we lie, cheat, steal, murder, drink and drive, divorce, engage in illicit sex, abort our babies, fight wars, pollute, buy and sell drugs, ignore the needy, commit suicide, and all the other wrong things we do. ■ So what is the remedy for ruptured relationships? In a nutshell: *Jesus Christ can repair our broken-down relationships!* ■ First, Jesus pardons our sins, bringing us into a right relationship with God. (Get this—by faith in Christ we are adopted into God's family! We become his children . . . eternally!) Then Christ gives us the wisdom and the power to build stronger horizontal ties—with parents, friends, bosses . . . even enemies! ■ Can your relationships stand a little improving? Check out Ephesians. The first three chapters explain how Jesus has made it possible for us to know God in a personal way. The rest of the book provides practical tips for getting along with people. ■ Hey, it just might change your life!

STATS

PURPOSE: To strengthen the Christian faith of the believers in Ephesus by explaining the nature and purpose of the church, the body of Christ

AUTHOR: Paul

TO WHOM WRITTEN: The church at Ephesus, and all believers everywhere

DATE WRITTEN: About A.D. 60, from Rome, during Paul's imprisonment there

SETTING: The letter was not written to confront any heresy or problem. It was sent with Tychicus to strengthen and encourage area churches. Paul spent over three years with the Ephesian church; he was very close to them. His last meeting with the Ephesian elders was at Miletus (Acts 20:17-38)—a meeting filled with great sadness because Paul was leaving them forever. There are no specific references to people or problems in the Ephesian church, so Paul may have intended this letter to be read to all the area churches.

KEY PEOPLE: Paul, Tychicus

Ephesians

CHAPTER 1 **PAUL: A LOYAL FOLLOWER OF CHRIST.** Dear Christian friends at Ephesus, ever loyal to the Lord: This is Paul writing to you, chosen by God to be Jesus Christ's messenger. ²May his blessings and peace be yours, sent to you from God our Father and Jesus Christ our Lord.

³How we praise God, the Father of our Lord Jesus Christ, who has blessed us with every blessing in heaven because we belong to Christ.

⁴Long ago, even before he made the world, God chose us to be his very own through what Christ would do for us; he decided then to make us holy in his eyes, without a single fault—we who stand before him covered with his love. ⁵His unchanging plan has always been to adopt us into his own family by sending Jesus Christ to die for us. And he did this because he wanted to!

⁶Now all praise to God for his wonderful kindness to us and his favor that he has poured out upon us because we belong to his dearly loved Son. ⁷So overflowing is his kindness toward us that he took away all our sins through the blood of his Son, by whom we are saved; ⁸and he has showered down upon us the richness of his grace—for how well he understands us and knows what is best for us at all times.

⁹God has told us his secret reason for sending Christ, a plan he decided on in mercy long ago; ¹⁰and this was his purpose: that when the time is ripe he will gather us all together from wherever we are—in heaven or on earth—to be with him in

Ephesus was a strategic city, ranking in importance with Alexandria in Egypt and Antioch in Syria as a port. It lay on the westernmost edge of Asia Minor (modern-day Turkey), the most important port on the Aegean Sea on the main route from Rome to the east.

GOOD

2:3 The fact that all people, without exception, commit sin proves that they share in the sinful nature. Does this mean there are no good people who are not Christians? Of course not—many people do good to others. On a relative scale, many are moral, kind, keep the laws, and so on. Comparing these people to criminals, we would say they are very good indeed. But on God's absolute scale, *no one* is good. Only through uniting our life to Christ's perfect life can we become good in God's sight.

Christ forever. [11]Moreover, because of what Christ has done, we have become gifts to God that he delights in, for as part of God's sovereign plan we were chosen from the beginning to be his, and all things happen just as he decided long ago. [12]God's purpose in this was that we should praise God and give glory to him for doing these mighty things for us, who were the first to trust in Christ.

[13]And because of what Christ did, all you others too, who heard the Good News about how to be saved, and trusted Christ, were marked as belonging to Christ by the Holy Spirit, who long ago had been promised to all of us Christians. [14]His presence within us is God's guarantee that he really will give us all that he promised; and the Spirit's seal upon us means that God has already purchased us and that he guarantees to bring us to himself. This is just one more reason for us to praise our glorious God.

[15]That is why, ever since I heard of your strong faith in the Lord Jesus and of the love you have for Christians everywhere, [16,17]I have never stopped thanking God for you. I pray for you constantly, asking God, the glorious Father of our Lord Jesus Christ, to give you wisdom to see clearly and really understand who Christ is and all that he has done for you. [18]I pray that your hearts will be flooded with light so that you can see something of the future he has called you to share. I want you to realize that God has been made rich because we who are Christ's have been given to him! [19]I pray that you will begin to understand how incredibly great his power is to help those who believe him. It is that same mighty power [20]that raised Christ from the dead and seated him in the place of honor at God's right hand in heaven, [21]far, far above any other king or ruler or dictator or leader. Yes, his honor is far more glorious than that of anyone else either in this world or in the world to come. [22]And God has put all things under his feet and made him the supreme Head of the Church—[23]which is his body, filled with himself, the Author and Giver of everything everywhere.

CHAPTER 2 OUR LIFE BEFORE AND AFTER CHRIST.

Once you were under God's curse, doomed forever for your sins. ²You went along with the crowd and were just like all the others, full of sin, obeying Satan, the mighty prince of the power of the air, who is at work right now in the hearts of those who are against the Lord. ³All of us used to be just as they are, our lives expressing the evil within us, doing every wicked thing that our passions or our evil thoughts might lead us into. We started out bad, being born with evil natures, and were under God's anger just like everyone else.

⁴But God is so rich in mercy; he loved us so much ⁵that even though we were spiritually dead and doomed by our sins, he gave us back our lives again when he raised Christ from the dead—only by his undeserved favor have we ever been saved—⁶and lifted us up from the grave into glory along with Christ, where we sit with him in the heavenly realms—all because of what Christ Jesus did. ⁷And now God can always point to us as examples of how very, very rich his kindness is, as shown in all he has done for us through Jesus Christ.

⁸Because of his kindness, you have been saved through trusting Christ. And even trusting is not of yourselves; it too is a gift from God. ⁹Salvation is not a reward for the good we have done, so none of us can take any credit for it. ¹⁰It is God himself who has made us what we are and given us new lives from Christ Jesus; and long ages ago he planned that we should spend these lives in helping others.

¹¹Never forget that once you were heathen and that you were called godless and "unclean" by the Jews. (But their hearts, too, were still unclean, even though they were going through the ceremonies and rituals of the godly, for they circumcised themselves as a sign of godliness.) ¹²Remember that in those days you were living utterly apart from Christ; you were enemies of God's children, and he had promised you no help. You were lost, without God, without hope.

¹³But now you belong to Christ Jesus, and though you once were far away from God, now you have been brought very near to him because of what Jesus Christ has done for you with his blood.

¹⁴For Christ himself is our way of peace. He has made peace between us Jews and you Gentiles by making us all one family, breaking down the wall of contempt that used to separate us. ¹⁵By his death he ended the angry resentment between us, caused by the Jewish laws that favored the Jews and excluded the Gentiles, for he died to annul that whole system of Jewish laws. Then he took the two groups that had been opposed to each other and made them parts of himself; thus he fused us together to become one new person, and at last there was peace. ¹⁶As parts of the same body, our anger against each other has disappeared, for both of us have been reconciled to God. And so the feud ended at last at the cross. ¹⁷And he has brought this Good News of peace to

GUILTY

2:11-13 Jews and Gentiles alike could be guilty of spiritual pride—Jews for thinking their ceremonies elevated them above everyone else, Gentiles for forgetting the hopelessness of their condition apart from Christ. Spiritual pride blinds us to our own faults and magnifies the faults of others. Be careful not to become proud of your salvation. Instead, humbly thank God for what he has done and encourage others who might be struggling in their faith.

OUR LIFE BEFORE AND AFTER CHRIST

Before	After
Under God's curse	Loved by God
Doomed because of our sins	Shown God's mercy and given salvation
Went along with the crowd	Stand for Christ and truth
God's enemies	God's children
Enslaved to Satan	Free to love and serve Christ
Followed our evil thoughts and passions	Seated with Christ in glory
Under God's anger	Given undeserved favor
Spiritually dead	Given new spiritual life in Christ

MARRIAGE

Maria was 23 years old, bright, attractive—and headed for divorce. She and Danny had been married two years. Now she sat in her former youth pastor's office and dissolved into tears. **"I**t's not working out," she choked out between sobs. "I don't know what happened. We were really in love, but we've lost something. I don't think we're going to make it. . . ." **T**ragically, this scene is repeated over and over.

Why is it that two people who are "made for each other" so often end up looking for the escape hatch labeled "divorce"? Maybe a better question is: What does it take to keep a marriage from becoming a casualty? **I**f marriage were just another human institution—like a corporation or a university—then getting out of it would be no more significant or painful than changing jobs or switching schools. Indeed, many people have tried to treat marriage that way, as something to enjoy when it's good or helpful and to terminate when it isn't. But those who have experienced a divorce will explain that a failed marriage is infinitely more painful. There's more to marriage than the human dimension. **M**arriage was God's holy and sacred idea. He performed the first "wedding" in the garden of Eden (Gen. 2:18-25), thus setting up guidelines for all people to follow: marriage is for one man and one woman for life. There are valid reasons for sometimes breaking this pattern (for example, death or adultery). But the intended pattern is one man, one woman, for life. Unfortunately, in a fallen world it often is difficult to submit to God's standards, especially since his standards do not change. **M**arriage is a covenant between a husband and wife. A covenant is an agreement between two people (or groups) that has benefits for keeping the arrangement and penalties for breaking it. Our relationship to God is described in covenant language throughout Scripture. The marriage relationship is described as a covenant (Malachi 2:14-15), and is used as an illustration of our relationship with God (Hosea 1:2; Ephesians 5:22-33). Just as our relationship with God is built on his steadfast, unchanging love and commitment toward us, so a marriage relationship is designed to be solid, faithful, and committed. Therein lies another extremely important—but often overlooked—principle for a successful marriage: commitment. **M**arriage is based on commitment, not emotions. The emotional rush two people experience when they "fall in love" and when they decide to marry is wonderful. It also is a terribly inadequate basis for marriage. That "rush," as powerful and enjoyable as it may be, will undoubtedly wear off at some point. If that's what the relationship is based on—physical attraction, romantic ideals, passion—the flame may burn brightly, but it will not burn for long. **R**omance, sexual attraction, and passion are tremendous God-given elements of a love relationship. But do not mistake them for the foundation of a lifelong commitment. They are like icing on a cake. Icing makes the cake much sweeter, but a diet of 100 percent refined sugar doesn't make for good health. **T**o survive the pressure and temptations that attack a marriage, both husband and wife have to be totally committed to making it work. Even when the romance is gone (as it sometimes will be in any marriage when the money is tight, or the urge to run out is overwhelming, Christians must stand strong on the commitment they have made. Instead of allowing the stresses to divide them, they must cling that much more tightly together. "What God has joined together, let no one"—and no thing—"separate." **M**arriage, when seen from God's perspective, can be one of his greatest gifts to his children. It can also, as Maria and millions of others have unfortunately discovered, be a source of deepest pain. Whether or not to marry—and what happens if you do marry—is up to you.

you Gentiles who were very far away from him, and to us Jews who were near. [18]Now all of us, whether Jews or Gentiles, may come to God the Father with the Holy Spirit's help because of what Christ has done for us.

[19]Now you are no longer strangers to God and foreigners to heaven, but you are members of God's very own family, citizens of God's country, and you belong in God's household with every other Christian.

[20]What a foundation you stand on now: the apostles and the prophets; and the cornerstone of the building is Jesus Christ himself! [21]We who believe are carefully joined together with Christ as parts of a beautiful, constantly growing temple for God. [22]And you also are joined with him and with each other by the Spirit and are part of this dwelling place of God.

CHAPTER **3** **SALVATION IS FOR EVERYONE.** I, Paul, the servant of Christ, am here in jail because of you—for preaching that you Gentiles are a part of God's house. [2,3]No doubt you already know that God has given me this special work of showing God's favor to you Gentiles, as I briefly mentioned before in one of my letters. God himself showed me this secret plan of his, that the Gentiles, too, are included in his kindness. [4]I say this to explain to you how I know about these things. [5]In olden times God did not share this plan with his people, but now he has revealed it by the Holy Spirit to his apostles and prophets.

[6]And this is the secret: that the Gentiles will have their full share with the Jews in all the riches inherited by God's sons; both are invited to belong to his Church, and all of God's promises of mighty blessings through Christ apply to them both when they accept the Good News about Christ and what he has done for them. [7]God has given me the wonderful privilege of telling everyone about this plan of his; and he has given me his power and special ability to do it well.

[8]Just think! Though I did nothing to deserve it, and though I am the most useless Christian there is, yet I was the one chosen for this special joy of telling the Gentiles the Glad News of the endless treasures available to them in Christ; [9]and to explain to everyone that God is the Savior of the Gentiles too, just as he who made all things had secretly planned from the very beginning.

[10]And his reason? To show to all the rulers in heaven how perfectly wise he is when all of his family—Jews and Gentiles alike—are seen to be joined together in his Church [11]in just the way he had always planned it through Jesus Christ our Lord.

[12]Now we can come fearlessly right into God's presence, assured of his glad welcome when we come with Christ and trust in him.

[13]So please don't lose heart at what they are doing to me here. It is for you I am suffering, and you should feel honored and encouraged.

[14,15]When I think of the wisdom and scope of his plan, I fall down on my knees and pray to the Father of all the great family of God—some of them already in heaven and some down here on earth—[16]that out of his glorious, unlimited resources he will give you the mighty inner strengthening of his Holy Spirit. [17]And I pray that Christ will be more and more at home in your hearts, living within you as you trust in him. May your roots go down deep into the soil of God's marvelous love; [18,19]and may you be able to feel and understand, as all God's children should, how long, how wide, how deep, and how high his love really is; and to experience this love for yourselves, though it is so great that you will never see the end of it or fully know or understand it. And so at last you will be filled up with God himself.

[20]Now glory be to God, who by his mighty

May you be able to feel and understand,

as all God's children should,

HOW L O N G

HOW WIDE

HOW DEEP

and HOW HIGH

HIS LOVE *really is;*

and to experience this LOVE for yourselves....

AND SO AT L A S T

you will be filled up with

GOD HIMSELF.

EPHESIANS 3:18-19

power at work within us is able to do far more than we would ever dare to ask or even dream of—infinitely beyond our highest prayers, desires, thoughts, or hopes. [21]May he be given glory forever and ever through endless ages because of his master plan of salvation for the Church through Jesus Christ.

CHAPTER 4 SPECIAL ABILITIES.

I beg you—I, a prisoner here in jail for serving the Lord—to live and act in a way worthy of those who have been chosen for such wonderful blessings as these. [2]Be humble and gentle. Be patient with each other, making allowance for each other's faults because of your love. [3]Try always to be led along together by the Holy Spirit and so be at peace with one another.

[4]We are all parts of one body, we have the same Spirit, and we have all been called to the same glorious future. [5]For us there is only one Lord, one faith, one baptism, [6]and we all have the same God and Father who is over us all and in us all, and living through every part of us. [7]However, Christ has given each of us special abilities—whatever he wants us to have out of his rich storehouse of gifts.

[8]The psalmist tells about this, for he says that when Christ returned triumphantly to heaven after his resurrection and victory over Satan, he gave generous gifts to men. [9]Notice that it says he returned to heaven. This means that he had first come down from the heights of heaven, far down to the lowest parts of the earth. [10]The same one who came down is the one who went back up, that he might fill all things everywhere with himself, from the very lowest to the very highest.

[11]Some of us have been given special ability as apostles; to others he has given the gift of being able to preach well; some have special ability in winning people to Christ, helping them to trust him as their Savior; still others have a gift for caring for God's people as a shepherd does his sheep, leading and teaching them in the ways of God.

[12]Why is it that he gives us these special abilities to do certain things best? It is that God's people will be equipped to do better work for him, building up the Church, the body of Christ, to a position of strength and maturity; [13]until finally we all believe alike about our salvation and about our Savior, God's Son, and all become full-grown in the Lord—yes, to the point of being filled full with Christ.

[14]Then we will no longer be like children, forever changing our minds about what we believe because someone has told us something different or has cleverly lied to us and made the lie sound like the truth. [15,16]Instead, we will lovingly follow the truth at all times—speaking truly, dealing truly, living truly—and so become more and more in every way like Christ who is the Head of his body, the Church. Under his direction, the whole body is fitted together perfectly, and each part in its own special way helps the other parts, so that the whole body is healthy and growing and full of love.

[17,18]Let me say this, then, speaking for the Lord: Live no longer as the unsaved do, for they are blinded and confused. Their closed hearts are full of darkness; they are far away from the life of God because they have shut their minds against him, and they cannot understand his ways. [19]They don't care anymore about right and wrong and have given themselves over to impure ways. They stop at nothing, being driven by their evil minds and reckless lusts.

[20]But that isn't the way Christ taught you! [21]If you have really heard his voice and learned from him the truths concerning himself, [22]then throw off your old evil nature—the old you that was a partner in your evil ways—rotten through and through, full of lust and sham.

[23]Now your attitudes and thoughts must all be constantly changing for the better. [24]Yes, you must be a new and different person, holy and good. Clothe yourself with this new nature.

[25]Stop lying to each other; tell the truth, for we are parts of each other and when we lie to each other we are hurting ourselves. [26]If you are angry, don't sin by nursing your grudge. Don't let the sun go down with you still angry—get over it quickly; [27]for when you are angry, you give a mighty foothold to the devil.

[28]If anyone is stealing he must stop it and begin using those hands of his for honest work so he can give to others in need. [29]Don't use bad language. Say only what is good and helpful to those you are talking to, and what will give them a blessing.

DATING

Michelle met Greg at a party during the holidays, and they've been going out ever since. She fell in love with his quick wit, and he fell right into her baby blue eyes.

In some ways, theirs is a really positive relationship. They both have trusted Christ as their Savior. They share a lot of the same interests and goals. They even attend a campus Bible study together.

But there are also some negative aspects to the "Michelle-n-Greg" romance. For instance, on the weekends the two have gradually gotten into the habit of watching whatever movies happen to be on cable TV (that usually means a large dose of skin, sex, and raw language). At the same time, Michelle has noticed that four-letter words are slipping out of her mouth with increasing frequency (she never used to say such things)! And, as if that weren't enough to deal with, Michelle and Greg suddenly seem powerless to resist the constant sexual pressures they feel (they haven't gone all the way, but they've come awfully close).

"What's happened to us?" Michelle asks. "It's like we've thrown our standards out the window!"

What would you do in Michelle's situation? Find help in Ephesians 5:3-11.

[30]Don't cause the Holy Spirit sorrow by the way you live. Remember, he is the one who marks you to be present on that day when salvation from sin will be complete.

[31]Stop being mean, bad-tempered, and angry. Quarreling, harsh words, and dislike of others should have no place in your lives. [32]Instead, be kind to each other, tenderhearted, forgiving one another, just as God has forgiven you because you belong to Christ.

CHAPTER 5 LEARN WHAT PLEASES GOD. Follow

God's example in everything you do just as a much loved child imitates his father. [2]Be full of love for others, following the example of Christ who loved you and gave himself to God as a sacrifice to take away your sins. And God was pleased, for Christ's love for you was like sweet perfume to him.

[3]Let there be no sex sin, impurity or greed among you. Let no one be able to accuse you of any such things. [4]Dirty stories, foul talk, and coarse jokes—these are not for you. Instead, remind each other of God's goodness, and be thankful.

[5]You can be sure of this: The Kingdom of Christ and of God will never belong to anyone who is impure or greedy, for a greedy person is really an idol worshiper—he loves and worships the good things of this life more than God. [6]Don't be fooled by those who try to excuse these sins, for the terrible wrath of God is upon all those who do them. [7]Don't even associate with such people. [8]For though once your heart was full of darkness, now it is full of light from the Lord, and your behavior should show it! [9]Because of this light within you, you should do only what is good and right and true.

[10]Learn as you go along what pleases the Lord. [11]Take no part in the worthless pleasures of evil and darkness, but instead, rebuke and expose them. [12]It would be shameful even to mention here those pleasures of darkness that the ungodly do. [13]But when you expose them, the light shines in upon their sin and shows it up, and when they see how wrong they really are, some of them may even become children of light! [14]That is why God says in the Scriptures, "Awake, O sleeper, and rise up from the dead; and Christ shall give you light."

[15,16]So be careful how you act; these are difficult days. Don't be fools; be wise: make the most of every opportunity you have for doing good. [17]Don't act thoughtlessly, but try to find out and do whatever the Lord wants you to. [18]Don't drink too much wine, for many evils lie along that path; be filled instead with the Holy Spirit and controlled by him.

[19]Talk with each other much about the Lord, quoting psalms and hymns and singing sacred songs, making music in your hearts to the Lord. [20]Always give thanks for everything to our God and Father in the name of our Lord Jesus Christ.

[21]Honor Christ by submitting to each other. [22]You wives must submit to your husbands' leadership in the same way you submit to the Lord. [23]For a husband is in charge of his wife in the same way

---

What does it mean to "grow as a Christian"?

Spiritual growth is a lot like physical growth. To stay healthy and grow physically, we must eat the right foods, exercise, and get plenty of rest. You've heard that since you were a child. According to Scripture, especially in verses such as Ephesians 4:14-15, growing spiritually involves the same formula.

Christians must eat the right "spiritual food": God's Word. Many Christians are trying to survive on spiritual "fast food." That is, they watch Christian TV, read Christian magazines, and listen to Christian music, but they rarely give attention to God's Word. There is only one food that will nourish our souls—reading the Bible. Everything else is only meant to be supplementary.

Christians exercise through resisting temptation, enduring trials, serving others, and telling others about our faith. We need to be pushed to stay strong. This means exercise. Temptation and problems test our character; serving others stretches our faith; telling people about Christ strengthens our devotion.

Christians rest through worship. Our world has a tendency to tighten us, like a rubber band pulled to the limit. Unless we take time weekly (and daily!) to recognize and worship God, he won't have the opportunity to minister to our needs.

We need sleep, rest, and times of vacation to get our physical batteries recharged. In the same way, we need worship to keep us spiritually renewed.

Spiritual growth takes time—a lifetime! This means growing in a relationship, not just changing our behavior. Growing a strong Christian life means learning how to love the person of Jesus Christ more each day, staying close to him and getting to know him better.

Christ is in charge of his body the Church. (He gave his very life to take care of it and be its Savior!) [24]So you wives must willingly obey your husbands in everything, just as the Church obeys Christ.

[25]And you husbands, show the same kind of love to your wives as Christ showed to the Church when he died for her, [26]to make her holy and clean, washed by baptism and God's Word; [27]so that he could give her to himself as a glorious Church without a single spot or wrinkle or any other blemish, being holy and without a single fault. [28]That is how husbands should treat their wives, loving them as parts of themselves. For since a man and his wife are now one, a man is really doing himself a favor and loving himself when he loves his wife! [29,30]No one hates his own body but lovingly cares for it, just as Christ cares for his body the Church, of which we are parts.

[31](That the husband and wife are one body is

proved by the Scripture, which says, "A man must leave his father and mother when he marries so that he can be perfectly joined to his wife, and the two shall be one.") ³²I know this is hard to understand, but it is an illustration of the way we are parts of the body of Christ.

³³So again I say, a man must love his wife as a part of himself; and the wife must see to it that she deeply respects her husband—obeying, praising, and honoring him.

CHAPTER **6** **FAMILY ADVICE.** Children, obey your parents; this is the right thing to do because God has placed them in authority over you. ²Honor your father and mother. This is the first of God's Ten Commandments that ends with a promise. ³And this is the promise: that if you honor your father and mother, yours will be a long life, full of blessing.

⁴And now a word to you parents. Don't keep on scolding and nagging your children, making them angry and resentful. Rather, bring them up with the loving discipline the Lord himself approves, with suggestions and godly advice.

⁵Slaves, obey your masters; be eager to give them your very best. Serve them as you would Christ. ⁶,⁷Don't work hard only when your master is watching and then shirk when he isn't looking; work hard and with gladness all the time, as though working for

---

GOD'S ARMOR FOR US

We are engaged in a spiritual battle—all believers find themselves subject to Satan's attacks because they are no longer on Satan's side. Thus, Paul tells us to use every piece of God's armor to resist Satan's attacks and to stand true to God in the midst of them.

Piece of Armor	Use	Application
STRONG BELT	Truth	Satan fights with lies, and sometimes his lies sound like truth; but believers have God's truth, which can defeat Satan's lies.
BREASTPLATE	God's approval	Satan often attacks our heart—the seat of our emotions, self-worth, and trust. God's approval is the breastplate that protects our heart. He approves of us because we have trusted Christ to save us and cleanse our hearts from sin.
SHOES	Readiness to spread the Good News	Satan wants us to think that telling others the Good News is a worthless and hopeless task—the size of the task is too big, and the negative responses are too much to handle. But the "shoes" God gives us are the motivation to continually proclaim the true peace that is available in God—news everyone needs to hear.
SHIELD	Faith	The shield of faith protects us from Satan's flaming arrows in the form of insults, setbacks, and temptations. With God's perspective, we can see beyond our circumstances and know that ultimate victory is ours.
HELMET	Salvation	Satan wants to make us doubt God, Jesus, and our salvation. The helmet protects our mind from doubting God's saving work for us.
SWORD	The Word of God	The sword is the only weapon of offense in this list of armor. There are times when we need to take the offensive against Satan. When we are tempted, we need to trust in the truth of God's Word.

So *use*
EVeRy PieCe
of GOD'S **ARMOR**
to RESIST
the **enemy**
W H E N E V E R
he *attacks*
and when
it is a l l o v e r
YOU *will*
STILL BE
STANDING UP.

EPHESIANS 6:13

peace with God. [16]In every battle you will need faith as your shield to stop the fiery arrows aimed at you by Satan. [17]And you will need the helmet of salvation and the sword of the Spirit—which is the Word of God.

[18]Pray all the time. Ask God for anything in line with the Holy Spirit's wishes. Plead with him, reminding him of your needs, and keep praying earnestly for all Christians everywhere. [19]Pray for me, too, and ask God to give me the right words as I boldly tell others about the Lord and as I explain to them that his salvation is for the Gentiles too. [20]I am in chains now for preaching this message from God. But pray that I will keep on speaking out boldly for him even here in prison, as I should.

[21]Tychicus, who is a much-loved brother and faithful helper in the Lord's work, will tell you all about how I am getting along. [22]I am sending him to you for just this purpose: to let you know how we are and be encouraged by his report.

[23]May God give peace to you, my Christian brothers, and love, with faith from God the Father and the Lord Jesus Christ. [24]May God's grace and blessing be upon all who sincerely love our Lord Jesus Christ.

Sincerely, Paul

Christ, doing the will of God with all your hearts. [8]Remember, the Lord will pay you for each good thing you do, whether you are slave or free.

[9]And you slave owners must treat your slaves right, just as I have told them to treat you. Don't keep threatening them; remember, you yourselves are slaves to Christ; you have the same Master they do, and he has no favorites.

[10]Last of all I want to remind you that your strength must come from the Lord's mighty power within you. [11]Put on all of God's armor so that you will be able to stand safe against all strategies and tricks of Satan. [12]For we are not fighting against people made of flesh and blood, but against persons without bodies—the evil rulers of the unseen world, those mighty satanic beings and great evil princes of darkness who rule this world; and against huge numbers of wicked spirits in the spirit world.

[13]So use every piece of God's armor to resist the enemy whenever he attacks, and when it is all over, you will still be standing up.

[14]But to do this, you will need the strong belt of truth and the breastplate of God's approval. [15]Wear shoes that are able to speed you on as you preach the Good News of

"Here's what I did..."

"Greg, what have you decided about going to the college we talked about? The deadline is coming up, isn't it?" Though my dad was trying to be casual, I could tell he wanted an answer.

"Yeah, I've decided. I don't want to go to that school, but you won't take that for an answer," I said.

"Greg," Dad began, but I could tell by his tone what he was going to say. We'd been through this too many times before. I didn't want to go; he wanted me to—and his pressuring me just made me angry.

I talked to my youth pastor about it the next day. "What do you think the Bible says about your situation?" Les asked me.

"Well, I know I'm not supposed to be angry at my dad, but I can't stand him pressuring me."

"Read Ephesians and let me know what you discover," Les suggested. So I read the book of Ephesians—and I saw that I can't always do what I want. Loving God means wanting to do *his* will, not mine. When I read Ephesians 6:1-3, I realized that God often chooses to work through my earthly parents. I tried to think through all the reasons Dad wanted me to go to that particular college and why I didn't want to go. Finally I decided it would be best to trust God and believe that he was leading me there.

God did bless my decision to attend this college. I am really growing in my faith here.

Greg
AGE 19

SATAN

April, 1989—Matamoros, Mexico: Police unearth thirteen bodies, all showing signs of torture and mutilation. The cause? The murders were part of satanic sacrificial rites. Satan, the deceiver, the evil one, the tempter. The Bible has many names for the devil. And today, interest in Satan and satanism—and activities performed in Satan's name—are on the rise. What does the Bible teach about this dark creature?

In the Old Testament, the Hebrew word from which we get "Satan" primarily means "adversary." Passages such as 1 Chronicles 21:1, Job 1–2, and Zechariah 3 portray him as an accuser of God's people. It is historically believed that Satan was behind the serpent that deceived Eve in Genesis 3. Many interpret Isaiah 14 (a prophecy about the "king of Babylon") as a veiled reference to Satan: "How you are fallen from heaven, O Lucifer, son of the morning!" The New Testament is filled with references to Satan. Matthew 4:1-11 and Mark 1:12-13 tell of Jesus' being tempted by Satan. In Matthew 12 Jesus describes Satan as "the evil prince of this world" (John 12:31, 14:30, and 16:11). Passages such as Matthew 13:19; 2 Corinthians 4:4; and Ephesians 6:16 show that Satan's goal is to keep people from hearing, understanding, and believing God's Word and the good news of salvation through Christ. Ultimately, Satan wants to destroy us: "Satan, your great enemy . . . prowls around like a hungry, roaring lion, looking for some victim to tear apart" (1 Peter 5:8. See also 2 Thessalonians 2:1-12 and Revelation 13). Satan is a powerful enemy, but the universe is not a cosmic tug-of-war contest between God and Satan. For all Satan's power and cunning, he is not God's equal; he is one of God's creatures, given some freedom to cause evil for a period of time. Satan is like a mean dog on a leash. If you get close to him he can hurt you; but his Master can always rein him in. (Just turn to the last book of the Bible, the Revelation, to see how the battle turns out.) Some find it difficult to believe in Satan. Others, like many heavy metal bands, display an obsessive preoccupation with the satanic world and the occult. Over 50 years ago, in The Screwtape Letters, C. S. Lewis wrote: "There are two equal and opposite errors into which our race can fall about the devils. One is to disbelieve in their existence. The other is to believe, and to feel an excessive and unhealthy interest in them. They themselves are equally pleased by both errors." The Bible clearly teaches that there is a literal, personal evil being called Satan. He is not to be taken lightly, but neither does the Christian need to be afraid. We know the one who holds Satan's leash securely in his nail-scarred hands.

MEGA *Themes*

GOD'S PURPOSE FOR A LIVING CHURCH

According to God's eternal, loving plan, he directs, carries out, and sustains our salvation.

When we respond to Christ's love by trusting in him, his purpose becomes our mission. Have you committed yourself to fulfilling God's purpose? We should always be seeking to understand more of who God created us to be and what he wants us to do with our life.

1. What does God want to accomplish through his children (the body of Christ) working together?
2. What attitudes and actions are necessary for the body to function as it should? (Check Romans 12 and 1 Corinthians 12 for similar teaching on "Body Life.")
3. In what ways can these attitudes be displayed and these actions lived out in your church and among your Christian friends?
4. What do you think God wants to accomplish through you for other believers?

CHRIST, THE CENTER

Christ is exalted as the central meaning of the universe and the focus of history. He is the Head of his body, the church.

Because Christ is central to everything, his power must be central in us. Begin by placing all your priorities under his control. Your life decisions should be based on who you are as his disciple.

1. According to 1:3-15, what do we have in Christ?
2. According to 2:11-21, how does Christ change human relationships?
3. According to 4:11-16, what role does Christ play in the body?
4. Review your responses to questions 1–3. Why is it so important to make Jesus, in our heart and mind, the central focus of our life?
5. Where is your focus today? (At home, by yourself, with your best friends, at school, at church.) In what sense are you "on center" in your commitment to Christ? In what sense are you "off center"?

NEW FAMILY

Because God through Christ paid our penalty for sin and forgave us, we have been reconciled and brought near to him. We are a new society, a new family. Being united with Christ means that we are to treat each other as family members.

We are one family in Christ; so there should be no barriers, no divisions, and no discrimination. Because we all belong to him, we should live in harmony with one another. We have a responsibility toward each other as brothers and sisters in Christ.

1. Check out 2:11–3:13. What does God desire concerning relationships between Jews and Gentiles?
2. Who are the people in your community who do not relate well to each other because of difference in color, race, culture, social status, or other personal barriers?
3. From what people are you most separated or alienated in your personal life? What does this study teach you about those relationships?
4. What can you do to change those relationships because of your faith in Christ?

CHRISTIAN CONDUCT

Paul encourages all Christians to make wise, dynamic Christian living a goal.

God provides his Holy Spirit to enable us to live his way. To utilize his power, we must lay aside our evil desires and draw upon the power of his new life. Submit your will to Christ and seek to love with *his* love by the power of the Spirit.

1. Ephesians gives several specific commands to obey in following Christ (for instance 3:25—tell the truth!). Make a quick list of these commands.
2. Now consider each item on your list in light of this question: "How does doing this action relate to my loving God?"
3. Read 5:1-2. How does God's love become the motivation for Christian conduct?
4. As you look at your list from question one, which actions are areas of strength in your life? Which ones are weaknesses? How can you strengthen your areas of weaknesses so that your life is a greater "walk in the light"?

*T*ime for a little daydreaming: ■ Scenario #1—A high-powered attorney calls to inform you that a distant relative has left you her entire estate worth *several million bucks!* ■ Scenario #2—You ace all of your midterm exams! ■ Scenario #3—In the biggest game of the year, you score with one second left to give your school an upset victory. ■ Scenario #4—You learn that the most attractive member of the opposite sex (in your whole school!) likes you. ■ Some dreams, huh? So, do you think you could get *excited* about those situations? OK, let's daydream some more: ■ Scenario #5—Your dad accidentally throws away your term paper—the one you worked on for over a month—the one that is due *today.* ■ Scenario #6—You develop a huge pimple on the end of your nose the night before the most important date of your life. ■ Scenario #7—You've trained for months for track team tryouts. On the way to school, you get in a wreck and break your ankle. ■ Scenario #8—Your boyfriend/girlfriend dumps you—for your best friend! ■ OK, so these are more like nightmares. Is it possible to be *joyful* in bad situations like these? ■ Believe it or not, it *is* possible to be content—even in the midst of horrible, terrible circumstances. ■ Facing problems or trials? Get a fresh perspective. Read Philippians, Paul's letter to a group of Christians. The message is clear: Joy and contentment really *can* be ours . . . as long as we keep trusting God through life's hard times.

STATS

PURPOSE: To thank the Philippians and to strengthen them by showing that true joy comes from Jesus Christ

AUTHOR: Paul

TO WHOM WRITTEN: Christians at Philippi and all believers

DATE WRITTEN: About A.D. 61, from Rome, during Paul's imprisonment there

SETTING: Paul and his companions founded the church at Philippi on his second missionary journey (Acts 16:11-40). This was the first church established on the European continent. The Philippian church had sent a gift with Epaphroditus (one of their members) to be delivered to Paul (4:18).

KEY PEOPLE: Paul, Timothy, Epaphroditus, Euodias, Syntyche

KEY PLACE: Philippi

Philippians

CHAPTER 1 PAUL'S PRAYER: KEEP GROWING.
From: Paul and Timothy, slaves of Jesus Christ.
To: The pastors and deacons and all the Christians in the city of Philippi.

²May God bless you all. Yes, I pray that God our Father and the Lord Jesus Christ will give each of you his fullest blessings and his peace in your hearts and your lives.

³All my prayers for you are full of praise to God! ⁴When I pray for you, my heart is full of joy ⁵because of all your wonderful help in making known the Good News about Christ from the time you first heard it until now. ⁶And I am sure that God who began the good work within you will keep right on helping you grow in his grace until his task within you is finally finished on that day when Jesus Christ returns.

⁷How natural it is that I should feel as I do about you, for you have a very special place in my heart. We have shared together the blessings of God, both when I was in prison and when I was out, defending the truth and telling others about Christ. ⁸Only God knows how deep is my love and longing for you—with the tenderness of Jesus Christ. ⁹My prayer for you is that you will overflow more and more with love for others, and at the same time

JOY SOURCE

1:4 This is the first of many times Paul uses the word *joy* in his letter. Here he says that the Philippians were a source of joy when he prayed. By helping Paul, they were helping Christ's cause. The Philippians were willing to be used by God for whatever task he had in store for them. When others think about you, are you a source of joy for them?

Philippi sat on the Egnatian Way, the main transportation route in Macedonia, an extension of the Appian Way, which joined the eastern empire with Italy.

SUFFERING

1:29 Suffering, in and of itself, is not a privilege. But when we suffer because we faithfully represent Christ, we know that our message and example are having an effect and that God considers us worthy to represent him (see Acts 5:41). Suffering has these additional benefits: (1) it takes our eyes off of earthly comforts; (2) it weeds out superficial believers; (3) it strengthens the faith of those who endure; (4) it serves as an example to others who may follow us. Suffering for our faith doesn't mean we have done something wrong. In fact, the opposite is often true—it may verify that we have been faithful.

keep on growing in spiritual knowledge and insight, ¹⁰for I want you always to see clearly the difference between right and wrong, and to be inwardly clean, no one being able to criticize you from now until our Lord returns. ¹¹May you always be doing those good, kind things that show you are a child of God, for this will bring much praise and glory to the Lord.

¹²And I want you to know this, dear brothers: Everything that has happened to me here has been a great boost in getting out the Good News concerning Christ. ¹³For everyone around here, including all the soldiers over at the barracks, knows that I am in chains simply because I am a Christian. ¹⁴And because of my imprisonment, many of the Christians here seem to have lost their fear of chains! Somehow my patience has encouraged them, and they have become more and more bold in telling others about Christ.

¹⁵Some, of course, are preaching the Good News because they are jealous of the way God has used me. They want reputations as fearless preachers! But others have purer motives, ¹⁶,¹⁷preaching because they love me, for they know that the Lord has brought me here to use me to defend the Truth. And some preach to make me jealous, thinking that their success will add to my sorrows here in jail!

¹⁸But whatever their motive for doing it, the fact remains that the Good News about Christ is being preached, and I am glad.

¹⁹I am going to keep on being glad, for I know that as you pray for me, and as the Holy Spirit helps me, this is all going to turn out for my good. ²⁰For I live in eager expectation and hope that I will never do anything that will cause me to be ashamed of myself but that I will always be ready to speak out boldly for Christ while I am going through all these trials here, just as I have in the past; and that I will always be an honor to Christ, whether I live or whether I must die. ²¹For to me, living means opportunities for Christ, and dying—well, that's better yet! ²²But if living will give me more opportunities to win people to Christ, then I really don't know which is better, to live or die! ²³Sometimes I want to live, and at other times I don't, for I long to go and be with Christ. How

much happier for *me* than being here! [24]But the fact is that I can be of more help to *you* by staying!

[25]Yes, I am still needed down here, and so I feel certain I will be staying on earth a little longer, to help you grow and become happy in your faith; [26]my staying will make you glad and give you reason to glorify Christ Jesus for keeping me safe when I return to visit you again.

[27]But whatever happens to me, remember always to live as Christians should, so that whether I ever see you again or not, I will keep on hearing good reports that you are standing side by side with one strong purpose—to tell the Good News [28]fearlessly, no matter what your enemies may do. They will see this as a sign of their downfall, but for you it will be a clear sign from God that he is with you, and that he has given you eternal life with him. [29]For to you has been given the privilege not only of trusting him but also of suffering for him. [30]We are in this fight together. You have seen me suffer for him in the past; and I am still in the midst of a great and terrible struggle now, as you know so well.

CHAPTER **2** **A CHRIST-LIKE ATTITUDE.** Is there any such thing as Christians cheering each other up? Do you love me enough to want to help me? Does it mean anything to you that we are brothers in the Lord, sharing the same Spirit? Are your hearts tender and sympathetic at all? [2]Then make me truly happy by loving each other and agreeing wholeheartedly with each other, working together with one heart and mind and purpose.

[3]Don't be selfish; don't live to make a good impression on others. Be humble, thinking of others as better than yourself. [4]Don't just think about your own affairs, but be interested in others, too, and in what they are doing.

[5]Your attitude should be the kind that was shown us by Jesus Christ, [6]who, though he was God, did not demand and cling to his rights as God, [7]but laid aside his mighty power and glory, taking the disguise of a slave and becoming like men. [8]And he humbled himself even further, going so far as actually to die a criminal's death on a cross.

[9]Yet it was because of this that God raised him up to the heights of heaven and gave him a name which is above every other name, [10]that at the name of Jesus every knee shall bow in heaven and on earth and under the earth, [11]and every tongue shall confess that Jesus Christ is Lord, to the glory of God the Father.

[12]Dearest friends, when I was there with you, you were always so careful to follow my instructions. And now that I am away you must be even more careful to do the good things that result from being saved, obeying God with deep reverence, shrinking back from all that might displease him. [13]For God is at work within you, helping you want to obey him, and then helping you do what he wants.

[14]In everything you do, stay away from complaining and arguing [15]so that no one can speak a word of blame against you. You are to live clean,

---

Before I became a Christian, I put some real garbage through my mind. How do I clean up my thought-life?

I WONDER . . .

Almost every school in America is equipped with computers. Most businesses remain competitive because they're able to access and store large amounts of information. Computers are serving nearly every segment of society. But they have one flaw—they are dependent on the programs and information put in them.

Your mind works like a computer. If it's programmed to think about crud, that's what will happen. If it's programmed to think about things that are healthy, you will think healthy thoughts. It's as simple as that.

The hard part comes in trying to keep out the unhealthy thoughts. It doesn't take much to pollute a mind.

So what's God's solution? Reprogram the mind! For this job, there are no shortcuts. The more exposure to things that have polluted us, whether from bad movies, magazines, TV, music, concerts, or just the everyday conversation of friends who don't care what they say, the longer it will take to clear our minds and reprogram them.

The reprograming process begins when we realize that destructive thoughts and images are trying to get a foothold in our minds, and then kick them out. The next step, as we see from Philippians 4:8, is choosing to dwell on what is "true and good and right . . . pure and lovely, and . . . fine."

---

innocent lives as children of God in a dark world full of people who are crooked and stubborn. Shine out among them like beacon lights, [16]holding out to them the Word of Life.

Then when Christ returns, how glad I will be that my work among you was so worthwhile. [17]And if my lifeblood is, so to speak, to be poured out over your faith, which I am offering up to God as a sacrifice—that is, if I am to die for you—even then I will be glad and will share my joy with each of you. [18]For you should be happy about this, too, and rejoice with me for having this privilege of dying for you.

[19]If the Lord is willing, I will send Timothy to see you soon. Then when he comes back, he can cheer me up by telling me all about you and how you are getting along. [20]There is no one like Timothy for having a real interest in you; [21]everyone else seems to be worrying about his own plans and not those of Jesus Christ. [22]But you know Timothy. He has been just like a son to me in helping me preach

the Good News. ²³I hope to send him to you just as soon as I find out what is going to happen to me here. ²⁴And I am trusting the Lord that soon I myself may come to see you.

²⁵Meanwhile, I thought I ought to send Epaphroditus back to you. You sent him to help me in my need; well, he and I have been real brothers, working and battling side by side. ²⁶Now I am sending him home again, for he has been homesick for all of you and upset because you heard that he was ill. ²⁷And he surely was; in fact, he almost died. But God had mercy on him and on me, too, not allowing me to have this sorrow on top of everything else.

²⁸So I am all the more anxious to get him back to you again, for I know how thankful you will be to see him, and that will make me happy and lighten all my cares. ²⁹Welcome him in the Lord with great joy, and show your appreciation, ³⁰for he risked his life for the work of Christ and was at the point of death while trying to do for me the things you couldn't do because you were far away.

CHAPTER 3 KNOW HIM.

Whatever happens, dear friends, be glad in the Lord. I never get tired of telling you this, and it is good for you to hear it again and again.

²Watch out for those wicked men—dangerous dogs, I call them—who say you must be circumcised to be saved. ³For it isn't the *cutting of our bodies* that makes us children of God; it is *worshiping him with our spirits*. That is the only true "circumcision." We Christians glory in what Christ Jesus has done for

SELF

Marie's favorite topic for discussion, her major concern, the number one thing on her mind is . . . Marie. Seriously, when we say she's stuck on herself, we're talking really stuck—super-glue style.

Just look:

- When Beth was extremely upset at not being asked to Homecoming, Marie responded by going on and on about her date.
- When anyone asks, "How was your weekend?" Marie gives a twenty-minute discourse. (Funny how she never asks anyone else that question.)
- When her favorite daytime TV show was interrupted last summer by a live news report about a four-alarm apartment fire, Marie got emotional. Not at the fact that people were dying and losing their homes, but at the fact that she had to miss her program.
- When Marie's neighbor called, desperately needing a baby-sitter at the last minute, Marie wouldn't go, even though she had no other plans. She ended up going to work out at the health club.
- When Marie receives money (allowance, pay, or cash from an unexpected source), she immediately goes to the mall and buys something for herself.

Do you know anyone like Marie? Are you like Marie? See Philippians 2:3-11 for a better way.

I CAN DO EVERYTHING GOD asks ME to with the help of CHRIST who gives gives gives gives ME the STRENGTH and POWER

PHILIPPIANS 4:13

us and realize that we are helpless to save ourselves.

⁴Yet if anyone ever had reason to hope that he could save himself, it would be I. If others could be saved by what they are, certainly I could! ⁵For I went through the Jewish initiation ceremony when I was eight days old, having been born into a pure-blooded Jewish home that was a branch of the old original Benjamin family. So I was a real Jew if there ever was one! What's more, I was a member of the Pharisees who demand the strictest obedience to every Jewish law and custom. ⁶And sincere? Yes, so much so that I greatly persecuted the Church; and I tried to obey every Jewish rule and regulation right down to the very last point.

⁷But all these things that I once thought very worthwhile—now I've thrown them all away so that I can put my trust and hope in Christ alone. ⁸Yes, everything else is worthless when compared with the priceless gain of knowing Christ Jesus my Lord. I have put aside all else, counting it worth less than nothing, in order that I can have Christ, ⁹and become one with him, no longer counting on

being saved by being good enough or by obeying God's laws, but by trusting Christ to save me; for God's way of making us right with himself depends on faith—counting on Christ alone. ¹⁰Now I have given up everything else—I have found it to be the only way to really know Christ and to experience the mighty power that brought him back to life again, and to find out what it means to suffer and to die with him. ¹¹So whatever it takes, I will be one who lives in the fresh newness of life of those who are alive from the dead.

¹²I don't mean to say I am perfect. I haven't learned all I should even yet, but I keep working toward that day when I will finally be all that Christ saved me for and wants me to be.

¹³No, dear brothers, I am still not all I should be, but I am bringing all my energies to bear on this one thing: Forgetting the past and looking forward to what lies ahead, ¹⁴I strain to reach the end of the race and receive the prize for which God is calling us up to heaven because of what Christ Jesus did for us.

¹⁵I hope all of you who are mature Christians will see eye-to-eye with me on these things, and if you disagree on some point, I believe that God will make it plain to you— ¹⁶if you fully obey the truth you have.

¹⁷Dear brothers, pattern your lives after mine, and notice who else lives up to my example. ¹⁸For I have told you often before, and I say it again now with tears in my eyes, there are many who walk along the Christian road who are really enemies of the cross of Christ. ¹⁹Their future is eternal loss, for their god is their appetite: they are proud of what they should be ashamed of; and all they think about is this life here on earth. ²⁰But our homeland is in heaven, where our Savior, the Lord Jesus Christ, is; and we are looking forward to his return from there. ²¹When he comes back, he will take these dying bodies of ours and change them into glorious bodies like his own, using the same mighty power that he will use to conquer all else everywhere.

CHAPTER **4** **THINK ABOUT THE GOOD.** Dear brother Christians, I love you and long to see you, for you are my joy and my reward for my work. My beloved friends, stay true to the Lord.

²And now I want to plead with those two dear women, Euodias and Syntyche. Please, please, with the Lord's help, quarrel no more—be friends again. ³And I ask you, my true teammate, to help these women, for they worked side by side with me in telling the Good News to others; and they worked with Clement, too, and the rest of my fellow workers whose names are written in the Book of Life.

⁴Always be full of joy in the Lord; I say it again, rejoice! ⁵Let everyone see that you are unselfish and considerate in all you do. Remember that the Lord is coming soon. ⁶Don't worry about anything; instead, pray about everything; tell God your needs, and don't forget to thank him for his

"Here's what I did..."

My grandmother was in the hospital. I heard my mom say over the phone to someone that the doctors weren't sure whether Grandma would make it; things looked pretty serious.

I went to my room feeling agitated. As far as I knew, Grandma didn't know that Jesus died for her sins. I had always wanted to tell her, but how do I do it? I felt so unsure of myself. What would I say? Would she even listen to me?

I prayed about this for quite a while. I knew God would want my grandmother to hear that God loves her and wants to save her for eternity. I tried to think through what I could say to her. Then I started reading my Bible. I read in Philippians, and the thirteenth verse in chapter four leaped out at me. "I can do everything God asks me to do with the help of Christ who gives me the strength and the power." It seemed like God was giving me direct encouragement that I would know what to say to my grandmother.

I went to the hospital and I told my grandmother about Jesus. And she listened and accepted Christ as her Lord and Savior!

One week later, she died. But I knew she was now with the Lord.

Jeff

AGE 17

answers. ⁷If you do this, you will experience God's peace, which is far more wonderful than the human mind can understand. His peace will keep your thoughts and your hearts quiet and at rest as you trust in Christ Jesus.

⁸And now, brothers, as I close this letter, let me say this one more thing: Fix your thoughts on what is true and good and right. Think about things that are pure and lovely, and dwell on the fine, good things in others. Think about all you can praise God for and be glad about. ⁹Keep putting into practice all you learned from me and saw me doing, and the God of peace will be with you.

¹⁰How grateful I am and how I praise the Lord that you are helping me again. I know you have always been anxious to send what you could, but

NO WORRIES

4:6-18 Imagine never having to worry about anything! It seems like an impossibility—we all have worries on the job, in our homes, at school. But Paul's advice is to turn your worries into prayers. Do you want to worry less? Then pray more! Whenever you start to worry, stop and pray.

for a while you didn't have the chance. [11]Not that I was ever in need, for I have learned how to get along happily whether I have much or little. [12]I know how to live on almost nothing or with everything. I have learned the secret of contentment in every situation, whether it be a full stomach or hunger, plenty or want; [13]for I can do everything God asks me to with the help of Christ who gives me the strength and power. [14]But even so, you have done right in helping me in my present difficulty.

[15]As you well know, when I first brought the Gospel to you and then went on my way, leaving Macedonia, only you Philippians became my partners in giving and receiving. No other church did this. [16]Even when I was over in Thessalonica you sent help twice. [17]But though I appreciate your gifts, what makes me happiest is the well-earned reward you will have because of your kindness.

[18]At the moment I have all I need—more than I need! I am generously supplied with the gifts you sent me when Epaphroditus came. They are a sweet-smelling sacrifice that pleases God well. [19]And it is he who will supply all your needs from his riches in glory because of what Christ Jesus has done for us. [20]Now unto God our Father be glory forever and ever. Amen.

Sincerely, Paul

P.S. [21]Say hello for me to all the Christians there; the brothers with me send their greetings, too. [22]And all the other Christians here want to be remembered to you, especially those who work in Caesar's palace. [23]The blessings of our Lord Jesus Christ be upon your spirits.

SECRET

4:23 In many ways the Philippian church was a model congregation. It was made up of different kinds of people who were learning to work together. But Paul knew problems could arise, so he prepared the Philippians for possible difficulties. Though a prisoner in Rome, Paul had learned the true secret of joy and peace—imitating Christ and serving others. By focusing on Christ we learn unity, humility, joy, and peace.

MEGA *Themes*

HUMILITY Christ showed true humility when he laid aside his rights and privileges as God to become human. He poured out his life to pay the penalty we deserve. Laying aside self-interest is essential to all our relationships.

We are to take Christ's attitude in serving others. We must not be concerned about personal recognition. When we give up the need to receive credit and praise, we will be able to serve with joy, love, and kindness.

1. If a person was described to you as "humble," what would be your impression of that person? Positive or negative? Weak or strong? Unique or average?
2. How did Jesus display his attitude of humility?
3. If Jesus were to attend your school, how do you think people would respond to him as he humbly served others?
4. What would it mean for you to display humility toward kids at school?

SELF-SACRIFICE Christ suffered and died so that we might have eternal life. With courage and

faithfulness, Paul sacrificed himself for the ministry, preaching the gospel even while he was in prison.

Christ gives us power to lay aside our personal needs and concerns. To utilize his power, we must imitate those leaders who deny themselves and serve others. We dare not be self-centered in view of such a self-sacrificing Savior.

1. What are the differences between a self-sacrificing person and a self-centered one?
2. What makes it difficult for a person to be self-sacrificing?
3. What was the connection between the self-sacrifice of Jesus and the self-sacrifice of Paul?
4. How could you overcome areas of self-centeredness through the help of Jesus and the work of his Spirit? What will you do to begin this work?

UNITY In every church, in every generation, there are problems that divide people (issues, loyalties, and conflicts). It is easy to turn against each other. Paul encouraged the Philippians to agree with one another, stop complaining, and work together.

As believers, we should fight against a common enemy, not each other. United in love, we become aware of Christ's strength. Always remember teamwork, consideration, and unselfishness. Keep your focus on the model of Jesus Christ.

1. What are some of the things that cause anger, hurt, and division among God's people?
2. What specific principles do you find in Philippians that could prevent or help resolve such conflict?
3. As you examine these principles, what truth is the key to maintaining unity in the body of believers?
4. What can you do to apply these principles in relationships with your Christian friends—specifically those in your church?

CHRISTIAN LIVING Paul shows us how to live successful Christian lives. We can become mature by being so identified with Christ that his attitude of humility and sacrifice rules us. Christ is both our source of power and our guide.

Developing our character begins with God's work in us, but it also requires discipline, obedience, and continual concentration on our part.

1. Read 3:1-16. If you had never heard of Paul before, what would be your impression of him after reading these verses? Do you agree or disagree with this statement: "Paul thought the Christian life was basically easy." Explain your response based on Philippians.
2. Summarize the key points you find in Paul's testimony of himself and his life in Christ. What can you do to develop godly character?
3. Describe your life as a Christian. In what ways is your experience similar to Paul's? In what ways is it different?

JOY Believers can have profound contentment, serenity, and peace no matter what happens. This joy comes from knowing Christ personally and from depending on his strength rather than on our own.

Joy does not come from outward circumstances but from inner strength. As Christians, we must not rely on what we have or what we experience to give us joy, but on Christ within us. His joy is greater than life's trials.

1. Based on Paul's circumstances and the content of his letter to the Philippians, how do you think Paul would have described being "joyful"?
2. How can a Christian find joy in apparently unhappy circumstances?
3. If a Christian friend were to say to you, "How can I possibly find joy in the Lord when life seems so unfair?" what would you say?
4. How will you find joy in Jesus this week?

Will the Real Jesus Please Stand Up ■ Sometimes it's hard to know what to think about Jesus Christ. ■ Christians say he is God with skin on—the second person of the Trinity and the carpenter from Nazareth all rolled into one. Others insist he never even existed. Still others regard Jesus as a troublesome politician with a Messiah complex, who ended up being executed. Then there is the Hollywood Jesus—weak, wishy-washy, misguided, filled with contradictions, and surrounded by controversy. ■ How about the increasingly popular "New Age" Jesus who is but one of many ways to God? And don't forget some cults who claim that Christ is *now living on the earth* in the person of their leader! ■ So, was Jesus just a good man and great moral teacher? Or was he, as Islam teaches, a prophet like Moses, Buddha, and Mohammed? Was he just one of many gods? Was he truly divine, or was he just more than human, or was he simply one manifestation of a divine, universal force? ■ There are hundreds of conflicting ideas floating around about who Jesus is. But only one of the views can be true—which makes the others wrong . . . and extremely dangerous! ■ Don't fall for lies about Christ. Meet him as he really is. See for yourself how superior he is to everything and everyone else in the universe. See what it means to know him in a personal way. ■ See all of this and more in the book of Colossians.

STATS

PURPOSE: To combat errors in the church and to show that believers have everything they need in Christ

AUTHOR: Paul

TO WHOM WRITTEN: The church at Colosse, a city in Asia Minor, and all believers everywhere

DATE WRITTEN: About A.D. 60, during Paul's imprisonment in Rome

SETTING: Paul had never visited Colosse—evidently the church had been founded by Epaphras and other converts from Paul's missionary travels. The church, however, had been infiltrated by religious relativism with some believers attempting to combine elements of paganism and secular philosophy with Christian doctrine. Paul confronts these false teachings and affirms the sufficiency of Christ.

KEY PEOPLE: Paul, Timothy, Tychicus, Onesimus, Aristarchus, Mark, Epaphras

KEY PLACES: Colosse, Laodicea (4:15-16)

Colossians

CHANGED

1:6 Wherever Paul went, he preached the gospel—to Gentile audiences, to hostile Jewish leaders, and even to his Roman guards. Whenever people believed in the message he spoke, they were changed. God's Word is not just for our information, it is for our transformation! Becoming a Christian means beginning a whole new relationship with God, not just turning over a new leaf or determining to do right. New believers have a changed purpose, direction, attitude, and behavior. They no longer seek to serve themselves but to serve God. In what areas has hearing God's Word changed your life? Where should it do so?

CHAPTER **1** **PAUL: CHOSEN BY GOD.** *From:* Paul, chosen by God to be Jesus Christ's messenger, and from Brother Timothy.

²*To:* The faithful Christian brothers—God's people—in the city of Colosse.

May God our Father shower you with blessings and fill you with his great peace.

³Whenever we pray for you, we always begin by giving thanks to God the Father of our Lord Jesus Christ, ⁴for we have heard how much you trust the Lord, and how much you love his people. ⁵And you are looking forward to the joys of heaven, and have been ever since the Gospel first was preached to you. ⁶The same Good News that came to you is going out all over the world and changing lives everywhere, just as it changed yours that very first day you heard it and understood about God's great kindness to sinners.

⁷Epaphras, our much-loved fellow worker, was the one who brought you this Good News. He is Jesus Christ's faithful slave, here to help us in your place. ⁸And he is the one who has told us about the great love for others that the Holy Spirit has given you.

⁹So ever since we first heard about you we have kept on praying and asking God to help

Paul had undoubtedly been through Laodicea on his third missionary journey because it lay on the main route to Ephesus, but he had never been to Colosse. Though a large city with a significant population, Colosse was smaller and less important than the nearby cities of Laodicea and Hieropolis.

you understand what he wants you to do; asking him to make you wise about spiritual things; [10]and asking that the way you live will always please the Lord and honor him, so that you will always be doing good, kind things for others, while all the time you are learning to know God better and better.

[11]We are praying, too, that you will be filled with his mighty, glorious strength so that you can keep going no matter what happens—always full of the joy of the Lord, [12]and always thankful to the Father who has made us fit to share all the wonderful things that belong to those who live in the Kingdom of light. [13]For he has rescued us out of the darkness and gloom of Satan's kingdom and brought us into the Kingdom of his dear Son, [14]who bought our freedom with his blood and forgave us all our sins.

[15]Christ is the exact likeness of the unseen God. He existed before God made anything at all, and, in fact, [16]Christ himself is the Creator who made everything in heaven and earth, the things we can see and the things we can't; the spirit world with its kings and kingdoms, its rulers and authorities; all were made by Christ for his own use and glory. [17]He was before all else began and it is his power that holds every-

thing together. [18]He is the Head of the body made up of his people—that is, his Church—which he began; and he is the Leader of all those who arise from the dead, so that he is first in everything; [19]for God wanted all of himself to be in his Son.

[20]It was through what his Son did that God cleared a path for everything to come to him—all things in heaven and on earth—for Christ's death on the cross has made peace with God for all by his blood. [21]This includes you who were once so far away from God. You were his enemies and hated him and were separated from him by your evil thoughts and actions, yet now he has brought you back as his friends. [22]He has done this through the death on the cross of his own human body, and now as a result Christ has brought you into the very presence of

HOW TO PRAY

1:9-14 Sometimes we wonder how to pray for missionaries and other leaders we have never met. Paul had never met the Colossians, but he faithfully prayed for them. His prayers teach us how to pray for others, whether we know them or not. We can request that they (1) understand God's will, (2) gain spiritual wisdom, (3) live lives pleasing and honoring to God, (4) do kind things for others, (5) know God better and better, (6) be filled with God's strength, (7) endure in faith, (8) stay full of Christ's joy, and (9) always be thankful. All believers have these same basic needs. When you don't know how to pray for someone, remember Paul's prayer pattern for the Colossians.

God, and you are standing there before him with nothing left against you—nothing left that he could even chide you for; [23]the only condition is that you fully believe the Truth, standing in it steadfast and firm, strong in the Lord, convinced of the Good News that Jesus died for you, and never shifting from trusting him to save you. This is the wonderful news that came to each of you and is now spreading all over the world. And I, Paul, have the joy of telling it to others.

[24]But part of my work is to suffer for you; and I am glad, for I am helping to finish up the remainder of Christ's sufferings for his body, the Church.

[25]God has sent me to help his Church and to tell his secret plan to you Gentiles. [26,27]He has kept this secret for centuries and generations past, but now at last it has pleased him to tell it to those who love him and live for him, and the riches and glory of his plan are for you Gentiles, too. And this is the secret: *Christ in your hearts is your only hope of glory.*

[28]So everywhere we go we talk about Christ to all who will listen, warning them and teaching them as well as we know how. We want to be able to present each one to God, perfect because of what Christ has done for each of them. [29]This is my work, and I can do it only because Christ's mighty energy is at work within me.

CHAPTER **2** **A NEW LIFE IN CHRIST.** I wish you could know how much I have struggled in prayer for you and for the church at Laodicea, and for my many other friends who have never known me personally. [2]This is what I have asked of God for you: that you will be encouraged and knit together by strong ties of love, and that you will have the rich experience of knowing Christ with real certainty and clear understanding. *For God's secret plan, now at last made known, is Christ himself.* [3]In him lie hidden all the mighty, untapped treasures of wisdom and knowledge.

[4]I am saying this because I am afraid that someone may fool you with smooth talk. [5]For though I am far away from you my heart is with you, happy because you are getting along so well, happy because of your strong faith in Christ. [6]And now just as you trusted Christ to save you, trust him, too, for each day's problems; live in vital union with him. [7]Let your roots grow down into him and draw up nourishment from him. See that you go on growing in the Lord, and become strong and vigorous in the truth you were taught. Let your lives overflow with joy and thanksgiving for all he has done.

[8]Don't let others spoil your faith and joy with their philosophies, their wrong and shallow answers built on men's thoughts and ideas, instead of on what Christ has said. [9]For in Christ there is all of God in a human body; [10]*so you have everything when you have Christ,* and you are filled with God through your union with

---

I have been a Christian for about two months and I feel so far behind spiritually, compared to friends who have been Christians for a lot longer. Sometimes it gets pretty discouraging. How do I catch up?

I WONDER . . .

We live in a world that makes it nearly impossible not to compare ourselves with others.

Sometimes we even compare our life as a Christian to others. However, you must fight this urge and recognize two essential facts.

First, receiving forgiveness for our sin and asking Christ to come into our lives is like a seed being planted in our hearts (see 1 Corinthians 3:6). Any seed planted must first take root before it grows and blossoms.

Do you remember in first grade when you planted a seed in a clear plastic cup? If the seed was planted close enough to the edge, you would see that the roots would grow downward first; then a few days later a plant would appear above the dirt. It was miraculous!

The only difference between you and your friends is that they have had more time to spread their roots down deep. They have lived longer in "vital union with him" and have drawn up more "nourishment from him" for a longer period of time.

When you took the first step of faith to trust Christ with your life, that was like the seed being planted. From this point it is up to you and God to nourish the seed and let the roots grow deep (see Colossians 2:6-7).

Your faith is nourished by rooting your new relationship with Christ. This means getting to know God better through reading and obeying his Word in the Bible (Romans 10:17). As with any relationship, time together helps you to appreciate God's character and will lead to a greater love for him (2 Peter 3:18).

Second, God doesn't compare one Christian to another. So you shouldn't, either. That would be like a father wanting his two-year-old son to throw a baseball as well as his nine-year-old. He can't!

As Christians, we never get to a point where we have arrived and are totally mature. Our love and appreciation for God can always grow deeper as he shows us new areas in our lives to trust him with.

Enjoy these beginning stages of your faith by taking in all of the spiritual nourishment you can handle. Remember, the stronger and deeper your roots grow below the surface, the more beautiful and fruitful you will be as a Christian (see John 15:4-5).

Christ. He is the highest Ruler, with authority over every other power.

[11]When you came to Christ, he set you free from your evil desires, not by a bodily operation of circumcision but by a spiritual operation, the baptism

of your souls. ¹²For in baptism you see how your old, evil nature died with him and was buried with him; and then you came up out of death with him into a new life because you trusted the Word of the mighty God who raised Christ from the dead.

¹³You were dead in sins, and your sinful desires were not yet cut away. Then he gave you a share in the very life of Christ, for he forgave all your sins, ¹⁴and blotted out the charges proved against you, the list of his commandments which you had not obeyed. He took this list of sins and destroyed it by nailing it to Christ's cross. ¹⁵In this way God took away Satan's power to accuse you of sin, and God openly displayed to the whole world Christ's triumph at the cross where your sins were all taken away.

¹⁶So don't let anyone criticize you for what you eat or drink, or for not celebrating Jewish holidays and feasts or new moon ceremonies or Sabbaths. ¹⁷For these were only temporary rules that ended when Christ came. They were only shadows of the real thing—of Christ himself. ¹⁸Don't let anyone declare you lost when you refuse to worship angels, as they say you must. They have seen a vision, they say, and know you should. These proud men (though they claim to be so humble) have a very clever imagination. ¹⁹But they are not connected to Christ, the Head to which all of us who are his body are joined; for we are joined together by his strong sinews, and we grow only as we get our nourishment and strength from God.

²⁰Since you died, as it were, with Christ and this has set you free from following the world's ideas of how to be saved—by doing good and obeying various rules—why do you keep right on following

LUST

Last year, thirteen-year-old Danny found a secret stash of pornographic magazines in his older brother's bedroom. Since then, he's developed a system. Each time his brother goes out for the evening, Danny sneaks one of the magazines into his own bedroom. There he'll stay for long hours fantasizing about being with each of the beautiful models. After a few days, he smuggles the much-studied magazine back into its place, whereupon he takes another one and repeats the process.

Each time he yields to these lustful temptations, Danny is overcome by a wave of guilt. After the short-term pleasure, Danny experiences only feelings of emptiness and loneliness. Even so, he rationalizes it this way:

"It's better to do what I'm doing than to be like my friends and actually go out and have sex! At least this way, I don't get myself or anybody else in trouble. Besides, I can't help it if I have a healthy sex drive. And anyway, I'm not sure I can stop."

What about Danny's ideas on lust? Are they sound arguments? Is it OK to stare at pictures (or real people) and imagine having sex with them? Take a look at Colossians 3:5 for God's thoughts on the issue.

COLOSSIANS 3:23

WORK hard and cheerfully at A L L *you do,* just as though *you were* **working** for THE LORD.

them anyway, still bound by such rules as ²¹not eating, tasting, or even touching certain foods? ²²Such rules are mere human teachings, for food was made to be eaten and used up. ²³These rules may seem good, for rules of this kind require strong devotion and are humiliating and hard on the body, but they have no effect when it comes to conquering a person's evil thoughts and desires. They only make him proud.

CHAPTER **3** SOME RULES TO OBEY. Since you became alive again, so to speak, when Christ arose from the dead, now set your sights on the rich treasures and joys of heaven where he sits beside God in the place of honor and power. ²Let heaven fill your thoughts; don't spend your time worrying about things down here. ³You should have as little desire for this world as a dead person does. Your real life is in heaven with Christ and God. ⁴And when Christ who is our real life comes back again, you will shine with him and share in all his glories.

⁵Away then with sinful, earthly things; deaden the evil desires lurking within you; have nothing to do with sexual sin, impurity, lust, and shameful desires; don't worship the good things of life, for that is idolatry. ⁶God's terrible anger is upon those who do such things.

DIFFERENCE

2:20-23 People should be able to see a difference between the way Christians and non-Christians live. Still, we should not expect instant maturity of new Christians. The Christian life is a process. Although we have a new nature, we don't automatically have all good thoughts and attitudes when we become new people in Christ. But if we keep listening to God, we will be changing all the time. As you look over the last year, what changes for the better have you seen in your thoughts and attitudes? Change may be slow, but your life will change significantly if you trust God to change you.

⁷You used to do them when your life was still part of this world; ⁸but now is the time to cast off and throw away all these rotten garments of anger, hatred, cursing, and dirty language.

⁹Don't tell lies to each other; it was your old life with all its wickedness that did that sort of thing; now it is dead and gone. ¹⁰You are living a brand new kind of life that is continually learning more and more of what is right, and trying constantly to be more and more like Christ who created this new life within you. ¹¹In this new life one's nationality or race or education or social position is unimportant; such things mean nothing. Whether a person has Christ is what matters, and he is equally available to all.

¹²Since you have been chosen by God who has given you this new kind of life, and because of his deep love and concern for you, you should practice tenderhearted mercy and kindness to others. Don't worry about making a good impression on them, but be ready to suffer quietly and patiently. ¹³Be gentle and ready to forgive; never hold grudges. Remember, the Lord forgave you, so you must forgive others.

¹⁴Most of all, let love guide your life, for then the whole church will stay together in perfect harmony. ¹⁵Let the peace of heart that comes from Christ be always present in your hearts and lives, for this is your responsibility and privilege as members of his body. And always be thankful.

¹⁶Remember what Christ taught, and let his words enrich your lives and make you wise; teach them to each other and sing them out in psalms and hymns and spiritual songs, singing to the Lord with thankful hearts. ¹⁷And whatever you do or say, let it be as a representative of the Lord Jesus, and come with him into the presence of God the Father to give him your thanks.

¹⁸You wives, submit yourselves to your husbands, for that is what the Lord has planned for you. ¹⁹And you husbands must be loving and kind to your wives and not bitter against them nor harsh.

²⁰You children must always obey your fathers and mothers, for that pleases the Lord. ²¹Fathers, don't scold your children so much that they become discouraged and quit trying.

²²You slaves must always obey your earthly masters, not only trying to please them when they are watching you but all the time; obey them willingly because of your love for the Lord and because you want to please him. ²³Work hard and cheerfully at all you do, just as though you were working for the Lord and not merely for your masters, ²⁴remembering that it is the Lord Christ who is going to pay you, giving you your full portion of all he owns. He is the one you are really working for. ²⁵And if you don't do your best for him, he will pay you in a way that you won't like—for he has no special favorites who can get away with shirking.

"Here's what I did..."

For a couple of years in high school, I didn't get along very well with my dad. I'm not sure why, now. It just seemed like everything he said irritated me. Dad seemed old-fashioned, too restrictive. I began to rebel, not openly, but more in my heart and on the sly. For instance, I would tell him that I'd do something he had asked me to, but then I never would get around to doing it. Then when he'd get angry, I'd tune him out. Or I would tell Dad I was going somewhere that I knew he'd approve, when I really was with friends he didn't like very much.

I knew things weren't great between us, but I didn't think much about it until our youth group was doing a study on relationships. When we talked about parents, we studied Colossians 3:20 and Ephesians 6:1-3. We talked about why we should obey our parents, and what it means to obey.

I felt cut to the heart. I realized that Dad was a good dad, and suddenly I understood that his restrictions were because he loved me. If I was honest with myself, a lot of them (not all, but a lot) made sense. I was being disobedient and rebellious. I cried some, knowing that I had been hurting my dad for a long time.

That evening I asked Dad to forgive me for all the ways I'd gone against him. It was hard to apologize, but it cleared the air. Dad took my apology well—he even admitted to some areas where he might have been too hard on me. That was the start of a much better father-son relationship, which has continued.

Brad

AGE 18

CHAPTER **4** **PAUL SAYS GOOD-BYE.** You slave owners must be just and fair to all your slaves. Always remember that you, too, have a Master in heaven who is closely watching you.

²Don't be weary in prayer; keep at it; watch for God's answers, and remember to be thankful when they come. ³Don't forget to pray for us too, that God will give us many chances to preach the Good News of Christ for which I am here in jail. ⁴Pray that I will be bold enough to tell it freely and fully

LIFELONG

4:2-8 The Christian is in a continuing education program. The more we know of Christ and his work, the more we will be changed to be like him. Because this process is lifelong, we must never stop learning and obeying. This should not be a justification for drifting along, but an incentive to find the rich treasures of growing in Christ. It takes practice, review, patience, and concentration to stay in line with his will.

and make it plain, as, of course, I should.

⁵Make the most of your chances to tell others the Good News. Be wise in all your contacts with them. ⁶Let your conversation be gracious as well as sensible, for then you will have the right answer for everyone.

⁷Tychicus, our much-loved brother, will tell you how I am getting along. He is a hard worker and serves the Lord with me. ⁸I have sent him on this special trip just to see how you are and to comfort and encourage you. ⁹I am also sending Onesimus, a faithful and much-loved brother, one of your own people. He and Tychicus will give you all the latest news.

¹⁰Aristarchus, who is with me here as a prisoner, sends you his love, and so does Mark, a relative of Barnabas. And as I said before, give Mark a hearty welcome if he comes your way. ¹¹Jesus Justus also sends his love. These are the only Jewish Christians working with me here, and what a comfort they have been!

¹²Epaphras, from your city, a servant of Christ Jesus, sends you his love. He is always earnestly praying for you, asking God to make you strong and perfect and to help you know his will in everything you do. ¹³I can assure you that he has worked hard for you with his prayers, and also for the Christians in Laodicea and Hierapolis.

¹⁴Dear Doctor Luke sends his love, and so does Demas.

¹⁵Please give my greeting to the Christian friends at Laodicea, and to Nymphas, and to those who meet in his home. ¹⁶By the way, after you have read this letter, will you pass it on to the church at Laodicea? And read the letter I wrote to them. ¹⁷And say to Archippus, "Be sure that you do all the Lord has told you to."

¹⁸Here is my own greeting in my own handwriting: Remember me here in jail. May God's blessings surround you.

Sincerely, Paul

ONLY SOURCE

4:18 The Colossian church was facing pressure from a cult-like teaching that promised deeper spiritual life through secret knowledge. But Paul makes it clear in Colossians that Christ alone is the source of our spiritual life. He is the Head of the body, the Lord of all. The path to deeper spiritual life is not through spiritual duties, special knowledge, or secrets; it is only through a clear connection with the Lord Jesus Christ. We must never let anything come between us and our Savior.

MEGA *Themes*

CHRIST IS GOD Jesus Christ is God in the flesh, Lord of all creation, and Lord of the new creation. He is the exact reflection of the invisible God. He is eternal, preexistent, all-powerful, and equal with the Father. Christ is supreme and complete.

Because Christ is supreme, our lives must be Christ centered. To recognize Jesus as God means to regard our relationship with him as most vital and to make his interests our top priority. He must become the navigator of our life's voyage.

1. List the words and phrases that are used to describe Jesus Christ in chapters 1 and 2. What do you

learn about Christ as God in these descriptions?
2. Why is it important to understand that Christ is both God and man?
3. Based on the fact that Christ is truly God, how should you respond to his lordship (control and leadership)?
4. How are you responding to his lordship in your life at the present? What can you do to be more submissive to Christ's role as your Lord?

CHRIST IS THE HEAD OF THE CHURCH
Because Christ is God, he is the Head of the Church, his true believers. Christ is the founder and leader of

the Church and the highest authority on earth. He requires first place in all our thoughts and activities.

To acknowledge Christ as our Head, we must welcome his leadership in all we do or think. No person, group, or church should have more loyalty from us than Christ.

1. What does this phrase mean: "Christ is the Head of the Church"?
2. If you were starting a local church, what kinds of things would you insist on in order to keep Christ as the central leader of that church?
3. Write a statement for yourself and other young people that challenges them to respond to Christ's headship of your local church.

UNION WITH CHRIST Because our sin has been forgiven and we have been reconciled to God, we have a union with Christ that can never be broken. In our faith connection with Christ, we identify with his death, burial, and resurrection.

We should live in constant contact and communication with God. When we do, we will be unified with Christ and with our fellow believers. We are a part of each other's "spiritual life-support system."

1. Read 2:6-15. What does it mean to have new life in Christ?
2. From what things were you set free when you were united with Christ?
3. Read 3:1-17. What things were you called to be and do when you were united to Christ?

4. In what specific ways has your union with Christ made a difference in your past? In your present? In your future?

MAN-MADE RELIGION False teachers were promoting a heresy that stressed man-made rules (legalism). They also sought spiritual growth by denying themselves personal contacts and by mysterious rules. This search created pride in their self-centered efforts.

We must not hold on to our own ideas and try to blend them into Christianity. Nor should we let our hunger for a more fulfilling Christian experience cause us to trust in a teacher, group, or system of thought more than in Christ himself. Christ is our hope and our true source of wisdom. We must reject any teacher whose message is not based absolutely on the truth of Christ.

1. What lie was behind the legalism that the false teachers taught to the Colossians?
2. What is the danger of promoting a religion that is based on man's responsibility to save himself with good works?
3. What are some current examples of the false teachings of legalism? Why are these harmful? How does this hinder non-Christians from understanding and accepting the gospel?
4. What can you do to make sure you don't get trapped by false teachings such as legalism?

*P*hobias are "phascinating" phenomena. Psychiatrists and psychologists have catalogued hundreds of them. Check out this list: ■ Anthophobia—the fear of flowers ■ Belonophobia—the fear of pins and needles ■ Decidophobia—the fear of making decisions ■ Mysophobia—the fear of dirt ■ Trichophobia—the fear of hair ■ Would you believe that some people are even terrified about *peanut butter sticking to the roof of their mouths?* That's called arachibutyrophobia. ■ You may not struggle with such odd fears, but you probably *do* worry about more common stuff. Every day, the media spotlights a different concern: ■ Is the environment damaged beyond repair? ■ Will researchers ever find a cure for AIDS? How many people are infected without knowing it? ■ Are we on the brink of a worldwide economic collapse? ■ How are we going to deal with a generation of drug-addicted babies? ■ Can we confront and correct our country's epidemic of violent crimes? ■ How has war affected our lives? ■ These are scary issues, but the Christian has real hope and genuine peace—even in uncertain times. ■ That's the message of this book: Be comforted, for no matter what happens, God is with us. Rest in the reassuring truth that Jesus Christ is coming back soon to . . . . ■ Aw, that's enough blabbering. Read it yourself. You won't believe your eyes.

STATS

PURPOSE: To strengthen the Thessalonian Christians in their faith and give them assurance of Christ's return

AUTHOR: Paul

TO WHOM WRITTEN: The church at Thessalonica and all believers everywhere

DATE WRITTEN: About A.D. 51 from Corinth; one of Paul's earliest letters

SETTING: The church at Thessalonica had been established only two or three years before this letter was written. The Christians needed to mature in their faith. Also, there was a misunderstanding about Christ's second coming—some thought he would return immediately, others wondered if the dead would experience a bodily resurrection at his return.

KEY PEOPLE: Paul, Timothy, Silas

KEY PLACE: Thessalonica

1**T**hessalonians

CHAPTER 1 CHOSEN BY GOD. *From:* Paul, Silas, and Timothy.

To: The church at Thessalonica—to you who belong to God the Father and the Lord Jesus Christ: May blessing and peace of heart be your rich gifts from God our Father and from Jesus Christ our Lord.

²We always thank God for you and pray for you constantly. ³We never forget your loving deeds as we talk to our God and Father about you, and your strong faith and steady looking forward to the return of our Lord Jesus Christ.

⁴We know that God has chosen you, dear brothers, much beloved of God. ⁵For when we brought you the Good News, it was not just meaningless chatter to you; no, you listened with great interest. What we told you produced a powerful effect upon you, for the Holy Spirit gave you great and full assurance that what we said was true. And you know how our very lives were further proof to you of the truth of our message. ⁶So you became our followers and the Lord's; for you received our message with joy from the Holy Spirit in spite of the trials and sorrows it brought you.

⁷Then you yourselves became an example to all the other Christians in Greece. ⁸And now the Word of the Lord has spread out from you to others everywhere, far beyond your boundaries, for wherever we go we find people telling us about your remarkable faith in God. We don't need to tell *them*

about it, [9]for *they* keep telling *us* about the wonderful welcome you gave us, and how you turned away from your idols to God so that now the living and true God only is your Master. [10]And they speak of how you are looking forward to the return of God's Son from heaven—Jesus, whom God brought back to life—and he is our only Savior from God's terrible anger against sin.

SEX

Melanie is confused about sex—not how (she learned that a long time ago), but when. Her mom tells her to wait. Her youth director gives her the same advice. But everywhere else the message is clearly, "Go for it!" Or, "If you're still a virgin, you're a total loser!"

•Friends at school tell her how great it is and how experienced they are.

•All the glamorous stars in TV shows and movies seem to be hopping from bed to bed—both on- and off-screen.

•In a health class lecture on birth control two weeks ago, the teacher stated, "Now, most normal young people are sexually active. I'm assuming you all are normal, so . . ."

•Melanie's boyfriend keeps telling her how much sex will strengthen their relationship.

•Almost every ad and billboard Melanie sees has a sexual twist or theme.

•A talk show featured live-in lovers talking about their "great" life-style.

"What am I supposed to think?" Melanie asks. "I feel like everybody else in the world is enjoying this really fantastic experience . . . and I'm like a nun or something. I want to wait, at least I think I do. Tell me, is it really worth saving yourself till marriage?"

The Bible says it's definitely wiser to wait until marriage for sex. Think hard about the message in 1 Thessalonians 4:1-8.

CHAPTER 2

PAUL'S FRIENDS. You yourselves know, dear brothers, how worthwhile that visit was. [2]You know how badly we had been treated at Philippi just before we came to you and how much we suffered there. Yet God gave us the courage to boldly repeat the same message to you, even though we were surrounded by enemies. [3]So you can see that we were not preaching with any false motives or evil purposes in mind; we were perfectly straightforward and sincere.

[4]For we speak as messengers from God, trusted by him to tell the truth; we change his message not one bit to suit the taste of those who hear it; for we serve God alone, who examines our hearts' deepest thoughts. [5]Never once did we try to win you with flattery, as you very well know, and God knows we were not just pretending to be your friends so that you would give us money! [6]As for praise, we have never asked for it from you or anyone else, although as apostles of Christ we certainly had a right to some honor from you. [7]But we were as gentle among you as a mother feeding and caring for her own children. [8]We loved you dearly—so dearly that we

gave you not only God's message, but our own lives too.

[9]Don't you remember, dear brothers, how hard we worked among you? Night and day we toiled and sweated to earn enough to live on so that our expenses would not be a burden to anyone there, as we preached God's Good News among you. [10]You yourselves are our witnesses—as is God—that we have been pure and honest and faultless toward every one of you. [11]We talked to you as a father to his own children—don't you remember?—pleading with you, encouraging you and even demanding [12]that your daily lives should not embarrass God but bring joy to him who invited you into his Kingdom to share his glory.

[13]And we will never stop thanking God for this: that when we preached to you, you didn't think of the words we spoke as being just our own, but you accepted what we said as the very Word of God—which, of course, it was—and it changed your lives when you believed it.

[14]And then, dear brothers, you suffered what the churches in Judea did, persecution from your own countrymen, just as they suffered from their own people, the Jews. [15]After they had killed their own prophets, they even executed the Lord Jesus; and now they have brutally persecuted us and driven us out. They are against both God and man, [16]trying to keep us from preaching to the Gentiles for fear some might be saved; and so their sins continue to grow. But the anger of God has caught up with them at last.

[17]Dear brothers, after we left you and had been away from you but a very little while (though our hearts never left you), we tried hard to come back to see you once more. [18]We wanted very much to come, and I, Paul, tried again and again, but Satan stopped us. [19]For what is it we live for, that gives us hope and joy and is our proud reward and crown? It is you! Yes, you will bring us much joy as we stand together before our Lord Jesus Christ when he comes back again. [20]For you are our trophy and joy.

OPPOSED

2:14 Just as the Jewish Christians in Jerusalem were persecuted by their own people, so the Gentile Christians in Thessalonica were persecuted by their fellow Gentiles. It is discouraging to face persecution, especially when it comes from your own people. But when we take a stand for Christ, we will face opposition, disapproval, ridicule, and even persecution from our neighbors, friends, and even family members.

CHAPTER **3** **A JOB WELL DONE.** Finally, when I could stand it no longer, I decided to stay alone in Athens [2,3]and send Timothy, our brother and fellow worker, God's minister, to visit you to strengthen your faith and encourage you and to keep you from becoming fainthearted in all the troubles you were

going through. (But of course you know that such troubles are a part of God's plan for us Christians. [4]Even while we were still with you we warned you ahead of time that suffering would soon come—and it did.)

[5]As I was saying, when I could bear the suspense no longer, I sent Timothy to find out whether your faith was still strong. I was afraid that perhaps Satan had gotten the best of you and that all our work had been useless. [6]And now Timothy has just returned and brings the welcome news that your faith and love are as strong as ever and that you remember our visit with joy and want to see us just as much as we want to see you. [7]So we are greatly comforted, dear brothers, in all of our own crushing troubles and suffering here, now that we know you are standing true to the Lord. [8]We can bear anything as long as we know that you remain strong in him.

[9]How can we thank God enough for you and for the joy and delight you have given us in our praying for you? [10]For night and day we pray on and on for you, asking God to let us see you again, to fill up any little cracks there may yet be in your faith.

[11]May God our Father himself and our Lord Jesus send us back to you again. [12]And may the Lord make your love to grow and overflow to each other and to everyone else, just as our love does toward you. [13]This will result in your hearts being made strong, sinless, and holy by God our Father so that you may stand before him guiltless on that day when our Lord Jesus Christ returns with all those who belong to him.

CHAPTER 4 HOW CAN I PLEASE GOD? Let me add this, dear brothers: You already know how to please God in your daily living, for you know the commands we gave you from the Lord Jesus himself. Now we beg you—yes, we demand of you in the name of the Lord Jesus—that you live more and more closely to that ideal. [3,4]For God wants you to be holy and pure and to keep clear of all sexual sin so that each of you will marry in holiness and honor— [5]not in lustful passion as the heathen do, in their ignorance of God and his ways.

[6]And this also is God's will: that you never cheat in this matter by taking another man's wife because the Lord will punish you terribly for this, as we have solemnly told you before. [7]For God has not called us to be dirty-minded and full of lust but to be holy and clean. [8]If anyone refuses to live by these rules, he is not disobeying the rules of men but of God who gives his *Holy* Spirit to you.

[9]But concerning the pure brotherly love that there should be among God's people, I don't need to say very much, I'm sure! For God himself is teaching you to love one another. [10]Indeed, your love is already strong toward all the Christian brothers throughout your whole nation. Even so, dear friends, we beg you to love them more and more. [11]This should be your ambition: to live a quiet life, minding your own business and doing your own work, just as we told you before. [12]As a

Even though I know I'm going to heaven, I'm still afraid of dying. How can I quit being so afraid of death?

I WONDER...

Extreme fear of the unknown can cripple a person. Unfortunately, death is an unknown for everyone, even for Christians.

What will we find on the other side? How is God going to take me? Will the people left behind be able to adjust? What if I die before I have a chance to get married or experience what I want to experience?

There are a lot of questions that don't have concrete answers. That can be frustrating. Someone once said that trying to explain to another person what God and heaven are like is similar to one dog telling another dog what it's like to be a human. It's impossible!

But death is not something that Christians have to fear, because—for them—death is not the end of the story. It is the gateway to a place of indescribable joy and beauty. It's the beginning of a new life!

Fear is a learned emotion. Through the years we are conditioned to fear certain things. Little kids aren't afraid of death because they don't understand it. Yet as they grow and see the response of adults and the media to death, they learn that it's something awful and to be avoided at all costs.

After we become Christians, we need to go through a relearning process about death. Paul, the author of half the books in the New Testament, said this about death, "For to me, living means opportunities [to win people to] Christ, and dying—well, that's better yet!" (Philippians 1:21).

Paul had learned that death would actually put an end to the struggles he faced on earth. He looked forward to the day when he could see Christ face-to-face. In the meantime, though, he had work to do: winning people to Christ. Life wasn't a chore—it was a privilege!

Fear of dying doesn't disappear instantly. But as you spend time in the Bible and with other Christians who have the same hope you do, you will grow to realize that death is only a door to an eternity far better than your wildest dreams (see 1 Thessalonians 4:13-14).

result, people who are not Christians will trust and respect you, and you will not need to depend on others for enough money to pay your bills.

[13]And now, dear brothers, I want you to know what happens to a Christian when he dies so that when it happens, you will not be full of sorrow, as those are who have no hope. [14]For since we believe that Jesus died and then came back to life again, we can also believe that when Jesus returns, God will bring back with him all the Christians who have died.

PRAYER

Imagine that you were about to meet someone famous—maybe the queen of England or the president of the United States. Chances are you'd be nervous, wondering what to say and how to act. You wouldn't want to make a fool of yourself by doing or saying something inappropriate. Now imagine you're just sitting around gabbing with your best friend. You don't worry about what to say or do. You can just be yourself; the talk flows freely and naturally. These two situations illustrate something about the nature of prayer. On the one hand, prayer brings you into the presence of the King of the universe, the Lord and Creator of everything. That's fairly intimidating! No wonder people feel awkward and tongue-tied when they pray. On the other hand, prayer is simply talking with your heavenly Father, the person who knows you better and loves you more than anyone else does. He is, in a very real way, your best friend; you can talk with him openly and honestly—about anything. Prayer has inspired countless books, debates, songs, poems, and lives. Though there is little to be said about prayer that is new, consider the following perspectives: Prayer is simply communication with God. Christianity talks about a personal God, not a "force," "concept," or "abstract idea." God is a person—we can know him. When you want to get to know a person, there really is only one way to do it: spend time together. The same is true of God. Imagine that! Small, limited, finite human beings are invited to know God in a personal way. What happens when we spend time with God? Basically, three things: First, we can tell God what is on our mind: our worries, joys, pains, fears, hopes—everything. Nothing is too big or too trivial to tell God. He is a loving Father, and good fathers want to hear what is on the heart of their children. We can be ourselves with God; we don't need to change how we talk when we talk with him, or say "thee," "thou," "beseecheth," etc. We can speak to God the way we would to our most trusted friend. Second, in prayer we can hear what God has to say to us. Listening to God requires more patience and more practice than talking to him. That shouldn't be surprising—most of us are better talkers than listeners—but listening to God can be a very rewarding experience. It is one more way God can give us guidance as we seek his will (other ways include the Bible, the counsel of other Christians, and knowing our own particular gifts and limitations). One caution: if you ever feel God is telling you to do something that runs contrary to Scripture, you have misunderstood. God never contradicts himself or his inspired Word. Third, where we may present our requests, praise, confessions, etc. This time spent in the presence of God will begin to have an effect on us: we will begin to become more like him. Have you ever noticed that when two people spend a lot of time together, they begin to talk, act, and even think alike? The same principle applies to our relationship with God. The more we're with him, the more we become like him. It's easy to get discouraged when we pray, to feel our prayers are having no effect. Remember, though, that prayer is more than simply asking God to give us what we want. It is living, active, and powerful communication with the Lord of all. That's much more significant than meeting with the queen or the president. And, through prayer, we always have access to the One who knows us, loves us, hears us, and is molding us into his image.

ALWAYS KEEP ON PRAYING
ALWAYS KEEP ON PRAYING
ALWAYS KEEP ON PRAYING
ALWAYS KEEP ON PRAYING
ALWAYS KEEP ON PRAYING
ALWAYS KEEP ON PRAYING
ALWAYS KEEP ON PRAYING
ALWAYS KEEP ON PRAYING
ALWAYS KEEP ON

a woman's birth pains begin when her child is born. And these people will not be able to get away anywhere—there will be no place to hide.

⁴But, dear brothers, you are not in the dark about these things, and you won't be surprised as by a thief when that day of the Lord comes. ⁵For you are all children of the light and of the day, and do not belong to darkness and night. ⁶So be on your guard, not asleep like the others. Watch for his return and stay sober. ⁷Night is the time for sleep and the time when people get drunk. ⁸But let us who live in the light keep sober, protected by the armor of faith and love, and wearing as our helmet the happy hope of salvation.

⁹For God has not chosen to pour out his anger upon us but to save us through our Lord Jesus Christ; ¹⁰he died for us so that we can live with him forever, whether we are dead or alive at the time of his return. ¹¹So encourage each other to build each other up, just as you are already doing.

¹²Dear brothers, honor the officers of your church who work hard among you and warn you against all that is wrong. ¹³Think highly of them and give them your wholehearted love because they are straining to help you. And remember, no quarreling among yourselves.

¹⁴Dear brothers, warn those who are lazy, comfort those who are frightened, take tender care of those who are weak, and be patient with everyone. ¹⁵See that no one pays back evil for evil, but always try to do good to each other and to everyone else. ¹⁶Always be joyful. ¹⁷Always keep on praying. ¹⁸No matter what happens, always be thankful, for this is God's will for you who belong to Christ Jesus.

¹⁹Do not smother the Holy Spirit. ²⁰Do not scoff at those who prophesy, ²¹but test everything that is said to be sure it is true, and if it is, then accept it. ²²Keep away from every kind of evil. ²³May the God of peace himself make you entirely pure and devoted to God; and may your spirit and soul and body be kept strong and blameless until that day when our Lord Jesus Christ comes back again. ²⁴God, who called you to become his child, will do all this for you, just as he promised. ²⁵Dear brothers, pray for us. ²⁶Shake hands for me with all the brothers there. ²⁷I command you in the name of the Lord to read this letter to all the Christians. ²⁸And may rich blessings from our Lord Jesus Christ be with you, every one.

Sincerely, Paul

¹⁵I can tell you this directly from the Lord: that we who are still living when the Lord returns will not rise to meet him ahead of those who are in their graves. ¹⁶For the Lord himself will come down from heaven with a mighty shout and with the soul-stirring cry of the archangel and the great trumpet-call of God. And the believers who are dead will be the first to rise to meet the Lord. ¹⁷Then we who are still alive and remain on the earth will be caught up with them in the clouds to meet the Lord in the air and remain with him forever. ¹⁸So comfort and encourage each other with this news.

CHAPTER 5 ARE YOU READY FOR CHRIST'S RETURN?

When is all this going to happen? I really don't need to say anything about that, dear brothers, ²for you know perfectly well that no one knows. That day of the Lord will come unexpectedly, like a thief in the night. ³When people are saying, "All is well; everything is quiet and peaceful"—then, all of a sudden, disaster will fall upon them as suddenly as

ENCOURAGE!

5:9-11 As you near the end of a foot race, your legs ache, your throat burns, and your whole body cries out for you to stop. This is when friends and fans are most valuable. Their encouragement helps you push through the pain to the finish. In the same way, Christians are to encourage one another. A word of encouragement offered at the right moment can be the difference between finishing well and collapsing along the way. Look around you. Be sensitive to others' need for encouragement and offer supportive words or actions.

Paul visited Thessalonica on his second and third missionary journeys. It was a seaport and trade center located on the Egnatian Way, a busy international highway. Paul probably wrote his two letters to the Thessalonians from Corinth.

MEGA *Themes*

PERSECUTION Paul and the new Christians at Thessalonica experienced persecution because of their faith in Christ. We can expect trials and troubles as well. We need to stand firm in our faith during our trials, being strengthened by the Holy Spirit.

The Holy Spirit helps us to remain strong in faith; he enables us to show genuine love to others and to maintain our moral character even when we are being persecuted, slandered, or oppressed.

1. How did the Thessalonians respond to pressure and opposition that came because of their faith in Christ?

2. During this persecution, where did they get their strength?

3. What pressures and/or opposition have you faced as a Christian? How did you feel when that happened? How have you responded to such situations?

4. What does it mean to "stand firm" when you are persecuted?

5. What can you do to prepare yourself so that you will stand firm throughout your life, even during intense persecution?

PAUL'S MINISTRY Paul expressed his concern for this church even while he was being slandered. Paul's commitment to share the gospel in spite of difficult circumstances is an example that we should follow.

Paul not only gave his message, he also gave himself. In our ministries, we must become like Paul—faithful and bold, yet sensitive and self-sacrificing. Achieving such maturity results from years of commitment to God's will—the younger you begin, the deeper your growth will be.

1. What qualities do you see in Paul's wonderful example of godly ministry that enabled his

message to be so powerful?

2. If you were Paul's companion in ministry, what would you most want to learn from him?

3. Who are the people closest to you who need to hear God's message? How will you follow Paul's example and do this?

4. What thoughts, attitudes, or actions do you have as a result of the hope that is within you in Christ? What can you do to comfort and encourage others with this truth?

BEING PREPARED No one knows when Christ will return. In the meantime, we are to live moral and holy lives, ever watching for his coming. Believers must not neglect their daily responsibilities, but always work and live as unto the Lord.

The gospel tells us not only what we should believe, but also how we must live. The Holy Spirit leads us in faithfulness, so we can avoid lust and fraud. Live as though you expect Christ's return at any time. Don't be caught unprepared.

1. Summarize the events of Christ's return as revealed in 1 Thessalonians.

2. What does it mean to be prepared for these events? Why is this so important? (Check Matthew 25 for Jesus' teaching.)

3. What are you doing to be ready for Christ's return?

A prominent author's best-selling new book has predicted that Christ is coming back in a few days. ■ Anne: "It's supposed to happen *this* weekend." ■ Sandra: "I guess I'm ready, but if it *does* happen, I'll never get my license—and I'll never get to . . . well, you know." ■ (Everyone but Pam giggles.) ■ Karen: "I think it's *great*. I've got a *huge* algebra test on Monday that I can't possibly pass. *Now* I can just relax and forget about it."

■ Sandra: "Right, and no more abuse from Steve Hampton and his atheist friends!" ■ Anne: "Omigosh, I never even thought about that. *That* will be the best!" ■ Pam: "You guys *cannot* be serious! You talk like you actually *believe* that stuff!" ■ Anne: "Of course we do! It all fits together, and it's in the Bible, Pam. It's going to be this weekend—you better get ready." ■ Jesus *is* coming back. And his return *will* radically change things. It *will* be great, just as the girls imagine. ■ But that doesn't mean we should start picking dates and sitting around waiting. The prospect of Christ's return should motivate us to action, not laziness. He is coming back, so let's live for him—and encourage others to do the same. ■ That's the message of 2 Thessalonians. Yes, the world is gross. Yes, the Christian life is hard. But Jesus is coming back soon to make everything right. So keep watching, waiting—and working. ■ (And by all means, study for your algebra exam!)

STATS

PURPOSE: To clear up the confusion about the second coming of Christ

AUTHOR: Paul

TO WHOM WRITTEN: The church at Thessalonica and all believers everywhere

DATE WRITTEN: About A.D. 51 or 52, a few months after 1 Thessalonians, from Corinth

SETTING: Many in the church were confused about the timing of Christ's return. Because of increasing persecution, they thought the Lord must return soon, so they interpreted Paul's first letter to say that the Second Coming would be at any moment. In light of this misunderstanding, some became lazy and disorderly.

KEY PEOPLE: Paul, Silas, Timothy

KEY PLACE: Thessalonica

SPECIAL FEATURES: This is a follow-up letter to 1 Thessalonians. In this epistle, Paul tells of various events that must precede the second coming of Christ.

2Thessalonians

CHAPTER 1 PATIENCE IN SUFFERING. *From:* Paul, Silas, and Timothy.

To: The church of Thessalonica—kept safe in God our Father and in the Lord Jesus Christ.

[2]May God the Father and the Lord Jesus Christ give you rich blessings and peace-filled hearts and minds.

[3]Dear brothers, giving thanks to God for you is not only the right thing to do, but it is our duty to God because of the really wonderful way your faith has grown and because of your growing love for each other. [4]We are happy to tell other churches about your patience and complete faith in God, in spite of all the crushing troubles and hardships you are going through.

[5]This is only one example of the fair, just way God does things, for he is using your sufferings to make you ready for his Kingdom, [6]while at the same time he is preparing judgment and punishment for those who are hurting you.

[7]And so I would say to you who are suffering, God will give you rest along with us when the Lord Jesus appears suddenly from heaven in flaming fire with his mighty angels, [8]bringing judgment on those who do not wish to know God and who refuse to accept his plan to save them through our Lord Jesus Christ. [9]They will be punished in everlasting hell, forever separated from the Lord, never to see the glory of his power [10]when he comes to receive praise and admiration because of all he has done for his people, his saints. And you will be among those praising him because you have believed what we told you about him.

[11]And so we keep on praying for you, that our God will make you the kind of children he wants to have—will make you as good as you wish you could be!—rewarding your faith with his power. [12]Then everyone will be praising the name of the Lord Jesus Christ because of the results they see in you; and your greatest glory will be that you belong to him. The tender mercy of our God and of the Lord Jesus Christ has made all this possible for you.

TROUBLES

1:5 As we live for Christ, we will experience troubles and hardships. Some say that troubles are a result of sin or lack of faith; Paul teaches that they may be a part of God's plan for believers. Our problems help us look upward and forward, not inward (Mark 13:35-36); help build strong character (Romans 5:3-4); and help us to be sensitive to others (2 Corinthians 1:3-5).

CHAPTER **2** THE ANTICHRIST. And now, what about the coming again of our Lord Jesus Christ and our being gathered together to meet him? Please don't be upset and excited, dear brothers, by the rumor that this day of the Lord has already begun. If you hear of people having visions and special messages from God about this, or letters that are supposed to have come from me, don't believe them. ³Don't be carried away and deceived regardless of what they say.

For that day will not come until two things happen: first, there will be a time of great rebellion against God, and then the man of rebellion will come—the son of hell. ⁴He will defy every god there is and tear down every other object of adoration and worship. He will go in and sit as God in the temple of God, claiming that he himself is God. ⁵Don't you remember that I told you this when I was with you? ⁶And you know what is keeping him from being here already; for he can come only when his time is ready.

⁷As for the work this man of rebellion and hell will do when he comes, it is already going on, but he himself will not come until the one who is holding him back steps out of the way. ⁸Then this wicked one will appear, whom the Lord Jesus will burn up with the breath of his mouth and destroy by his presence when he returns. ⁹This man of sin will come as Satan's tool, full of satanic power, and will trick everyone with strange demonstrations, and will do great miracles. ¹⁰He will completely fool those who are on their way to hell because they have said no to the Truth; they

have refused to believe it and love it and let it save them, ¹¹so God will allow them to believe lies with all their hearts, ¹²and all of them will be justly judged for believing falsehood, refusing the Truth, and enjoying their sins.

¹³But we must forever give thanks to God for you, our brothers loved by the Lord, because God chose from the very first to give you salvation, cleansing you by the work of the Holy Spirit and by your trusting in the Truth. ¹⁴Through us he told you the Good News. Through us he called you to share in the glory of our Lord Jesus Christ.

¹⁵With all these things in mind, dear brothers, stand firm and keep a strong grip on the truth that we taught you in our letters and during the time we were with you.

¹⁶May our Lord Jesus Christ himself and God our Father, who has loved us and given us everlasting comfort and hope, which we don't deserve, ¹⁷comfort your hearts with all comfort, and help you in every good thing you say and do.

CHAPTER **3** GOD MAKES US STRONG. Finally, dear brothers, as I come to the end of this letter, I ask you to pray for us. Pray first that the Lord's message will spread rapidly and triumph wherever it goes, winning converts everywhere as it did when it came to you. ²Pray, too, that we will be saved out of the clutches of evil men, for not everyone loves the Lord. ³But the Lord is faithful; he will make you strong and guard you from satanic attacks of every kind. ⁴And we trust the Lord that you are putting into practice the things we taught you, and that you always will. ⁵May the Lord bring you into an ever deeper understanding of the love of God and of the patience that comes from Christ.

⁶Now here is a command, dear brothers, given in the name of our Lord Jesus Christ by his authority: Stay away from any Christian who spends his days in laziness and does not follow the ideal of hard work we set up for you. ⁷For you well know that you ought to follow our example: you never saw us loafing; ⁸we never accepted food from any-

LAZINESS

Trip walks in the door, drops his books on the couch, and heads straight for the kitchen. Opening the pantry, he scans the shelves and scowls. "How come there's never anything to eat in this stupid house?" he mutters to no one in particular.

Grabbing a banana, he settles back in the recliner, remote control in hand. *Click . . . Click . . . Click.*

The phone rings. Trip doesn't budge.

A voice from the hallway: "Trip, can you get the phone? I've got shaving cream all over my hands."

Trip sits impassively, staring at the TV.

The phone continues to ring. The voice from the rear of the house gets louder. "Trip! Answer the phone!"

Just as the mystery caller gives up, Trip's mom staggers through the door, her arms loaded with grocery sacks.

Trip watches her struggle from his easy chair and greets her by saying, "I hope you bought something decent to eat."

"Go get the other sacks and I'll get supper started."

"Sheesh!" Trip complains as he grudgingly leaves his comfortable throne. "Why do I always have to do everything around here? You and Dad treat me like a slave!"

Are you a lazy person? See what the Bible says about individuals who are unwilling to pull their share of the load— 2 Thessalonians 3:6-13.

EVIL

2:3 Throughout history there have been antichrists— individuals who epitomized evil (see 1 John 2:18; 4:3; 2 John 1:7). Antichrists will occur until a "man of rebellion" arises just before the Second Coming. This evil individual will be Satan's tool—perhaps even Satan himself (2:9). This "son of hell" will be *the* Antichrist.

It is dangerous, however, to label certain individuals *antichrists* and try to predict Christ's coming based on those assumptions. Paul mentions the Antichrist, not necessarily to help us recognize him, but to urge us to ready ourselves for anything that might threaten our faith. If our faith is strong, we needn't fear what lies ahead. God is in control; he will be victorious. We must ready ourselves for Christ, spreading his Good News to help others be prepared also.

one without buying it; we worked hard day and night for the money we needed to live on, in order that we would not be a burden to any of you. [9]It wasn't that we didn't have the right to ask you to feed us, but we wanted to show you firsthand how you should work for your living. [10]Even while we were still there with you, we gave you this rule: "He who does not work shall not eat."

[11]Yet we hear that some of you are living in laziness, refusing to work, and wasting your time in gossiping. [12]In the name of the Lord Jesus Christ we appeal to such people—we command them—to quiet down, get to work, and earn their own living. [13]And to the rest of you I say, dear brothers, never be tired of doing right.

[14]If anyone refuses to obey what we say in this letter, notice who he is and stay away from him, that he may be ashamed of himself. [15]Don't think of him as an enemy, but speak to him as you would to a brother who needs to be warned.

[16]May the Lord of peace himself give you his peace no matter what happens. The Lord be with you all.

[17]Now here is my greeting, which I am writing with my own hand, as I do at the end of all my letters, for proof that it really is from me. This is in my own handwriting. [18]May the blessing of our Lord Jesus Christ be upon you all.

Sincerely, Paul

MEGA Themes

PERSECUTION Paul encouraged the church to have patience in spite of troubles and hardships. God will bring victory to his faithful followers, and he will judge those who persecute them.

God promises to reward our faith with his power and to help us bear persecution. Suffering for our faith will strengthen us to serve Christ. God never will allow us to experience suffering apart from his power and presence.

1. How did the Thessalonians respond to persecution?
2. What did Paul say to encourage them?
3. What was the basis of Paul's belief that the Thessalonians could stand firm in their faith in spite of these painful experiences?
4. In what ways can Paul's words help you?

CHRIST'S RETURN Paul had said that Christ would come back at any moment, so some of the Thessalonian believers had stopped work to wait.

Christ will return and bring total victory to all who trust in him. If we stand firm and keep working, we will be ready. If we are ready, we don't have to be concerned about *when* he will return. Our lives are already eternally secure in Christ.

1. What concerns did Paul express in chapter 3? What false ideas had developed about what it means to prepare for Christ's coming?
2. How did the promise of Christ's ultimate reign affect Paul's attitude toward life? How did he challenge the Thessalonians to live in light of Christ's coming?
3. How does thinking about the promise of Christ's ultimate reign affect your feelings? Thoughts? Actions?

4. What is your plan of preparation? How does this relate to Paul's prayer request in 3:5?

GREAT REBELLION Before Christ's return, there will be a great rebellion against God led by the man of rebellion (the Antichrist). God will remove all the restraints on evil before he brings judgment on the rebels. The Antichrist will attempt to deceive many.

We should not be afraid when we see evil increase. God is in control, no matter how evil the world becomes. God guards us from satanic attack. We can have victory over evil by remaining faithful to God. Satan and all evil are subject to God.

1. What is the danger of the Antichrist?
2. In light of the fact that the Antichrist will impact the world and that evil is already present, how should we live?
3. How should you live in an evil world? How can this give you the confidence to endure even the dangers of the Antichrist?

PERSISTENCE Because church members had quit working and become disorderly and disobedient, Paul criticized them for their laziness. He told them to show courage and to live as Christians should.

We must never get so tired of doing right that we quit. We can be persistent by making the most of our time and talent. Our endurance will be rewarded.

1. Why is laziness so negative for a Christian?
2. In what areas do you struggle most with laziness? What does this tell you about the root of laziness?
3. Developing self-discipline is a learned quality. It is easy and natural to do only what we want to do. What does it take to develop self-discipline?
4. Outline a plan for developing self-discipline in one specific, weak area in your life.

What does it take to be a leader? Brains? Good looks? A magnetic personality? The ability to speak persuasively? A ruthless obsession for power? That's what the world says. ■ The world is wrong. Leadership is not about being tall, tan, and telegenic. Leadership has nothing to do with impressive resumés or rousing speeches. Leadership is far more than being well-born or highly-educated or multitalented. Jesus defined leadership as servanthood. It involves compassion, courage, and conviction. ■ So here's the shocker: *Anyone who takes the time to develop those qualities can be a leader.* ■ Even you. ■ "Who? Me?! You must be kidding. I don't have any special talents. Besides, I'm young and kind of shy. I could never lead anyone." ■ Funny you should say that. A young man by the name of Timothy once felt the exact same way. He found himself facing big responsibilities and even bigger challenges. He wondered what to do and whether he had what leadership requires. ■ Then he got the following letter from his friend and mentor, Paul. More than a mere letter, the Epistle of 1 Timothy is also an essay on leadership. ■ Hey, you may never be a major politician or the president of a big company, but you'll always have friends, relatives, neighbors, and acquaintances who need to be influenced. People you can (and should) influence for Christ. ■ So read about the character, compassion, courage, and conviction that leadership involves. ■ Then give it a try. Be a leader.

STATS

PURPOSE: To encourage and instruct Timothy

AUTHOR: Paul

TO WHOM WRITTEN: Timothy, young church leaders, and all believers everywhere

DATE WRITTEN: About A.D. 64, from Rome or Macedonia (possibly Philippi), probably just prior to Paul's final imprisonment in Rome

SETTING: Timothy was one of Paul's closest companions. Paul had sent him to the church at Ephesus to counter the false teaching that had arisen there (1 Timothy 1:3-4). Timothy probably served for a time as a leader in the church at Ephesus. Paul hoped to visit Timothy (3:14-15; 4:13), but in the meantime, he wrote this letter to give Timothy practical advice for the ministry.

KEY PEOPLE: Paul, Timothy

KEY PLACE: Ephesus

1 **T**imothy

CHAPTER 1 PAUL'S SON IN THE LORD. *From:* Paul, a missionary of Jesus Christ, sent out by the direct command of God our Savior and by Jesus Christ our Lord—our only hope.

[2]*To:* Timothy.

Timothy, you are like a son to me in the things of the Lord. May God our Father and Jesus Christ our Lord show you his kindness and mercy and give you great peace of heart and mind.

[3,4]As I said when I left for Macedonia, please stay there in Ephesus and try to stop the men who are teaching such wrong doctrine. Put an end to their myths and fables, and their idea of being saved by finding favor with an endless chain of angels leading up to God—wild ideas that stir up questions and arguments instead of helping people accept God's plan of faith. [5]What I am eager for is that all the Christians there will be filled with love that comes from pure hearts, and that their minds will be clean and their faith strong.

[6]But these teachers have missed this whole idea and spend their time arguing and talking foolishness. [7]They want to become famous as teachers of the laws of Moses when they haven't the slightest idea what those laws really show us. [8]Those laws are good when used as God intended. [9]But they were not made for us, whom God has saved; they are for sinners who hate God, have rebellious hearts, curse and swear, attack their fathers and mothers, and murder. [10,11]Yes, these laws are made to identify as sinners all who are immoral and impure: homosexuals, kidnappers, liars, and all others who do things that contradict the glorious Good News of our blessed God, whose messenger I am.

[12]How thankful I am to Christ Jesus our Lord for choosing me as one of his messengers, and giving me the strength to be faithful to him, [13]even though

ALLEGIANCE

1:3-11 The world is filled with people demanding our allegiance. Many would have us turn from Christ to follow them. Often their influence is subtle. How can you recognize false teaching before it does irreparable damage? (1) It stirs up questions and arguments instead of helping people come to Jesus (1:4). (2) It is often promoted by teachers whose motivation is to make a name for themselves (1:7). (3) It is contrary to the true teaching of the Scriptures (1:6-7; 4:1-3). Instead of listening to false teachers, we should learn what the Bible teaches and remain strong in our faith in Christ alone.

I used to scoff at the name of Christ. I hunted down his people, harming them in every way I could. But God had mercy on me because I didn't know what I was doing, for I didn't know Christ at that time. [14]Oh, how kind our Lord was, for he showed me how to trust him and become full of the love of Christ Jesus.

[15]How true it is, and how I long that everyone should know it, that Christ Jesus came into the world to save sinners—and I was the greatest of them all. [16]But God had mercy on me so that Christ Jesus could use me as an example to show everyone how patient he is with even the worst sinners, so that others will realize that they, too, can have everlasting life. [17]Glory and honor to God forever and ever. He is the King of the ages, the unseen one who never dies; he alone is God, and full of wisdom. Amen.

[18]Now, Timothy, my son, here is my command to you: Fight well in the Lord's battles, just as the Lord told us through his prophets that you would. [19]Cling tightly to your faith in Christ and always keep your conscience clear, doing what you know is right. For some people have disobeyed their consciences and have deliberately done what they knew was wrong. It isn't surprising that soon they lost their faith in Christ after defying God like that. [20]Hymenaeus and Alexander are two examples of this. I had to give them over to Satan to punish them until they could learn not to bring shame to the name of Christ.

CHAPTER 2 GUIDELINES FOR WORSHIP.

Here are my directions: Pray much for others; plead for God's mercy upon them; give thanks for all he is going to do for them.

[2]Pray in this way for kings and all others who are in authority over us, or are in places of high responsibility, so that we can live in peace and quietness, spending our time in godly living and thinking much about the Lord. [3]This is good and pleases God our Savior, [4]for he longs for all to be saved and to understand this truth: [5]*That God is on one side and all the people on the other side, and Christ Jesus, himself man, is between them to bring them together, [6]by giving his life for all mankind.*

This is the message that at the proper time God gave to the world. [7]And I have been chosen—this is the absolute truth—as God's minister and missionary to teach this truth to the Gentiles and to show them God's plan of salvation through faith.

[8]So I want men everywhere to pray with holy hands lifted up to God, free from sin and anger and resentment. [9,10]And the women should be the same way, quiet and sensible in manner and clothing. Christian women should be noticed for being kind and good, not for the way they fix their hair or because of their jewels or fancy clothes. [11]Women should listen and learn quietly and humbly.

[12]I never let women teach men or lord it over them. Let them be silent in your church meetings. [13]Why? Because God made Adam first, and afterwards he made Eve. [14]And it was not Adam who was fooled by Satan, but Eve, and sin was the result. [15]So God sent pain and suffering to women when their children are born, but he will save their souls if they trust in him, living quiet, good, and loving lives.

CHAPTER 3 GUIDELINES FOR CHURCH LEADERS.

It is a true saying that if a man wants to be a pastor he has a good ambition. [2]For a pastor must be a good man whose life cannot be spoken against. He must have only one wife, and he must be hard working and thoughtful, orderly, and full of good deeds. He must enjoy having guests in his home and must be a good Bible teacher. [3]He must not be a drinker or quarrelsome, but he must be gentle and kind and not be one who loves money. [4]He must have a well-behaved family, with children who obey quickly and quietly. [5]For if a man can't make his own little family behave, how can he help the whole church?

[6]The pastor must not be a new Christian because he might be proud of being chosen so soon, and pride comes before a fall. (Satan's downfall is an example.) [7]Also, he must be well spoken of by people outside the church—those who aren't Christians—so that Satan can't trap him with many accusations and leave him without freedom to lead his flock.

[8]The deacons must be the same sort of good, steady men as the pastors. They must not be heavy drinkers and must not be greedy for money. [9]They must be earnest, wholehearted followers of Christ, who is the hidden Source of their faith. [10]Before they are asked to be deacons, they should be given other jobs in the church as a test of their character

INNER TUGS

1:19 How can you keep your conscience clear? Treasure your faith in Christ more than anything else and do what you know is right. Each time you deliberately ignore your conscience, you are hardening your heart. Soon your capacity to tell right from wrong will disappear. But when you walk with God, he is able to speak to you through your conscience, letting you know the difference between right and wrong. Be sure to act on those inner tugs to do what is right—then your conscience will remain clear.

MAKE PEACE

2:8 Besides being displeasing to God, it is difficult to pray when we have sinned or when we feel angry and resentful. That is why Jesus told us to interrupt worship, if necessary, to make peace with others (Matthew 5:23-24). Our goal is to have a right relationship with God and also with others.

and ability, and if they do well, then they may be chosen as deacons.

[11]Their wives must be thoughtful, not heavy drinkers, not gossipers, but faithful in everything they do. [12]Deacons should have only one wife, and they should have happy, obedient families. [13]Those who do well as deacons will be well rewarded both by respect from others and also by developing their own confidence and bold trust in the Lord.

[14]I am writing these things to you now, even though I hope to be with you soon, [15]so that if I don't come for awhile, you will know what kind of men you should choose as officers for the church of the living God, which contains and holds high the truth of God.

[16]It is quite true that the way to live a godly life is not an easy matter. But the answer lies in Christ, who came to earth as a man, was proved spotless and pure in his Spirit, was served by angels, was preached among the nations, was accepted by men everywhere, and was received up again to his glory in heaven.

CHAPTER 4 IGNORE FALSE TEACHERS: THEY LIE. But
the Holy Spirit tells us clearly that in the last times some in the church will turn away from Christ and become eager followers of teachers with devil-inspired ideas. [2]These teachers will tell lies with straight faces and do it so often that their consciences won't even bother them.

[3]They will say it is wrong to be married and wrong to eat meat, even though God gave these things to well-taught Christians to enjoy and be thankful for. [4]For everything God made is good, and we may eat it gladly if we are thankful for it, [5]and if we ask God to bless it, for it is made good by the Word of God and prayer.

[6]If you explain this to the others you will be doing your duty as a worthy pastor who is fed by faith and by the true teaching you have followed.

[7]Don't waste time arguing over foolish ideas and silly myths and legends. Spend your time and energy in the exercise of keeping spiritually fit. [8]Bodily exercise is all right, but spiritual exercise is much more important and is a tonic for all you do. So exercise yourself spiritually, and

TIMOTHY

Real leadership abilities are sometimes buried under a person's shyness. It takes a friend with understanding and patience to uncover those strengths. That's what happened between the apostle Paul and a young man named Timothy. Timothy probably became a Christian when Paul visited his hometown of Lystra during his first missionary journey (Acts 14:8-20). Timothy's Jewish mother and grandmother had prepared him by teaching him from the Old Testament. By the time Paul visited Lystra again, Timothy was known as a growing Christian. When invited, Timothy jumped at the chance to travel with Paul and Silas.

Away from home, Timothy struggled with his shyness. Unfortunately, shy people are often written off as being unable to carry much responsibility. But Paul chose to give Timothy important responsibilities in the ministry. Paul even made Timothy his personal representative on several occasions. Sometimes Timothy failed on his missions, but Paul never gave up on him. Timothy became a "son" to Paul.

Our last pictures of Timothy come from the most personal letters in the New Testament: 1 and 2 Timothy. They were written by Paul in such a way that his deep friendship with Timothy is obvious; they had traveled, suffered, cried, and laughed together. The letters were intended to encourage and direct Timothy in Ephesus, where Paul had left him in charge of a young church (1 Timothy 1:3-4). These same letters have helped and encouraged countless other "Timothys" through the years. When you face a challenge that is beyond your abilities, read 1 and 2 Timothy. Remember, others have shared your experience.

KEY VERSES: "There is no one like Timothy for having a real interest in you; everyone else seems to be worrying about his own plans and not those of Jesus Christ. But you know Timothy. He has been just like a son to me in helping me preach the Good News" (Philippians 2:20-22).

LESSONS: Youthfulness should not be an excuse for ineffectiveness
Our inadequacies and inabilities should not keep us from being available to God
Timothy's story is told in Acts, starting in chapter 16. He is also mentioned in Romans 16:21; 1 Corinthians 4:17; 16:10-11; 2 Corinthians 1:1,19; Colossians 1:1; Philippians 1:1; 2:19-23; Colossians 1:1-2; 1 Thessalonians 1:1-10; 2:3-4; 3: 2-6; 1 and 2 Timothy; Philemon 1:1; Hebrews 13:23.

UPS:
• Became a believer after Paul's first missionary journey and joined him for his other two journeys
• Was a respected Christian in his hometown
• Was Paul's special representative on several occasions
• Received two personal letters from Paul
• Probably knew Paul better than any other person, becoming like a son to him

DOWNS:
• Struggled with a timid and reserved nature
• Allowed others to look down on his youthfulness
• Was apparently unable to correct some of the problems in the church at Corinth when Paul sent him there

STATS:
• Where: Lystra
• Occupation: Missionary-in-training
• Relatives: Mother: Eunice; Grandmother: Lois; Greek father.
• Contemporaries: Paul, Silas, Luke, Mark, Peter, Barnabas

practice being a better Christian because that will help you not only now in this life, but in the next life too. [9,10]This is the truth and everyone should accept it. We work hard and suffer much in order that people will believe it, for our hope is in the living God who died for all, and particularly for those who have accepted his salvation.

[11]Teach these things and make sure everyone learns them well. [12]Don't let anyone think little of you because you are young. Be their ideal; let them follow the way you teach and live; be a pattern for them in your love, your faith, and your clean thoughts. [13]Until I get there, read and explain the Scriptures to the church; preach God's Word.

[14]Be sure to use the abilities God has given you through his prophets when the elders of the church laid their hands upon your head. [15]Put these abilities to work; throw yourself into your tasks so that everyone may notice your improvement and progress. [16]Keep a close watch on all you do and think. Stay true to what is right and God will bless you and use you to help others.

CHAPTER 5 YOUR PART.
Never speak sharply to an older man, but plead with him respectfully just as though he were your own father. Talk to the younger men as you would to much-loved brothers. [2]Treat the older women as mothers, and the girls as your sisters, thinking only pure thoughts about them.

[3]The church should take loving care of women whose husbands have died if they don't have anyone else to help them. [4]But if they have children or grandchildren, these are the ones who should take the responsibility, for kindness should begin at home, supporting needy parents. This is something that pleases God very much.

[5]The church should care for widows who are poor and alone in the world if they are looking to God for his help and spending much time in prayer; [6]but not if they are spending their time running around gossiping, seeking only pleasure and thus ruining their souls. [7]This should be your church rule so that the Christians will know and do what is right.

[8]But anyone who won't care for his own relatives when they need help, especially those living in his own family, has no right to say he is a Christian. Such a person is worse than the heathen.

[9]A widow who wants to become one of the special church workers should be at least sixty years old and have been married only once. [10]She must be well thought of by everyone because of the good she has done. Has she brought up her children well? Has she been kind to strangers as well as to other Christians? Has she helped those who are sick and hurt? Is she always ready to show kindness?

[11]The younger widows should not become members of this special group because after awhile they are likely to disregard their vow to Christ and marry again. [12]And so they will stand condemned because they broke their first promise. [13]Besides,

DON'T let a n y o n e think little of YOU because YOU are young. BE their IDEAL; let them follow the way you teach and live; BE a PATTERN for them in YOUR LOVE YOUR FAITH and YOUR CLEAN THOUGHTS

1 TIMOTHY 4:12

they are likely to be lazy and spend their time gossiping around from house to house, getting into other people's business. [14]So I think it is better for these younger widows to marry again and have children and take care of their own homes; then no one will be able to say anything against them. [15]For I am afraid that some of them have already turned away from the church and been led astray by Satan.

[16]Let me remind you again that a widow's relatives must take care of her and not leave this to the church to do. Then the church can spend its money for the care of widows who are all alone and have nowhere else to turn.

[17]Pastors who do their work well should be paid well and should be highly appreciated, especially those who work hard at both preaching and teaching. [18]For the Scriptures say, "Never tie up the mouth of an ox when it is treading out the grain—let him eat as he goes along!" And in another place, "Those who work deserve their pay!"

[19]Don't listen to complaints against the pastor unless there are two or three witnesses to accuse him. [20]If he has really sinned, then he should be rebuked in front of the whole church so that no one else will follow his example.

[21]I solemnly command you in the presence of God and the Lord Jesus Christ and of the holy angels to do this whether the pastor is a special friend of yours or not. All must be treated exactly the same. [22]Never be in a hurry about choosing a pastor; you may overlook his sins, and it will look as if you approve of them. Be sure that you yourself stay away from all sin. [23](By the way, this doesn't mean you should completely give up drinking wine. You ought to take a little sometimes as medicine for your stomach because you are sick so often.)

[24]Remember that some men, even pastors, lead sinful lives, and everyone knows it. In such situations you can do something about it. But in other cases only the judgment day will reveal the terrible truth. [25]In the same way, everyone knows how much good some pastors do, but sometimes their good deeds aren't known until long afterward.

CHAPTER **6** **MONEY ISN'T EVERYTHING.** Christian slaves should work hard for their owners and respect them; never let it be said that Christ's people are poor workers. Don't let the name of God or his teaching be laughed at because of this.

[2]If their owner is a Christian, that is no excuse for slowing down; rather they should work all the harder because a brother in the faith is being helped by their efforts.

Teach these truths, Timothy, and encourage all to obey them.

[3]Some may deny these things, but they are the sound, wholesome teachings of the Lord Jesus Christ and are the foundation for a godly life. [4]Anyone who says anything different is both proud and stupid. He is quibbling over the meaning of Christ's words and stirring up arguments ending in

Trying to stay pure and not sin seems like a full-time job. How can anyone stay pure? Why would anyone want to?

I WONDER . . .

Jesus talked a lot about the Pharisees. These men had created long lists of dos and don'ts about behavior of every kind. They wanted to be pure! Many of them were very, very good.

But in Matthew 5:20, Jesus made an incredible statement! "I warn you—unless your goodness is greater than that of the Pharisees and other Jewish leaders, you can't get into the Kingdom of Heaven at all!"

Wow! If the Pharisees couldn't make it, who can?

Those who make it into the Kingdom of Heaven are not just pure on the outside, like the Pharisees. Anyone can make sure their behavior is correct (at least for a while).

Jesus was talking about being pure on the inside. This begins by accepting Christ's death on the cross as punishment for our sins. When we do this, we take on Christ's goodness, and, in God's eyes, we are pure and worthy of eternity in heaven! Now that's a pretty good deal!

It doesn't stop there, of course. God wants us to be like Jesus. This is a lifetime process of allowing God to mold us and change us (see 1 Timothy 6:11-12). It happens by staying close to Christ and living like he wants us to. It's what keeps the Christian life fun, interesting, and challenging.

A Christian who's really alive realizes that his eternity is settled. But he also genuinely wants to be more like the one who paid such a high price for his soul—Jesus. His motivation is not to parade his goodness in front of others, but rather to please God.

Staying pure and growing as a Christian are "full-time jobs." But they are also natural by-products of staying close to Christ.

jealousy and anger, which only lead to name-calling, accusations, and evil suspicions. [5]These arguers—their minds warped by sin—don't know how to tell the truth; to them the Good News is just a means of making money. Keep away from them.

[6]Do you want to be truly rich? You already are if you are happy and good. [7]After all, we didn't bring any money with us when we came into the world, and we can't carry away a single penny when we die. [8]So we should be well satisfied without money if we have enough food and clothing. [9]But people who long to be rich soon begin to do all kinds of wrong things to get money, things that hurt them and make them evil-minded and finally send them to hell itself. [10]For the love of money is the first step toward all kinds of sin. Some people

have even turned away from God because of their love for it, and as a result have pierced themselves with many sorrows.

[11]O Timothy, you are God's man. Run from all these evil things, and work instead at what is right and good, learning to trust him and love others and to be patient and gentle. [12]Fight on for God. Hold tightly to the eternal life that God has given you and that you have confessed with such a ringing confession before many witnesses.

[13]I command you before God, who gives life to all, and before Christ Jesus, who gave a fearless testimony before Pontius Pilate, [14]that you fulfill all he has told you to do so that no one can find fault with you from now until our Lord Jesus Christ returns. [15]For in due season Christ will be revealed from heaven by the blessed and only Almighty God, the King of kings and Lord of lords, [16]who alone can never die, who lives in light so terrible that no human being can approach him. No mere man has ever seen him nor ever will.

Unto him be honor and everlasting power and dominion forever and ever. Amen.

[17]Tell those who are rich not to be proud and not to trust in their money, which will soon be gone, but their pride and trust should be in the living God who always richly gives us all we need for our enjoyment. [18]Tell them to use their money to do good. They should be rich in good works and should give happily to those in need, always being ready to share with others whatever God has given them. [19]By doing this they will be storing up real treasure for themselves in heaven—it is the only safe investment for eternity! And they will be living a fruitful Christian life down here as well.

[20]Oh, Timothy, don't fail to do these things that God entrusted to you. Keep out of foolish arguments with those who boast of their "knowledge" and thus prove their lack of it. [21]Some of these people have missed the most important thing in life—they don't know God. May God's mercy be upon you.

Sincerely, Paul

YOU'RE RICH

6:17-19 Ephesus was a wealthy city and the Ephesian church probably had many wealthy members. Paul advised Timothy to deal with a potential problem by teaching that the possession of riches carries great responsibility. Those who have money must be generous, not arrogant. They must be careful not to put their trust in money instead of in the living God. Even if we don't have material wealth, we can be rich in good works toward others. No matter how poor we are, we have something to share with someone.

MONEY LOVE

6:6-10 Despite almost overwhelming evidence to the contrary, some people still believe money brings happiness. Rich people craving greater riches can be caught in an endless cycle that only ends in ruin and desperation. How can we avoid the love of money? Paul gives us some principles: (1) realize that one day material riches will all be gone (6:7,17); (2) be content with what you have (6:8); (3) watch what you are willing to do to get more money (6:9-10); (4) love people and God's work more than money (6:11,18); (5) freely share what you have with others (6:18).

MEGA *Themes*

SOUND DOCTRINE Paul instructed Timothy to preserve the Christian faith by teaching sound doctrine and modeling right living. Timothy had to oppose false teachers who were leading church members away from belief in salvation by faith in Jesus Christ alone.

We must know the truth to defend it. And the truth is that Christ came to save us. We should stay away from those who twist the words of the Bible for their own purposes. Therefore, we must study and know the Bible ourselves.

1. What do you consider to be the main points in the Bible concerning God and man, sin and salvation, life and death?
2. Why are these truths so important to the Bible's message?
3. Paul greatly opposed those who taught against the truth of the gospel. What did Paul tell Timothy to do about false teachers?
4. Based on this study, how should you respond to the message of a false teacher? What can you do to be able to discern the truth from error?

PUBLIC WORSHIP In public worship, prayer must be done with a proper attitude toward God and fellow believers.

Christian character must be evident in every aspect of worship. We must rid ourselves of any anger, resentment, or offensive attire that might disrupt worship or damage church unity. Christian unity begins with your own attitude and actions toward others.

1. What were Paul's instructions to Timothy about worship?
2. What aspects of public, congregational worship do you most enjoy? Least enjoy? How do you feel about worship overall?
3. What should be a Christian's attitude in worship? What actions should be a part of worship services?
4. What steps can you take to deepen your worship as well as to encourage others in your church to do the same?

CHURCH LEADERSHIP Paul gives specific instructions concerning the qualifications for church leaders so that the church might honor God and run smoothly.

Church leaders must be wholly committed to Christ. If you are a new or young Christian, don't be anxious to become a leader in your church. Develop your Christian character first. Be sure to consider God, not your own ambition.

1. Describe the overall character of the persons who are qualified to serve in church leadership according to 3:1-16.
2. In what specific ways does Paul challenge Timothy to mature and develop personally?
3. How can a young person who is a Christian prepare now to be a man or woman of God later, as he or she matures?
4. Praise God for your areas of personal strength. Design a plan to work on your personal

weaknesses so that, by his grace, you will be a godly leader throughout your life.

PERSONAL DISCIPLINE It takes discipline to be a leader in the church. Timothy, like all church leaders, had to guard his motives, minister faithfully, and live right. Any pastor must keep morally and spiritually fit.

To stay in good spiritual shape, you must discipline yourself to study God's Word and to live a godly life. Put your spiritual abilities to work!

1. What areas of personal discipline would Timothy have to develop as a result of what Paul told him?
2. How do you think Timothy felt as he read this letter? Read chapters 4 and 6 and describe how you would have felt if this letter had been written to you.
3. What beginning steps can you take to deepen your faith?
4. How will the Holy Spirit of God help you to deal with the personal difficulties you may face as you attempt to step out?

CARING CHURCH The church has a responsibility to care for the needs of all its members, especially the sick, the poor, and the widowed.

Caring for the family of believers demonstrates our Christlike attitude and genuine love. We are Christ's touch of love in one another's lives.

1. What did Paul think about the church's responsibility for reaching out to others?
2. Why is this so important for the church as Christ's body?
3. On a scale of A-B-C-D-F, give your church a grade in terms of Paul's descriptions of what it means to serve those in need.
4. Grade yourself on the above scale. What can you do to improve your grade? What can you do to get involved with your church to improve its grade?

*T*rivia is "unimportant matters." It's all that information that's often interesting but doesn't really matter much. For instance, did you know that: ■ Grasshoppers are approximately three times more nutritious than rib-eye steak? ■ Kangaroos can't jump when their tails are lifted off the ground? ■ France's King Louis XIV feared water so much that he never took a bath and rarely washed more than the tip of his nose? ■ It's impossible to sneeze with your eyes open? ■ Benjamin Franklin invented swim fins and the rocking chair? ■ Mozart wrote the tune "Twinkle, Twinkle, Little Star" when he was five? ■ Eating too many carrots can make your skin turn yellow? ■ Nine-hundred-and-twenty-eight average size fleas will fit inside a Ping-Pong ball. ■ Though amusing—and helpful for filling the silence in an awkward conversation—the facts just cited are worthless. They won't change your life. They're trivia. *Trivial* trivia. ■ Not so the book of 2 Timothy. ■ The apostle Paul's Second Letter to Timothy is serious stuff. History says that these were Paul's last words; he died shortly after penning them. ■ Perhaps the aged saint recognized that his time was running out. If so, it's not surprising that he talked about important matters. Consider carefully Paul's final thoughts. He is, after all, one of the most influential individuals in history. ■ And Paul's challenge to Timothy is just as appropriate 2,000 years later. ■ The bottom line? 2 Timothy is no trivial pursuit!

STATS

PURPOSE: To give final instructions and encouragement to Timothy, an elder of the church at Ephesus

AUTHOR: Paul

TO WHOM WRITTEN: Timothy

DATE WRITTEN: About A.D. 66 or 67 from prison in Rome. After a year or two of freedom, Paul was arrested again and executed under Emperor Nero.

SETTING: Paul was virtually alone in prison, only Luke was with him. He wrote this letter to pass the torch to the new generation of church leaders. He also asked for visits from his friends, for his books, and especially the parchments—possibly parts of the Old Testament, the Gospels, and other biblical manuscripts.

KEY PEOPLE: Paul, Timothy, Luke, Mark, and others

KEY PLACES: Rome, Ephesus

2 T*imothy*

CHAPTER 1 A LETTER TO ENCOURAGE TIMOTHY.

From: Paul, Jesus Christ's missionary, sent out by God to tell men and women everywhere about the eternal life he has promised them through faith in Jesus Christ.

[2]*To:* Timothy, my dear son. May God the Father and Christ Jesus our Lord shower you with his kindness, mercy, and peace.

[3]How I thank God for you, Timothy. I pray for you every day, and many times during the long nights I beg my God to bless you richly. He is my fathers' God and mine, and my only purpose in life is to please him.

[4]How I long to see you again. How happy I would be, for I remember your tears as we left each other.

[5]I know how much you trust the Lord, just as your mother Eunice and your grandmother Lois do; and I feel sure you are still trusting him as much as ever.

[6]This being so, I want to remind you to stir into flame the strength and boldness that is in you, that entered into you when I laid my hands upon your head and blessed you. [7]For the Holy Spirit, God's gift, does not want you to be afraid of people, but to be wise and strong, and to love them and enjoy being with them.

[8]If you will stir up this inner power, you will

BE BOLD

1:6-7 Timothy was experiencing great opposition to his message and to himself as a leader. Timothy's youth, his association with Paul, and his leadership had come under fire. Paul urged Timothy to be bold. When we allow people to intimidate us, we neutralize our effectiveness for God. The power of the Holy Spirit can help us overcome our fear of what some might say or do to us so we can continue to do God's work.

never be afraid to tell others about our Lord or to let them know that I am your friend even though I am here in jail for Christ's sake. You will be ready to suffer with me for the Lord, for he will give you strength in suffering.

⁹It is he who saved us and chose us for his holy work not because we deserved it but because that was his plan long before the world began—to show his love and kindness to us through Christ. ¹⁰And now he has made all of this plain to us by the coming of our Savior Jesus Christ, who broke the power of death and showed us the way of everlasting life through trusting him. ¹¹And God has chosen me to be his missionary, to preach to the Gentiles and teach them.

¹²That is why I am suffering here in jail, and I am certainly not ashamed of it, for I know the one in whom I trust, and I am sure that he is able to safely guard all that I have given him until the day of his return. ¹³Hold tightly to the pattern of truth I taught you, especially concerning the faith and love Christ Jesus offers you. ¹⁴Guard well the splendid, God-given ability you received as a gift from the Holy Spirit who lives within you.

¹⁵As you know, all the Christians who came here from Asia have deserted me; even Phygellus and Hermogenes are gone. ¹⁶May the Lord bless Onesiphorus and all his family because he visited me and encouraged me often. His visits revived me like a breath of fresh air, and he was never ashamed of my being in jail. ¹⁷In fact, when he came to Rome, he searched everywhere trying to find me, and finally

did. ¹⁸May the Lord give him a special blessing at the day of Christ's return. And you know better than I can tell you how much he helped me at Ephesus.

CHAPTER 2 BE A GOOD SOLDIER. O Timothy, my son, be strong with the strength Christ Jesus gives you. ²For you must teach others those things you and many others have heard me speak about. Teach these great truths to trustworthy men who will, in turn, pass them on to others.

³Take your share of suffering as a good soldier of Jesus Christ, just as I do; ⁴and as Christ's soldier, do not let yourself become tied up in worldly affairs, for then you cannot satisfy the one who has enlisted you in his army. ⁵Follow the Lord's rules for doing his work, just as an athlete either follows the rules or is disqualified and wins no prize. ⁶Work hard like a farmer who gets paid well if he raises a large crop. ⁷Think over these three illustrations, and may the Lord help you to understand how they apply to you.

⁸Don't ever forget the wonderful fact that Jesus Christ was a man, born into King David's family; and that he was God, as shown by the fact that he rose again from the dead. ⁹It is because I have preached these great truths that I am in trouble here and have been put in jail like a criminal. But the Word of God is not chained, even though I am. ¹⁰I am more than willing to suffer if that will bring salvation and eternal glory in Christ Jesus to those God has chosen.

¹¹I am comforted by this truth, that when we suffer and die for Christ it only means that we will begin living with him in heaven. ¹²And if we think that our present service for him is hard, just remember that some day we are going to sit with him and rule with him. But if we give up when we suffer, and turn against Christ, then he must turn against us. ¹³Even when we are too weak to have any faith left, he remains faithful to us and will help us, for he cannot disown us who are part of himself, and he will always carry out his promises to us.

¹⁴Remind your people of these great facts, and command them in the name of the Lord not to argue over unimportant things. Such arguments are

POPULAR MUSIC

It's guaranteed to be the most spectacular concert tour ever. The members of Oozing Tumors are getting back together for one last fling.

People line up to camp out for tickets—a week in advance! Among the O.T. faithful are three teenagers who happen to be Christians. Let's ask Em, Donny, and Brad a few questions.

"So you guys are pretty cranked, huh?"

Donny: "Oh, yeah! This is gonna be awesome! I saw O.T. on their last tour, and they were unbelievable. During the last song, the guitarist shattered nine guitars!"

"Isn't he the same guy who pulls the ears off rabbits?"

Em: "Only once . . . and he apologized later. I'd give anything for a front row seat. I want to see what he wears."

"You mean almost wears?" (Em giggles.)

"Does it bother you that these guys constantly brag about how many chicks they've slept with?"

Brad: "Oh, I just like their music."

"But should Christians support people who laugh at our beliefs and values?"

Em: "Whoa, dude! It's just a concert!"

What about popular music? Whether it's rock, metal, rap, country & western, or whatever? Read 2 Timothy 3:1-5, noting especially the end of verse five.

LIFE CHANGE

2:9 When Paul said Jesus was God, he angered the Jews who had condemned Jesus for blasphemy—but many Jews became Christians (1 Corinthians 1:24); he angered the Romans who worshiped the emperor as God, but even some in Caesar's palace turned to Jesus (Philippians 4:22). When Paul said Jesus was man, he angered the Greeks who thought divinity was soiled if it had any contact with humanity; still many Greeks accepted the faith (Acts 11:20-21). The truth that Jesus is one person with two united natures has never been easy to accept, but it *is* being accepted by people every day. Are you one of those who has accepted this life-changing message?

confusing and useless and even harmful. [15]Work hard so God can say to you, "Well done." Be a good workman, one who does not need to be ashamed when God examines your work. Know what his Word says and means. [16]Steer clear of foolish discussions that lead people into the sin of anger with each other. [17]Things will be said that will burn and hurt for a long time to come. Hymenaeus and Philetus, in their love of argument, are men like that. [18]They have left the path of truth, preaching the lie that the resurrection of the dead has already occurred; and they have weakened the faith of some who believe them.

[19]But God's truth stands firm like a great rock, and nothing can shake it. It is a foundation stone with these words written on it: "The Lord knows those who are really his," and "A person who calls himself a Christian should not be doing things that are wrong."

[20]In a wealthy home there are dishes made of gold and silver as well as some made from wood and clay. The expensive dishes are used for guests, and the cheap ones are used in the kitchen or to put garbage in. [21]If you stay away from sin you will be like one of these dishes made of purest gold—the very best in the house—so that Christ himself can use you for his highest purposes.

[22]Run from anything that gives you the evil thoughts that young men often have, but stay close to anything that makes you want to do right. Have faith and love, and enjoy the companionship of those who love the Lord and have pure hearts.

[23]Again I say, don't get involved in foolish arguments, which only upset people and make them angry. [24]God's people must not be quarrelsome; they must be gentle, patient teachers of those who are wrong. [25]Be humble when you are trying to teach those who are mixed up concerning the truth. For if you talk meekly and courteously to them, they are more likely, with God's help, to turn away from their wrong ideas and believe what is true. [26]Then they will come to their senses and escape from Satan's trap of slavery to sin, which he uses to catch them whenever he likes, and then they can begin doing the will of God.

CHAPTER 3 BEING A CHRISTIAN CAN BE TOUGH.

You may as well know this too, Timothy, that in the last days it is going to be very difficult to be a Christian. [2]For people will love only themselves and their money; they will be proud and boastful, sneering at God, disobedient to their parents, ungrateful to them, and thoroughly bad. [3]They will be hardheaded and never give in to others; they will be constant liars and troublemakers and will think nothing of immorality. They will be rough and cruel, and sneer at those who try to be good. [4]They will betray their friends; they will be hotheaded, puffed up with pride, and prefer good times to worshiping God. [5]They will go to church, yes, but they won't really believe anything they hear. Don't be taken in by people like that.

A friend of mine stopped coming to church because he said that God had stopped answering his prayers. How do I answer him?

I WONDER . . .

Like Demas, who deserted Paul (see 2 Timothy 4:10), many Christians have a what-have-you-done-for-me-lately type of faith in God. They are willing to trust him in the good times, but when trouble hits they figure God has "checked out on them"—so they "check out on God."

Because we live in a society where we often can get what we want, when we want it, we may begin to think that God's only purpose is to meet our needs. Then when something doesn't work out—when we think that God hasn't come through for us, we turn away from him.

God is in the business of molding our character. One way he does this is by allowing us to go through tough times. When Paul wrote this letter, the church was going through intense persecution. Demas got tired of it and left. He wanted his comforts more than he wanted God's will.

Encourage your friend to change the what-have-you-done-for-me-lately attitude. Help him realize that God wants to build his character. His goal is not to make us feel good, but to develop us into the kind of people he wants.

---

[6]They are the kind who craftily sneak into other people's homes and make friendships with silly, sin-burdened women and teach them their new doctrines. [7]Women of that kind are forever following new teachers, but they never understand the truth. [8]And these teachers fight truth just as Jannes and Jambres fought against Moses. They have dirty minds, warped and twisted, and have turned against the Christian faith.

[9]But they won't get away with all this forever. Someday their deceit will be well known to everyone, as was the sin of Jannes and Jambres.

[10]But you know from watching me that I am not that kind of person. You know what I believe and the way I live and what I want. You know my faith in Christ and how I have suffered. You know my love for you, and my patience. [11]You know how many troubles I have had as a result of my preaching the Good News. You know about all that was done to me while I was visiting in Antioch, Iconium, and Lystra, but the Lord delivered me. [12]Yes, and those who decide to please Christ Jesus by

THE WHOLE BIBLE WAS GIVEN TO US BY INSPIRATION FROM GOD

and is useful to teach us what is TRUE *and to make us realize what is* Wrong *in our lives;* IT straightens us out *and helps us do what is* RIGHT.

living godly lives will suffer at the hands of those who hate him. [13]In fact, evil men and false teachers will become worse and worse, deceiving many, they themselves having been deceived by Satan.

[14]But you must keep on believing the things you have been taught. You know they are true, for you know that you can trust those of us who have taught you. [15]You know how, when you were a small child, you were taught the holy Scriptures; and it is these that make you wise to accept God's salvation by trusting in Christ Jesus. [16]The whole Bible was given to us by inspiration from God and is useful to teach us what is true and to make us realize what is wrong in our lives; it straightens us out and helps us do what is right. [17]It is God's way of making us well prepared at every point, fully equipped to do good to everyone.

CHAPTER 4 SHARE YOUR FAITH. And so I solemnly urge you before God and before Christ Jesus—who will someday judge the living and the dead when he appears to set up his Kingdom— [2]to preach the Word of God urgently at all times, whenever you get the chance, in season and out, when it is convenient and when it is not. Correct and rebuke your people when they need it, encourage them to do right, and all the time be feeding them patiently with God's Word.

[3]For there is going to come a time when people won't listen to the truth but will go around looking for teachers who will tell them just what they want to hear. [4]They won't listen to what the Bible says but will blithely follow their own misguided ideas.

[5]Stand steady, and don't be afraid of suffering for the Lord. Bring others to Christ. Leave nothing undone that you ought to do.

[6]I say this because I won't be around to help you very much longer. My time has almost run out. Very soon now I will be on my way to heaven. [7]I have fought long and hard for my Lord, and through it all I have kept true to him. And now the time has come for me to stop fighting and rest. [8]In heaven a crown is waiting for me, which the Lord, the righteous Judge, will give me on that great day of his return. And not just to me but to all those whose lives show that they are eagerly looking forward to his coming back again.

[9]Please come as soon as you can, [10]for Demas has left me. He loved the good things of this life and went to Thessalonica. Crescens has gone to Galatia, Titus to Dalmatia. [11]Only Luke is with me. Bring Mark with you when you come, for I need him. [12](Tychicus is gone too, as I sent him to Ephesus.) [13]When you come, be sure to bring the coat I left at Troas with Brother Carpus, and also the books, but especially the parchments.

[14]Alexander the coppersmith has done me much harm. The Lord will punish him, [15]but be careful of him, for he fought against everything we said.

[16]The first time I was brought before the judge, no one was here to help me. Everyone had run away. I hope that they will not be blamed for it. [17]But the Lord stood with me and gave me the opportunity to boldly preach a whole sermon for all the world to hear. And he saved me from being thrown to the lions. [18]Yes, and the Lord will always deliver me from all evil and will bring me into his heavenly Kingdom. To God be

THE SOURCE

3:16 The whole Bible is God's inspired Word. Because it is inspired and trustworthy, we should *read* it carefully, with the intent of *applying* it to our lives. The Bible can help us in every situation we encounter. It is our standard for testing everything else that claims to be true. It is our safeguard against false teaching and our source of guidance for how we should live, regardless of circumstances. The Bible is our only source of knowledge about how we can be saved. God wants to show you what is true and equip you to live for him. How much time do you spend in God's Word? Read it regularly to discover God's truth and to become confident in your life and faith. Develop a plan for reading the whole Bible, not just the same familiar passages.

the glory forever and ever. Amen.

[19]Please say hello for me to Priscilla and Aquila and those living at the home of Onesiphorus. [20]Erastus stayed at Corinth, and I left Trophimus sick at Miletus.

[21]Do try to be here before winter. Eubulus sends you greetings, and so do Pudens, Linus, Claudia, and all the others. [22]May the Lord Jesus Christ be with your spirit.

Farewell, Paul

MEGA Themes

BOLDNESS In the face of opposition and persecution, Timothy was told to carry out his ministry unashamed and unafraid. Paul urged Timothy to use the gifts of preaching and teaching that the Holy Spirit had given him.

God honors our confident testimony even when we suffer. To get over our fear of what people might say or do, we must take our eyes off people and look only to God. People will disappoint us, God will always be faithful.
1. Why was boldness important in Timothy's ministry? How did Paul challenge Timothy to find this boldness?
2. Describe a time in your life when you felt bold in your faith. Describe a time in your life when you felt timid about your faith.
3. What caused the difference between the time of boldness and the time of timidity?
4. What is your level of boldness for Christ at church? In your neighborhood? At home? In school? At social activities? In which areas is it most difficult for you to be boldly honest about your faith and life-style?

FAITHFULNESS Jesus was faithful to all of us when he died for our sins. Paul was a faithful minister even when he was in prison. Paul urged Timothy to maintain not only sound doctrine, but also loyalty, diligence, and endurance.

We can count on opposition, suffering, and hardship as we serve Christ. But that will show that our faithfulness is having an effect on others. As we trust Christ, he counts us worthy to suffer and will give us the strength we need to be steadfast.
1. How did Paul challenge Timothy to live out his faithfulness to God?
2. What reasons do you have for being faithful to God? What struggles do you face in trying to be faithful?
3. When you find yourself drifting away from God,

what can you do to remember your commitment of faithfulness to God?
4. How are you being faithful today?

PREACHING AND TEACHING Paul and Timothy were active in preaching and teaching the Good News about Jesus Christ. Paul encouraged Timothy not only to carry the torch of truth but also to train others, passing on to them sound doctrine and enthusiasm for Christ's mission.

We must prepare people to pass on God's Word to others. Does your church carefully train others to teach? Each of us should look for ways to become better equipped to serve, as well as for ways to teach others what we have learned.
1. Why do you think Paul stressed to Timothy the importance of training others to carry out preaching and teaching?
2. How was Paul a good example of this?
3. Who are the preachers and teachers in your church? How are they training others? (Are they training others?)
4. What type of ministry training would you want to receive? Who could provide this training?

ERROR In the final days before Christ returns, there will be false teachers, spiritual dropouts, and heresy. The remedy for error is to have a solid program for teaching Christians.

Because of deception and false teaching, we must be disciplined and ready to reject error by knowing God's Word. Knowing the Bible is your sure defense against error and confusion.
1. What are the dangers of deceptive teachers?
2. According to 3:14-17, how does God use his Word to prevent his people from being deceived?
3. Based on this study, how should you respond to Bible teaching?
4. What can you do to improve yourself as a student of God's Word?

*I*n many of life's situations—whether from natural instinct, repeated instruction, or unpleasant experience—you know precisely what to do. ■ For instance: • If your clothing catches fire, drop to the ground and roll. • In case of emergency, call 911. • Never stare at the sun during an eclipse. • Always wash your hands after using the restroom and before eating. • On a romantic first date, never order pizza with extra garlic and onions. • Don't run while carrying sharp objects. • Never swim right after eating. • When attacked by a bear, fall face down and play dead. • Look both ways before crossing a street. • Make certain you know the price of an object before you agree to buy it. • Never sign *anything* until you read the fine print.

■ You've probably heard these rules before; no doubt you could handle each situation with ease. But what about the millions of other life circumstances where it's really *hard* to know what to do? ■ That's why the next book of the Bible is so important. The apostle Paul's Epistle to Titus gives us plenty of practical advice for living a pure life in an impure world. Commitment, discipline, self-control, moral purity, solid relationships, civic duties—you'll learn about all those important topics and more. By the way—as you prepare to dive into this dynamite little letter, here's a reminder of one more famous rule of life (It's one our moms pounded into our heads!): Never read in dim light, unless you want to ruin your eyesight.

STATS

PURPOSE: To advise Titus in his responsibility of supervising the churches on the island of Crete

AUTHOR: Paul

TO WHOM WRITTEN: Titus, a Greek convert, who had become Paul's special representative to the island of Crete

DATE WRITTEN: About A.D. 64, around the same time 1 Timothy was written; probably from Macedonia when Paul traveled in between his Roman imprisonments

SETTING: Paul sent Titus to organize and oversee the churches on Crete. This letter tells him how to do this job.

KEY PEOPLE: Paul, Titus

KEY PLACES: Crete, Nicopolis

SPECIAL FEATURES: Titus is very similar to 1 Timothy with its instructions to pastors (elders).

Titus

CHAPTER **1** **PAUL IS SENT TO BRING FAITH.**

From: Paul, the slave of God and the messenger of Jesus Christ.

I have been sent to bring faith to those God has chosen and to teach them to know God's truth—the kind of truth that changes lives—so that they can have eternal life, which God promised them before the world began—and he cannot lie. ³And now in his own good time he has revealed this Good News and permits me to tell it to everyone. By command of God our Savior, I have been trusted to do this work for him.

⁴*To:* Titus, who is truly my son in the affairs of the Lord.

May God the Father and Christ Jesus our Savior give you his blessings and his peace.

⁵I left you there on the island of Crete so that you could do whatever was needed to help strengthen each of its churches, and I asked you to appoint pastors in every city who would follow the instructions I gave you. ⁶The men you choose must be well thought of for their good lives; they must have only one wife and their children must love the Lord and not have a reputation for being wild or disobedient to their parents.

⁷These pastors must be men of blameless lives because they are God's ministers. They must not be

NO LIE

1:1-2 The foundation of our faith is trust in God's character. Because he is truth, he is the source of all truth and cannot lie. The eternal life he has promised will be ours because he keeps his promises. Build your faith on the foundation of a trustworthy God who will not lie.

proud or impatient; they must not be drunkards or fighters or greedy for money. [8]They must enjoy having guests in their homes and must love all that is good. They must be sensible men, and fair. They must be clean minded and level headed. [9]Their belief in the truth that they have been taught must be strong and steadfast so that they will be able to teach it to others and show those who disagree with them where they are wrong.

[10]For there are many who refuse to obey; this is especially true among those who say that all Christians must obey the Jewish laws. But this is foolish talk; it blinds people to the truth, [11]and it must be stopped. Already whole families have been turned away from the grace of God. Such teachers are only after your money. [12]One of their own men, a prophet from Crete, has said about them, "These men of Crete are all liars; they are like lazy animals, living only to satisfy their stomachs." [13]And this is true. So speak to the Christians there as sternly as necessary to make them strong in the faith [14]and to stop them from listening to Jewish folk tales and the demands of men who have turned their backs on the truth.

[15]A person who is pure of heart sees goodness and purity in everything; but a person whose own heart is evil and untrusting finds evil in everything, for his dirty mind and rebellious heart color all he sees and hears. [16]Such persons claim they know God, but from seeing the way they act, one knows they don't. They are rotten and disobedient, worthless so far as doing anything good is concerned.

*I*NTEGRITY

When Dawn sticks her head into her youth pastor's office, it's plain to see she is troubled.

"Mike, can I talk to you?"

"Sure, Dawn, come in."

"It's this whole youth group leadership team thing."

"What do you mean?"

"Well, you know Kelly, the girl who's been coming with me to church the last few weeks?"

"Yeah."

"Well, she told me that she wants to be on the team. She wants to be in charge of publicity for the youth group."

"That's great. We've been looking for someone to fill that—"

"No, that's not great! You don't know Kelly. She's pretty wild . . . I mean, she's not exactly living like a Christian."

"I see."

"Don't get me wrong. I really love Kelly, and I'm trying to be a good influence on her and everything. I just don't think it's a very good idea to have her out there in charge of publicizing our group. At least not when she's living like she is. People might get the wrong idea, you know?"

"I agree. So, are you going to talk to her?"

"Oh, I guess so. Any advice?"

"Sure. If I were you, I'd . . ." Christians in leadership positions are expected to adhere to the highest standards of godly character. Read Titus 1:5-8; 2:11–3:8 for a quick glimpse at the integrity Christian leaders must possess.

CHAPTER **2** **SPECIAL GUIDELINES.** But as for you, speak up for the right living that goes along with true Christianity. [2]Teach the older men to be serious and unruffled; they must be sensible, knowing and believing the truth and doing everything with love and patience.

[3]Teach the older women to be quiet and respectful in everything they do. They must not go around speaking evil of others and must not be heavy drinkers, but they should be teachers of goodness. [4]These older women must train the younger women to live quietly, to love their husbands and their children, [5]and to be sensible and clean minded, spending their time in their own homes, being kind and obedient to their husbands so that the Christian faith can't be spoken against by those who know them.

A PERSON who is PURE of heart SEES GOODNESS and PURITY in everything EVERYTHING everything EVERYTHING everything; BUT A PERSON whose own heart is evil and untrusting finds EVERYTHING INevilTHING INeEVERY eEvviIL INTeHING EVERYTHING

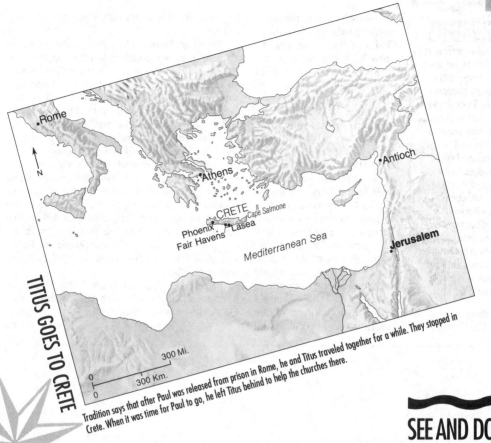

TITUS GOES TO CRETE

Tradition says that after Paul was released from prison in Rome, he and Titus traveled together for a while. They stopped in Crete. When it was time for Paul to go, he left Titus behind to help the churches there.

Rome

Athens

CRETE Cape Salmone
Phoenix Lasea
Fair Havens

Antioch

Jerusalem

Mediterranean Sea

300 Mi.

300 Km.

N

⁶In the same way, urge the young men to behave carefully, taking life seriously. ⁷And here you yourself must be an example to them of good deeds of every kind. Let everything you do reflect your love of the truth and the fact that you are in dead earnest about it. ⁸Your conversation should be so sensible and logical that anyone who wants to argue will be ashamed of himself because there won't be anything to criticize in anything you say!

⁹Urge slaves to obey their masters and to try their best to satisfy them. They must not talk back, ¹⁰nor steal, but must show themselves to be entirely trustworthy. In this way they will make people want to believe in our Savior and God.

¹¹For the free gift of eternal salvation is now being offered to everyone; ¹²and along with this gift comes the realization that God wants us to turn from godless living and sinful pleasures and to live good, God-fearing lives day after day, ¹³looking forward to that wonderful time we've been expecting, when his glory shall be seen—the glory of our great God and Savior Jesus Christ. ¹⁴He died under God's judgment against our sins so that he could rescue us from

constant falling into sin and make us his very own people, with cleansed hearts and real enthusiasm for doing kind things for others. ¹⁵You must teach these things and encourage your people to do them, correcting them when necessary as one who has every right to do so. Don't let anyone think that what you say is not important.

CHAPTER **3** OBEY THE GOVERNMENT. Remind
your people to obey the government and its officers, and always to be obedient and ready for any honest work. ²They must not speak evil of anyone, nor quarrel, but be gentle and truly courteous to all.

³Once we, too, were foolish and disobedient; we were misled by others and became slaves to many evil pleasures and wicked desires. Our lives were full of resentment and envy. We hated others and they hated us.

SEE AND DO

2:6-8 Paul urged Titus to be a good example to those around him so that others might see his good deeds and imitate him. Titus's life would give his words greater impact. If you want someone to act a certain way, be sure to live that way yourself. Then you will earn the right to be heard.

⁴But when the time came for the kindness and love of God our Savior to appear, ⁵then he saved us—not because we were good enough to be saved but because of his kindness and pity—by washing away our sins and giving us the new joy of the indwelling Holy Spirit, ⁶whom he poured out upon us with wonderful fullness—and all because of what Jesus Christ our Savior did ⁷so that he could declare us good in God's eyes—all because of his great kindness; and now we can share in the wealth of the eternal life he gives us, and we are eagerly looking forward to receiving it. ⁸These things I have told you are all true. Insist on them so that Christians will be careful to do good deeds all the time, for this is not only right, but it brings results.

⁹Don't get involved in arguing over unanswerable questions and controversial theological ideas; keep out of arguments and quarrels about obedience to Jewish laws, for this kind of thing isn't worthwhile; it only does harm. ¹⁰If anyone is causing divisions among you, he should be given a first and second warning. After that have nothing more to do with him, ¹¹for such a person has a wrong sense of values. He is sinning, and he knows it.

¹²I am planning to send either Artemas or Tychicus to you. As soon as one of them arrives, please try to meet me at Nicopolis as quickly as you can, for I have decided to stay there for the winter. ¹³Do everything you can to help Zenas the lawyer and Apollos with their trip; see that they are given everything they need. ¹⁴For our people must learn to help all who need their assistance, that their lives will be fruitful.

¹⁵Everybody here sends greetings. Please say hello to all of the Christian friends there. May God's blessings be with you all.

Sincerely, Paul

MEGA Themes

A GOOD LIFE The Good News of salvation is that we can't be saved by living a good life; we are saved only by faith in Jesus Christ. But the gospel transforms people's lives, so that they eventually perform good works. Our service won't save us, but we are saved to serve.

A good life is a witness to the gospel's power. As Christians, we must have commitment and discipline to serve. Each of us is to be a living servant; none of us is to consider himself or herself inactive.

1. Why do you think it is important for a Christian to live a good and pure life even though this is not the basis of salvation?
2. Describe a life that would be pleasing to God.
3. What areas of your life do you think are pleasing to God? In what areas of your life do you need to make changes in order to be more like the life you described in question 2?
4. Outline your personal plan for improving these areas for God's glory.

CHARACTER Titus's responsibility on Crete was to appoint pastors (elders) to maintain proper organization and discipline, so Paul listed the qualities that elders should have. Their conduct in their homes revealed their fitness for service in the church.

It's not enough to be educated or have a following to be Christ's kind of leader. You must have self-control, spiritual and moral fitness, and Christian character. Who you are is just as important as what you can do.

1. Summarize Paul's description of those who are qualified to serve as church leaders.
2. Describe the person you want to be when you are older. What will be your personal qualities? What will be your priorities? What will be the impact of your life? How will you be serving God?
3. What choices are you making now that will help you fulfill the above description one day?

CHURCH RELATIONSHIPS Church teaching was supposed to relate to various groups. Older Christians were to teach and to be examples to younger men and women. Every age and group has a lesson to learn and a role to play.

Right living and right relationship go along with right doctrine. Treat relationships with other believers as important parts of your relationship with God.

1. Summarize Paul's teaching on church relationships in 2:1-15.
2. What groups in your church seem to be the most "distant" in their personal relationships (young-old, wealthy-average-poor, liberal ideas-conservative ideas, traditional worshipers-nontraditional worshipers, etc.)?
3. What would Paul say to those groups if he were to write a letter to your church leaders about this distance? From your perspective, how could this gap be bridged?
4. What might you do to be a "bridge builder" in your church?

CITIZENSHIP Christians must be good citizens in society, not just in church. Believers must obey the government and work honestly.

How you fulfill your civic duties is a witness to the watching world. Your community life should reflect Christ's love as much as your church life does. You must guard against trying to separate your walk with God from the way you live each day.

1. Why is it important for Christians to obey the government?
2. Do you agree or disagree with this statement: "Being a good citizen involves more than just not breaking the law." Explain your response.
3. What are the biggest issues facing your community? How would you apply this study to your role as a member of the community?
4. How can a Christian have an impact for Christ by simply being a citizen who contributes positively? How can you provide this impact in your community?

I could *never* forgive her!" ■ "He'll *never* get serious about God!" ■ "I wish things would work out, but they won't. My situation is *impossible!*" ■ Ever heard—or made—statements like those? If so, take this hint! Never say, "Never." Many of the hard-to-believe things we declare "impossible!" eventually do come to pass . . . right before our embarrassed eyes. ■ Consider the Munich elementary school teacher who told ten-year-old Albert Einstein, "You will never amount to very much." ■ Or the misguided executive with the Decca Recording Company in the early '60s who decided *not* to offer a contract to an obscure musical group called The Beatles. ■ And you can be sure Simon Newcomb is red-faced in his grave. He's the guy who asserted in the 1800s that "flight by machines heavier than air is . . . utterly impossible." ■ Never say, "Never." Don't end that friendship or relationship just because you've been wronged. Don't give up on that friend who claims to be an atheist. Don't throw in the towel on your dream. Don't write off your future just because you've made some bad choices in the past. ■ Never say, "Never." The Gospel of Matthew states that same principle ("With God all things are possible") and the book of Philemon illustrates it—describing how a poor slave and his rich master ended up as Christian brothers. You are about to read a story of betrayal and forgiveness, and of how Jesus Christ breaks down all barriers. ■ So before you say, "That's *impossible!*" Or, "That could *never* happen!" take five minutes to read Paul's postcard to Philemon.

STATS

PURPOSE: To convince Philemon to forgive—and accept as a brother in the faith—his runaway slave, Onesimus

AUTHOR: Paul

TO WHOM WRITTEN: Philemon, who probably was a wealthy member of the Colossian church

DATE WRITTEN: About A.D. 60, during Paul's first imprisonment in Rome, at about the same time the books of Ephesians and Colossians were written

SETTING: Slavery was very common in the Roman Empire. Evidently some Christians had slaves. Paul makes a radical statement by calling this slave Philemon's brother in Christ.

KEY PEOPLE: Paul, Philemon, Onesimus

KEY PLACES: Colosse, Rome

Philemon

CHAPTER 1 ONESIMUS COMES HOME. *From:* Paul, in jail for preaching the Good News about Jesus Christ, and from Brother Timothy.

To: Philemon, our much-loved fellow worker, and to the church that meets in your home, and to Apphia our sister, and to Archippus who, like myself, is a soldier of the cross.

³May God our Father and the Lord Jesus Christ give you his blessings and his peace.

⁴I always thank God when I am praying for you, dear Philemon, ⁵because I keep hearing of your love and trust in the Lord Jesus and in his people. ⁶And I pray that as you share your faith with others it will grip their lives too, as they see the wealth of good things in you that come from Christ Jesus. ⁷I myself have gained much joy and comfort from your love, my brother, because your kindness has so often refreshed the hearts of God's people.

⁸,⁹Now I want to ask a favor of you. I could demand it of you in the name of Christ because it is the right thing for you to do, but I love you and prefer just to ask you—I,

GOOD DEAL

1:8-9 Because Paul was an elder and an apostle, he could have used his authority with Philemon, commanding him to deal kindly with his runaway slave. But Paul based his request not on his own authority, but on Philemon's Christian commitment. Paul wanted Philemon's heartfelt obedience. When you know something is right and you have the power to demand it, do you appeal to your authority or the other person's commitment? Here Paul provides a good example of how to deal with a possible conflict between Christian friends.

Paul, an old man now, here in jail for the sake of Jesus Christ. ¹⁰My plea is that you show kindness to my child Onesimus, whom I won to the Lord while here in my chains. ¹¹Onesimus (whose name means "Useful") hasn't been of much use to you in the past, but now he is going to be of real use to both of us. ¹²I am sending him back to you, and with him comes my own heart.

¹³I really wanted to keep him here with me while I am in these chains for preaching the Good News, and you would have been helping me through him, ¹⁴but I didn't want to do it without your consent. I didn't want you to be kind because you had to but because you wanted to. ¹⁵Perhaps you could think of it this way: that he ran away from you for a little while so that now he can be yours forever, ¹⁶no longer only a slave, but something much better—a beloved brother, especially to me. Now he will mean much more to you too, because he is not only a servant but also your brother in Christ.

¹⁷If I am really your friend, give him the same welcome you would give to me if I were the one who was coming. ¹⁸If he has harmed you in any way or stolen anything from you, charge me for it. ¹⁹I will pay it back (I, Paul, personally guarantee this by writing it here with my own hand) but I won't mention how much you owe me! The fact is, you even owe me your very soul! ²⁰Yes, dear brother, give me joy with this loving act and my weary heart will praise the Lord.

²¹I've written you this letter because I am posi-tive that you will do what I ask and even more!

²²Please keep a guest room ready for me, for I am hoping that God will answer your prayers and let me come to you soon.

²³Epaphras my fellow prisoner, who is also here for preaching Christ Jesus, sends you his greetings. ²⁴So do Mark, Aristarchus, Demas, and Luke, my fellow workers.

²⁵The blessings of our Lord Jesus Christ be upon your spirit.

Paul

FORGIVEN

1:10ff Paul asked Philemon not only to forgive his runaway slave who had become a Christian, but to accept him as a brother. As Christians, we should forgive as we have been forgiven (Matthew 6:5-15; Ephesians 4:31-32). True forgiveness means that we treat the person we've forgiven as we would want to be treated. Is there someone you say you have forgiven, but who still needs your kindness?

I KEEP HEARING
KEEP HEARING
KEEP HEARING of your love and trust in the LORD and JESUS and in his people. AND I pray that as you share your faith with OTHERS OTHERS OTHER IT WILL GRIP THEIR LIVES TOO, AS THEY SEE THE THE WEALTH OF WEALTH OF GOOD THINGS GOOD THING in YOU that come from CHRIST JESUS.

PHILEMON 1:5-6

RECONCILIATION

As roommates (and total opposites), college freshmen Melanie and Laura had a very awkward relationship:

- Laura was short and stout; Melanie was tall and thin.
- Laura was refined and reserved; Melanie was loud and obnoxious.
- Laura was upper-class prep; Melanie was a middle-class freak.
- Laura was a conservative; Melanie was a liberal.
- Laura was a morning person; Melanie was a night owl.
- Laura was a Christian; Melanie clearly was not.

At the end of the fall semester, Melanie moved out of the dorm into an apartment. Right about that same time, Laura couldn't find her diamond pendant. She suspected Melanie, but she never said a word.

The following summer, Laura got a letter from Melanie. The first part of the letter told how she had come to Christ during a beach outreach. The second half was a confession. Melanie had indeed taken the pendant and pawned it for some needed cash. She was pleading for forgiveness.

Laura immediately wrote back—welcoming Melanie to the family of God, granting the requested forgiveness, and asking if the girls could get together first thing in the fall.

Could you have responded to Melanie as Laura did? Their story isn't a fairy tale. Read Philemon to see for yourself the amazing reconciliation that is possible in Jesus Christ.

MEGA *Themes*

FORGIVENESS Philemon was Paul's friend and Onesimus's owner. Paul asked Philemon not to punish Onesimus, but to forgive and restore him as a new Christian brother.

Christian relationships must be full of forgiveness and acceptance. Forgiving those who have wronged you is the appropriate response to Christ's forgiveness of you.

1. How would you have felt if you were Philemon before you received the letter? How would Paul's letter have changed your attitude? What verses in the letter would have had the most impact on your thinking?

2. How is Paul's request for Onesimus in 1:18-20 a reflection of what Christ has done for all of us?

3. As you reflect on this study and the people involved, what do you learn about the importance of forgiveness in Christian relationships? What is the basis of this forgiveness? How is this forgiveness lived out when someone has been wronged?

4. What difference does it make whether or not you forgive a Christian friend who wrongs you? If there is such a wrong that you have not forgiven, how can you go to that friend and make things right?

BARRIERS Slavery was widespread in the Roman Empire. Slavery was a barrier between people, but Christian love and fellowship can overcome such barriers.

In Christ we are one family. No walls of race, economic status, or political differences should separate believers. Let Christ work through you to remove barriers between Christian brothers and sisters. Take steps to act out the love of Christ in you.

1. What are some of the differences and prejudices which separate and alienate people from one another?

2. Why are such conflicts offensive to God?

3. In your community, what groups of people do not relate to each other simply because of external differences?

4. What can you do to demonstrate to your school or church that God is greater than all barriers?

RESPECT Paul was a friend of both Philemon and Onesimus. He had the authority as an apostle to tell Philemon what to do. Yet Paul chose to appeal to his friend in Christian love rather than to order him to do what he wished.

When dealing with people, tactful persuasion accomplishes a great deal more than commands. Remember to exhibit courtesy and respect in dealing with people.

1. What do you think it means to respect a person?

2. Who are the people you most respect? What are the qualities that lead you to respect them?

3. Which of these qualities do you most want to develop as you grow into an adult who can be respected by others?

4. What about now? What leads others to respect you as a young person?

*F*our Very Uncool Activities You Can Do ■ 1. Wear a diaper to school and suck on a pacifier during all your classes. ■ 2. Treat yourself to a lunch of jars of baby food: strained carrots, creamed spinach, and milk (out of a baby bottle, of course). ■ 3. Drool all over yourself. ■ 4. Crawl from class to class. Anytime anything doesn't go your way, kick your legs, flail your arms, and cry uncontrollably. ■ Such behavior is uncool for a teenager—it's immature, the kind of things we expect *babies* to do. We would never tolerate such immaturity in an older person. ■ So why do we tolerate such infantile behavior in the spiritual realm? ■ The church has far too many "baby Christians." Some have only been believers in Christ a short time, so it's understandable that *they* might do silly or immature things. But for those Christians who have been in God's family for years and who still act like infants—well, there's just no excuse. ■ In the same way that little kids grow up physically, "baby" Christians need to grow up in their relationship with Christ. ■ That's what Hebrews is all about—growing up spiritually. You should know up front that Hebrews contains some tough statements and some sobering challenges. It's a risky book to read—especially if you apply it. ■ Neglect its powerful message, and you face an even greater risk—remaining a spiritual infant. ■ You can't get more uncool than that.

STATS

PURPOSE: To present Christ's sufficiency and superiority

AUTHOR: Unknown. Paul, Luke, Barnabas, Apollos, Silas, Philip, Priscilla, and others have been suggested. Whoever the author was speaks of Timothy as "brother" (13:23).

TO WHOM WRITTEN: Hebrew Christians who may have been considering a return to Judaism, perhaps because of immaturity due to their lack of understanding of biblical truths. They seem to be "second-generation" Christians (2:3). And to all believers everywhere.

DATE WRITTEN: Probably before the destruction of the Temple in Jerusalem in A.D. 70; the religious sacrifices and ceremonies are referred to, but not the Temple's destruction

SETTING: These Jewish Christians were probably undergoing fierce persecution, socially and physically, both from Jews and from Romans. The people needed to be reassured that Christianity was true and that Jesus was the Messiah.

KEY PEOPLE: Old Testament men and women of faith (chapter 11)

Hebrews

CHAPTER 1 **JESUS CHRIST IS GOD'S SON.** Long ago God spoke in many different ways to our fathers through the prophets [in visions, dreams, and even face to face], telling them little by little about his plans.

²But now in these days he has spoken to us through his Son to whom he has given everything and through whom he made the world and everything there is.

³God's Son shines out with God's glory, and all that God's Son is and does marks him as God. He regulates the universe by the mighty power of his command. He is the one who died to cleanse us and clear our record of all sin, and then sat down in highest honor beside the great God of heaven.

⁴Thus he became far greater than the angels, as proved by the fact that his name "Son of God," which was passed on to him from his Father, is far greater than the names and titles of the angels.

⁵,⁶For God never said to any angel, "You are my Son, and today I have given you the honor that goes with that name." But God said it about Jesus. Another time he said, "I am his Father and he is my Son." And still another time—when his firstborn Son came to earth—God said, "Let all the angels of God worship him."

⁷God speaks of his angels as messengers swift as the wind and as servants made of flaming fire; ⁸but of his Son he says, "Your Kingdom, O God, will last forever and ever; its commands are always just and right. ⁹You love right and hate wrong; so God, even your God, has poured out more gladness upon you than on anyone else."

JESUS

1:2-3 Not only is Jesus God's spokesman; he is God himself—the very God who spoke in Old Testament times. Christ is eternal; he worked with the Father in creating the world (John 1:3; Colossians 1:16). He is the full revelation of God. You can have no clearer view of God than by looking at him. Jesus Christ is the complete embodiment of God.

¹⁰God also called him "Lord" when he said, "Lord, in the beginning you made the earth, and the heavens are the work of your hands. ¹¹They will disappear into nothingness, but you will remain forever. They will become worn out like old clothes, ¹²and some day you will fold them up and replace them. But you yourself will never change, and your years will never end."

¹³And did God ever say to an angel, as he does to his Son, "Sit here beside me in honor until I crush all your enemies beneath your feet"?

¹⁴No, for the angels are only spirit-messengers sent out to help and care for those who are to receive his salvation.

CHAPTER 2 LISTEN CAREFULLY AND OBEY GOD.

So we must listen very carefully to the truths we have heard, or we may drift away from them. ²For since the messages from angels have always proved true and people have always been punished for disobeying them, ³what makes us think that we can escape if we are indifferent to this great salvation announced by the Lord Jesus himself and passed on to us by those who heard him speak?

STABILITY

2:9 God has put Jesus in charge of everything, and Jesus has revealed himself to us. We do not yet see Jesus reigning on earth, but we can picture him in his heavenly glory. When confused by tomorrow and anxious about the future, keep a clear view of Jesus Christ—who he is, what he has done, and what he is doing for you right now. This will give stability to your decisions day by day.

⁴God always has shown us that these messages are true by signs and wonders and various miracles and by giving certain special abilities from the Holy Spirit to those who believe; yes, God has assigned such gifts to each of us.

⁵And the future world we are talking about will not be controlled by angels. ⁶No, for in the book of Psalms David says to God, "What is mere man that you are so concerned about him? And who is this Son of Man you honor so highly? ⁷For though you made him lower than the angels for a little while, now you have crowned him with glory and honor. ⁸And you have put him in complete charge of everything there is. Nothing is left out."

We have not yet seen all of this take place, ⁹but we do see Jesus—who for awhile was a little lower than the angels—crowned now by God with glory and honor because he suffered death for us. Yes, because of God's great kindness, Jesus tasted death for everyone in all the world.

¹⁰And it was right and proper that God, who made everything for his own glory, should allow Jesus to suffer, for in doing this he was bringing

For since
HE HIMSELF
has now
been through
and suffering
HE temptation,
knows
what
it is like
when
WE suffer
and are tempted
and
HE is
wonderfully able
to help us.

HEBREWS 2:18

vast multitudes of God's people to heaven; for his suffering made Jesus a perfect Leader, one fit to bring them into their salvation.

¹¹We who have been made holy by Jesus, now have the same Father he has. That is why Jesus is not ashamed to call us his brothers. ¹²For he says in the book of Psalms, "I will talk to my brothers about God my Father, and together we will sing his praises." ¹³At another time he said, "I will put my trust in God along with my brothers." And at still another time, "See, here am I and the children God gave me."

¹⁴Since we, God's children, are human beings—made of flesh and blood—he became flesh and blood too by being born in human form; for only as a human being could he die and in dying break the power of the devil who had the power of death. ¹⁵Only in that way could he deliver those who through fear of death have been living all their lives as slaves to constant dread.

¹⁶We all know he did not come as an angel but as a human being—yes, a Jew. ¹⁷And it was necessary for Jesus to be like us, his brothers, so that he

could be our merciful and faithful High Priest before God, a Priest who would be both merciful to us and faithful to God in dealing with the sins of the people. [18]For since he himself has now been through suffering and temptation, he knows what it is like when we suffer and are tempted, and he is wonderfully able to help us.

CHAPTER 3 JESUS: GREATER THAN MOSES.

Therefore, dear brothers whom God has set apart for himself—you who are chosen for heaven—I want you to think now about this Jesus who is God's Messenger and the High Priest of our faith.

[2]For Jesus was faithful to God who appointed him High Priest, just as Moses also faithfully served in God's house. [3]But Jesus has far more glory than Moses, just as a man who builds a fine house gets more praise than his house does. [4]And many people can build houses, but only God made everything.

[5]Well, Moses did a fine job working in God's house, but he was only a servant; and his work was mostly to illustrate and suggest those things that would happen later on. [6]But Christ, God's faithful Son, is in complete charge of God's house. And we Christians are God's house—he lives in us!—if we keep up our courage firm to the end, and our joy and our trust in the Lord.

[7,8]And since Christ is so much superior, the Holy Spirit warns us to listen to him, to be careful to hear his voice today and not let our hearts become set against him, as the people of Israel did. They steeled themselves against his love and complained against him in the desert while he was testing them. [9]But God was patient with them forty years, though they tried his patience sorely; he kept right on doing his mighty miracles for them to see. [10]"But," God says, "I was very angry with them, for their hearts were always looking somewhere else instead of up to me, and they never found the paths I wanted them to follow."

[11]Then God, full of this anger against them, bound himself with an oath that he would never let them come to his place of rest.

[12]Beware then of your own hearts, dear brothers, lest you find that they, too, are evil and unbelieving and are leading you away from the living God. [13]Speak to each other about these things every day while there is still time so that none of you will become hardened against God, being blinded by the glamor of sin. [14]For if we are faithful to the end, trusting God just as we did when we first became Christians, we will share in all that belongs to Christ.

[15]But *now* is the time. Never forget the warning, "*Today* if you hear God's voice speaking to you, do not harden your hearts against him, as the people of Israel did when they rebelled against him in the desert."

[16]And who were those people I speak of, who heard God's voice speaking to them but then rebelled against him? They were the ones who came out of Egypt with Moses their leader. [17]And who was it who made God angry for all those forty

---

I have heard so many different opinions on what God is really like that I'm beginning to wonder if someone can ever know. Is there any way to know for sure?

I WONDER...

Have you ever assembled a complicated jigsaw puzzle? If so, you know how important the picture on the box is. As you put the puzzle together, you use the picture as a reference, your guide.

But what if you had the wrong box top, and the picture didn't match the puzzle? The puzzle would be nearly impossible to assemble (at least until you realized the mistake).

People throughout the world are trying to put the "God puzzle" together. But often they are trying to match the pieces to the wrong picture!

God is not trying to hide. As Hebrews 1:1-3 tells us, God has clearly shown the world what he is like, through nature, through the Bible, and especially through Christ.

Jesus said it plainly, "I and the Father are one" (John 10:30).

Even when he was asked pointblank by Philip, he was straightforward in his reply. "Don't you even yet know who I am, Philip, even after all this time I have been with you? Anyone who has seen me has seen the Father! So why are you asking to see him?" (John 14:9).

It doesn't get more obvious than that! To know what God is like, all you have to do is look at Jesus.

People get their God-pictures from TV preachers; friends who say they believe in God, but never act like it; religious relatives; coaches who pray before games and then swear the paint off of the walls at halftime; and so forth. These are pictures of God that aren't anything like what he's really like. No wonder they can't put the puzzle together.

That's why it's so important not to settle for hearsay when it comes to finding out what God is like. Instead, look at the right picture—look at Christ.

---

years? These same people who sinned and as a result died in the wilderness. [18]And to whom was God speaking when he swore with an oath that they could never go into the land he had promised his people? He was speaking to all those who disobeyed him. [19]And why couldn't they go in? Because they didn't trust him.

CHAPTER 4 GOD'S PROMISE OF REST.

Although God's promise still stands—his promise that all may enter his place of rest—we ought to tremble with fear because some of you may be on the verge of failing to get there after all. [2]For this wonderful news—the message that God wants to save us—has been given to us just as it was to those who lived in the time of Moses. But it didn't do them any good because they didn't believe it. They didn't mix it with faith. ³For only we who believe God can enter into his place of rest. He has said, "I have sworn in my anger that those who don't believe me will never get in," even though he has been ready and waiting for them since the world began.

⁴We know he is ready and waiting because it is written that God rested on the seventh day of creation, having finished all that he had planned to make.

⁵Even so they didn't get in, for God finally said, "They shall never enter my rest." ⁶Yet the promise remains and some get in—but not those who had the first chance, for they disobeyed God and failed to enter.

⁷But he has set another time for coming in, and that time is now. He announced this through King David long years after man's first failure to enter, saying in the words already quoted, "Today when you hear him calling, do not harden your hearts against him."

⁸This new place of rest he is talking about does not mean the land of Israel that Joshua led them into. If that were what God meant, he would not have spoken long afterwards about "today" being the time to get in. ⁹So there is a full complete rest *still waiting* for the people of God. ¹⁰Christ has already entered there. He is resting from his work, just as God did after the creation. ¹¹Let us do our best to go into that place of rest, too, being careful not to disobey God as the children of Israel did, thus failing to get in.

¹²For whatever God says to us is full of living power: it is sharper than the sharpest dagger, cutting swift and deep into our innermost thoughts and desires with all their parts, exposing us for what we really are. ¹³He knows about everyone, everywhere. Everything about us is bare and wide open to the all-seeing eyes of our living God; nothing can be hidden from him to whom we must explain all that we have done.

¹⁴But Jesus the Son of God is our great High Priest who has gone to heaven itself to help us; therefore let us never stop trusting him. ¹⁵This High Priest of ours understands our weaknesses since he had the same temptations we do, though he never once gave way to them and sinned. ¹⁶So let us come

TURN BACK

4:1-3 Some of the Jewish Christians who received this letter may have been on the verge of turning back from their promised rest in Christ, just as the people in Moses' day turned back from the Promised Land. In both cases, the difficulties of the present moment overshadowed the reality of God's promise, and people stopped believing that God was able to fulfill his promises. When we trust our own efforts instead of Christ, we too are in danger of turning back. Our own efforts are never adequate; only Christ can see us through.

boldly to the very throne of God and stay there to receive his mercy and to find grace to help us in our times of need.

CHAPTER **5** JESUS CHRIST IS OUR HIGH PRIEST. The Jewish high priest is merely a man like anyone else, but he is chosen to speak for all other men in their dealings with God. He presents their gifts to God and offers to him the blood of animals that are

SO LET US COME BOLDLY TO THE VERY THRONE OF GOD and stay there to receive his mercy and to find grace grace grace to help us in our times of need.

sacrificed to cover the sins of the people and his own sins too. And because he is a man, he can deal gently with other men, though they are foolish and ignorant, for he, too, is surrounded with the same temptations and understands their problems very well.

⁴Another thing to remember is that no one can be a high priest just because he wants to be. He has to be called by God for this work in the same way God chose Aaron.

⁵That is why Christ did not elect himself to the honor of being High Priest; no, he was chosen by God. God said to him, "My Son, today I have honored you." ⁶And another time God said to him, "You have been chosen to be a priest forever, with the same rank as Melchizedek."

⁷Yet while Christ was here on earth he pleaded with God, praying with tears and agony of soul to the only one who would save him from [premature] death. And God heard his prayers because of his strong desire to obey God at all times.

⁸And even though Jesus was God's Son, he had to learn from experience what it was like to obey when obeying meant suffering. ⁹It was after he had proved himself perfect in this experience that Jesus became the Giver of eternal salvation to all those who obey him. ¹⁰For remember that God has chosen him to be a High Priest with the same rank as Melchizedek.

¹¹There is much more I would like to say along these lines, but you don't seem to listen, so it's hard to make you understand.

¹²,¹³You have been Christians a long time now, and you ought to be teaching others, but instead you have dropped back to the place where you need someone to teach you all over again the very first principles in God's Word. You are like babies who can drink only milk, not old enough for solid food. And when a person is still living on milk it shows he isn't very far along in the Christian life, and doesn't know much about the difference between right and wrong. He is still a baby Christian! ¹⁴You will never be able to eat solid spiritual food and understand the deeper things of God's Word until you become better Christians and learn right from wrong by practicing doing right.

CHAPTER **6** **COUNT ON GOD'S PROMISES.** Let us stop going over the same old ground again and again, always teaching those first lessons about Christ. Let us go on instead to other things and become mature in our understanding, as strong Christians ought to be. Surely we don't need to speak further about the foolishness of trying to be saved by being good, or about the necessity of faith in God; ²you don't need further instruction about

baptism and spiritual gifts and the resurrection of the dead and eternal judgment.

³The Lord willing, we will go on now to other things.

⁴There is no use trying to bring you back to the Lord again if you have once understood the Good News and tasted for yourself the good things of heaven and shared in the Holy Spirit, ⁵and know how good the Word of God is, and felt the mighty powers of the world to come, ⁶and then have turned against God. You cannot bring yourself to repent again if you have nailed the Son of God to the cross again by rejecting him, holding him up to mocking and to public shame.

⁷When a farmer's land has had many showers upon it and good crops come up, that land has experienced God's blessing upon it. ⁸But if it keeps on having crops of thistles and thorns, the land is considered no good and is ready for condemnation and burning off.

⁹Dear friends, even though I am talking like this I really don't believe that what I am saying applies to you. I am confident you are producing the good fruit that comes along with your salvation. ¹⁰For God is not unfair. How can he forget your hard work for him, or forget the way you used to show your love for him—and still do—by helping his children? ¹¹And we are anxious that you keep right on loving others as long as life lasts, so that you will get your full reward.

¹²Then, knowing what lies ahead for you, you won't become bored with being a Christian nor become spiritually dull and indifferent, but you will be anxious to follow the example of those who receive all that God has promised them because of their strong faith and patience.

¹³For instance, there was God's promise to Abraham: God took an oath in his own name, since there was no one greater to swear by, ¹⁴that he would bless Abraham again and again, and give him a son and make him the father of a great nation of people. ¹⁵Then Abraham waited patiently until finally God gave him a son, Isaac, just as he had promised.

¹⁶When a man takes an oath, he is calling upon someone greater than himself to force him to do what he has promised or to punish him if he later refuses to do it; the oath ends all argument about it. ¹⁷God also bound himself with an oath, so that those he promised to help would be perfectly sure and never need to wonder whether he might change his plans.

EVIDENCE

6:7-8 Land that produces good fruit receives loving care, but land that produces thistles and thorns has to be burned off so that the farmer can start over. God condemns an unproductive Christian life. We are not saved by works or conduct, but what we do is the *evidence* of our faith. Being productive for Christ is serious business.

[18]He has given us both his promise and his oath, two things we can completely count on, for it is impossible for God to tell a lie. Now all those who flee to him to save them can take new courage when they hear such assurances from God; now they can know without doubt that he will give them the salvation he has promised them.

[19]This certain hope of being saved is a strong and trustworthy anchor for our souls, connecting us with God himself behind the sacred curtains of heaven, [20]where Christ has gone ahead to plead for us from his position as our High Priest, with the honor and rank of Melchizedek.

CHAPTER 7 MELCHIZEDEK: JUSTICE AND PEACE.

This Melchizedek was king of the city of Salem and also a priest of the Most High God. When Abraham was returning home after winning a great battle against many kings, Melchizedek met him and blessed him; [2]then Abraham took a tenth of all he had won in the battle and gave it to Melchizedek.

Melchizedek's name means "Justice," so he is the King of Justice; and he is also the King of Peace because of the name of his city, Salem, which means "Peace." [3]Melchizedek had no father or mother and there is no record of any of his ancestors. He was never born and he never died but his life is like that of the Son of God—a priest forever.

[4]See then how great this Melchizedek is:

(a)Even Abraham, the first and most honored of all God's chosen people, gave Melchizedek a tenth of the spoils he took from the kings he had been fighting. [5]One could understand why Abraham would do this if Melchizedek had been a Jewish priest, for later on God's people were required by law to give gifts to help their priests because the priests were their relatives. [6]But Melchizedek was not a relative, and yet Abraham paid him.

(b)Melchizedek placed a blessing upon mighty Abraham, [7]and as everyone knows, a person who has the power to bless is always greater than the person he blesses.

[8](c)The Jewish priests, though mortal, received tithes; but we are told that Melchizedek lives on. [9](d)One might even say that Levi himself (the ancestor of all Jewish priests, of all who receive tithes), paid tithes to Melchizedek through Abraham. [10]For although Levi wasn't born yet, the seed from which he came was in Abraham when Abraham paid the tithes to Melchizedek.

[11](e)If the Jewish priests and their laws had been able to save us, why then did God need to send Christ as a priest with the rank of Melchizedek, instead of sending someone with the rank of Aaron—the same rank all other priests had?

[12-14]And when God sends a new kind of priest, his law must be changed to permit it. As we all know, Christ did not belong to the priest-tribe of Levi, but came from the tribe of Judah, which had not been chosen for priesthood; Moses had never given them that work.

[15]So we can plainly see that God's method changed, for Christ, the new High Priest who came with the rank of Melchizedek, [16]did not become a priest by meeting the old requirement of belonging to the tribe of Levi, but on the basis of power flowing from a life that cannot end. [17]And the psalmist points this out when he says of Christ, "You are a priest forever with the rank of Melchizedek."

[18]Yes, the old system of priesthood based on family lines was canceled because it didn't work. It was weak and useless for saving people. [19]It never made anyone really right with God. But now we have a far better hope, for Christ makes us acceptable to God, and now we may draw near to him.

[20]God took an oath that Christ would always be a Priest, [21]although he never said that of other priests. Only to Christ he said, "The Lord has sworn and will never change his mind: You are a Priest forever, with the rank of Melchizedek." [22]Because of God's oath, Christ can guarantee forever the success of this new and better arrangement.

[23]Under the old arrangement there had to be many priests so that when the older ones died off, the system could still be carried on by others who took their places.

[24]But Jesus lives forever and continues to be a Priest so that no one else is needed. [25]He is able to save completely all who come to God through him. Since he will live forever, he will always be there to remind God that he has paid for their sins with his blood.

[26]He is, therefore, exactly the kind of High Priest we need; for he is holy and blameless, unstained by sin, undefiled by sinners, and to him has been given the place of honor in heaven. [27]He never needs the daily blood of animal sacrifices, as other priests did, to cover over first their own sins and then the sins of the people; for he finished all sacrifices, once and for all, when he sacrificed himself on the cross. [28]Under the old system, even the high priests were weak and sinful men who could not keep from doing wrong, but later God appointed by his oath his Son who is perfect forever.

PAID

7:25 What does it mean that Jesus is able to save completely? No one else can add to what Jesus did to save us; our past, present, and future sins are all forgiven. Jesus is with the Father as a sign that our sins are forgiven. If you are a Christian, remember that Christ has paid the price for your sins once and for all. (See also 9:25-26.)

CHAPTER 8 OUR NEW HIGH PRIEST.

What we are saying is this: Christ, whose priesthood we have just described, is our High Priest and is in heaven at the place of greatest honor next to God himself. [2]He ministers in the temple in heaven, the true place of worship built by the Lord and not by human hands.

[3]And since every high priest is appointed to offer gifts and sacrifices, Christ must make an offering too. [4]The sacrifice he offers is far better than those offered by the earthly priests. (But even so, if he were here on earth he wouldn't even be permitted to be a priest because down here the priests still follow the old Jewish system of sacrifices.) [5]Their work is connected with a mere earthly model of the real tabernacle in heaven; for when Moses was getting ready to build the tabernacle, God warned him to follow exactly the pattern of the heavenly tabernacle as shown to him on Mount Sinai. [6]But Christ, as a Minister in heaven, has been rewarded with a far more important work than those who serve under the old laws because the new agreement that he passes on to us from God contains far more wonderful promises.

[7]The old agreement didn't even work. If it had, there would have been no need for another to replace it. [8]But God himself found fault with the old one, for he said, "The day will come when I will make a new agreement with the people of Israel and the people of Judah. [9]This new agreement will not be like the old one I gave to their fathers on the day when I took them by the hand to lead them out of the land of Egypt; they did not keep their part in that agreement, so I had to cancel it. [10]But this is the new agreement I will make with the people of Israel, says the Lord: I will write my laws in their minds so that they will know what I want them to do without my even telling them, and these laws will be in their hearts so that they will want to obey them, and I will be their God and they shall be my people. [11]And no one then will need to speak to his friend or neighbor or brother, saying, 'You, too, should know the Lord,' because everyone, great and small, will know me already. [12]And I will be merciful to them in their wrongdoings, and I will remember their sins no more."

[13]God speaks of these new promises, of this new agreement, as taking the place of the old one; for the old one is out of date now and has been put aside forever.

CHAPTER 9 OLD RULES ABOUT WORSHIP.

Now in that first agreement between God and his people there were rules for worship and there was a sacred tent down here on earth. Inside this place of worship there were two rooms. The first one contained the golden candlestick and a table with special loaves of holy bread upon it; this part was called the Holy Place. [3]Then there was a curtain, and behind the curtain was a room called the Holy of Holies. [4]In that room there were a golden incense-altar and the golden chest, called the ark of the covenant, completely covered on all sides with pure gold. Inside the ark were the tablets of stone with the Ten Commandments written on them, and a golden jar with some manna in it, and Aaron's wooden cane that budded. [5]Above the golden chest were statues of angels called the cherubim—the guardians of God's glory—with their wings stretched out over the ark's golden cover, called the mercy seat. But enough of such details.

[6]Well, when all was ready, the priests went in and out of the first room whenever they wanted to, doing their work. [7]But only the high priest went into the inner room, and then only once a year, all alone, and always with blood that he sprinkled on the mercy seat as an offering to God to cover his own mistakes and sins and the mistakes and sins of all the people.

[8]And the Holy Spirit uses all this to point out to us that under the old system the common people could not go into the Holy of Holies as long as the outer room and the entire system it represents were still in use.

[9]This has an important lesson for us today. For under the old system, gifts and sacrifices were offered, but these failed to cleanse the hearts of the people who brought them. [10]For the old system dealt only with certain rituals—what foods to eat and drink, rules for washing themselves, and rules about this and that. The people had to keep these rules to tide them over until Christ came with God's new and better way.

[11]He came as High Priest of this better system that we now have. He went into that greater, perfect tabernacle in heaven, not made by men nor part of this world, [12]and once for all took blood into that inner room, the Holy of Holies, and sprinkled it on the mercy seat; but it was not the blood of goats and calves. No, he took his own blood, and with it he, by himself, made sure of our eternal salvation.

[13]And if under the old system the blood of bulls and goats and the ashes of young cows could cleanse men's bodies from sin, [14]just think how much more surely the blood of Christ will transform our lives and

LOAD

9:9-14 Though you know Christ, you may still be trying to make yourself good enough for God. But rules and rituals have never cleansed people's hearts. By Jesus' blood alone: (1) our consciences are cleared, (2) we are freed from death and can live to serve God, and (3) we are freed from sin's power. If you are carrying a load of guilt because you can't be good enough for God, take another look at Jesus' death and what it means for you.

hearts. His sacrifice frees us from the worry of having to obey the old rules and makes us want to serve the living God. For by the help of the eternal Holy Spirit, Christ willingly gave himself to God to die for our sins—he being perfect, without a single sin or fault. [15]Christ came with this new agreement so that all who are invited may come and have forever all the wonders God has promised them. For Christ died to rescue them from the penalty of the sins they had committed while still under that old system.

[16]Now, if someone dies and leaves a will—a list of things to be given away to certain people when he dies—no one gets anything until it is proved that the person who wrote the will is dead. [17]The will goes into effect only after the death of the person who wrote it. While he is still alive no one can use it to get any of those things he has promised them.

[18]That is why blood was sprinkled [as proof of Christ's death] before even the first agreement could go into effect. [19]For after Moses had given the people all of God's laws, he took the blood of calves and goats, along with water, and sprinkled the blood over the book of God's laws and over all the people, using branches of hyssop bushes and scarlet wool to sprinkle with. [20]Then he said, "This is the blood that marks the beginning of the agreement between you and God, the agreement God commanded me to make with you." [21]And in the same way he sprinkled blood on the sacred tent and on whatever instruments were used for worship. [22]In fact we can say that under the old agreement almost everything was cleansed by sprinkling it with blood, and without the shedding of blood there is no forgiveness of sins.

[23]That is why the sacred tent down here on earth and everything in it—all copied from things in heaven—all had to be made pure by Moses in this way, by being sprinkled with the blood of animals. But the real things in heaven, of which these down here are copies, were made pure with far more precious offerings.

[24]For Christ has entered into heaven itself to appear now before God as our Friend. It was not in the earthly place of worship that he did this, for that was merely a copy of the real temple in heaven. [25]Nor has he offered himself again and again, as the high priest down here on earth offers animal blood in the Holy of Holies each year. [26]If that had been necessary, then he would have had to die again and again, ever since the world began. But no! He came once for all, at the end of the age, to put away the power of sin forever by dying for us.

[27]And just as it is destined that men die only once, and after that comes judgment, [28]so also Christ died only once as an offering for the sins of many people; and he will come again, but not to deal again with our sins.

This time he will come bringing salvation to all those who are eagerly and patiently waiting for him.

CHAPTER 10 FORGIVENESS: ONCE AND FOR ALL

The old system of Jewish laws gave only a dim foretaste of the good things Christ would do for us. The sacrifices under the old system were repeated again and again, year after year, but even so they could never save those who lived under their rules. [2]If they could have, one offering would have been enough; the worshipers would have been cleansed once for all and their feeling of guilt would be gone.

[3]But just the opposite happened: those yearly sacrifices reminded them of their disobedience and guilt instead of relieving their minds. [4]For it is not possible for the blood of bulls and goats really to take away sins.

[5]That is why Christ said as he came into the world, "O God, the blood of bulls and goats cannot satisfy you, so you have made ready this body of mine for me to lay as a sacrifice upon your altar. [6]You were not satisfied with the animal sacrifices, slain and burnt before you as offerings for sin. [7]Then I said, 'See, I have come to do your will, to lay down my life, just as the Scriptures said that I would.'"

[8]After Christ said this about not being satisfied with the various sacrifices and offerings required under the old system, [9]he then added, "Here I am. I have come to give my life."

He cancels the first system in favor of a far better one. [10]Under this new plan we have been forgiven and made clean by Christ's dying for us once and for all.

[11]Under the old agreement the priests stood before the altar day after day offering sacrifices that

---

VALUE

9:15 Value, in our human way of thinking, is not measured by how *many* people can have something good, but by how *few*. "Limited edition" means "valuable" because only a few can have it. God's great plan of redemption, however, is dramatically different. It is the most valuable of all treasures, yet it is available to all. The more who have it, and the more they use it, the greater its value! Exercise your faith by sharing it and using it to serve God, and so increase its value.

BE THERE!

10:25 To neglect Christian meetings is to give up the encouragement and help of other Christians. We gather together to share our faith and strengthen each other in the Lord. As we get closer to the time of Christ's return, we may face many spiritual struggles, tribulations, and even persecution.
Anti-Christian forces will grow in strength. Difficulties should never be excuses for missing church services. Rather, as difficulties arise, we should make an even greater effort to be faithful in attendance.

could never take away our sins. [12]But Christ gave himself to God for our sins as one sacrifice for all time and then sat down in the place of highest honor at God's right hand, [13]waiting for his enemies to be laid under his feet. [14]For by that one offering he made forever perfect in the sight of God all those whom he is making holy.

[15]And the Holy Spirit testifies that this is so, for he has said, [16]"This is the agreement I will make with the people of Israel, though they broke their first agreement: I will write my laws into their minds so that they will always know my will, and I will put my laws in their hearts so that they will want to obey them." [17]And then he adds, "I will never again remember their sins and lawless deeds."

[18]Now, when sins have once been forever forgiven and forgotten, there is no need to offer more sacrifices to get rid of them.

[19]And so, dear brothers, now we may walk right into the very Holy of Holies, where God is, because of the blood of Jesus. [20]This is the fresh, new, life-giving way that Christ has opened up for us by tearing the curtain—his human body—to let us into the holy presence of God.

[21]And since this great High Priest of ours rules over God's household, [22]let us go right in to God himself, with true hearts fully trusting him to receive us because we have been sprinkled with Christ's blood to make us clean and because our bodies have been washed with pure water.

[23]Now we can look forward to the salvation God has promised us. There is no longer any room for doubt, and we can tell others that salvation is ours, for there is no question that he will do what he says.

[24]In response to all he has done for us, let us outdo each other in being helpful and kind to each other and in doing good.

[25]Let us not neglect our church meetings, as some people do, but encourage and warn each other, especially now that the day of his coming back again is drawing near.

[26]If anyone sins deliberately by rejecting the Savior after knowing the truth of forgiveness, this sin is not covered by Christ's death; there is no way to get rid of it. [27]There will be nothing to look forward to but the terrible punishment of God's awful anger, which will consume all his enemies. [28]A man who refused to obey the laws given by Moses was killed without mercy if there were two or three witnesses to his sin. [29]Think how much more terrible the punishment will be for those who have trampled underfoot the Son of God and treated his cleansing blood as though it were common and unhallowed, and insulted and outraged the Holy Spirit who brings God's mercy to his people.

[30]For we know him who said, "Justice belongs to me; I will repay them"; who also said, "The Lord himself will handle these cases." [31]It is a fearful thing to fall into the hands of the living God.

[32]Don't ever forget those wonderful days when you first learned about Christ. Remember how you kept right on with the Lord even though it meant terrible suffering. [33]Sometimes

I like the idea about having a personal faith in God. What I don't like is having to go to church. It seems boring and a waste of time. I have been to other churches and it all seems the same. Why can't there be a church with just kids my own age?

I WONDER . .

Imagine growing up without a family. It's tough to think of life without at least one parent who really cares.

Now imagine growing up with just brothers and sisters in the house and no parents at all! For a day or two it may seem like heaven, but very soon you would see that it is chaos! Eventually you would miss not having someone take care of your basic needs.

Families are designed to take care of your daily needs and to give you the continual love and guidance you need as you are growing up. Because Mom and Dad have been around longer, they often know what to do when a tough circumstance comes up (as much as you may hate to admit it!).

In Hebrews 10:24-25, we are warned against neglecting "our church meetings." Church is our spiritual family. If we stay away, we are left to try to survive by ourselves. If all we had around were other kids, church would be like a house with no adults. Pretty soon we would recognize that many of our needs would not be getting met.

The church, like the family, can often be underappreciated for the role it plays in our spiritual growth. Some Christians do not recognize its influence until years later, then they realize they would still be spiritual babies without the church's influence and love.

you were laughed at and beaten, and sometimes you watched and sympathized with others suffering the same things. [34]You suffered with those thrown into jail, and you were actually joyful when all you owned was taken from you, knowing that better things were awaiting you in heaven, things that would be yours forever.

[35]Do not let this happy trust in the Lord die away, no matter what happens. Remember your reward! [36]You need to keep on patiently doing God's will if you want him to do for you all that he has promised. [37]His coming will not be delayed much longer. [38]And those whose faith has made them good in God's sight must live by faith, trusting him

in everything. Otherwise, if they shrink back, God will have no pleasure in them.

³⁹But we have never turned our backs on God and sealed our fate. No, our faith in him assures our souls' salvation.

CHAPTER 11 GREAT HEROES OF THE FAITH.

What is faith? It is the confident assurance that something we want is going to happen. It is the certainty that what we hope for is waiting for us, even though we cannot see it up ahead. ²Men of God in days of old were famous for their faith.

³By faith—by believing God—we know that the world and the stars—in fact, all things—were made at God's command; and that they were all made from things that can't be seen.

⁴It was by faith that Abel obeyed God and brought an offering that pleased God more than Cain's offering did. God accepted Abel and proved it by accepting his gift; and though Abel is long dead, we can still learn lessons from him about trusting God.

⁵Enoch trusted God too, and that is why God took him away to heaven without dying; suddenly he was gone because God took him. Before this happened God had said how pleased he was with Enoch. ⁶You can never please God without faith, without depending on him. Anyone who wants to come to God must believe that there is a God and that he rewards those who sincerely look for him.

⁷Noah was another who trusted God. When he heard God's warning about the future, Noah believed him even though there was then no sign of a flood, and wasting no

time, he built the ark and saved his family. Noah's belief in God was in direct contrast to the sin and disbelief of the rest of the world—which refused to obey—and because of his faith he became one of those whom God has accepted.

⁸Abraham trusted God, and when God told him to leave home and go far away to another land that he promised to give him, Abraham obeyed. Away he went, not even knowing where he was going. ⁹And even when he reached God's promised land, he lived in tents like a mere visitor as did Isaac and Jacob, to whom God gave the same promise. ¹⁰Abraham did this because he was confidently waiting for God to bring him to that strong heavenly city whose designer and builder is God.

¹¹Sarah, too, had faith, and because of this she was able to become a mother in spite of her old age, for she realized that God, who gave her his promise, would certainly do what he said. ¹²And so a whole nation came from Abraham, who was too old to have even one child—a nation with so many millions of people that, like the stars of the sky and the sand on the ocean shores, there is no way to count them.

¹³These men of faith I have mentioned died without ever receiving all that God had promised them; but they saw it all awaiting them on ahead and were glad, for they agreed that this earth was not their real home but that they were just strangers visiting down here. ¹⁴And quite obviously when they talked like that, they were looking forward to their real home in heaven.

¹⁵If they had wanted to, they could have gone back to the good things of this world. ¹⁶But they didn't want to. They were living for heaven. And now God is not ashamed to be called their God, for he has made a heavenly city for them.

¹⁷While God was testing him, Abraham still trusted in God and his promises, and so he offered up his son Isaac and was ready to slay him on the altar of sacrifice; ¹⁸yes, to slay even Isaac, through whom God had promised to give Abraham a whole nation of descendants!

¹⁹He believed that if Isaac died God would bring him back to life again; and that is just about what happened, for as far as Abraham was concerned, Isaac was doomed to death, but he came back again

CONSISTENCY

Follow for six months the paths of Ramsey and Tyrone, two guys who made commitments to Christ in August at youth camp:

September: Both guys begin attending a midweek Bible study sponsored by a local church.

October: Both guys are taught how to have a morning devotional time and start digging into God's Word.

November: Ramsey shares his newfound faith in Christ with two friends on the football team. Tyrone, claiming a busy schedule, begins skipping Bible study.

December: Ramsey decides to nix his habit of weekend carousing with the boys. Tyrone is no longer reading his Bible.

January: Ramsey has signed up to go to a Christian discipleship conference over spring break. Tyrone doesn't want to go to the conference, and he acts weird whenever Ramsey tries to talk to him about spiritual matters.

February: Ramsey leads his girlfriend to Christ. Tyrone's girlfriend is pregnant and planning to get an abortion.

Why the difference in the two guys? Why was Ramsey able to be so consistent and why did Tyrone fall away. For a possible answer, read Hebrews 12:1-4.

VISION

11:13-16 The people of faith listed here died without receiving all that God had promised, but they never lost their vision of heaven. Many Christians become frustrated and defeated because their needs, wants, expectations, and demands were not immediately met when they believed in Christ. They become impatient and want to quit. Are you discouraged because your goal seems far away? Take courage from these heroes of faith who lived and died without seeing the fruit of their faith on earth, yet they continued to believe.

alive! ²⁰It was by faith that Isaac knew God would give future blessings to his two sons, Jacob and Esau.

²¹By faith Jacob, when he was old and dying, blessed each of Joseph's two sons as he stood and prayed, leaning on the top of his cane.

²²And it was by faith that Joseph, as he neared the end of his life, confidently spoke of God bringing the people of Israel out of Egypt; and he was so sure of it that he made them promise to carry his bones with them when they left!

²³Moses' parents had faith too. When they saw that God had given them an unusual child, they trusted that God would save him from the death the king commanded, and they hid him for three months and were not afraid.

²⁴,²⁵It was by faith that Moses, when he grew up, refused to be treated as the grandson of the king, but chose to share ill-treatment with God's people instead of enjoying the fleeting pleasures of sin. ²⁶He thought that it was better to suffer for the promised Christ than to own all the treasures of Egypt, for he was looking forward to the great reward that God would give him. ²⁷And it was because he trusted God that he left the land of Egypt and wasn't afraid of the king's anger. Moses kept right on going; it seemed as though he could see God right there with him. ²⁸And it was because he believed God would save his people that he commanded them to kill a lamb as God had told them to and sprinkle the blood on the doorposts of their homes so that God's terrible Angel of Death could not touch the oldest child in those homes as he did among the Egyptians.

²⁹The people of Israel trusted God and went right through the Red Sea as though they were on dry ground. But when the Egyptians chasing them tried it, they all were drowned.

³⁰It was faith that brought the walls of Jericho tumbling down after the people of Israel had walked around them seven days as God had commanded them. ³¹By faith—because she believed in God and his power—Rahab the harlot did not die

with all the others in her city when they refused to obey God, for she gave a friendly welcome to the spies.

³²Well, how much more do I need to say? It would take too long to recount the stories of the faith of Gideon and Barak and Samson and Jephthah and David and Samuel and all the other prophets. ³³These people all trusted God and as a result

"Here's what I did..."

Money and material things used to be very important to me. I cared a lot about the clothes I wore. I liked it that my parents had a nice home and nice cars—and I wasn't very interested in people who didn't have nice clothes or nice things. I just didn't think I had much in common with people who didn't have as much money as I did.

Then I met Cathy. She attended my school, but I didn't know her because we hung around different groups. I got to know Cathy at a Christian camp. She and I were worlds apart in lots of ways. Her parents didn't have much money and she didn't care about fashion at all, but Cathy was the most caring person I had ever met. She knew how to listen, and that summer she turned out to be a good friend to me as I went through a rough time. Some other kids at the camp spread some untrue rumors about me, and it hurt me a lot. But Cathy was always there, to listen and encourage.

That fall when we returned to school, I began to see how shallow some of my other friendships were compared to what I'd experienced with Cathy. I began to do more things with her and her friends, and I found that I liked her friends, even though they weren't "cool." My old friends started making fun of me for hanging around Cathy, but that only showed me more that those people weren't true friends.

I asked Cathy once why she didn't seem to care about money. She said, "Sometimes I do care that I don't have nice clothes like you. But I found a Bible verse that says we're not to love money, but to be satisfied with what we have. I try to do that." She showed me the verse: Hebrews 13:5. What struck me was that she seemed to be more satisfied with what she had than I was, even though she owned much less. I knew she had something that I was just beginning to appreciate: the sense that God really was with her.

My attitude toward money and toward people started to change as I prayed that God would help me to be satisfied with what I had and not to care so much about externals. I saw that God—and true friends—look on the heart, not on whether you wear the latest fashions.

Katie
AGE 16

won battles, overthrew kingdoms, ruled their people well, and received what God had promised them; they were kept from harm in a den of lions ³⁴and in a fiery furnace. Some, through their faith, escaped death by the sword. Some were made strong again after they had been weak or sick. Others were given great power in battle; they made whole armies turn and run away. ³⁵And some women, through faith, received their loved ones back again from death. But others trusted God and were beaten to death, preferring to die rather than turn from God and be free—trusting that they would rise to a better life afterwards.

[36]Some were laughed at and their backs cut open with whips, and others were chained in dungeons. [37,38]Some died by stoning and some by being sawed in two; others were promised freedom if they would renounce their faith, then were killed with the sword. Some went about in skins of sheep and goats, wandering over deserts and mountains, hiding in dens and caves. They were hungry and sick and ill-treated—too good for this world. [39]And these men of faith, though they trusted God and won his approval, none of them received all that God had promised them; [40]for God wanted them to wait and share the even better rewards that were prepared for us.

CHAPTER 12 LET GOD TRAIN YOU.

Since we have such a huge crowd of men of faith watching us from the grandstands, let us strip off anything that slows us down or holds us back, and especially those sins that wrap themselves so tightly around our feet and trip us up; and let us run with patience the particular race that God has set before us.

[2]Keep your eyes on Jesus, our leader and instructor. He was willing to die a shameful death on the cross because of the joy he knew would be his afterwards; and now he sits in the place of honor by the throne of God.

[3]If you want to keep from becoming faint-hearted and weary, think about his patience as sinful men did such terrible things to him. [4]After all, you have never yet struggled against sin and temp-

tation until you sweat great drops of blood.

[5]And have you quite forgotten the encouraging words God spoke to you, his child? He said, "My son, don't be angry when the Lord punishes you. Don't be discouraged when he has to show you where you are wrong. [6]For when he punishes you, it proves that he loves you. When he whips you, it proves you are really his child."

[7]Let God train you, for he is doing what any loving father does for his children. Whoever heard of a son who was never corrected? [8]If God doesn't punish you when you need it, as other fathers punish their sons, then it means that you aren't really God's son at all—that you don't really belong in his family. [9]Since we respect our fathers here on earth, though they punish us, should we not all the more cheerfully submit to God's training so that we can begin really to live?

[10]Our earthly fathers trained us for a few brief years, doing the best for us that they knew how, but God's correction is always right and for our best good, that we may share his holiness. [11]Being punished isn't enjoyable while it is happening—it hurts! But afterwards we can see the result, a quiet growth in grace and character.

[12]So take a new grip with your tired hands, stand firm on your shaky legs, [13]and mark out a straight, smooth path for your feet so that those who follow you, though weak and lame, will not fall and hurt themselves but become strong.

[14]Try to stay out of all quarrels, and seek to live a clean and holy life, for one who is not holy will not see the Lord. [15]Look after each other so that not one of you will fail to find God's best blessings. Watch out that no bitterness takes root among you, for as it springs up it causes deep trouble, hurting many in their spiritual lives. [16]Watch out that no one becomes involved in sexual sin or becomes careless about God as Esau did: he traded his rights as the oldest son for a single meal. [17]And afterwards, when he wanted those rights back again, it was too late, even though he wept bitter tears of repentance. So remember, and be careful.

[18]You have not had to stand face to face with terror, flaming fire, gloom, darkness, and a terrible storm as the Israelites did at Mount Sinai when God gave them his laws. [19]For there was an awesome trumpet blast and a voice with a

*R*EPUTATION

There's a time-out on the floor, and the varsity cheerleaders are building a pyramid at midcourt. Their complicated stunt, however, is not the most fascinating thing taking place in Butler Gymnasium.

Far more interesting are the thoughts that fill the minds of those in the student section. What if you could crawl through each set of watching eyes into each churning brain? What would you discover?

Well, you'd find that most of the students, when they glance at Tammy (the girl at the apex of the pyramid), are thinking words like "conceited," "snotty," "snob," "fake," and "back-stabber." Her reputation is, frankly, not the best.

Meanwhile the girl doing the splits out in front of the others, Amy, is regarded by almost everyone in the stands as "sweet," "nice," "friendly," "fun-to-be-with," and "likable."

Three quick questions:
1. Why would you suppose there is such a sharp contrast in reputations?
2. Do you know any people like Tammy and Amy?
3. How do other people regard you?

Read Hebrews 13 for a fast lesson in reputation making. How was Gaius regarded by others? Diotrephes? Demetrius?

OUR COACH

12:12-13 God is not only a disciplining parent, he is also a demanding coach who pushes us to our limits and requires of us a disciplined life. Although we may not feel strong enough to push on to victory, we will be able to continue as we follow Christ and draw upon his strength. Then we can use our growing strength to help those around us who are weak and struggling.

message so terrible that the people begged God to stop speaking. [20]They staggered back under God's command that if even an animal touched the mountain it must die. [21]Moses himself was so frightened at the sight that he shook with terrible fear.

[22]But you have come right up into Mount Zion, to the city of the living God, the heavenly Jerusalem, and to the gathering of countless happy angels; [23]and to the church, composed of all those registered in heaven; and to God who is Judge of all; and to the spirits of the redeemed in heaven, already made perfect; [24]and to Jesus himself, who has brought us his wonderful new agreement; and to the sprinkled blood, which graciously forgives instead of crying out for vengeance as the blood of Abel did.

[25]So see to it that you obey him who is speaking to you. For if the people of Israel did not escape when they refused to listen to Moses, the earthly messenger, how terrible our danger if we refuse to listen to God who speaks to us from heaven! [26]When he spoke from Mount Sinai his voice shook the earth, but, "Next time," he says, "I will not only shake the earth but the heavens too." [27]By this he means that he will sift out everything without solid foundations so that only unshakable things will be left.

[28]Since we have a Kingdom nothing can destroy, let us please God by serving him with thankful hearts and with holy fear and awe. [29]For our God is a consuming fire.

CHAPTER **13** LIVE GOOD AND OBEDIENT LIVES.

Continue to love each other with true brotherly love. [2]Don't forget to be kind to strangers, for some who have done this have entertained angels without realizing it! [3]Don't forget about those in jail. Suffer with them as though you were there yourself. Share the sorrow of those being mistreated, for you know what they are going through.

[4]Honor your marriage and its vows, and be pure; for God will surely punish all those who are immoral or commit adultery.

[5]Stay away from the love of money; be satisfied with what you have. For God has said, "I will never, *never* fail you nor forsake you." [6]That is why we can say without any doubt or fear, "The Lord is my Helper, and I am not afraid of anything that mere man can do to me."

[7]Remember your leaders who have taught you the Word of God. Think of all the good that has come from their lives, and try to trust the Lord as they do.

[8]Jesus Christ is the same yesterday, today, and forever. [9]So do not be attracted by strange, new ideas. Your spiritual strength comes as a gift from God, not from ceremonial rules about eating certain foods—a method which, by the way, hasn't helped those who have tried it!

[10]We have an altar—the cross where Christ was sacrificed—where those who continue to seek sal-

My grandma has been a Christian for 40 years. She has faced so much trouble during those years I can't believe it. Why would God allow so much trouble to come into one person's life?

I WONDER . . .

No doubt you've seen weight lifters on TV or have friends who work out with weights.

The goal of lifting weights is to develop the muscles and make them stronger. But this muscle-building process involves the muscles being constantly broken down!

At first, the strain of lifting causes the person to feel weak. In the long run, however, it makes him or her strong.

Like a muscle, faith grows stronger when it is exercised. That's why James 1:2-4 says to be happy when facing difficult trials and temptations. The entire book of Hebrews is about faith—how to strengthen it, how it can help you endure. In Hebrews 11, you will find the "Hall of Faith," a list of those who suffered for their faith . . . and who will one day receive wonderful rewards for standing firm!

One of God's goals for us is to learn to trust him more. When a Christian asks God for more faith, he or she is really asking for more trials. God knows that only through exercise can our faith be strengthened.

Eventually, James says, we will be "ready for anything, strong in character, full and complete" (1:4).

Another reason for trials and problems is found in 2 Corinthians 1:3-5: helping others.

"What a wonderful God we have—he is the Father of our Lord Jesus Christ, the source of every mercy, and the one who so wonderfully comforts and strengthens us in our hardships and trials. And why does he do this? So that when others are in trouble, needing our sympathy and encouragement, we can pass on to them this same help and comfort God has given us. You can be sure that the more we undergo sufferings for Christ, the more he will shower us with his comfort and encouragement."

Helping someone else is probably the last thing we are thinking about when we are going through problems. But our success at coming through trials is very important to God. Then he can use us to pass along comfort and encouragement to others.

Some Christians are glad that they have few problems. Unfortunately, they won't have the opportunity to see their character grow stronger. And they won't receive the joy that comes when they help others.

vation by obeying Jewish laws can never be helped. [11]Under the system of Jewish laws, the high priest brought the blood of the slain animals into the sanctuary as a sacrifice for sin, and then the bodies of the animals were burned outside the city.

¹²That is why Jesus suffered and died outside the city, where his blood washed our sins away.

¹³So let us go out to him beyond the city walls [that is, outside the interests of this world, being willing to be despised] to suffer with him there, bearing his shame. ¹⁴For this world is not our home; we are looking forward to our everlasting home in heaven.

¹⁵With Jesus' help we will continually offer our sacrifice of praise to God by telling others of the glory of his name. ¹⁶Don't forget to do good and to share what you have with those in need, for such sacrifices are very pleasing to him. ¹⁷Obey your spiritual leaders and be willing to do what they say. For their work is to watch over your souls, and God will judge them on how well they do this. Give them reason to report joyfully about you to the Lord and not with sorrow, for then you will suffer for it too.

¹⁸Pray for us, for our conscience is clear and we want to keep it that way. ¹⁹I especially need your prayers right now so that I can come back to you sooner.

^{20,21}And now may the God of peace, who brought again from the dead our Lord Jesus, equip you with all you need for doing his will. May he who became the great Shepherd of the sheep by an everlasting agreement between God and you, signed with his blood, produce in you through the power of Christ all that is pleasing to him. To him be glory forever and ever. Amen.

²²Brethren, please listen patiently to what I have said in this letter, for it is a short one. ²³I want you to know that Brother Timothy is now out of jail; if he comes here soon, I will come with him to see you. ^{24,25}Give my greetings to all your leaders and to the other believers there. The Christians from Italy who are here with me send you their love. God's grace be with you all. Good-bye.

UNCHANGING

13:1-21 We must keep our eyes on Christ, our ultimate leader, who, unlike human leaders, will never change. He has been and will be the same forever. In a changing world we can trust our unchanging Lord.

MATURITY

13:24-25 Hebrews is a call to Christian maturity. This book was addressed to first-century Jewish Christians, but it applies to Christians of any age or background. Christian maturity means making Christ the beginning and end of our faith. To mature, we must center our lives on him, not depending on religious ritual, not falling back into sin, not trusting in ourselves, and not letting anything come between us and Christ.

MEGA *Themes*

CHRIST IS SUPERIOR Hebrews reveals Jesus' true identity as God. Christ is the ultimate authority. He is greater than any religion or any angel, and superior to any Jewish leader (such as Abraham, Moses, or Joshua) or priest. Christ is the complete revelation of God.

Jesus alone can forgive your sin. He has secured your forgiveness and salvation by his death on the cross. With Christ you can find peace with God and real meaning for life. Without him, there is no hope for true life.

1. What was unique about Jesus Christ?
2. Why did the first-century Jews have difficulty accepting these truths about Jesus?

3. How do the majority of people in your school feel about being a Christian? What are their misconceptions about Jesus?
4. If you could explain one thing about Christ to those who do not understand him, what would you tell them?

HIGH PRIEST In the Old Testament, the high priest represented the Jews before God. Jesus Christ links us with God. There is no other way to reach God. Because Jesus Christ lived a sinless life, he is the perfect substitute to die for our sin. Christ is our perfect representative with God.

Jesus guarantees our access to God the Father. He intercedes for us so that we can boldly come to the

Father with our needs. When we are weak we can come confidently to God for forgiveness and help. He never shuts us out or refuses to respond to our needs.

1. In Hebrews, what do you learn about the role of a high priest?
2. Based on 4:14-16 and 7:19-28, what are the ways that Jesus is the perfect High Priest?
3. What benefits do you have because Jesus is your High Priest?
4. What hurts, needs, or wants do you want to bring to God, your Father? How does Jesus, your High Priest, provide the way for you to present these to God? Express your needs to God and share with him your feelings about the perfect High Priest he has provided in Jesus.

SACRIFICE Christ's sacrifice was the ultimate fulfillment of all that the Old Testament sacrifices represented—God's forgiveness for sin. Because Christ was the perfect sacrifice, our sins have been completely forgiven—past, present, and future.

Christ removed sin that kept us from God's presence and fellowship. But we must accept Christ's sacrifice for us. By believing in him we are declared "not guilty," cleansed, and made whole. Christ's sacrifice provided the way for us to have eternal life.

1. What qualified Jesus to be the perfect, once-and-for-all fulfillment of the Old Testament sacrificial requirements?
2. What blessings do you have as a result of Jesus' sacrifice?
3. Contrast the difference for those who reject Christ's sacrifice and those who accept it (check 10:26-39).
4. What have you personally received from the one who sacrificed himself for your sins? What difference has Jesus' sacrifice made in your life?

FAITH Faith is confident trust in God. God's salvation is in his son Jesus, who is the only one who can save us from sin.

If you trust in Jesus Christ for your salvation, he will transform you completely. Then you should live a life of faith.

1. Rewrite 11:3 in your own words.
2. Explain what you think is meant by this statement: "Faith is not just knowing, it is doing."
3. Read chapter 11. What do you learn about the life of faith from the great men and women listed there?
4. If someone were to write a couple of verses describing your life of faith, what would they include?
5. In what ways would you like to see your faith grow? How do you develop this growth in faith?

MATURITY THROUGH ENDURANCE Faith enables Christians to face trials. Genuine faith includes the commitment to stay true to God when we are under fire. Endurance builds character and leads to victory.

You can have victory in your trials if you don't give up or turn your back on Christ. Stay true to Christ and pray for endurance. He will never grow tired of supporting you.

1. Hebrews 12 describes what it means to grow through endurance and discipline. Why is discipline necessary for growth?
2. Based on 12:1-5, what are the keys to endurance? How can you apply these principles to where you are in "the race" at this point in your life?
3. What are the main points of Hebrews' teaching concerning God's discipline?
4. If someone were to ask you, "Why should I take obedience to God so seriously?" how would you respond?

You've been feeling strange all week. At first you had trouble sleeping. Then came the headaches. Yesterday your teeth began hurting and your fingernails turned blue for several hours. This morning you realized it was time to consult your family doctor when, after a morning jog, your mom asked if you'd been sprayed by a skunk. ■ The doctor tries to hold her breath as she asks you questions. She nods knowingly as you tick off your symptoms. After looking in your eyes and noting your swollen eardrums, she orders some lab work. ■ A few hours later she returns to tell you, "Just what I suspected— you have an extremely high number of antibiomolecularsucrothyamin microbes in your liver." ■ "Huh?" you gulp. ■ "Oh, don't worry. You have a common ailment we call odoramonia. We'll put you on an antibiotic and get you eating a balanced diet, and you'll be fine." ■ Aren't doctors amazing? By examining us and noting our symptoms, they're usually able to diagnose our physical ailments and prescribe the proper treatment. ■ God does the same thing in our spiritual realm. ■ By looking at our actions (or lack of action) God can tell us exactly what attitudes and desires need healing. His Word gives detailed prescriptions for curing wrong behavior patterns. ■ Is your spiritual life on the sick side? Are you fighting worldly infections or possibly even the disease of disobedience? ■ Follow the advice of the Great Physician. No matter what your ailment, the Epistle of James has the cure.

STATS

PURPOSE: To expose unethical practices and to teach right Christian behavior

AUTHOR: James, Jesus' brother, a leader in the Jerusalem church

TO WHOM WRITTEN: First-century Jewish Christians residing in Gentile communities outside Palestine and to all Christians everywhere

DATE WRITTEN: Probably A.D. 49, prior to the Jerusalem Council held in A.D. 50

SETTING: This letter expresses James's concern for persecuted Christians who were once part of the Jerusalem church

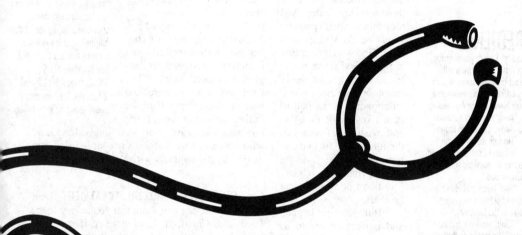

James

CHAPTER 1 **JAMES: A SERVANT OF GOD.** *From:* James, a servant of God and of the Lord Jesus Christ.

To: Jewish Christians scattered everywhere. Greetings!

²Dear brothers, is your life full of difficulties and temptations? Then be happy, ³for when the way is rough, your patience has a chance to grow. ⁴So let it grow, and don't try to squirm out of your problems. For when your patience is finally in full bloom, then you will be ready for anything, strong in character, full and complete.

⁵If you want to know what God wants you to do, ask him, and he will gladly tell you, for he is always ready to give a bountiful supply of wisdom to all who ask him; he will not resent it. ⁶But when you ask him, be sure that you really expect him to tell you, for a doubtful mind will be as unsettled as a wave of the sea that is driven and tossed by the wind; ⁷,⁸and every decision you then make will be uncertain, as you turn first this way and then that. If you don't ask with faith, don't expect the Lord to give you any solid answer.

⁹A Christian who doesn't amount to much in this world should be glad, for he is great in the Lord's sight. ¹⁰,¹¹But a rich man should be glad that

ROUGH TIMES

1:2-4 We can't really know the depth of our character until we see how we react under pressure. It is easy to be kind when everything is going well, but can we still be kind when others are treating us unfairly? Instead of complaining about our struggles, we should see them as opportunities for growth. Thank God for promising to be with you in rough times. Ask him to help you solve your problems or give you the strength to endure them. Then be patient. God will not leave you; he will stay close by and help you grow.

his riches mean nothing to the Lord, for he will soon be gone, like a flower that has lost its beauty and fades away, withered—killed by the scorching summer sun. So it is with rich men. They will soon die and leave behind all their busy activities.

[12]Happy is the man who doesn't give in and do wrong when he is tempted, for afterwards he will get as his reward the crown of life that God has promised those who love him. [13]And remember, when someone wants to do wrong it is never God who is tempting him, for God never wants to do wrong and never tempts anyone else to do it. [14]Temptation is the pull of man's own evil thoughts and wishes. [15]These evil thoughts lead to evil actions and afterwards to the death penalty from God. [16]So don't be misled, dear brothers.

[17]But whatever is good and perfect comes to us from God, the Creator of all light, and he shines forever without change or shadow. [18]And it was a happy day for him when he gave us our new lives through the truth of his Word, and we became, as it were, the first children in his new family.

[19]Dear brothers, don't ever forget that it is best to listen much, speak little, and not become angry; [20]for anger doesn't make us good, as God demands that we must be.

[21]So get rid of all that is wrong in your life, both inside and outside, and humbly be glad for the wonderful message we have received, for it is able to save our souls as it takes hold of our hearts.

[22]And remember, it is a message to obey, not just to listen to. So don't fool yourselves. [23]For if a person just listens and doesn't obey, he is like a man looking at his face in a mirror; [24]as soon as he walks away, he can't see himself anymore or remember what he looks like. [25]But if anyone keeps looking steadily into God's law for free men, he will not only remember it but he will do what it says, and God will greatly bless him in everything he does.

[26]Anyone who says he is a Christian but doesn't control his sharp tongue is just fooling himself, and his religion isn't worth much. [27]The Christian who is pure and without fault, from God the Father's point of view, is the one who takes care of orphans and widows, and who remains true to the Lord—not soiled and dirtied by his contacts with the world.

CHAPTER **2** **NO SPECIAL TREATMENT.** Dear brothers, how can you claim that you belong to the Lord Jesus Christ, the Lord of glory, if you show favoritism to rich people and look down on poor people?

[2]If a man comes into your church dressed in expensive clothes and with valuable gold rings on his fingers, and at the same moment another man comes in who is poor and dressed in threadbare clothes, [3]and you make a lot of fuss over the rich man and give him the best seat in the house and say to the poor man, "You can stand over there if you like or else sit on the floor"—well, [4]judging a man by his wealth shows that you are guided by wrong motives.

[5]Listen to me, dear brothers: God has chosen poor people to be rich in faith, and the Kingdom of

SNOWBALL

1:12-15 Temptation comes from evil desires inside us, not from God. It begins with an evil thought and becomes sin when we dwell on the thought and allow it to become an action. Like a snowball rolling downhill, sin's destruction grows the more we let sin have its way. The best time to stop a snowball is at the top of the hill, before it is too big or moving too fast to control. See Matthew 4:1-11; 1 Corinthians 10:13; and 2 Timothy 2:22 for more about escaping temptation.

OBEDIENCE

The First Church youth group has just heard a great talk about the importance of serving others. On the way home, three friends discuss the meeting:

"Andy is a great speaker! He always makes me laugh!"

"His talk was awesome."

"I know! I feel so convicted. I never do anything for my mom or dad."

"That was a cool idea he gave about doing a project down in the inner city."

"Yeah, wouldn't that be great? We should do that sometime."

Now, let's listen in on the conversation a few minutes later:

"So, what are you guys going to do this weekend?"

"Probably the same old stuff—go to a movie, sit around and be bored."

"That drives me nuts! How come there is nothing for kids our age to do? If I have to go to the mall one more time, I'm going to puke!"

"I agree!"

What's wrong with that conversation? Anything? Read over it again.

Less than 30 minutes after being challenged to serve others, these teens are complaining they don't have anything to do.

The point? Christians should never be bored! We always have opportunities to serve others. In fact, if we're not putting our faith into practice on a regular basis, the Bible says our religion isn't worth very much. See James 1:21-27.

DON'T EVER FORGET

that it is BEST to LISTEN MUCH SPEAK LITTLE and not become ANGRY.

Heaven is theirs, for that is the gift God has promised to all those who love him. [6]And yet, of the two strangers, you have despised the poor man. Don't you realize that it is usually the rich men who pick on you and drag you into court? [7]And all too often they are the ones who laugh at Jesus Christ, whose noble name you bear.

[8]Yes indeed, it is good when you truly obey our Lord's command, "You must love and help your neighbors just as much as you love and take care of yourself." [9]But you are breaking this law of our Lord's when you favor the rich and fawn over them; it is sin.

[10]And the person who keeps every law of God but makes one little slip is just as guilty as the person who has broken every law there is. [11]For the God who said you must not marry a woman who already has a husband also said you must not murder, so even though you have not broken the marriage laws by committing adultery, but have murdered someone, you have entirely broken God's laws and stand utterly guilty before him.

[12]You will be judged on whether or not you are doing what Christ wants you to. So watch what you do and what you think; [13]for there will be no mercy to those who have shown no mercy. But if you have been merciful, then God's mercy toward you will win out over his judgment against you.

[14]Dear brothers, what's the use of saying that you have faith and are Christians if you aren't proving it by helping others? Will *that* kind of faith save anyone? [15]If you have a friend who is in need of food and clothing, [16]and you say to him, "Well, good-bye and God bless you; stay warm and eat hearty," and then don't give him clothes or food, what good does that do?

[17]So you see, it isn't enough just to have faith. You must also do good to prove that you have it. Faith that doesn't show itself by good works is no faith at all—it is dead and useless.

[18]But someone may well argue, "You say the way to God is by faith alone, plus nothing; well, I say that good works are important too, for without good works you can't prove whether you have faith or not; but anyone can see that I have faith by the way I act."

[19]Are there still some among you who hold that "only believing" is enough? Believing in one God? Well, remember that the demons believe this too—so strongly that they tremble in terror! [20]Fool! When will you ever learn that "believing" is useless without *doing* what God wants you to? Faith that does not result in good deeds is not real faith.

[21]Don't you remember that even our father Abraham was declared good because of what he *did* when he was willing to obey God, even if it meant offering his son Isaac to die on the altar? [22]You see, he was trusting God so much that he was willing to do whatever God told him to; his faith was made complete by what he did—by his actions, his good deeds. [23]And so it happened just as the Scriptures say, that Abraham trusted God, and the Lord declared him good in God's sight, and he

"Here's what I did..."

I went to a special school where several classes were held in a zoo two days a week. Because of this, I didn't always feel a part of the high school student body. Even worse, I didn't know any other Christians at the high school or in my classes at the zoo. Then I started studying the book of James. My Bible notes said that the book was written to Christians who were scattered everywhere. That's how I felt: scattered among a couple thousand students who didn't know or care about God.

One day I was working with a friend on an assignment at the zoo. As he and I talked about life, I found out he was a Christian. But he said his faith was weak. He was going through all these trials—his mom was sick, he was feeling pressured about taking the SAT and choosing a school, and other things were going wrong in his life.

I had a Bible in my book bag, so I opened it to James 1 and showed him the verses I had been studying. The look on his face when he finished reading it clearly said, "Wow, this fits!" Later he thanked me and told me that the Scripture I'd shared had helped him a lot.

I knew what he meant. James 1 always encourages me, too. But it encouraged me even more to be able to share it with him, and to see God speaking so clearly to him through his Word. Plus, I now had a Christian friend at school!

Shea
AGE 15

was even called "the friend of God." [24]So you see, a man is saved by what he does, as well as by what he believes.

[25]Rahab, the prostitute, is another example of this. She was saved because of what she did when she hid those messengers and sent them safely away by a different road. [26]Just as the body is dead when there is no spirit in it, so faith is dead if it is not the kind that results in good deeds.

CHAPTER 3 CONTROL WHAT YOU SAY.

Dear brothers, don't be too eager to tell others their faults, for we all make many mistakes; and when we teachers of religion, who should know better, do wrong, our punishment will be greater than it would be for others.

If anyone can control his tongue, it proves that he has perfect control over himself in every other way. [3]We can make a large horse turn around and go wherever we want by means of a small bit in his mouth. [4]And a tiny rudder makes a huge ship turn wherever the pilot wants it to go, even though the winds are strong.

[5]So also the tongue is a small thing, but what enormous damage it can do. A great forest can be set on fire by one tiny spark. [6]And the tongue is a flame of fire. It is full of wickedness, and poisons every part of the body. And the tongue is set on fire by hell itself and can turn our whole lives into a blazing flame of destruction and disaster.

[7]Men have trained, or can train, every kind of animal or bird that lives and every kind of reptile and fish, [8]but no human being can tame the tongue. It is always ready to pour out its deadly poison. [9]Sometimes it praises our heavenly Father, and sometimes it breaks out into curses against men who are made like God. [10]And so blessing and cursing come pouring out of the same mouth. Dear brothers, surely this is not right! [11]Does a spring of water bubble out first with fresh water and then with bitter water? [12]Can you pick olives from a fig tree, or figs from a grape vine? No, and you can't draw fresh water from a salty pool.

[13]If you are wise, live a life of steady goodness so that only good deeds will pour forth. And if you don't brag about them, then you will be truly wise! [14]And by all means don't brag about being wise and good if you are bitter and jealous and selfish; that is the worst sort of lie. [15]For jealousy and selfishness are not God's kind of wisdom. Such things are earthly, unspiritual, inspired by the devil. [16]For wherever there is jealousy or selfish ambition, there will be disorder and every other kind of evil.

[17]But the wisdom that comes from heaven is first of all pure and full of quiet gentleness. Then it is peace-loving and courteous. It allows discussion and is willing to yield to others; it is full of mercy and good deeds. It is wholehearted and straightfor-

ward and sincere. [18]And those who are peacemakers will plant seeds of peace and reap a harvest of goodness.

CHAPTER 4 HOW CAN YOU GET CLOSE TO GOD?

What is causing the quarrels and fights among you? Isn't it because there is a whole army of evil desires within you? [2]You want what you don't have, so you kill to get it. You long for what others have, and can't afford it, so you start a fight to take it away from them. And yet the reason you don't have what you want is that you don't ask God for it. [3]And even when you do ask you don't get it because your whole aim is wrong—you want only what will give *you* pleasure.

[4]You are like an unfaithful wife who loves her husband's enemies. Don't you realize that making friends with God's enemies—the evil pleasures of this world—makes you an enemy of God? I say it again, that if your aim is to enjoy the evil pleasure of the unsaved world, you cannot also be a friend of God. [5]Or what do you think the Scripture means when it says that the Holy Spirit, whom God has placed within us, watches over us with tender jealousy? [6]But he gives us more and more strength to stand against all such evil longings. As the Scripture says, God gives strength to the humble but sets himself against the proud and haughty.

[7]So give yourselves humbly to God. Resist the devil and he will flee from you. [8]And when you draw close to God, God will draw close to you. Wash your hands, you sinners, and let your hearts be filled with God alone to make them pure and true to him. [9]Let there be tears for the wrong things you have done. Let there be sorrow and sincere grief. Let there be sadness instead of laughter, and gloom instead of joy. [10]Then when you realize your worthlessness before the Lord, he will lift you up, encourage and help you.

[11]Don't criticize and speak evil about each other, dear brothers. If you do, you will be fighting against God's law of loving one another, declaring it is wrong. But your job is not to decide whether this law is right or wrong, but to obey it. [12]Only he who made the law can rightly judge among us. He alone decides to save us or destroy. So what right do you have to judge or criticize others?

SAY WHAT?

3:2-3 What you say and what you *don't* say are both important. Proper speech is not only saying the right words at the right time, but also controlling your desire to say what you shouldn't. Examples of wrongly using the tongue include gossiping, putting others down, bragging, manipulating, false teaching, exaggerating, complaining, flattering, and lying. Before you speak, ask, "Is it true, is it necessary, and is it kind?"

BUILD UP

4:11-12 Jesus summarized the law as loving God and your neighbor (Matthew 22:37-40), and Paul said love demonstrated toward a neighbor fully satisfies the law (Romans 13:6-10). When we fail to love, we break God's law. Examine your attitude and actions. Do you build people up or tear them down? Instead of criticizing someone, remember God's law of love and say something good instead. If you make this a habit, your tendency to find fault with others will decrease and your ability to obey God will increase.

[13]Look here, you people who say, "Today or tomorrow we are going to such and such a town, stay there a year, and open up a profitable business." [14]How do you know what is going to happen tomorrow? For the length of your lives is as uncertain as the morning fog—now you see it; soon it is gone. [15]What you ought to say is, "If the Lord wants us to, we shall live and do this or that." [16]Otherwise you will be bragging about your own plans, and such self-confidence never pleases God.

[17]Remember, too, that knowing what is right to do and then not doing it is sin.

CHAPTER **5** A WARNING TO THE RICH. Look here, you rich men, now is the time to cry and groan with anguished grief because of all the terrible troubles ahead of you. [2]Your wealth is even now rotting away, and your fine clothes are becoming mere moth-eaten rags. [3]The value of your gold and silver is dropping fast, yet it will stand as evidence against you and eat your flesh like fire. That is what you have stored up for yourselves to receive on that coming day of judgment. [4]For listen! Hear the cries of the field workers whom you have cheated of their pay. Their cries have reached the ears of the Lord of Hosts.

[5]You have spent your years here on earth having fun, satisfying your every whim, and now your fat hearts are ready for the slaughter. [6]You have condemned and killed good men who had no power to defend themselves against you.

[7]Now as for you, dear brothers who are waiting for the Lord's return, be patient, like a farmer who waits until the autumn for his precious harvest to ripen. [8]Yes, be patient. And take courage, for the coming of the Lord is near.

[9]Don't grumble about each other, brothers. Are you yourselves above criticism? For see! The great Judge is coming. He is almost here. [Let him do whatever criticizing must be done.]

[10]For examples of patience in suffering, look at the Lord's prophets. [11]We know how happy they are now because they stayed true to him then, even though they suffered greatly for it. Job is an example of a man who continued to trust the Lord in sorrow; from his experiences we can see how the Lord's plan finally ended in good, for he is full of tenderness and mercy.

[12]But most of all, dear brothers, do not swear either by heaven or earth or anything else; just say a simple yes or no so that you will not sin and be condemned for it.

[13]Is anyone among you suffering? He should keep on praying about it. And those who have reason to be thankful should continually be singing praises to the Lord.

[14]Is anyone sick? He should call for the elders of the church and they should pray over him and pour a little oil upon him, calling on the Lord to heal him. [15]And their prayer, if offered in faith, will heal him, for the Lord will make him well; and if his sickness was caused by some sin, the Lord will forgive him.

I feel guilty more often now that I'm a Christian. Sometimes the guilt comes on for just little stuff that I used to never give a second thought about. When do I need to ask God for forgiveness?

I WONDER . . .

God's goal is not to overwhelm us with our sin so that we become discouraged. He knows when to point out sin in our lives.

Some people are basically pretty "good" people when they come to faith in Christ. They don't have many destructive habits to overcome, and their parents have tried to teach them right from wrong. Others come with a lot of sin "baggage."

Although each person is unique, we're the same when it comes to our nature—we're sinners. In fact, we were born with a sinful nature. This is called "original sin." And throughout our lives, we do all sorts of things that are wrong.

When we accept Christ as Savior, God declared us "not guilty." But this doesn't mean that we're perfect and don't sin anymore. We must daily deal with sin while we're still alive on earth. It's part of being human. Christians, like everyone, have two types of sin to deal with. Past sins and present sins.

As I said, when we become Christians, all of our past sins are wiped away. "He has removed our sins as far away from us as the east is from the west" (Psalm 103:12). That's a distance that can't be measured!

Ideally, having past sins removed should also take away our guilt feelings. We can put the past behind us. We're forgiven!

But what about present sin? One of the roles of the Holy Spirit is to remind us when we sin. He doesn't do this to condemn us, but to prompt us to confess it, forsake it, and move on. God has forgiven us for these present sins, too. We confess them to him to keep the communication channels open and to keep the relationship close. So we should talk to God about our lives, and confess, whenever we need to. And remember, sins aren't limited to doing what is wrong. They also include not doing what is right.

The passage in James 4:17 is plain. "Remember, too, that knowing what is right to do and then not doing it is sin."

If we know we should help someone stop gossiping; give our parents the whole truth, instead of only part of it; turn off the TV and spend time with God . . . and don't do it—we sin!

Let God do the convicting in your life, not others, and you'll be glad to confess your sins to him. He's eager to clear away the barriers between you and himself and start fresh.

¹⁶Admit your faults to one another and pray for each other so that you may be healed. The earnest prayer of a righteous man has great power and wonderful results. ¹⁷Elijah was as completely human as we are, and yet when he prayed earnestly that no rain would fall, none fell for the next three and a half years! ¹⁸Then he prayed again, this time that it *would* rain, and down it poured, and the grass turned green and the gardens began to grow again.

¹⁹Dear brothers, if anyone has slipped away from God and no longer trusts the Lord and someone helps him understand the Truth again, ²⁰that person who brings him back to God will have saved a wandering soul from death, bringing about the forgiveness of his many sins.

Sincerely, James

MEGA Themes

LIVING FAITH James wants believers to hear the truth *and* to do it. He contrasts empty faith ("claims without conduct") with faith that works. Commitment to love and to serve is evidence of true faith.

Living faith makes a difference. Make sure your faith results in action. Be alert to ways of putting your faith to work. Be certain that you not only "talk" the gospel, but that you "walk" the gospel as well.

1. Contrast "living faith" with "dead faith."
2. What would it mean to have a dead faith in your school? What would it mean to have a living faith in your school?
3. How are your vital signs? Identify evidence of life in your faith.
4. In what ways can you become more alive as a doer of God's Word in your school? With your friends? In your relationships at church? In response to the needy in your community?

TRIALS In the Christian life there are trials and temptations. Successfully overcoming these adversities produces maturity and strong character.

Don't resent troubles when they come. Pray for wisdom; God will supply all you need to face persecution or adversity. He will give you patience and keep you strong.

1. What attitude does James teach you to have concerning trials?
2. What trials and problems have you recently experienced?
3. How did you feel when you were facing these trials and problems? How did you feel towards God?
4. Describe how you can choose to respond with an appropriate attitude the next time you face a trial or problem. Why is developing such responses important for a Christian? (Check the results of enduring trials in chapter 1.)

LAW OF LOVE We are saved by God's gracious mercy, not by keeping the law. But Christ gave us a special command, "love your neighbor as yourself"

(Matthew 19:19). We are to love and serve those around us.

Keeping the law of love shows that our faith is vital and real. To show love to others, we must root out our own selfishness. This begins by acting on what we know to be true about God's will in our lives.

1. What does James teach in chapter 2 about the life of faith?
2. What would happen if every Christian in your community lived with the attitude and actions described in 2:2-16?
3. Why are the acts of giving to those in need and not showing favoritism important expressions of living faith?
4. What does it mean in your life not to show favoritism? (home, school, church) Who are the needy who can benefit from your resources? (time, love, food, money, work)

WISE SPEECH Wisdom shows itself in speech. We are responsible for the destructive results of our talk. The wisdom of God that helps control the tongue can help control all our actions.

Accepting God's wisdom will affect your speech because your words will reveal their godly source. Think of God and others before you speak, and allow God to strengthen your self-control.

1. Why does James devote so much of this book to the issue of controlling the tongue?
2. When did someone's words hurt you or a person you really care about? How did you feel? What were the results?
3. When did your words hurt another person? How did you feel? What were the results?
4. Taking the principles from James, what could have been done differently in those situations that would have led to positive communication?

WEALTH James teaches Christians not to compromise with worldly attitudes about wealth. Because the glory of wealth fades, Christians should store up God's treasures through sincere service. Christians must not show partiality to the wealthy or be prejudiced against the poor.

We all are accountable for how we use what we have. We should be generous toward others. We are to see one another as God sees us—created as equals in his image.

1. What does James think about rich people? What is it about these wealthy men in chapter 5 that causes James to react so strongly?

2. After studying James 2 and 5, what should be the Christian life-style of a person who is blessed with great wealth?

3. How can you make your possessions a part of your life of faith? Why is it important that you not separate what you have from your responsibility to God?

*E*ach year a few individuals compete in what may be the most grueling athletic competition of all: a bicycle race across the U.S. ■ Consider the obstacles: blazing deserts, towering mountain ranges, inclement weather, 18- to 20-hour stretches of pedaling, flat tires, potholes, skin-scraping spills, inconsiderate motorists, and sheer fatigue. It's *amazing* anyone ever finishes. The fact that some complete the 2,000-plus mile trip in *just over a week* is downright unbelievable! ■ How do they do it? ■ With the help of carefully trained support teams. These support teams follow the cyclists in specially equipped recreational vehicles, providing whatever the rider needs—food, drink, a repair job, a replacement bike, medical attention, a rubdown, a short nap, coaching, or a few shouts of encouragement. These support teams make an otherwise impossible trip very possible. ■ The Christian life is similar to that grueling bicycle marathon. The occasional joys of gliding downhill are obscured by the more frequent times of having to churn our way up steep mountain peaks. We get weary. We feel like quitting. The finish line seems far, far away. ■ Fortunately God has given us a first-rate support team to help us go the distance. With the Holy Spirit, the Word of God, and other believers to encourage us, we can not only finish the race, we can *win!* ■ Find out more about your spiritual support team in the book that follows, the book called 1 Peter. ■ (But don't wait too long. The race has already started!)

STATS

PURPOSE: To offer encouragement to suffering Christians

AUTHOR: Peter

TO WHOM WRITTEN: Jewish Christians who had been driven out of Jerusalem and scattered throughout Asia Minor and to all believers everywhere

DATE WRITTEN: About A.D. 62—64 from Rome

SETTING: Peter was probably in Rome when the great persecution under Emperor Nero began (Peter was eventually executed during the persecution). Throughout the Roman Empire, Christians were being tortured and killed for their faith, and the church in Jerusalem was being scattered throughout the Mediterranean world.

KEY PEOPLE: Peter, Silvanus, Mark

KEY PLACES: Jerusalem, Rome, and the regions of Pontus, Galatia, Cappadocia, Asia Minor, and Bithynia

1Peter

CHAPTER 1 **GOD'S MISSIONARY.** *From:* Peter, Jesus Christ's missionary.

To: The Jewish Christians driven out of Jerusalem and scattered throughout Pontus, Galatia, Cappadocia, Asia Minor, and Bithynia.

²Dear friends, God the Father chose you long ago and knew you would become his children. And the Holy Spirit has been at work in your hearts, cleansing you with the blood of Jesus Christ and making you to please him. May God bless you richly and grant you increasing freedom from all anxiety and fear.

³All honor to God, the God and Father of our Lord Jesus Christ; for it is his boundless mercy that has given us the privilege of being born again so that we are now members of God's own family. Now we live in the hope of eternal life because Christ rose again from the dead. ⁴And God has reserved for his children the priceless gift of eternal life; it is kept in heaven for you, pure and undefiled, beyond the reach of change and decay. ⁵And God, in his mighty power, will make sure that you get there safely to receive it because you are trusting him. It will be yours in that coming last day for all to see. ⁶So be truly glad! There is wonderful joy ahead, even though the going is rough for a while down here.

⁷These trials are only to test your faith, to see whether or not it is strong and pure. It is being tested as fire tests gold and purifies it—and your faith is far more precious to God than mere gold; so if your faith remains strong after being tried in the test tube of fiery trials, it will bring you much praise and glory and honor on the day of his return.

⁸You love him even though you have never seen him; though not seeing him, you trust him; and even now you are happy with the inexpressible joy that comes from heaven itself. ⁹And your further reward for trusting him will be the salvation of your souls.

LIVE IN HOPE

1:3-6 Do you need encouragement? Peter's words offer joy and hope in times of trouble, and he bases his confidence on what God has done for us in Christ Jesus. We're called to *live* in the hope of eternal life (1:3). Our hope is not only for the future; eternal life begins when we believe in God and join his family. The eternal life we now have gives us hope and enables us to live with confidence in God.

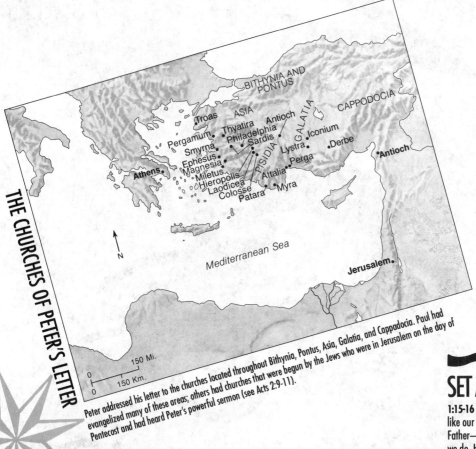

BITHYNIA AND PONTUS

CAPPODOCIA

ASIA

GALATIA

Troas
Pergamum
Thyatira Antioch
Philadelphia
Smyrna Sardis
Ephesus
Magnesia
Miletus
Hieropolis
Laodicea
Colosse
Patara

Iconium
Lystra Derbe
PSIDIA Perga
Attalia
Myra

Athens

Antioch

Jerusalem.

Mediterranean Sea

N

0   150 Mi.
0   150 Km.

Peter addressed his letter to the churches located throughout Bithynia, Pontus, Asia, Galatia, and Cappadocia. Paul had evangelized many of these areas; others had churches that were begun by the Jews who were in Jerusalem on the day of Pentecost and had heard Peter's powerful sermon (see Acts 2:9-11).

[10]This salvation was something the prophets did not fully understand. Though they wrote about it, they had many questions as to what it all could mean. [11]They wondered what the Spirit of Christ within them was talking about, for he told them to write down the events which, since then, have happened to Christ: his suffering, and his great glory afterwards. And they wondered when and to whom all this would happen.

[12]They were finally told that these things would not occur during their lifetime, but long years later, during yours. And now at last this Good News has been plainly announced to all of us. It was preached to us in the power of the same heaven-sent Holy Spirit who spoke to them; and it is all so strange and wonderful that even the angels in heaven would give a great deal to know more about it.

[13]So now you can look forward soberly and intelligently to more of God's kindness to you when Jesus Christ returns.

[14]Obey God because you are his children; don't slip back into your old ways—doing evil because you knew no better. [15]But be holy now in everything you do, just as the Lord is holy, who invited you to be his child. [16]He himself has said, "You must be holy, for I am holy."

[17]And remember that your heavenly Father to whom you pray has no favorites when he judges. He will judge you with perfect justice for everything you do; so act in reverent fear of him from now on until you get to heaven. [18]God paid a ransom to save you from the impossible road to heaven which your fathers tried to take, and the ransom he paid was not mere gold or silver as you very well know. [19]But he paid for you with the precious lifeblood of Christ, the sinless, spotless Lamb of God. [20]God chose him for this purpose long before the world began, but only recently was he brought into public view, in these last days, as a blessing to you.

[21]Because of this, your trust can be in God who raised Christ from the dead and gave him great glory. Now your faith and hope can rest in him alone. [22]Now you can have real love for everyone because your souls have been cleansed from selfishness and hatred when you trusted

SET APART

1:15-16 Peter tells us to be like our heavenly Father—holy in everything we do. Holiness means being totally devoted or dedicated to God, set aside for his special use, and set apart from sin and its influence. We're not to blend in with the crowd, yet we shouldn't be different just to be different. What makes us different are God's qualities in our lives. Our focus and priorities must be his. All this is in direct contrast to our old ways (1:14). We cannot become holy on our own, but God gives us his Holy Spirit to help us obey and to give us power to overcome sin. Don't use the excuse that you can't help slipping into sin. Ask all-powerful God to free you from sin's grip.

Christ to save you; so see to it that you really do love each other warmly, with all your hearts.

²³For you have a new life. It was not passed on to you from your parents, for the life they gave you will fade away. This new one will last forever, for it comes from Christ, God's ever-living Message to men. ²⁴Yes, our natural lives will fade as grass does when it becomes all brown and dry. All our greatness is like a flower that droops and falls; ²⁵but the Word of the Lord will last forever. And his message is the Good News that was preached to you.

CHAPTER 2 A LIVING STONE FOR GOD'S HOUSE.

So get rid of your feelings of hatred. Don't just pretend to be good! Be done with dishonesty and jealousy and talking about others behind their backs. ²,³ Now that you realize how kind the Lord has been to you, put away all evil, deception, envy, and fraud. Long to grow up into the fullness of your salvation; cry for this as a baby cries for his milk.

⁴Come to Christ, who is the living Foundation of Rock upon which God builds; though men have spurned him, he is very precious to God who has chosen him above all others.

⁵And now you have become living building-stones for God's use in building his house. What's more, you are his holy priests; so come to him—[you who are acceptable to him because of Jesus Christ]—and offer to God those things that please him. ⁶As the Scriptures express it, "See, I am sending Christ to be the carefully chosen, precious Cornerstone of my church, and I will never disappoint those who trust in him."

⁷Yes, he is very precious to you who believe; and to those who reject him, well—"The same Stone that was rejected by the builders has become the Cornerstone, the most honored and important part of the building." ⁸And the Scriptures also say,

---

It's hard to believe in anything you can't see. Why has God made it so difficult for people who would believe in him if they could only see him?

I WONDER...

God is big, strong, powerful, and able to appear to anyone he wants. But if he did that, most people would feel forced or intimidated into following him, rather than loved into it. God wants us to respond out of love for him, not fear!

The truth is that people *can* see God . . . through the eyes of faith. This means taking God at his word—opening ourselves up to him. Some people say "seeing is believing." The truth is that "believing is seeing."

All of us believe in things we have never seen. A person in history. Gravity. The wind. Everyone has the capacity to believe things that aren't seen. The bottom line for most who say, "I can't believe in something I haven't seen," is "I won't believe in God, because I want to run my own life." God doesn't work that way. Each person must trust in Christ, acknowledging him as Savior.

Peter said that loving God, even though we have never seen him, will bring us "inexpressible joy" (1 Peter 1:8). Jesus said, "Blessed are those who haven't seen me and believe anyway" (John 20:29).

We live by faith, then we meet God.

"He is the Stone that some will stumble over, and the Rock that will make them fall." They will stumble because they will not listen to God's Word nor obey it, and so this punishment must follow—that they will fall.

⁹But you are not like that, for you have been chosen by God himself—you are priests of the King, you are holy and pure, you are God's very own—all this so that you may show to others how God called you out of the darkness into his wonderful light. ¹⁰Once you were less than nothing; now you are God's own. Once you knew very little of God's kindness; now your very lives have been changed by it.

¹¹Dear brothers, you are only visitors here. Since your real home is in heaven, I beg you to keep away from the evil pleasures of this world; they are not for you, for they fight against your very souls.

¹²Be careful how you behave among your unsaved neighbors; for then, even if they are suspicious of you and talk against you, they will end up praising God for your good works when Christ returns.

¹³For the Lord's sake, obey every law of your government: those of the king as head of the state, ¹⁴and those of the king's officers, for he has sent

THE WORD OF THE LORD WILL LAST FOREVER

them to punish all who do wrong, and to honor those who do right.

[15]It is God's will that your good lives should silence those who foolishly condemn the Gospel without knowing what it can do for them, having never experienced its power. [16]You are free from the law, but that doesn't mean you are free to do wrong. Live as those who are free to do only God's will at all times.

[17]Show respect for everyone. Love Christians everywhere. Fear God and honor the government.

[18]Servants, you must respect your masters and do whatever they tell you—not only if they are kind and reasonable, but even if they are tough and cruel. [19]Praise the Lord if you are punished for doing right! [20]Of course, you get no credit for being patient if you are beaten for doing wrong; but if you do right and suffer for it, and are patient beneath the blows, God is well pleased.

[21]This suffering is all part of the work God has given you. Christ, who suffered for you, is your example. Follow in his steps: [22]He never sinned, never told a lie, [23]never answered back when insulted; when he suffered he did not threaten to get even; he left his case in the hands of God who always judges fairly. [24]He personally carried the load of our sins in his own body when he died on the cross so that we can be finished with sin and live a good life from now on. For his wounds have healed ours! [25]Like sheep you wandered away from God, but now you have returned to your Shepherd, the Guardian of your souls who keeps you safe from all attacks.

PARTIES

It's prom time, and Courtney and Shelby are getting nervous.

Their problem?

Getting their dates, Terry and Peter, to forget the idea of an unchaperoned party in a hotel suite after the prom.

Maybe that situation seems simple to solve, but consider the facts:

•The girls are freshmen. Their dates are seniors and so are expected at the hotel.

•The party will feature an open bar and several available beds.

•Terry and Peter each have already kicked in $75 to pay for this private affair.

•A similar party last year featured some unbelievably wild activities.

"What are we gonna do?" Courtney pleads.

"Well, we could just tell our parents and let them get us out of this."

"Oh, right, Shelby! And get laughed out of school? We can't do that!"

"OK, what if we fake like we're sick or something?"

"Shelby!! And miss the whole prom? It's our first one—and I don't want it to be our last. Look, this whole mess isn't our fault. Let's just pray about it. Maybe God wants us to go and be good examples or something."

"OK," Shelby agrees.

The girls bow their heads.

Do Courtney and Shelby need to pray about such a decision? Especially when God's Word is pretty clear about Christians avoiding wild parties? See 1 Peter 4:3-6.

CHAPTER 3 ADVICE FOR HUSBANDS AND WIVES.

Wives, fit in with your husbands' plans; for then if they refuse to listen when you talk to them about the Lord, they will be won by your respectful, pure behavior. Your godly lives will speak to them better than any words.

[3]Don't be concerned about the outward beauty that depends on jewelry, or beautiful clothes, or hair arrangement. [4]Be beautiful inside, in your hearts, with the lasting charm of a gentle and quiet spirit that is so precious to God. [5]That kind of deep beauty was seen in the saintly women of old, who trusted God and fitted in with their husbands' plans.

[6]Sarah, for instance, obeyed her husband Abraham, honoring him as head of the house. And if you do the same, you will be following in her steps like good daughters and doing what is right; then you will not need to fear [offending your husbands].

[7]You husbands must be careful of your wives, being thoughtful of their needs and honoring them as the weaker sex. Remember that you and your wife are partners in receiving God's blessings, and if you don't treat her as you should, your prayers will not get ready answers.

[8]And now this word to all of you: You should be like one big happy family, full of sympathy toward each other, loving one another with tender hearts and humble minds. [9]Don't repay evil for evil. Don't snap back at those who say unkind things about you. Instead, pray for God's help for them, for we are to be kind to others, and God will bless us for it.

[10]If you want a happy, good life, keep control of your tongue, and guard your lips from telling lies. [11]Turn away from evil and do good. Try to live in peace even if you must run after it to catch and hold it! [12]For the Lord is watching his children, listening to their prayers; but the Lord's face is hard against those who do evil.

[13]Usually no one will hurt you for wanting to do good. [14]But even if they should, you are to be envied, for God will

CUT DOWN

3:9 In our sinful world, it is acceptable to tear people down verbally or to get back at them if we feel hurt. Remembering Jesus' teaching to turn the other cheek (Matthew 5:39), Peter encourages his readers to pay back wrongs by praying for the offenders. In God's Kingdom, revenge is unacceptable behavior. So is insulting a person, no matter how indirectly it is done. Rise above getting back at those who hurt you. Instead, pray for them.

SPEAK UP

3:15 Some Christians believe that faith is a personal matter and should be kept to oneself. It is true that we shouldn't be boisterous or obnoxious in sharing our faith, but we should always be ready to answer, gently and respectfully, when asked about our beliefs, our lifestyle, or our Christian perspective. Will you tell others what Christ has done in your life?

reward you for it. [15]Quietly trust yourself to Christ your Lord, and if anybody asks why you believe as you do, be ready to tell him, and do it in a gentle and respectful way.

[16]Do what is right; then if men speak against you, calling you evil names, they will become ashamed of themselves for falsely accusing you when you have only done what is good. [17]Remember, if God wants you to suffer, it is better to suffer for doing good than for doing wrong!

[18]Christ also suffered. He died once for the sins of all us guilty sinners although he himself was innocent of any sin at any time, that he might bring us safely home to God. But though his body died, his spirit lived on, [19]and it was in the spirit that he visited the spirits in prison and preached to them—[20]spirits of those who, long before in the days of Noah, had refused to listen to God, though he waited patiently for them while Noah was building the ark. Yet only eight persons were saved from drowning in that terrible flood. [21](That, by the way, is what baptism pictures for us: In baptism we show that we have been saved from death and doom by the resurrection of Christ; not because our bodies are washed clean by the water but because in being baptized we are turning to God and asking him to cleanse our *hearts* from sin.) [22]And now Christ is in heaven, sitting in the place of honor next to God the Father, with all the angels and powers of heaven bowing before him and obeying him.

CHAPTER **4** CONTINUE TO LOVE ONE ANOTHER.

Since Christ suffered and underwent pain, you must have the same attitude he did; you must be ready to suffer, too. For remember, when your body suffers, sin loses its power, [2]and you won't be spending the rest of your life chasing after evil desires but will be anxious to do the will of God. [3]You have had enough in the past of the evil things the godless enjoy—sex, sin, lust, getting drunk, wild parties, drinking bouts, and the worship of idols, and other terrible sins.

[4]Of course, your former friends will be very surprised when you don't eagerly join them anymore in the wicked things they do, and they will laugh at you in contempt and scorn. [5]But just remember that they must face the Judge of all, living and dead; they will be punished for the way they have lived. [6]That is why the Good News was

"Here's what I did..."

I attended a Christian school during junior high and the first year of high school. But after three years at Christian schools, I felt led to go back to a public school. I talked it over in depth with my parents. They supported me, but reminded me of how difficult it could be because of all the pressures to live for yourself, not for God.

They were right—the pressures and temptations were greater. I didn't know quite how to be a Christian in that atmosphere. I was afraid people would make fun of me once they found out I was a Christian, yet I was determined not to hide my faith. After all, I knew Jesus, the one person in this life who will never let me down. I wanted to share my faith with the new friends I was making.

I decided to adopt 1 Peter 3:15 as my key verse to get me through public school. It shows me how to live my life in that setting, among people who really need to hear some Good News.

This verse helps me keep in line in difficult situations. For instance, if I'm at a party and drinking only Coke, often someone will ask me why I'm not drinking any alcohol. I tell them that I don't need alcohol to help me have a good time, and that Jesus helps to enjoy life and people just as they are. Most people respect me when I say that. (Even when they don't, as it says in 1 Peter 3:16-17, it's better that they mock me for doing something right than for making a fool of myself for getting drunk.)

1 Peter 3:15 helps me overcome temptations like this and reminds me of my purpose for being in a public school: to be ready to tell people of the hope I have in Jesus.

Jenny

AGE 16

preached even to those who were dead—killed by the flood—so that although their bodies were punished with death, they could still live in their spirits as God lives.

[7]The end of the world is coming soon. Therefore be earnest, thoughtful men of prayer. [8]Most important of all, continue to show deep love for each other, for love makes up for many of your faults. [9]Cheerfully share your home with those who need a meal or a place to stay for the night.

[10]God has given each of you some special abilities; be sure to use them to help each other, passing on to others God's many kinds of blessings. [11]Are you called to preach? Then preach as though God himself were speaking through you. Are you called to help others? Do it with all the strength and energy that God supplies so that God will be glori-

GOOD MARKS

4:16 It is not shameful to suffer for being a Christian. When Peter and John were persecuted for preaching the Good News, they rejoiced because such persecution was a mark of God's approval of their work (Acts 5:41). Don't seek out suffering, and don't try to avoid it. Instead, keep on doing what is right regardless of the suffering it might bring.

fied through Jesus Christ—to him be glory and power forever and ever. Amen.

[12]Dear friends, don't be bewildered or surprised when you go through the fiery trials ahead, for this is no strange, unusual thing that is going to happen to you. [13]Instead, be really glad—because these trials will make you partners with Christ in his suffering, and afterwards you will have the wonderful joy of sharing his glory in that coming day when it will be displayed.

[14]Be happy if you are cursed and insulted for being a Christian, for when that happens the Spirit of God will come upon you with great glory. [15]Don't let me hear of your suffering for murdering or stealing or making trouble or being a busybody and prying into other people's affairs. [16]But it is no shame to suffer for being a Christian. Praise God for the privilege of being in Christ's family and being called by his wonderful name! [17]For the time has come for judgment, and it must begin first among God's own children. And if even we who are Christians must be judged, what terrible fate awaits those who have never believed in the Lord? [18]If the righteous are barely saved, what chance will the godless have?

[19]So if you are suffering according to God's will, keep on doing what is right and trust yourself to the God who made you, for he will never fail you.

CHAPTER 5 ADVICE FOR TEACHERS AND STUDENTS.

And now, a word to you elders of the church. I, too, am an elder; with my own eyes I saw Christ dying on the cross; and I, too, will share his glory and his honor when he returns. Fellow elders, this is my plea to you: [2]Feed the flock of God; care for it willingly, not grudgingly; not for what you will get out of it but because you are eager to serve the Lord. [3]Don't be tyrants, but lead them by your good example, [4]and when the Head Shepherd comes, your reward will be a never-ending share in his glory and honor.

[5]You younger men, follow the leadership of those who are older. And all of you serve each other with humble spirits, for God gives special blessings to those who are humble, but sets himself against those who are proud. [6]If you will humble yourselves under the mighty hand of God, in his good time he will lift you up.

[7]Let him have all your worries and cares, for he is always thinking about you and watching everything that concerns you.

[8]Be careful—watch out for attacks from Satan, your great enemy. He prowls around like a hungry, roaring lion, looking for some victim to tear apart. [9]Stand firm when he attacks. Trust the Lord; and remember that other Christians all around the world are going through these sufferings too.

[10]After you have suffered a little while, our God, who is full of kindness through Christ, will give you his eternal glory. He personally will come and pick you up, and set you firmly in place, and make you stronger than ever. [11]To him be all power over all things, forever and ever. Amen.

[12]I am sending this note to you through the courtesy of Silvanus who is, in my opinion, a very faithful brother. I hope I have encouraged you by this letter, for I have given you a true statement of the way God blesses. What I have told you here should help you to stand firmly in his love.

[13]The church here in Rome—she is your sister in the Lord—sends you her greetings; so does my son Mark. [14]Give each other the handshake of Christian love. Peace be to all of you who are in Christ.

BOTH WAYS

5:5 Both young and old can benefit from Peter's instructions. Pride often keeps elders from trying to understand young people and young people from listening to their elders. Peter's instructions go both ways: he told both young and old to be humble, to serve each other. Young men should follow the leadership of older men, who should lead by example. Respect your elders, listen to those younger than you, and be humble enough to admit that you can learn from each other.

MEGA Themes

SALVATION Salvation is a gracious gift from God. God chose us out of his love for us, Jesus died to pay the penalty for our sin, and the Holy Spirit cleansed us from sin when we believed. Eternal life is a wonderful privilege for those who trust in Christ.

Our safety and security are in God. If we experience joy in relationship with Christ now, how much greater will our joy be when he returns and we see him face-to-face! Such a hope should motivate us to serve Christ even more.

1. What are the blessings of our salvation that have been revealed to us through Jesus?
2. Why would this be such an important message for Jewish Christians who had been suffering for their faith?
3. What does it mean to you to be saved? Include your feelings, the present benefits, and your hope for the future.
4. How can you communicate this through your life to someone who is without Christ? Why is it important that others come to know Christ?

PERSECUTION Peter offers faithful believers comfort and hope. We should expect ridicule, rejection, and suffering because we are Christians. Persecution makes us stronger because it refines our faith. We can face persecution victoriously as Christ did, if we rely on him.

We don't have to be terrified by persecution. The fact that we will live eternally with Christ should give us the confidence, patience, and hope to stand firm even when we are persecuted. Suffering can glorify God.

1. Read 2:21-25. Describe Jesus' response to suffering.
2. How does Jesus' example provide encouragement and inspiration during suffering?
3. How do fellow believers provide encouragement and inspiration during suffering?
4. When you face ridicule or oppression for your faith, what are the specific ways that you can cope with this suffering?

GOD'S FAMILY We are privileged to belong to God's family, a community with Christ as the Founder and Foundation. Everyone in this community is related—we are all brothers and sisters, loved equally by God.

We must be devoted, loyal, and faithful to Christ, the foundation of our family. Through obedience, we show that we are his children. We must live differently from the society around us. Our relationships are to be patterned by what we see in Christ, not by what we see in the world.

1. List the specific teachings concerning Christian fellowship in 4:7-11.

2. Who are the people who have ministered Christ's love and grace to you? In what ways have they provided this love and grace?
3. Why is it necessary for you and other believers to be providers of his love to one another?
4. In what two ways will you become a part of God's love and grace in the life of fellow believers this week?

FAMILY LIFE Peter encouraged the wives of unbelievers to submit to the authority of their husbands as a means of winning them to Christ. He urged all family members to treat others with sympathy, love, tenderness, and humility.

We must treat our families lovingly. Though it's never easy, willing service is the best way to influence our loved ones. To gain the needed strength, we must pray for God's help. Relationships with parents, brothers and sisters, and spouses are important aspects of Christian discipleship.

1. In 1 Peter, what principles do you find for a godly marriage?
2. How could 3:6 be misused by a domineering husband? What corrective does God's Word provide against misusing this husband-wife relationship? (Also check Ephesians 5.)
3. What qualities do you want in a marriage partner some day?
4. What qualities do you think your mate will desire in you? How can you develop those qualities so that you bring godliness and maturity to your marriage?

JUDGMENT God will judge everyone with perfect justice. He will punish evildoers and those who persecute his people; those who love God will be rewarded with life forever in his presence.

Because all are accountable to God, we can leave judgment of others to him. We must not hate or resent those who persecute us. We should realize that we will be held responsible for how we live each day.

1. What will happen to those without Christ when they face God's judgment?
2. What difference will having Jesus as your Lord make when you face God's judgment?
3. Review 1:14-25. If you will not be condemned because of Jesus, why should God's holiness continue to be your motivation for living a holy life?
4. What are the specific areas of your life that still need to become holy through obedience to Christ? How can this be accomplished?

We've all come face-to-face with life's ironies: ■ One man, noting the regularity (and certainty) of these quirks, decided to make a list. The result? The famous "Murphy's Laws." ■ Some of Murphy's more interesting observations: •If anything *can* go wrong it *will*. •"Broken" gadgets will operate perfectly in the presence of a repairman. •Saying "Watch this!" guarantees that the behavior you want others to witness will not happen. •A poorly-thrown Frisbee will always come to rest under the exact center of a parked car. •Stored objects are never needed . . . until immediately after they are discarded. •The bowl that breaks is never the one that was already chipped. •The other line always moves faster. •If you put a napkin in your lap you will not spill; failure to use a napkin ensures spillage. •You will only be forced to wait when you do not have time to wait. ■ We nod and smile at those "laws" because we've lived them. They're amazingly true to life. How about some other laws of life? Perhaps not as humorous, but just as true—and much more life-changing: •Spiritual growth only happens when we get to know God and make the effort to serve him. •The world is full of people who will try to lead you astray. •Jesus Christ is coming back. ■ Would you like to know more about these critical principles? They're all contained in the book that follows, the Bible book we call 2 Peter.

STATS

PURPOSE: To warn Christians about false teachers and to exhort them to grow in their faith and knowledge of Christ

AUTHOR: Peter

TO WHOM WRITTEN: The church at large

DATE WRITTEN: About A.D. 67, three years after 1 Peter was written, possibly from Rome

SETTING: Peter knew that his time on earth was limited (1:13-14), so he was writing about what was on his heart, warning believers of what would happen when he was gone—especially about false teachers. He reminded believers of the unchanging truth of the gospel.

KEY PEOPLE: Peter, Paul

SPECIAL FEATURES: The date and destination are uncertain, and the authorship has been disputed. Because of this, 2 Peter was the last epistle admitted to the canon of the New Testament Scripture. Also, there are similarities between 2 Peter and Jude.

2 Peter

CHAPTER 1 STEPS TO SPIRITUAL GROWTH.

From: Simon Peter, a servant and missionary of Jesus Christ.

To: All of you who have our kind of faith. The faith I speak of is the kind that Jesus Christ our God and Savior gives to us. How precious it is, and how just and good he is to give this same faith to each of us.

²Do you want more and more of God's kindness and peace? Then learn to know him better and better. ³For as you know him better, he will give you, through his great power, everything you need for living a truly good life: he even shares his own glory and his own goodness with us! ⁴And by that same mighty power he has given us all the other rich and wonderful blessings he promised; for instance, the promise to save us from the lust and rottenness all around us, and to give us his own character.

⁵But to obtain these gifts, you need more than faith; you must also work hard to be good, and even that is not enough. For then you must learn to know God better and discover what he wants you to do. ⁶Next, learn to put aside your own desires so that you will become patient and godly, gladly letting God have his way with you. ⁷This will make possible the next step, which is for

TRY

1:6 False teachers were saying that self-control was not needed because works do not help the believer anyway (2:19). It is true that works cannot save us, but it is absolutely false to think they are unimportant. We are saved so that we can grow to resemble Christ and so that we can serve others. God wants to produce his character in us. But to do this, he demands effort from us. To grow spiritually, we must develop self-control.

you to enjoy other people and to like them, and finally you will grow to love them deeply. [8]The more you go on in this way, the more you will grow strong spiritually and become fruitful and useful to our Lord Jesus Christ. [9]But anyone who fails to go after these additions to faith is blind indeed, or at least very shortsighted and has forgotten that God delivered him from the old life of sin so that now he can live a strong, good life for the Lord.

[10]So, dear brothers, work hard to prove that you really are among those God has called and chosen, and then you will never stumble or fall away. [11]And God will open wide the gates of heaven for you to enter into the eternal kingdom of our Lord and Savior Jesus Christ.

[12]I plan to keep on reminding you of these things even though you already know them and are really getting along quite well! [13,14]But the Lord Jesus Christ has shown me that my days here on earth are numbered, and I am soon to die. As long as I am still here I intend to keep sending these reminders to you, [15]hoping to impress them so clearly upon you that you will remember them long after I have gone.

[16]For we have not been telling you fairy tales when we explained to you the power of our Lord Jesus Christ and his coming again. My own eyes have seen his splendor and his glory: [17,18]I was there on the holy mountain when he shone out with honor given him by God his Father; I heard that glorious, majestic voice calling down from heaven, saying, "This is my much-loved Son; I am well pleased with him." [19]So we have seen and

proved that what the prophets said came true. You will do well to pay close attention to everything they have written, for, like lights shining into dark corners, their words help us to understand many things that otherwise would be dark and difficult. But when you consider the wonderful truth of the prophets' words, then the light will dawn in your souls and Christ the Morning Star will shine in your hearts. [20,21]For no prophecy recorded in Scripture was ever thought up by the prophet himself. It was the Holy Spirit within these godly men who gave them true messages from God.

CHAPTER 2 BEWARE OF FALSE TEACHERS. But there were false prophets, too, in those days, just as there will be false teachers among you. They will cleverly tell their lies about God, turning against even their Master who bought them; but theirs will be a swift and terrible end. [2]Many will follow their evil teaching that there is nothing wrong with sexual sin. And because of them Christ and his way will be scoffed at.

[3]These teachers in their greed will tell you anything to get hold of your money. But God condemned them long ago and their destruction is on the way. [4]For God did not spare even the angels

2 PETER 3:10,12

FREEDOM

2:19 Many people believe that freedom means doing anything you want. But no one is ever completely free in that way. If we refuse to follow God, we will follow our own sinful desires and become enslaved to what our bodies want. If we submit our lives to Christ, he will free us from slavery to sin. Christ frees us to serve him, and that will always result in our ultimate good.

THE DAY OF THE LORD IS SURELY COMING

as unexpectedly as a *thief*... You should look forward to that day and hurry it along.

CULTS

A month ago, while on a city bus, Patricia picked up a discarded leaflet advertising a free music festival and complimentary vegetarian meal. She called her friend Elaine, and the two of them went to see what it was all about.

The whole afternoon Elaine was whispering, "Let's get out of here. This is weird!" But Patricia kept replying, "Lighten up, Elaine! You're too intense."

On the way home, Elaine made it clear what she thought. "Look, I don't care what you say. That group is some kind of cult or something."

"Why? Name one thing they did or said that was bad."

"Well, I don't know—they gave me the creeps."

"Aw, I think you're paranoid. Who knows? I just might go to one of their classes."

Patricia did go back. And now she's a full-fledged member of the "church," The Society of Enlightened Minds. The people there accept her and make her feel special.

Elaine's parents did some checking. Patricia's "church" doesn't accept the Bible; nor does it believe that Christ is God. It teaches that each of us is a god and that together, we can recreate the world.

With their popular, feel-good philosophies, dangerous cult groups are capturing millions of hungry hearts and uncritical minds. No wonder we are told in 2 Peter 2:17-22 to carefully consider the ideas that we hear every day. Read it and heed it!

who sinned, but threw them into hell, chained in gloomy caves and darkness until the judgment day. ⁵And he did not spare any of the people who lived in ancient times before the flood except Noah, the one man who spoke up for God, and his family of seven. At that time God completely destroyed the whole world of ungodly men with the vast flood. ⁶Later, he turned the cities of Sodom and Gomorrah into heaps of ashes and blotted them off the face of the earth, making them an example for all the ungodly in the future to look back upon and fear.

⁷,⁸But at the same time the Lord rescued Lot out of Sodom because he was a good man, sick of the terrible wickedness he saw everywhere around him day after day. ⁹So also the Lord can rescue you and me from the temptations that surround us, and continue to punish the ungodly until the day of final judgment comes. ¹⁰He is especially hard on those who follow their own evil, lustful thoughts, and those who are proud and willful, daring even to scoff at the Glorious Ones without so much as trembling, ¹¹although the angels in heaven who stand in the very presence of the Lord, and are far greater in power and strength than these false teachers, never speak out disrespectfully against these evil Mighty Ones.

¹²But false teachers are fools— no better than animals. They do whatever they feel like; born only to be caught and killed, they laugh at the terrifying powers of the underworld which they know so little about; and they will be destroyed along with all the demons and powers of hell.

¹³That is the pay these teachers will have for their sin. For they live in evil pleasures day after day. They are a disgrace and a stain among you, deceiving you by living in foul sin on the side while they join your love feasts as though they were honest men. ¹⁴No woman can escape their sinful stare, and of adultery they never have enough. They make a game of luring unstable women. They train themselves to be greedy; and are doomed and cursed. ¹⁵They have gone off the road and become lost like Balaam, the son of Beor, who fell in love with the money he could make by doing wrong; ¹⁶but Balaam was stopped from his mad course when his donkey spoke to him with a human voice, scolding and rebuking him.

¹⁷These men are as useless as dried-up springs of water, promising much and delivering nothing; they are as unstable as clouds driven by the storm winds. They are doomed to the eternal pits of darkness. ¹⁸They proudly boast about their sins and conquests, and, using lust as their bait, they lure back into sin those who have just escaped from such wicked living.

"Here's what I did..."

I didn't want to break up with my girlfriend, but the more I prayed about the relationship, the more I saw that it was interfering with my relationship with God. My girlfriend wasn't a Christian; her values were completely different from mine. I cared about her, but it came down to a choice: either her or God.

The clincher came when I read 2 Peter 1:5-8. It says: "But to obtain these gifts, you need more than faith; you must also work hard to be good, and even that is not enough. For then you must learn to know God better and discover what he wants you to do. Next, learn to put aside your own desires so that you will become patient and godly, gladly letting God have his way with you. This will make possible the next step, which is for you to enjoy other people and to like them, and finally you will grow to love them deeply. The more you go on in this way, the more you will grow strong spiritually and become fruitful and useful to our Lord Jesus Christ."

I didn't need anymore guidance; I knew I had to break up and concentrate on strengthening my relationship with the Lord. Though I felt bad after breaking up, I was confident that I had done the right thing and that the Lord still cared about me and my decisions.

I also was encouraged. God was showing me that I was slowly but surely becoming stronger spiritually. Every verse of that passage fit a part of my life. As I put God first and determined to obey him, I could see times when I put aside my own desires and how I was becoming more patient, etc. Yes, breaking up was hard, but knowing that I did it to obey God made all the difference.

Joel
AGE 16

¹⁹"You aren't saved by being good," they say, "so you might as well be bad. Do what you like; be free."

But these very teachers who offer this "freedom" from law are themselves slaves to sin and destruction. For a man is a slave to whatever controls him. ²⁰And when a person has escaped from the wicked ways of the world by learning about our Lord and Savior Jesus Christ, and then gets tangled up with sin and becomes its slave again, he is worse off than he was before. ²¹It would be better if he had never known about Christ at all than to learn of him and then afterwards turn his back on the holy commandments that were given to him. ²²There is an old saying that "A dog comes back to what he has vomited, and a pig is washed only to come back and wallow in the mud again." That is the way it is with those who turn again to their sin.

CHAPTER 3 HOPE FOR GROWING CHRISTIANS.

This is my second letter to you, dear brothers, and in both of them I have tried to remind you—if you will let me—about facts you already know: facts you learned from the holy prophets and from us apostles who brought you the words of our Lord and Savior.

[3]First, I want to remind you that in the last days there will come scoffers who will do every wrong they can think of and laugh at the truth. [4]This will be their line of argument: "So Jesus promised to come back, did he? Then where is he? He'll never come! Why, as far back as anyone can remember, everything has remained exactly as it was since the first day of creation."

[5,6]They deliberately forget this fact: that God did destroy the world with a mighty flood long after he had made the heavens by the word of his command and had used the waters to form the earth and surround it. [7]And God has commanded that the earth and the heavens be stored away for a great bonfire at the judgment day, when all ungodly men will perish.

[8]But don't forget this, dear friends, that a day or a thousand years from now is like tomorrow to the Lord. [9]He isn't really being slow about his promised return, even though it sometimes seems that way. But he is waiting, for the good reason that he is not willing that any should perish, and he is giving more time for sinners to repent. [10]The day of the Lord is surely coming, as unexpectedly as a thief, and then the heavens will pass away with a terrible noise, and the heavenly bodies will disappear in fire, and the earth and everything on it will be burned up.

[11]And so since everything around us is going to melt away, what holy, godly lives we should be living! [12]You should look forward to that day and hurry it along—the day when God will set the heavens on fire, and the heavenly bodies will melt and disappear in flames. [13]But we are looking forward to God's promise of new heavens and a new earth afterwards, where there will be only goodness.

[14]Dear friends, while you are waiting for these things to happen and for him to come, try hard to live without sinning; and be at peace with everyone so that he will be pleased with you when he returns.

[15,16]And remember why he is waiting. He is giving us time to get his message of salvation out to others. Our wise and beloved brother Paul has talked about these same things in many of his letters. Some of his comments are not easy to understand, and there are people who are deliberately stupid, and always demand some unusual interpretation—they have twisted his letters around to mean something quite different from what he meant, just as they do the other parts of the Scripture—and the result is disaster for them.

[17]I am warning you ahead of time, dear brothers, so that you can watch out and not be carried away by the mistakes of these wicked men, lest you yourselves become mixed up too. [18]But grow in spiritual strength and become better acquainted with our Lord and Savior Jesus Christ. To him be all glory and splendid honor, both now and forevermore. Good-bye.

Peter

TOUGH GUY

2:10-12 The "Glorious Ones" may be angels, the glories of the unseen world, or fallen angels. A similar passage is found in Jude 1:8-10. Either way, the false teachers laughed at spiritual realities they didn't understand, taking Satan's power lightly, thinking they could judge evil. Many today mock the supernatural, denying the reality of the spiritual world. They say only what can be seen and felt is real. Like all false teachers, they are fools who will be proven wrong. Don't take Satan and his supernatural powers lightly or feel arrogant about his defeat. Satan will be destroyed completely—but he is working now, luring complacent or arrogant Christians over to his side.

BE EAGER?

3:14 We should not become lazy and complacent because Christ has not yet returned. Instead, our lives should express our eager expectation of his coming. What would you like to be doing when Christ returns? Is that the way you are living each day?

MEGA *Themes*

DILIGENCE If our faith is real, it will be evident in our faithful behavior. If people are diligent in Christian growth, they won't backslide or be deceived by false teachers.

Growth is essential. It begins with faith and culminates in love for others. To keep growing, we need to know God, keep on following him, and remember what he taught us. It may not always be easy, but it will always be worthwhile.

1. According to chapter 1, what are the attitudes and actions that lead to maturity?
2. If a Christian friend were to ask you, "How are you growing?" what would be your response?
3. Based on this study, identify five practical steps to personal spiritual growth.
4. How and when will you apply these five steps to your relationship with God?

FALSE TEACHERS Peter warns the church to beware of false teachers. These teachers were proud of their position, promoted sexual sin, and advised against keeping the Ten Commandments. Peter countered them by pointing to the Spirit-inspired Scriptures as our authority.

Christians need discernment to resist false teachers. God can rescue us from their lies if we stay true to his Word, the Bible, and reject those who twist the truth. The truth is our best defense because it exposes the lies of those who try to deceive us.

1. Contrast the lives of the false teachers with the lives of those who follow God's truth.
2. Why can God's Word be trusted more than all teachers?
3. What false teaching have you heard about God and Jesus?
4. What would you say to someone who wanted to be certain not to fall into the deception of a false teacher?

CHRIST'S RETURN One day Christ will create a new heaven and earth where we will live forever. As Christians, our hope is in this promise. But with Christ's return comes his judgment on all who refuse to believe.

The cure for complacency, lawlessness, and heresy is found in the confident assurance that Christ will return. God is still giving unbelievers time to repent. To be ready, Christians must keep on trusting Christ and resist the pressure to give up waiting for his return.

1. What reason does Peter give for Christ's patience in waiting to return?
2. How does Peter say we should live in light of Christ's expected return?
3. How do most Christians view Christ's eventual return?

*L*ove. ■ We can't touch it, count it, bottle it, or even see it. But who among us would argue that love isn't real? ■ Love. ■ It makes sane people do and say crazy things. It prompts snobby, selfish people to do noble things. It turns boring people into exciting, unpredictable creatures. What else on earth has that kind of power? ■ Love. ■ It can hurt like nothing else in the world. And yet, paradoxically, *not* loving is much more painful. ■ Love. ■ The most talked-about and sung-about and thought-about theme in all the world. And also the most misunderstood. ■ Love. ■ Would you like to know more about it and see it in a brand new light? Then read *1 John,* the most eloquent description of love ever penned. ■ Love. ■ It's not everything you think it is. It's more . . . much, much more.

STATS

PURPOSE: To reassure Christians in their faith and to counter false teachings

AUTHOR: The apostle John

TO WHOM WRITTEN: The letter is untitled and was written to no particular church. It was sent as a pastoral letter to several Gentile congregations. It was also written to all believers everywhere.

DATE WRITTEN: Probably between A.D. 85 and 90 from Ephesus

SETTING: John was an older man and perhaps the only surviving apostle at this time. He had not yet been banished to the island of Patmos where he would live in exile. As an eyewitness of Christ, he wrote authoritatively to give this new generation of believers assurance and confidence in God and in their faith.

KEY PEOPLE: John, Jesus

SPECIAL FEATURES: John is the apostle of love, and love is mentioned throughout this letter. There are a number of similarities in vocabulary, style, and main ideas between this letter and John's Gospel. John uses brief statements and simple words, and he features sharp contrasts—light and darkness, truth and error, God and Satan, life and death, love and hate.

1John

CHAPTER 1 JESUS CHRIST IS ETERNAL LIFE. Christ was alive when the world began, yet I myself have seen him with my own eyes and listened to him speak. I have touched him with my own hands. He is God's message of life. ²This one who is life from God has been shown to us, and we guarantee that we have seen him; I am speaking of Christ, who is eternal Life. He was with the Father and then was shown to us. ³Again I say, we are telling you about what we ourselves have actually seen and heard, so that you may share the fellowship and the joys we have with the Father and with Jesus Christ his son. ⁴And if you do as I say in this letter, then you, too, will be full of joy, and so will we.

⁵This is the message God has given us to pass on to you: that God is Light and in him is no darkness at all. ⁶So if we say we are his friends but go on living in spiritual darkness and sin, we are lying. ⁷But if we are living in the light of God's presence, just as Christ does, then we have wonderful fellowship and joy with each other, and the blood of Jesus his Son cleanses us from every sin.

⁸If we say that we have no sin, we are only fooling ourselves and refusing to accept the truth. ⁹But if we confess our sins to him, he can be depended on to forgive us and to cleanse us from every wrong. [And it is perfectly proper for God to do this for us because Christ died to wash away our sins.] ¹⁰If we claim we have not sinned, we are lying and calling God a liar, *for he says we have sinned.*

CHAPTER 2 LOVE GOD, NOT THIS WORLD. My little children, I am telling you this so that you will stay away from sin. But if you sin, there is someone to plead for you before the Father. His name is Jesus Christ, the one who is all that is good and who pleases God completely. ²He is the one who took God's wrath against our sins upon himself and brought us into fellowship with God; and he is the forgiveness for our sins, and not only ours but all the world's.

³And how can we be sure that we belong to him? By looking within ourselves: are we really trying to do what he wants us to?

⁴Someone may say, "I am a Christian; I am on my way to heaven; I belong to Christ." But if he doesn't do what Christ tells him to, he is a liar. ⁵But those who do what Christ tells them to will learn to love God more and more. That is the way to know whether or not you are a Christian. ⁶Anyone who says he is a Christian should live as Christ did.

⁷Dear brothers, I am not writing out a new rule for you to obey, for it is an old one you have always had, right from the start. You have heard it all before. ⁸Yet it is always new, and works for you just as it did for Christ; and as we obey this commandment, *to love one another,* the darkness in our lives disappears and the new light of life in Christ shines in.

⁹Anyone who says he is walking in the light of Christ but dislikes his fellow man is still in darkness. ¹⁰But whoever loves his fellow man is "walking in the light" and can see his way without stumbling around in darkness and sin. ¹¹For he who dislikes his brother is wandering in spiritual darkness and doesn't know where he is going, for the darkness has made him blind so that he cannot see the way.

¹²I am writing these things to all of you, my little children, because your sins have been forgiven in the name of Jesus our Savior. ¹³I am saying these things to you older men because you really know Christ, the one who has been alive from the beginning. And you young men, I am talking to you because you have won your battle with Satan. And I am writing to you younger boys and girls because you, too, have learned to know God our Father.

¹⁴And so I say to you fathers who know the eternal God, and to you young men who are strong with God's Word in your hearts, and have won your struggle against Satan: ¹⁵Stop loving this evil world and all that it offers you, for when you love these things you show that you do not really love God; ¹⁶for all these worldly things, these evil desires—the craze for sex, the ambition to buy everything that appeals to you, and the pride that comes from wealth and importance—these are

LOVE

At a slumber party, Wendy makes the terrible mistake of being the first to fall asleep. A few hours later she is awakened by a funny smell and a damp feeling on her head. Staggering into the bathroom, she discovers her hair is filled with petroleum jelly, shaving cream, eggs, honey, and flour . . . all great products, but not exactly the sort of things you want to wear in your hair.

As she tries (in vain) to wash all the glop out, Wendy hears giggles and whispers coming from the living room.

Guess how Wendy feels?
(a) angry
(b) sad
(c) hurt
(d) rejected
(e) all of the above
You guessed it: (e) describes *exactly* how she feels.

Guess what Wendy wants to do?
(a) leave
(b) tell her friends off
(c) get back at them
(d) cry
(e) all of the above
That's right: (e) again. You are *so* smart!

So what does Wendy *actually* do? Here's the shocker: She prays and asks the Lord to give her the strength to love her friends in spite of what they have done. Later, when she has the chance to get back at them, she refuses.

Why is Wendy being so kind when her friends are being so mean? Because 1 John 4:7-21 is real to her. Check it out.

A CHOICE

2:9-11 Does this mean if you dislike anyone you aren't a Christian? These verses are not talking about disliking a disagreeable Christian brother. There will always be people we will not like as well as others. John's words focus on the attitude that causes us to ignore or despise others, to treat them as irritants, competitors, or enemies. Fortunately, Christian love is not a feeling but a choice. We can choose to be concerned with people's well-being and to treat them with respect, whether or not we feel affection toward them. If we choose to love others, God will give us the necessary strength and will show us how to express our love.

SEE HOW VERY MUCH OUR HEAVENLY FATHER LOVES Us for he allows us to be CALLED his children *Think of it—* and WE *REALLY are!*

1 JOHN 3:1

not from God. They are from this evil world itself. [17]And this world is fading away, and these evil, forbidden things will go with it, but whoever keeps doing the will of God will live forever.

[18]Dear children, this world's last hour has come. You have heard about the Antichrist who is coming—the one who is against Christ—and already many such persons have appeared. This makes us all the more certain that the end of the world is near. [19]These "against-Christ" people used to be members of our churches, but they never really belonged with us or else they would have stayed. When they left us it proved that they were not of us at all.

[20]But you are not like that, for the Holy Spirit has come upon you, and you know the truth. [21]So I am not writing to you as to those who need to know the truth, but I warn you as those who can discern the difference between true and false.

[22]And who is the greatest liar? The one who says that Jesus is not Christ. Such a person is antichrist, for he does not believe in God the Father and in his Son. [23]For a person who doesn't believe in Christ, God's Son, can't have God the Father either. But he who has Christ, God's Son, has God the Father also.

[24]So keep on believing what you have been taught from the beginning. If you do, you will always be in close fellowship with both God the Father and his Son. [25]And he himself has promised us this: *eternal life*.

[26]These remarks of mine about the Antichrist are pointed at those who would dearly love to blindfold you and lead you astray. [27]But you have received the Holy Spirit, and he lives within you, in your hearts, so that you don't need anyone to teach you what is right. For he teaches you all things, and he is the Truth, and no liar; and so, just as he has said, you must live in Christ, never to depart from him.

[28]And now, my little children, stay in happy fellowship with the Lord so that when he comes you will be sure that all is well and will not have to be ashamed and shrink back from meeting him. [29]Since we know that God is always good and does only right, we may rightly assume that all those who do right are his children.

CHAPTER **3** WE ARE GOD'S CHILDREN. See how very much our heavenly Father loves us, for he allows us to be called his children—think of it—and we really *are!* But since most people don't know God, naturally they don't understand that we are his children. [2]Yes, dear friends, we are already God's children, right now, and we can't even imagine what it is going to be like later on. But we do know this, that when he comes we will be like him,

"Here's what I did..."

I was the master of rationalization—at least in some areas of my life. When I got into an argument with my parents, I always knew they were totally wrong. If I talked about someone behind their back, I told myself that it wasn't gossip, it was information the person really needed to know. When my boyfriend and I started having sex, I rationalized that it was OK because we loved each other, and didn't the Bible say that love was what it was all about?

Then I heard my pastor preach on 1 John 1:8-10, and suddenly I knew I was just fooling myself. God called these things—rebelliousness toward my parents, gossip, premarital sex—sins. I was kidding myself, but not God. The preacher said we are calling God a liar when we don't acknowledge our sins! That shook me up pretty bad.

I reread the passage after church, when I was alone in my room, and I cried. Not only because I'd been lying to myself and to God, but because this passage also talks about how willing God is to forgive us and cleanse us.

Before God that day, I owned up to the sins I had been rationalizing away. It was hard to do because I knew I had to be willing to change, not just to say "I'm sorry." Change would be hard, particularly in my relationship with my boyfriend. But verse 9 encouraged me that God would not only forgive, but also give me the strength to make a clean new start.

I did end up breaking up with my boyfriend; it proved impossible to start over in our physical relationship. The breakup hurt a lot. But underneath the pain, something felt very good, very right: I knew I was no longer lying to myself or to God. A new, clear conscience is helping me through the pain of change.

Tricia

AGE 16

as a result of seeing him as he really is. [3]And everyone who really believes this will try to stay pure because Christ is pure.

[4]But those who keep on sinning are against God, for every sin is done against the will of God. [5]And you know that he became a man so that he could take away our sins, and that there is no sin in him, no missing of God's will at any time in any way. [6]So if we stay close to him, obedient to him, we won't be sinning either; but as for those who keep on sinning, they should realize this: They sin because they have never really known him or become his.

FOOTHOLD

3:8-9 We all have areas where temptation is strong and habits are hard to break. However, John is not talking about people who are working to overcome a particular sin; he is talking about people who make a practice of sinning and look for ways to justify it. Use these three steps to overcome prevailing sin: (1) seek the power of the Holy Spirit and God's Word; (2) flee lustful desires; and (3) talk to other Christians.

[7]Oh, dear children, don't let anyone deceive you about this: if you are constantly doing what is good, it is because you *are* good, even as he is. [8]But if you keep on sinning, it shows that you belong to Satan, who since he first began to sin has kept steadily at it. But the Son of God came to destroy these works of the devil. [9]The person who has been born into God's family does not make a practice of sinning because now God's life is in him; so he can't keep on sinning, for this new life has been born into him and controls him—he has been *born again.*

[10]So now we can tell who is a child of God and who belongs to Satan. Whoever is living a life of sin and doesn't love his brother shows that he is not in God's family;[11]for the message to us from the beginning has been that we should love one another.

[12]We are not to be like Cain, who belonged to Satan and killed his brother. Why did he kill him? Because Cain had been doing wrong and he knew very well that his brother's life was better than his. [13]So don't be surprised, dear friends, if the world hates you.

[14]If we love other Christians, it proves that we have been delivered from hell and given eternal life. But a person who doesn't have love for others is headed for eternal death. [15]Anyone who hates his Christian brother is really a murderer at heart; and you know that no one wanting to murder has eternal life within. [16]We know what real love is from Christ's example in dying for us. And so we also ought to lay down our lives for our Christian brothers.

[17]But if someone who is supposed to be a Christian has money enough to live well, and sees a brother in need, and won't help him—how can God's love be within *him*? [18]Little children, let us stop just *saying* we love people; let us *really* love them, and *show it* by our *actions.* [19]Then we will know for sure, by our actions, that we are on God's side, and our consciences will be clear, even when we stand before the Lord. [20]But if we have bad consciences and feel that we have done wrong, the Lord will surely feel it even more, for he knows everything we do.

[21]But, dearly loved friends, if our consciences are clear, we can come to the Lord with perfect assurance and trust, [22]and get whatever we ask for because we are obeying him and doing the things that please him. [23]And this is what God says we must do: Believe on the name of his Son Jesus

Christ, and love one another. [24]Those who do what God says—they are living with God and he with them. We know this is true because the Holy Spirit he has given us tells us so.

I became a Christian at a big youth rally last fall. Afterwards, I felt great for a few days— I knew that having a relationship with God was something I wanted—but soon my good feelings went away. Did I lose God? Why didn't the good feelings stay around?

I WONDER

Picture yourself meeting your favorite TV or music superstar face-to-face. It would be an experience that you would likely never forget. Yet over time you would forget the intensity of the emotion you once felt. Would it mean that you did not actually meet this person? Of course not, but it does illustrate that our feelings often come and go based on current experience.

Asking Jesus Christ into your life is far better than meeting another human, famous or not! What you have begun is a lifelong relationship with God, who created everything! He actually wants to live in you so that you will live forever *and* so others can see that he really loves them, too.

In John 14:23 Jesus says, "I will only reveal myself to those who love me and obey me. The Father will love them too, and we will come to them and live with them." The phrase *live with them* actually means "build a mansion" in them. God wants to come into your life and make something extraordinary out of it. God has begun a process of molding your character to become more like that of Jesus Christ. Within this lifelong process will be some good feelings, but more often we will not have, or want, continual, intense excitement.

The wonder of getting to know someone as loving and forgiving as Jesus Christ has similarities to other relationships you enjoy. There is the initial experience of meeting a person, followed by months and years of growing to appreciate his or her friendship and influence. Anything worthwhile takes time.

First John 5:10-12 assures us that "whoever has God's Son has life." Once you have genuinely chosen to follow Jesus Christ you can never lose him. He will always be there in your life to guide and love you, even in the midst of all our world may throw your way. This should outweigh your tendency to base your relationship with God on your up and down feelings.

CHAPTER 4 WHAT'S TRUE AND WHAT'S NOT?

Dearly loved friends, don't always believe everything you hear just because someone says it is a message from God: test it first to see if it really is. For there are many false teachers around, [2]and the way to find out if their message is from the Holy Spirit is to ask: Does it really agree that Jesus Christ, God's Son, actually became man with a human body? If so, then the message is from God. ³If not, the message is not from God but from one who is against Christ, like the "Antichrist" you have heard about who is going to come, and his attitude of enmity against Christ is already abroad in the world.

⁴Dear young friends, you belong to God and have already won your fight with those who are against Christ because there is someone in your hearts who is stronger than any evil teacher in this wicked world. ⁵These men belong to this world, so, quite naturally, they are concerned about worldly affairs and the world pays attention to them. ⁶But we are children of God; that is why only those who have walked and talked with God will listen to us. Others won't. That is another way to know whether a message is really from God; for if it is, the world won't listen to it.

⁷Dear friends, let us practice loving each other, for love comes from God and those who are loving and kind show that they are the children of God, and that they are getting to know him better. ⁸But if a person isn't loving and kind, it shows that he doesn't know God—for God is love.

⁹God showed how much he loved us by sending his only Son into this wicked world to bring to us eternal life through his death. ¹⁰In this act we see what real love is: it is not our love for God but his love for us when he sent his Son to satisfy God's anger against our sins.

¹¹Dear friends, since God loved us as much as that, we surely ought to love each other too. ¹²For though we have never yet seen God, when we love each other God lives in us, and his love within us grows ever stronger. ¹³And he has put his own Holy Spirit into our hearts as a proof to us that we are living with him and he with us. ¹⁴And furthermore, we have seen with our own eyes and now tell all the world that God sent his Son to be their Savior. ¹⁵Anyone who believes and says that Jesus is the Son of God has God living in him, and he is living with God.

¹⁶We know how much God loves us because we have felt his love and because we believe him when he tells us that he loves us dearly. God is love, and anyone who lives in love is living with God and God is living in him. ¹⁷And as we live with Christ, our love grows more perfect and complete; so we will not be ashamed and embarrassed at the day of judgment, but can face him with confidence and joy because he loves us and we love him too.

¹⁸We need have no fear of someone who loves us perfectly; his perfect love for us eliminates all dread of what he might do to us. If we are afraid, it is for fear of what he might do to us and shows that we are not fully convinced that he really loves us. ¹⁹So you see, our love for him comes as a result of his loving us first.

²⁰If anyone says "I love God," but keeps on hating his brother, he is a liar; for if he doesn't love his brother who is right there in front of him, how can he love God whom he has never seen?

CAIN

and his brother Abel worshiped God. In some way, God let them know that Abel's worship was right and Cain's was wrong. God told Cain to start over. Cain got angry. God saw his anger and warned him to be careful. Cain was angry at God, but he took it out on his brother. Instead of making things right with God by changing his attitude, he chose to kill his brother.

Anger is a powerful human reaction. When something happens to us that we didn't expect, we get angry! It starts like a small, hot flame. Unless it is put out, the flame destroys as much as it can. Cain was an angry person whose anger got out of control. But he wasn't in trouble until he acted out his anger in a wrong way. His attitude could have been corrected, but his actions couldn't.

When we get angry, we're in the same danger. We may not react the same as Cain, but we act just like him. We get angry. We see that we have a choice to make between right and wrong. And we often chose wrong. Being angry should remind us that we need God's help. Asking for his help to do the right thing may keep us from making mistakes we can't correct.

LESSONS: Anger is not sin; what causes our anger or what we do with our anger can be sinful.

What we offer to God must be from the heart—the best we are and have

The consequences of sin are sometimes for life

KEY VERSE: "[Your face] can be bright with joy if you will do what you should! But if you refuse to obey, watch out. Sin is waiting to attack you, longing to destroy you. But you can conquer it!" (Genesis 4:7)

Cain's story is told in Genesis 4:1-17. He is also mentioned in Hebrews 11:4; 1 John 3:12; Jude 1:11.

UPS:
- First human child
- First to follow in father's profession: farming

DOWNS:
- When disappointed, reacted out of anger and discouragement
- Took the negative choice even when a positive possibility was offered
- Was the first murderer

STATS:
- Where: Near Eden, which was probably located in the present-day countries of Iraq or Iran
- Occupation: Farmer at first; later, nomad
- Relatives: Parents: Adam and Eve. Brothers and sisters: Abel, Seth, and others not mentioned by name.

²¹And God himself has said that one must love not only God but his brother too.

CHAPTER 5 LOVE GOD AND OBEY HIM.

If you believe that Jesus is the Christ—that he is God's Son and your Savior—then you are a child of God. And all who love the Father love his children too. ²So you can find out how much you love God's children—your brothers and sisters in the Lord—by how much you love and obey God. ³Loving God means doing what he tells us to do, and really, that isn't hard at all; ⁴for every child of God can obey him, defeating sin and evil pleasure by trusting Christ to help him.

⁵But who could possibly fight and win this battle except by believing that Jesus is truly the Son of God?⁶⁻⁸And we know he is, because God said so with a voice from heaven when Jesus was baptized, and again as he was facing death—yes, not only at his baptism but also as he faced death. And the Holy Spirit, forever truthful, says it too. So we have these three witnesses: the voice of the Holy Spirit in our hearts, the voice from heaven at Christ's baptism, and the voice before he died. And they all say the same thing: that Jesus Christ is the Son of God. ⁹We believe men who witness in our courts, and so surely we can believe whatever God declares. And God declares that Jesus is his Son. ¹⁰All who believe this know in their hearts that it is true. If anyone doesn't believe this, he is actually calling God a liar because he doesn't believe what God has said about his Son.

¹¹And what is it that God has said? That he has given us eternal life and that this life is in his Son.

¹²So whoever has God's Son has life; whoever does not have his Son, does not have life.

¹³I have written this to you who believe in the Son of God so that you may know you have eternal life. ¹⁴And we are sure of this, that he will listen to us whenever we ask him for anything in line with his will. ¹⁵And if we really know he is listening when we talk to him and make our requests, then we can be sure that he will answer us.

¹⁶If you see a Christian sinning in a way that does not end in death, you should ask God to forgive him, and God will give him life unless he has sinned that one fatal sin. But there is that one sin which ends in death, and if he has done that, there is no use praying for him. ¹⁷Every wrong is a sin, of course. I'm not talking about these ordinary sins; I am speaking of that one that ends in death.

¹⁸No one who has become part of God's family makes a practice of sinning, for Christ, God's Son, holds him securely, and the devil cannot get his hands on him. ¹⁹We know that we are children of God and that all the rest of the world around us is under Satan's power and control. ²⁰And we know that Christ, God's Son, has come to help us understand and find the true God. And now we are in God because we are in Jesus Christ his Son, who is the only true God; and he is eternal Life.

²¹Dear children, keep away from anything that might take God's place in your hearts. Amen.

Sincerely, John

A TEST

4:20-21 It is easy to say we love God when it doesn't cost us anything more than weekly attendance at religious services. But the real test of our love for God is how we treat the people right in front of us—our family members and fellow believers. We cannot truly love God while neglecting to love those who are created in his image.

YOU KNOW IT!

5:13 Some people *hope* they will be given eternal life. John says that we can *know* we have it. Our certainty is based on God's promise that he has given us eternal life through his Son. This is true whether you feel close to God or distant from him. Eternal life is not based on feelings, but on facts. You can know you have eternal life if you believe God's truth. If you lack assurance as to whether you are a Christian, ask yourself if you have honestly committed your life to Christ as your Savior and Lord. If so, you know by faith that you are indeed a child of God.

MEGA *Themes*

SIN Even Christians sin. Sin requires God's forgiveness, which Christ's death provides. Determining to live according to God's biblical standards shows we are forgiven and that our lives are being transformed.

We cannot deny our sinful nature or minimize the consequences of sin in our relationship with God. We must resist the attraction of sin, yet we must confess when we do sin. Sin is our fault—Christ is our redeemer.

1. What happened when the sinless Christ entered the sinful world?
2. What happens when the sinless Christ enters the life of a sinful person?
3. What does John say we should do about our sins?
4. What is happening in your life in terms of dealing with sin? Are you dealing with your sin with the action and attitude of 1:9? Explain.

LOVE Christ commands us to love others as he did. This love is evidence that we are truly saved. God is the creator of love; and he wants his children to love each other.

Love means putting others first. Love is action—showing others we care, not just saying it. To show love, we must give our time and money to meet the needs of others.

1. Describe God's love for you as described in 1 John.
2. Why is knowing and experiencing God's love essential to living a full life?
3. Who are the people you love most? How does your "love life" compare to your description of God's love? What are your strengths and weaknesses?
4. Whom do you have difficulty loving? How can you apply God's love to those relationships? Why should you do this?

FAMILY OF GOD We become God's children by believing in Christ. God's life in us enables us to love our fellow family members.

How we treat others shows who our Father is. Live as a faithful, loving family member. Remember whose child you are!

1. Who are the children of God according to 1 John?

2. What privileges do these children have? What responsibilities?
3. Complete this statement with specific responses from your own life: "Being a child of God enables me to _____."
4. How would those who know you describe your Father based on their knowledge of you as his child?

TRUTH AND ERROR False teachers encouraged believers to throw off moral restraints, teaching that the body does not matter. They also taught that Christ wasn't really a man and that we must be saved by having some special mystical knowledge. The result was that people became indifferent to sin.

God is truth and light, so the more we get to know him, the better we can keep focused on the truth. Don't be led astray by any teaching that denies Christ's deity or humanity. Check the message; test the claims.

1. Identify several false teachings that John was correcting in his letter.
2. What are our resources for discerning and dealing with false teachings?
3. How can you live so that others can see the difference between God's truth and the false messages in the world?
4. How would you describe your commitment to God's truth? What will you do this week? *Do* what you answered for question number 3.

ASSURANCE God is in control of heaven and earth. Because God's Word is true, we can have assurance of eternal life and victory over sin. By faith we can be certain of our eternal destiny with him.

Assurance of our relationship with God is a promise, but it is also a way of life. We build our confidence by trusting in God's Word and in Christ's provision for our sin.

1. If a young Christian were to ask you, "How can I be sure I am saved?" what would be your response?
2. How could you use 3:12-16 in your answer?
3. How do you know that *you* are saved? What impact does this assurance have in the way you are currently living?

*P*ractical jokes have been around a long time. The Old Testament, for example, is full of sneaky characters. There's Abraham, trying to pass off his wife Sarah as his sister—*twice*. There's Jacob donning a goatskin disguise to snatch his big brother's inheritance and blessing. (And that's just in the first half of the first book—Genesis!) ■ Most people have tried shocking or embarrassing someone with a joy buzzer or a whoopee cushion. Others have short sheeted beds or done various phone pranks. Perhaps you have attempted a more complicated stunt—turning a friend's dresser drawers upside down, freezing your brother's underwear, toilet papering a house. (It's reported that some university pals lined a dorm mate's room with plastic and turned it into a giant aquarium—complete with a shark!) ■ As long as no one gets hurt, no laws are broken, and there's no property damage, pranks are no big deal. It's fun to fool people—or even be fooled. ■ Except in the spiritual dimension. There we can't afford to be deceived because our enemy the devil packs his pranks with disaster! ■ One of Satan's favorite methods of suckering us is to get us to listen to *false teaching*. This can come in many different forms, some very pleasing—but no matter how pleasant it may seem, false teaching is always deadly. ■ The book of 2 John warns us against false teaching. That's a warning we need to heed because the enemy's tricks aren't just for amusement—they're meant for destruction!

STATS

PURPOSE: To emphasize the basics of following Christ—truth and love—and to warn against false teachers

AUTHOR: The apostle John

TO WHOM WRITTEN: To a woman called "Cyria" or "the elect lady" and her household (some think that the greeting refers instead to a local church) and to Christians everywhere.

DATE WRITTEN: About the same time as 1 John, around A.D. 90, from Ephesus

SETTING: Evidently this woman and her family were involved in one of the churches that John was overseeing—they had developed a strong friendship. John was warning her of the false teachers that were becoming prevalent in some of the churches.

KEY PEOPLE: John, Cyria and her children

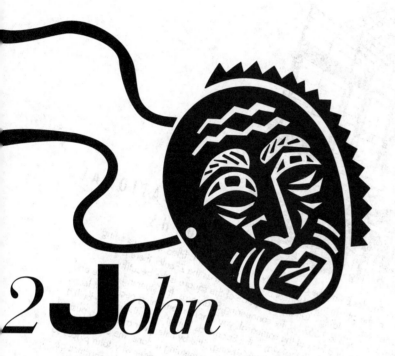

2 John

CHAPTER 1 **BEWARE OF FALSE TEACHERS.** *From:* John, the old Elder of the church.

To: That dear woman Cyria, one of God's very own, and to her children whom I love so much, as does everyone else in the church. ²Since the Truth is in our hearts forever, ³God the Father and Jesus Christ his Son will bless us with great mercy and much peace, and with truth and love.

⁴How happy I am to find some of your children here and to see that they are living as they should, following the Truth, obeying God's command.

⁵And now I want to urgently remind you, dear friends, of the old rule God gave us right from the beginning, that Christians should love one another. ⁶If we love God, we will do whatever he tells us to. And he has told us from the very first to love each other.

⁷Watch out for the false leaders—and there are many of them around—who don't believe that Jesus Christ came to earth as a human being with a body like ours. Such people are against the truth and against Christ. ⁸Beware of being like them and losing the prize that you and I have been working so hard to get. See to it that you win your full reward from the Lord. ⁹For if you wander beyond the teaching of Christ, you will leave God behind; while if you are loyal to Christ's teachings, you will have God too. Then you will have both the Father and the Son.

¹⁰If anyone comes to teach you, and he doesn't believe what Christ taught, don't even invite him into your home. Don't encourage him in any way. ¹¹If you do, you will be a partner with him in his wickedness.

¹²Well, I would like to say much more, but I don't want to say it in this letter, for I hope to come to see you soon, and then we can talk over these things together and have a joyous time.

¹³Greetings from the children of your sister—another choice child of God.

Sincerely, John

SHOW LOVE

1:5-6 The love that Christians should have for one another is a recurrent New Testament theme. Yet love for one's neighbor is an old command first appearing in the third book of Moses (Leviticus 19:18). We can show love in many ways: by avoiding prejudice and discrimination; by accepting people; by listening, helping, giving, serving, and refusing to judge. Just knowing God's command is not enough. We must obey the command and put it into practice. (See also Matthew 22:37-39 and 1 John 2:7-8.)

FOUNDATIONAL TRUTHS

Mexico City is a fascinating place. Besides being the biggest city in the world, it is filled with interesting historical sights. At the very center of the city, in the historical district known as the Zocalo, there is a huge square plaza surrounded by magnificent buildings. On the north side of the square is the beautiful metropolitan cathedral, built from A.D. 1573 to 1667 by the conquering Spaniards. It is stunning, inside and out. **B**ut if you stand back in the square and look at the cathedral, you'll notice something peculiar. It leans. The entire building slopes to the right. It wasn't built that way—the Spaniards built it straight. But they built it on a dry lake bed (formerly Lake Texcoco). The church has been sinking, little by little, year after year, pushed into the soft ground by its own enormous weight. Sooner or later, unless something is done, the cathedral will crack and crumble into rubble just like many of the Aztec ruins nearby. **D**o you wonder why John places so much emphasis on knowing the Bible? Well, he's not alone—many biblical authors stress the importance of knowing God's word. In Psalm 119, the longest chapter in the Bible, all but three of the 176 verses refer specifically to God's word. The writer uses various terms, such as law, instructions, rules—not exactly favorites for any of us—but they all refer to the Scriptures. Likewise, John refers to the Truth—which comes only from God's word—throughout this short letter. Why is knowing the Bible so important? And what in the world does this have to do with Mexico City's metropolitan cathedral? **J**ust this: Like any structure, your life needs a foundation. The bigger the structure, the stronger the foundation has to be. To build a skyscraper or a massive cathedral, you must build on a deep, lasting, rock-solid foundation. If you just want to pitch a tent or throw together a wooden shack, it doesn't really matter where you build. Any place will do. **L**ikewise, if you want to build a life worthy of God, a life that's big, bold, and reflective of his glory, you need a firm base from which to start. The only place to find such a support structure is in the word of God. It is the only platform that will never buckle under the pressure of living for Christ in a very non-Christian world. When you spend time reading the Bible—even when you don't feel like it—you're working on laying your solid foundation. **I**f you don't care what kind of life you're offering up to the Lord, sleep in or watch soap operas all day. But don't be surprised when your life's structure begins to sink and tilt. If you want to have a life worthy of the high calling of following Jesus, start digging. You're already in the right place.

MEGA *Themes*

TRUTH Following God's Word, the Bible, is essential to Christian living because God is truth. Christ's true followers consistently obey his truth.

To be loyal to Christ's teaching we must know the Bible, but we must never twist the Bible's message to our own needs or purposes, nor encourage others who misuse it. We should be servants to the truth of the Word.

1. According to John, why is truth important?
2. How do we know truth?
3. Who are the enemies of the truth? What should be our response to these enemies?
4. How does your life compare with the enemies of the truth in your world?

LOVE Christ's command is for Christians to love one another. This is the basic ingredient of true Christianity.

To obey Christ fully, we must believe his command to love others. Helping, giving, and meeting needs puts love into practice. Love in deed is love indeed.

1. How does John connect love for one another with love for God?

2. What seems to be the connection between love and truth?
3. Identify the people in your life who do not know Christ and his love. What can you do for them that will be a witness concerning the reality of the truth and love of God?

FALSE LEADERS We must be wary of religious leaders who are not true to Christ's teachings. We should not give them a platform to spread false teachings.

Don't encourage those who are contrary to Christ. Politely remove yourself from association with false leaders. Be aware of what's being taught in the church.

1. How can you tell who is a false teacher?
2. What do you see as the main dangers of false teachings?
3. What passages of Scripture would you use to correct the error of these false teachers?
4. Why is it important, based on this study, to be a student of God's Word?
5. What steps are you taking to be led by the truth and to avoid error?

*I*t was over before it got started!" "Blink and you'll miss it." "Short, sweet, and to the point." ■ Those are just some of the expressions you might use to describe: ■ The 1896 war between the United Kingdom and Zanzibar. (It lasted a mere 38 minutes!) ■ Boxer Al Couture's 1946 knockout of opponent Ralph Walton in only 10 1/2 seconds (and that included a 10-second count by the referee)! ■ The 20-minute reign of King Dom Luis III of Portugal in 1908. ■ Montana's Roe River. (Its length? A measley 201 feet!) ■ The 10-yard-long (or should we say "10-yard-*short)* McKinley Street in Bellefontaine, Ohio. ■ But just because things are brief or small or short doesn't mean they're unimportant. ■ Take 3 John for instance. With only 15 verses, it is one of the shortest books of the Bible—a quick contrast between godly living and worldly behavior. ■ In fact, this introduction is about as long as the book itself! So go ahead and read this warm, personal note from the apostle John to his friend Gaius. ■ When you do, another familiar expression may come to mind: ■ "Good things come in little packages."

STATS

PURPOSE: To commend Gaius for his hospitality and to encourage him in his Christian life

AUTHOR: The apostle John

TO WHOM WRITTEN: Gaius, a prominent Christian in one of the churches known to John, and to all Christians everywhere

DATE WRITTEN: About A.D. 90, from Ephesus

SETTING: Church leaders traveled from town to town helping to establish new congregations. They depended on the hospitality of fellow believers. Gaius was one who welcomed them into his home.

KEY PEOPLE: John, Gaius, Diotrephes, Demetrius

3John

CHAPTER 1 HOSPITALITY PLEASES GOD. *From:* John, the Elder.

To: Dear Gaius, whom I truly love.

²Dear friend, I am praying that all is well with you and that your body is as healthy as I know your soul is. ³Some of the brothers traveling by have made me very happy by telling me that your life stays clean and true and that you are living by the standards of the Gospel. ⁴I could have no greater joy than to hear such things about my children.

⁵Dear friend, you are doing a good work for God in taking care of the traveling teachers and missionaries who are passing through. ⁶They have told the church here of your friendship and your loving deeds. I am glad when you send them on their way with a generous gift. ⁷For they are traveling for the Lord and take neither food, clothing, shelter, nor money from those who are not Christians, even though they have preached to them. ⁸So we ourselves should take care of them in order that we may become partners with them in the Lord's work.

⁹I sent a brief letter to the church about this, but proud Diotrephes, who loves to push himself forward as the leader of the Christians

HOSPITALITY

1:5 In the church's early days, traveling prophets, evangelists, and teachers were helped on their way by people like Gaius who housed and fed them. Hospitality is a lost art in many churches today. We would do well to invite more people into our homes for meals—fellow church members, young people, traveling missionaries, those in need, visitors. This is an active and much appreciated way to show your love. In fact, it probably is more important today than ever because of our individualistic, self-centered society. There are many lonely people who wonder if anyone cares whether they live or die. If you find such a lonely person, show him or her that *you* care!

THE NEW AGE MOVEMENT

Following Christ isn't easy. Consider John's words: "Dear friend. . . . Follow only what is good. . . . Follow only what is good. In Remember that those who do what is right prove they are God's children." Follow only what is good. In today's world, that's difficult! Now take a look at Luke 9:23, where Jesus tells us "anyone who wants to follow me must . . . carry his cross . . . . Whoever loses his life for my sake will save it." That's quite a price tag for following Jesus! Isn't there an easier path to God—one that doesn't make such tough demands on us?

Yes! At least, that's what those in the "New Age movement" say. And lots of people are listening. But are New Agers right? Just what is the New Age movement and what does it have to do with Jesus? New religions researchers Bob and Gretchen Passantino describe the New Age movement as "the fastest growing alternative belief system" in the U.S. Alternative to what? To the Jewish-Christian tradition that most Americans have been raised in. J. Gordon Melton, another new religions expert, defines New Age as "a vision of a world transformed, a heaven on earth, a society in which the problems of today are overcome and a new existence emerges." New Agers believe that we stand on the threshold of a new era, a "new age," a major transitional shift into humanity's next evolutionary stage. Sound vague? Well, you're not alone. Even New Agers have difficulty defining who and what they are. But there are some general New Age principles that have been pinned down. The overridding philosophy of the New Age movement is the belief that "all is one." There is no distinction between right or wrong, male or female, good or bad. There isn't even a division between God and man. Everything is divine. This philosophy isn't new. It's been around for thousands of years and is called "pantheism." Pantheism is the basis for all Eastern mystical religions (Hinduism, Buddhism, Confucianism, etc.). But New Agers differ from these religions in that they see this unity from a positive and optimistic view. The New Age is kind of an "eastern-religion-meets-American-positive-thinking." This blend of exotic religious thought and popular psychology attracts many people to New Age teachings. But there's a catch. A big one. If all is one, then there's no difference between right and wrong—or God and man. If there's no difference between God and man, the next logical step is that man is god. No one can tell me "no"; I can do whatever I want. After all, I'm god. (Sound far-fetched? That's exactly what Shirley MacLaine, the "high priestess" of the New Age movement, claims in her autobiography, Out On A Limb. And she is not alone.) The New Age movement is growing rapidly. The belief in the oneness of all things (along with things like ecological harmony, reincarnation, unlimited human potential) appeals to modern, "enlightened" people. The idea that I can be my own god is very seductive. However, history is littered with the atrocities committed by people who thought they answered to no one—Hitler, Pol Pot, Idi Amin, Saddam Hussein. In fact, this was Lucifer's sin, which resulted in his expulsion from heaven. Don't be deceived. There is only one true God— the God of Abraham, Moses, David, Peter, James, and John. He will not share his throne with anyone, and he has certain demands for his followers, like carrying your cross and losing your life for his sake. It's a high price, but Jesus promises us it is worth it. And he is worthy of our sacrificial commitment. The god of the New Age—the god that looks like us—doesn't ask anything of us. But that kind of god can't deliver us from our sins, show us how to love, or die on a cross for us. That god isn't real— he's a lie. Someone has said, "History is filled with men who would be gods; but only one God who would be man." His name is Jesus. Take up your cross and follow him.

there, does not admit my authority over him and refuses to listen to me. [10]When I come I will tell you some of the things he is doing and what wicked things he is saying about me and what insulting language he is using. He not only refuses to welcome the missionary travelers himself but tells others not to, and when they do he tries to put them out of the church.

[11]Dear friend, don't let this bad example influence you. Follow only what is good. Remember that those who do what is right prove that they are God's children; and those who continue in evil prove that they are far from God. [12]But everyone, including Truth itself, speaks highly of Demetrius. I myself can say the same for him, and you know I speak the truth.

[13]I have much to say, but I don't want to write it, [14]for I hope to see you soon and then we will have much to talk about together. [15]So good-bye for now. Friends here send their love, and please give each of the folks there a special greeting from me.

Sincerely, John

MEGA Themes

HOSPITALITY John wrote to encourage those who were kind to others. Genuine hospitality for traveling Christian workers was needed then and is still important.

Faithful Christian teachers and missionaries need our support. Whenever you can extend hospitality to others, it will make you a partner in their ministry.

1. Why is Christian hospitality important?
2. In what specific ways can you and your friends at church extend Christian hospitality?
3. How might your actions of hospitality enable you to become partners in God's work in and through others?
4. What attitudes are required in order to be truly hospitable? How are you doing in terms of these attitudes?
5. Develop a hospitality plan of action based on this study.

PRIDE Diotrephes not only refused to offer hospitality, but he set himself up as a church boss. Pride disqualified him as a real leader.

Christian leaders must shun pride and its effects on them. Be careful not to misuse your position of leadership. The best leaders are always the best servants.

1. What were Diotrephes's sinful actions?
2. Why does John label Diotrephes as prideful?
3. How can a person who is prideful learn to be more humble?
4. Do you struggle with sinful pride? If so, how can you apply your responses in number 3 to your pride?

FAITHFULNESS Gaius and Demetrius were commended for their faithful work in the church. They were held up as examples of faithful, selfless servants.

Don't take for granted Christian workers who serve faithfully. Be sure to encourage these workers so they won't grow weary of serving.

1. What do you learn about Gaius in 3 John?
2. What Christians do you know who live faithfully in their relationship with God? What qualities do you see in them that reflect faithfulness to God? How could you encourage them in their ministry and leadership?
3. Why is faithfulness such an essential quality in the Christian life?
4. What is currently reflecting faithfulness in your life? Identify the ways that your faithfulness, like that of Gaius and those you listed in number 2, makes a difference to others.

*I*s your faith fit for a (spiritual) fight? ■ What would you say if the school agnostic called the resurrection of Christ a myth? Or if a minister you respect admitted that he believes the Bible contains errors and contradictions? ■ What if your favorite teacher announced, "It is insensitive and downright *wrong* for one group of people to try to force its views on another group! Right and wrong is a relative concept, and we cannot legislate morality"? ■ Imagine meeting someone full of joy and peace, a person *seemingly* very much in touch with God. As you converse, this person tells you that she is content and fulfilled because of daily yoga exercises, meditation, and also because of an experience she recently had in which she journeyed back through her previous incarnations. She nods when you mention Jesus Christ and says, "If that works for you, great! But I found the truth another way." ■ If you haven't already had encounters like the ones just described, then just wait. Your time is definitely coming! ■ The fact of the matter is that our world is *full* of confused people who are eagerly spreading their confusing ideas. ■ Don't get caught off-guard! Get your Christian beliefs and behavior ready for spiritual battle by understanding what you believe and why. There's no better place to start your Bible Bootcamp Training than in Jude, the brief book that follows.

STATS

PURPOSE: To remind the church of the need for constant vigilance—to keep strong in the faith and to defend it against heresy

AUTHOR: Jude, James's brother and Jesus' half brother

TO WHOM WRITTEN: Jewish Christians and all believers everywhere

DATE WRITTEN: About A.D. 65

SETTING: From the first century on, the church has been threatened by heresy and false teaching—we must always be on our guard.

KEY PEOPLE: Jude, James, Jesus

Jude

CHAPTER 1 TO CHRISTIANS EVERYWHERE.

From: Jude, a servant of Jesus Christ, and a brother of James.

To: Christians everywhere—beloved of God and chosen by him. ²May you be given more and more of God's kindness, peace, and love.

³Dearly loved friends, I had been planning to write you some thoughts about the salvation God has given us, but now I find I must write of something else instead, urging you to stoutly defend the truth that God gave once for all to his people to keep without change through the years. ⁴I say this because some godless teachers have wormed their way in among you, saying that after we become Christians we can do just as we like without fear of God's punishment. The fate of such people was written long ago, for they have turned against our only Master and Lord, Jesus Christ.

⁵My answer to them is: Remember this fact—which you know already—that the Lord saved a whole nation of people out of the land of Egypt and then killed every one of them who did not trust and obey him. ⁶And I remind you of those angels who were once pure and holy but turned to a life of sin. Now God has them chained up in prisons of darkness, waiting for the judgment day. ⁷And don't forget the cities of

Sodom and Gomorrah and their neighboring towns, all full of lust of every kind, including lust of men for other men. Those cities were destroyed by fire and continue to be a warning to us that there is a hell in which sinners are punished.

[8]Yet these false teachers carelessly go right on living their evil, immoral lives, degrading their bodies and laughing at those in authority over them, even scoffing at the Glorious Ones. [9]Yet Michael, one of the mightiest of the angels, when he was arguing with Satan about Moses' body, did not dare to accuse even Satan, or jeer at him, but simply said, "The Lord rebuke you." [10]But these men mock and curse at anything they do not understand, and like animals, they do whatever they feel like, thereby ruining their souls.

[11]Woe upon them! For they follow the example of Cain who killed his brother; and like Balaam, they will do anything for money; and like Korah, they have disobeyed God and will die under his curse.

[12]When these men join you at the love feasts of the church, they are evil smears among you, laughing and carrying on, gorging and stuffing themselves without a thought for others. They are like clouds blowing over dry land without giving rain, promising much, but producing nothing. They are like fruit trees without any fruit at picking time. They are not only dead, but doubly dead, for they have been pulled out, roots and all, to be burned.

[13]All they leave behind them is shame and disgrace like the dirty foam left along the beach by the wild waves. They wander around looking as bright as stars, but ahead of them is the everlasting gloom and darkness that God has prepared for them.

[14]Enoch, who lived seven generations after Adam, knew about these men and said this about them: "See, the Lord is coming with millions of his holy ones. [15]He will bring the people of the world before him in judgment, to receive just punishment and to prove the terrible things they have done in rebellion against God, revealing all they have said against him." [16]These men are constant gripers, never satisfied, doing whatever evil they feel like; they are loud-mouthed "show-offs," and when they show respect for others, it is only to get something from them in return.

[17]Dear friends, remember what the apostles of our Lord Jesus Christ told you, [18]that in the last times there would come these scoffers whose whole purpose in life is to enjoy themselves in every evil way imaginable. [19]They stir up arguments; they love the evil things of the world; they do not have the Holy Spirit living in them.

[20]But you, dear friends, must build up your lives ever more strongly upon the foundation of our holy faith, learning to pray in the power and strength of the Holy Spirit.

[21]Stay always within the boundaries where God's love can reach and bless you. Wait patiently for the eternal life that our Lord Jesus Christ in his mercy is going to give you. [22]Try to help those who argue against you. Be merciful to those who doubt. [23]Save some by snatching them as from the very flames of hell itself. And as for others, help them to find the Lord by being kind to them, but be careful that you yourselves aren't pulled along into their sins. Hate every trace of their sin while being merciful to them as sinners.

[24,25]And now—all glory to him who alone is God, who saves us through Jesus Christ our Lord; yes, splendor and majesty, all power and authority are his from the beginning; his they are and his they evermore shall be. And he is able to keep you from slipping and falling away, and to bring you, sinless and perfect, into his glorious presence with mighty shouts of everlasting joy. Amen.

Jude

PERSEVERANCE

Cindy and Kate met way back in 8th grade. Not only did the girls become fast friends, but by the end of that school year Cindy had helped Kate find a personal relationship with Jesus Christ.

Throughout high school Cindy always did her best to help Kate grow in the Christian faith. It was sometimes comical—Cindy practically dragging Kate to retreats and youth functions. Had you known the girls in those years, you would have predicted that Cindy was destined to do great things for God. And you would have seriously doubted the long-term stability of Kate's faith.

Boy, would you have been wrong!

During their first year of college, Cindy got too physically involved with her boyfriend. When she had a baby out of wedlock, she married a non-Christian guy and dropped out of sight. Meanwhile, Kate has continued to mature in her walk with God. She's the one with the dynamic ministry on campus.

Yogi Berra said, "It ain't over till it's over." Another sports figure quipped, "The opera isn't over until the fat lady sings." The point? The Christian life is a long, long race.

Read about perseverance in the Epistle of Jude, and ask God to give you the grace and strength to hang in there for God all the days of your life.

WATCH OUT!

1:10 False teachers were claiming that they possessed secret knowledge that gave them authority. Their "knowledge" of God was mystical and beyond human understanding. In reality, the nature of God *is beyond* our understanding. But God in his grace has chosen to reveal himself to us—in his Word, and supremely in Jesus Christ. Therefore, we must seek to know all we can about what God has revealed, even though we cannot fully comprehend God with our finite human minds. Beware of those who claim to have all the answers and who belittle what they do not understand.

GOD *is able to keep you from* sl*i*pp*i*ng *and* fa*l*\i*n*g *awa*y*, and to bring you,* SINLESS *and* PERFECT, *into* HIS GLORIOUS PRESENCE *with* MIGHTY SHOUTS *of* e v e r l a s t i n g · j o y · e v e r l a s t i n g · j o y · e v e r l a s t i n g · j o y

---

MEGA Themes

JUDE WARNS against false teachers and leaders who reject the lordship of Christ, undermine the faith of others, and lead people astray. These leaders and any who follow them will be punished.

We must stoutly defend Christian truth. Make sure that you avoid leaders and teachers who change the Bible to suit their own purposes. Genuine servants of God will faithfully portray Christ in their words and conduct.

1. How does Jude describe the false teachers?
2. What were the negative results of their teachings?
3. How were the Christians supposed to respond to teachings of error?
4. What safeguards can you build into your life to insure that you are not deceived by false teachings?
5. What are you doing to serve as a living testimony of the truth of God?

APOSTASY Jude warns against apostasy—turning away from Christ. We are to remember that God punishes rebellion against him. We must be careful not to drift away from a firm commitment to Christ.

Those who do not study God's Word are susceptible to apostasy. Christians must guard against any false teachings that would distract them from the truth preached by the apostles and written in God's Word.

1. Contrast those who are led by God with those who are living in rebellion.
2. What are the principles found in verses 20-23 for dealing with the rebellious?
3. How would you apply those principles to your life at school? In church? In your social life?
4. What confidence do you find in verses 24-25 that tells you God will remain faithful to you as you follow him? Take time to praise God for who he is and for how he keeps you in his love.

*F*airy tales always end perfectly. The frog turns into a prince, the unloved stepsister becomes a beloved bride, and mean and greedy people get paid back for the rotten things they've done. ■ Unfortunately, fairy tales aren't true. "Happily ever after"? No way! The real world doesn't work that way. ■ Or does it? ■ We are near the end of the Bible. One book left to read: The Revelation. This strange vision of the apostle John's is one of the most discussed, mysterious, and controversial books ever written. It's labeled "prophecy" and "theology." ■ And it's like a fairy tale. ■ *"A fairy tale"?!* ■ That's right. According to The Revelation, those who have become God's children by faith in Christ will have the happiest of all endings: being in the very presence of God, enjoying an existence untouched by sorrow or death. ■ And every bad and wicked creature (including the devil himself) will "face the music." All injustices will be righted; all unforgiven sin will be judged. ■ That, in a nutshell, is the message of The Revelation: happiness and reward for the good, punishment and justice for all the guilty. A picture-perfect ending. ■ You must admit it *does* sound like a fairy tale. There is, however, one important difference: this too-good-to-be-true story is truer than anything that ever existed. It *is* going to happen. ■ You can count on it.

STATS

PURPOSE: To reveal the full identity of Christ and to give warning and hope to believers

AUTHOR: The apostle John

TO WHOM WRITTEN: Seven Asian churches; all believers

DATE WRITTEN: About A.D. 95, from the island of Patmos

SETTING: Most scholars believe that the seven churches of Asia to whom John wrote were experiencing the persecution that took place under Emperor Domitian (A.D. 90-95). Apparently the Roman authorities had exiled John to the island of Patmos (off the coast of Asia). John, an eyewitness of the incarnate Christ, has a vision of the glorified Christ. God also revealed to him what is to take place in the future—judgment and the ultimate triumph of God over evil.

KEY PEOPLE: John, Jesus

KEY PLACES: Island of Patmos, the seven churches, the new Jerusalem

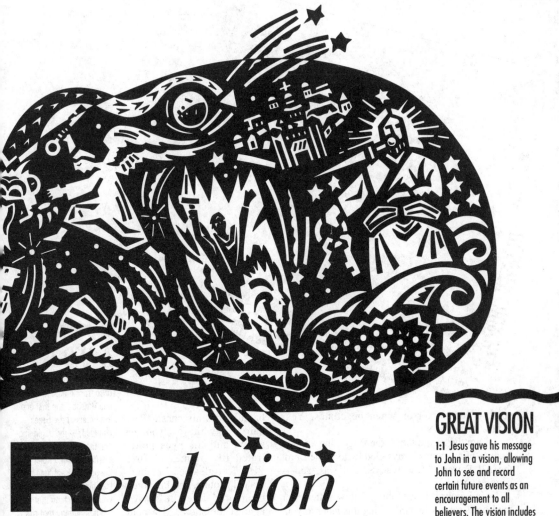

Revelation

CHAPTER **1** **A REVELATION ABOUT THE FUTURE.**
This book unveils some of the future activities soon to occur in the life of Jesus Christ. God permitted him to reveal these things to his servant John in a vision; and then an angel was sent from heaven to explain the vision's meaning. [2]John wrote it all down—the words of God and Jesus Christ and everything he heard and saw.

[3]If you read this prophecy aloud to the church, you will receive a special blessing from the Lord. Those who listen to it being read and do what it says will also be blessed. For the time is near when these things will all come true.

[4]*From:* John

To: The seven churches in Turkey.

Dear Friends:

May you have grace and peace from God who is, and was, and is to come; and from the seven-fold Spirit before his throne; [5]and from Jesus Christ who faithfully reveals all truth to us. He was the first to rise from death, to die no more. He is far greater than any king in all the earth. All praise to him who always loves us and who set us free from our sins by pouring out his life-blood for us. [6]He has gathered us into his Kingdom and made us priests of God his Father. Give to him everlasting glory! He rules forever! Amen!

[7]See! He is arriving, surrounded by clouds; and every eye shall see him—yes, and those who pierced him. And the nations will weep in

GREAT VISION

1:1 Jesus gave his message to John in a vision, allowing John to see and record certain future events as an encouragement to all believers. The vision includes many signs and symbols to effectively show what will happen. What John saw, in most cases, was indescribable, so he used illustrations to show what it was *like*. When reading this symbolic language, don't try to understand every detail—John didn't. Instead, let the imagery show you that Christ is the glorious, victorious Lord of all.

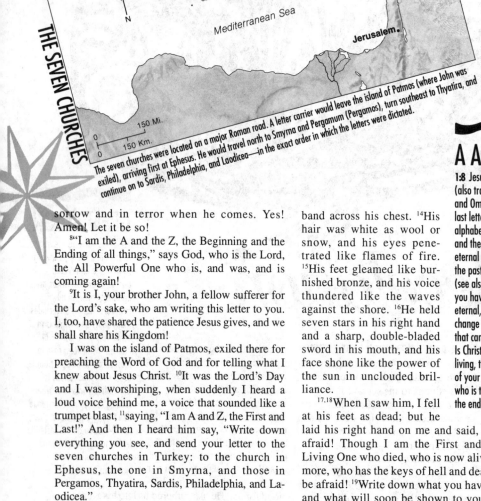

150 Mi.

0

0   150 Km.

The seven churches were located on a major Roman road. A letter carrier would leave the island of Patmos (where John was exiled), arriving first at Ephesus. He would travel north to Smyrna and Pergamum (Pergamos), turn southeast to Thyatira, and continue on to Sardis, Philadelphia, and Laodicea—in the exact order in which the letters were dictated.

A AND Z

1:8 Jesus is the A and the Z (also translated, "the Alpha and Omega," the first and last letters of the Greek alphabet)—the beginning and the end. Jesus is the eternal Lord and Ruler of the past, present, and future (see also 4:8). Without Christ you have nothing that is eternal, nothing that can change your life, nothing that can save you from sin. Is Christ your reason for living, the "first and last" of your life? Honor the One who is the beginning and the end of all existence.

sorrow and in terror when he comes. Yes! Amen! Let it be so!

[8]"I am the A and the Z, the Beginning and the Ending of all things," says God, who is the Lord, the All Powerful One who is, and was, and is coming again!

[9]It is I, your brother John, a fellow sufferer for the Lord's sake, who am writing this letter to you. I, too, have shared the patience Jesus gives, and we shall share his Kingdom!

I was on the island of Patmos, exiled there for preaching the Word of God and for telling what I knew about Jesus Christ. [10]It was the Lord's Day and I was worshiping, when suddenly I heard a loud voice behind me, a voice that sounded like a trumpet blast, [11]saying, "I am A and Z, the First and Last!" And then I heard him say, "Write down everything you see, and send your letter to the seven churches in Turkey: to the church in Ephesus, the one in Smyrna, and those in Pergamos, Thyatira, Sardis, Philadelphia, and Laodicea."

[12]When I turned to see who was speaking, there behind me were seven candlesticks of gold. [13]And standing among them was one who looked like Jesus, who called himself the Son of Man, wearing a long robe circled with a golden band across his chest. [14]His hair was white as wool or snow, and his eyes penetrated like flames of fire. [15]His feet gleamed like burnished bronze, and his voice thundered like the waves against the shore. [16]He held seven stars in his right hand and a sharp, double-bladed sword in his mouth, and his face shone like the power of the sun in unclouded brilliance.

[17,18]When I saw him, I fell at his feet as dead; but he laid his right hand on me and said, "Don't be afraid! Though I am the First and Last, the Living One who died, who is now alive forevermore, who has the keys of hell and death—don't be afraid! [19]Write down what you have just seen and what will soon be shown to you. [20]This is the meaning of the seven stars you saw in my right hand and the seven golden candlesticks: The seven stars are the leaders of the seven churches, and the seven candlesticks are the churches themselves.

CHAPTER **2** JOHN WRITES TO SEVEN CHURCHES.
"Write a letter to the leader of the church at Ephesus and tell him this:

"I write to inform you of a message from him who walks among the churches and holds their leaders in his right hand.

"He says to you: [2]I know how many good things you are doing. I have watched your hard work and your patience; I know you don't tolerate sin among your members, and you have carefully examined the claims of those who say they are apostles but aren't. You have found out how they lie. [3]You have patiently suffered for me without quitting.

[4]"Yet there is one thing wrong; you don't love me as at first! [5]Think about those times of your first love (how different now!) and turn back to me again and work as you did before; or else I will come and remove your candlestick from its place among the churches.

[6]"But there is this about you that is good: You hate the deeds of the licentious Nicolaitans, just as I do.

[7]"Let this message sink into the ears of anyone who listens to what the Spirit is saying to the churches: To everyone who is victorious, I will give fruit from the Tree of Life in the Paradise of God.

[8]*"To the leader of the church in Smyrna write this letter:*

"This message is from him who is the First and Last, who was dead and then came back to life.

[9]"I know how much you suffer for the Lord, and I know all about your poverty (but you have heavenly riches!). I know the slander of those opposing you, who say that they are Jews—the children of God—but they aren't, for they support the cause of Satan. [10]Stop being afraid of what you are about to suffer—for the devil will soon throw some of you into prison to test you. You will be persecuted for 'ten days.' Remain faithful even when facing death and I will give you the crown of life—an unending, glorious future. [11]Let everyone who can hear listen to what the Spirit is saying to the churches: He who is victorious shall not be hurt by the Second Death.

[12]*"Write this letter to the leader of the church in Pergamos:*

"This message is from him who wields the sharp and double-bladed sword. [13]I am fully aware that you live in the city where Satan's throne is, at the center of satanic worship; and yet you have remained loyal to me and refused to deny me even when Antipas, my faithful witness, was martyred among you by Satan's devotees.

[14]"And yet I have a few things against you. You tolerate some among you who do as Balaam did when he taught Balak how to ruin the people of Israel by involving them in sexual sin and encouraging them to go to idol feasts. [15]Yes, you have

some of these very same followers of Balaam among you!

[16]"Change your mind and attitude, or else I will come to you suddenly and fight against them with the sword of my mouth.

Because of my shyness and my family situation, I find it difficult to let people get close to me. As a Christian, I hear all the time how much God loves me. How close does God want to get with me?

I W O N D E R . .

As close as you'll let him.

God knows everything about us, and yet he still wants to be a Father to us. Isn't that amazing? King David wrote about how close God wants to be.

"How precious it is, Lord, to realize that you are thinking about me constantly! I can't even count how many times a day your thoughts turn toward me. And when I waken in the morning, you are still thinking of me!" (Psalms 139:17-18).

Knowing how much God thinks about us (especially in light of how little we think of him) should give us an incredible feeling of worth. Our response to God's constant attentiveness, however, should never be out of obligation. God does not want us to come close to him only because we feel we have to.

Revelation 2:4 warns us not to allow our love for God to grow weaker. God wants us to progress and grow beyond our initial commitment to him, just like in a marriage where love should continue to grow. Unfortunately, this doesn't always happen. Many people who become Christians are really excited about their new relationship with God. But as problems come up, the excitement often wears off (just like what happens in some marriages!).

To maintain a growing relationship with God, the key word is time: daily time with him, time with others who know him, and time (in years) to grow to appreciate his love for you.

Though God is anxious for an intimate relationship with us, he will wait for the day when we'll experience for ourselves what loving him really means. And what a wonderful day that will be!

[17]"Let everyone who can hear, listen to what the Spirit is saying to the churches: Everyone who is victorious shall eat of the hidden manna, the secret nourishment from heaven; and I will give to each a white stone, and on the stone will be engraved a new name that no one else knows except the one receiving it.

[18]*"Write this letter to the leader of the church in Thyatira:*

"This is a message from the Son of God, whose eyes penetrate like flames of fire, whose feet are like glowing brass.

[19]"I am aware of all your good deeds—your kindness to the poor, your gifts and service to them;

also I know your love and faith and patience, and I can see your constant improvement in all these things.

²⁰"Yet I have this against you: You are permitting that woman Jezebel, who calls herself a prophetess, to teach my servants that sex sin is not a serious matter; she urges them to practice immorality and to eat meat that has been sacrificed to idols. ²¹I gave her time to change her mind and attitude, but she refused. ²²Pay attention now to what I am saying: I will lay her upon a sickbed of intense affliction, along with all her immoral followers, unless they turn again to me, repenting of their sin with her; ²³and I will strike her children dead. And all the churches shall know that I am he who searches deep within men's hearts, and minds; I will give to each of you whatever you deserve.

^{24,25}"As for the rest of you in Thyatira who have not followed this false teaching ('deeper truths,' as they call them—depths of Satan, really), I will ask nothing further of you; only hold tightly to what you have until I come.

²⁶"To everyone who overcomes—who to the very end keeps on doing things that please me—I will give power over the nations. ²⁷You will rule them with a rod of iron just as my Father gave me the authority to rule them; they will be shattered like a pot of clay that is broken into tiny pieces. ²⁸And I will give you the Morning Star!

²⁹"Let all who can hear listen to what the Spirit says to the churches.

CHAPTER 3 *"To the leader of the church in Sardis write this letter:*

"This message is sent to you by the one who has the seven-fold Spirit of God and the seven stars.

"I know your reputation as a live and active church, but you are dead. ²Now wake up! Strengthen what little remains—for even what is left is at the point of death. Your deeds are far from right in the sight of God. ³Go back to what you heard and believed at first; hold to it firmly and turn to me again. Unless you do, I will come suddenly upon you, unexpected as a thief, and punish you.

⁴"Yet even there in Sardis some haven't soiled their garments with the world's filth; they shall walk with me in white, for they are worthy. ⁵Everyone who conquers will be clothed in white, and I will not erase his name from the Book of Life, but I will announce before my Father and his angels that he is mine.

⁶"Let all who can hear listen to what the Spirit is saying to the churches.

⁷*"Write this letter to the leader of the church in Philadelphia.*

"This message is sent to you by the one who is holy and true and has the key of David to open what no one can shut and to shut what no one can open.

⁸"I know you well; you aren't strong, but you have tried to obey and have not denied my Name. Therefore I have opened a door to you that no one can shut.

⁹"Note this: I will force those supporting the causes of Satan while claiming to be mine (but they aren't—they are lying) to fall at your feet and acknowledge that you are the ones I love.

¹⁰"Because you have patiently obeyed me despite the persecution, therefore I will protect you from the time of Great Tribulation and temptation, which will come upon the world to test everyone alive. ¹¹Look, I am coming soon! Hold tightly to the little strength you have—so that no one will take away your crown.

¹²"As for the one who conquers, I will make him a pillar in the temple of my God; he will be secure and will go out no more; and I will write my God's Name on him, and he will be a citizen in the city of my God—the New Jerusalem, coming down from heaven from my God; and he will have my new Name inscribed upon him.

¹³"Let all who can hear listen to what the Spirit is saying to the churches.

¹⁴*"Write this letter to the leader of the church in Laodicea:*

"This message is from the one who stands firm, the faithful and true Witness [of all that is or was or evermore shall be], the primeval source of God's creation:

¹⁵"I know you well—you are neither hot nor cold; I wish you were one or the other! ¹⁶But since you are merely lukewarm, I will spit you out of my mouth!

¹⁷"You say, 'I am rich, with everything I want; I don't need a thing!' And you don't realize that

SEX SIN

2:20 Why is sex sin serious? Sex outside marriage always hurts someone. It hurts God because it shows that we prefer to follow our own desires instead of God's Word. It hurts others because it violates the commitment so necessary to a marriage relationship. It hurts us because it often brings disease to our bodies and harms our personalities. Sex sin has tremendous power to destroy families, communities, and even nations because it destroys the relationships upon which these institutions are built. God wants to protect us from hurting ourselves and others, so we should have no part in sex sin, even if our society says it's all right.

KNOCKING

3:20 Jesus is knocking on the door of our hearts every time we sense that we should turn to him. He wants to have fellowship with us, and he wants us to open up to him. Jesus is patient and persistent in trying to get through to us—not breaking and entering, but knocking. He allows us to decide whether or not to open our lives to him. Do you intentionally keep Christ's life-changing presence and power on the other side of the door?

spiritually you are wretched and miserable and poor and blind and naked.

[18]"My advice to you is to buy pure gold from me, gold purified by fire—only then will you truly be rich. And to purchase from me white garments, clean and pure, so you won't be naked and ashamed; and to get medicine from me to heal your eyes and give you back your sight. [19]I continually discipline and punish everyone I love; so I must punish you unless you turn from your indifference and become enthusiastic about the things of God.

[20]"Look! I have been standing at the door, and I am constantly knocking. If anyone hears me calling him and opens the door, I will come in and fellowship with him and he with me. [21]I will let everyone who conquers sit beside me on my throne, just as I took my place with my Father on his throne when I had conquered. [22]Let those who can hear listen to what the Spirit is saying to the churches."

CHAPTER 4   THE GLORIOUS THRONE.

Then as I looked, I saw a door standing open in heaven, and the same voice I had heard before, which sounded like a mighty trumpet blast, spoke to me and said, "Come up here and I will show you what must happen in the future!"

[2]And instantly I was in spirit there in heaven and saw—oh, the glory of it!—a throne and someone sitting on it! [3]Great bursts of light flashed forth

I HAVE BEEN STANDING AT THE DOOR AND I AM CONSTANTLY KNOCKING.

If anyone hears me CALLING HIM and opens the door, I will come in and fellowship with him and with ME.

from him as from a glittering diamond or from a shining ruby, and a rainbow glowing like an emerald encircled his throne. [4]Twenty-four smaller thrones surrounded his, with twenty-four Elders sitting on them; all were clothed in white, with golden crowns upon their heads. [5]Lightning and thunder issued from the throne, and there were voices in the thunder. Directly in front of his throne were seven lighted lamps representing the seven-fold Spirit of God. [6]Spread out before it was a shiny crystal sea. Four Living Beings, dotted front and back with eyes, stood at the throne's four sides. [7]The first of these Living Beings was in the form of a lion; the second looked like an ox; the third had the face of a man; and the fourth, the form of an eagle, with wings spread out as though in flight. [8]Each of these Living Beings had six wings, and the central sections of their wings were covered with eyes. Day after day and night after night they kept on saying, "Holy, holy, holy, Lord God Almighty—the one who was, and is, and is to come."

[9]And when the Living Beings gave glory and honor and thanks to the one sitting on the throne, who lives forever and ever, [10]the twenty-four Elders fell down before him and worshiped him, the Eternal Living One, and cast their crowns before the throne, singing, [11]"O Lord, you are worthy to receive the glory and the honor and the power, for you have created all things. They were created and called into being by your act of will."

CHAPTER 5   THE SEALED SCROLL AND THE LAMB.

And I saw a scroll in the right hand of the one who was sitting on the throne, a scroll with writing on the inside and on the back, and sealed with seven seals. [2]A mighty angel with a loud voice was shouting out this question: "Who is worthy to break the seals on this scroll and to unroll it?" [3]But no one in all heaven or earth or from among the dead was permitted to open and read it.

[4]Then I wept with disappointment because no one anywhere was worthy; no one could tell us what it said.

[5]But one of the twenty-four Elders said to me, "Stop crying, for look! The Lion of the tribe of Judah, the Root of David, has conquered, and proved himself worthy to open the scroll and to break its seven seals."

NO FEAR

4:1 Chapters 4 and 5 are a glimpse into Christ's glory. Here we see into the throne room of heaven. God is orchestrating all the events that John will record. The world is not spinning out of control; the God of creation will carry out his plans as Christ initiates the final battle with the forces of evil. John shows us heaven before showing us earth so we will not be frightened by future events.

[6]I looked and saw a Lamb standing there before the twenty-four Elders, in front of the throne and the Living Beings, and on the Lamb were wounds that once had caused his death. He had seven horns and seven eyes, which represent the seven-fold Spirit of God, sent out into every part of the world. [7]He stepped forward and took the scroll from the right hand of the one sitting upon the throne. [8]And as he took the scroll, the twenty-four Elders fell down before the Lamb, each with a harp and golden vials filled with incense—the prayers of God's people!

[9]They were singing him a new song with these words: "You are worthy to take the scroll and break its seals and open it; for you were slain, and your blood has bought people from every nation as gifts for God. [10]And you have gathered them into a kingdom and made them priests of our God; they shall reign upon the earth."

[11]Then in my vision I heard the singing of millions of angels surrounding the throne and the Living Beings and the Elders: [12]"The Lamb is worthy" (loudly they sang it!) "—the Lamb who was slain. He is worthy to receive the power, and the riches, and the wisdom, and the strength, and the honor, and the glory, and the blessing."

[13]And then I heard everyone in heaven and earth, and from the dead beneath the earth and in the sea, exclaiming, "The blessing and the honor and the glory and the power belong to the one sitting on the throne, and to the Lamb forever and ever." [14]And the four Living Beings kept saying, "Amen!" And the twenty-four Elders fell down and worshiped him.

CHAPTER 6 BREAKING THE SEALS ONE BY ONE.

As I watched, the Lamb broke the first seal and began to unroll the scroll. Then one of the four Living Beings, with a voice that sounded like thunder, said, "Come!"

[2]I looked, and there in front of me was a white horse. Its rider carried a bow, and a crown was placed upon his head; he rode out to conquer in many battles and win the war.

[3]Then he unrolled the scroll to the second seal and broke it open, too. And I heard the second Living Being say, "Come!"

[4]This time a red horse rode out. Its rider was given a long sword and the authority to banish peace and bring anarchy to the earth; war and killing broke out everywhere.

[5]When he had broken the third seal, I heard the third Living Being say, "Come!" And I saw a black horse, with its rider holding a pair of balances in his hand. [6]And a voice from among the four Living Beings said, "A loaf of bread for $20, or three pounds of barley flour, but there is no olive oil or wine."

[7]And when the fourth seal was broken, I heard the fourth Living Being say, "Come!" [8]And now I saw a pale horse, and its rider's name was Death. And there followed after him another horse whose rider's name was Hell. They were given control of one-fourth of the earth, to kill with war and famine and disease and wild animals.

[9]And when he broke open the fifth seal, I saw an altar, and underneath it all the souls of those who had been martyred for preaching the Word of God and for being faithful in their witnessing. [10]They called loudly to the Lord and said, "O Sovereign Lord, holy and true, how long will it be before you judge the people of the earth for what they've done to us? When will you avenge our blood against those living on the earth?" [11]White robes were given to each of them, and they were told to rest a little longer until their other brothers, fellow servants of Jesus, had been martyred on the earth and joined them.

[12]I watched as he broke the sixth seal, and there was a vast earthquake; and the sun became dark like black cloth, and the moon was blood-red. [13]Then the stars of heaven appeared to be falling to earth—like green fruit from fig trees buffeted by mighty winds. [14]And the starry heavens disappeared as though rolled up like a scroll and taken away; and every mountain and island shook and shifted. [15]The kings of the earth, and world leaders, and rich men, and high-ranking military officers, and all men great and small, slave and free, hid themselves in the caves and rocks of the mountains, [16]and cried to the mountains to crush them. "Fall on us," they pleaded, "and hide us from the face of the one sitting on the throne, and from the anger of the Lamb, [17]because the great day of their anger has come, and who can survive it?"

ALL TYPES

5:9-10 People from every nation are praising God before his throne. The gospel is not limited to a specific culture, race, or country. Anyone who comes in repentance and faith is accepted by God and will be part of his Kingdom. Don't allow prejudice or bias to stop you from sharing Christ with others. Christ welcomes all types of people into his Kingdom.

GOD'S TIME

6:9-11 The martyrs are eager for God to bring justice to the earth, but they are told to wait. Those who suffer and die for their faith will not be forgotten, nor do they die in vain. Rather, they will be singled out by God for special honor. We may wish for justice immediately, as these martyrs did, but we must be patient. God works on his own timetable, and he promises justice. No suffering for the sake of God's Kingdom is wasted effort.

THE NAMES OF JESUS

JESUS' NAME	REFERENCE
THE **A** AND THE **Z** THE BEGINNING AND ENDING	1:8
LORD	1:8
ALL POWERFUL ONE	1:8
Son of Man	1:13
FIRST AND LAST	1:18
The Living One	1:18
Son of GOD	2:18
WITNESS	3:14
CREATOR	4:11
Lion of Judah	5:5
ROOT OF DAVID	5:5
Lamb	5:6
Shepherd	7:17
CHRIST	12:10
FAITHFUL FAITHFUL FAITHFUL FAITHFUL AND TRUE	19:11
WORD OF GOD	19:13
KING of KINGS	19:16
LORD of LORDS	19:16
THE MORNING STAR	22:16

Scattered among the vivid images of the book of Revelation is a large collection of names for Jesus. Each one tells something of his character and highlights a particular aspect of his role within God's plan of redemption.

CHAPTER 7 **THE 144,000 CHOSEN BY GOD.** Then I saw four angels standing at the four corners of the earth, holding back the four winds from blowing so that not a leaf rustled in the trees, and the ocean became as smooth as glass. ²And I saw another angel coming from the east, carrying the Great Seal of the Living God. And he shouted out to those four angels who had been given power to injure earth and sea, ³"Wait! Don't do anything yet—hurt neither earth nor sea nor trees—until we have placed the Seal of God upon the foreheads of his servants."

⁴⁻⁸How many were given this mark? I heard the number—it was 144,000; out of all twelve tribes of Israel, as listed here:

Judah	12,000	Naphtali	12,000	Issachar	12,000
Reuben	12,000	Manasseh	12,000	Zebulun	12,000
Gad	12,000	Simeon	12,000	Joseph	12,000
Asher	12,000	Levi	12,000	Benjamin	12,000

⁹After this I saw a vast crowd, too great to count, from all nations and provinces and languages, standing in front of the throne and before the Lamb, clothed in white, with palm branches in their hands. ¹⁰And they were shouting with a mighty shout, "Salvation comes from our God upon the throne, and from the Lamb."

¹¹And now all the angels were crowding around the throne and around the Elders and the four Living Beings, and falling face down before the throne and worshiping God. ¹²"Amen!" they said. "Blessing, and glory, and wisdom, and thanksgiving, and honor, and power, and might, be to our God forever and forever. Amen!"

¹³Then one of the twenty-four Elders asked me, "Do you know who these are, who are clothed in white, and where they come from?"

¹⁴"No, sir," I replied. "Please tell me."

"These are the ones coming out of the Great Tribulation," he said; "they washed their robes and whitened them by the blood of the Lamb. ¹⁵That is why they are here before the throne of God, serving him day and night in his temple. The one sitting on the throne will shelter them; ¹⁶they will never be fully hungry again, nor thirsty, and they will be fully protected from the scorching noontime heat. ¹⁷For the Lamb standing in front of the throne will feed them and be their Shepherd and lead them to the springs of the Water of Life. And God will wipe their tears away."

THE ONLY WAY

7:10 People try many methods to remove the guilt of sin—good works, intellectual pursuits, and even placing blame. The crowd in heaven, however, praises God, saying, "Salvation comes from our God upon the throne, and from the Lamb." Salvation from sin's penalty can come only through Jesus Christ. Have you had the guilt of sin removed in the only way possible?

CHAPTER 8 THE SEVENTH SEAL IS BROKEN.

When the Lamb had broken the seventh seal, there was silence throughout all heaven for what seemed like half an hour. [2]And I saw the seven angels that stand before God, and they were given seven trumpets.

[3]Then another angel with a golden censer came and stood at the altar; and a great quantity of incense was given to him to mix with the prayers of God's people, to offer upon the golden altar before the throne. [4]And the perfume of the incense mixed with prayers ascended up to God from the altar where the angel had poured them out.

[5]Then the angel filled the censer with fire from the altar and threw it down upon the earth; and thunder crashed and rumbled, lightning flashed, and there was a terrible earthquake.

[6]Then the seven angels with the seven trumpets prepared to blow their mighty blasts.

[7]The first angel blew his trumpet, and hail and fire mixed with blood were thrown down upon the earth. One-third of the earth was set on fire so that one-third of the trees were burned, and all the green grass.

MAKE SURE

8:6 The trumpet blasts have three purposes: (1) to warn that judgment is certain, (2) to call the forces of good and evil to battle, and (3) to announce the return of the King, the Messiah. These warnings urge us to make sure our faith is firmly fixed on Christ.

[8,9]Then the second angel blew his trumpet, and what appeared to be a huge burning mountain was thrown into the sea, destroying a third of all the ships; and a third of the sea turned red as blood; and a third of the fish were killed.

[10]The third angel blew, and a great flaming star fell from heaven upon a third of the rivers and springs. [11]The star was called "Bitterness" because it poisoned a third of all the water on the earth and many people died.

[12]The fourth angel blew his trumpet, and immediately a third of the sun was blighted and darkened, and a third of the moon and the stars so that the daylight was dimmed by a third, and the nighttime darkness deepened. [13]As I watched, I saw a solitary eagle flying through the heavens crying loudly, "Woe, woe, woe to the people of the earth because of the terrible things that will soon happen when the three remaining angels blow their trumpets."

CHAPTER 9

Then the fifth angel blew his trumpet, and I saw one who was fallen to earth from heaven, and to him was given the key to the bottomless pit. [2]When he opened it, smoke poured out as though from some huge furnace, and the sun and air were darkened by the smoke.

[3]Then locusts came from the smoke and descended onto the earth and were given power to sting like scorpions. [4]They were told not to hurt the grass or plants or trees, but to attack those people who did not have the mark of God on their foreheads. [5]They were not to kill them, but to torture them for five months with agony like the pain of scorpion stings. [6]In those days men will try to kill themselves but won't be able to—death will not come. They will long to die—but death will flee away!

[7]The locusts looked like horses armored for battle. They had what looked like golden crowns on their heads, and their faces looked like men's. [8]Their hair was long like women's, and their teeth were those of lions. [9]They wore breastplates that seemed to be of iron, and their wings roared like an army of chariots rushing into battle. [10]They had stinging tails like scorpions, and their power to hurt, given to them for five months, was in their tails. [11]Their king is the Prince of the bottomless pit whose name in Hebrew is Abaddon, and in Greek, Apollyon [and in English, the Destroyer].

[12]One terror now ends, but there are two more coming!

[13]The sixth angel blew his trumpet, and I heard a voice speaking from the four horns of the golden altar that stands before the throne of God, [14]saying to the sixth angel, "Release the four mighty demons held bound at the great River Euphrates." [15]They had been kept in readiness for that year and month and day and hour, and now they were turned loose to kill a third of all mankind. [16]They led an army of 200,000,000 warriors—I heard an announcement of how many there were.

[17,18]I saw their horses spread out before me in my vision; their riders wore fiery-red breastplates, though some were sky-blue and others yellow. The horses' heads looked much like lions', and smoke and fire and flaming sulphur billowed from their mouths, killing one-third of all mankind. [19]Their power of death was not only in their mouths, but in their tails as well, for their tails were similar to serpents' heads that struck and bit with fatal wounds.

[20]But the men left alive after these plagues *still refused to worship God!* They would not renounce their demon-worship, nor their idols made of gold and silver, brass, stone, and wood—which neither

SLIPPING

9:20-21 These men were so hardhearted that even plagues did not drive them to God. People don't usually fall into immorality and evil suddenly—they slip into it a little at a time until they are entangled in their wicked ways. Any person who allows sin to take root in his life can find himself in this predicament. Temptation entertained today becomes sin tomorrow, a habit the next day, then death and separation from God forever (see James 1:15). To think you could never become this evil is the first step toward a hard heart.

see nor hear nor walk! ²¹Neither did they change their mind and attitude about all their murders and witchcraft, their immorality and theft.

CHAPTER 10 AN ANGEL WITH A SCROLL TO EAT.

Then I saw another mighty angel coming down from heaven, surrounded by a cloud, with a rainbow over his head; his face shone like the sun and his feet flashed with fire. ²And he held open in his hand a small scroll. He set his right foot on the sea and his left foot on the earth ³and gave a great shout—it was like the roar of a lion—and the seven thunders crashed their reply.

⁴I was about to write what the thunders said when a voice from heaven called to me, "Don't do it. Their words are not to be revealed."

⁵Then the mighty angel standing on the sea and land lifted his right hand to heaven ⁶and swore by him who lives forever and ever, who created heaven and everything in it and the earth and all that it contains and the sea and its inhabitants, that there should be no more delay, ⁷but that when the seventh angel blew his trumpet, then God's veiled plan—mysterious through the ages ever since it was announced by his servants the prophets—would be fulfilled.

⁸Then the voice from heaven spoke to me again, "Go and get the unrolled scroll from the mighty angel standing there upon the sea and land."

⁹So I approached him and asked him to give me the scroll. "Yes, take it and eat it," he said. "At first it will taste like honey, but when you swallow it, it will make your stomach sour!" ¹⁰So I took it from his hand, and ate it! And just as he had said, it was sweet in my mouth, but it gave me a stomachache when I swallowed it.

¹¹Then he told me, "You must prophesy further about many peoples, nations, tribes, and kings."

CHAPTER 11 TWO PROPHETS. Now I was given

a measuring stick and told to go and measure the temple of God, including the inner court where the altar stands, and to count the number of worshipers. ²"But do not measure the outer court," I was told, "for it has been turned over to the nations. They will trample the Holy City for forty-two months. ³And I will give power to my two witnesses to prophesy 1,260 days clothed in sackcloth."

⁴These two prophets are the two olive trees, and two candlesticks standing before the God of all the earth. ⁵Anyone trying to harm them will be killed by bursts of fire shooting from their mouths. ⁶They have power to shut the skies so that no rain will fall during the three and a half years they prophesy, and to turn rivers and oceans to blood, and to send every kind of plague upon the earth as often as they wish.

⁷When they complete the three and a half years of their solemn testimony, the tyrant who comes out of the bottomless pit will declare war against them and conquer and kill them; ⁸,⁹and for three and a half days their bodies will be exposed in the streets of Jerusalem (the city fittingly described as "Sodom" or "Egypt")—the very place where their Lord was crucified. No one will be allowed to bury them, and people from many nations will crowd around to gaze at them. ¹⁰And there will be a worldwide holiday—people everywhere will rejoice and give presents to each other and throw parties to celebrate the death of the two prophets who had tormented them so much!

¹¹But after three and a half days, the spirit of life from God will enter them, and they will stand up! And great fear will fall on everyone. ¹²Then a loud voice will shout from heaven, "Come up!" And they will rise to heaven in a cloud as their enemies watch.

¹³The same hour there will be a terrible earthquake that levels a tenth of the city, leaving 7,000 dead. Then everyone left will, in their terror, give glory to the God of heaven.

¹⁴The second woe is past, but the third quickly follows:

¹⁵For just then the seventh angel blew his trumpet, and there were loud voices shouting down from heaven, "The Kingdom of this world now belongs to our Lord, and to his Christ; and he shall reign forever and ever."

¹⁶And the twenty-four Elders sitting on their thrones before God threw themselves down in worship, saying, ¹⁷"We give thanks, Lord God Almighty, who is and was, for now you have assumed your great power and have begun to reign. ¹⁸The nations were angry with you, but now it is your turn to be angry with them. It is time to judge the dead and reward your servants—prophets and people alike, all who fear your Name, both great and small—and to destroy those who have caused destruction upon the earth."

¹⁹Then, in heaven, the temple of God was opened and the ark of his covenant could be seen inside. Lightning flashed and thunder crashed and roared, and there was a great hailstorm, and the world was shaken by a mighty earthquake.

LIVE NOW!

10:4 Throughout history people have wanted to know what would happen in the future, and God reveals some of it in this book. But John was stopped from revealing certain parts of his vision. An angel also told the prophet Daniel that some things he saw were not to be revealed yet to everyone (Daniel 12:9), and Jesus told his disciples that the time of the end is known by no one but God (Mark 13:32-33). God has revealed all we need to know to live for him now. In our desire to be ready for the end, we must not place more emphasis on speculation about the last days than on living godly lives while waiting.

CHAPTER **12** THE WOMAN AND THE DRAGON.

Then a great pageant appeared in heaven, portraying things to come. I saw a woman clothed with the sun, with the moon beneath her feet, and a crown of twelve stars on her head. ²She was pregnant and screamed in the pain of her labor, awaiting her delivery.

SEEK THE TRUTH

"Dana, are you still planning to talk to Rhonda?"

"I've got to. Those people she's been hanging around are weird. My mom even thinks they're a cult!"

"So why don't her parents say something? I mean, my folks would kill me if I came home spouting all that junk!"

"Oh, Mr. and Mrs. Jordan don't care what she does. He's all wrapped up in his business, and she's got some pretty strange religious ideas herself. Their basic attitude is, 'Whatever makes you happy, Rhonda.'"

"What do you think she'll say?"

"I don't know."

"What are you going to say?"

"I'm going to tell her that what she's been hearing from those people isn't true. I'll show her what the Bible says about false teachers. And I'll challenge her to quit seeking some kind of ooey-gooey feeling, and start seeking the truth."

We need more people like Dana—people who cling doggedly to the truth and who encourage others to do the same. Would you have the courage to confront a friend who was caught up in a false religion? Would you know what to say?

As you read Revelation, notice the constant emphasis on seeking the truth.

³Suddenly a red Dragon appeared, with seven heads and ten horns, and seven crowns on his heads. ⁴His tail drew along behind him a third of the stars, which he plunged to the earth. He stood before the woman as she was about to give birth to her child, ready to eat the baby as soon as it was born.

⁵She gave birth to a boy who was to rule all nations with a heavy hand, and he was caught up to God and to his throne. ⁶The woman fled into the wilderness, where God had prepared a place for her, to take care of her for 1,260 days.

⁷Then there was war in heaven; Michael and the angels under his command fought the Dragon and his hosts of fallen angels. ⁸And the Dragon lost the battle and was forced from heaven. ⁹This great Dragon—the ancient serpent called the devil, or Satan, the one deceiving the whole world—was thrown down onto the earth with all his army.

¹⁰Then I heard a loud voice shouting across the heavens, "It has happened at last! God's salvation and the power and the rule, and the authority of his Christ are finally here; for the Accuser of our brothers has been thrown down from heaven onto earth—he accused them day and night before our God. ¹¹They defeated him by the blood of the Lamb and by their testimony; for they did not love their lives but laid them down for him. ¹²Rejoice, O heavens! You citizens of heaven, rejoice! Be glad! But woe to you people of the world, for the devil has come down to you in great anger, knowing that he has little time."

¹³And when the Dragon found himself cast down to earth, he persecuted the woman who had given birth to the child. ¹⁴But she was given two wings like those of a great eagle, to fly into the wilderness to the place prepared for her, where she was cared for and protected from the Serpent, the Dragon, for three and a half years.

¹⁵And from the Serpent's mouth a vast flood of water gushed out and swept toward the woman in an effort to get rid of her; ¹⁶but the earth helped her by opening its mouth and swallowing the flood! ¹⁷Then the furious Dragon set out to attack the rest of her children—all who were keeping God's commandments and confessing that they belong to Jesus. He stood waiting on an ocean beach.

CREATURES

13:1ff Satan has two evil accomplices: (1) the Creature that comes out of the sea (13:1ff) and (2) the strange animal that comes out of the earth (13:11ff). Together, the three form an unholy trinity in direct opposition to the holy Trinity.

When Satan tempted Jesus in the wilderness, he wanted Jesus to show his power (see Matthew 4:1-11). Satan wanted to rule the world through Jesus, but Jesus refused to do what Satan asked. Thus Satan turns to the fearsome creatures of Revelation, giving them special powers. This unholy trinity—the Dragon, the evil Creature, and the false prophet—then unites in a desperate attempt to overthrow God. To find out what becomes of them, read Revelation 19:19-21 and 20:10.

CHAPTER **13** THE TWO STRANGE CREATURES.

And now, in my vision, I saw a strange Creature rising up out of the sea. It had seven heads and ten horns, and ten crowns upon its horns. And written on each head were blasphemous names, each one defying and insulting God. ²This Creature looked like a leopard but had bear's feet and a lion's mouth! And the Dragon gave him his own power and throne and great authority.

³I saw that one of his heads seemed wounded beyond recovery—but the fatal wound was healed! All the world marveled at this miracle and followed the Creature in awe. ⁴They worshiped the Dragon for giving him such power, and they worshiped the strange Creature. "Where is there anyone as great as he?" they exclaimed. "Who is able to fight against him?"

⁵Then the Dragon encouraged the Creature to speak great blasphemies against the Lord; and gave him authority to control the earth for forty-two months. ⁶All that time he blasphemed God's Name

and his temple and all those living in heaven. ⁷The Dragon gave him power to fight against God's people and to overcome them, and to rule over all nations and language groups throughout the world. ⁸And all mankind—whose names were not written down before the founding of the world in the slain Lamb's Book of Life —worshiped the evil Creature.

⁹Anyone who can hear, listen carefully: ¹⁰The people of God who are destined for prison will be arrested and taken away; those destined for death will be killed. But do not be dismayed, for here is your opportunity for endurance and confidence.

¹¹Then I saw another strange animal, this one coming up out of the earth, with two little horns like those of a lamb but a fearsome voice like the Dragon's. ¹²He exercised all the authority of the Creature whose death-wound had been healed, whom he required all the world to worship. ¹³He did unbelievable miracles such as making fire flame down to earth from the skies while everyone was watching. ¹⁴By doing these miracles, he was deceiving people everywhere. He could do these marvelous things whenever the first Creature was there to watch him. And he ordered the people of the world to make a great statue of the first Creature, who was fatally wounded and then came back to life. ¹⁵He was permitted to give breath to this statue and even make it speak! Then the statue ordered that anyone refusing to worship it must die!

¹⁶He required everyone—great and small, rich and poor, slave and free—to be tattooed with a certain mark on the right hand or on the forehead. ¹⁷And no one could get a job or even buy in any store without the permit of that mark, which was either the name of the Creature or the code number of his name. ¹⁸Here is a puzzle that calls for careful thought to solve it. Let those who are able, interpret this code: the numerical values of the letters in his name add to 666!

CHAPTER **14** **THE LAMB AND A GREAT CHOIR.** Then I saw a Lamb standing on Mount Zion in Jerusalem, and with him were 144,000 who had his Name and his Father's Name written on their foreheads. ²And I heard a sound from heaven like the roaring of a great waterfall or the rolling of mighty thunder. It was the singing of a choir accompanied by harps.

³This tremendous choir—144,000 strong—sang a wonderful new song in front of the throne of God and before the four Living Beings and the twenty-four Elders; and no one could sing this song except those 144,000 who had been redeemed from the earth. ⁴For they are spiritually undefiled, pure as virgins, following the Lamb wherever he goes. They have been purchased from among the men on the earth as a consecrated offering to God and the Lamb. ⁵No falsehood can be charged against them; they are blameless.

⁶And I saw another angel flying through the heavens, carrying the everlasting Good News to preach to those on earth—to every nation, tribe, language, and people.

⁷"Fear God," he shouted, "and extol his greatness. For the time has come when he will sit as Judge. Worship him who made the heaven and the earth, the sea and all its sources."

⁸Then another angel followed him through the skies, saying, "Babylon is fallen, is fallen—that

"Here's what I did..."

I struggle with apathy. I guess you can say I'm not very self-disciplined. This affects both my schoolwork and my Christian life: I have trouble applying myself to what I need to do if I don't feel like doing it at the moment.

In my youth group we studied 2 Timothy and one verse has really challenged me directly: verse 15 of chapter 2. It says, "Work hard so God can say to you, 'Well done.' Be a good workman, one who does not need to be ashamed when God examines your work. Know what his Word says and means." These words remind me that my actions and attitudes are significant, and someday I'll have to answer to God for them. Revelation tells about when that will happen (14:7). That helps me to make an extra effort to do the right thing, whether it's reading my Bible regularly or turning off the TV and opening a textbook.

Sue

AGE 15

great city—because she seduced the nations of the world and made them share the wine of her intense impurity and sin."

⁹Then a third angel followed them shouting, "Anyone worshiping the Creature from the sea and his statue, and accepting his mark on the forehead or the hand ¹⁰must drink the wine of the anger of God; it is poured out undiluted into God's cup of wrath. And they will be tormented with fire and burning sulphur in the presence of the holy angels and the Lamb. ¹¹The smoke of

PASSED OUT

14:14-17 This is an image of judgment: Christ is separating the faithful from the unfaithful like a farmer harvesting his crops. This will be a time of joy for the Christians who have been persecuted and martyred—they will receive their long awaited reward. Christians should not fear the last judgment. Jesus said, "I say emphatically that anyone who listens to my message and believes in God who sent me has eternal life, and will never be damned for his sins, but has already passed out of death into life" (John 5:24).

their torture rises forever and ever, and they will have no relief day or night, for they have worshiped the Creature and his statue, and have been tattooed with the code of his name. [12]Let this encourage God's people to endure patiently every trial and persecution, for they are his saints who remain firm to the end in obedience to his commands and trust in Jesus."

[13]And I heard a voice in the heavens above me saying, "Write this down: At last the time has come for his martyrs to enter into their full reward. Yes, says the Spirit, they are blessed indeed, for now they shall rest from all their toils and trials; for their good deeds follow them to heaven!" [14]Then the scene changed, and I saw a white cloud and someone sitting on it who looked like Jesus, who was called "The Son of Man," with a crown of solid gold upon his head and a sharp sickle in his hand.

[15]Then an angel came from the temple and called out to him, "Begin to use the sickle, for the time has come for you to reap; the harvest is ripe on the earth." [16]So the one sitting on the cloud swung his sickle over the earth, and the harvest was gathered in. [17]After that another angel came from the temple in heaven, and he also had a sharp sickle.

[18]Just then the angel who has power to destroy the world with fire, shouted to the angel with the sickle, "Use your sickle now to cut off the clusters of grapes from the vines of the earth, for they are fully ripe for judgment." [19]So the angel swung his sickle on the earth and loaded the grapes into the great winepress of God's wrath. [20]And the grapes were trodden in the winepress outside the city, and blood flowed out in a stream 200 miles long and as high as a horse's bridle.

CHAPTER 15

And I saw in heaven another mighty pageant showing things to come: Seven angels were assigned to carry down to earth the seven last plagues—and then at last God's anger will be finished.

[2]Spread out before me was what seemed to be an ocean of fire and glass, and on it stood all those who had been victorious over the Evil Creature and his statue and his mark and number. All were holding harps of God, [3,4]and they were singing the song of Moses, the servant of God, and the song of the Lamb:

> "Great and marvelous
> Are your doings,
> Lord God Almighty.
> Just and true
> Are your ways,
> O King of Ages.
> Who shall not fear,
> O Lord,
> And glorify your Name?
> For you alone are holy.
> All nations will come
> And worship before you,
> For your righteous deeds
> Have been disclosed."

[5]Then I looked and saw that the Holy of Holies of the temple in heaven was thrown wide open!
[6]The seven angels who were assigned to pour out the seven plagues then came from the temple, clothed in spotlessly white linen, with golden belts across their chests. [7]And one of the four Living Beings handed each of them a golden flask filled with the terrible wrath of the Living God who lives forever and forever. [8]The temple was filled with smoke from his glory and power; and no one could enter until the seven angels had completed pouring out the seven plagues.

CHAPTER 16 SEVEN FLASKS OF WRATH.

And I heard a mighty voice shouting from the temple to the seven angels, "Now go your ways and empty out the seven flasks of the wrath of God upon the earth."

[2]So the first angel left the temple and poured out his flask over the earth, and horrible, malignant sores broke out on everyone who had the mark of the Creature and was worshiping his statue.

[3]The second angel poured out his flask upon the oceans, and they became like the watery blood of a dead man; and everything in all the oceans died.

[4]The third angel poured out his flask upon the rivers and springs and they became blood. [5]And I heard this angel of the waters declaring, "You are just in sending this judgment, O Holy One, who is and was, [6]for your saints and prophets have been martyred and their blood poured out

READY?

16:15 Christ will return unexpectedly (1 Thessalonians 5:1-6), so we must be ready when he returns. We can prepare ourselves by resisting temptation and by being committed to God's moral standards. In what ways does your life show your readiness for Christ's return?

upon the earth; and now, in turn, you have poured out the blood of those who murdered them; it is their just reward."

[7]And I heard the angel of the altar say, "Yes, Lord God Almighty, your punishments are just and true."

[8]Then the fourth angel poured out his flask upon the sun, causing it to scorch all men with its fire. [9]Everyone was burned by this blast of heat, and they cursed the name of God who sent the plagues—they did not change their mind and attitude to give him glory.

[10]Then the fifth angel poured out his flask upon the throne of the Creature from the sea, and his kingdom was plunged into darkness. And his subjects gnawed their tongues in anguish, [11]and cursed the God of heaven for their pains and sores, but they refused to repent of all their evil deeds.

[12]The sixth angel poured out his flask upon the great River Euphrates and it dried up so that the kings from the east could march their armies westward without hindrance. [13]And I saw three evil spirits disguised as frogs leap from the mouth of the Dragon, the Creature, and his False Prophet. [14]These miracle-working demons conferred with all the rulers of the world to gather them for battle against the Lord on that great coming Judgment Day of God Almighty.

[15]"Take note: I will come as unexpectedly as a thief! Blessed are all who are awaiting me, who keep their robes in readiness and will not need to walk naked and ashamed."

[16]And they gathered all the armies of the world near a place called, in Hebrew, Armageddon—the Mountain of Megiddo.

[17]Then the seventh angel poured out his flask into the air; and a mighty shout came from the throne of the temple in heaven, saying, "It is finished!" [18]Then the thunder crashed and rolled, and lightning flashed; and there was a great earthquake of a magnitude unprecedented in human history. [19]The great city of "Babylon" split into three sections, and cities around the world fell in heaps of rubble; and so all of "Babylon's" sins were remembered in God's thoughts, and she was punished to the last drop of anger in the cup of the wine of the fierceness of his wrath. [20]And islands vanished, and mountains flattened out, [21]and there was an incredible hailstorm from heaven; hailstones weighing a hundred pounds fell from the sky onto the people below, and they cursed God because of the terrible hail.

CHAPTER 17 A DRUNKEN WOMAN.

One of the seven angels who had poured out the plagues came over and talked with me. "Come with me," he said,

"and I will show you what is going to happen to the Notorious Prostitute, who sits upon the many waters of the world. [2]The kings of the world have had immoral relations with her, and the people of the earth have been made drunk by the wine of her immorality."

[3]So the angel took me in spirit into the wilderness. There I saw a woman sitting on a scarlet animal that had seven heads and ten horns, written all over with blasphemies against God. [4]The woman wore purple and scarlet clothing and beautiful jewelry made of gold and precious gems and pearls, and held in her hand a golden goblet full of obscenities:

[5]A mysterious caption was written on her forehead: "Babylon the Great, Mother of Prostitutes and of Idol Worship Everywhere around the World."

[6]I could see that she was drunk—drunk with the blood of the martyrs of Jesus she had killed. I stared at her in horror.

[7]"Why are you so surprised?" the angel asked. "I'll tell you who she is and what the animal she is riding represents. [8]He was alive but isn't now. And yet, soon he will come up out of the bottomless pit and go to eternal destruction; and the people of earth, whose names have not been written in the Book of Life before the world began, will be dumbfounded at his reappearance after being dead.

[9]"And now think hard: his seven heads represent a certain city built on seven hills where this woman has her residence. [10]They also represent seven kings. Five have already fallen, the sixth now reigns, and the seventh is yet to come, but his reign will be brief. [11]The scarlet animal that died is the eighth king, having reigned before as one of the seven; after his second reign, he too, will go to his doom. [12]His ten horns are ten kings who have not yet risen to power; they will be appointed to their kingdoms for one brief moment, to reign with him. [13]They will all sign a treaty giving their power and strength to him. [14]Together they will wage war against the Lamb, and the Lamb will conquer them; for he is Lord over all lords, and King of kings, and his people are the called and chosen and faithful ones.

[15]"The oceans, lakes, and rivers that the woman is sitting on represent masses of people of every race and nation.

[16]"The scarlet animal and his ten horns—which represent ten kings who will reign with him—all hate the woman, and will attack her and leave her naked and ravaged by fire. [17]For God will put a plan

IN CHARGE

17:17 No matter what happens, we must trust that God is still in charge, and his plans will happen just as he says. He even uses people opposed to him to execute his will. Although he allows evil to permeate this present world, the new earth will never know sin.

into their minds, a plan that will carry out his purposes: They will mutually agree to give their authority to the scarlet animal so that the words of God will be fulfilled. [18]And this woman you saw in your vision represents the great city that rules over the kings of the earth."

CHAPTER 18 THE FALL OF BABYLON. After all this I saw another angel come down from heaven with great authority, and the earth grew bright with his splendor.

[2]He gave a mighty shout, "Babylon the Great is fallen, is fallen; she has become a den of demons, a haunt of devils and every kind of evil spirit. [3]For all the nations have drunk the fatal wine of her intense immorality. The rulers of earth have enjoyed themselves with her, and businessmen throughout the world have grown rich from all her luxurious living."

[4]Then I heard another voice calling from heaven, "Come away from her, my people; do not take part in her sins, or you will be punished with her. [5]For her sins are piled as high as heaven, and God is ready to judge her for her crimes. [6]Do to her as she has done to you, and more—give double penalty for all her evil deeds. She brewed many a cup of woe for others—give twice as much to her. [7]She has lived in luxury and pleasure—match it now with torments and with sorrows. She boasts, 'I am queen upon my throne. I am no helpless widow. I will not experience sorrow.' [8]Therefore the sorrows of death and mourning and famine shall overtake her in a single day, and she shall be utterly consumed by fire; for mighty is the Lord who judges her."

[9]And the world leaders who took part in her immoral acts and enjoyed her favors will mourn for her as they see the smoke rising from her charred remains. [10]They will stand far off, trembling with fear and crying out, "Alas, Babylon, that mighty city! In one moment her judgment fell."

[11]The merchants of the earth will weep and mourn for her, for there is no one left to buy their goods. [12]She was their biggest customer for gold and silver, precious stones, pearls, finest linens, purple silks, and scarlet; and every kind of perfumed wood, and ivory goods, and most expensive wooden carvings, and brass, and iron, and marble; [13]and spices, and perfumes, and incense, ointment, and frankincense, wine, olive oil, and fine flour; wheat, cattle, sheep, horses, chariots, and slaves—and even the souls of men.

GREED GUARD

18:11-19 God's people should not live for money. Instead, they should keep on guard constantly against greed, which is always ready to take over their lives. Money will be worthless in eternity, and God calls greed sinful.

THE BEGINNING AND THE END

The Bible records for us the beginning of the world and the end of the world. The story of mankind, from beginning to end–from the fall into sin to the redemption of Christ and God's ultimate victory over evil–is found in the pages of the Bible.

GENESIS
The sun is created
Satan is victorious
Sin enters the human race
People run and hide from God
Tears are shed, with sorrow for sin
The Garden and earth are cursed
The fruit from the Tree of Life is not to be eaten
Paradise is lost
People are doomed to death

REVELATION
The sun is not needed
Satan is defeated
Sin is banished
People are invited to live with God forever
The curse is removed
No more sin, no more tears or sorrow
God's city is glorified, the earth is made new
God's people may eat from the Tree of Life
Paradise is regained
Death is defeated, believers live forever with God

14"All the fancy things you loved so much are gone," they cry. "The dainty luxuries and splendor that you prized so much will never be yours again. They are gone forever."

15And so the merchants who have become wealthy by selling her these things shall stand at a distance, fearing danger to themselves, weeping and crying, 16"Alas, that great city, so beautiful—like a woman clothed in finest purple and scarlet linens, decked out with gold and precious stones and pearls! 17In one moment, all the wealth of the city is gone!"

And all the shipowners and captains of the merchant ships and crews will stand a long way off, 18crying as they watch the smoke ascend, and saying, "Where in all the world is there another city such as this?" 19And they will throw dust on their heads in their sorrow and say, "Alas, alas, for that great city! She made us all rich from her great wealth. And now in a single hour all is gone. . . ."

20But you, O heaven, rejoice over her fate; and you, O children of God and the prophets and the apostles! For at last God has given judgment against her for you.

21Then a mighty angel picked up a boulder shaped like a millstone and threw it into the ocean and shouted, "Babylon, that great city, shall be thrown away as I have thrown away this stone, and she shall disappear forever. 22Never again will the sound of music be there—no more pianos, saxophones, and trumpets. No industry of any kind will ever again exist there, and there will be no more milling of the grain. 23Dark, dark will be her nights; not even a lamp in a window will ever be seen again. No more joyous wedding bells and happy voices of the bridegrooms and the brides. Her businessmen were known around the world, and she deceived all nations with her sorceries. 24And she was responsible for the blood of all the martyred prophets and the saints."

CHAPTER **19** A HALLELUJAH CHORUS.

After this I heard the shouting of a vast crowd in heaven, "Hallelujah! Praise the Lord! Salvation is from our God. Honor and authority belong to him alone; 2for his judgments are just and true. He has punished the Great Prostitute who corrupted the earth with her sin; and he has avenged the murder of his servants."

3Again and again their voices rang, "Praise the Lord! The smoke from her burning ascends forever and forever!"

4Then the twenty-four Elders and four Living Beings fell down and worshiped God, who was sitting upon the throne, and said, "Amen! Hallelujah! Praise the Lord!"

5And out of the throne came a voice that said, "Praise our God, all you his servants, small and great, who fear him."

6Then I heard again what sounded like the shouting of a huge crowd, or like the waves of a hundred oceans crashing on the shore, or like the mighty rolling of great thunder, "Praise the Lord. For the Lord our God, the Almighty, reigns. 7Let us be glad and rejoice and honor him; for the time has come for the wedding banquet of the Lamb, and his bride has prepared herself. 8She is permitted to wear the cleanest and whitest and finest of linens." (Fine linen represents the good deeds done by the people of God.)

9And the angel dictated this sentence to me: "Blessed are those who are invited to the wedding feast of the Lamb." And he added, "God himself has stated this."

10Then I fell down at his feet to worship him, but he said, "No! Don't! For I am a servant of God just as you are, and as your brother Christians are, who testify of their faith in Jesus. Worship God. The purpose of all prophecy and of all I have shown you is to tell about Jesus."

HEARTFELT

19:1-10 Praise is the heartfelt response to God by those who love him. The more you get to know God and realize what he has done, the more you will respond with praise. Praise is at the heart of true worship. Let your praise of God flow out of your realization of who he is and how much he loves you.

11Then I saw heaven opened and a white horse standing there; and the one sitting on the horse was named Faithful and True—the one who justly punishes and makes war. 12His eyes were like flames, and on his head were many crowns. A name was written on his forehead, and only he knew its meaning. 13He was clothed with garments dipped in blood, and his title was "The Word of God." 14The armies of heaven, dressed in finest linen, white and clean, followed him on white horses.

15In his mouth he held a sharp sword to strike down the nations; he ruled them with an iron grip; and he trod the winepress of the fierceness of the wrath of Almighty God. 16On his robe and thigh was written this title: "King of Kings and Lord of Lords."

17Then I saw an angel standing in the sunshine, shouting loudly to the birds, "Come! Gather together for the supper of the Great God! 18Come and eat the flesh of kings, and captains, and great generals; of horses and riders; and of all humanity, both great and small, slave and free."

19Then I saw the Evil Creature gathering the governments of the earth and their armies to fight against the one sitting on the horse and his army. 20And the Evil Creature was captured, and with him the False Prophet, who could do mighty miracles when the Evil Creature was present—miracles that deceived all who had accepted the Evil Creature's mark, and who worshiped his statue. Both of them—the Evil Creature and his False Prophet—were thrown alive into the Lake of Fire that burns with sulphur. [21]And their entire army was killed with the sharp sword in the mouth of the one riding the white horse, and all the birds of heaven were gorged with their flesh.

CHAPTER 20

THE 1,000 YEARS. Then I saw an angel come down from heaven with the key to the bottomless pit and a heavy chain in his hand. [2]He seized the Dragon—that old Serpent, the devil, Satan—and bound him in chains for a thousand years, [3]and threw him into the bottomless pit, which he then shut and locked so that he could not fool the nations any more until the thousand years were finished. Afterwards he would be released again for a little while.

[4]Then I saw thrones, and sitting on them were those who had been given the right to judge. And I saw the souls of those who had been beheaded for their testimony about Jesus, for proclaiming the Word of God, and who had not worshiped the Creature or his statue, nor accepted his mark on their foreheads or their hands. They had come to life again and now they reigned with Christ for a thousand years.

[5]This is the First Resurrection. (The rest of the dead did not come back to life until the thousand years had ended.) [6]Blessed and holy are those who share in the First Resurrection. For them the Second Death holds no terrors, for they will be priests of God and of Christ, and shall reign with him a thousand years.

[7]When the thousand years end, Satan will be let out of his prison. [8]He will go out to deceive the nations of the world and gather them together, with Gog and Magog, for battle—a mighty host, numberless as sand along the shore. [9]They will go up across the broad plain of the earth and surround God's people and the beloved city of Jerusalem on every side. But fire from God in heaven will flash down on the attacking armies and consume them.

[10]Then the devil who had betrayed them will again be thrown into the Lake of Fire burning with sulphur where the Creature and False Prophet are, and they will be tormented day and night forever and ever.

[11]And I saw a great white throne and the one who sat upon it, from whose face the earth and sky fled away, but they found no place to hide. [12]I saw the dead, great and small, standing before God; and The Books were opened, including the Book of Life. And the dead were judged according to the things written in The Books, each according to the deeds he had done. [13]The oceans surrendered the bodies buried in them; and the earth and the underworld gave up the dead in them. Each was judged according to his deeds. [14]And Death and Hell were thrown into the Lake of Fire. This is the Second Death—the Lake of Fire. [15]And if anyone's name was not found recorded in the Book of Life, he was thrown into the Lake of Fire.

CHAPTER 21 A NEW HEAVEN AND NEW EARTH.

Then I saw a new earth (with no oceans!) and a new sky, for the present earth and sky had disappeared. [2]And I, John, saw the Holy City, the new Jerusalem, coming down from God out of heaven. It was a glorious sight, beautiful as a bride at her wedding.

[3]I heard a loud shout from the throne saying, "Look, the home of God is now among men, and he will live with them and they will be his people; yes, God himself will be among them. [4]He will wipe away all tears from their eyes, and there shall be no more death, nor sorrow, nor crying, nor pain. All of that has gone forever."

[5]And the one sitting on the throne said, "See, I am making all things new!" And then he said to me,

DESPAIR

Blood, violence, murder, mayhem, images of doom and gloom.

What have we got here? Some kind of horror movie?

No, just another edition of the nightly news.

With smiling faces and playful banter, the channel 2 news anchors recite one horror story after another: the ongoing drug war, tensions in the Middle East, 18 killed in a school bus tragedy, a psychotic killer on the loose, alarming new predictions about AIDS, a devastating flood in India, the growing nightmare of pollution, the possible consequences of the greenhouse effect.

As Wes turns off the TV, he sighs.

"I'm telling you," he mutters to himself, "this world is totally messed up. What's the point? I mean, what do I have to live for? The way things are going, we won't even make it to the year 2000."

Is it any wonder the guy's depressed? The human race does seem bent on self-destruction. Is there any hope in a world that seems to be spinning out of control?

Yes! One of the greatest, most encouraging passages in the whole Bible is found right at the end. Read Revelation 21 and 22 for a fascinating and faith-building look at what the future holds for those who know Christ. (If you don't know Christ as your Savior, now is a perfect time to ask him to forgive your sins and to give you eternal life.)

NO CONTEST

20:9 This is not a typical battle where the outcome is in doubt during the heat of the conflict. Here there is no contest. Two mighty forces of evil—those of the Creature (19:19) and of Satan (20:8)—unite to do battle against God. The Bible uses just two verses to describe each battle—the evil Creature and his forces are captured and thrown into the Lake of Fire (19:20-21), and fire from God consumes Satan and his attacking armies (20:9-10). There will be no doubt, no worry, and no second thoughts for believers about whether they have chosen the right side. If you choose God, you will experience this tremendous victory with Christ.

"Write this down, for what I tell you is trustworthy and true: [6]It is finished! I am the A and the Z—the Beginning and the End. I will give to the thirsty the springs of the Water of Life—as a gift! [7]Everyone who conquers will inherit all these blessings, and I will be his God and he will be my son. [8]But cowards who turn back from following me, and those who are unfaithful to me, and the corrupt, and murderers, and the immoral, and those conversing with demons, and idol worshipers and all liars—their doom is in the Lake that burns with fire and sulphur. This is the Second Death."

[9]Then one of the seven angels who had emptied the flasks containing the seven last plagues came and said to me, "Come with me and I will show you the bride, the Lamb's wife."

[10]In a vision he took me to a towering mountain peak, and from there I watched that wondrous city, the holy Jerusalem, descending out of the skies from God. [11]It was filled with the glory of God and flashed and glowed like a precious gem, crystal clear like jasper. [12]Its walls were broad and high, with twelve gates guarded by twelve angels. And the names of the twelve tribes of Israel were written on the gates. [13]There were three gates on each side—north, south, east, and west. [14]The walls had twelve foundation stones, and on them were written the names of the twelve apostles of the Lamb.

[15]The angel held in his hand a golden measuring stick to measure the city and its gates and walls. [16]When he measured it, he found it was a square as wide as it was long; in fact it was in the form of a cube, for its height was exactly the same as its other dimensions—1,500 miles each way. [17]Then he measured the thickness of the walls and found them to be 216 feet across (the angel called out these measurements to me, using standard units).

[18-20]The city itself was pure, transparent gold like glass! The wall was made of jasper, and was built on twelve layers of foundation stones inlaid with gems: the first layer with jasper; the second with sapphire; the third with chalcedony; the fourth with emerald; the fifth with sardonyx; the sixth layer with sardus; the seventh with chrysolite; the eighth with beryl; the ninth with topaz; the tenth with chrysoprase; the eleventh with jacinth; the twelfth with amethyst.

[21]The twelve gates were made of pearls—each gate from a single pearl! And the main street was pure, transparent gold, like glass.

[22]No temple could be seen in the city, for the Lord God Almighty and the Lamb are worshiped in it everywhere. [23]And the city has no need of sun or moon to light it, for the glory of God and of the Lamb illuminate it. [24]Its light will light the nations of the earth, and the rulers of the world will come and bring their glory to it. [25]Its gates never close; they stay open all day long—and there is no night! [26]And the glory and honor of all the nations shall be brought into it. [27]Nothing evil will be permitted in it—no one immoral or dishonest—but only those whose names are written in the Lamb's Book of Life.

CHAPTER **22** THE RIVER OF LIFE. And he pointed out to me a river of pure Water of Life, clear as crystal, flowing from the throne of God and the Lamb, [2]coursing down the center of the main street. On each side of the river grew Trees of Life, bearing twelve crops of fruit, with a fresh crop each month; the leaves were used for medicine to heal the nations.

[3]There shall be nothing in the city that is evil; for the throne of God and of the Lamb will be there, and his servants will worship him. [4]And they shall see his face; and his name shall be written on their

ETERNITY IS

21:3-4 Have you ever wondered what eternity will be like? The "Holy City, the new Jerusalem" is described as the place where God "will wipe away all tears." Forevermore, there will be no death, pain, sorrow, or crying. What a wonderful truth! No matter what you are going through, it's not the last word—God has written the final chapter, and it includes eternal joy for those who love him. We do not know as much as we would like, but it is enough to know that eternity with God will be more wonderful than we can imagine.

H E *will wipe away all tears from their eyes,* and there shall be **NO MORE DEATH,** nor sorrow, nor crying, nor pain. ALL OF THAT HAS GONE FOREVER

REVELATION 21:4

EYEWITNESS

22:8-9 Hearing or reading an eyewitness account is the next best thing to seeing the event yourself. John witnessed the events reported in Revelation and wrote them down so we could "see" and believe as he did. If you have read this far, you have "seen." Have you also believed?

foreheads. [5]And there will be no night there—no need for lamps or sun—for the Lord God will be their light; and they shall reign forever and ever.

[6,7]Then the angel said to me, "These words are trustworthy and true: 'I am coming soon!' God, who tells his prophets what the future holds, has sent his angel to tell you this will happen soon. Blessed are those who believe it and all else written in the scroll."

[8]I, John, saw and heard all these things, and fell down to worship the angel who showed them to me; [9]but again he said, "No, don't do anything like that. I, too, am a servant of Jesus as you are, and as your brothers the prophets are, as well as all those who heed the truth stated in this book. Worship God alone."

[10]Then he instructed me, "Do not seal up what you have written, for the time of fulfillment is near. [11]And when that time comes, all doing wrong will do it more and more; the vile will become more vile; good men will be better; those who are holy will continue on in greater holiness."

[12]"See, I am coming soon, and my reward is with me, to repay everyone according to the deeds he has done. [13]I am the A and the Z, the Beginning and the End, the First and Last. [14]Blessed forever are all who are washing their robes, to have the right to enter in through the gates of the city and to eat the fruit from the Tree of Life.

[15]"Outside the city are those who have strayed away from God, and the sorcerers and the immoral and murderers and idolaters, and all who love to lie, and do so.

[16]"I, Jesus, have sent my angel to you to tell the churches all these things. I am both David's Root and his Descendant. I am the bright Morning Star. [17]The Spirit and the bride say, 'Come.' Let each one who hears them say the same, 'Come.' Let the thirsty one come—anyone who wants to; let him come and drink the Water of Life without charge. [18]And I solemnly declare to everyone who reads this book: If anyone adds anything to what is written here, God shall add to him the plagues described in this book. [19]And if anyone subtracts any part of these prophecies, God shall take away his share in the Tree of Life, and in the Holy City just described.

[20]"He who has said all these things declares: Yes, I am coming soon!"

Amen! Come, Lord Jesus!

[21]The grace of our Lord Jesus Christ be with you all. Amen!

INVITED

22:17 When Jesus met the Samaritan woman at the well he told her of the Living Water that he could supply (John 4:10-15). This image is used again as Christ invites anyone to come and drink of the Water of Life. The gospel is unlimited in scope—all people, everywhere, may come. Salvation cannot be earned, but God gives it freely. We live in a world desperately thirsty for Living Water, and many are dying of thirst. But it's still not too late. Let us invite everyone to come and drink.

MEGA Themes

GOD'S SOVEREIGNTY God is sovereign. He is greater than any power in the universe, and not to be compared with any leader, government, or religion. He controls history for the purpose of uniting true believers in loving fellowship with him.

Though Satan's power may temporarily increase, we are not to be led astray. God is all-powerful. Satan is not equivalent to God. God is supreme, in control, and will safely bring his family into eternal life. God cares for us; we can trust him with our lives.

1. In what ways is God revealed as sovereign in Revelation?

2. How does God's sovereignty offer security to you?
3. Based on your security in God, what plans, dreams, worries, and/or problems can you bring to him today? How does trusting God with both hopes and fears enable you to experience his sovereignty?

CHRIST'S RETURN Christ came to earth as a "Lamb," the symbol of his perfect sacrifice for our sin. He will return as the triumphant "Lion," the rightful ruler and conqueror. Christ will defeat Satan, settle accounts with all those who rejected him, and bring his faithful people into eternity.

Assurance of Christ's return gives suffering Christians the strength to endure. We can look forward to Christ's return as King and Judge. Because no one knows the time when Christ will appear, we must be ready at all times by keeping our faith strong.

1. Contrast the nature of Christ's first coming with his second coming.
2. What impact did Christ's first coming have on the world? On you?
3. What impact will Christ's second coming have on the world? On you?
4. How can the reality of Christ's second coming have a positive impact on you now?

GOD'S FAITHFUL PEOPLE John wrote to encourage the church not to worship the Roman emperor. He warns all God's faithful people to be devoted only to Christ. Revelation identifies the faithful people and what they should be doing until Christ returns.

Take your place in the ranks of God's faithful people: believe in Christ. Victory is sure for those who resist temptation and make loyalty to Christ their top priority.

1. What were some of the problems facing the churches in chapters 2 and 3? How were they to correct those problems?
2. Which of these churches can you identify with? How would you apply the command for correction?
3. What is the reward of those who endure faithfully?
4. Why is the cost of being a Christian worth it? Explain how this motivates you to grow in Christ rather than just surrendering to your weaknesses.

JUDGMENT One day God's anger toward sin will be fully and completely unleashed. Satan will be defeated; false religion will be destroyed. God will reward the faithful with eternal life, but all who refuse to believe in him will face eternal punishment.

God's final judgment will put an end to evil and injustice. We must be certain of our commitment to Christ if we want to escape this great final judgment. No one who is uncommitted to Christ will escape God's punishment. All who belong to Christ will receive their full rewards based on what Christ has done.

1. What will happen in the final judgment? (chapter 20)
2. Whose names are written in the Book of Life?
3. How does knowledge of this final judgment affect the way you live your life? The way you view death?
4. What would you like to communicate to your friends about the final judgment? How can you do this?

HOPE One day God will create a new heaven and a new earth. All believers will live with God forever in perfect peace and security. Those who have already died will be raised to life. These promises for the future bring us hope.

Our greatest hope is that what Christ promises will be true. When we have confidence in our final destination, we will be able to follow Christ with unwavering dedication no matter what we must face. Because we belong to him, there is no room for despair.

1. What will God do after the final judgment?
2. What is your ultimate hope in Christ?
3. When do you find yourself most needing to rely on this ultimate hope? How does "final hope" provide hope in the present?
4. What would you like to communicate to your friends about the final hope? How can you do this?

PSALMS

& Proverbs

*E*motions. We experience countless feelings every day, ranging from exuberant joy to deep grief. We feel pain when someone we love dies. We feel anger when things go wrong. We feel confusion when we don't understand. And we feel joy when something good happens. Emotions add spice and color to life. ■ The book of Psalms is about emotions. The pages are filled with them: anger, confusion, joy, pain, humility, bewilderment, contentment—all directed toward God. God created us with emotions, and he knows they will be part of our dealings with him. ■ Many people read the book of Psalms because of its honesty. Rather than ignoring the "negative" emotions or condemning them as sinful, the writers faced their feelings and continued to talk with God. ■ Psalms also is loved because of the clear picture of God it presents. Our emotions change constantly, but God is constant. While we fret, worry, and shout about injustice, God remains calm. When we fall on our faces before him because of our awful sin, he isn't surprised—he is gentle and ready to forgive. Psalms reminds us that God is exalted, the Creator and Ruler of the world, and worthy of worship. He alone is God. ■ How are you feeling today? Angry? Afraid? Frustrated? Or are you joyful, happy, and excited? Read Psalms and express yourself honestly to God.

STATS

PURPOSE: To provide poetry for the expression of praise, worship, and confession to God

AUTHORS: David wrote 73 psalms; Asaph wrote 12; the sons of Korah wrote 9; Solomon wrote 2; Heman (with the sons of Korah), Ethan, and Moses each wrote 1; and 51 psalms are anonymous, though the New Testament ascribes two of the anonymous psalms—Psalms 2 and 95—to David. (See Acts 4:25; Hebrews 4:7.)

DATE WRITTEN: Between the time of Moses (around 1440 B.C.) and the Babylonian captivity (586 B.C.)

SETTING: For the most part, the psalms were not intended to be narrations of historical events. However, they often parallel events in history, such as David's flight from Saul and his sin with Bathsheba.

KEY PERSON: David

KEY PLACE: God's holy Temple

SPECIAL FEATURES: Psalms has a unified plan, but each psalm can be read and understood alone. Psalms is probably the most widely read book of the Bible, because it is easy to relate to the writers' emotions.

Psalms

PSALM 1 PLEASING GOD. Oh, the joys of those who do not follow evil men's advice, who do not hang around with sinners, scoffing at the things of God. ²But they delight in doing everything God wants them to, and day and night are always meditating on his laws and thinking about ways to follow him more closely.

³They are like trees along a riverbank bearing luscious fruit each season without fail. Their leaves shall never wither, and all they do shall prosper.

⁴But for sinners, what a different story! They blow away like chaff before the wind. ⁵They are not safe on Judgment Day; they shall not stand among the godly.

⁶For the Lord watches over all the plans and paths of godly men, but the paths of the godless lead to doom.

PSALM 2 GREAT GOD. What fools the nations are to rage against the Lord! How strange that men should try to outwit God! ²For a summit conference of the nations has been called to plot against the Lord and his Messiah, Christ the King. ³"Come, let us break his chains," they say, "and free ourselves from all this slavery to God."

⁴But God in heaven merely laughs! He is amused by all their puny plans. ⁵And then in fierce fury he rebukes them and fills them with fear.

⁶For the Lord declares, "This is the King of my choice, and I have enthroned him in Jerusalem, my holy city."

[7]His chosen one replies, "I will reveal the everlasting purposes of God, for the Lord has said to me, 'You are my Son. This is your Coronation Day. Today I am giving you your glory.'" [8]"Only ask and I will give you all the nations of the world. [9]Rule them with an iron rod; smash them like clay pots!"

[10]O kings and rulers of the earth, listen while there is time. [11]Serve the Lord with reverent fear; rejoice with trembling. [12]Fall down before his Son and kiss his feet before his anger is roused and you perish. I am warning you—his wrath will soon begin. But oh, the joys of those who put their trust in him!

FRIENDSHIP

Last year Rhonda moved from a small Midwest town to Chicago. She didn't want to leave her hometown, but her dad got a job offer he'd been wanting to get for years. Rhonda left behind close friends, a great youth group, a good school, and 14 years' worth of memories.

Chicago was a brand-new world. In Baxter everybody knew everybody else (not to mention everybody else's business). In Chicago Rhonda felt invisible. The first month, she cried almost every night.

Even when Rhonda's family found a church with a big youth group, things didn't improve. Nobody in the group really reached out. They were so into their own little circle of friends, they barely noticed Rhonda.

At about that same time, however, a group of kids at school began reaching out to "the new girl." One guy called himself an agnostic. Two of the girls claimed to have had abortions. Another guy had a police record. None of them went to church.

When Rhonda's parents expressed concern about her choice of friends, Rhonda retorted, "Well, they may be a little bit on the wild side, but at least they treat me like a person. I'd rather hang out with them than with those fakes at the church!"

What would you do in Rhonda's situation? Do friends really affect the direction of our lives? Read Psalm 1, noting especially the first verse.

PSALM 3 MY HOPE. *A Psalm of David when he fled from his son Absalom*

O Lord, so many are against me. So many seek to harm me. I have so many enemies. [2]So many say that God will never help me. [3]But Lord, you are my shield, my glory, and my only hope. You alone can lift my head, now bowed in shame.

[4]I cried out to the Lord, and he heard me from his Temple in Jerusalem. [5]Then I lay down and slept in peace and woke up safely, for the Lord was watching over me. [6]And now, although ten thousand enemies surround me on every side, I am not afraid. [7]I will cry to him, "Arise, O Lord! Save me, O my God!" And he will slap them in the face, insulting them and breaking off their teeth.

[8]For salvation comes from God. What joys he gives to all his people.

PSALM 4 WHO CAN KEEP US SAFE? O God, you have declared me perfect in your eyes; you have always cared for me in my distress; now hear me as I call again. Have mercy on me. Hear my prayer.

[2]The Lord God asks, "Sons of men, will you forever turn my glory into shame by worshiping these silly idols, when every claim that's made for them is false?"

[3]Mark this well: The Lord has set apart the redeemed for himself. Therefore he will listen to me and answer when I call to him. [4]Stand before the Lord in awe, and do not sin against him. Lie quietly upon your bed in silent meditation. [5]Put your trust in the Lord, and offer him pleasing sacrifices.

[6]Many say that God will never help us. Prove them wrong, O Lord, by letting the light of your face shine down upon us. [7]Yes, the gladness you have given me is far greater than their joys at harvest time as they gaze at their bountiful crops. [8]I will lie down in peace and sleep, for though I am alone, O Lord, you will keep me safe.

PSALM 5 GOD HATES LIES. O Lord, hear me praying; listen to my plea, O God my King, for I will never pray to anyone but you. [3]Each morning I will look to you in heaven and lay my requests before you, praying earnestly.

[4]I know you get no pleasure from wickedness and cannot tolerate the slightest sin. [5]Therefore, proud sinners will not survive your searching gaze, for how you hate their evil deeds. [6]You will destroy them for their lies; how you abhor all murder and deception.

[7]But as for me, I will come into your Temple protected by your mercy and your love; I will worship you with deepest awe.

[8]Lord, lead me as you promised me you would; otherwise my enemies will conquer me. Tell me clearly what to do, which way to turn. [9]For they cannot speak one truthful word. Their hearts are filled to the brim with wickedness. Their suggestions are full of the stench of sin and death. Their tongues are filled with flatteries to gain their wicked ends. [10]O God, hold them responsible. Catch them in their own traps; let them fall beneath

PRAYERS

4:3 David knew God heard his prayers and would answer him. We, too, can know that God listens and answers when we call on him. Sometimes we think God will not hear us because we have fallen short of his high standards for holy living. But God listens to us because we have been forgiven. When you feel that your prayers are bouncing off the ceiling, remember that as a believer you have been set apart by God, and he loves you. He hears and answers (although his answers may not be what we expect). Look at your problems in the light of God's power instead of looking at God in the light of your problems.

the weight of their own transgressions, for they rebel against you.

[11]But make everyone rejoice who puts his trust in you. Keep them shouting for joy because you are defending them. Fill all who love you with your happiness. [12]For you bless the godly man, O Lord; you protect him with your shield of love.

PSALM **6** GOD HEARS MY PRAYERS.

No, Lord! Don't punish me in the heat of your anger. [2]Pity me, O Lord, for I am weak. Heal me, for my body is sick, [3]and I am upset and disturbed. My mind is filled with apprehension and with gloom. Oh, restore me soon.

[4]Come, O Lord, and make me well. In your kindness save me. [5]For if I die, I cannot give you glory by praising you before my friends. [6]I am worn out with pain; every night my pillow is wet with tears. [7]My eyes are growing old and dim with grief because of all my enemies.

[8]Go, leave me now, you men of evil deeds, for the Lord has heard my weeping [9]and my pleading. He will answer all my prayers. [10]All my enemies shall be suddenly dishonored, terror-stricken, and disgraced. God will turn them back in shame.

PSALM **7** THE PERFECT JUDGE.

I am depending on you, O Lord my God, to save me from my persecutors. [2]Don't let them pounce upon me as a lion would and maul me and drag me away with no one to rescue me. [3]It would be different, Lord, if I were doing evil things— [4]if I were paying back evil for good or unjustly attacking those I dislike. [5]Then it would be right for you to let my enemies destroy me, crush me to the ground, and trample my life in the dust.

[6]But Lord! Arise in anger against the anger of my enemies. Awake! Demand justice for me, Lord! [7,8]Gather all peoples before you; sit high above them, judging their sins. But justify me publicly; establish my honor and truth before them all. [9]End all wickedness, O Lord, and bless all who truly worship God; for you, the righteous God, look deep within the hearts of men and examine all their motives and their thoughts.

[10]God is my shield; he will

REVENGE

7:1-6 Have you ever been falsely accused or badly hurt and wanted revenge? David wrote this psalm in response to the slanderous accusations of those who claimed he was trying to kill King Saul and seize the throne (1 Samuel 24:9-11). Instead of seeking revenge, David cried out to God for justice. The proper response to slander is prayer, not revenge. God says, "Justice belongs to me; I will repay them" (Deuteronomy 32:35-36; Hebrews 10:30). Instead of striking back, ask God to take your case, bring justice, and restore your reputation.

REASONS TO READ PSALMS

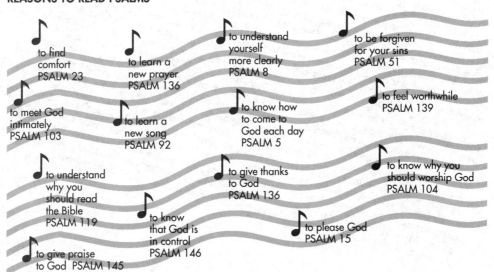

to find comfort PSALM 23

to learn a new prayer PSALM 136

to understand yourself more clearly PSALM 8

to be forgiven for your sins PSALM 51

to meet God intimately PSALM 103

to learn a new song PSALM 92

to know how to come to God each day PSALM 5

to feel worthwhile PSALM 139

to understand why you should read the Bible PSALM 119

to know that God is in control PSALM 146

to give thanks to God PSALM 136

to know why you should worship God PSALM 104

to give praise to God PSALM 145

to please God PSALM 15

God's word was written to be studied, understood, and applied, and the book of Psalms lends itself most directly to application. We may turn to Psalms looking for something, but sooner or later we will meet Someone. As we read and memorize the psalms, we will discover how much they are already part of us. They put our deepest hurts, longings, thoughts, and prayers into words. They gently push us toward being what God designed us to be—people who love and live for him.

MADE IN THE IMAGE OF GOD

"Van Gogh's *Irises* sells for $53.9 million." **A**rt sales don't usually make headlines, but occasionally you'll see a front-page story about a particular painting being sold for an astronomical sum. To the untrained eye, even such an extremely expensive work may seem to be only a few lines splashed across the canvas, holding no meaning or appeal. What makes such a picture worth so much? **T**he answer is found tucked away, almost unnoticeably, in the lower right-hand corner—the artist's signature. Even if the image on the canvas seems rather ordinary or commonplace, the name Van Gogh or Gauguin or Rembrandt scrawled somewhere on it makes the piece priceless. The reason the artwork is worth so much is simple: it came from the hands of a master. **T**he same is true of humanity. Some people think that human beings are valuable because we have somehow acquired dignity in a meaningless universe. Others think our value comes from being the most highly evolved creatures on this planet. But Psalm 8 teaches that what makes us worthwhile is the fact that we are made in the image of God. In spite of our sinfulness, we still bear the image of the One who made us. **I**t's easy to believe this of kind, attractive, thoughtful people. But it is just as true of the murderer on death row and the terrorist who bombs airports. We're not on our goodness—which is a good thing because we are full of sinfulness. We're like a masterpiece that has had mud and filth splattered on it. Underneath the dirt, we still have the Master's signature on us. That should help guide how we treat each other—even the people we don't like. **W**hen you are confronted by people who seem to exist only to make your life unpleasant—the classmate who majors in being obnoxious, the parent who seems only to criticize and put down, the teacher who takes pleasure in putting red marks on your papers—remember: that person bears the signature of the Master Artist. So do you. Regardless of our sinfulness, that fact makes each of us the most priceless object in the universe.

defend me. He saves those whose hearts and lives are true and right.

¹¹God is a judge who is perfectly fair, and he is angry with the wicked every day. ¹²Unless they repent, he will sharpen his sword and slay them.

He has bent and strung his bow ¹³and fitted it with deadly arrows made from shafts of fire.

¹⁴The wicked man conceives an evil plot, labors with its dark details, and brings to birth his treachery and lies; ¹⁵let him fall into his own trap. ¹⁶May the violence he plans for others boomerang upon himself; let him die.

¹⁷Oh, how grateful and thankful I am to the Lord because he is so good. I will sing praise to the name of the Lord who is above all lords.

PSALM **8** WHY GOD MADE US. O Lord our God, the majesty and glory of your name fills all the earth and overflows the heavens. ²You have taught the little children to praise you perfectly. May their example shame and silence your enemies!

³When I look up into the night skies and see the work of your fingers—the moon and the stars you have made— ⁴I cannot understand how you can bother with mere puny man, to pay any attention to him!

⁵And yet you have made him only a little lower than the angels and placed a crown of glory and honor upon his head.

⁶You have put him in charge of everything you made; everything is put under his authority: ⁷all sheep and oxen, and wild animals too, ⁸the birds and fish, and all the life in the sea. ⁹O Jehovah, our Lord, the majesty and glory of your name fills the earth.

PSALM **9** GOD HEARS US. O Lord, I will praise you with all my heart and tell everyone about the marvelous things you do. ²I will be glad, yes, filled with joy because of you. I will sing your praises, O Lord God above all gods.

³My enemies will fall back and perish in your presence; ⁴you have vindicated me; you have endorsed my work, declaring from your throne that it is good. ⁵ You have rebuked the nations and destroyed the wicked, blotting out their names forever and ever. ⁶O enemies of mine, you are doomed forever. The Lord will destroy your cities; even the memory of them will disappear.

⁷,⁸But the Lord lives on forever; he sits upon his throne to judge justly the nations of the world. ⁹All who are oppressed may come to him. He is a refuge for them in their times of trouble. ¹⁰All those who know your mercy, Lord, will count on you for help. For you have never yet forsaken those who trust in you.

¹¹Oh, sing out your praises to the God who lives in Jerusalem. Tell the world about his unforgettable deeds. ¹²He who avenges murder has an open ear to those who cry to him for justice. He does not ignore the prayers of men in trouble when they call to him for help.

¹³And now, O Lord, have mercy on me; see how I suffer at the hands of those who hate me. Lord, snatch me back from the jaws of death. ¹⁴Save me, so that I can praise you publicly before all the people at Jerusalem's gates and rejoice that you have rescued me.

¹⁵The nations fall into the pitfalls they have dug for others; the trap they set has snapped on them. ¹⁶The Lord is famous for the way he punishes the wicked in their own snares!

¹⁷The wicked shall be sent away to hell; this is the fate of all the nations forgetting the Lord. ¹⁸For the needs of the needy shall not be ignored forever; the hopes of the poor shall not always be crushed.

¹⁹O Lord, arise and judge and punish the nations; don't let them defy you! ²⁰Make them tremble in fear; put the nations in their place until at last they know they are but puny men.

WITNESSING

9:1-2 One of the natural results of praising God is witnessing. When we know God is wonderful, we naturally want to tell others and have them praise God with us.

"Here's what I did..."

There was a time a couple of years ago when I was really down on myself, depressed and very confused. I couldn't do anything to make myself feel better. I prayed about it and one night I opened my Bible looking for consolation. I leafed through the Psalms, remembering that a Christian friend had once told me that whenever he felt bad, it helped to read the Psalms.

What caught my eye that night was the heading for Psalm 6: "A prayer for deliverance in time of distress. God is able to deliver us." That's what I felt—distressed; and what I needed was deliverance. I read and reread that psalm. It spoke straight to my heart, and it showed me that God was there for me, as always. Do I ever love him!

Now whenever I'm in doubt about God's love and care, I turn to that Psalm. It reminds me that God is always there and that he will lead me through any dark time I experience, just as he did that one night when I first read Psalm 6.

Jenna

AGE 17

PSALM 10 WILL THE WICKED SUCCEED? Lord, why are you standing aloof and far away? Why do you hide when I need you the most?

²Come and deal with all these proud and wicked men who viciously persecute the poor. Pour upon these men the evil they planned for others! ³For these men brag of all their evil lusts; they revile God and congratulate those the Lord abhors, whose only goal in life is money.

⁴These wicked men, so proud and haughty, seem to think that God is dead. They wouldn't think of looking for him! ⁵Yet there is success in everything they do, and their enemies fall before them. They do not see your punishment awaiting them. ⁶They boast that neither God nor man can ever keep them down—somehow they'll find a way!

⁷Their mouths are full of profanity and lies and fraud. They are always boasting of their evil plans. ⁸They lurk in dark alleys of the city and murder passersby. ⁹Like lions they crouch silently, waiting to pounce upon the poor. Like hunters they catch their victims in their traps. ¹⁰The unfortunate are overwhelmed by their superior strength and fall beneath their blows. ¹¹"God isn't watching," they say to themselves; "he'll never know!"

¹²O Lord, arise! O God, crush them! Don't forget the poor or anyone else in need. ¹³Why do you let the wicked get away with this contempt for God? For they think that God will never call them to account. ¹⁴Lord, you see what they are doing. You have noted each evil act. You know what trouble and grief they have caused. Now punish them. O Lord, the poor man trusts himself to you; you are known as the helper of the helpless. ¹⁵Break the arms of these wicked men. Go after them until the last of them is destroyed.

¹⁶The Lord is King forever and forever. Those who follow other gods shall be swept from his land. ¹⁷Lord, you know the hopes of humble people. Surely you will hear their cries and comfort their hearts by helping them. ¹⁸You will be with the orphans and all who are oppressed, so that mere earthly man will terrify them no longer.

PSALM 11 GOD SEES IT ALL. How dare you tell me, "Flee to the mountains for safety," when I am trusting in the Lord?

²For the wicked have strung their bows, drawn their arrows tight against the bowstrings, and aimed from ambush at the people of God. ³"Law and order have collapsed," we are told. "What can the righteous do but flee?"

⁴But the Lord is still in his holy temple; he still rules from heaven. He closely watches everything that happens here on earth. ⁵He puts the righteous and the wicked to the test; he hates those loving violence. ⁶He will rain down fire and brimstone on the wicked and scorch them with his burning wind.

⁷For God is good, and he loves goodness; the godly shall see his face.

PSALM 12 CAN I TRUST GOD? Lord! Help! Godly men are fast disappearing. Where in all the world can dependable men be found? ²Everyone deceives and flatters and lies. There is no sincerity left.

³,⁴But the Lord will not deal gently with people who act like that; he will destroy those proud liars who say, "We will lie to our hearts' content. Our lips are our own; who can stop us?"

⁵The Lord replies, "I will arise and defend the oppressed, the poor, the needy. I will rescue them as they have longed for me to do." ⁶The Lord's promise is sure. He speaks no careless word; all he says is purest truth, like silver seven times refined. ⁷O Lord, we know that you will forever preserve your own from the reach of evil men, ⁸although they prowl on every side and vileness is praised throughout the land.

PSALM 13 I NEED HELP. How long will you forget me, Lord? Forever? How long will you look the other way when I am in need? ²How long must I be hiding daily anguish in my heart? How long shall my enemy have the upper hand?

³Answer me, O Lord my God; give me light in my darkness lest I die. ⁴Don't let my enemies say, "We have conquered him!" Don't let them gloat that I am down.

⁵But I will always trust in you and in your mercy and shall rejoice in your salvation. ⁶I will sing to the Lord because he has blessed me so richly.

PSALM 14 FOOLISH OR WISE? That man is a fool who says to himself, "There is no God!" Anyone who talks like that is warped and evil and cannot really be a good person at all.

²The Lord looks down from heaven on all man-

DOUBTS

10:1 To the psalmist, God seemed far away. "Why do you hide when I need you the most?" he asked God. But though he had honest doubts, he did not stop praying or assume that God no longer cared. He was not complaining but was asking God to hurry to his aid. It is during those times when we feel most alone or oppressed that we need to keep praying, telling God about our troubles.

LYING

12:2-4 We may be tempted to believe that lies are relatively harmless, even useful at times. But deceit, flattery, boasting, and lies are not overlooked by God. Each of these sins originates from a bad attitude that eventually is expressed in our speech. The tongue can be our greatest enemy because, though small, it can do great damage (James 3:5). Be careful how you use yours.

kind to see if there are any who are wise, who want to please God. ³But no, all have strayed away; all are rotten with sin. Not one is good, not one! ⁴They eat my people like bread and wouldn't think of praying! Don't they really know any better?

⁵Terror shall grip them, for God is with those who love him. ⁶He is the refuge of the poor and humble when evildoers are oppressing them. ⁷Oh, that the time of their rescue were already here, that God would come from Zion now to save his people. What gladness when the Lord has rescued Israel!

PSALM 15 WHAT MAKES SOMEONE GOOD? Lord,
who may go and find refuge and shelter in your tabernacle up on your holy hill?

²Anyone who leads a blameless life and is truly sincere. ³Anyone who refuses to slander others, does not listen to gossip, never harms his neighbor, ⁴speaks out against sin, criticizes those committing it, commends the faithful followers of the Lord, keeps a promise even if it ruins him, ⁵does not crush his debtors with high interest rates, and refuses to testify against the innocent despite the bribes offered him—such a man shall stand firm forever.

PSALM 16 GOD'S FRIEND.
Save me, O God, because I have come to you for refuge. ²I said to him, "You are my Lord; I have no other help but yours." ³I want the company of the godly men and women in the land; they are the true nobility. ⁴Those choosing other gods shall all be filled with sorrow; I will not offer the sacrifices they do or even speak the names of their gods.

⁵The Lord himself is my inheritance, my prize. He is my food and drink, my highest joy! He guards all that is mine. ⁶He sees that I am given pleasant brooks and meadows as my share! What a wonderful inheritance! ⁷I will bless the Lord who counsels me; he gives me wisdom in the night. He tells me what to do.

⁸I am always thinking of the Lord; and because he is so near, I never need to stumble or to fall.

⁹Heart, body, and soul are filled with joy. ¹⁰For you will not leave me among the dead; you will not allow your beloved one to rot in the grave. ¹¹You have let me experience the joys of life and the exquisite pleasures of your own eternal presence.

PSALM 17 SEEING GOD FACE-TO-FACE. I am
pleading for your help, O Lord; for I have been honest and have done what is right, and you must listen to my earnest cry! ²Publicly acquit me, Lord, for you are always fair. ³You have tested me and seen that I am good. You have come even in the night and found nothing amiss and know that I have told the truth. ⁴I have followed your commands and have not gone along with cruel and evil men. ⁵My feet have not slipped from your paths.

⁶Why am I praying like this? Because I know you will answer me, O God! Yes, listen as I pray. ⁷Show me your strong love in wonderful ways, O Savior of all those seeking your help against their foes. ⁸Protect me as you would the pupil of your eye; hide me in the shadow of your wings as you hover over me.

⁹My enemies encircle me with murder in their eyes. ¹⁰They are pitiless and arrogant. Listen to their boasting. ¹¹They close in upon me and are

"Here's what I did..."

I couldn't get out of my mind what my friend had told me. She said that when she was eight years old, her oldest brother raped her—more than once.

I felt angry, mainly at God. I just couldn't understand it. How could God let such a terrible thing happen to such a wonderful person? Why hadn't he done anything to stop it—like have the phone ring, or someone come to the door, or someone come home? Anything!

This really bothered me for a long time. Then I was reading in the Psalms, and I came across Psalm 13. I saw that the psalmist was angry at God, too—he was actually complaining to God! That gave me freedom to spill out my heart to God. I told God all my bitter and confused thoughts concerning what happened to my friend. I cried. I even lashed out at God. And the result of telling God what was on my mind and my heart was an incredible peace. Psalm 13 showed me that God always wants to hear what's on my mind, even when I'm angry with him. In the end, I found that God is there for me—even if I don't always understand all his ways.

Eric

AGE 16

ready to throw me to the ground. ¹²They are like lions eager to tear me apart, like young lions hiding and waiting their chance.

¹³,¹⁴Lord, arise and stand against them. Push them back! Come and save me from these men of the world whose only concern is earthly gain—these men whom you have filled with your treasures so that their children and grandchildren are rich and prosperous.

¹⁵But as for me, my contentment is not in wealth but in seeing you and knowing all is well between us. And when I awake in heaven, I will be fully satisfied, for I will see you face to face.

PSALM 18 GOD CARES FOR US. *This song of David was written at a time when the Lord had delivered him from his many enemies, including Saul.*

Lord, how I love you! For you have done such tremendous things for me.

²The Lord is my fort where I can enter and be safe; no one can follow me in and slay me. He is a rugged mountain where I hide; he is my Savior, a rock where none can reach me, and a tower of safety. He is my shield. He is like the strong horn of a mighty fighting bull. ³All I need to do is cry to him—oh, praise the Lord—and I am saved from all my enemies!

⁴Death bound me with chains, and the floods of ungodliness mounted a massive attack against me. ⁵Trapped and helpless, I struggled against the ropes that drew me on to death.

⁶In my distress I screamed to the Lord for his help. And he heard me from heaven; my cry reached his ears. ⁷Then the earth rocked and reeled, and mountains shook and trembled. How they quaked! For he was angry. ⁸Fierce flames leaped from his mouth, setting fire to the earth; smoke blew from his nostrils. ⁹He bent the heavens down and came to my defense; thick darkness was beneath his feet. ¹⁰Mounted on a mighty angel, he sped swiftly to my aid with wings of wind. ¹¹He enshrouded himself with darkness, veiling his approach with dense clouds dark as murky waters. ¹²Suddenly the brilliance of his presence broke through the clouds with lightning and a mighty storm of hail.

¹³The Lord thundered in the heavens; the God above all gods has spoken—oh, the hailstones; oh, the fire! ¹⁴He flashed his fearful arrows of lightning and routed all my enemies. See how they run! ¹⁵Then at your command, O Lord, the sea receded from the shore. At the blast of your breath the depths were laid bare.

¹⁶He reached down from heaven and took me and drew me out of my great trials. He rescued me from deep waters. ¹⁷He delivered me from my strong enemy, from those who hated me—I who was helpless in their hands.

¹⁸On the day when I was weakest, they attacked. But the Lord held me steady. ¹⁹He led me to a place of safety, for he delights in me.

²⁰The Lord rewarded me for doing right and being pure. ²¹For I have followed his commands and have not sinned by turning back from following him. ²²I kept close watch on all his laws; I did not refuse a single one. ²³I did my best to keep them all, holding myself back from doing wrong. ²⁴And so the Lord has paid me with his blessings, for I have done what is right, and I am pure of heart. This he knows, for he watches my every step.

²⁵Lord, how merciful you are to those who are merciful. And you do not punish those who run from evil. ²⁶You give blessings to the pure but pain to those who leave your paths. ²⁷You deliver the humble but condemn the proud and haughty ones. ²⁸You have turned on my light! The Lord my God has made my darkness turn to light. ²⁹Now in your strength I can scale any wall, attack any troop.

³⁰What a God he is! How perfect in every way! All his promises prove true. He is a shield for everyone who hides behind him. ³¹For who is God except our Lord? Who but he is as a rock?

³²He fills me with strength and protects me wherever I go. ³³He gives me the surefootedness of a mountain goat upon the crags. He leads me safely along the top of the cliffs. ³⁴He prepares me for battle and gives me strength to draw an iron bow!

³⁵You have given me your salvation as my shield. Your right hand, O Lord, supports me;

SHIELD

18:30 Many say belief in God is a crutch for weak people who cannot make it on their own. God is indeed a shield to protect us when we are too weak to face certain trials by ourselves. He strengthens, protects, and guides us in order to send us back into an evil world to fight for him. David was not a coward; he was a mighty warrior who, with all his armies and weapons, knew that only God could ultimately protect and save him.

GREATNESS

18:35 David offers an interesting twist to the concept of greatness, saying that God's gentleness made him great. Our society believes that greatness is attained through a combination of opportunity, talent, and aggressiveness. But true greatness comes from living according to God's laws and standards and recognizing that all we have comes from the gentleness of God's merc

The heavens heavens heavens heavens heavens ARE TELLING THE GLORY OF GOD THE GLORY OF GOD THE GLORY OF GOD They are a marvelous of his display CRAFTSMANSHIP.

your gentleness has made me great. [36]You have made wide steps beneath my feet so that I need never slip. [37]I chased my enemies; I caught up with them and did not turn back until all were conquered. [38]I pinned them to the ground; all were helpless before me. I placed my feet upon their necks. [39]For you have armed me with strong armor for the battle. My enemies quail before me and fall defeated at my feet. [40]You made them turn and run; I destroyed all who hated me. [41]They shouted for help, but no one dared to rescue them; they cried to the Lord, but he refused to answer them. [42]So I crushed them fine as dust and cast them to the wind. I threw them away like sweepings from the floor. [43-45]You gave me victory in every battle. The nations came and served me. Even those I didn't know before come now and bow before me. Foreigners who have never seen me submit instantly. They come trembling from their strongholds.

[46]God is alive! Praise him who is the great rock of protection. [47]He is the God who pays back those who harm me and subdues the nations before me.

[48]He rescues me from my enemies; he holds me safely out of their reach and saves me from these powerful opponents. [49]For this, O Lord, I will praise you among the nations. [50]Many times you have miraculously rescued me, the king you appointed. You have been loving and kind to me and will be to my descendants.

PSALM 19 MORE VALUABLE THAN GOLD.

The heavens are telling the glory of God; they are a marvelous display of his craftsmanship. [2]Day and night they keep on telling about God. [3,4]Without a sound or word, silent in the skies, their message reaches out to all the world. The sun lives in the heavens where God placed it [5]and moves out across the skies as radiant as a bridegroom going to his wedding, or as joyous as an athlete looking forward to a race! [6]The sun crosses the heavens from end to end, and nothing can hide from its heat.

[7,8]God's laws are perfect. They protect us, make us wise, and give us joy and light. [9]God's laws are pure, eternal, just. [10]They are more desirable than gold. They are sweeter than honey dripping from a honeycomb. [11]For they warn us away from harm and give success to those who obey them.

[12]But how can I ever know what sins are lurking in my heart? Cleanse me from these hidden faults. [13]And keep me from deliberate wrongs; help me to stop doing them. Only then can I be free of guilt and innocent of some great crime.

[14]May my spoken words and unspoken thoughts be pleasing even to you, O Lord my Rock and my Redeemer.

PSALM 20 GOD IS WITH US.

In your day of trouble, may the Lord be with you! May the God of Jacob keep you from all harm.[2]May he send you aid from his sanctuary in Zion. [3]May he remember with pleasure the gifts you have given him, your

A friend of mine is convinced that being good will get him into heaven. I'm starting to agree with him. God won't send people who live good lives to hell, will he? *I WONDER . . .*

Teachers have developed two systems for grading their students' performance. First, there is the "curve." Put simply, in a particular class 50 percent of the students will score above the average, 50 percent will score below. Often those who score below the average still have a chance to pass. That's why students seem to like this system best.

Then there is the "set" scale. With this system, a certain percentage determines your grade. If you get below a 75 percent grade, for example, you fail.

Most people would like to believe that God grades on a curve. In other words, if they're better than others, it will be all right with God. All they have to do to pass is not steal or kill anyone, mind their own business, and wait for heaven.

Unfortunately, God doesn't grade that way.

Psalm 14:1-3 is clear. There isn't anyone who is good. Not one! All of us have strayed away. This doesn't mean we're all murderers, it means our hearts are stained with the sin of Adam—the desire to be god of our life and run it ourselves. No one has a pure heart. (See Luke 18:18-26 for a great illustration.)

God has *one* method of salvation. In his wisdom, he gave everyone the opportunity to go to heaven by faith, not by works. All a person has to do to be saved is believe that Christ paid the penalty for sin and rose again from the dead: "Because of his kindness you have been saved through trusting Christ. And even trusting is not of yourselves; it too is a gift from God. Salvation is not a reward for the good we have done, so none of us can take any credit for it" (Ephesians 2:8-9).

Most people say this is too simple. But that's the whole idea! God isn't trying to make it tough on us. He wants us to be with him forever!

Throughout your life you will run into people who believe that simply living a good life means heaven awaits. A good life is important to point people to a holy God, but it will not buy you a ticket to heaven. That ticket has already been paid for by Jesus Christ! But you must come to him to get it.

sacrifices and burnt offerings. [4]May he grant you your heart's desire and fulfill all your plans. [5]May there be shouts of joy when we hear the news of your victory, flags flying with praise to God for all that he has done for you. May he answer all your prayers!

[6]"God save the king"—I know he does! He hears me from highest heaven and sends great

victories. [7]Some nations boast of armies and of weaponry, but our boast is in the Lord our God. [8]Those nations will collapse and perish; we will arise to stand firm and sure!

[9]Give victory to our king, O Lord; oh, hear our prayer.

PSALM 21 THANKING GOD FOR HIS ANSWERS.

How the king rejoices in your strength, O Lord! How he exults in your salvation. [2]For you have given him his heart's desire, everything he asks you for!

[3]You welcomed him to the throne with success and prosperity. You set a royal crown of solid gold upon his head. [4]He asked for a long, good life, and you have granted his request; the days of his life stretch on and on forever. [5]You have given him fame and honor. You have clothed him with splendor and majesty. [6]You have endowed him with eternal happiness. You have given him the unquenchable joy of your presence. [7]And because the king trusts in the Lord, he will never stumble, never fall; for he depends upon the steadfast love of the God who is above all gods.

[8]Your hand, O Lord, will find your enemies, all who hate you. [9,10]When you appear, they will be destroyed in the fierce fire of your presence. The Lord will destroy them and their children. [11]For these men plot against you, Lord, but they cannot possibly succeed. [12]They will turn and flee when they see your arrows aimed straight at them.

[13]Accept our praise, O Lord, for all your glorious power. We will write songs to celebrate your mighty acts!

PSALM 22 EVERYONE HATES ME—DOES GOD?

My God, my God, why have you forsaken me? Why do you refuse to help me or even to listen to my groans? [2]Day and night I keep on weeping, crying for your help, but there is no reply— [3,4]for *you are holy.*

The praises of our fathers surrounded your throne; they trusted you and you delivered them. [5]You heard their cries for help and saved them; they were never disappointed when they sought your aid.

[6]But I am a worm, not a man, scorned and despised by my own people and by all mankind. [7]Everyone who sees me mocks and sneers and shrugs. [8]"Is this the one who rolled his burden on the Lord?" they laugh. "Is this the one who claims the Lord delights in him? We'll believe it when we see God rescue him!"

[9-11]Lord, how you have helped me before! You took me safely from my mother's womb and brought me through the years of infancy. I have depended upon you since birth; you have always been my God. Don't leave me now, for trouble is near and no one else can possibly help.

[12]I am surrounded by fearsome enemies, strong as the giant bulls from Bashan. [13]They come at me with open jaws, like roaring lions attacking their prey. [14]My strength has drained away like water, and all my bones are out of joint. My heart melts like wax; [15]my strength has dried up like sun-baked clay; my tongue sticks to my mouth, for you have laid me in the dust of death. [16]The enemy, this gang of evil men, circles me like a pack of dogs; they have pierced my hands and feet. [17]I can count every bone in my body. See these men of evil gloat and stare; [18]they divide my clothes among themselves by a toss of the dice.

[19]O Lord, don't stay away. O God my Strength, hurry to my aid. [20]Rescue me from death; spare my precious life from all these evil men. [21]Save me from these lions' jaws and from the horns of these wild oxen. Yes, God will answer me and rescue me.

[22]I will praise you to all my brothers; I will stand up before the congregation and testify of the wonderful things you have done. [23]"Praise the Lord, each one of you who fears him," I will say. "Each of you must fear and reverence his name. Let all Israel sing his praises, [24]for he has not despised my cries of deep despair; he has not turned and walked away. When I cried to him, he heard and came."

[25]Yes, I will stand and praise you before all the people. I will publicly fulfill my vows in the presence of all who reverence your name.

[26]The poor shall eat and be satisfied; all who seek the Lord shall find him and shall praise his name. Their hearts shall rejoice with everlasting joy. [27]The whole earth shall see it and return to the Lord; the people of every nation shall worship him.

[28]For the Lord is King and rules the nations. [29]Both proud and humble together, all who are mortal—born to die— shall worship him. [30]Our children too shall serve him, for

LEADERS

21:7 A good leader trusts God and depends upon his steadfast love. Too often our leaders trust in their own cleverness and strength, or in the "god" of military power. But God is above all these gods. If you want to be a leader, keep the Lord God at the center of your life and depend on him.

GUIDANCE

23:2-3 When we allow God our Shepherd to guide us, we have contentment. When we choose to sin, however, we are choosing to go our own way and we cannot blame God for the environment in which we find ourselves. Our Shepherd knows the "meadow grass" and "quiet streams" that will restore us. We will reach these places only by following him obediently. Rebelling against the Shepherd's leading is actually rebelling against our own best interests for the future. We must remember this the next time we are tempted to go our way rather than the Shepherd's way.

Because

THE LORD

is

S H E P H E R D

M Y

I have

EVeRyTHing

I need!

they shall hear from us about the wonders of the Lord; [31]generations yet unborn shall hear of all the miracles he did for us.

PSALM 23 THE GOOD SHEPHERD. Because the Lord is my Shepherd, I have everything I need!

[2,3]He lets me rest in the meadow grass and leads me beside the quiet streams. He gives me new strength. He helps me do what honors him the most.

[4]Even when walking through the dark valley of death I will not be afraid, for you are close beside me, guarding, guiding all the way.

[5]You provide delicious food for me in the presence of my enemies. You have welcomed me as your guest; blessings overflow!

[6]Your goodness and unfailing kindness shall be with me all of my life, and afterwards I will live with you forever in your home.

PSALM 24 WHO OWNS THE WORLD? The earth belongs to God! Everything in all the world is his! [2]He is the one who pushed the oceans back to let dry land appear.

[3]Who may climb the mountain of the Lord and enter where he lives? Who may stand before the Lord? [4]Only those with pure hands and hearts, who do not practice dishonesty and lying. [5]They will receive God's own goodness as their blessing from him, planted in their lives by God himself, their Savior. [6]These are the ones who are allowed to stand before the Lord and worship the God of Jacob.

[7]Open up, O ancient gates, and let the King of Glory in. [8]Who is this King of Glory? The Lord, strong and mighty, invincible in battle. [9]Yes, open wide the gates and let the King of Glory in.

[10]Who is this King of Glory? The Commander of all of heaven's armies!

PSALM 25 GOD WILL BE MY GUIDE. To you, O Lord, I pray. [2]Don't fail me, Lord, for I am trusting you. Don't let my enemies succeed. Don't give them victory over me. [3]None of those who have faith in God will ever be disgraced for trusting him. But all who harm the innocent shall be defeated.

[4]Show me the path where I should go, O Lord; point out the right road for me to walk. [5]Lead me; teach me; for you are the God who gives me salvation. I have no hope except in you. [6,7]Overlook my youthful sins, O Lord! Look at me instead through eyes of mercy and forgiveness, through eyes of everlasting love and kindness.

[8]The Lord is good and glad to teach the proper path to all who go astray; [9]he will teach the ways that are right and best to those who humbly turn to him. [10]And when we obey him, every path he guides us on is fragrant with his loving-kindness and his truth.

[11]But Lord, my sins! How many they are. Oh, pardon them for the honor of your name.

[12]Where is the man who fears the Lord? God will teach him how to choose the best.

[13]He shall live within God's circle of blessing, and his children shall inherit the earth.

[14]Friendship with God is reserved for those who reverence him. With them alone he shares the secrets of his promises.

[15]My eyes are ever looking to the Lord for help, for he alone can rescue me. [16]Come, Lord, and show me your mercy, for I am helpless, overwhelmed, in deep distress; [17]my problems go from bad to worse. Oh, save me from them all! [18]See my sorrows; feel my pain; forgive my sins. [19]See how many enemies I have and how viciously they hate me! [20]Save me from them! Deliver my life from their power! Oh, let it never be said that I trusted you in vain!

[21]Assign me Godliness and Integrity as my bodyguards, for I expect you to protect me [22]and to ransom Israel from all her troubles.

ENEMIES

25:2 Seventy-two psalms—almost half the book—speak about enemies. Enemies are those who not only oppose us, but also oppose God's way of living. Enemies can also be temptations—money, success, prestige, lust. And our greatest enemy is Satan. David asked God to keep his enemies from overcoming him because they opposed what God stood for. If his enemies succeeded, David feared that many would think that living for God was futile. David did not question his own faith—he knew that God would triumph. But he didn't want his enemies' success to be an obstacle to the faith of others.

PSALM 26 ON GOD'S SIDE. Dismiss all the charges against me, Lord, for I have tried to keep your laws and have trusted you without wavering. [2]Cross-examine me, O Lord, and see that this is so;

test my motives and affections too. ³For I have taken your loving-kindness and your truth as my ideals.⁴I do not have fellowship with tricky, two-faced men; they are false and hypocritical. ⁵I hate the sinners' hangouts and refuse to enter them. ⁶I wash my hands to prove my innocence and come before your altar, ⁷singing a song of thanksgiving and telling about your miracles.

⁸Lord, I love your home, this shrine where the brilliant, dazzling splendor of your presence lives.

⁹,¹⁰Don't treat me as a common sinner or murderer who plots against the innocent and demands bribes.

¹¹No, I am not like that, O Lord; I try to walk a straight and narrow path of doing what is right; therefore in mercy save me.

¹²I publicly praise the Lord for keeping me from slipping and falling.

PSALM 27 WHY SHOULD I BE AFRAID? The Lord is my light and my salvation; he protects me from danger—whom shall I fear? ²When evil men come to destroy me, they will stumble and fall! ³Yes, though a mighty army marches against me, my heart shall know no fear! I am confident that God will save me.

⁴The one thing I want from God, the thing I seek most of all, is the privilege of meditating in his Temple, living in his presence every day of my life, delighting in his incomparable perfections and glory. ⁵There I'll be when troubles come. He will hide me. He will set me on a high rock ⁶out of reach of all my enemies. Then I will bring him sacrifices and sing his praises with much joy.

⁷Listen to my pleading, Lord! Be merciful and send the help I need.

⁸My heart has heard you say, "Come and talk with me, O my people." And my heart responds, "Lord, I am coming."

⁹Oh, do not hide yourself when I am trying to find you. Do not angrily reject your servant. You have been my help in all my trials before; don't leave me now. Don't forsake me, O God of my salvation. ¹⁰For if my father and mother should abandon me, you would welcome and comfort me.

¹¹Tell me what to do, O Lord, and make it plain because I am surrounded by waiting enemies. ¹²Don't let them get me, Lord! Don't let me fall into their hands! For they accuse me of things I never

did, and all the while are plotting cruelty. ¹³I am expecting the Lord to rescue me again, so that once again I will see his goodness to me here in the land of the living.

¹⁴Don't be impatient. Wait for the Lord, and he will come and save you! Be brave, stouthearted, and courageous. Yes, wait and he will help you.

PSALM 28 PRAYER IS POWERFUL. I plead with you to help me, Lord, for you are my Rock of safety. If you refuse to answer me, I might as well give up and die. ²Lord, I lift my hands to heaven and implore your help. Oh, listen to my cry.

³Don't punish me with all the wicked ones who speak so sweetly to their neighbors while planning to murder them. ⁴Give them the punishment they so richly deserve! Measure it out to them in proportion to their wickedness; paythem back for all their evil deeds. ⁵They care nothing for God or what he has done or what he has made; therefore God will dismantle them like old buildings, never to be rebuilt again.

⁶Oh, praise the Lord, for he has listened to my pleadings! ⁷He is my strength, my shield from every danger. I trusted in him, and he helped me. Joy rises in my heart until I burst out in songs of praise to him. ⁸The Lord protects his people and gives victory to his anointed king.

⁹Defend your people, Lord; defend and bless your chosen ones. Lead them like a shepherd and carry them forever in your arms.

PSALM 29 NATURE SPEAKS OF GOD. Praise the Lord, you angels of his; praise his glory and his strength. ²Praise him for his majestic glory, the glory of his name. Come before him clothed in sacred garments.

³The voice of the Lord echoes from the clouds. The God of glory thunders through the skies. ⁴So powerful is his voice; so full of majesty. ⁵,⁶It breaks down the cedars. It splits the giant trees of Lebanon. It shakes Mount Lebanon and Mount Sirion. They leap and skip before him like young calves! ⁷The voice of the Lord thunders through the lightning. ⁸It resounds through the deserts and shakes the wilderness of Kadesh. ⁹The voice of the Lord spins and topples the mighty oaks. It strips the forests bare. They whirl and sway beneath the

RELIANCE

27:5 We often run to God when we are experiencing difficulties. But David sought God's guiding presence *every day*. When troubles came his way, he was already in God's presence and prepared to handle any test. Believers can call to God for help at any time. How shortsighted it is to call on God only after trouble has come! Many of our problems could be avoided or handled far more easily by constantly relying on God's help and direction.

MASQUERADE

28:3-5 It's easy to pretend friendship. Wicked people often masquerade in goodness, pretending kindness or friendship to gain their own ends. David, in his royal position, may have met many who pretended friendship for selfish reasons. David knew God would punish them accordingly, but he prayed that their punishment would come swiftly. True believers live honest lives before God and others.

blast. But in his temple all are praising, "Glory, glory to the Lord."

[10]At the Flood the Lord showed his control of all creation. Now he continues to unveil his power. [11]He will give his people strength. He will bless them with peace.

PSALM 30 SAVED FROM THE GRAVE. I will

praise you, Lord, for you have saved me from my enemies. You refuse to let them triumph over me. [2]O Lord my God, I pleaded with you, and you gave me my health again. [3]You brought me back from the brink of the grave, from death itself, and here I am alive!

[4]Oh, sing to him you saints of his; give thanks to his holy name. [5]His anger lasts a moment; his favor lasts for life! Weeping may go on all night, but in the morning there is joy.

[6,7]In my prosperity I said, "This is forever; nothing can stop me now! The Lord has shown me his favor. He has made me steady as a mountain." Then, Lord, you turned your face away from me and cut off your river of blessings. Suddenly my courage was gone; I was terrified and panic-stricken. [8]I cried to you, O Lord; oh, how I pled: [9]"What will you gain, O Lord, from killing me? How can I praise you then to all my friends? How can my dust in the grave speak out and tell the world about your faithfulness? [10]Hear me, Lord; oh, have pity and help me." [11]Then he turned my sorrow into joy! He took away my clothes of mourning and clothed me with joy [12]so that I might sing glad praises to the Lord instead of lying in silence in the grave. O Lord my God, I will keep on thanking you forever!

PSALM 31 BELIEVE, NO MATTER WHAT. Lord, I

trust in you alone. Don't let my enemies defeat me. Rescue me because you are the God who always does what is right. [2]Answer quickly when I cry to you; bend low and hear my whispered plea. Be for me a great Rock of safety from my foes. [3]Yes, you are my Rock and my fortress; honor your name by leading me out of this peril. [4]Pull me from the trap my enemies have set for me. For you alone are strong enough. [5,6]Into your hand I commit my spirit.

You have rescued me, O God who keeps his promises. I worship only you; how you hate all those who worship idols, those imitation gods. [7]I am radiant with joy because of your mercy, for you have listened to my troubles and have seen the crisis in my soul. [8]You have not handed me over to my enemy but have given me open ground in which to maneuver.

[9,10]O Lord, have mercy on me in my anguish. My eyes are red from weeping; my health is broken from sorrow. I am pining away with grief; my years are shortened, drained away because of sadness. My sins have sapped my strength; I stoop with sorrow and with shame. [11]I am scorned by all my enemies and even more by my neighbors and friends. They dread meeting me and look the other way when I go by. [12]I am forgotten like a dead man, like a broken and discarded pot. [13]I heard the lies about me, the slanders of my enemies. Everywhere I looked I was afraid, for they were plotting against my life.

[14,15]But I am trusting you, O Lord. I said, "You alone are my God; my times are in your hands. Rescue me from those who hunt me down relentlessly. [16]Let your favor shine again upon your servant; save me just because you are so kind! [17]Don't disgrace me, Lord, by not replying when I call to you for aid. But let the wicked be shamed by what they trust in; let them lie silently in their graves, [18]their lying lips quieted at last—the lips of these arrogant men who are accusing honest men of evil deeds."

[19]Oh, how great is your goodness to those who publicly declare that you will rescue them. For you have stored up great blessings for those who trust and reverence you. [20]Hide your loved ones in the shelter of your presence, safe beneath your hand, safe from all conspiring men. [21]Blessed is the Lord, for he has shown me that his never-failing love protects me like the walls of a fort! [22]I spoke too hastily when I said, "The Lord has deserted me," for you listened to my plea and answered me.

[23]Oh, love the Lord, all of you who are his people; for the Lord protects those who are loyal to him, but harshly punishes all who haughtily reject him. [24]So cheer up! Take courage if you are depending on the Lord.

SECURITY

30:6-7 Prosperity had made David feel invincible. Although he knew his riches and power had come from God, they had gone to his head, making him proud. Wealth, power, and fame have an intoxicating effect on people, making them feel self-reliant, self-secure, and independent of God. But this is a false security that is shattered easily. Don't be trapped by the false security of prosperity. Depend on God for your security and you won't be shaken when worldly possessions disappear.

PSALM 32 GOD FORGIVES. What happiness for

those whose guilt has been forgiven! What joys when sins are covered over! What relief for those who have confessed their sins and God has cleared their record.

[3]There was a time when I wouldn't admit what a sinner I was. But my dishonesty made me miserable and filled my days with frustration. [4]All day and all night your hand was heavy on me. My

BELIEVING

33:4 A person's words are measured by the quality of his or her character. If your friends trust what you say, it is because they trust you. If you trust what God says, it is because you trust him to be the God he claims to be. If you doubt his words, you doubt the integrity of God himself. If you believe that God is truly God, then believe what he says!

strength evaporated like water on a sunny day [5]until I finally admitted all my sins to you and stopped trying to hide them. I said to myself, "I will confess them to the Lord." And you forgave me! All my guilt is gone.

[6]Now I say that each believer should confess his sins to God when he is aware of them, while there is time to be forgiven. Judgment will not touch him if he does.

[7]You are my hiding place from every storm of life; you even keep me from getting into trouble! You surround me with songs of victory. [8]I will instruct you (says the Lord) and guide you along the best pathway for your life; I will advise you and watch your progress. [9]Don't be like a senseless horse or mule that has to have a bit in its mouth to keep it in line!

[10]Many sorrows come to the wicked, but abiding love surrounds those who trust in the Lord. [11]So rejoice in him, all those who are his, and shout for joy, all those who try to obey him.

PSALM 33 WHO IS IN CHARGE?

Let all the joys of the godly well up in praise to the Lord, for it is right to praise him. [2]Play joyous melodies of praise upon the lyre and on the harp; [3]Compose new songs of praise to him, accompanied skillfully on the harp; sing joyfully.

[4]For all God's words are right, and everything he does is worthy of our trust. [5]He loves whatever is just and good; the earth is filled with his tender love. [6]He merely spoke, and the heavens were formed and all the galaxies of stars. [7]He made the oceans, pouring them into his vast reservoirs.

[8]Let everyone in all the world—men, women and children—fear the Lord and stand in awe of him. [9]For when he but spoke, the world began! It appeared at his command! [10]And with a breath he can scatter the plans of all the nations who oppose him, [11]but his own plan stands forever. His intentions are the same for every generation.

[12]Blessed is the nation whose God is the Lord, whose people he has chosen as his own. [13-15]The Lord gazes down upon mankind from heaven where he lives. He has made their hearts and closely watches everything they do.

[16,17]The best-equipped army cannot save a king—for great strength is not enough to save anyone. A war horse is a poor risk for winning victories—it is strong, but it cannot save.

[18,19]But the eyes of the Lord are watching over those who fear him, who rely upon his steady love.

He will keep them from death even in times of famine! [20]We depend upon the Lord alone to save us. Only he can help us; he protects us like a shield. [21]No wonder we are happy in the Lord! For we are trusting him. We trust his holy name. [22]Yes, Lord, let your constant love surround us, for our hopes are in you alone.

PSALM 34 HOW TO TRUST GOD.

I will praise the Lord no matter what happens. I will constantly speak of his glories and grace. [2]I will boast of all his kindness to me. Let all who are discouraged take heart. [3]Let us praise the Lord together and exalt his name.

[4]For I cried to him and he answered me! He freed me from all my fears. [5]Others too were radiant at what he did for them. Theirs was no downcast look of rejection! [6]This poor man cried to the Lord—and the Lord heard him and saved him out of his troubles. [7]For the Angel of the Lord guards and rescues all who reverence him.

[8]Oh, put God to the test and see how kind he is! See for yourself the way his mercies shower down on all who trust in him. [9]If you belong to the Lord, reverence him; for everyone who does this has everything he needs. [10]Even strong young lions sometimes go hungry, but those of us who reverence the Lord will never lack any good thing.

[11]Sons and daughters, come and listen and let me teach you the importance of trusting and fearing the Lord. [12]Do you want a long, good life? [13]Then watch your tongue! Keep your lips from lying. [14]Turn from all known sin and spend your time in doing good. Try to live in peace with everyone; work hard at it.

[15]For the eyes of the Lord are intently watching all who live good lives, and he gives attention when they cry to him. [16]But the Lord has made up his mind to wipe out even the memory of evil men from the earth. [17]Yes, the Lord hears the good man when he calls to him for help and saves him out of all his troubles.

[18]The Lord is close to those whose hearts are breaking; he rescues those who are humbly sorry for their sins. [19]The good

ENOUGH

34:9-10 "Those of us who reverence the Lord will never lack any good thing." This is not a blanket promise that all Christians will be rich. It is David's observation of God's goodness—all those who call upon God will be answered, sometimes in unexpected ways.

Remember, our deepest needs are spiritual. Many Christians face unbearable poverty and hardship. David was saying that to have God is to have all that a person needs. God is enough.

If you feel you don't have everything you need, ask yourself: (1) Is this really a need? (2) Is this really good for me? (3) Is this the best time for me to have what I desire? Even if you answer yes to all three questions, God may allow you to go without to help you grow more dependent on him. We may need to learn that we need *him* more than those things.

man does not escape all troubles—he has them too. But the Lord helps him in each and every one. [20]Not one of his bones is broken.

[21]Calamity will surely overtake the wicked; heavy penalties are meted out to those who hate the good. [22]But as for those who serve the Lord, he will redeem them; everyone who takes refuge in him will be freely pardoned.

PSALM 35 WHEN PEOPLE AREN'T FAIR. O Lord,

fight those fighting me; declare war on them for their attacks on me. [2]Put on your armor, take your shield and protect me by standing in front. [3]Lift your spear in my defense, for my pursuers are getting very close. Let me hear you say that you will save me from them. [4]Dishonor those who are trying to kill me. Turn them back and confuse them. [5]Blow them away like chaff in the wind— wind sent by the Angel of the Lord. [6]Make their path dark and slippery before them, with the Angel of the Lord pursuing them. [7]For though I did them no wrong, yet they laid a trap for me and dug a pitfall in my path. [8]Let them be overtaken by sudden ruin, caught in their own net and de-stroyed.

[9]But I will rejoice in the Lord. He shall rescue me! [10]From the bottom of my heart praise rises to him. Where is his equal in all of heaven and earth? Who else protects the weak and helpless from the strong, and the poor and needy from those who would rob them?

[11]These evil men swear to a lie. They accuse me of things I have never even heard about. [12]I do them good, but they return me harm. I am sinking down to death. [13]When they were ill, I mourned before the Lord in sackcloth, asking him to make them well; I refused to eat; I prayed for them with utmost earnestness, but God did not listen. [14]I went about sadly as though it were my mother, friend, or brother who was sick and nearing death. [15]But now that I am in trouble they are glad; they come together in meetings filled with slander against me—I didn't even know some of those who were there. [16]For they gather with the worthless fellows of the town and spend their time cursing me.

[17]Lord, how long will you stand there, doing nothing? Act now and rescue me, for I have but one life and these young lions are out to get it. [18]Save me, and I will thank you publicly before the entire congregation, before the largest crowd I can find.

[19]Don't give victory to those who fight me without any reason! Don't let them rejoice at my fall— let them die. [20]They don't talk of peace and doing good, but of plots against innocent men who are minding their own business. [21]They shout that they have seen *me* doing wrong! "Aha!" they say. "With our own eyes we saw him do it." [22]Lord, you know all about it. Don't stay silent! Don't desert me now!

[23]Rise up, O Lord my God; vindicate me. [24]Declare me "not guilty," for you are just. Don't let my enemies rejoice over me in my troubles. [25]Don't let them say, "Aha! Our dearest wish against him will soon be fulfilled!" and, "At last we have him!" [26]Shame them; let these who boast against me and who rejoice at my troubles be themselves overcome by misfortune that strips them bare of everything they own. Bare them to dishonor. [27]But give

"Here's what I did..."

There are two Scripture verses that sustain me daily. Because I have a disease called Epstein-Barr, I am always fatigued and often in pain. Psalm 34 reminds me that I can rely on God constantly for every ounce of strength I need, and it reminds me that God does hear the cry of those who are trusting him. I rely on these verses constantly for the "now" of every day.

Jeremiah 29:11 is my source of hope for the future. It reminds me that my constant worry about college and about ever getting over my illness is totally unnecessary; everything that happens is part of God's plan for my life. His plan is for good, not evil, and he intends to give me a future and a hope. He truly will take care of everything as I trust him.

I have memorized these passages and remind myself of the words whenever I need to—which is almost every day! They are a great source of comfort to me.

Anita

AGE 17

great joy to all who wish me well. Let them shout with delight, "Great is the Lord who enjoys helping his child!" [28]And I will tell everyone how great and good you are; I will praise you all day long.

PSALM 36 GOD'S GOODNESS IS GREAT. Sin

lurks deep in the hearts of the wicked, forever urging them on to evil deeds. They have no fear of God to hold them back. [2]Instead, in their conceit, they think they can hide their evil deeds and not get caught. [3]Everything they say is crooked and deceitful; they are no longer wise and good. [4]They lie awake at night to hatch their evil plots instead of planning how to keep away from wrong.

[5]Your steadfast love, O Lord, is as great as all the heavens. Your faithfulness reaches beyond the

clouds. [6]Your justice is as solid as God's mountains. Your decisions are as full of wisdom as the oceans are with water. You are concerned for men and animals alike. [7]How precious is your constant love, O God! All humanity takes refuge in the shadow of your wings. [8]You feed them with blessings from your own table and let them drink from your rivers of delight.

[9]For you are the Fountain of life; our light is from your light. [10]Pour out your unfailing love on those who know you! Never stop giving your blessings to those who long to do your will.

[11]Don't let these proud men trample me. Don't let their wicked hands push me around. [12]Look! They have fallen. They are thrown down and will not rise again.

PSALM 37 KEEP DOING GOOD. Never envy the

wicked! [2]Soon they fade away like grass and disappear. [3]Trust in the Lord instead. Be kind and good to others; then you will live safely here in the land and prosper, feeding in safety.

[4]Be delighted with the Lord. Then he will give you all your heart's desires. [5]Commit everything you do to the Lord. Trust him to help you do it, and he will. [6]Your innocence will be clear to everyone. He will vindicate you with the blazing light of justice shining down as from the noonday sun.

[7]Rest in the Lord; wait patiently for him to act. Don't be envious of evil men who prosper.

[8]Stop your anger! Turn off your wrath. Don't fret and worry—it only leads to harm. [9]For the wicked shall be destroyed, but those who trust the Lord shall be given every blessing. [10]Only a little while and the wicked shall disappear. You will look for them in vain. [11]But all who humble themselves before the Lord shall be given every blessing and shall have wonderful peace.

[12,13]The Lord is laughing at those who plot against the godly, for he knows their judgment day is coming. [14]Evil men take aim to slay the poor; they are ready to butcher those who do right. [15]But their swords will be plunged into their own hearts, and all their weapons will be broken.

[16]It is better to have little and be godly than to own an evil man's wealth; [17]for the strength of evil men shall be broken, but the Lord takes care of those he has forgiven.

[18]Day by day the Lord observes the good deeds done by godly men, and gives them eternal rewards. [19]He cares for them when times are hard; even in famine, they will have enough. [20]But evil men shall perish. These enemies of God will wither like grass and disappear like smoke. [21]Evil men borrow and "cannot pay it back"! But the good man returns what he owes with some extra besides. [22]Those blessed by the Lord shall inherit the earth, but those cursed by him shall die.

[23]The steps of good men are directed by the Lord. He delights in each step they take. [24]If they fall it isn't fatal, for the Lord holds them with his hand.

[25]I have been young and now I am old. And in all my years I have never seen the Lord forsake a man who loves him; nor have I seen the children of the godly go hungry. [26]Instead, the godly are able to be generous with their gifts and loans to others, and their children are a blessing.

[27]So if you want an eternal home, leave your evil, low-down ways and live good lives. [28]For the Lord loves justice and fairness; he will never abandon his people. They will be kept safe forever; but all who love wickedness shall perish.

[29]The godly shall be firmly planted in the land and live there forever. [30,31]The godly man is a good counselor because he is just and fair and knows right from wrong.

[32]Evil men spy on the godly, waiting for an excuse to accuse them and then demanding their death. [33]But the Lord will not let these evil men succeed, nor let the godly be condemned when they are brought before the judge.

[34]Don't be impatient for the Lord to act! Keep traveling steadily along his pathway and in due season he will honor you with every blessing, and you will see the wicked destroyed. [35,36]I myself have seen it happen: a proud and evil man, towering like a cedar of Lebanon, but when I looked again, he was gone! I searched but could not find him! [37]But the good man—what a different story! For the good man—the blameless, the upright, the man of peace—he has a wonderful future ahead of him. For him there is a happy ending. [38]But evil men shall be destroyed, and their posterity shall be cut off.

[39]The Lord saves the godly! He is their salvation

TREASURE

37:1 We should never envy the popularity or wealth of the wicked. No matter how much they have, it will fade and vanish like grass that withers and dies. Those who follow God live in a different manner than the wicked. And in the end, the godly will have far greater treasures in heaven. What the unbeliever gets lasts a lifetime, if he is lucky. What you get from following God lasts an eternity.

ON THE EDGE

38:17 In David's confession of sin, he acknowledged that he was *constantly* on the verge of sin. No matter how hard we try to follow God, we are sinners by nature and we often sin. It is difficult to escape situations in which we are tempted. We stand on the verge of sin as if we are walking along the edge of a cliff and could fall at any moment. Those who think they are beyond sin are sure to fall. Therefore, the first step toward avoiding sin is to acknowledge our tendency to sin. Only then will we be ready to say no.

and their refuge when trouble comes. [40]Because they trust in him, he helps them and delivers them from the plots of evil men.

PSALM 38 CONFESSING OUR SIN. O Lord,

don't punish me while you are angry! [2]Your arrows have struck deep; your blows are crushing me. [3,4]Because of your anger, my body is sick, my health is broken beneath my sins. They are like a flood, higher than my head; they are a burden too heavy to bear. [5,6]My wounds are festering and full of pus. Because of my sins, I am bent and racked with pain. My days are filled with anguish. [7]My loins burn with inflammation, and my whole body is diseased. [8]I am exhausted and crushed; I groan in despair.

[9]Lord, you know how I long for my health once more. You hear my every sigh. [10]My heart beats wildly, my strength fails, and I am going blind. [11]My loved ones and friends stay away, fearing my disease. Even my own family stands at a distance.

[12]Meanwhile my enemies are trying to kill me. They plot my ruin and spend all their waking hours planning treachery. [13,14]But I am deaf to all their threats; I am silent before them as a man who cannot speak. I have nothing to say. [15]For I am waiting for you, O Lord my God. Come and protect me. [16]Put an end to their arrogance, these who gloat when I am cast down!

[17]How constantly I find myself upon the verge of sin; this source of sorrow always stares me in the face. [18]I confess my sins; I am sorry for what I have done. [19]But my enemies persecute with vigor and continue to hate me—though I have done nothing against them to deserve it. [20]They repay me evil for good and hate me for standing for the right.

[21]Don't leave me, Lord; don't go away! [22]Come quickly! Help me, O my Savior.

PSALM 39 SO WHAT'S IMPORTANT? I said to

myself, I'm going to quit complaining! I'll keep quiet, especially when the ungodly are around me. [2,3]But as I stood there silently the turmoil within me grew to the bursting point. The more I mused, the hotter the fires inside. Then at last I spoke and pled with God: [4]Lord, help me to realize how brief my time on earth will be. Help me to know that I am here for but a moment more. [5,6]My life is no longer than my hand! My whole lifetime is but a moment to you. Proud man! Frail as breath! A shadow! And all his busy rushing ends in nothing. He heaps up riches for someone else to spend. [7]And so, Lord, my only hope is in you.

[8]Save me from being overpowered by my sins, for even fools will mock me then.

[9]Lord, I am speechless before you. I will not open my mouth to speak one word of complaint, for my punishment is from you.

[10]Lord, don't hit me anymore—I am exhausted beneath your hand. [11]When you punish a man for his sins, he is destroyed, for he is as fragile as a moth-infested cloth; yes, man is frail as breath. [12]Hear my prayer, O Lord; listen to my cry! Don't sit back, unmindful of my tears. For I am your guest. I am a traveler passing through the earth, as all my fathers were.

[13]Spare me, Lord! Let me recover and be filled with happiness again before my death.

PSALM 40 OBEYING BY WAITING. I waited pa-

tiently for God to help me; then he listened and heard my cry. [2]He lifted me out of the pit of despair, out from the bog and the mire, and set my feet on a hard, firm path, and steadied me as I walked along. [3]He has given me a new song to sing, of praises to our God. Now many will hear of the glorious things he did for me, and stand in awe before the Lord, and put their trust in him. [4]Many blessings are given to those who trust the Lord and have no confidence in those who are proud or who trust in idols.

[5]O Lord my God, many and many a time you have done great miracles for us, and we are ever in your thoughts. Who else can do such glorious things? No one else can be compared with you. There isn't time to tell of all your wonderful deeds.

[6]It isn't sacrifices and offerings that you really want from your people. Burnt animals bring no special joy to your heart. But you have accepted the offer of my life-long service. [7]Then I said, "See, I have come, just as all the prophets foretold. [8]And I delight to do your will, my God, for your law is written upon my heart!"

[9]I have told everyone the good news that you forgive people's sins. I have not been timid about it, as you well know, O Lord. [10]I have not kept this good news hidden in my heart, but have proclaimed your loving-kindness and truth to all the congregation.

[11]O Lord, don't hold back your tender mercies from me! My only hope is in your love and faithfulness. [12]Otherwise I perish, for problems far too big for me to solve are piled higher than my head. Meanwhile my sins, too many to count, have all caught up with me, and I am ashamed to look up. My heart quails within me.

LIFE

39:4 Life is short no matter how long we live. If there is something important we want to do, we must not put it off for a better day. Ask yourself, "If I had only six months to live, what would I do?" Tell someone that you love him or her? Deal with an undisciplined area in your life? Tell someone about Jesus? Life is short—don't neglect what is truly important.

[13]Please, Lord, rescue me! Quick! Come and help me! [14,15]Confuse them! Turn them around and send them sprawling—all these who are trying to destroy me. Disgrace these scoffers with their utter failure!

[16]But may the joy of the Lord be given to everyone who loves him and his salvation. May they constantly exclaim, "How great God is!"

[17]I am poor and weak, yet the Lord is thinking about me right now! O my God, you are my helper. You are my Savior; come quickly, and save me. Please don't delay!

PSALM 41 GOD: THE ONLY TRUE FRIEND.

God blesses those who are kind to the poor. He helps them out of their troubles. [2]He protects them and keeps them alive; he publicly honors them and destroys the power of their enemies. [3]He nurses them when they are sick and soothes their pains and worries.

[4]"O Lord," I prayed, "be kind and heal me, for I have confessed my sins." [5]But my enemies say, "May he soon die and be forgotten!" [6]They act so friendly when they come to visit me while I am sick; but all the time they hate me and are glad that I am lying there upon my bed of pain. And when they leave, they laugh and mock. [7]They whisper together about what they will do when I am dead. [8]"It's fatal, whatever it is," they say. "He'll never get out of that bed!"

[9]Even my best friend has turned against me—a man I completely trusted; how often we ate together. [10]Lord, don't you desert me! Be gracious, Lord, and make me well again so I can pay them back! [11]I know you are pleased with me because you haven't let my enemies triumph over me. [12]You have preserved me because I was honest; you have admitted me forever to your presence.

[13]Bless the Lord, the God of Israel, who exists from everlasting ages past—and on into everlasting eternity ahead. Amen and amen!

PSALM 42 WHY AM I SO SAD?

As the deer pants for water, so I long for you, O God. [2]I thirst for God, the living God. Where can I find him to come and stand before him? [3]Day and night I weep for his help, and all the while my enemies taunt me.

"Where is this God of yours?" they scoff.

[4,5]Take courage, my soul! Do you remember those times (but how could you ever forget them!) when you led a great procession to the Temple on festival days, singing with joy, praising the Lord? Why then be downcast? Why be discouraged and sad? Hope in God! I shall yet praise him again. Yes, I shall again praise him for his help.

[6]Yet I am standing here depressed and gloomy, but I will meditate upon your kindness to this lovely land where the Jordan River flows and where Mount Hermon and Mount Mizar stand. [7]All your waves and billows have gone over me, and floods of sorrow pour upon me like a thundering cataract.

[8]Yet day by day the Lord also pours out his steadfast love upon me, and through the night I sing his songs and pray to God who gives me life.

[9]"O God my Rock," I cry, "why have you forsaken me? Why must I suffer these attacks from my enemies?" [10]Their taunts pierce me like a fatal wound; again and again they scoff, "Where is that God of yours?" [11]But, O my soul, don't be discouraged. Don't be upset. Expect God to act! For I know that I shall again have plenty of reason to praise him for all that he will do. He is my help! He is my God!

PSALM 43 GOD MAKES ME SMILE AGAIN.

O God, defend me from the charges of these merciless, deceitful men. [2]For you are God, my only place of refuge. Why have you tossed me aside? Why must I mourn at the oppression of my enemies?

[3]Oh, send out your light and your truth—let them lead me. Let them lead me to your Temple on your holy mountain, Zion. [4]There I will go to the altar of God, my exceeding joy, and praise him with my harp. O God—my God! [5]O my soul, why be so gloomy and discouraged? Trust in God! I shall again praise him for his wondrous help; he will make me smile again, *for he is my God!*

PSALM 44 GOD ALONE CAN SAVE US.

O God, we have heard of the glorious miracles you did in the days of long ago. Our forefathers have told us how you drove the heathen nations from this land and gave it all to us, spreading Israel from one end of the country to the other. [3]They did not conquer by their own strength and skill, but by your mighty power and because you smiled upon them and favored them.

[4]You are my King and my God. Decree victories for your people. [5]For it is only by your power and through your name that we tread down our enemies; [6]I do not trust my weapons. They could never save me. [7]Only you can give us the victory over those who hate us.

[8]My constant boast is God. I can never thank you enough! [9]And yet for a time, O Lord, you have tossed us aside in dishonor and have not helped us in our battles. [10]You have actually fought against us and defeated us before our foes. Our enemies have invaded our land and pillaged the countryside. [11]You have treated us like sheep in a slaughter pen and scattered us among the nations. [12]You sold us for a pittance. You valued us at nothing at all. [13]The neighboring nations laugh and mock at us because of all the evil you have sent. [14]You have made the word *Jew* a byword of contempt and shame among the nations, disliked by all. [15,16]I am constantly despised, mocked, taunted, and cursed by my vengeful enemies.

[17]And all this has happened, Lord, despite our loyalty to you. We have not violated your covenant. [18]Our hearts have not deserted you! We have not left your path by a single step. [19]If we had, we could understand your punishing us in the barren wilderness and sending us into darkness and death. [20]If we had turned away from worshiping our God and were worshiping idols, [21]would God not know it? Yes, he knows the secrets of every heart. [22]But that is not our case. For we are facing death threats constantly because of serving you! We are like sheep awaiting slaughter.

[23]Waken! Rouse yourself! Don't sleep, O Lord! Are we cast off forever? [24]Why do you look the other way? Why do you ignore our sorrows and oppression? [25]We lie face downward in the dust. [26]Rise up, O Lord, and come and help us. Save us by your constant love.

PSALM 45 THE KING'S WEDDING.

My heart is overflowing with a beautiful thought! I will write a lovely poem to the King, for I am as full of words as the speediest writer pouring out his story:

[2]You are the fairest of all;
Your words are filled with grace;
God himself is blessing you forever.
[3]Arm yourself, O Mighty One,
So glorious, so majestic!
[4]And in your majesty
Go on to victory,
Defending truth, humility, and justice.
Go forth to awe-inspiring deeds!
[5]Your arrows are sharp
In your enemies' hearts;
They fall before you.
[6]Your throne, O God, endures forever.
Justice is your royal scepter.
[7]You love what is good
And hate what is wrong.
Therefore God, your God,
Has given you more gladness
Than anyone else.

"Here's what I did..."

Everything was going wrong in my life. My parents were getting a divorce. My boyfriend broke up with me. I couldn't concentrate in school, so my grades started going down.

It began to affect my faith. I couldn't understand why God was letting all this happen to me. When I prayed, I felt like I was talking to myself. I guess I was mad at God, blaming him in my heart for the things that were happening.

I tried to read the Bible anyway, even though I was struggling spiritually. One day I read Psalm 46. Verse 10 really made me stop and think. This verse seemed to say, "Stop looking at your problems and look at me. Look at who I am." I realized God was in charge—he knew exactly what he was doing and had a purpose in mind for what I was going through. I just needed to accept it and believe he is a loving God who would never do a thing to hurt me.

That changed my perspective. Instead of blaming God, I asked him to help me through my struggles. And he has. Things are still rough sometimes, but now I know that God is for me, and he will work things out for good. As Romans 8:31 says, "If God is on our side, who can ever be against us?"

Jodi
AGE 17

[8]Your robes are perfumed with myrrh, aloes, and cassia. In your palaces of inlaid ivory, lovely music is being played for your enjoyment. [9]Kings' daughters are among your concubines. Standing beside you is the queen, wearing jewelry of finest gold from Ophir.

[10,11]"I advise you, O daughter, not to fret about your parents in your homeland far away. Your royal husband delights in your beauty. Reverence him, for he is your lord. [12]The people of Tyre, the richest

CONFIDENCE

46:1-3 The fear of mountains or cities suddenly crumbling into the sea by a nuclear blast haunts many people today. But the psalmist says that even if the world ends, "We need not fear!" Even in the face of utter destruction, he expressed a quiet confidence in God's ability to save him. It seems impossible to face the end of the world without fear, but the Bible is clear: God is our eternal refuge, even in the face of total destruction.

people of our day, will shower you with gifts and entreat your favors."

¹³The bride, a princess, waits within her chamber, robed in beautiful clothing woven with gold. ¹⁴Lovely she is, led beside her maids of honor to the king! ¹⁵What a joyful, glad procession as they enter in the palace gates! ¹⁶"Your sons will some day be kings like their father. They shall sit on thrones around the world!

¹⁷"I will cause your name to be honored in all generations; the nations of the earth will praise you forever."

PSALM 46 GOD IS ON OUR SIDE.

God is our refuge and strength, a tested help in times of trouble. ²And so we need not fear even if the world blows up and the mountains crumble into the sea. ³Let the oceans roar and foam; let the mountains tremble!

⁴There is a river of joy flowing through the city of our God—the sacred home of the God above all gods. ⁵God himself is living in that city; therefore it stands unmoved despite the turmoil everywhere. He will not delay his help. ⁶The nations rant and rave in anger—but when God speaks, the earth melts in submission and kingdoms totter into ruin.

⁷The Commander of the armies of heaven is here among us. He, the God of Jacob, has come to rescue us.

⁸Come, see the glorious things that our God does, how he brings ruin upon the world ⁹and causes wars to end throughout the earth, breaking and burning every weapon. ¹⁰"Stand silent! Know that I am God! I will be honored by every nation in the world!"

¹¹The Commander of the heavenly armies is here among *us!* He, the God of Jacob, has come to rescue *us!*

PSALM 47 GOD IS THE GREAT KING.

Come, everyone, and clap for joy! Shout triumphant praises to the Lord! ²For the Lord, the God above all gods, is awesome beyond words; he is the great King of all the earth. ³He subdues the nations before us ⁴and will personally select his choicest blessings for his Jewish people—the very best for those he loves.

⁵God has ascended with a mighty shout, with trumpets blaring. ^{6,7}Sing out your praises to our God, our King. Yes, sing your highest praises to our King, the King of all the earth. Sing thoughtful

praises! ⁸He reigns above the nations, sitting on his holy throne. ⁹The Gentile rulers of the world have joined with us in praising him—praising the God of Abraham—for the battle shields of all the armies of the world are his trophies. He is highly honored everywhere.

PSALM 48 GOD PROTECTS JERUSALEM.

How great is the Lord! How much we should praise him. He lives upon Mount Zion in Jerusalem. ²What a glorious sight! See Mount Zion rising north of the city high above the plains for all to see—Mount Zion, joy of all the earth, the residence of the great King.

³God himself is the defender of Jerusalem. ⁴The kings of the earth have arrived together to inspect the city. ⁵They marvel at the sight and hurry home again, ⁶afraid of what they have seen; they are filled with panic like a woman in travail! ⁷For God destroys the mightiest warships with a breath of wind. ⁸We have heard of the city's glory—the city of our God, the Commander of the armies of heaven. And now we see it for ourselves! God has established Jerusalem forever.

⁹Lord, here in your Temple we meditate upon your kindness and your love. ¹⁰Your name is known throughout the earth, O God. You are praised everywhere for the salvation you have scattered throughout the world. ¹¹O Jerusalem, rejoice! O people of Judah, rejoice! For God will see to it that you are finally treated fairly. ¹²Go, inspect the city! Walk around and count her many towers! ¹³Note her walls and tour her palaces so that you can tell your children.

¹⁴For this great God is our God forever and ever. He will be our guide until we die.

PSALM 49 MONEY CAN'T SAVE YOU.

Listen, everyone! High and low, rich and poor, all around the world—listen to my words, ³for they are wise and filled with insight.

⁴I will tell in song accompanied by harps the answer to one of life's most perplexing problems:

⁵*There is no need to fear when times of trouble come,* even though surrounded by enemies! ⁶They trust in their wealth and boast about how rich they are, ⁷yet not one of them, though rich as kings, can ransom his own brother from the penalty of sin! For God's forgiveness does not come that way. ^{8,9}For a soul is far too pre-

MAP

48:14 We often pray for God's guidance as we strugg[l]e with decisions. What we need is both guidance and a guide—a map that gives us landmarks and directions an[d] a constant companion who has an intimate knowledge [of] the way and will make sure we interpret the map correctly. The Bible is just suc[h] a map, and God is our constant companion and guide. Lean upon both the map and the Guide.

cious to be ransomed by mere earthly wealth. There is not enough of it in all the earth to buy eternal life for just one soul, to keep it out of hell.

[10]Rich man! Proud man! Wise man! You must die like all the rest! You have no greater lease on life than foolish, stupid men. You must leave your wealth to others. [11]You name your estates after yourselves as though your lands could be forever yours and you could live on them eternally. [12]But man with all his pomp must die like any animal. [13]Such is the folly of these men, though after they die they will be quoted as having great wisdom.

[14]Death is the shepherd of all mankind. And "in the morning" those who are evil will be the slaves of those who are good. For the power of their wealth is gone when they die, they cannot take it with them.

[15]But as for me, God will redeem my soul from the power of death, for he will receive me. [16]So do not be dismayed when evil men grow rich and build their lovely homes. [17]For when they die, they carry nothing with them! Their honors will not follow them. [18]Though a man calls himself happy all through his life—and the world loudly applauds success— [19]yet in the end he dies like everyone else and enters eternal darkness.

[20]For man with all his pomp must die like any animal.

PSALM **50** GOD WANTS OUR TRUE THANKS. The mighty God, the Lord, has summoned all mankind from east to west!

[2]God's glory-light shines from the beautiful Temple on Mount Zion. [3]He comes with the noise of thunder, surrounded by devastating fire; a great storm rages round about him. [4]He has come to judge his people. To heaven and earth he shouts, [5]"Gather together my own people who by their sacrifice upon my altar have promised to obey me." [6]God will judge them with complete fairness, for all heaven declares that he is just.

[7]O my people, listen! For I am your God. Listen! Here are my charges against you: [8]I have no complaint about the sacrifices you bring to my altar, for you bring them regularly. [9]But it isn't sacrificial bullocks and goats that I really want from you. [10,11]For all the animals of field and forest are mine! The cattle on a thousand hills! And all the birds upon the mountains! [12]If I were hungry, I would not mention it to you—for all the world is mine and everything in it. [13]No, I don't need your sacrifices of flesh and blood. [14,15]What I want from you is your true thanks; I want your promises fulfilled. *I want you to trust me in your times of trouble, so I can rescue you and you can give me glory.*

[16]But God says to evil men: Recite my laws no

longer and stop claiming my promises, [17]for you have refused my discipline, disregarding my laws. [18]You see a thief and help him, and spend your time with evil and immoral men. [19]You curse and lie, and vile language streams from your mouths. [20]You slander your own brother. [21]I remained silent—you thought I didn't care—but now your time of punishment has come, and I list all the above charges

I heard something about a sin that God cannot forgive. What is it?

What you are referring to is sinning against the Holy Spirit. "Even blasphemy against me or any other sin, can be forgiven— all except one: speaking against the Holy Spirit shall never be forgiven, either in this world or in the world to come" (Matthew 12:31-32).

I WONDER . . .

As you read in Psalm 51, everyone is born a sinner (verse 5). Left to ourselves we certainly would die, because our sinful nature separates us from God and from life (Romans 3:23; 6:23).

The good news is God did not leave us on our own. He sent Jesus to pay the penalty for us and to die in our place. This way he killed sin forever. All who receive Christ into their life and accept his gift of forgiveness are forgiven—period (John 1:12).

The only sin that cannot be forgiven is when someone refuses to receive Christ, ignoring or rejecting the Holy Spirit's work in his or her life.

The incident that caused King David to pray the prayer in Psalm 51 is found in 2 Samuel 12:1-23. David not only committed adultery, but he had the woman's husband murdered so he could marry her! That's pretty bad behavior for anyone, let alone a king.

When confronted with his sin a year after those events, David repented. He asked God to forgive him and to renew their relationship once again.

Though David's sins were great, God forgave him. God is always willing to forgive those who admit their mistakes and who genuinely try not to repeat them.

It has been said that "the only sin God cannot forgive is the one we have not confessed."

By daily coming to God in humility, trust, and dependence, we show him that we mean business in keeping our relationship with him clean and growing.

David's prayer is the perfect example of a humble heart seeking after the only thing in life that really matters: a close relationship with God.

against you. [22]This is the last chance for all of you who have forgotten God, before I tear you apart— and no one can help you then.

[23]But true praise is a worthy sacrifice; this really honors me. Those who walk my paths will receive salvation from the Lord.

PSALM **51** A PRAYER OF FORGIVENESS. *Written after Nathan the prophet had come to inform David of God's judgment against him because of* *his adultery with Bathsheba, and his murder of Uriah, her husband.*

O loving and kind God, have mercy. Have pity upon me and take away the awful stain of my transgressions. ²Oh, wash me, cleanse me from this guilt. Let me be pure again. ³For I admit my shameful deed—it haunts me day and night. ⁴It is against you and you alone I sinned and did this terrible thing. You saw it all, and your sentence against me is just. ⁵But I was born a sinner, yes, from the moment my mother conceived me. ⁶You deserve honesty from the heart; yes, utter sincerity and truthfulness. Oh, give me this wisdom.

⁷Sprinkle me with the cleansing blood and I shall be clean again. Wash me and I shall be whiter than snow. ⁸And after you have punished me, give me back my joy again. ⁹Don't keep looking at my sins—erase them from your sight. ¹⁰Create in me a new, clean heart, O God, filled with clean thoughts and right desires. ¹¹Don't toss me aside, banished forever from your presence. Don't take your Holy Spirit from me. ¹²Restore to me again the joy of your salvation, and make me willing to obey you. ¹³Then I will teach your ways to other sinners, and they—guilty like me—will repent and return to you. ¹⁴,¹⁵Don't sentence me to death. O my God, you alone can rescue me. Then I will sing of your forgiveness, for my lips will be unsealed—oh, how I will praise you.

¹⁶You don't want penance; if you did, how gladly I would do it! You aren't interested in offerings burned before you on the altar. ¹⁷It is a broken spirit you want—remorse and penitence. A broken and a contrite heart, O God, you will not ignore.

¹⁸And Lord, don't punish Israel for my sins—help your people and protect Jerusalem.

¹⁹And when my heart is right, then you will rejoice in the good that I do and in the bullocks I bring to sacrifice upon your altar.

PSALM 52 GOD PUNISHES THE WICKED. *Written by David to protest against his enemy Doeg (1 Samuel 22), who later slaughtered eighty-five priests and their families.*

You call yourself a *hero*, do you? You *boast* about this evil deed of yours against God's people. ²You are sharp as a tack in plotting your evil tricks. ³How you love wickedness—far more than good! And lying more than truth! ⁴You love to slander—you love to say anything that will do harm, O man with the lying tongue.

⁵But God will strike you down, pull you from your home, and drag you away from the land of the living. ⁶The followers of God will see it happen. They will watch in awe. Then they will laugh and say, ⁷"See what happens to those who despise God and trust in their wealth, and become ever more bold in their wickedness."

⁸But I am like a sheltered olive tree protected by the Lord himself. I trust in the mercy of God forever and ever. ⁹O Lord, I will praise you forever and ever for your punishment. And I will wait for your mercies—for everyone knows what a merciful God you are.

PSALM 53 SIN KEEPS US FROM GOD. Only a fool would say to himself, "There is no God." And why does he say it? Because of his wicked heart, his dark and evil deeds. His life is corroded with sin.

²God looks down from heaven, searching among all mankind to see if there is a single one who does right and really seeks for God. ³But all have turned their backs on him; they are filthy with sin—corrupt and rotten through and through. Not one is good, not one! ⁴How can this be? Can't they understand anything? For they devour my people like bread and refuse to come to God. ⁵But soon unheard-of terror will fall on them. God will scatter the bones of these, your enemies. They are doomed, for God has rejected them.

⁶Oh, that God would come from Zion now and save Israel! Only when the Lord himself restores them can they ever be really happy again.

PSALM 54 MY KEEPER.
Written by David at the time the men of Ziph tried to betray him to Saul.

Come with great power, O God, and save me! Defend me with your might! ²Oh, listen to my prayer. ³For violent men have risen against me—ruthless men who care nothing for God are seeking my life.

⁴But God is my helper. He is a friend of mine! ⁵He will cause the evil deeds of my en-

VICTIMS

51:4 Although David sinned with Bathsheba, he said he had sinned against God. When someone steals, murders, or slanders, it is against someone else—a victim. According to the world's standards, sex between two "consenting adults" is acceptable because nobody "gets hurt." But people *do* get hurt—in David's case, a man was murdered and a baby died. All sin hurts us and others, and ultimately it offends God because sin in any form is a rebellion against his way of living. When tempted to do wrong, remember that you will be sinning against God. That may help you stay on the right track.

FOOLS

53:1 Echoing the message of Psalm 14, David proclaimed that "Only a fool would say to himself, 'There is no God'" (see also Romans 3:10). People may say there is no God to cover their sin, to have an excuse to continue in sin, and/or to ignore the Judge so they can avoid the judgment. A "fool" is not necessarily lacking intelligence; many atheists and unbelievers are highly learned. Fools are people who reject God, the only one who can save them.

emies to boomerang upon them. Do as you promised and put an end to these wicked men, O God. [6]Gladly I bring my sacrifices to you; I will praise your name, O Lord, for it is good.

[7]God has rescued me from all my trouble, and triumphed over my enemies.

PSALM **55** **WHEN FRIENDS HURT US.** Listen to my prayer, O God; don't hide yourself when I cry to you. [2]Hear me, Lord! Listen to me! For I groan and weep beneath my burden of woe.

[3]My enemies shout against me and threaten me with death. They surround me with terror and plot to kill me. Their fury and hatred rise to engulf me. [4]My heart is in anguish within me. Stark fear overpowers me. [5]Trembling and horror overwhelm me. [6]Oh, for wings like a dove, to fly away and rest! [7]I would fly to the far-off deserts and stay there. [8]I would flee to some refuge from all this storm.

[9]O Lord, make these enemies begin to quarrel among themselves—destroy them with their own violence and strife. [10]Though they patrol their walls night and day against invaders, their real problem is internal—wickedness and dishonesty are entrenched in the heart of the city. [11]There is murder and robbery there, and cheating in the markets and wherever you look.

[12]It was not an enemy who taunted me—then I could have borne it; I could have hidden and escaped. [13]But it was you, a man like myself, my companion and my friend. [14]What fellowship we had, what wonderful discussions as we walked together to the Temple of the Lord on holy days.

[15]Let death seize them and cut them down in their prime, for there is sin in their homes, and they are polluted to the depths of their souls.

[16]But I will call upon the Lord to save me—and he will. [17]I will pray morning, noon, and night, pleading aloud with God; and he will hear and answer. [18]Though the tide of battle runs strongly against me, for so many are fighting me, yet he will rescue me. [19]God himself—God from everlasting ages past—will answer them! For they refuse to fear him or even honor his commands.

[20]This friend of mine betrayed me—I who was at peace with him. He broke his promises. [21]His words were oily smooth, but in his heart was war. His words were sweet, but underneath were daggers.

[22]Give your burdens to the Lord. He will carry them. He will not permit the godly to slip or fall. [23]He will send my enemies to the pit of destruction. Murderers and liars will not live out half their days. But I am trusting you to save me.

PSALM **56** **GOD IS ON MY SIDE.** Lord, have mercy on me; all day long the enemy troops press in. So many are proud to fight against me;

how they long to conquer me.

[3,4]But when I am afraid, I will put my confidence in you. Yes, I will trust the promises of God. And since I am trusting him, what can mere man do to me? [5]They are always twisting what I say. All their thoughts are how to harm me. [6]They meet together to perfect their plans; they hide beside the trail, listening for my steps, waiting to kill me. [7]They expect to get away with it. Don't let them, Lord. In anger cast them to the ground.

[8]You have seen me tossing and turning through the night. You have collected all my tears and preserved them in your bottle! You have recorded every one in your book.

[9]The very day I call for help, the tide of battle turns. My enemies flee! This one thing I *know: God is for me!*

[10,11]I am trusting God—oh, praise his promises! I am not afraid of anything mere man can do to me! Yes, praise his promises. [12]I will surely do what I have promised, Lord, and thank you for your help. [13]For you have saved me from death and my feet from slipping, so that I can walk before the Lord in the land of the living.

REAL FRIENDS

55:12-14 Nothing hurts as much as a wound from a "friend." Real friends, however, stick by you in times of trouble and bring healing, love, acceptance, and understanding. There will be times when friends lovingly confront us, but their motives will be to help. What kind of friend are you? Faithful or fickle? Don't betray those you love.

PSALM **57** **GREATER THAN HEAVEN.** O God, have pity, for I am trusting you! I will hide beneath the shadow of your wings until this storm is past. [2]I will cry to the God of heaven who does such wonders for me. [3]He will send down help from heaven to save me because of his love and his faithfulness. He will rescue me from these liars who are so intent upon destroying me. [4]I am surrounded by fierce lions—hotheads whose teeth are sharp as spears and arrows. Their tongues are like swords. [5]Lord, be exalted above the highest heavens! Show your glory high above the earth. [6]My enemies have set a trap for me. Frantic fear grips me. They have dug a pitfall in my path. But look! They themselves have fallen into it!

[7]O God, my heart is quiet and confident. No wonder I can sing your praises! [8]Rouse yourself, my soul! Arise, O harp and lyre! Let us greet the dawn with song! [9]I will thank you publicly throughout the land. I will sing your praises among the nations. [10]Your kindness and love are as vast as the heavens. Your faithfulness is higher than the skies.

[11]Yes, be exalted, O God, above the heavens. May your glory shine throughout the earth.

PSALM 58 GOD CARES.

Justice? You high and mighty politicians don't even know the meaning of the word! Fairness? Which of you has any left? Not one! All your dealings are crooked: you give "justice" in exchange for bribes. [3]These men are born sinners, lying from their earliest words! [4,5]They are poisonous as deadly snakes, cobras that close their ears to the most expert of charmers.

[6]O God, break off their fangs. Tear out the teeth of these young lions, Lord. [7]Let them disappear like water into thirsty ground. Make their weapons useless in their hands. [8]Let them be as snails that dissolve into slime and as those who die at birth, who never see the sun. [9]God will sweep away both old and young. He will destroy them more quickly than a cooking pot can feel the blazing fire of thorns beneath it.

[10]The godly shall rejoice in the triumph of right; they shall walk the blood-stained fields of slaughtered, wicked men. [11]Then at last everyone will know that good is rewarded, and that there is a God who judges justly here on earth.

PSALM 59 SAFETY IN A WICKED WORLD.

Written by David at the time King Saul set guards at his home to capture and kill him. (1 Samuel 19:11)
O my God, save me from my enemies. Protect me from these who have come to destroy me. [2]Preserve me from these criminals, these murderers. [3]They lurk in ambush for my life. Strong men are out there waiting. And not, O Lord, because I've done them wrong. [4]Yet they prepare to kill me. Lord, waken! See what is happening! Help me! [5](And O Jehovah, God of heaven's armies, God of Israel, arise and punish the heathen nations surrounding us.) Do not spare these evil, treacherous men. [6]At evening they come to spy, slinking around like dogs that prowl the city. [7]I hear them shouting insults and cursing God, for "No one will hear us," they think. [8]Lord, laugh at them! (And scoff at these surrounding nations too.)

[9]O God my Strength! I will sing your praises, for you are my place of safety. [10]My God is changeless in his love for me, and he will come and help me. He will let me see my wish come true upon my

enemies. [11]Don't kill them—for my people soon forget such lessons—but stagger them with your power and bring them to their knees. Bring them to the dust, O Lord our shield. [12,13]They are proud, cursing liars. Angrily destroy them. Wipe them out. (And let the nations find out, too, that God rules in Israel and will reign throughout the world.) [14,15]Let these evil men slink back at evening and prowl the city all night before they are satisfied, howling like dogs and searching for food.

[16]But as for me, I will sing each morning about your power and mercy. For you have been my high tower of refuge, a place of safety in the day of my distress. [17]O my Strength, to you I sing my praises; for you are my high tower of safety, my God of mercy.

PSALM 60 REAL HELP COMES FROM GOD.

Written by David at the time he was at war with Syria, with the outcome still uncertain; this was when Joab, captain of his forces, slaughtered twelve thousand men of Edom in the Valley of Salt.
O God, you have rejected us and broken our defenses; you have become angry and deserted us. Lord, restore us again to your favor. [2]You have caused this nation to tremble in fear; you have torn it apart. Lord, heal it now, for it is shaken to its depths. [3]You have been very hard on us and made us reel beneath your blows.

[4,5]But you have given us a banner to rally to; all who love truth will rally to it; then you can deliver your beloved people. Use your strong right arm to rescue us. [6,7]God has promised to help us. He has vowed it by his holiness! No wonder I exult! "Shechem, Succoth, Gilead, Manasseh—still are mine!" he says. "Judah shall continue to produce kings, and Ephraim great warriors. [8]Moab shall become my lowly servant, and Edom my slave. And I will shout in triumph over the Philistines."

[9,10]Who will bring me in triumph into Edom's strong cities? God will! He who cast us off! He who abandoned us to our foes! [11]Yes, Lord, help us against our enemies, for man's help is useless.

[12]With God's help we shall do mighty things, for he will trample down our foes.

PSALM 61 GOD ALWAYS HEARS US.

O God, listen to me! Hear my prayer! [2]For wherever I am, though far away at the ends of the earth, I will cry

---

CHANGELESS

59:10 David was hunted by those whose love had turned to jealousy, which was driving them to want to murder him. Trusted friends and his own son had turned against him. What changeable love these people had! But David knew that God's love for him was *changeless*. God's love for everyone who trusts him is changeless. When the love of others fails or disappoints us, we can rest in God's changeless love.

PRAISE

61:5 David continually praised God through both the good and difficult times of his life. His commitment to praise God every day showed his reverence for God. Do you find something to praise God for each day? As you do, you will find your heart elevated from daily distractions to lasting confidence.

---

to you for help. When my heart is faint and overwhelmed, lead me to the mighty, towering Rock of safety. ³For you are my refuge, a high tower where my enemies can never reach me. ⁴I shall live forever in your tabernacle; oh, to be safe beneath the shelter of your wings! ⁵For you have heard my vows, O God, to praise you every day, and you have given me the blessings you reserve for those who reverence your name.

⁶You will give me added years of life, as rich and full as those of many generations, all packed into one. ⁷And I shall live before the Lord forever. Oh, send your loving-kindness and truth to guard and watch over me, ⁸and I will praise your name continually, fulfilling my vow of praising you each day.

PSALM 62 GOD'S CONTROL. I
stand silently before the Lord, waiting for him to rescue me. For salvation comes from him alone. ²Yes, he alone is my Rock, my rescuer, defense and fortress. Why then should I be tense with fear when troubles come?

³,⁴But what is this? They pick on me at a time when my throne is tottering; they plot my death and use lies and deceit to try to force me from the throne. They are so friendly to my face while cursing in their hearts!

⁵But I stand silently before the Lord, waiting for him to rescue me. For salvation comes from him alone. ⁶Yes, he alone is my Rock, my rescuer, defense, and fortress—why then should I be tense with fear when troubles come?

⁷My protection and success come from God alone. He is my refuge, a Rock where no enemy can reach me. ⁸O my people, trust him all the time. Pour out your longings before him, for he can help! ⁹The greatest of men or the lowest—both alike are nothing in his sight. They weigh less than air on scales.

¹⁰Don't become rich by extortion and robbery; if your riches increase, don't be proud. ¹¹,¹²God has said it many times, that power belongs to him (and also, O Lord, steadfast love belongs to you). He rewards each one of us according to what our works deserve.

PSALM 63 I WANT TO BE NEAR GOD. *A Psalm of David when he was hiding in the wilderness of Judea.*

O God, my God! How I search for you! How I thirst for you in this parched and weary land where there is no water. How I long to find you! ²How I wish I could go into your sanctuary to see your strength and glory, ³for your love and kindness are better to me than life itself. How I praise you! ⁴I will bless you as long as I live, lifting up my hands to you in prayer. ⁵At last I shall be fully satisfied; I will praise you with great joy.

"Here's what I did..."

I'll never forget the day my father collapsed and was rushed to the hospital. The doctor told my mother and me that he'd suffered a severe heart attack and was now teetering between life and death; it could go either way. Standing with my mother by his bed, I prayed harder than I'd ever prayed before. I thought about how my father always reached out to others for Jesus, and I couldn't believe that God would be done with him yet. It almost seemed that God was reassuring me of this, but I asked him for a promise from his word. I didn't want to go just on feelings. The verse he brought to mind is Psalm 57:1: "O God, have pity, for I am trusting you! I will hide beneath the shadow of your wings until this storm is past."

I felt God was saying through this verse that if I took refuge in him and trusted him completely to be in control of the doctors and everything involved in my father's care, he would answer my prayer and make my father well. I was not to worry and not to try to make anything happen; hands off. I was to leave everything absolutely in God's hands and trust him for the outcome.

That's what I did. And I discovered that God is so faithful: my father did recover. God has continued to use Dad in marvelous ways to bring others to trust in Christ. And I learned something invaluable about trusting God and leaving everything in his hands when I'm facing life's storms.

David

AGE 17

⁶I lie awake at night thinking of you—⁷of how much you have helped me—and how I rejoice through the night beneath the protecting shadow of your wings. ⁸I follow close behind you, protected by your strong right arm. ⁹But those plotting to destroy me shall go down to the depths of hell. ¹⁰They are doomed to die by the sword, to become the food of jackals. ¹¹But I will rejoice in God. All who trust in him exult, while liars shall be silenced.

PSALM 64 WHEN PEOPLE MAKE TRAPS. Lord,
listen to my complaint: Oh, preserve my life from the conspiracy of these wicked men, these gangs of criminals. ³They cut me down with sharpened tongues; they aim their bitter words like arrows straight at my heart. ⁴They shoot from ambush at the innocent. Suddenly the deed is done, yet they are not afraid. ⁵They encourage each other to do

evil. They meet in secret to set their traps. "He will never notice them here," they say. [6]They keep a sharp lookout for opportunities of crime. They spend long hours with all their endless evil thoughts and plans.

[7]But God himself will shoot them down. Suddenly his arrow will pierce them. [8]They will stagger backward, destroyed by those they spoke against. All who see it happening will scoff at them. [9]Then everyone shall stand in awe and confess the greatness of the miracles of God; at last they will realize what amazing things he does. [10]And the godly shall rejoice in the Lord, and trust and praise him.

PSALM 65 GIVING THANKS TO GOD. O God in Zion, we wait before you in silent praise, and thus fulfill our vow. And because you answer prayer, all mankind will come to you with their requests. [3]Though sins fill our hearts, you forgive them all. [4]How greatly to be envied are those you have chosen to come and live with you within the holy tabernacle courts! What joys await us among all the good things there. [5]With dread deeds and awesome power you will defend us from our enemies, O God who saves us. You are the only hope of all mankind throughout the world and far away upon the sea.

[6]He formed the mountains by his mighty strength. [7]He quiets the raging oceans and all the world's clamor. [8]In the farthest corners of the earth the glorious acts of God shall startle everyone. The dawn and sunset shout for joy! [9]He waters the earth to make it fertile. The rivers of God will not run dry! He prepares the earth for his people and sends them rich harvests of grain. [10]He waters the furrows with abundant rain. Showers soften the earth, melting the clods and causing seeds to sprout across the land. [11,12]Then he crowns it all with green, lush pastures in the wilderness; hillsides blossom with joy. [13]The pastures are filled with flocks of sheep, and the valleys are carpeted with grain. All the world shouts with joy and sings.

PSALM 66 WE ARE IN GOD'S HAND. Sing to the Lord, all the earth! [2]Sing of his glorious name! Tell the world how wonderful he is.

[3]How awe-inspiring are your deeds, O God! How great your power! No wonder your enemies surrender! [4]All the earth shall worship you and sing of your glories. [5]Come, see the glorious things God

FORGIVEN

65:3 Although sins fill our hearts, God will forgive them all if we ask sincerely. Do you feel as though God could never forgive you, that your sins are too many, or that some of them are too great? Don't worry! God can and will forgive them all. Nobody is beyond redemption, and nobody is so full of sin that he cannot be made clean.

has done. What marvelous miracles happen to his people! [6]He made a dry road through the sea for them. They went across on foot. What excitement and joy there was that day!

[7]Because of his great power he rules forever. He watches every movement of the nations. O rebel lands, he will deflate your pride.

[8]Let everyone bless God and sing his praises; [9]for he holds our lives in his hands, and he holds our feet to the path. [10]You have purified us with fire, O Lord, like silver in a crucible. [11]You captured us in your net and laid great burdens on our backs. [12]You sent troops to ride across our broken bodies. We went through fire and flood. But in the end, you brought us into wealth and great abundance.

[13]Now I have come to your Temple with burnt offerings to pay my vows. [14]For when I was in trouble, I promised you many offerings. [15]That is why I am bringing you these fat male goats, rams, and calves. The smoke of their sacrifice shall rise before you.

[16]Come and hear, all of you who reverence the Lord, and I will tell you what he did for me: [17]For I cried to him for help with praises ready on my tongue. [18]He would not have listened if I had not confessed my sins. [19]But he listened! He heard my prayer! He paid attention to it!

[20]Blessed be God, who didn't turn away when I was praying and didn't refuse me his kindness and love.

PROMISES

66:14-15 People sometimes make bargains with God, saying, "If you heal me (or get me out of this mess), I'll obey you for the rest of my life." Soon after they recover, however, the vow is often forgotten and the old life-style resumes. This writer had made a promise to God, but he remembered the promise and paid his vow. God always keeps his promises, and wants us to follow his example. Be careful to follow through on whatever you promise to do.

PSALM 67 A MISSIONARY PSALM. O God, in mercy bless us; let your face beam with joy as you look down at us.

[2]Send us around the world with the news of your saving power and your eternal plan for all mankind. [3]How everyone throughout the earth will praise the Lord! [4]How glad the nations will be, singing for joy because you are their King and will give true justice to their people! Praise God, O world! May all the peoples of the earth give thanks to you. [6,7]For the earth has yielded abundant harvests. God, even our own God, will bless us. And peoples from remotest lands will worship him.

PSALM 68 THE GREAT PROVIDER. Arise, O God, and scatter all your enemies! Chase them away! Drive them off like smoke before the wind;

melt them like wax in fire! So let the wicked perish at the presence of God. 3But may the godly man exult. May he rejoice and be merry. 4Sing praises to the Lord! Raise your voice in song to him who rides upon the clouds! Jehovah is his name—oh, rejoice in his presence. 5He is a father to the fatherless; he gives justice to the widows, for he is holy. 6He gives families to the lonely, and releases prisoners from jail, singing with joy! But for rebels there is famine and distress.

7O God, when you led your people through the wilderness, 8the earth trembled and the heavens shook. Mount Sinai quailed before you—the God of Israel. 9,10You sent abundant rain upon your land, O God, to refresh it in its weariness! There your people lived, for you gave them this home when they were destitute.

11-13The Lord speaks. The enemy flees. The women at home cry out the happy news: "The armies that came to destroy us have fled!" Now all the women of Israel are dividing the booty. See them sparkle with jewels of silver and gold, covered all over as wings cover doves! 14God scattered their enemies like snowflakes melting in the forests of Zalmon.

15,16O mighty mountains in Bashan! O splendid many-peaked ranges! Well may you look with envy at Mount Zion, the mount where God has chosen to live forever. 17Surrounded by unnumbered chariots, the Lord moves on from Mount Sinai and comes to his holy temple high upon Mount Zion. 18He ascends the heights, leading many captives in his train. He receives gifts for men, even those who once were rebels. God will live among us here.

19What a glorious Lord! He who daily bears our burdens also gives us our salvation.

20He frees us! He rescues us from death. 21But he will crush his enemies, for they refuse to leave their guilty, stubborn ways. 22The Lord says, "Come," to all his people's enemies; they are hiding on Mount Hermon's highest slopes and deep within the sea! 23His people must destroy them. Cover your feet with their blood; dogs will eat them.

24The procession of God my King moves onward to the sanctuary— 25singers in front, musicians behind, girls playing the timbrels in between. 26Let all the people of Israel praise the Lord, who is Israel's fountain. 27The little tribe of Benjamin leads the way. The princes and elders of Judah, and the princes of Zebulun and Naphtali are right behind. 28Summon your might; display your strength, O God, for you have done such mighty things for us.

29The kings of the earth are bringing their gifts to your temple in Jerusalem. 30Rebuke our enemies, O Lord. Bring them—submissive, tax in hand.

Scatter all who delight in war. 31Egypt will send gifts of precious metals. Ethiopia will stretch out her hands to God in adoration. 32Sing to the Lord, O kingdoms of the earth—sing praises to the Lord, 33to him who rides upon the ancient heavens, whose mighty voice thunders from the sky.

34Power belongs to God! His majesty shines down on Israel; his strength is mighty in the heavens. 35What awe we feel, kneeling here before him in the sanctuary. The God of Israel gives strength and mighty power to his people. Blessed be God!

PSALM 69   A SEA OF TROUBLE.

Save me, O my God. The floods have risen. Deeper and deeper I sink in the mire; the waters rise around me. 3I have wept until I am exhausted; my throat is dry and hoarse; my eyes are swollen with weeping, waiting for my God to act. 4I cannot even count all those who hate me without cause. They are influential men, these who plot to kill me though I am innocent. They demand that I be punished for what I didn't do.

5O God, you know so well how stupid I am, and you know all my sins. 6O Lord God of the armies of heaven, don't let me be a stumbling block to those who trust in you. O God of Israel, don't let me cause them to be confused, 7though I am mocked and cursed and shamed for your sake. 8Even my own brothers pretend they don't know me! 9My zeal for God and his work burns hot within me. And because I advocate your cause, your enemies insult me even as they insult you. 10How they scoff and mock me when I mourn and fast before the Lord! 11How they talk about me when I wear sackcloth to show my humiliation and sorrow for my sins! 12I am the talk of the town and the song of the drunkards. 13But I keep right on praying to you, Lord. For now is the time—you are bending down to hear! You are ready with a plentiful supply of love and kindness. Now answer my prayer and rescue me as you promised. 14Pull me out of this mire. Don't let me sink in. Rescue me from those who hate me, and from these deep waters I am in.

15Don't let the floods overwhelm me or the ocean swallow me; save me from the pit that threatens me. 16O Jehovah, answer my prayers, for your loving-kindness is wonderful; your mercy is so plentiful, so tender and so kind. 17Don't hide from me, for I am in deep trouble. Quick! Come and save

BREATHLESS

68:34-35 We should feel an overwhelming sense of awe as we kneel before the Lord in his sanctuary. Surrounding us are countless signs of his wonderful power; shining down upon us are countless signs of his majesty. Unlimited power and unspeakable majesty leave us breathless in his presence. When you catch your breath, praise the Lord!

me. ¹⁸Come, Lord, and rescue me. Ransom me from all my enemies. ¹⁹You know how they talk about me, and how they so shamefully dishonor me. You see them all and know what each has said.

²⁰Their contempt has broken my heart; my spirit is heavy within me. If even one would showsome pity, if even one would comfort me! ²¹For food they gave me gall; for my awful thirst they offered vinegar. ²²Let their joys turn to ashes and their peace disappear; ²³let darkness, blindness, and great feebleness be theirs. ²⁴Pour out your fury upon them; consume them with the fierceness of your anger. ²⁵Let their homes be desolate and abandoned. ²⁶For they persecute the one you have smitten and scoff at the pain of the one you have pierced. ²⁷Pile their sins high and do not overlook them. ²⁸Let these men be blotted from the list of the living; do not give them the joys of life with the righteous.

²⁹But rescue me, O God, from my poverty and pain. ³⁰Then I will praise God with my singing! My thanks will be his praise—³¹that will please him more than sacrificing a bullock or an ox. ³²The humble shall see their God at work for them. No wonder they will be so glad! All who seek for God shall live in joy. ³³For Jehovah hears the cries of his needy ones and does not look the other way.

³⁴Praise him, all heaven and earth! Praise him, all the seas and everything in them! ³⁵For God will save Jerusalem; he rebuilds the cities of Judah. His people shall live in them and not be dispossessed. ³⁶Their children shall inherit the land; all who love his name shall live there safely.

INJUSTICE

"It isn't fair!" Joyce sobs. "I try really hard to live for the Lord. I go to church, read my Bible, pray every day, try to be a witness to my friends—everything! But does it do any good? No way! My life is still the worst. My family is awful, my fat body is a wreck, I never get asked out, I have only two friends, and I can't even pass geometry! You'd think God would at least reward me a little bit.

"On the other hand, Amy has it made! She's tan and beautiful. She has dates every weekend. She makes straight A's without even trying. Her family is rich—I mean, how many other kids get their own Miata convertible? She never has any problems. Her life is totally perfect . . . and here's the big rip-off: she's not even a Christian! In fact, she couldn't care less about God. She's wild!

"It doesn't make any sense. Why do I get shot down for doing what's right, and she gets rewarded for being 'Miss Party'?

"Doesn't God see what's going on? Doesn't he care? I'm serious . . . there is absolutely no justice in this world. I might as well live like a heathen for all the good it does me."

Ever feel like Joyce? Ever wonder why some non-Christians seem to have perfect lives, while so many of God's people struggle and have lives full of pain? A follower of God named Asaph once asked some of the very same questions. Psalm 73 describes the answers he found.

PSALM **70** A SHORT PRAYER FOR HELP.

Rescue me, O God! Lord, hurry to my aid! ^{2,3}They are after my life and delight in hurting me. Confuse them! Shame them! Stop them! Don't let them keep on mocking me! ⁴But fill the followers of God with joy. Let those who love your salvation exclaim, "What a wonderful God he is!" ⁵But I am in deep trouble. Rush to my aid, for only you can help and save me. O Lord, don't delay.

PSALM **71** YOUNG OR OLD—GOD HELPS.

Lord, you are my refuge! Don't let me down! ²Save me from my enemies, for you are just! Rescue me! Bend down your ear and listen to my plea and save me. ³Be to me a great protecting Rock, where I am always welcome, safe from all attacks. For you have issued the order to save me. ⁴Rescue me, O God, from these unjust and cruel men. ⁵O Lord, you alone are my hope; I've trusted you from childhood. ⁶Yes, you have been with me from birth and have helped me constantly—no wonder I am always praising you! ⁷My success—at which so many stand amazed—is because you are my mighty protector. ⁸All day long I'll praise and honor you, O God, for all that you have done for me.

⁹And now, in my old age, don't set me aside. Don't forsake me now when my strength is failing. ¹⁰My enemies are whispering, ¹¹"God has forsaken him! Now we can get him. There is no one to help him now!" ¹²O God, don't stay away! Come quickly! Help! ¹³Destroy them! Cover them with failure and disgrace—these enemies of mine.

¹⁴I will keep on expecting you to help me. I praise you more and more. ¹⁵I cannot count the times when you have faithfully rescued me from danger. I will tell everyone how good you are, and of your constant, daily care. ¹⁶I walk in the strength of the Lord God. I tell everyone that you alone are just and good. ¹⁷O God, you have helped me from my earliest childhood—and I have constantly testified to others of the wonderful things you do. ¹⁸And now that I am old and gray, don't forsake me. Give me time to tell this new generation (and their children too) about all your mighty miracles. ¹⁹Your power and goodness, Lord, reach to the highest heavens. You have done such wonderful things. Where is there another God like you? ²⁰You have let me sink down deep in desperate

PANIC

70:4 This short psalm was David's plea for God to rush to his aid. Yet even in this moment of panic, praise was not forgotten. Praise is important because it helps us remember who God is. Often our prayers are filled with requests for ourselves and others; we forget to thank God for what he has done and to worship him for who he is. Don't take God for granted or treat him as a vending machine. Even in the midst of his fear, David praised God.

problems. But you will bring me back to life again, up from the depths of the earth. ²¹You will give me greater honor than before and turn again and comfort me.

²²I will praise you with music, telling of your faithfulness to all your promises, O Holy One of Israel. ²³I will shout and sing your praises for redeeming me. ²⁴I will talk to others all day long about your justice and your goodness. For all who tried to hurt me have been disgraced and dishonored.

PSALM 72 THE PERFECT KING.

O God, help the king to judge as you would, and help his son to walk in godliness. ²Help him to give justice to your people, even to the poor. ³May the mountains and hills flourish in prosperity because of his good reign. ⁴Help him to defend the poor and needy and to crush their oppressors. ⁵May the poor and needy revere you constantly, as long as sun and moon continue in the skies! Yes, forever!

⁶May the reign of this son of mine be as gentle and fruitful as the springtime rains upon the grass—like showers that water the earth! ⁷May all good men flourish in his reign with abundance of peace to the end of time.

⁸Let him reign from sea to sea and from the Euphrates River to the ends of the earth. ⁹The desert nomads shall bow before him; his enemies shall fall face downward in the dust. ¹⁰Kings along the Mediterranean coast—the kings of Tarshish and the islands—and those from Sheba and from Seba—all will bring their gifts. ¹¹Yes, kings from everywhere! All will bow before him! All will serve him!

¹²He will take care of the helpless and poor when they cry to him; for they have no one else to defend them. ¹³He feels pity for the weak and needy and will rescue them. ¹⁴He will save them from oppression and from violence, for their lives are precious to him.

¹⁵And he shall live; and to him will be given the gold of Sheba, and there will be constant praise for him. His people will bless him all day long. ¹⁶Bless us with abundant crops throughout the land, even on the highland plains; may there be fruit like that of Lebanon; may the cities be as full of people as the fields are of grass. ¹⁷His name will be honored forever; it will continue as the sun; and all will be blessed in him; all nations will praise him.

¹⁸Blessed be Jehovah God, the God of Israel, who only does wonderful things! ¹⁹Blessed be his glorious name forever! Let the whole earth be filled with his glory. Amen and amen!

²⁰(This ends the psalms of David, son of Jesse.)

PSALM 73 WHY ARE WICKED PEOPLE RICH?

How good God is to Israel—to those whose hearts are pure. ²But as for me, I came *so* close to the edge of the cliff! My feet were slipping and I was almost gone. ³For I was envious of the prosperity of the proud and wicked. ⁴Yes, all through life their road is smooth! They grow sleek and fat. ⁵They aren't always in trouble and plagued with problems like everyone else, ⁶so their pride sparkles like a jeweled necklace, and their clothing is woven of cruelty! ⁷These fat cats have everything their hearts could ever wish for! ⁸They scoff at God and threaten his people. How proudly they speak! ⁹They boast against the very heavens, and their words strut through the earth.

¹⁰And so God's people are dismayed and confused and drink it all in. ¹¹"Does God realize what is going on?" they ask. ¹²"Look at these men of arrogance; they never have to lift a finger—theirs is a life of ease; and all the time their riches multiply."

¹³Have I been wasting my time? Why take the trouble to be pure? ¹⁴All I get out of it is trouble and woe—every day and all day long! ¹⁵If I had really said that, I would have been a traitor to your people. ¹⁶Yet it is so hard to explain it—this prosperity of those who hate the Lord. ¹⁷Then one day I went into God's sanctuary to meditate and thought about the future of these evil men. ¹⁸What a slippery path they are on—suddenly God will send them sliding over the edge of the cliff and down to their destruction: ¹⁹an instant end to all their happiness, an eternity of terror. ²⁰Their present life is only a dream! They will awaken to the truth as one awakens from a dream of things that never really were!

²¹When I saw this, what turmoil filled my heart! ²²I saw myself so stupid and so ignorant; I must seem like an animal to you, O God. ²³But even so, you love me! You are holding my right hand! ²⁴You will keep on guiding me all my life with your wisdom and counsel, and afterwards receive me into the glories of heaven! ²⁵Whom have I in heaven but you? And I desire no one on earth as much as you! ²⁶My health fails; my spirits droop, yet God remains! He is the strength of my heart; he is mine forever!

²⁷But those refusing to worship God will perish, for he destroys those serving other gods.

²⁸But as for me, I get as close to him as I can! I have chosen him, and I will tell everyone about the wonderful ways he rescues me.

HELPLESS

72:12-14 God cares for the helpless and poor because they are precious to him. If God feels so strongly about the poor and loves them so deeply, how can we ignore their plight? Examine what you are doing to reach out with God's love to the poor, weak, and needy in the world. Are you ignoring them?

PSALM 74 RECALL YOUR PROMISES, O LORD.

O God, why have you cast us away forever? Why is your anger hot against us—the sheep of your own pasture? [2]Remember that we are your people—the ones you chose in ancient times from slavery and made the choicest of your possessions. You chose Jerusalem as your home on earth!

[3]Walk through the awful ruins of the city and see what the enemy has done to your sanctuary. [4]There they shouted their battle cry and erected their idols to flaunt their victory. [5,6]Everything lies in shambles like a forest chopped to the ground. They came with their axes and sledgehammers and smashed and chopped the carved paneling; [7]they set the sanctuary on fire, and razed it to the ground—your sanctuary, Lord. [8]"Let's wipe out every trace of God," they said, and went through the entire country burning down the assembly places where we worshiped you.

[9,10]There is nothing left to show that we are your people. The prophets are gone, and who can say when it all will end? How long, O God, will you allow our enemies to dishonor your name? Will you let them get away with this forever? [11]Why do you delay? Why hold back your power? Unleash your fist and give them a final blow.

[12]God is my King from ages past; you have been actively helping me everywhere throughout the land. [13,14]You divided the Red Sea with your strength; you crushed the sea-god's heads! You gave him to the desert tribes to eat! [15]At your command the springs burst forth to give your people water; and then you dried a path for them across the ever-flowing Jordan. [16]Day and night alike belong to you; you made the starlight and the sun. [17]All nature is within your hands; you make the summer and the winter too. [18]Lord, see how these enemies scoff at you. O Jehovah, an arrogant nation has blasphemed your name.

[19]O Lord, save me! Protect your turtledove from the hawks. Save your beloved people from these beasts. [20]Remember your promise! For the land is full of darkness and cruel men. [21]O Lord, don't let your downtrodden people be constantly insulted. Give cause for these poor and needy ones to praise your name![22]Arise, O God, and state your case against our enemies. Remember the insults these rebels have hurled against you all day long. [23]Don't

overlook the cursing of these enemies of yours; it grows louder and louder.

PSALM 75 WICKED PEOPLE WILL BE JUDGED.

How we thank you, Lord! Your mighty miracles give proof that you care.

[2]"Yes," the Lord replies, "and when I am ready, I will punish the wicked! [3]Though the earth shakes and all its people live in turmoil, yet its pillars are firm, for I have set them in place!"

[4]I warned the proud to cease their arrogance! I told the wicked to lower their insolent gaze [5]and to stop being stubborn and proud. [6,7]For promotion and power come from nowhere on earth, but only from God. He promotes one and deposes another. [8]In Jehovah's hand there is a cup of pale and sparkling wine. It is his judgment, poured out upon the wicked of the earth. They must drain that cup to the dregs.

[9]But as for me, I shall forever declare the praises of the God of Jacob. [10]"I will cut off the strength of evil men," says the Lord, "and increase the power of good men in their place."

PSALM 76 GOD IS GREAT.

God's reputation is very great in Judah and in Israel. [2]His home is in Jerusalem. He lives upon Mount Zion. [3]There he breaks the weapons of our enemies.

[4]The everlasting mountains cannot compare with you in glory! [5]The mightiest of our enemies are conquered. They lie before us in the sleep of death; not one can lift a hand against us. [6]When you rebuked them, God of Jacob, steeds and riders fell. [7]No wonder you are greatly feared! Who can stand before an angry God? [8]You pronounce sentence on them from heaven; the earth trembles and stands silently before you. [9]You stand up to punish the evil-doers and to defend the meek of the earth. [10]Man's futile wrath will bring you glory. You will use it as an ornament!

[11]Fulfill all your vows that you have made to Jehovah your God. Let everyone bring him presents. He should be reverenced and feared, [12]for he cuts down princes and does awesome things to the kings of the earth.

PSALM 77 GOD HELPS IN HARD TIMES.

I cry to the Lord; I call and call to him. Oh, that he would listen! [2]I am in deep trouble and I need his help so

HATE

74:8 When enemy armies defeated Israel, they sacked Jerusalem, trying to wipe out every trace of God. This has often been the response of people who hate God. Today many are trying to erase all traces of God from traditions in our society and subjects taught in our schools. Do what you can to help maintain a Christian influence, but don't become discouraged when others appear to make great strides in eliminating all traces of God. They cannot eliminate his presence in the lives of believers.

TIMING

75:2 Children have difficulty grasping the concept of time "It's not time yet" is not a reason they easily understand. They only comprehend the present. As limited human beings, we can't comprehend God's perspective on time. We want everything now, not recognizing that God's timing is better for us. When God is ready, he will do what needs to be done, not what we would like him to do. We may be impatient as children, but it is clear that God's timing is perfect, so we should accept much. All night long I pray, lifting my hands to heaven, pleading. There can be no joy for me until he acts. ³I think of God and moan, overwhelmed with longing for his help. ⁴I cannot sleep until you act. I am too distressed even to pray!

⁵I keep thinking of the good old days of the past, long since ended. ⁶Then my nights were filled with joyous songs. I search my soul and meditate upon the difference now. ⁷Has the Lord rejected me forever? Will he never again be favorable? ⁸Is his loving-kindness gone forever? Has his promise failed? ⁹Has he forgotten to be kind to one so undeserving? Has he slammed the door in anger on his love? ¹⁰And I said: This is my fate, that the blessings of God have changed to hate. ¹¹I recall the many miracles he did for me so long ago. ¹²Those wonderful deeds are constantly in my thoughts. I cannot stop thinking about them.

¹³O God, your ways are holy. Where is there any other as mighty as you? ¹⁴You are the God of miracles and wonders! You still demonstrate your awesome power.

¹⁵You have redeemed us who are the sons of Jacob and of Joseph by your might. ¹⁶When the Red Sea saw you, how it feared! It trembled to its depths! ¹⁷The clouds poured down their rain, the thunder rolled and crackled in the sky. Your lightning flashed. ¹⁸There was thunder in the whirlwind; the lightning lighted up the world! The earth trembled and shook.

¹⁹Your road led by a pathway through the sea— a pathway no one knew was there! ²⁰You led your people along that road like a flock of sheep, with Moses and Aaron as their shepherds.

PSALM **78** **HISTORY TEACHES US.** O my people, listen to my teaching. Open your ears to what I am saying. ²,³For I will show you lessons from our history, stories handed down to us from former generations. ⁴I will reveal these truths to you so that you can describe these glorious deeds of Jehovah to your children and tell them about the mighty miracles he did. ⁵For he gave his laws to Israel and commanded our fathers to teach them to their children, ⁶so that they in turn could teach their children too. Thus his laws pass down from generation to generation. ⁷In this way each generation has been able to obey his laws and to set its hope anew on God and not forget his glorious miracles. ⁸Thus they did not need to be as their fathers were—stubborn, rebellious, unfaithful, refusing to give their hearts to God.

⁹The people of Ephraim, though fully armed, turned their backs and fled when the day of battle came ¹⁰because they didn't obey his laws. They refused to follow his ways. ¹¹,¹²And they forgot about the wonderful miracles God had done for them and for their fathers in Egypt. ¹³For he divided the sea before them and led them through! The water stood banked up along both sides of them! ¹⁴In the daytime he led them by a cloud, and at night by a pillar of fire. ¹⁵He split open the rocks in the wilderness to give them plenty of water, as though gushing from a spring. ¹⁶Streams poured from the rock, flowing like a river!

¹⁷Yet they kept on with their rebellion, sinning against the God who is above all gods. ¹⁸They murmured and complained, demanding other food than God was giving them. ¹⁹,²⁰They even spoke against God himself. "Why can't he give us decent food as well as water?" they grumbled. ²¹Jehovah heard them and was angry; the fire of his wrath burned against Israel ²²because they didn't believe in God or trust in him to care for them, ²³even though he commanded the skies to open—he opened the windows of heaven—²⁴and rained down manna for their food. He gave them bread from heaven! ²⁵They ate angels' food! He gave them all they could hold.

²⁶And he led forth the east wind and guided the south wind by his mighty power. ²⁷He rained down birds as thick as dust, clouds of them like sands along the shore! ²⁸He caused the birds to fall to the ground among the tents. ²⁹The people ate their fill. He gave them what they asked for. ³⁰But they had hardly finished eating, and the meat was yet in their mouths, ³¹when the anger of the Lord rose against them and killed the finest of Israel's young men. ³²Yet even so the people kept on sinning and refused to believe in miracles. ³³So he cut their lives short and gave them years of terror and disaster.

³⁴Then at last, when he had ruined them, they walked awhile behind him; how earnestly they turned around and followed him! ³⁵Then they remembered that God was their Rock—that their Savior was the God above all gods. ³⁶But it was only with their words they followed him, not with their hearts; ³⁷their hearts were far away. They did not keep their promises. ³⁸Yet he was merciful and forgave their sins and didn't destroy them all. Many and many a time he held back his anger. ³⁹For he remembered that they were merely mortal men, gone in a moment like a breath of wind.

⁴⁰Oh, how often they rebelled against him in those desert years and grieved his heart. ⁴¹Again and again they turned away and tempted God to kill them, and limited the Holy One of Israel from

TALK

78:36-37 Over and over the children of Israel said they would follow God, but then they turned away from him. The problem was that they followed God with words and not with their hearts, thus their repentance was empty. Talk is cheap. God wants our lives to back up our spiritual claims and promises—he wants us to be true believers.

READY

78:71-72 Although David had been on the throne when this psalm was written, he is called a shepherd and not a king. Shepherding, a common profession in biblical times, was a highly responsible job. The flocks were completely dependent upon shepherds for guidance, provision, and protection. David had spent his early years as a shepherd (1 Samuel 16:10-11). This was a training ground for the future responsibilities God had in store for him. When he was ready, God took him from caring for sheep to caring for Israel, God's people. Don't treat your present situation lightly or irresponsibly; it may be God's training ground for your future.

giving them his blessings. [42]They forgot his power and love and how he had rescued them from their enemies; [43]they forgot the plagues he sent upon the Egyptians in Tanis—[44]how he turned their rivers into blood so that no one could drink, [45]how he sent vast swarms of flies to fill the land, and how the frogs had covered all of Egypt!

[46]He gave their crops to caterpillars. Their harvest was consumed by locusts. [47]He destroyed their grapevines and their sycamores with hail. [48]Their cattle died in the fields, mortally wounded by huge hailstones from heaven. Their sheep were killed by lightning. [49]He loosed on them the fierceness of his anger, sending sorrow and trouble. He dispatched against them a band of destroying angels. [50]He gave free course to his anger and did not spare the Egyptians' lives, but handed them over to plagues and sickness. [51]Then he killed the eldest son in each Egyptian family—he who was the beginning of its strength and joy.

[52]But he led forth his own people like a flock, guiding them safely through the wilderness. [53]He kept them safe, so they were not afraid. But the sea closed in upon their enemies and overwhelmed them. [54]He brought them to the border of his land of blessing, to this land of hills he made for them. [55]He drove out the nations occupying the land and gave each tribe of Israel its apportioned place as its home.

[56]Yet though he did all this for them, they still rebelled against the God above all gods and refused to follow his commands. [57]They turned back from entering the Promised Land and disobeyed as their fathers had. Like a crooked arrow, they missed the target of God's will. [58]They made him angry by erecting idols and altars to other gods.

[59]When God saw their deeds, his wrath was strong and he despised his people. [60]Then he abandoned his Tabernacle at Shiloh, where he had lived among mankind, [61]and allowed his Ark to be captured; he surrendered his glory into enemy hands. [62]He caused his people to be butchered because his anger was intense. [63]Their young men were killed by fire, and their girls died before they were old enough to sing their wedding songs. [64]The priests were slaughtered, and their widows died before they could even begin their lament. [65]Then the Lord

rose up as though awakening from sleep, and like a mighty man aroused by wine, [66]he routed his enemies; he drove them back and sent them to eternal shame. [67]But he rejected Joseph's family, the tribe of Ephraim, [68]and chose the tribe of Judah—and Mount Zion, which he loved. [69]There he built his towering temple, solid and enduring as the heavens and the earth. [70]He chose his servant David, taking him from feeding sheep [71,72]and from following the ewes with lambs; God presented David to his people as their shepherd, and he cared for them with a true heart and skillful hands.

PSALM 79 LIFE IS NOT FAIR, BUT GOD IS.

O God, your land has been conquered by the heathen nations. Your Temple is defiled, and Jerusalem is a heap of ruins. [2]The bodies of your people lie exposed—food for birds and animals. [3]The enemy has butchered the entire population of Jerusalem; blood has flowed like water. No one is left even to bury them. [4]The nations all around us scoff. They heap contempt on us.

[5]O Jehovah, how long will you be angry with us? Forever? Will your jealousy burn till every hope is gone? [6]Pour out your wrath upon the godless nations—not on us—on kingdoms that refuse to pray, that will not call upon your name! [7]For they have destroyed your people Israel, invading every home. [8]Oh, do not hold us guilty for our former sins! Let your tenderhearted mercies meet our needs, for we are brought low to the dust. [9]Help us, God of our salvation! Help us for the honor of your name. Oh, save us and forgive our sins. [10]Why should the heathen nations be allowed to scoff, "Where is their God?" Publicly avenge this slaughter of your people! [11]Listen to the sighing of the prisoners and those condemned to die. Demonstrate the greatness of your power by saving them. [12]O Lord, take sevenfold vengeance on these nations scorning you.

[13]Then we your people, the sheep of your pasture, will thank you forever and forever, praising your greatness from generation to generation.

BE PREPARED

79:10 Can we expect God to care for us so others won't scoff at our beliefs? In the end, God will bring himself glory (Psalm 76:10), but in the meantime, we must endure suffering with patience and allow God to purify us through it. For reasons that we do not know, the heathen are allowed to scoff at believers. We should be prepared for criticism, jokes, and unkind remarks because God does not place us beyond the attacks of scoffers.

PSALM 80 GOD WILL HELP US TRUST HIM.

O Shepherd of Israel who leads Israel like a flock; O God enthroned above the Guardian Angels, bend down your ear and listen as I plead. Display your power and radiant glory. [2]Let Ephraim, Benjamin, and Manasseh see you rouse yourself and use your mighty power to rescue us.

[3]Turn us again to yourself, O God. Look down on us in joy and love; only then shall we be saved.

[4]O Jehovah, God of heaven's armies, how long will you be angry and reject our prayers? [5]You have fed us with sorrow and tears [6]and have made us the scorn of the neighboring nations. They laugh among themselves.

[7]Turn us again to yourself, O God of Hosts. Look down on us in joy and love; only then shall we be saved. [8]You brought us from Egypt as though we were a tender vine and drove away the heathen from your land and planted us. [9]You cleared the ground and tilled the soil, and we took root and filled the land. [10]The mountains were covered with our shadow; we were like the mighty cedar trees, [11]covering the entire land from the Mediterranean Sea to the Euphrates River. [12]But now you have broken down our walls, leaving us without protection. [13]The boar from the forest roots around us, and the wild animals feed on us.

[14]Come back, we beg of you, O God of the armies of heaven, and bless us. Look down from heaven and see our plight and care for this your vine! [15]Protect what you yourself have planted, this son you have raised for yourself. [16]For we are chopped and burned by our enemies. May they perish at your frown. [17]Strengthen the man you love, the son of your choice, [18]and we will never forsake you again. Revive us to trust in you.

[19]Turn us again to yourself, O God of the armies of heaven. Look down on us, your face aglow with joy and love—only then shall we be saved.

PSALM **81** A PSALM FOR SPECIAL TIMES.

The Lord makes us strong! Sing praises! Sing to Israel's God!

[2]Sing, accompanied by drums; pluck the sweet lyre and harp. [3]Sound the trumpet! Come to the joyous celebrations at full moon, new moon, and all the other holidays. [4]For God has given us these times of joy; they are scheduled in the laws of Israel. [5]He gave them as reminders of his war against Egypt where we were slaves on foreign soil.

I heard an unknown voice that said, [6]"Now I will relieve your shoulder of its burden; I will free your hands from their heavy tasks." [7]He said, "You cried to me in trouble, and I saved you; I answered from Mount Sinai where the thunder hides. I tested your faith at Meribah, when you complained there was no water. [8]Listen to me, O my people, while I give you stern warnings. O Israel, if you will only listen! [9]*You must never worship any other god* nor ever have an idol in your home. [10]For it was I,

Jehovah your God, who brought you out of the land of Egypt. Only test me! Open your mouth wide and see if I won't fill it. You will receive every blessing you can use!

[11]"But no, my people won't listen. Israel doesn't want me around. [12]So I am letting them go their blind and stubborn way, living according to their own desires.

[13]"But oh, that my people would listen to me! Oh, that Israel would follow me, walking in my paths! [14]How quickly then I would subdue her enemies! How soon my hands would be upon her foes! [15]Those who hate the Lord would cringe before him; their desolation would last forever. [16]But he would feed you with the choicest foods. He would satisfy you with honey for the taking."

PSALM **82** GOD WILL JUDGE.

God stands up to open heaven's court. He pronounces judgment on the judges. [2]How long will you judges refuse to listen to the evidence? How long will you shower special favors on the wicked? [3]Give fair judgment to the poor man, the afflicted, the fatherless, the destitute. [4]Rescue the poor and helpless from the grasp of evil men. [5]But you are so foolish and so ignorant! Because you are in darkness, all the foundations of society are shaken to the core. [6]I have called you all "gods" and "sons of the Most High." [7]But in death you are mere men. You will fall as any prince—for all must die.

[8]Stand up, O God, and judge the earth. For all of it belongs to you. All nations are in your hands.

PSALM **83** TELL THE WORLD GOD IS GOOD.

O God, don't sit idly by, silent and inactive when we pray. Answer us! Deliver us!

[2]Don't you hear the tumult and commotion of your enemies? Don't you see what they are doing, these proud men who hate the Lord? [3]They are full of craftiness and plot against your people, laying plans to slay your precious ones. [4]"Come," they say, "and let us wipe out Israel as a nation—we will destroy the very memory of her existence." [5]This was their unanimous decision at their summit conference—they signed a treaty to ally themselves against Almighty God—[6]these Ishmaelites and Edomites and Moabites and Hagrites; [7]people from the lands of Gebal, Ammon, Amalek, Philistia and Tyre; [8]Assyria has

HOLIDAYS

81:4-5 Israel's holidays reminded the nation of God's great miracles. It was a time of rejoicing and a time to renew one's strength for life's daily struggles. At Christmas, do most of your thoughts revolve around presents? Is Easter only a warm anticipation of spring, and Thanksgiving only a good meal? Remember the spiritual origins of these special days, and use them as opportunities to worship God for his goodness to you, your family, and your nation.

THE RULER

83:13-18 The rulers of the nations exercise great power, changing the course of history and its peoples. Surrounding Judah were heathen nations that sought its downfall. Asaph prayed that God would blow his hot breath of judgment upon them until, in their defeat, they recognized that the Lord is above all rulers of the earth. Sometimes we must be dragged in the dust before we will look up and see the Lord; we must be defeated before we can have the ultimate victory. Wouldn't it be better to seek the Lord in times of prosperity than to wait until his judgment is upon us?

joined them too, and is allied with the descendants of Lot.

[9]Do to them as once you did to Midian, or as you did to Sisera and Jabin at the river Kishon, [10]and as you did to your enemies at Endor, whose decaying corpses fertilized the soil. [11]Make their mighty nobles die as Oreb did, and Zeeb; let all their princes die like Zebah and Zalmunna, [12]who said, "Let us seize for our own use these pasturelands of God!"

[13]O my God, blow them away like dust; like chaff before the wind—[14]as a forest fire that roars across a mountain. [15]Chase them with your fiery storms, tempests, and tornados. [16]Utterly disgrace them until they recognize your power and name, O Lord. [17]Make them failures in everything they do; let them be ashamed and terrified [18]until they learn that you alone, Jehovah, are the God above all gods in supreme charge of all the earth.

PSALM 84 OUR TRUST DELIGHTS GOD.

How lovely is your Temple, O Lord of the armies of heaven.

[2]I long, yes, faint with longing to be able to enter your courtyard and come near to the Living God. [3]Even the sparrows and swallows are welcome to come and nest among your altars and there have their young, O Lord of heaven's armies, my King and my God! [4]How happy are those who can live in your Temple, singing your praises.

[5]Happy are those who are strong in the Lord, who want above all else to follow your steps. [6]When they walk through the Valley of Weeping, it will become a place of springs where pools of blessing and refreshment collect after rains! [7]They will grow constantly in strength, and each of them is invited to meet with the Lord in Zion.

[8]O Jehovah, God of the heavenly armies, hear my prayer! Listen, God of Israel. [9]O God, our Defender and our Shield, have mercy on the one you have anointed as your king.

[10]A single day spent in your Temple is better than a thousand anywhere else! I would rather be a doorman of the Temple of my God than live in palaces of wickedness. [11]For Jehovah God is our Light and our Protector. He gives us grace and glory. No good thing will he withhold from those who walk along his paths.

[12]O Lord of the armies of heaven, blessed are those who trust in you.

PSALM 85 FOLLOW GOD: FIND PEACE.

Lord, you have poured out amazing blessings on this land! You have restored the fortunes of Israel, [2]and forgiven the sins of your people—yes, covered over each one, [3]so that all your wrath, your blazing anger, is now ended.

[4]Now bring us back to loving you, O Lord, so that your anger will never need rise against us again. [5](Or will you be always angry—on and on to distant generations?) [6]Oh, revive us! Then your people can rejoice in you again. [7]Pour out your love and kindness on us, Lord, and grant us your salvation.

[8]I am listening carefully to all the Lord is saying—for he speaks peace to his people, his saints, if they will only stop their sinning. [9]Surely his salvation is near to those who reverence him; our land will be filled with his glory.

[10]Mercy and truth have met together. Grim justice and peace have kissed! [11]Truth rises from the earth, and righteousness smiles down from heaven. [12]Yes, the Lord pours down his blessings on the land, and it yields its bountiful crops. [13]Justice goes before him to make a pathway for his steps.

PSALM 86 THERE IS ONLY ONE TRUE GOD.

Bend down and hear my prayer, O Lord, and answer me, for I am deep in trouble.

[2]Protect me from death, for I try to follow all your laws. Save me, for I am serving you and trusting you. [3]Be merciful, O Lord, for I am looking up to you in constant hope. [4]Give me happiness, O Lord, for I worship only you. [5]O Lord, you are so good and kind, so ready to forgive, so full of mercy for all who ask your aid.

[6]Listen closely to my prayer, O God. Hear my urgent cry. [7]I will call to you whenever trouble strikes, and you will help me.

[8]Where among the heathen gods is there a god like you? Where are their miracles? [9]All the nations—and you made each one—will come and bow before you, Lord, and praise your great and holy name. [10]For you are great and do great miracles. You alone are God.

[11]Tell me where you want me to go and I will go there. May every fiber of my being unite in reverence to your name. [12]With all my heart I will praise you. I will give glory to your name forever,

WHOLEHEARTE

86:11-12 Wholehearted reverence means appreciating God and honoring him in all areas of life. We need to show our loyalty to him in every part of our lives, not just in going to church. If we reverence God with our whole heart, then our work, relationships, use of money, and desires will be in keeping with his will.

13for you love me so much! You are constantly so kind! You have rescued me from deepest hell.

14O God, proud and insolent men defy me; violent, godless men are trying to kill me. 15But you are merciful and gentle, Lord, slow in getting angry, full of constant loving-kindness and of truth; 16so look down in pity and grant strength to your servant and save me. 17Send me a sign of your favor. When those who hate me see it, they will lose face because you help and comfort me.

PSALM 87 JERUSALEM: A CITY GOD LOVES. High
on his holy mountain stands Jerusalem, the city of God, the city he loves more than any other!

3O city of God, what wondrous tales are told of you! 4Nowadays when I mention among my friends the names of Egypt and Babylonia, Philistia and Tyre, or even distant Ethiopia, someone boasts that he was born in one or another of those countries. 5But someday the highest honor will be to be a native of Jerusalem! For the God above all gods will personally bless this city. 6When he registers her citizens, he will place a checkmark beside the names of those who were born here. 7And in the festivals they'll sing, "All my heart is in Jerusalem."

PSALM 88 GOD UNDERSTANDS YOUR HURTS. O
Jehovah, God of my salvation, I have wept before you day and night. 2Now hear my prayers; oh, listen to my cry, 3for my life is full of troubles, and death draws near. 4They say my life is ebbing out—a hopeless case. 5They have left me here to die, like those slain on battlefields from whom your mercies are removed.

6You have thrust me down to the darkest depths. 7Your wrath lies heavy on me; wave after wave engulfs me. 8You have made my friends to loathe me, and they have gone away. I am in a trap with no way out. 9My eyes grow dim with weeping. Each day I beg your help; O Lord, I reach my pleading hands to you for mercy.

10Soon it will be too late! Of what use are your miracles when I am in the grave? How can I praise you then? 11Can those in the grave declare your loving-kindness? Can they proclaim your faithfulness? 12Can the darkness speak of your miracles? Can anyone in the Land of Forgetfulness talk about your help?

13O Lord, I plead for my life and will keep on pleading day by day. 14O Jehovah, why have you thrown my life away? Why are you turning your face from me and looking the other way?

15From my youth I have been sickly and ready to die. I stand helpless before your terrors. 16Your fierce wrath has overwhelmed me. Your terrors have cut me off. 17They flow around me all day long. 18Lover, friend, acquaintance—all are gone. There is only darkness everywhere.

PSALM 89 GOD KEEPS PROMISES FOREVER.
Forever and ever I will sing about the tender kindness of the Lord! Young and old shall hear about your blessings. 2Your love and kindness are forever; your truth is as enduring as the heavens.

3,4The Lord God says, "I have made a solemn agreement with my chosen servant David. I have taken an oath to establish his descendants as kings forever on his throne, from now until eternity!"

5All heaven shall praise your miracles, O Lord; myriads of angels will praise you for your faithfulness. 6For who in all of heaven can be compared with God? What mightiest angel is anything like him? 7The highest of angelic powers stand in dread and awe of him. Who is as revered as he by those surrounding him? 8O Jehovah, Commander of the heavenly armies, where is there any other Mighty One like you? Faithfulness is your very character.

9You rule the oceans when their waves arise in fearful storms; you speak, and they lie still. 10You have cut haughty Egypt to pieces. Your enemies are scattered by your awesome power. 11The heavens are yours, the world, everything—for you created them all. 12You created north and south! Mount Tabor and Mount Hermon rejoice to be signed by your name as their maker! 13Strong is your arm! Strong is your hand! Your right hand is lifted high in glorious strength.

14,15Your throne is founded on two strong pillars—the one is Justice and the other Righteousness. Mercy and Truth walk before you as your attendants. Blessed are those who hear the joyful blast of the trumpet, for they shall walk in the light of your presence. 16They rejoice all day long in your wonderful reputation and in your perfect righteousness. 17You are their strength. What glory! Our power is based on your favor! 18Yes, our protection is from the Lord himself and he, the Holy One of Israel, has given us our king.

19In a vision you spoke to your prophet and said, "I have chosen a splendid young man from the common people to be the king—20he is my servant David! I have anointed him with my holy oil. 21I will steady him and make him strong. 22His enemies shall not outwit him, nor shall the wicked overpower him. 23I will beat down his adversaries

AMBASSADOR

89:14-15 God's throne is pictured with pillars of Justice and Righteousness, and he is attended by Mercy and Truth. These describe fundamental aspects of the way God deals with people. As God's ambassadors, we should deal with people similarly. Make sure your actions flow out of justice, righteousness, mercy, and truth because any unfair, unloving, or dishonest action cannot come from God.

DOWN IN THE DUMPS

In the movie The Accidental Tourist, the main characters are a husband and wife named Macon and Sarah Leary. Their son Ethan has died tragically, leaving them in despair, struggling to pull their lives back together. In one particularly touching scene, Sarah says to her husband: "I should have agreed to teach summer school or something. I open my eyes in the morning and I think, why bother getting up? Why bother eating? Why bother breathing?" This isn't just a scene from a movie—it's an experience common to people everywhere. Life can be terribly unfair, terribly tragic. When we're in the depths of despair, we feel like Sarah Leary: Why bother going on at all? There are those who feel that Christians are—or should be—immune to depression. "After all," they say, "what have you got to be depressed about? You have a relationship with God, a family of brothers and sisters who love you, and a guaranteed ticket to heaven." When the person carrying the weight of gloom hears this, he is not only depressed, he feels guilty as well because it's "unspiritual" to be down in the dumps. For those who struggle with feelings of depression, there is good news and bad news. The bad news is that such feelings are a fact of life in this broken world. Man's fall into sin in the Garden of Eden affected every area of human existence. Look at it this way: when you inhabit a planet in open rebellion against its Creator, it's not surprising that sometimes you get caught in the crossfire. Depression is just one of the ways that we can be wounded. Now the good news: you are not alone. As Psalm 73 (and many other passages) clearly shows, even God's chosen people experience anxiety, despair, and darkness in their souls. (If Psalm 73 doesn't convince you, check out the accounts of Jesus' experience in Gethsemane. Matthew 26 speaks of Jesus' soul being "crushed with horror and sadness to the point of death." Feeling down—really down—seems to be an occasional fact of life. Don't be surprised when you face grief.) Feeling down—really down—seems to be an occasional fact of life. Obviously, depression that is too deep or lasts too long indicates a need for counseling; but there is nothing unusual or unspiritual about "walking through the dark valley" from time to time. There's nothing wrong with being in one of those unpleasant times, don't add guilt to your load. And know for certain that the Captain is sailing through stormy seas, expect a little motion discomfort. And know for certain that the Captain is not asleep on the bridge. He'll guide you safely through.

before him and destroy those who hate him. ²⁴I will protect and bless him constantly and surround him with my love; he will be great because of me. ²⁵He will hold sway from the Euphrates River to the Mediterranean Sea. ²⁶And he will cry to me, 'You are my Father, my God, and my Rock of Salvation.'

²⁷"I will treat him as my firstborn son and make him the mightiest king in all the earth. ²⁸I will love him forever and be kind to him always; my covenant with him will never end. ²⁹He will always have an heir; his throne will be as endless as the days of heaven. ³⁰⁻³²If his children forsake my laws and don't obey them, then I will punish them, ³³but I will never completely take away my loving-kindness from them, nor let my promise fail. ³⁴No, I will not break my covenant; I will not take back one word of what I said. ³⁵,³⁶For I have sworn to David (and a holy God can never lie) that his dynasty will go on forever, and his throne will continue to the end of time. ³⁷It shall be eternal as the moon, my faithful witness in the sky!"

³⁸Then why cast me off, rejected? Why be so angry with the one you chose as king? ³⁹Have you renounced your covenant with him? For you have thrown his crown in the dust. ⁴⁰You have broken down the walls protecting him and laid in ruins every fort defending him. ⁴¹Everyone who comes along has robbed him while his neighbors mock. ⁴²You have strengthened his enemies against him and made them rejoice. ⁴³You have struck down his sword and refused to help him in battle. ⁴⁴You have ended his splendor and overturned his throne. ⁴⁵You have made him old before his time and publicly disgraced him.

⁴⁶O Jehovah, how long will this go on? Will you hide yourself from me forever? How long will your wrath burn like fire? ⁴⁷Oh, remember how short you have made man's lifespan. Is it an empty, futile life you give the sons of men? ⁴⁸No man can live forever. All will die. Who can rescue his life from the power of the grave?

⁴⁹Lord, where is the love you used to have for me? Where is your kindness that you promised to David with a faithful pledge? ⁵⁰Lord, see how all the people are despising me. ⁵¹Your enemies joke about me, the one you anointed as their king.

⁵²And yet—blessed be the Lord forever! Amen and amen!

PSALM 90 GOD'S ETERNAL KINGDOM. *A prayer of Moses, the man of God.*

Lord, through all the generations you have been our home! ²Before the mountains were created, before the earth was formed, you are God without beginning or end.

³You speak, and man turns back to dust. ⁴A thousand years are but as yesterday to you! They are like a single hour! ⁵,⁶We glide along the tides of time as swiftly as a racing river and vanish as quickly as a dream. We are like grass that is green in the morning but mowed down and withered before the evening shadows fall. ⁷We die beneath

Does God get tired of hearing about our troubles? I get frustrated when I struggle with the same problems over and over.

I WONDER . . .

Do you know someone who complains a lot? Perhaps you have a little brother or sister, a friend, or an acquaintance at school who is always complaining. Complainers aren't much fun to be around.

Complaining means that we aren't happy with what is going on around us and we think that by telling others we want something to change, it will happen. It also means we want attention. Complaining shines the spotlight on us for a while, and people give us attention. Sometimes, that's all we really wanted in the first place!

If you have been reading through Psalms, you can see that David seems to complain a lot! He is always in some sort of trouble, and he always wants God to get him out of it (see Psalm 88). Sound familiar?

The motivation behind our complaining is the key issue. When surrounded by enemies, David cried to God for protection. He had nowhere else to turn. Although this may seem like complaining, it actually is a very honest way to pray. God never gets tired of hearing us and coming to our rescue if we need his help.

But sometimes we complain or ask God for help because we have made wrong choices that have gotten us into trouble. Our natural response is to ask God to get us out of it. Although God always listens to us, he knows that the solution is not found in his coming to the rescue.

Instead, we must ask for forgiveness and then change the behavior that caused the problem in the first place. Some troubles are best solved by being humble and admitting we were wrong.

But if trouble comes from people or situations that are beyond our control, God is not only quick to hear, but also quick to answer. Either he will provide the internal resources necessary to handle the problem (peace "far more wonderful than the human mind can understand" [Philippians 4:7]) or he will provide the way of escape. Remember, "many others have faced exactly the same problems before you. And no temptation is irresistible. You can trust God to keep the temptation from becoming so strong that you can't stand up against it, for he has promised this and will do what he says. He will show you how to escape temptation's power so that you can bear up patiently against it" (1 Corinthians 10:13).

your anger; we are overwhelmed by your wrath. ⁸You spread out our sins before you—our secret sins—and see them all. ⁹No wonder the years are long and heavy here beneath your wrath. All our days are filled with sighing.

¹⁰Seventy years are given us! And some may even live to eighty. But even the best of these years

are often emptiness and pain; soon they disappear, and we are gone. [11]Who can realize the terrors of your anger? Which of us can fear you as he should?

[12]Teach us to number our days and recognize how few they are; help us to spend them as we should.

[13]O Jehovah, come and bless us! How long will you delay? Turn away your anger from us. [14]Satisfy us in our earliest youth with your loving-kindness, giving us constant joy to the end of our lives. [15]Give us gladness in proportion to our former misery! Replace the evil years with good. [16]Let us see your miracles again; let our children see glorious things, the kind you used to do, [17]and let the Lord our God favor us and give us success. May he give permanence to all we do.

PSALM 91 SAFE FROM DANGER. We live within the shadow of the Almighty, sheltered by the God who is above all gods.

[2]This I declare, that he alone is my refuge, my place of safety; he is my God, and I am trusting him. [3]For he rescues you from every trap and protects you from the fatal plague. [4]He will shield you with his wings! They will shelter you. His faithful promises are your armor. [5]Now you don't need to be afraid of the dark any more, nor fear the dangers of the day; [6]nor dread the plagues of darkness, nor disasters in the morning.

THE PROTECTOR

91:5-6 God is a refuge, a shelter when we are afraid. The writer's faith in God as Protector would carry him through all the dangers and fears of life. This should be a picture of our trust—trading all our fears for faith in him, no matter what kind of fear it may be.

[7]Though a thousand fall at my side, though ten thousand are dying around me, the evil will not touch me. [8]I will see how the wicked are punished, but I will not share it. [9]For Jehovah is my refuge! I choose the God above all gods to shelter me. [10]How then can evil overtake me or any plague come near? [11]For he orders his angels to protect you wherever you go. [12]They will steady you with their hands to keep you from stumbling against the rocks on the trail. [13]You can safely meet a lion or step on poisonous snakes, yes, even trample them beneath your feet!

[14]For the Lord says, "Because he loves me, I will rescue him; I will make him great because he trusts in my name. [15]When he calls on me, I will answer; I will be with him in trouble and rescue him and honor him. [16]I will satisfy him with a full life and give him my salvation."

PSALM 92 A SONG FOR THE LORD'S DAY. A song to sing on the Lord's Day.

It is good to say thank you to the Lord, to sing praises to the God who is above all gods.

[2]Every morning tell him, "Thank you for your kindness," and every evening rejoice in all his faithfulness. [3]Sing his praises, accompanied by music from the harp and lute and lyre. [4]You have done so much for me, O Lord. No wonder I am glad! I sing for joy.

[5]O Lord, what miracles you do! And how deep are your thoughts! [6]Unthinking people do not understand them! No fool can comprehend this: [7]that although the wicked flourish like weeds, there is only eternal destruction ahead of them. [8]But the Lord continues forever, exalted in the heavens, [9]while his enemies—all evil-doers—shall be scattered.

[10]But you have made me as strong as a wild bull. How refreshed I am by your blessings! [11]I have heard the doom of my enemies announced and seen them destroyed. [12]But the godly shall flourish like palm trees and grow tall as the cedars of Lebanon. [13]For they are transplanted into the Lord's own garden and are under his personal care. [14]Even in old age they will still produce fruit and be vital and green. [15]This honors the Lord and exhibits his faithful care. He is my shelter. There is nothing but goodness in him!

PSALM 93 OUR ALMIGHTY GOD. Jehovah is King! He is robed in majesty and strength. The world is his throne.

[2]O Lord, you have reigned from prehistoric times, from the everlasting past. [3]The mighty oceans thunder your praise. [4]You are mightier than all the breakers pounding on the seashores of the world! [5]Your royal decrees cannot be changed. Holiness is forever the keynote of your reign.

PSALM 94 GOD WILL DEAL WITH THE WICKED. Lord God, to whom vengeance belongs, let your glory shine out. Arise and judge the earth; sentence the proud to the penalties they deserve. [3]Lord, how long shall the wicked be allowed to triumph and exult? [4]Hear their insolence! See their arrogance! How these men of evil boast! [5]See them oppressing your people, O Lord, afflicting those you love. [6,7]They murder widows, immigrants, and orphans, for "The Lord isn't looking," they say, "and besides, he doesn't care."

[8]Fools! [9]Is God deaf and blind—he who makes

ELDERLY

92:14 Honoring God is not limited to young people who are still blessed with physical strength and vitality. Even in old age, devoted believers can produce spiritual fruit. There are many faithful older people who have much to share and teach from a lifetime of living with God. Seek out an elderly friend or relative to tell you about life experiences with the Lord and challenge you to new heights of spiritual living.

ears and eyes? [10]He punishes the nations—won't he also punish you? He knows everything—doesn't he also know what you are doing?

[11]The Lord is fully aware of how limited and futile the thoughts of mankind are, [12,13]so he helps us by punishing us. This makes us follow his paths and gives us respite from our enemies while God traps them and destroys them. [14]The Lord will not forsake his people, for they are his prize. [15]Judgment will again be just, and all the upright will rejoice.

[16]Who will protect me from the wicked? Who will be my shield? [17]I would have died unless the Lord had helped me. [18]I screamed, "I'm slipping, Lord!" and he was kind and saved me.

[19]Lord, when doubts fill my mind, when my heart is in turmoil, quiet me and give me renewed hope and cheer. [20]Will you permit a corrupt government to rule under your protection—a government permitting wrong to defeat right? [21,22]Do you approve of those who condemn the innocent to death? No! The Lord my God is my fortress—the mighty Rock where I can hide. [23]God has made the sins of evil men to boomerang upon them! He will destroy them by their own plans. Jehovah our God will cut them off.

PSALM 95 LET'S WORSHIP GOD.

Oh, come, let us sing to the Lord! Give a joyous shout in honor of the Rock of our salvation!

[2]Come before him with thankful hearts. Let us sing him psalms of praise. [3]For the Lord is a great God, the great King of all gods. [4]He controls the formation of the depths of the earth and the mightiest mountains; all are his. [5]He made the sea and formed the land; they too are his. [6]Come, kneel before the Lord our Maker, [7]for he is our God. We are his sheep, and he is our Shepherd. Oh, that you would hear him calling you today and come to him!

[8]Don't harden your hearts as Israel did in the wilderness at Meribah and Massah. [9]For there your fathers doubted me, though they had seen so many of my miracles before. My patience was severely tried by their complaints. [10]"For forty years I watched them in disgust," the Lord God says. "They were a nation whose thoughts and heart were far away from me. They refused to accept my laws. [11]Therefore, in mighty wrath I swore that they would never enter the Promised Land, the place of rest I planned for them."

PSALM 96 HOW CAN I PRAISE GOD?

Sing a new song to the Lord! Sing it everywhere around the world! [2]Sing out his praises! Bless his name. Each day tell someone that he saves.

[3]Publish his glorious acts throughout the earth. Tell everyone about the amazing things he does. [4]For the Lord is great beyond description and greatly to be praised. Worship only him among the gods! [5]For the gods of other nations are merely idols, but our God made the heavens! [6]Honor and majesty surround him; strength and beauty are in his Temple.

[7]O nations of the world, confess that God alone is glorious and strong. [8]Give him the glory he deserves! Bring your offering and come to worship him. [9]Worship the Lord with the beauty of holy lives. Let the earth tremble before him. [10]Tell the nations that Jehovah reigns! He rules the world. His power can never be overthrown. He will judge all nations fairly.

[11]Let the heavens be glad, the earth rejoice; let the vastness of the roaring seas demonstrate his glory. [12]Praise him for the growing fields, for they display his greatness. Let the trees of the forest rustle with praise. [13]For the Lord is coming to judge the earth; he will judge the nations fairly and with truth!

PSALM 97 GOD IS AWESOME AND JUST.

Jehovah is King! Let all the earth rejoice! Tell the farthest islands to be glad.

[2]Clouds and darkness surround him. Righteousness and justice are the foundation of his throne. [3]Fire goes forth before him and burns up all his foes. [4]His lightning flashes out across the world. The earth sees and trembles. [5]The mountains melt like wax before the Lord of all the earth. [6]The heavens declare his perfect righteousness; every nation sees his glory.

[7]Let those who worship idols be disgraced—all who brag about their worthless gods—for every god must bow to him! [8,9]Jerusalem and all the cities of Judah have heard of your justice, Lord, and are glad that you reign in majesty over the entire earth and are far greater than these other gods.

[10]The Lord loves those who hate evil; he protects the lives of his people and rescues them from the wicked. [11]Light is sown for the godly and joy for the good. [12]May all who are godly be happy in the Lord and crown him, our holy God.

HATE EVIL

97:10 A sincere desire to please God will result in an alignment of your desires with God's desires. You will love what God loves and hate what God hates. Here we read that God loves those who hate evil. If you do not despise the actions of people who take advantage of others, if you admire people who look out only for themselves, or if you envy those who get ahead using any means to accomplish their ends, then your primary desire in life is not to please God. Learn to love God's ways and hate evil in every form— not only the obvious sins, but the socially acceptable ones as well.

PSALM 98 **A SONG OF JOY AND VICTORY.** Sing a new song to the Lord telling about his mighty deeds! For he has won a mighty victory by his power and holiness. ^{2,3}He has announced this victory and revealed it to every nation by fulfilling his promise to be kind to Israel. The whole earth has seen God's salvation of his people. ⁴That is why the earth breaks out in praise to God and sings for utter joy!

⁵Sing your praise accompanied by music from the harp. ⁶Let the cornets and trumpets shout! Make a joyful symphony before the Lord, the King! ⁷Let the sea in all its vastness roar with praise! Let the earth and all those living on it shout, "Glory to the Lord."

^{8,9}Let the waves clap their hands in glee and the hills sing out their songs of joy before the Lord, for he is coming to judge the world with perfect justice.

PSALM 99 **GOD IS FAIR AND HOLY.** Jehovah is King! Let the nations tremble! He is enthroned between the Guardian Angels. Let the whole earth shake.

²Jehovah sits in majesty in Zion, supreme above all rulers of the earth. ³Let them reverence your great and holy name.

⁴This mighty King is determined to give justice. Fairness is the touchstone of everything he does. He gives justice throughout Israel. ⁵Exalt the Lord our holy God! Bow low before his feet.

⁶When Moses and Aaron and Samuel, his prophet, cried to him for help, he answered them. ⁷He spoke to them from the pillar of cloud, and they followed his instructions. ⁸O Jehovah our God! You answered them and forgave their sins, yet punished them when they went wrong.

⁹Exalt the Lord our God and worship at his holy mountain in Jerusalem, for he is holy.

PSALM 100 **COME BEFORE GOD WITH PRAISE.** Shout with joy before the Lord, O earth! ²Obey him gladly; come before him, singing with joy.

³Try to realize what this means—the Lord is God! He made us—we are his people, the sheep of his pasture.

⁴Go through his open gates with great thanksgiving; enter his courts with praise. Give thanks to him and bless his name. ⁵For the Lord is always good. He is always loving and kind, and his faithfulness goes on and on to each succeeding generation.

PSALM 101 **LIVING A CLEAN LIFE FOR GOD.** I will sing about your loving-kindness and your justice, Lord. I will sing your praises!

²I will try to walk a blameless path, but how I need your help, especially in my own home, where I long to act as I should.

³Help me to refuse the low and vulgar things; help me to abhor all crooked deals of every kind, to have no part in them. ⁴I will reject all selfishness and stay away from every evil. ⁵I will not tolerate anyone who secretly slanders his neighbors; I will not permit conceit and pride. ⁶I will make the godly of the land my heroes and invite them to my home. Only those who are truly good shall be

HIS NAME

99:3 Everyone, even kings and rulers, should reverence God's great and holy name because his name symbolizes his nature, his personage, and his reputation. But the name of God is used so often in vulgar conversation that we have lost sight of its holiness. How easy it is to treat God lightly in everyday life! If you claim him as your father, live in a way that is worthy of the family name. Reverence God's name by both your *words* and your *life.*

HEROES

101:6 David set different standards for heroes than most. He said that he would make the "godly of the land'" his heroes. Our heroes, those we set up in our minds as models to copy, have a great influence on our lives. Choose your heroes with care.

GO
THROUGH
H I S
O P E N
G A T E S
with **GREAT**
thanksgiving

ENTER HIS COURTS
with
P R A I S E
P R A I S E
P R A I S

Give thanks to HIM
and
BLESS BLESS BLESS BLESS
HIS NAME

my servants. ⁷But I will not allow those who deceive and lie to stay in my house. ⁸My daily task will be to ferret out criminals and free the city of God from their grip.

PSALM **102** WHEN WE NEED HELP. *A prayer when overwhelmed with trouble.*

Lord, hear my prayer! Listen to my plea!

²Don't turn away from me in this time of my distress. Bend down your ear and give me speedy answers, ³,⁴for my days disappear like smoke. My health is broken, and my heart is sick; it is trampled like grass and is withered. My food is tasteless, and I have lost my appetite. ⁵I am reduced to skin and bones because of all my groaning and despair. ⁶I am like a vulture in a far-off wilderness or like an owl alone in the desert. ⁷I lie awake, lonely as a solitary sparrow on the roof.

⁸My enemies taunt me day after day and curse at me. ⁹,¹⁰I eat ashes instead of bread. My tears run down into my drink because of your anger against me, because of your wrath. For you have rejected me and thrown me out. ¹¹My life is passing swiftly as the evening shadows. I am withering like grass, ¹²while you, Lord, are a famous King forever. Your fame will endure to every generation.

¹³I know that you will come and have mercy on Jerusalem—and now is the time to pity her—the time you promised help. ¹⁴For your people love every stone in her walls and feel sympathy for every grain of dust in her streets. ¹⁵Now let the nations and their rulers tremble before the Lord, before his glory. ¹⁶For Jehovah will rebuild Jerusalem! He will appear in his glory!

¹⁷He will listen to the prayers of the destitute, for he is never too busy to heed their requests. ¹⁸ I am recording this so that future generations will also praise the Lord for all that he has done. And a people that shall be created shall praise the Lord. ¹⁹Tell them that God looked down from his temple in heaven ²⁰and heard the groans of his people in slavery—they were children of death—and released them, ²¹,²²so that multitudes would stream to the Temple in Jerusalem to praise him, and his praises were sung throughout the city; and many rulers throughout the earth came to worship him.

²³He has cut me down in middle life, shortening my days. ²⁴But I cried to him, "O God, you live forever and forever! Don't let me die half through my years! ²⁵In ages past you laid the foundations of the earth and made the heavens with your hands! ²⁶They shall perish, but you go on forever. They will grow old like worn-out clothing, and you will change them like a man putting on a new shirt and throwing away the old one! ²⁷But you yourself never grow old. You are forever, and your years never end.

²⁸"But our families will continue; generation after generation will be preserved by your protection."

PSALM **103** GOD'S GREAT LOVE FOR US. I

bless the holy name of God with all my heart. ²Yes, I will bless the Lord and not forget the glorious things he does for me.

³He forgives all my sins. He heals me. ⁴He ransoms me from hell. He surrounds me with loving-kindness and tender mercies. ⁵He fills my life with good things! My youth is renewed like the eagle's! ⁶He gives justice to all who are treated unfairly. ⁷He revealed his will and nature to Moses and the people of Israel.

⁸He is merciful and tender toward those who don't deserve it; he is slow to get angry and full of kindness and love. ⁹He never bears a grudge, nor remains angry forever. ¹⁰He has not punished us as we deserve for all our sins, ¹¹for his mercy toward those who fear and honor him is as great as the height of the heavens above the earth. ¹²He has removed our sins as far away from us as the east is from the west. ¹³He is like a father to us, tender and sympathetic to those who reverence him. ¹⁴For he knows we are but dust ¹⁵and that our days are few and brief, like grass, like flowers, ¹⁶blown by the wind and gone forever.

¹⁷,¹⁸But the loving-kindness of the Lord is from everlasting to everlasting to those who reverence him; his salvation is to children's children of those who are faithful to his covenant and remember to obey him!

¹⁹The Lord has made the heavens his throne; from there he rules over everything there is. ²⁰Bless the Lord, you mighty angels of his who carry out his orders, listening for each of his commands. ²¹Yes, bless the Lord, you armies of his angels who serve him constantly. ²²Let everything everywhere bless the Lord. And how I bless him too!

PLENTY

103:1ff David's praise focused on God's glorious acts. It is easy to complain about life, but David's list gives us plenty for which to praise God—his love, forgiveness, salvation, kindness, mercy, justice, patience, tenderness—we receive all of these without deserving any of them. No matter how difficult your life's journey, you can always count your blessings—past, present, and future. When you feel as though you have nothing for which to praise God, read David's list.

PSALM **104** GOD TAKES CARE OF HIS WORLD. I

bless the Lord: O Lord my God, how great you are! You are robed with honor and with majesty and light! You stretched out the starry curtain of the heavens, ³and hollowed out the surface of the earth to form the seas. The clouds are his chariots. He

CREATION

104:24 Creation is filled with stunning variety, revealing the rich creativity, goodness, and wisdom of our loving God. As you observe your natural surroundings, thank God for his creativity. Take a fresh look at people, seeing each one as his unique creation, each with his or her own special talents, abilities, and gifts.

rides upon the wings of the wind. [4]The angels are his messengers—his servants of fire!

[5]You bound the world together so that it would never fall apart. [6]You clothed the earth with floods of waters covering up the mountains. [7,8]You spoke, and at the sound of your shout the water collected into its vast ocean beds, and mountains rose and valleys sank to the levels you decreed. [9]And then you set a boundary for the seas so that they would never again cover the earth.

[10]He placed springs in the valleys and streams that gush from the mountains. [11]They give water for all the animals to drink. There the wild donkeys quench their thirst, [12]and the birds nest beside the streams and sing among the branches of the trees. [13]He sends rain upon the mountains and fills the earth with fruit. [14]The tender grass grows up at his command to feed the cattle, and there are fruit trees, vegetables, and grain for man to cultivate, [15]and wine to make him glad, and olive oil as lotion for his skin, and bread to give him strength. [16]The Lord planted the cedars of Lebanon. They are tall and flourishing. [17]There the birds make their nests, the storks in the firs. [18]High in the mountains are pastures for the wild goats, and rock-badgers burrow in among the rocks and find protection there.

[19]He assigned the moon to mark the months and the sun to mark the days. [20]He sends the night and darkness, when all the forest folk come out. [21]Then the young lions roar for their food, but they are dependent on the Lord. [22]At dawn they slink back into their dens to rest, [23]and men go off to work until the evening shadows fall again. [24]O Lord, what a variety you have made! And in wisdom you have made them all! The earth is full of your riches.

[25]There before me lies the mighty ocean, teeming with life of every kind, both great and small. [26]And look! See the ships! And over there, the whale you made to play in the sea. [27]Every one of these depends on you to give them daily food. [28]You supply it, and they gather it. You open wide your hand to feed them, and they are satisfied with all your bountiful provision.

[29]But if you turn away from them, then all is lost. And when you gather up their breath, they die and turn again to dust.

[30]Then you send your Spirit, and new life is born to replenish all the living of the earth. [31]Praise God forever! How he must rejoice in all his work! [32]The earth trembles at his glance; the mountains burst into flame at his touch.

[33]I will sing to the Lord as long as I live. I will praise God to my last breath! [34]May he be pleased by all these thoughts about him, for he is the source of all my joy. [35]Let all sinners perish—all who refuse to praise him. But I will praise him. Hallelujah!

PSALM 105 REMEMBER GOD'S MIRACLES.

Thank the Lord for all the glorious things he does; proclaim them to the nations. [2]Sing his praises and tell everyone about his miracles. [3]Glory in the Lord; O worshipers of God, rejoice.

[4]Search for him and for his strength, and keep on searching!

[5,6]Think of the mighty deeds he did for us, his chosen ones—descendants of God's servant Abraham, and of Jacob. Remember how he destroyed our enemies. [7]He is the Lord our God. His goodness is seen everywhere throughout the land. [8,9]Though a thousand generations pass he never forgets his promise, his covenant with Abraham and Isaac [10,11]and confirmed with Jacob. This is his never-ending treaty with the people of Israel: *"I will give you the land of Canaan as your inheritance."* [12]He said this when they were but few in number, very few, and were only visitors in Canaan. [13]Later they were dispersed among the nations and were driven from one kingdom to another; [14]but through it all he would not let one thing be done to them apart from his decision. He destroyed many a king who tried! [15]"Touch not these chosen ones of mine," he warned, "and do not hurt my prophets."

[16]He called for a famine on the land of Canaan, cutting off its food supply. [17]Then he sent Joseph as a slave to Egypt to save his people from starvation. [18]There in prison they hurt his feet with fetters and placed his neck in an iron collar [19]until God's time finally came—how God tested his patience! [20]Then the king sent for him and set him free. [21]He was put in charge of all the king's possessions. [22]At his pleasure he could imprison the king's aides and teach the king's advisors.

[23]Then Jacob (Israel) arrived in Egypt and lived there with his sons. [24]In the years that followed, the people of Israel multiplied explosively until they were a greater nation than their rulers. [25]At that point God turned the Egyptians against the Israelis; they hated and enslaved them.

[26]But God sent Moses as his representative, and

SEEK

105:4 If God seems far away, keep searching for him. God rewards those who sincerely look for him (Hebrews 11:6). Jesus promised "seek, and you will find" (Matthew 7:7). David suggested a valuable way to search out God— become familiar with the way he has helped his people in the past. The Bible records the history of God's people. In searching its pages we will discover a loving God who is waiting for us to find him.

Aaron with him, ²⁷to call down miracles of terror upon the land of Egypt. ²⁸They followed his instructions. He sent thick darkness through the land ²⁹and turned the nation's water into blood, poisoning the fish. ³⁰Then frogs invaded in enormous numbers; they were found even in the king's private rooms. ³¹When Moses spoke, the flies and other insects swarmed in vast clouds from one end of Egypt to the other. ³²Instead of rain he sent down murderous hail, and lightning flashes overwhelmed the nation. ³³Their grape vines and fig trees were ruined; all the trees lay broken on the ground. ³⁴He spoke, and hordes of locusts came ³⁵and ate up everything green, destroying all the crops. ³⁶Then he killed the oldest child in each Egyptian home, their pride and joy—³⁷and brought his people safely out from Egypt, loaded with silver and gold; there were no sick and feeble folk among them then. ³⁸Egypt was glad when they were gone, for the dread of them was great.

³⁹He spread out a cloud above them to shield them from the burning sun and gave them a pillar of flame at night to give them light. ⁴⁰They asked for meat, and he sent them quail and gave them manna—bread from heaven. ⁴¹He opened up a rock, and water gushed out to form a river through the dry and barren land; ⁴²for he remembered his sacred promises to Abraham his servant.

⁴³So he brought his chosen ones singing into the Promised Land. ⁴⁴He gave them the lands of the Gentiles, complete with their growing crops; they ate what others planted. ⁴⁵This was done to make them faithful and obedient to his laws. Hallelujah!

PSALM **106** **GOD ALWAYS FORGIVES.** Hallelujah! Thank you, Lord! How good you are! Your love for us continues on forever. ²Who can ever list the glorious miracles of God? Who can ever praise him half enough?

³Happiness comes to those who are fair to others and are always just and good.

⁴Remember me too, O Lord, while you are blessing and saving your people. ⁵Let me share in your chosen ones' prosperity and rejoice in all their joys, and receive the glory you give to them.

⁶Both we and our fathers have sinned so much. ⁷They weren't impressed by the wonder of your miracles in Egypt and soon forgot your many acts of kindness to them. Instead they rebelled against you at the Red Sea. ⁸Even so you saved them—to defend the honor of your name and demonstrate your power to all the world. ⁹You commanded the Red Sea to divide, forming a dry road across its bottom. Yes, as dry as any desert! ¹⁰Thus you rescued them from their enemies. ¹¹Then the water returned and covered the road and drowned their foes; not one survived.

¹²Then at last his people believed him. Then they finally sang his praise.

¹³Yet how quickly they forgot again! They wouldn't wait for him to act ¹⁴but demanded better food, testing God's patience to the breaking point. ¹⁵So he gave them their demands but sent them leanness in their souls. ¹⁶They were envious of Moses, yes, and Aaron too, the man anointed by God as his priest. ¹⁷Because of this, the earth opened and swallowed Dathan, Abiram, and his friends; ¹⁸and fire fell from heaven to consume these wicked men. ^{19,20}For they preferred a statue of an ox that eats grass to the glorious presence of God himself. ^{21,22}Thus they despised their Savior who had done such mighty miracles in Egypt and at the Sea. ²³So the Lord declared he would destroy them. But Moses, his chosen one, stepped into the breach between the people and their God and begged him to turn from his wrath and not destroy them.

²⁴They refused to enter the Promised Land, for they wouldn't believe his solemn oath to care for them. ²⁵Instead, they pouted in their tents and mourned and despised his command. ²⁶Therefore he swore that he would kill them in the wilderness ²⁷and send their children away to distant lands as exiles. ²⁸Then our fathers joined the worshipers of Baal at Peor and even offered sacrifices to the dead! ²⁹With all these things they angered him— and so a plague broke out upon them ³⁰and continued until Phineas executed those whose sins had caused the plague to start. ³¹(For this good deed Phineas will be remembered forever.)

³²At Meribah, too, Israel angered God, causing Moses serious trouble, ³³for he became angry and spoke foolishly.

³⁴Nor did Israel destroy the nations in the land as God had told them to, ³⁵but mingled in among the heathen and learned their evil ways, ³⁶sacrificing to their idols, and were led away from God. ^{37,38}They even sacrificed their little children to the demons— the idols of Canaan—shedding innocent blood and polluting the land with murder. ³⁹Their evil deeds defiled them, for their love of idols was adultery in the sight of God. ⁴⁰That is why Jehovah's anger burned against his people, and he abhorred them. ^{41,42}That is why he let the heathen nations crush them. They were ruled by those who hated them and oppressed by their enemies.

TROUBLES

106:40-42 God allowed trouble to come to the Israelites to help them. Our troubles can be helpful because they (1) humble us, (2) pull us from the allurements of the world and drive us back to God, (3) quicken our prayers, (4) allow us to experience more of God's faithfulness, (5) make us more dependent upon God, (6) encourage us to submit to God's purpose for our lives, and (7) make us more compassionate to others in trouble.

⁴³Again and again he delivered them from their slavery, but they continued to rebel against him and were finally destroyed by their sin. ⁴⁴Yet, even so, he listened to their cries and heeded their distress; ⁴⁵he remembered his promises to them and relented because of his great love, ⁴⁶and caused even their enemies who captured them to pity them.

⁴⁷O Lord God, save us! Regather us from the nations so we can thank your holy name and rejoice and praise you.

⁴⁸Blessed be the Lord, the God of Israel, from everlasting to everlasting. Let all the people say, "Amen!" Hallelujah!

PSALM 107 GIVE THANKS ALWAYS. Say thank you to the Lord for being so good, for always being so loving and kind. ²Has the Lord redeemed you? Then speak out! Tell others he has saved you from your enemies.

³He brought the exiles back from the farthest corners of the earth. ⁴They were wandering homeless in the desert, ⁵hungry and thirsty and faint. ⁶"Lord, help!" they cried, and he did! ⁷He led them straight to safety and a place to live. ⁸Oh, that these men would praise the Lord for his loving-kindness, and for all of his wonderful deeds! ⁹For he satisfies the thirsty soul and fills the hungry soul with good.

¹⁰Who are these who sit in darkness, in the shadow of death, crushed by misery and slavery? ¹¹They rebelled against the Lord, scorning him who is the God above all gods. ¹²That is why he broke them with hard labor; they fell and none could help them rise again. ¹³Then they cried to the Lord in their troubles, and he rescued them! ¹⁴He led them from the darkness and shadow of death and snapped their chains. ¹⁵Oh, that these men would praise the Lord for his loving-kindness and for all of his wonderful deeds! ¹⁶For he broke down their prison gates of brass and cut apart their iron bars.

¹⁷Others, the fools, were ill because of their sinful ways. ¹⁸Their appetites were gone, and death was near. ¹⁹Then they cried to the Lord in their troubles, and he helped them and delivered them. ²⁰He spoke, and they were healed—snatched from the door of death. ²¹Oh, that these men would praise the Lord for his loving-kindness and for all of his wonderful deeds! ²²Let them tell him thank you as their sacrifice and sing about his glorious deeds.

²³And then there are the sailors sailing the seven seas, plying the trade routes of the world. ²⁴They, too, observe the power of God in action. ²⁵He calls to the storm winds; the waves rise high. ²⁶Their ships are tossed to the heavens and sink again to the depths; the sailors cringe in terror. ²⁷They reel and stagger like drunkards and are at their wit's end. ²⁸Then they cry to the Lord in their trouble, and he saves them. ²⁹He calms the storm and stills the waves. ³⁰What a blessing is that stillness as he brings them safely into harbor! ³¹Oh, that these men would praise the Lord for his loving-kindness and for all of his wonderful deeds! ³²Let them praise him publicly before the congregation and before the leaders of the nation.

³³He dries up rivers ³⁴and turns the good land of the wicked into deserts of salt. ³⁵Again, he turns deserts into fertile, watered valleys. ³⁶He brings the hungry to settle there and build their cities, ³⁷to sow their fields and plant their vineyards, and reap their bumper crops! ³⁸How he blesses them! They raise big families there and many cattle.

³⁹But others become poor through oppression, trouble, and sorrow. ⁴⁰For God pours contempt upon the haughty and causes princes to wander among ruins; ⁴¹but he rescues the poor who are godly and gives them many children and much prosperity. ⁴²Good men everywhere will see it and be glad, while evil men are stricken silent.

⁴³Listen, if you are wise, to what I am saying. Think about the loving-kindness of the Lord!

PSALM 108 WITH GOD, WE CAN. O God, my heart is ready to praise you! I will sing and rejoice before you.

²Wake up, O harp and lyre! We will meet the dawn with song. ³I will praise you everywhere around the world, in every nation. ⁴For your loving-kindness is great beyond measure, high as the heavens. Your faithfulness reaches the skies. ⁵His glory is far more vast than the heavens. It towers above the earth. ⁶Hear the cry of your beloved child—come with mighty power and rescue me.

⁷God has given sacred promises; no wonder I exult! He has promised to give us all the land of Shechem and also Succoth Valley. ⁸"Gilead is mine to give to you," he says, "and Manasseh as well; the land of Ephraim is the helmet on my head. Judah is my scepter. ⁹But Moab and Edom are despised; and I will shout in triumph over the Philistines."

¹⁰Who but God can give me strength to conquer

STRENGTH

107:28-32 Sometimes we feel as though all is hopeless. But trouble can lead us to depend on God as we cry to him for help. When he saves us, we will praise him for the good he has done. Then we understand that God can bring good out of troubles because our afflictions strengthen our faith.

STAKE A CLAIM

108:13 Do our prayers end with requests just to make it through stressful situations? David prayed not just for rescue, but for victory. With God's help we can claim more than just survival, we can claim victory! Look for ways God can use your distress as an opportunity to show his mighty power.

these fortified cities? Who else can lead me into Edom?

[11]Lord, have you thrown us away? Have you deserted our army? [12]Oh, help us fight against our enemies, for men are useless allies. [13]But with the help of God we shall do mighty acts of valor. For he treads down our foes.

PSALM 109 HELP ME, O LORD!

O God of my praise, don't stand silent and aloof [2]while the wicked slander me and tell their lies. [3]They have no reason to hate and fight me, yet they do! [4]I love them, but even while I am praying for them, they are trying to destroy me. [5]They return evil for good, and hatred for love.

[6]Show him how it feels! Let lies be told about him, and bring him to court before an unfair judge. [7]When his case is called for judgment, let him be pronounced guilty. Count his prayers as sins. [8]Let his years be few and brief; let others step forward to replace him. [9,10]May his children become fatherless and his wife a widow; may they be evicted from the ruins of their home. [11]May creditors seize his entire estate and strangers take all he has earned. [12,13]Let no one be kind to him; let no one pity his fatherless children. May they die. May his family name be blotted out in a single generation. [14]Punish the sins of his father and mother. Don't overlook them. [15]Think constantly about the evil things he has done, and cut off his name from the memory of man.

[16]For he refused all kindness to others, and persecuted those in need, and hounded brokenhearted ones to death. [17]He loved to curse others; now you curse him. He never blessed others; now don't you bless him. [18]Cursing is as much a part of him as his clothing, or as the water he drinks, or the rich food he eats.

[19]Now may those curses return and cling to him like his clothing or his belt. [20]This is the Lord's punishment upon my enemies who tell lies about me and threaten me with death.

[21]But as for me, O Lord, deal with me as your child, as one who bears your name! Because you are so kind, O Lord, deliver me.

[22,23]I am slipping down the hill to death; I am shaken off from life as easily as a man brushes a grasshopper from his arm. [24]My knees are weak from fasting, and I am skin and bones. [25]I am a symbol of failure to all mankind; when they see me they shake their heads.

[26]Help me, O Lord my God! Save me because you are loving and kind. [27]Do it publicly, so all will see that you yourself have done it. [28]Then let them curse me if they like—I won't mind that if you are blessing me! For then all their efforts to destroy me will fail, and I shall go right on rejoicing!

[29]Make them fail in everything they do. Clothe them with disgrace. [30]But I will give repeated thanks to the Lord, praising him to everyone. [31]For he stands beside the poor and hungry to save them from their enemies.

PSALM 110 JESUS CHRIST, THE MESSIAH.

Jehovah said to my Lord the Messiah, "Rule as my regent—I will subdue your enemies and make them bow low before you."

[2]Jehovah has established your throne in Jerusalem to rule over your enemies. [3]In that day of your power your people shall come to you willingly, dressed in holy altar robes. And your strength shall be renewed day by day like morning dew. [4]Jehovah has taken oath and will not rescind his vow that you are a priest forever like Melchizedek. [5]God stands beside you to protect you. He will strike down many kings in the day of his anger. [6]He will punish the nations and fill them with their dead. He will crush many heads. [7]But he himself shall be refreshed from springs along the way.

MESSIAH

110:1-7 Many people have a vague belief in God, but refuse to accept Jesus as anything more than a great human teacher. But the Bible does not allow that option. Both the Old and New Testaments proclaim the deity of the One who came to save and to reign. This psalm shows God's promise of sending the Messiah. The New Testament clearly shows that Jesus is God's Son, the Messiah. You can't straddle the fence, calling Jesus "just a good teacher," because the Bible clearly calls him the Messiah.

PSALM 111 ALL GOD DOES IS GOOD.

Hallelujah! I want to express publicly before his people my heartfelt thanks to God for his mighty miracles. All who are thankful should ponder them with me. [3]For his miracles demonstrate his honor, majesty, and eternal goodness.

[4]Who can forget the wonders he performs—deeds of mercy and of grace? [5]He gives food to those who trust him; he never forgets his promises. [6]He has shown his great power to his people by giving them the land of Israel, though it was the home of many nations living there. [7]All he does is just and good, and all his laws are right, [8]for they are formed from truth and goodness and stand firm forever. [9]He has paid a full ransom for his people; now they are always free to come to Jehovah (what a holy, awe-inspiring name that is).

[10]How can men be wise? The only way to begin is by reverence for God. For growth in wisdom comes from obeying his laws. Praise his name forever.

PSALM 112 HAPPY ARE THOSE WHO OBEY.

Praise the Lord! For all who fear God and trust in him are blessed beyond expression. Yes, happy is the man who delights in doing his commands.

²His children shall be honored everywhere, for good men's sons have a special heritage. ³He himself shall be wealthy, and his good deeds will never be forgotten. ⁴When darkness overtakes him, light will come bursting in. He is kind and merciful—⁵and all goes well for the generous man who conducts his business fairly.

⁶Such a man will not be overthrown by evil circumstances. God's constant care of him will make a deep impression on all who see it. ⁷He does not fear bad news, nor live in dread of what may happen. For he is settled in his mind that Jehovah will take care of him. ⁸That is why he is not afraid but can calmly face his foes. ⁹He gives generously to those in need. His deeds will never be forgotten. He shall have influence and honor.

¹⁰Evil-minded men will be infuriated when they see all this; they will gnash their teeth in anger and slink away, their hopes thwarted.

FEARLESS

112:7-8 We all want to live without fear; our heroes are fearless people who face dangers and overcome them. The psalmist teaches us that *fear* of God can lead to a *fearless* life. To fear God means to respect and reverence him as the almighty Lord. When we trust God completely to take care of us, we will find that our other fears—even of death itself—will subside.

PSALM 113 GOD CARES ABOUT EVERYONE.

Hallelujah! O servants of Jehovah, praise his name. ²Blessed is his name forever and forever. ³Praise him from sunrise to sunset! ⁴For he is high above the nations; his glory is far greater than the heavens.

⁵Who can be compared with God enthroned on high? ⁶Far below him are the heavens and the earth; he stoops to look, ⁷and lifts the poor from the dirt and the hungry from the garbage dump, ⁸and sets them among princes! ⁹He gives children to the childless wife, so that she becomes a happy mother.

Hallelujah! Praise the Lord.

PSALM 114 CELEBRATE GOD'S GREAT WORKS.

Long ago when the Israelis escaped from Egypt, from that land of foreign tongue, ²then the lands of Judah and of Israel became God's new home and kingdom.

³The Red Sea saw them coming and quickly broke apart before them. The Jordan River opened up a path for them to cross. ⁴The mountains skipped like rams, the little hills like lambs! ⁵What's wrong, Red Sea, that made you cut yourself in two? What happened, Jordan River, to your waters? Why were they held back? ⁶Why, mountains, did you skip like rams? Why, little hills, like lambs?

⁷Tremble, O earth, at the presence of the Lord, the God of Jacob. ⁸For he caused gushing streams to burst from flinty rock.

PSALM 115 GOD LIVES.

Glorify your name, not ours, O Lord! Cause everyone to praise your loving-kindness and your truth. ²Why let the nations say, "Their God is dead!"

³For he is in the heavens and does as he wishes. ⁴Their gods are merely manmade things of silver and of gold. ⁵They can't talk or see, despite their eyes and mouths! ⁶Nor can they hear, nor smell, ⁷nor use their hands or feet, nor speak! ⁸And those who make and worship them are just as foolish as their idols are.

⁹O Israel, trust the Lord! He is your helper. He is your shield. ¹⁰O priests of Aaron, trust the Lord! He is your helper; he is your shield. ¹¹All of you, his people, trust in him. He is your helper; he is your shield.

¹²Jehovah is constantly thinking about us, and he will surely bless us. He will bless the people of Israel and the priests of Aaron, ¹³ and all, both great and small, who reverence him.

¹⁴May the Lord richly bless both you and your children. ¹⁵Yes, Jehovah who made heaven and earth will personally bless you! ¹⁶The heavens belong to the Lord, but he has given the earth to all mankind.

¹⁷The dead cannot sing praises to Jehovah here on earth, ¹⁸but we can! We praise him forever! Hallelujah! Praise the Lord!

THOUGHTS

115:12 "Jehovah is constantly thinking about us" says the psalm writer. What a fantastic truth! There are many times when we feel isolated, alone, and abandoned, even by God. In reality, he sees, understands, and is thinking about us. When depressed or struggling, be encouraged that God keeps you in his thoughts. If he thinks about you, surely his help is near.

PSALM 116 GOD SAVES US; LET'S WORSHIP HIM.

I love the Lord because he hears my prayers and answers them. ²Because he bends down and listens, I will pray as long as I breathe!

³Death stared me in the face—I was frightened and sad. ⁴Then I cried, "Lord, save me!" ⁵How kind he is! How good he is! So merciful, this God of ours! ⁶The Lord protects the simple and the childlike; I was facing death, and then he saved me. ⁷Now I can relax. For the Lord has done this wonderful miracle for me. ⁸He has saved me from death, my eyes from tears, my feet from stumbling. ⁹I shall live! Yes, in his presence—here on earth!

¹⁰,¹¹ In my discouragement I thought, "They are lying when they say I will recover." ¹²But now what

can I offer Jehovah for all he has done for me? [13]I will bring him an offering of wine and praise his name for saving me. [14]I will publicly bring him the sacrifice I vowed I would. [15]His loved ones are very precious to him, and he does not lightly let them die.

[16]O Lord, you have freed me from my bonds, and I will serve you forever. [17]I will worship you and offer you a sacrifice of thanksgiving. [18,19]Here in the courts of the Temple in Jerusalem, before all the people, I will pay everything I vowed to the Lord. Praise the Lord.

PSALM 117 PRAISE GOD FOR HIS LOVE.

Praise the Lord, all nations everywhere. Praise him, all the peoples of the earth. [2]For he loves us very dearly, and his truth endures. Praise the Lord.

PSALM 118 GOD'S LOVE NEVER FAILS.

Oh, thank the Lord, for he's so good! His loving-kindness is forever.

[2]Let the congregation of Israel praise him with these same words: "His loving-kindness is forever." [3]And let the priests of Aaron chant, "His loving-kindness is forever." [4]Let the Gentile converts chant, "His loving-kindness is forever."

[5]In my distress I prayed to the Lord, and he answered me and rescued me. [6]He is for me! How can I be afraid? What can mere man do to me? [7]The Lord is on my side; he will help me. Let those who hate me beware.

[8]It is better to trust the Lord than to put confidence in men. [9]It is better to take refuge in him than in the mightiest king!

[10]Though all the nations of the world attack me, I will march out behind his banner and destroy them. [11]Yes, they surround and attack me; but with his flag flying above me I will cut them off. [12]They swarm around me like bees; they blaze against me like a roaring flame. Yet beneath his flag I shall destroy them. [13]You did your best to kill me, O my enemy, but the Lord helped me. [14]He is my strength and song in the heat of battle, and now he has given me the victory. [15,16]Songs of joy at the news of our rescue are sung in the homes of the godly. The strong arm of the Lord has done glorious things! [17]I shall not die but live to tell of all his deeds. [18]The Lord has punished me but not handed me over to death.

[19]Open the gates of the Temple—I will go in and give him my thanks. [20]Those gates are the way into the presence of the Lord, and the godly enter there. [21]O Lord, thank you so much for answering my prayer and saving me.

[22]The stone rejected by the builders has now become the capstone of the arch! [23]This is the Lord's doing, and it is marvelous to see! [24]This is the day the Lord has made. We will rejoice and be glad in it. [25]O Lord, please help us. Save us. Give us success. [26]Blessed is the one who is coming, the one sent by the Lord. We bless you from the Temple.

[27,28]Jehovah God is our light. I present to him my sacrifice upon the altar, for you are my God, and I shall give you this thanks and this praise. [29]Oh, give thanks to the Lord, for he is so good! For his loving-kindness is forever.

PSALM 119 HAPPINESS IS OBEYING GOD.

Happy are all who perfectly follow the laws of God. [2]Happy are all who search for God and always do his will, [3]rejecting compromise with evil and walking only in his paths. [4]You have given us your laws to obey—[5]oh, how I want to follow them consistently. [6]Then I will not be disgraced, for I will have a clean record.

[7]After you have corrected me, I will thank you by living as I should! [8]I *will* obey! Oh, don't forsake me and let me slip back into sin again.

[9]How can a young man stay pure? By reading your Word and following its rules. [10]I have tried my best to find you—don't let me wander off from your instructions. [11]I have thought much about your words and stored them in my heart so that they would hold me back from sin.

DETERRENT

119:11 Storing God's word in our hearts and minds is a deterrent to sin. This alone should inspire us to want to memorize Scripture. But memorization alone will not keep us from sin; we must also put God's word to work in our lives, making it a vital guide to everything we do.

[12]Blessed Lord, teach me your rules. [13]I have recited your laws [14]and rejoiced in them more than in riches. [15]I will meditate upon them and give them my full respect. [16]I will delight in them and not forget them.

[17]Bless me with life so that I can continue to obey you. [18]Open my eyes to see wonderful things in your Word. [19]I am but a pilgrim here on earth: how I need a map—and your commands are my chart and guide. [20]I long for your instructions more than I can tell.

[21]You rebuke those cursed proud ones who refuse your commands—[22]don't let them scorn me for obeying you. [23]For even princes sit and talk against me, but I will continue in your plans. [24]Your laws are both my light and my counselors.

[25]I am completely discouraged—I lie in the dust. Revive me by your Word. [26]I told you my plans and you replied. Now give me your instructions. [27]Make me understand what you want; for then I shall see your miracles.

[28]I weep with grief; my heart is heavy with sorrow; encourage and cheer me with your words.

^{29,30}Keep me far from every wrong; help me, undeserving as I am, to obey your laws, for I have chosen to do right. ³¹I cling to your commands and follow them as closely as I can. Lord, don't let me make a mess of things. ³²If you will only help me to want your will, then I will follow your laws even more closely.

^{33,34}Just tell me what to do and I will do it, Lord. As long as I live I'll wholeheartedly obey. ³⁵Make me walk along the right paths, for I know how delightful they really are.

³⁶Help me to prefer obedience to making money! ³⁷Turn me away from wanting any other plan than yours. Revive my heart toward you. ³⁸Reassure me that your promises are for me, for I trust and revere you.

³⁹How I dread being mocked for obeying, for your laws are right and good. ⁴⁰⁻⁴²I long to obey them! Therefore in fairness renew my life, for this was your promise—yes, Lord, to save me! Now spare me by your kindness and your love. Then I will have an answer for those who taunt me, for I trust your promises.

⁴³May I never forget your words, for they are my only hope. ⁴⁴⁻⁴⁶Therefore I will keep on obeying you forever and forever, free within the limits of your laws. I will speak to kings about their value, and they will listen with interest and respect.

⁴⁷How I love your laws! How I enjoy your commands! ⁴⁸"Come, come to me," I call to them, for I love them and will let them fill my life.

^{49,50}Never forget your promises to me your servant, for they are my only hope. They give me strength in all my troubles; how they refresh and revive me! ⁵¹Proud men hold me in contempt for obedience to God, but I stand unmoved. ⁵²From my earliest youth I have tried to obey you; your Word has been my comfort.

⁵³I am very angry with those who spurn your commands. ⁵⁴For these laws of yours have been my source of joy and singing through all these years of my earthly pilgrimage. ⁵⁵I obey them even at night and keep my thoughts, O Lord, on you. ⁵⁶What a blessing this has been to me—to constantly obey.

⁵⁷Jehovah is mine! And I promise to obey! ⁵⁸With all my heart I want your blessings. Be merciful just as you promised. ^{59,60}I thought about the wrong direction in which I was headed, and turned around and came running back to you. ⁶¹Evil men have tried to drag me into sin, but I am firmly anchored to your laws.

RULES

119:12-18 Most of us don't like rules because we think they keep us from doing what we want. So it may seem strange to hear the psalmist talk of rejoicing in God's laws more than in riches (119:14). But God's laws were given to free us to be all he wants us to be. They restrict us from doing those things that will cripple us and keep us from being our best. God's laws are guidelines to help us follow in his path and not wander onto paths that would lead to destruction.

⁶²At midnight I will rise to give my thanks to you for your good laws. ⁶³Anyone is my brother who fears and trusts the Lord and obeys him. ⁶⁴O Lord, the earth is full of your loving-kindness! Teach me your good paths.

⁶⁵Lord, I am overflowing with your blessings, just as you promised. ⁶⁶Now teach me good judgment as well as knowledge. For your laws are my guide. ⁶⁷I used to wander off until you punished me; now I closely follow all you say. ⁶⁸You are good and do only good; make me follow your lead.

⁶⁹Proud men have made up lies about me, but the truth is that I obey your laws with all my heart. ⁷⁰Their minds are dull and stupid, but I have sense enough to follow you.

^{71,72}The punishment you gave me was the best thing that could have happened to me, for it taught me to pay attention to your laws. They are more valuable to me than millions in silver and gold!

⁷³You made my body, Lord, now give me sense to heed your laws. ⁷⁴All those who fear and trust in you will welcome me because I am trusting in your Word.

⁷⁵⁻⁷⁷I know, O Lord, that your decisions are right and that your punishment was right and did me good. Now let your loving-kindness comfort me, just as you promised. Surround me with your tender mercies that I may live. For your law is my delight.

⁷⁸Let the proud be disgraced, for they have cut me down with all their lies. But I will concentrate my thoughts upon your laws.

⁷⁹Let all others join me who trust and fear you, and we will discuss your laws. ⁸⁰Help me to love your every wish; then I will never have to be ashamed of myself.

⁸¹I faint for your salvation; but I expect your help, for you have promised it. ⁸²My eyes are straining to see your promises come true. When will you comfort me with your help? ⁸³I am shriveled like a wineskin in the smoke, exhausted with waiting. But still I cling to your laws and obey them. ⁸⁴How long must I wait before you punish those who persecute me? ^{85,86}These proud men who hate your truth and laws have dug deep pits for me to fall in. Their lies have brought me into deep trouble. Help me, for you love only truth. ⁸⁷They had almost finished me off, yet I refused to yield and disobey your laws. ⁸⁸In your kindness, spare my life; then I can continue to obey you.

⁸⁹Forever, O Lord, your Word stands firm in

WISER

119:96-104 God's word makes us wise—wiser than our enemies, wiser than any teachers who ignore it. True wisdom is not amassing knowledge, but *applying* knowledge in a life-changing way. Intelligent or experienced people are not necessarily wise. Wisdom comes from allowing what God teaches to make a difference in our lives.

heaven. ⁹⁰,⁹¹Your faithfulness extends to every generation, like the earth you created; it endures by your decree, for everything serves your plans.

⁹²I would have despaired and perished unless your laws had been my deepest delight. ⁹³I will never lay aside your laws, for you have used them to restore my joy and health. ⁹⁴I am yours! Save me! For I have tried to live according to your desires. ⁹⁵Though the wicked hide along the way to kill me, I will quietly keep my mind upon your promises.

⁹⁶Nothing is perfect except your words. ⁹⁷Oh, how I love them. I think about them all day long. ⁹⁸They make me wiser than my enemies because they are my constant guide. ⁹⁹Yes, wiser than my teachers, for I am ever thinking of your rules. ¹⁰⁰They make me even wiser than the aged.

¹⁰¹I have refused to walk the paths of evil, for I will remain obedient to your Word. ¹⁰²,¹⁰³No, I haven't turned away from what you taught me; your words are sweeter than honey. ¹⁰⁴And since only your rules can give me wisdom and understanding, no wonder I hate every false teaching.

¹⁰⁵Your words are a flashlight to light the path ahead of me and keep me from stumbling. ¹⁰⁶I've said it once and I'll say it again and again: I will obey these wonderful laws of yours.

¹⁰⁷I am close to death at the hands of my enemies; oh, give me back my life again, just as you promised me. ¹⁰⁸Accept my grateful thanks and teach me your desires. ¹⁰⁹My life hangs in the balance, but I will not give up obedience to your laws. ¹¹⁰The wicked have set their traps for me along your path, but I will not turn aside. ¹¹¹Your laws are my joyous treasure forever. ¹¹²I am determined to obey you until I die.

¹¹³I hate those who are undecided whether or not to obey you; but my choice is clear—I love your law. ¹¹⁴You are my refuge and my shield, and your promises are my only source of hope. ¹¹⁵Begone, you evil-minded men! Don't try to stop me from obeying God's commands. ¹¹⁶Lord, you promised to let me live! Never let it be said that God failed me. ¹¹⁷Hold me safe above the heads of all my enemies; then I can continue to obey your laws.

¹¹⁸But you have rejected all who reject your laws. They are only fooling themselves. ¹¹⁹The wicked are the scum you skim off and throw away; no wonder I love to obey your laws! ¹²⁰I tremble in fear of you; I fear your punishments.

¹²¹Don't leave me to the mercy of my enemies, for I have done what is right; I've been perfectly fair. ¹²²Commit yourself to bless me! Don't let the proud oppress me! ¹²³My eyes grow dim with longing for you to fulfill your wonderful promise to rescue me. ¹²⁴Lord, deal with me in loving-kindness, and teach me, your servant, to obey; ¹²⁵for I am your servant; therefore give me common sense to apply your rules to everything I do.

¹²⁶Lord, it is time for you to act. For these evil men have violated your laws, ¹²⁷while I love your commandments more than the finest gold. ¹²⁸Every law of God is right, whatever it concerns. I hate every other way.

¹²⁹Your laws are wonderful; no wonder I obey them. ¹³⁰As your plan unfolds, even the simple can understand it. ¹³¹No wonder I wait expectantly for each of your commands.

¹³²Come and have mercy on me as is your way with those who love you. ¹³³Guide me with your laws so that I will not be overcome by evil. ¹³⁴Rescue me from the oppression of evil men; then I can obey you. ¹³⁵Look down in love upon me and teach me all your laws. ¹³⁶I weep because your laws are disobeyed.

¹³⁷O Lord, you are just and your punishments are fair. ¹³⁸Your demands are just and right. ¹³⁹I am indignant and angry because of the way my enemies have disregarded your laws. ¹⁴⁰I have thoroughly tested your promises, and that is why I love them so much. ¹⁴¹I am worthless and despised, but I don't despise your laws.

¹⁴²Your justice is eternal for your laws are perfectly fair. ¹⁴³In my distress and anguish your commandments comfort me. ¹⁴⁴Your laws are always fair; help me to understand them, and I shall live.

¹⁴⁵I am praying with great earnestness; answer me, O Lord, and I will obey your laws. ¹⁴⁶"Save me," I cry, "for I am obeying." ¹⁴⁷Early in the morning before the sun is up, I am praying and pointing out how much I trust in you. ¹⁴⁸I stay awake through the night to think about your promises. ¹⁴⁹Because you are so loving and kind, listen to me and make me well again.

¹⁵⁰Here come these lawless men to attack me, ¹⁵¹but you are near, O Lord; all your commandments are based on truth. ¹⁵²I have known from earliest days that your will never changes.

¹⁵³Look down upon my sorrows and rescue me, for I am obeying your commands. ¹⁵⁴Yes, rescue me and give me back my life again just as you have promised. ¹⁵⁵The wicked are far from salvation, for they do not care for your laws. ¹⁵⁶Lord, how great is your mercy; oh, give me back my life again.

¹⁵⁷My enemies are so many. They try to make me disobey, but I have not swerved from your will. ¹⁵⁸I loathed these traitors because they care nothing for your laws. ¹⁵⁹Lord, see how much I really love your demands. Now give me back my life and

MEDICINE

119:125 Faith comes alive at the points where we apply Scripture to our lives. Like the psalmist, we need the common sense and the desire to apply Scripture where we need help. The Bible is similar to medicine—it goes to work only when you put it on the infected areas. As you read the Bible, be on the alert for lessons, commands, or examples that you can apply to situations in your life.

health because you are so kind. ¹⁶⁰There is utter truth in all your laws; your decrees are eternal.

¹⁶¹Great men have persecuted me, though they have no reason to, but I stand in awe of only your words. ¹⁶²I rejoice in your laws like one who finds a great treasure. ¹⁶³How I hate all falsehood, but how I love your laws. ¹⁶⁴I will praise you seven times a day because of your wonderful laws.

¹⁶⁵Those who love your laws have great peace of heart and mind and do not stumble. ¹⁶⁶I long for your salvation, Lord, and so I have obeyed your laws. ¹⁶⁷I have looked for your commandments, and I love them very much; ¹⁶⁸yes, I have searched for them. You know this because everything I do is known to you.

¹⁶⁹O Lord, listen to my prayers; give me the common sense you promised. ¹⁷⁰Hear my prayers; rescue me as you said you would. ¹⁷¹I praise you for letting me learn your laws. ¹⁷²I will sing about their wonder, for each of them is just. ¹⁷³Stand ready to help me because I have chosen to follow your will. ¹⁷⁴O Lord, I have longed for your salvation, and your law is my delight. ¹⁷⁵If you will let me live, I will praise you; let your laws assist me.

¹⁷⁶I have wandered away like a lost sheep; come and find me, for I have not turned away from your commandments.

PEACEMAKER

120:7 Peacemaking is not very popular because it is more human to "fight for what is right." The glory of battle is the hope of winning, but someone must be a loser. The glory of peacemaking is that it may actually produce two winners. Peacemaking is God's way, so we should carefully and prayerfully attempt to be peacemakers.

PSALM 120 GOD WILL HELP.

In my troubles I pled with God to help me and he did!

²Deliver me, O Lord, from liars. ³O lying tongue, what shall be your fate? ⁴You shall be pierced with sharp arrows and burned with glowing coals.

⁵,⁶My troubles pile high among these haters of the Lord, these men of Meshech and Kedar. I am tired of being here among these men who hate peace. ⁷I am for peace, but they are for war, and my voice goes unheeded in their councils.

PSALM 121 GOD GUARDS US.

Shall I look to the mountain gods for help? ²No! My help is from Jehovah who made the mountains! And the heavens too! ³,⁴He will never let me stumble, slip, or fall. For he is always watching, never sleeping.

⁵Jehovah himself is caring for you! He is your defender. ⁶He protects you day and night. ⁷He keeps you from all evil and preserves your life. ⁸He keeps his eye upon you as you come and go and always guards you.

PSALM 122 WORSHIPING.

I was glad for the suggestion of going to Jerusalem, to the Temple of the Lord. ²,³Now we are standing here inside the crowded city. ⁴All Israel—Jehovah's people—have come to worship as the law requires, to thank and praise the Lord. ⁵Look! There are the judges holding court beside the city gates, deciding all the people's arguments.

⁶Pray for the peace of Jerusalem. May all who love this city prosper. ⁷O Jerusalem, may there be peace within your walls and prosperity in your palaces. ⁸This I ask for the sake of all my brothers and my friends who live here; ⁹and may there be peace as a protection to the Temple of the Lord.

FOR OTHERS

122:6-9 The psalmist was not praying for his own peace and prosperity, but for his fellow citizens of Jerusalem. This is intercessory prayer, prayer on the behalf of others. Such prayer is unselfish. Too often we pray for our own needs and desires when we should be interceding for others. Will you pray for someone in need today?

PSALM 123 GOD IS MERCIFUL.

O God enthroned in heaven, I lift my eyes to you.

²We look to Jehovah our God for his mercy and kindness just as a servant keeps his eyes upon his master or a slave girl watches her mistress for the slightest signal.

³,⁴Have mercy on us, Lord, have mercy. For we have had our fill of contempt and of the scoffing of the rich and proud.

PSALM 124 GOD IS ON OUR SIDE.

If the Lord had not been on our side (let all Israel admit it), if the Lord had not been on our side, ²,³we would have been swallowed alive by our enemies, destroyed by their anger. ⁴,⁵We would have drowned beneath the flood of these men's fury and pride.

⁶Blessed be Jehovah who has not let them devour us. ⁷We have escaped with our lives as a bird from a hunter's snare. The snare is broken and we are free!

⁸Our help is from the Lord who made heaven and earth.

PSALM 125 GOD IS OUR PROTECTOR.

Those who trust in the Lord are steady as Mount Zion, unmoved by any circumstance.

²Just as the mountains surround and protect Jerusalem, so the Lord surrounds and protects his people. ³For the wicked shall not rule the godly, lest the godly be forced to do wrong. ⁴O Lord, do good to those who are good, whose hearts are right with the Lord; ⁵but lead evil men to execution. And let Israel have quietness and peace.

PSALM 126 TEARS TURN TO JOY. When Jehovah brought back his exiles to Jerusalem, it was like a dream! [2]How we laughed and sang for joy. And the other nations said, "What amazing things the Lord has done for them."

[3]Yes, glorious things! What wonder! What joy! [4]May we be refreshed as by streams in the desert.

[5]Those who sow tears shall reap joy. [6]Yes, they go out weeping, carrying seed for sowing, and return singing, carrying their sheaves.

PSALM 127 GOD MAKES LIFE WORTHWHILE. Unless the Lord builds a house, the builders' work is useless. Unless the Lord protects a city, sentries do no good. [2]It is senseless for you to work so hard from early morning until late at night, fearing you will starve to death; for God wants his loved ones to get their proper rest.

[3]Children are a gift from God; they are his reward. [4]Children born to a young man are like sharp arrows to defend him.

[5]Happy is the man who has his quiver full of them. That man shall have the help he needs when arguing with his enemies.

PSALM 128 A FAMILY BLESSING. Blessings on all who reverence and trust the Lord—on all who obey him!

[2]Their reward shall be prosperity and happiness. [3]Your wife shall be contented in your home. And look at all those children! There they sit around the dinner table as vigorous and healthy as young olive trees. [4]That is God's reward to those who reverence and trust him.

[5]May the Lord continually bless you with heaven's blessings as well as with human joys. [6]May you live to enjoy your grandchildren! And may God bless Israel!

PSALM 129 LEAVE YOUR ENEMIES TO GOD. Persecuted from my earliest youth (Israel is speaking), [2]and faced with never-ending discrimination—but not destroyed! My enemies have never been able to finish me off!

[3,4]Though my back is cut to ribbons with their whips, the Lord is good. For he has snapped the chains that evil men had bound me with.

[5]May all who hate the Jews be brought to ignominious defeat. [6,7]May they be as grass in shallow soil, turning sere and yellow when half grown, ignored by the reaper, despised by the binder. [8]And may those passing by refuse to bless them by saying, "Jehovah's blessings be upon you; we bless you in Jehovah's name."

PSALM 130 GOD FORGIVES. O Lord, from the depths of despair I cry for your help: [2]"Hear me! Answer! Help me!"

[3,4]Lord, if you keep in mind our sins, then who can ever get an answer to his prayers? But you forgive! What an awesome thing this is! [5]That is why I wait expectantly, trusting God to help, for he has promised. [6]I long for him more than sentinels long for the dawn.

[7]O Israel, hope in the Lord; for he is loving and kind and comes to us with armloads of salvation. [8]He himself shall ransom Israel from her slavery to sin.

PSALM 131 A PSALM OF CONTENTMENT. Lord, I am not proud and haughty. I don't think myself better than others. I don't pretend to "know it all." [2]I am quiet now before the Lord, just as a child who is weaned from the breast. Yes, my begging has been stilled.

[3]O Israel, you too should quietly trust in the Lord—now, and always.

PSALM 132 HONOR GOD. Lord, do you remember that time when my heart was so filled with turmoil? [2-5]I couldn't rest, I couldn't sleep, thinking

PRIORITY

127:1 Families establish homes, and sentries guard cities, but both of these activities are futile unless God is with them. A family without God can never experience the spiritual bond God brings to relationships. A city without God will crumble from evil and corruption on the inside. Don't make the mistake of leaving God out of your life—if you do, it will be lived in vain. Make God your highest priority and let him do the building.

Shall I look to the **mountain gods** for help? **NO!**

My help is from JEHOVAH

who made the mountains! And the heavens too!

PSALM 121:1-2

how I ought to build a permanent home for the Ark of the Lord, a Temple for the mighty one of Israel. Then I vowed that I would do it; I made a solemn promise to the Lord.

⁶First the Ark was in Ephrathah, then in the distant countryside of Jaar. ⁷But now it will be settled in the Temple, in God's permanent home here on earth. That is where we will go to worship him. ⁸Arise, O Lord, and enter your Temple with the Ark, the symbol of your power.

⁹We will clothe the priests in white, the symbol of all purity. May our nation shout for joy.

¹⁰Do not reject your servant David—the king you chose for your people. ¹¹For you promised me that my son would sit on my throne and succeed me. And surely you will never go back on a promise! ¹²You also promised that if my descendants will obey the terms of your contract with me, then the dynasty of David shall never end.

¹³O Lord, you have chosen Jerusalem as your home: ¹⁴"This is my permanent home where I shall live," you said, "for I have always wanted it this way. ¹⁵I will make this city prosperous and satisfy her poor with food. ¹⁶I will clothe her priests with salvation; her saints shall shout for joy. ¹⁷David's power shall grow, for I have decreed for him a mighty Son. ¹⁸I'll clothe his enemies with shame, but he shall be a glorious King."

PSALM 133 LIVING TOGETHER IN PEACE.

How wonderful it is, how pleasant, when brothers live in harmony! ²For harmony is as precious as the fragrant anointing oil that was poured over Aaron's head and ran down onto his beard and onto the border of his robe. ³Harmony is as refreshing as the dew on Mount Hermon, on the mountains of Israel. And God has pronounced this eternal blessing on Jerusalem, even life forevermore.

PSALM 134 WORSHIP THE LORD.

Oh, bless the Lord, you who serve him as watchmen in the Temple every night. ²Lift your hands in holiness and bless the Lord.

³The Lord bless you from Zion—the Lord who made heaven and earth.

PSALM 135 OUR GOD IS REAL.

Hallelujah! ²Yes, let his people praise him as they stand in his Temple courts. ³Praise the Lord because he is so good; sing to his wonderful name. ⁴For the Lord has chosen Israel as his personal possession.

⁵I know the greatness of the Lord—that he is greater far than any other god. ⁶He does whatever pleases him throughout all of heaven and earth and in the deepest seas. ⁷He makes mists rise throughout the earth; he sends the lightning to bring down the rain and sends the winds from his treasuries. ⁸He destroyed the eldest child in each Egyptian home, along with the firstborn of the flocks. ⁹He did great miracles in Egypt before Pharaoh and all his people. ¹⁰He smote great nations, slaying mighty kings—¹¹Sihon, king of Amorites; and Og, the king of Bashan; and the kings of Canaan—¹²and gave their land as an eternal gift to his people Israel.

¹³O Jehovah, your name endures forever; your fame is known to every generation. ¹⁴For Jehovah will vindicate his people and have compassion on his servants.

¹⁵The heathen worship idols of gold and silver made by men—¹⁶idols with speechless mouths, sightless eyes, ¹⁷and ears that cannot hear; they cannot even breathe. ¹⁸Those who make them become like them! And so do all who trust in them!

¹⁹O Israel, bless Jehovah! High priests of Aaron, bless his name. ²⁰O Levite priests, bless the Lord Jehovah! Oh, bless his name, all of you who trust and reverence him. ²¹All people of Jerusalem, praise the Lord, for he lives here in Jerusalem. Hallelujah!

PSALM 136 NEVER-ENDING LOVE.

Oh, give thanks to the Lord, for he is good; his loving-kindness continues forever.

²Give thanks to the God of gods, for his loving-kindness continues forever. ³Give thanks to the Lord of lords, for his loving-kindness continues forever. ⁴Praise him who alone does mighty miracles, for his loving-kindness continues forever. ⁵Praise him who made the heavens, for his loving-kindness continues forever. ⁶Praise him who planted the water within the earth, for his loving-kindness continues forever. ⁷Praise him who made the heavenly lights, for his loving-kindness continues forever: ⁸the sun to rule the day, for his loving-kindness continues forever; ⁹and the moon and stars at night, for his loving-kindness continues forever. ¹⁰Praise the God who smote the firstborn of Egypt, for his loving-kindness to Israel continues forever.

WORSHIP

135:18 In subtle, imperceptible ways we become like the "gods" we worship. So if the true God is your God, you will become more like him as you worship him. What are your gods? What takes priority in your life? Choose carefully, because you will take on the characteristics of whatever you worship.

PLANS

138:8 Each of us makes plans for our future. We work hard to see those dreams come true. But to truly make the most of life, we must include God's plans in our plans. He alone knows what is best for us. As you make plans and dream dreams, talk with God about them.

¹¹,¹²He brought them out with mighty power and upraised fist to strike their enemies, for his loving-kindness to Israel continues forever. ¹³Praise the Lord who opened the Red Sea to make a path before them, for his loving-kindness continues forever, ¹⁴and led them safely through, for his loving-kindness continues forever—¹⁵but drowned Pharaoh's army in the sea, for his loving-kindness to Israel continues forever.

¹⁶Praise him who led his people through the wilderness, for his loving-kindness continues forever. ¹⁷Praise him who saved his people from the power of mighty kings, for his loving-kindness continues forever, ¹⁸and killed famous kings who were their enemies, for his loving-kindness to Israel continues forever: ¹⁹Sihon, king of Amorites—for God's loving-kindness to Israel continues forever—²⁰and Og, king of Bashan—for his loving-kindness to Israel continues forever. ²¹God gave the land of these kings to Israel as a gift forever, for his loving-kindness to Israel continues forever; ²²yes, a permanent gift to his servant Israel, for his loving-kindness continues forever.

²³He remembered our utter weakness, for his loving-kindness continues forever. ²⁴And saved us from our foes, for his loving-kindness continues forever.

²⁵He gives food to every living thing, for his loving-kindness continues forever. ²⁶Oh, give thanks to the God of heaven, for his loving-kindness continues forever.

PSALM **137** SONG OF THE CAPTIVES. Weeping, we sat beside the rivers of Babylon thinking of Jerusalem. ²We have put away our lyres, hanging them upon the branches of the willow trees, ³,⁴for how can we sing? Yet our captors, our tormentors, demand that we sing for them the happy songs of Zion! ⁵,⁶If I forget you, O Jerusalem, let my right hand forget its skill upon the harp. If I fail to love her more than my highest joy, let me never sing again.

⁷O Jehovah, do not forget what these Edomites did on that day when the armies of Babylon captured Jerusalem. "Raze her to the ground!" they yelled. ⁸O Babylon, evil beast, you shall be destroyed. Blessed is the man who destroys you as you have destroyed us. ⁹Blessed is the man who takes your babies and smashes them against the rocks!

PSALM **138** GOD HEARS AND ANSWERS US. Lord, with all my heart I thank you. I will sing your praises before the armies of angels. ²I face your Temple as I worship, giving thanks to you for all your loving-kindness and your faithfulness, for your promises are backed by all the honor of your name. ³When I pray, you answer me and encourage me by giving me the strength I need.

⁴Every king in all the earth shall give you thanks, O Lord, for all of them shall hear your voice. ⁵Yes, they shall sing about Jehovah's glorious ways, for his glory is very great. ⁶Yet though he is so great, he respects the humble, but proud men must keep their distance. ⁷Though I am surrounded by troubles, you will bring me safely through them. You will clench your fist against my angry enemies! Your power will save me. ⁸The Lord will work out his plans for my life—for your loving-kindness, Lord, continues forever. Don't abandon me—for you made me.

PSALM **139** GOD KNOWS ALL ABOUT YOU.
O Lord, you have examined my heart and know everything about me. ²You know when I sit or stand. When far away you know my every thought. ³You chart the path ahead of me and tell me where to stop and rest. Every moment you know where I am. ⁴You know what I am going to say before I even say it. ⁵You both precede and follow me and place your hand of blessing on my head.

⁶This is too glorious, too wonderful to believe! ⁷I can *never* be lost to your Spirit! I can *never* get away from my God! ⁸If I go up to heaven, you are there; if I go down to the place of the dead, you are there. ⁹If I ride the morning winds to the farthest oceans, ¹⁰even there your hand will guide me, your strength will support me. ¹¹If I try to hide in the darkness, the night becomes light around me. ¹²For even darkness cannot hide from God; to you the night shines as bright as day. Darkness and light are both alike to you.

¹³You made all the delicate, inner parts of my body and knit them together in my mother's womb. ¹⁴Thank you for making me so wonderfully complex! It is amazing to think about. Your workmanship is marvelous—and how well I know it. ¹⁵You were there while I was being formed in utter seclusion! ¹⁶You saw me before I was born and scheduled each day of my life before I began to breathe. Every day was recorded in your book!

¹⁷,¹⁸How precious it is, Lord, to realize that you are thinking about me constantly! I can't even count how many times a day your thoughts turn toward me. And when I waken in the morning, you are still thinking of me!

RESPECT

139:13-15 God's character goes into the creation of every person. When you feel worthless or even begin to hate yourself, remember that God's Spirit is ready and willing to work within you to make your character all God meant it to be. God thinks of you constantly (139:17-18). We should have as much respect for ourselves as our Maker has for us.

¹⁹Surely you will slay the wicked, Lord! Away, bloodthirsty men! Begone! ²⁰They blaspheme your name and stand in arrogance against you—how silly can they be? ²¹O Lord, shouldn't I hate those who hate you? Shouldn't I be grieved with them? ²²Yes, I hate them, for your enemies are my enemies too.

²³Search me, O God, and know my heart; test my thoughts. ²⁴Point out anything you find in me that makes you sad, and lead me along the path of everlasting life.

ABORTION

"Maybe you made a mistake—or maybe the test is wrong."

"I don't think so. . . . Oh, Kris, what am I gonna do?" The tears begin to roll down Sarah's face. "I'm pregnant!"

Kris hugs her friend. "Look, don't panic. Everything's gonna work out. My sister will help us. She knows about this clinic. The doctors are good, and nobody else has to find out."

Sarah is shocked. "You mean an abortion?"

"Well, do you have any better ideas? C'mon, Sarah, you're only 17. What are you gonna do with a kid? And what would you tell your mom?"

"I don't know . . . I'm so confused." Sarah sighs, wiping her eyes on her sleeve. "What would you do? I mean, could you kill your own baby?"

"What do you mean, 'kill'? It's just a bunch of cells! It's not a person yet. If you were six or seven months pregnant, I'd tell you not to do it. But you're probably only about five weeks along. I don't see what else you can do."

"You really think it's right?"

"Well, let's just say I don't think it's wrong."

Sarah is obviously in deep thought. "Well, how soon can you call your sister?"

Kris picks up the phone. "I bet she's at her dorm right now."

Is Sarah making the right decision? Is Kris right about when life begins? See Psalm 139:13-18.

PSALM 140
PRAYER FOR PROTECTION.

O Lord, deliver me from evil men. Preserve me from the violent, ²who plot and stir up trouble all day long. ³Their words sting like poisonous snakes. ⁴Keep me out of their power. Preserve me from their violence, for they are plotting against me. ⁵These proud men have set a trap to catch me, a noose to yank me up and leave me dangling in the air; they wait in ambush with a net to throw over and hold me helpless in its meshes.

⁶⁻⁸O Jehovah, my Lord and Savior, my God and my shield—hear me as I pray! Don't let these wicked men succeed; don't let them prosper and be proud. ⁹Let their plots boomerang! Let them be destroyed by the very evil they have planned for me. ¹⁰Let burning coals fall down upon their heads, or throw them into the fire or into deep pits from which they can't escape.

¹¹Don't let liars prosper here in our land; quickly punish them. ¹²But the Lord will surely help those they persecute; he will maintain the rights of the poor. ¹³Surely the godly are thanking you, for they shall live in your presence.

PSALM 141 WHEN TEMPTED AND CRITICIZED.

Quick, Lord, answer me—for I have prayed. Listen when I cry to you for help! ²Regard my prayer as my evening sacrifice and as incense wafting up to you.

³Help me, Lord, to keep my mouth shut and my lips sealed. ⁴Take away my lust for evil things; don't let me want to be with sinners, doing what they do, sharing their delicacies. ⁵Let the godly smite me! It will be a kindness! If they reprove me, it is medicine! Don't let me refuse it. But I am in constant prayer against the wicked and their deeds. ⁶,⁷When their leaders are condemned, and their bones are strewn across the ground, then these men will finally listen to me and know that I am trying to help them.

⁸I look to you for help, O Lord God. You are my refuge. Don't let them slay me. ⁹Keep me out of their traps. ¹⁰Let them fall into their own snares, while I escape.

PSALM 142 WHEN YOU FEEL TRAPPED.

How I plead with God, how I implore his mercy, pouring out my troubles before him. ³For I am overwhelmed and desperate, and you alone know which way I ought to turn to miss the traps my enemies have set for me. ⁴(There's one—just over there to the right!) No one gives me a passing thought. No one will help me; no one cares a bit what happens to me. ⁵Then I prayed to Jehovah. "Lord," I pled, "you are my only place of refuge. Only you can keep me safe.

⁶"Hear my cry, for I am very low. Rescue me from my persecutors, for they are too strong for me. ⁷Bring me out of prison so that I can thank you. The godly will rejoice with me for all your help."

PSALM 143 WHEN WEAK AND SCARED.

Hear my prayer, O Lord; answer my plea because you are faithful to your promises. ²Don't bring me to trial! For as compared with you, no one is perfect.

³My enemies chased and caught me. They have knocked me to the ground. They force me to live in the darkness like those in the grave. ⁴I am losing all hope; I am paralyzed with fear.

⁵I remember the glorious miracles you did in days of long ago. ⁶I reach out for you. I thirst for

TONGUE

141:3 James wrote that "the tongue is a small thing, but what enormous damage it can do" (James 3:5). On the average, a person opens his mouth approximately 700 times a day to speak. David wisely asked God to help him keep his mouth shut—sometimes even as he underwent persecution. Jesus himself was silent before his accusers (Matthew 26:63). Knowing the power of the tongue, we would do well to ask God to guard what we say so that our words will bring honor to his name.

you as parched land thirsts for rain. ⁷Come quickly, Lord, and answer me, for my depression deepens; don't turn away from me or I shall die. ⁸Let me see your kindness to me in the morning, for I am trusting you. Show me where to walk, for my prayer is sincere. ⁹Save me from my enemies. O Lord, I run to you to hide me. ¹⁰Help me to do your will, for you are my God. Lead me in good paths, for your Spirit is good.

¹¹Lord, saving me will bring glory to your name. Bring me out of all this trouble because you are true to your promises. ¹²And because you are loving and kind to me, cut off all my enemies and destroy those who are trying to harm me; for I am your servant.

PSALM **144** REJOICE IN GOD'S CARE. Bless the

Lord who is my immovable Rock. He gives me strength and skill in battle. ²He is always kind and loving to me; he is my fortress, my tower of strength and safety, my deliverer. He stands before me as a shield. He subdues my people under me.

³O Lord, what is man that you even notice him? Why bother at all with the human race? ⁴For man is but a breath; his days are like a passing shadow.

⁵Bend down the heavens, Lord, and come. The mountains smoke beneath your touch.

⁶Let loose your lightning bolts, your arrows, Lord, upon your enemies, and scatter them.

⁷Reach down from heaven and rescue me; deliver me from deep waters, from the power of my enemies. ⁸Their mouths are filled with lies; they swear to the truth of what is false.

⁹I will sing you a new song, O God, with a ten-stringed harp. ¹⁰For you grant victory to kings! You are the one who will rescue your servant David from the fatal sword. ¹¹Save me! Deliver me from these enemies, these liars, these treacherous men.

¹²⁻¹⁵Here is my description of a truly happy land where Jehovah is God:

Sons vigorous and tall as growing plants.
Daughters of graceful beauty like the
    pillars of a palace wall.
Barns full to the brim with crops of every
    kind.
Sheep by the thousands out in our fields.
Oxen loaded down with produce.

No enemy attacking the walls, but peace
    everywhere.
No crime in our streets.
Yes, happy are those whose God is Jehovah.

PSALM **145** A MAGNIFICENT GOD. I will

praise you, my God and King, and bless your name each day and forever.

³Great is Jehovah! Greatly praise him! His greatness is beyond discovery! ⁴Let each generation tell its children what glorious things he does. ⁵I will meditate about your glory, splendor, majesty, and miracles. ⁶Your awe-inspiring deeds shall be on every tongue; I will proclaim your greatness. ⁷Everyone will tell about how good you are and sing about your righteousness.

⁸Jehovah is kind and merciful, slow to get angry, full of love. ⁹He is good to everyone, and his compassion is intertwined with everything he does.

"Here's what I did..."

I had an unusual, frightening experience at the beginning of tenth grade: I ate an apple that some disturbed person had tampered with. It wasn't poisonous—not like it would have killed me—but it did make me pretty sick. Most of all, the experience scared me. For about a year and a half, I wouldn't eat anything unless I shared it with someone, or someone else tried a bite first and was OK.

Finally the fear got to me. I talked to my youth worker about it. She encouraged me to read Psalm 140, and to realize that God was there to help and protect me—no matter what! Then she pointed out that God didn't want me to give in to a spirit of fear, and she showed me 2 Timothy 1:7. That verse became very meaningful to me. I memorized it and reminded myself of it over and over, until eventually I began to believe that most people could be trusted, that most people weren't out to hurt me. God is helping me to "be wise and strong, and to love people and enjoy being with them." I'm very thankful for this verse; God is using it to deliver me from my fear.

Melinda AGE 18

¹⁰All living things shall thank you, Lord, and your people will bless you. ¹¹They will talk together about the glory of your kingdom and mention examples of your power. ¹²They will tell about your miracles and about the majesty and glory of your reign. ¹³For your kingdom never ends. You rule generation after generation.

¹⁴The Lord lifts the fallen and those bent beneath their loads. ¹⁵The eyes of all mankind look up to you for help; you give them their food as they need it. ¹⁶You constantly satisfy the hunger and thirst of every living thing.

[17]The Lord is fair in everything he does and full of kindness. [18]He is close to all who call on him sincerely. [19]He fulfills the desires of those who reverence and trust him; he hears their cries for help and rescues them. [20]He protects all those who love him, but destroys the wicked.

[21]I will praise the Lord and call on all men everywhere to bless his holy name forever and forever.

PSALM 146 GOD'S HELP IS ALL YOU NEED.

Praise the Lord! Yes, really praise him! [2]I will praise him as long as I live, yes, even with my dying breath.

[3]Don't look to men for help; their greatest leaders fail; [4]for every man must die. His breathing stops, life ends, and in a moment all he planned for himself is ended. [5]But happy is the man who has the God of Jacob his helper, whose hope is in the Lord his God—[6]the God who made both earth and heaven, the seas and everything in them. He is the God who keeps every promise, [7]who gives justice to the poor and oppressed and food to the hungry. He frees the prisoners [8]and opens the eyes of the blind; he lifts the burdens from those bent down beneath their loads. For the Lord loves good men. [9]He protects the immigrants and cares for the orphans and widows. But he turns topsy-turvy the plans of the wicked.

[10]The Lord will reign forever. O Jerusalem, your God is King in every generation! Hallelujah! Praise the Lord!

PSALM 147 YES, PRAISE THE LORD!

Hallelujah! Yes, praise the Lord! How good it is to sing his praises! How delightful, and how right!

[2]He is rebuilding Jerusalem and bringing back the exiles. [3]He heals the brokenhearted, binding up their wounds. [4]He counts the stars and calls them all by name. [5]How great he is! His power is absolute! His understanding is unlimited. [6]The Lord supports the humble, but brings the wicked into the dust.

[7]Sing out your thanks to him; sing praises to our God, accompanied by harps. [8]He covers the heavens with clouds, sends down the showers, and makes the green grass grow in mountain pastures. [9]He feeds the wild animals, and the young ravens cry to him for food. [10]The speed of a horse is nothing to him. How puny in his sight is the strength of a man. [11]But his joy is in those who reverence him, those who expect him to be loving and kind.

[12]Praise him, O Jerusalem! Praise your God, O Zion! [13]For he has fortified your gates against all enemies and blessed your children. [14]He sends peace across your nation and fills your barns with plenty of the finest wheat. [15]He sends his orders to the world. How swiftly his word flies. [16]He sends the snow in all its lovely whiteness, scatters the frost upon the ground, [17]and hurls the hail upon the earth. Who can stand before his freezing cold? [18]But then he calls for warmer weather, and the spring winds blow and all the river ice is broken. [19]He has made known his laws and ceremonies of worship to Israel—[20]something he has not done with any other nation; they have not known his commands.

Hallelujah! Yes, praise the Lord!

PSALM 148 LET ALL CREATION GIVE PRAISE.

Praise the Lord, O heavens! Praise him from the skies! [2]Praise him, all his angels, all the armies of heaven. [3]Praise him, sun and moon and all you twinkling stars. [4]Praise him, skies above. Praise him, vapors high above the clouds.

[5]Let everything he has made give praise to him. For he issued his command, and they came into being; [6]he established them forever and forever. His orders will never be revoked.

[7]And praise him down here on earth, you creatures of the ocean depths. [8]Let fire and hail, snow, rain, wind, and weather, all obey. [9]Let the mountains and hills, the fruit trees and cedars, [10]the wild animals and cattle, the snakes and birds, [11]the kings and all the people with their rulers and their judges, [12]young men and maidens, old men and children—[13]all praise the Lord together. For he alone is worthy. His glory is far greater than all of earth and heaven. [14]He has made his people strong, honoring his godly ones—the people of Israel, the people closest to him.

Hallelujah! Yes, praise the Lord!

PSALM 149 GOD ENJOYS US.

Hallelujah! Yes, praise the Lord! Sing him a new song. Sing his praises, all his people.

UNLIMITED

147:5 Sometimes we feel as though we don't understand ourselves—what we want, how we feel, what's wrong with us, or what we should do about it. But God's understanding is unlimited and therefore he understands us fully. If you feel troubled and don't understand yourself, remember that God understands you perfectly. Take your mind off yourself and focus it on God. Strive to become more and more like him. The more you learn about God and his ways, the better you will understand yourself.

ENJOY GOD

149:3-5 Although the Bible invites us to praise God, we often aren't sure how to go about it. Here, several ways are suggested—with your voice, in music, in your actions. God enjoys his people. We should enjoy praising him as well.

WHERE TO GET HELP
IN THE BOOK OF PSALMS

When you feel . . .

Afraid 3, 4, 27, 46, 49, 56, 91, 118

Alone 9, 10, 12, 13, 27, 40, 43

"Burned Out" 6, 63

Cheated 41

Confused 10, 12, 73

Depressed 27, 34, 42, 43, 88, 143

Distressed 13, 25, 31, 40, 107

Elated 19, 96

Guilty 19, 32, 38, 51

Hateful 11

Impatient 13, 27, 37, 40

Insecure 3, 5, 12, 91

Insulted 41, 70

Jealous 37

Like Quitting 29, 43, 145

Lost 23, 139

Overwhelmed 25, 69, 142

Penitent/Sorry 32, 51, 66

Proud 14, 30, 49

Purposeless 14, 25, 39, 49, 90

Sad 13

Self-confident 24

Tense 4

Thankful 118, 136, 138

Threatened 3, 11, 17

Tired/Weak 6, 13, 18, 28, 29, 40, 86

Trapped 7, 17, 42, 88, 142

Unimportant 8, 90, 139

Vengeful 3, 7, 109

Worried 37

Worshipful 8, 19, 27, 29, 150

When you're facing . . .

Atheists 10, 14, 19, 52, 53, 115

Competition 133

Criticism 35, 56, 120

Danger 11

Death 6, 71, 90

Decisions 1, 119

Discrimination 54

Doubts 34, 37, 94

Evil people 10, 35, 36, 49, 52, 109, 140

Enemies 3, 25, 35, 41, 56, 59

Handicap/Illness 6, 139

Heresy 14

Hypocrisy 26, 28, 40, 50

Lies 5, 12, 120

Old Age 71, 92

Persecution 1, 3, 7, 56

Poverty 9, 10, 12

Punishment 6, 38, 39

Slander/Insults 7, 15, 35, 43, 120

Slaughter 6, 46, 83

Sorrow 23, 34

Success 18, 112, 127, 128

Temptation 38, 141

Troubles 34, 55, 86, 102, 142, 145

Verbal Cruelty 35, 120

When you want . . .

Acceptance 139

Answers 4, 17

Confidence 47, 71

Courage 11, 42

Fellowship with God 5, 16, 25, 27, 37, 133

Forgiveness 32, 38, 40, 51, 69, 86, 103, 130

Friendship 16

Godliness 15, 25

Guidance 1, 5, 15, 19, 25, 32, 48

Healing 6, 41

Hope 16, 17, 18, 23, 27

Humility 19, 147

Illumination 19

Integrity 24, 25

Joy 9, 16, 28, 126

Justice 2, 7, 14, 26, 37, 49, 58, 82

Knowledge 2, 8, 18, 19, 25, 29, 97, 103

Leadership 72

Miracles 60, 111

Money 15, 16, 17, 49

Peace 3, 4

Perspective 2, 11

Prayer 5, 17, 27, 61

Protection 3, 4, 7, 16, 17, 18, 23, 27, 31, 91, 121, 125

Provision 23

Rest 23, 27

Salvation 26, 37, 49, 126

Stability 11, 33, 46

Vindication 9, 14, 28, 35, 109

Wisdom 1, 16, 19, 64, 111

²O Israel, rejoice in your Maker. O people of Jerusalem, exult in your King. ³Praise his name with dancing, accompanied by drums and lyre.

⁴,⁵For Jehovah enjoys his people; he will save the humble. Let his people rejoice in this honor. Let them sing for joy as they lie upon their beds.

⁶,⁷Adore him, O his people! And take a double-edged sword to execute his punishment upon the nations. ⁸Bind their kings and leaders with iron chains, ⁹and execute their sentences.

He is the glory of his people. Hallelujah! Praise him!

PSALM 150 PRAISE THE LORD, ONE AND ALL.

Hallelujah! Yes, praise the Lord!

Praise him in his Temple and in the heavens he made with mighty power. ²Praise him for his mighty works. Praise his unequaled greatness. ³Praise him with the trumpet and with lute and harp. ⁴Praise him with the drums and dancing. Praise him with stringed instruments and horns. ⁵Praise him with the cymbals, yes, loud clanging cymbals.

⁶Let everything alive give praises to the Lord! *You* praise him!

Hallelujah!

MEGA Themes

PRAISE Psalms are songs of praise to God as our Creator, Sustainer, and Redeemer. Praise is recognizing, appreciating, and expressing God's greatness.

When we think about God, we want to praise him. The more we know of him, the more we will appreciate what he has done for us. We should focus on the specific, unique attributes of who God is as we worship him.

1. Read Psalm 145. How do you think the psalmist was feeling toward God when he wrote these verses? How did you feel when you read them?
2. What specific characteristics of God are praised?
3. Does praise always begin with feeling positive toward God? Explain your response.
4. How can praising God lead to a change of attitude, thoughts, and feelings?
5. List the ways you can live a life of praise to God. In other words, how can you become a living psalm of praise?

GOD'S POWER God is all-powerful, and he always acts at the right time. He is sovereign (in control) over every situation. God's power is shown by the ways he reveals himself in creation, history, and the Bible.

When we feel powerless, God can help us. His strength can overcome the despair of any pain or trial. We can always pray that he will deliver, protect, and sustain. And he will answer.

1. How is God's power revealed in the following psalms: 19, 21, 78?
2. How have you seen God's power at work in your life?

3. In what ways do you need God's power at the present time? How do you think you may need him in the future?
4. What do you learn from Psalms about relying on God's power during these times of need?

FORGIVENESS Many psalms are intense prayers asking God for forgiveness. God forgives us when we confess our sin and turn from it.

Because God forgives us, we can pray to him honestly and directly. When we receive God's forgiveness, we move from being separated from him to being close to him, from feeling guilty to feeling loved.

1. Psalm 51 is David's prayer after his sin with Bathsheba. Read this prayer with the following questions in mind: How was David feeling about himself? How was David feeling toward God?
2. What are David's specific prayer requests?
3. When you are facing a sin that you need to confess and repent of, how do you feel about yourself? About God?
4. Take a few moments to seek God's forgiveness in areas in which you have sinned.

THANKFULNESS We should be grateful to God for his personal concern, help, and mercy. He protects, guides, and forgives us, and he provides everything we need.

When we realize how much we benefit from knowing God, we can fully express our thanks to him. By thanking him often, we will develop spontaneity in our prayer life.

1. Read Psalms 100 and 136.
2. Make your own "Thanksgiving" list using the following statements:

I thank God that he is: _____.

I thank God for showing me his love by: _____.

I thank God for the people I love, including: _____.

I thank God for providing me with: _____.

I thank God for helping me: _____.

I thank God that I am: _____.

3. Write a prayer of thanksgiving to help you remember that God is your source of all that is good and eternal.

TRUST God is faithful and just. When we put our trust in him, he calms our hearts. Because he has been faithful throughout history, we can trust him in times of trouble.

People can be unfair and friends may desert us, but we can trust in God. Knowing God intimately drives away doubt, fear, and loneliness. We should remember that he is God, even when our feelings seem to be saying something else.

1. Psalm 23 is a psalm of trust in God. Complete this sentence: Psalm 23 shows that David trusts God because God _____.

2. Psalm 91 also expresses trust in God. Describe the relationship that the psalmist seems to have with God.

3. What is the basis of your trust in God?

4. In what area of your life do you find it the most difficult to trust God? What truth do you find in Psalms that can build your trust in God?

*T*homas has a problem. He worked all summer to earn the money he now holds in his hands. It isn't a lot, a few hundred dollars, but it represents two months of long hours doing odd jobs. Thomas wonders what he should do with the money. Mom and Dad want him to put it into the bank. But his friends urge him to spend it. ("After all," they say, "it's *his* money.") Thomas isn't sure what to do. He wishes he were wiser about such things.

■ There are lots of areas where most of us would like to have more wisdom, the ability to make good (wise) decisions. Lots of people are smart (book knowledge), but only a few are wise. ■ Proverbs was written by Solomon, the wisest man who ever lived. In this book he shares his wisdom on such varied topics as money, marriage, family life, discipline, friends, laziness, speech, relationships, temptation, and leadership. Solomon's purpose was "to teach his people how to live—how to act in every circumstance." ■ Proverbs is a book of answers—answers to our questions about everyday life. As you read, ask God to make the wisdom of Solomon your wisdom too. And ask God to help you begin your steps toward wisdom by trusting him.

STATS

PURPOSE: To teach people how to be understanding, just, and fair in everything they do; to make the simple-minded wise; to warn young men about some problems they will face; and to help the wise become good leaders (see 1:2-6). In short, to help people apply divine wisdom to daily life and to provide them with moral instruction.

AUTHOR: Solomon wrote most of this book; Agur and Lemuel contributed some of the later sections

DATE WRITTEN: Solomon wrote and compiled most of these proverbs early in his reign

SETTING: This is a book of wise sayings, a textbook for teaching people how to live godly lives through the repetition of wise thought

SPECIAL FEATURES: The book uses varied *literary forms:* poems, brief parables, pointed questions, and couplets. Other *literary devices* include antithesis, comparison, and personification.

₽roverbs

CHAPTER **1** **THE REASON FOR PROVERBS.** These are the proverbs of King Solomon of Israel, David's son:

²He wrote them to teach his people how to live—how to act in every circumstance, ³for he wanted them to be understanding, just and fair in everything they did. ⁴"I want to make the simple-minded wise!" he said. "I want to warn young men about some problems they will face. ⁵,⁶I want those already wise to become the wiser and become leaders by exploring the depths of meaning in these nuggets of truth."

⁷⁻⁹How does a man become wise? The first step is to trust and reverence the Lord!

Only fools refuse to be taught. Listen to your father and mother. What you learn from them will stand you in good stead; it will gain you many honors.

¹⁰If young toughs tell you, "Come and join us"—turn your back on them! ¹¹"We'll hide and rob and kill," they say. ¹²"Good or bad, we'll treat them all alike. ¹³And the loot we'll get! All kinds of stuff! ¹⁴Come on, throw in your lot with us; we'll split with you in equal shares."

¹⁵Don't do it, son! Stay far from men like that, ¹⁶for crime is their way of life, and murder is their specialty. ¹⁷When a bird sees a trap being set, it stays away, ¹⁸but not these men; they trap themselves! They lay a booby trap for their own lives. ¹⁹Such is the fate of all who live by violence and murder. They will die a violent death.

²⁰Wisdom shouts in the streets for a hearing. ²¹She calls out to the crowds along Main Street, and to the judges in their courts, and to everyone in all the land: ²²"You simpletons!" she cries. "How long will you go on being fools? How long will you scoff at wisdom and fight the facts? ²³Come here and listen to me! I'll pour out the spirit of wisdom upon you and make you

SIN

1:10-19 Sin is attractive because it offers a quick route to prosperity and makes us feel like "one of the crowd." When we go along with others and refuse to listen to the truth, our own appetites become our masters. We'll do anything to satisfy them. But sin is deadly. We must learn to make choices not on the basis of flashy appeal or short-range pleasure, but in view of the long-range effects. Sometimes this means steering clear of people who want to draw us into activities we know are wrong. We can't be friendly with sin and expect our lives to remain unaffected. Turn and run—this is not cowardly; it is both brave and smart.

wise. [24]I have called you so often, but still you won't come. I have pleaded, but all in vain. [25]For you have spurned my counsel and reproof. [26]Some day you'll be in trouble, and I'll laugh! Mock me, will you?—I'll mock you! [27]When a storm of terror surrounds you, and when you are engulfed by anguish and distress, [28]then I will not answer your cry for help. It will be too late though you search for me ever so anxiously.

[29]"For you closed your eyes to the facts and did not choose to reverence and trust the Lord, [30]and you turned your back on me, spurning my advice. [31]That is why you must eat the bitter fruit of having your own way and experience the full terrors of the pathway you have chosen. [32]For you turned away from me—to death; your own complacency will kill you. Fools! [33]But all who listen to me shall live in peace and safety, unafraid."

If YOU want FAVOR with BOTH GOD and man, and a REPUTATION for GOOD JUDGMENT and common sense, THEN trust THE LORD COMPLETELY DON'T EVER TRUST YOURSELF. In everything YOU do PUT GOD FIRST and HE will direct YOU and CROWN YOUR EFFORTS with SUCCESS

CHAPTER 2 WISDOM COMES FROM GOD. Every young man who listens to me and obeys my instructions will be given wisdom and good sense. [3-5]Yes, if you want better insight and discernment, and are searching for them as you would for lost money or hidden treasure, then wisdom will be given you and knowledge of God himself; you will soon learn the importance of reverence for the Lord and of trusting him.

[6]For the Lord grants wisdom! His every word is a treasure of knowledge and understanding. [7,8]He grants good sense to the godly—his saints. He is their shield, protecting them and guarding their pathway. [9]He shows how to distinguish right from wrong, how to find the right decision every time. [10]For wisdom and truth will enter the very center of your being, filling your life with joy. [11-13]You will be given the sense to stay away from evil men who want you to be their partners in crime—men who turn from God's ways to walk down dark and evil paths [14]and exult in doing wrong, for they thoroughly enjoy their sins. [15]Everything they do is crooked and wrong.

[16,17]Only wisdom from the Lord can save a man from the flattery of prostitutes; these girls have abandoned their husbands and flouted the laws of God. [18]Their houses lie along the road to death and hell. [19]The men who enter them are doomed. None of these men will ever be the same again.

[20]Follow the steps of the godly instead, and stay on the right path, [21]for only good men enjoy life to the full; [22]evil men lose the good things they might have had, and they themselves shall be destroyed.

CHAPTER 3 WISDOM IS PRICELESS. My son, never forget the things I've taught you. If you want a long and satisfying life, closely follow my instructions. [3]Never tire of loyalty and kindness. Hold these virtues tightly. Write them deep within your heart. [4,5]If you want favor with both God and man, and a reputation for good judgment and common sense, then trust the Lord completely; don't ever trust yourself. [6]In everything you do, put God first, and he will direct you and crown your efforts with success.

[7,8]Don't be conceited, sure of your own wisdom. Instead, trust and reverence the Lord, and turn your

CHOICES

2:9-10 Wisdom comes through a constant process of growth. First, we must trust and honor God. Second, we must realize that the Bible reveals God's wisdom to us. Third, we must learn to make right choices. Fourth, when we make sinful or mistaken choices, we must learn from our errors. People don't develop all aspects of wisdom at once. For example, some people have more insight than discretion; others have more knowledge than common sense. But we can pray for all the aspects of wisdom and seek to develop them in our lives.

back on evil; when you do that, then you will be given renewed health and vitality.

9,10Honor the Lord by giving him the first part of all your income, and he will fill your barns with wheat and barley and overflow your wine vats with the finest wines.

11,12Young man, do not resent it when God chastens and corrects you, for his punishment is proof of his love. Just as a father punishes a son he delights in to make him better, so the Lord corrects you.

13-15The man who knows right from wrong and has good judgment and common sense is happier than the man who is immensely rich! For such wisdom is far more valuable than precious jewels. Nothing else compares with it. 16,17Wisdom gives: a long, good life, riches, honor, pleasure, peace. 18Wisdom is a tree of life to those who eat her fruit; happy is the man who keeps on eating it.

19The Lord's wisdom founded the earth; his understanding established all the universe and space. 20The deep fountains of the earth were broken open by his knowledge, and the skies poured down rain.

21Have two goals: wisdom—that is, knowing and doing right—and common sense. Don't let them slip away, 22for they fill you with living energy and bring you honor and respect. 23They keep you safe from defeat and disaster and from stumbling off the trail. 24-26With them on guard you can sleep without fear; you need not be afraid of disaster or the plots of wicked men, for the Lord is with you; he protects you.

27,28Don't withhold repayment of your debts. Don't say "some other time," if you can pay now. 29Don't plot against your neighbor; he is trusting you. 30Don't get into needless fights. 31Don't envy violent men. Don't copy their ways. 32For such men are an abomination to the Lord, but he gives his friendship to the godly.

33The curse of God is on the wicked, but his blessing is on the upright. 34The Lord mocks at mockers, but helps the humble. 35The wise are promoted to honor, but fools are promoted to shame!

CHAPTER **4** **YOU CAN LEARN WISDOM.** Young men, listen to me as you would to your father. Listen, and grow wise, for I speak the truth—don't turn away. 3For I, too, was once a son, tenderly loved by my mother as an only child, and the companion of my father. 4He told me never to forget his words. "If you follow them," he said, "you will have a long and happy life. 5*Learn to be wise,*" he said, "*and develop good judgment and common sense! I cannot overemphasize this point.*" 6Cling to wisdom—she will protect you.

Love her—she will guard you.

7Getting wisdom is the most important thing you can do! And with your wisdom, develop common sense and good judgment. 8,9If you exalt wisdom, she will exalt you. Hold her fast, and she will

I'm always giving in to my friends. Lots of times this goes against what I think a Christian should do. How do I withstand the pressure?

I WONDER . . .

If every young person had a dollar for every time friends asked him or her to "come along," most could pay for four years of college!

Being included feels great, and everyone needs friends. But friends don't always have our welfare at heart. In fact, sometimes they only want us to join them so they can feel better about doing whatever it is they want to do.

But is this really pressure?

When someone invites you to go along with a questionable (or bad) situation and you give in, you haven't succumbed to peer pressure. You have chosen to do something wrong and have concealed your true identity.

Too often we hide our real character, hoping to be liked by a group or person. We want to be accepted. Unfortunately, this often works. If it didn't, people wouldn't do it!

Everyone is tempted to bend their rules or beliefs in order to teach someone to like them. During the teenage years, this kind of pressure can be intense, and it can generate a hungry urge to do what others are doing in order to fit in.

But God wants to provide the inner muscle you'll need to combat the outer pressure you feel. Ask him to give you the courage and strength to say no.

He also wants to teach you what to do. Remember when Mom or Dad taught you to do something like bake cookies or start a lawnmower? They didn't just tell you to do it, they showed you how.

God shows us how to act through the teachings and stories in the Bible.

Commands like "Don't copy the behavior and customs of this world, but be a new and different person with a fresh newness in all you do and think" (Romans 12:2) need to be read to understand God's heart. But examples from throughout the Bible can help.

Consider these: Joseph ran from temptation (Genesis 39:12), and Daniel prayed his way through it (Daniel 6:10). And like the counsel in Proverbs 1:10, sometimes we just have to realize that the consequences are not worth the risk.

lead you to great honor; she will place a beautiful crown upon your head. 10My son, listen to me and do as I say, and you will have a long, good life.

11I would have you learn this great fact: that a life of doing right is the wisest life there is. 12If you live that kind of life, you'll not limp or stumble as you run. 13Carry out my instructions; don't forget

AFFECTIONS

them, for they will lead you to real living.

¹⁴Don't do as the wicked do. ¹⁵Avoid their haunts—turn away, go somewhere else, ¹⁶for evil men can't sleep until they've done their evil deed for the day. They can't rest unless they cause someone to stumble and fall. ¹⁷They eat and drink wickedness and violence!

¹⁸But the good man walks along in the ever-brightening light of God's favor; the dawn gives way to morning splendor, ¹⁹while the evil man gropes and stumbles in the dark.

²⁰Listen, son of mine, to what I say. Listen carefully. ²¹Keep these thoughts ever in mind; let them penetrate deep within your heart, ²²for they will mean real life for you and radiant health.

²³*Above all else, guard your affections.* For they influence everything else in your life. ²⁴Spurn the careless kiss of a prostitute. Stay far from her. ²⁵Look straight ahead; don't even turn your head to look. ²⁶Watch your step. Stick to the path and be safe. ²⁷Don't sidetrack; pull back your foot from danger.

CHAPTER 5 RUN FROM SIN.

Listen to me, my son! I know what I am saying; *listen!* ²Watch yourself, lest you be indiscreet and betray some vital information. ³For the lips of a prostitute are as sweet as honey, and smooth flattery is her stock in trade. ⁴But afterwards only a bitter conscience is left to you, sharp as a double-edged sword. ⁵She leads you down to death and hell. ⁶For she does not know the path to life. She staggers down a crooked trail and doesn't even realize where it leads.

⁷Young men, listen to me, and never forget what I'm about to say: *⁸Run from her! Don't go near her house,* ⁹lest you fall to her temptation and lose your honor, and give the remainder of your life to the cruel and merciless; ¹⁰lest strangers obtain your wealth, and you become a slave of foreigners. ¹¹Lest afterwards you groan in anguish and in shame when syphilis consumes your body, ¹²and you say, "Oh, if only I had listened! If only I had not demanded my own way! ¹³Oh, why wouldn't I take advice? Why was I so stupid? ¹⁴For now I must face public disgrace."

¹⁵Drink from your own well, my son—be faith-ful and true to your wife. ¹⁶Why should you beget children with women of the street? ¹⁷Why share your children with those outside your home? ¹⁸Be happy, yes, rejoice in the wife of your youth. ¹⁹Let her breasts and tender embrace satisfy you. Let her love alone fill you with delight. ²⁰Why delight yourself with prostitutes, embracing what isn't yours? ²¹*For God is closely watching you,* and he weighs carefully everything you do.

²²The wicked man is doomed by his own sins; they are ropes that catch and hold him. ²³He shall die because he will not listen to the truth; he has let himself be led away into incredible folly.

CHAPTER 6 RUN FROM FOOLISHNESS.

Son, if you endorse a note for someone you hardly know, guaranteeing his debt, you are in serious trouble. ²You may have trapped yourself by your agreement. ³Quick! Get out of it if you possibly can! Swallow your pride; don't let embarrassment stand in the way. Go and beg to have your name erased. ⁴Don't put it off. Do it now. Don't rest until you do. ⁵If you can get out of this trap you have saved yourself like a deer that escapes from a hunter or a bird from the net.

⁶Take a lesson from the ants, you lazy fellow. Learn from their ways and be wise! ⁷For though they have no king to make them work, ⁸yet they labor hard all summer, gathering food for the winter. ⁹But you—all you do is sleep. When will you wake up? ¹⁰"Let me sleep a little longer!" Sure, just a little more! ¹¹And as you sleep, poverty creeps upon you like a robber and destroys you; want attacks you in full armor.

^{12,13}Let me describe for you a worthless and a wicked man; first, he is a constant liar; he signals his true intentions to his friends with eyes and feet and fingers. ¹⁴He is always thinking up new schemes to swindle people. He stirs up trouble everywhere. ¹⁵But he will be destroyed suddenly, broken beyond hope of healing.

¹⁶⁻¹⁹For there are six things the Lord hates—no, seven: haughtiness, lying, murdering, plotting evil, eagerness to do wrong, a false witness, sowing discord among brothers.

²⁰Young man, obey your father and your mother. ²¹Take to heart all of their advice; keep in mind everything they tell you. ²²Every day and all

EXPERIENCE

STRATEGY FOR EFFECTIVE LIVING

Begins with
GOD'S WISDOM
Respecting and appreciating who God is. Reverence and awe in recognizing the Almighty God.

Requires
MORAL APPLICATION
Trusting in God and his word. Allowing his word to speak to us personally. Being willing to obey.

Requires
PRACTICAL APPLICATION
Acting on God's direction in daily devotions.

Results in
EFFECTIVE LIVING
Experiencing what God does with our obedience.

night long their counsel will lead you and save you from harm; when you wake up in the morning, let their instructions guide you into the new day. ²³For their advice is a beam of light directed into the dark corners of your mind to warn you of danger and to give you a good life. ²⁴Their counsel will keep you far away from prostitutes, with all their flatteries, and unfaithful wives of other men.

²⁵Don't lust for their beauty. Don't let their coyness seduce you. ²⁶For a prostitute will bring a man to poverty, and an adulteress may cost him his very life. ²⁷Can a man hold fire against his chest and not be burned? ²⁸Can he walk on hot coals and not blister his feet? ²⁹So it is with the man who commits adultery with another's wife. He shall not go unpunished for this sin. ³⁰Excuses might even be found for a thief if he steals when he is starving! ³¹But even so, he is fined seven times as much as he stole, though it may mean selling everything in his house to pay it back.

³²But the man who commits adultery is an utter fool, for he destroys his own soul. ³³Wounds and constant disgrace are his lot, ³⁴for the woman's husband will be furious in his jealousy, and he will have no mercy on you in his day of vengeance. ³⁵You won't be able to buy him off no matter what you offer.

CHAPTER **7** **KEEP YOURSELF PURE.** Follow my advice, my son; always keep it in mind and stick to it. ²Obey me and live! Guard my words as your most precious possession. ³Write them down, and also keep them deep within your heart. ⁴Love wisdom like a sweetheart; make her a beloved member of your family. ⁵Let her hold you back from affairs with other women—from listening to their flattery.

⁶I was looking out the window of my house one day ⁷and saw a simple-minded lad, a young man

lacking common sense, ⁸,⁹walking at twilight down the street to the house of this wayward girl, a prostitute. ¹⁰She approached him, saucy and pert, and dressed seductively. ¹¹,¹²She was the brash, coarse type, seen often in the streets and markets, soliciting at every corner for men to be her lovers.

¹³She put her arms around him and kissed him, and with a saucy look she said, "I was just coming

"Here's what I did..."

Sometimes reading Scripture is like getting a good swift kick in the pants! That's what happened to me, anyway.

I've had this problem with procrastination and laziness. Basically I just don't make an effort with things that bore me (like school or chores my parents want me to do). One day I was reading along in Proverbs 6:6-11, which describes what a lazy person is like—and I knew that it was talking about me! Those verses taught me that putting things off isn't just a bad habit, it's a sin that can lead to some pretty bad consequences. This passage helped motivate me to quit sitting around, to take some action even if I don't feel like it.

John
AGE 14

to look for you and here you are! ¹⁴⁻¹⁷Come home with me, and I'll fix you a wonderful dinner, and after that—well, my bed is spread with lovely, colored sheets of finest linen imported from Egypt, perfumed with myrrh, aloes, and cinnamon. ¹⁸Come on, let's take our fill of love until morning, ¹⁹for my husband is away on a long trip. ²⁰He has taken a wallet full of money with him and won't return for several days."

²¹So she seduced him with her pretty speech, her coaxing and her wheedling, until he yielded to her. He couldn't resist her flattery. ²²He followed her as an ox going to the butcher or as a stag that is trapped, ²³waiting to be killed with an arrow through its heart. He was as a bird flying into a snare, not knowing the fate awaiting it there.

²⁴Listen to me, young men, and not only listen

but obey; ²⁵don't let your desires get out of hand; don't let yourself think about her. Don't go near her; stay away from where she walks, lest she tempt you and seduce you. ²⁶For she has been the ruin of multitudes—a vast host of men have been her victims. ²⁷If you want to find the road to hell, look for her house.

CHAPTER 8 WISDOM GIVES GOOD ADVICE.

Can't you hear the voice of wisdom? She is standing at the city gates and at every fork in the road, and at the door of every house. Listen to what she says: ⁴,⁵"Listen, men!" she calls. "How foolish and naive you are! Let me give you understanding. O foolish ones, let me show you common sense! ⁶,⁷Listen to me! For I have important information for you. Everything I say is right and true, for I hate lies and every kind of deception. ⁸My advice is wholesome and good. There is nothing of evil in it. ⁹My words are plain and clear to anyone with half a mind—if it is only open! ¹⁰My instruction is far more valuable than silver or gold."

¹¹For the value of wisdom is far above rubies; nothing can be compared with it. ¹²Wisdom and good judgment live together, for wisdom knows where to discover knowledge and understanding. ¹³If anyone respects and fears God, he will hate evil. For wisdom hates pride, arrogance, corruption, and deceit of every kind.

¹⁴⁻¹⁶"I, Wisdom, give good advice and common sense. Because of my strength, kings reign in power, and rulers make just laws. ¹⁷I love all who love me. Those who search for me shall surely find me.

¹⁸Unending riches, honor, justice, and righteousness are mine to distribute. ¹⁹My gifts are better than the purest gold or sterling silver! ²⁰My paths are those of justice and right. ²¹Those who love and follow me are indeed wealthy. I fill their treasuries. ²²The Lord formed me in the beginning, before he created anything else. ²³From ages past, I am. I existed before the earth began. ²⁴I lived before the oceans were created, before the springs bubbled forth their waters onto the earth, ²⁵before the mountains and the hills were made. ²⁶Yes, I was born before God made the earth and fields and the first handfuls of soil.

²⁷⁻²⁹"I was there when he established the heavens and formed the great springs in the depths of the oceans. I was there when he set the limits of the seas and gave them his instructions not to spread beyond their boundaries. I was there when he made the blueprint for the earth and oceans. ³⁰I was the craftsman at his side. I was his constant delight, rejoicing always in his presence. ³¹And how happy I was with what he created—his wide world and all his family of mankind! ³²And so, young men, listen to me, for how happy are all who follow my instructions.

³³"Listen to my counsel—oh, don't refuse it—and be wise. ³⁴Happy is the man who is so anxious to be with me that he watches for me daily at my gates, or waits for me outside my home! ³⁵For whoever finds me finds life and wins approval from the Lord. ³⁶But the one who misses me has injured himself irreparably. Those who refuse me show that they love death."

CHAPTER 9 KNOWING GOD RESULTS IN WISDOM.

Wisdom has built a palace supported on seven pillars, ²and has prepared a great banquet, and mixed the wines, ³and sent out her maidens inviting all to come. She calls from the busiest intersections in the city, ⁴"Come, you simple ones without good judgment; ⁵come to wisdom's banquet and drink the wines that I have mixed. ⁶Leave behind your foolishness and begin to live; learn how to be wise."

⁷,⁸If you rebuke a mocker, you will only get a smart retort; yes, he will snarl at you. So don't bother with him; he will only hate you for trying to help him. But a wise man, when rebuked, will love you all the more. ⁹Teach a wise man, and he will be the wiser; teach a good man, and he will learn more. ¹⁰*For the reverence and fear of God are basic to all wisdom. Knowing God*

results in every other kind of understanding. ¹¹"I, Wisdom, will make the hours of your day more profitable and the years of your life more fruitful." ¹²Wisdom is its own reward, and if you scorn her, you hurt only yourself.

¹³A prostitute is loud and brash and never has enough of lust and shame. ¹⁴She sits at the door of her house or stands at the street corners of the city, ¹⁵whispering to men going by and to those minding their own business. ¹⁶"Come home with me," she urges simpletons. ¹⁷"Stolen melons are the sweetest; stolen apples taste the best!" ¹⁸But they don't realize that her former guests are now citizens of hell.

CHAPTER 10 GOD'S WISDOM IS FOR EVERYONE.
Happy is the man with a level-headed son; sad the mother of a rebel.

²Ill-gotten gain brings no lasting happiness; right living does.

³The Lord will not let a good man starve to death, nor will he let the wicked man's riches continue forever.

⁴Lazy men are soon poor; hard workers get rich.

⁵A wise youth makes hay while the sun shines, but what a shame to see a lad who sleeps away his hour of opportunity.

⁶The good man is covered with blessings from head to foot, but an evil man inwardly curses his luck.

⁷We all have happy memories of good men gone to their reward, but the names of wicked men stink after them.

⁸The wise man is glad to be instructed, but a self-sufficient fool falls flat on his face.

⁹A good man has firm footing, but a crook will slip and fall.

¹⁰Winking at sin leads to sorrow; bold reproof leads to peace.

¹¹There is living truth in what a good man says, but the mouth of the evil man is filled with curses.

¹²Hatred stirs old quarrels, but love overlooks insults.

¹³Men with common sense are admired as counselors; those without it are beaten as servants.

¹⁴A wise man holds his tongue. Only a fool blurts out everything he knows; that only leads to sorrow and trouble.

¹⁵The rich man's wealth is his only strength. The poor man's poverty is his only curse.

¹⁶The good man's earnings advance the cause of righteousness. The evil man squanders his on sin.

¹⁷Anyone willing to be corrected is on the pathway to life. Anyone refusing has lost his chance.

¹⁸To hide hatred is to be a liar; to slander is to be a fool.

¹⁹Don't talk so much. You keep putting your foot in your mouth. Be sensible and turn off the flow!

²⁰When a good man speaks, he is worth listening to, but the words of fools are a dime a dozen.

²¹A godly man gives good advice, but a rebel is destroyed by lack of common sense.

²²The Lord's blessing is our greatest wealth. All our work adds nothing to it!

²³A fool's fun is being bad; a wise man's fun is being wise!

²⁴The wicked man's fears will all come true and so will the good man's hopes.

²⁵Disaster strikes like a cyclone and the wicked are whirled away. But the good man has a strong anchor.

²⁶A lazy fellow is a pain to his employers—like smoke in their eyes or vinegar that sets the teeth on edge.

²⁷Reverence for God adds hours to each day; so how can the wicked expect a long, good life?

²⁸The hope of good men is eternal happiness; the hopes of evil men are all in vain.

²⁹God protects the upright but destroys the wicked.

³⁰The good shall never lose God's blessings, but the wicked shall lose everything.

³¹The good man gives wise advice, but the liar's counsel is shunned.

³²The upright speak what is helpful; the wicked speak rebellion.

TIME
10:4-5 Every day has 24 hours filled with opportunities to grow, serve, and be productive. It is so easy to waste time, letting life slip from our grasp. Instead, refuse to be a lazy person, sleeping or squandering the hours meant for productive work. See time as God's gift, and seize the opportunities to live for him.

CHAPTER 11 GOD HATES CHEATING.
The Lord hates cheating and delights in honesty.

²Proud men end in shame, but the meek become wise.

³A good man is guided by his honesty; the evil man is destroyed by his dishonesty.

⁴Your riches won't help you on Judgment Day; only righteousness counts then.

⁵Good people are directed by their honesty; the wicked shall fall beneath their load of sins.

⁶The good man's goodness delivers him; the evil man's treachery is his undoing.

⁷When an evil man dies, his hopes all perish, for they are based upon this earthly life.

⁸God rescues good men from danger while letting the wicked fall into it.

⁹Evil words destroy; godly skill rebuilds.

¹⁰The whole city celebrates a good man's success—and also the godless man's death.

¹¹The good influence of godly citizens causes a

city to prosper, but the moral decay of the wicked drives it downhill.

¹²To quarrel with a neighbor is foolish; a man with good sense holds his tongue.

¹³A gossip goes around spreading rumors, while a trustworthy man tries to quiet them.

¹⁴Without wise leadership, a nation is in trouble; but with good counselors there is safety.

¹⁵Be sure you know a person well before you vouch for his credit! Better refuse than suffer later.

¹⁶Honor goes to kind and gracious women, mere money to cruel men.

¹⁷Your own soul is nourished when you are kind; it is destroyed when you are cruel.

¹⁸The evil man gets rich for the moment, but the good man's reward lasts forever.

¹⁹The good man finds life; the evil man, death.

²⁰The Lord hates the stubborn but delights in those who are good.

²¹You can be very sure the evil man will not go unpunished forever. And you can also be very sure God will rescue the children of the godly.

²²A beautiful woman lacking discretion and modesty is like a fine gold ring in a pig's snout.

²³The good man can look forward to happiness, while the wicked can expect only wrath.

²⁴²⁵It is possible to give away and become richer! It is also possible to hold on too tightly and lose everything. Yes, the liberal man shall be rich! By watering others, he waters himself.

²⁶People curse the man who holds his grain for higher prices, but they bless the man who sells it to them in their time of need.

²⁷If you search for good, you will find God's favor; if you search for evil, you will find his curse.

²⁸Trust in your money and down you go! Trust in God and flourish as a tree!

²⁹The fool who provokes his family to anger and resentment will finally have nothing worthwhile left. He shall be the servant of a wiser man.

³⁰Godly men are growing a tree that bears life-giving fruit, and all who win souls are wise.

³¹Even the godly shall be rewarded here on earth; how much more the wicked!

CAUGHT

11:31 Contrary to popular opinion, no one sins and gets away with it. Ultimately, the faithful are rewarded for their faith and the wicked are punished for their sins. Don't think for a moment that "it won't matter" or "nobody will know" or "we won't get caught." (See also 1 Peter 4:18.)

CHAPTER **12** GAIN WISDOM: AVOID MISTAKES.

To learn, you must want to be taught. To refuse reproof is stupid.

²The Lord blesses good men and condemns the wicked.

³Wickedness never brings real success; only the godly have that.

⁴A worthy wife is her husband's joy and crown; the other kind corrodes his strength and tears down everything he does.

⁵A good man's mind is filled with honest thoughts; an evil man's mind is crammed with lies.

⁶The wicked accuse; the godly defend.

⁷The wicked shall perish; the godly shall stand.

⁸Everyone admires a man with good sense, but a man with a warped mind is despised.

⁹It is better to get your hands dirty—and eat, than to be too proud to work—and starve.

¹⁰A good man is concerned for the welfare of his animals, but even the kindness of godless men is cruel.

¹¹Hard work means prosperity; only a fool idles away his time.

¹²Crooks are jealous of each other's loot, while good men long to help each other.

¹³Lies will get any man into trouble, but honesty is its own defense.

¹⁴Telling the truth gives a man great satisfaction, and hard work returns many blessings to him.

¹⁵A fool thinks he needs no advice, but a wise man listens to others.

¹⁶A fool is quick-tempered; a wise man stays cool when insulted.

¹⁷A good man is known by his truthfulness; a false man by deceit and lies.

¹⁸Some people like to make cutting remarks, but the words of the wise soothe and heal.

¹⁹Truth stands the test of time; lies are soon exposed.

²⁰Deceit fills hearts that are plotting for evil; joy fills hearts that are planning for good!

²¹No real harm befalls the good, but there is constant trouble for the wicked.

²²God delights in those who keep their promises and abhors those who don't.

²³A wise man doesn't display his knowledge, but a fool displays his foolishness.

²⁴Work hard and become a leader; be lazy and never succeed.

²⁵Anxious hearts are very heavy, but a word of encouragement does wonders!

²⁶The good man asks advice from friends; the wicked plunge ahead—and fall.

²⁷A lazy man won't even dress the game he gets while hunting, but the diligent man makes good use of everything he finds.

²⁸The path of the godly leads to life. So why fear death?

COOL

12:16 When someone insults you, it is natural to insult in return. But this solves nothing and only encourages trouble. Instead, "keep your cool" and answer slowly and quietly. Your positive response will achieve positive results.

CHAPTER **13** **THE WAY TO SUCCESS.** A wise youth accepts his father's rebuke; a young mocker doesn't.

²The good man wins his case by careful argument; the evil-minded only wants to fight.

³Self-control means controlling the tongue! A quick retort can ruin everything.

⁴Lazy people want much but get little, while the diligent are prospering.

⁵A good man hates lies; wicked men lie constantly and come to shame.

⁶A man's goodness helps him all through life, while evil men are being destroyed by their wickedness.

⁷Some rich people are poor, and some poor people have great wealth!

⁸Being kidnapped and held for ransom never worries the poor man!

⁹The good man's life is full of light. The sinner's road is dark and gloomy.

¹⁰Pride leads to arguments; be humble, take advice, and become wise.

¹¹Wealth from gambling quickly disappears; wealth from hard work grows.

¹²Hope deferred makes the heart sick; but when dreams come true at last, there is life and joy.

¹³Despise God's Word and find yourself in trouble. Obey it and succeed.

¹⁴The advice of a wise man refreshes like water from a mountain spring. Those accepting it become aware of the pitfalls on ahead.

¹⁵A man with good sense is appreciated. A treacherous man must walk a rocky road.

¹⁶A wise man thinks ahead; a fool doesn't and even brags about it!

¹⁷An unreliable messenger can cause a lot of trouble. Reliable communication permits progress.

¹⁸If you refuse criticism, you will end in poverty and disgrace; if you accept criticism, you are on the road to fame.

¹⁹It is pleasant to see plans develop. That is why fools refuse to give them up even when they are wrong.

²⁰Be with wise men and become wise. Be with evil men and become evil.

²¹Curses chase sinners, while blessings chase the righteous!

²²When a good man dies, he leaves an inheritance to his grandchildren; but when a sinner dies, his wealth is stored up for the godly.

²³A poor man's farm may have good soil, but injustice robs him of its riches.

²⁴If you refuse to discipline your son, it proves you don't love him; for if you love him, you will be prompt to punish him.

²⁵The good man eats to live, while the evil man lives to eat.

CHAPTER **14** **ANGER CAUSES MISTAKES.** A wise woman builds her house, while a foolish woman tears hers down by her own efforts.

²To do right honors God; to sin is to despise him.

³A rebel's foolish talk should prick his own pride! But the wise man's speech is respected.

⁴An empty stable stays clean—but there is no income from an empty stable.

⁵A truthful witness never lies; a false witness always lies.

⁶A mocker never finds the wisdom he claims he is looking for, yet it comes easily to the man with common sense.

⁷If you are looking for advice, stay away from fools.

⁸The wise man looks ahead. The fool attempts to fool himself and won't face facts.

⁹The common bond of rebels is their guilt. The common bond of godly people is good will.

¹⁰Only the person involved can know his own bitterness or joy—no one else can really share it.

¹¹The work of the wicked will perish; the work of the godly will flourish.

¹²Before every man there lies a wide and pleasant road that seems right but ends in death.

¹³Laughter cannot mask a heavy heart. When the laughter ends, the grief remains.

¹⁴The backslider gets bored with himself; the godly man's life is exciting.

¹⁵Only a simpleton believes everything he's told! A prudent man understands the need for proof.

¹⁶A wise man is cautious and avoids danger; a fool plunges ahead with great confidence.

¹⁷A short-tempered man is a fool. He hates the man who is patient.

¹⁸The simpleton is crowned with folly; the wise man is crowned with knowledge.

¹⁹Evil men shall bow before the godly.

²⁰,²¹Even his own neighbors despise the poor man, while the rich have many "friends." But to despise the poor is to sin. Blessed are those who help them.

²²Those who plot evil shall wander away and be lost, but those who plan good shall be granted mercy and quietness.

²³Work brings profit; talk brings poverty!

GOODWILL

14:9 How rarely we find goodwill around us today! Angry drivers scowl at each other. People fight to be first in line. Disgruntled employers and employees demand their rights. But the common bond of God's people should be goodwill. Those with goodwill think the best of others and assume that others have good motives and intend to do what is right. When someone crosses you and your blood pressure starts to rise, ask yourself, "How can I show goodwill to this person?"

²⁴Wise men are praised for their wisdom; fools are despised for their folly.

²⁵A witness who tells the truth saves good men from being sentenced to death, but a false witness is a traitor.

²⁶Reverence for God gives a man deep strength; his children have a place of refuge and security.

²⁷Reverence for the Lord is a fountain of life; its waters keep a man from death.

²⁸A growing population is a king's glory; a dwindling nation is his doom.

²⁹A wise man controls his temper. He knows that anger causes mistakes.

³⁰A relaxed attitude lengthens a man's life; jealousy rots it away.

³¹Anyone who oppresses the poor is insulting God who made them. To help the poor is to honor God.

³²The godly have a refuge when they die, but the wicked are crushed by their sins.

³³Wisdom is enshrined in the hearts of men of common sense, but it must shout loudly before fools will hear it.

³⁴Godliness exalts a nation, but sin is a reproach to any people.

³⁵A king rejoices in servants who know what they are doing; he is angry with those who cause trouble.

QUIET

15:1 Have you ever tried to argue in a whisper? It is hard to argue with someone who insists on answering softly. On the other hand, a rising voice almost always triggers an angry response. If the most important goal is to win the argument, then you had better warm up your vocal cords. But if your goal is to seek peace, then a consistently quiet response is your best choice.

CHAPTER **15** **GOD DELIGHTS IN OUR PRAYERS.** A gentle answer turns away wrath, but harsh words cause quarrels.

²A wise teacher makes learning a joy; a rebellious teacher spouts foolishness.

³The Lord is watching everywhere and keeps his eye on both the evil and the good.

⁴Gentle words cause life and health; griping brings discouragement.

⁵Only a fool despises his father's advice; a wise son considers each suggestion.

⁶There is treasure in being good, but trouble dogs the wicked.

⁷Only the good can give good advice. Rebels can't.

⁸The Lord hates the gifts of the wicked but delights in the prayers of his people.

^{9,10}The Lord despises the deeds of the wicked but loves those who try to be good. If they stop trying, the Lord will punish them; if they rebel against that punishment, they will die.

¹¹The depths of hell are open to God's knowledge. How much more the hearts of all mankind!

¹²A mocker stays away from wise men because he hates to be scolded.

¹³A happy face means a glad heart; a sad face means a breaking heart.

¹⁴A wise man is hungry for truth, while the mocker feeds on trash.

¹⁵When a man is gloomy, everything seems to go wrong; when he is cheerful, everything seems right!

¹⁶Better a little with reverence for God than great treasure and trouble with it.

¹⁷It is better to eat soup with someone you love than steak with someone you hate.

¹⁸A quick-tempered man starts fights; a cool-tempered man tries to stop them.

¹⁹A lazy fellow has trouble all through life; the good man's path is easy!

²⁰A sensible son gladdens his father. A rebellious son saddens his mother.

²¹If a man enjoys folly, something is wrong! The sensible stay on the pathways of right.

²²Plans go wrong with too few counselors; many counselors bring success.

²³Everyone enjoys giving good advice, and how wonderful it is to be able to say the right thing at the right time!

²⁴The road of the godly leads upward, leaving hell behind.

²⁵The Lord destroys the possessions of the proud but cares for widows.

²⁶The Lord hates the thoughts of the wicked but delights in kind words.

²⁷Dishonest money brings grief to all the family, but hating bribes brings happiness.

²⁸A good man thinks before he speaks; the evil man pours out his evil words without a thought.

²⁹The Lord is far from the wicked, but he hears the prayers of the righteous.

³⁰Pleasant sights and good reports give happiness and health.

^{31,32}If you profit from constructive criticism, you will be elected to the wise men's hall of fame. But to reject criticism is to harm yourself and your own best interests.

³³Humility and reverence for the Lord will make you both wise and honored.

NEW IDEAS

15:22 Those with tunnel vision, people who are locked into one way of thinking, are likely to miss the right road because they have closed their minds to any new options. We need the help of those who can enlarge our vision and broaden our perspective. Seek out the advice of those who know you and have a wealth of experience. Build a network of counselors. Then be willing to weigh their suggestions carefully. Your plans will be strengthened, your chances for success increased.

CHAPTER 16 PRIDE LEADS TO TROUBLE.

We can make our plans, but the final outcome is in God's hands.

²We can always "prove" that we are right, but is the Lord convinced?

³Commit your work to the Lord, then it will succeed.

⁴The Lord has made everything for his own purposes—even the wicked, for punishment.

⁵Pride disgusts the Lord. Take my word for it—*proud men shall be punished.*

⁶Iniquity is atoned for by mercy and truth; evil is avoided by reverence for God.

⁷When a man is trying to please God, God makes even his worst enemies to be at peace with him.

⁸A little gained honestly is better than great wealth gotten by dishonest means.

⁹We should make plans—counting on God to direct us.

¹⁰God will help the king to judge the people fairly; there need be no mistakes.

¹¹The Lord demands fairness in every business deal. He established this principle.

¹²It is a horrible thing for a king to do evil. His right to rule depends upon his fairness.

¹³The king rejoices when his people are truthful and fair.

¹⁴The anger of the king is a messenger of death, and a wise man will appease it.

¹⁵Many favors are showered on those who please the king.

¹⁶How much better is wisdom than gold, and understanding than silver!

¹⁷The path of the godly leads away from evil; he who follows that path is safe.

¹⁸Pride goes before destruction and haughtiness before a fall.

¹⁹Better poor and humble than proud and rich.

²⁰God blesses those who obey him; happy the man who puts his trust in the Lord.

²¹The wise man is known by his common sense, and a pleasant teacher is the best.

²²Wisdom is a fountain of life to those possessing it, but a fool's burden is his folly.

²³From a wise mind comes careful and persuasive speech.

²⁴Kind words are like honey—enjoyable and healthful.

²⁵Before every man there lies a wide and pleasant road he thinks is right, but it ends in death.

²⁶Hunger is good—if it makes you work to satisfy it!

²⁷Idle hands are the devil's workshop; idle lips are his mouthpiece.

²⁸An evil man sows strife; gossip separates the best of friends.

²⁹Wickedness loves company—and leads others into sin.

³⁰The wicked man stares into space with pursed lips, deep in thought, planning his evil deeds.

³¹White hair is a crown of glory and is seen most among the godly.

I hear Christians talk a lot about God's will. Has God planned out everything I'll ever do?

I WONDER...

Follow these instructions: Put your right hand straight up in the air. Next place your index finger in your left ear (come on, your left ear). Now clap your hands.

Who controlled your hand and fingers?

Tough question. Especially if you were silly enough to do what we asked. But we know from experience that when people give us instructions, we choose whether or not we obey.

The question, however, is who has ultimate control—you or God. This question has been debated for centuries, and the discussion can get quite complicated. For now, let's keep it as simple as possible.

We each have a will, a part within our brains that is the "chooser." Because we are human, the things we do sometimes don't match up with what God wants us to do. It isn't God's will for us to sin.

Of course, God is strong enough to force his will on us. But because he loves us, he allows us to have choices. What loving, earthly father would force his child to say, "I love you, Daddy"? There would be no satisfaction at all in forced expressions of love.

God does not force us to follow him. And it is obvious that many use their will to reject Christ. In essence, they choose to go to hell!

Putting all of these facts together points to the conclusion that God has allowed us to use our will to sometimes go against his will. One of the highest acts of love you can give someone is the opportunity to reject you. This is exactly what God has done.

So what *is* God's will for us? First, it is to know him. Second, it is to help others. "It is God himself who has made us what we are and given us new lives from Christ Jesus: and long ages ago he planned that we should spend these lives in helping others" (Ephesians 2:10).

Third, it is to be filled with the Holy Spirit. "So be careful how you act; these are difficult days. Don't be fools; be wise: make the most of every opportunity you have for doing good. Don't act thoughtlessly, but try to find out and do whatever the Lord wants you to. Don't drink too much wine, for many evils lie along that path; be filled instead with the Holy Spirit, and controlled by him" (Ephesians 5:15-18).

By allowing God to fill you, you are really saying, "God, take my will and help me do what you want." You are following the good advice of Proverbs 16:9.

³²It is better to be slow-tempered than famous; it is better to have self-control than to control an army.

³³We toss the coin, but it is the Lord who controls its decision.

CHAPTER 17 TRUE FRIENDS ARE LOYAL.

A dry crust eaten in peace is better than steak every day along with argument and strife.

²A wise slave will rule his master's wicked sons and share their estate.

³Silver and gold are purified by fire, but God purifies hearts.

⁴The wicked enjoy fellowship with others who are wicked; liars enjoy liars.

⁵Mocking the poor is mocking the God who made them. He will punish those who rejoice at others' misfortunes.

⁶An old man's grandchildren are his crowning glory. A child's glory is his father.

⁷Truth from a rebel or lies from a king are both unexpected.

⁸A bribe works like magic. Whoever uses it will prosper!

⁹Love forgets mistakes; nagging about them parts the best of friends.

¹⁰A rebuke to a man of common sense is more effective than a hundred lashes on the back of a rebel.

¹¹The wicked live for rebellion; they shall be severely punished.

¹²It is safer to meet a bear robbed of her cubs than a fool caught in his folly.

¹³If you repay evil for good, a curse is upon your home.

¹⁴It is hard to stop a quarrel once it starts, so don't let it begin.

¹⁵The Lord despises those who say that bad is good and good is bad.

¹⁶It is senseless to pay tuition to educate a rebel who has no heart for truth.

¹⁷A true friend is always loyal, and a brother is born to help in time of need.

¹⁸It is poor judgment to countersign another's note, to become responsible for his debts.

¹⁹Sinners love to fight; boasting is looking for trouble.

²⁰An evil man is suspicious of everyone and tumbles into constant trouble.

²¹It's no fun to be a rebel's father.

²²A cheerful heart does good like medicine, but a broken spirit makes one sick.

²³It is wrong to accept a bribe to twist justice.

²⁴Wisdom is the main pursuit of sensible men, but a fool's goals are at the ends of the earth!

²⁵A rebellious son is a grief to his father and a bitter blow to his mother.

²⁶How shortsighted to fine the godly for being good! And to punish nobles for being honest!

²⁷,²⁸The man of few words and settled mind is wise; therefore, even a fool is thought to be wise when he is silent. It pays him to keep his mouth shut.

CHAPTER 18 GET THE FACTS BEFORE DECIDING.

The selfish man quarrels against every sound principle of conduct by demanding his own way.

²A rebel doesn't care about the facts. All he wants to do is yell.

³Sin brings disgrace.

⁴A wise man's words express deep streams of thought.

⁵It is wrong for a judge to favor the wicked and condemn the innocent.

⁶,⁷A fool gets into constant fights. His mouth is his undoing! His words endanger him.

⁸What dainty morsels rumors are. They are eaten with great relish!

⁹A lazy man is brother to the saboteur.

¹⁰The Lord is a strong fortress. The godly run to him and are safe.

¹¹The rich man thinks of his wealth as an impregnable defense, a high wall of safety. What a dreamer!

¹²Pride ends in destruction; humility ends in honor.

¹³What a shame—yes, how stupid!—to decide before knowing the facts!

¹⁴A man's courage can sustain his broken body, but when courage dies, what hope is left?

¹⁵The intelligent man is always open to new ideas. In fact, he looks for them.

¹⁶A gift does wonders; it will bring you before men of importance!

¹⁷Any story sounds true until someone tells the other side and sets the record straight.

¹⁸A coin toss ends arguments and settles disputes between powerful opponents.

¹⁹It is harder to win back the friendship of an offended brother than to capture a fortified city. His anger shuts you out like iron bars.

²⁰Ability to give wise advice satisfies like a good meal!

²¹Those who love to talk will suffer the consequences. Men have died for saying the wrong thing!

MOCKING

17:5 Few acts are as cruel as mocking those who are less fortunate, but many people do it because it makes them feel good to be better off or more successful than someone else. Mocking the poor is mocking the God who made them. We also mock God when we mock the weak, or those who are different, or anyone who is an easy target. When you catch yourself putting down others just for fun, stop. If you don't, you will drag yourself down and anger God.

TRUE FRIEND

18:24 Many people today feel cut off and alienated from others. Being in a crowd just makes people more aware of their isolation. Lonely people don't need to hear "Have a nice day." They need friends who will stick close, listen, care, and offer help when it is needed—in good and bad times. It is better to have one such friend than dozens of superficial acquaintances. Instead of wishing you could find a true friend, seek to become one yourself. There are people who need your friendship. Ask God to reveal them to you, and then take on the challenge of being a true friend.

²²The man who finds a wife finds a good thing; she is a blessing to him from the Lord.

²³The poor man pleads, and the rich man answers with insults.

²⁴There are "friends" who pretend to be friends, but there is a friend who sticks closer than a brother.

CHAPTER 19 A LAZY MAN GOES HUNGRY. Better be poor and honest than rich and dishonest.

²It is dangerous and sinful to rush into the unknown.

³A man may ruin his chances by his own foolishness and then blame it on the Lord!

⁴A wealthy man has many "friends"; the poor man has none left.

⁵Punish false witnesses. Track down liars.

⁶Many beg favors from a man who is generous; everyone is his friend!

⁷A poor man's own brothers turn away from him in embarrassment; how much more his friends! He calls after them, but they are gone.

⁸He who loves wisdom loves his own best interest and will be a success.

⁹A false witness shall be punished, and a liar shall be caught.

¹⁰It doesn't seem right for a fool to succeed or for a slave to rule over princes!

¹¹A wise man restrains his anger and overlooks insults. This is to his credit.

¹²The king's anger is as dangerous as a lion's. But his approval is as refreshing as the dew on grass.

¹³A rebellious son is a calamity to his father, and a nagging wife annoys like constant dripping.

¹⁴A father can give his sons homes and riches, but only the Lord can give them understanding wives.

¹⁵A lazy man sleeps soundly—and he goes hungry!

¹⁶Keep the commandments and keep your life; despising them means death.

¹⁷When you help the poor you are lending to the Lord—and he pays wonderful interest on your loan!

¹⁸Discipline your son in his early years while there is hope. If you don't you will ruin his life.

¹⁹A short-tempered man must bear his own penalty; you can't do much to help him. If you try once you must try a dozen times!

²⁰Get all the advice you can and be wise the rest of your life.

²¹Man proposes, but God disposes.

²²Kindness makes a man attractive. And it is better to be poor than dishonest.

²³Reverence for God gives life, happiness, and protection from harm.

²⁴Some men are so lazy they won't even feed themselves!

²⁵Punish a mocker and others will learn from his example. Reprove a wise man, and he will be the wiser.

²⁶A son who mistreats his father or mother is a public disgrace.

²⁷Stop listening to teaching that contradicts what you know is right.

²⁸A worthless witness cares nothing for truth—he enjoys his sinning too much.

²⁹Mockers and rebels shall be severely punished.

LOOKS

19:22 You can't do much about the body with which you were born. However, you can do a lot about what is on the inside. Inwardly, you can be as attractive as you want to be. You can have kindness, for example, in any amount you choose. You can control your most important asset: the attractiveness of your character.

CHAPTER 20 YOUR ACTIONS TELL ABOUT YOU.

Wine gives false courage; hard liquor leads to brawls; what fools men are to let it master them, making them reel drunkenly down the street!

²The king's fury is like that of a roaring lion; to rouse his anger is to risk your life.

³It is an honor for a man to stay out of a fight. Only fools insist on quarreling.

⁴If you won't plow in the cold, you won't eat at the harvest.

⁵Though good advice lies deep within a counselor's heart, the wise man will draw it out.

⁶Most people will tell you what loyal friends they are, but are they telling the truth?

⁷It is a wonderful heritage to have an honest father.

There are "friends" who pretend to be friends, BUT there is a *Friend* who sticks closer than a brother

PROVERBS 18:24

⁸A king sitting as judge weighs all the evidence carefully, distinguishing the true from false.

⁹Who can ever say, "I have cleansed my heart; I am sinless"?

¹⁰The Lord despises every kind of cheating.

¹¹The character of even a child can be known by the way he acts—whether what he does is pure and right.

¹²If you have good eyesight and good hearing, thank God who gave them to you.

¹³If you love sleep, you will end in poverty. Stay awake, work hard, and there will be plenty to eat!

¹⁴"Utterly worthless!" says the buyer as he haggles over the price. But afterwards he brags about his bargain!

¹⁵Good sense is far more valuable than gold or precious jewels.

¹⁶It is risky to make loans to strangers!

¹⁷Some men enjoy cheating, but the cake they buy with such ill-gotten gain will turn to gravel in their mouths.

¹⁸Don't go ahead with your plans without the advice of others; don't go to war until they agree.

¹⁹Don't tell your secrets to a gossip unless you want them broadcast to the world.

²⁰God puts out the light of the man who curses his father or mother.

²¹Quick wealth is not a blessing in the end.

²²Don't repay evil for evil. Wait for the Lord to handle the matter.

²³The Lord loathes all cheating and dishonesty.

²⁴Since the Lord is directing our steps, why try to understand everything that happens along the way?

²⁵It is foolish and rash to make a promise to the Lord before counting the cost.

²⁶A wise king stamps out crime by severe punishment.

²⁷A man's conscience is the Lord's searchlight exposing his hidden motives.

²⁸If a king is kind, honest, and fair, his kingdom stands secure.

²⁹The glory of young men is their strength; of old men, their experience.

³⁰Punishment that hurts chases evil from the heart.

CHAPTER **21** **LEARN BY LISTENING.** Just as water is turned into irrigation ditches, so the Lord directs the king's thoughts. He turns them wherever he wants to.

²We can justify our every deed, but God looks at our motives.

³God is more pleased when we are just and fair than when we give him gifts.

⁴Pride, lust, and evil actions are all sin.

⁵Steady plodding brings prosperity; hasty speculation brings poverty.

⁶Dishonest gain will never last, so why take the risk?

⁷Because the wicked are unfair, their violence boomerangs and destroys them.

⁸A man is known by his actions. An evil man lives an evil life; a good man lives a godly life.

⁹It is better to live in the corner of an attic than with a crabby woman in a lovely home.

¹⁰An evil man loves to harm others; being a good neighbor is out of his line.

¹¹The wise man learns by listening; the simpleton can learn only by seeing scorners punished.

¹²God, the Righteous One, knows what is going on in the homes of the wicked and will bring the wicked to judgment.

¹³He who shuts his ears to the cries of the poor will be ignored in his own time of need.

¹⁴An angry man is silenced by giving him a gift!

¹⁵A good man loves justice, but it is a calamity to evil-doers.

¹⁶The man who strays away from common sense will end up dead!

¹⁷A man who loves pleasure becomes poor; wine and luxury are not the way to riches!

¹⁸The wicked will finally lose; the righteous will finally win.

¹⁹Better to live in the desert than with a quarrel-

DRINKING

The first time 13-year-old Paul drank with his friends, Mario and Cleve, it was kind of exciting. With the help of a college student, the three guys managed to get a six-pack—two beers each. It wasn't enough to get smashed, but it was enough to get a slight buzz. Sipping slowly as they sat around a campfire, the boys laughed for several hours. The next day Mario suggested, "We should do this more often!"

So each weekend they played the game, always coming up with a new scheme to acquire alcohol. Once they stumbled upon a block party where there were three "unguarded" kegs just sitting there. Another time they swiped a bottle of vodka from a neighbor's liquor cabinet. Another time a high school senior bought them some tequila and showed them how to shoot it.

Every now and then one of the guys would overdo it and end up with a mean hangover. But they never got caught. It didn't affect their grades at school since they only did it on weekends. Everything was cool . . . until Paul went on a church retreat one weekend.

Now Paul won't go with Mario and Cleve anymore. He thinks they're headed for trouble. And they think he's turned into a religious fanatic.

See one of the passages that changed Paul's mind about drinking. Read Proverbs 23:29-35.

MOTIVES

21:2 People can find an excuse for doing almost anything, but God looks behind the excuse to the motives. We often have to make difficult choices in areas of life where the right action is hard to discern. We can help ourselves make such decisions by trying to identify our motives first, and then asking, "Would God be pleased with my real reasons for doing this?" God is not pleased when we do good deeds only to receive something back.

some, complaining woman.

20The wise man saves for the future, but the foolish man spends whatever he gets.

21The man who tries to be good, loving, and kind finds life, righteousness, and honor.

22The wise man conquers the strong man and levels his defenses.

23Keep your mouth closed and you'll stay out of trouble.

24Mockers are proud, haughty, and arrogant.

25,26The lazy man longs for many things, but his hands refuse to work. He is greedy to get, while the godly love to give!

27God loathes the gifts of evil men, especially if they are trying to bribe him!

28No one believes a liar, but everyone respects the words of an honest man.

29An evil man is stubborn, but a godly man will reconsider.

30No one, regardless of how shrewd or well-advised he is, can stand against the Lord.

31Go ahead and prepare for the conflict, but victory comes from God.

CHAPTER 22 GIVING CAN MAKE YOU HAPPY.

If you must choose, take a good name rather than great riches; for to be held in loving esteem is better than silver and gold.

2The rich and the poor are alike before the Lord who made them all.

3A prudent man foresees the difficulties ahead and prepares for them; the simpleton goes blindly on and suffers the consequences.

4True humility and respect for the Lord lead a man to riches, honor, and long life.

5The rebel walks a thorny, treacherous road; the man who values his soul will stay away.

6Teach a child to choose the right path, and when he is older, he will remain upon it.

7Just as the rich rule the poor, so the borrower is servant to the lender.

8The unjust tyrant will reap disaster, and his reign of terror shall end.

9Happy is the generous man, the one who feeds the poor.

10Throw out the mocker, and you will be rid of tension, fighting, and quarrels.

11He who values grace and truth is the king's friend.

12The Lord preserves the upright but ruins the plans of the wicked.

13The lazy man is full of excuses. "I can't go to work!" he says. "If I go outside, I might meet a lion in the street and be killed!"

14A prostitute is a dangerous trap; those cursed of God are caught in it.

15A youngster's heart is filled with rebellion, but

punishment will drive it out of him.

16He who gains by oppressing the poor or by bribing the rich shall end in poverty.

17-19Listen to this wise advice; follow it closely, for it will do you good, and you can pass it on to others: *Trust in the Lord.*

20,21In the past, haven't I been right? Then believe what I am telling you now and share it with others.

22,23Don't rob the poor and sick! For the Lord is their defender. If you injure them, he will punish you.

24,25Keep away from angry, short-tempered men, lest you learn to be like them and endanger your soul.

26,27Unless you have the extra cash on hand, don't countersign a note. Why risk everything you own? They'll even take your bed!

28Do not move the ancient boundary marks. That is stealing.

29Do you know a hard-working man? He shall be successful and stand before kings!

CHAPTER 23 CRITICISM CAN HELP YOU.

When dining with a rich man, be on your guard and don't stuff yourself, though it all tastes so good; for he is trying to bribe you, and no good is going to come of his invitation.

4,5Don't weary yourself trying to get rich. Why waste your time? For riches can disappear as though they had the wings of a bird!

6-8Don't associate with evil men; don't long for their favors and gifts. Their kindness is a trick; they want to use you as their pawn. The delicious food they serve will turn sour in your stomach, and you will vomit it and have to take back your words of appreciation for their "kindness."

9Don't waste your breath on a rebel. He will despise the wisest advice.

10,11Don't steal the land of defenseless orphans by moving their ancient boundary marks, for their Redeemer is strong; he himself will accuse you.

12Don't refuse to accept criticism; get all the help you can.

13,14Don't fail to correct your children; discipline won't hurt them! They won't die if you use a stick on them! Punishment will keep them out of hell.

15,16My son, how I will rejoice if you become a man of common sense. Yes, my heart will thrill to your thoughtful, wise words.

17,18Don't envy evil men but continue to reverence the Lord all the time, for surely you have a wonderful future ahead of you. There is hope for you yet!

COMPANIONS

22:24-25 People tend to become like those around them. Even the negative characteristics sometimes rub off. The Bible exhorts us to be cautious in our choice of companions. Choose companions who have the characteristics you would like to develop in your own life.

¹⁹⁻²¹O my son, be wise and stay in God's paths; don't carouse with drunkards and gluttons, for they are on their way to poverty. And remember that too much sleep clothes a man with rags. ²²Listen to your father's advice and don't despise an old mother's experience. ²³Get the facts at any price, and hold on tightly to all the good sense you can get. ^{24,25}The father of a godly man has cause for joy—what pleasure a wise son is! So give your parents joy!

²⁶⁻²⁸O my son, trust my advice—stay away from prostitutes. For a prostitute is a deep and narrow grave. Like a robber, she waits for her victims as one after another become unfaithful to their wives.

^{29,30}Whose heart is filled with anguish and sorrow? Who is always fighting and quarreling? Who is the man with bloodshot eyes and many wounds? It is the one who spends long hours in the taverns, trying out new mixtures. ³¹Don't let the sparkle and the smooth taste of strong wine deceive you. ³²For in the end it bites like a poisonous serpent; it stings like an adder. ³³You will see hallucinations and have delirium tremens, and you will say foolish, silly things that would embarrass you no end when sober. ³⁴You will stagger like a sailor tossed at sea, clinging to a swaying mast. ³⁵And afterwards you will say, "I didn't even know it when they beat me up. . . . Let's go and have another drink!"

ALCOHOL

23:29-30 The soothing comfort of alcohol is only temporary. Real relief comes from dealing with the cause of anguish and sorrow, and turning to God for peace. Don't lose yourself in alcohol; find yourself in God.

CHAPTER 24 PLANS ARE AS BAD AS ACTIONS.

Don't envy godless men; don't even enjoy their company. ²For they spend their days plotting violence and cheating.

^{3,4}Any enterprise is built by wise planning, becomes strong through common sense, and profits wonderfully by keeping abreast of the facts.

⁵A wise man is mightier than a strong man. Wisdom is mightier than strength.

⁶Don't go to war without wise guidance; there is safety in many counselors.

⁷Wisdom is too much for a rebel. He'll not be chosen as a counselor!

⁸To plan evil is as wrong as doing it.

⁹The rebel's schemes are sinful, and the mocker is the scourge of all mankind.

¹⁰You are a poor specimen if you can't stand the pressure of adversity.

^{11,12}Rescue those who are unjustly sentenced to death; don't stand back and let them die. Don't try to disclaim responsibility by saying you didn't know about it. For God, who knows all hearts, knows yours, and he knows you knew! And he will reward everyone according to his deeds.

^{13,14}My son, honey whets the appetite and so does wisdom! When you enjoy becoming wise, there is hope for you! A bright future lies ahead!

^{15,16}O evil man, leave the upright man alone and quit trying to cheat him out of his rights. Don't you know that this good man, though you trip him up seven times, will each time rise again? But one calamity is enough to lay you low.

¹⁷Do not rejoice when your enemy meets trouble. Let there be no gladness when he falls— ¹⁸for the Lord may be displeased with you and stop punishing him!

^{19,20}Don't envy the wicked. Don't covet his riches. For the evil man has no future; his light will be snuffed out.

^{21,22}My son, watch your step before the Lord and the king, and don't associate with radicals. For you will go down with them to sudden disaster, and who knows where it all will end?

²³It is wrong to sentence the poor and let the rich go free. ²⁴He who says to the wicked, "You are innocent," shall be cursed by many people of many nations; ²⁵but blessings shall be showered on those who rebuke sin fearlessly.

²⁶It is an honor to receive a frank reply.

²⁷Develop your business first before building your house.

^{28,29}Don't testify spitefully against an innocent neighbor. Why lie about him? Don't say, "Now I can pay him back for all his meanness to me!"

^{30,31}I walked by the field of a certain lazy fellow and saw that it was overgrown with thorns; it was covered with weeds, and its walls were broken down. ^{32,33}Then, as I looked, I learned this lesson:

LYING

25:18 Lying is vicious. Its effects can be as permanent as those of a stab wound. The next time you are tempted to pass on a bit of gossip, imagine yourself striking the victim of your remarks with an axe. This image may shock you into silence.

> "A little extra sleep,
> A little more slumber,
> A little folding of the hands to rest"

³⁴means that poverty will break in upon you suddenly like a robber and violently like a bandit.

CHAPTER 25 KEEP YOUR PROMISES.

These proverbs of Solomon were discovered and copied by the aides of King Hezekiah of Judah:

^{2,3}It is God's privilege to conceal things, and the king's privilege to discover and invent. You cannot understand the height of heaven, the size of the earth, or all that goes on in the king's mind!

^{4,5}When you remove dross from silver, you have

sterling ready for the silversmith. When you remove corrupt men from the king's court, his reign will be just and fair.

⁶,⁷Don't demand an audience with the king as though you were some powerful prince. It is better to wait for an invitation rather than to be sent back to the end of the line, publicly disgraced!

⁸⁻¹⁰Don't be hot-headed and rush to court! You may start something you can't finish and go down before your neighbor in shameful defeat. So discuss the matter with him privately. Don't tell anyone else, lest he accuse you of slander and you can't withdraw what you said.

¹¹Timely advice is as lovely as gold apples in a silver basket.

¹²It is a badge of honor to accept valid criticism.

¹³A faithful employee is as refreshing as a cool day in the hot summertime.

¹⁴One who doesn't give the gift he promised is like a cloud blowing over a desert without dropping any rain.

¹⁵Be patient and you will finally win, for a soft tongue can break hard bones.

¹⁶Do you like honey? Don't eat too much of it, or it will make you sick!

¹⁷Don't visit your neighbor too often, or you will outwear your welcome!

¹⁸Telling lies about someone is as harmful as hitting him with an axe, or wounding him with a sword, or shooting him with a sharp arrow.

¹⁹Putting confidence in an unreliable man is like chewing with a sore tooth, or trying to run on a broken foot.

²⁰Being happy-go-lucky around a person whose heart is heavy is as bad as stealing his jacket in cold weather or rubbing salt in his wounds.

²¹,²²If your enemy is hungry, give him food! If he is thirsty, give him something to drink! This will make him feel ashamed of himself, and God will reward you.

²³As surely as a wind from the north brings cold, just as surely a retort causes anger!

²⁴It is better to live in a corner of an attic than in a beautiful home with a cranky, quarrelsome woman.

²⁵Good news from far away is like cold water to the thirsty.

²⁶If a godly man compromises with the wicked, it is like polluting a fountain or muddying a spring.

²⁷Just as it is harmful to eat too much honey, so also it is bad for men to think about all the honors they deserve!

²⁸A man without self-control is as defenseless as a city with broken-down walls.

CHAPTER **26** REBELS ARE IMPOSSIBLE. Honor doesn't go with fools any more than snow with summertime or rain with harvesttime!

²An undeserved curse has no effect. Its intended victim will be no more harmed by it than by a sparrow or swallow flitting through the sky.

³Guide a horse with a whip, a donkey with a bridle, and a rebel with a rod to his back!

⁴,⁵When arguing with a rebel, don't use foolish arguments as he does, or you will become as foolish as he is! Prick his conceit with silly replies!

⁶To trust a rebel to convey a message is as foolish as cutting off your feet and drinking poison!

⁷In the mouth of a fool a proverb becomes as useless as a paralyzed leg.

⁸Honoring a rebel will backfire like a stone tied to a slingshot!

⁹A rebel will misapply an illustration so that its point will no more be felt than a thorn in the hand of a drunkard.

¹⁰The master may get better work from an untrained apprentice than from a skilled rebel!

¹¹As a dog returns to his vomit, so a fool repeats his folly.

¹²There is one thing worse than a fool, and that is a man who is conceited.

¹³The lazy man won't go out and work. "There might be a lion outside!" he says. ¹⁴He sticks to his bed like a door to its hinges! ¹⁵He is too tired even to lift his food from his dish to his mouth! ¹⁶Yet in his own opinion he is smarter than seven wise men.

¹⁷Yanking a dog's ears is no more foolish than interfering in an argument that isn't any of your business.

¹⁸,¹⁹A man who is caught lying to his neighbor and says, "I was just fooling," is like a madman throwing around firebrands, arrows, and death!

²⁰Fire goes out for lack of fuel, and tensions disappear when gossip stops.

²¹A quarrelsome man starts fights as easily as a match sets fire to paper.

²²Gossip is a dainty morsel eaten with great relish.

²³Pretty words may hide a wicked heart, just as a pretty glaze covers a common clay pot.

²⁴⁻²⁶A man with hate in his heart may sound pleasant enough, but don't believe him; for he is cursing you in his heart. Though he pretends to be so kind, his hatred will finally come to light for all to see.

LAZINESS

26:13-16 If a person is not willing to work, he can find endless excuses to avoid it. But laziness is more dangerous than a prowling lion. The less you do, the less you want to do, and the more useless you become. To overcome laziness, take a few small steps toward change. Set a concrete, realistic goal. Figure out the steps needed to reach it. Pray for strength and persistence. And follow those steps. To keep your excuses from making you useless, stop making useless excuses.

²⁷The man who sets a trap for others will get caught in it himself. Roll a boulder down on someone, and it will roll back and crush you.

²⁸Flattery is a form of hatred and wounds cruelly.

CHAPTER 27 JEALOUSY IS DANGEROUS. Don't brag about your plans for tomorrow—wait and see what happens.

²Don't praise yourself; let others do it!

³A rebel's frustrations are heavier than sand and rocks.

⁴Jealousy is more dangerous and cruel than anger.

⁵Open rebuke is better than hidden love!

⁶Wounds from a friend are better than kisses from an enemy!

⁷Even honey seems tasteless to a man who is full; but if he is hungry, he'll eat anything!

⁸A man who strays from home is like a bird that wanders from its nest.

⁹Friendly suggestions are as pleasant as perfume.

¹⁰Never abandon a friend—either yours or your father's. Then you won't need to go to a distant relative for help in your time of need.

¹¹My son, how happy I will be if you turn out to be sensible! It will be a public honor to me.

¹²A sensible man watches for problems ahead and prepares to meet them. The simpleton never looks and suffers the consequences.

¹³The world's poorest credit risk is the man who agrees to pay a stranger's debts.

¹⁴If you shout a pleasant greeting to a friend too early in the morning, he will count it as a curse!

¹⁵A constant dripping on a rainy day and a cranky woman are much alike! ¹⁶You can no more stop her complaints than you can stop the wind or hold onto anything with oil-slick hands.

¹⁷A friendly discussion is as stimulating as the sparks that fly when iron strikes iron.

¹⁸A workman may eat from the orchard he tends; anyone should be rewarded who protects another's interests.

¹⁹A mirror reflects a man's face, but what he is really like is shown by the kind of friends he chooses.

²⁰Ambition and death are alike in this: neither is ever satisfied.

²¹The purity of silver and gold can be tested in a crucible, but a man is tested by his reaction to men's praise.

²²You can't separate a rebel from his foolishness though you crush him to powder.

²³,²⁴Riches can disappear fast. And the king's crown doesn't stay in his family forever—so watch your business interests closely. Know the state of your flocks and your herds; ²⁵⁻²⁷then there will be lambs' wool enough for clothing and goats' milk enough for food for all your household after the hay is harvested, and the new crop appears, and the mountain grasses are gathered in.

CHAPTER 28 ADMIT YOUR MISTAKES. The wicked flee when no one is chasing them! But the godly are bold as lions!

²When there is moral rot within a nation, its government topples easily; but with honest, sensible leaders there is stability.

³When a poor man oppresses those even poorer, he is like an unexpected flood sweeping away their last hope.

⁴To complain about the law is to praise wickedness. To obey the law is to fight evil.

⁵Evil men don't understand the importance of justice, but those who follow the Lord are much concerned about it.

⁶Better to be poor and honest than rich and a cheater.

⁷Young men who are wise obey the law; a son who is a member of a lawless gang is a shame to his father.

⁸Income from exploiting the poor will end up in the hands of someone who pities them.

⁹God doesn't listen to the prayers of those who flout the law.

¹⁰A curse on those who lead astray the godly. But men who encourage the upright to do good shall be given a worthwhile reward.

¹¹Rich men are conceited, but their real poverty is evident to the poor.

¹²When the godly are successful, everyone is glad. When the wicked succeed, everyone is sad.

¹³A man who refuses to admit his mistakes can never be successful. But if he confesses and forsakes them, he gets another chance.

¹⁴Blessed is the man who reveres God, but the man who doesn't care is headed for serious trouble.

¹⁵A wicked ruler is as dangerous to the poor as

NAGGING

27:15-16 Nagging, a steady stream of unwanted advice, is a form of torture. People nag because they think they're not getting through, but nagging hinders communication more than it helps. When tempted to engage in this destructive habit, stop and examine your motives. Are you more concerned about yourself— about getting your way or being right—than about the person you are pretending to help? If you truly are concerned about other people, is there a more effective way to get through to them? Surprise them with words of love and patience, and see what happens.

INTENTIONS

28:9 God does not listen to our prayers if we intend to go back to our sin as soon as we get off our knees. If we want to forsake our sin and follow him, however, he willingly listens—no matter how bad our sin has been. What closes his ears is not the depth of our sin, but the shallowness of our "repentance."

a lion or bear attacking them.

¹⁶Only a stupid prince will oppress his people, but a king will have a long reign if he hates dishonesty and bribes.

¹⁷A murderer's conscience will drive him into hell. Don't stop him!

¹⁸Good men will be rescued from harm, but cheaters will be destroyed.

¹⁹Hard work brings prosperity; playing around brings poverty.

²⁰The man who wants to do right will get a rich reward. But the man who wants to get rich quick will quickly fail.

²¹Giving preferred treatment to rich people is a clear case of selling one's soul for a piece of bread.

²²Trying to get rich quick is evil and leads to poverty.

²³In the end, people appreciate frankness more than flattery.

²⁴A man who robs his parents and says, "What's wrong with that?" is no better than a murderer.

²⁵Greed causes fighting; trusting God leads to prosperity.

²⁶A man is a fool to trust himself! But those who use God's wisdom are safe.

²⁷If you give to the poor, your needs will be supplied! But a curse upon those who close their eyes to poverty.

²⁸When the wicked prosper, good men go away; when the wicked meet disaster, good men return.

CHAPTER **29** **GOD REWARDS FAIRNESS.** The man who is often reproved but refuses to accept criticism will suddenly be broken and never have another chance.

²With good men in authority, the people rejoice; but with the wicked in power, they groan.

³A wise son makes his father happy, but a lad who hangs around with prostitutes disgraces him.

⁴A just king gives stability to his nation, but one who demands bribes destroys it.

⁵,⁶Flattery is a trap; evil men are caught in it, but good men stay away and sing for joy.

⁷The good man knows the poor man's rights; the godless don't care.

⁸Fools start fights everywhere while wise men try to keep peace.

⁹There's no use arguing with a fool. He only rages and scoffs, and tempers flare.

¹⁰The godly pray for those who long to kill them.

¹¹A rebel shouts in anger; a wise man holds his temper in and cools it.

¹²A wicked ruler will have wicked aides on his staff.

¹³Rich and poor are alike in this: each depends on God for light.

"Here's what I did..."

I went to England with a missions group to do street evangelism right after I graduated from high school. Once I got out on the street, supposedly ready to talk to someone, I froze. I was struck with fear and couldn't say a word.

It really bothered me. That evening I looked up "fear" in a concordance, and read through several Scriptures. The verse that helped me most was Proverbs 29:25: "Fear of man is a dangerous trap, but to trust in God means safety." I realized that I had fallen into Satan's trap because I was afraid of people—what they would think of me, even what they might do to me, if I tried to share the gospel. I vowed that I would trust in God.

The next day I was still nervous, but I asked God to keep me from falling into the trap of fear and to help me know what to say. Things went much better. As I trusted God to help and protect me during that missions trip, I grew more and more bold in sharing my faith. I actually came to enjoy it! But I might have stayed stuck in fear if I hadn't found that verse and really applied it to my situation.

Kristen
AGE 19

¹⁴A king who is fair to the poor shall have a long reign.

¹⁵Scolding and spanking a child helps him to learn. Left to himself, he brings shame to his mother.

¹⁶When rulers are wicked, their people are too; but good men will live to see the tyrant's downfall.

¹⁷Discipline your son and he will give you happiness and peace of mind.

¹⁸Where there is ignorance of God, crime runs wild; but what a wonderful thing it is for a nation to know and keep his laws.

¹⁹Sometimes mere words are not enough—discipline is needed. For the words may not be heeded.

²⁰There is more hope for a fool than for a man of quick temper.

²¹Pamper a servant from childhood, and he will expect you to treat him as a son!

²²A hot-tempered man starts fights and gets into all kinds of trouble.

²³Pride ends in a fall, while humility brings honor.

²⁴A man who assists a thief must really hate himself! For he knows the consequence but does it anyway.

LOOKING FOR A PERFECT 10

WANTED: LIFE PARTNER. Must have a body that can stop traffic, money to last two lifetimes (mine and yours), hair that looks like it belongs in a shampoo commercial, great sense of humor, high IQ (just below mine), well-paying job, your own (hot) car. Must love my kind of music (loud), sports, and everything about me. Send resume and photo to: Is That Too Much to Ask? Inc. P.O. Box 101010 FantasyLand, U.S.A. 12345 **S**ound familiar? Everybody seems to have an image of the perfect guy or girl. Perfect looks, perfect personality, perfect relationship . . . But think about it. What really makes someone a perfect 10? **L**ooks: Thanks to *Playboy*, *MTV*, *Seventeen* and a million other influences today, we are bombarded by images of unbelievably attractive men and women. The message is as subtle as a sledge hammer: Use our product and you will not only look as good as our models do, but you will find yourself surrounded by other beautiful people. You will be happy, popular, and adored. **L**ooks are important. Anyone who says otherwise is kidding him or herself. There's nothing wrong with wanting to look your best, or with being attracted to good-looking people. But when looking good becomes an obsession—when you have to wear certain clothes, spend hours getting ready for school or a date, throw down a small fortune on cosmetics, colognes, hair products, etc.—you've bought into the Madison Avenue lie. You are more than your looks. You're beautiful, not because of your physical appearance, but because you were made in the image of God! **P**ersonality: Everybody knows the joke. You've been set up for a blind date, you ask what he (or she) looks like and they say, "He (or she) has a great personality." Which tells you one thing: you're going to the movies with either Godzilla or Frankenstein's Bride. **B**ut there's another side: an attractive guy or girl who has the personality of a dead squid. If you've encountered this, you know personality is important. Or kills it. **S**pirituality: *Hmmm, you may be thinking. Looks and personality, OK. But what is "spirituality"?* Everyone has a spiritual nature. That's what makes you more than a mass of oxygen-absorbing molecules, glands, and hormones. If you belong to Christ, you are spiritually alive. If not, you're spiritually dead. (For more on this, see Romans 3; Galatians 5:16-26; Ephesians 2:1-10.) When you're thinking about spending the rest of your life with someone, you need to look for more than looks and personality. You need to be spiritually compatible, too. **P**roverbs 31:10-31 gives a vivid, lively picture of what a truly spiritual woman is like. And she's no plastic saint, sitting home reading the Bible till her husband shows up. She's strong, intelligent, industrious, compassionate, wise: "She is a woman of strength and dignity . . . (vs. 25)." (When you get right down to it, that's a good description of a godly man, too.) **S**ure, good looks are great. But everyone—everyone—grows old, gets wrinkles, and adds a few pounds. A relationship based on looks or personality is doomed to failure. Don't believe it? Try to find a successful, faithful marriage in Hollywood, Body Beautiful capital of the world. **T**he only cement that can bond two people together for life is mutual commitment to God and to each other. When you're ready to find a partner for life, make the spiritual dimension your primary requirement. There's nothing wrong with looking for a perfect 10. Just remember, it takes more than beauty or a pleasant temperament to add up to someone whose love will last. So take a look at Proverbs 31. It's a great snapshot image of a person who has that something more. (For more on the subject of marriage itself, see the Ultimate Issue on marriage in Ephesians.)

[25]Fear of man is a dangerous trap, but to trust in God means safety.

[26]Do you want justice? Don't fawn on the judge, but ask the Lord for it!

[27]The good hate the badness of the wicked. The wicked hate the goodness of the good.

CHAPTER 30 WONDERFUL THINGS. *These are the messages of Agur, son of Jakeh, addressed to Ithiel and Ucal:*

[2]I am tired out, O God, and ready to die. I am too stupid even to call myself a human being! [3]I cannot understand man, let alone God. [4]Who else but God goes back and forth to heaven? Who else holds the wind in his fists and wraps up the oceans in his cloak? Who but God has created the world? If there is any other, what is his name—and his Son's name—if you know it?

[5]Every word of God proves true. He defends all who come to him for protection. [6]Do not add to his words, lest he rebuke you, and you be found a liar.

[7]O God, I beg two favors from you before I die: [8]First, help me never to tell a lie. Second, give me neither poverty nor riches! Give me just enough to satisfy my needs! [9]For if I grow rich, I may become content without God. And if I am too poor, I may steal and thus insult God's holy name.

[10]Never falsely accuse a man to his employer, lest he curse you for your sin.

[11,12]There are those who curse their father and mother and feel themselves faultless despite their many sins. [13,14]They are proud beyond description, arrogant, disdainful. They devour the poor with teeth as sharp as knives!

[15,16]There are two things never satisfied, like a leech forever craving more: no, three things! no, four! Hell, the barren womb, a barren desert, fire.

[17]A man who mocks his father and despises his mother shall have his eye plucked out by ravens and eaten by vultures.

[18,19]There are three things too wonderful for me to understand—no, four!

How an eagle glides through the sky.
How a serpent crawls upon a rock.
How a ship finds its way across the
    heaving ocean.
The growth of love between a man and a girl.

[20]There is another thing too: how a prostitute can sin and then say, "What's wrong with that?"

[21-23]There are three things that make the earth tremble—no, four it cannot stand:

A slave who becomes a king.
A rebel who prospers.
A bitter woman when she finally marries.
A servant girl who marries her mistress'
    husband.

[24-28]There are four things that are small but unusually wise:

Ants: they aren't strong, but store up food for
    the winter.
Cliff badgers: delicate little animals who
    protect themselves by living among the
    rocks.
The locusts: though they
    have no leader, they
    stay together in
    swarms.
The lizards: they are easy
    to catch and kill, yet
    are found even in
    king's palaces!

[29-31]There are three stately monarchs in the earth—no, four:

The lion, king of the
    animals. He won't turn
    aside for anyone.
The peacock.
The male goat.
A king as he leads his
    army.

[32]If you have been a fool by being proud or plotting evil, don't brag about it—cover your mouth with your hand in shame.

[33]As the churning of cream yields butter, and a blow to the nose causes bleeding, so anger causes quarrels.

CHAPTER 31 These are the wise sayings of King Lemuel of Massa, taught to him at his mother's knee:

[2]O my son, whom I have dedicated to the Lord, [3]do not spend your time with women—the royal pathway to destruction.

[4]And it is not for kings, O Lemuel, to drink wine and whiskey. [5]For if they drink they may forget their duties and be unable to give justice to those who are oppressed. [6,7]Hard liquor is for sick men at the brink of death, and wine for those in deep depression. Let them drink to forget their poverty and misery.

IDEAL WOMAN

31:10-31 Proverbs has a lot to say about women. How fitting that the book ends with a picture of "the best of them all"—a woman of strong character, great wisdom, many skills, and great compassion.

Some people have the mistaken idea that the ideal woman in the Bible is retiring, servile, and entirely domestic. Not so! This woman is an excellent wife and mother. She also is a manufacturer, importer, manager, realtor, farmer, seamstress, upholsterer, and merchant. Her strength and dignity do not come from her amazing achievements, however. They are a result of her reverence for God. In our society where physical appearance counts for so much, it may surprise us to realize that her appearance is never mentioned. Her attractiveness comes entirely from her character.

The woman described in this chapter has outstanding abilities. Her family's social position is high. In fact, she may not be one woman at all—she may be a composite portrait of ideal womanhood. Do not see her as a model to imitate in every detail; your days are not long enough to do everything she does! See her instead as an inspiration to be all you can be. We can't be just like her, but we can learn from her industry, integrity, and resourcefulness.

[8]You should defend those who cannot help themselves. [9]Yes, speak up for the poor and helpless, and see that they get justice.

[10]If you can find a truly good wife, she is worth more than precious gems! [11]Her husband can trust her, and she will richly satisfy his needs. [12]She will not hinder him but help him all her life. [13]She finds wool and flax and busily spins it. [14]She buys imported foods brought by ship from distant ports. [15]She gets up before dawn to prepare breakfast for her household and plans the day's work for her servant girls. [16]She goes out to inspect a field and buys it; with her own hands she plants a vineyard. [17]She is energetic, a hard worker, [18]and watches for bargains. She works far into the night!

[19,20]She sews for the poor and generously helps those in need. [21]She has no fear of winter for her household, for she has made warm clothes for all of them. [22]She also upholsters with finest tapestry; her own clothing is beautifully made—a purple gown of pure linen. [23]Her husband is well known, for he sits in the council chamber with the other civic leaders. [24]She makes belted linen garments to sell to the merchants.

[25]She is a woman of strength and dignity and has no fear of old age. [26]When she speaks, her words are wise, and kindness is the rule for everything she says. [27]She watches carefully all that goes on throughout her household and is never lazy. [28]Her children stand and bless her; so does her husband. He praises her with these words: [29]"There are many fine women in the world, but you are the best of them all!"

[30]Charm can be deceptive and beauty doesn't last, but a woman who fears and reverences God shall be greatly praised. [31]Praise her for the many fine things she does. These good deeds of hers shall bring her honor and recognition from people of importance.

HOW GOD IS DESCRIBED IN PROVERBS

Proverbs is a book about wise living. It often focuses on a person's response and attitude toward God, who is the source of wisdom. And a number of proverbs point out aspects of God's character. Knowing God helps us on the way to wisdom.

GOD . . .
is aware of all that happens 15:3
knows all people 15:11; 16:2; 21:2
is the maker of all things 16:4; 21:30
controls all things 16:33
is a strong fortress 18:10
rescues good people from danger 11:8, 21
rewards the godly 11:31
blesses good people, condemns the wicked 12:2
delights in our prayers 15:8, 29
loves those who obey him 11:27; 15:9-10; 16:20; 22:12
cares for poor, sick, and widows 15:25; 22:22-23
purifies hearts 17:3
hates evil 17:5; 21:27; 28:9

OUR RESPONSE SHOULD BE . . .
to reverence God 10:27; 14:26-27; 15:16; 16:6; 19:23; 28:14
to obey God's word 13:13; 19:16
to please God 16:7; 20:12; 21:3
to trust God 22:17-19; 29:25

MEGA *Themes*

WISDOM God wants his people to be wise. Two kinds of people portray two contrasting paths of life: The fool is the wicked, stubborn person who hates or ignores God; the wise person seeks to know and love God.

When we choose God's way, he grants us wisdom. His word, the Bible, leads us to live right, have right relationships, and make right decisions.
1. Read 1:7 and 9:10. What did Solomon teach was the key to being wise?
2. What will be the results of wisdom in a person's life? (Check 3:13-26.)
3. How has knowing God and learning about his Word increased your personal wisdom?
4. In what areas of your life would you like to have more wisdom? Based on your study of Proverbs, how will you find that wisdom?

RELATIONSHIPS Proverbs gives us advice for developing our personal relationships with others, including friends, family members, and co-workers. In every relationship, we must show love, dedication, and high moral standards.

To relate to people, we need consistency, sensitivity, and discipline to use the wisdom God gives us. If we don't treat others according to the wisdom God gives, our relationships will suffer.
1. What type of relationships does Proverbs encourage? Discourage?
2. Why does the writer devote so much attention to avoiding sexual immorality? What wisdom is given regarding sex outside of marriage?
3. What seem to be the qualities that make relationships, including friendships and marriages, deeper and stronger? What ruins such relationships?
4. List three important relationships in your life. From what you've read in Proverbs, what should you change in those relationships?

SPEECH What we say shows our real attitude toward others. How we talk reveals what we're really like. Our speech is a test of how wise we've become.

To be wise in our speech we need to use self-control. Our words should be honest and well chosen. We need to remember that what we say affects others.
1. When is it hardest to control what you say?

2. What circumstances can cause you to lose control of your words? How do you feel after you blow it? How does this usually affect others?
3. Proverbs encourages speaking honestly, but with self-control. When have you been hurt by someone who did not speak with wisdom? How did it affect your relationship with that person?
4. List some specific actions you could take to develop honesty and self-control in your speech.

WORK God controls the final outcome of all we do. However, we must carry out our work with diligence and discipline, not laziness.

Because God evaluates how we live, we should work purposefully. We must never be lazy or self-satisfied. We don't always have to be the best in comparison to others, but we should always do our best with what God has given us.
1. What does Proverbs teach about the person who is lazy and unwilling to work?
2. What does Proverbs teach about the person who is diligent and self-disciplined?
3. How does being disciplined help you as a student?
4. How does being disciplined help you in your Christian life?
5. What is one area where you need to develop this discipline? Write out a specific plan for this development. (Be diligent in carrying it out!)

SUCCESS Although people work very hard for money and fame, God considers a good reputation, moral character, and spiritual devotion to obey him to be the true measures of success.

A successful relationship with God counts for eternity. Everything else is only temporary. All our resources, time, and talents come from God. We should do our best to use them wisely.
1. According to Proverbs, what is the value of riches? How important is wealth to most people who want to be successful?
2. How do your friends measure success? How do you think they will measure success when they are adults?
3. Do you agree or disagree with your friends' values? Explain.
4. How do you think God measures success?

NEW TESTAMENT, PSALMS, AND PROVERBS READING PLAN

BEFORE YOU BEGIN

Notice that each reading has a title and a question. These are important application questions that will help you as you read. Always pray before you read and ask God to help you understand, apply, and obey his Word. And remember, this is only the start of the great adventure of reading God's Word and getting to know him.

NEW TESTAMENT

You will be reading various parts of the four Gospels in order to have a fairly chronological biography of Jesus' life.

Luke 1:1-4; John 1:1-18 Beginnings
Have you personally received Jesus as your Savior and become a child of God?
Luke 1:5-25 The Angel and Zacharias
How would you react to an angel's visit?
Luke 1:26-56 Mary and Elizabeth
What gives you joy in your life?
Luke 1:57-80 John the Baptist Is Born
When did you last say thank you to your parents?
Matthew 1:1-25 A Family Tree
Which of these people have you read about in the Old Testament?
Luke 2:1-20 Jesus Is Born!
What does Christmas mean to you?
Luke 2:21-39 Jesus' First Trip to Church
How would you react to holding Jesus when he was a baby?
Matthew 2:1-12 Foreign Visitors
What gifts have you ever given Christ?
Matthew 2:13-23 Escape and Return
How has knowing God brought excitement into your life?
Luke 2:41-52 Jesus in the Temple Again
What four words would summarize your teenage years?
Mark 1:1-13 Baptism and Temptation
What are your most difficult temptations? Compare them to Jesus' temptations.
John 1:19-34 John the Baptist and Jesus
To whom did you last talk about Christ?
John 1:35-51 Jesus' First Disciples
How would someone know that you're a disciple of Jesus?
John 2:1-25 Jesus and Surprises
How has Christ been unpredictable in your life?
John 3:1-21 Jesus and Nicodemus
When did you first meet Jesus? How?
John 3:22-36; Luke 3:19-20 John Gets into Trouble
When has knowing Christ ever gotten you into trouble?
John 4:1-42 Jesus Changes a Town

In what ways has Jesus affected your town?
John 4:43-54 Jesus Preaching and Healing
Why do you believe in Christ?
Luke 4:16-30 Jesus Rejected
How would Jesus be received in your church next Sunday?
Mark 1:16-39 Jesus Calls People to Follow
What specific things have you left behind to follow Christ?
Luke 5:1-39 Miracles and Questions
How do Jesus' miracles affect you today?
John 5:1-47 Jesus Demonstrates He Is God's Son
What do you find most attractive about Jesus?
Mark 2:23–3:19 Jesus and Disciples
How would Jesus treat your personal traditions?
Matthew 5:1-16 Jesus Gives the Beatitudes
Which of these attitudes most needs to be in your life today?
Matthew 5:17-30 Jesus on Law, Anger, and Lust
How do Jesus' views compare with yours?
Matthew 5:31-48 Jesus on Relationships
What part of your life could be most radically changed by these words?
Matthew 6:1-18 Jesus on Doing Good Things
How do your public and private lives compare?
Matthew 6:19-34 Jesus on Money and Worry
In what ways are money and worry related in your life?
Matthew 7:1-12 Jesus on Criticizing and Praying
Which one are you most persistent in doing? Why?
Matthew 7:13-29 How Jesus Looks at Us
What is your foundation in life?
Luke 7:1-17 Jesus and Foreigners
What is your attitude toward foreigners? How can you show them God's love?
Matthew 11:1-30 Jesus Describes John
How would you want Jesus to summarize your life?
Luke 7:36–8:3 Jesus and Women
How would you have fit into the group that followed Jesus?

```
WELCOME TO BEST BUY   # 505
HORROW, GA 30260
770 968-0884

                    03/16/97    17:6
       537057  SALE         6773 0505 00

420422 13.98 C/B      RGC 1        9.99
             SUBTOTAL             9.99
    5.0000 % SALES TAX             .50
               TOTAL             10.49

    CASH TENDER                  20.00
                CHANGE            9.51


A 15% RESTOCKING FEE APPLIES
TO ALL NON-DEFECTIVE NOTEBOOK
COMPUTER, RADAR DETECTOR, AND
CAMCORDER RETURNS & EXCHANGES.

>>>>>>>>>> CUSTOMER COPY <<<<<<<<<<
```

Matthew 20:1-19 A Parable about Equal Pay
How often are you jealous of what God has given to someone else?

Mark 10:35-52 Jesus on Serving Others
In what ways are you learning to be a servant?

Luke 19:1-27 Jesus and Zacchaeus
What personal physical characteristic has most affected how you feel about yourself?

John 12:1-11 A Woman Anoints Jesus
What have you ever "wasted" as an expression of love for Christ?

Matthew 21:1-17 Jesus Rides into Jerusalem
If you had been part of the crowd that day, what would have been your most lasting memory?

John 12:20-36 Jesus Explains Why He Must Die
How would you explain to someone why Jesus had to die on the cross?

John 12:37-50 Jesus and His Message
What kinds of pressures make you hesitant to tell others about your belief in Christ?

Mark 11:20-33 Permission to Pray for Anything
How bold is your prayer life?

Matthew 21:28-46 Two Parables
Which son do you resemble most?

Matthew 22:1-14 Jesus Tells about the Wedding Feasts
At what point in your life did you realize that you were invited? How did you respond?

Luke 20:20-40 Jesus Answers Questions
How do you really feel about living forever?

Mark 12:28-37 Questions Given and Taken
Whom do you know who is not far from the Kingdom of God?

Matthew 23:1-39 Jesus: Warnings and Grieving
Which of these seven warnings most directly relate to your life?

Luke 21:1-24 Jesus Talks about the Future
What do your giving habits say about your level of trust in God?

Luke 21:25-38 Jesus on Being Prepared
What does your schedule today say about your watchfulness?

Matthew 25:1-30 Parables about Being Prepared
With which of the people in these two stories do you identify most?

Matthew 25:31-46 Jesus on the Final Judgment
What people in your life are you treating in ways you would want to treat Christ?

Luke 22:1-13 Preparing the Last Supper
How do you prepare yourself for Communion?

John 13:1-20 Jesus Washes His Disciples' Feet
What is the greatest service someone has done for you? How do you serve others?

John 13:21-38 A Sad Prediction
How well do you feel Christ knows you?

John 14:1-14 Jesus Is the Way
How would you rate your present level of understanding of Christ and his teachings?

John 14:15-31 Jesus Promises the Comforter
How have you experienced the Comforter?

John 15:1-16 Jesus on the Vine and the Branches
What kind of fruit has the Gardener produced in you?

John 15:17–16:4 Jesus Warns about Troubles
What have you learned recently about loving others?

John 16:5-33 Jesus on the Holy Spirit and Prayers
Where in these verses do you find peace of heart and mind?

John 17:1-26 Jesus Prays
Where do you find yourself in this prayer?

Mark 14:26-52 A Repeated Prediction
What practical prayer problems do you need to work on?

John 18:1-24 Jesus Betrayed and Abandoned
How close have you come to Peter's denial of Christ?

Matthew 26:57-75 Trial and Denial
In what ways has being a follower of Jesus complicated your life?

Matthew 27:1-10 The Religious Trial and Judas's Death
When you think of sin's consequences, what personal examples come to mind?

Luke 23:1-12 Two Political Trials
In what ways did your childhood and background prepare you to respond to Jesus?

Mark 15:6-24 Sentencing and Torture
Was there a time you chose to do the wrong thing on purpose? Why? What happened?

Luke 23:32-49 Jesus Crucified
What do you feel when you read the description of the Crucifixion?

Matthew 27:57-66 Jesus' Body Laid in a Guarded Tomb
What have you seen people do in their resistance to Christ?

John 20:1-18 Jesus Is Alive!
What makes Easter an important celebration in your life?

Matthew 28:8-15 Reactions to the Resurrection
What would be your first words to Jesus if he appeared to you?

Luke 24:13-43 Appearances of Jesus
Would you recognize Jesus if you saw him today? How?

John 20:24–21:14 More Appearances of Jesus
How has Christ answered your doubts?

John 21:15-25 Jesus Talks with Peter
What difference would it make to you to read these verses with your name in the place of Simon Peter's?

Matthew 28:16-20 Jesus Gives the Great Commission
What are you doing specifically to obey Christ's words?

Luke 24:44-53 Jesus Says Farewell
How do you find Christ opening your mind as you read the Bible?

Acts 1:1-11 The Departure of Jesus
What one thing would you be sure to do if you knew Jesus was coming back today?

Acts 1:12-26 First Things First
What is your idea of the right amount of time for prayer?

Acts 2:1-13 An Amazing Gift
What is the main purpose of any gift God might have given you?

Romans 8:19-39 How God Loves
What things do you sometimes feel might be able to separate you from the love of Christ?

Romans 12:1-21 Living Sacrifice
What act of a living sacrifice might God allow you to do today?

1 Corinthians 13:1-13 Real Love
Which quality of real love do you most need to ask God to increase in your life?

1 Corinthians 15:1-20 The Basic Gospel
What parts of the gospel are especially helpful to you in times of doubt or stress?

1 Corinthians 15:42-58 Destiny!
How much are you looking forward to all Christ has planned for you?

2 Corinthians 4:1-18 Weak Containers; Strong Contents
With which of the four difficult situations Paul mentions do you identify most clearly?

Galatians 5:13-26 Two Radically Different Lives
Who comes to mind as someone who you need to love as you love yourself?

Ephesians 1:3-23 God's Action
In what ways has God marked your life?

Ephesians 2:1-22 God's Plan
When have you recently reminded yourself and God that you want your life to be used for his purposes?

Ephesians 4:1-16 Picture of the Church
What is your role in Christ's body?

Ephesians 6:10-20 Armor of God
Which of these weapons do you need to learn to use better?

Philippians 2:1-18 The Mind of Jesus
In what ways would having Christ's attitude make you face this day differently?

Philippians 3:1-21 Learning Joy
What areas of your life could God be using to teach you joy?

Colossians 2:1-15 What We Have in Christ
What dangerous philosophy is present in your environment that could affect your relationship with Christ?

Colossians 3:1-17 Christian Relationships
What do you envision when you think about heaven?

1 Thessalonians 1:1-10 Spiritual Reputation
How do you think others would evaluate your spiritual life?

1 Thessalonians 4:1-18 Living for God
What specific action could you take today simply out of obedience to God?

2 Thessalonians 1:1-12 Encouragement
What other Christians could you encourage today?

2 Thessalonians 3:1-18 Final Requests
How aware and involved are you in the worldwide spread of the gospel?

1 Timothy 4:1-16 Always Going Forward

Which of these positive commands need to be given a higher priority in your life?

1 Timothy 6:3-21 A Friend's Final Words
How does your attitude toward money match Paul's advice?

2 Timothy 1:1-18 The Importance of Examples
Who has been a good spiritual example for you? How can you thank him or her?

2 Timothy 3:1-17 Last Days
How many of these characteristics are part of your world today?

Titus 3:1-11; Philemon 1:4-7 Good Counsel
Which of these commands apply directly to your life?

Hebrews 10:19-39 The New Life
What do your prayer habits and church habits say about the real importance of faith in your life?

Hebrews 11:1-40 A Review of Faith
How deep is your commitment to Christ?

Hebrews 12:1-13 Our Turn
Which of these directions would have a significant impact on your faith?

James 1:2-27 Tough Times, Happy People
In what difficulty could you use the "James plan" right now?

James 2:1-13 Valuing Other People
Which tendencies do you have to watch out for in how you treat others?

James 3:1-12 Words as Weapons
How sharp would others consider your tongue?

1 Peter 2:1-25 Living Stones
Which would you choose as the biggest personal challenge in these verses?

1 Peter 3:1-22 Relationships and Pain
How willing are you to carry out your relationships God's way, even when there are difficulties?

2 Peter 1:2-21 Knowing God
How would you answer someone who asked you what it means to know God?

1 John 1:1-10 The Way of Forgiveness
What part does confession have in your life?

1 John 3:1-24 God Is Love
How can you tell if your love is growing?

1 John 5:1-21 The Life God Gives
How do you know that you have eternal life?

2 John 1:4-6; 3 John 1:5-8; Jude 1:17-25 Family Matters
How often do you go out of your way to meet the needs of other Christians?

Revelation 1:1-20 Jesus the King
How would you describe your mental picture of Jesus?

Revelation 21:1-27 Everything Made New
What difference do you think you will most notice between the new world and the old?

Revelation 22:1-21 Life in the New City
When was the last time you were excited about heaven?

PSALMS & PROVERBS

Psalm 1:1-6 Two Kinds of Lives
What kind of person do you really want to be?

Psalm 8:1-9 The Value of Humans
How do you know you have worth?

Psalm 23:1-6 A Sheep's Song
What is the most comforting phrase to you in this psalm?

Psalm 51:1-19 A Confession
What examples of repentance have been part of your life?

Psalm 103:1-22 What God Is Like
Which picture in this psalm helps you understand God better?

Psalm 119:1-16 A Hunger for the Word
How can you stay pure?

Psalm 139:1-24 How Well God Knows Us
What do you feel when you read this psalm?

Psalm 145:1-21 God for All People and Time
Which of God's qualities do you most need today?

Proverbs 4:1-27 Wise Words about Life
What priority have you given finding wisdom?

Proverbs 5:1-23 Wise Words about Sex
How do these words match what you hear around you every day?

FOLLOW-UP FOR NEW CHRISTIANS

"Now we rejoice in our wonderful new relationship with God—all because of what our Lord Jesus Christ has done in dying for our sins—making us friends of God" (Romans 5:11).

You have just helped someone become a new Christian or you have been given the responsibility to do the follow-up of a new Christian . . . so now what do you do?

First of all, you can be excited about this opportunity. Second, you need to be serious about this responsibility. Read Romans 5:11 again. You have the privilege of helping someone grow in his or her new relationship with your friend Jesus Christ. Here are some ways you can help a new Christian and Jesus grow closer. Remember, we all need FRIENDS:

Follow up with your new Christian friend by getting together regularly. Get together within 48 hours after your friend receives Christ, and at least once a week during the next six weeks (Matthew 28:20).

Reinforce what Christ has done in your friend's life. Do this by looking at Scriptures that affirm God's commitment to Christians (John 14:20; Hebrews 13:5; Colossians 2:13-14; 1 John 5:13; Galatians 5:25).

Involve your friend in a Bible-teaching church. Take your friend with you and help answer any of his or her questions (Hebrews 10:24-25).

Exhibit Christ in your life through your actions and words. You don't have to be perfect, just someone who wants to obey and please God (Colossians 3:17).

Nurture your friend's spiritual growth. A new Christian is like a newborn baby who needs spiritual food and care. Try using the 14 appointments with God included in this section (1 Peter 2:2-3).

Do things together. Spending time together will give you opportunities to encourage your friend and put your faith into practice (Acts 14:21-22).

Stand by your friend in both the good and bad times. Your friend will fall down spiritually. Get ready to help him or her to get up and go again (Ephesians 4:11-16).

You have recently trusted Jesus Christ to be your Savior . . . so now what do you do?

First of all, you must know that through Christ you have become friends with God. Read Romans 5:11. Remember:

■ You realized that your sin was keeping you from a relationship with God;

- You understood that Jesus Christ died on the cross to pay the penalty for your sin and that he rose again from the dead;
- You prayed, asking Jesus to forgive your sins and be your Savior.

Next, please understand that you have begun an exciting and lasting friendship. As in any relationship, getting to know someone takes time—it doesn't just happen by itself. (Make sure you have a friend who has been a Christian for a while who can help you grow in your new faith. If no one has contacted you, you should go back to the person who helped you become a Christian and ask for help.)

You can grow closer to God just like you grow closer to people. God created you to have a relationship with him, to be his very own son or daughter. Now that you're his child and friend, he will patiently help you get to know him better and better.

Here are some ideas you can use to help you and God become close friends. Remember, all it takes is TIME:

Talk to God through prayer. To help you learn how to talk to God, the 14 appointments with God include ideas for prayer. Give them a try. God will listen when you talk to him.

Investigate God's Word. Decide on a time and place to read the Bible each day. The schedule for 14 appointments with God will help you know what to read. This will help you grow.

Make it practical. One of the best ways to learn is by doing. The 14-appointment schedule includes action steps to help you make your friendship with God active and practical.

Express your thoughts. You know how important it is to show appreciation to a friend. As you finish your daily time with God, tell him thank you. During the next 14 appointments with God, try to keep a personal journal. Simply write down your thoughts, your questions, and, most important of all, why you're thankful to God!

Finally, to get to know God better, try using the following "14 Appointments with God." These appointments are great ways to spend some time with God and find out more about who he is and who he wants you to be.

14 APPOINTMENTS WITH GOD

APPOINTMENT

1

*It's
Guaranteed*
■ ASSURANCE

You recently became a Christian. Have you had any doubts about whether or not Jesus really came into your life? Do you wonder if you'll really go to heaven someday?

Talk to God: "Father, thank you for giving me a relationship with you. Jesus, thank you for giving me life. Please teach me and help me learn more about you. Amen."

Investigate God's Word: Read 1 John 5:11-13. Memorize verse 13.

Make it practical: Check out "I Wonder"—1 John 5:10-12, page 356, or "Here's What I Did"—Matthew 7:24-27, page 13. How can you put the ideas presented here into action in your own life?

Express your thoughts: In your journal, write a description of when, where, and how you became a Christian. Say thanks to God!

APPOINTMENT

2

*Part of
the Family*
■ GOD,
   OUR FATHER

Everyone knows what it's like to not feel totally accepted by others. Did you know that when you became a Christian, God adopted you into his family and accepted you unconditionally?

Talk to God: "Dear God, thanks for making me part of your family. You accept me. That's awesome! Amen."

Investigate God's Word: Ephesians 1:3-8. Memorize verse 5.

Make it practical: "I Wonder"—Hebrews 1:1-3, page 317, or "Here's What I Did"—Mark 9:35, page 55.

Express your thoughts: In your journal, make a list of what you like about being part of God's family. Don't forget to thank him.

APPOINTMENT

3

*New Life
in Christ*
■ GROWTH

OK, now that you're a new Christian, what's next? Well, the best relationships are those that grow and deepen. It's the same way in your relationship with Jesus Christ. It's time for growth.

Talk to God: "Lord, help me to let my roots sink down into you. Thanks for helping me grow. Amen."

Investigate God's Word: Colossians 2:6-7. Memorize verse 7a.

Make it practical: "I Wonder"—Colossians 2:6-7, page 273, or "Here's What I Did"—2 Peter 1:5-8, page 349.

Express your thoughts: Think of one way that you'd like to grow spiritually, share it with one friend, and write it in your journal. Then ask God to help you do what you've decided to do.

APPOINTMENT 4

Time to Talk
■ PRAYER

You know how good friends love to talk with each other. God, our heavenly Father, is ready for a heart-to-heart talk all the time. Conversation with God is a must!

Talk to God: "God, I'm so glad we can talk anytime. Thank you that you'll listen to my needs. Help me learn to listen to you. Amen."

Investigate God's Word: Philippians 4:6-7. Memorize verse 6.

Make it practical: "Incantation"—Matthew 6:7-8, page 10, or "Find Time"— Mark 1:35, page 42.

Express your thoughts: Commit yourself to spending at least three minutes in prayer every day. In your journal, keep a record of your prayer requests and answers. Tell God thanks for those answers.

APPOINTMENT 5

Dig In
■ BIBLE

When you get something new, you often receive an instruction manual. With your new life in Christ, you need God's instruction manual, the Bible. God communicates to us through his Word.

Talk to God: "Dear God, thank you for showing me what you're like through your Word. Help me to read it, study it, and obey it. Amen."

Investigate God's Word: 2 Timothy 3:14-17. Memorize verse 16.

Make it practical: "I Wonder"—John 20:30-31, page 137, or "The Source"— 2 Timothy 3:16, page 302.

Express your thoughts: Commit yourself to spending five minutes a day reading the Bible. As a result of something you read, write down in your journal something you will do. Ask God to help you.

APPOINTMENT 6

Jesus Did It All
■ JESUS, OUR SAVIOR

Friendships get stronger when you really get to know the other person. You have trusted Christ to be your Savior and to give you new life. Really get to know who he is and what he has done! It's incredible!

Talk to God: "Jesus, you are so powerful! I'm thankful that you hold everything together, including me! Amen."

Investigate God's Word: Colossians 1:15-23. Memorize verse 17.

Make it practical: "I Wonder"—Psalm 14:1-3, page 403.

Express your thoughts: Ask a friend to tell you what he or she really likes about Jesus. In your journal, write a note to Jesus about what you really appreciate about him.

APPOINTMENT 7

Solid Rock
■ OBEDIENCE

A good foundation is essential for a house to stand strong. Jesus wants you to realize that obeying God will give your life a solid foundation.

Talk to God: "Dear God, you know what's best for me. Help me to be strong and obey you in each area of my life. Amen."

Investigate God's Word: Luke 6:46-49. Memorize verse 47a.

Make it practical: "Here's What I Did"—Ephesians 6:1-3, page 259.

Express your thoughts: In your journal, list one area of your life where you are obeying God and one where you are not. Say thanks to God for helping you to want to obey.

APPOINTMENT

8

You Have In-sight
■ HOLY SPIRIT

Nobody in this world knows you better than you know yourself. Nobody knows God like God's Spirit knows God. As a new Christian, you have been given God's Holy Spirit. He will give you insight into what God is like and what he wants you to do.

T*alk to God:* "Thank you, God, for giving me your Spirit. You know me so well, and I will trust your Spirit to help me know more about you. Amen."

I*nvestigate God's Word:* 1 Corinthians 2:9-16. Memorize verse 12.

M*ake it practical:* "I Wonder"—Romans 7:15–8:2, page 193, or "The Holy Spirit"—Acts 2:14-36, page 144.

E*xpress your thoughts:* In your journal, write down one question that you'd like the Holy Spirit to help you with. Now take a couple of minutes and just listen to God. Tell him thanks.

APPOINTMENT

9

Don't Give In
■ TEMPTATION

The Bible says in 1 Peter 5:8 that our enemy Satan is like a lion that wants to rip us apart. Satan will tempt us to disobey God, but God will show us a way out!

T*alk to God:* "Dear God, you know the temptations I struggle with. Thank you that you have promised me a way to escape. Amen."

I*nvestigate God's Word:* 1 Corinthians 10:13. Memorize verse 13.

M*ake it practical:* "I Wonder"—Matthew 18:7-9, page 25, or "Here's What I Did"—1 Peter 3:15, page 343.

E*xpress your thoughts:* List the three temptations that Satan really uses on you. Now thank God ahead of time that he will show you how to not give in next time.

APPOINTMENT

10

I'm Sorry
■ FORGIVENESS

As a child in God's family, you'll still mess up. But God's love for you is so great that he will forgive you! He can do that because he loves you!

T*alk to God:* "Dear God, I confess to you my sin of _____. I admit that it was wrong. Thank you that Jesus died on the cross to forgive me for this sin. Amen."

I*nvestigate God's Word:* 1 John 1:8-10. Memorize verse 9.

M*ake it practical:* "I Wonder"—James 4:17, page 335, or "Here's What I Did"—Romans 12:19, page 197.

E*xpress your thoughts:* Write down ways that you have disobeyed God recently. Look at each one and confess it through prayer. Cross out each sin. Let this remind you of God's loving forgiveness. Be sure to thank him!

APPOINTMENT

11

Worship Him
■ CHURCH

Christians are part of the body of Christ, which is called his church. Be sure you get together with other believers, members of the "body." It's an opportunity to love God and each other.

T*alk to God:* "Dear God, thank you for your body of believers, the church. Teach me how to get involved with other Christians and really worship you. Amen."

I*nvestigate God's Word:* Hebrews 10:22-25. Memorize verse 25.

M*ake it practical:* "I Wonder"—Hebrews 10:24-25, page 323, or "Here's What I Did"—James 1, page 333.

E*xpress your thoughts:* Go with some friends or family to church this week. List two ways you worshiped God.

APPOINTMENT

12

*I Gotta Tell
You Something*
■ WITNESSING

If you have a close friend, you can't keep from talking about that person. When you love someone, you can hardly contain yourself! Let your love for Christ motivate you to tell others about him.

Talk to God: "Lord, you have changed my life. Give me the courage and opportunities to tell others about you. Amen."

Investigate God's Word: Romans 1:16-17. Memorize verse 16.

Make it practical: "I Wonder"—Luke 22:54-66, page 103, or "Here's What I Did"—Acts 4:13, page 147.

Express your thoughts: Write down the name of one person who needs to know Jesus Christ. Start praying for that person to become a Christian. Ask a Christian friend to pray with you for the person and to help you learn how to share your faith with him or her.

APPOINTMENT

13

*Do You
Remember*
■ BIBLE
MEMORY

To fight a battle you need powerful equipment. The Holy Spirit will use the power of God's Word like a sword to defeat Satan. So a great strategy is to memorize Scripture! What verses have you already learned?

Talk to God: "Lord, I need your power! Help me to memorize Scripture verses. I know this will help me live for you. Amen."

Investigate God's Word: Ephesians 6:10-17. Memorize verse 17.

Make it practical: "I Wonder"—Philippians 4:8, page 265, or "Here's What I Did"—Psalm 34, page 409.

Express your thoughts: Review your memory verses from the past 12 days. In your journal, write down your favorite verse.

APPOINTMENT

14

Be like Christ
■ SPIRITUAL
GOAL

You've been a Christian for a short time now, and you're learning that you have a lifelong relationship with Christ. So what's your long-range plan? Becoming like Christ is the ultimate goal.

Talk to God: "Dear Jesus, more than anything else I want to become more like you. Thanks that you'll be patient and help me. Amen."

Investigate God's Word: Colossians 3:10-11. Memorize verse 10.

Make it practical: "I Wonder"—Mark 5:1-20, page 47, or "Here's What I Did"—Matthew 5:39, page 9.

Express your thoughts: Make a list of at least five ways you want to become more like Jesus. Spend time asking God to help you. Remind yourself to read this part of your journal in one month to check on your spiritual growth.

LIFE-CHANGER INDEX

(Look up notes by referring to Scripture location or page number.)

INDEX TO THE MORAL DILEMMAS

(Look up notes by referring to Scripture location or page number.)

INDEX TO "I WONDER"

(Look up notes by referring to Scripture location or page number.)

INDEX TO THE ULTIMATE ISSUES

(Look up notes by referring to Scripture location or page number.)

INDEX TO THE CHARTS

(Look up charts by referring to Scripture location or page number.)

INDEX TO THE PERSONALITY PROFILES

(Look up profiles by referring to Scripture location or page number.)

INDEX TO THE MAPS

(Look up maps by referring to Scripture location or page number.)